MIDDLE EAST CONFLICTS FROM ANCIENT EGYPT TO THE 21ST CENTURY

MIDDLE EAST CONFLICTS FROM ANCIENT EGYPT TO THE 21ST CENTURY

An Encyclopedia and Document Collection

VOLUME 1: A–F

Dr. Spencer C. Tucker

Editor

ABC-CLIO®

An Imprint of ABC-CLIO, LLC
Santa Barbara, California • Denver, Colorado

Copyright © 2019 by ABC-CLIO, LLC

All rights reserved. No part of this publication may be reproduced, stored in a retrieval system, or transmitted, in any form or by any means, electronic, mechanical, photocopying, recording, or otherwise, except for the inclusion of brief quotations in a review, without prior permission in writing from the publisher.

Every reasonable effort has been made to trace the owners of copyright materials in this book, but in some instances this has proven impossible. The editors and publishers will be glad to receive information leading to more complete acknowledgments in subsequent printings of the book and in the meantime extend their apologies for any omissions.

Library of Congress Cataloging-in-Publication Data

Names: Tucker, Spencer, 1937– editor.
Title: Middle East conflicts from Ancient Egypt to the 21st century : an encyclopedia and document collection / Spencer C. Tucker, Editor.
Description: Santa Barbara, CA : ABC-CLIO, [2019] | Includes bibliographical references and index. |
Identifiers: LCCN 2019020655 (print) | LCCN 2019021604 (ebook) | ISBN 9781440853531 (ebook) | ISBN 9781440853524 (set : alk. paper) | ISBN 9781440853548 (volume 1 : alk. paper) | ISBN 9781440853555 (volume 2 : alk. paper) | ISBN 9781440853562 (volume 3 : alk. paper) | ISBN 9781440853579 (volume 4 : alk. paper)
Subjects: LCSH: Middle East—History, Military. | Arab countries—History, Military. | Middle East—History, Military—Encyclopedias. | Arab countries—History, Military—Encyclopedias.
Classification: LCC DS63.15 (ebook) | LCC DS63.15 .M53 2019 (print) | DDC 355.020956/03—dc23
LC record available at https://lccn.loc.gov/2019020655

ISBN: 978-1-4408-5352-4 (set)
    978-1-4408-5354-8 (vol. 1)
    978-1-4408-5355-5 (vol. 2)
    978-1-4408-5356-2 (vol. 3)
    978-1-4408-5357-9 (vol. 4)
    978-1-4408-5353-1 (ebook)

23 22 21 20 19   1 2 3 4 5

This book is also available as an eBook.

ABC-CLIO
An Imprint of ABC-CLIO, LLC

ABC-CLIO, LLC
147 Castilian Drive
Santa Barbara, California 93117
www.abc-clio.com

This book is printed on acid-free paper ∞
Manufactured in the United States of America

To Laurent Boetsch:
Gentleman scholar, linguist, university president,
leader in international education, and esteemed friend.

About the Editors

Spencer C. Tucker, PhD, has been senior fellow in military history at ABC-CLIO since 2003. He is the author or editor of 66 books and encyclopedias, many of which have won prestigious awards. Tucker's last academic position before his retirement from teaching was the John Biggs Chair in Military History at the Virginia Military Institute. He has been a Fulbright scholar, a visiting research associate at the Smithsonian Institution, and, as a U.S. Army captain, an intelligence analyst in the Pentagon. His recently published works include *World War I: The Definitive Encyclopedia and Document Collection, Wars That Changed History: 50 of the World's Greatest Conflicts,* and *Enduring Controversies in Military History: Critical Analyses and Context,* all published by ABC-CLIO.

Priscilla Roberts, PhD, is an associate professor of business at the City University of Macau and codirector of the university's Asia-Pacific Business Research Centre. With Spencer C. Tucker and others, she has coedited and contributed the documents volumes to 11 ABC-CLIO encyclopedias on the Korean War, World War I, World War II, the Cold War, the Arab-Israeli conflict, and Middle East wars. Roberts is the editor of *Cuban Missile Crisis: The Essential Reference Guide, World War II: The Essential Reference Guide, Voices of World War II: Contemporary Accounts of Daily Life, Arab-Israeli Conflict: The Essential Reference Guide, Arab-Israeli Conflict: A Documentary and Reference Guide,* and *The Cold War: Interpreting Conflict through Primary Documents.* In addition, she is the author of numerous other books and articles in international history. Roberts spent 2003 at George Washington University as a Fulbright scholar and has received numerous other academic awards for research in the United States, Great Britain, Australia, Canada, Hong Kong, and Macao. She earned her PhD at King's College, Cambridge, England, and specializes in 20th-century diplomatic and international history.

Contents

Volume 1: A–F
List of Entries   ix
List of Maps   xxiii
Preface   xxv
Introduction   xxvii
General Maps   xxxv
Entries   1

Volume II: G–N
List of Entries   ix
List of Maps   xxiii
General Maps   xxv
Entries   441

Volume III: O–Z
List of Entries   ix
List of Maps   xxiii
General Maps   xxv
Entries   901
Chronology   1383
Glossary   1389
Selective Bibliography   1391
Editors and Contributors   1397

Volume IV: Documents
List of Documents   ix
Documents   1405
Index   1775

List of Entries

Abadi, Haider al- (1952–)
Abbas, Abu (1948–2004)
Abbas, Mahmoud (1935–)
Abbasid Caliphate (750–1258, 1261–1517)
Abbasid Revolution (747–751)
Abbas Mirza (1789–1833)
Abbas I the Great (1571–1629)
Abd Allah ibn al-Zubair (624–692)
Abdel-Rahman, Omar (1938–2017)
Abdulhamid II (1842–1918)
Abdullah I (1882–1951)
Abdullah II (1962–)
Abizaid, John Philip (1951–)
Aboukir, First Battle of (July 25, 1799)
Aboukir, Second Battle of (March 8, 1801)
Aboukir Bay, Battle of (August 1, 1798)
Abu Abbas (1948–2004)
Abu Ghraib
Abulustayn, Battle of (April 15, 1277)
Abu Muslim Khorasani (718?–755)
Abu Nidal (1937–2002)
Achaemenid Empire (550–330 BCE)
Acre, Battle of (November 3, 1840)
Acre, 1189 Siege of (August 28, 1189–July 12, 1191)
Acre, 1291 Siege of (April 6–May 28, 1291)
Acre, 1799 Siege of (March 17–May 20, 1799)
Actium, Battle of (September 2, 31 BCE)
Adan, Avraham "Bren" (1926–2012)

Adana Massacre (April 1909)
Aden Emergency (1963–1967)
Adrianople, Battle of (August 9, 378)
Adrianople, Crusades Battle of (April 14–15, 1205)
Adrianople, 1444 Treaty of (June 12, 1444)
Adrianople, 1713 Treaty of (June 24, 1713)
Adrianople, 1829 Treaty of (September 14, 1829)
Aegospotami, Battle of (405 BCE)
Ager Sanguinis, Battle of (June 28, 1119)
Agha Muhammad Khan Qajar (1742–1797)
Agranat Commission (November 18, 1973–January 30, 1975)
Ajnadain, Battle of (July 30? 634)
Akkad
Akroinon, Battle of (740)
Al-Adil (1145–1218)
Al-Afdal (?–1122)
Alam el Halfa, Battle of (August 31–September 7, 1942)
Al-Amin, Muhammad (787–813)
Al-Anfal Campaign (1987–1988)
al-Aqsa Martyrs Brigades
Al-Aqsa Mosque Massacre (October 8, 1990)
al-Atrash, Sultan (1891–1982)
Alawites
Aleppo, Battle for (July 19, 2012–December 22, 2016)
Alexander I Balas (ca. 173–145 BCE)
Alexander III the Great (356–323 BCE)
Alexander III's Invasion of the Persian Empire (334–323 BCE)

Alexander Severus, Roman Emperor (ca. 208–235)
Alexandria, Bombardment of (July 11, 1882)
Alexandria, Sack of (October 9–12, 1365)
Alexandropol, Treaty of (December 2, 1920)
Alexios I Komnenos (1048–1118)
Alexios III Angelos (ca. 1153–1211)
Alexios V Doukas Mourtzouphlos (1140–1204)
Algiers Agreement (March 6, 1975)
Algiers Declaration (November 15, 1988)
Ali, Ahmad Ismail (1917–1974)
Ali Bey al-Kabir (1728–1773)
Ali ibn Abi Talib (ca. 600–661)
Aliya Bet
Allawi, Ayad (1944–)
Allenby, Sir Edmund Henry Hynman (1861–1936)
Allon, Yigal (1918–1980)
Allon Plan (July 26, 1967)
Al-Mamun, Abd Allah (786–833)
Al-Nusra Front
Alp Arslan (ca. 1030–1072)
Al Qaeda
Al Qaeda in Iraq
Al Qaeda in the Arabian Peninsula
Al-Sabah, Jaber al-Ahmad (1926–2006)
al-Sannabra, Battle of (June 28, 1113)
Altalena Incident (June 23, 1948)
Amalric of Jerusalem (1136–1174)
Amara, Battle of (June 3, 1915)
Amasya, Treaty of (May 29, 1555)
Ambush Alley
Amer, Abdel Hakim (December 11, 1919–
 September 14, 1967)
Amiriyah Shelter Bombing (February 13, 1991)
Amman Campaign (March 21–September 25, 1918)
Amr ibn al-As (ca. 585–664)
Anbar Awakening Movement
Anglo-American Committee of Inquiry (1946)
Anglo-Egyptian Treaty (August 26, 1936)
Anglo-Egyptian War (1882)
Anglo-Iranian Oil Crisis (1951–1953)
Anglo-Iraqi Treaties of 1922 and 1930
Anglo-Jordanian Defense Treaty (March 15, 1948)
Anglo-Ottoman Treaty (1838)
Anglo-Ottoman War (1807–1809)
Anglo-Persian War (1856–1857)
Anglo-Sudan War (1883–1899)
Ankara, Battle of (July 20, 1402)
Ankara, Pact of (October 19, 1939)

Ansar al-Islam
Anti-Arab Attitudes and Discrimination
Antigonus I Monophthalmus (382–301 BCE)
Antioch, Principality of
Antioch, Sieges of (1097–1098)
Antioch on the Meander, Battle of (1211)
Antiochus I Soter (ca. 324–261 BCE)
Antiochus III Megas (ca. 241–187 BCE)
Antiochus IV Epiphanes (ca. 215–164 BCE)
Antiochus VII Sidetes (ca. 159–129 BCE)
Antiochus Hierax (ca. 260–226 BCE)
Anti-Semitism
Aoun, Michel (1935–)
Aqaba, Capture of (July 6, 1917)
Aqaba, Gulf of
Arab Economic Boycott of Israel
Arabi, Ahmed (1841–1911)
Arabia, Roman
Arab-Jewish Communal War (November 30, 1947–
 May 14, 1948)
Arab League
Arab Legion
Arab Liberation Army
Arab Nationalism
Arab Oil Embargo (October 17, 1973–March 18, 1974)
Arab Revolt in Palestine (1936–1939)
Arab Revolt of World War I (June 5, 1916–
 October 31, 1918)
Arab Riots, Jerusalem (April 4–8, 1920)
Arab Spring (December 17, 2010–Mid-2012)
Arafat, Yasser (1929–2004)
Ardashir I (180–240)
Arif, Abd al-Salam (1921–1966)
Armenians and the Armenian Genocide
Army of Islam
ARROWHEAD RIPPER, Operation (June 19–August 19, 2007)
Arsuf, Battle of (September 7, 1191)
Artah, Battle of (August 11, 1164)
Artaxerxes I (?–424 BCE)
Artaxerxes II (435 or 445–358)
Artaxerxes III (359–338 BCE)
Artemisia I (5th Century BCE)
Artuqid Dynasty (1101–1408)
Asabiyya
Ascalon, Battle of (August 12, 1099)
Ashkenazic Judaism
Ashurbanipal (ca. 693–627 BCE)
Assad, Bashar al- (1965–)

Assad, Hafez al- (1930–2000)
Assassins
Assyrian Empire
Ataturk, Mustafa Kemal (1881–1938)
Auchinleck, Sir Claude John Eyre (1884–1981)
Aurelian, Emperor (214–275)
Auspicious Incident (June 15, 1826)
AUTUMN CLOUDS, Operation (November 1–8, 2006)
Ayn Jalut, Battle of (September 3, 1260)
Ayyubid Dynasty

Baath Party
Babylon, Siege of (539–538 BCE)
Babylonian Empire, Neo- (626–539 BCE)
Babylonian Empire, Old (ca. 1894–911 BCE)
Badr, Battle of (March 15, 624)
Badr al-Jamali (1015–1094)
Baghavard, First Battle of (June 14, 1735)
Baghavard, Second Battle of (August 9, 1745)
Baghdad, Capture of (March 11, 1917)
Baghdad, 812–813 Siege of (August 812–September 813)
Baghdad, 1258 Siege of
Baghdad, 1401 Siege of
Baghdad, 1638 Siege of
Baghdad, 1733 Battle of (July 19, 1733)
Baghdad, 2003 Battle of (April 5–10, 2003)
Baghdadi, Abu Bakr al- (1971–)
Baghdad Pact (February 4, 1955)
Bahrain
Bakhchisarai, Treaty of (January 3, 1681)
Bakr, Ahmad Hassan al- (1914–1982)
Balak ibn Bahram ibn Ortok (?–1124)
Baldat al-Shaykh Massacre (January 31, 1947)
Baldwin I of Constantinople (1171–1206)
Baldwin I of Jerusalem (ca. 1061–1118)
Baldwin II of Constantinople (1217–1273)
Baldwin II of Jerusalem (1060–1131)
Baldwin III of Jerusalem (1130–1163)
Baldwin IV of Jerusalem (1161–1185)
Balfour Declaration (November 2, 1917)
Balkans, Ottoman Conquest of the (1350s–1593)
Balkan Wars (1912–1913)
Balta Liman, Convention of (May 1, 1849)
Baltim, Battle of (October 12–13, 1973)
Bapheus, Battle of (July 27, 1301)
Barak, Ehud (1942–)
Barkiyaruq (1079/1080–1105)
Bar Kochba Revolt (132–135)

Bar-Lev Line
Basian, Battle of (1203)
Basil II Bulgaroctonos (958–1025)
Basra, Battle for (March 23–April 7, 2003)
Bassorah, Battle of (November 7, 656)
Baybars I (1223–1277)
Bayezid I (1360–1403)
Bayezid II (1447–1512)
Bedouins
Beersheba, Battle of (October 31, 1917)
Begin, Menachem (1913–1992)
Belisarius (ca. 505–565)
Ben-Gurion, David (1886–1973)
Bernadotte, Folke (1895–1948)
Beth-Horon, Battle of (October 66 CE)
Bible
Bin Laden, Osama (1957–2011)
Bithynia
Black September (September 6, 1970–July 1971)
Black September Organization
Bohemund I of Antioch (ca. 1054–1111)
Bohemund VI of Antioch-Tripoli (ca. 1237–1275)
Bohemund VII of Antioch-Tripoli (1261–1287)
Bonaparte, Napoleon (1769–1821)
Boniface I of Montferrat (ca. 1150–1207)
Border War (1949–1956)
Bremer, Lewis Paul, III (1941–)
Bubiyan Island, Battle of (January 29–30, 1991)
Burqan, Battle of (February 25, 1991)
Bush Doctrine
Byzantine Empire (330–1453)
Byzantine Empire Civil War (1341–1347)
Byzantine-Muslim Wars (629–1035)
Byzantine-Ottoman Wars (1280–1479)
Byzantine-Sassanid War (602–628)
Byzantine-Seljuk Wars (1048–1308)

Caesar, Gaius Julius (100–44 BCE)
Caesar's Campaign in Egypt (48–47 BCE)
Cairo Accord (May 4, 1994)
Cairo Agreement (November 3, 1969)
Cairo Declaration, Palestine Liberation Organization (November 7, 1985)
Cambyses II (?–522 BCE)
Camp David Accords (September 17, 1978)
Camp Speicher Massacre (June 12, 2014)
Carrhae, Battle of (June 9, 53 BCE)
Carter Doctrine (January 23, 1980)

Caucasus Front, World War I
Cezayirli Gazi Hasan Pasha (1713–1790)
Chaldiran, Battle of (August 23, 1514)
Chamoun, Camille (1900–1987)
Chancellor, Sir John Robert (1870–1952)
Chemical Weapons and Warfare
Chesma, Battle of (July 5–7, 1770)
Chinese Farm, Battle of the (October 14–18, 1973)
Cleopatra VII (69–30 BCE)
Clermont, Council of (1095)
Climate of the Middle East
Cold War in the Middle East
Cole, USS, Attack on (October 12, 2000)
Conrad III, King of Germany (1093–1152)
Constantine I (ca. 277–286–337)
Constantine XI Palaiologos (1405–1453)
Constantinople, Crusader Siege and Capture of (April 8–13, 1204)
Constantinople, Latin Empire of (1204–1261)
Constantinople, Muslim Siege of (August 15, 717–August 15, 718)
Constantinople, 1590 Treaty of (May 21, 1590)
Constantinople, 1700 Treaty of (July 3, 1700)
Constantinople, 1720 Treaty of (November 16, 1720)
Constantinople, 1832 Treaty of (July 21, 1832)
Constantinople, 1913 Treaty of (September 29, 1913)
Constantinople, Ottoman Siege of (April 6–May 29, 1453)
Constantius II, Emperor (317–361)
Copts
Corupedium, Battle of (281 BCE)
Crassus, Marcus Licinius (ca. 115–53 BCE)
Cresson, Battle of (May 1, 1187)
Croesus of Lydia (ca. 595–547 BCE)
Crusades in the Holy Land, Christian (1096–1291)
Ctesiphon, 363 Battle of (May 29, 363)
Ctesiphon, 1915 Battle of (November 22–25, 1915)
Cunaxa, Battle of (401 BCE)
Cunningham, Sir Alan Gordon (1887–1983)
Cyprus
Cyprus, Athenian Expedition to (450–449 BCE)
Cyprus, Ottoman Conquest of (1570–1571)
Cyrus II the Great (ca. 601/590–530 BCE)
Cyrus the Younger (ca. 423–401 BCE)

Damascus, Allied Capture of (October 1, 1918)
Damascus, Siege of (634–635)
Damascus Agreement (December 28, 1985)
Damietta
Danishmendid Dynasty (1071–1178)
Daoud, Abu (1937–2010)
Dar al-Islam and Dar al-Harb
Dardanelles Campaign (February–March 1915)
Darius I (ca. 549–486 BCE)
Darius II (?–404 BCE)
Darius III (ca. 380–330 BCE)
Dawud Pasha (1767–1851)
Dayan, Moshe (1915–1981)
Debecka Pass, Battle of (April 6, 2003)
DEFENSIVE SHIELD, Operation (April 3–May 10, 2002)
Definitive Treaty (March 14, 1812)
Degania, Battle of (May 20, 1948)
Deir Yassin Massacre (April 9–11, 1948)
Demetrius I Poliorcetes (336–282 BCE)
Demetrius II Nicator (ca. 160–125 BCE)
DESERT FOX, Operation (December 16–19, 1998)
DESERT THUNDER I, Operation (1998)
DESERT THUNDER II, Operation (1998)
Devshirme System
Dhahran, Scud Missile Attack on (February 25, 1991)
Dhofar Rebellion (1962–1976)
Diadochi, Wars of the (323–275 BCE)
Diaspora
Djemal Pasha, Ahmed (1872–1922)
Doha Agreement (May 21, 2008)
Donkey Island, Battle of (June 30–July 1, 2007)
Dorylaion, Battle of (July 1, 1097)
Druze-Ottoman Wars
Druzes

EARNEST WILL, Operation (1987–1989)
Edessa, County of
Edward I, King of England (1239–1307)
Egypt
Egypt, Ancient
Egypt, Arab Conquest of (640–642)
Egypt, Athenian Intervention in (460–454 BCE)
Egypt, British Invasion of (1807)
Egypt, French Invasion and Occupation of (1798–1801)
Egypt, Ptolemaic and Roman Periods
Egyptian-Arab Wars (1811–1840)
Egyptian-Ottoman Wars (1831–1833 and 1838–1841)
Egyptian Revolution of 2011
Egyptian-Soviet Arms Deal (Summer 1955)
Egypt under British Rule (1882–1936)
Eilat, Israel

Eilat, Sinking of (October 21, 1967)
Eisenhower Doctrine (1957)
Eitan, Rafael (1929–2004)
El Alamein, First Battle of (July 1–27, 1942)
El Alamein, Second Battle of (October 23–November 11, 1942)
Elazar, David (1925–1976)
Entebbe Hostage Rescue (July 3–4, 1976)
Enver Pasha (1881–1922)
Erdoğan, Recep Tayyip (1954–)
Erzincan, 1230 Battle of (August 10–12, 1230)
Erzincan, 1916 Battle of (July 25–26, 1916)
Erzurum, First Treaty of (July 28, 1823)
Erzurum, Second Treaty of (May 31, 1847)
Erzurum Offensive (January 10–March 25, 1916)
Eshkol, Levi (1895–1969)
Eumenes of Cardia (ca. 361–316 BCE)
Eumenes I of Pergamum (r. 263–241 BCE)
Eumenes II of Pergamum (r. 197–159 BCE)
Euphrates River
Eurymedon, Battle of (ca. 468–466 BCE)
Eustace III of Boulogne (ca. 1058–1125)
Evagoras I (ca. 435–374 BCE)
Exodus Incident (July 11–August 22, 1947)
Expellees and Refugees, Palestinian

Fahd, ibn Abd al-Aziz al-Saud (1922–2005)
Faisal I, King of Iraq (1885–1933)
Faisal II, King of Iraq (1935–1958)
Fallujah, First Battle of (April 4–May 1, 2004)
Fallujah, Second Battle of (November 7–December 23, 2004)
Fallujah, Third Battle of (May 23–June 28, 2016)
Fao Peninsula
Farouk I, King of Egypt (1920–1965)
Fatah, al-
Fatimid Dynasty (909–1171)
Fatwa
Fedayeen
Finckenstein, Treaty of (May 4, 1807)
Forbie, Battle of (October 17, 1244)
Franco-Lebanese Treaty (November 13, 1936)
Franco-Syrian Treaty (September 9, 1936)
Franco-Turkish War (1920)
Franks, Tommy (1945–)
Frederick I or Frederick Barbarossa (1122–1190)
Frederick II, Holy Roman Emperor (1194–1250)
Frederick V, Duke of Swabia (1167–1191)

Gabiene, Battle of (316 BCE)
Galerius, Roman Emperor (ca. 250s–311)
Galilee
Gallipoli Campaign (April 25, 1915–January 9, 1916)
Gamaat Islamiya
Ganja, Treaty of (March 10, 1735)
Gaugamela, Battle of (October 1, 331 BCE)
Gaza, Battle of (November 13, 1239)
Gaza, First Battle of (March 26–27, 1917)
Gaza, Second Battle of (April 17–19, 1917)
Gaza, Third Battle of (October 31–November 7, 1917)
Gaza Raid (February 28, 1955)
Gaza Strip
Gaza Strip Disengagement (August 15–September 12, 2005)
Gaza War of 2006 (June 27–November 26, 2006)
Gaza War of 2008–2009 (December 27, 2008–January 18, 2009)
Gaza War of 2012 (November 14–22, 2012)
Gaza War of 2014 (July 8–August 26, 2014)
General Treaty of Peace (1820)
Geneva Accord (December 1, 2003)
Geneva Peace Conference (December 21, 1973–January 9, 1974)
Geography of the Middle East
Georgian-Seljuk Wars (11th–13th centuries)
Ghazi
Ghulams
Giddi Pass
Glubb, Sir John Bagot (1897–1986)
Godfrey of Bouillon (ca. 1060–1100)
Gog and Magog
Golan Heights
Golden Horde–Ilkhanid Wars (1261–1323)
Goltz, Wilhelm Leopold Colmar von der (1843–1916)
Gordian III, Emperor (225–244)
Gouraud, Henri Joseph Eugène (1867–1946)
Granicus, Battle of the (May 334 BCE)
Greco-Persian Wars (499–479 BCE)
Greco-Turkish War (1919–1922)
Green Line
Green Zone, Iraq
Grivas, Georgios (1898–1974)
Gulf Cooperation Council
Gulistan, Treaty of (October 24, 1813)
Gulnabad, Battle of (March 8, 1772)
Guy of Lusignan (ca. 1150–1194)

xiv List of Entries

Haditha, Battle of (August 1–4, 2005)
Hadrian, Emperor (76–138)
Haganah
Haifa Street, Battle of (January 6–9, 2007)
Hama Massacre (February 3–28, 1982)
Hamas
Hammurabi (ca. 1810–1750 BCE)
Hanit, Attack on the (July 21, 2006)
HARD SURFACE, Operation (June 12, 1963–January 1964)
Haredim
Harim, Battle of (August 12, 1164)
Hariri, Rafik (1944–2005)
Harran, Battle of (May 7, 1104)
Harun al-Rashid (763–809)
Hashemites
Hashomer
Hasidic Judaism
Hasmonean Tunnel Incident (September 23–28, 1996)
Hattin, Battle of (July 3–4, 1187)
Havlaga
Hayreddin Barbarossa (ca. 1483–1546)
Hebron Massacre (August 23–24, 1929)
Hebron Mosque Massacre (February 25, 1994)
Hejaz Railroad, Attacks on (1916–1918)
Hellespont
Hellespont Campaign (411–410 BCE)
Henry of Constantinople (ca. 1178–1216)
Henry VI of Germany (1165–1197)
Heraclius (ca. 575–641)
Herzl, Theodor (1860–1904)
Hezbollah
Holocaust (1941–1945)
Homs, First Battle of (December 11, 1260)
Homs, Second Battle of (October 29, 1281)
Homs, Third Battle of (December 23, 1299)
Hormuz, Strait of
Houthi, Hussein Badr al-Din al- (?–2004)
Houthis
Hrawi, Elias (1925–2006)
Hulegu (1218–1265)
Hunkar Iskelesi, Treaty of (July 8, 1833)
Husaybah, Battle of (April 17, 2004)
Hussein, Saddam (1937–2006)
Husseini, Haj Amin al- (1895–1974)
Hussein ibn Ali ibn Mohammed (1856–1931)
Hussein ibn Talal, King of Jordan (1935–1999)
Hyksos

Ibelin, Battle of (May 29, 1123)
Ibn Saud, King (1875–1953)
Ibrahim Pasha (1789–1848)
Ikhwan
Ilghazi ibn Artuq, Najm al-Din (ca. 1062–1122)
Ilkhan Dynasty (ca. 1261–1353)
IMMINENT THUNDER, Operation (November 15–21, 1990)
Improvised Explosive Devices
Inab, Battle of (June 29, 1149)
INHERENT RESOLVE, Operation (August 8, 2014–)
İnönü, İsmet (1884–1973)
Intifada, First (1987–1993)
Intifada, Second (2000–2004)
Ionian Revolt (499–493 BCE)
Ipsus, Battle of (Spring, 301 BCE)
Iran
Iran, Islamic Revolution in (1978–1979)
Iran Air Flight 655, Downing of (July 3, 1988)
Iran Hostage Crisis (November 4, 1979–January 20, 1981)
Iran Hostage Rescue Mission (Operation EAGLE CLAW, April 25, 1980)
Iran-Iraq War (1980–1988)
Iran Nuclear Deal (July 14, 2015)
Iraq
Iraq, Sanctions on
Iraq Insurgency (2003–)
Iraq No-Fly Zones
Iraq War (March 19, 2003–December 15, 2011)
Irgun Tsvai Leumi
Isfahan, Siege of (March–October 23, 1722)
Islamic Army of Aden
Islamic Civil War, First (656–661)
Islamic Civil War, Second (680–692)
Islamic Radicalism in the 20th and 21st Centuries
Islamic State of Iraq and Syria
Ismail, Khedive (1830–1895)
Ismail Ali, Ahmad (1917–1974)
Ismail I, Shah (1487–1524)
Ismailis
Israel
Israel-Egypt Peace Treaty (March 26, 1979)
Israeli Air Strikes Beginning the Six-Day War (June 5, 1967)
Israeli Air Strike on Presumed Syrian Nuclear Facility (September 6, 2007)
Israeli Security Fence
Israeli War of Independence (1948–1949)

Israeli War of Independence, Truce Agreements (February 24, 1949–July 20, 1949)
Israel-Jordan Peace Treaty (October 26, 1994)
Issus, Battle of (November 333 BCE)
Italo-Ottoman War (1911–1912)
IVORY JUSTICE, Operation (July 24–August 1990)
Izz ad-Din al-Qassam Brigades

Jabotinsky, Vladimir Yevgenyevich (1880–1940)
Jadid, Salah al- (1926–1993)
Jaffa, Battle of (August 5, 1192)
Jaffa, Treaty of (September 2, 1192)
Jam, Battle of (September 24, 1528)
Janissaries
Jarring Mission (December 9, 1967–October 1973)
Jassy, Treaty of (January 9, 1792)
Jawhar (?–992)
Jeddah, Siege of (February 10–December 17, 1925)
Jenin, Battle of (April 3–11, 2002)
Jericho Conference (December 1, 1948)
Jerusalem, Capture of (December 9, 1917)
Jerusalem, Crusader Siege of (June 7–July 15, 1099)
Jerusalem, Latin Kingdom of
Jerusalem, Roman Siege of (70 CE)
Jewish Brigade
Jewish Legion
Jewish-Roman War, First (66–73 CE)
Jihad
John of Brienne (ca. 1170–1237)
Jordan
Jordan River
Joscelin I of Edessa (?–1131)
Jovian (331–364)
Judaea
Judas Maccabeus (ca. 190–130 BCE)
Julian, Emperor (331–363)
Justinian I the Great, Emperor (483–565)

Kabakchi Incident (May 25, 1807)
Kadesh, Battle of (1274 BCE)
Kafr Qasim Massacre (October 29, 1956)
Kafur, Abu al-Misk (905–968)
Kapikulu Corps
Karameh, Battle of (March 21, 1968)
Karbala, Battle of (October 10, 680)
Karbala, First Battle of (March 31–April 6, 2003)
Karbala, Second Battle of (August 27–29, 2007)

Karbala Gap
Karbugha (d. 1102)
Karim Khan Zand, Muhammad (ca. 1705–1779)
Karlowitz, Treaty of (January 26, 1699)
Kars, Battle of (August 9–19, 1745)
Kars, Treaty of (October 13, 1921)
Kassites
Khadairi Bend, Battle of (December 13, 1916–January 29, 1917)
Khafji, Battle of (January 29–February 1, 1991)
Khalid bin Sultan, Prince (1949–)
Khalid ibn al-Walid (ca. 592–642)
Khanaqin, Battle of (June 3, 1916)
Khandaq, Battle of the (January–February 627)
Khan Yunis
Kharijites
Khartoum Resolution (September 1, 1967)
Khirokitia, Battle of (July 7, 1426)
Khobar Towers Bombing (June 25, 1996)
Khomeini, Ruhollah (1900–1989)
Khosrow I Anushiravan (496?–579)
Kirkuk
Kobanî, Siege of (September 27, 2014–January 26, 2015)
Kobanî Massacre (June 25–26, 2015)
Konya, Battle of (December 21, 1832)
Köprülü Abdullah Pasha (1694–1735)
Köprülü Fazil Ahmed Pasha (1635–1676)
Köprülü Mehmed Pasha (1583?–1661)
Köse Dağ, Battle of (June 26, 1243)
Kress von Kressenstein, Friedrich Sigismund Georg (1870–1948)
Kuchuk Kainardji, Treaty of (July 21, 1774)
Kurdan, Treaty of (September 4, 1746)
Kurds
Kurds, Massacres of
Kutahya Convention (May 4, 1833)
Kut al-Amara, Siege of (December 7, 1915–April 29, 1916)
Kuwait
Kuwait, Iraqi Invasion of (August 2, 1990)
Kuwait, Iraqi Occupation of (August 2, 1990–February 27, 1991)
Kuwait, Liberation of (February 27, 1991)

Lahoud, Émile Jamil (1936–)
Latakia, Battle of (October 6, 1973)
Latrun, Battles of (May 25–July 18, 1948)
Lausanne, First Treaty of (October 18, 1912)

Lausanne, Second Treaty of (July 24, 1923)
Lavon Affair (July–December 11, 1954)
Lawrence, Thomas Edward (1888–1935)
League of Nations Covenant Article 22
Lebanon
Lebanon, First U.S. Intervention in (July 15–October 25, 1958)
Lebanon, Israeli Operations against (July 13–August 14, 2006)
Lebanon, Israeli Security Zone in
Lebanon, Second U.S. Intervention in (August 24, 1982–February 26, 1984)
Lebanon Civil War (April 13, 1975–August 1990)
Lebanon-Israeli War (June 6–September 1982)
Leilan, Battle of (November 9, 1733)
Leo III the Isaurian (ca. 680–741)
Leopold V of Austria (1157–1194)
Lepanto, Battle of (October 7, 1571)
Liberty Incident (June 8, 1967)
Libyan-Egyptian War (July 21–24, 1977)
Liman von Sanders, Otto (1855–1929)
LITANI, Operation (March 14–21, 1978)
Lod Airport Massacre (May 30, 1972)
Lohamei Herut Israel
London, 1840 Treaty of (July 15, 1840)
London, 1913 Treaty of (May 30, 1913)
London Round Table Conference (February 7–March 17, 1939)
London Straits Convention (July 13, 1841)
Long Campaign in Hungary (1443–1444)
Long War in Hungary (1593–1606)
Louis VII, King of France (1120–1180)
Louis IX, King of France (1214–1270)
Lucius Verus (130–169)
Lydia
Lysimachus (ca. 355–281 BCE)

Ma'an, Siege of (April 17–September 28, 1918)
Maccabean Revolt (167–160 BCE)
MacMichael, Sir Harold (1882–1969)
Madrid Conference (October 30–November 1, 1991)
Magnesia, Battle of (December 190 BCE)
Mahmud, Muhammad Sidqi (1923–)
Mahmud II, Sultan (1785–1839)
Majid al-Tikriti, Ali Hassan al- (1941–2010)
Makarios III, Archbishop (1913–1977)
Maliki, Nuri Muhammed Kamil al- (1950–)
Malik Shah I (1055–1092)

Mamluk-Ilkhanid Wars (1260–1323)
Mamluk-Ottoman Wars (1485–1491 and 1516–1517)
Mamluk Sultanate (1250–1517)
Mandates, League of Nations
Mansurah, Battle of (February 8–11, 1250)
Manuel I Komnenos, Emperor (1118–1180)
Manuel II Palaiologos, Emperor (1350–1425)
Manzikert, Battle of (August 26, 1071)
Marcus, David (1901–1948)
Marcus Aurelius, Emperor (121–180)
Marj Dabiq, Battle of (August 24, 1516)
Maronites
Marsh Arabs
Martyrdom
Masada
Mashal, Khaled (1956–)
Massacre at the Citadel (March 1, 1811)
Maududi, Abul A'Ala (1903–1979)
Mawdud (?–1113)
Maysalun, Battle of (July 24, 1920)
McMahon-Hussein Correspondence
Medina, Siege of (1916–1919)
Medina Ridge, Battle of (February 27, 1991)
Megiddo, Ancient Battle of (1479 BCE)
Megiddo, Battle of (September 19–21, 1918)
Mehmed Ali (1769–1849)
Mehmed II, Sultan (1432–1481)
Meir, Golda Mabovitch (1898–1978)
Mersa Matruh, First Battle of (June 26, 1942)
Mersa Matruh, Second Battle of (November 7, 1942)
Mesopotamia
Mesopotamian Theater, World War I
Michael VIII Palaiologos (1223–1282)
Miletus, Battle of (411 BCE)
Mithridates VI Eupator Dionysius (ca. 134–63 BCE)
Mithridatic Wars (89–84, 83–81, and 73–63 BCE)
Mitla Pass
Mizrahi Judaism
Mongol Invasion of the Middle East (1256–1280)
Montenegrin-Ottoman Wars (1852–1913)
Mont Giscard, Battle of (November 25, 1177)
Montgomery, Bernard Law (1887–1976)
Morrison-Grady Plan (July 31, 1946)
Morsi, Mohamed (1951–2019)
Mosul, First Battle of (November 8–16, 2004)
Mosul, Second Battle of (October 17, 2016–July 9, 2017)
"Mother of All Battles"

Moudros, Armistice of (October 30, 1918)
Mount Lebanon Civil War (1860)
Muawiyah I (602–680)
Mubarak, Hosni (1928–)
Müezzinzade Ali Pasha (?–1571)
Mughal-Safavid Wars (1622–1623 and 1648–1653)
Muhammad, Campaigns of the Prophet (622–632)
Muhammad, Prophet of Islam (ca. 569–632)
Multinational Force and Observers in the Sinai
Multi-National Force–Iraq (2004–2009)
Murad II, Sultan (1404–1451)
Murray, Sir Archibald James (1860–1945)
Muslim Brotherhood
Muslim Wars of Expansion (623–732)
Mutla Ridge (February 25–27, 1991)
Mwawi, Ahmad Ali al- (1897–ca. 1979)
Mycale, Battle of (479)
Myriokephalon, Battle of (September 17, 1176)

NACHSHON, Operation (April 5–20, 1948)
Nadir Shah (1688–1747)
Naguib, Mohammad (1901–1984)
Nahr al-Bared Refugee Camp, Siege of (May 20–September 2, 2007)
Najaf, First Battle of (August 5–27, 2004)
Najaf, Second Battle of (January 28, 2007)
Nasar, Mustafa bin Abd al-Qadir Setmariam (1958–)
Nasiriyah, Battle of (March 23–29, 2003)
Nasser, Gamal Abdel (1918–1970)
Nasuh Pasha, Treaty of (1612)
Nebuchadnezzar II (ca. 634–562 BCE)
Nelson, Horatio (1758–1805)
NEMESIS, Operation (1920–1922)
Netanyahu, Benjamin (1949–)
Nicaea, Empire of (1204–1261)
Nika Uprising (January 13–18, 532)
Nikopolis, Crusade in (1396)
Nile River
NIMBLE ARCHER, Operation (October 19, 1987)
Nineveh, Battle of (December 12, 627)
Nisibis, Battle of (217)
Nissa, Treaty of (October 3, 1739)
Nixon, Sir John Eccles (1857–1921)
Nixon Doctrine (November 3, 1969)
Nizip, Battle of (June 24, 1839)
Norfolk, Battle of (February 26–27, 1991)
NORTHERN WATCH Operation (January 1, 1997–March 17, 2003)

Nur al-Din (1118–1174)
Nuri al-Said (1888–July 15, 1958)

O'Connor, Richard Nugent (1889–1981)
Odenathus (ca. 220–268)
Olmert, Ehud (1945–)
Oman
Organization of Petroleum Exporting Countries
Osiraq Raid (June 7, 1981)
Oslo Accords (September 13, 1993)
Osman I (ca. 1254–1324/1326)
Osman Nuri Pasha (1832–1900)
Otlukbeli, Battle of (August 11, 1473)
Ottoman Empire (1299–1922)
Ottoman Empire, Entry into World War I
Ottoman Empire, Post–World War I Revolution in
Ottoman-Habsburg Wars (1529–1791)
Ottoman-Hungarian Wars (1437–1526)
Ottoman-Persian Wars of the 18th and 19th Centuries
Ottoman-Polish Wars of the 17th Century
Ottoman-Safavid Wars (1526–1639)
Outremer

Palestine, British Mandate for (1922–1948)
Palestine, Partition of
Palestine, Pre-1918 History of
Palestine and Syria Campaign, World War I (1915–1918)
Palestine Liberation Army
Palestine Liberation Front
Palestine Liberation Organization
Palestinian Islamic Jihad
Palestinian National Authority
Palmach
Palmyra
Pan-Arab Congress (September 8, 1937)
Pan-Arabism and Pan-Arabist Thought
Paraetacene, Battle of (317 BCE)
Parthian Empire (247 BCE–224 CE)
Passarowitz, Treaty of (July 21, 1718)
Patria, Destruction of (November 25, 1940)
Patrona Halil Revolt (September 28, 1730)
Peel Commission (August 1936–July 7, 1937)
Pelagius of Albano (ca. 1165–1230)
Pelekanon, Battle of (June 10–11, 1329)
Pelusium, Battle of (525 BCE)
Perdiccas (365–321 BCE)
Pergamum
Persia, Arab Conquest of (642–671)

Persia, 18th-Century Wars of Succession
Persian Cossack Brigade
Persian Front, World War I
Persian Gulf
Persian Gulf War, Air Campaign (January 17–February 28, 1991)
Persian Gulf War, Cease-Fire Agreement (April 6, 1991)
Persian Gulf War, Ground Campaign (February 24–28, 1991)
Persian Gulf War, Naval Operations (January 17–February 28, 1991)
Persian Gulf War, Overview (January 17–February 28, 1991)
Peshmerga
Peter the Hermit (1050?–1115)
Petraeus, David Howell (1952–)
PHANTOM STRIKE, Operation (August 15, 2007–January 2008)
PHANTOM THUNDER, Operation (June 16–August 14, 2007)
Pharnabazus (?–ca. 370 BCE)
Phase Line Bullet, Battle of (February 26, 1991)
Philippe II, King (1165–1223)
Philomelion, Battle of (1116)
Phoenicia
Pompeius Magnus, Gnaeus (106–48 BCE)
Pontus (281 BCE–62 CE)
Popular Front for the Liberation of Palestine
Popular Front for the Liberation of Palestine–General Command
Popular Front for the Liberation of the Occupied Arabian Gulf
Portuguese Colonial Wars in Arabia (1507–1650)
PRAYING MANTIS, Operation (April 18, 1988)
PRIME CHANCE, Operation (1987–1989)
PROVIDE COMFORT, Operation (1991)
Pruth, Treaty of (July 23, 1711)
Ptolemaic Kingdom (305–30 BCE)
Ptolemy Ceraunus (ca. 320–279 BCE)
Ptolemy I Soter (367–282 BCE)
Ptolemy II Philadelphus (308–246 BCE)
Ptolemy III Euergetes (r. 246–221 BCE)
Ptolemy IV Philopator (ca. 244–205 BCE)
Ptolemy V Epiphanes (ca. 210–180)
Ptolemy VI Philometor (ca. 186–145 BCE)
Pyramids, Battle of the (July 21, 1798)

Qaboos bin Said al-Said (1940–)
Qadisiyya, Battle of (November 16–19, 636)
Qalawun (ca. 1222–1290)
Qarmatians
Qasim, Abdul Karim (1914–1963)
Qassam, Izz ad-Din al- (1882–1935)
Qatar
Qawuqji, Fawzi al- (1890–1976)
Qibya Massacre (October 14, 1953)
Qilij Arslan I of Rum (1079–1107)
Qilij Arslan II of Rum (ca. 1115–1192)
Quran
Qurna, Battle of (December 4–9, 1915)
Qutb, Sayyid Ibrahim Husayn Shadhili (1906–1966)
Quwatli, Shukri al- (1891–1967)

Rabat Summit (October 26–29, 1974)
Rabin, Yitzhak (1922–1995)
Rafah Tunnels
Ramadi, Fall of (November 21, 2014–May 17, 2015)
Ramadi, First Battle of (April 6–10, 2004)
Ramadi, Recapture of (November 25, 2015–February 9, 2016)
Ramadi, Second Battle of (June 17–November 15, 2006)
Ramesses II the Great (ca. 1303–1213 BCE)
Ramla, First Battle of (September 7, 1101)
Ramla, Second Battle of (May 17, 1102)
Ramla, Third Battle of (August 27, 1105)
Raphia, Battle of (June 22, 217 BCE)
Reagan Plan (September 1, 1982)
Red Sea
Reform Judaism and Zionism
Regime Change, Iraq War
Religious Sites in the Middle East, Christian
Religious Sites in the Middle East, Jewish
Religious Sites in the Middle East, Muslim
Republican Guard, Iraq
Resht, Treaty of (February 1, 1732)
Revisionist Zionism
Reza Shah Pahlavi (1878–1944)
Rhodes, Demetrius's Siege of (305–304 BCE)
Rhodes, Suleiman's Siege of (July 28–December 21, 1522)
Richard I, King (1157–1199)
Richard of Cornwall (1209–1272)
Ridda Wars (632–633)
Right of Return, Palestinian
Rogers Plan (December 9, 1969)
Rognvald Kali Kolsson (ca. 1099–1158)
Romani, Battle of (August 4–5, 1916)
Roman-Parthian Wars (53 BCE–215 CE)

Roman-Sassanid Wars (232–440)
Rommel, Erwin Johannes Eugen (1891–1944)
Rum, Sultanate of (1080–1307)
Russo-Ottoman Wars (1676–1911)
Russo-Persian Wars (1722–1911)

Saadabad Pact (July 8, 1937)
Sabra and Shatila Massacre (September 16–18, 1982)
Sadat, Anwar (1918–1981)
Saddam Line, Persian Gulf War
Sadeh, Yitzhak (1890–1952)
Sadr, Muqtada al- (1973–)
Sadr City, Battle of (March 26–May 11, 2008)
Safavid Dynasty (1501–1722 and 1729–1736)
Saif al-Dawla (926–967)
Sakarya, Battle of the (August 23–September 13, 1921)
Saladin (1138–1193)
Salafism
Saleh, Ali Abdullah (1942–2017)
Samawah, Battle of (March 30–April 4, 2003)
Samita Incident (December 1972–April 1973)
Samu Raid, West Bank (November 13, 1966)
Sanchez, Ricardo S. (1951–)
San Remo Conference (April 19–26, 1920)
San Stefano, Treaty of (March 3, 1878)
Saracen
Sargon of Akkad (ca. 2350–2279 BCE)
Sarikamish, Battle of (December 22, 1914–January 17, 1915)
Sassanid Empire (224–651)
Saudi Arabia
Saudi-Hashemite War (1919–1925)
Saudi King as Custodian of the Two Holy Mosques
Saudi-Kuwaiti War (1921–1922)
Saudi-Ottoman War (1911–1913)
Saudi-Rashidi Wars (1887–1921)
Saudi-Yemeni War (1934)
SCATHE MEAN, Operation (January 17, 1991)
Schwarzkopf, H. Norman, Jr. (1934–2012)
SCORPION, Operation
Seleucid Empire (312–63 BCE)
Seleucus I Nicator (ca. 358–281 BCE)
Selim I, Sultan (1470–1520)
Selim III, Sultan (1761–1808)
Seljuk Dynasty (1016–1153)
Seljuk War of Succession (1092–1105)
Sennacherib (?–681 BCE)
Sephardic Judaism

September 11, 2001, Attacks on the United States
Septimius Severus, Emperor (ca. 145–211)
Serbian-Ottoman War (1876)
Settlements, Israeli
73 Easting, Battle of (February 26, 1991)
Sèvres, Treaty of (August 10, 1920)
Shakur, Yusuf bin Raghib (1928–)
Shallah, Ramadan Abdullah Mohammad (1958–)
Shamir, Yitzhak (1915–2012)
Shapur I the Great (ca. 215–270)
Shapur II the Great (309–379)
Sharia
Sharm El Sheikh
Sharon, Ariel (1928–2014)
Shatt al-Arab Waterway
Shaw Commission (August 1929–March 31, 1930)
Shazly, Saad el- (1922–2011)
Shia Islam
Shiqaqi, Fathi (1951–1995)
Shishakli, Adib al- (1909–1964)
Shomron, Dan (1937–2008)
Shultz Plan (March 4, 1988)
Siffin, Battle of (July 26–28, 657)
Sinai Campaign of 1916–1917 (March 1916–January 1917)
Sinai Campaign of 1956 (October 29–November 6, 1956)
Sinai I and Sinai II Agreements (January 19 and September 4, 1974)
Sinai Peninsula
Siniura, Fuad (1943–)
Sinope, Battle of (November 30, 1853)
Sisi, Abdel Fattah el- (1954–)
Sistani, Sayyid Ali Hisayn al- (1930–)
Six-Day War (June 5–10, 1967)
Smyrna Crusade (1344–1348)
SOUTHERN WATCH, Operation (1992–2003)
South Lebanon Army
South Yemen Civil War (January 13–24, 1986)
Special Night Squads
Special Republican Guards
Stark Incident (May 17, 1987)
STEEL CURTAIN, Operation (November 5–22, 2005)
Stern, Avraham (1907–1942)
St. Petersburg, Treaty of (September 12, 1723)
Strait of Tiran Crisis (1956–1967)
St. Sabas, War of (1256–1270)
Suez Canal

Suez Canal, World War I Ottoman Operations against
Suez Canal and Egypt, World War II Campaigns for Control of (1940–1942)
Suez Crisis (July 26, 1956–March 6, 1957)
Suicide Bombings
Suleiman I (1494–1566)
Sumer
Sunni Islam
Sunni Triangle
Sykes-Picot Agreement (May 16, 1916)
Syria
Syria and Lebanon Campaign (June 8–July 14, 1941)
Syrian Civil War (March 25, 2011–)
Syrian-Egyptian Wars (274–168 BCE)
Syrian-Roman War (192–188 BCE)

Taalat Pasha, Mehmed (1874–1921)
Tahmasp I, Shah (1514–1576)
Taif Accords (October 22, 1989)
Taji Bunkers, Attacks on (January 17–February 27, 1991)
Talmud
Tamerlane (1336–1405)
Tammuz I Reactor
Tancred (ca. 1076–1112)
Tanzimat
Task Force Normandy (January 17, 1991)
Tehran Treaty (November 25, 1814)
Tel el-Kebir, Battle of (September 13, 1882)
Ten Thousand, March of the (401–399 BCE)
Terrorism
Thani, Khalifa bin Hamad al- (1932–2016)
Theodore I Laskaris (ca. 1174–1221)
Thutmose III, Pharaoh (ca. 1504–1425 BCE)
Thymbra, Battle of (546 BCE)
Tiglath-Pileser I (?–1077 BCE)
Tiglath-Pileser III (?–727 BCE)
Tigris and Euphrates Valley
Tigris River
Titus, Emperor (39–81)
Townshend, Sir Charles Vere Ferrers (1861–1924)
Trajan (53–117)
Transjordan Campaign (1918)
Trebizond, Empire of (1204–1461)
Tripartite Declaration (May 25, 1950)
Tripoli, County of
Troop Surge, U.S., Iraq War

Troy, Siege of (1194–1184 BCE)
Turan Shah (?–1250)
Turcopoles
Turkey
Turki ibn Abdullah, Campaigns of (1823–1833)
Turkish-Armenian War (1920)
Tutush I (1066–1095)
Tuwaitha Nuclear Facility
Tyre and Gaza, Sieges of (332 BCE)

Umayyad Caliphate (661–750)
Umm Qasr, Battle of (March 21–23, 2003)
United Arab Emirates
United Arab Republic (1958–1961)
United Nations Palestine Partition Plan (November 29, 1947)
United Nations Special Commission on Palestine (May 13–August 31, 1947)
Uzun Hasan (1425–1478)

Valens, Emperor (ca. 328–378 CE)
Valerian, Emperor (ca. 193–260/264)
Valley of Tears, Battle of the (October 6–9, 1973)
Varna Crusade (1444)
Vasvár, Treaty of (August 10, 1664)
Venetian-Ottoman Wars (1416–1718)
Vespasian, Emperor (9–79)
VIGILANT WARRIOR, Operation (October 8, 1994–December 8, 1994)
VIKING HAMMER, Operation (March 28–30, 2003)

Wadi al-Batin, Battle of (February 26, 1991)
Wahhabism
War of Attrition (July 1969–August 1970)
Wauchope, Sir Arthur Grenfell (1874–1947)
West Bank
White Paper of 1922 (June 3, 1922)
White Paper of 1930 (October 31, 1930)
White Paper of 1939 (May 17, 1939)
Wingate, Orde Charles (1903–1944)
Woodhead Report (November 9, 1938)
World War I, Impact on the Middle East
World War II, Impact on the Middle East
Wye River Agreement (October 23, 1998)

Xenophon (ca. 431–ca. 354 BCE)
Xerxes I (519–465 BCE)

Yarmouk River, Battle of (August 15–20, 636)
Yazidis
Yemen
Yemen, Civil War in the North (1962–1970)
Yemen, Civil War in the South (May 4–July 7, 1994)
Yemen Civil War (2015–Present)
Yemen Hotel Bombings (December 29, 1992)
Yemenite War (February 24–March 19, 1979)
Yom Kippur War (October 6–25, 1973)
Young Turks
Yudenich, Nikolai Nikolaevich (1862–1933)

Zab, Battle of (February 26, 750)
Zangi, Imad ad-Din (1084/1085–1146)
Zanj Slave Revolts
Zarqawi, Abu Musab al- (1966–2006)
Zayed bin Sultan Al Nahyan (1918–2004)
Zenobia (240–274?)
Zionism
Zoroastrianism
Zsitvatorok, Peace of (November 11, 1606)
Zuhab, Treaty of (May 17, 1639)
Zuravno, Treaty of (October 16, 1676)

List of Maps

General Maps
Ancient Near East, ca. 1400 BCE
The East, ca. 600 BCE
Middle East, 1945–1990

Entry Maps
Battle of the Nile, August 1, 1798
Naval Battle of Actium, September 2, 31 BCE
The Empire of Alexander the Great
Drive on Baghdad, March 20–April 12, 2003
Bahrain
Byzantine Empire, 1355
Siege of Constantinople, April 6–May 29, 1453
The Crusades
Cyprus
Egypt
Ancient Egypt
Gallipoli Campaign, April 25, 1915–January 9, 1916
Persian Empire, ca. 500 BCE
Greece during the Persian Wars
Iran
Iraq
Israel
Israeli War of Independence, 1948–1949
Jordan
Kuwait
Lebanon
Expansion of Islam, 814
Oman
Expansion of the Ottoman Empire, 1361–1571
Asia Minor in 189 BCE
Israel and Phoenicia, 860 BCE
Qatar
Saudi Arabia
Balance of Forces, May 14–24, 1967
Syria
Battle of Tel el-Kebir, September 13, 1882
Turkey
United Arab Emirates
Yemen

Preface

The Middle East traditionally has included the areas of Iran (Persia), Asia Minor, Mesopotamia, the Levant, the Arabian Peninsula, and Egypt. In modern-day country terms these areas embrace Bahrain, Cyprus, Egypt, Iran, Iraq, Israel (including the occupied territories), Jordan, Kuwait, Lebanon, Oman, Qatar, Saudi Arabia, Syria, Turkey, the United Arab Emirates, and Yemen. This is an immense geographic area with a considerable history, and word count constraints, even in a multivolume work, have necessitated some parameters.

I have therefore not been able to include entries on weapons, armies, and tactics. The encyclopedia is not limited specifically to leaders, wars, and battles, however. Geography, climate, and topography have played important roles in warfare in the Middle East. These topics are covered here, with entries on specific choke points and key geographical features such as the Strait of Hormuz, the Shatt al-Arab waterway, the Strait of Tiran, and the Suez Canal. And with religion central to much of the conflict in the region, there are also entries on the important religions and sects as well as on the most important religious shrines for Christianity, Judaism, and Islam. Key political figures, diplomacy, and treaties are also included, as these relate to warfare.

The encyclopedia begins chronologically with the Sumerians of Mesopotamia, the land between the rivers and present-day Iraq, which is regarded by most scholars as the cradle of civilization. Because the encyclopedia is limited specifically to the Middle East, I have elected to cover warfare involving the Middle Eastern powers that carries into territories outside the Middle East but not to have separate entries on battles that are beyond the Middle East geographically. Thus, the Battle of Marathon in 490 BCE, so important for the development of Western civilization, is included in the entry on the Greco-Persian Wars but not as a separate battle entry. Conversely, the major battles in the Middle East fought by Alexander III of Macedon, a non–Middle Eastern actor, are covered although not his battles in India, launched from Persian territory.

The country entries on the 16 individual states comprising the Middle East today provide important context with an overview of that nation's history but emphasize the 20th century and contemporary events in some detail. They also provide such information as population figures, religious composition, and an overview of their political structures and have longer lists of reference works. The reader will probably find it useful to delve into these first or to refer to them subsequently when reading related material.

Individuals, however great, who might have played a major role in the history of the Middle East but outside its territory and nearby waters are not covered here. Thus, the great Byzantine general Narses, who campaigned with such success in Italy, is omitted here, as is the great Athenian leader Themistocles, who defeated the Persians in the decisive naval Battle of Salamis in 480 BCE.

Events outside the Middle East are generally not covered simply because of space constraints. Thus, various peace plans advanced by governments apart from the Middle East are often omitted. The Holocaust and the September 11 attacks on the United States are included, however, because of the tremendous impact they have had in shaping today's Middle East.

I have chosen to use the name "Persia" throughout rather than "Iran" for the earlier period until 1935, when the government in Tehran requested that those countries with which it had diplomatic relations call Persia "Iran," the name of the country in Persian.

I am very grateful to Professor Priscilla Roberts for her usual fine work in the documents volume and to Dr. Paul Pierpaoli Jr. of ABC-CLIO for helping me with the entry list and writing a number of entries. I very much hope that the encyclopedia will prove a useful reference work and instructive to those seeking to understand this immensely important part of the world.

Because of time constraints necessary on bringing such an extensive work as this encyclopedia to publication, I was forced to end most contemporary entries with the beginning of 2019.

SPENCER C. TUCKER

Introduction

The Middle East has been called the cradle of civilization. The region saw the first city-states, kingdoms, and empires. Three of the world's great religions—Judaism, Islam, and Christianity—originated in the region, and the Middle East also produced the world's first intensive agriculture, the first writing, the first centralized governments, and the first law codes. The Middle East has made numerous important contributions to the arts, architecture, mathematics, and astronomy. The region also witnessed the first rigid societal stratification and slavery and the first wars between states. In warfare the Middle East experienced the first battle recorded by an eyewitness and saw numerous military innovations, such as the introduction of the horse-drawn chariot. The region has also experienced more than its share of conflict and warfare, which continues there today. Certainly the region as a whole is one of the world's most dangerous hot spots.

The term "Middle East" may have originated with the British India Office in the 1850s, but it can certainly be credited to U.S. Navy strategist Rear Admiral Alfred Thayer Mahan, who employed the term in an article in 1902 to designate the region between Arabia and India. "Middle East" has been in general use since the 1930s, when the British military established its Middle East Command in Cairo.

The actual area encompassed by the term has fluctuated. Today the Middle East is said to extend from Turkey in the north to Yemen and the Persian Gulf states in the south and from Egypt and Cyprus in the west to Syria and Lebanon in the east. Put simply, the Middle East may be thought of as Western Asia without the Caucasus and Egypt without the rest of North Africa, known as the Maghreb. The Middle East encompasses 16 states: Bahrain, Cyprus, Egypt, Iran, Iraq, Israel (including the occupied territories), Jordan, Kuwait, Lebanon, Oman, Qatar, Saudi Arabia, Syria, Turkey, the United Arab Emirates, and Yemen. The administration of President George W. Bush employed the term "Greater Middle East," which harked back to some earlier usages that included Pakistan and Afghanistan.

Göbekli Tepe in present-day southeastern Anatolia is the earliest discovered Neolithic sanctuary. Dating to about 10,000 BCE, it also boasts the world's oldest megaliths. The first human settlements are at Nevali Cori, also in Turkey, and date from circa 8400–8100. The peoples of the Middle East were also the first to enter the Bronze Age (ca. 3300–1200) and the Iron Age (ca. 1200–500).

Early civilizations developed around bodies of water, and in the case of the Middle East it was the Tigris and Euphrates Rivers in Mesopotamia and the Nile in Egypt. Around 6000 BCE these areas saw the first systematic irrigation and flood control, while the world's earliest civilization was that of the Sumerians in present-day southern Iraq about 3500. The Sumerians gave the world its first written language.

The first wheeled vehicles date from about 3500, as do the first Egyptian cities. Around 3150, Lower and Upper Egypt were united into one kingdom in the First Dynasty. Dates for dynasties in the ancient world vary widely depending on source, but the three high points of Egyptian civilization were the Old Kingdom (2686–2181), the Middle Kingdom (2055–1650), and the New Kingdom (1550–1069). Ancient Egypt ended in the Late Period (664–332 BCE) and its conquest by Alexander III the Great of Macedon. Ptolemaic Egypt began in 305 and ended in 30 BCE, when it fell to Julius Caesar and Rome.

Contemporaneous with that of ancient Egypt, civilizations developed in the so-called Fertile Crescent (the land between the Tigris and Euphrates Rivers in Mesopotamia), the Levant (the area of the eastern Mediterranean), and Anatolia. In the Levant these included the kingdoms of Israel and Judah, among many others. Phoenician civilization, comprising a number of city-states, also developed along the eastern coast.

Sargon the Great founded the Akkadian Empire of 2334–2154. All the Akkadian-speaking Mesopotamian Semites (as well as the Sumerians) came under the rule of the city-state of Akkad in central Mesopotamia. Most notable for its military prowess were the Old Assyrian Empire of 2025–1378 and the Neo-Assyrian Empire of 912–612. At its peak the Assyrian Empire was the largest in history to that point, controlling the territory of present-day Iraq, Syria, Lebanon, Israel, Palestine, Kuwait, Jordan, Egypt, Cyprus, and Bahrain as well as large swaths of Iran, Turkey, Armenia, Georgia, Sudan, and Arabia.

Brutal in war, with captured soldiers tortured and slain and cities destroyed, Assyria nonetheless allowed its conquered peoples considerable autonomy, providing tribute was paid promptly. This loose administrative system fostered rebellion and the need to repeatedly conquer the subject states. In the end, the nearly constant wars deleted Assyrian manpower and diluted the quality of Assyrian military because the Assyrians lacked sufficient manpower on their own and found it necessary to utilize foreign levies to garrison and control the vast empire.

Other states in the region ultimately challenged Assyrian rule. These included the Babylonian and Persian Empires. The Old Babylonian Empire held sway circa 1894–911 BCE, while the Neo-Babylonian Empire (Chaldean Empire) of 626–539 formed an alliance with the Chaldeans and the Iranian peoples of the Medes, Persians, Sagartians, and Parthians to bring finis to the Assyrian Empire with the capture and sack of Nineveh in 612.

In 538 BCE, however, Cyrus II of Media, who had established himself as king of all Persia, invaded Babylonia and captured Babylon. The Persians then took Egypt. This Achaemenid Empire (First Persian Empire) of 550–330 BCE was in turn conquered by Alexander III, king of Macedon. Alexander died young, and his lieutenants (the Diadochi, or Successors) were soon at war with one another (323–275 BCE). Although Alexander's empire was broken up (two large components were the Ptolemaic Empire of Egypt and the Seleucid Empire in Western Asia), they did, however, complete his work of Hellenizing the region.

The next major Middle Eastern powers were both centered on Persia: the Parthian Empire (Arsacid Empire) of 247 BCE–224 CE and the Sassanid Empire of 224–651 CE. From the first century BCE the Middle East was dominated by Romans, Parthians, and Sassanids, who for much of the time were at war with one another until the seventh century.

In the first century BCE, Rome took possession of the entire eastern Mediterranean (Julius Caesar conquered Egypt in 47 BCE). Greek culture, which the Romans had largely absorbed, continued to predominate. Egypt became the empire's breadbasket for its production of grain. Christianity was the dominant religion.

In 330 Emperor Constantine I (the Great), already sole ruler of the Roman Empire, transferred its capital from Rome to the city of Byzantium (popularly known as Constantinople). This date is held by many historians to mark the beginning of the Byzantine Empire, which lasted until 1453. At its greatest territorial extent in 555 under Emperor Justinian I, the empire included the former western half of the old Roman Empire, with Italy, parts of southern Spain and France, all of the Mediterranean islands, North Africa, Egypt, the Levant, Anatolia, and the Balkans.

Centuries of warfare between the Byzantines and Sassanids, however, weakened both empires and aided the emergence in the seventh century of a new power in the Arabs. Strongly motivated by their Islamic faith, the Arab armies swept over the region, completing the conquest of Persia and seizing perhaps half of the Byzantine territory, including—with the aid of the Bulgarians—much of Anatolia. The Arab armies also swept across North Africa and absorbed Spain, although they were halted in their drive north into Western Europe as a consequence of the Battle of Tours in Gaul in 732. The Arab caliphates were in fact the first to control the entire Middle East.

In the 11th century the Seljuk Turks (their dynasty lasted from 1016 to 1153) arrived from Central Asia. They conquered Persia, Iraq, Syria, Palestine, and the Hejaz. Egypt held out under the Fatimid caliphs until 1169, when it too fell to the Seljuks. Despite its considerable earlier territorial losses to the Arabs, the Byzantine Empire had remained a major military force. The subsequent Seljuk defeat of the

Byzantines and ensuing control of much of Anatolia marked the beginning of the end of Byzantine influence in the region, although the Seljuk Empire broke up into a number of smaller sultanates.

Motivated by religion, trade, and territorial ambition, during 1096–1291 the rulers of much of Christian Europe launched a series of military efforts to seize the Christian shrines of the Holy Land from Muslim control. Although the crusaders captured Jerusalem in 1099 and established a series of small Christian enclaves in the Levant, these were soon lost again. Regardless of this failure, the clash of the Christian and Muslim civilizations had profound impacts on both.

In the early 13th century a new wave of Asiatic invaders, the Mongols, swept through the region. They sacked Baghdad in 1258 and reached Egypt, where they were defeated in the Battle of Ayn Jalut by the army of the Mamluk Sultanate (1250–1517), which had recently taken power in Egypt.

It was not Egypt but rather a new state that would dominate the Middle East. Established in 1299 by Osman I, ruler of a small Turkic state in Anatolia, the Ottoman Empire was by far the major power in the region until after World War I. Already having made serious inroads into the Balkans, after several earlier failures and now led by the young sultan Suleiman I, in 1453 the Ottomans ended what remained an empire in name alone by taking the Byzantine capital of Constantinople (the city was then renamed Istanbul).

The Ottomans steadily expanded their holdings. Syria was taken in 1516 and Egypt in 1517, with the empire reaching the zenith of its power and territorial extent during the 16th and 17th centuries, when it controlled a vast swath of the Mediterranean basin including Asia Minor, the Balkans, much of Hungary, North Africa, and the Middle East. Indeed, for the first time since the Abbasid Caliphate in the 10th century, the entire Middle East was under one ruler.

Ottoman reform efforts largely failed to arrest a steady decline, however, as the empire was buffeted by outside forces. By 1700 the Ottomans had been driven out of Hungary, and considerable areas in the Balkans were never fully converted to Islam. The rise of European nationalism played a major role, and aided by Russia, in the 19th century Greece, Serbia, Romania, and Bulgaria all became independent. Although the Ottomans were aided by Britain, France, and the Kingdom of Sardinia (Sardinia-Piedmont) in the Crimean War of 1853–1856 that blocked Russian efforts to secure control of the Dardanelles Straits, this success proved short-lived. Russia returned to defeat the Ottomans in the Russo-Turkish War of 1877–1878, and the first Balkan War of 1912–1913 saw the Ottomans driven from the Balkans altogether except for Istanbul and its hinterland.

Much of the remaining Ottoman holdings outside of Anatolia were also lost. The French annexed Algeria in 1830 and Tunisia in 1878. The Ottomans had ceded Cyprus to the British in 1878, and in 1882 the British invaded Egypt on the pretext of quashing a revolt there, although Egypt (and Cyprus) remained under nominal Ottoman suzerainty until 1914. Control of Egypt was immensely important to Britain, as its trade with India now passed by way of the Suez Canal, opened in 1869. Not to be left out, Italy took Libya and the Dodecanese Islands as a consequence of its victory in the Italo-Ottoman War of 1911–1912. The British also established effective control of the Persian Gulf, and the French extended their influence in the Levant.

During 1905–1911 the Persian Constitutional Revolution (Constitutional Revolution of Iran) occurred, leading to the establishment of a parliament. In the Ottoman Empire, the losses sustained in the First Balkan War greatly discredited the sultan and led reformers known as the Young Turks, who had already forced the establishment of a constitution and parliament there, to seize power in a coup d'état in January 1913. In November 1914 a triumvirate of new Ottoman leaders took the empire into World War I on the side of Germany.

A major development in the Middle East was the discovery of oil, first in Persia in 1908 and then in 1938 in Saudi Arabia but also subsequently in other Persian Gulf states as well as Libya and Algeria. The Middle East was found to possess the world's largest easily accessible crude oil reserves. The leaders of the oil states used the immense wealth thus generated to consolidate their hold on power. Western dependence on oil and the decline of British influence also brought growing American interest in the region. Initially Western oil companies pumped and exported nearly all of the oil, but this shifted after World War II when Arab nationalists demanded control, and the Organization of Petroleum Exporting Countries (OPEC), established in 1960, came to exert considerable influence over the Western economies.

World War I meanwhile had immense impact on the Middle East. Although Ottoman leaders entered the war with high hopes of expanding their territory, this was soon dashed. Some notable successes were registered against the British and French in the Dardanelles and Gallipoli Campaigns, in Mesopotamia, and—late in the war after the Russian Revolution—in Armenia and Azerbaijan. These accomplishments were overshadowed by failed expeditions against the Suez Canal and British Empire victories in Mesopotamia and the Levant. The Ottoman government was also guilty of undertaking genocidal policies against the Armenians, who sought independence.

The British government actively encouraged and supported the Arab Revolt (1916–1918) against the Ottomans during World War I, with the promise of the creation of an Arab state, while at the same time in the Balfour Declaration pledging its support for a Jewish homeland in Palestine. The British and French were actively double-dealing, for in the secret 1916 Sykes-Picot Agreement they reached agreement to carve up the Ottoman Arab territories among themselves. There was little military activity in Persia, but in 1921 with the Soviet Red Army attempting to seize power, the British, who then had a substantial presence, elevated Reza Khan to command the Cossack Brigade. He ended the Russian threat, overthrew the government in Tehran, and in 1925 became Reza Shah, inaugurating the Pahlavi dynasty.

British, French, and Greek troops occupied Ottoman territory at the end of the war. The Greeks hoped to cut away Smyrna in western Anatolia, home to a great many Greeks. In the 1919–1922 Greco-Turkish War (or as it is known in Turkey, the War of Turkish Independence), the Turks defeated a Greek offensive into eastern Anatolia and ultimately forced the Greeks to evacuate Anatolia altogether. In 1920 the Turks also defeated the Armenians. In 1922 the new government abolished the sultanate, and on October 29, 1923, the Republic of Turkey was officially proclaimed, with Ankara as its capital.

With the defeat of the Ottomans in the war, Britain and France soon established control and rearranged the Middle East to suit themselves. Syria and Lebanon became French protectorates, or mandates, under the League of Nations, while the British secured Palestine (Transjordan, later simply Jordan, was subsequently split off) and Iraq, also as mandates. Meanwhile, in a series of wars beginning in 1918 British ally Ibn Saud defeated the Hashemites and created the Kingdom of Saudi Arabia in 1932.

Palestine became a major problem for the British, for the Arab majority vehemently opposed the arrival there of Jewish immigrants and their purchase of property, financed by wealthy European Jews, from absentee Arab landowners. By the 1930s this had led to considerable violence and a three-way conflict involving the British, militant Jews, and Arab nationalists, culminating in the Arab Revolt of 1936–1939.

Violence also occurred elsewhere as Middle Eastern peoples sought to throw off foreign rule, notably in Egypt and Syria. In the latter, French forces had to be called in but defeated the nationalists in the Battle of Maysalun (July 24, 1920). Iraqi nationalists also revolted against British rule and were crushed, largely by British airpower. In 1922 the British supposedly granted Egypt independence, but little changed there. Indeed, a 1936 treaty gave the British the right to maintain troops in Egypt to protect the Suez Canal.

During World War II, Egypt was a major base for British military operations. A nationalist coup in Iraq in 1941 saw Germany actively supporting the new Axis-aligned Iraqi government, leading to British military intervention that ended the new government. British and Free French forces then invaded Vichy France–controlled Syria and Lebanon, which had been the conduit for planned German military assistance to Iraq. In September 1941 the British and Soviets forced the abdication of Reza Shah in Iran, who had declared Iranian neutrality and had refused to permit Iran to be used as a military staging area. British and Soviet forces then occupied much of that country to protect Allied supply lines to the Soviet Union. U.S. forces also became involved. During the war and afterward British warships turned away ships carrying European Jews seeking to reach Palestine to escape the Holocaust.

World War II marked the end of the era of European colonialism, although some of the colonial powers were slow to come to this realization. Lebanon became independent in November 1943, Syria in January 1944, and Jordan in May 1946. Iraq secured its independence in 1947 and Egypt in 1947, when British forces were withdrawn into the Suez Canal Zone. Pressure from the new United Nations (UN) also helped force a Soviet withdrawal from northern Iran.

In Palestine the British tried to work out a partition agreement that would see the creation of Jewish and Arab states, but this agreement and one advanced by the UN both failed. London then simply announced a date for the end of its mandate. Immediately upon the British departure, the Jews on May 14, 1948, proclaimed establishment of the new State of Israel, and the Arab states declared war against it. The Jews won the war, although the Arab states refused to recognize Israeli independence. The war also saw the exodus—both self-imposed and forced—of some 800,000 Palestinians from land in the new State of Israel and their relocation to refugee camps in the Arab lands. The right of the Palestinians to return to their land and territorial issues have continued to be stumbling blocks to peace between Israel and many of the Arab states to this day.

In 1960 Britain granted Cyprus independence, but tensions between Greeks, minority Turks, and the first president of the Republic of Cyprus, Greek Orthodox archbishop

Makarios III, who increasingly advanced his own interests, brought fighting. This in turn led to the decision by the junta then ruling Greece to strengthen their waning prestige by annexing the island. This brought a Turkish invasion of Cyprus in 1974. The Turks then forced out many Greeks and took control of a larger share of the island's territory, a situation that remains to the present.

With the departure of France and Britain from the Middle East, the United States and the Soviet Union vied for influence, with the United States endeavoring to balance the fact that it was the chief supporter of Israel while also being the major foreign player in the growing Middle East oil industry. Meanwhile, in the 1950s–1960s revolutions occurred throughout the region, with Arab nationalist regimes taking power in Egypt in 1952, Syria in 1963, Iraq in 1968, and Libya in 1969. Seeking to take advantage, the Soviet Union became a major arms supplier for these new regimes, including those of strongmen Gamal Abdel Nasser in Egypt, Hafez al-Assad in Syria, and Saddam Hussein in Iraq.

Concern in the West over growing Soviet influence led the United States to push the formation in 1955 of the Central Treaty Organization (CENTO), known as the Baghdad Pact. CENTO involved Iran, Iraq, Pakistan, Turkey, and the United Kingdom but was dissolved in 1979.

In 1956 the Suez Crisis erupted. Nasser had pledged to build a high dam at Aswan on the Nile as part of his economic development program for Egypt, but the Western powers withdrew funding when he made substantial arms purchases from the Soviet bloc. Nasser's response was to nationalize the Suez Canal. This led the governments of Britain, France, and Israel to conclude a secret agreement whereby Israeli forces would invade the Sinai, while Britain and France would intervene militarily with the supposed intent to protect the Suez Canal but in reality to topple Nasser and reassert control over the canal. The ensuing Suez Crisis was one of the greatest of the Cold War, but strong U.S. financial pressure on Britain brought the withdrawal of the invaders, which strengthened Nasser.

Events in 1967 were extremely consequential for the Middle East. Having lent strong support of terrorist raids against Israel, Nasser believed a false Soviet report that Israel was mobilizing forces on the Syrian border. He then endeavored to bluff the Israelis to back down but went too far in his closure of the Strait of Tiran to Israeli shipping. The Israelis then mounted a preemptive strike. The resulting Six-Day War of June 5–10 fundamentally changed the Middle East. Involving Israeli forces against Egypt, Syria, and Jordan, it saw the Israelis seize substantial Arab-held territory in the Sinai, East Jerusalem, the West Bank of the Jordan River, the Gaza Strip, and the Golan Heights. These territorial acquisitions would make reaching a peace settlement in the Middle East infinitely more difficult.

Nasser died in 1970. His successor as Egyptian president, Anwar Sadat, was determined to end the status quo and in the Yom Kippur War (Ramadan War) of October 6–25, 1973 did just that. The Israelis were taken by surprise when Egyptian forces crossed the Suez Canal and Syrian troops invaded the Golan Heights. After hard fighting the war was brought to a close under international pressure, with Israeli forces in position to inflict major damage on their opponents, but Sadat had proven his point. He later traveled to Israel and concluded a peace settlement that saw Israeli forces withdrawn from the Sinai in 1979.

In the 1970s the Palestinians, led by Yasser Arafat's Palestine Liberation Organization (PLO), resorted to a prolonged campaign of violence against Israel but also against American, Jewish, and Western targets. The goals were to weaken Israeli resolve and undermine Western support for Israel.

In addition to its staunch support of Israel, the United States strongly supported Iranian ruler Mohammad Reza Shah Pahlavi, seeing him as a bulwark against the Soviet Union. Indeed, when he was briefly toppled in August 1953, the U.S. Central Intelligence Agency and British intelligence orchestrated a coup that restored him to power. Although the shah embarked on a reform program, this largely failed, and anger against the West helped drive him from power in the 1979 Islamic Revolution. The new Islamic Republic of Iran, proclaimed on April 1, 1979, by Ayatollah Ruhollah Khomeini, saw Shiite clergy running Iranian affairs. Iran was now strongly anti-Western. The United States was forced into close alliance with Sunni Muslim Saudi Arabia, the Persian Gulf states, Egypt, and Jordan. Syria, ruled by Shiite-associated Alawite Muslims, drew closer to Iran and the Soviet Union, which secured a naval base on Syrian territory on the Mediterranean.

The impasse over the Israeli-Palestinian issue continued. Continued military actions by the PLO from Lebanon led to an Israeli invasion of southern Lebanon and the Lebanon-Israeli War of 1982 that culminated in a siege of Beirut and the departure of the PLO for Tunis. This did not bring peace, however, for the Islamist Hezbollah organization in Lebanon continued actions against Israel.

Meanwhile, by 1979 Saddam Hussein controlled Iraqi affairs. Seeking to take advantage of disorder in Iran following its Islamic revolution, in 1980 he sent Iraqi forces into Iran with the aim of territorial expansion. The Iraqis failed to press home their initial invasion, and the war soon settled into a costly stalemate, not ending until 1988.

The great costs of the Iran-Iraq War led Hussein to send his army into his small oil-rich neighbor of Kuwait in August 1990, long claimed as an Iraqi province. The threat that this posed to Saudi Arabia led to the formation of a formidable international coalition headed by the United States that included the Arab states of Saudi Arabia, Egypt, and Syria. Completely dominant in the air, the coalition forces drove those of Iraq from Kuwait in the brief Persian Gulf War early in 1991. U.S. president George H. W. Bush stopped the war with the liberation of Kuwait, fearful that Iraq—needed as a counterweight to Iran—might break up into Shiite, Sunni, and Kurdish states. Hussein thus remained in power.

The now seemingly permanent U.S. military presence in the region had other consequences, for it led Saudi citizen Osama bin Laden to direct the Al Qaeda terrorist organization to attack U.S. interests in Africa and the Middle East and then the United States in the attacks of September 11, 2001, the worst terrorist action in U.S. history.

The collapse of the Soviet Union in 1991 had major impact on the Middle East. A great many Jews were now able to immigrate to Israel from Russia and other former Soviet territories, strengthening the Jewish state. Financial constraints led to the curtailment of Russian credit and armaments to the anti-Western Arab regimes, and increased Russian oil production produced lower prices and reduced Western dependence on oil from the Arab states.

Despite the best efforts of the diplomats to secure a peace deal between the Israelis and Palestinians, major violence occurred in the First Intifada (1987–1993) and the Second Intifada (al-Aqsa Intifada, 2000–2005) that included suicide bombings of Israeli civilian targets.

The failure of the Islamist Taliban in Afghanistan to meet U.S. demands regarding the surrender of Al Qaeda in that country led the administration of President George W. Bush to launch an invasion of that country in 2001. The invasion overthrew the Taliban but failed to capture bin Laden or stabilize the country, thanks in large part to support rendered to the Islamists from Pakistan. Fighting there continued, with the Afghanistan War—still ongoing in 1919, the longest armed struggle in U.S. history.

With the Afghanistan War still unwon and falsely convinced that Iraq was developing nuclear weapons, Bush led the United States into an even more costly war, in Iraq in 2003. Unlike the Persian Gulf War, this venture did not have UN support, and the invading coalition paled in comparison to that of 1991. The goals were to end the threat of weapons of mass destruction and turn Iraq into a model democracy with a free market economy that would be a model for the entire Middle East. This proved to be a chimera. Although Hussein was overthrown, stability was not achieved, and sectarian violence between Shiites and Sunnis became the norm. U.S. and coalition forces were withdrawn by the end of 2011, but the violence continued, as did doubts as to whether Iraq could indeed survive as one nation.

The Israeli government's decision to withdraw from the Gaza Strip in 2005 did not end Arab violence against the Jewish state. Israeli economic constraints and terrorist raids and rockets launched into Israeli territory from Gaza led to a spate of "Gaza Wars" in which Israeli forces carried out major military actions against the Gaza Strip.

Beginning in late 2010 a revolutionary wave, which came to be known as the Arab Spring, swept much of the Middle East, with protesters taking to the streets with demands for democratic rule and an end to endemic corruption. In 2011 this brought revolution in Egypt and also the beginning of the Syrian Civil War, which at the end of 2017 was still continuing, having brought with it vast humanitarian and refugee crises as well as military intervention by Iran and Russia.

The breakdown of order in Iraq and Syria provided the opportunity for the Islamic State of Iraq and Syria (ISIS), a new Islamist terrorist organization that had the stated goal of reestablishing the caliphate and spreading Islam by the sword throughout the world. ISIS took control of large swaths of northern and eastern Syria and northern and central Iraq including Mosul, Iraq's second-largest city. This brought an Iraqi government request for the reintroduction of some U.S. forces, principally airpower, and the formation of a U.S. coalition that included some 40 nations in Operation INHERENT RESOLVE to fight ISIS. Iraqi and coalition forces recovered Mosul in July 2017.

One bright spot in the chaotic and violent Middle East was an agreement reached in July 2015 between Western states and Iran whereby that country agreed to an inspection regime regarding its nuclear program designed to prevent Iran from developing an atomic bomb. On March 24, 2019, the last ISIS held village in Syria fell, erasing the Caliphate. This did not mean the end of ISIS, however, as was made clear by the bombings of Christian churches in Sri Lanka the next month.

Yemen, which had undergone civil wars in 1962–1970 and 1994, was again in full-blown civil war beginning in 2015, with Houthi rebels aided by Iran battling the internationally recognized Yemeni government supported by an Arab coalition headed by Saudi Arabia. Now, in 2019, peace and stability in the Middle East seem as elusive as ever. Seeking to increase pressure on Iran and already a strong critic of the agreement, President Donald Trump withdrew the United States from the nuclear deal in 2018, leaving its future very much in doubt. Indeed, in April 2019 as the Trump administration also applied sanctions and heightened military pressure on that country, Iranian president Hassan Rouhani announced that his nation would partially withdraw from its commitments under the landmark nuclear deal, rendering its future very much in doubt.

Spencer C. Tucker

References

Asbridge, Thomas. *The Crusades: The Authoritative History of the War for the Holy Land.* New York: Ecco, 2010.

Cleveland, William, and Martin P. Bunton. *A History of the Modern Middle East.* 6th ed. Boulder, CO: Westview, 2017.

Fromkin, David. *A Peace to End All Peace: The Fall of the Ottoman Empire and the Creation of the Modern Middle East.* New York: Avon Books, 1989.

Goldschmidt, Arthur, Jr. *A Concise History of the Middle East.* Boulder, CO: Westview, 1991.

Lewis, Bernard. *The Middle East: A Brief History of the Last 2,000 Years.* New York: Scribner, 1995.

Mansfield, Peter, and Nicolas Pelham. *A History of the Middle East.* New York: Penguin Books, 2013.

Smith, Dan. *The State of the Middle East: An Atlas of Conflict and Resolution.* Berkeley: University of California Press, 2006.

Van de Mieroop, Marc. *A History of the Ancient Near East: ca. 3000–323 BC.* Chichester, West Sussex, UK: Wiley, 2015.

General Maps

Ancient Near East, ca. 1400 BCE

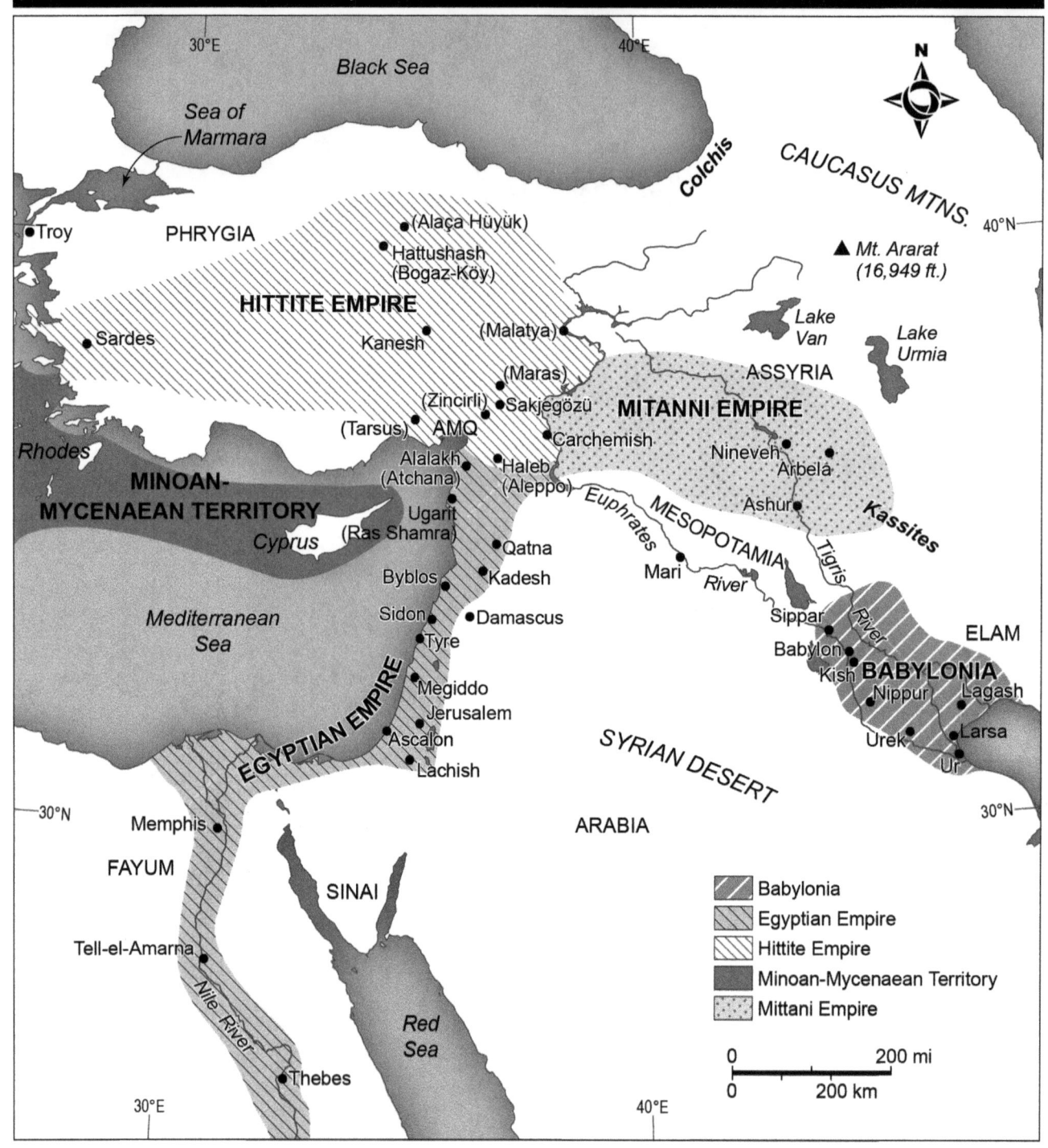

The East, ca. 600 BCE

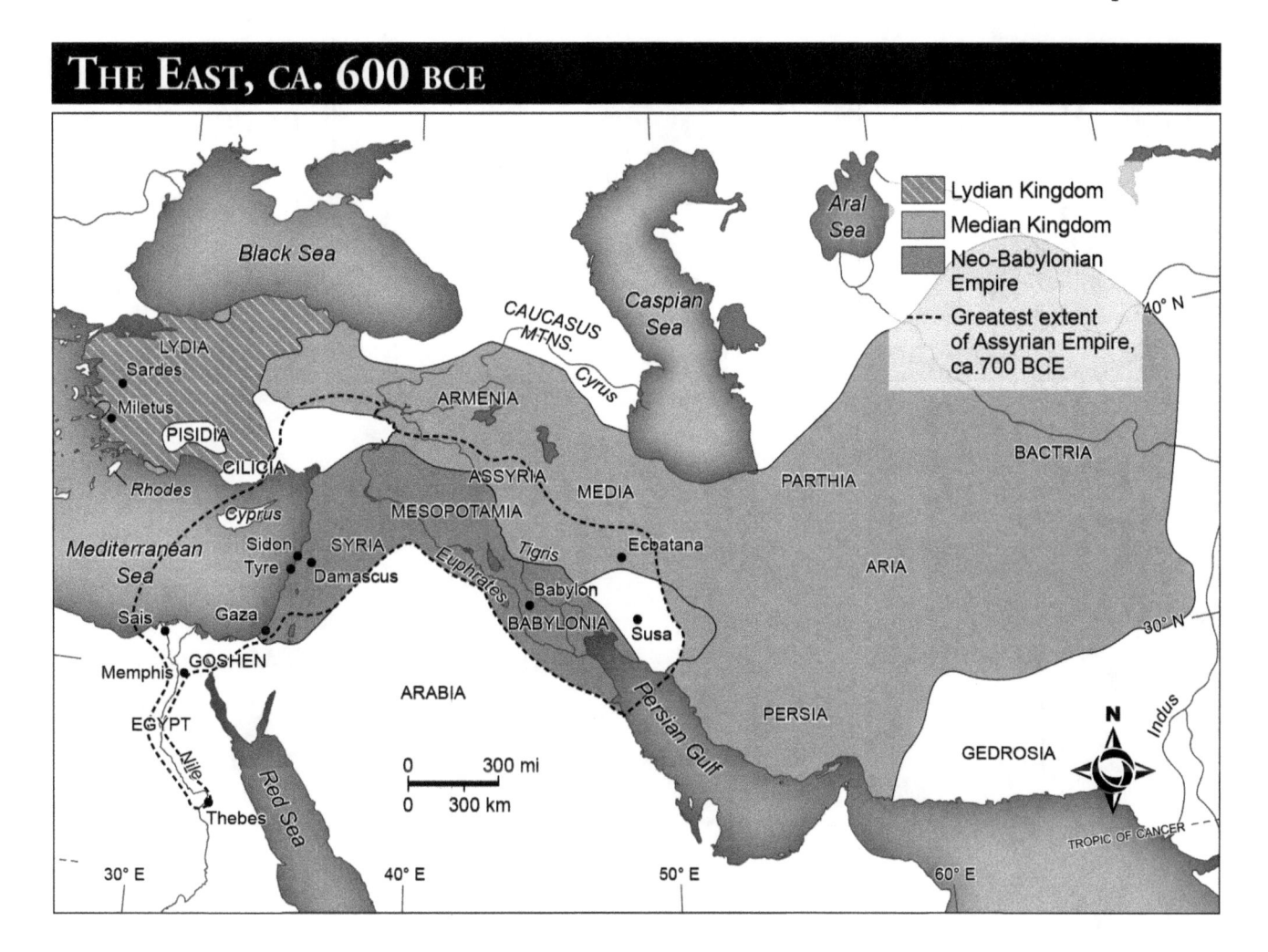

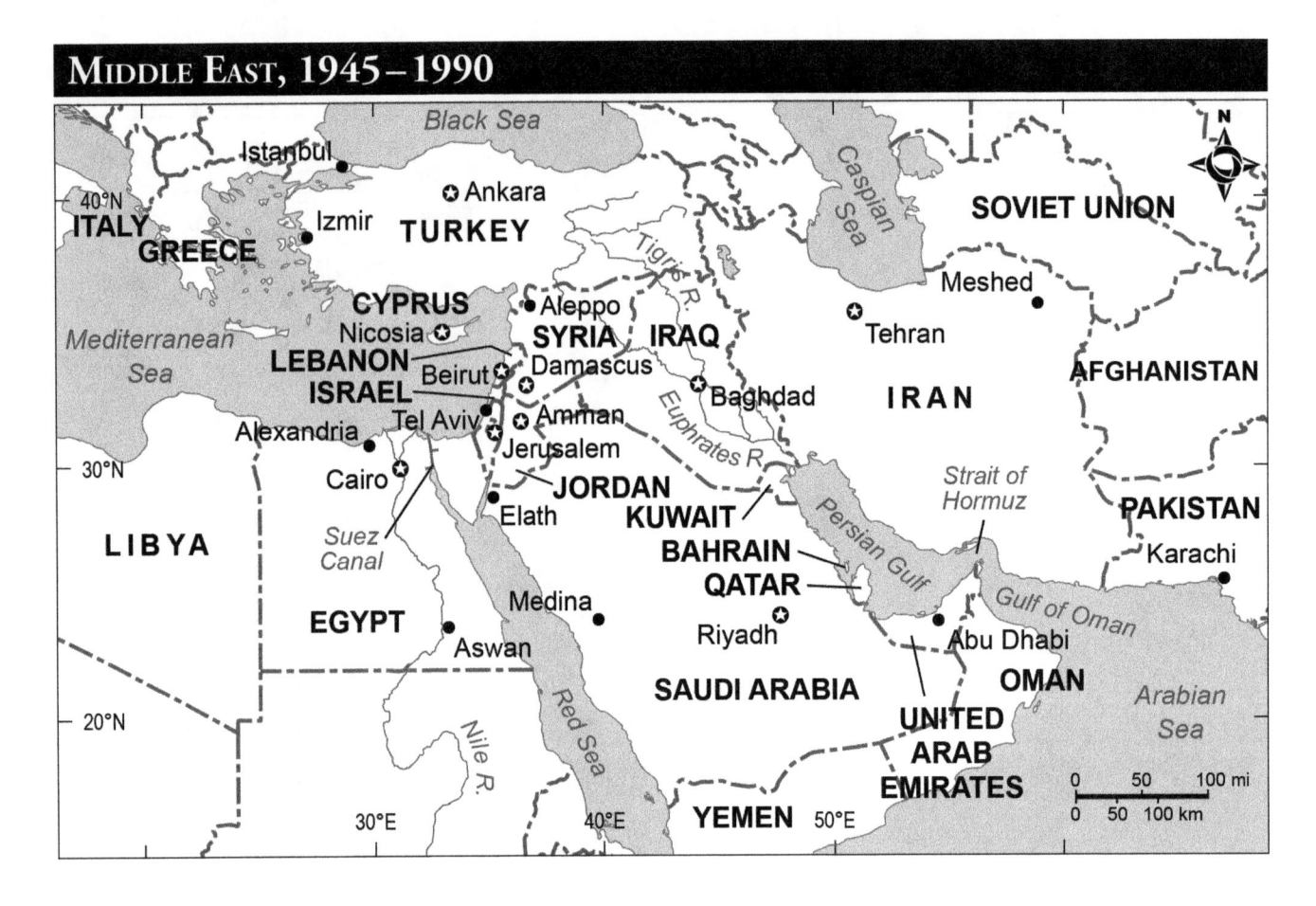

Middle East, 1945–1990

A

Abadi, Haider al- (1952–)

Iraqi engineer, politician, and prime minister of Iraq since September 8, 2014. Haider al-Abadi was born in Baghdad on April 25, 1952. He earned an undergraduate degree in electrical engineering from the University of Technology in Baghdad in 1975 and a PhD in electrical engineering from the University of Manchester in England in 1980. Abadi was active in the Iraqi Dawa Party, having joined in 1967, and in 1977 while a student in London, he was named party head. The Dawa Party was outlawed by Iraqi president Saddam Hussein's government in 1979, however, and in 1983 Hussein's government revoked Abadi's passport. Abadi chose to remain in London and did not return to Iraq until 2003. He worked as an engineering consultant in both the public and private sectors in England between 1980 and 2003.

Abadi returned to Iraq in the summer of 2003 after Hussein's ouster following the Anglo-American military invasion. Abadi then agreed to serve as minister of communications in the Iraqi interim government, the Coalition Provisional Authority (CPA). His tenure, which began on September 1, was a rocky one, however, as he continually clashed with CPA administrator American L. Paul (Jerry) Bremer. Refusing to be a mere "rubber-stamp" functionary, Abadi vigorously disagreed with Bremer's policy that all state-owned companies should be immediately privatized prior to elections that would form a new Iraqi government. Abadi left his post on June 1, 2004, several weeks before Bremer left his CPA position.

In January 2005 Abadi agreed to serve as a consultant to the Iraqi government, chiefly on issues relating to reconstruction and infrastructure. In December 2005, running on the Islamic Dawa Party ticket, he won a seat in the Iraqi parliament. In 2007 he was elected deputy leader of the Islamic Dawa Party. Abadi was reelected to Parliament in 2010, having now gained a reputation for even-handedness and impartiality. In 2006 and again in 2010 his name had been mentioned as a potential candidate for the Iraqi premiership, which ultimately went to Nuri al-Maliki. Meanwhile, many Iraqis admired Abadi's tough stance toward the continued stationing of coalition troops in Iraq. Indeed, he became one of the chief architects of the Iraqi status of forces agreement with the United States, finally approved in December 2008.

Maliki's tenure as prime minister quickly turned into disaster. Once U.S. troops left Iraq in late 2011, Maliki, a Shiite Muslim, engaged in a campaign of repression against Iraq's Sunni Muslim population. He alienated large portions of the Iraqi population and permitted the Iraqi military to languish. This aided the rise of Islamic extremist groups, particularly the Islamic State of Iraq and Syria (ISIS), which began seizing control and unleashing terror over large portions of northern and eastern Iraq by early 2014. Despite the fact that Maliki had lost the support of key international allies, including the United States, as well as the backing of many within his own party and government, he stubbornly clung to power. Finally, with the situation in Iraq steadily deteriorating, Maliki agreed to step down on August 14, 2014.

Meanwhile, Iraqi president Fuad Masum had nominated Abadi as Maliki's replacement on August 11, a move that was widely hailed as a positive step toward the Iraqi government regaining control of its territory. On September 8, 2014, the Iraqi parliament confirmed Abadi's appointment, and he took office that same day.

A Shiite Muslim, Abadi vowed to reinvigorate Iraq's army and work closely with the new coalition formed to stop and eventually eradicate ISIS. He also promised more governmental transparency, and although he, like Maliki, is a Shiite Muslim, Abadi pledged to bridge the gaping chasm between Iraq's Sunni and Shiite populations.

On November 12, 2014, Abadi announced the removal of 36 senior military commanders in a sweeping move to improve Iraqi Army fighting ability as it attempted to take the offensive and retake territory lost to ISIS. Despite having received more than $35 billion in U.S. training and equipment in the past decade, the Iraqi Army had performed abysmally in losing immense swaths of the country to ISIS, with much of the blame for this falling on an inept Iraqi military leadership. Abadi also installed 18 other commanders in order to promote professionalism and to "counter corruption."

Since becoming prime minister, Abadi has traveled abroad. This includes visits to Egypt, Jordan, Turkey, and the United States (with both President Barack Obama and President Donald Trump) to discuss combating ISIS. Abadi was critical of Obama, claiming that he was not doing enough against ISIS. U.S. officials in the Obama administration were concerned, however, about Abadi welcoming cooperation with Russia and Iran in the fight against ISIS. Nonetheless, the U.S. government pledged substantial assistance to the Iraqi government, including humanitarian assistance and military aid in increased numbers of U.S. troops in Iraq and substantial air support in operations against ISIS-held Iraqi territory, especially valuable in the Iraqi Army effort to retake the city of Mosul.

In 2015, Abadi unveiled a plan to eliminate security details for senior officials and cut benefits for certain high-level officials. In April 2016, however, the dysfunctional nature of the Iraqi government and Abadi's difficulties in implementing meaningful political reforms brought the storming of the Iraqi parliament by followers of Shia cleric Muqtada al-Sadr. The protesters breached the heavily fortified Green Zone in Baghdad, which contained key government officers and foreign embassies, and disrupted the parliament itself.

In the fall of 2017, Abadi bitterly denounced the Iraqi Kurds' September 25 independence vote. He quickly moved to secure oil fields in Iraqi Kurdistan and placed sanctions on the Kurdistan Regional Government. In December 2017 Abadi declared victory over ISIS, although this by no means marked the end of insurgency activities in Iraq. In the summer of 2018, Abadi rejected calls for the May 2018 Iraqi parliamentary elections to be set aside amid criticism by some Iraqis that the results had been tainted. Meanwhile, in the wake of the victory over ISIS, Abadi has made a number of decisions designed to further weaken extremist insurgents, unite the Iraq people, and pave the way for the final exit of U.S. troops from Iraq.

PAUL G. PIERPAOLI JR. AND SPENCER C. TUCKER

See also
Bremer, Lewis Paul, III; Iraq; Islamic State of Iraq and Syria; Maliki, Nuri Muhammed Kamil al-; Sadr, Muqtada al-

References
Alawi, Ali A. *The Occupation of Iraq: Winning the War, Losing the Peace.* New Haven, CT: Yale University Press, 2007.
Jaffe, Greg. "Protests in Baghdad Throw Administration's Iraq Plan into Doubt." *Washington Post*, April 30, 2016.

Abbas, Abu (1948–2004)

Leader of the Palestine Liberation Front (PLF). Abu Abbas, the nom de guerre of Muhammad Zaidan, was born in Safed, Palestine, on December 10, 1948. His family fled to Syria that same year along with 12,000–15,000 Arab residents after the Haganah attacks. In 1968 he joined the Popular Front for the Liberation of Palestine General Command (PFLP-GC), led by Ahmad Jibril. Abu Abbas disagreed with Jibril over the PFLP-GC's strong support for Syria and its failure to criticize Syrian support of the Lebanese Phalangist Party against the Palestine Liberation Organization (PLO) in Lebanon. In April 1977, Abu Abbas and Talat Yaqub left the PFLP-GC to form the PLF.

During the 1970s Abu Abbas advocated armed struggle against Israel, chiefly in the form of attacks mounted from southern Lebanon. He was wounded in fighting during the 1982 Israeli invasion of Lebanon. The following year when the PLF split into three factions, he led the largest pro-Iraqi group. In 1984 he became a member of the PLO Executive Committee.

On October 7, 1985, Abu Abbas masterminded the PLF's most dramatic terrorist action, the hijacking of the Italian cruise ship *Achille Lauro,* which at the time was steaming from Alexandria to Port Said, Egypt. The hijacking resulted in the death of U.S.-born Jew Leon Klinghoffer. Although the Egyptian aircraft carrying Abbas and the other three hijackers to asylum in Tunisia was diverted by U.S. aircraft to a North Atlantic Treaty Organization (NATO) air base in Sicily, the Italian government allowed the passengers to depart, and Abu Abbas escaped among them.

There was, however, much criticism of Abbas for the PLF's attempted terrorist attack on Nizamim Beach near Tel Aviv on May 30, 1990, which was designed to torpedo the possibility of PLO-Israeli peace talks. Nonetheless, the Israeli government alleged that the PLF had regularly received funding from PLO chairman Yasser Arafat. Indeed, in January 1996 the PLO agreed to provide an undisclosed sum to finance the Leon and Marilyn Klinghoffer Memorial Foundation of the U.S. Anti-Defamation League, in return for which Klinghoffer's daughters dropped a lawsuit brought against the PLO. In 1989 Abu Abbas had supported the PLO's acceptance of United Nations Security Council Resolution 242, and these militant actions betrayed that stance.

Following the 1993 Oslo Accords, Abu Abbas returned to Gaza. He then moved to Iraq. There was a standing U.S. warrant for his arrest, and in 2003 during the U.S.-led invasion of Iraq, he was taken into custody by U.S. forces. He died in Iraq, reportedly of natural causes, on March 8, 2004, while in U.S. custody.

Spencer C. Tucker

See also

Lebanon-Israeli War; Oslo Accords; Palestine Liberation Organization

References

Alexander, Yonah. *Palestinian Secular Terrorism.* Ardsley, NY: Transnational Publishers, 2003.

Bohn, Michael K. *The Achille Lauro Hijacking: Lessons in the Politics and Prejudice of Terrorism.* Dulles, VA: Potomac Books, 2004.

Cassese, Antonio. *Terrorism, Politics and Law: The Achille Lauro Affair.* Princeton, NJ: Princeton University Press, 1989.

Nassar, Jamal R. *The Palestine Liberation Organization: From Armed Struggle to the Declaration of Independence.* New York: Praeger, 1991.

Abbas, Mahmoud (1935–)

First prime minister of the Palestinian [National] Authority (PNA or PA) March–October 2003; chairman of the Palestine Liberation Organization (November 2004–present); and president of the PNA, January 2005–present. Mahmoud Abbas (Abu Mazen) was born on March 26, 1935, in Safed, British mandatory Palestine. During the 1948 Arab-Israeli war, his family fled Palestine and settled in Syria. Abbas graduated from the University of Damascus and studied law in Egypt and Syria before earning a PhD in history in 1982 from the Oriental College in Moscow.

In 1984, Abbas published in Arabic *The Other Side: The Secret Relationship between Nazism and Zionism.* Based on his dissertation, Abbas dismissed as a "myth" and a "fantastic lie" that 6 million Jews had died in the Holocaust. He put the figure at a few hundred thousand or at most 890,000 and said that the larger figure had been presented to curry world support for Zionism. In 2006, however, he said that the Holocaust "was a terrible thing and nobody can claim I denied it."

Abbas was the civil service director of personnel for Qatar when he began his involvement in Palestinian politics in the mid-1950s. He was one of the founders of Fatah (1957) and was part of the leadership of Yasser Arafat's Palestine Liberation Organization (PLO) in exile in Jordan, Lebanon, and Tunisia during the 1960s through the 1980s. During this time Abbas cultivated relationships with left-wing and pacifist Jewish groups. He joined the Palestine National Council in 1968 and was the funding source for Black September's attack on Israeli athletes at the 1972 Summer Olympics in Munich, Germany. Abbas asserts, however, that he was unaware of the intended use of the funds.

Abbas assumed the leadership of the PLO's Department for National and International Relations in 1980. He began his leadership of the PLO's Negotiations Affairs Department that same year. In May 1988 he assumed chairmanship of the division treating the Occupied Territories. When PLO support for Iraq's 1990 invasion of Kuwait harmed relationships with Arab states that had joined the U.S.-led coalition in the 1991 Persian Gulf War, it was Abbas who repaired the damage. He was also the major architect of the 1993 Oslo Accords between the PLO and Israel. In 1996 Abbas was elected secretary-general of the PLO Executive Committee, headed the first session of the Israeli-Palestinian final status negotiations, led the Central Election Commission for the Palestine Legislative Council (PLC), and then was elected to the PLC.

On March 19, 2003, Arafat appointed the more moderate and pragmatically perceived Abbas as the first prime minister of the Palestinian Authority. Arafat's unwillingness to share significant power, persistent conflicts with militant Palestinian groups such as Hamas and Islamic Jihad, Israeli-targeted assignations of Palestinian militants, and a perceived lack of support from the United States led Abbas to resign as prime minister on September 4, 2003, effective October 7, 2003.

Palestinian leader Mahmoud Abbas. The chairman of the Executive Committee of the Palestinian Liberation Organization since November 2004, he has been president of the Palestinian National Authority since January 2005. (European Community)

Following Arafat's death, Abbas became chairman of the PLO on November 11, 2004. Abbas's authority and attempts to reengage the Road Map to Peace were challenged by most of the militant Palestinian groups, however. On January 15, 2005, Abbas became president of the PNA. A May 2005 pledge of $50 million and continued support of a free Palestinian state from the United States coupled with the Israeli withdrawal from Gaza on August 23, 2005, led Abbas to set PLC elections for January 20, 2006. However, when Hamas fared well in local elections in December 2005, Abbas sought to postpone the PLC election. He nevertheless proceeded with the January elections in which Hamas won a majority of seats in the PA parliament. This reduced Abbas's Fatah party to a minority.

Abbas has been dogged by claims of embezzlement of public funds by officials of the Palestinian Authority, including himself, these same charges having bedeviled his mentor and predecessor, Arafat. This perceived corruption on the part of Fatah leadership is believed to have been a major factor in the convincing Hamas victory in the January 2006 parliamentary election.

Although Abbas remains as PNA president, Hamas controls the parliament, governmental services, and the security forces. Israel has made it clear that Abbas and the PNA are expected to fulfill all agreements made prior to the 2006 elections, including the agreement to disarm Palestinian militants. The United States and many European countries withdrew their financial support of the PNA in view of Hamas's refusal to disavow its commitment to the destruction of Israel. This financial crisis and Hamas's militancy continued to challenge Abbas's leadership and presidency.

With tensions between Hamas and Fatah virtually paralyzing the PNA, Abbas called for a unity government between the two factions, which was effected in March 2007. By June, however, Abbas had dissolved the coalition government in the wake of continued violence between Hamas and Fatah in Gaza and Hamas's refusal to deal in good faith. Indeed, a virtual civil war had broken out between the two parties. Abbas declared a state of emergency, and on June 14 Hamas seized control of all of Gaza. Abbas's move, which essentially denounced Hamas, resulted in the restoration of economic aid to the PNA from the European Union and the United States. Israel followed suit on July 1, 2007.

Meanwhile, Abbas was locked in contentious peace negotiations with Israel. These went nowhere, and several times Abbas threatened to resign if a peace deal was not arrived at "within six months." The Israeli incursion into the Gaza Strip beginning in late December 2008, designed to punish Hamas militants and end their rocket attacks on southern Israel, threatened to derail the shaky peace process and only further widened the chasm between Fatah and Hamas.

In 2015, Abbas admitted that in September 2008 he turned down an Israeli offer for a Palestinian state comprising virtually all of the West Bank. He claimed that Israeli prime minister Ehud Olmert had presented him with a proposal whereby Israel would annex only 6.3 percent of the West Bank but also compensate the Palestinians with 5.8 percent taken from pre-1967 Israel. Abbas said that he had rejected this out of hand, insisting instead on the June 4, 1967, borders of Palestine. He said that Olmert did not give a map of the proposal and that he could not sign without seeing the proposal. Abbas said in October 2011 that he made a counteroffer to let Israel annex 1.9 percent of the West Bank.

In the meantime, Abbas's presidential term had ended on January 9, 2009, but he extended it, arguing that the Basic Law permitted this and that he needed more time to better prepare the PNA for forthcoming elections. Hamas rejected this outright and claimed that his presidential term had ended and that Abdel Aziz Duwaik, Speaker of the Palestinian Legislative Council, was acting president. Abbas remains president, however.

According to a report by the International Crisis Group, most Israeli officials see Abbas not as a partner in the peace process but rather as a "nonthreatening, violence-abhorring, strategic asset."

In June 2016, Abbas repeated to the European Parliament a false report that rabbis in Israel were calling for Palestinian wells to be poisoned. Although he soon retracted the statement and said that he did not intend "to do harm to Judaism or to offend Jewish people around the world," the incident permitted Prime Minister Benjamin Netanyahu, no advocate of the peace process, to brand Abbas's statement as a "blood libel." Abbas loudly protested the Donald Trump administration's December 2017 decision to relocate the U.S. embassy to Jerusalem, claiming that this placed an irrevocable obstacle to any future peace negotiations between the Palestinians and Israelis.

By the summer of 2018 a true unity government involving Fatah and Hamas remained elusive, although the two factions had by then narrowed their differences to some extent. In the summer of 2018, Abbas slammed the Trump administration's decision to freeze U.S. funding for the PNA and claimed to have thwarted the administration's efforts to broker a lasting peace deal, which had yet to be unveiled.

RICHARD M. EDWARDS AND SPENCER C. TUCKER

See also

Arafat, Yasser; Fatah, al-; Hamas; Holocaust; Intifada, Second; Netanyahu, Benjamin; Olmert, Ehud; Palestine Liberation Organization; Palestinian Islamic Jihad

References

Abbas, Mahmud. *Through Secret Channels: The Road to Oslo; Senior PLO Leader Abu Mazen's Revealing Story of the Negotiations with Israel.* Reading, UK: Garnet Publishing, 1997.

Doaud, Abu. *Memoirs of a Palestinian Terrorist.* New York: Arcade Publishing, 2002.

Gelvin, James L. *The Israel-Palestine Conflict: One Hundred Years of War.* Cambridge: Cambridge University Press, 2005.

Makovsky, David. *Making Peace with the PLO: The Rabin Government's Road to the Oslo Accord.* Boulder, CO: Westview, 1996.

Pappe, Ilan. *A History of Modern Palestine: One Land, Two Peoples.* Cambridge: Cambridge University Press, 2003.

Rubin, Barry. *Revolution until Victory? The Politics and History of the PLO.* Reprint ed. Cambridge, MA: Harvard University Press, 2003.

Abbasid Caliphate (750–1258, 1261–1517)

An Arab dynasty that reigned in present-day Iraq (750–1258) and Egypt (1261–1517). By the mid-eighth century the Umayyad caliphal dynasty (661–750) had made many enemies, including both Shiites and other members of the Muslim community who felt that the Umayyads were too concerned with worldly issues and not sufficiently focused on Islam itself. The Umayyads were also weakened by rivalries among the tribes supporting them in their chosen power base, Syria. Eventually a rebellion broke out in Khurasan (eastern Persia, Afghanistan, and other lands east of the Oxus River). This spread to Iraq, where a descendant of Prophet Muhammad's uncle al-Abbas was proclaimed caliph with the regnal title of al-Saffa. The last Umayyad army was defeated in 750 in Egypt, with the Umayyad caliph, Marwan II, being killed in the fighting.

The inhabitants of al-Saffa's dynasty became known as Abbasids, after their ancestor. As with their predecessors, the Abbasid caliphs were both the religious and secular leaders of the Muslim world. Initially they based their particular claims to the caliphate on both their kinship with Prophet Muhammad and the fact that unlike others, they had taken action against a regime that was perceived as unjust. Later they also presented themselves as patrons of orthodoxy, stressing their position as guardians of Islam. They made their capital at Baghdad in Iraq, from which most of the caliphs reigned until 1258.

The reign of Harun al-Rashid (786–809) is generally regarded as the high point of the Abbasid caliphate, particularly when contrasted with later events. His death was followed by a civil war between his sons. This was soon followed by a gradual decline in caliphal power exacerbated by financial problems, increasing domination of the caliphs by their subordinates, and rebellions by Shiites and other disaffected elements.

During this period much of the Muslim world fragmented such that the provinces came to acknowledge only nominal allegiance to the caliphs. Finally, in 945 Baghdad was taken by the Buyids (Buwayhids), a Shiite dynasty from the mountains of Daylam in Persia. They maintained the existence of the Sunni caliphate, ruling as the caliphs' nominal subordinates until 1055. Meanwhile Egypt was taken by the Fatimids (969), who also temporarily extended their influence into parts of Palestine, Syria, and Arabia, although by the period of the Christian crusades much of these gains had again been lost.

In 1055, Sunni rule was restored in Baghdad when the Seljuks took control of the city. This did little to change the situation in the city itself, for while the Seljuks became embroiled in the struggle for the Levant with the Fatimids and crusaders, the caliphs remained largely impotent.

However, the collapse of Seljuk authority enabled some of the more vigorous caliphs to exercise their own authority somewhat. In particular, al-Muqtafi (1136–1160) asserted caliphal independence from the Seljuks in Iraq. His great-grandson al-Nair (1180–1225) not only overthrew the Seljuks but also, through a mixture of diplomacy, military action, and a little luck, extended caliphal territories and warded off potential attacks from other enemies, including the Mongols. He also made several other social, political, and religious reforms, emphasizing in particular the primacy of the caliph and even coming to a certain degree of understanding with the Shiites. The resurgence of caliphal authority was brief, however. The end came in 1258, when the Mongols took Baghdad and put the reigning caliph, al-Musta'im, to death.

Not all the caliph's family died in the Mongol onslaught, and in 1261 the Mamluk sultan Baybars restored the caliphate in Cairo. From here the Abbasid caliphs reigned, albeit in name only, until the Ottoman conquest. The last caliph died as a prisoner of war in Istanbul (Constantinople) in 1517.

Niall Christie

See also
Abbasid Revolution; Baghdad, 1258 Siege of; Seljuk Dynasty; Umayyad Caliphate

References
Holt, Peter M. *The Age of the Crusades.* London: Longman, 1986.
Kennedy, Hugh. *The Prophet and the Age of the Caliphates.* London: Longman, 1986.
Kurpalidis, G. M. "The Seljuqids and the Sultan's Power." In *Altaica Berolinensia: The Concept of Sovereignty in the Altaic World,* ed. Barbara Kellner-Heinkele, 133–137. Wiesbaden: Harrassowitz, 1993.
Lassner, Jacob. *The Shaping of 'Abbasid Rule.* Princeton, NJ: Princeton University Press, 1980.
Moammad, Alsheikh al-Amin. *The Role of Saljuks on the Abbasid's Caliphate.* Ankara: Türk Tarih Kurumu Basimevi, 1994.

Abbasid Revolution (747–751)

The Abbasid Revolution of 747–751 overthrew the Umayyad Caliphate. The Umayyad family had assumed the leadership of the Islamic realm following the assassination of Caliph Ali in 661. During the next 80 years, Umayyad caliphs presided over a rapid expansion of the empire that ultimately stretched from the Indus Valley in the east to the Pyrenees mountains in the west. Despite establishing a centralized state and developing a vigorous commerce, the Umayyads also generated widespread hostility for their constant military campaigns and privileged treatment of Muslim Arabs. Non-Arab Muslims opposed discriminatory taxes, while Shia Muslims denounced the Umayyads as usurpers and continued to support the descendants of Ali.

The Abbasids, descendants of Prophet Muhammad's uncle Abbas, successfully exploited these animosities against the Umayyads. Their anti-Umayyad propaganda proved especially appealing in Khurasan, the northeastern frontier of Persia, where both Arab and non-Arab Muslims harbored intense grudges against the state. The Abbasids developed an intricate network of supporters throughout the caliphate, particularly in present-day Iraq, Palestine, and Syria.

In 747 in Khurasan the Abbasids launched their revolt, unfurling black flags, symbols of the Mahdi, a messianic figure in popular Islam. After capturing the town of Merv in February 748, Abbasid commanders Abu Salama and Abu Muslim advanced westward, securing control of central Persia by the end of the year. In 749, having captured most of Persia, the head of the movement, Abu al-Abbas, was declared caliph at Kufa.

In January 750, Abbasid forces defeated Ummayad Caliph Marwan's army on the banks of the Great Zab River in northern Iraq; the caliph escaped to Egypt but was assassinated there seven months later. The Umayyad family and its supporters were massacred, with a few survivors rallying in Spain. Caliph Abu al-Abbas and his successor, Caliph al-Mansur, ended ethnic and economic discriminations against non-Arab Muslims, upholding the fundamental principle of equality for all Muslims. The Abbasids abandoned the Umayyad capital of Damascus in Syria and shifted the political center of the caliphate to the newly built city of Baghdad in Iraq.

Alexander Mikaberidze

See also
Abbasid Caliphate; Abu Muslim Khorasani

References
Kennedy, Hugh. *The Early Abbasid Caliphate: A Political History.* London: Taylor & Francis, 1986.
Lassner, Jacob. *The Shaping of 'Abbasid Rule.* Princeton, NJ: Princeton University Press, 1980.
Shaban, M. A. *The Abbasid Revolution.* Cambridge: Cambridge University Press, 1970.

Abbas Mirza (1789–1833)

Persian general and military reformer. The eldest son of Fath Ali Shah, Abbas Mirza was born on August 26, 1789, at Nava, Mazandaran. When he was only 10 years old, Abbas Mirza became governor (*beglerbegi*) of the province of Azerbaijan, where he ruled as crown prince and heir (*na'ib al-Saltana*) to the Qajar throne until 1831. When war began between Russia and Persia in 1804 he received command of the Persian Army, which he led on a disastrous campaign against the Russians, suffering a series of defeats at Gumry, Kalagiri, on the Aras (Araxes) and Zagam Rivers in 1805; Karakapet in 1806; Karababa in 1808; Ganja in 1809; Meghri, the Aras River, and Akhalkalaki in 1810; and Aslanduz in 1812.

The war resulted in Persia losing most of southeast Caucasia and also convinced Abbas Mirza of the need of military reforms. He believed that the introduction of European-style regiments would enable Iran to gain the upper hand over Russia and reclaim lost territory. Influenced by Sultan Selim III's reform, Abbas Mirza set out to create an Iranian version of the Ottoman Nizam-i Cedid troops and reduce the Qajar dependence on tribal and provincial forces. After the war, he began sending students to Europe to learn Western tactics and employed British and French officers (as well as a few renegade Russian officers) to raise and drill troops; the number of foreign instructors particularly increased after the end of the Napoleonic Wars in 1815, when many unemployed European officers traveled far afield in search of positions.

Abbas Mirza established a printing press to translate and publish European military textbooks. He built a gunpowder factory and an artillery foundry in Tabriz. He also tried to introduce a new recruitment system to create a more predictable supply of manpower and to make himself independent of the local elite. In the new *bunichah* system, Abbas Mirza established a form of conscription under which each province was called upon to provide recruits, the number calculated on the basis of the amount of land under cultivation and supplemented by voluntary enlistment and incorporation of small tribal contingents. Abbas Mirza had to overcome public resistance to reforms, as the population and the ulema opposed change, the European appearance of new regiments, and the presence of infidel instructors. Although he received British subsidies to defray the cost of military reforms, training and equipping new regiments proved very expensive, affecting the Qajar finances.

The reformed army had some success in campaigns against the Ottomans in 1821–1823 but proved to be ill-prepared for the second Russo-Iranian war (1826–1828). Although Abbas Mirza was able to seize initiative and regain considerable territory in southern Caucasia in the first months of the war, the Russian counteroffensive soon shattered the Iranian forces on the banks of the Shamkhor River near Ganja. In 1827 the Russians drove Abbas Mirza back into Iran, occupying eastern Armenia and capturing Tabriz, the capital of the Azerbaijan province, itself. At the end of the war in 1828, Iran had lost all its Georgian and southeast Caucasian territories.

The war had an important psychological effect on Abbas Mirza, who accepted responsibility for its outcome. Still, he remained undeterred in military reforms and maintained the reformed forces in his province; by 1831, this force consisted of about 12,000 infantry, 1,200 horse artillery, and 1 regiment of lancers, organized into 10 regiments of Persian troops and 2 units of Russian deserters (*bahaduran*). These units played an important role in maintaining order and defending Qajar authority in Persia.

Abbas Mirza spent the last years of his life feuding with his many brothers, who sought to replace him as an heir apparent. He died at age 44 on October 25, 1833, at Mashhad while leading an expedition against rebel tribes in Khorasan.

ALEXANDER MIKABERIDZE

See also
Ottoman-Persian Wars of the 18th and 19th Centuries; Russo-Persian Wars

References
Avery, Peter, et al., eds. *The Cambridge History of Iran: From Nadir Shah to the Islamic Republic,* Vol. 7. Cambridge: Cambridge University Press, 1991.
Baddeley, John Frederick. *The Russian Conquest of the Caucasus.* London: Longmans, Green, 1908.
Farmanfarmaian, Roxane. *War and Peace in Qajar Persia: Implications Past and Present.* New York: Routledge, 2008.

Abbas I the Great (1571–1629)

Shah (king) of Persia. Born in Herat (now in Afghanistan) on January 27, 1571, Abbas was the son of Shah Mohammed Khudabanda of the Safavid dynasty. Persia was then in turmoil, riven by divisions within the Qizibash Army and under threat from the Ottoman Empire, the Uzbeks, and the Mogul rulers of India, all of whom had taken advantage of the internal Persian turmoil to seize large chunks of its territory. Perhaps half of Persian territory was under foreign control, and many provinces were virtually independent.

On October 1, 1587, Murshid Qoli Khan, one of the Qizibash leaders, mounted a coup d'état, forcing the abdication of weak-willed Shah Mohammed and bringing to power his son Abbas at age 16. Abbas consolidated power and caused the murder of Murshid in 1589, securing full authority. In 1590 Abbas signed the humiliating Treaty of

Constantinople (also known as the Treaty of Ferdhad Pasha) to end the Ottoman-Safavid War of 1578–1590 in order to secure a free hand for internal reorganization. Abbas then reformed the government, reducing the influence of the Qizibash in affairs of state and beginning the modernization of the army, which he modeled after those of the Ottoman Empire and the West. A great builder, Abbas also transferred the Persian capital from Qazvin to Isfahan in 1598.

After having carried out army reforms, Abbas attacked his foreign enemies piecemeal, moving first against the Uzbeks (1590–1598) who, under Abdullah II, had captured Herat, Meshed, and much of Khorasan from the Safavid Empire. Abbas made peace with the Ottomans, abandoning several provinces to them in order to concentrate on the Uzbeks. He drove the Uzbeks from most of Khorasan before suffering a major defeat near Balkh in 1598. With both sides exhausted, Abbas concluded peace that same year, with the Uzbeks retaining a small bit of Khorasan.

During the next several years Shah Abbas completely reorganized the Safavid Army, employing European military advisers sent out by Western nations to try to bring Persia into combination against the Ottomans. Thus, English artillerist Robert Shirley completely reorganized the Persian artillery. Abbas also employed Armenians and Georgians in his army. He then used this force to restore order in his own realm, bringing the rebellious provinces to heel. By 1600 Abbas had at his disposal the nucleus of a modern professional military force solely dependent on him and able to compete on equal footing with the Ottoman Turks.

In 1602, taking advantage of internal problems in the Ottoman Empire and its involvement in Europe, Abbas invaded the eastern Ottoman Empire. In October 1603 he captured Tabriz following a prolonged siege, and in 1604 he secured Yerevan (Erevan, Erivan) after a six-month siege. Shirvan and Kars also fell. Abbas thus regained the territory lost to the Ottomans the decade before.

Determined to recapture the territory lost to Abbas during the previous two years, Ottoman sultan Ahmed now advanced against the Safavids with some 100,000 men and joined battle with Abbas and his army of some 62,000 men on September 9, 1606, at Sis near Lake Urmia in present-day Azerbaijan. Abbas utilized his predominantly cavalry force to great advantage, decisively defeating the Ottomans, who reportedly suffered some 20,000 dead. As a consequence of the battle, Shah Abbas secured Azerbaijan, Kurdistan, Baghdad, Mosul, and Diarbekh.

In 1613 Abbas sent an army into Georgia to force it to acknowledge his suzerainty. Because the Ottomans

Portrait of Shah of Persia Abbas I the Great (1571–1629). Assuming full power in 1589, he was the greatest ruler of the Safavid dynasty. Abbas proved an excellent administrator, and during his reign Persian territory reached its greatest extent in antiquity. His reign also saw a flowering of Persian arts and culture. (The Walters Art Museum)

considered Georgia within their sphere of influence, the Safavid occupation led to renewed war between the two empires in 1616. The Ottomans invaded Armenia with a large army and laid siege to its largest city, Yerevan (Erevan), but were forced to raise the siege in the winter of 1616–1617, suffering major casualties from both the cold and the Safavid forces. A year later, the Ottomans again invaded and moved against Tabriz. The Safavids ambushed part of the invading army, leading to peace talks in which the Ottomans agreed to recognize Safavid control of both Azerbaijan and Georgia.

In 1622 Abbas led a Safavid army into present-day Afghanistan, capturing Kandahar. A rebellion by his second son, Khurram, prevented Mughal emperor Jahangir from intervening. Also in 1622 with the assistance of four English ships, Abbas captured Hormuz, retaking Hormuz from the Portuguese. He sought to replace it with a new port on the mainland, Bandar Abbas, but it was not a success.

In 1623 the Ottomans again went to war against the Safavids in an effort to retake the territory lost to Abbas in the two earlier wars. This time the Ottomans focused on recapturing Baghdad. Their effort there during 1625–1626 was unsuccessful and led to heavy losses, especially during their withdrawal in 1626 when they were subjected to Safavid attacks. Although there are no major battles during the next several years, border warfare continued.

Abbas's last years were troubled. Three of his sons survived into adulthood. Believing that they were plotting against him, Abbas had them either killed or blinded. Abbas died in Mazandaran, Iran, on January 19, 1629. He was succeeded by his grandson, Sam Mirza, who took the title Shah Safi.

Abbas I was the greatest ruler of the Safavid dynasty. An excellent administrator and organizer, he used his modernized army to extend the territory of his kingdom to what it had occupied in antiquity. Abbas also presided over a flowering of Persian culture and the arts. A Shiite Muslim, he was generally tolerant of other religions, including Christianity, although he did persecute Sunni Muslims living in Persia's western provinces.

Spencer C. Tucker

See also
Constantinople, 1590 Treaty of; Iran; Nasuh Pasha, Treaty of; Ottoman-Safavid Wars; Safavid Dynasty; Shia Islam

References
Blow, David. *Shah Abbas: The Ruthless King Who Became an Iranian Legend.* New York: I. B. Tauris, 2009.
Eskander Beg Monshi. *History of Shah Abbas the Great.* 2 vols. Translated by Roger M. Savory. Boulder, CO: Westview, 1978.
Nahavandi, H., and Y. Bomati. *Shah Abbas, Empereur de Perse (1587–1629).* Paris: Perrin, 1998.
Newman, Andrew J. *Safavid Iran: Rebirth of a Persian Empire.* London: I. B. Tauris, 2006.
Savory, Roger. *Iran under the Safavids.* Cambridge: Cambridge University Press, 2007.

Abd Allah ibn al-Zubair (624–692)

Abd Allah ibn al-Zubair was an Arab general who contested the Umayyad Caliphate for nine years. Born in Medina, Arabia, in 624, Abd Allah was the son of Zubair ibn al-Awwam, one of the most prominent of Prophet Muhammad's companions and a member of one of the noble families of the Quraysh tribe. Abd Allah accompanied his father in the early Arab conquests, participating in the Arab victory over the Byzantines at Yarmouk in 636. In 639 Abd Allah served in Amr al-As's army that conquered Egypt and also played a prominent part in the Arab conquest of Ifrikiya (North Africa). In 648–649 Abd Allah distinguished himself in the Battle of Sufetula, where he routed and killed Gregory the Patrician, the self-proclaimed emperor of the Byzantine province of Africa. In the early 650s Abd Allah served in expeditions to Khurasan (northern Persia) before returning to Arabia, where he supported Caliph Uthman ibn Affan (Osman) against the malcontents, valiantly defending him during the siege in the summer of 656.

Abd Allah opposed Caliph Ali and commanded infantry at the Battle of the Camel (Bassorah) in December 656. Following Ali's death in 661, Abd Allah supported Muawiyah but avoided political life until the accession of Yazid I, when Abd Allah refused to pledge allegiance to the new caliph. Instead Abd Allah, who aspired to be caliph, declared openly against Yazid. Some sources suggest that Abd Allah advised Husayn, the son of Caliph Ali and his rival for the supreme authority, to travel to Kufa despite knowing that the trip would be treacherous and potentially fatal.

After Husayn's death at Karbala in 680, Abd Allah had himself proclaimed caliph in Mecca and assumed the title *amir al-muminin*. His authority was recognized in much of Hejaz (western Arabia) but prompted the Umayyad invasion led by Muslim ibn Okba, who routed Abd Allah's forces at al-Harrah and captured Medina, and Husayn ibn Numair al-Sakuni, who besieged Mecca in September 683. The death of Caliph Yazid saved Abd Allah, since the Umayyad army raised the siege and departed. He then sent out delegations to various corners of the Arab world seeking recognition as caliph. His authority was recognized in Arabia, Iraq, and parts of Syria and Egypt, effectively splitting the caliphate into two parts.

Abd Allah's attempts to overthrow the Umayyad caliphs Marwan I and Abd al-Malik failed in 684–690; Abd Allah's troops were defeated at Kufa in 685, Harura in 687, and Maskin on the Lesser Tigris in 690. By early 690, the Umayyads reclaimed most of the regions and reduced Abd Allah's authority to Mecca alone. In 692, al-Hajjaj ibn Yusuf led a new Umayyad invasion of the Hejaz and laid siege to Mecca for the second time. The town was bombarded and its holy sites damaged, but Abd Allah resisted for six and a half months before he died in battle in November 692. His head was cut off and publicly displayed.

Alexander Mikaberidze

See also
Amr ibn al-As; Bassorah, Battle of; Umayyad Caliphate

References
Donner, Fred M. *The Early Islamic Conquests.* Princeton, NJ: Princeton University Press, 1981.
Madelung, Wilferd. *The Succession to Muhammad: A Study of the Early Caliphate.* Cambridge: Cambridge University Press, 1998.

Abdel-Rahman, Omar (1938–2017)

Omar Abdel-Rahman (aka the Blind Sheikh) was a militant Muslim. Born in Fayyum, Egypt, on May 3, 1938, he suffered from childhood diabetes, which resulted in blindness when he was 10 months old. By age 11, he had memorized the Quran and devoted himself to preaching the Muslim faith. Graduating in Quranic studies from Al-Azhar University in Cairo, he became a professor at the Theological College in Asyut and soon had gained a large militant following in Cairo's southern slums and villages after speaking out against Egyptian government violations of traditional Islamic sharia law.

Abdel-Rahman became the spiritual leader of the loosely knit, highly militant al-Gama'a al-Islamiyya (Islamic Group) umbrella organization and the Egyptian Islamic Jihad. Both organizations opposed the Egyptian government's policies and preached militant jihad. Islamic Jihad was responsible for the 1981 assassination of Egyptian president Anwar Sadat.

In 1981, Abdel-Rahman and 23 other Islamic militants were arrested in connection with Sadat's assassination. Abdel-Rahman spent three years in Egyptian jails, where he was tortured. Although acquitted of conspiracy in the assassination of Sadat, Abdel-Rahman was expelled from Egypt and went to Afghanistan, where he reportedly made contact with Al Qaeda leader Osama bin Laden. Abdel-Rahman then traveled widely, recruiting mujahideen to fight in Afghanistan against the Soviet Union. Returning to Egypt, he was again arrested in 1989 for inciting antigovernment clashes in Fayyum but was again acquitted.

Abdel-Rahman fled Egypt after being linked to further terrorist attacks on Coptic Christians in northern Egypt and illegally entered the United States in 1990 on a tourist visa obtained in Sudan. He gained permanent U.S. residency as a religious worker in 1991, an action that the U.S. Immigration and Naturalization Service (INS) now says was erroneous. However, Abdel-Rahman's marriage to an American Muslim convert enabled him to avoid deportation despite Egypt's calls for his extradition and his status as a prominent figure on the official U.S. terrorist list.

In January 1993, Abdel-Rahman was discovered to be actively preaching militant Islamic fundamentalist sermons to thousands of Egyptian, Yemeni, Sudanese, and other Muslim immigrants in New York's mosques. The sheikh's messages, secretly recorded on tape cassettes and funneled to his followers in the Egyptian underground, advocated the "eradication of all those who stand in the way of Islam" because "the laws of God have been usurped by Crusaders' laws. The hand of a thief is not cut off, the drinker of liquor is not whipped, the adulterer is not stoned. Islamic holy law should be followed to the letter."

Abdel-Rahman was arrested in the United States in July 1993 for his suspected involvement in the World Trade Center bombing, but insufficient evidence forced the INS to initially hold him on lesser charges of illegal immigration and polygamy. He was held in a U.S. federal prison while he appealed the deportation order against him and was awarded limited preferential treatment because of his ill health and blindness.

On October 1, 1995, in the largest terrorism trial to that point in U.S. history, Abdel-Rahman was convicted of 48 of 50 charges, including seditious conspiracy, for leading a four-year terrorist campaign of bombings and assassinations intended to destroy the United Nations building and other landmarks in the New York area. He was also convicted of conspiring to assassinate Egyptian president Hosni Mubarak and of solicitation to attack U.S. military installations. Abdel-Rahman was sentenced to life imprisonment on January 17, 1996. He is currently serving his life sentence at the Federal Administrative Maximum Penitentiary Hospital in Florence, Colorado. Abdel-Rahman is also believed to have ordered the November 1990 assassination in New York of militant Zionist leader Rabbi Meir Kahane. In 2005 members of Rahman's legal team, including lawyer Lynne Stewart, were convicted of facilitating communication between the imprisoned sheikh and members of the terrorist organization al-Gama'a al-Islamiyya in Egypt. They received long federal prison sentences based on their violated obligation to keep the sheikh incommunicado while providing him with legal counsel. In 2012 it was rumored that Egypt's new president, Mohamed Morsi, had begun negotiations with the United States to have the sheikh extradited to Egypt, but Morsi's ouster in July 2013 put an end to such efforts.

Adbdel-Rahman died at a medical center at a federal prison compound in Butner, North Carolina, of natural causes on February 18, 2017.

SPENCER C. TUCKER

See also
Al Qaeda; Bin Laden, Osama; Sadat, Anwar; Sharia

References
Fried, Joseph P. "Sheik Sentenced to Life in Prison in Bombing Plot." *New York Times,* January 18, 1996.
Hedges, Chris. "A Cry of Islamic Fury Tape in Brooklyn for Cairo." *New York Times,* January 7, 1993.
Kohlmann, Evan F. *Al-Qaida's Jihad in Europe.* London: Berg Publishers/Bloomsbury Academic, 2004.

Lance, Peter. *1000 Years for Revenge: International Terrorism and the FBI.* New York: HarperCollins, 2003.

Macfarquhar, Neil. "In Jail or Out, Sheik Preaches Views of Islam." *New York Times,* October 2, 1995.

Abdulhamid II (1842–1918)

Ottoman sultan. The son of Sultan Abdulmecid, Abdulhamid (Abdul Hamid II) was born on September 21, 1842. He succeeded to the throne on the deposition of his brother Murad on August 31, 1876, and ruled until April 27, 1909. Abdulhamid II enjoyed near absolutist rule. He attempted to carry out reforms, but these latter proved impossible. His reign came to be marked by war, internal violence, upheaval, and pressure on the empire from outside powers. A revolt occurred in Bosnia and Herzegovina in 1875, and war with Serbia and Montenegro followed, leading to Russian intervention and the Russo-Turkish War of 1877–1878. The latter was a disaster for the empire, although the harsh effects of the Treaty of San Stefano were somewhat mitigated by the 1878 Congress of Berlin. In gratitude for London's assistance at that conference, Turkey ceded Cyprus to Britain in 1878. In 1881 the French seized Tunis in North Africa, and in 1882 British forces occupied Egypt. Despite the Ottoman wartime victory over Greece in 1897, the Great Powers insisted that Turkey yield Crete. Further territorial losses for the Ottoman Empire occurred during the Balkan Wars of 1912–1913.

Agitation by Armenians within the empire for reforms promised them by the Great Powers at the 1885 Conference of Berlin led Abdulhamid to grant semiofficial recognition to Kurdish bandits already actively involved in violence against the Armenians. Made up largely of Kurds but also other minorities such as Turkomans and armed by the government, these Hamidiye Alaylari (Hamidian Regiments) actively attacked the Armenians and seized their grain, foodstuffs, and livestock. To protect themselves, the Armenians established the Social Democrat Hunchakian Party in 1887 and the Armenian Revolutionary Federation in 1890. Following clashes at Merzifon in 1892 and at Tokat in 1893, Abdulhamid employed force against the Armenians, utilizing local Muslims, mostly Kurds. Reportedly as many as 300,000 Armenians died in what became known as the Hamidian Massacres. Widely reported in the West, the massacres led to Abdulhamid being known as the "Bloody Sultan." On July 21, 1905, the Armenian Revolutionary Federation attempted to assassinate Abdulhamid with a car bombing during a public appearance, but with the sultan briefly delayed, the bomb went off early, killing 26 and wounding 58, 4 mortally.

Perhaps surprisingly, Abdulhamid pursued a liberal policy toward the Jews. In 1876 he allowed Jews of the empire full equality before the law. Jews were elected to the Ottoman parliament, and Abdulhamid named two Jews as senators. Another Jew was made an admiral in the Turkish Navy. In Palestine, Abdulhamid introduced administrative reforms that improved the situation for the people there, and during his reign the Hejaz railroad was constructed to Medina and Mecca.

Abdulhamid strongly opposed Zionist aspirations for a state in Palestine, however. This was at least in part because he feared that increased immigration from the European states, especially from Turkey's historic enemy Russia, would lead to further European influence in the empire. Following expanded Jewish emigration from Russia after the 1881 pogroms, in 1882 Abdulhamid prohibited Jewish immigration to Palestine. He rescinded the order in 1883 but reinstated it in 1891. Nonetheless, the regulations against immigration were not stringently enforced, and Jews were still able to settle in Palestine.

In June 1896 Abdulhamid awarded Zionist leader Theodor Herzl the Commander's Cross of the Majidiyya Order. In May 1891 the sultan received Herzl in private audience, although this brought no tangible advantages to Zionism. Abdulhamid rejected Herzl's effort to secure a charter that would have established an autonomous Jewish settlement in Palestine in return for cash payments to help reduce the Turkish national debt. Abdulhamid suggested instead that Jewish immigrants settle in various parts of the Ottoman Empire.

Dissatisfaction with continued deterioration of the Ottoman domestic situation coupled with the loss of Ottoman territory brought the rise of the Young Turk movement and the Revolution of 1908. Suspected of sympathies with a counterrevolutionary coup attempt of April 23, 1909, Abdulhamid was deposed on April 27. Banished to Salonica, he was permitted to return to Istanbul in 1912 and passed his last years studying and working at his hobby of carpentry. Abdulhamid died in Istanbul on February 10, 1918.

Spencer C. Tucker

See also

Armenians and the Armenian Genocide; Balkan Wars; Cyprus; Egypt, Athenian Intervention in; Herzl, Theodor; Ottoman Empire; Palestine, Pre-1918 History of; Russo-Ottoman Wars; San Stefano, Treaty of; World War I, Impact on the Middle East; Young Turks; Zionism

References

Fromkin, David. *A Peace to End All Peace: The Fall of the Ottoman Empire and the Creation of the Modern Middle East.* New York: Avon, 1989.

Kent, Marian, ed. *The Great Powers and the End of the Ottoman Empire.* London: Routledge, 1996.

Palmer, Alan. *The Decline and Fall of the Ottoman Empire.* London: John Murray, 1992.

Abdullah I (1882–1951)

Emir of Transjordan under the British mandate from 1921 to 1946 and, following Jordan's independence in 1946, king of Jordan from 1946 until his assassination in 1951. Abdullah bin Hussein, a 40th-generation direct descendant of Muhammad ibn Abdullah, the founder of Islam, was born in Mecca (now Saudi Arabia) sometime in 1882, the eldest son of Hussein bin Ali, emir of Mecca during 1908–1917. In 1917 Hussein, a Hashemite, proclaimed himself king of the Hejaz. He ruled until 1924, when he was defeated in a power struggle with Abdul Aziz al-Saud, who founded Saudi Arabia.

During World War I, Abdullah led several Arab revolts against Ottoman rule. Because of his assistance to the British in the war, in 1921 he secured the throne of Transjordan, an autonomous political division of the British Mandate for Palestine. The British government recognized Transjordan as a state in May 1923 and agreed to limit British control to military, financial, and foreign policy concerns. At the same time, the British placed Abdullah's brother Faisal (1883–1933) on the throne of Iraq. In 1928 Abdullah promulgated a constitution for Jordan, making him one of the first Arab leaders to establish a constitutional monarchy.

During World War II, Abdullah strongly opposed the Axis powers. This outlook reflected Abdullah's overall foreign policy stance, which was generally pro-Western and prodemocratic. On March 22, 1946, the British granted Jordan complete independence, and on May 25, 1946, the Jordanian parliament proclaimed Abdullah king of the Hashemite Kingdom of Transjordan.

During the Israeli-Arab War of 1948–1949, Jordan's Arab Legion, which had been trained by the British, was the most effective Arab fighting force, defeating the Israelis at Bab al-Wad, Latrun, and East Jerusalem. In April 1949, Abdullah changed his country's name to the Hashemite Kingdom of Jordan. In 1950, the Jordanian parliament formally annexed the West Bank. Abdullah's neighbors, particularly the Saudis, opposed his goal of uniting Jordan, Iraq, and Syria under the Hashemite dynasty. Some also looked askance at his pro-Western positions and generally moderate foreign and domestic policies, viewing them as akin to subservience to colonialist nations.

On July 20, 1951, Abdullah paid a visit to the Al-Aqsa Mosque in Jerusalem and there was assassinated by Mustapha Shukri Usho, a Palestinian, who shot the king three times. The king was accompanied by his young grandson and future Jordanian king Hussein ibn Talal (1935–1999), who was also shot and wounded. Hussein survived because the bullet had been deflected by a medal pinned on his chest at Abdullah's insistence earlier in the day. The assassin, who was immediately shot by security guards, was part of a conspiracy led by Colonel Abdullah Tell, former military governor of Jerusalem and a hero of the first Israeli-Arab war. Palestinians, angered by the possibility that Jordan and Lebanon might sign a separate peace treaty with Israel, had orchestrated Abdullah's assassination. A Jordanian court sentenced six men to death for the king's murder. The death sentence was in absentia for Tell and another accomplice, who had managed to flee to Egypt immediately after the shooting.

Abdullah was briefly succeeded by his son, Talal (1909–1972). Talal, who suffered from mental illness, abdicated the throne on August 11, 1952, whereupon Hussein became king.

MICHAEL R. HALL

See also

Al-Aqsa Mosque Massacre; Arab Legion; Arab Revolt of World War I; Faisal I, King of Iraq; Hussein ibn Ali ibn Mohammed; Hussein ibn Talal, King of Jordan; Ibn Saud, King; Israeli War of Independence; Jordan; Latrun, Battles of; Muhammad, Prophet of Islam; World War I, Impact on the Middle East

References

Milton-Edwards, Beverly, and Peter Hinchcliffe. *Jordan: A Hashemite Legacy.* London: Routledge, 2001.

Paris, Timothy. *Britain, the Hashemites, and Arab Rule, 1920–1925: The Sherifian Solution.* London: Frank Cass, 2003.

Abdullah II (1962–)

King of Jordan. Born in Amman, Jordan, on January 30, 1962, Abdullah ibn al-Hussein was the eldest son of King Hussein and Princess Muna al-Hussein. Abdullah and his 10 brothers and sisters are 43rd-generation direct descendants of Prophet Muhammad. Abdullah attended the Islamic Educational College in Amman and St. Edmund's School in Surrey, England. His secondary education occurred at Eaglebrook School and Deerfield Academy in the United States.

In 1980 Abdullah entered the Royal Military Academy, Sandhurst. Commissioned a second lieutenant in the British Army upon his graduation in 1981, he served in West Germany and in Britain. During 1982–1983 he completed a course in Middle Eastern affairs at Oxford University. Returning to Jordan, he served as a junior officer in the 40th Armored Brigade of the Jordanian Army. In 1985 he attended the Armored Officers Advanced Course at Fort Knox, Kentucky, returning to Jordan to take command as a captain of a tank company in the 91st Armored Brigade. He also served with the Anti-Tank Wing of the Jordanian Air Force, where he earned his wings as a helicopter pilot and also became a qualified parachutist.

During 1987–1988 Abdullah earned a master's degree in the School of Foreign Service at Georgetown University in Washington, D.C. Resuming his military career, he commanded the Jordanian Special Forces in 1989. Attending the British Staff College at Camberley, he was promoted to major in 1990. He next served as the Armored Corps representative in the Office of the Inspector General of the Jordanian Armed Forces.

In 1992 Abdullah took command of a battalion in the 2nd Armored Cavalry Regiment. The next year he was promoted to colonel and served with the 40th Brigade. In 1994 as a brigadier general, he reorganized the special forces and other elite Jordanian units into the Special Operations Command. Promoted to major general in 1998, he attended a course in defense resources management at the U.S. Naval Postgraduate School at Monterey, California.

On occasion during the 1990s Abdullah had acted as regent on the absence of King Hussein from Jordan, but for the most part this duty was performed by Hussein's younger brother, Crown Prince El Hassan bin Talal, whom Hussein had designated in 1965 as his successor. Hussein was diagnosed with cancer in 1992 and underwent several periods of medical treatment in the United States. Upon his return to Jordan after a six-month medical absence in late 1998, he publicly criticized Hassan's management of Jordanian affairs and accused him of abusing his power as regent and crown prince. On January 24, 1999, to the surprise of many, Hussein shifted the line of succession to Abdullah, naming him crown prince and heir to the throne. Abdullah became king following the death of his father two weeks later on February 7, 1999.

Since his accession to the throne, Abdullah has continued his father's work in seeking to find a solution to the seemingly intractable Arab-Israeli conflict. This quest can be seen in the title of his autobiography, *Our Last Best Chance: The Pursuit of Peace in a Time of Peril* (2010). Jordan seeks the

Abdullah II, king of Jordan since February 1999. He is shown here on April 5, 2001, during a visit to the United States. (U.S. Department of Defense)

establishment of an independent Palestinian state, with the 1967 borders. Toward that end, he has met frequently with world leaders, including U.S. presidents. Reportedly, a trip by Abdullah to Washington and meeting there with President Donald Trump in early February 2017 helped convince the new U.S. president to change his position regarding the construction of new Israel settlements in the West Bank and support for Israel moving its capital from Tel Aviv to Jerusalem.

Abdullah has also committed himself to the continued development of democratic institutions and pluralism in Jordan as well as to improving the lot of its citizens through economic development, advancing education, and protecting and furthering civil liberties. During Abdullah's reign, Jordan has been admitted to the World Trade Organization and has ratified free trade agreements with a number of countries, including the United States.

Islamic extremists have viewed Jordan with contempt because of its peace treaty with Israel and strong orientation toward the West. On November 9, 2015, Al Qaeda carried out a terrorist attack in Amman, the deadliest such attack in the kingdom's history. The terrorists struck three hotels, killing 60 people and wounding 115. Jordan then tightened its internal security. There have been no terrorist attacks in Jordan since, although at least one has been foiled.

The Arab Spring that began with a revolution in Tunisia in December 2010 saw unrest in Jordan, largely prompted by economic concerns brought on by sharp prices for basic commodities and high unemployment. Unrest led by the Muslim Brotherhood as well as leftist and other opposition groups led Abdullah to make a succession of leadership changes and pledge democratic reforms. Indeed, Jordan was the first regime to offer political concessions during the Arab Spring. These included a number of constitutional amendments and an early election in January 2013 that nonetheless led to proregime candidates winning a majority of the seats. The November 2016 general election saw a form of proportional representation, and reforms encouraged the participation of opposition parties. Many see this as a step toward establishing parliamentary governments in which parliamentary blocs instead of the king choose the prime minister.

Jordan has historically welcomed refugees, and the beginning of civil war in Syria in March 2011 led to a massive influx of refugees from that country across their 233-mile common border. By 2017 the number of refugees there had grown to some 629,000. The kingdom is among those states involved in covert operations to train and arm Syrian rebel forces, and in September 2014 it joined the international coalition against the extremist Islamic State of Iraq and Syria (ISIS).

In December 2014 when a Jordanian F-16 crashed near Raqqa, Syria, during a bombing mission, ISIS captured the pilot and in early February 2015 released a video showing him being burned to death in a cage. This sparked widespread outrage across Jordan and the world. Abdullah cut short a visit to the United States and authorized 56 air strikes against ISIS targets during the following week. In early 2017 Abdullah traveled to Washington, D.C., and met with Trump. There Abdullah convinced Trump to disavow support for the continued building of Israeli settlements in areas contested with the Palestinians.

Abdullah is today certainly regarded as one of the most respected leaders of the Arab world.

Spencer C. Tucker

See also
Arab Spring; Hussein ibn Talal, King of Jordan; Islamic State of Iraq and Syria; Jordan; Syrian Civil War

References
Robbins, Philip. *A History of Jordan*. Cambridge: Cambridge University Press, 2004.
Wagner, Heather Lehr. *King Abdullah II*. New York: Chelsea House, 2005.

Abizaid, John Philip (1951–)

U.S. Army officer and commander in chief of the U.S. Central Command (CENTCOM) from July 7, 2003, to March 16, 2007. John Philip Abizaid was born on April 1, 1951, in Coleville, California, into a Christian Lebanese family that had immigrated to the United States in the 1880s. He graduated from the U.S. Military Academy, West Point, in 1973 and was commissioned as a second lieutenant. He served initially in a parachute regiment as platoon leader before moving to the U.S. Army Rangers as a company commander.

Abizaid won a prestigious Olmsted Scholarship, which entitled him to study at a foreign university. After a year of training in Arabic, he enrolled in the University of Jordan–Amman in 1978. Political tension in Jordan resulted in the shutdown of the university, and Abizaid then trained with the Jordanian Army instead. In 1980 he earned a master of arts in Middle Eastern studies from Harvard University.

Abizaid led a ranger company during the U.S. invasion of Grenada in 1983. During the Persian Gulf crisis he commanded a battalion of the 325th Airborne Infantry Regiment. In 1991 the battalion was deployed in northern Iraq during Operation PROVIDE COMFORT, which followed the end of the Persian Gulf War (Operation DESERT STORM).

Abizaid subsequently studied peacekeeping at Stanford University's Hoover Institution and commanded the 504th Parachute Infantry Regiment of the 82nd Airborne Division before serving as assistant division commander of the 1st Armored Division in Bosnia-Herzegovina. Numerous staff appointments along the way included a tour as a United Nations observer in Lebanon and several European staff tours.

In 1997, Abizaid became commandant of cadets at West Point as a newly promoted brigadier general. There he played a major role in reforming some of the more egregious requirements of the plebe system. Promoted to major general in 1999, Abizaid assumed command of the 1st Infantry Division, which contributed troops to Operation JOINT GUARDIAN, the NATO campaign in Kosovo.

Abizaid's appointment as director of the Joint Staff brought with it advancement to lieutenant general. In January 2003 he became deputy commander of CENTCOM, which has responsibility for covering 27 countries of the Middle East and Central Asia. During the Iraq War (Operation IRAQI FREEDOM), which began in March 2003, Abizaid served as deputy commander (Forward), Combined Force Command. He succeeded General Tommy Franks as CENTCOM commander when the latter retired in July 2003. At the same time, Abizaid was promoted to full (four-star) general.

When Abizaid took command of CENTCOM, insurgent violence in Iraq was rapidly escalating. He had already expressed reservations about poor planning for the postwar era in Iraq and the competence of Pentagon officials in charge of the arrangements. Abizaid believed that most Iraqis would not welcome a U.S. occupation of their country and that widespread terrorism and guerrilla activity would likely follow a U.S. invasion.

Abizaid used the opportunity of his first press conference to state that the United States was now fighting a classic guerrilla insurgency in Iraq, an opinion directly opposite the views held by Secretary of Defense Donald Rumsfeld, who bristled at Abizaid's comments. The contradiction quickly made headlines and resulted in Abizaid receiving a private reprimand from Rumsfeld.

Abizaid also disagreed with the decision by Paul Bremer, head of the Coalition Provisional Authority, to disband the Iraqi Army, and advocated rehiring select Sunni officers. Abizaid was also critical of Bremer's de-Baathification policy. In addition, Abizaid realized that the U.S. intelligence apparatus in Iraq was in total disarray. On October 1, 2003, he issued orders reorganizing intelligence operations so that in the future all reports would be passed through a single intelligence fusion center.

During the summer of 2004, Abizaid informed his superiors that a military victory in Iraq was unlikely. Instead of pursuing an elusive victory, Abizaid favored a policy of shifting the burden of the war to Iraqi security forces and minimizing the U.S. presence. He also supported research into the situation in Iraq and on the global war on terror. However, publicly and in interviews with the press Abizaid presented an optimistic version of events, despite having privately expressed doubts. In keeping with his public optimism, he appeared before the Senate Armed Services Committee on March 16, 2006, and gave another positive review of progress in Iraq. During a break in the proceedings, Abizaid approached Congressman John Murtha (D-Pa.), a former marine who had been highly critical of the Iraq War, and indicated to Murtha that Murtha's views were close to his own.

Abizaid's retirement as head of CENTCOM was announced in December 2006. On March 16, 2007, he was replaced by Admiral William Fallon. On May 1, 2007, Abizaid retired from the army and became a research fellow at the Hoover Institution. In 2008, he became a member of the board of directors of RPM International.

PAUL WILLIAM DOERR

See also
Baath Party; Bremer, Lewis Paul, III; Franks, Tommy; Iraq Insurgency; Iraq War; Persian Gulf War, Overview; PROVIDE COMFORT, Operation

References
Gordon, Michael R., and Bernard E. Trainor. *Cobra II: The Inside Story of the Invasion and Occupation of Iraq.* New York: Pantheon Books, 2006.
Ricks, Thomas E. *Fiasco: The American Military Adventure in Iraq.* New York: Penguin, 2006.
Woodward, Bob. *State of Denial: Bush at War, Part III.* New York: Simon and Schuster, 2006.

Aboukir, First Battle of (July 25, 1799)

In May 1798, French general Napoleon Bonaparte had set sail from Toulon, France, for Egypt with a vast armada of some 400 ships. The project was not new, but the Directory hoped that Napoleon could secure Egypt, then march overland and threaten the British in India. The planners had hoped that the Ottoman Empire would not intervene militarily. After taking the island of Malta and seizing its ample treasury, the French arrived at Alexandria on July 1.

The British were well aware that the French were mounting a major expedition, and Royal Navy rear admiral Horatio Nelson had correctly guessed its destination to be Egypt, but sailing faster than the French, his squadron had arrived at Alexandria before them and then sailed elsewhere. He finally caught up with the French, and in the Battle of Aboukir Bay near Alexandria (the Battle of the Nile as the British know it) on August 1, 1798, the British destroyed the bulk of the French fleet, in effect cutting Napoleon off in Egypt.

This British naval victory and adroit British diplomacy led the Ottoman Empire to declare war on France on September 9, 1798. Meanwhile, Bonaparte had defeated the Mamluk forces in the Battle of the Pyramids (Embabeh) on July 21, 1798, and in other engagements. The French had also seized Cairo and then put down a revolt there, effectively securing control of Egypt.

The first serious Ottoman military effort came in 1799. One Ottoman army was to move overland from Syria to attack Egypt by means of the Sinai. A second Ottoman army was to assemble on the island of Rhodes and then be assisted by the Royal Navy in mounting a seaborne invasion. In February 1799 Bonaparte took the initiative and marched into Palestine, capturing El Arish and Jaffa and then laying siege to Acre (Acco). There he suffered rebuff, unable to take the city owing to the capture by the British of his heavy siege guns, which he had sent by ship. On May 10 Bonaparte broke off the siege and returned to Cairo, falsely trumpeting a victory, on June 14.

On July 14, the second Ottoman army arrived in Egypt. It had seen service at Acre helping to repulse the French infantry assaults. It had then proceeded southward, supported by a combined Anglo-Ottoman fleet, to land at Aboukir Bay. Storming ashore, the Ottomans had easily overwhelmed the small French garrison there of some 300 men. But Ottoman commander Mustapha Bey had then decided to dig in rather than advance toward Alexandria.

Lacking sufficient numbers to attack the Ottoman force, French commander at Alexandria General Auguste de Marmont put up such defenses as he could and appealed for assistance from Bonaparte. Securing manpower in Cairo, Bonaparte quickly created a new army and set out for Alexandria, where he was delighted to find the Ottoman army still encamped at Aboukir Bay.

There is no agreement on numbers of men engaged in the Battle of July 25. Some accounts give the Ottomans 18,000 men, which is no doubt too high. Although it had initially numbered some 15,000 men, it had suffered casualties from the fighting at Acre and from disease and may have numbered as few as 7,000 men, probably the key factor in Mustapha Bey's decision to fight a defensive battle close to the support of the allied fleet. Napoleon's field force probably numbered some 6,000–9,000 men.

The Ottoman forces were drawn up in two lines: the forward line was inland on a plain about a mile from the coast, while the second line was at Mount Vizir near the sea. This division of manpower was a great advantage for Bonaparte, as it allowed him the opportunity to engage and defeat his enemy in detail. In other battles in Egypt, Bonaparte had taken a defensive posture. At Aboukir, however, he took the offensive.

While the French infantry attacked the center of the Ottoman first line, General Joachim Murat's cavalry struck both its flanks. The Ottoman first line was soon rolled up and forced back onto the second line. Notable in this phase of the battle was the personal combat between Murat and Mustapha Ali. Murat suffered a pistol shot to his jaw, while the Ottoman commander lost two fingers and his pistol to Murat's saber blow. After the French success here, Bonaparte rested his men before renewing the battle at 3:00 that same afternoon.

The second phase of the battle saw the French force the Ottomans back to the sea. Thousands of Ottoman soldiers are said to have drowned while trying to escape to the ships offshore, with the seamen rescuing all they could. Among those escaping was future Egyptian ruler Mohammed Ali. Ottoman casualties are said to have been as many as 2,000 killed, 4,000 drowned, 1,500 taken prisoner, and 2,000 missing. French casualties were reported as 220 killed and 600 wounded.

The Battle of Aboukir secured the French occupation of Egypt, at least for the time being. Shortly after the battle, French officers went aboard the British flagship to arrange an exchange of prisoners. The British presented them with French newspapers, which painted a dire picture of the situation in France—now threatened by the forces of the Second Coalition. Despite not having received orders to this effect (they had, however, been issued), Bonaparte decided to abandon his army and return to France. He departed in a fast frigate on August 23 and reached France on October 9. A month later he took part in the coup d'état in Paris that overthrew the Directory.

The French Army of Egypt remained in place for two more years. The Second Battle of Aboukir (March 8, 1801) brought its defeat. Under the terms of capitulation, the British agreed to transport the survivors back to France.

Spencer C. Tucker

See also

Aboukir, Second Battle of; Aboukir Bay, Battle of; Acre, 1799 Siege of; Bonaparte, Napoleon; Egypt, French Invasion and Occupation of; Nelson, Horatio; Pyramids, Battle of the

References

Chandler, David G. *The Campaigns of Napoleon.* New York: Macmillan, 1966.

Markham, J. David. *Napoleon's Road to Glory: Triumphs, Defeats & Immortality.* London: Brassey's, 2003.

Schur, Nathan. *Napoleon in the Holy Land.* London: Greenhill, 1999.

Strathern, Paul. *Napoleon in Egypt.* New York: Bantam, 2007.

Aboukir, Second Battle of (March 8, 1801)

Battle between the British and French forces in Egypt that made British victory over the French possible. A French Army under general Napoleon Bonaparte had arrived in Egypt on July 1, 1798. The French Directory, then ruling France, hoped to secure Egypt and then send Bonaparte's

Army of the Orient overland to threaten the British in India. While Bonaparte's forces were successful on land and defeated both the Mamluks of Egypt and then the Ottoman Turks when the latter joined the Second Coalition against France, the French had been essentially cut off in Egypt by Rear Admiral Horatio Nelson's brilliant victory in the Battle of the Nile on August 1, 1798. With the Ottomans preparing to invade Egypt, Bonaparte took the initiative and invaded Palestine but was unable to advance past Acre (Akko) owing to British capture of his siege artillery, sent by sea. Bonaparte was forced to break off the siege and withdraw. He then engaged and defeated a second Ottoman army landed by British and Ottoman ships at Aboukir near Alexandria on July 25, 1799. The British, however, made Bonaparte aware through French newspapers of the unrest in France, and shortly thereafter he abandoned his army and returned to France aboard a fast French frigate. In November he seized power in a coup d'état in Paris.

French general Jean-Baptiste Kléber then assumed command of French forces in Egypt. The French repelled a second landing of Ottoman troops at Damietta in early November but then faced combined Anglo-Ottoman forces, which included European-style Ottoman troops. Kléber negotiated a French withdrawal with the Ottomans in January 24, 1800, but the agreement depended on British ships transporting the French army back to France, which the British rejected. Fighting then resumed.

On March 20, 1800, Kléber defeated an Ottoman army at Heliopolis, then reclaimed Cairo and much of Lower Egypt. During March–April the French suppressed a second major uprising in Cairo. To secure more manpower, Kléber also organized the Coptic Christian Legion. On June 14, 1800, however, Kléber was stabbed to death in Cairo. His successor was the far less capable General Jacques Menou, who converted to Islam and took the name Abdallah Menou.

Menou failed to take adequate precautions to meet a British invasion, for in early March 1801 a powerful British naval force arrived in Aboukir Bay near Alexandria and the Nile Delta. Commanded by Viscount George Keith, it included seven ships of the line, five frigates, and a dozen corvettes escorting a large number of troop transports. Unfortunately for the invaders, strong gales and heavy seas delayed the disembarkation for several days; however, Menou failed to move promptly.

On March 8 with the weather now allowing, some 5,000 British troops under Sir Ralph Abercromby began coming

Illustration depicting the Second Battle of Aboukir, Egypt. Fought on March 8, 1801, it saw some 5,000 British troops come ashore and defeat 2,000 French defenders, making possible the ultimate British victory over the French in Egypt. (Print Collector/Getty Images)

ashore at Aboukir. These were the first wave in an invasion force of some 17,500 British troops with which the British intended to defeat the remaining French troops in Egypt.

In this Second Battle of Aboukir, French general Louis Friant's had only 2,000 men and 10 artillery pieces. These proved wholly insufficient to contain the British, although artillery fire on the boats as they came ashore from the transports sank some of them and killed or wounded 600 British soldiers and sailors. But the invaders established a lodgement ashore and then, with fixed bayonets, stormed the steep cliffs, driving off the far smaller force of French defenders and enabling the remainder of the invasion force and its artillery and equipment to come ashore. Success here made everything that followed possible.

Leaving a smaller force in place to reduce Fort Aboukir, Abercromby then advanced with the main body. The fort's garrison of 200 men surrendered on March 20. Meanwhile, in a major clash near Alexandria on March 13, the British sustained 130 killed and 600 wounded or missing. However, the French withdrew, having suffered the loss of at least 300 dead or wounded along with eight guns.

It was now essential that Menou strike quickly with all available forces against the British. This is what Bonaparte or Kléber would have done, but Menou was far too slow in his response and even then left half his force at Cairo. Even if Cairo had risen again, as indeed it did, he could have retaken it later. In any case, he gave Abercromby time to consolidate and lay siege to Alexandria. Another Ottoman force marched through Syria to Egypt, and a third major uprising against the French occurred in Cairo. Mamluk forces also continued to harass the French in Lower Egypt.

On March 21, Menou did battle with the British in the decisive battle near ancient Canopus, between Aboukir and Alexandria. Abercromby disposed of some 15,000 men; Menou's force was slightly inferior in numbers, perhaps 12,000, but he attacked. The result was costly for both sides. The French lost perhaps 4,000 dead, wounded, or captured. During the days after the battle, the British buried 1,040 Frenchmen. British losses were probably in excess of a reported 140 killed and 1,040 wounded. Abercromby was among the wounded. He became delirious and died a week later.

On June 27, 1801, the French garrison of Cairo surrendered. The terms of capitulation allowed the nearly 13,000 French soldiers and officials, not counting women and children, to depart the city with their weapons, equipment, and such personal possessions as they could carry. They marched to Rosetta, from where they were evacuated in British transports and returned to France in October.

Menou, who had withdrawn with his remaining forces from Canopus to Alexandria, capitulated there, the treaty being signed on August 30, with Admiral Keith coming ashore on September 2 to ratify it. The French scientists were allowed to keep their collections but not the Rosetta Stone, which proved to be the key to unlocking Egyptian hieroglyphics and which the British insisted upon taking.

Under the terms of the capitulation, those men surrendering at Alexandria were also returned to France by the British. Bonaparte had arrived in Egypt with some 34,000 land troops and some 16,000 sailors. Of this number only about 23,000 (3,000 of them sick or wounded) ever returned to France. The French Egyptian adventure was over.

SPENCER C. TUCKER

See also
Aboukir Bay, Battle of; Aboukir, First Battle of; Acre, 1799 Siege of; Bonaparte, Napoleon; Egypt, French Invasion and Occupation of; Mamluk Sultanate; Nelson, Horatio

References
Chandler, David G. *The Campaigns of Napoleon.* New York: Macmillan, 1966.
Herold, J. Christopher. *Bonaparte in Egypt.* New York: Harper & Row, 1962.
Markham, J. David. *Napoleon's Road to Glory: Triumphs, Defeats & Immortality.* London: Brassey's, 2003.
Schur, Nathan. *Napoleon in the Holy Land.* London: Greenhill, 1999.
Strathern, Paul. *Napoleon in Egypt.* New York: Bantam, 2007.

Aboukir Bay, Battle of (August 1, 1798)

In 1798 the French mounted a major expedition under General Napoleon Bonaparte to capture Egypt and threaten British interests in India. The French force sailed on May 19. It numbered some 35,000 men in 400 transports, accompanied by 13 ships of the line and a number of smaller frigates. En route to Egypt the French took Malta, ruled by the Knights of St. John, and its sizable treasury. London dispatched a small fleet under Rear Admiral Horatio Nelson to seek out the French invasion force that had sailed east from Toulon to a then unknown destination. In pursuit, Nelson actually passed close by the French ships on the night of June 22–23 without realizing it. He guessed Bonaparte's objective to be Alexandria. With all sails set, Nelson's ships arrived there on June 28, but not seeing the French there, Nelson departed. Slower than the British because of their transports and supply ships, the French ships dropped anchor in Alexandria on July 1. Believing that the French might have made for Sicily,

BATTLE OF THE NILE, AUGUST 1, 1798

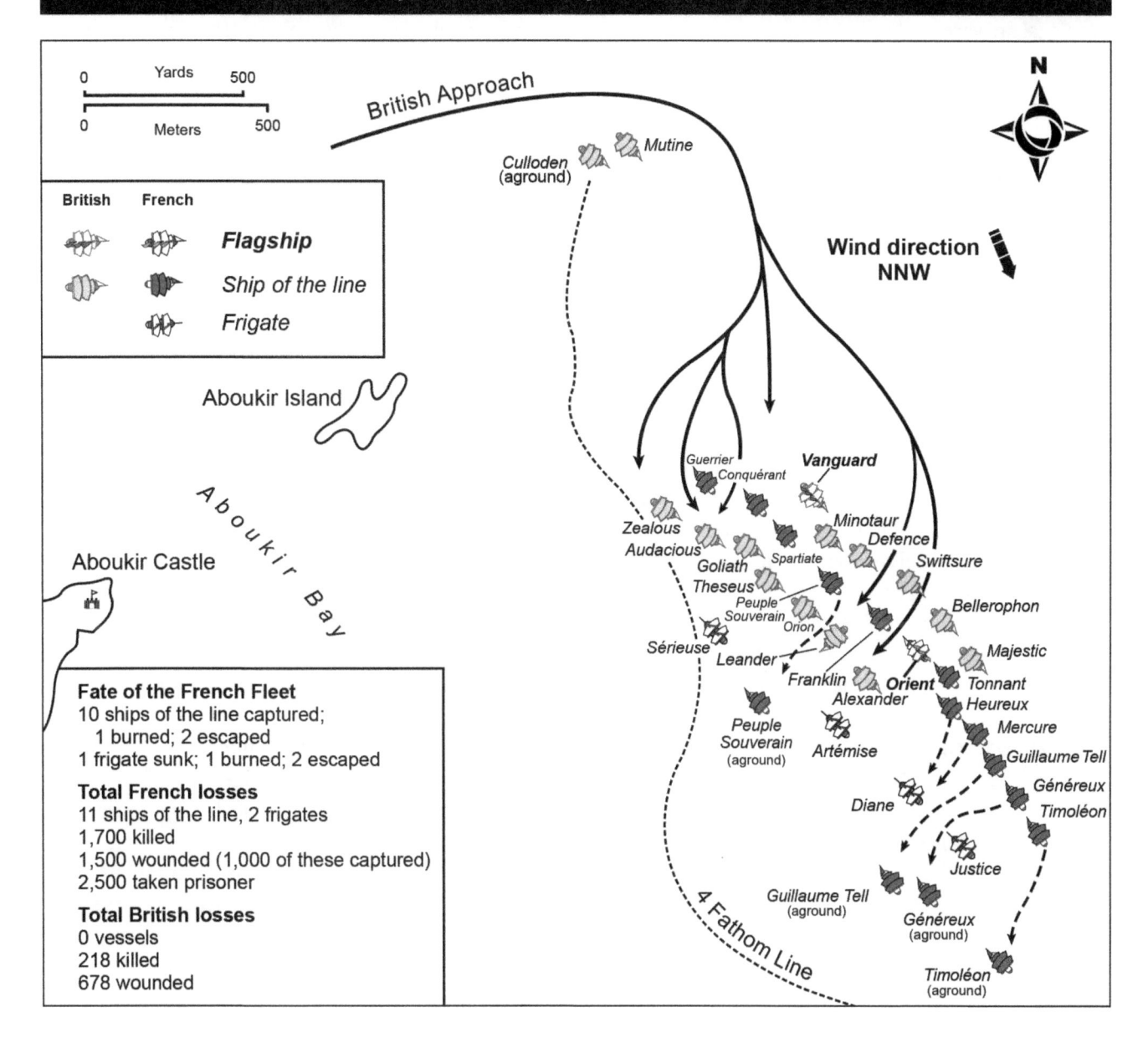

Fate of the French Fleet
10 ships of the line captured;
  1 burned; 2 escaped
1 frigate sunk; 1 burned; 2 escaped

Total French losses
11 ships of the line, 2 frigates
1,700 killed
1,500 wounded (1,000 of these captured)
2,500 taken prisoner

Total British losses
0 vessels
218 killed
678 wounded

Nelson sailed for that island, only to learn that he had been correct in his original surmise.

Finally, at Aboukir Bay, Egypt, on August 1, 1798, Nelson and his 13 74-gun ships of the line caught up with the French fleet commanded by Vice Admiral François Brueys d'Aigalliers. Although the two sides were equal in number of capital ships, many of the French ships were larger than those of the English. The English had 13 ships of the line of 74 guns each, 1 ship of 50 guns, and 1 sloop. The French had 13 ships of the line: 1 of 120 guns, 3 of 80 guns each, and 9 of 74 guns. They also had 4 frigates of 36–40 guns each, 2 brigs, 3 bomb vessels, and several gunboats. The French crews, however, had been decimated by disease, and they were short of water and supplies. Some of the French ships were also weakly armed, so the French battle line was considerably less formidable than it appeared.

The French were also unprepared for battle. Brueys, who flew his flag in the 120-gun *Orient,* thought his position secure. His 13 ships of the line were anchored in a single line, protected by shoals, gunboats, and shore batteries, but part of his crews were ashore. He had not ordered cables strung between the ships to prevent penetration by opposing vessels, nor did the French ships have springs attached to their anchor cables to prevent an opposing vessel from engaging them stern to stern. Also, the nearest French land batteries were three miles distant and thus quite unable to provide additional firepower to the fleet.

On seeing the French ships, Nelson ordered the general signal "Prepare for Battle" hoisted. As the British ships closed on the French, over dinner Nelson announced to his officers, "Before this time tomorrow, I shall have gained a Peerage or Westminster Abbey." He had foreseen the situation and already explained to his captains what he expected; no new orders were needed, and the attack occurred that same afternoon. The resulting Battle of Aboukir Bay, which the British remember as the Battle of the Nile, was a disaster for the French.

The French ships were anchored to allow them to swing with the current. Noting that if there was room for a French ship to swing there was sufficient space for a British ship to maneuver and guessing that the French ships were unprepared to fight on their port sides, Nelson sent his leading ships in from that direction. The risk was revealed when the first British ship, the *Culloden,* grounded. Three of Nelson's ships of the line led by the *Goliath* managed to get in between the French battle line and the shore, however, where they anchored. Nelson, in the *Vanguard,* took the remainder of his force down the outside of the French line.

Brueys's ships were now under attack from two sides. Such fighting was difficult in the best of circumstances, but it was made more so for the French because their ships were shorthanded. Systematically moving down the line, the British doubled up on one French ship after another.

The battle continued well into the night. The *Orient,* which was being painted when the British arrived, caught fire. The flames finally reached the magazine, whereupon the ship went up in a great explosion that rocked the coast for miles. The flagship took down with it most of Bonaparte's treasury, some £600,000 in gold and diamonds alone.

By dawn only two French ships of the line remained; the rest had been burned, sunk, or captured. One that did get away carried Admiral Pierre Charles Villeneuve, Nelson's opponent at the later Battle of Trafalgar; the other took Admiral Denis Decrès, subsequently Bonaparte's minister of marine. Admiral Brueys was among those killed. More important from a strategic standpoint than the loss of the French ships, Bonaparte's army was now cut off in Egypt. The British victory also led to the formation of a new coalition against France that included Russia, Austria, some of the Italian states, and the Ottoman Empire. Bonaparte was in effect the prisoner of his conquest.

British sea power had ended Bonaparte's dreams of a Middle Eastern empire. In early October 1799, made aware of the turmoil in France, he abandoned his army in Egypt and sailed to France in a fast frigate. The next month Bonaparte took power as first consul in a coup d'état.

SPENCER C. TUCKER

See also
Aboukir, First Battle of; Bonaparte, Napoleon; Egypt, French Invasion and Occupation of; Nelson, Horatio

References
Foreman, Laura. *Napoleon's Lost Fleet: Bonaparte, Nelson, and the Battle of the Nile.* New York: Discovery Books, 1999.
Gardiner, Robert, ed. *Nelson against Napoleon.* London: Chatham Publishing, 1997.
Lavery, Brian. *Nelson and the Nile: The Naval War against Bonaparte, 1798.* London: Chatham Publishing, 1998.
Tracy, Nicholas. *Nelson's Battles: The Art of Victory in the Age of Sail.* London: Chatham, 1996.

Abu Abbas (1948–2004)

Leader of the Palestine Liberation Front (PLF). Born Muhammed Zaidan in Safed, Palestine, in 1948, he moved with his family to Syria that same year. In 1968, Abu Abbas (his nom de guerre) joined the Popular Front for the Liberation of Palestine–General Command (PFLP-GC) led by Ahmad Jibril. Abu Abbas disagreed with Jibril over the PFLP-GC's strong support for Syria and its failure to criticize Syrian support of the Phalange against the Palestine Liberation Organization (PLO) in Lebanon. In April 1977, Abu Abbas and Tal'at Ya'qub left the PFLP-GC to form the PLF.

During the 1980s, Abu Abbas advocated armed struggle against Israel, chiefly in the form of terrorism mounted from southern Lebanon. He was wounded in fighting during the 1982 Israeli invasion of Lebanon. In 1983 when the PLF split into three factions, Abu Abbas led the largest, a pro-Iraqi group. He became a member of the PLO's Executive Committee in 1984.

On October 7, 1985, Abu Abbas masterminded the PLF's most dramatic terrorist action, the hijacking of the Italian cruise ship the *Achille Lauro* that resulted in the death of American Jew Leon Klinghoffer. Although the Egyptian aircraft carrying Abu Abbas and the other three hijackers to asylum in Tunisia was diverted by U.S. aircraft to a NATO air base in Sicily, the Italian government let the passengers depart, and Abu Abbas escaped among them. There was, however, much criticism of Abu Abbas for the

PLF attempted terrorist attack on Nizamim Beach near Tel Aviv on May 30, 1990, which was designed to torpedo the possibility of PLO-Israeli peace talks. Nonetheless, the PLF had regularly received funding from PLO chairman Yasser Arafat. Indeed, in January 1996 the PLO agreed to provide an undisclosed sum to finance the Leon and Marilyn Klinghoffer Memorial Foundation of the U.S. Anti-Defamation League, in return for which Klinghoffer's daughters dropped a lawsuit brought against the PLO. In 1989, Abu Abbas supported the PLO's acceptance of United Nations Security Council Resolution 242.

Following the 1993 Oslo Accords, Abu Abbas returned to the Gaza Strip. He then moved to Iraq. There was a U.S. warrant for his arrest, and in 2003 during the U.S.-led invasion of Iraq, Abu Abbas was taken by U.S. forces. He died in Iraq while in U.S. custody on March 8, 2004, reportedly of natural causes.

Spencer C. Tucker

See also

Arafat, Yasser; Palestine Liberation Organization; Terrorism

References

Alexander, Yonah. *Palestinian Secular Terrorism*. Ardsley, NY: Transnational Publishers, 2003.

Bohn, Michael K. *The Achille Lauro Hijacking: Lessons in the Politics and Prejudice of Terrorism*. Dulles, VA: Potomac Books, 2004.

Cassese, Antonio. *Terrorism, Politics and Law: The Achille Lauro Affair*. Princeton, NJ: Princeton University Press, 1989.

Nassar, Jamal R. *The Palestine Liberation Organization: From Armed Struggle to the Declaration of Independence*. New York: Praeger, 1991.

Abu Ghraib

Notorious Iraqi prison facility. Located about 20 miles west of the Iraqi capital of Baghdad and known during the regime of Saddam Hussein as an infamous place of torture and execution, Abu Ghraib prison later drew international attention when photographs of inmate abuse and reports of torture at the hands of coalition troops were made public in 2004.

Abu Ghraib, officially called the Baghdad Central Confinement Facility (BCCF) under the Hussein regime, was built by British contractors hired by the Iraqi government in the 1960s. Covering an area of about one square mile, the prison housed five different types of prisoners during the Hussein regime: those with long sentences, those with short sentences, those imprisoned for capital crimes, those imprisoned for so-called special offenses, and foreign detainees. Cells, which are about 51 square feet in area, held as many as 40 people each.

During the 1980–1988 Iran-Iraq War, the Iraqi Baathist regime used the facility to imprison political dissidents and members of ethnic or religious groups seen as threats to the central government. In particular, hundreds of Arab and Kurdish Shiites and Iraqis of Iranian heritage were arrested and housed in the BCCF; torture and executions became routine. Among the tactics used by prison guards was the feeding of shredded plastic to inmates, and it has been speculated that prisoners were used as guinea pigs for biological and chemical weapons. Although the Iraqi government kept its actions within the complex secret from Iraqi citizens and the international community alike, Amnesty International reported several specific incidents, including the 1996 execution of hundreds of political dissidents and the 1998 execution of many people who had been involved in the 1991 Shiite revolt. The prison, which contained thousands of inmates who were completely cut off from outside communication and held without conviction, was also used to house coalition prisoners of war during the 1991 Persian Gulf War.

With the 2003 U.S.-led Iraq War and subsequent fall of the Hussein government in Iraq, coalition troops took control of Abu Ghraib prison. The U.S. military used the complex for holding Iraqi insurgents and terrorists accused of anti-U.S. attacks, although by 2004 it had released several hundred prisoners and shared use of the facility with the Iraqi government. Because of the disarray in the Iraqi criminal system, many common criminals uninvolved in the war were held at the facility as well.

Abu Ghraib became a household name in April 2004, when the television program *60 Minutes II* aired photographs of prisoner abuse at the hands of U.S. troops. Just two days later, the photographs were posted online with Seymour Hersh's article in the *New Yorker* magazine. The photos, which showed prisoners wearing black hoods, attached to wires with which they were threatened with electrocution, and placed in humiliating sexual positions, sparked worldwide outrage and calls for the investigation and conviction of the military personnel involved.

The abuse was immediately decried by U.S. president George W. Bush and Defense Secretary Donald Rumsfeld, who on May 7, 2004, took responsibility for the acts occurring during his tenure. The Pentagon, which had been investigating reports of abuse since 2003, launched a further investigation into the incidents documented in the photographs. Previously, detainee abuse had been investigated by U.S. Army major general Antonio Taguba, who had been given digital images of the abuse by Sergeant Joseph Darby in January 2004. Major General Taguba concluded in his 53-page report that U.S. military personnel had violated international law. More than a dozen U.S. soldiers and officers were removed from the prison as a result of the internal investigation.

More details emerged following the *60 Minutes II* broadcast. Photographs that the U.S. government would not allow to be released earlier were circulated in 2006. Most importantly, it appeared that the senior U.S. military officer, Lieutenant General Ricardo Sanchez, had authorized treatment "close to" torture, such as the use of military dogs, temperature extremes, and sensory and sleep deprivation, thus making it more difficult to locate responsibility for the general environment leading to abuse. In addition to charging certain troops and contractors with torture, the United States made an effort to reduce the number of detainees—estimated at 7,000 prior to the scandal's outbreak—by several thousand. However, many argued that the measures taken were not harsh enough to fit the crime, and some demanded Rumsfeld's resignation. Meanwhile, in August 2004 a military panel confirmed 44 cases of prisoner abuse at the facility and identified 23 soldiers as being responsible. The so-called ringleader of the operation, Army Specialist Charles Graner, was convicted and sentenced to 10 years in prison. In January 2005, Abu Ghraib was twice attacked by insurgents attempting to free prisoners held there.

The United States held detainees in the portion of the prison known as Camp Redemption, built in 2004. In September 2006, the United States handed over control of Abu Ghraib to the Iraqi government. The Iraqi government holds convicted criminals in the older area known as the Hard Site, although efforts were made to release those who might be innocent.

The terrorist organization Al Qaeda in Iraq claimed responsibility for two coordinated assaults on July 23, 2013, that freed 500–600 militants being held at Abu Ghraib and Taji. This action greatly enhanced the Al Qaeda affiliate's fortunes in Iraq and Syria. At least 26 members of the Iraqi security forces and more than a dozen prisoners died.

JESSICA BRITT

See also
Al Qaeda in Iraq; Bush Doctrine; Hussein, Saddam; Iran-Iraq War; Iraq; Kurds

References
Danner, Mark. *Torture and Truth: America, Abu Ghraib, and the War on Terror.* New York: New York Review Books, 2004.
Graveline, Christopher, and Michael Clemens. *The Secrets of Abu Ghraib Revealed.* Dulles, VA: Potomac Books, 2010.
Greenberg, Karen J., and Joshua L. Dratel, eds. *The Torture Papers: The Road to Abu Ghraib.* Cambridge, MA: Cambridge University Press, 2005.
Strasser, Steven, ed. *The Abu Ghraib Investigations: The Official Independent Panel and Pentagon Reports on the Shocking Prisoner Abuse in Iraq.* New York: PublicAffairs, 2004.

Abulustayn, Battle of (April 15, 1277)

Major battle between the Mamluks and the Mongols on April 15, 1277. The initial Mongol invasion of Syria and Palestine, organized by Hulegu Khan, resulted in the Mamluk victories at Ayn Jalut and Homs in 1260. For a variety of reasons, neither Hulegu nor his successor made any serious attempts to exact revenge on the Mamluks and their allies or attempt to reconquer Syria for the next 21 years. The Mamluks used this period to reform their forces and establish political alliances (e.g., with the Christian crusader states and the Golden Horde) to be better prepared for the future wars against the Ilkhan Mongols.

Between 1261 and 1277 the Mamluks and the Mongols were engaged in prolonged border skirmishing, with neither side willing or able to undertake a major attack. In 1277, however, Mamluk leader Baybars, concerned by Mongol expansion into the Sultanate of Rum, launched a preemptive invasion into Asia Minor. Marching through Palestine and Syria, Baybars led his army across the Taurus Mountains via the Aqcha Darband Pass. During the crossing, the Mamluk advance guard under Sunqur al-Ashqar surprised a Mongol detachment and captured a few prisoners who informed Baybars that the main Mongol army under Tudawun, supported by the contingents from the Rum Sultanate and Georgia, was bivouacked near the town of Abulustayn (Elbistan).

On April 15 the Mamluks descended from the mountain passes onto the plain of Abulustayn, where the Mongol army was already arranged. According to surviving sources (e.g., Bar Hebraeus, al-Mansuri), the Mongol army was deployed in 11 units (*atlab*), each of about 1,000 men. The Georgian contingent of some 3,000 men was kept as a separate *tulb*, while the Rumi troops were separated from the main force because the Mongols did not trust them.

The battle commenced with a spirited Mongol and Georgian attack that smashed through the Mamluk army center, drove back the left wing, and threatened to turn the right wing. In this critical moment Baybars demonstrated remarkable composure, as he exploited his numerical superiority by bringing up reinforcements, strengthening threatened sectors, and launching a counterattack. The Mongols and Georgians were driven back, but instead of retreating, they dismounted and continued to fight to the death.

Most of the Mongol army perished, including its leaders. Contemporary sources disagree on precise numbers but refer to some 6,000–10,000 losses; Bar Hebraeus states that some 5,000 Mongols and 2,000 Georgians died in the fighting. The victory allowed Baybars to limit Mongol authority and extend his influence to the Sultanate of Rum. It also provoked open hostilities between the Mamluk Sultanate and the Mongol Ilkhanate, which resulted in the Battle of Homs.

ALEXANDER MIKABERIDZE

See also
Baybars I; Homs, First Battle of; Homs, Second Battle of; Homs, Third Battle of

References
Amitai-Preiss, Reuven. *Mongols and Mamluks: The Mamluk-Ilkhanid War, 1260–1281*. Cambridge: Cambridge University Press, 1995.
Boyle, J. A. *The Mongol World Empire, 1206–1370*. London: Variorum, 1977.
Morgan, D. O. "The Mongols in Syria 1260–1300." In *Crusade and Settlement*, ed. Peter W. Edbury. Cardiff: University College of Cardiff Press, 1985.

Abu Muslim Khorasani (718?–755)

Prominent Arab military commander and one of the key leaders in the Abbasid Revolution. Abu Muslim Khorasani's early life is obscure owing to a paucity of sources, which disagree on the date (718 to 727) and place of his birth (Merv or Isfahan) and family origins. Most sources, however, agree that he grew up in Kufa, which in the early eighth century became a center of anti-Umayyad unrest.

The Abbasids, descendants of Prophet Muhammad's uncle, exploited this in their favor, asserting that the caliphate was restricted to Muhammad's family. Exposed to such ideas, Abu Muslim was recruited by the Abbasid agents, and in 745–746 he went to Khorasan to garner support for the Abbasid cause. In early 746, Abu Muslim received instructions to openly proclaim the Abbasid cause and raised the black standards in Sefidanj, signaling the beginning of the revolt.

During the course of the next few months, Abu Muslim strengthened his position through continued propagandizing. His defeat of an army sent by the Ummayad governor of Khorasan only further enhanced his reputation and garnered new support. In 746–747 Abu Muslim's forces captured Herat, Balk, and Nesa and by early 748 the city of Merv itself. In 748–749, he repeatedly defeated the Umayyad forces sent against him and captured Nishapur, Gorgan, Hamadan, and Nehavand.

Invading northern Iraq, Abu Muslim's forces inflicted a decisive defeat on the Umayyad caliph Marwan on the banks of the Greater Zab River and declared the Abbasid Abu al-Abbas as Caliph al-Saffah. After the Abbasid Revolution, Abu Muslim remained in Khorasan, where he exercised absolute authority. Suspicious and jealous of Abu Muslim's power, the caliph even considered assassinating him but died in 754 before he could do so.

Upon ascending the throne, new caliph al-Mansur faced a revolt, which Abu Muslim suppressed in late 754. Yet, relations between Mansur and Abu Muslim quickly deteriorated. In early 755, the caliph promised to guarantee Abu Muslim safe passage if he returned to court to ask forgiveness. Arriving at the palace, Abu Muslim was assassinated by Mansur's agents on February 755. After his death he became a legendary figure and was even regarded in some regions as a messiah.

ALEXANDER MIKABERIDZE

See also
Abbasid Caliphate; Abbasid Revolution; Zab, Battle of

References
Kennedy, Hugh. *The Prophet and the Age of the Caliphates: The Islamic Near East from the Sixth to the Eleventh Century*. 2nd ed. Harlow, UK: Longman, 2004.
Shaban, M. A. *The Abbasid Revolution*. Cambridge: Cambridge University Press, 1970.

Abu Nidal (1937–2002)

Radical Palestinian and founder of the Fatah Revolutionary Council (FRC), also known as the Abu Nidal Organization, a notorious international terrorist group. Abu Nidal, which translates as "the father of struggle," was the nom de guerre of Sabri Khalil al-Banna, who was born in May 1937 in Jaffa, Palestine (now Tel Aviv–Yafo), which at the time was under the British mandate. In 1948, the Arab nations in the region rejected the United Nations Partition Plan, which ultimately led to war between the Jews and Arabs. Jaffa soon became a battle zone. During the conflict, the new Israeli government confiscated Abu Nidal's father's expansive orange groves, and Abu Nidal and his family fled to refugee camps in Gaza. Abu Nidal later moved on to Nablus, which was under Jordanian governance.

While in Jordan, Abu Nidal joined the Arab nationalist Baath Party. He soon landed in a Jordanian prison for his political views. When Baathists were suppressed by Jordanian king Hussein in 1957, Abu Nidal fled to Saudi Arabia. There in 1967 he founded the Palestine Secret Organization. After the Israelis won the 1967 Six-Day War, he was jailed again, this time by the Saudis, for his radical views.

In Saudi Arabia, Abu Nidal joined al-Fatah, Yasser Arafat's faction within the Palestine Liberation Organization (PLO), whose stated objective was to free Palestine from Israeli control. Abu Nidal, apparently dissatisfied with certain members of Fatah who sought diplomatic solutions, including a two-state solution to the Jewish problem, left Fatah in 1973. He became enamored with the rejectionist position held by the Iraqi government, which opposed any solution to the Palestinian problem that allowed for the existence of a Jewish state. Abu Nidal soon accused the PLO of treason, formed the FRC, and became Arafat's bitter rival. Meanwhile, Fatah sentenced Abu Nidal to death in absentia.

The FRC, operating out of Iraq, burst onto the international scene on September 5, 1973, when FRC gunmen took control of the Saudi embassy in Paris. This was followed by a number of spectacular acts of violence that were remarkable primarily because they seemed to show no concern for their effect on innocent civilians. The FRC also assassinated a number of key PLO diplomats.

In 1981, Abu Nidal switched bases from Iraq to Syria because Damascus was interested in utilizing his brand of terrorism. Just one year later, the FRC critically wounded Israeli ambassador to the United Kingdom Shlomo Argov. The Israeli government wasted no time in retaliating and, only three days later, used the failed assassination attempt as a justification to invade Lebanon and attempt to destroy the PLO there.

By the mid-1980s, Abu Nidal was considered the world's most lethal terrorist and was a principal target of the U.S. Central Intelligence Agency (CIA) and other counterterrorist organizations. At the same time, he became increasingly paranoid, subjecting his followers to endless security checks and bloody purges.

In 1985 Abu Nidal moved his base to Tripoli, Libya, where he became close friends with Libyan strongman Muammar Gaddafi. As with the Syrians, Gaddafi also found many ways to employ Abu Nidal's services. After American warplanes struck Tripoli in April 1986 as punishment for a West Berlin nightclub bombing, Gaddafi convinced Abu Nidal to strike the United States and Britain. The result was staggering. After a kidnapping that left 3 hostages dead, an FRC team hijacked Pan Am Flight 73 in Karachi, Pakistan, in September 1986, killing 22 people. The FRC also provided the explosives that brought down Pan Am Flight 103 en route to New York City over Lockerbie, Scotland, on December 21, 1988, killing 270 people.

The FRC was also responsible for the 1988 attack on the Greek cruise ship *City of Poros* that killed 9 people and left 80 others injured. The attack was roundly criticized in Arab circles because its savagery did not serve either the Palestinian or the Arab political cause. As a result, some theorists accused Abu Nidal of being a Mossad agent or at least being on the Israeli payroll. Some have even argued that the FRC was Arafat's supreme deception in that it allowed Arafat to pose as a moderate while Abu Nidal carried out all of the PLO's truly violent acts.

In 1999 after being expelled by Gaddafi when the Libyan leader began to mend relations with the United States, Abu Nidal returned to Iraq, where he lived in open defiance of the Jordanian government that had sentenced him to death in absentia. He was living in a Baghdad home owned by the Iraqi Mukhabbarat (Secret Service) when on August 16, 2002, he allegedly committed suicide, suffering multiple gunshot wounds, after being detained by Iraq's internal security force.

From a Western perspective, Abu Nidal's violence may have seemed to be targeted at just Israeli interests. However, the bulk of his victims were Arabs. In fact, most of his killings were not even ideologically driven per se in that he served as a mercenary for such states as Iraq, Syria, and Libya, killing these nations' political enemies for financial gain. Abu Nidal's activities tended to put Palestinian demands in the worst possible light and diminish any hope of gaining broader international support. As a result, it should come as no surprise that the FRC was never popular among most Palestinians. Abu Nidal and the FRC were believed to have carried out some 90 terrorist attacks in 20 nations that may have killed as many as 1,000 people.

B. Keith Murphy

See also
Arafat, Yasser; Baath Party; Fatah, al-; Palestine Liberation Organization; Terrorism

References
Melman, Yossi. *The Master Terrorist: The True Story of Abu Nidal.* Translated by Shmuel Himmelstein. New York: Adama, 1986.

Seale, Patrick. *Abu Nidal, a Gun for Hire: The Secret Life of the World's Most Notorious Arab Terrorist.* New York: Random House, 1992.

Tibi, Bassam. *Arab Nationalism: Between Islam and the Nation-State.* New York: St. Martin's, 1997.

Achaemenid Empire (550–330 BCE)

The Achaemenid Empire, also known as the First Persian Empire, was named for Achaemenes, the seventh-century BCE ruler of the kingdom of Media. Centered on the territory of modern-day Iran, the Achaemenid period of the Persian Empire lasted from 550 to 330 BCE. (In its other forms, the empire extended to 642 CE, when it was conquered by the Arabs). One of history's truly great empires, it was renowned for its immense wealth.

Aryan tribesmen from the Caspian Sea region settled the Persian plateau around 2,000 BCE. This region in modern south-central Iran was known as Fars, also called Farsistan and Persis, which gave name to Persia. The valleys of the plateau were immensely fertile, and agriculture formed the basis of the wealth that led to the building of urban centers and the development of a sophisticated culture.

The Medes played an important role in the end of the Assyrian Empire and in the establishment of the Persian Empire. These people lived in Media in modern northwestern Iran. They first entered the historical record in 831 BCE when the Assyrians mounted a military campaign there. The Medes first posed a threat to the Assyrians in the seventh century BCE under their first great king, Deicoes. Their most powerful ruler, however, was Cyaxares (r. 625–585), who established both the Median Empire and its dynasty. He took and destroyed the Assyrian capital of Nineveh in 612 and then went on to secure all Assyrian territory east of the Tigris River. By the time of his death, the Median Empire included Media proper, Assyria, and Persia.

Cyaxares was followed by Astyages (r. 575–550) who, according to Greek historian Herodotus, was a particularly cruel and inept ruler. He was overthrown by Cyrus, the Achaemenid dynasty king of the Persian dependency of Media. Astyages was so despised by his own people that many of his generals went over to Cyrus, and the Persian people also largely rallied to Cyrus. Cyrus was victorious in 550. Media was no longer the ruler of Persia; rather, Persia was the ruler of Media.

Cyrus II (r. 550–530), known as Cyrus the Great, founded the Achaemenian Empire. Having secured control of Persia, he organized the military establishments of Media and Persia into a seemingly invincible army and went on to defeat Croesus, the ruler of Lydia and of fabled wealth. Cyrus secured control of the Aegean coast of Asia Minor and Armenia. He then turned east, taking Parthia, Chorasmis, and Bactria. He besieged and captured Babylon in 539 and released the Jews who had been held captive there. Cyrus made the Persian Empire the largest political organization of the pre-Roman period and among the best governed in all history. Truly a great ruler, he was well known for his generosity toward conquered foes, reversing the practice in the Middle East at the time whereby the victor in battle slew all captured enemy soldiers. This proved to be a formidable asset, for soldiers would not fight the Persians with the same desperation as when they knew that it was kill or be killed. He also departed from conventional practice in allowing conquered peoples to worship the gods of their choosing. In this he recognized that religion could be more powerful than the state. Cyrus was, however, slain in his effort to expand the empire even farther while battling peoples along the southern reaches of the Caspian Sea.

Cyrus's half-mad son, Cambyses II (r. 530–521), reversed his father's wise policies of toleration and clemency but in his short reign conquered Egypt and added Cyprus to the empire. He was overthrown while on campaign, succeeded by the third king in the Achaemenian line, Darius I (r. 521–486). He became another legendary ruler of Persia. A strong leader, he quelled revolts against Persian control in a number of lands. He retook Babylon following a long siege and then had some 3,000 of its leading citizens crucified as a lesson to any would-be rebels. After his successes on the battlefield and restoring order with a ruthless hand, he devoted himself to establishing a highly effective administrative system that made Persia the model empire until the time of Rome. He also caused to be built an impressive capital at Persepolis, established a reliable postal service, and introduced a system of standardized weights and measures for the empire.

Again taking up the sword, Darius I invaded southern Russia, crossing the Bosporus and the Danube and reaching the Volga. He also campaigned in Afghanistan, and he conquered areas of western India. Fatefully, Darius also expanded the Persian Empire west against Greece. This was probably prompted by fears that the Greek city-states and their colonies posed a potential threat to Persian control over Western Asia. This seemed confirmed when Ionia in Asia Minor revolted against Persia and received assistance from both Athens and Sparta. Although he met fierce resistance by some of the Greek city-states, the Persians were able to conquer Thrace. Darius sent a strong expeditionary force across the Aegean Sea to Greece, but this met defeat in the Battle of Marathon in 490. Darius was preparing a new invasion of Greece when he died in 486.

Darius's son and successor Xerxes I (r. 486–465 BCE) took up his father's cause and sent a vast host on a bridge across the Hellespont (Dardanelles) that he caused to be built and that was one of the wonders of ancient engineering.

View of the ruins of the center of the ancient city of Persepolis in modern-day southwestern Iran. Persepolis was built in the sixth century BCE and was a residence for the kings of the Achaemenid dynasty. (steba1/iStockphoto.com)

Successful on land in northern Greece at Thermopylae and having taken Athens, Xerxes watched from shore as his fleet met defeat in the naval Battle of Salamis in 480. This decisive reverse forced his army to withdraw. His rule of two decades was ended when he was murdered by a courtier in 465.

The period that followed was largely one of intrigue and murder. Artaxerxes I (r. 465–424) had the murderer of his father put to death and enjoyed a long reign. His son and successor, Xerxes II, however, enjoyed a reign of only 45 days in 424, being murdered by his brother Sogdianus. Sogdianus's illegitimate brother, Ochus, satrap of Hyrcania, then rebelled against and killed Sogdianus. Ochus then became king, taking the throne name Darius II. He ruled from 423 to 404, putting down a revolt by the Medes in 409.

Darius II was followed by his son Artaxerxes II (r. 404–358), who in 401 had to fight his brother Cyrus when the latter tried to take power. Artaxerxes II also killed his son Darius for conspiring against him and is said to have died of a broken heart on learning that another son was bent on overthrowing him. That son, Ochus, became king as Artaxerxes III (r. 358–338). His first attempt to recover Egypt, which had been lost during his father's reign, failed, but a strong Greek mercenary force brought success in a second effort in 343.

Artaxerxes died in 338, poisoned by one of his generals, Bagoas, who then placed Artaxerxes III's son Arses on the throne as Artasxerxes IV (r. 338–336). Bagoas then had Arses's brother slain to solidify the throne before killing Arses himself and giving the throne to a close associate, Artashata, known to the Greeks as Codomannus, who became king as Darius III. He ruled for only six years (336–330). Defeated by Macedonian king Alexander III the Great in the Battle of Gaugamela (Arbela), he was murdered by his generals in 330. His death brought end to the Achaemenid dynasty.

The Persian kings referred to themselves as the "king of kings," and the ancient world did not dispute that claim. The king held absolute power and could kill without reason. He also had the right to choose his successor, although frequently this was dictated by assassination.

The Achaemenid Empire was based on agriculture. Industry was little developed, with Persian rulers content to let other nations provide the finished goods needed, paid for with their tribute. The Persians left commerce to foreigners. Engineering, however, was highly developed. The Persian rulers caused the construction of great roads to unite the component parts of their vast empire. These had way stations at regular intervals with horse relays to provide a rapid and efficient mail service. Persian attention was centered on land transport. The Persians had no fleet of their own, choosing to rely for that on the Phoenicians and Greeks.

At its height, the Persian Empire included 20 provinces or satrapies in what was the largest empire to that point in history. It was a diverse empire of many different peoples, languages, and religions. The Persians had no literature of their own and did not even use their own language for the business of government. Scribes and interpreters conveyed orders in languages unfamiliar to Persians. Architecture, medicine, shipping, and military matters were all left to foreign experts. During the course of its two centuries, these divisions were not lessened so that any weakening of the central power was bound to encourage revolt by ambitious satraps or provincial governors. Persia's vast wealth also invited foreign invasion, and unfortunately for them the Persian kings failed to keep pace with military advances made by the Greeks. Indeed, the best Persian troops were Greek mercenaries, but these were only a small minority of the Persian military. Thus, while his own forces were vastly outnumbered, Alexander the Great's defeat of Persia on the battlefield was almost inevitable.

Spencer C. Tucker

See also
Alexander III the Great; Alexander III's Invasion of the Persian Empire; Cyrus II the Great; Cyrus the Younger; Darius III; Gaugamela, Battle of; Greco-Persian Wars

References
Cook, J. M. *The Persian Empire.* London: Dent, 1983.
Curtis, John, ed. *Forgotten Empire: The World of Ancient Persia.* Berkeley: University of California Press, 2005.
Sykes, Percy M. *History of Persia.* New York: Routledge, 2003.

Acre, Battle of (November 3, 1840)

Important battle during the Second Egyptian-Ottoman War of 1839–1841. The Ancient seaport and fortress of Acre (Akko), located on the Mediterranean coast of modern-day Israel, had been an important strategic position since ancient times. In a region where land transport was poor because of adverse geography of mountains, deserts, and lack of water for draft animals, it provided a vital link between armies moving north or south and their seaborne supplies. Consequently, Acre was heavily fortified and subject to many sieges.

In 1840 the British and the Ottomans were active on the Syrian coast, facing the powerful armies of Muhammad Ali (Mehmed Ali), pasha of Egypt. In the First Egyptian-Ottoman War (1831–1833) Muhammad Ali's son Ibrahim Pasha had captured Acre in May 1832, along with the area now constituting Israel, Lebanon, and Syria. In 1839 Muhammad Ali, who sought an independent throne, had annihilated Ottoman land forces and threatened to overthrow the empire.

Anxious to maintain the Ottoman Empire as a regional power and an economic client, the British sent a small fleet to the Syrian coast. This force, although commanded by Admiral Sir Robert Stopford, was largely directed by Foreign Secretary Lord Palmerston and driven by his friend Commodore Sir Charles Napier. The British warships soon cut Egyptian logistics by blockading Alexandria and sweeping the seas of Egyptian shipping. The British then landed Ottoman troops and raised a rebellion in Lebanon before storming Sidon from the sea and forcing the Egyptians out of Beirut in combined operations. Acre was the remaining Egyptian stronghold on the eastern Mediterranean. The British had to act quickly before the weather on the coast deteriorated in mid-November.

On November 3, 1840, a British, Austrian, and Ottoman force of eight ships of the line, six frigates, three smaller sailing warships, and four steamers attacked the fortress. The plan was for a heavy naval bombardment to open a breach in the seawalls for an assault by marines. The ships fired shot and shell into the city. However, after two hours, a shell from one of the steamers penetrated Acre's main powder magazine in the southern part of the city, resulting in a massive explosion that killed as many as 1,200 people and destroyed much of Acre. Defensive fire quickly subsided, and the Egyptians evacuated the city that night. In the action the allied ships suffered 14 British and 4 Ottoman sailors killed and 42 wounded.

Early on November 4, realizing that the Egyptians had withdrawn, landing parties were sent ashore. These soon linked up with 5,000 troops sent from Beirut by land. Muhammad Ali now accepted the inevitable and on November 27 agreed to the Alexandria Convention presented by Napier.

Andrew Lambert and Spencer C. Tucker

See also
Egyptian-Ottoman Wars; Ibrahim Pasha

References

Clowes, William Laird. *The Royal Navy: A History from the Earliest Times to 1900*, Vol. 6. 1901; reprint, London: Sampson Low, Marston, 1997.

Lambert, Andrew. *The Last Sailing Battlefleet: Maintaining Naval Mastery, 1815–1850*. London: Conway, 1991.

Pocock, Tom. *A Thirst for Glory: The Life of Admiral Sir Sidney Smith*. London: Aurum, 1996.

Acre, 1189 Siege of (August 28, 1189–July 12, 1191)

One of the great sieges in history, the two-year-long operation by Christian crusaders against the port city of Acre in Palestine during 1189–1191 halted the reconquest of the Holy Land by Egyptian sultan Saladin (Salan-al-din) and helped ensure the survival of a truncated crusader kingdom there for another century.

In the months following Saladin's great victory over the crusaders in the Battle of Hattin on July 4, 1187, the Muslims reconquered much of the territory of the Latin Kingdom of Jerusalem. Acre surrendered without a fight on July 10; Jerusalem followed on October 2 after resisting for less than two weeks. Saladin had taken as prisoner Guy of Lusignan, king of Jerusalem and ruler of the Latin Kingdom since 1186, but had freed him on the promise that he would not again fight against the Muslims. Although Guy was able to secure a ruling from the Catholic Church that the oath he had taken in captivity was null and void, he was literally without a kingdom.

The fall of Jerusalem prompted the Third Crusade, however, and brought Christian reinforcements under Archbishop Ubaldo of Pisa as well as Sicilian mercenaries. On August 28, 1189, Guy began an ineffectual siege of Acre. An assault several days later failed, and he appealed to the Christian states for additional assistance. A Danish fleet arrived in September and placed Acre under blockade from the sea. Ships from other European states joined this effort, and Conrad of Montferrat, who had established a kingdom at Tyre, lent troops. In October the crusaders assaulted Acre again but were halted in bitter fighting.

Saladin sought reinforcements from Muslim powers as far away as Spain. With this support, in both October and December he was able to pass ships through the Christian naval blockade and bring supplies and men into Acre. He also began a land countersiege of King Guy's forces. Both sides built extensive trench systems and fortifications, with those of the crusaders facing in two directions. Conrad was nevertheless able to get vital supplies to Guy by sea past the Saracen fleet.

Using these supplies, during the winter of 1189 the Christians built three large siege towers and moved them against the city walls on May 1, 1190. On May 11, Saladin launched an attack on the Christian siege lines. The fighting was intense, and Saladin's attacks forced the crusaders to fight on both fronts, which enabled the defenders of Acre to burn the crusaders' siege towers.

During the summer of 1190 more Christian reinforcements arrived, chiefly from France. The most important figure among the new crusaders was Henry of Troyes, count of Champagne, who took command of siege operations. In October, Germans from the army of Holy Roman emperor Frederick Barbarossa arrived but without Frederick, who had drowned in June in Cilicia. The besieging crusaders constructed both rams and trebuchets for another assault on Acre, but the defenders were again able to destroy the siege engines with inflammatory devices, beating back several major assaults.

In November the crusaders succeeded in opening a land supply route. That winter, however, Saladin was able to close it off and again isolate the crusaders. The winter of 1190–1191 was especially severe and hard on the crusaders, now suffering from disease and famine. Among the victims were Guy's wife Sybelle and their daughters. The Christians would have broken off the siege had it not been for the hope of English and French reinforcements that spring.

As promised, additional Christian manpower, ships, supplies, and money arrived under French king Philippe II Augustus on April 20, 1191, and English king Richard I (the Lionheart) on June 8. Their arrival created a new sense of hope and enthusiasm among the crusaders. With additional warships, the crusader forces were at last able to cut off Acre entirely from the seaborne resupply. On land, the crusaders constructed a large number of trebuchets and other artillery pieces and a large siege tower. The crusaders concentrated their attacks on one tower, known as "the Accursed Tower."

With Acre in dire straits, Saladin attempted to draw off the crusaders on July 3. This attack, led by his nephew, failed. The crusaders had now opened a number of breaches in the city walls. Although the defenders repulsed three assaults, the city finally surrendered on July 12, 1191.

Acre served as the chief military base for King Richard I and his reconquest of much of the coast of Palestine to Jaffa thereafter. Almost exactly 100 years later, there was another siege of Acre. This time the crusaders defended the city against Muslim Turkish attack. The Ottomans were victorious, capturing this last Christian enclave in Palestine in May 1291. The victors then filled in the harbor. Acre was again the site of a famous siege in 1799, when Napoleon Bonaparte and his Army of Egypt tried unsuccessfully to take the city. Failure here forced Napoleon to retreat back to Cairo. A fourth notable siege of Acre occurred in 1840.

Spencer C. Tucker

See also
Acre, Battle of; Acre, 1291 Siege of; Acre, 1799 Siege of; Frederick I or Frederick Barbarossa; Guy of Lusignan; Hattin, Battle of; Philippe II, King; Richard I, King; Saladin

References
Gillingham, J. *Richard I*. 2nd ed. New Haven, CT: Yale University Press, 2000.
Hosler, John D. *The Siege of Acre, 1189–91: Saladin, Richard the Lionheart, and the Battle That Decided the Third Crusade*. New Haven, CT: Yale University Press, 2018.
Lyons, M., and D. Jackson. *Saladin: The Politics of Holy War*. Cambridge: Cambridge University Press, 1982.
Rogers, R. *Latin Siege Warfare in the Twelfth Century*. Oxford, UK: Clarendon, 1992.

Acre, 1291 Siege of (April 6– May 28, 1291)

The Muslim siege of Acre (modern-day Akko, Israel) by the Mamluks of Egypt lasted from April 6 to May 28, 1291. Following an attack by Italian crusaders on the Muslim population of Acre in August 1290, Egyptian sultan Qalawun revoked a 10-year truce concluded with the Latin Kingdom of Jerusalem in 1283 and moved against Acre. Although Qalawun died on October 10 shortly after leaving Cairo, his son al-Ashraf Khalil continued the plan. He arrived before Acre with a large Mamluk army on April 5, 1291.

Siege operations began the next day. The Mamluks concentrated their attacks on the St. Anthony's Gate complex linking Montmusard with the old city and on the northeastern point, which was fortified by a barbican (King Hugh's Tower) and a tower (King Henry's Tower) at the outer wall and another tower (the Accursed Tower) at the inner wall. Sorties by the Templars and Hospitallers in mid-April failed, resulting in heavy Frankish casualties. On May, King Hugh's Tower had to be abandoned; it collapsed on May 15. The following day, the Muslims attempted to storm the city but were beaten back by a sortie of the Hospitallers. On May 18, the Mamluks attacked the fortifications between St. Anthony's Gate and the Accursed Tower with full force and managed to enter the city.

There were insufficient ships for the inhabitants of Acre to escape by sea. Those unable to escape found refuge in the Templar castle and were offered unhindered departure in exchange for its surrender. On May 25, Muslim troops entered the castle to supervise the Franks' departure, but as they supposedly molested the Frankish women and children, they were killed by the Templar garrison. When Marshal Peter of Sevrey went to Khalil to explain the incident, he was seized and beheaded. Meanwhile, Muslim mining collapsed the castle walls on May 28, ending the siege.

The Muslim victory at Acre brought the end of the Latin Kingdom of Jerusalem. The subsequent systematic Mamluk destruction of Acre and other coastal cities made any future return of the Frankish population unviable.

Jochen Burgtorf

See also
Mamluk Sultanate; Qalawun

References
Marshall, Christopher. *Warfare in the Latin East, 1192–1291*. Cambridge: Cambridge University Press, 1992.
Runciman, Steven. *A History of the Crusades*. 3 vols. Cambridge: Cambridge University Press, 1951–1954.

Acre, 1799 Siege of (March 17– May 20, 1799)

French Army siege of the Mediterranean port city of Acre held by Ottoman forces in the War of the Second Coalition (1799–1802) during the Wars of the French Revolution. In July 1798 French general Napoleon Bonaparte had invaded Egypt with an army of 35,000 men and defeated the Ottoman forces there, even though he had been cut off owing to destruction of most of his fleet in the Battle of the Nile (Aboukir Bay, August 1, 1798). In early 1799, Bonaparte had embarked on a campaign up the coast with the intention of proceeding overland to British India. He had a ridiculously small force of 13,000 men and 52 field guns. On March 3, 1799, he took Jaffa after a three-day fight, taking some 2,000–2,500 prisoners. Considering the size of his own force and learning that many of the Ottoman soldiers had been paroled from earlier battles on condition that they would not again fight against France, he ordered them killed, a decision made easier by the Ottoman treatment of French prisoners.

Bonaparte then proceeded farther up the Mediterranean coast to the ancient fortress city of Acre. Securing it was essential to the campaign, as it controlled the land route between Egypt and Syria. On March 17, 1799, Bonaparte instituted siege operations.

Acre was well constructed for defensive purposes with massive stone walls, and the defenders, who numbered some 30,000, also possessed some 250 cannon. The Ottomans had a capable commander in French emigré Colonel Antoine Le Picard de Phélippeaux, who had been a student with Bonaparte at the École Militaire. Unfortunately for Bonaparte, he sent his siege guns by sea, and they were there intercepted by British warships under Commodore Sir William Sidney Smith. Brought into Acre, they were then turned against the French. Bonaparte's light field guns were unable to inflict material damage, and his only recourse was infantry assault. Despite the fact that he had only some 13,000 men, Bonaparte was confident of success, expecting to seize Acre within two weeks.

All of the French infantry assaults failed at considerable cost, however. Given these casualties and others of his men falling prey to the plague, a shortage of ammunition, and reports that Smith was preparing to transport a large Ottoman ground force to Egypt, Bonaparte broke off the siege and quit Acre on May 30. He left behind the worst-off French plague victims. Of the original 13,000-man force, 2,500 were dead (half from disease); another 2,500 were sick or wounded, and half of these did not reach Egypt.

SPENCER C. TUCKER

See also
Bonaparte, Napoleon; Egypt, French Invasion and Occupation of

References
Connelly, Owen. *Blundering to Glory: Napoleon's Military Campaigns.* Rev. ed. Wilmington, DE: Scholarly Resources, 1999.

Laurens, Henry. *La Question de Palestine: L'invention de la terre sainte, 1799–1922.* Paris: Fayard, 1999.

Actium, Battle of (September 2, 31 BCE)

The naval Battle of Actium in 31 BCE ended the civil wars of the late Roman Republic and allowed Octavian (later Augustus) to establish the Roman Empire. On March 15, 44 BCE, in Rome, assassins stabbed to death Julius Caesar shortly after he had extended his dictatorship to life. Caesar's lieutenant, Marc Antony, turned the Senate against the murderers, who then fled for their lives. Encouraged by Cicero, the Senate rallied against Mark Antony's effort to succeed Caesar, and its forces defeated him in pitched battle in 43.

Antony though had allied himself with the 20-year-old Octavian, who had been adopted in his great-uncle Caesar's will as his principal heir and probably also as his son. They formed a partnership to "reform the state" and avenge Caesar's murder. Among some 2,000 executed were 300 senators and Cicero. Antony and Octavian also defeated the republican forces in the Battle of Philippi in Macedonia in 42, after which both Brutus and Cassius, two of the principal conspirators in the death of Caesar, committed suicide.

Octavian and Antony then battled to see who would hold power. Octavian controlled Italy and the Western provinces, while Antony's strength was in the Eastern provinces. Antony ignored his wife, Octavia (Octavian's sister), and withdrew into Egypt with a large army. While there he fell in love with the beautiful Queen Cleopatra, which allowed Octavian to portray Antony as sacrificing Roman interests to those of Egypt. Octavian also induced the Senate to declare war on Cleopatra.

Gathering their forces in Antioch, in 32 Antony and Cleopatra brought some 500 ships (including transports) and a large land force to northwestern Greece, apparently planning an invasion of Italy. Octavian was fortunate in having as his naval commander Marcus Vipsanius Agrippa, probably the greatest naval tactician of the era. In a series of actions, Agrippa secured important coastal bases in Greece and used these to disrupt Antony's sea routes of supply and communication.

Antony stationed his forces at Actium, just south of the entrance to the Gulf of Ambracia in Epirus. Octavian then transferred his army from Italy to north of Actium and, during the summer of 31, established both a naval and a land blockade of Antony's forces. Antony lost so many men to desertion and disease that he could not fully man his ships. Apparently the resulting sea battle was more an effort to extricate his forces than an attempt to secure a victory.

The battle occurred on September 2. Octavian, without his detached light squadrons, had at his disposal perhaps 200 ships, while Antony had perhaps 170. Each commander added legionnaires to bolster the ship crews and thus may have shipped as many as 60,000 or more men. As evidence that Antony's chief goal was escape, however, his crews did not stow their masts and sails on shore but instead kept them on board their galleys so they might take advantage of the usual later daily breeze and outrun their opponent's galleys powered only by oars. Given that Antony's larger ships were quite fast under sail, this plan appeared to be a wise one. Agrippa's smaller ships, however, enjoyed a speed advantage under oars, and their attacks prevented Antony from fully implementing his plan. Agrippa also made effective use of a new harpoon-like weapon, the harpax. It had a

Naval Battle of Actium, September 2, 31 BCE

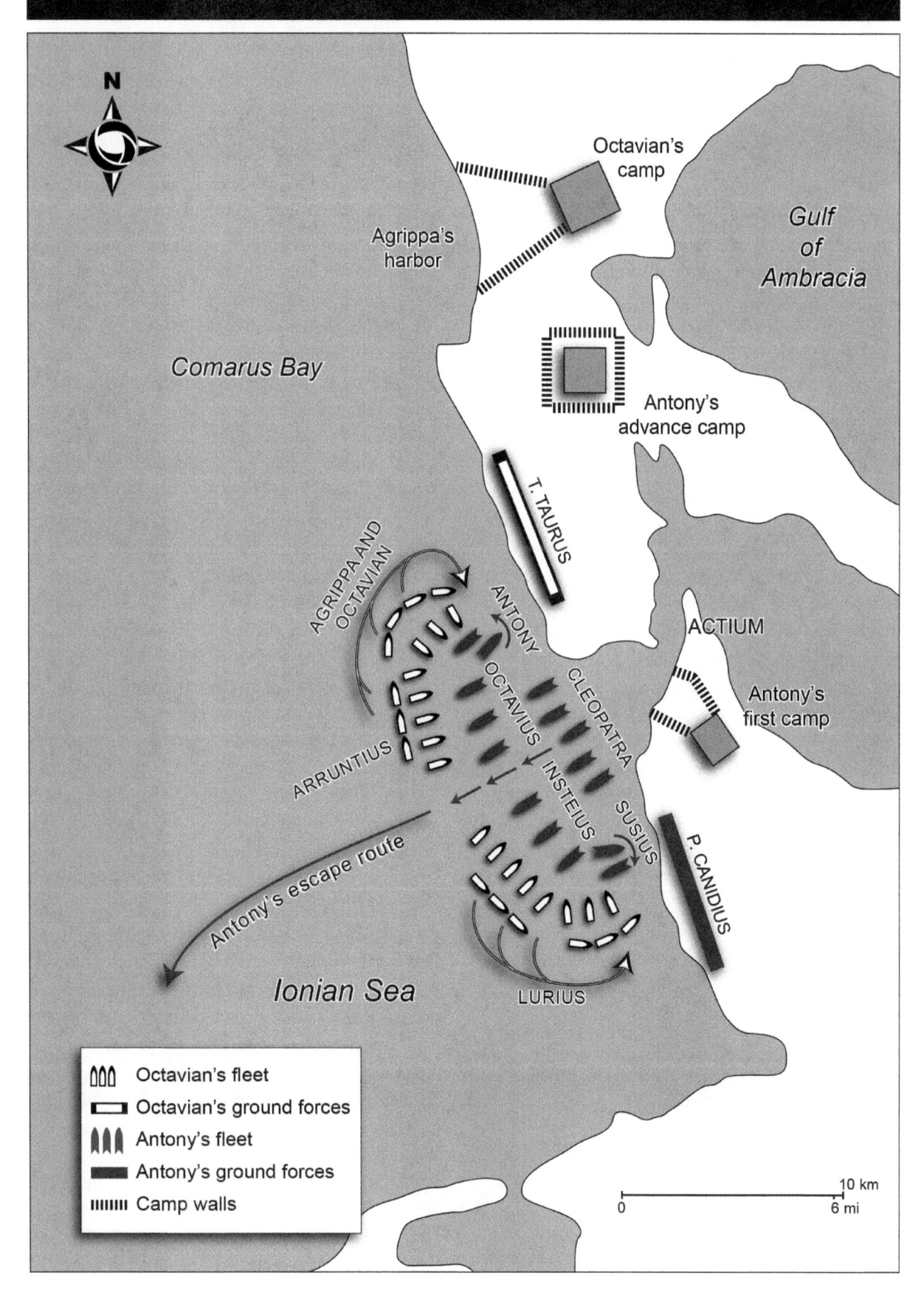

hook at one end and a line attached to the other. Projected by a catapult against an enemy vessel, it was used to draw the ship close so that it could be boarded.

The principal fighting occurred on the northern flank. Antony initially had the upper hand, but his crews in the center and the left wing had been sapped by propaganda attacking Cleopatra, and they fell back or failed to fight with much enthusiasm. Antony signaled to Cleopatra to escape, then tried to get to the open sea. When his own vessel was secured with a harpax, he escaped to another ship and broke free with a few of his ships to join Cleopatra. In the end, only Cleopatra's Egyptian squadron of 60 vessels made a clean breakthrough under sail, followed by the few ships led by Antony. Most of Antony's fleet surrendered, as did his land force a short time later. Octavian subsequently ordered the construction of Nicopolis (Victory City) on the site of his former headquarters.

Antony never recovered from Actium. Octavian invaded Egypt in July 30. Although Antony initially repulsed Octavian's forces before Alexandria, he was misinformed that Cleopatra had killed herself and stabbed himself, only to die a lingering death in Cleopatra's presence. Cleopatra held out hope that she might beguile Octavian as she had done with both Caesar and Antony. He was not interested, however. When it became obvious that he intended to exhibit her in a triumphant procession through Rome, Cleopatra too committed suicide at age 39 by means of a snake smuggled to her in a basket of figs.

Octavian now controlled the immense wealth of Egypt as well as being master of the entire Mediterranean. He secured the Roman Eastern provinces largely by confirming Antony's appointments there and returned to Rome to declare the civil wars at an end. In October 27, the Senate proclaimed him augustus princeps (revered first citizen).

SPENCER C. TUCKER

See also
Caesar, Gaius Julius; Cleopatra VII

References
Adcock, Frank Ezra. *The Roman Art of War under the Republic.* New York: Barnes & Noble, 1960.

Carter, John M. *The Battle of Actium: The Rise and Triumph of Augustus Caesar.* London: Hamilton, 1970.

Gurval, Robert Alan. *Actium and Augustus: The Politics and Emotions of Civil War.* Ann Arbor: University of Michigan Press, 1995.

Morrison, J. S. *Greek and Roman Oared Warships.* Oxford, UK: Oxbow Books, 1996.

Starr, Chester G. *The Roman Imperial Navy, 31 B.C.–A.D. 324.* New York: Barnes & Noble, 1960.

Adan, Avraham "Bren" (1926–2012)

Israel Defense Forces (IDF) general. Born in Kfar Gileadi in the British Mandate for Palestine in 1926, Avraham Adan participated in all of the major Arab-Israeli conflicts that have marked the recent history of the Middle East. Adan joined the Palmach Jewish strike force in 1943. In the Israeli War of Independence (1948–1949), he was a captain in the Negev Brigade that captured the port of Eilat on the Red Sea.

Adan remained in the IDF after the war, and by the time of the Sinai Campaign during the Suez Crisis of 1956, he was a lieutenant colonel in command of the 7th Armored Brigade in the Sinai. He remained in the Sinai as part of the Armored Corps. During the 1967 Six-Day War he was deputy commander of an armored division. By war's end, he was a major general.

The Six-Day War was concluded with a cease-fire, but a permanent settlement proved elusive between the Arabs and Israel. The Israeli capture of the Sinai during the war was particularly galling to the Egyptians, who continued to engage in hostile actions along the frontier of the Suez Canal and the deserts of the Sinai. What became known as the War of Attrition gradually developed, which forced the IDF to devise a new defensive strategy.

Lieutenant General Chaim Bar-Lev appointed General Adan to preside over the military committee that would come up with this new policy. Until then, the most important element in Israeli strategy was that any war between Israel and an Arab state had to be short and fought on foreign soil. This strategy had encouraged the armed forces to concentrate on the development of rapid offensive capabilities and a high degree of mobility, which had worked brilliantly during the 1967 conflict. Adan was now in charge of modifying these basic precepts.

The plan that Adan submitted to the General Staff required 35 small strongpoints located every seven miles, between which IDF patrols would maintain constant observation of Egyptian forces on the other side. Strong, armored formations were positioned in assembly areas some distance from the canal, ready to counterattack any Egyptian attempt to cross. The strongpoints were designed to prevent any surprise attack by the Egyptians crossing the canal and only expose a small number of men to the danger of artillery barrage.

Although many Israeli generals, including Israel Tal and Ariel Sharon, disapproved of this plan because its static defensive line deviated so sharply from the traditional adherence to mobility, Bar-Lev approved the plan, and construction of what became known as the Bar-Lev Line was more or less complete by 1969.

Israeli general Avraham "Bren" Adan, shown here on October 22, 1972. Adan drew up the controversial static defense plan along the Suez Canal and commanded the Israel Defense Forces's Armored Corps in the 1973 War. (Israeli Government Press Office)

In 1972 Adan became head of the Armored Corps and was thus a key commander when in October 1973, the armed forces of Egypt and Syria mounted their successful surprise attack on Israel to begin the Yom Kippur War (Ramadan War). Caught off guard, the IDF stumbled badly at the beginning of the war. The standard strategy of the Armored Corps had been developed by General Tal and called for all-tank attacks without infantry. This was the Israeli strategy in place as the IDF responded to the Egyptian crossing of the Suez Canal.

Adan's 162nd Armored Division of 250 tanks was charged with liberating the posts along the Bar-Lev Line that had been captured by the Egyptians. On the morning of October 8, his division set out but was surprised by the full fury of Egyptian antitank missiles, for which they were unprepared and which savaged the Israeli tank crews. Adan's division in the northern Sinai quickly lost three-quarters of its tanks and was not able to regain even one of the Israeli canal strongpoints.

After regrouping, Adan's division eventually crossed the Suez Canal, although significantly behind schedule. By October 14, however, the Israelis had recovered, and Adan's unit was engaged in heavy fighting on the Egyptian side of the canal, taking out many of the missile sites that had caused such heavy damage earlier. At Suez City, his division cut off the Egyptian Third Army. A cease-fire took place shortly thereafter. Adan's unit, on orders from the IDF Southern Command, violated the cease-fire by continuing to fight on until October 25.

Although the IDF emerged from the war with a tactical victory, it had suffered heavy losses in the first days of the fighting. Analysts evaluated the wisdom of the Bar-Lev Line, the emphasis on all-tank battalions, and the difficulties that Adan and others had encountered in trying to carry out their orders. Generally speaking, the official Agranat Commission report found that Adan had acquitted himself correctly on most specific counts and that in situations where a different approach was indicated, he had erred in a "good faith misinterpretation" of orders. He was absolved of any blame for the early setbacks.

During 1974–1977 Adan served as the Israeli military attaché in Washington, D.C. In 1980 he published his own account of the Yom Kippur War. Adan died on September 28, 2012, at Ramat HaSharon, Israel.

Spencer C. Tucker

See also
Agranat Commission; Bar-Lev Line; Eilat, Israel; Israeli War of Independence; Palmach; Sharon, Ariel; Sinai Campaign of 1956; Six-Day War; Suez Crisis; War of Attrition

References
Adan, Avraham. *On the Banks of the Suez: An Israeli General's Personal Account of the Yom Kippur War.* Novato, CA: Presidio, 1980.
Rabinovich, Abraham. *The Yom Kippur War: An Epic Encounter That Transformed the Middle East.* New York: Schocken Books, 2004.
Shazli, Saad al. *The Crossing of the Suez.* San Francisco: Mideast Research, 1980.

Adana Massacre (April 1909)

The mass killings of some 30,000 Armenians during April 1909 in the city and province of Adana, then part of the Ottoman Empire. The city of Adana is located in southern Anatolia, along the eastern Mediterranean coast. The Adana Massacre resulted from the civil war between nationalist-minded Turks, known as the Young Turks, and supporters of Ottoman sultan Abdul Hamid II (r. 1876–1909). There were also economic, religious, and cultural components that led to the atrocities.

The Armenians, who were Christians in an overwhelmingly Muslim state, had backed the ouster of Abdul Hamid, which had outraged the sultan and his supporters. At the time of the massacre, supporters of the sultanate were engaged in a civil conflict with those supporting the Young Turk movement, embodied in the Committee of Union and Progress (CUP), in an effort to restore Abdul Hamid to power. The CUP, however, also had reason to dislike the Armenians because of strong support from within this minority for an autonomous Armenian state, a scenario that the CUP was determined to quash. In essence, the Armenians found themselves caught in the middle of a power struggle within the Ottoman Empire. They were further vilified because of their religion, European roots, and economic prosperity.

The massacre began in the city of Adana, where reportedly 4,437 Armenian homes were burned along with about half the city. Within days, the violence had spread to adjoining areas and the countryside beyond. Two Armenian towns in the countryside—Hadjin (Hajen) and Dortyol (Chorkmarzban)—mounted a successful resistance, but many of the outlying Armenian villages were destroyed. It is believed that some 1,300 Assyrians (Christians of Syrian origins) also died in the massacre.

Both the Young Turks and the sultan's supporters were responsible for the killings. The CUP made a feeble attempt to investigate the mass murders at Adana, but nothing came of this. Indeed, many in the CUP suspected that the killings had been undertaken by the loyalists in an attempt to discredit the Young Turks, but there is ample evidence to suggest culpability on both sides. The massacre clearly showed that the Young Turks embraced both modern liberal and reactionary nationalist sentiments. It also proved to many people in the Young Turk movement that long-standing ethnic and religious animosities could be used to advance political ends. Above all, the Adana events demonstrated that the Ottoman Empire's Armenian population—and Christian population in general—could be easily conquered or compelled to leave. This set the stage for the Armenian Genocide of 1915–1917, resulting in the deaths of some 1.5 million people.

Paul G. Pierpaoli Jr.

See also
Abdulhamid II; Armenians and the Armenian Genocide; Ottoman Empire; Young Turks

References
Bobelian, Michael. *Children of Armenia: A Forgotten Genocide and the Century-Long Struggle for Justice.* New York: Simon & Schuster, 2009.

Dadrian, Vahakn N. "The Circumstances Surrounding the 1909 Adana Holocaust." *Armenian Review* 41, no. 4 (1988): 1–16.

Kevorkian, Raymond. *The Armenian Genocide: A Complete History.* London: I. B. Tauris, 2011.

Aden Emergency (1963–1967)

Insurgency in the British crown colony of Aden during 1963–1967. Now part of the Republic of Yemen, Aden is located at the southern tip of the Arabian Peninsula. The port there was of great interest to the British as an antipiracy station to protect shipping lanes to India, and the British East India Company landed forces there in 1839. With the opening of the Suez Canal, Aden also served as a coaling station. It became a crown colony in 1937.

The British established the Federation of Arab Emirates of the South in 1959. It subsequently added nine states, and in April 1962 this polity became the Federation of South Arabia. Aden joined in January 1963. Inspired by the Pan-Arabism and socialism of Egyptian president Gamal Abdel Nasser, in June 1963 a Marxist insurgent organization was established in Aden. Known as the National Liberation Front (NLF), it enjoyed Egyptian support. Shortly thereafter a rival insurgent group came into being, known as the Front for the Liberation of South Yemen (FLOSY).

There had been considerable unrest in Aden for a number of years, and a United Nations Observer Force had been dispatched there in June 1963. The insurgency began there with the December 10, 1963, grenade attack on the British high commissioner that killed 1 person and injured 50. This led the British to declare a state of emergency.

The ensuing Aden Emergency pitted the British and local sheikhs against the NLF and FLOSY, but the situation was complicated by the fact that the two insurgent groups often fought one another. Indeed, when the NLF became more Marxist, Nasser switched Egyptian support to FLOSY. The insurgents engaged largely in hit-and-run attacks. The British moved in troops as well as aircraft, and by 1965 when the British suspended the Federation of South Arabia government and imposed direct British rule, the Royal Air Force had nine squadrons of fixed-wing aircraft and helicopters there.

The situation in Aden was exacerbated by the June 1967 Six-Day War. Nasser charged that the British had assisted the Israelis during that war, and this led to a mutiny on June 20 among the South Arabian Federation Army and police in Aden's Crater district, resulting in the deaths of 23 British servicemen. Following two weeks of insurgent control, on July 5 in Operation STIRLING CASTLE, Lieutenant Colonel Colin Campbell "Mad Mitch" Mitchell's 1st Battalion, Argyll, and Sutherland Highlanders restored order in the district.

Guerrilla attacks against the British soon resumed, however. British casualties went from 2 on 1964 to 44 in 1967. In all, 382 people died as a result of terrorist incidents during 1964–1967, with 57 of them being British military personnel. Despite these relatively modest casualties, the British Labour government of Prime Minister Harold Wilson announced in February 1967 that it would quit Aden. Major fighting then occurred in Aden between the NLF and FLOSY, with heavy casualties on both sides. In November 1967 London withdrew all British troops from Aden and south Arabia. On November 30, the federation came to an end.

With the precipitous British departure having occurred without agreement on governance, the Marxist NLF secured the support of the Yemeni Federal Army and defeated FLOSY, now bereft of Egyptian military support as a consequence of the Six-Day War.

The NLF then proclaimed the People's Republic of South Yemen. The closure of the naval base meant hard times economically for Aden for a number of years thereafter, however. In 1978 the NLF changed its name to the Yemeni Socialist Party. It became the only legal political party. There was renewed fighting in the brief South Yemen Civil War of January 1986. In May 1990 the People's Republic of South Yemen united with the Yemen Arab Republic, commonly known as North Yemen, to form the current Republic of Yemen.

SPENCER C. TUCKER

See also
Nasser, Gamal Abdel; South Yemen Civil War; Yemen

References
Kostiner, Joseph. *The Struggle for South Yemen.* New York: St. Martin's, 1984.
Naumkin, Vitaly. *Red Wolves of Yemen: The Struggle for Independence.* Cambridge, UK: Oleander, 2004.
Walker, Jonathan. *Aden Insurgency: The Savage War in Yemen, 1962–1967.* Barnsley, South Yorkshire, UK: Pen & Sword Military, 2011.

Adrianople, Battle of (August 9, 378)

The Battle of Adrianople (Hadrianopolis, Edirne), fought between the Byzantines (Eastern Romans) and the Goths on August 9, 378, at modern-day Edirne in European Turkey, was one of the worst military defeats sustained by the Roman Empire. Following the death of Constantine the Great in 337, the Roman Empire underwent a series of succession struggles. In 364 Valentian, a successful general, became emperor. Valentian I (r. 364–375) appointed his brother Valens as coemperor and sent him to Constantinople to deal with the Persians while he himself concentrated on shoring up the empire's Danubian defenses against the Barbarians. Valens's realm then included Greece, Egypt, Syria and Anatolia as far east as Persia. Valentian died in 375 and was succeeded by his 16-year-old son Gratian, who proved too young and inexperienced to deal with the incursions of large numbers of Goths in the Balkan portions of the empire.

The movement of the Huns west from China drove other peoples before them. As the Huns forced the Ostrogoths (Eastern Goths) westward, they in turn pushed against the Visigoths (Western Goths), driving them into the Danube River Valley, the northern border of the Roman Empire. When the Visigoths arrived in Byzantine territory, they asked to be allowed to settle there. Valens (r. 364–378) agreed on condition that they surrender their weapons to Byzantine authorities and give up as hostage all males under military age. Valens held the Visigoths in utter contempt; had he been more accommodating, he might well have won their loyalty and secured a large loyal population from which he could draw soldiers.

In 377 Valens campaigned against the Persians. He left two generals, Luppicinus and Maximus, in charge of disarming the Visigoths. They chose to enrich themselves and, in return for bribes and sexual favors, allowed the Visigoths to keep their weapons. Meanwhile, the Ostrogoths arrived. When their request for sanctuary was denied, they simply crossed into Roman territory anyway, pillaging widely.

King Fritigern, one of the Visigoth leaders pressed too far by Luppicinus and Maximus, made common cause with the Ostrogoths. When the two Roman generals attempted to assassinate Fritigern, the Goths went to war and soon inflicted several defeats on the Eastern Romans.

Valens responded by concluding a truce with the Persians and returning to Europe. He then sent a sizable force against Fritigern, pushing the Goths back into a marshy area near the mouth of the Danube. The resulting battle proved inconclusive, with most of the Goths escaping through the marsh. The Goths then raided northern Greece, and Valens pursued, marching into Thrace, northeast of Greece.

Valens sought reinforcements from his nephew Gratian in Italy, for the Goths had concluded a series of alliances with German tribes against Rome. German uprisings along the Rhine forced Gratian to campaign there. Defeating the

Germanic tribes, he then moved down the Danube River Valley to join up with his uncle.

In the summer of 378 Valens's generals drove the Goths back in Thrace toward the city of Adrianople, west of Constantinople on the Maritza River. Valens's principal general, Sebastian, had trained a small reliable force and conducted a series of successful hit-and-run attacks with it. He recommended a continuation of this strategy, believing that it would eventually force the Goths to depart. Valens disagreed. He favored a large pitched battle, believing that his forces would have the advantage against what he believed were poorly trained Goth levies.

Some eight miles from Adrianople, Fritigern and the Visigoths set up camp in an excellent defensive position on high ground with a perimeter circle of wagons. The Visigoths were primarily an infantry force, while the Ostrogoths provided the bulk of the cavalry. The Goth cavalry then departed to forage for provisions to feed the camp population of perhaps 100,000 warriors and 200,000 women and children.

Jealous of Gratian's success and anxious to achieve a glorious victory before his nephew could arrive, Varens decided to press the issue. He departed Adrianople with his legions at dawn on August 9, having left behind under suitable guard his treasury and baggage. After a rapid advance in extreme heat over rough ground, at about 2:00 p.m. Valens and his legions came on Fritigern's camp. Valens commanded some 50,000 men; Fritigern had twice that number, the majority of them cavalry.

Fritigern sent negotiators to Valens to purchase time for the Ostrogoth cavalry to return. Valens stalled in order to rest and deploy his men but finally broke off negotiations. Before the Romans had completed their deployment of infantry in the center and cavalry on the wings, however, the Goth cavalry returned and fell on the cavalry on the Byzantine right wing. Although the Byzantine cavalry fought well, it was badly outnumbered; when it broke, the cavalry under Ostrogoth chieftains Alatheus and Saphrax drove against the still not completely deployed infantry. Blinded by dust kicked up by the cavalry, the foot soldiers were driven back into a mass so tight that many could not even draw their swords, let alone use them.

The Ostrogoths then subjected the Roman infantry to attack by arrows. Seeing the situation, Fritigern passed his own infantry from inside the ring of wagons. Their long slashing swords and battle-axes exacted a terrible toll on the Byzantine infantry: some 40,000 reportedly perished in the battle, Valens and Sebastian among them.

Called by one Roman historian the greatest defeat for Rome since Cannae (216 BCE), the battle did not immediately affect the Roman Empire. Although the Goths rampaged through the Balkans for a time, Gratian and new Byzantine emperor Theodosius I (r. 379–395) eventually drove back across the Danube those Goths who would not swear loyalty to the empire. In 382, Theodosius extended official recognition to the German communities within his territory in return for a pledge of military service. Influenced by the large number of Goths in the army, the army of the Byzantine Empire became predominantly a cavalry force.

Peter S. Noble

See also
Byzantine Empire; Valens, Emperor

References
Burns, Thomas S. *Barbarians within the Gates of Rome.* Bloomington: Indiana University Press, 1994.
Ferrill, Arthur. *The Fall of the Roman Empire: The Military Explanation.* London: Thames & Hudson, 1986.
Gibbon, Edward. *The History of the Decline and Fall of the Roman Empire,* Vol. 3. Ed. J. B. Bury. London: Methuen, 1909.
Grant, Michael. *The Army of the Caesars.* New York: Scribner, 1974.

Adrianople, Crusades Battle of (April 14–15, 1205)

Battle between the Bulgarians under their ruler, Kalojan, and an army of Frankish Christian crusaders under Baldwin I, the new Latin emperor of Constantinople (modern-day Istanbul), who was trying to suppress a revolt by the Greeks in Thrace.

Without waiting for the return of all the Franks then campaigning in Asia Minor, Baldwin led a small army (140 knights and their followers) from Constantinople, accompanied by Enrico Dandolo, doge of Venice, and Louis of Blois, duke of Nicaea, and joined up with a small force under Geoffrey of Villehardouin. The Frankish army took up a position outside Adrianople (modern-day Edirne, Turkey) on March 29, 1205, but was able to blockade only two gates and was very short of supplies. On April 13, Kalojan arrived with a large army including 14,000 Cumans to help the besieged.

The fighting on the first day (April 14) was inconclusive, but the crusaders suffered many losses when the Cumans feigned flight to draw their enemy into pursuit. That evening a Frankish war council issued strict orders that the army should await the enemy attack without moving. On April 15, the Cumans rode right up to the Franks' lines, and despite the agreed battle plan, Louis of Blois led his men in pursuit of them and called on Baldwin to follow. The Franks were picked off individually, and the battle ended in a disastrous defeat, with Louis dead and the emperor captive. The survivors joined the rear guard under Geoffrey of Villehardouin, who led a disciplined retreat to Rodosto.

News of the battle provoked a mass flight of Latins from Constantinople (7,000 according to Villehardouin) and encouraged further revolts by the Greeks. The Latin Empire was seriously weakened by the loss of manpower and the interregnum, which lasted until news of the death of Emperor Baldwin in captivity reached Constantinople.

PETER S. NOBLE

See also
Baldwin I of Constantinople; Constantinople, Latin Empire of

References
Dufournet, Jean. "La bataille d'Andrinople dans la Chronique de Villehardouin." *L'Information littéraire* 25 (1973): 81–92.
Primov, Borislav. "The Third and Fourth Crusades and Bulgaria." *Etudes historiques* 7 (1975): 43–68.

Adrianople, 1444 Treaty of (June 12, 1444)

An armistice negotiated between the Ottoman sultan Murad II and Hungarian leader John Hunyadi at Adrianople (Edirne) on June 12, 1444. Later ratified by the Treaty of Szegedin, it followed in the wake of the failed Christian crusade of Varna (1443–1444) against the Ottomans. Under the terms of this 10-year truce, Murad agreed to return to Anatolia and restore Serbian territory captured since 1427 to exiled Serbian leader George Brankovic. Ottoman rule was acknowledged in Bulgaria in return for Murad's recognition of the autonomous state of Serbia and Hungarian control over Walacia.

ALEXANDER MIKABERIDZE

See also
Murad II, Sultan; Varna Crusade

Reference
Shaw, Stanford Jay. *History of the Ottoman Empire and Modern Turkey: Empire of the Gazis; The Rise and Decline of the Ottoman Empire, 1280–1808*. Cambridge: Cambridge University Press, 1991.

Adrianople, 1713 Treaty of (June 24, 1713)

The Treaty of Adrianople, signed at Adrianople (Edirne) on June 24, 1713, ended the Russo-Ottoman War of 1711–1713. Its main articles repeated provisions of the Pruth Treaty of 1711, which compelled Russia to surrender Azov and the territory along the Orel River to the Ottoman Empire. The Treaty of Adrianople was quite advantageous to Russia, since it allowed the Russian government to divert resources to the struggle against Sweden. The treaty remained in effect under the Treaty of Constantinople of 1720.

ALEXANDER MIKABERIDZE

See also
Constantinople, 1720 Treaty of; Pruth, Treaty of; Russo-Ottoman Wars

Reference
Shaw, Stanford Jay. *History of the Ottoman Empire and Modern Turkey: Empire of the Gazis; The Rise and Decline of the Ottoman Empire, 1280–1808*. Cambridge: Cambridge University Press, 1991.

Adrianople, 1829 Treaty of (September 14, 1829)

Treaty concluding the Russian-Ottoman War of 1828–1829 and signed on September 14, 1829, in Adrianople by Russia's Count Aleksey Orlov and the Ottoman Empire's Abdul Kadyr-Bey. Russia, the forces of which had advanced as far as Adrianople during the war, abandoned most of its conquests beyond the Danube but gained territory at the mouth of the Danube and acquired substantial territories in the Caucasus and southern Georgia. The Porte recognized Russia's possession of western Georgia and of the Khanates of Yerivan and Nakhichevan, which had been ceded to Russia by Persia in the Treaty of Turkmenchay (1828).

The Ottomans recognized the autonomy of Serbia and agreed to the removal of their troops, except for frontier garrisons, and to end Ottoman collection of taxes in return for a fixed annual Serbian tribute to the sultan. The treaty also provided for autonomy of the Principalities of Moldavia and Walacia under Russian protection and fixed the border between the Ottoman Empire and Walacia on the *thalweg* of the Danube. The Porte also recognized the autonomy of Greece, which achieved full independence in 1830. The treaty opened the Dardanelles to all commercial vessels, and

Russia was granted the same capitulatory rights enjoyed by other European states.

ALEXANDER MIKABERIDZE

See also
Russo-Ottoman Wars

References
Finkel, Caroline. *Osman's Dream: The Story of the Ottoman Empire, 1300–1923.* New York: Basic Books, 2006.
Karsh, Inari. *Empires of the Sand: The Struggle for Mastery in the Middle East, 1789–1923.* Cambridge MA: Harvard University Press, 2001.

Aegospotami, Battle of (405 BCE)

Decisive naval victory by the Peloponnesian side over Athens during the Second Peloponnesian War (431–404 BCE). The battle was fought in the Hellespont (Dardanelles) in 405 BCE off Aegospotami (Goat's Rivers), and its outcome led directly to the defeat of Athens in the war.

Some 180 Athenian triremes took station off a beach at Aegospotami on the European side of the Hellespont. On the Asian side from Lampsacus—a better anchorage—Spartan commander Lysander was operating with probably a like number of triremes against the Black Sea grain route vital to Athens's food supply. The Athenian anchorage was open and lacked nearby supplies of food, which the exiled Athenian general Alcibiades vainly pointed out.

The Athenians sailed out for four days in a row to tempt Lysander to fight. When he refused, they returned and landed, and the ships' crews went in search of food. In an excellent example of deception, throughout this Lysander kept his anchored ships fully crewed but with the men concealed. When the Athenians left, fast ships shadowed them, and Lysander kept his fleet manned until they reported. On the fifth day when the scout ships signaled from midchannel and the Athenian crews were scattered looking for food, Lysander attacked. Of the Athenian ships, only the state trireme, the *Paralus,* and eight ships under Conon escaped. The rest were captured, along with most of the sailors.

In retaliation for recent atrocities by the Athenians, Lysander had all the captives executed except for Adeimantus (who had argued against them). He apparently freed all non-Athenian captives. The loss of 171 triremes and their skilled crews crippled Athens. Byzantium and Chalcedon deserted, and Lysander closed the grain route to Athens and later blockaded the city, a major factor in its surrender in 404 BCE.

IAIN SPENCE

See also
Hellespont

References
Strauss, Barry S. "A Note on the Topography and Tactics of the Battle of Aegospotami." *American Journal of Philology* 108 (1987): 741–745.
Tritle, Lawrence A. *A New History of the Peloponnesian War.* Malden, MA: Wiley-Blackwell, 2010.

Ager Sanguinis, Battle of (June 28, 1119)

A battle fought in the Ruj Valley (Syria) in 1119 between the Franks of Antioch, led by Roger of Salerno, and an Ottoman coalition led by the Artuqid leader Ilghazi. The name of the battle (Ager Sanguinis means "Field of Blood") reflects its disastrous outcome for the Christian forces. The most detailed account of the fray was written by the chancellor of Antioch, Walter, an eyewitness to events. In the spring of 1119, Ilghazi collected a large army, said to have numbered some 40,000 men, to attack Antioch as part of a campaign to secure Aleppo. It is likely that Roger's victory in the Battle of Tell Danith (September 14, 1115) had made him overconfident.

Although he appealed for help from King Baldwin II of Jerusalem and Count Pons of Tripoli when he learned of the Ottoman threat, Roger did not wait for reinforcements. On June 20 he led out the army of Antioch. Informed by his scouts of his opponents' weakness, Ilghazi decided on an immediate attack. He surrounded the enemy camp on the night of June 27, and Roger was forced to give battle the next day. Few of his knights escaped the slaughter, and Roger himself was killed.

The Ottomans treated their Christian prisoners with great brutality both on the battlefield and in Aleppo. Most were put to death in ways graphically described by Walter the Chancellor. However, the Ottomans failed to follow up their victory. The principality of Antioch was effectively defenseless, with its army destroyed and its prince killed, but the Latin patriarch, Bernard of Valence, rallied the inhabitants and sent an urgent appeal to Baldwin II of Jerusalem. Meanwhile, Ilghazi devoted himself to celebrating his victory, so much so (his detractors reported) that he became ill, giving time for Baldwin to bring up his troops. Baldwin brought the Ottomans to battle at Hab (August 14, 1119); the outcome was inconclusive, but it ended the Ottoman threat for the near future.

SUSAN B. EDGINGTON

See also
Baldwin II of Jerusalem; Crusades, Christian in the Holy Land

References
Asbridge, Thomas S. *The Creation of the Principality of Antioch, 1098–1130.* Woodbridge, UK: Boydell, 2000.
Asbridge, Thomas S. "The Significance and Causes of the Battle of the Field of Blood." *Journal of Medieval History* 23 (1997): 301–316.

Agha Muhammad Khan Qajar (1742–1797)

Shah of Iran (r. 1789–1797) and founder of the Qajar dynasty. Born in 1742, Agha Muhammad Khan was the eldest son of the chief of the Qavanlu clan of the Qajars, who played an important role in Persia political life of the early 18th century. Muhammad's grandfather was executed by Shah Tahmasp II. and his father became a fugitive; in one of the skirmishes, a rival clan captured young Muhammad and had him castrated, hence his title *agha*, which was usually given to court eunuchs.

Agha Muhammad Khan grew up in a Persia torn apart by ongoing rivalries between various tribes and groups. In 1759, his father lost control of western Iran to Karim Khan Zand, and Agha Muhammad Khan was captured and kept at the Zand court in Shiraz. He spent 16 years at Karim Khan's court, well treated but a prisoner nevertheless. In 1779 upon Karim Khan's death, an internecine war broke out over the succession, allowing Agha Muhammad Khan to escape. For the next decade he was involved in a prolonged struggle for power and gradually succeeded in establishing his authority over Persia's northern provinces.

In 1781, Agha Muhammad Khan repelled a Russian naval expedition seeking to establish a fort near Ashraf. In 1782–1784 he conducted a successful campaign against Ali-Morad Khan Zand, one of the claimants of the Zand throne, thereby becoming the undisputed ruler of the northern half of Persia. Agha Muhammad moved his capital to Tehran, where he was enthroned (but not crowned) by 1789, laying the foundation for the Qajar dynasty.

In 1790–1794, Agha Muhammad continued his struggle against other pretenders. Although his army suffered repeated defeats at the hand of young Zand prince Lotf Ali Khan, Agha Muhammad Khan eventually triumphed over the Zands, sacking their last refuge in Kerman, where all males were either killed or blinded and as many as 20,000 women and children were enslaved. By then Agha

Portrait of Shah of Persia Agha Muhammad Khan Qajar (1742–1797). Done around 1840, the portrait is in the collection of the Victoria and Albert Museum in London. (Fine Art Images/Heritage Images/Getty Images)

Muhammad Khan controlled most of Persia, which allowed him to move to secure the former Safavid territories as well.

Agha Muhammad Khan first turned to the Caucasus, where the Georgian kingdom of Kartli-Kakheti, once a Safavid tributary, had sought an alliance with Russia against Persia and the Ottoman Empire. Agha Muhammad Khan demanded Georgian recognition of his sovereignty. Upon rejection of this demand, he invaded southern Caucasia in 1796. He defeated the heavily outnumbered Georgian army at Krtsanisi in September 1795 and then razed the Georgian capital of Tiflis (Tbilisi). After capturing Erivan, Agha Muhammad crowned himself as shah of Persia in March 1796, girding himself with a sword of Safavid Shah Ismail.

Also in 1796 Agha Muhammad Khan Qajar planned a campaign to reclaim Khurasan, but this was never implemented because of fresh troubles in Georgia. The Georgians refused to accept his control, and late in 1796 Russian troops had finally arrived to conquer the Caspian littoral. Although the Russian troops were soon recalled, Agha Muhammad Khan Qajar decided to conduct a second campaign in Caucasia to resolve the situation there. As he was camped north of the Araz River at Shusha, two of his servants, one of whom was a Georgian, got into an argument, and the shah condemned both of them to death. However, he postponed their execution owing to it being the Muslim holy day of Friday and ordered them back to their duties. That night, knowing that the shah would keep his word and joined by another servant, the three men crept into Agha Muhammad Khan Qajar's tent and assassinated him. His nephew, crowned as Fath-Ali Shah Qajar, succeeded him.

Through his ruthlessness, austerity, military competence, and political shrewdness, Agha Muhammad Khan Qajar had reclaimed much of Persia. Yet his failed campaigns in eastern Georgia resulted in the Russian annexation of this kingdom and opened the way for the Russian expedition into southern Caucasia.

ALEXANDER MIKABERIDZE

See also
Karim Khan Zand, Muhammad; Persia, 18th-Century Wars of Succession; Russo-Persian Wars

References
Farmanfarmaian, Roxane. *War and Peace in Qajar Persia: Implications Past and Present.* New York: Routledge, 2008.

Hambly, Gavin. "Agha Muhammad Khan and the Establishment of the Qajar Dynasty." In *The Cambridge History of Iran*, Vol. 7, ed. Peter Avery, Gavin Hambly, and C. P. Melville, 101–144. Cambridge: Cambridge University Press, 1991.

Tsintsadze, Iase. *Agha-Mahmad-Khanis tavdaskhma sakartveloze.* Tbilisi: Tsodna, 1963.

Agranat Commission (November 18, 1973–January 30, 1975)

Israeli government commission appointed by Prime Minister Golda Meir to investigate the circumstances under which Israel Defense Forces (IDF) and the Israeli government were caught by surprise in the Egyptian-Syrian attacks that began the Yom Kippur War (Ramadan War) of October 1973. The commission was named for its chairman, chief justice of the Israeli Supreme Court Shimon Agranat. Other members were Justice Moshe Landau, State Comptroller Yitzhak Nebenzahl, and former IDF chiefs of staff General Yigal Yadin and General Haim Laskov.

The commission, which held 140 sessions and heard 58 witnesses, issued an interim report on April 1, 1974, and its final report on January 30, 1975. The report chiefly blamed a failure of Israeli military intelligence and basic operational assumptions that in order for a war to occur, the Arab states would first have to unite and Egypt would not attack without first achieving air superiority. The committee noted the failure to assess political motivations present in the Egyptian decision to initiate hostilities.

The commission report found fault with six individuals, including IDF chief of staff Lieutenant General David Elazar and chief of the Southern Command Major General Shmuel Gonen. The report held that Elazar, who had primary responsibility for the entire IDF, should be dismissed and recommended that Gonen, who commanded the Egyptian Front and whose forces had been unable to prevent the Egyptians from crossing the Suez Canal, be relieved from active duty. The report also recommended the same for director of military intelligence Major General Eli Zeira and his deputy, Brigadier General Aryeh Shalev. The commission recommended that two other intelligence officers, the head of the Egyptian desk Lieutenant Colonel Bandman and the chief of Southern Command intelligence Lieutenant Colonel Gedelia, both be transferred from intelligence duties. Elazar subsequently resigned as chief of staff, and Gonen and Zeira were removed from active duty.

The report was controversial in that it absolved both Defense Minister Moshe Dayan and Prime Minister Meir of all responsibility. The commission held that it could not take into account Dayan's military background and should judge him only as a civilian defense minister acting in a political capacity. Dayan offered his resignation, but Meir refused to accept it. Strong adverse public opinion following publication of the interim report, however, forced Meir and her entire cabinet to resign on April 11, 1974, although she did not formally leave office until the formation of a new government on June 3.

SPENCER C. TUCKER

See also
Dayan, Moshe; Elazar, David; Meir, Golda Mabovitch; Yom Kippur War

References
Herzog, Chaim. *The War of Atonement: October, 1973.* Boston: Little, Brown, 1975.

Rabinovich, Abraham. *The Yom Kippur War: The Epic Encounter That Transformed the Middle East.* New York: Schocken, 2005.

Ajnadain, Battle of (July 30? 634)

Major battle between Byzantine forces defending Syria and Palestine and Arab forces pushing northward from the Arabian Peninsula at the start of the Islamic conquests. Little is known about the battle itself. It was probably fought around July 30, 634, southwest of Jerusalem. The initial Arab thrust toward Syria was stopped by Byzantine forces under Theodorus, brother of Emperor Heraclius. However, Khalid ibn al-Walid made a dramatic forced march across the Syrian desert with reinforcements and decisively defeated the Byzantine army.

The battle opened the route for the Arab advance into Syria and marked the escalation of an Arab-Byzantine conflict that eventually led to the decisive Battle of the Yarmouk River, which ended Byzantine dominance of the region.

ALEXANDER MIKABERIDZE

See also
Khalid ibn al-Walid; Yarmouk River, Battle of

Reference
Donner, Fred M. *The Early Islamic Conquests.* Princeton, NJ: Princeton University Press, 1981.

Akkad

Situated in the area of modern-day central Iraq, Akkad was the northernmost area of ancient Babylonia and was a thriving region in the second millennium BCE. The people of Akkad were most famous for their language, which became the predominant lingua franca of Mesopotamian cultures for some 2,000 years.

By the fourth millennium BCE, Akkad was well populated with many city-states. The region of Akkad was named around 2300 BCE at the juncture of the Tigris and Euphrates Rivers. Founded by Sargon of Akkad, the first king of the Mesopotamians, Akkad was the home to a mostly Semitic population. Their southern neighbors were the Sumerians; together, those regions made up the ancient Babylonian kingdom.

During Sargon's reign, the people of Akkad became consolidated into a powerful state. Ruling from his capital, Agade, Sargon forged his empire. Akkad remained the preeminent region of his dynasty until around 2150 BCE. At that time, Sargon's descendants were conquered by the Gutians, who were invaders and conquerors of both Akkad and Sumer.

The Akkadians continued to influence Mesopotamian culture with their language. A Semitic language, Akkadian was written on cuneiform tablets in the same script as Sumerian using more than 600 syllabic and word symbols. The Akkadians were also renowned for their artistry, and even today their naturalistic sculptures, including those found on the celebrated stela of Sumerian king Naram-Sin, speak to their sophisticated artistic abilities. They often depicted their mythologies and histories with well-defined graphics that showcased their achievement as masters of glyptic art.

Victory stele of Naram-Sin. The fourth king of the First Dynasty of Akkad in Mesopotamia, Naram-Sin was the first in the dynasty to claim divinity. The stele celebrates Naram-Sin's victory over a mountain people and dates from approximately 2254–2218 BCE. It is housed at the Louvre Museum in Paris. (G. Dagli Orti/De Agostini/Getty Images)

An almost constant state of war characterized Sargon's reign. His army featured seasoned professionals. As in Sumer, Sargon's Akkadian Army was composed of nine battalions of 600 men. Even if they had begun their military experience as conscripts, within a short time Sargon's soldiers would have become battle-experienced veterans. Equipping an army of this size would have undoubtedly required a high degree of military organization.

An innovation introduced by Sargon was the *niskum*, the class of soldiers who held plots of land by favor of the king and received allotments of fish and salt every three months. The intent was to create a body of loyal semiprofessionals, much along the later model of the Roman Republic. The Akkadian system worked to provide significant numbers of loyal trained soldiers who could be used in war or to suppress local revolts.

During the period of Sargon's rule, the Sumerians/Akkadians contributed a major innovation in weaponry—the composite bow. The introduction of this revolutionary weapon may have occurred during the reign of Naram-Sin (2254–2218 BCE), Sargon's grandson. Like his grandfather, Naram-Sin fought continuous wars of conquest against foreign enemies. Although the simple bow could kill at ranges from 50 to 100 yards, it would not penetrate even simple leather armor at those ranges. The composite bow, with a pull and distance of at least twice that of the simple bow, could easily penetrate leather armor and perhaps even the early prototypes of bronze armor that were emerging at the time. So important was this weapon that it became a basic implement of war in all armies of the Middle East for the next 1,500 years.

RICHARD A. GABRIEL AND NANCY L. STOCKDALE

See also
Mesopotamia; Sargon of Akkad; Sumer

References
Gabriel, Richard A. *Great Armies of Antiquity*. Westport, CT: Praeger, 2002.
Pollack, Susan. *Ancient Mesopotamia*. Cambridge: Cambridge University Press, 1990.

Akroinon, Battle of (740)

Major battle fought between forces of the Umayyad Caliphate and those of the Byzantine Empire in Asia Minor. Caliph Hisham ibn Abd al-Malik (r. 723–743) assigned command of a Muslim expeditionary force invading Asia Minor to his son Sulayman, who divided it into three bodies. Byzantine forces under Emperor Leo III the Isaurian (r. 717–741) and his son, the future Constantine V, surrounded the force under Abdallah al-Battal and al-Malik ibn Shu'ai at Akroinon and destroyed it. Reportedly only 6,800 men in the Umayyad force of 20,000 escaped. Both Arab commanders were among the dead.

Although Sulayman's remaining forces devastated the countryside, they failed to capture any towns or forts, and the Muslim defeat at Akroinon forced the Arabs to withdraw from western Asia Minor, ending Arab incursions there for three decades. The failed Umayyad offensive weakened the dynasty and helped bring its end a decade later.

SPENCER C. TUCKER

See also
Byzantine-Muslim Wars; Umayyad Caliphate

References
Blankinship, Khalid Yahya. *The End of the Jihad State: The Reign of Hisham ibn Abd al-Malik and the Collapse of the Umayyads*. Albany: State University of New York Press, 1994.
Bréhier, Louis. *The Life and Death of Byzantium*. Translated by Margaret Vaughan. Amsterdam, NY: North-Holland, 1977.

Al-Adil (1145–1218)

Prominent Muslim military leader, lord of Upper Mesopotamia (r. 1193–1198) and of Damascus (r. 1198–1200), and sultan of Egypt and Syria (r. 1200–1218). Born al-Adil Abu Bakr in June 1145, he was the brother of Saladin. Al-Adil earned the title *sayf ad-din* (the sword of religion) and was known as Saphadin in the West. Al-Adil was a capable administrator who provided essential support for the campaigns of his more famous brother. Also a capable general and strategist, al-Adil played an essential role in the success of the Ayyubid state.

Al-Adil came to prominence during Saladin's conquest of Egypt in 1174–1175, and after his brother's departure to Syria, al-Adil replaced him in Egypt, demonstrating considerable administrative and military talents as he suppressed domestic revolts and dealt with the threat posed by the Christian crusaders. He energetically supported from Egypt the policies of his brother and contributed to his success against the Franks during the Third Crusade. Al-Adil was present at the conquest of Jerusalem and participated in Saladin's negotiations with King Richard I (the Lionheart).

In early 1190, al-Adil assumed rule over Upper Mesopotamia. Following the death of Saladin in 1193, al-Adil tried to mediate between his nephews who became embroiled in the struggle for the sovereignty. After failing to secure peace, he actively participated in the power struggle and developed a series of shifting alliances that led to dispossessing his nephews of their lands and power. After seizing Damascus in 1198, al-Adil was able to establish his authority over the Ayyubid Empire by 1200 when he reclaimed Egypt from Saladin's grandson, al-Mansur. This success was partially owing to the period between the Fourth and Fifth Crusades that allowed al-Adil to concentrate resources on consolidating his power. Yet in 1217–1218 he faced the crusader invasion of Egypt (the Fifth Crusade) and was unable to prevent the loss of Damietta. He died in August 1218 before its fall, however. The sultanate then passed to his son, al-Kamil, who brought the war against the crusaders in the Nile Delta to a successful conclusion.

Alexander Mikaberidze

See also

Crusades in the Holy Land, Christian; Saladin

References

Phillips, Jonathan. *The Crusades: 1095–1197.* New York: Longman, 2002.

Regan, Geoffrey. *Lionhearts: Saladin, Richard I, and the Era of the Third Crusade.* New York: Walker, 1999.

Reston, James, Jr. *Warriors of God: Richard the Lionheart and Saladin in the Third Crusade.* New York: Doubleday, 2001.

Al-Afdal (?–1122)

Muslim vizier and effective dictator of Fatimid Egypt (1094–1122). A Muslim convert of Armenian origin, al-Afdal was the son and successor of Badr al-Jamalii, whose military intervention in 1073 in the civil war then ravaging Egypt restored order in the country and kept the Fatimids in power. Al-Afdal misjudged the aims of the Christian First Crusade (1096–1099) and offered the crusaders cooperation against the Seljuks. He was slow to offer a military response to the crusader advance on Jerusalem, and the army he dispatched to Ascalon (modern-day Tel Ashqelon, Israel) was defeated by the crusaders (August 12, 1099).

In the wake of the defeat, al-Afdal introduced military reforms and incorporated Ottoman slaves into the Fatimid Army. Under his rule Egypt enjoyed a period of stability and prosperity, but the privileged position of Ismaili Islam in the country was eroded. In 1122 al-Amir, the ruling caliph, caused the assassination of al-Afdal and took the reins of power himself.

Yaacov Lev

See also

Crusades in the Holy Land, Christian; Fatimid Dynasty

References

Brett, Michael. "The Battles of Ramla (1099–1105)." In *Egypt and Syria in the Fatimid, Ayyubid and Mamluk Eras,* ed. Urbain Vermeulen and Daniel De Smet, 17–39. Leuven: Peeters, 1995.

Lev, Yaacov. *State and Society in Faimid Egypt.* Leiden: Brill, 1991.

Alam el Halfa, Battle of (August 31–September 7, 1942)

Battle in north-central Egypt south of El Alamein fought between German field marshal Erwin Rommel's Afrika Korps and British lieutenant general Bernard Law Montgomery's Eighth Army. Fearful that he would permanently lose the initiative to the Eighth Army after his advance was halted at the First Battle of El Alamein during July 1–27, 1942, Rommel reorganized his forces with the intention of resuming his advance toward Suez. Meanwhile, Montgomery assumed command of the British Eighth Army on August 13 and began planning for the offensive, all the while expecting Rommel to attack first.

Late on the evening of August 30, Rommel attempted as at Gazala, although his force was weak in armor, to get around the Eighth Army's left flank. With diversionary attacks designed to hold British forces along the coast, Rommel ordered the Afrika Korps east and south of Alam Halfa Ridge with the aim of swinging north to the Mediterranean coast behind Montgomery and enveloping the Eighth Army.

The Eighth Army had established a defense in depth, including strong positions on the Alam Halfa and Ruweisat Ridges, and Montgomery rejected any withdrawal. The 10th Armored Division, 22nd Armored Brigade, and 44th Division defended Alam Halfa, while the 7th Armored Division was south of the ridge. Montgomery ordered his armored units to defend from their current positions rather than advancing to meet Rommel's panzers.

Slowed by British minefields and fuel shortages, Rommel's tanks did not reach Alam Halfa until the evening of August 31. Daylight brought vicious Desert Air Force attacks against the Axis advance, and the 7th Armored Division's placement forced Rommel to swing north prematurely, into the teeth of a tank brigade on Alam Halfa Ridge. Fuel shortages prevented the Afrika Korps from outflanking Alam Halfa to the east, forcing Rommel onto the defensive there.

On September 1 after a flank assault on the 22nd Armored Brigade failed and having suffered severe losses, Rommel ordered his forces to retire to their original positions. The withdrawal, which began the next day, exposed the Afrika Korps to further devastating British aerial attacks. Rommel repulsed a counterattack by the 2nd New Zealand Division on the evening of September 3, and Montgomery believed that he lacked the resources to force a general Axis withdrawal, so he decided not to press his advantage for the time being. Certainly Rommel's past successes made Montgomery wary of pushing too far forward. Montgomery had fought his first battle as commander of the Eighth Army with great skill. Rommel now had no choice but to go on the defensive. He established positions between the Mediterranean and the Qattara Depression as both sides prepared for the Eighth Army's upcoming offensive: the Second Battle of El Alamein (October 23–November 4, 1942).

THOMAS D. VEVE

See also
El Alamein, Second Battle of; Montgomery, Bernard Law; Rommel, Erwin Johannes Eugen; World War II, Impact on the Middle East

References
Lucas, James. *Panzer Army Africa.* San Rafael, CA: Presidio, 1977.
Montgomery, Bernard L. *The Memoirs of Field-Marshal the Viscount Montgomery of Alamein, K.G.* Cleveland, OH: World Publishing, 1958.
Stewart, Adrian. *Eighth Army's Greatest Victories: Alam Halfa to Tunis, 1942–1943.* Barnsley, South Yorkshire, UK: Leo Cooper, 1999.
Thompson, R. W. *Churchill and the Montgomery Myth.* New York: J. B. Lippincott, 1967.

Al-Amin, Muhammad (787–813)

The sixth Abbasid caliph who ruled during 809–813. Born Muhammad ibn Harun al-Rashid in April 787 but better known by his regnal name of al-Amin, his short reign was highlighted by the Abbasid civil war of 1810–1833 fought between him and his half brother Abd Allah al-Mamun from 810 up to al-Amin's death in 813. Al-Amin's mother was the legitimate wife of fifth caliph Harun al-Rashid and of Arab blood. His half brother was born of the union of al-Rashid and an Iranian concubine and was born six months before his half brother.

Caliph Harun al-Rashid named al-Amin as his heir and also named al-Amin's half brother al-Mamun as al-Amin's successor and ruler of an autonomous Khurasan. The two brothers swore to uphold their father's succession arrangements. Within a year of his father's death in March 1909, however, al-Amin started to undermine al-Mamun's rule in Khurasan and tried to bring that region under central control. When al-Mamun refused to comply with al-Amin's wishes, al-Amin removed him from the succession and sent an army of 40,000 men commanded by Ali ibn Isa against him. Tahir ibn Husayn, a Persian, commanded al-Mamun's far smaller Khurasani army. The two armies met near Rayy in May 811, and in the ensuing battle Ali ibn Isa was killed, and his army was routed.

Tahir then marched westward, defeating every army al-Amin sent against him. Tahir was also joined by another of al-Mamun's commanders, Harthama Ibn Ayan, and together they laid siege to Baghdad in August 812. The siege lasted for a year, during which most of al-Amin's soldiers defected to Tahir. In response, al-Amin armed the populace of Baghdad in a final bid to salvage his position. Despite this, Tahir and Harthama's forces overwhelmed the defenders and took Baghdad in September 813. Al-Amin hoped to deal with Harthama, who had been his father's friend, but Tahir intercepted the fleeing caliph and caused him to be executed on September 27.

ADAM ALI AND SPENCER C. TUCKER

See also
Abbasid Caliphate; al-Mamun, Abd Allah

References
Hodgson, Marshall G. S. *The Venture of Islam: Conscience and History in a World Civilization.* Chicago: University of Chicago Press, 1977.
Kennedy, Hugh. *The Prophet and the Age of the Caliphates: The Islamic Near East from the Sixth to the Eleventh Century.* 2nd ed. Harlow: Longman, 2004.
Saunders, J. J. *A History of Medieval Islam.* London: Routledge and K. Paul, 1965.

Al-Anfal Campaign (1987–1988)

A military campaign undertaken by Iraqi leader Saddam Hussein against the Kurdish population of Iraq during 1987–1988. Embroiled in a prolonged conflict with Iran, the Iraqi government considered the Kurds a major domestic threat and potential "fifth column" for Iran because of the Kurdish demands of autonomy in northern Iraq. In early spring 1987, Hussein named his cousin Ali Hassan al-Majid as secretary-general of the administrative zone called the Northern Bureau that controlled Iraqi Kurdistan. Al-Majid, who soon earned the grisly moniker "Chemical Ali," launched a series of attacks on Kurdish villages, destroying settlements and resettling thousands of Kurds to detention centers in other regions of Iraq. The Kurds resisted this forcible relocation and clashes occurred between them and government forces. In response, the Baathist regime sanctioned mass killing of anyone who refused to leave their villages.

The Al-Anfal (The Spoils) campaign consisted of eight major stages between February 23 and September 6, 1988, and featured ground offensives with summary executions, aerial attacks, and the widespread use of chemical warfare. The SF/4008 directive, issued by al-Majid in June 1987, specified that "all persons captured in [Kurdish] villages shall be detained and interrogated by the security services and those between the ages of 15 and 70 shall be executed after any useful information has been obtained from them." A principal goal of the campaign was the Arabization of Iraq's north, and the depopulated Kurdish villages were settled by Arabs from Iraq's southern regions.

There is no precise figure for the number of Kurds who were killed, but the best estimates are 100,000 to 150,000, many of them the victims of poison gas. Some 4,000 Kurdish villages and towns, more than 1,700 schools, and hundreds of mosques were destroyed. Following the U.S.-led invasion of Iraq in 2003, Hussein and 6 other government members were tried for crimes committed during the al-Anfal Campaign. Found guilty of crimes against humanity, Hussein was executed by hanging in December 2006 and al-Majid in January 2010.

ALEXANDER MIKABERIDZE

See also
Hussein, Saddam; Kurds, Massacres of

References
Black, George, ed. *Genocide in Iraq: the Anfal Campaign against the Kurds.* New York: Human Rights Watch, 1993.
McDowall, David. *A Modern History of the Kurds.* London: I. B. Tauris, 2004.

al-Aqsa Martyrs Brigades

An amalgamation of militias in the West Bank, sometimes affiliated with the late Palestinian leader Yasser Arafat's Fatah movement, and branded a terrorist organization by the European Union, Israel, and the United States. The al-Aqsa Martyrs Brigades are a Palestinian nationalist group formed in 2002 to force Israel from the West Bank and the Gaza Strip through militant action, including suicide bombings. Unlike Hamas and the Palestinian Islamic Jihad, the al-Aqsa Martyrs Brigades is not rooted in political Islam. It is a secular organization, the primary goal of which is the creation of an autonomous Palestinian state (but not necessarily an Islamic state).

The al-Aqsa Martyrs Brigades were born out of the turbulent violence of the Second Intifada (also known as the al-Aqsa Intifada) of 2000–2005. The intifada (or uprising) was triggered partly by the breakdown in the Arab-Israeli peace process in the late 1990s. The actual fuse was lit, however, by Likud Party leader Ariel Sharon's controversial visit in September 2000 to Haram al-Sharif (Noble Sanctuary), known to Jews as the Temple Mount. (Sharon would become Israel's prime minister in February 2001.)

Haram al-Sharif/the Temple Mount is sacred to both Jews and Muslims. It is claimed both as the site of Prophet Muhammad's ascension to Heaven and the location of both King Solomom's (First) Temple and Zerubbabel's (Second) Temple and as the Mosque of Umar and the Aqsa Mosque. At the base of the Temple Mount is the Western Wall, a retaining wall built about the time of King Herod the Great, circa 19 BCE. The only physical remnant that connects to the biblical Jewish temples, the "Wailing Wall" as it is called is the holiest site in Judaism today. Sharon's actions enraged Palestinians, and the al-Aqsa Martyrs Brigades arose from this outrage. The name is taken from the al-Aqsa Mosque and symbolizes their commitment to the al-Aqsa Intifada and resistance to Israeli oppression. They became one of the most active players in the al-Aqsa Intifada, which erupted shortly after Sharon's visit.

Initially, the group's strategy was to target Israeli military outposts and Jewish settlers within the West Bank and the Gaza Strip. However, in response to increased Israeli retaliation, the al-Aqsa Martyrs Brigades stepped up their activities to include targets in Israel itself. The group cites Lebanon's militant Hezbollah group as the inspiration for its style of violence. And although they do not have any documented links to Al Qaeda, they sometimes mirrored the actions of other militant organizations. The brigades do not exclusively target Israelis; they have been known to attack Palestinians of differing factions and have likewise been targeted by them. For more than a year they fought Palestinian Authority (PA) leaders who attacked them, and some of these were associated with Fatah. For example, Fatah PA authorities captured and tortured brigade members in Jericho in June 2005. In some cities the brigades, or certain brigade leaders, are regarded in a positive light for their attacks on criminals and gangs.

The al-Aqsa Martyrs Brigades have also fought with Palestinians regarding rights to establish launching sites of attacks near their homes. In July 2004, for example, militants reportedly shot and killed a 15-year-old Palestinian Arab after he and his family had tried to stop the erection of Qassam rocket launchers in their neighborhood. Most attacks have come from Gaza into places such as Sderot and were led by the Izz ad-Din al-Qassam Brigade.

Israeli sources claim that many al-Aqsa Martyrs Brigades members are known to have come from Fatah's militant youth group Tanzim (an Israeli identification for Fatah's

Masked members of the al-Aqsa Martyrs Brigades, an offshoot of Palestinian leader Yasser Arafat's Fatah organization, during a rally in support of Arafat in Gaza City on August 14, 2002. (Fayez Nureldine/AFP/Getty Images)

militias). Subsequently, Tanzim was identified by Israeli authorities as a "youth organization" and attributed to Marwan Barghuti after Yasser Arafat's death. Israelis also accused Barghuti of organizing the brigades. Indeed, one of the local brigades acknowledged him as their leader, which his defenders took to mean as their source of inspiration but earned him a prison sentence.

In November 2003, reporters for the British Broadcasting Company (BBC) investigated the PA, looking for some solid proof of a link to the al-Aqsa Martyrs Brigades. The BBC soon unearthed documents authorizing monthly payments of $50,000 from the PA to the militant group. The United States and Israel promptly denounced the PA for sponsoring terrorism. PA officials, however, insisted that the money—roughly $250 per group member—was actually intended to deter potential suicide bombers by providing them with financial assistance, thus reducing the lucrative appeal of terrorism.

Following the BBC investigation and resultant criticism, on December 18, 2003, Fatah officially recognized its connection to the al-Aqsa Martyrs Brigades by inviting the group to join the Fatah Council. Arafat's personal involvement with planning the group's activities is open to conjecture. Some acknowledged him as the head of the group who directly ordered its movements, while others maintained that he was not involved in day-to-day planning or operations.

Typically, al-Aqsa Martyrs Brigades attacks have been carried out via shootings and suicide bombings. The bombings have included female suicide bombers, and several children have also been involved. As well, the brigades have resorted to Qassam rocket attacks on Israel launched from Palestinian territory. Among the worst of the attacks charged to the brigades have been twin suicide bombings in downtown Tel Aviv in January 2003 that killed 23 and wounded 100, a March 2002 suicide bombing of a Jerusalem café that killed 11 and wounded 50, and a sniper assault at an Israeli checkpoint in the West Bank that killed 10 Israelis in March 2002. However, the Al-Aqsa Martyrs Brigades are not committed to the destruction of Israel; their goal is that Israel should recognize the 1967 borders, and they are loyal to Fatah's two-state solution.

Yasser Arafat died on November 11, 2004, and in commemoration of his passing, the al-Aqsa Martyrs Brigades changed their name to al-Shahid Yasser Arafat (the Martyr Yasser Arafat) Brigades, although the organization is still widely known as the al-Aqsa Martyrs Brigades. The group is reportedly integrated into the PA's official security forces and supported Fatah candidate Mahmoud Abbas in the January 2005 Palestinian presidential election, although had Marwan Barghuti not withdrawn they probably would have supported him.

On July 26, 2007, PA chairman Abbas announced the disarmament of "all the armed militias and irregular military or paramilitary groups" existing in the Palestinian Authority. This included the al-Aqsa Martyrs Brigades and occurred after Hamas took over the Gaza Strip in June–July 2007. Israel then pardoned close to 200 Fatah fugitives in return for their signing a commitment to abandon terrorism, give up their weapons to the PA, and undergo a transition period in PA prisons and then Palestinian towns, upon completion of which they would be absorbed into the Palestinian police.

Then in the midst of the 2014 Israeli-Gaza conflict, known to Israelis as Operation PROTECTIVE EDGE undertaken in response to rocket fire from Gaza into Israel, the headquarters of the al-Aqsa Martyrs Brigades in the West Bank announced on July 22, 2014, an "open war against the Zionist enemy in all ways with [operational] surprises, in accordance with all the laws and international conventions that bestow on us the right to armed struggle so as to remove this occupation from all the Palestinian land." On August 16, the al-Aqsa Martyrs Brigades published a summation of more than 30 terror attacks that it claimed it had carried out in July and the first half of August in the West Bank and Jerusalem.

Sherifa Zuhur and Spencer C. Tucker

See also
Abbas, Mahmoud; Arafat, Yasser; Hamas; Hezbollah; Intifada, Second; Israel; Palestinian National Authority; Religious Sites in the Middle East, Jewish; Religious Sites in the Middle East, Muslim; Sharon, Ariel

References
Jones, Clive, and Ami Pedahzur, eds. *Between Terrorism and Civil War: The Al-Aqsa Intifada*. London: Routledge, 2005.
Parsons, Nigel. *The Politics of the Palestinian Authority: From Oslo to Al-Aqsa*. London: Routledge, 2005.

Al-Aqsa Mosque Massacre (October 8, 1990)

The killing of Palestinian Arabs in and around the al-Aqsa Mosque on the Temple Mount (Haram al-Sharif) by Israeli troops on October 8, 1990. In the attack, some 23 Palestinians died and another 850 were injured. The Temple Mount is considered the third-holiest site in Islam. The confrontation there emerged from the activities of a Jewish organization that called itself the Temple Trustees. Its members sought to occupy the Temple Mount and to begin construction on the Third Temple there. Quite naturally, Arabs and Palestinians were outraged by what they viewed as the potential desecration of a significant holy shrine.

In the days leading up to October 8, the Temple Trustees announced plans for a mass march to the Temple Mount, the objective of which would be the laying of a cornerstone for a new temple. The well-publicized march soon drew a large Jewish contingent. The Israeli government did little to prevent the march, so the demonstration went forward despite the obvious threats it might pose to civil order. To make matters worse, the leader of the Temple Trustees, Ghershon Salomon, publicly exhorted Israelis to rally to the cause, reestablish their "sacred ties" to the Temple Mount, and terminate Arab claims to the area, including the al-Aqsa Mosque. Such rhetoric only stoked Arab enmity toward the marchers and the Israeli government.

By the time the march had reached its peak, as many as 200,000 Israelis may have joined the fray. (Israeli estimates are lower.) Israeli security forces, in an attempt to separate Palestinians and Jews during the march, began cordoning off roads leading to Jerusalem and Haram al-Sharif. The idea was to prevent Palestinians from assembling their own counterdemonstrations. Furthermore, Israeli officials closed the doors to the al-Aqsa Mosque to prevent even more people from entering. Unfortunately, this was a move that came too late, for there were already perhaps 2,000–3,000 Muslims assembled in the mosque, gathered there by the imam in a show of force to prevent Jews from entering the sanctuary.

When the marchers converged on the Temple Mount and attempted to lay the foundation stone of the Third Temple, mayhem ensued, and Israeli security forces lost control of the situation. Many in the al-Aqsa Mosque attempted to leave, but at around 10:00 a.m. an Israeli soldier opened fire on the crowd. The result was utter chaos. For almost 30 minutes, the Israelis attempted to quell the crowd by firing into it indiscriminately. The tragic result was the deaths of 23 Palestinians and the wounding of 850 others, some of them Israelis but most Palestinians.

Internal and international pressure on the government in Tel Aviv compelled Israeli prime minister Yitzhak Shamir to establish a fact-finding committee, headed by former Mossad director Tu'fi Zamir. After months of investigations, the Zamir Committee found no specific fault with the Israeli security forces present at the mosque that day. Instead, the committee blamed extremists on both sides, although the implication was that Arab extremism had largely contributed to the showdown. This begs the question, however, as to why the Israelis had not anticipated such violence and why they had not attempted to stop the march in the first place.

PAUL G. PIERPAOLI JR.

See also
Religious Sites in the Middle East, Muslim; Shamir, Yitzhak

References
Journalists of Reuters. *The Israeli-Palestinian Conflict: Crisis in the Middle East.* New York: Reuters/Prentice Hall, 2002.

Qumsiyeh, Mazin B. *Sharing the Land of Canaan: Human Rights and the Israeli-Palestinian Struggle.* London: Pluto, 2004.

Tessler, Mark. *A History of the Israeli-Palestinian Conflict.* Bloomington: Indiana University Press, 1994.

al-Atrash, Sultan (1891–1982)

Prominent Arab Druze leader, Syrian nationalist and leader of the Syrian Revolution forces (1925–27). Sultan al-Atrash, commonly known as Sultan Pasha al-Atrash, was born on March 5, 1891, in the village of al-Qrayya in the Druze area of Syria. His father had fought the Ottomans in 1910 and was captured and executed in 1911.

Sultan al-Atrash was among a number of young Druze men conscripted by the Ottomans and sent to fight in the Balkans. During World War I the Ottoman Empire sided with the Central Powers but, fearing rebellion, left the Druzes in peace. Sultan al-Atrash was in touch with other Arab nationalists and raised forces to join the Arab Revolt (1916–1918), recruiting and then leading some 1,300 men in that effort. His forces were among the first to enter Damascus on September 29, 1918. Al-Atrash became a close friend of Hashemite Emir Faisal, leader of the Arab forces, and was awarded the rank of general, the equivalent of pasha in the Ottoman Army.

During the war the British and French governments had concluded the Sykes-Picot Agreement, effectively dividing up much of the Ottoman holdings in the Middle East among themselves. France was to secure a mandate over Syria and Lebanon. The British had promised Faisal that he would be king of an Arab state in the event of an Allied victory, and he sought this in Syria. It did not last long, however. Despite widespread native support, the French moved in substantial forces and defeated the poorly equipped Arab forces in the Battle of Maysalun on July 24, 1920. Al-Atrash was gathering his men to fight the French, but events cut that short. French forces entered Damascus and subsequently divided Syria into five autonomous regions, one of them being Jabal el Druze.

On July 7, 1922, the French captured Adham Khanjar, a Lebanese Shiite rebel who had attempted to assassinate French Army commander in Syria General Henri Gouraud and had taken refuge at al-Atrash's home while he was absent. The French rejected al-Atrash's subsequent demands for the release of Khanjar. Al-Atrash subsequently led an attack on a French convoy that was assumed to be transporting Khanjar, who actually was sent to Damascas by aircraft. The French then leveled al-Atrash's home and ordered his arrest. He, however, escaped to British-controlled Transjordan and launched raids from there against the French posts in Syria. Pardoned by the French, he returned to Syria in late 1923.

Al-Atrash continued to support a united Syrian state and opposed French rule, and on August 23, 1925, he officially proclaimed the start of a revolution against the French. Fighting soon occurred in Damascus, Homs, and Hama. A major threat to French rule, the fighting came to encompass all of Syria and parts of Lebanon. Al-Atrash won a number of battles against the French at the beginning of the armed struggle in 1925, most notably al-Kafr (July 21) and al-Mazraa (August 2). The French government ordered substantial reinforcements to Syria from Morocco and Senegal. French artillery, tanks, and aircraft proved decisive. The French soon regained control of most of the cities and wore down their opponents, although resistance continued until the spring of 1927. The French sentenced al-Atrash to death, but he escaped with others to Transjordan. Eventually pardoned by the French, he returned to Syria in 1937 after the signing in 1936 of a Franco-Syrian treaty that called for immediate recognition of Syrian independence as a sovereign republic but with full emancipation to occur during a 25-year period, which nonetheless did not go into effect.

Al-Atrash participated actively in the Syrian uprising against the French in 1945 that bought their withdrawal and full Syrian independence the next year, but he refused to accept a political office. Al-Atrash opposed the policies of General Adib bin Hassan al-Shishakli, who seized power in a coup and became president of Syria in 1953. Al-Atrash moved to Jordan, returning only after al-Shishakli was forced out in yet another coup the next year. Al-Atrash supported the 1958 union of Egypt and Syria in the United Arab Republic and opposed its breakup by Syria three years later.

Sultan Pasha al-Atrash died in al-Qrayya, Syria, on March 26, 1982, at age 91. Widely regarded as a Syrian national hero, especially among the Druzes, he is respected for his patriotism, secularism, and humility.

SPENCER C. TUCKER

See also

Arab Revolt of World War I; Faisal I, King of Iraq; Gouraud, Henri Joseph Eugène; Maysalun, Battle of; Shishakli, Adib al-; Sykes-Picot Agreement; Syria

References

McHugo, John. *Syria: A Recent History.* London: Saqi, 2014.

Provence, Michael. *The Great Syrian Revolt and the Rise of Arab Nationalism.* Austin: University of Texas Press, 2005.

Alawites

Alawites, also known as Alawis, are part of Alawi Islam, a branch of Islam centered in Syria. Alawites are self-described Shia Muslims and follow the Twelver school of Shia Islam but with syncretistic elements. Alawites revere Ali (Ali ibn Abi Talib), the cousin, son-in-law, and first male follower of Muhammad, prophet of Islam. Ali ruled over the caliphate from 656 to 661 and was imam of Shia Islam from 632 to 661. The name "Alawi" means "follower of Ali."

The origins of the Alawite sect are disputed, but it is believed to have been founded by Ibn Nusayr in the ninth century, and for this reason Alawites are sometimes known as Nusayris. Alawites number some 2.5 million worldwide. Most live in Syria, but there are significant Alawite minority communities in Turkey and in northern Lebanon.

Alawites have historically kept their beliefs secret, a practice that has led to many misconceptions regarding them. Alawites hold that they were originally stars or divine lights but were cast out of Heaven through disobedience and must undergo repeated reincarnation (metempsychosis) before returning to Heaven. They can be reincarnated as Christians or others through sin and as animals should they become infidels. Among other beliefs and practices, Alawites consecrate wine in a secret form of mass only open to males. They frequently have Christian names and observe some Christian feast days. They bury their dead in sarcophagi aboveground (their only religious structures). They also believe that women lack souls.

Alawites believe in a divine triad comprising three aspects of one God. These aspects or emanations appear cyclically in human form throughout history, the last emanations being Ali, Muhammad, and Salman the Persian. Some tenets of the faith are known only to a select few Alawites, leading to Alawites being called a mystical sect. Sunnis, who make up the majority of the Muslim population in Syria and also worldwide, have historically persecuted Alawites for their beliefs, whereas Shiites (notably Shiite Iran) have supported them.

Alawites have frequently been persecuted. Christian crusaders killed many when they invaded Syria in 1097, although the crusaders seem to have subsequently concluded that the Alawites were not truly an Islamic sect. During the reign of Ottoman sultan Selim I (r. 1512–1520), the Alawites underwent significant persecution. When the Ottomans attempted to convert them to Sunni Islam, the Alawites mounted several revolts, managing to survive in their mountain regions.

With the defeat of the Ottoman Empire in World War I, France secured a League of Nations mandate over Syria. During this mandate period (1918–1938), the Alawites initially rebelled against the French but then came to favor a continuation of French rule. This was because the French created exclusive minority areas in Syria, which brought an Alawite state in the Mediterranean coastal area. The Alawites later sought unsuccessfully to convert this into actual independence. Alawites feared persecution by the Sunnis, and in 1936, 80 prominent Alawi leaders appealed to the French government that the Alawite people not be part of Syria but remain under French protection. Among the signatories was Sulayman Ali al-Assad, father of future Syrian president Hafez al-Assad. It was not to be, for in December of that year the Alawite state was reincorporated into Syria in a concession by the French to the Syrian National Bloc, the Syrian political party in power in the nascent Syrian government.

In order to create a counter to the majority Sunnis in Syria, who tended to be hostile to their rule, the French brought a number of Alawites into the Syrian Army. Although their state was dismantled, Alawites continued to be prominent in the Syrian Army.

Syria became fully independent in April 1946. Political instability was the rule, and a number of military coups followed. In 1970 in a great shock to the majority Sunnis who had dominated Syria for so long, Syrian Air Force general and minister of defense Hafez al-Assad, an Alawite, seized power. In 1971 Assad declared himself president of Syria, a position restricted at the time by the constitution to Sunni Muslims. Assad introduced a new constitution in 1973 that specified only that the president be a Muslim. Assad and then his son Bashar al-Assad have ruled Syria ever since, with Alawites occupying prominent positions. A subsequent fatwa by Musa as-Sadr, a leader of the Twelvers of Lebanon and founder of the Amal Movement, proclaimed Alawites to be a community of Twelver Shiite Muslims.

Although there was greater toleration of religious minorities under Hafez al-Assad, this was not the case with political dissidents. In 1976 Sunni Muslim fundamentalists began challenging the Syrian Baath Party's secular outlook, and in February 1982 Assad sent in the army to crush an uprising by the Muslim Brotherhood in Hama. In what is known as the Hama Massacre, large parts of the city were destroyed, and probably some 20,000 people, most of them innocent civilians, were killed.

Hafez al-Assad died in 2000 and was succeeded as president by his son Bashar al-Assad. In 2011, however, civil war began in Syria with Sunni Muslims—both fundamentalists and moderates—taking up arms against the government in an ongoing and bloody conflict that has seen Shiite Iran support its coreligionists in the Alawite regime, joined by Russia, which seeks to retain its important naval base at Tartus on the Syrian Mediterranean coast.

The pre–civil war Alawite population of Syria was about 2.6 million, or 12 percent of Syria's 22 million people (by 2018 the Syrian population had shrunk to some 18.2 million). The civil war has proven especially costly for the Alawites. Some estimates have perhaps a third of young Alawite males killed in the fighting. For good reason, Alawites greatly fear a government defeat and the effect it would have on their community.

The Alawite population is concentrated in the An-Nusayriyah Mountain region on the Mediterranean coast, with Latakia and Tartus being the principal population centers. There are also numbers of Alawites around Hama and Homs.

The number of Alawites in Turkey is unknown, but there were some 700,000 there in 1970, suggesting a figure of more than twice that today. There are another 180,000–200,000 Alawites in Lebanon, primarily in the area of Tripoli. Several thousand Alawites living in the village of Ghajar in the Golan Heights chose to become Israeli citizens after that area was seized by Israel as a consequence of the 1967 Arab-Israeli War.

Spencer C. Tucker

See also
Ali ibn Abi Talib; Assad, Bashar al-; Assad, Hafez al-; Iran; Lebanon; Shia Islam; Sunni Islam; Syria; Syrian Civil War

References
Friedman, Yaron. *The Nusayri-'Alawis: An Introduction to the Religion, History and Identity of the Leading Minority in Syria.* Leiden: Brill, 2010.

Procházka, Stephan, and Gisela Procházka-Eisl. *The Plain of Saints and Prophets: The Nusayri-Alawi Community of Cilicia (Southern Turkey) and Its Sacred Places.* Wiesbaden-Erbenheim, Germany: Harrassowitz Verlag, 2010.

Winter, Stefan. *A History of the 'Alawis: From Medieval Aleppo to the Turkish Republic.* Princeton, NJ: Princeton University Press, 2016.

Worth, Robert F. *A Rage for Order: The Middle East in Turmoil, from Tahrir Square to ISIS.* London: Pan Macmillan, 2016.

Aleppo, Battle for (July 19, 2012–December 22, 2016)

Major military engagement fought for control of the largest city in Syria, with a population of some 2.5 million. This Battle for Aleppo during the long, ongoing Syrian Civil War (2011 to the present) began on July 19, 2012. Repeated efforts by international relief agencies to provide aid to civilians or facilitate evacuation were routinely disrupted by continued combat and mistrust on both sides. United Nations attempts to end the carnage saw the Syrian government turn down plans that would grant eastern Aleppo autonomy, and the battle settled into a struggle of attrition ultimately decided by force of arms on December 22, 2016.

Nationwide protests in Syria against the regime of President Bashar al-Assad began in mid-March 2011, part of the so-called Arab Spring throughout much of the Arab world that demanded an end to corruption and more democratic governments. Aleppo, known as a multicultural city, remained largely unaffected by these developments and indeed was generally supportive of the Syrian government until the beginning of large-scale protests there in May 2012. Then on July 22, rebel fighters opposing the Assad regime entered Aleppo from neighboring communities. The government response was heavy-handed and indiscriminate.

Initial rebel strength was perhaps 6,000–7,000 men, with the largest contingent being the al-Tawhid Brigade and the most prominent the Free Syrian Army (FSA), which was largely composed of men who had deserted from the regular Syrian armed forces. Although most of the initial antigovernment forces were drawn from the immediate Aleppo countryside, they were later joined by Islamic extremists and foreign fighters, many of whom had taken part in the ongoing insurgency in neighboring Iraq. The long battle that followed pitted the FSA and other Sunni Muslim groups such as the Levant Front and the Al Qaeda-affiliated Al-Nusra Front but also the Kursih Protection Units against the Syrian government armed forces, supported by Hezbollah (Shia Muslims from Lebanon), various Shia Muslim militias, Iran, and then Russia. Russian air strikes, which began in late September 2015, were key in turning the battle in the government's favor.

Late in the battle, Syrian president Assad likened the fighting in Aleppo to that of Stalingrad during World War II, and in the destruction wrought there certainly is a parallel. Government forces, having lifted the rebel siege of Aleppo in October 2013, continued their offensive in 2014. This culminated in their capture of the Sheikh Najjar industrial district

Destruction in Aleppo's old city on October 2, 2013. This protracted battle in the ongoing Syrian Civil War was fought during July 19, 2012–December 22, 2016, and left much of Syria's largest city in ruins. (Richard Harvey/Dreamstime.com)

north of Aleppo and the raising on May 22, 2014, of the rebel siege of Aleppo Central Prison, where government soldiers had held out since 2012.

The battle was largely a stalemate for its first four years, with the government controlling west Aleppo and opposition forces holding much of east Aleppo. This phase ended in July 2016 when, greatly aided by Lebanese Hezbollah Shiite militiamen, heavy Syrian artillery, and indiscriminate Syrian government air strikes, Syrian government forces were able to seal off east Aleppo, closing the last rebel supply lines into the city and essentially trapping there some 250,000 civilians, a third of them children.

In early August, the rebels led by Jabhat Fateh al-Sham, formerly the al-Nusra Front (which had only two weeks before broken its long-standing ties with Al Qaeda in order to build closer alliances with other jihadist and rebel groups), opened an offensive and seized a government military complex in the Ramouseh district, securing the weaponry stored there. This success did not take. Other rebel offensives in September and October failed. Syrian government forces, again greatly aided by Russian air strikes, turned back the rebel attacks and then began a major offensive operation of their own that ultimately brought victory.

The fighting saw widespread atrocities against civilians, with the targeting of clearly marked hospitals and schools by both the Syrian and Russian air forces as well as extensive artillery shelling of civilian areas, the indiscriminate use of antipersonnel "barrel bombs" and cluster munitions by the Syrian and Russian air forces as well as residual air strikes designed to target rescue workers after a first strike. There were also charges that the Syrian government had employed chemical weapons. Improvised and wildly inaccurate artillery employed by the rebel forces also resulted in civilian casualties.

On December 13 following two weeks of steady government advances and with only some 5 percent of the city still in rebel hands, a cease-fire agreement was reached following talks between Assad's main ally of Russia and Turkey, a leading backer of the rebels. After some hitches and a resumption of shelling by the government side, on December 22 the evacuation of tens of thousands of civilians and fighters from the remaining rebel-held areas of Aleppo came to an end, leaving what remained of the city in government hands.

Although certainly Assad's biggest victory in the civil war to date, much of Aleppo lay in ruins, with some 33,500 buildings demolished. A third of the Old City of Aleppo, a UNESCO World Heritage site, had been destroyed. Some 31,000 people had died in the fighting, two-thirds of them civilians, including a large number of children. Hundreds of thousands of city residents were also displaced. Whether this was a turning point in the long-running Syrian Civil War remained unclear.

SPENCER C. TUCKER

See also
Arab Spring; Assad, Bashar al-; Syria; Syrian Civil War

References
The Battle of Aleppo: The History of the Ongoing Siege at the Center of the Syrian Civil War. Waltham, MA: Charles River Editors, 2016.
Beehner, Lionel, and Mike Jackson. "What the Siege of Sarajevo Can Teach Us about Aleppo." *Washington Post,* May 9, 2016.
Dehghanpisheh, Babak, and Liz Sly. "Iran Pledges Support for Syria as Battle Rages for Aleppo." *Washington Post,* August 7, 2012.
Hubbard, Ben. "Turning Point in Syria as Assad Regains All of Aleppo." *New York Times,* December 22, 2016.
Sorenson, David S. *Syria in Ruins: The Dynamics of the Syrian Civil War.* Santa Barbara, CA: Praeger Security International, 2016.

Alexander I Balas (ca. 173–145 BCE)

Seleucid ruler. Alexander I Balas was born around 173 BCE. His origins remain largely a mystery. The name Balas may be Semitic in origin. Allegedly of obscure lower-class birth, around 152 Balas was used by the kings of Pergamum and Egypt against their common enemy, Seleucid king Demetrius II Nicator (ca. 336–283 BCE). Balas was purportedly a son of Antiochus IV (r. 175–163) and had earlier secured the backing of Rome. In a two-year war using foreign troops, Balas won the support of the population of Antioch, the Seleucid capital in 150, defeating and killing Demetrius Soter, who was deserted in battle by his own troops. At the age of 23 Balas took the regal name of Alexander, and among other titles styled himself Theopater Euergetes (meaning "with a God for his father, benefactor"). To the populace, however, he remained Balas.

Alexander I Balas's reign during 150–145 was discredited by factionalism and intrigue at court. Genial and pleasure-loving, Balas did not command respect. When Demetrius, son of the late king, invaded with an army of mercenaries (ca. 147), Balas's only solid support was from the Jewish leader Jonathan. Successes won by Jewish forces and concessions that Balas granted to Jonathan further alienated his Greek subjects. Balas also lost the support of his former backer Egyptian king Ptolemy VI (r. 180–145), who was instrumental in having Demetrius accepted as king. After Balas was driven out of the capital, in 145 he attempted an assault on Antioch with an army raised in Cilicia but was defeated, betrayed, and murdered.

Balas is a puzzling figure. Before becoming king he showed remarkable diplomatic persuasiveness but was unable to secure the loyalty of the army or the population of Antioch, both essential for a Seleucid ruler.

DOUGLAS KELLY

See also
Demetrius II Nicator; Egypt; Maccabean Revolt; Ptolemy VI Philometor; Seleucid Empire; Syria

Reference
Green, Peter. *Alexander to Actium.* Berkeley: University of California Press, 2008.

Alexander III the Great (356–323 BCE)

King of Macedonian and ruler of Persia. Alexander III's conquest of the Persian Empire, his military ability as one of history's truly great captains, his vision of a unified people, and his role in spreading Greek culture that changed the Mediterranean world and ushered in the Hellenistic period all warrant the appellation of "Great." Alexander was born in Pella, Macedonia, in 356 BCE to Philip II, king of Macedonia, and Olympias of Epirus. Bright and charismatic, Alexander had the philosopher Aristotle as his teacher after 342.

Although Alexander had a tumultuous relationship with his father, much of his later success is attributable to Philip's training and generals. Philip created the superb Macedonian Army that his son used to conquer the known world. Philip also secured control of Greece, an essential prelude to an invasion of the Persian Empire.

Alexander proved himself as a military commander, having charge of the Macedonian left-wing cavalry in Philip's victory over the allied Greeks in the Battle of Chaeronea (August 338). In 337 Alexander fled with Olympias to Epirus following a violent quarrel between her and Philip. Both returned to Pella some months later.

Philip was preparing to invade Persia when he was assassinated in July 336. Suspicions swirled around Alexander and Olympias, but the succession was not contested, and Alexander became king. Before he could carry out his father's plan of invading Persia, Alexander first shored up his power base in northern Greece. In 335 he won a series of victories in Thessaly, Boeotia, and Illyria, and he brutally suppressed a revolt in Thebes, after which he razed the city.

In 334 Alexander set out to invade the Persian Empire, the world's largest. Departing Macedonia with an army of Macedonian and Greek soldiers drawn from the League of Corinth, the confederation Philip had created after his victory at Chaeronea in 338, Alexander crossed the Hellespont (Dardanelles) into Asia Minor with the aim of first liberating the small Greek city-states of Asia Minor. His army was small for the task ahead of it: only some 30,000 infantry and 5,000 cavalry. What moved his men was Alexander's leadership. He shared their hardships and was always in the thick of the fray.

The Persian satraps (governors) of Asia Minor assembled a much larger force to fight Alexander and waited for him on the east bank of the Granicus River. In May 334 Alexander personally led his cavalry across the river into the Persian line, and the Macedonians achieved a stunning victory. This dramatic triumph established Alexander as a bold commander and inspired fanatical devotion to him among his men.

After freeing the Ionian cities from Persian control, Alexander won successive battles and sieges in central Turkey, and in September the swift-moving Alexander surprised the Persian defenders of the Cilician Gates (near Bolkar Daglari) and seized that vital pass without a fight. Alexander then moved against the main Persian army under Emperor Darius III. The decisive Battle of Issus (November 333) again proved Alexander's reputation. Darius escaped, but Alexander captured his family and all of his baggage, later marrying one of Darius's daughters. Alexander refused an offer from Darius of 10,000 talents (300 tons) in gold.

Alexander then pushed south. In one of the great siege operations in all of history, he took Tyre and Gaza at the end of 332 BCE. All Phoenicia passed under his control, an essential prelude to a new invasion of Persia as far as his lines of communication back to Greece were concerned. He then occupied Egypt, traveling into the desert to consult the oracle of Ammon at Siwa (331), where he was greeted by the priest as the son of Ammon (Zeus to the Greeks). It is not clear whether Alexander believed in his own divinity.

Learning that Darius had put together a huge new army, Alexander departed Egypt and marched north into southern Mesopotamia in the spring of 331. Alexander and his army crossed the Tigris River that September, and in the Battle of Gaugamela (Arbela, October 331) with about 50,000 men he again defeated King Darius III's force, variously estimated at between 250,000 and 1 million men. Alexander's victory ended the Persian Empire.

Later in 331 Alexander captured Babylon and then Susa. Cities rallied to him, knowing of his leniency and toleration of their gods if they surrendered and of terrible punishments if they resisted. In December in a lightning strike, Alexander secured the Persian Gates and then occupied and sacked the Persian capital of Persepolis, one of the blemishes on his career (the reasons remain in dispute). When Darius was killed in 330 by members of his own entourage, Alexander became king.

Alexander shocked his Macedonians by adopting Persian dress and ceremonies and by advancing Persians to high posts. He insisted that his generals take Persian wives. Aristotle had told him to treat the Persians as slaves, but Alexander had a wider vision in which all men would be bound by a common culture (that of Greece) and have equal opportunity based on their deeds.

Alexander now ruled the greatest empire of antiquity, but he wanted more. He campaigned along the southern shores of the Caspian Sea. Suppressing a plot from among his senior officers, he ordered the execution of both Philotas and his father Parmenion in December 330. In 329 Alexander invaded southern Afghanistan and Badakshan. Wherever he went he founded new cities, many of them named for him (the most famous was Alexandria in Egypt). He then campaigned along the Oxus River before besieging and capturing the reputedly impregnable fortresses of the Sogdian Rock and the Chiorenes Rock in 327. He then married Roxanne, daughter of the lord of the Sogdian Rock, reportedly to secure an heir, for he had a male lover in his general Hephaestion. That same year Alexander crushed a plot against him from among the corps of pages, executing its leader.

Alexander invaded India by the Khyber Pass, crossed the Indus River (April 326 BCE), and defeated King Porus in the Battle of the Hydaspes (May). That July Alexander's army mutinied, refusing to proceed farther. Alexander then led his army in a difficult and nearly disastrous march across the Gedrosian Desert in Buluchistan during September–November 325, returning to Persepolis in January 324. He then crushed another mutiny against his assimilationist policies in the army. Alexander arrived in Babylon (spring 323), evidently intent on making it his capital. In June 323 after a night of heavy drinking, Alexander took ill. He died several days later of a fever, perhaps malaria, on June 13, 323, at only age 32. Reportedly, when asked on his deathbed to whom he would leave the empire, he whispered "Kratisto" (meaning "to the strongest").

Following Alexander's death, first Perdiccas and then Antigonus the One-Eyed endeavored to maintain the unity of the empire. Soon, however, a dozen of Alexander's leading generals (the Diadochi, or successors) were fighting for control of the state. Although skillful generals, none had Alexander's vision or genius. By 309 BCE Alexander's direct family had been eliminated, and the contenders believed themselves strong enough to claim the title of king in their own areas of the Hellenistic world. Alexander's vision of a universal commonwealth was thus lost. By 276 BCE the three major power centers of the Hellenistic empire were Macedon, Egypt, and the Seleucid Empire.

Despite the breakup of the empire, the cultural impact of Alexander's conquests was immense. The fusion of Greek and non-Greek culture, known as Hellenistic, impacted virtually all areas, including the arts but also education, government, and even city planning, and was still evident in the Byzantine Empire of the mid-15th century.

Spencer C. Tucker

See also
Alexander III's Invasion of the Persian Empire; Darius III; Gaugamela, Battle of; Granicus, Battle of the; Issus, Battle of; Tyre and Gaza, Sieges of

References
Bosworth, Albert B. *Alexander and the East: The Tragedy of Triumph.* Oxford: Oxford University Press, 2001.

Bosworth, Albert B. *Conquest and Empire: The Reign of Alexander the Great.* Cambridge: Cambridge University Press, 1988.

Daskalakis, A. *Alexander the Great and Hellenism.* Thessaloniki: Institute for Balkan Studies, 1966.

Green, Peter. *Alexander of Macedon, 356–323 B.C.: A Historical Biography.* Berkeley: University of California Press, 1991.

Hammond, Nicholas. *Alexander the Great: King, Commander, and Statesman.* London: Duckworth, 1981.

Lane Fox, Robin. *Alexander the Great.* London: Penguin, 1973.

Alexander III's Invasion of the Persian Empire (334–323 BCE)

Following the successful defense of their homeland by the Greek city-states against invasions by forces of the vast Persian Empire in the Greco-Persian Wars of 499–479 BCE, a number of Greeks harbored visions of turning the tables and conquering the Persian Empire, then the world's largest empire. Among these was Philip II, king of Macedon, who ruled that territory in the northeastern part of the Greek peninsula during 359–336. Inaugurating a new period in Greek history, Philip organized Macedonia for war and turned its army into a formidable military force, transforming it into arguably the finest military establishment the world had yet seen. Philip studied and understood the strengths, limitations, and utility of each type of military formation and melded these into a combined-arms team that included strong cavalry and artillery elements whereby the particular strength of each contributed to the success of the whole. Commanded by the king in person and upon his death by his son Alexander III (the Great), the army was not only well trained but also efficiently organized and brilliantly administered, triumphing over all other forces it encountered.

Taking advantage of the sharp divisions and rivalries among the Greek city-states to the south, Philip expanded Macedonian territory in Illyria and toward the Danube and then in Thrace and Thessaly. He also greatly increased his influence in Greece. Philip had long planned to invade Persia. He hoped to be able to do so at the head of an army that would include an allied Greek force, but the leading Greek city-states stole a march on him and concluded an alliance with King Artaxerxes of Persia. This forced Philip to move quickly against his Greek adversaries before he could invade Persia.

In May 338 BCE Philip defeated the forces of Athens, Thebes, and their allies in the Battle of Chaeronea in Boeotia in central Greece. One of the most decisive battles in Greek history, it extinguished the independence of the city-states and made Philip master of all Greece. He then established a federal system in the so-called League of Corinth that united most of the city-states and ended the struggles that had distracted them for so long. Sparta, however, refused to participate.

Philip then prepared to launch his invasion of the Persian Empire. This was ostensibly to free the Greek city-states of Asia Minor, but his grand design was to conquer Persia and secure the wealth of that vast empire. In 336 he sent his trusted general Parmenio to Asia Minor with an advance force. Philip was preparing to follow with the main invasion force when he was assassinated, possibly with the complicity of Olympias, his estranged wife. In any case, Philip was succeeded by his son Alexander, who now prepared to implement his father's plan.

The accession to the throne of Macedon of young Alexander (he was but 20 years old at the time) appeared to present an opportunity for the Greek city-states to reassert their independence, but Alexander quickly marched an army southward and, at Corinth, secured election as captain

The Empire of Alexander the Great

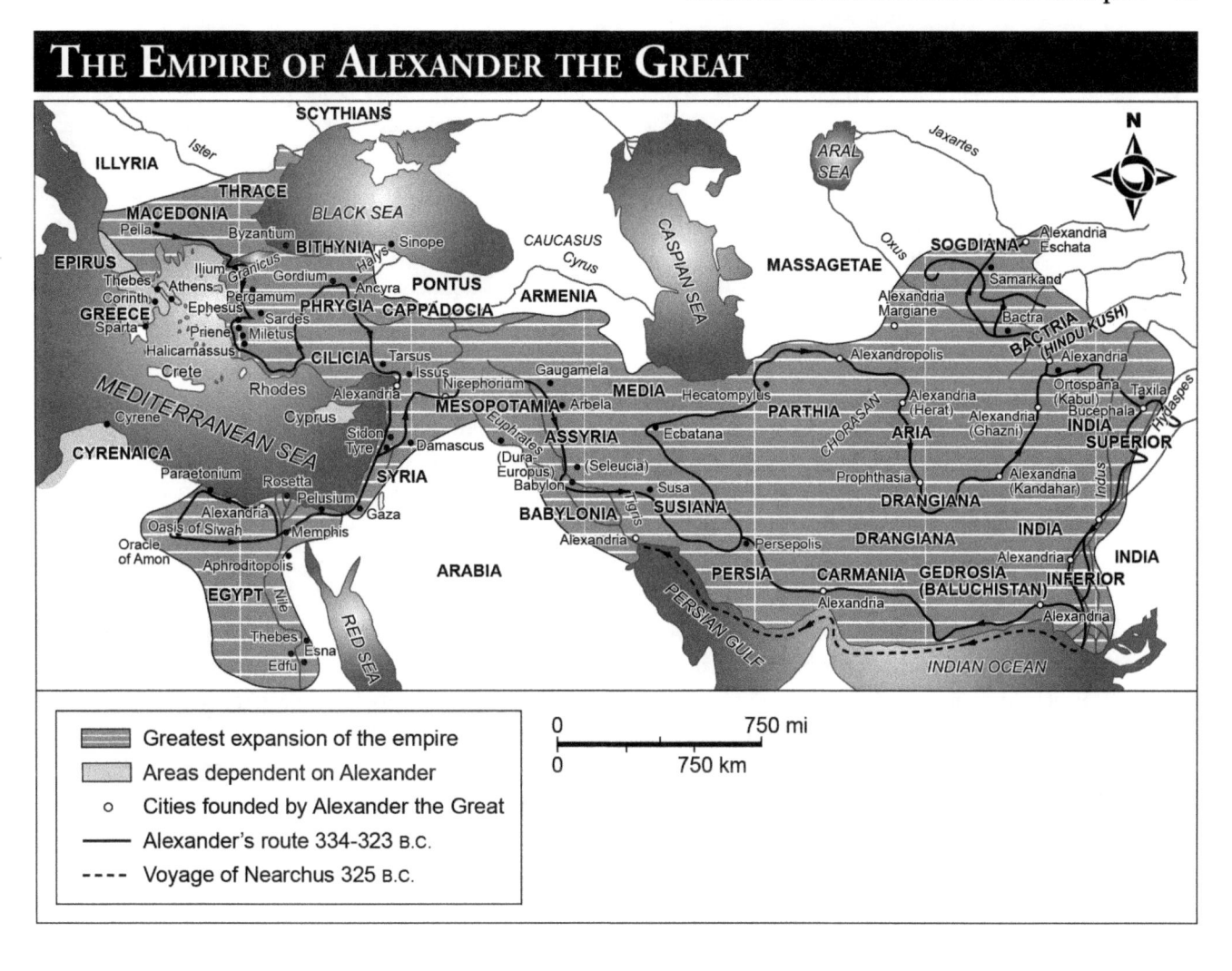

general of the Hellenic League, the same position held by his father. In 335 Alexander moved against areas under Macedonian control to the north that also had become restive, crushing a revolt in southern Illyria. There he learned that Athens and Thebes had risen against him, probably under the influence of Darius III, the new king of Persia. Alexander immediately marched south into Greece with a sizable force. Moving quickly, he surprised and took Thebes, sacking and virtually destroying it. Athens surrendered and was treated generously, ending opposition in Greece to Alexander's rule.

His base of operations secure, in 334 BCE Alexander proceeded to invade the Persian Empire with what was a relatively small army of some 30,000 infantry and 5,000 cavalry. This included soldiers from the Greek states. Alexander left behind in Macedon his trusted general Antipater and 10,000 men to hold Macedonia and Greece in his absence. During the next decade Alexander not only conquered Persia but also campaigned in Egypt and as far as Uzbekistan, Afghanistan, and the Punjab. Everywhere victorious, his conquests created what became known as the Hellenistic world.

Alexander's army reached the Hellespont (present-day Dardanelles) in just three weeks and crossed without Persian opposition. His fleet numbered only about 160 ships supplied by the allied Greeks. The Persian fleet included perhaps 400 Phoenician triremes, and its crews were far better trained, yet the Persian ships did not contest the crossing.

Alexander instructed his men that there was to be no looting in what was now, he said, their land. The invaders received the submission of a number of Greek towns in Asia Minor. Persian king Darius III was, however, gathering forces to oppose Alexander. Memnon, a Greek mercenary general in the Great King's employ, knew that Alexander was short of supplies and cash; he therefore favored a scorched-earth policy to eventually force Alexander to withdraw. At the same time, Darius would use his fleet to transport the army across the Aegean and invade Macedonia. Memnon advised that the Persians should avoid a pitched battle with Alexander at all costs. This, however, wounded Persian pride, influencing Darius to reject Memnon's wise advice.

The two armies met in May along the Granicus River. The Persian force was approximately the same size as that of Alexander and included as many as 6,000 Greek hoplite mercenaries. Alexander routed the Persians in the Battle of the Granicus.

Following the battle, Alexander proceeded to liberate the Greek coastal cities of Asia Minor. His only real opposition came at Miletus, which he captured following a brief siege. Alexander then took the momentous decision of disbanding his fleet of some 160 triremes. He kept only the Athenian detachment, to serve as transports and provide hostages, and a squadron in the Hellespont. With the Persian fleet of more than 400 triremes dominating the eastern Mediterranean, he could not hope to win a sea battle, and maintaining the fleet was expensive. His commanders opposed this decision. The Persians might now easily cut off the army in Asia Minor and prevent both its resupply and its return to Macedonia and Greece. The Persians could also raid Greece and stir up revolts against Alexander there. Alexander, however, believed that his men would fight harder knowing that retreat was not possible. He also seems to have profoundly distrusted his Greek allies, so much so that he was prepared to risk his entire campaign rather than entrust its safety to a Greek fleet. Alexander told his generals that he intended to move against the Persian fleet from the land instead, taking the Persian and Phoenician naval bases along the eastern Mediterranean coast. Indeed, during 334–333 he conquered much of the coast of Asia Minor.

Alexander's early military successes owed much to his reputation for mercy, justice, and toleration. It certainly helped his cause that his rule brought improved administration, lower taxes, and public works projects. The only difficult operation in this campaign occurred at Halicarnassus, where the defenders were led by Memnon. Alexander only took the city following a siege.

While Alexander secured the remaining coastal cities, Darius III now loosed Memnon, his only first-class general, against Alexander's lines of communication. Memnon soon took sick and died, however. Darius was busy gathering yet another army for another military test with the invader when he learned that Alexander had moved south into Syria. This news caused Darius to move before he was fully ready. Crossing the Amarnus Mountains, Darius positioned his forces behind Alexander, cutting off his line of communications. With the potentially hostile cities of Phoenicia to the south, Alexander had no choice but to break off this campaign to turn and fight.

The two armies came together at Issus in southern Anatolia in early November 333 (possibly November 5). The size of the armies remains in dispute. Darius had more men, probably 75,000 and perhaps as many as 100,000, while Alexander had about 47,000. Alexander was again victorious, and Darius fled the field. Persian losses may have been as high as half of the force, or 50,000 men, while Alexander reported some 450 dead. Among the captives were Darius's wife, mother, and two daughters. The loot taken included some 3,000 talents in gold.

Issus was a glorious victory, but it was not decisive. More than 10,000 Greek mercenaries escaped and would form the nucleus of yet another Persian army against Alexander. Darius also still lived, and as long as this was the case, the fight would continue.

After Issus, Alexander returned to his strategy of capturing the Persian Mediterranean naval bases in order to secure his southern flank prior to resuming his eastward march to the extremities of the Persian Empire. His sieges of Tyre and Gaza in 332 are two of the great military operations in history. Certainly they demonstrated Alexander's thorough mastery of siege warfare and greatly added to his mystique of invincibility. Alexander was, however, fortunate that Darius had not moved against the Macedonian lines of communication.

Darius offered Alexander 10,000 talents in gold, the territory of the empire west of the Euphrates River, and his daughter in marriage. Alexander rejected this overture, replying that he intended to conquer all Persia.

Having secured both Syria and Palestine, during 332–331 Alexander occupied Egypt. While there he founded Alexandria, only one of many cities to bear his name. While in Egypt, Alexander also traveled 200 miles into the desert to visit the Temple of Zeus Ammon and there received confirmation of his divinity as the son of Zeus.

Taking advantage of Alexander's absence and with funds supplied by Persia, during 331 King Agis III of Sparta led a revolt in Greece. Most of the southern Greek states joined it and laid siege to Megalopolis (present-day Megalopoli) in the southwestern Peloponnesus. Antipater marched south, however, and defeated the rebels outside Megalopolis. Antipater then sent Alexander reinforcements, who joined him in Egypt.

In April 331 Alexander departed Egypt with his army, marching north to Tyre and then east across the territory he had carved out of Asia Minor. This time, however, he moved directly against the distant cities of Persia, crossing the Euphrates on a bridge constructed by some of his men under his general and alleged lover Hephaestion.

Darius III had assembled a new army of perhaps 100,000 men. Alexander had a maximum of 47,000. Darius awaited Alexander on the plain at Gaugamela, some 60 miles from the city of Arbela (modern-day Erbil). Most probably the

A mosaic ca. 100, perhaps based on an earlier Greek painting, depicting the victory in 333 BCE of Macedonian king Alexander III the Great over the Persians at Issus. This mosaic from Pompeii shows Persian ruler Darius III about to flee as Alexander (on horseback at left) seeks to reach him from the flank. (Jupiterimages)

battle occurred east of the city of Mosul in present-day northern Iraq. Battle was joined on October 1, 331. Again Alexander was in the thick of the fray, and again he was victorious and Darius escaped. Macedonian casualties were reported as some 500 killed and up to 3,000 wounded, while Persian losses were close to 50,000.

Alexander did not rest and after the battle advanced rapidly toward the Persian capital of Persepolis so as not to allow the Persian generals time to reorganize their forces. Bessus and other Persian generals, disgusted by Darius's conduct, murdered him in mid-330. Alexander caught such regicides as he could and executed them.

Alexander sent most of his men by the long route, while he led about a third of his force through the mountains on a shorter route through the Persian Gates (the strategic pass now known as Tang-e Meyran in modern-day Iran), held by a Persian army under Ariobarzan. The Persians halted the Macedonians at the narrow pass and reportedly inflicted heavy casualties. Either through a shepherd or prisoners, Alexander learned of a path that flanked the Persian position and, in a highly dangerous move, led a number of his men by it at night and turned the Persian position. As a result, Alexander reached Persepolis before the guards of the treasury could hide its reputed 3,000 tons of gold and silver, the greatest known treasury in the world. He then destroyed the great palace, perhaps as a sign of the end of Persian power.

Alexander was now 25 years old. In 4 years he had broken the power of Persia forever and now ruled an empire of 1 million square miles. No one in the world could come close to him in wealth or power. The speed of what he accomplished stands unequaled before or since.

Alexander's tutor, Aristotle, had urged him to treat the Persians as slaves. Instead Alexander treated them as equals and employed them in administrative positions, something many of his troops could not understand. After organizing his new empire, in 329 Alexander campaigned in Parthia and Bactria. He then turned north across the Oxus River into Sogdiana. In 328 he subdued Sogdiana and then fought his way through the mountain passes north of the Kabul Valley and across the Indus River into India.

In May 326 Alexander triumphed over King Porus of the Punjab in the Battle of the Hydaspes River, leaving Porus as a vassal king. Alexander then conquered the Punjab and sailed down the Indus River to the Indian Ocean.

Alexander planned to continue campaigning in north-central India and to proceed to the Ganges. He reached only the Hyphasis (Beas) River when in July 326 his men mutinied and refused to go farther. Reluctantly Alexander agreed to halt. Returning to Persia and then to Mesopotamia in 324, Alexander concentrated on restoring order in his vast empire and attempting to combine the best of Greek and Persian cultures. He did not have the time necessary to make this work, as he died in 323 at only age 32.

SPENCER C. TUCKER

See also
Achaemenid Empire; Alexander III the Great; Darius III; Gaugamela, Battle of; Granicus, Battle of the; Issus, Battle of; Tyre and Gaza, Sieges of

References
Burn, A. *Alexander the Great and the Hellenistic Empire.* 2nd ed. London: English Universities Press, 1951.
Engels, Donald W. *Alexander the Great and the Logistics of the Macedonian Army.* Berkeley: University of California Press, 1978.
Green, Peter. *Alexander of Macedon, 356–323 B.C.: A Historical Biography.* Berkeley: University of California Press, 1991.
Hammond, N. G. L. *Alexander the Great: King, Commander, and Statesman.* 3rd ed. London: Bristol Classical Press, 1996.
Hammond, N. G. L. *The Genius of Alexander the Great.* Chapel Hill: University of North Carolina Press, 1997.
Kern, Paul Bentley. *Ancient Siege Warfare.* Bloomington: Indiana University Press, 1999.
Sekunda, Nick, and John Warry. *Alexander the Great: His Armies and Campaigns, 332–323 B.C.* London: Osprey, 1988.

Alexander Severus, Roman Emperor (ca. 208–235)

Born Gessius Iulius Bassianus Alexianus in Syria around 208, Severus Alexander (also Alexander Severus) was Roman emperor during 222–235. His mother Iulia Mamaea was the niece of Iulia Domna, wife of Emperor Septimius Severus (r. 193–211). The young Alexianus lived at Emesa in Syria until his cousin Elagabalus became emperor in 218. In 221, Elagabalus adopted Alexianus as his heir. Less than a year later Elagabalus was assassinated, and Alexianus ascended to the throne as Marcus Aurelius Severus Alexander.

Alexander encountered serious problems at court. Praetorian prefect Ulpian was murdered in a power struggle in 223, while Alexander's mother Mamaea earned a reputation for greed and cruelty. In 225, Alexander married a woman from a senatorial family, Seia Herennia Sallustia Barbia Orbiana, but she was exiled by Mamaea less than two years later. Orbiana's father was accused of treason and put to death.

War dominated the last years of Alexander's reign, beginning in the east with the Sassanids under Ardashir I (r. 224–242), who established the Sassanian Empire. Accounts differ sharply on the war, but apparently the Romans suffered early reversals. In 230 the Sassanid Persians attacked Roman settlements along the eastern frontier, and the next year Alexander took the field himself against them. Making Antioch his base, he marched toward Ctesiphon, but another of his armies suffered defeat by the Persians, and the Romans suffered other losses in withdrawing in Armenia. In 232 there was a mutiny in the Roman forces in Syria, leading to them proclaiming Taurinus as emperor. Alexander crushed this threat to his rule, and Taurinus drowned while attempting to flee across the Euphrates. Alexander was able to check the Sassanid advances in 233 and that same year celebrated a triumph in Rome.

The next year Alexander campaigned in Germany against the Alamanni, who had crossed the Rhine frontier. However, another mutiny resulted in the murders of both Alexander and Mamaea in their tent on March 19, 235. Alexander was only 26 years old.

CAILLAN DAVENPORT AND SPENCER C. TUCKER

See also
Septimius Severus, Emperor

References
Campbell, J. B. *The Emperor and the Roman Army 31 BC–AD 235.* Oxford, UK: Clarenden, 1984.
Potter, David S. *The Roman Empire at Bay: AD 180–395.* New York: Routledge, 2004.
Southern, Pat. *The Roman Empire from Severus to Constantine.* New York: Routledge, 2001.

Alexandria, Bombardment of (July 11, 1882)

Khedive Ismail of Egypt, saddled with growing debts to European banks, decided to sell the British government Egypt's shares in the Suez Canal Company. He was also forced to accept an Anglo-French debt commission to control Egyptian finances. The growing Western influence in Egyptian affairs created a strong Egyptian nationalist movement, and in February 1881 Egyptian colonel Ahmet Arabi (Urabi) led a revolt under the slogan "Egypt for the Egyptians." Arabi subsequently became minister of war and the key figure in the new government.

Their position in Egypt threatened, the British and French governments then planed a joint military intervention. Both nations dispatched powerful naval squadrons to Alexandria in May, but a change of government in France led to the belated decision in Paris not to participate. London then proceeded alone. The goal was to overthrow the revolutionaries and restore the nominal authority of Khedive Tewfik (Tawfiq).

On June 11, 1882, antiforeign riots in Alexandria resulted in the deaths of 68 Europeans and more than that number of Egyptians. Anticipating a reaction, Arabi strengthened the defenses of Alexandria. British admiral Sir Frederick Beauchamp Paget Seymour assembled 14 warships, led by the battleship *Inflexible*. Small Austrian and Ottoman naval contingents also participated. Seymour demanded a halt to the Egyptian effort to strengthen Alexandria's defenses. When it continued, Seymour insisted that the Egyptians surrender the shore batteries of Ras el Tin and that the south side of the harbor be disarmed.

Following an unsatisfactory Egyptian reply, the British ships opened fire at 7:00 a.m. on July 11. Firing was halted at 5:30 p.m. In the exchange of fire, the British suffered 5 killed, 28 wounded, and slight damage to their ships. Egyptian casualties were estimated at between 300 and 2,000 people.

Considerable damage was inflicted on the largely antiquated Egyptian shore defenses. Subsequent fires, some set by Egyptians, burned much of the city. Seymour sent 600 marines and seamen ashore to keep order in Alexandria, and they drove Egyptian troops from the city. The British then landed an expeditionary force and defeated the Egyptians on land in the September 13 Battle of Tel el-Kebir, which led to their occupation of Cairo and takeover of Egypt.

SPENCER C. TUCKER

See also
Anglo-Egyptian War; Egypt under British Rule; Tel el-Kebir, Battle of

References
Clowes, William Laird. *The Royal Navy: A History from the Earliest Times to 1900*, Vol. 7. London: Sampson Low, Marston, 1903.
Farwell, Byron. *Queen Victoria's Little Wars*. New York: Norton, 1972.
Hopkins, A. G. "The Victorians and Africa: A Reconsideration of the Occupation of Egypt, 1882." *Journal of African History* 27, no. 2 (July 1986): 363–391.

Alexandria, Sack of (October 9–12, 1365)

The capture of the port city of Alexandria, Egypt, was the climax of a Christian crusade launched by King Peter I of Cyprus. The last major Christian stronghold in the Holy Land, Acre, had fallen to the Mamluk Sultanate in 1291. Thereafter, there was much talk of a major crusade. King Peter, whether out of practical concern for the economy of Cyprus and security or religious zeal, actively promoted the idea of renewed crusading. In 1362 he visited several European courts seeking support for a crusade, and by 1365 he managed to gather French, English, Cypriot, Hospitaller, and other forces at the Island of Rhodes.

Peter set the city of Alexandria as the objective of the crusade because it was the greatest and richest port of the Mamluk Sultanate and the gateway to Cairo. The Christian fleet approached the city on October 9 and attacked the same day. By the following day the crusaders had broken through the Egyptian defenses, and the city was then ruthlessly pillaged and laid waste over the next three days. Defenders and townspeople were indiscriminately slaughtered, irrespective of age or sex.

Although Guillaume de Machaut's claim of 20,000 Alexandrians slain is no doubt exaggerated, the city itself was reduced to rubble, and thousands of its citizens were killed; some 5,000 were carried off as slaves, while loot filled more than 70 of the attackers' ships. As the crusaders pondered their next move, they learned of the approach of a large Mamluk army. King Peter argued for defending Alexandria, but most of the crusaders preferred to abandon it, which was immediately done.

The sack of Alexandria was the last significant crusade to carry out an actual attack on a major target in or near the Holy Land. Despite its initial success, it brought no long-term strategic benefits for the crusaders.

ALEXANDER MIKABERIDZE

See also
Mamluk Sultanate

References
Edbury, Peter W. *The Kingdom of Cyprus and the Crusades, 1191–1374*. Cambridge: Cambridge University Press, 1991.
Machaut, Guillaume de. *The Capture of Alexandria*. Translated by Janet Shirley. Introduction and notes by Peter W. Edbury. Aldershot, UK: Ashgate, 2001.

Alexandropol, Treaty of (December 2, 1920)

Treaty signed at Alexandropol on December 2, 1920, that ended war between the Turkish revolutionary government (the Grand National Assembly of Turkey) and Armenia and led to the end of a separate Armenia state. The Treaty of Brest-Litovsk of March 3, 1918, that ended Russian participation in World War I forced Russia to return territories captured from the Ottoman Empire after 1877. Before the Ottomans could reestablish their authority in this region, however, they were forced to conclude an armistice with the victorious Allied Powers.

In these circumstances an independent Democratic Republic of Armenia was established in December 1918 and quickly recognized by the victorious Allies. In June 1920, however, Armenian troops clashed with Turkish tribes along the border. In response, Turkish soldiers under General Kazim Karabekir invaded western Armenia on September 20. Despite strong resistance, the Armenians were driven from the prewar Ottoman territory and in response massacred local Muslim populations.

The European powers refused to help the Armenians, and Karabekir captured the important city of Alexandropol on November 6. Karabekir's terms for peace included the cession of half of Armenian territory and the virtual disarming of the state. When the Armenians refused, Karabekir threatened to occupy all of Armenia, forcing the Armenians to sign the treaty in Alexandropol.

Under the terms of the treaty, Armenia renounced the provisions of the Treaty of Sèvres, which called for establishment of a large Armenian state and accepted the territorial division established in the Treaty of Brest-Litovsk. Two days later, a Bolshevik army invaded remaining Armenian territory and established a soviet republic. In 1921 Turkey and the Soviet Union signed the Treaties of Moscow and Kars, which formalized the situation and established the present borders.

TIM J. WATTS

See also
Kars, Treaty of; Sèvres, Treaty of; Turkish-Armenian War

Reference
Walker, Christopher. *Armenia, the Survival of a Nation*. London: Croom Helm, 1980.

Alexios I Komnenos (1048–1118)

Byzantine emperor. Born in Constantinople (Istanbul) in 1048, Alexios (Alexius) was a great-nephew of Byzantine emperor Isaac I Komnenos (Comnenus). As a member of the military aristocracy, Alexios went to war at a young age and established himself as a successful general while in his early 20s. He distinguished himself in fighting the Seljuk Turks during 1068–1069 and 1070–1071. Alexios also took

Twelfth-century illustration depicting Byzantine ruler Alexios I Komnenos (1048–1118) appearing before Christ. It is from the collection of the Biblioteca Apostolica Vaticana. (Fine Art Images/Heritage Images/Getty Images)

part in the Byzantine Civil War of 1071–1081 and won an important victory at Kalavryta in Thrace (1079).

The incompetence of Emperor Nicephorus III Botaniates (r. 1078–1081) led Alexios and his brother Isaac to seize the imperial throne in April 1081. At that time the Byzantine Empire was under heavy pressure from the Seljuk Turks in Anatolia and from the Norman rulers in southern Italy, who threatened Byzantine territory in the Balkans. Alexios concentrated first on the Normans.

Norman leader Robert Guiscard had already defeated Byzantine forces in southern Italy when he occupied the island of Corfu and laid siege to Dracchium in present-day Albania, the chief Byzantine Adriatic port. Alexios secured some troops from the Turkish sultan of Nicaea and rushed to defend Dracchium but was forced to surrender the port to Guiscard (February 1082). Guiscard then advanced into Epirus and Thessaly, laying siege to Larissa in Thessaly. In the Battle of Larissa (1084), Alexios defeated a large Norman force and looted their camp. This victory and the death of Guiscard in 1085 ended the Norman threat.

Next pressured along the lower Danube by the nomadic Pechenegs and Cumans who raided into Thrace, Alexios secured an understanding with the Cumans in order to defeat the Pechenegs in the Battle of Mount Levounion (April 1091). Then in 1094 Alexios defeated the Cumans.

In March 1095 Alexios requested the help of Pope Urban II at Rome against the Seljuk Turks in order to recover Asia Minor with the Holy Land. Urban II urged the Christian West to provide assistance, and in November 1095 at Clermont he called for a Crusade against the Turks. The various European armies traveled through Byzantine territory to Constantinople, where they were to set off for the Holy Land. In the process they plundered and clashed with Byzantine forces. Fearful that the crusaders would turn on Constantinople itself (as indeed happened in the Fourth Crusade), Alexios bribed their leaders and got them to swear an oath of loyalty to him and promise the return of Byzantine lands taken by the Turks. Finally, the crusaders departed and aided Alexios in capturing Nicaea (June 19, 1097) following a 45-day siege. The defenders surrendered to the Byzantines on the condition that the crusaders not be allowed to plunder the city. These terms strained relations between Alexios and the crusaders, who had very different goals. Alexios sought to capture the important coastal cities of western Anatolia and strengthen them against the Seljuks, while the crusaders wanted to plunder these cities in order to finance their goal of an advance on Jerusalem (which they finally took in 1099). These divergent views became all too apparent in the siege of Antioch (October 1097–June 1098). Meanwhile, Alexios was able to achieve his goal of retaking Smyrna (Izmir), Ephesus, and Sardis and other cities in western Asia Minor.

The final years of Alexios's reign saw the Seljuks attempt to regain territories they had lost. Seljuk successes led Alexios to launch a major campaign in central Anatolia, culminating in his great victory at Philomelion (1117). Alexios died on August 15, 1118, in Constantinople. He had ruled Byzantium for 37 years. A capable general and an outstanding diplomat, he adroitly blended war and diplomacy to maximum advantage and left the empire far stronger, although this success proved temporary.

SPENCER C. TUCKER

See also
Antioch, Sieges of; Clermont, Council of; Philomelion, Battle of

References
Angold, Michael. *The Byzantine Empire, 1025–1204: A Political History.* 2nd ed. London: Longman, 1997.
Commena, Anna. *The Alexiad.* 1969; reprint, Harmondsworth, UK: Penguin, 1979.
Norwich, John Julius. *Byzantium: The Decline and Fall.* New York: Knopf, 1996.

Alexios III Angelos (ca. 1153–1211)

Byzantine emperor (1195–1203). Alexios was born around 1153, the elder brother of Isaac II, first ruler of the Angelos dynasty, whom he deposed on April 8, 1195, and subsequently had blinded and imprisoned.

Generally ranked among the most incompetent Byzantine sovereigns, Alexios III oppressed his people through extravagance and heavy taxes, among them a German tax (*alamanikon*) in 1197, reputedly required to ward off German emperor Henry VI's crusading plans against Byzantium. Several Greek and Balkan local rulers rebelled against Alexios, among them Leo Sgouros and Manuel Kammytzes, who proclaimed their independence in the northeastern Peloponnese and northern Thessaly, while Alexios almost lost his throne in a court coup led by John Axouchos Komnenos Pachys (1200/1201).

In the summer of 1203 the Fourth Crusade arrived before the walls of Constantinople, and on July 17–18 Alexios ignominiously fled from his capital with the imperial treasury and the crown jewels, escaping to Mosynopolis in Thrace, while the crusaders installed Isaac II and the latter's son Alexios IV as coemperors. In the summer of 1204, Alexios III allied himself with Alexios V Doukas Mourtzouphlos, who had overthrown the coemperors (January 1204) but fled again after the second capture of Constantinople by the crusaders (April 12–13). Alexios III gave his daughter Eudokia Angelina to Mourtzouphlos in marriage but aspired to regain the throne for himself; in August 1204 Alexios had Mourtzouphlos blinded, and Eudokia was married to the nobleman Leo Sgouros, whose power was still in the ascendant. Soon afterward, in late 1204 Alexios III and his wife Euphrosyne Doukaina were captured by Boniface I of Montferrat and detained in Thessaly. Ransomed in 1209 or 1210 by his relative Michael I of Epiros, Alexios was sent to the Seljuk sultan of Rum, Kay-Khusraw I, with whose help he hoped to regain his crown. However, after the defeat of the Seljuks by Theodore I Laskaris in the spring of 1211, Alexios was seized and incarcerated in the Hyakinthos monastery in Nicaea, where he died on August 15, 1211.

ALEXIOS G. C. SAVVIDES

See also

Alexios V Doukas Mourtzouphlos; Boniface I of Montferrat; Byzantine Empire; Seljuk Dynasty; Theodore I Laskaris

References

Angold, Michael. *The Byzantine Empire, 1025–1204: A Political History.* 2nd ed. London: Longman, 1997.

Brand, Charles. *Byzantium Confronts the West, 1180–1204.* Cambridge, MA: Harvard University Press, 1968.

Harris, Jonathan. *Byzantium and the Crusades.* London: Hambledon, 2003.

Ostrogorsky, George. *History of the Byzantine State,* 2nd ed. Oxford: Blackwell, 1968.

Alexios V Doukas Mourtzouphlos (1140–1204)

Byzantine emperor (January–April 1204) and the last ruler of the empire before the conquest of Constantinople (Istanbul) during the Fourth Crusade (1202–1204). Alexios (Alexius) V Doukas (Ducas) was born in 1140. A scion of the noble Doukas family, he was nicknamed Mourtzouphlos (Greek for "bushy-browed," "sullen," or "morose") and joined the abortive coup in 1200–1201 of John Axouchos Komnenos against Alexios III Angelos, for which he was incarcerated until July 1203, when Isaac II and Alexios IV were jointly brought to the throne with the assistance of the Christian crusaders.

On his release, Mourtzouphlos was given the position of protovestiarios, a high Byzantine court post, which did not, however, prevent him from manifesting his anti-Latin feelings, thus undermining the pro-Latin policies of Alexios IV. On January 27, 1204, Byzantine popular discontent against Alexios IV resulted in the brief proclamation of the unwilling Nicholas Kanabos as emperor, a development exploited by Mourtzouphlos, who encouraged Alexios IV to seek crusader aid to oust Kanabos and then used this as a pretext to overthrow him during January 28–29, 1204.

After being crowned on February 5, Alexios V tried to fortify parts of his capital and dictate demands for an immediate crusader withdrawal, which soon provoked an attack by the latter. He and his supporters repelled a first crusader assault on February 9 but were eventually overwhelmed, and he fled just before Constantinople was stormed and captured by the crusaders during April 12–13. In the summer of 1204 Alexios V sought refuge at Mosynopolis in Thrace with Alexios III, who gave him in marriage his daughter Eudokia Angelina; however, Alexios III had evidently not forgiven his new son-in-law's previous plots against him and had him blinded in August 1204. Alexios V ended up in the hands of the Franks, who had him tried and found guilty of treason against Alexios IV; Alexios V was then cast to his death from the top of the Theodosian Column in Constantinople in December 1204.

Alexios V was the last Byzantine emperor to reign in Constantinople before the establishment of the Latin Empire, which would control the city for the next 57 years until it was recovered by Nicaean emperor Michael VIII Palaiologos.

Alexios G. C. Savvides

See also

Alexios III Angelos; Michael VIII Palaiologos

References

Brand, Charles. *Byzantium Confronts the West, 1180–1204.* Cambridge, MA: Harvard University Press, 1968.

Harris, Jonathan. *Byzantium and the Crusades.* 2nd ed. New York: Bloomsbury Academic, 2014.

Phillips, Jonathan. *The Fourth Crusade and the Sack of Constantinople.* New York: Penguin Books, 2005.

Queller, Donald E., and Thomas F. Madden. *The Fourth Crusade: The Conquest of Constantinople.* 2nd ed. Philadelphia: University of Pennsylvania Press, 1997.

Algiers Agreement (March 6, 1975)

Diplomatic accord between Iraq and Iran designed to settle outstanding issues between the two nations and avert war. The Algiers Agreement of March 6, 1975, also known as the Algiers Accord, was an agreement mediated by Algerian president Houari Boumedienne at a meeting of the Organization of Petroleum Exporting Countries (OPEC). The accord was approved by Shah Reza Pahlavi II of Iran and President Saddam Hussein of Iraq.

Essentially, the agreement attempted to resolve territorial disputes between the two countries involving common borders as well as water and navigation rights. It provided for continuing Algerian participation in an ongoing Iranian-Iraqi dialogue that would occur at alternating meetings in Tehran and Baghdad. The agreement also established an Iraqi-Iranian joint commission intended to refine and monitor the agreement's provisions and resolve any further disputes.

The Algiers Agreement resulted in a formal treaty signed on June 13, 1975, which stipulated the Constantinople Protocol of 1913 and the Proceedings of the Border Delimitation Commission of 1914 as the basis of the determination of the Iranian-Iraqi border. Iran and Iraq agreed that the *thalweg* (median course) of the Shatt El Arab River, Iraq's only outlet to the sea, formed the river border between the two countries even though the shifting course of the Shatt-El-Arab had given rise to some of the original disputes. They further consented to resolve ownership of disputed islands and other territories related to the waterway, end subversive infiltration of each other's country, and resolve issues related to other border disputes, such as Khuzestan. Although not part of the agreement, the shah used the agreement's termination of subversive activities clause to withdraw Iranian support for the Kurdish rebellion against Iraq.

In the end both parties failed to comply with the terms of the accord, and the festering, unresolved territorial issues that it was designed to address led in part to the destructive Iran-Iraq War (1980–1988). This in turn led to a general destabilization in the Middle East.

RICHARD M. EDWARDS

See also
Hussein, Saddam; Iran-Iraq War; Iraq; Reza Shah Pahlavi

References
Coughlin, Con. *Saddam: His Rise and Fall.* New York: HarperCollins, 2002.
Hiro, Dilip. *The Longest War: The Iran-Iraq Military Conflict.* London: Routledge, 1991.
Karsh, Efraim. *The Iran-Iraq War 1980–1988.* Northwarts, UK: Osprey, 2002.

Algiers Declaration (November 15, 1988)

Formal proclamation of a Palestinian state made by Palestine Liberation Organization (PLO) chairman Yasser Arafat in Algiers, Algeria, on November 15, 1988. The declaration was made in conjunction with a meeting of the Palestinian National Council (PNC). Contrary to popular perception, Arafat's declaration was not the first such proclamation. A similar declaration of the existence of a Palestinian nation was made on October 1, 1948, in Gaza. This had occurred in the throes of the Israeli War of Independence (1948–1949). Despite the considerable press coverage that the proclamation engendered, Arafat's move was largely symbolic, as the PLO did not then control any of the territory it hoped to govern. Yet the Algiers Declaration was well-timed in that it coincided with the outbreak of the First Intifada (in 1987), came on the heels of Jordan's renouncement of its claims in the West Bank, and clearly signaled the future intent of the PLO.

Regarding the 1947 United Nations (UN) General Assembly Resolution 181 (which codified the 1947 UN partition plan), the PNC's 1988 proclamation was risky. By basing its declaration on Resolution 181, the PNC—and thus the PLO and Fatah—were accepting what the Arab states had overwhelmingly rejected in 1947–1948. Even more risky was the tacit acceptance of the State of Israel, for the 1948 resolution had called for a Jewish state and a Palestinian state. Thus, in cleaving to Resolution 181, Arafat and the PNC were essentially recognizing Israel's existence. This was a marked turn of events, for the PLO had never before been willing to make such a concession. Not surprisingly, Palestinian hard-liners balked at this approach.

Nevertheless, on December 15, 1988, the PLO's permanent representative to the UN presented the Algiers Declaration to the UN General Assembly for a vote. The body enthusiastically adopted the declaration by a vote of 104 to 2 (with Israel and the United States voting no and with 36 abstentions). In so doing, the UN specifically affirmed that the Palestinians had the right to form their own nation, per Resolution 181. All UN references to the Palestinians would now read "Palestine" rather than "Palestine Liberation Organization," thereby strengthening their UN observer status.

During the months that followed, 89 countries moved to formally recognize the state of Palestine, if in theory only. Although the Algiers Declaration did not, of course, create a bona fide Palestinian nation, it was an important leap of faith for the PLO. Since its inception in the early 1960s, the organization had steadfastly refused to abandon its goal of the destruction of Israel. The United States in turn refused to enter into any talks with the PLO. Thus, the PNC's and Arafat's move toward greater accommodation was clearly an effort to court U.S. favor. It was also no doubt an attempt by the PLO to break out of its doldrums dating back to its banishment from Lebanon in 1982. In relative isolation in Tunisia since then, the organization sought to make itself relevant again by jump-starting efforts to secure a Palestinian homeland by nonviolent means.

PAUL G. PIERPAOLI JR.

See also
Arafat, Yasser; Intifada, First; Palestine Liberation Organization; United Nations Palestine Partition Plan

References
Aburish, Said K. *Arafat: From Defender to Dictator.* New York: Bloomsbury, 1998.
Nassar, Jamal R. *The Palestine Liberation Organization: From Armed Struggle to the Declaration of Independence.* New York: Praeger, 1991.
Norton, Augustus Richard, and Martin H. Greenberg, eds. *Th International Relations of the Palestine Liberation Organization.* Carbondale: Southern Illinois University Press, 1989.

Ali, Ahmad Ismail (1917–1974)

Egyptian minister of defense during the Yom Kippur War (Ramadan War) of October 6–25, 1973. Born in Egypt on October 14, 1917, Ali graduated from the Egyptian Royal Military Academy in 1938 and was commissioned an officer in a cavalry regiment. Advancing through the ranks, he fought with the British Eighth Army in the Western Desert during World War II.

Ali commanded a tank battalion in the 1948–1959 Israeli War of Independence. Following advanced training in the United Kingdom, he took part in the fighting following the invasion of Egypt by Israeli and then British and French forces in the Suez Crisis of 1956. Following further military training, this time in the Soviet Union, he commanded a division during the Six-Day War in 1967.

Egyptian president Gamal Abdel Nasser appointed Ali chief of staff of the Egyptian Army in March 1969 but then dismissed him that September following successful Israeli raids against Egypt during the so-called War of Attrition. After Nasser's death in September 1970, however, new Egyptian president Anwar Sadat named Ali chief of intelligence in 1971, a post he held until 1972.

In October 1972, Ali thwarted a coup attempt against Sadat and was then named minister of defense and promoted to full general. In this capacity Ali helped plan the surprise Egyptian and Syrian attacks that began the Yom Kippur War on October 6, 1973. Ali was promoted to field marshal in November 1973. He died of cancer on December 26, 1974.

Spencer C. Tucker

See also
Israeli War of Independence; Nasser, Gamal Abdel; Sadat, Anwar; Six-Day War; Suez Crisis; War of Attrition; Yom Kippur War

References
El-Gamasy, Mohamed Abdul Ghani. *The October War: Memoirs of Field Marshal El-Gamasy of Egypt*. Translated by Gillian Potter, Nadra Morcos, and Rosette Frances. Cairo: American University in Cairo Press, 1993.
Heikal, Mohammed Hasanyn. *The Road to Ramadan*. New York: Quadrangle/New York Times Book Company, 1975.
Shazli, Saad al. *The Crossing of the Suez*. San Francisco: Mideast Research, 1980.

Ali Bey al-Kabir (1728–1773)

Mamluk ruler of Egypt during 1760–1773. Ali Bey al-Kabir was born in northwestern Georgia in 1728, the son of a priest in the Georgian Orthodox Church. Ali Bey was kidnapped and sold into slavery in 1741. Two years later, he was purchased in Cairo and gradually rose in influence, reaching the top office of *sheikh al-balad* in 1763.

During the Russo-Ottoman War of 1768–1774, Ali Bey broke the Mamluk-Ottoman Treaty of 1517 and deposed the Ottoman governor in 1768. The following year, Ali Bey proclaimed Egyptian independence, stopped the annual tribute to the Ottoman Empire, proclaimed himself sultan, and had his name struck on local coins.

During 1770–1771, Ali Bey successfully campaigned in the Hejaz, Palestine, and Syria, capturing Damascus in June 1771. However, his initial success faltered when the Mamluks turned against each other, and in 1772 Ali Bey was defeated. He fled to Acco in Syria. After rallying his forces, he attempted to regain power but was again defeated at al-Salihiyya in April 1773. Captured in battle, Ali Bey was executed in Cairo on May 8, 1773.

Alexander Mikaberidze

See also
Mamluk Sultanate; Russo-Ottoman Wars

References
Crecelius, Daniel, and Gotcha Djaparidze. "Georgians in the Military Establishment in Egypt in the Seventeenth and Eighteenth Centuries." *Annales islamologique* 42 (2008): 313–339.
Hathaway, Jane. *Politics of Households in Ottoman Egypt: Rise of the Qazdaglis*. Cambridge: Cambridge University Press, 1997.

Ali ibn Abi Talib (ca. 600–661)

Fourth caliph, during 656–661. Born around 600, Ali ibn Abi Talib was the cousin and son-in-law of Prophet Muhammad and played an important role in the history of the caliphate. The prophet took him into his household when Ali was age six in order to relieve Ali's uncle, Abi Talib, from financial difficulties. Ali was thus brought up as if he had been a son of Muhammad.

At the age of 10, Ali was the first male to accept Islam. His military career commenced after the immigration of Muhammad and his followers to Medina in 622. Ali proved himself in battle on several occasions during the lifetime of the prophet and is looked upon as a champion of Islam. Ali distinguished himself in combat in the Battles of Badr (624) and Khandaq (627) and the conquest of Khaybar (629). In the Battles of Uhud (625) and Hunayn (630) he stood near the prophet and defended him when the tide turned against the Muslims. Thus, through his courage and conduct on the battlefield, Ali gained a legendary reputation among Muslims.

Ali did not participate in the Riddah Wars or in the great conquests during the reigns of the first three caliphs but retired to a life of religious studies and compiling the Quran. He also aided the caliphs in legal matters from his vast knowledge of the Quran and the sunna.

The First Islamic Civil War, or First Fitna (656–661), followed the assassination of the third caliph, Uthman ibn Affan, and led to permanent divisions in the Islamic world. Although Ali was recognized as caliph in Medina, there was considerable opposition elsewhere to him and his policies. Many prominent Muslims condemned him for not punishing Uthman's murderers.

Ali marched to Basra, where Talha, Zubayr, and Aisha, the prophet's wife, had mustered an army to oppose him. Ali was victorious in the Battle of the Camel (also known as the Battle of Bassorah and the Battle of Jamal) on November 7, 656. The next year he faced Muawiyah, governor of Syria and the late caliph's cousin, at Siffin in Syria. As the battle (July 26–28, 657) turned in the favor of Ali, the Syrians raised pages of the Quran on their spears and demanded to resolve the religious quarrel through arbitration. Ali agreed but in the process lost not only his most zealous supporters, who wished to fight and believed that he had sinned and betrayed Islam, but also the arbitration, with Muawiyah proclaimed caliph. He and Ali ruled different parts of the empire until Ali's death in 661, after which Muawiyah became the sole ruler.

Ali was at prayer at the mosque of Kufa on the 21st of Ramadan in 661 when he was mortally wounded by a poison-coated sword wielded by a Kharijite, Abd al-Rahman ibn Mulijam, who was seeking revenge for the massacre of thousands of Kharijites at Nahrawan in 658 and for accepting arbitration at Siffin. Ali died two days later.

ADAM ALI AND SPENCER C. TUCKER

See also
Badr, Battle of; Bassorah, Battle of; Islamic Civil War, First; Khandaq, Battle of the; Muawiyah I; Muhammad, Prophet of Islam; Siffin, Battle of

References
Hodgson, Marshall G. S. *The Venture of Islam: Conscience and History in a World Civilization*. Chicago: University of Chicago Press, 1977.
Ibn Hisham, and Abd al-Malik. *The Life of Muhammad; a Translation of Ishaq's Sirat Rasul Allah*. Introduction and notes by A. Guillaume. Lahore: Oxford University Press, 1967.
Madelung, Wilferd. *The Succession to Muhammad: A Study of the Early Caliphate*. Cambridge: Cambridge University Press, 1997.

Aliya Bet

Aliya Bet is the term for the illegal immigration of Jews from Europe to the British Mandate for Palestine. *Aliya* means "immigration" in Hebrew, while *Bet* is "B" and implied nonofficial immigration. The operation was part of the Beri'hah (Hebrew for "flight" or "escape") underground operation during 1944–1948 that moved Jews from displaced persons'(DP) camps in Europe to Palestine. Jews were not supposed to leave the camps, and the British sought to prevent the illegal immigration. The British had unofficially upped the yearly immigration limit to 18,000 Jews, but this hardly addressed the matter of the hundreds of thousands of Jews in DP camps who wished to settle in Israel.

Beri'hah (the organized effort to help Jews escape to Palestine) had been established in Warsaw beginning in late 1944 and soon merged with similar undertakings by Haganah and the Jewish Brigade. Illegal immigration accelerated in 1946, with some 100,000 Jews leaving Europe in a three-month span. Through 1948 more than 250,000 Holocaust survivors were moved in extensive smuggling networks into Italy and France. The French were especially helpful, in part because of resentment at being pushed out of the Levant by the British during the war and the influence of highly placed French Jews in the government.

The Jews sailed in ships from Italian and French Mediterranean ports. Even during World War II and the height of the Holocaust the British had turned back illegal immigrants, but after the war they increased their naval and air presence off the coast to intercept the ships and take the refugees to Cyprus. Armed clashes occurred and there were deaths on both sides. By 1946–1947, the British also had 80,000 troops in Palestine. Haganah did what it could to learn British plans and decoy the British from the actual landing sites.

During late 1945 and early 1946 some half dozen small ships landed 4,000 Jewish refugees in Palestine. The British then intensified their efforts, and between 1945 and 1948 intercepted most of the 65 ships employed and interned 28,000 DPs in Cyprus.

Despite daunting odds, the illegal immigration operation continued until the establishment of the State of Israel, when immigration became legal. Nonetheless, a number of nation states continued to block Jews from leaving for Palestine, including the Arab countries and the Soviet Union and its Eastern bloc satellites.

SPENCER C. TUCKER

Allawi, Ayad (1944–)

Iraqi politician and prime minister of Iraq's appointed interim government that assumed the governance of Iraq on June 28, 2004. Ayad Allawi held the premiership until April 7, 2005. He also held the vice presidency of Iraq from September 8, 2014, to August 11, 2015, and began serving as vice president again as of October 10, 2016. He has shared that post with two other co–vice presidents. As of August 2018, he continued in that post. Allawi was born into a well-to-do family in Baghdad on May 31, 1944. His father and uncle were physicians. His father was also a member of Iraq's parliament, and his grandfather had participated in the negotiations that granted Iraq its independence in 1932. Also, the family had long-standing commercial and political ties to both the British and the Americans.

Allawi graduated from the American Jesuits' Baghdad College, an intermediate and senior-level preparatory school, and entered the Baghdad University College of Medicine in 1961, the same year he joined the Baath Party, met future Iraqi dictator Saddam Hussein, and became active in the Iraqi National Students' Union. Allawi organized strikes and other activities against the government of Abdul Karim Qasim. On February 8, 1963, Qasim was overthrown in a Baathist coup, which resulted in General Ahmad Hassan al-Bakr becoming prime minister. Allawi was eventually placed in charge of the central security office at the presidential palace and was given the nickname "palace doctor."

Although unproven, there are charges that Allawi participated in intense interrogations and torture that led to the deaths of trade union officials, students, and political leaders. Allawi was arrested on these charges, but he was released after al-Bakr intervened. Allawi participated in the July 17, 1968, coup that made al-Bakr president and excluded all but Baathists from government positions. Al-Bakr then pressured the minister of health, Ezzat Mustafa, to expedite Allawi's graduation from the college of medicine.

Iraqi prime minister Ayad Allawi, shown here during a meeting of the European Union in Brussels on November 5, 2004. A moderate, Allawi sought to bridge the vast divisions in Iraq during the interim government and held office from June 28, 2004 to April 7, 2005. (Council of the European Union)

Opposition to Allawi grew within the government, and he was sent to Beirut in 1971 before moving to London in 1972 to head the Baath National Students Union and to pursue advanced medical studies. Allawi left the Baath Party in 1975 and supposedly began working for MI6, the British foreign intelligence service. In 1976, he earned a masters of science in medicine from London University. Allawi's name was placed on an assassination list in 1978 after Iraqi president Saddam Hussein failed to convince him to rejoin the Baathists. In February 1978, Allawi and his wife were attacked by an ax-bearing intruder in their Surrey home but escaped serious injury. Allawi earned a doctorate in medicine in 1979 from London University before being certified as a neurologist in 1982.

In 1979, Allawi had begun gathering alienated former Iraqi Baathists together into a group that grew into a Hussein opposition party. It was formalized in December 1990 as the Iraqi National Accord (INA). The INA received backing from Britain, the United States, Jordan, Saudi Arabia, and Turkey. It fomented dissent among the disaffected in Iraq and committed acts of terror and sabotage in that country in an attempt to bring down the Hussein regime. Allawi and the INA were recruited by the U.S. Central Intelligence Agency (CIA) after the 1991 Persian Gulf War and paid $5 million in 1995 and $6 million in 1996. The CIA supported the INA's 1996 failed military coup, code-named DBACHILLES, which led to the execution of many Iraqis and to the confiscation or destruction of approximately $250 million of Allawi family assets.

The INA and Allawi gathered intelligence establishing the alleged existence of weapons of mass destruction in Iraq that formed the core of the MI6 dossier released in September 2002. This dossier formed a major part of the rationale for the U.S.- and British-led coalition invasion of Iraq in March 2003. On July 13, 2003, Allawi was appointed by Coalition Provisional Authority administrator L. Paul Bremer to the 25-member Iraqi Governing Council (IGC), where he served as minister of defense and assumed the rotating presidency for October 2003. He resigned as head of the IGC Security Committee in April 2004 over alleged concerns about U.S. tactics used to subdue the 2004 Fallujah insurgency.

The coalition-led IGC transferred authority to the Iraqi Interim Government, with Allawi as the appointed interim prime minister on June 28, 2004. During his tenure in this position, he created a domestic spy agency named the General Security Directorate to counter the Iraqi insurgency, closed the Iraqi office of the television network Al Jazeera, attempted to marginalize radical Shiite cleric Muqtada al-Sadr and his militia, and assumed the power to declare martial law. Allawi tried to draw Baathists who had not committed criminal acts during Hussein's rule into the government and considered pardoning insurgents who surrendered their weapons. Allawi stepped down as premier on April 7, 2005, the day the Islamic Dawa Party leader Ibrahim al-Jaafari was elected to lead the transitional Iraqi National Assembly.

Allawi's INA won just 25 seats in the December 2005 elections establishing the permanent Iraqi National Assembly. This placed the party a distant third in the assembly, with only 14 percent of the vote. In 2007, the INA boycotted the Iraqi government altogether, and Allawi refused to take a cabinet position in it. Allawi retains his dual British citizenship, and his wife and children reside in the United Kingdom for security reasons. In January 2009, Allawi excoriated the George W. Bush administration for its mismanagement of the Iraq War since 2003 and criticized Bush for his insistence on elections and democratic institutions in Iraq before first having achieved stability. Allawi was also highly critical of the Iraqi government led by Nuri al-Maliki. In December 2017, Allawi slammed the Donald Trump administration's decision to relocate the U.S. embassy in Tel Aviv, Israel, to Jerusalem, warning that the move would greatly complicate the peace process between Israel and the Palestinians.

RICHARD M. EDWARDS

See also
Baath Party; Bakr, Ahmad Hassan al-; Bremer, Lewis Paul, III; Fallujah, Second Battle of; Hussein, Saddam; Iraq; Iraq Insurgency; Maliki, Nuri Muhammed Kamil al-; Qasim, Abdul Karim

References
Allawi, Ali. *Winning the War, Losing the Peace: The Occupation of Iraq.* New Haven, CT: Yale University Press, 2006.
Keegan, John. *The Iraq War: The Military Offensive, from Victory in 21 Days to the Insurgent Aftermath.* New York: Vintage, 2005.
Polk, William R. *Understanding Iraq: The Whole Sweep of Iraqi History, from Genghis Khan's Mongols to the Ottoman Turks to the British Mandate to the American Occupation.* New York: Harper Perennial, 2006.

Allenby, Sir Edmund Henry Hynman (1861–1936)

British Army field marshal. Born on April 23, 1861, at Brackenhurst, Nottinghamshire, England, Edmund Henry Hynman Allenby was educated at Haileybury College. At first he expressed no interest in the military, but after failing the entrance exam for the Indian Civil Service, he passed the examination for the Royal Military College, Sandhurst, leaving there as a lieutenant in the 6th Inniskilling Dragoons in 1881.

Reporting to his regiment in South Africa in 1882, Allenby first saw combat in the Bechuanaland Expedition of 1884–1885. Returning to Britain with his unit in 1890, in 1895 he entered the Staff College at Camberley. Before leaving Camberley in 1897, he was promoted to major.

In 1898 Allenby served with the 3rd Cavalry Brigade in Ireland. The next year on the beginning of the South African (Boer) War (1899–1902), he returned to his Inniskilling Regiment and sailed to South Africa, where he helped defend the frontier against Boer attack and aided in the relief of Kimberley in February 1900. Allenby assumed temporary command of the regiment when its commander was invalided home, and he then led a cavalry column of the Cavalry Division in the Transvaal.

Colonel Allenby returned to Britain in 1902, recognized as a promising officer. He commanded the 5th Lancers during

One of the ablest British generals of World War I, British field marshal Edmund Allenby commanded the troops that defeated Ottoman Empire forces in the Middle East and secured control of Palestine. The photograph dates from around 1921. (Library of Congress)

1902–1905. This was followed by promotion to brigadier general (1905) and command of the 4th Cavalry Brigade at Colchester, then promotion to major general (1910) and the post of inspector of cavalry. Here his abrupt manner and imposing physical appearance led to Allenby being known as "The Bull."

In August 1914 Allenby commanded the single cavalry division in the British Expeditionary Force (BEF) sent to France to serve on the Western Front. His unit distinguished itself covering the British retreat after the Battle of Mons (August 23). In November 1914 on the expansion of the BEF to two armies, Allenby received command of the Cavalry Corps. He commanded the V Corps in the Second Battle of Ypres (April 22–May 25, 1915) and that October assumed command of the Third Army. Allenby was promoted to lieutenant general in 1916.

Allenby's troops performed well in the Second Battle of Arras (April 9–May 16, 1917), although his aggressive style rankled more cautious and conservative senior officers. On June 9, 1917, Allenby was replaced in command of the Third Army by General Sir Julian Byng and transferred to Egypt. Allenby's leadership and battlefield skills fitted perfectly with the dynamics of the desert theater, but a principal reason for his transfer was his ongoing feud over tactics with BEF commander Field Marshal Sir Douglas Haig.

On June 27, 1917, Allenby replaced Lieutenant General Sir Archibald Murray as commander of British and imperial forces in Egypt. Murray had failed to break through the Ottoman defenses in two battles at Gaza in March and April 1917. The War Office charged Allenby with capturing Jerusalem by Christmas.

Arab forces fighting alongside the British and imperial forces played an important role, but Allenby's bold and proactive leadership buoyed sagging morale as operations commenced against the Ottoman forces. The capture of Beersheba on October 31, 1917, by surprise attack, made possible by artful operational deception, broke the stalemate on the Gaza-Beersheba Line that had so stymied Murray. On the night of November 1–2, Allied forces broke through the Ottoman lines in the Third Battle of Gaza.

Allenby's aggressive attacks on Ottoman forces resulted in victories at Junction Station (November 13–15, 1917) and the occupation of Jerusalem (December 9), all despite water and logistics problems complicated by stiffening Turkish defenses. Allenby and his officers entered Jerusalem on foot (December 11) through the Jaffa Gate out of respect for Jerusalem's status as a religious shrine for Christianity, Judaism, and Islam.

The loss of troops taken for Western Front service handicapped offensive operations through the spring of 1918, but reinforcements allowed Allenby to resume vigorous summer actions. Rapid attacks coordinated with Lieutenant Colonel T. E. Lawrence's Arab guerrillas in September and October resulted in smashing the Turkish defensive lines at Megiddo (September 19–21) and the occupation of the key cities of Damascus (October 1), Homs (October 16), and Aleppo (October 25). Faced with the collapse of their southern imperial front, the Ottomans withdrew from the war (October 30), which further stimulated the armistice of November.

Created a field marshal in 1919 and made Viscount Allenby of Megiddo and Felixstowe that October 7, Allenby remained in the Middle East as British high commissioner for Egypt (1919–1925), overseeing a trying transition to a nominally sovereign state. Returning to Britain, he died in London on May 14, 1936.

Allenby was the consummate professional soldier. As a theater commander, his qualities of bold, aggressive leadership resulted in rapid and overwhelming victory with relatively few casualties, making him among the most successful of all British major commanders of the war. His masterful employment of combined arms in the Battle of Megiddo is considered to be a precursor to the German blitzkrieg tactics of World War II.

Stanley D. M. Carpenter and Spencer C. Tucker

See also
Arab Revolt of World War I; Beersheba, Battle of; Gaza, First Battle of; Gaza, Second Battle of; Gaza, Third Battle of; Jerusalem, Capture of; Lawrence, Thomas Edward; Megiddo, Battle of; World War I, Impact on the Middle East

References
Bullock, David L. *Allenby's War: The Palestine-Arabian Campaigns, 1916–1918.* New York: Blandford, 1988.
Gardner, Brian M. *Allenby.* London: Cassell, 1965.
Hughes, Matthew. *Allenby and British Strategy in the Middle East, 1917–1919.* London: Frank Cass, 1999.
James, Lawrence. *Imperial Warrior: The Life and Times of Field Marshal Viscount Allenby, 1861–1936.* London: Weidenfeld & Nicolson, 1993.
War Office, Great Britain. *Brief Record of the Egyptian Force under the Command of General Sir Edmund H. H. Allenby: July 1917 to October 1918, Egyptian Expeditionary Force.* 2nd ed. London: HMSO, 1919.
Wavell, A. P. *Allenby: A Study in Greatness.* London: Harrap, 1940.
Wavell, A. P. *Allenby in Egypt.* London: Harrap, 1943. Allenby,

Allon, Yigal (1918–1980)

Israeli politician, military officer, and foreign minister (1974–1977). Yigal Allon was born at Kfar Tavor in Galilee on October 10, 1918. In 1936 he joined the Haganah defense forces. Allon gained valuable military training while serving with Orde Wingate's Special Night Squads, organized in 1938. In 1941 Yitzhak Sadeh, founder of the new elite commando unit Palmach, personally selected Allon for command of its 1st Company. In 1943 Sadeh promoted Allon to deputy command of Palmach, and in 1945 Allon assumed command of the strike force.

During World War II, Allon led Allied-sponsored Palmach raids into Syria and Lebanon. Following the war, he organized Palmach operations against Arab guerrillas and subverted attempts by the British mandate forces to restrict the flow of Jews into Palestine. He was promoted to major general in 1948.

A bold and imaginative leader, Allon ranks among the best field commanders during the Israeli War of Independence (1948–1949). In May 1948 after Palmach was absorbed into the newly organized Israel Defense Forces (IDF), Allon led military operations that captured Upper Galilee. In June 1948 he planned the operations that captured Lydda and Ramla. In October Allon, now commanding the southern front, forced the Egyptian Army to retreat into the Sinai, a success that ultimately gave Israel control of the Negev Desert and the port city of Eilat after the final armistice. In 1950 after Prime Minister David Ben-Gurion had dissolved Palmach and passed Allon over as IDF chief of staff, he decided to retire from the military.

Allon subsequently helped found the Zionist Socialist Workers political party and won a seat in the Knesset in 1954. Joining the Labor government of Ben-Gurion in 1961 as minister of labor, Allon remained in the cabinet until 1977. He rose to deputy prime minister and minister for immigration absorption in 1967. He remained deputy prime minister until 1977. When Levi Eshkol died in 1969, Allon served for a brief time as acting prime minister. After Labor chose Golda Meir as Eshkol's replacement, Allon accepted the post of minister of education and culture. When Yitzhak Rabin became prime minister in 1974, he named Allon foreign minister.

Among his accomplishments while in the Israeli government, Allon was a member of the war cabinet that planned the dramatic victory of the Six-Day War in 1967. In 1972 he developed the so-called Allon Plan for the occupied West Bank. It offered a return of most of a demilitarized Judaea and Samaria to Jordanian rule, while a series of protective Jewish paramilitary settlements would be built along the Jordan River. Although the plan was never instituted, it showed the flexibility with which Allon was prepared to engage the Arabs. He also served as a member of the Israeli delegation that negotiated the separation of forces with Egypt and Syria in 1974.

Leaving government in 1977 when the Likud Party won control of the Knesset, Allon maintained an active public life, remaining in the Knesset and chairing the World Labor Zionist Movement. He died at Afula, Israel, on February 29, 1980.

Thomas D. Veve

See also
Ben-Gurion, David; Haganah; Israeli War of Independence; Palmach; Six-Day War; Wingate, Orde Charles

References

Allon, Yigal. *Shield of David: The Story of Israel's Armed Forces.* New York: Random House, 1970.

Herzog, Chaim. *Heroes of Israel: Profiles of Jewish Courage.* London: Little, Brown, 1989.

Rosenblum, Morris. *Heroes of Israel.* New York: Fleet, 1972.

Allon Plan (July 26, 1967)

Peace plan authored by Israeli military officer and politician Yigal Allon, initially presented to the Israeli cabinet in July 1967. At the time Allon was serving as deputy prime minister, and he would subsequently serve as foreign minister (1974–1977). The Allon Plan was a proposal to negotiate the partitioning of West Bank territories between Israel and Jordan in the immediate aftermath of the June 1967 Six-Day War. It was also aimed at providing Israel safe and defensible borders against potential future attacks from the east through the West Bank and the Jordan River Valley. A brilliant and well-respected military strategist whose experience dated back to Palmach, Allon hoped to define and establish secure borders while at the same time extending an olive branch of sorts to the Jordanians.

Under the terms of the plan, the Israelis would turn over to the Jordanians those areas in Judaea and Samaria that encompassed Arab majority populations. Meanwhile, Israel was to control a thin strip of relatively unpopulated territory along the Jordan River for defensive purposes. This piece of land would begin near the Syrian border to the north and run south through the Jordan River Valley and the Judaean Desert and eventually converge with the Negev. Included in this was a sliver of territory along the western shore of the Dead Sea and a large area surrounding Jerusalem.

Allon reasoned that this barrier territory in the eastern part of the West Bank would provide the Israelis with enough space to buy time in the event of a concerted Arab attack. Under the proposed plan, Israel would ultimately retain control over some 700 square miles in the West Bank, or approximately 35 percent of the entire landmass. For the Israeli-controlled areas, Allon proposed the building of settlements and military installations. In other areas, local leaders would be involved in the creation of a semiautonomous Palestinian-Jordanian region that would maintain close economic ties to the State of Israel. The Israelis would retain sole control of Jerusalem with the possibility of a Jordanian-administered Muslim section within the Old City of Jerusalem.

Submitted to several Israeli cabinets, the Allon Plan never was formally adopted as a plan of action, but nor was it fully rejected. Indeed, it shaped to a significant extent Israeli settlement policies until 1977 and was the basis of Israeli negotiations with the Egyptians in 1978 and 1979 and during the Oslo Accords in 1993. In September 1968, Israeli officials entered into secret talks with King Hussein of Jordan during which they unveiled the Allon Plan to him. Hussein politely rejected the plan because he believed that it presented an infringement of Jordan's sovereignty. The Israelis still allowed for the construction of settlements beyond the confines of the Allon-proposed West Bank territories, and modern military analysts have argued that control of the area would afford virtually no protection from attack in the age of ballistic missiles and rockets.

PAUL G. PIERPAOLI JR.

See also

Allon, Yigal; Hussein ibn Talal, King of Jordan; Jordan; Six-Day War; West Bank

References

Hillel, Frisch. *Countdown to Statehood: Palestinian State Formation in the West Bank and Gaza.* Ithaca, NY: SUNY Press, 1998.

Parker, Richard B., ed. *The Six-Day War: A Retrospective.* Gainesville: University Press of Florida, 1996.

Roth, Stephen J. *The Impact of the Six-Day War: A Twenty-Year Assessment.* London: Palgrave Macmillan, 1988.

Al-Mamun, Abd Allah (786–833)

The seventh Abbasid caliph, who ruled from 813 to 833. Born in 786 in Baghdad, he is best known by his throne name Abd Allah al-Mamun, but his full name was Abu Ja'far Abdullah al-Mamun ibn Harun al-Rashid. The son of the fifth caliph Harun al-Rashid and an Iranian concubine, al-Mamun was born six months before his half brother, Abd Allah al-Amin, whose mother was a legitimate wife of Arab blood.

In 802 on the occasion of a pilgrimage to Mecca, al-Rashid named al-Amin his successor as caliph but gave al-Mamun rule of an autonomous Khorasan (now in Turkmenistan) and also designated him al-Amin's successor. Harun al-Rashid's death in March 809 and the succession of al-Amin nevertheless soon led to conflict between the two men, as al-Amin attempted to assert control over his half brother and stripped him of his rights to the succession.

In 1811 al-Amin sent an army of 40,000 men commanded by Ali ibn Isa against al-Mamun. Tahir ibn Husayn, a Persian, commanded al-Mamun's far smaller Khurasani army.

The two armies came together near Rayy in May 811. Ali ibn Isa was killed in the battle and his army routed. Thanks to this victory, al-Mamun's army went on to occupy western Persia. Al-Amin drew additional troops from among the Arabs of Syria but sustained other defeats, and in April 1812 Tahir laid siege to him at Baghdad. Following desperate fighting, the city fell in September 813. Al-Amin, who had in the meantime been declared deposed as caliph in parts of the Abbasid Empire, was captured and killed.

The struggle over the succession was not merely a personal rivalry between the two brothers but rather a conflict between different politico-religious trends. Al-Amin had emphasized traditionalism and Arab culture, while al-Mamun was open to new movements of thought and outside influences and sought to secure the support of the Persians and the eastern provinces.

While caliph of the entire Abbasid Empire, al-Mamun continued to reside at Merv rather than Baghdad. Determined to end the Islamic world split between Sunni and Shiite Islam and reconcile the two families, he designated as his heir not a member of his own family but rather Ali al-Ridha, a descendant of Prophet Muhammad and the eighth Shia imam after his father Musa al-Kadhim and before his son Muhammad al-Jawad. Al-Mamun gave Ali al-Ridha his own daughter as a wife. As a further symbol of reconciliation, al-Mamun adopted the green flag in place of the traditional black flag of the Abbasid family. This inspired effort failed, for it proved insufficient for the Shiite extremists and embittered partisans of Abbasid legitimism and of Sunnism, particularly in Iraq. The Sunnis in Baghdad declared al-Mamun deposed and proclaimed Abbasid prince Ibrahim, son of the third caliph al-Mahdi, as caliph.

On receipt of what had transpired, al-Mamun left Merv for Baghdad. Arriving there in August 819, he reestablished his authority by abandoning his efforts to achieve reconciliation with the descendants of Ali, symbolized by reinstating the traditional black Abbasid flag. As caliph, al-Mamun sought to maintain strict control of his provincial governors, although he was forced to allow Tahir a degree of latitude in Khorasan.

In 825–826, Tahir secured Egypt for al-Mamun. At the same time an uprising in Qum regarding high taxes was crushed. In 827–828 there was an uprising in Yemen. Egypt continued in unrest, as did Sindh.

Abbasid relations with the Byzantine Empire had settled into raids back and forth across their common border, the Arabs raiding deep into Anatolia in order to secure slaves and booty. This situation changed with the accession in 820 of Michael II as emperor. He ruled until 829. Forced to deal with a rebellion against his rule, Michael had few resources available to counter an Andalusian invasion and conquest of Crete in 824. A Byzantine counterinvasion of 826 was a failure. In 827 Berbers from Tunis invaded Sicily but were expelled by stiff Byzantine resistance. Michael II was succeeded on his death in 829 by his son Theophilos. The next year, the Berbers from Tunis returned to Sicily and following a yearlong siege captured Palermo.

Taking advantage of Byzantine weakness, al-Mamun launched an invasion of Anatolia in 830 and captured a number of Byzantine forts, sparing those who surrendered. Theophilos continued the fight and in 831 captured Tarsus. The next year on learning that the Byzantines had killed some 1,600 Muslims, al-Mamun returned, won several battles, and captured several dozen Byzantine forts. He was preparing a major invasion of the Byzantine Empire when he died at Raqqa in present-day Syria on August 7, 833.

A man of high intelligence, Caliph al-Mamun showed a keen interest in Greek and Hellenistic philosophy and in science, especially astronomy to which he made notable contribution.

Spencer C. Tucker

See also
Abbasid Caliphate; Al-Amin, Muhammad

References
Hodgson, Marshall G. S. *The Venture of Islam: Conscience and History in a World Civilization.* Chicago: University of Chicago Press, 1977.
Kennedy, Hugh. *The Prophet and the Age of the Caliphates: The Islamic Near East from the Sixth to the Eleventh Century.* 2nd ed. Harlow: Longman, 2004.
Saunders, J. J. *A History of Medieval Islam.* London: Routledge and K. Paul, 1965.

Al-Nusra Front

Sunni Islamist organization that operated as an antigovernment Syrian rebel group from January 2012 until January 2017 during the Syrian Civil War. The al-Nusra Front (also known as Jabhat al-Nusra) was led by Abu Mohammed al-Julani and functioned as Al Qaeda's branch in Syria. After July 2016, it was renamed the Front for the Conquest of Syria (Jabhat Fatah al-Sham). Following violent clashes with Ahrar al-Sham and other rebel groups, on January 28, 2017, Jabhat Fatah al-Sham merged with four other groups to become Tahrir al-Sham. It is not known precisely how many fighters were associated with the al-Nusra Front, but by 2013 it was considered one of most effective rebel groups involved in operations against Syrian government forces.

In the summer of 2011 Al Qaeda's leadership, along with that of the fledgling Islamic State of Iraq and Syria (ISIS), then a branch of Al Qaeda in Iraq (AQI), decided to form an Al Qaeda offshoot in Syria, with the goal of ousting from power Syrian president Bashar al-Assad and creating an Islamic-based state within Syria. On January 23, 2012, the al-Nusra Front became operational, with al-Julani as its leader. Within weeks, however, numerous world powers designated it a terrorist organization. Unlike the diverse memberships of ISIS and Al Qaeda, most al-Nusra fighters hailed from Syria.

Contrary to ISIS, the al-Nusra Front sought to cooperate with other like-minded rebel groups and did not unduly antagonize local populations. Neither did it resort to beheadings and the mass killings of civilians, which became one of ISIS's most notorious hallmarks. Not surprisingly, al-Julani became disillusioned with ISIS and formally ended al-Nusra's lose affiliation with it in November 2013. By early 2014, al-Nusra fighters were engaged in combat with ISIS rebels. There were also signs that al-Julani was seeking to disassociate his group from Al Qaeda.

In 2015, Qatar and several other Persian Gulf states allegedly offered financial support for the al-Nusra Front if it disavowed Al Qaeda. The group also joined forces with several other rebel organizations, forming the powerful Army of Conquest, which secured much of northwestern Syria by the summer of that year. Russia entered the civil war in late September 2015 and began a punishing bombing campaign against al-Nusra interests. As the group came under more pressure from external actors, it increased the level and frequency of terror attacks against government targets; some of these involved the deaths of Syrian civilians.

In July 2016 when al-Julani formally split from Al Qaeda, he asserted that the Jabhat Fatah al-Sham (Front for the Conquest of Syria), a new name for the al-Nusra Front, would eschew all ties to international Islamist groups and would seek to unite other antigovernment rebel groups. He also said that his organization would focus less on global jihad and more on creating an Islamic-based government in Syria.

PAUL G. PIERPAOLI JR.

See also
Al Qaeda; Assad, Bashar al-; Islamic State of Iraq and Syria; Syria; Syrian Civil War

References
Sherlock, Ruth. "Inside Jabhat al-Nusra: The Most Extreme Wing of Syria's Struggle." *The Telegraph*, December 2, 2012, http://www.telegraph.co.uk/news/worldnews/middleeast/syria/9716545/Inside-Jabhat-al-Nusra-the-most-extreme-wing-of-Syrias-struggle.html.

Yassin-Kassab, Robin, and Leila al-Shami. *Burning Country: Syrians in Revolution and War.* London: Pluto, 2016.

Alp Arslan (ca. 1030–1072)

Second sultan of the Seljuk dynasty (r. 1063–1072). Born around 1030, Alp Arslan was the son of Chagri Beg and the nephew and heir of Toghrul Beg. Leading his father's armies at an early age, Alp Arslan defeated the Ghaznavids several times and raided Buyid territories in the west. He also assisted Toghrul Beg against Ibrahim Inal's rebellion in Persia, defeating him near Rayy in 1059.

Alp Arslan succeeded his father as the ruler of Khurasan and also succeeded Tughrul Beg, who died childless in 1063. Alp Arslan thus united all the Seljuk domains under his rule. Abbasid caliph al-Qaim confirmed Alp Arslan as sultan. Despite this, Alp Arslan had to deal with several relatives who challenged his rule and centralizing policies. In 1063–1664 he defeated and killed Qutlumish, a cousin, who led a rebellion in the Caspian region. Alp Arslan also dispatched his half brother, Sulaymany. Alp Arslan's uncle Quward led a revolt in Kerman in 1064, but Alp Arslan forced him to submit and later pardoned him.

After securing his control of the sultanate, Alp Arslan embarked on a series of military campaigns on both the eastern and western frontiers of the Seljuk Empire. Marching against the Qarakhanids, he reinforced their submission while maintaining his father's peace agreement with the Ghaznavids. Alp Arslan's major military efforts were launched from Azerbaijan against the Byzantines, Armenians, and Georgians, leading the Turkomans who formed a large part of his army in attacks against these Christian states. These successful military campaigns helped to secure Azerbaijan's borders and also occupied the energies of the Turkoman tribesmen, who might otherwise have been disturbing the peace within the Seljuk domains.

As a devout Sunni Muslim, Alp Arslan planned to conquer Syria and Egypt and put an end to the Ismaili Fatimid Caliphate. While he was campaigning in Syria, he learned that Byzantine emperor Romanus Diogenes was marching eastward with a large army. Securing the submission of Aleppo, Alp Arslan then abandoned his plans to march on Egypt and gathered his forces to meet this new threat. Despite being outnumbered, the Seljuks were victorious in the subsequent Battle of Manzikert (August 26, 1071). Romanus was taken prisoner, but Alp Arslan released him shortly after the battle. This victory opened Anatolia for future Turkic conquests.

Alp Arslan was campaigning against the Qarakhanids in Transoxania when he was mortally wounded in 1072 by a prisoner who was brought before him. Before his death Alp Arslan named his son, Malik Shah, as his successor.

ADAM ALI

See also
Byzantine-Seljuk Wars; Georgian-Seljuk Wars; Malik Shah I; Seljuk Dynasty

References
Bosworth, C. Edmund. "The Political and Dynastic History of the Iranian World." In *The Cambridge History of Iran,* Vol. 5, *The Saljuq and Mongol Periods,* ed. J. A. Boyle, 1–202. Cambridge: Cambridge University Press, 1968.

Cahen, Claude. *Pre-Ottoman Turkey.* London: Sidgwick and Jackson, 1968.

Donner, Fred M. "Muhammad and the Caliphate: Political History of the Islamic Empire Up to the Mongol Conquest." In *The Oxford History of Islam,* ed. John Esposito, 1–61. Oxford: Oxford University Press, 1999.

Groussett, Rene. *The Empire of the Steppes: A History of Central Asia.* Translated by Naomi Walford. New Brunswick, NJ: Rutgers University Press, 1970.

Al Qaeda

Al Qaeda is an international radical Islamic organization, the hallmark of which is the perpetration of terrorist attacks against Western interests in the name of Islam. Although initially based in Afghanistan, its activities are worldwide, with much of this located in the Middle East.

In the late 1980s, Al Qaeda (meaning the "base" or "foundation") fought against the Soviet occupation of Afghanistan. The organization is, however, best known for the September 11, 2001, terrorist attacks in the United States, the worst such attacks in U.S. history. The founding of Al Qaeda, which is composed chiefly of Sunni Muslims, is shrouded in controversy. Research from a number of Arabic scholars indicates that Al Qaeda was created sometime between 1987 or 1988 by Sheikh Abdullah Azzam, a mentor to Osama bin Laden. Azzam was a professor at Jeddah University in Saudi Arabia. Bin Laden attended Jeddah University, where he met and was strongly influenced by Azzam.

Al Qaeda grew out of the Afghan Service Bureau, also known as the Maktab al-Khidmat lil-mujahidin al-Arab (MaK). Azzam founded the MaK, and bin Laden funded it and was considered the deputy director. This organization recruited, trained, and transported Muslim soldiers from any Muslim nation into Afghanistan to wage jihad (holy war) against the Soviet armies in the 1980s. Sayyid Qutb, a philosopher of the Muslim Brotherhood, developed the credo for Al Qaeda, which is to arm all Muslims in the world and to overthrow any government that does not support traditional Muslim practice and Islamic law.

Following the mysterious death of Sheikh Azzam in November 1989, bin Laden took over the leadership of Al Qaeda. He continued to work toward Azzam's goal of creating an international organization composed of mujahideen (soldiers) who will fight the oppression of Muslims throughout the world. Al Qaeda actually has several goals: to destroy Israel, to rid the Islamic world of the influence of Western civilization, to reestablish a caliphate form of government throughout the world, to fight against any government viewed as contrary to the ideals of Islamic law and religion, and to aid all Islamic groups trying to establish an Islamic form of government in their countries.

The organization of Al Qaeda follows the Shur majlis, or consultative council form of leadership. The emir general's post was held by bin Laden, who was succeeded by Ayman al-Zawahiri upon bin Laden's death in May 2011. Several other generals are under the emir general, and then there are additional leaders of related groups. There are 24 related groups in the consultative council. The council consists of four committees—military, religious-legal, finance, and media. Each leader of these committees was personally selected by bin Laden or Zawahiri and reported directly to them. All levels of Al Qaeda are highly compartmentalized, and secrecy is the key to all its operations.

Al Qaeda's ideology has appealed to both Middle Eastern and non–Middle Eastern groups who adhere to Islam. There are also a number of radical Islamic terrorist groups associated with Al Qaeda that have established a history of violence and terrorism in numerous countries in the world today. The Islamic State of Iraq and Syria (ISIS) has taken center stage in recent years. Nevertheless, Al Qaeda continues to be a major force of world terrorism because of its opposition to Western domination.

Bin Laden was able to put most of the radical Islamic terrorist groups under the umbrella of Al Qaeda. Indeed, its leadership spread throughout the world, and its influence penetrated many religious, social, and economical structures in most Muslim communities. Today, the upper-echelon leadership of Al Qaeda continues to elude American intelligence and Western armies in Afghanistan and Pakistan.

The strength of Al Qaeda's membership remains difficult to determine because of its decentralized organizational structure. By early 2005, U.S. officials claimed to have killed or taken prisoner two-thirds of the Al Qaeda leaders behind the September 11 attacks. However, some of these prisoners have been shown to have had no direct connection with the attacks. Al Qaeda periodically released audio recording and videotapes, some featuring bin Laden himself, to comment on current issues, exhort followers to keep up the fight, and prove to Western governments that it was still a force with which to be reckoned.

Despite the decimation of Al Qaeda's core leadership in Afghanistan and Pakistan, it continues to be a major threat. Al Qaeda morphed from a centralized organization to a series of local-actor organizations forming a terrorist network. Al Qaeda in Iraq was decimated by the end of the Iraq War in 2011, but it then regained control of many of its former staging areas and the ability to launch car bomb attacks.

On May 1, 2011, bin Laden was killed in an attack mounted by U.S. special forces on his compound in Pakistan. Nonetheless, in July 2013 more than 1,000 people were killed in Iraq in terrorist actions, the highest monthly death toll in five years. Most of the attacks were led by Al Qaeda and its affiliates. That same year in Syria, Al Qaeda affiliate Jabhat al-Nusra, a combat force that has been fighting with some success against the regime of Syrian president Bashar al-Assad, rose to prominence. The force reports directly to the Al Qaeda leadership. Between 2009 and 2013 in Libya, Al Qaeda–affiliated terror groups were blamed for scores of attacks, many of them including civilians. Indeed, Al Qaeda has been blamed for the September 11, 2012, attack on the U.S. consulate in Benghazi that left the U.S. ambassador and three other Americans dead. In Yemen, Al Qaeda leaders in strongholds in the country's south have not been vanquished by a Yemeni military backed by U.S. forces and drone strikes. Al Qaeda affiliates in Iraq, Syria, Yemen, and West Africa have dramatically expanded their operating areas and capabilities and appear poised to continue their expansion, with the exception of ISIS, which was largely defeated in Iraq and Syria by early 2018.

By early 2014, ISIS and Al Qaeda had secured much of Iraq's Anbar Province, including Fallujah, and Al Qaeda was making significant headway in Afghanistan, often colluding with a resurgent Taliban. Al Qaeda has also successfully established itself in parts of Lebanon, Egypt, Algeria, and Mali. By early 2014, the U.S. Barack Obama administration had begun shipping Hellfire missiles and other weaponry to Prime Minister Nuri al-Maliki's government in Iraq to help suppress the growing insurgency there, which was dominated by Al Qaeda.

In June 2015 Al Qaeda's second-in-command, Nasir al-Wuhayshi, died in a U.S. air strike in Yemen. The Obama administration trumpeted this as a major blow to the Al Qaeda leadership, but the organization appeared not to have suffered unduly because of it. In Afghanistan meanwhile, Obama reluctantly agreed to keep a force of more than 8,000 troops there into 2018, in part because of Taliban battlefield successes and increased activity by Al Qaeda and its affiliates. In 2017 and 2018, President Donald Trump increased troop deployments to Afghanistan to help stem the tide of a mounting insurgency driven by the Taliban, Al Qaeda, and its affiliates, including ISIS. Saudi Arabia mounted a major military intervention in the Yemeni Civil War in 2015, which was designed in large measure to defeat Al Qaeda in the Arabian Peninsula (AQAP). That intervention, which is ongoing, has been limited chiefly to air strikes, however. In 2016 and 2017 as ISIS suffered more military defeats and lost more territory in Syria and Iraq, it markedly increased terror attacks, not just in the Middle East. ISIS sponsored major attacks that killed hundreds in Baghdad and other Iraqi cities as well as in Syria; it also carried out attacks in Turkey, Afghanistan, Egypt, Saudi Arabia, Iran, Bangladesh, Indonesia, France, Spain, Great Britain, Germany, Belgium, and the United States.

By early 2017 Al Qaeda in Syria, like other antigovernment rebel groups, had suffered major losses. In March 2017, Al Qaeda's leadership called upon its rank and file to kill Americans after a U.S. air strike damaged a mosque and killed civilians in a town just west of Aleppo.

Although Al Qaeda has endured many setbacks since 2001, it remains a potent force for worldwide terrorism. Perhaps its greatest influence in recent years has been its ability to form spin-off organizations such as ISIS and to encourage such allied groups as Boko Haram. And despite its more diffuse leadership, Al Qaeda remained a central focus of the war on terror well into 2018.

Harry Raymond Hueston II and Paul G. Pierpaoli Jr.

See also
Al Qaeda in Iraq; Al Qaeda in the Arabian Peninsula; Bin Laden, Osama; Islamic Radicalism in the 20th and 21st Centuries; Jihad; Maliki, Nuri Muhammed Kamil al-; Mubarak, Hosni; Muslim Brotherhood; Salafism; September 11, 2001, Attacks on the United States; Terrorism

References
Atwan, Abdel Bari. *The Secret History of al Qaeda*. Berkeley: University of California Press, 2006.

Bergen, Peter L. *Holy War, Inc.* New York: Touchstone, 2002.
Bergen, Peter L. *The Longest War: The Enduring Conflict between America and Al-Qaeda.* New York: Free Press, 2011.
Gunaratna, Rohan. *Inside Al Qaeda.* New York: Columbia University Press, 2002.
Hueston, Harry R., and B. Vizzin. *Terrorism 101.* 2nd ed. Ann Arbor, MI: XanEdu, 2004.
Mura, Andrea. *The Symbolic Scenarios of Islamism: A Study in Islamic Political Thought.* London: Routledge, 2015.

Al Qaeda in Iraq

Al Qaeda in Iraq (al-Qa'ida fi Bilad al-Rafhidayn, AQI) is a violent Sunni jihadist organization that took root in Iraq after the 2003 Anglo-American–led invasion of that nation. It later became subsumed by the Islamic State of Iraq and Syria (ISIS) and by 2015 was no longer a stand-alone organization. The U.S. government characterized AQI, sometimes referred to as Al Qaeda in Mesopotamia, as the most deadly Sunni jihadist insurgent force in Iraq. Other sources and experts argue that this designation is exaggerated, as the group is among more than 40 similar organizations, and that the claim was made symbolically to rationalize the idea that coalition forces are fighting terrorism in Iraq and thus should not withdraw precipitously.

Some knowledgeable observers have argued that the 2003 invasion sparked the growth of Salafi jihadism and suicide terrorism in Iraq and its export to other parts of the Islamic world. The AQI first formed following the invasion and toppling of the Iraqi regime under the name Jama'at al-Tawhid wal-Jihad (Organization of Monotheism and Jihad), led by Abu Musab al-Zarqawi, born in Jordan.

Zarqawi's organization was blamed for or took credit for numerous attacks, including bombings of the Jordanian embassy, the Canal Hotel that killed 23 at the United Nations headquarters, and the Imam Ali mosque in Najaf. It is also credited with the killing of Italian paramilitary police and civilians at Nasiriyah and numerous suicide attacks that continued through 2005. The group also seized hostages and beheaded them. A video of the savage execution of U.S. businessman Nicholas Berg, murdered in Iraq on May 7, 2004, reportedly by Zarqawi himself, was followed by other killings of civilians.

The AQI targeted Iraqi governmental and military personnel and police because of their cooperation with the occupying force. Estimates of AQI members ranged from 850 to several thousand. Also under dispute is the number of foreign fighters, although it is believed that some 90 percent have been native Iraqis.

In October 2004 Zarqawi's group issued a statement acknowledging the leadership of Al Qaeda under Osama bin Laden and adopted the name al-Qa'ida fi Bilad al-Rafhidayn. The Iraqi city of Fallujah, in western Anbar Province, became an AQI stronghold. U.S. forces twice tried to capture the city, first in the prematurely terminated Operation VIGILANT RESOLVE from April 4 to May 1, 2004. The Fallujah Guard then controlled the city. U.S. military and Iraqi forces conquered the city in Operation PHANTOM FURY (AL-FAJR) during November 7–December 23, 2004, in extremely bloody fighting.

Zarqawi formed relationships with other Salafist jihad organizations, announcing an umbrella group, the Mujahideen Shura Council, in 2006. After Zarqawi was reportedly killed by a U.S. air strike at a safe house in June 2006, the new AQI leader, Abu Ayyub al-Masri, announced a new coalition, the Islamic State of Iraq, that included the Mujahideen Shura Council.

Al Qaeda, along with other Sunni Salafist and nationalist groups, strongly resisted Iraqi and coalition forces in Baghdad, Ramadi, and Baqubah and continued staging very damaging attacks into 2007. However, by mid-2008 U.S. commanders claimed control of these areas. Nevertheless, the AQI was acknowledged to still be operative southeast of Baghdad in Jabour, Mosul, Samarra, Hawijah, and Miqdadiyah. The AQI's diminished presence was attributable by U.S. analysts to the Anbar Awakening, which enlisted numerous tribes, including some former AQI members, to fight Al Qaeda. The U.S. troop surge strategy that began in early 2007 many also have been a factor.

The AQI strongly influenced other jihadist groups and actors, particularly through its Internet presence. The group tapped into the intolerance of many Salafi groups as well as other Sunni Iraqis and Sunni Muslims outside of Iraq who felt threatened by the emergence of Shia political parties and institutions that had been suppressed during the Baathist regime of Saddam Hussein.

The AQI claimed responsibility for the July 23, 2013, jailbreak from the infamous Abu Ghraib prison that unleashed 500 to 600 militants into an already unstable environment and boosted the group's resurgent fortunes in Iraq and Syria. At least 26 members of the Iraqi security forces and more than a dozen prisoners were killed.

Iraqi security forces struggled to cope with a resurgent AQI after U.S. forces withdrew in December 2011, taking with them much of the expertise and technology that had been used to hold extremists at bay. Iraqi fears about a resurgent Al Qaeda were realized when the AQI, now affiliated with ISIS, helped that organization take control of Fallujah and Ramadi and much of Anbar Province by January 2014. Meanwhile, car bombings, kidnappings, and other violence perpetrated by Al Qaeda and ISIS accelerated rapidly during 2014 and 2015.

By 2014 the AQI was virtually indistinguishable from ISIS, as it had become ISIS's de facto affiliate operating within Iraq. By 2015, the AQI had been entirely subsumed by ISIS. ISIS was also fighting a bloody insurgency in neighboring Syria and has operatives in Lebanon, Egypt, and other Middle Eastern nations. In the late summer of 2014, the Barack Obama administration cobbled together an international coalition designed to take back territory gained by ISIS and the AQI and ultimately to defeat them. The United States also dispatched a small contingent of special forces soldiers to bolster Iraq's ground campaign against the insurgents. Iraq and its allies still faced a daunting task in their quest to vanquish ISIS militarily. Meanwhile, in 2014 Al Qaeda's worldwide leader Ayman al-Zawahiri disavowed Al Qaeda's ties to ISIS, citing its wanton brutality and unwillingness to yield to authority.

Sherifa Zuhur and Paul G. Pierpaoli Jr.

See also
Al Qaeda; Bin Laden, Osama; Fallujah, Second Battle of; Zarqawi, Abu Musab al-

References
Associated Press. "In Motley Array of Iraqi Foes, Why Does U.S. Spotlight al-Qaida?" *International Herald Tribune,* June 8, 2007.

Brisard, Jean-Charles, and Damien Martinez. *Zarqawi: The New Face of Al-Qaeda.* New York: Other Press, 2005.

Burns, John, and Melissa Rubin. "U.S. Arming Sunnis in Iraq to Battle Old Qaeda Allies." *New York Times,* June 11, 2007.

Congressional Research Service, Report to Congress. *Iraq: Post-Saddam Governance and Security, September 6, 2007.* Washington, DC: U.S. Government Printing Office, 2007.

Al Qaeda in the Arabian Peninsula

Muslim extremist group based in Saudi Arabia that is loosely affiliated with Osama bin Laden's and Ayman al-Zawahiri's transnational Al Qaeda network. Al Qaeda in the Arabian Peninsula (al-Qaida fi Jazirat al-Arabiyya, AQAP) was organized in 2001–2002 and emerged publicly in 2003 when it carried out a series of deadly bombings against the Saudi government and expatriate residences in the kingdom's major cities, including the capital city of Riyadh and the key Red Sea port city of Jeddah. The group came under attack in 2004 and 2005 during a series of arrests and shootouts with Saudi police and soldiers. These resulted in the deaths of several top AQAP leaders and operatives including its founder, Yusuf Salah Fahd al-Uyayri (Ayiri) (d. 2003) and his two successors, Abd al-Aziz bin Issa bin Abd al-Muhsin al-Muqrin (d. 2004) and Salah al-Alawi al-Awfi (d. 2005).

AQAP's primary goal was to overthrow the House of Saud, the kingdom's ruling family, which the group sees as corrupt and anathema to the "pure" society that the group's members and other unaffiliated and nonmilitant opponents of the monarchy seek to establish. The monarchy is harshly criticized by both the opposition and many of its own supporters among the ranks of the kingdom's official religious scholars (the ulema) as being too closely aligned with foreign powers, such as the United States, to the detriment of Saudi interests and social values. AQAP members proved to be adept users of the Internet, creating websites and widely read online publications such as the online magazine *Sawt al-Jihad* (Voice of Jihad).

Despite a series of small-scale attacks on Europeans and Americans in the kingdom during 2002 and early 2003, Saudi authorities did not acknowledge the existence of AQAP as a fully operational group until May 12, 2003. On that day, the group carried out three simultaneous suicide vehicle bombings at the Hamra, Vinnell, and Jedewahl housing compounds used by foreign (mainly Western) expatriates. The attacks killed 35 people, including 9 of the terrorists, and wounded 200 others. According to senior U.S. diplomats and Saudi intellectuals, this attack drove home to Crown Prince Abdullah (King Abdullah from 2005 to 2015) the need to vigorously combat homegrown Saudi radicalism.

In response to the attacks, hundreds of suspects were arrested by Saudi authorities, many of them with ties to AQAP and to the resistance in Iraq, although many were also probably figures from the nonmilitant religious opposition whom the authorities wished to silence under the guise of combating terrorism. Al-Uyayri (or Ayiri), AQAP's founder and first leader, was killed in June 2003 at the height of this sweep by Saudi authorities. He was succeeded by Abd al-Aziz al-Muqrin.

On November 3, 2003, Saudi security forces had a shootout with AQAP operatives in the city of Mecca, the location of the Kaaba, Islam's holiest shrine, that resulted in the deaths of 2 militants and the capture of a large weapons cache. Five days later AQAP launched a successful suicide bombing attack against the Muhayya housing complex in Riyadh, which was home to many non-Saudi Arab expatriate workers; the attack killed 18 people and wounded scores of others.

The group continued to launch attacks on Saudi and foreign targets, including a Riyadh government building on April 21, 2004, and an oil company office in Yanbu on May 1 that resulted in the killing of five Western workers. AQAP suffered another setback on March 15, 2004, when Khalid Ali bin Ali al-Haj, a Yemeni national and senior AQAP leader, was killed in a shootout with Saudi police along with his companion, AQAP member Ibrahim al-Muzayni. The group retaliated with a host of deadly attacks on expatriates, killing Herman Dengel (a German, on May 22, 2004), BBC cameraman Simon Cumbers (on June 6), Robert Jacob (an American, on June 8), Kenneth Scroggs (an American, on June 12), Irish engineer Tony Christopher (on August 3), British engineer Edward Muirhead-Smith (on September 15), and Laurent Barbot (a Frenchman, on September 26).

The most widely publicized attack, however, was the June 12, 2004, kidnapping and June 18 beheading of Paul M. Johnson Jr., an American employee of U.S. defense contractor Lockheed Martin. His kidnappers demanded the release of all detainees held by Saudi authorities, which was denied. The beheading was filmed and released on websites associated with and sympathetic to AQAP. That same day, Muqrin was killed by Saudi security forces during a raid on an AQAP safe house. Meanwhile, on May 29 the group carried out attacks on three targets in the city of Khobar, taking hostages in oil business offices and housing complexes associated with foreign companies. Saudi police and soldiers stormed the buildings the next day and rescued many of the hostages but not before the attackers had killed 22 others. Shortly after this attack, the U.S. Department of State issued a statement that urged U.S. citizens to leave the kingdom. The year was capped off with a spectacular attack on December 6 on the U.S. consulate in Jeddah in which 5 consulate employees, 4 Saudi national guardsmen, and 3 AQAP members were killed.

The Saudi government waged a successful campaign against AQAP throughout 2004 and into 2005, killing dozens of the group's members and nearly wiping out its senior leadership. In April 2005 several senior operatives were killed in a shootout in Rass, and in August Saudi security forces killed Muqrin's successor and AQAP leader Salah al-Alawi al-Awfi in the holy city of Medina. Other AQAP members were arrested.

Most of the group's members remain at large, and Saudi and foreign intelligence agencies continue to warn that AQAP poses a serious threat. The Saudi government has responded with antiterrorist measures, such as conferences and public pronouncements, a highly structured in-prison

Onlookers watch smoke billowing from the U.S. consulate in the Saudi Arabian city of Jeddah on December 6, 2004. The first attack on a foreign consulate in Saudi Arabia, it saw gunmen of Al Qaeda in the Arabian Peninsula storm the consulate, triggering a bloody three-hour engagement that left five non-American staffers and three attackers dead. Four Saudi guards were also killed in the shootout. (AFP/Getty Images)

counseling program designed to deradicalize detainees, and the Sakinah program that analyzes and engages Internet postings. In 2007 and 2008 Saudi security forces detained and imprisoned hundreds of people, some of them suspected militants and others in a variety of incidents, including those planning an attack during hajj, the annual Islamic pilgrimage to Mecca.

On September 30, 2011, a U.S. drone attack in Yemen resulted in the death of Anwar al-Awlaki, one of the group's leaders, and Samir Khan, the editor of *Inspire,* its English-language magazine. Both men were U.S. citizens. AQAP claimed responsibility for the May 21, 2012, suicide attack at a parade rehearsal for Yemen's Unity Day, killing more than 120 people and injuring 200 others. The attack was the deadliest in Yemeni history.

The pace of U.S. drone attacks quickened significantly beginning in 2012, with more than 20 strikes in the first five months of the year, compared to only 10 strikes in all 2011. During 2013 targeted killings by U.S. drones and special forces increased in number, thanks in part to the erection of secret U.S. bases in the Horn of Africa and the Arabian Peninsula. Meanwhile, on October 4, 2012, the United Nations 1267/1989 Al Qaeda Sanctions Committee and the U.S. State Department designated Ansar al-Sharia as an alias for Al Qaeda in the Arabian Peninsula. Meanwhile, U.S. drone strikes have continued and intensified, and 2017 saw a record number of such attacks as the Donald Trump administration sought to increase support for the Saudis and degrade AQAP and other Yemeni rebels.

In the summer of 2013 in response to news that AQAP was planning an offensive against U.S. diplomatic posts abroad, the American government temporarily closed more than two dozen embassies and legations as a precaution. This corresponded with an uptick in U.S. drone attacks, which now began to target lower-level AQAP members and other militant jihadists.

In 2014 AQAP launched several attacks against Yemeni government targets, and in early December of that year it released a video of kidnapped American journalist Luke Somers and demanded an unspecified ransom for his return. The Barack Obama administration mounted a military rescue effort, but the AQAP terrorists murdered Somers on December 6 before U.S. commandos could reach him. In January 2015, AQAP claimed responsibility for the *Charlie Hebdo* shootings in Paris that left 11 people dead. Three months later, the group seized the Yemeni port city of Al Mukalla after a protracted battle with Yemeni armed forces. Meanwhile, U.S. drone strikes killed dozens of AQAP militants during April 19–20, 2015, part of a much larger American campaign that has witnessed drone and air strikes against extremist fighters within Yemen. That campaign continued into 2018.

Yemen has been plagued by a costly civil war since 2011, and AQAP has been heavily involved in that struggle. Iran, which supports the Houthi rebels in that civil strife, has essentially been fighting a proxy war with the Yemeni government and its allies, including the United States and Saudi Arabia. Meanwhile, in late March 2015 the Saudis, now leading a nine-nation Arab coalition to aid the Yemeni government, intervened in the conflict by way of air strikes and a blockade of key ports. Although the chief target remained the Houthi fighters, AQAP also fell within the coalition's crosshairs. By the end of April, however, the Saudis had scaled back their air strikes and began to seek a diplomatic end to the fighting. Peace talks were under way by September 2015, but that effort suffered a setback when the exiled Yemeni government pulled out of the negotiations. During 2017 and 2018 Yemeni rebels, including AQAP fighters, fired missiles at Saudi targets within Saudi Arabia and at sea. In 2018, the Saudi government came under international scrutiny for attacks it initiated in Yemen that resulted in considerable civilian deaths. As of 2019, the civil war in Yemen continued virtually unabated.

Christopher Paul Anzalone

See also
Al Qaeda; Saudi Arabia; Terrorism; Yemen

References
Al-Rasheed, Madawi. *Contesting the Saudi State: Islamic Voices from a New Generation.* Cambridge: Cambridge University Press, 2006.
Cordesman, Anthony H., and Nawaf Obaid. *Al-Qaeda in Saudi Arabia: Asymmetric Threats and Islamist Extremists.* Washington, DC: Center for Strategic and International Studies, 2005.
Murphy, Caryle. "Saudi Arabia Indicts 991 Suspected Al Qaeda Militants." *Christian Science Monitor,* October 22, 2008.
Riedel, Bruce, and Bilal Y. Saab. "Al Qaeda's Third Front: Saudi Arabia." *Washington Quarterly* 21 (2008): 33–46.
Zuhur, Sherifa. "Decreasing Violence in Saudi Arabia and Beyond." In *Home-Grown Terrorism: Understanding and Addressing the Root Causes of Radicalisation among Groups with an Immigrant Heritage in Europe,* Vol. 60, ed. Thomas M. Pick, Anne Speckard, and Beatrice Jacuch, 74–98. NATO Science for Peace and Security Series. Amsterdam: IOS Press, 2010.
Zuhur, Sherifa. *Saudi Arabia: Islamic Threat, Political Reform and the Global War on Terror.* Carlisle Barracks, PA: Strategic Studies Institute, 2005.

Al-Sabah, Jaber al-Ahmad (1926–2006)

Thirteenth emir of Kuwait (1977–2006) and a member of the ruling family of al-Sabah. Born in Kuwait City on June 29, 1926, Jaber al-Ahmad al-Sabah was the third son of the late Sheikh Ahmad al-Jaber Al-Sabah, who was emir of Kuwait (head of state) from 1921 to 1950. It is believed that Sheikh Jaber was educated at the Al-Mubarakiya School, the Al-Ahmediya School, and the Al-Sharqiya School, and he was further tutored privately in Arabic, English, religion, and science.

In 1949, Jaber served as chief of public security in the al-Ahmadi oil fields. In 1962 he was appointed minister of finance, and under his direction Kuwait was transformed into a prosperous state with one of the world's highest per capita incomes. In 1965, he was appointed prime minister of Kuwait and was subsequently named crown prince in 1966. He was thereby officially recognized as the heir apparent to the throne of Kuwait. In December 1977 Jaber succeeded his uncle, Sheikh Sabah al-Salim al-Sabah, as emir.

A confluence of external and internal events dominated Jaber's rule. During the 1980s, a marked increase in political violence in Kuwait had disturbed this historically peaceful country. This violence included the bombing of the U.S. and French embassies in December 1983 and an assassination attempt on the emir by a suicide bomber in 1985. In 1986, prompted by such events, Jaber dissolved the National Assembly, exercising his powers as stipulated in Kuwait's constitution. Almost immediately he took measures to curb civil and political rights. In 1991, however, after the Persian Gulf War, Jaber reinstated the National Assembly; by 1992 many press and civil restrictions were lifted.

On August 2, 1990, following a long-running border dispute between Kuwait and Iraq, Iraq invaded and occupied Kuwait with the stated intent of annexing it. This was the first time in Kuwait's history that it had been placed under direct foreign rule. During and after the occupation, Jaber was subjected to severe criticism for immediately fleeing to Saudi Arabia and for setting up a government-in-exile there. In March 1991 after the conclusion of the Persian Gulf War, the emir returned to Kuwait. He assumed his former role as head of state, in spite of the fact that he had all but removed himself from the struggle to liberate Kuwait from Iraqi occupation.

In 1999 despite opposition from tribal and Islamist factions in parliament, Jaber approved an amendment allowing women the right to vote and run for office; the bill was rejected by a vote of 41 to 21 in the National Assembly. The bill was reintroduced and approved in June 2005, however, when parliament finally granted Kuwaiti women political rights.

Jaber also helped found the Cooperation Council for the Arab States of The Gulf, or the Gulf Cooperation Council (GCC), in 1981, an organization composed of Kuwait, Saudi Arabia, Bahrain, Qatar, Oman, and the United Arab Emirates. The GCC provided vital support during the Iraqi occupation of Kuwait.

In September 2000, Jaber suffered a stroke and traveled to the United Kingdom for medical treatment, returning four months later. Under his watch, Kuwait remained a staunch ally of the United States and the West. His government fully supported the U.S.-led invasion of Afghanistan after the September 11, 2001, terror attacks on the United States, and Kuwait also supported the Anglo-American–led invasion of Iraq in 2003. Indeed, Kuwait continued to serve as a major staging area for coalition troops in the Middle East.

In July 2003, Jaber announced that his brother—Prime Minister Sheik Sabah al-Ahmad al-Jaber al-Sabah—would lead the formation of a new government. Sabah was already the country's de facto leader because of the emir's failing health. Jaber al-Ahmad died on January 15, 2006, in Kuwait City. He was automatically succeeded by Crown Prince Saad al-Abdullah al-Salim al-Sabah, who resigned within nine days. On January 29, 2006, Jaber's brother was confirmed as the new emir of Kuwait.

Kirsty Anne Montgomery

See also
Gulf Cooperation Council; Kuwait

References
Casey, Michael. *The History of Kuwait.* Westport, CT: Greenwood, 2007.
Countrywatch. *Kuwait: 2006 Country Review.* Houston, TX: Countrywatch, 2006.
Mansfield, Peter. *Kuwait: Vanguard of the Gulf.* London: Hutchinson, 1990.
Metz, Helen Chapin. *Persian Gulf States: Country Studies.* 3rd ed. Washington, DC: Federal Research Division, Library of Congress, 1994.
Zahlan, Rosemarie Said. *The Making of the Modern Gulf States: Kuwait, Bahrain, Qatar, the United Arab Emirates, and Oman.* London: Unwin Hyman, 1989.

al-Sannabra, Battle of (June 28, 1113)

Battle fought between a Christian army led by King Baldwin I of Jerusalem and Muslim forces dispatched by the Seljuk sultan Muhammad I (r. 1105–1118) and led by Mawdud ibn Altuntash, *atabeg* of Mosul, and Tughtigin, *atabeg* of Damascus. The fighting occurred near the village of al-Sannabra (al-Sinnabrah), south of Lake Tiberias.

Muhammad had ordered an offensive against the Kingdom of Jerusalem, and his combined forces invaded Galilee in late May 1113. Baldwin I summoned assistance from the principality of Antioch and the county of Tripoli. Without waiting for the reinforcements to arrive, he immediately moved against the invaders with some 700 knights and 4,000 foot soldiers. The two sides came together on June 28, 1113, near the village of al-Sannabra as the Muslim force was about to cross the Jordan River south of the Sea of Galilee. Mawdud feigned retreat, and Baldwin rashly ordered a charge, only to encounter the main Muslim force. The Christians suffered heavy casualties, with the survivors withdrawing to a hilltop position west of Tiberias (modern-day Teverya, Israel). Although joined there by contingents under Prince Roger of Antioch and Count Pons of Tripoli, Baldwin did not dare attack, and for the next two months much of the countryside of the kingdom was under the effective control of the Turks, who sacked Nablus and ravaged as far as Jaffa (modern-day Tel Aviv–Yafo, Israel) and Jerusalem. The Seljuk forces finally withdrew at the end of August when the Frankish ranks were swelled by a large number of Christian pilgrims.

ALAN V. MURRAY AND SPENCER C. TUCKER

See also
Mawdud

References
Röhricht, Reinhold. *Geschichte des Königsreich Jerusalem (1100–1291)*. Innsbruck: Wagner, 1898.
Smail, R. C. *Crusading Warfare 1097–1193*. New York: Barnes & Noble Books, 1995.

al-Suri, Abu Mus'ab
See Nasar, Mustafa bin Abd al-Qadir Setmariam

Altalena Incident (June 23, 1948)

The intentional shelling by Israel Defense Forces (IDF) of the *Altalena*, a ship carrying Irgun Tsvai Leumi (National Military Organization) troops and arms, off the coast of Tel Aviv on June 23, 1948. The *Altalena* Incident brought the infant State of Israel to the brink of civil war and remained a festering wound in Israeli politics for years thereafter. The incident must be understood in the related contexts of the military exigencies of the Israeli War of Independence (1948–1949) and the long-standing struggle for supremacy between the Right and the Left within the Yishuv (Zionist settlement in Palestine).

The *Altalena* bore the pen name of Irgun founder Vladimir Jabotinsky. A World War II landing ship tank (LST) of 4,500 tons, purchased in New York in 1947 by American Irgunists, it was expected to make a number of trips to Israel transporting arms for the new Jewish state. Originally scheduled to arrive in Palestine by the end of the British mandate, it belatedly sailed in early June 1948 from Port-de-Bouc (near Marseille, France) with 940 militia fighters under the command of Eliahu Lankin. This, however, coincided with the beginning of the first truce in the Israeli War of Independence on June 11. The timing would prove to be fateful.

David Ben-Gurion, acting as both prime minister and defense minister, had ordered the dissolution of all militias and their subordination to a single command, that of the IDF. On the one hand, the IDF was exhausted and desperately needed the arms aboard the *Altalena*, which French premier Georges Bidault had insisted be provided to Israel free of charge. These weapons were sufficient to equip 8 to 10 battalions and included several hundred machine guns, 5,000 rifles, 4 million rounds of ammunition, thousands of grenades and bombs, 5 Bren carriers, and several tons of other war matériel. On the other hand, their importation would be a visible violation of the truce. Of even greater concern to Ben-Gurion was the proposition that the arms would be under Irgun control.

Unable to halt or delay the arrival of the ship, Irgun leader Menachem Begin won government permission for it to dock in Israel. Negotiations faltered, however, over demands that a portion of the weapons go to Irgun troops within the IDF and to autonomous units in Jerusalem. The cabinet authorized the use of force as a last resort if negotiations failed to bring the arms under effective IDF control.

Following sporadic fighting during June 20–21 around the first landing site at isolated Kfar Vitkin, Begin ordered the *Altalena* to Tel Aviv, where it attracted Irgun supporters, some of whom deserted IDF units. As crews attempted to unload the ship there, fighting broke out anew on June 22. Now no longer able to seize the ship, IDF forces shelled and destroyed it on June 23. In the process 3 IDF soldiers died, while the Irgun side suffered 16 killed and 70 wounded. On June 28 all members of the armed forces took an oath of allegiance, and Irgun ceased to exist as a separate entity.

Members of Irgun uniformly depicted themselves as blameless victims in the confrontation. Although it is true that Begin himself planned no revolt and that Ben-Gurion's tactics and timing made compromise impossible and violence inevitable, the threat posed by Irgun was not entirely fanciful. More than likely, a showdown would have come sooner or later. Ben-Gurion was unrepentant, often declaring that the cannon that sank the *Altalena* belonged in a museum exhibition. Whether because he had to or simply because he knew he could, Ben-Gurion followed other revolutionary leaders including Vladimir Lenin (whom he admired) by striking out against both rightists and leftists in order to consolidate power. He subsequently ordered the arrest of some 250 Irgunists, and the assassination of United Nations mediator Folke Bernadotte by Lehi (the Stern Gang)

The intentional shelling and burning of the *Altalena* off Tel Aviv, Israel, by the Israel Defense Forces on June 6, 1948. The ship was carrying troops and arms of the militant Jewish Irgun Tsvai Leumi, and its destruction brought the new Israeli state to the brink of civil war. (Israeli Government Press Office)

provided Ben-Gurion with an excuse to complete the purge. He also broke the power of Palmach.

Begin claimed that the arrival of the ship in May would have ended the war by enabling Israel to advance to the Jordan River and that its unloading in June would have lowered Israeli casualties and increased territorial gains. Principal IDF officers in the affair—Yigal Yadin, Moshe Dayan, and Yitzhak Rabin—went on to play leading roles in Israeli military and political life. After years of bitter rivalry, Begin was among those who implored Ben-Gurion to lead the government before the 1967 Six-Day War, which, under Defense Minister Dayan and Chief of Staff Rabin, resulted in Israeli control of eastern Jerusalem and the West Bank.

Because the *Altalena* Incident was the closest Israel came to civil war, it figured prominently in the discourse of those trying to either foment or prevent one. For the Right, it represented betrayal. Months before the Rabin assassination in November 1995, Ariel Sharon recalled the *Altalena* while accusing the government of abandoning the settlers in disputed territories. A decade later, the same allusion was applied to Sharon's government when he withdrew from Gaza. For the Left, the ship's arms were lost, but the battle for principle was won, as prompt and vigorous action was taken against extremists.

JAMES WALD

See also
Begin, Menachem; Ben-Gurion, David; Bernadotte, Folke; Dayan, Moshe; Eshkol, Levi; Haganah; Irgun Tsvai Leumi; Israeli War of Independence; Lohamei Herut Israel; Rabin, Yitzhak; Sharon, Ariel

References
Begin, Menachem. *The Revolt.* Los Angeles: Nash Publishing, 1972.
Kurzman, Dan. *Ben-Gurion: Prophet of Fire.* New York: Simon and Schuster, 1983.

Lankin, Eliahu. *To Win the Promised Land: Story of a Freedom Fighter.* Translated by Artziah Hershberg. Walnut Creek, CA: Benmir Books, 1992.

Sprinzak, Ehud. *Brother against Brother: Violence and Extremism in Israeli Politics from Altalena to the Rabin Assassination.* New York: Free Press, 1999.

Amalric of Jerusalem (1136–1174)

King of Jerusalem (1163–1174) and the younger son of Queen Melisende and Fulk of Anjou. Born in 1136, Amalric was the younger brother of Baldwin III, king of Jerusalem (r. 1145–1163) who made him count of Jaffa (modern-day Tel Aviv–Yafo, Israel) in 1151. Amalric seems to have lost these lands in 1152 because he sided with Melisende in a civil dispute between Baldwin and the queen mother. The brothers evidently reconciled by 1154, for at that time Baldwin III restored Jaffa to him and also made Amalric count of Ascalon (modern-day Tel Ashqelon, Israel). In 1157 Amalric married Agnes of Courtenay, daughter of Count Joscelin II of Edessa. She bore him two children, Sibyl (before 1161) and Baldwin (in 1161).

Amalric succeeded to the throne in 1163 when his brother Baldwin died childless, but the magnates and patriarch of Jerusalem, fearing that Agnes's family would grow too powerful, insisted that he divorce her before he could be crowned. Amalric agreed to do so on the condition that their children remain legitimate.

Amalric's policies aimed at strengthening the crown legislatively and financially. In judicial matters, his most famous achievement was the *Assise sur la ligèce,* which determined that all fief holders in the kingdom had to take an oath of homage to the king. But court decisions based on this assize seem to have favored the upper nobility rather than the crown. The same held true of Amalric's fiscal ambitions: his campaigns in Egypt, though creatively financed, ultimately ended in military and economic losses.

Fatimid Egypt was a tempting target owing to its immense wealth and shaky political situation where two viziers vied for control. Nur al-Din, the ruler of Muslim Syria, might intervene there if Jerusalem failed to do so, but equally, he could not allow the Franks to dominate Egypt. In 1163 Nur al-Din sent his general Shirkuh to assist one of the two viziers, Shawar, who, however, soon sought military aid against him from Amalric. The king invaded Lower Egypt, andCed Nur al-Din countered with campaigns against Christian Syria. He captured Prince Bohemund III of Antioch and Count Raymond III of Tripoli while seizing Harenc, Banyas, and parts of the principality of Antioch in 1164.

Expeditions in 1167 turned the tables. Nur al-Din sent Shirkuh back to Egypt, which meant that Amalric also had to launch a campaign. The king summoned the High Court but could not convince his nobles to support an attack outside the kingdom. He then secured financing for it through a 10 percent tax paid by the church and vassals who would not go to Egypt. Shawar greeted the Frankish army with 400,000 dinars in exchange for an alliance. The two armies then besieged Alexandria until Shirkuh came to terms, and he and the Franks withdrew from Egypt.

Amalric's agreement with Shawar remained in force: Amalric pledged military assistance as long as Shawar paid an annual tribute of 100,000 dinars. The royal treasury benefited from this arrangement, and as long as Amalric remained content with a nominal protectorship over Egypt, Nur al-Din probably would not have reacted.

Amalric, however, dreamed of conquering Egypt with Byzantine help. In 1167 he cemented his alliance with Manuel I Komnenos by marrying the emperor's niece, Maria. The following year Amalric planned a joint assault on Egypt, with the Byzantine fleet blockading Egyptian Mediterranean ports while the Franks invaded by land. The king moved too quickly, though, and marched out before the Byzantine Navy could provide backup. He could not convince the Templars to join him, despite the inducement of rich lands. Shawar turned to Nur al-Din for assistance, and Shirkuh returned to Egypt for the last time. Although Amalric won some important victories at first, he could not take Cairo and finally withdrew. Shirkuh then marched in, had Shawar killed, and installed himself as vizier. Shirkuh died two months later, to be succeeded by his nephew Saladin, who quickly built up a strong government in the name of the Fatimids.

Amalric invaded Egypt once more, in 1168, this time waiting for Byzantine ships to support his attack on Damietta, but he withdrew without having received Byzantine support and having gained nothing. Once back in Jerusalem, Amalric patched up his relationship with Manuel Komnenos, culminating in a state visit to Constantinople (modern-day Istanbul) in 1171.

Saladin was able to topple the Fatimids in 1171, restoring Sunni Islam in Egypt, and Nur al-Din's death in May 1174 allowed Saladin to move into Syria. The military orders were increasingly acting as free agents within Outremer, negotiating or overturning truces with Islamic powers.

Amalric died on July 11, 1174. His heir, Baldwin IV, came to the throne as a minor suffering from leprosy, and

Baldwin's sisters Sibyl and Isabella (Maria's daughter) became pawns in the hands of rival factions at court.

DEBORAH GERISH

See also
Baldwin III of Jerusalem; Baldwin IV of Jerusalem; Crusades in the Holy Land, Christian; Fatimid Dynasty; Manuel I Komnenos, Emperor; Nur al-Din; Saladin

References
Edbury, Peter W., and John G. Rowe. *William of Tyre: Historian of the Latin East.* Cambridge: Cambridge University Press, 1988.
Lilie, Ralph-Johannes. *Byzantium and the Crusader States, 1096–1204.* Oxford, UK: Clarendon, 1993.
Loud, Graham A. "The *Assise sur la ligèce* and Ralph of Tiberias." In *Crusade and Settlement,* ed. Peter W. Edbury, 404–412. Cardiff: University College Cardiff Press, 1985.
Lyons, Malcolm C., and D. E. P. Jackson. *Saladin: The Politics of Holy War.* Cambridge: Cambridge University Press, 1982.
Phillips, Jonathan. *Defenders of the Holy Land: Relations between the Latin East and the West, 1119–1187.* Oxford, UK: Clarendon, 1996.
Runciman, Steven. "The Visit of King Amalric I to Constantinople in 1171." In *Outremer: Studies in the History of the Crusading Kingdom of Jerusalem,* ed. Hans Eberhard Mayer, Benjamin Z. Kedar, and R. C. Smail, 153–158. Jerusalem: Yad Izhak Ben-Zvi Institute, 1982.

Amara, Battle of (June 3, 1915)

World War I battle during the 1915 Mesopotamian Campaign. On May 31, 1915, the British began an offensive operation up the Tigris River to secure the Tigris Valley and its oil pipeline. This operation, commanded by Major General Sir Charles V. F. Townshend, involved about 14,000 men moving by water and land supported by several gunboats on the Tigris commanded by Royal Navy captain Wilfred Nunn.

Townshend first seized key positions south of the city of Amara along the Tigris, including Norfolk Hill, One Tree Hill, One Tower Hill, and Gun Hill. On June 3 he halted his forces 12 miles from Amara to wait for reinforcements because he believed that Ottoman forces would defend the city. Later that same day, he changed his mind and ordered his forces to proceed into Amara.

Royal Navy lieutenant Mark Singleton's gunboat *Shaitan* led the advance, reconnoitering ahead of the main British forces. Singleton's action was an important element in the capture of the city that same day, as many Ottomans fled on the gunboat's approach. Townshend arrived in Amara later that same afternoon in the gunboat *Comet.*

As British forces came ashore, large numbers of Ottoman troops surrendered. Fewer than 50 British soldiers were at Amara initially. The speed and intensity of the British attack had caught the Ottoman defenders off guard, and the British easily secured Amara at little cost on June 3. The next day, the 2nd Battalion of the Norfolk Regiment arrived and completed the British occupation of the city.

British casualties in the capture of Amara were only 4 killed and 21 wounded, while the Ottoman defenders suffered 120 killed or wounded and 2,000 captured. Townshend's troops also took a number of weapons, including 5 naval guns and 12 fieldpieces. General Sir John Nixon, commanding the Indian Expeditionary Force, praised Townshend for his quick action in taking Amara and the effective coordination that he and Captain Nunn maintained throughout the operation. With Amara taken, Nixon began planning an attack against Nasiriyah on the Euphrates River.

ANTHONY J. SCHMAUS

See also
Nixon, Sir John Eccles; Townshend, Sir Charles Vere Ferrers

References
Moberly, F. J. *The Campaign in Mesopotamia, 1914–1918.* 3 vols. Nashville: Battery Press, 1997–1998.
Nunn, Wilfred. *Tigris Gunboats: The Forgotten War in Iraq, 1914–1917.* Annapolis, MD: Naval Institute Press, 2007.
The Times History of the War, Vol. 10. London: The Times, 1917.

Amasya, Treaty of (May 29, 1555)

Peace treaty signed between the Ottoman and Safavid Empires on May 29, 1555, that ended the Ottoman-Safavid War of 1532–1555. Under the terms of the Treaty of Amasya (Amasia), southern Caucasia and Asia Minor were divided into two parts, with Persia receiving Azerbaijan, eastern Armenia, eastern Kurdistan, the Georgian kingdoms of Kartli-Kakheti, and the eastern part of Samtskhe, while the Ottomans secured all of western Georgia, Arabia, Iraq, and western Armenia and Kurdistan. Kars was declared neutral, and its fortress was destroyed. The peace lasted until an Ottoman offensive in 1578 sought to take advantage of a period of Persian weakness under Shah Muhammad Khudabanda (1578–1587).

ALEXANDER MIKABERIDZE

See also
Ottoman-Safavid Wars

Reference
Jackson, Peter. *The Cambridge History of Iran: The Timurid and Safavid Periods,* Vol. 6. Cambridge: Cambridge University Press, 1986.

Ambush Alley

A stretch of road, including two bridges, located at the edge of Nasiriyah, Iraq. "Ambush Alley" gained its nickname in March 2003 during the initial stages of the Iraq War (Operation IRAQI FREEDOM) owing to two incidents. The first was the ambush of the U.S. Army 507th Maintenance Company, which had been ensnared and captured on March 21.

The second more notable incident occurred on March 23. In this engagement, Iraqi forces attacked a force of U.S. marines seeking to capture two bridges over the Saddam Canal and the Euphrates River and the roadway between them. The ensuing battle became the costliest single engagement for American forces during the initial invasion of Iraq. The battle eventually involved the bulk of Task Force Tarawa, including the 1st and 3rd Battalions of the 2nd Marine Regiment; Alpha Company, 8th Tank Battalion; and Marine Aircraft Group 29.

The marine mission had seemed straightforward. Invasion planners recognized that the two bridges and the road between them represented a vital supply artery on the road to Baghdad. Once the bridges and the road were secured, the way would be open for the Americans to drive north toward Kut and from there to Baghdad.

Neither the marine field commanders entrusted with the capture of the bridges—Lieutenant Colonel Rick Grabowski, commander of the 1st Battalion, 2nd Marine Regiment, and his immediate superior, Colonel Ronald Bailey, commander of the regiment—nor the senior U.S. military leadership expected any difficulty here. Nasiriyah lay in one of the areas of Iraq considered the least hostile. Senior U.S. commanders believed that the Shia population, traditionally hostile to the Iraqi regime, would welcome them. Moreover, they believed that the Iraqi regular army soldiers in the city, mostly from the 11th Infantry Division, were second rate and would flee or blend into the civilian population as soon as the Americans approached. Unknown to the marines, however, Fedayeen Saddam commandos were present in the city. Word of the 507th Maintenance Company's mishap either had not reached the Americans on the ground or, if it had, the possible implications had not registered.

Based on these assumptions and the perceived need to capture the two bridges quickly, Grabowski planned to take the southern Euphrates bridge with Alpha Company. Bravo Company would then cross the bridge onto Route Moe (Ambush Alley), turn immediately to the east, and push to the northern Saddam Canal bridge with close artillery, air, and armored support. Charlie Company of the 1st Battalion, 2nd Marines, was to move through Alpha and Bravo's lines and seize the northern Saddam Canal bridge. The tank company was included in the initial attack, but some of its M1 Abrams tanks were refueling, so the initial attacks were launched without armored support.

The American assumptions proved incorrect. As the marines approached the southern Euphrates bridge, Iraqi forces on both sides of the road opened fire on Alpha Company. Shortly thereafter, Charlie Company also reported that it was taking fire from the area around the Saddam Canal bridge. Bravo Company, following Alpha Company near the south bridge, was soon pinned down by heavy fire from automatic weapons and rocket-propelled grenades. The marines were trapped in narrow streets surrounding the bridges where it was difficult to bring their supporting arms to bear. Although they held the southern bridge, their foothold was tenuous.

The fighting involved U.S. efforts to relieve the embattled 1st Battalion and secure the road. The greatest difficulties proved to be getting armored support and reinforcements to the marines through the narrow streets and coordinating air support. The process proved to be costly. The marines faced a maze of Iraqi roadblocks. A field south of the Euphrates bridge that seemed promising as a route for the tanks proved to be a sewage disposal bog that would not support heavy tanks. Mounting casualties made medical evacuation urgent, but it was impossible to get medevac helicopters to the marine positions because of intense ground fire. In the early afternoon, an air strike by Fairchild-Republic A-10 Thunderbolt II ground attack aircraft went awry and struck Charlie Company's position instead of the Iraqis.

By the evening of March 23 the 2nd Marine Regiment had seized both bridges, and the firing from the Iraqi positions had slackened. But the marines still had not completely secured Ambush Alley. It would take another two days to completely clear the roadway.

Events at Nasiriyah shook the marines. The official casualty count was 18 dead and 55 wounded, but many American officers privately thought the count was much higher. Despite many acts of heroism, the Ambush Alley fight was not an impressive beginning to IRAQI FREEDOM. The intelligence on Iraqi strength and fortifications here was faulty, and the marine plan, which involved coordination among multiple commands, was too complicated. The tactics employed by the Iraqis at Nasiriyah indicated that they would not use conventional tactics but would fight instead with ambushes and hit-and-run attacks. The Battle of Ambush Alley portended the nature of the fighting for the rest of the initial Iraq invasion and the ensuing Iraqi insurgency.

WALTER F. BELL

See also

Fedayeen; Iraq War; Nasiriyah, Battle of

References

Gordon, Michael R., and Bernard E. Trainor. *Cobra II: The Inside Story of the Invasion and Occupation of Iraq.* New York: Random House, 2006.

Pritchard, Tim. *Ambush Alley: The Most Extraordinary Battle of the Iraq War.* New York: Presidio, 2005.

Amer, Abdel Hakim (December 11, 1919–September 14, 1967)

Egyptian Army field marshal and leading figure in the Gamal Abdel Nasser government during 1952–1967. Born in Minya Province, Egypt, on December 11, 1919, Abdel Hakim Amer graduated from the Egyptian Military Academy in 1938. At the academy, he became acquainted with Nasser. Following graduation, both officers served briefly in the Egyptian town of Mankabad in the district of Asyut. Both Amer and Nasser were later transferred to Khartoum and then Jabal al-Awliyya, Sudan, where they served in an infantry unit together. There they became especially close friends.

Following service in the Sudan, Amer returned to Egypt and served as a military instructor at the Army School of Administration. Both Amer and Nasser took part in the Israeli War of Independence (1948–1949), and they were equally appalled by Egypt's lack of preparedness for this conflict. Later, Amer helped Nasser form the Free Officers Movement, which overthrew King Faruq in July 1952. Amer's warm and jovial nature complemented the personality of the often dour Nasser.

Field Marshal Abdel Hakim Amer, vice president of the United Arab Republic (UAR), addressing Egyptian troops and pilots during a visit to UAR military outposts near the Israeli border on May 20, 1967. (Bettmann/Getty Images)

In June 1953, Amer was promoted directly from major to major general and became commander of the Egyptian Armed Forces. In 1954 he became minister of defense with the rank of full general. He is widely reported to have quarreled with Nasser over strategy during the 1956 Suez Crisis and Sinai Campaign but nevertheless remained in office. Amer was appointed to the rank of field marshal in 1958 and became head of the Joint Military Command established by Egypt and Syria when the two countries merged as the United Arab Republic (1958–1961).

In March 1964 Amer was appointed first vice president of Egypt and deputy supreme commander of the armed forces (under Nasser). In May 1964 both Nasser and Amer were awarded the Soviet Union's Order of Lenin for their roles in improving Egyptian-Soviet relations. In May 1966 Amer was named to head the Committee for the Liquidation of Feudalism, an investigative body that was designed to discipline wealthy landholders deemed to be exploiting the peasantry by appropriating their landholdings. He gave up the position of minister of defense but arranged to have his protégé, Shams Badran, appointed to that position in the summer of 1966. Badran continued to function as one of Amer's most loyal subordinates.

Throughout his time in office, Amer was known for ensuring that only officers of complete loyalty to the regime were retained and promoted. His brilliance at political maneuvering was nevertheless not matched by even the most basic understanding of modern warfare. He displayed exceptional confidence during Cairo's buildup to the 1967 Six-Day War and by most accounts believed that Egypt would score an easy victory against the Israelis. In the aftermath of the massively successful preemptive Israeli air strike against Egyptian airfields on June 5, 1967, Amer went from supreme confidence to a state of almost total despair and ordered an immediate withdrawal of Egyptian units from the Sinai. It is not clear if he issued the order on his own authority or if the order had originated with Nasser, but Amer alone is usually blamed for this decision, which proved disastrous. Egyptian units did not retreat in an organized military withdrawal, with some units covering others, but instead made a mad scramble for the Suez Canal while being continually mauled by Israeli airpower. The Egyptian Armed Forces therefore suffered the most humiliating defeat in its modern history under Amer's leadership. In the aftermath of the war, Nasser sent word to Amer through Anwar Sadat that he would not be permitted to remain in Egypt but would not be pursued were he to go into exile. Amer chose to stay in Egypt and was later accused of attempting to seize control of the government.

Arrested by Egyptian authorities along with some 50 other officers, Amer was reported to have committed suicide on September 14, 1967, while in custody. The precise location of this event is not clear. Widespread speculation persists that he was either executed in prison or was told that his conviction and execution for treason were inevitable. In that case, he may have seen suicide as his only option. A subsequent investigation suggests that Amer died by poison, which may indicate the involvement of Egyptian security forces in his death.

W. Andrew Terrill

See also

Egypt; Israeli War of Independence; Nasser, Gamal Abdel; Sadat, Anwar; Sinai Campaign of 1956; Six-Day War; Suez Crisis

References

Aburish, Said K. *Arafat: From Defender to Dictator.* New York: Bloomsbury, 1998.

El-Gamasy, Mohamed Abdel Ghani. *The October War: Memoirs of Field Marshal El-Gamasy of Egypt.* Cairo: American University in Cairo Press, 1989.

Nutting, Anthony. *Nasser.* New York: Dutton, 1972.

Oren, Michael B. *Six Days of War: June 1967 and the Making of the Modern Middle East.* Novato, CA: Presidio, 2003.

Amiriyah Shelter Bombing (February 13, 1991)

Controversial U.S. air strike during the Persian Gulf War. The U.S. military asserted that Public Shelter No. 25 in the Amiriyah district of Baghdad was an Iraqi command shelter, or backup communications bunker. It was, however, consistently publicized by the Iraqi government as the civilian air shelter for Amiriyah. The bunker was attacked by the U.S. Air Force in the early morning hours of February 13, 1991, during INSTANT THUNDER, the air campaign component of Operation DESERT STORM. The attack, which occurred 11 days before the beginning of the allied ground offensive began, killed or wounded a large number of Iraqi civilians.

Coalition air war planners developed a plan for an air campaign that would destroy 84 strategic targets in Iraq in the opening week of the air campaign, which began on January 17, 1991. The planners held that destruction of these targets would paralyze Iraqi leadership, degrade Iraq's military and communications capabilities, and neutralize the Iraqi will to fight. Additionally, the planners included other targets such as Iraq's nuclear, biological, and chemical warfare facilities; ballistic missile production and storage facilities; key bridges; railroads and ports that enabled

Iraq to supply its forces in Kuwait; and the Iraqi air defense system. Finally, at the insistence of coalition commander U.S. Army general H. Norman Schwarzkopf Jr., the air campaign envisaged attacks against Iraqi forces in Kuwait to reduce their effectiveness and compel their surrender or evacuation.

On January 17, 1991, coalition air forces opened Operation DESERT STORM with a massive air campaign, with more than 1,000 sorties launched per day. After several weeks, the emphasis of the bombing moved from attacking Baghdad and leadership sites to other targets and Iraq's fielded military forces. Other priorities also intruded on the leadership focus, such as new intelligence on Iraq's weapons of mass destruction and tactical ballistic missiles that could carry chemical warheads and had the potential of provoking an Israeli overreaction to Iraqi missile attacks that in turn might cause Arab coalition partners to leave the fight. The initial attacks swept away much of Iraq's ability to defend against further air assaults, including radar installations, command and control centers in Baghdad, air bases and hangars, and the Iraqi air defense system.

In early February 1991, U.S. war planners added to the target list what was alleged to be the "Al-Firdos command, control, and communications bunker" as a newly activated Iraqi command shelter. They claimed that they had intercepted signals traffic and that daytime satellite photography of limousines and trucks parked outside the bunker suggested leadership activity there.

On the evening of February 12 hundreds of Baghdad residents, possibly families of higher-ranking government and intelligence personnel, entered the bunker's upper levels to escape the nighttime bombing raids of Baghdad. In the early morning of February 13, two U.S. Air Force Lockheed F-117 Nighthawk stealth fighters dropped two 2,000-pound laser-guided bombs on the hardened shelter, piercing the concrete- and steel-reinforced roof. No warning had been issued.

Some 400 Iraqi civilians, mostly women and children, died in the attack. Another 200 were severely injured. The U.S. Department of Defense admitted that it knew the shelter had been used as a civilian air shelter during the Iran-Iraq war. Human Rights Watch conducted interviews with the neighborhood residents and affirmed that the facility was clearly marked as a civilian air shelter and that it was known to be operating in that capacity. Supposedly, a single human source claimed that the Iraqi military had begun using the facility. Schwarzkopf and General Colin L. Powell, chairman of the U.S. Joint Chiefs of Staff, considered the site a valid military objective and believed that the coalition had adhered to its legal obligations for limiting civilian casualties. Human Rights Watch, however, noted that bombing the facility without warning and knowing that civilians were housed there was a serious violation of international law. Schwarzkopf and Powell explained the attack as an unfortunate mistargeting problem and as an inevitable civilian tragedy brought on by wartime conditions. The attack brought condemnation from the Arab world. Certainly the attack on the Amiriyah air shelter was the most glaring instance of civilian losses during the Persian Gulf War air campaign.

ROBERT B. KANE

See also
Persian Gulf War, Overview; Schwarzkopf, H. Norman, Jr.

References
Conduct of the Persian Gulf War: Final Report to Congress, Washington, DC: Department of Defense, April 1992.
Davis, Richard C. *On Target Organizing and Executing the Strategic Air Campaign against Iraq.* Washington, DC: Air Force History and Museums Program, 2002.
Human Rights Watch. "Needless Deaths in the Gulf War: Civilian Casualties during the Air Campaign and Violations of the Laws of War." 1991.
Keaney, Thomas A., and Cohen, Eliot A. *Gulf War Air Power Survey Summary Report.* Washington, DC: Department of the Air Force, 1993.
Mann, Edward C., III. *Thunder and Lightning: Desert Storm and the Airpower Debates.* Maxwell Air Force Base, AL: Air University Press, 1995.

Amman Campaign (March 21–September 25, 1918)

British attempts to seize Amman, Jordan, led by commander of the Egyptian Expeditionary Force (EEF) Lieutenant General Edmund Allenby. The initial attempt to secure Amman, a key installation on the Hejaz railroad, occurred in March 1918. Amman was of such importance because the Hejaz railroad was a vital Ottoman supply line, and securing it would ease the progress of British troops toward Damascus.

The first British raid on Amman began on March 21. The Australian 1st and 7th Light Horse Brigades attacked, supported by the Camel Brigade. The raiders' mission was to destroy two key structures in the railroad line, a viaduct and a tunnel, and then withdraw back to the Jordan River. During the 11-day span through March 30, British forces advanced toward Amman but were unable to complete the mission because of unfamiliar terrain, torrential downpours, and fierce resistance from Ottoman troops.

The second raid on Amman, mounted by the Australian 3rd and 4th Light Horse Brigades, began on April 29, 1918. It also ended in failure. By May 5, the entire British force had withdrawn west of the Jordan River.

After suffering two setbacks, Allenby devised a new plan. Having now convinced the Ottoman military that his intention was to push toward Amman, he decided instead to carry out an infantry attack on the opposite flank, moving northward. Once he had broken that line, he planned to send cavalry to outflank and surround Ottoman troops to the east.

To mask his plan, Allenby ordered his men to construct a mock camp along the Jaffa-Jerusalem line on the banks of the Jordan. The ruse included 15,000 dummy horses made of canvas. He also moved his Indian troops across the river during the day and brought them secretly back each night to make it seem as if he was massing troops for another attack on Amman. Allenby further secretly doubled the number of his troops on the opposite flank. By the time the battle began there, Allenby enjoyed a manpower advantage of two to one.

At 4:30 a.m. on September 19, 1918, Allenby began the attack in the Battle of Megiddo. Royal Air Force bombing destroyed the communications center at Nazareth, hampering Ottoman redeployment efforts. Once the line broke, 9,000 cavalry troops of the 4th Cavalry Division pushed through the hole and rode northeast to Jenin and Megiddo. By that night, these forces had taken 2,500 Ottoman prisoners. Ottoman commander German general of cavalry Otto Liman von Sanders narrowly escaped capture.

Following this successful advance into the Jordan River Valley, Allenby's next two tasks were to prevent the Ottoman army at Amman from retreating northward and capture the town itself. On the morning of September 25, Major General Edward W. C. Chaytor's division (the Australian and New Zealand Mounted Division, first formed in Egypt in March 1916) moved into position around Amman. The 2nd Light Horse Brigade and the New Zealand Brigade carried out the initial assault; the 1st Light Horse Brigade was held in reserve.

Ottoman forces repelled the initial British attack with machine-gun fire. Then the 2nd Light Horse Brigade overran the stone fortifications surrounding Amman, and by 1:30 p.m. British forces had seized the railroad station. In taking Amman, the Anzacs captured 2,563 Ottoman soldiers and 10 guns.

The British also secured the surrender of 5,000–6,000 Ottoman reinforcements advancing from Ma'an to the south to Amman. Chaytor's troops smoothed the way to Damascus for the main army. In all, during the period from September 19 the EEF had taken 45,000 prisoners and 260 guns.

LAURA J. HILTON

See also
Allenby, Sir Edmund Henry Hynman; Liman von Sanders, Otto; Ma'an, Siege of; Megiddo, Battle of; Palestine and Syria Campaign, World War I; Transjordan Campaign

References
Bruce, Anthony P. C. *The Last Crusade: The Palestine Campaign in the First World War.* London: John Murray, 2002.

Falls, Cyril. *Armageddon, 1918: The Final Palestinian Campaign of World War I.* Philadelphia: University of Pennsylvania Press, 2003.

MacMunn, George, and Cyril Falls. *Official History of the Great War: Military Operations, Egypt and Palestine, from the Outbreak of the War with Germany to June 1917.* London: HMSO, 1928.

Preston, R. M. P. *The Desert Mounted Corps.* Boston: Houghton Mifflin, 1922.

Amr ibn al-As (ca. 585–664)

Arab general who conquered Egypt during the period of early Arab expansion. Born on February 14, 585, at Mecca, Arabia, Amr ibn al-As (al-Aasi) was a contemporary of Prophet Muhammad who converted to Islam before the fall of Mecca and became a leading Arab general. Throughout his career Amr undertook numerous important missions. His first major expedition saw him travel to Oman on behalf of the prophet to convince the local rulers to convert to Islam. Amr succeeded on this mission, but during his stay in Oman the prophet died, prompting Amr to return to Medina.

Abu Bakr, the successor of Muhammad, gave Amr command of the army to invade Palestine in 633. Although there are conflicting reports regarding this invasion, Amr was responsible for the conquest of the Byzantine territories west of the Jordan River. In addition, Amr took part in the victory over the Byzantines in the Battle of Yarmouk (August 15, 636) and the capture of Damascus.

Amr's major achievement came in 640 when he led an army into Egypt. There remains some debate on whether he did this on his own initiative or whether Caliph Umar directed him to do so. In any case, Umar ostensibly approved of it, as Amr did receive reinforcements, and the conquest was completed in 642 with the capture of Alexandria. Afterward, Amr contributed greatly to the administration of Egypt and oversaw construction of the city that became Cairo. His career in Egypt, however, was short-lived, as Caliph Uthman recalled him to Medina.

Amr remained absent from major military events until the Battle of Siffin in 657, when Muawiyah and Ali ibn Abi Talib battled for control of the caliphate. Amr sided with Muawiyya, leading the cavalry in the battle, which ended more or less in a draw with the dispute settled through arbitration. Before the decision came, however, Amr was able to occupy Egypt and remove Ali's factions from power there in 658. Amr remained governor of Egypt until his death there in 664.

TIMOTHY MAY

See also
Byzantine-Muslim Wars; Egypt, Arab Conquest of; Muawiyah I; Muhammad, Campaigns of the Prophet; Siffin, Battle of; Yarmouk River, Battle of

References
Belyaev, E. A. *Arabs, Islam, and the Arab Caliphate in the Early Middle Ages.* London: Pall Mall, 1969.
Donner, Fred M. *The Early Islamic Conquests.* Princeton, NJ: Princeton University Press, 1981.
Shaban, M. A. *Islamic History: A New Interpretation.* New York: Cambridge University Press, 1971.

Anbar Awakening Movement

A U.S. operation to obtain or regain the loyalties of Sunni Arab tribes of Anbar Province, Iraq, that began in the provincial capital of Ramadi in September 2006. Tribal sheikhs who had been marginalized or who sought revenge against Al Qaeda in Iraq (AQI) began cooperating with U.S. forces to root out the AQI network from the province. The Anbar Awakening restored a degree of order to a region that appeared on the verge of slipping irrevocably under insurgent control. It is credited as being a major factor in the diminution of violence in Iraq, which began in earnest in 2007.

That the Sunni tribes of Anbar would serve as the catalyst for such a transformative development was a carefully planned movement, based on the sentiments expressed by U.S. ambassador Zalmay Khalilzad and General David Petraeus as well as others that the Sunni population must be granted a stake in the outcome. However, the province's recent engagement in violent opposition to the U.S.-led coalition and differences with the new Iraqi government were obstacles to be surmounted. Anbar, the largest of Iraq's 18 provinces with its predominantly Sunni population, became a hotspot of insurgent activity following the fall of Baghdad in 2003. Disaffected sheikhs and their tribal followers gravitated to the insurgency, driven by anger at seeing their lands occupied by foreign soldiers, resentment over the loss of jobs and prestige, and distrust of the new Shiite-dominated political order, among other things. The porous border that Anbar shared with Syria at the far western end of the province also provided an easy point of entry for fighters from other nations, who filtered into Fallujah, Ramadi, and the smaller population centers along the upper Euphrates River. Many joined the organization founded by Jordanian extremist Abu Musab al-Zarqawi, which evolved into the AQI.

Tribal insurgents had formed an alliance of convenience with AQI jihadists in Anbar, and the AQI itself was actually an overwhelmingly Iraqi, not foreign, organization. By the middle of 2006, the insurgency had grown so strong that Anbar outpaced even Baghdad in terms of the number of violent incidents, with 30–40 attacks occurring daily in the province. Conditions in Ramadi were particularly grim: public services were negligible, and the Iraqi security presence was almost nonexistent, enabling insurgent fighters to operate freely in most sections of the city. A classified assessment completed by the U.S. Marine Corps in August 2006 concluded that the province was all but lost to the insurgency.

Yet the AQI laid the groundwork for its own demise by demanding control of the insurgency and reducing Anbar's tribal chiefs to subordinate status. AQI operatives punished in brutal fashion any who opposed them, with bombings and murders that targeted not only the sheikhs but also their family members and supporters. The vicious tactics used by the AQI to cow the tribes also alienated them and opened up a rift within the insurgency. In what in retrospect can be seen as a precursor to the Anbar Awakening movement, several tribes around Ramadi in January 2006 formed the al-Anbar People's Council, a breakaway group that sought to distance itself from the AQI while continuing to resist the coalition. The council soon collapsed after seven of its members were assassinated and a suicide bomber killed dozens at a police recruiting event.

The demise of the al-Anbar People's Council demonstrated that the Ramadi tribes lacked the strength and cohesion to stand up against the AQI on their own. A few months later, the sheikhs gained a powerful new benefactor when Colonel Sean MacFarland arrived with the U.S. Army's 1st Brigade Combat Team to take charge of Ramadi's security. MacFarland and his brigade had deployed first in January 2006 to Tal Afar, the city in northern Iraq that had been pacified the previous year by Colonel H. R. McMaster in what was widely hailed as a textbook counterinsurgency operation. Moving to Ramadi in June 2006,

MacFarland was determined to apply some of the same counterinsurgency practices that had proven so effective at Tal Afar.

As one of the first steps in his plan to win back the city, MacFarland launched an outreach program aimed at gaining the trust and support of Ramadi's leaders. Among the earliest to respond was a charismatic young sheikh of relatively junior stature named Abd al-Sattar Buzaigh al-Rishawi. His record was far from clean, however. He was reputed to be a smuggler and highway bandit who had cooperated with the AQI in the past. More recently, he had lost his father and three brothers to the AQI's campaign of terror against the tribes, so he was receptive to American overtures. With Sattar's help in gathering recruits, MacFarland was able to begin the process of rebuilding Ramadi's embattled police force, which numbered only about 400 officers at the beginning of his tour. The sheikh also assisted with MacFarland's efforts to persuade other tribal leaders to shift their allegiance from the AQI to the coalition.

Sattar expanded his opposition to the AQI into a full-fledged movement after AQI agents bombed one of the new Iraqi police stations that had been set up in the city and murdered the sheikh whose tribesmen were staffing the post. In response, Sattar convened a meeting of over 50 sheikhs and MacFarland at his home on September 9, 2006. At the gathering Sattar announced the launching of the Anbar Awakening, an alliance of tribes dedicated to expelling the AQI from the region. Initially, only a handful of tribes signed on to the movement. However, over the next few months the movement acquired new converts in and around Ramadi once those related to Sattar saw that MacFarland was committed to using his troops to protect the tribes that rejected the AQI. The American commander also supported the tribes' efforts to defend themselves through the organization of armed tribal auxiliary groups, later known as Concerned Local Citizens or Sons of Iraq. MacFarland arranged for militia members to receive training and ensured that as many as possible were incorporated into the Iraqi police force. By the end of 2006, some 4,000 recruits had been added to police ranks.

The AQI did not allow itself to be swept aside by the Anbar Awakening movement without a fight. Violence levels in Anbar peaked in October 2006 and remained high through March 2007. But the movement acquired its own momentum, spreading from Ramadi and gaining adherents in Fallujah and other parts of the province throughout 2007. Insurgent activity dropped sharply after March, a trend that reflected not only the diminishing strength of the AQI but also the fact that once sheikhs joined the Anbar Awakening, they directed their followers to cease all attacks on American troops. Sattar himself was killed in a bombing outside his Ramadi home on September 13, 2007, a mere 10 days after he had met with President George W. Bush at a military base in Anbar. Nonetheless, Sattar's death did not reverse or slow the progress that had been made in the province, nor did it diminish local support for the Awakening Councils and their militia offshoots, which had sprouted up in Sunni areas outside of Anbar.

On September 1, 2008, Anbar completed its own remarkable turnaround from the most volatile region in Iraq to a more stable environment, and security for the province was officially transferred to the Iraqi government.

Growing tensions between the Awakening Councils and the government over late pay and a lack of jobs led in March 2009 to an uprising in the Sunni-dominated Fahdil section of Baghdad and the disarmament by Iraqi and U.S. troops of the Awakening Council there. The government retained a number of members of the Fahdi Council but subsequently announced that the 150 members of the council would be offered jobs in the Iraqi security forces.

Unfortunately, after the withdrawal of U.S. and coalition troops from Iraq in 2011, Anbar Province was convulsed by a renewal of sectarian and insurgent violence. By early 2014 Islamist groups, including AQI, had seized control of both Fallujah and Ramadi, and by the spring of that year the Iraqi government no longer controlled Anbar Province. By late 2014 the Islamic State of Iraq and Syria (ISIS) controlled Anbar, and the U.S. government began carrying out air strikes there in an attempt to assist the Iraqi government. With Anbar virtually lost, the future of Iraq remained very much in question. Only in late 2015 did the Iraqi government, with substantial military assistance from Iran, the United States, and other allies, begin major offensive operations to retake the province. Ramadi was secured in February 2016, and Fallujah was retaken in June. By early 2018, Anbar was firmly under Iraqi control.

Jeff Seiken

See also
Al Qaeda in Iraq; Fallujah, Third Battle of; Iraq; Iraq Insurgency; Islamic State of Iraq and Syria; Ramadi, Fall of; Ramadi, Recapture of

References
Lubin, Andrew. "Ramadi: From the Caliphate to Capitalism." *Proceedings* 134 (April 2008): 54–61.
McCary, John A. "The Anbar Awakening: An Alliance of Incentives." *Washington Quarterly* 32 (January 2009): 43–59.

Smith, Major Niel, and Colonel Sean MacFarland. "Anbar Awakens: The Tipping Point." *Military Review* (March–April 2008): 41–52.

West, Bing. *The Strongest Tribe: War, Politics, and the Endgame in Iraq.* New York: Random House, 2008.

Anglo-American Committee of Inquiry (1946)

Committee composed of American and British delegates that recommended the creation of a single Arab-Jewish state under the trusteeship of the United Nations (UN) and the admission of 100,000 Jewish refugees to Palestine.

The conclusion of World War II presented new difficulties for Great Britain in the Middle East. The stabilizing influence by Britain, long considered the dominant colonial power in the Arab world, in the region rapidly dissipated with the depletion of its economic resources from the war. Compounding the problem was the fierce nationalistic sentiment of its former wards. Both Egypt and Iraq were far less receptive to their prewar alliances. Transjordan soon became independent, fueling the debate among Arabs in Palestine regarding their own freedom. Britain's divergent past promises to both Zionists and Arabs quickly came unraveled when the U.S. government called for displaced Jews to live in Palestine. The Arabs outnumbered the Jews about two to one in Palestine and relied on Britain to honor its established immigration quotas.

U.S. president Harry S. Truman was sympathetic toward the Jews in light of their terrible losses in the Holocaust. But politics may have played a larger role than Truman's humanitarianism. Apart from the fact that the United States wanted to secure Middle Eastern oil for the West as well as bases in the Middle East to check Soviet expansionism, Truman was very much concerned about securing the Jewish American vote, particularly in New York, for the forthcoming presidential election of 1948. The front-runner for the Republican nomination and the eventual nominee was New York governor Thomas E. Dewey. Toward that end, Truman began urging British prime minister Winston Churchill and his successor Clement Attlee to admit as many Jews to Palestine as possible.

Arabs living in the region were determined to keep the Jewish refugees out. Truman had notified the British that he had no intention of using American military forces to suppress any violence that might result from unrestricted immigration. Knowing that U.S. assistance would be minimal and understanding the volatility of the situation, in a speech to the House of Commons on October 26, 1945, and in remarks in a letter to Truman on November 13, Attlee proposed the creation of a joint Anglo-American committee to investigate the immigration matter. The committee was actually a British attempt to deflect American pressure to admit refugees into Palestine. Truman accepted the idea of a joint committee but with the qualification that immigration into Palestine alone be the focus of the inquiry. The British grudgingly agreed.

The Anglo-American Committee of Inquiry first met in Washington and then heard from both Jewish and Arab representatives in New York. Neither side was willing to compromise. The Arabs claimed that U.S. interest in Jewish immigration to Palestine was driven solely by politics, while Jews savagely attacked British immigration policies almost to the point of making the British government appear to have been responsible for the Holocaust. The committee moved on to London in January 1946. There it heard dire predictions from representatives of the British Colonial and Foreign Offices of a bloodbath in Palestine should large numbers of Jewish immigrants be admitted there.

After a stay in London and a trip to Vienna, in February 1946 committee members visited several displaced persons camps in Europe. No doubt this had a powerful influence. Commission member and Labour Party member of Parliament Richard Crossman later wrote that the visits to the camps made arguments about Zionism abstract and that a Jewish state seemed "curiously remote after this experience of human degradation."

The committee also traveled to Cairo and Jerusalem and then proceeded to Lausanne, Switzerland, where it drafted its recommendations. On May 1, 1946, the committee issued a unanimous report of fewer than 100 pages. The report called for the admission of 100,000 Jewish refugees and the creation of a single Arab-Jewish state under the trusteeship of the UN. To maximize the possibility for the success of its recommendations, the commission rejected partition for Palestine. Despite the committee's conclusion that there was little or no evidence of cooperation between Jews and Arabs and its failure to make any recommendations as to how this might be achieved, it recommended that Jews and Arabs continue to live in a single state in which neither would dominate the other.

The commission did express concerns. Among these was the belief, later proven false, that Palestine could not support a much larger population. This was based on the belief that the amount of water in the area could not be increased by pumping water from the Jordan River. The commission also noted the economic imbalance between Arabs and Jews. Although during the years of the British mandate there had been an unprecedented growth in the size and prosperity of the Arab population in Palestine, generally speaking economic conditions for the Arabs were inferior to those for the Jews.

Extremists on both sides rejected the commission's recommendations, and subsequent attempts by the UN at partition failed. On May 14, 1947, Israel declared its independence, and that same day Arab forces invaded, beginning the Israeli War of Independence (May 14, 1948–January 7, 1949).

CHARLES FRANCIS HOWLETT AND SPENCER C. TUCKER

See also
Israeli War of Independence; Palestine, British Mandate for; United Nations Special Commission on Palestine

References
Donovan, Robert J. *Conflict and Crisis: The Presidency of Harry S. Truman, 1945–1948.* New York: Norton, 1977.
Goodwin, Geoffrey L. *Britain and the United Nations.* London: Oxford University Press, 1957.
Hurewitz, J. C. *The Struggle for Palestine.* New York: Schocken, 1976.
Manuel, Frank E. *The Realities of American-Palestine Relations.* Washington, DC: PublicAffairs, 1949.
Ryan, Stephen. *The United Nations and International Politics.* New York: St. Martin's, 2000.
Sachar, Howard M. *A History of Israel: From the Rise of Zionism to Our Time.* 3rd ed. New York: Knopf, 2007.
Safran, Nadav. *The United States and Israel.* Cambridge, MA: Harvard University Press, 1963.

Anglo-Egyptian Treaty (August 26, 1936)

Treaty signed in London that spelled out the relationship between Britain and Egypt. Driven by strategic and economic interests in the Suez Canal as well as economic interests in cotton production, the British secured control of Egypt in 1882. The British government had promised to withdraw "once order had been restored" but remained in Egypt. In December 1914 after the Ottoman Empire had entered World War I on the side of the Central Powers, Britain declared Egypt a protectorate.

In response to anti-British riots following the war, the British in February 1922 ended the protectorate and declared Egypt to be a sovereign, independent kingdom. This was mere window dressing, however, for Britain continued to dominate Egyptian affairs through its advisers, who controlled the key organs of state, including internal security.

Nonetheless, the threat posed to the security of the region by Italy's invasion of Ethiopia in September 1935 led to negotiations between London and Cairo and a treaty between the two nations, signed in London on August 26, 1936.

According to this treaty, Britain and Egypt entered into an alliance whereby Britain pledged to defend Egypt against outside aggression and Egypt promised to place its facilities at Britain's disposal in case of war. Recognizing the vital importance of the Suez Canal to Britain, Egypt allowed Britain to garrison 10,000 troops and 400 pilots in the Canal Zone and to provide for their barracks at Egyptian expense. In return, Britain would evacuate all other Egyptian bases except the naval base at Alexandria, which it would be allowed to maintain for eight more years.

All British personnel in the Egyptian Army and police force were to be withdrawn, but a British military mission would remain to advise the Egyptian Army to the exclusion of any other foreigners. Also, Egyptian officers were to train abroad only in Britain. Egypt had the full right to expand the size of its armed forces.

On the thorny matter of the Sudan, Britain promised to allow unrestricted immigration of Egyptians into the Sudan. Egyptian troops were also allowed to return there. Britain agreed to work for the removal of the capitulations and for the admission of Egypt to the League of Nations. The British high commissioner would be replaced by an ambassador. The treaty was to be of indefinite duration, but negotiations for any changes would be permitted after a 20-year period.

In effect, Britain retained its right to protect security through the canal and compromised on a number of other issues, including that of the protection of British citizens and foreigners. Left unresolved was the question of the future status of the Sudan. Despite some criticism of it, the Egyptian parliament ratified the treaty on December 11, 1936. Although many Egyptians thought of this treaty as marking their independence because the action of 1922 had been a unilateral one by Britain alone, in fact the British continued to exercise considerable control over the Egyptian government.

In May 1937 the powers that had enjoyed capitulatory privileges in Egypt agreed to renounce these treaties, with the proviso that the mixed courts in Cairo and Alexandria were to remain in effect for another 12 years. That same month, Egypt was officially admitted to the League of Nations.

Relations with Britain dominated post–World War II Egyptian foreign policy, with Cairo determined to revise the 1936 treaty. The chief points of grievance for the Egyptians were the continued presence of British troops in the country; the matter of the future of the Sudan, which Egypt sought to regain; and the sovereignty of the Egyptian government. Egyptian leaders were determined that all British troops be withdrawn from Egyptian territory.

In October 1946, Egyptian prime minister Sidqi Pasha concluded an agreement with British foreign secretary Ernest Bevin providing for the withdrawal of British forces from the Canal Zone and for a formula regarding the Sudan. The Sudanese would themselves determine their own future government and decide whether they would be independent or part of Egypt. In the winter of 1950–1951, there were further talks over modification of the 1936 treaty. The arrival of the Cold War produced British intransigence on the matter of treaty revision, however, for the West came to regard Egypt as the most suitable military base in the Middle East.

Following the Egyptian Revolution of July 1952, however, on October 19, 1954, Egyptian strongman Gamal Abdel Nasser concluded a new treaty with Britain whereby the British gave up all rights to the Suez Canal base and agreed to evacuate the Canal Zone entirely within 20 months. In return, Egypt promised to keep the base in combat readiness and allow the British to return in case of an attack by an outside power against Turkey or any Arab state. The British right of defense of the canal under the treaty was, of course, London's justification for its attempt to intervene militarily in Egypt following Nasser's nationalization of the Suez Canal and the Israeli invasion of the Sinai (mounted with British collusion) during the 1956 Suez Crisis.

SPENCER C. TUCKER

See also
Egypt; Nasser, Gamal Abdel; Pan-Arabism and Pan-Arabist Thought; Suez Canal; Suez Crisis

References
Dawisha, A. I. *Egypt in the Arab World*. New York: Wiley, 1976.
Gorst, Anthony, and Lewis Johnman. *The Suez Crisis*. London: Routledge, 1997.
Jankowski, James P. *Nasser's Egypt, Arab Nationalism, and the United Arab Republic*. Boulder, CO: Lynne Rienner, 2001.
Waterbury, John. *The Egypt of Nasser and Sadat: Political Economy of Two Regimes*. Princeton, NJ: Princeton University Press, 1983.

Anglo-Egyptian War (1882)

In 1798 during the wars of the French Revolution, a French army landed in Egypt, defeated the Egyptian Army, and established French control of Egypt that lasted until 1801. After the French withdrawal, the Ottoman Empire reclaimed its authority in the region, and in 1805 Muhammad Ali (Mehmed Ali) became a governor of Egypt. He sought to modernize Egypt by adopting Western technology and military techniques. Ultimately he created a large state that included Egypt, Sudan, and western Arabia; in the late 1830s, the Egyptian Army defeated the Ottoman forces and seized control of Syria and Palestine as well.

After Muhammad Ali's death in 1849, his successors struggled to maintain Egyptian predominance in the region. The American Civil War (1861–1865) caused a cotton shortage in Europe but also resulted in a windfall for Egypt, where cotton cultivation rapidly expanded and attracted European capital. Borrowing for investment and their own lavish spending, the Egyptian rulers soon incurred heavy debts that further increased with the Union victory in the American Civil War and an end to the Egyptian cotton boom market. The construction of the Suez Canal, which was completed in 1869, vastly increased the strategic value of Egypt to European powers, particularly Britain, which sought to protect this shorter passage to India.

Khedive Ismail, a grandson of Muhammad Ali who came to power in 1863, became saddled with growing debts to European banks that led him to selling to the British government Egypt's shares in the Suez Canal Company. He was also forced to accept an Anglo-French debt commission to control Egyptian finances. The growing Western influence in Egyptian affairs led by 1880 to a strong nationalist movement. In February 1881 Egyptian colonel Ahmet Arabi (Urabi) led a revolt under the slogan "Egypt for the Egyptians." Arabi subsequently became minister of war and the key figure in the new government.

Their position in Egypt threatened, the British and French governments then planned a joint military intervention. Both nations dispatched powerful naval squadrons to Alexandria in May, but a change of government in France led to the belated decision in Paris not to participate. London then proceeded alone. The goal was to overthrow the revolutionaries and restore the nominal authority of Khedive Tewfik (Tawfiq).

On June 11, antiforeign riots in Alexandria resulted in the deaths of 68 Europeans. Anticipating a reaction, Arabi strengthened the defenses of Alexandria. British admiral Sir Frederick Beauchamp Paget Seymour now assembled a squadron of warships, including Austrian and Ottoman ships, off Alexandria. When Arabi rejected demands to halt efforts to strengthen Alexandria's defenses, on July 11 Seymour ordered a bombardment of Alexandria. Lasting more than 10 hours, it ended with much of the city burning and destroyed. Marines and seamen then came ashore and secured control of Alexandria.

The British then assembled an expeditionary force of 24,000 men at Malta and Cyprus and 7,000 Indian Army troops at Aden. Lieutenant General Garnet Wolseley had overall command. Wolseley landed at Ismailia at the mouth of the Suez Canal on August 20 and then advanced on Cairo. On September 13, the British forces defeated the Egyptians under Arabi, drawn up in a defensive position along the Tel el-Kebir ridge line.

British cavalry entered Cairo two days later. Arabi surrendered, and the revolt quickly ended. Arabi was subsequently tried and condemned to death but was spared and exiled to Ceylon. Although British prime minister William Gladstone's government formally notified other powers that British forces would be withdrawn "as soon as the state of the country, and the organization of the proper means for the maintenance of the Khedive's authority, will admit of it," British troops remained in Egypt. The real ruler of the country for the next 23 years was the British consul general and high commissioner Evelyn Baring, Lord Cromer. British imperialists now considered the Nile Valley part of the British Empire. The last British troops did not leave Egypt until June 1956.

Spencer C. Tucker and Robert B. Kane

See also
Alexandria, Bombardment of; Egypt; Tel el-Kebir, Battle of

References
Farwell, Byron. *Queen Victoria's Little Wars.* New York: Norton, 1972.
Featherstone, Donald. *Tel el Kebir 1882: Wolseley's Conquest of Egypt.* London: Osprey, 1993.
Hopkins, A. G. "The Victorians and Africa: A Reconsideration of the Occupation of Egypt, 1882." *Journal of African History* 27 (2) (July 1986): 363–391.
Pakenham, Edward. *The Scramble for Africa, 1876–1912.* New York: Random House, 1991.
Robinson, Ronald, and John Gallagher. *Africa and the Victorians: The Official Mind of Imperialism.* London: Macmillan, 1961.

Anglo-Iranian Oil Crisis (1951–1953)

The Anglo-Iranian oil crisis began on April 26, 1951, when Iran's new nationalist leader, Mohammad Mossadegh, moved to nationalize his nation's oil reserves. Mossadegh's nationalization measures came largely at the expense of the British-controlled Anglo-Iranian Oil Company, which had been exploiting Iranian oil reserves for years. The crisis highlighted the differing communist containment policies carried out by the British Foreign Office and the U.S. State Department in the Middle East. It can also be viewed as an early attempt by a developing nation to break free from Western imperialism and colonial control. The fact that the crisis involved oil also showcases just how critical cheap and abundant oil supplies were to the West.

During 1951–1953 there was an ongoing diplomatic crisis among Iran, the United Kingdom, and the United States over Mossadegh's actions. Beginning in November 1951, Mossadegh requested that Western nations that had purchased Iranian oil in the past confirm their current orders with the newly nationalized Iranian oil industry. The British took immediate action by pressuring purchasing nations not to cooperate with Mossadegh's request.

At first the United States took a rather neutral stance in the crisis, siding completely with neither London nor Tehran. The Americans' chief concern was keeping Iranian oil out of Soviet control rather than saving the Anglo-Iranian Oil Company. U.S. secretary of state Dean Acheson urged Britain to accept Iran's nationalization and instead aim at maintaining control over the technical aspects of oil production. Throughout much of 1951, the United States regarded Iran's continued alliance with the West as a priority over British economic interests.

President Harry Truman sought to broker a settlement between Tehran and London based on the acceptance of Iranian nationalization in return for British control over oil production and drilling. At the same time, British officials were divided over whether launching a war against Iran was a viable option to ending the standoff. The British Foreign Office seemed willing to entertain the idea of military force, while British prime minister Clement Attlee steadfastly opposed it.

Nevertheless, the British government refused to negotiate with the Iranians and instead opted to impose economic sanctions on Mossadegh's regime. On September 10, 1951, Britain took measures to prevent purchases of Iranian oil on the international market.

Meanwhile, the United States and Britain were moving closer together on ending the crisis. Throughout the autumn of 1951, the Truman administration became less neutral. As time went on, the U.S. State Department trusted Mossadegh less and less. From January 1952 on, the United States became increasingly concerned about Iran's internal economic stability. Washington maintained that Mossadegh was now increasingly likely to turn to Moscow to stabilize Iran's economy. By the spring of 1952, these concerns led the Americans to view regime change as a viable path to ending the crisis. Between the end of 1951 and July 1952, the Americans hoped that this would happen as a result of the

Demonstrators in Tehran, Iran, most of them students, confronting police and troops during a 1951 protest rally against British government policies during the Anglo-Iranian oil crisis. (Library of Congress)

dispute between Shah Mohammad Reza Pahlavi of Iran and Mossadegh over which of the two would control the Persian Army. In the fall of 1952, Tehran broke diplomatic relations with London.

In January 1953, Dwight D. Eisenhower became president of the United States. The failure of diplomacy coupled with the Eisenhower administration's eagerness to end the crisis opened the door for the coup d'état of August 1953. The Eisenhower administration supported regime change in Iran in a coup organized by the U.S. Central Intelligence Agency (CIA). U.S. policy makers were particularly alarmed at the possibility that Mossadegh would bring the communists to power in Iran. Supported by the British government as well and carried out on August 19 of that year, the coup returned Shah Pahlavi to power. The British and U.S. governments then established an Anglo-American oil consortium on April 12, 1954.

SIMONE SELVA

See also
Iran; Reza Shah Pahlavi

References
Bamberg, James. *British Petroleum and Global Oil, 1950–75: The Challenge to Nationalism.* Cambridge: Cambridge University Press, 2000.
Heiss, Mary Ann. *Empire and Nationhood: The United States, Great Britain, and Iranian Oil, 1950–54.* New York: Columbia University Press, 1997.
Marsh, Steve. *Anglo-American Relations and Cold War Oil.* London: Palgrave MacMillan, 2003.

Anglo-Iraqi Treaties of 1922 and 1930

Signed at Baghdad on June 30, 1930, the treaty between Great Britain and Iraq went into force on November 16, 1930. A redrafting on the Anglo-Iraqi Treaty of 1922, the 1930 treaty gave the British exclusive commercial and military rights in

Iraq once that nation became independent in 1932. Neither agreement offered the Iraqis anything in return, and both engendered much antipathy in Iraq. The 1922 treaty was the result of the newly created British League of Nations mandate that encompassed modern-day Iraq and political unrest among various Iraqi factions. Angered that Iraq was not to become independent but rather a British-administered mandate after World War I, a coalition of Shia and Sunni Muslims precipitated a major revolt in 1920 against British occupation forces. The Kurds in northern Iraq also revolted against the British presence, hoping to form their own nation.

In 1921 Iraqi and British leaders convened in Cairo in an attempt to bring the Iraqi revolt to an end. The leaders agreed to allow Iraq more (but still limited) autonomy under a newly installed Hashemite king, Faisal Ibn Hussein. The arrangement was a clear compromise that was to allow for continued British influence in Iraq while appeasing—to a limited extent—the Iraqi nationalists who had fomented the 1920 uprising. The agreement resulted in the 1922 Anglo-Iraqi Treaty. Signed by the British on October 10 of that year, it was not ratified by the Iraqi assembly until 1924. Iraqi nationalists were displeased by the lack of specificity regarding independence as well as continuing British influence in Iraqi affairs. Nevertheless, after British authorities threatened to circumvent the new Iraqi constitution and rule by decree, the Iraqis reluctantly acceded to the agreement.

Between 1924 and 1930 the situation in Iraq stabilized, with King Faisal I ruling so as to keep the British contented and the nationalists from fomenting revolt. Beginning in 1927, British-owned oil companies discovered massive petroleum reserves in Iraq, which made the nation all the more important to London. Because of this and the impending end of the British mandate in 1932, London sought a new treaty with the Iraqis that would secure continued British control of Iraqi oil production as well as keep out potential adversaries there (Germany and the Soviet Union in particular).

In a sop to Iraqi nationalists, the 1930 Anglo-Iraqi Treaty mapped a path toward independence after 1932. However, London clearly held most of the cards during the negotiations and insisted that Britain be granted wide-reaching commercial rights, including ownership of Iraqi oil fields. Equally important, the treaty gave London extensive military rights in Iraq, allowing it to garrison troops there an/or use it as a base for future military operations. Iraqi nationalists were incensed by the treaty, which appeared to offer the Iraqis nothing in return for the commercial and military concessions.

The 1930 treaty was invoked by the British in 1941, when they moved troops into Iraq and occupied it during much of World War II. This move had been necessitated by an Iraqi coup that saw its leaders attempt to ally Iraq with the Axis powers. The British did not vacate Iraq until 1947. At that point, London attempted to foist another agreement on the Iraqis that would have given it even more influence in Iraqi affairs, but the Iraqis refused, and nothing came of it.

The Anglo-Iraqi Treaties of 1922 and 1930 clearly sowed the seeds of great nationalist resentment in Iraq and helped set the stage for the political instability there that endures to the present.

PAUL G. PIERPAOLI JR.

See also
Iraq; Mandates, League of Nations

References
Abdullah, Thabit. *A Short History of Iraq*. London: Pearson, 2003.
Dodge, Toby. *Inventing Iraq*. New York: Columbia University Press, 2003.
Polk, William R. *Understanding Iraq*. New York: Harper Perennial, 2005.

Anglo-Jordanian Defense Treaty (March 15, 1948)

Mutual defense agreement between the British and Jordanian governments signed on March 15, 1948. The 20-year accord bound each country to come to the other's aid if attacked, permitted British air bases on Jordanian soil, provided British military officers for Jordan's Arab Legion, and granted Jordan a £10 million annual subsidy.

Although independent from British mandatory rule in 1946, Jordan remained a functional British colony. The defense treaty, which built on the 1923, 1928, and 1946 Anglo-Transjordanian Agreements, fully codified Jordan's military and financial dependence on Great Britain.

Most importantly, John Bagot Glubb (Glubb Pasha), an Arabic-speaking British officer, commanded the Arab Legion, which protected British interests by defending the Hashemite monarchy from external and internal threats. The annual subsidy was paid directly to Glubb, while British officers held all Arab Legion command positions and made all decisions regarding financing, training, equipping, and expanding the Jordanian military.

In spite of the treaty, Britain remained aloof during the Israeli War of Independence (1948–1949). However, the British did support the Jordanian annexation of the West

Bank in 1950. This move doubled Jordan's population, but the predominantly Palestinian newcomers upset the kingdom's delicate ethnic balance. From 1952 to 1956, Israeli attacks on the West Bank, mounted in retaliation for infiltration and fedayeen raids, did not activate the treaty, and Britain turned down numerous Jordanian requests for offensive military assistance.

Jordan became more strategically vital to Britain following the withdrawal of the latter's troops from Egypt in 1954. The success of Egyptian president Gamal Abdel Nasser in negotiating this withdrawal prompted King Hussein of Jordan to seek a similar agreement. This desire became embroiled in 1955 negotiations urging Jordan to join the regional defense alliance of the Baghdad Pact. Accession to the pact contained the promise of revising the increasingly unpopular defense treaty.

In January 1956, however, the Jordanian parliament publicly declared its opposition to the kingdom joining the Baghdad Pact. Pressure from Egypt, Saudi Arabia, and Syria along with Palestinian and nationalist domestic opinion instead provoked calls to repeal the Anglo-Jordanian treaty and remove British officers and influence. Egyptian propaganda reminded the Jordanian people of the loss of much of Palestine, the Arab Legion's weak response to Israeli retaliatory attacks, and Britain's behind-the-scenes control of Jordan.

To protect his position, Hussein dismissed Glubb and 11 other British officers on March 1, 1956. The Jordanian Army then began a process of Arabization. On October 25, 1956, Jordan allied itself with Egypt and Syria.

March 1957 brought Jordan's official abrogation of the Anglo-Jordanian Defense Treaty. The British evacuated their forces, Jordan officially purchased their bases, and the Egyptians and Saudis replaced the annual subsidy. Following the 1958 coup in Iraq, British soldiers temporarily returned to Jordan at the king's request, but the other Arab countries and the United States soon superseded Britain as Jordan's benefactors.

Andrew Theobald

See also
Arab Legion; Baghdad Pact; Fedayeen; Glubb, Sir John Bagot; Israeli War of Independence

References
Faddah, Mohammed Ibrahim. *The Middle East in Transition: A Study of Jordan's Foreign Policy*. London: Asia Publishing House, 1974.
Glubb, John Bagot. *A Soldier with the Arabs*. New York: Harper and Brothers, 1959.
Oren, Michael B. "A Winter of Discontent: Britain's Crisis in Jordan, December 1955-March 1956." *International Journal of Middle East Studies* 22, no. 2 (1990): 171–184.

Satloff, Robert B. *From Abdullah to Hussein: Jordan in Transition*. New York: Oxford University Press, 1993.

Anglo-Ottoman Treaty (1838)

The Anglo-Ottoman Treaty (also known as the Balta Liman Treaty) of 1838 was a major trade agreement. Myriad attempts by the European Great Powers to expand their influence and especially trade into the Ottoman Empire in the early 19th century led to various treaties imposing European hegemony in the region. Known collectively as the Capitulations, these treaties forced the Ottoman Empire to agree to European commercial demands at the expense of its own sovereignty. A weakened Ottoman Empire, already fraught with regional unrest, particularly in Egypt, was forced to comply with British commercial demands.

The Anglo-Ottoman Treaty of 1838 expanded British merchant rights within Ottoman territories. These included the right of travel and free trade. It also provided for direct relations with producers of goods and the right to have commercial disputes resolved by tribunals and not Islamic law or courts. By allowing British merchants direct access to producers, the treaty did not allow establishment of Ottoman state monopolies regarding particular products and manufactures, which eliminated potential sources of revenue for the Ottoman government. Moreover, the provision regarding the courts ensured extraterritorial privileges for British merchants. The treaty also compelled the Ottoman state to enforce higher duties on exports, which benefited British imports while not allowing the Ottomans to compete effectively in the international economy.

Mehmet Ali, ruling in Egypt, had sought independence for Egypt from the Ottoman Empire. His forces defeated the Ottomans in Syria in 1838. However, the Great Powers, primarily the British, forced an Egyptian withdrawal in 1841. British pressure forced Egypt to comply with the terms of the Anglo-Ottoman Treaty as well.

Abraham O. Mendoza

See also
Egyptian-Ottoman Wars; Russo-Ottoman Wars

References
Fattah, Hala Mundhir. *The Politics of Regional Trade in Iraq, Arabia, and the Gulf, 1745–1900*. Albany, NY: SUNY Press, 1997.
Fromkin, David. *A Peace to End All Peace: The Fall of the Ottoman Empire and the Creation of the Modern Middle East*. New York: Holt, 1989.

Anglo-Ottoman War (1807–1809)

In the War of the Fourth Coalition (1806–1807) during the Napoleonic Wars, the British government as early as November 1806 grew concerned that Ottoman naval assets would be added to those of France. Britain was then allied with Russia against France. Royal Navy Mediterranean commander Vice Admiral Cuthbert Collingwood, alarmed by reports from Istanbul (Constantinople), had in November 1806 detached a squadron of five ships (three of the line) under Rear Admiral Sir Thomas Louis from his own forces monitoring Cádiz to reconnoiter the Dardanelles in case it should be necessary to force those straits and proceed to Istanbul. Louis flew his flag in the 80-gun ship of the line *Canopus*. Leaving the bulk of his squadron in the Dardanelles, Louis proceed to Istanbul, where he joined the frigate *Endymion*, which had brought out British ambassador Charles Arbuthnot.

Meanwhile, Russian forces had invaded Ottoman Moldavia. This development ended Ottoman negotiations with Russia, and French ambassador to the Sublime Porte General Horace-François Sébastiani was able to convince Sultan Selim III to declare war on Russia on December 27, 1806. The French promised to help the sultan put down a rebellion in Serbia and recover Ottoman territory lost to the Russians. With the declaration of war, the British warships at Istanbul hastily evacuated the British commercial colony there, fearful that they would become hostages.

As early as November 22, 1806, the British government had been sufficiently alarmed about developments in Istanbul to order Collingwood to detach a large squadron and send it to the Dardanelles, with Vice Admiral Sir John Duckworth in command. Collingwood did not receive the orders until mid-January 1807, however. He instructed Duckworth to proceed to Istanbul and there consult with Ambassador Arbuthnot to demand surrender of the Ottoman fleet, along with sufficient naval stores to maintain it. Should negotiations fail, Duckworth was empowered to bombard Istanbul and capture or destroy the Ottoman fleet. Collingwood also sent a message to Vice Admiral Dimitri Seniavin, then commanding a Russian squadron in the eastern Mediterranean, asking that he detach four ships to join Duckworth.

Duckworth flew his flag in the 100-gun ship of the line *Royal George*. He sailed from Gibraltar on January 17 and ultimately had at his disposal an entirely British squadron of 8 ships of the line, 2 frigates, and 2 bomb vessels. He arrived off the island of Tenedos at the mouth of the Dardanelles on February 10. Although named to a command that would call for "much ability and firmness," Duckworth

British vice admiral Cuthbert Collingwood commanded British naval forces in the Mediterranean during the Anglo-Ottoman War of 1807–1809, but his effort to sail to Istanbul and force the Ottoman government into submission proved a failure. (Georgios Art/iStockphoto.com)

wrote Collingwood that he had learned that the Ottomans had erected batteries in the Dardanelles that would flank the British ships and that he had serious reservations about the strength of his force and probable success of his mission.

Nonetheless, Duckworth weighed anchor on February 11 and proceeded into the Dardanelles, but on February 14 a fire broke out in the 74-gun ship of the line *Ajax*. The flames spread rapidly, and the ship blew up; only 381 of its crew of 633 survived. Although Duckworth's ships met in the Sea of Marmara and defeated and drove ashore an Ottoman squadron of one 64-gun ship and three frigates, four small corvettes, two brigs, and three gunboats with scant casualties and damage to his own ships, he also wasted valuable time, and his dilatory advance had given the Ottomans more time to strengthen their defenses. Duckworth's squadron passed through the Dardanelles only on February 17. With the British warships finally before Istanbul three days later, Ottoman sultan Selim III rejected the British ultimatum. The Ottomans had placed some 1,000 guns along the shore and opened fire on the British ships. Some of the Ottoman guns were quite large, firing shot weighing up to 800 pounds.

Duckworth's ships sustained considerable damage in the exchange of fire, and two were lost. Unable to accomplish his aims, he withdrew on March 3, with his ships sustaining further damaged in repassing the Dardanelles. Vice Admiral Dimitri Seniavin's Russian squadron, which had far more success against the Ottomans in the eastern Mediterranean, then joined him.

Duckworth rejected Seniavin's suggestion that they combine their squadrons and return to Istanbul, while a second Russian squadron blockaded that city from the northern end of the Bosporus. The British expedition against Istanbul was thus a total failure.

The British had more success elsewhere. Seeking to support Duckworth's squadron operating against Istanbul by opening another front against the Ottomans, London dispatched an expedition to Egypt, where Muhammad Ali had in 1805 established himself as ruler under Ottoman suzerainty. On March 3, 1807, the British departed Messina, Sicily, with a naval squadron escorting 33 transports lifting 5,000 troops under Major General A. Mackenzie Fraser to Alexandria. The troops came ashore two weeks later.

On March 20 the British secured Aboukir Castle, and the next day Alexandria surrendered. Duckworth appeared with part of his squadron on March 22, and Fraser then decided to attack Rosetta but was repulsed there on April 20 with 400 casualties. By September, the British position had deteriorated to the point that they concluded a convention allowing them to evacuate Egypt on September 14.

Having secured little support from France in its war against Russia, however, on January 5, 1809, the Ottoman government concluded at Çanak the Treaty of the Dardanelles with Britain. The Ottomans restored the extensive British commercial and legal privileges in the empire, while Britain promised to protect the integrity of the Ottomans against France, both through supplies of weapons and with its own fleet. The treaty affirmed the principle that no warships of any power were to enter the Straits of the Dardanelles or the Bosporus. Thus, the treaty anticipated the London Straits Convention concluded in 1841, by which the major powers bound themselves to this same principle.

SPENCER C. TUCKER

See also
Ottoman Empire; Russo-Ottoman Wars

References
Clowes, William. *The Royal Navy: A History from the Earliest Times to 1900*, Vol. 5. London: Chatham, 1996.

Macksey, Piers. *The War in the Mediterranean, 1803–1810*. New York: Longmans, Green, 1957.

Anglo-Persian War (1856–1857)

A conflict fought between Great Britain and Persia over sphere of influence in Afghanistan. The immediate cause for the war was a Persian attempt to take control of Herat, which historically recognized the suzerainty of the Iranian shahs. As Herat was located on key military and trade routes, it was also the object of interest of British authorities in India in the context of the Great Game, the Anglo-Russian rivalry in Central Asia.

In light of the Russo-Persian wars of the early 19th century, British leaders believed that Persia could fall under Russian influence, and for this reason the British opposed Nasser al-Din Shah's attempt to take control of Herat. Britain declared war on Persia on November 1, 1856, and dispatched a naval force with a 10,000-man expeditionary force into the Persian Gulf. The British captured Kharg island on December 4, and on December 9 they came ashore and the following day occupied the port town of Bushire.

Learning of larger Persian forces at Shiraz, British expeditionary force commander Major General Foster Stalker remained at Bushire and requested reinforcements. A second division, led by Brigadier General Henry Havelock, landed in Persia in January 1857, and the entire expeditionary force came under the command of Major General James Outram. On February 7, 1857, the British defeated the Persians under Khanlar Mirza at Khushab (Khoosh-Ab) but did not pursue the enemy and instead retired back on Bushire.

Changing their direction of attack, the British then advanced up the Shatt al-Arab waterway to Mohammerah (Khorramshahr), not far from Basra, where they arrived by March 24. The Persian garrison withdrew without a fight, and after occupying Basra on March 27, the British advanced to Ahvaz, upstream on the Karun River, where Khanlar Mirza's forces were deployed. However, the Persians again withdrew, and the British occupied Ahvaz on April 1.

Just days later the British forces learned that a peace treaty had been signed between Persia and Britain in Paris on March 4. Persia was to withdraw from Herat, refrain from further interference in Afghan affairs, and cooperate in suppressing the slave trade in the Persian Gulf region. The British agreed not to shelter opponents of the shah in their embassy and received the right to appoint consuls at their discretion. The British expeditionary force soon left occupied Persian territory and returned to India, then in the midst of the Indian Rebellion of 1857.

ALEXANDER MIKABERIDZE

See also
Iran

References
Greaves, Rose. "Iranian Relations with Great Britain and British India, 1798–1821." In *The Cambridge History of Iran*, Vol. 6, *From Nadir Shah to the Islamic Republic*, ed. Peter Avery et al., 374–425. Cambridge: Cambridge University Press, 1991.

Hunt, Capt. G. H., and George Townsend. *Outram & Havelock's Persian Campaign*. London: G. Routledge, 1858.

Kelly, J. B. *Britain and the Persian Gulf, 1795–1880*. Oxford: Oxford University Press, 1968.

Anglo-Sudan War (1883–1899)

The Anglo-Sudan War (also known as the Mahdist War) saw Anglo-Egyptian forces invade and ultimately conquer the Sudan. As a consequence of the 1882 Anglo-Egyptian War, the British had established control of Egypt. This meant, however, that the British inherited Egypt's problems, one of which was Egypt's relationship with its southern neighbor, Sudan.

Egyptian leaders had long sought to establish their authority over this vast region along the Upper Nile. Sudanese opposition to this arose regarding prohibitions against the slave trade and heavy Egyptian taxes. A nationalist leader came to the fore in 1881 in Muhammad Ahmad ibn Abdullah, who claimed to be the Mahdi, the prophesied redeemer of Islam who would rule before the Day of Judgment. Soon the Mahdi had raised thousands of followers, known as Dervishes.

The Mahdi's forces besieged the Egyptian military base at El Obeid in the Sudan. In an effort to relieve El Obeid, British colonel William Hicks led a force of some 8,000 Egyptian troops, 1,000 cavalry, and some 2,000 camp followers. Hicks also had some artillery pieces and Maxim guns. Unaware that El Obeid had already fallen and its military stores had been secured by the Mahdi, the Egyptian force encountered the Mahdi and perhaps 40,000 Dervishes near El-Obeid on November 3, 1883, and was destroyed, suffering some 7,000 dead, including Hicks and other British officers.

The Mahdi's victory at El Obeid greatly strengthened the Sudanese revolt. Egyptian leaders begged the British for assistance, and at last Liberal Party leader and British prime minister William Gladstone moved. He decided that the Sudan must be evacuated, and to accomplish this he sent out British Army general Charles Gordon.

Gordon was the worst possible choice. In the 1860s he had commanded the imperial army in China that had helped put down the great Taiping Rebellion, from which he had earned the nickname "Chinese Gordon." He had also once been governor of the Sudan for the Egyptians. Eccentric and deeply religious, he had ended the slave trade in the Sudan. Gordon had a martyr fixation and thus was the wrong person to carry out a withdrawal. Arriving in Cairo, Gordon deliberately disobeyed his orders. He planned to defeat the Mahdi and become governor of the Sudan again. Gordon convinced the Egyptian administration of his plan and then traveled up the Nile to Khartoum, where he delayed and then came under siege by the Mahdi's forces.

Although the British press clamored for a rescue force to be dispatched, a furious Gladstone delayed for five months before ordering it. General Garnet Wolseley, who had charge of the relief expedition, spent excessive time in preparation, and his progress up the Nile was slow. The expedition arrived at Khartoum on January 28, 1885, but only two days before the Dervishes had overcome Khartoum's defenses and stormed the palace. They killed Gordon, then presented his severed head at the feet of the Mahdi. Wolseley withdrew, and the British and Egyptians completely evacuated the Sudan.

In 1896 French expansion from the west had begun to threaten the Sudan and with it the Lower Nile and British Egypt. Establishing British control over Sudan became essential to keeping the French at bay. Under orders from the Conservative government in London headed by Benjamin Disraeli, the British returned in force to the Sudan. General Sir Horatio Herbert Kitchener headed the attempt. He made careful preparations and then set out in June 1896, building a rail line southward as he proceeded.

On September 1, 1898, Kitchener and his well-armed force of 20,000 men arrived at Omdurman, across the Nile from Khartoum. Kitchener had river gunboats mounting 100 guns and a considerable supply train of camels and horses. The next morning at dawn, 50,000 Dervishes attacked the British along a four-mile-long line and were massacred. Kitchener employed his six Maxim guns to great effect and killed 10,000 Dervishes at a cost of only 28 dead on his own side. Surveying the battlefield from horseback, Kitchener announced in a considerable understatement that the enemy had been given "a good dusting."

The Mahdi and his remaining forces fled southward. The Mahdi died six months later of typhus, and the British now controlled the Sudan.

SPENCER C. TUCKER

See also
Egypt

References
Farwell, Byron. *Queen Victoria's Little Wars.* New York: Norton, 1972.
Pekenham, Thomas. *The Scramble for Africa: The White Man's Conquest of the Dark Continent from 1876–1912.* New York: Random House, 1991.
Vandervort, Bruce. *Wars of Imperial Conquest in Africa, 1830–1914.* Bloomington: Indiana University Press, 1998.

Ankara, Battle of (July 20, 1402)

A decisive military confrontation between the armies of Ottoman sultan Bayezid I and Mongol ruler of Central Asia Timur Lenk (Tamer-lane). Timur had secured Georgia and Azerbaijan in 1390 and Syria in 1399, thus expanding his own territory to the borders of the Ottoman Empire. When Bayezid demanded tribute from an Anatolian beylik who had pledged his loyalty to Timur, Timur took this as a personal insult and in 1400 sacked the Ottoman city of Sebaste (modern-day Sivas). Both leaders also exchanged insulting letters.

In 1402 while Bayezid was occupied attempting to conquer Hungary, Timur took this as propitious to mount a full-scale invasion of Anatolia. Bayezid rushed back from Hungary in hopes of confronting Timur to the east, but with an entirely mounted army, Timur's forces were able to move swiftly into Anatolia, sacking cities and towns and leaving a swath of destruction in their wake.

There is considerable controversy over the size of the forces involved. A figures of 1 million men on each side has been put forward, but more recent scholarship suggests perhaps 600,00 men for Timur, with Bayezid having no more than 120,000. Certainly Bayezid was badly outnumbered, with a number of his supporters switching sides and joining Timur in the battle.

Battle was joined near the Chubuk (Çubuk-ovasi) River north of Ankara on July 20, 1402. Occupying a defensive hilly position, the heterogeneous Ottoman army sustained a fierce attack by the Mongol cavalry and was eventually overrun, owing largely to the defection of Turkoman and despite the heroic defense of Bayezid's Christian vassals, particularly the Serbs who held the sultan's left flank.

Timur, reputedly in a secret plot with the Byzantine regent John VII Palaiologos, took Bayezid prisoner (he would die in captivity in 1403) along with one of his sons, Musa Çelebi. Timur then captured the town of Brusa, along with Bayezid's treasures, and consequently ended Ottoman domination over much of northwestern and southern Anatolia, reestablishing several of the Turkoman emirates (beyliks). The commencement of a fierce civil war among Bayezid's sons (1402/1403–1413) put a temporary halt to the expansion of the Ottoman Empire and gave the beleaguered Byzantine Empire breathing space for another half century.

ALEXIOS G. C. SAVVIDES AND SPENCER C. TUCKER

See also
Bayezid I

References
Alexandrescu-Dersca, Marie-Mathilde. *La campagne de Timur en Anatolie, 1402.* London: Variorum, 1977.
Matschke, Klaus-Peter. *Die Schlacht bei Ankara und das Schicksal von Byzanz.* Weimar: Böhlaus Nachfolger, 1981.
Roloff, G. "Die Schlacht bei Angora." *Historische Zeitschrift* 161 (1940): 244–262.

Ankara, Pact of (October 19, 1939)

Treaty concluded at Ankara, Turkey, on October 19, 1939, a month and a half after the beginning of World War II in Europe. Concluded between Britain, France, and Turkey, the Pact of Ankara pledged "mutual assistance in resistance to aggression should the necessity arise." The Turkish government promised not to enter into any conflict with the Soviet Union, while the British and French governments agreed to loan Turkey £25 million to purchase military supplies from them and £18.5 million to release their frozen balances with Turkey. The agreement provided for repayment of both loans, at 4 percent and 3 percent, respectively, during a 20-year period.

ALEXANDER MIKABERIDZE

See also
Kars, Treaty of

Reference
Zurcher, Erik Jan. *Turkey: A Modern History.* London: I. B. Tauris, 2004.

Ansar al-Islam

A radical Kurdish Islamist separatist movement formed in 2001 in northern Iraq (Kurdistan). The U.S. government has held that the group was founded by Mullah Krekar, with assistance and funds from Al Qaeda leader Osama bin Laden. The complicated history of Ansar al-Islam (Supporters of Islam) dates back to the Islamic Movement in Kurdistan (IMK), formed in 1987 of various factions, some of whose members had trained and fought in Afghanistan. Some others apparently returned to Kurdistan after the fall of the Taliban in late 2001, which is the basis of arguments that the group has links to Al Qaeda, a claim also made by its enemies in the larger Kurdish factions.

The IMK fought with the Popular Union of Kurdistan (PUK) and eventually had to retreat to the Iranian border before returning to its base in Halabja. In 2001 the IMK splintered, and various new groupings formed the Jund al-Islam in September of that year, declaring jihad (holy war) on those Kurdish parties that had left the Islamic path. The PUK fought Jund al-Islam, which dissolved and renamed itself Ansar al-Islam in December 2001, under the leadership of Amir Mullah Krekar, also known as Najumddin Faraj Ahmad. Since then, however, Krekar has been living in Norway and faces various indictments and deferred deportation for supporting terrorism.

While still operating under the name of Jund al-Islam, Ansar al-Islam tried to quash non-Islamic practices. It banned music, television, and alcohol; imposed the veil on women and beards on men; closed schools and employment to women; and tried to force a minority religious group called the Ahl al-Haqq to convert and then drove its members out of their villages. The group cracked down on the Naqshabandi Sufis and also pursued individuals, and some were held and tortured. Ansar al-Islam's strict Salafi stance makes it akin to various Sunni nationalist resistance groups that developed after 2003 and accentuate its differences with the principal Kurdish political factions.

The struggle between the PUK and Ansar al-Islam has also involved human rights violations, the assassination of the governor of Arbil, and fighting that has continued for years. In December 2002, Ansar al-Islam forces took two PUK outposts and killed about 50 people; more than half of these reportedly died after they had surrendered. On the other hand, Ansar al-Islam prisoners have been mistreated by the PUK.

When the U.S.- and British-led invasion of Iraq occurred in March 2003, Ansar al-Islam mounted various small attacks and carried out actions against those it called "collaborators" with the Americans, including civilians. The group mounted a much larger attack in 2004, when its suicide bombers attacked the PUK and Kurdistan Democratic Party (KDP) headquarters and killed 109 people, among them the KDP's deputy prime minister, Sami Abd al-Rahman. In 2005, the group assassinated an aide to Grand Ayatollah Sayyid Ali Husayn al-Sistan, Sheikh Mahmud al-Madayini, in Baghdad.

In 2003, fighters from Ansar al-Islam joined with other Sunni Salafi fighters in the central region of Iraq, forming Jama'at Ansar al-Sunna (formerly Jaysh Ansar al-Sunna). But the Ansar al-Islam elements returned to their earlier name in 2007. Also in 2007, Ansar al-Sunna, along with Ansar al-Islam, the Islamic Army of Iraq, and the Army of the Mujahideen, formed a new grouping called the Jihad and Reformation Front. In any event, its remains unclear what links Ansar al-Islam has to Al Qaeda, and there is some evidence to suggest that it might have received aid from Iran.

Ansar al-Islam continued its operations after the withdrawal of U.S. and other coalition forces from Iraq by the end of 2011, claiming to have participated in the insurgency against the central government with attacks against Iraqi security forces. The group has also taken part in the Syrian Civil War that began in March 2011, initially taking the name Ansar al-Sham and then under its own name. Reportedly it cooperates with other Islamic-bassed rebel groups such as the al-Nusra Front and the Islamic Front. Among Ansar al-Islam's combat operations was the Battle for Aleppo. Reportedly most of the Ansar al-Islam operation joined the Islamic State of Iraq and Syria in 2014.

Sherifa Zuhur and Spencer C. Tucker

See also
Aleppo, Battle for; Al Qaeda; Al Qaeda in Iraq; Bin Laden, Osama; Iraq; Iraq Insurgency; Iraq War; Islamic State of Iraq and Syria; Jihad; Syrian Civil War

References
Gunaratna, Rohan. *Inside al-Qaeda: Global Network of Terror.* New York: Columbia University Press, 2002.
Schanzer, Jonathan. *Al-Qaeda's Armies: Middle East Affiliate Groups & the Next Generation of Terror.* New York: Specialist Press International, 2005.
Tucker, Mike, and Charles Faddis. *Operation Hotel California: The Clandestine War inside Iraq.* Guilford, CT: Lyons, 2008.

Anti-Arab Attitudes and Discrimination

Anti-Arab attitudes, especially toward Muslim Arabs, as well as formal and informal policies and codes of conduct that unfairly target Arabs and are sometimes known as anti-Arabism have been virulent in Israel since 1948. However, prejudice against Arabs has certainly manifested itself in other areas of the world and has seen a widespread expansion in the West since 1973 that intensified following the Iranian Revolution and then again after September 11, 2001. People with anti-Arab attitudes often stereotype Arabs as uneducated, dirty, brutal, untrustworthy, and fanatical terrorists or supporters of terrorism.

In Israel, anti-Arabism dates to 1948, when the country was first established. But anti-Arab discrimination among Jews certainly predates the modern State of Israel, as Arabs and Jews had been in conflict since at least the early part of the 20th century. On May 15, 1948, the Arab League declared jihad (holy war) against Israel that led to even stronger enmity of Israelis toward Arabs. Israelis tend to view Arabs as religious fanatics who insist on war with an internationally recognized country that favors peace. After the numerous conflicts between the Arabs and Israel in the 20th and early 21st centuries, anti-Arab attitudes now exist at both the personal and political levels in Israel. This bias is directed toward Arab citizens of Israel as well as those living in other Middle Eastern and North African countries.

In recent years, the most notable public manifestations in Israel that showcased anti-Arab attitudes were the October 2000 riots. During the riots, Israeli Jews assaulted Arabs by stone throwing, property destruction, and chants of "Death to Arabs." The worst of the rioting occurred in Tel Aviv and Nazareth. Two Arabs were killed and many more were injured in the attacks.

At the political level in Israel, anti-Arab attitudes include discriminatory language frequently used by politicians or party leaders and by government policies that are clearly discriminatory in nature. For example, Yehiel Hazan, a Knesset (Israeli parliament) member, speaking on the floor of that body, bluntly stated that "the Arabs are worms." Another example of anti-Arabism can be found in the rightist political party Yisrael Beytenu (Our Home). The party dedicates itself chiefly to the purpose of redrawing the Israeli border, which would force many Arab citizens of Israel to lose their citizenship.

The Israeli government also shows hostility toward Arabs. The 2005 U.S. State Department country reports on human rights practices noted that the 2003 report of the Orr Commission, which was established following the police killing of 12 Israeli-Arab demonstrators and a Palestinian in October 2000, stated that government handling of the Arab sector was "primarily neglectful and discriminatory" and was not sufficiently sensitive to Arab needs and that the government did not allocate state resources equally. As a result, "serious distress prevailed in the Arab sector," including poverty, unemployment, land shortages, an inadequate educational system, and a substantially defective infrastructure.

Problems also exist in the health and social services sectors. According to 2004 reports by Mossawa (Advocacy Center for Arab Citizens of Israel) and the Arab Association for Human Rights, racist violence against Arab citizens of Israel was on the increase, and the government has not acted to prevent this problem.

Anti-Arab attitudes continue to exist in Israel. According to one recent Israeli poll, more than two-thirds of Jews would refuse to live in the same building with an Arab, 41 percent were in favor of segregation, and 63 percent believed Arabs to be a "security and demographic threat" to Israel. Such attitudes, it should be noted, are fueled by terrorist attacks made by a small minority of Arabs.

Anti-Arab bias is not, of course, confined to Israel. A significant amount of Arab discrimination exists in Iran, for example, in which Arabs are an ethnic minority. Some critics of the hard-line fundamentalist regime there assert that the Iranian government is actively pursuing an anti-Arab campaign that smacks of ethnic cleansing.

Throughout the West there also exists considerable anti-Arab bias. In Western Europe these anti-Arab attitudes vary from country to country, as some were former colonial powers over Arab lands. Nevertheless, even in those nations anti-Arab bias is troublesome at best and dangerous at worst. Examples of this were the widespread riots in France in 2005 that virtually paralyzed the country. Suffering from extreme poverty, segregation, poor health services, and unemployment rates of 25 percent or more, thousands of French Muslims—Arab and non-Arab alike—took to the streets in demonstrations in many French cities.

Anti-Arab attitudes and discrimination also widely exist in the United States and have grown in recent years. The primary reason for such attitudes in the West is considered to be the terrorist attacks carried out by or related to Arabs or Muslims. After the terrorist attacks on September 11, 2001, in the United States and the London subway bombings on July 7, 2005, anti-Arab attitudes became more widespread in the United States, Britain, and other Western countries. According to a poll of Arab Americans conducted by the Arab American Institute in 2001, 32 percent of Arab Americans reported being subjected to some form of ethnic-based discrimination during their lifetimes, and 20 percent reported having experienced ethnic-based discrimination since September 11, 2001.

Anti-Arabism in the United States takes many forms, including hate crimes and discrimination in schools and company hiring policies. Sometimes, non-Muslim Americans have blamed Arabs or Muslims for attacks in which they had no involvement. This was clearly the case in the immediate aftermath of the April 19, 1995, bombing of the

A controversial poster in a New York City subway station on September 27, 2012. Already defaced, it condemns radical Islam. These posters were funded by Pamela Geller, who had sued and lost in court to prevent establishment of an Islamic center near the September 11, 2001, terrorist attack site. The poster reads, "In any war between the civilized man and the savage, support the civilized man. Support Israel. Defeat Jihad." (Spencer Platt/Getty Images)

Alfred P. Murrah Federal Building in Oklahoma City. Several supposed eyewitnesses claimed to have seen an Arab lurking about the scene before the attack, and the national media quickly picked up on this. As it turned out, there were no such persons on the scene that day, and the bombing was carried out by a non-Arab American citizen.

The Western media—and Hollywood in particular—has often resorted to ethnic stereotypes when depicting Arabs. Most Arabs in U.S. films are portrayed in a negative light, and most play the role of villain. The 2000 film *Rules of Engagement* has been heavily criticized for its anti-Arab slant. In a recent review of more than 900 Hollywood films released over a long span, just 12 depicted Arabs in positive terms, and only 50 were considered balanced portrayals of Arabs.

More recently, anti-Muslim sentiment has surged in much of the West. This latest crescendo of discrimination has been fueled chiefly by the acts of extremist Islamic groups such as the Islamic State of Iraq and Syria (ISIS) and Boko Haram. These radical groups have targeted both Muslims and non-Muslims, but terrorist attacks reportedly sponsored or encouraged by ISIS in Europe and the United States in recent years resulted in considerable anti-Muslim and anti-Arab sentiments in Western Europe and the United States. This has been compounded by a huge influx of Syrian and Libyan refugees into Southern and Western Europe.

Anti-Muslim sentiments even became a major issue in the 2016 U.S. presidential campaign, with a number of Republican nominees arguing that America should not take in any Syrian refugees. The blustery businessman Donald Trump, while campaigning for the Republican nomination in late 2015, went so far as to assert that all Muslims in the United States should be required to register with the government and that no Muslims should be allowed into the country. His extreme position, however, was not supported by the other candidates.

After Trump unexpectedly prevailed in the 2016 election, he took office in January 2017 and immediately moved to ban refugees from seven predominantly Muslim nations in the Middle East and North Africa. Among the nations included in the ban was Iraq, which angered the U.S.-backed Iraqi government. The executive order caused much consternation domestically and internationally and was promptly blocked by a U.S. court. The Trump administration issued a revised order, this time exempting Iraq, but it too was blocked by a U.S. court. The courts have contended that the travel bans appeared to be religiously motivated and invoked Trump's own incendiary views on Islam as proof of that conclusion.

During his first foreign trip as president, in late May 2017, Trump met with a number of Muslim leaders and gave a speech in Saudi Arabia. In it, he sought to soft-pedal his prior views toward Islam and tried to strike a conciliatory tone, but on his return to the United States he again called for approval of a travel ban, clearly directed against Muslim states. Anti-Arabism continues to plague diplomacy in the Middle East.

Yuanyuan Ding and Paul G. Pierpaoli Jr.

See also
Jihad; Terrorism

References
Herzog, Chaim. *The Arab-Israeli Wars: War and Peace in the Middle East from the War of Independence to Lebanon.* Westminster, MD: Random House, 1984.
Rabinovich, Itamar. *Waging Peace: Israel and the Arabs, 1948–2003.* Princeton, NJ: Princeton University Press, 2004.
Salaita, Steven. *Anti-Arab Racism in the USA: Where It Comes from and What It Means for Politics Today.* London: Pluto, 2006.

Antigonus I Monophthalmus (382–301 BCE)

A Macedonian noble, Antigonus Monophthalmus (One-eye, so named for the loss of one of his eyes in battle) served under King Alexander III the Great and became one of the Diadochi (successors) who competed to control the vast territory Alexander had conquered after his death. Born in Elimeia, Macedon, in 382 BCE, Antigonus served under Alexander's father, King Philip II of Macedon, and was one of Alexander's generals during the invasion of Persia in 334.

Antigonus was satrap of Phrygia from 333 and repelled several Persian attacks. In 323 following the death of Alexander, Perdiccas, acting as regent for the infant Alexander IV, also granted him Lycia and Pamphylia. Two years later, though, Antigonus fled when Perdiccas threatened him for not following orders.

Antigonus played a major role in the Wars of the Diadochi that followed when he persuaded two other generals, Antipater and Cassander, that Perdiccas was plotting against them as well. In 320 Antipater appointed Antigonus to command against Eumenes of Cardia in Asia Minor. In 319 Antigonus overran Eumenes's territory, besieged him in Nora, and defeated a relief force. On Antipater's death (also in 319), Antigonus allied with Cassander, Lysimachus, and Ptolemy I Soter to fight Polyperchon, Antipater's successor. Antigonus's immediate task was to defeat Eumenes, now Polyperchon's commander in Asia Minor. Antigonus fought two indecisive battles against Eumenes—Paraetacene (317) and Gabiene (316)—but at the latter Eumenes was betrayed to him, and Antigonus had him executed.

Antigonus seized the treasury at Susa and occupied Babylon; its satrap, Seleucus, fled to join Ptolemy in Egypt. Antigonus's success in securing most of Alexander's Asian possessions led the other Diadochi (Cassander, Lysimachus, Ptolemy, and Seleucus) to join forces against him. Despite this, Antigonus enjoyed several years of success. He supplied financial support to Polyperchon to allow him to fight Cassander and secured local support in Asia Minor and the Aegean by declaring all Greek cities free and establishing the League of Islanders. This league was a maritime arrangement that had the additional benefit of remedying his weakness in naval power. Antigonus also conducted successful campaigns in Phoenicia and Syria. However, in 312 Antigonus's son Demetrius (later Demetrius I Poliorcetes) was defeated by Ptolemy at the Battle of Gaza.

This defeat led to peace with Cassander, Lysimachus, and Ptolemy (311) but also allowed Seleucus to regain his satrapy and rebuild his power base. Seleucus not only held out but also decisively defeated Antigonus's forces at an unknown location in 309. Antigonus then turned his attention west, to the Aegean and mainland Greece, leading to a long-running naval conflict with Ptolemy. In 307 Demetrius liberated Athens, and in 306 Antigonus defeated Ptolemy's fleet off Cyprus and seized that strategically located island. Antigonus then proclaimed himself and Demetrius as kings—the other Diadochi soon followed suit.

However, Demetrius failed to take Rhodes and in 304 had to return to Greece to prevent Cassander from occupying

Athens. Building on this successful operation, in 302 Antigonus reestablished the Hellenic League of Philip II and came close to defeating Cassander. Once again, Antigonus's success caused Cassander, Lysimachus, Ptolemy, and Seleucus to band together. In 301, the 80-year-old and very overweight Antigonus was killed at the Battle of Ipsus, left in the lurch when Demetrius's overly eager cavalry pursuit took him too far from the battlefield.

IAIN SPENCE

See also
Demetrius I Poliorcetes; Diadochi, Wars of the; Eumenes of Cardia; Gabiene, Battle of; Ipsus, Battle of; Lysimachus; Paraetacene, Battle of; Perdiccas; Ptolemy I Soter

References
Billows, Richard A. *Antigonos the One-Eyed and the Creation of the Hellenistic State.* Berkeley: University of California Press, 1990.
Bosworth, A. Brian. *The Legacy of Alexander: Politics, Warfare and Propaganda under the Successors.* Oxford: Oxford University Press, 2002.

Antioch, Principality of

A Frankish state in northern Syria. Established in 1098 by the armies of the First Crusade (1096–1099), the Antioch principality survived until 1268. With its capital at the city of Antioch (modern-day Antakya, Turkey), the principality comprised much of the northwest of the modern-day state of Syria as well as the province of Hatay in present-day southeastern Turkey.

Upon his arrival in Constantinople in 1097, one of the crusade leaders Bohemund, prince of Taranto, took the oath required by Byzantine emperor Alexios I Komnenos and promised not to lay claim to any former part of the empire that the crusade might conquer. However, during the siege of the city of Antioch (1097–1098), Bohemund obtained a pledge from the other crusade leaders that he would be allowed to keep Antioch if he could take it and if Alexios would not come in person to reclaim it. Bohemund then used his contacts with Firuz, a military commander in Antioch, to enter and take the city except for the citadel. After the crusaders' victory over Karbugha of Mosul (June 28, 1098), the citadel surrendered. On November 5, 1098, the crusade leaders confirmed Bohemund's claim to Antioch, and when the main army of the crusade resumed its march south in January 1099, Bohemund stayed in Antioch.

Bohemund's new territory was the second Frankish state established in the east after only the county of Edessa that same year, 1098. It had been a Byzantine province until the Arab conquest in the seventh century, and in 1085 the Seljuks had seized the region. The principality of Antioch was bordered in the north by the plains of Cilicia and the Taurus Mountains; in the west by the Mediterranean Sea; in the south by the future county of Tripoli, the Muslim emirate of Homs, and the lands of the Assassins; and in the east by the county of Edessa and the Muslim emirate of Aleppo.

The principality of Antioch remained the target of Muslim reconquest until the 1170s, when Saladin shifted his attention to the south. Antioch, the capital city, was well fortified, with its 360 towers dating back to the Byzantine period. It was connected to the Mediterranean Sea through the port of St. Simeon (modern-day Süveydiye, Turkey). As a commercial center Antioch was not as important as Acre or the coastal cities of Cilicia, however. Antioch was known for the good relationship between its various ethnic and religious groups: Franks, Syrians, Greeks, Jews, Armenians, and Muslim Arabs.

In 1100 Bohemund was taken prisoner in fighting with the Danishmendids. Bohemund's nephew Tancred then became regent. Tancred expanded the principality's territory, seizing Tarsus and Latakia from the Byzantine Empire. These and other territories were lost after the crusader defeat in the Battle of Harran (May 7, 1104), when Baldwin II of Edessa was captured. Following payment of a ransom, Bohemund was released in 1103. He then traveled to Italy to raise more manpower, during which time Tancred remained regent of Antioch. Bohemund attacked the Byzantines in 1107 but was defeated at Dyrrhachium in 1108 and forced that same year by Emperor Alexios I Komnenos in the Treaty of Devol to make Antioch a vassal state of the Byzantine Empire. Bohemund returned to Italy, where he died in 1111. Tancred was again regent in Antioch.

Tancred died in 1112 and was succeeded by Bohemund II under the regency of Tancred's nephew Roger of Salerno, who defeated a Seljuk attack on the principality in 1113. Roger was killed in the Battle of Ager Sanguinis (Field of Blood, June 28, 1119), and Antioch became a vassal state of Jerusalem with King Baldwin II as regent until 1126. Bohemund II, who married Baldwin's daughter Alice, ruled for only four years, and the principality was inherited by his young daughter Constance. Baldwin II was again regent until his death in 1131, when Fulk of Jerusalem took power. In 1136 Constance, then 10 years old, married Raymond of Poitiers, age 36.

Raymond attacked the Byzantine province of Cilicia. Arriving with an army at Antioch in 1138, Byzantine emperor John II Komnenos forced Raymond to swear fealty. John then led the armies of Byzantium, Antioch, and Edessa against Muslim Syria. Aleppo proved too strong to attack, but the allied force took the fortresses of Balat, Biza'a, Atherib, Maarat al-Numan, and Kafartabt, this despite the fact that most of the effort was by the Byzantines, while Raymond and Count Joscelin II of Edessa did little. Following a siege, Emperor John took the city of Shaizar, although the citadel held out. The emir of Shaizar finally agreed to pay a large indemnity, become John's vassal, and pay yearly tribute. While John reluctantly accepted the terms, on the armies' return to Antioch a riot instigated by Joscelin II of Edessa forced the emperor to leave without having secured the citadel. John II had hoped to recover Antioch and become overlord of the remaining crusader states, but he died in 1143.

After the fall of Edessa in 1144, Muslim leader Nur al-Din attacked Antioch during the Second Crusade (1147–1149), securing much of the eastern part of the principality. Raymond was killed at the Battle of Inab (June 29, 1149), and Baldwin III of Jerusalem became regent for Raymond's widow Constance until 1153, when she married Raynald of Châtillon. Raynald was soon fighting the Byzantines, this time in Cyprus.

Raynald made peace with Manuel I Komnenos in 1158, and in 1159 Manuel arrived to take personal control of the principality. From that point on until Manual's death in 1180 the Antioch principality was a vassal of Byzantium. As such, the principality had to provide troops for the Byzantine Army and indeed took part in an attack on the Seljuk Turks in 1176. Byzantine forces also helped to protect Antioch against Nur al-Din at a time when it was in serious danger of being overrun.

Raynald was taken prisoner by the Muslims in 1160 (not released until 1176, he never returned to Antioch), and the patriarch of Antioch became regent. Meanwhile, Manuel married Constance's daughter Maria. Constance, who really had no power in Antioch, was deposed in 1163, replaced by her son Bohemund III. Bohemund was taken captive by Nur al-Din at the Battle of Harim (August 12, 1164), however, and the Orontes River became the boundary between Antioch and Aleppo. Bohemund returned to Antioch in 1165 and married one of Manuel's nieces.

With the death of Manuel I in 1180, the Byzantine alliance that had protected Antioch against Nur al-Din came to an end. Thanks to fleets of the Italian trading cities, Antioch survived Saladin's assault on the Kingdom of Jerusalem in 1187. Neither Antioch nor Tripoli participated in the Third Crusade (1189–1192), although what was left of Emperor Frederick I Barbarossa's army briefly stopped in Antioch in 1190 to bury him.

Bohemund III's death in 1201 brought a struggle for control of Antioch between his son Bohemund, who had earlier become count of Tripoli, and Armenia, represented by Bohemund III's grandson Raymond-Roupen. Bohemund of Tripoli secured control of Antioch, ruling as Bohemund IV by 1207, but Raymond briefly ruled as a rival from 1216 to 1219. Bohemund died in 1233, and Antioch, now ruled by his son Bohemund V, played no important role in the subsequent Christian crusades.

The power struggle between Antioch and Armenia came to an end in 1254 when Bohemund VI married an Armenian princess. Both of these states were soon a part of the conflict between the Mamluks and the Mongols. In 1260 under the influence of his father-in-law, the Armenian king Hetoum I, Bohemund VI submitted to Mongol general Hulegu, and Antioch became a tributary state of the Mongol Empire. Bohemund and Hetoum fought on the Mongol side during the latter's conquests of Muslim Syria, helping to capture both Aleppo and Damascus.

Following the Mamluk defeat of the Mongols in the Battle of Ayn Jalut (September 3, 1260), Mamluk sultan of Egypt Baybars I began to threaten Antioch, which had supported the Mongols. Baybars finally took Antioch in 1268; all of northern Syria also fell. In 1291 Acre fell, and the crusader states of Outremer ceased to exist. The empty title "Prince of Antioch" passed to the kings of Cyprus.

JOCHEN BURGTORF AND SPENCER C. TUCKER

See also
Ager Sanguinis, Battle of; Alexios I Komnenos; Antioch, Sieges of; Ayn Jalut, Battle of; Baybars I; Bohemund I of Antioch; Bohemund VI of Antioch-Tripoli; Bohemund VII of Antioch-Tripoli; Danishmendid Dynasty; Edessa, County of; Frederick I or Frederick Barbarossa; Harim, Battle of; Harran, Battle of; Karbugha; Manuel I Komnenos, Emperor; Nur al-Din; Seljuk Dynasty; Tancred; Tripoli, County of

References
Asbridge, Thomas S. *The Creation of the Principality of Antioch, 1098–1130*. Woodbridge, UK: Boydell, 2000.

Cahen, Claude. *La Syrie du Nord à l'époque des croisades et la principauté franque d'Antioche*. Paris: Geuthner, 1940.

Hamilton, Bernard. *Crusaders, Cathars, and Holy Places*. Aldershot, UK: Ashgate, 1999.

Hiestand, Rudolf. "Antiochia, Sizilien und das Reich am Ende des 12. Jahrhunderts." *Quellen und Forschungen aus italienischen Archiven und Bibliotheken* 73 (1993): 70–121.

Lilie, Ralph-Johannes. *Byzantium and the Crusader States, 1096–1204*. Oxford, UK: Clarendon, 1993.

Mayer, Hans Eberhard. *Varia Antiochena: Studien zum Kreuz-fahrerfürstentum Antiochia im 12. und frühen 13. Jahrhundert.* Hannover: Hahn, 1993.

Antioch, Sieges of (1097–1098)

Two consecutive sieges of the city of Antioch (modern-day Antakya, Turkey) during the First Crusade (1096–1099). In the course of these sieges, the crusaders invested and captured the Seljuk-held city (October 21, 1097–June 3, 1098) but were then themselves besieged by a relieving Seljuk army, which they defeated four weeks later on June 28, 1098.

The crusaders recognized the importance of Antioch in order to proceed against Jerusalem. Their hope of speedy progress was based on their knowledge of the fragmentation of the Seljuk sultanate after the death in 1095 of the ruler of Syria, Tutush I, which left his territories divided between his sons Riwan at Aleppo and Duqaq at Damascus. Their rivalry enabled men such as Yaghisiyan, Seljuk governor of Antioch, to enjoy great independence, while the sultan, Barkiyaruq (r. 1095–1105), was viewed with deep suspicion by all the powers of Syria.

The siege of Antioch began on October 21, 1097. The crusaders could count on support from the Armenian lands to the north, east, and west that they had secured during their march, a process solidified when Baldwin of Boulogne seized Edessa (modern-day Sanliurfa, Turkey) in March 1098. An English fleet had captured St. Symeon, the port for Antioch, and Laodikeia in Syria, a major maritime city to the south, establishing close connections with Byzantine Cyprus that would serve as a supply base throughout the siege.

When a Genoese fleet put into St. Symeon on November 17, the skills and equipment it brought enabled the army to build a fortified bridge of boats across the Orontes River and a fortress called Malregard to protect their camp north of the city. On March 4, 1098, another English fleet arrived, enabling the besiegers to build the crucial Mahommeries Tower, which blockaded the Bridge Gate. Yet, when the crusade first reached Antioch, the idea was floated (perhaps by the imperial representative, Tatikios) of a distant blockade, the method used when the Byzantines had reconquered Antioch from the Arab Hamdanid dynasty in 969. However, the crusaders rejected this idea, probably because of the need to keep the army together, and established themselves along the north wall in front of the gates between Mount Staurin and the Bridge Gate. Communications with St. Symeon were precarious, depending on the bridge of boats and subject to attack from the Bridge Gate.

A mid-13th century illuminated manuscript depicting the successful siege by Christian crusaders in 1097 of the Muslim stronghold of Antioch during the First Crusade (1096–1099). (The British Library)

Although the Western sources present the siege as a noble and continuous struggle, it was effectively a close blockade, probably punctuated by a series of truces, and there was never a general assault. The crusader army had suffered extensive losses crossing Asia Minor, and its mounted knights were reduced to about 700. It had come under attack from Seljuk outposts to the north and feared relief expeditions.

By December 1097 the army was starving, and a foraging expedition was mounted into Syria. On December 31, the crusaders encountered a relief expedition sent by Duqaq of Damascus in an effort to undermine Riwan. In a drawn battle near Albara, the crusaders halted this expedition, but their failure to gather booty plunged the army into a profound supply crisis, prompting Tatikios to return to Constantinople to hasten imperial assistance. Riwan moved to reassert his control over Antioch, but on February 9, 1098, Bohemund led all the surviving crusader cavalry and successfully ambushed Riwan's great army as it approached the city.

The crusaders had thus survived a great crisis, and by early March they had built the Mahommeries Tower outside the Bridge Gate and blockaded the St. George Gate to the south. Under this severe pressure, in late May one of the Seljuk commanders, Piruz, agreed to betray his section of the wall to Bohemund (late May). At the same time, news arrived of the approach of a huge relief army sent by the sultan under Karbugha of Mosul; this enabled Bohemund to extort a promise from the other leaders that he could have possession of the city if the Byzantine emperor did not come to their relief. On the night of June 2–3 the crusaders entered the city, which was then sacked. The citadel within Antioch continued to hold out under its Seljuk garrison, however.

Two days after its fall, on June 5 Karbugha appeared before Antioch, having wasted time in a fruitless three-week siege of Edessa designed to please some of his allies. He established a camp some three miles north of the city and drove in all the crusader outposts. Another camp was then set up close to the citadel, and an effort was made on June 7 to storm the city through the citadel, but this attempt failed because the crusaders were able to block the narrow route down to Antioch. By June 9 Karbugha had established his own siege of the city. The crusaders were starving and frightened to such an extent that there were substantial desertions, including that of Stephen of Blois, and Bohemund set part of the city on fire to flush out the timorous.

In this hour of crisis a series of visionaries came forward proclaiming God's trust in his people. These events culminated on June 14 in the discovery of the Holy Lance (the weapon used to pierce Jesus's side during the crucifixion) in the cathedral by a Provençal pilgrim named Peter Bartholomew. This greatly lifted crusader morale.

On June 28, the crusaders sortied from the Bridge Gate escorted by so many clergy that it seemed like a religious procession. Religious ardor played a major role in the ensuing crusader victory, but so did the military prudence of Bohemund, who had been placed in command and held back his own men as a reserve. But the decisive factor was that Karbugha had dispersed his forces: as his troops near the Bridge Gate were pushed back, those from outside other gates were drawn piecemeal into the battle. It took time for Karbugha to realize what was happening and mobilize his massive cavalry forces in the main camp; by the time they arrived the battle was lost, and the bulk of his forces never engaged.

The siege of Antioch had been an enormous strain on the crusader army, but its capture ensured the continuation of the crusade. The city remained in Christian hands until 1268.

JOHN FRANCE

See also
Antioch, Principality of; Bohemund I of Antioch; Karbugha

References
Bachrach, Bernard S. "The Siege of Antioch: A Study in Military Demography." *War in History* 6 (1999): 127–146.
France, John. "The Fall of Antioch during the First Crusade." In *Dei Gesta per Francos: Etudes sur les croisades dédiées à Jean Richard*, ed. Michel Balard, Benjamin Z. Kedar, and Jonathan Riley-Smith, 13–20. Aldershot, UK: Ashgate, 2001.
France, John. *Victory in the East: A Military History of the First Crusade.* Cambridge: Cambridge University Press, 1994.
Morris, Colin. "Policy and Visions: The Case of the Holy Lance Found at Antioch." In *War and Government in the Middle Ages: Essays in Honour of J. O. Prestwich*, ed. J. Gillingham and J. C. Holt, 33–35. Woodbridge: Boydell, 1984.
Riley-Smith, Jonathan, *The First Crusade and the Idea of Crusading.* London: Athlone, 1986.
Rogers, Randall. "Peter Bartholomew and the Role of 'the Poor' in the First Crusade." In *Warriors and Churchmen in the High Middle Ages: Essays Presented to Karl Leyser,* ed. Timothy Reuter, 109–122. London: Hambledon, 1992.

Antioch on the Meander, Battle of (1211)

The Battle of Antioch on the Meander (also known as the Battle of Alasehir) occurred in 1211 in western Anatolia near the present-day town Yamalak in the Kuyucak district, Aydin Province. It was fought between the Seljuks and the Empire of Nicaea. Sultan Kaykhusraw led the Seljuk forces in attacking Theodore Laskaris (Lascaris), who claimed the imperial throne. Former Byzantine emperor Alexios III, who had been deposed after the capture of Constantinople by Christian forces of the Fourth Crusade in 1204, had promised Kaykhusraw rich rewards to help him recover his throne and accompanied the army in the field.

Lascaris's army consisted of 2,000 cavalry, including 800 Latin mercenaries. Kaykhusraw's army was considerably larger, probably between 5,000 and 11,000 men. (Exaggerated figures ranging to more than 100,000 men are given for the Seljuks in some sources.) The Nicaeans won the battle thanks to the bravery and hardiness of the Latin mercenaries who, however, were almost completely annihilated in the fighting.

Kaykhusraw's son and successor, Kaykaus I, concluded a truce with Nicaea in June 1211. Laskaris secured western Anatolia, and the border between the two states then was largely unchallenged until the 1260s. Former emperor Alexios, Laskaris's father-in-law, was taken prisoner during the battle. Laskaris treated him well but sent him to a monastery, where he ended his days.

ADAM ALI AND SPENCER C. TUCKER

See also
Seljuk Dynasty

References
Bartusis, Mark C. *The Late Byzantine Army: Arms and Society, 1204–1453*. Philadelphia: University of Pennsylvania Press, 1992.
Rice, Tamara Talbot. *The Saljuks in Asia Minor*. London: Thames and Hudson, 1961.

Antiochus I Soter (ca. 324–261 BCE)

Antiochus I Soter was a king of the Hellenistic Seleucid Empire. Born around 324 BCE in Mesopotamia or Persia, he reigned from 292 to 261 (as coregent until 281). Antiochus I was the son of King Seleucus I Nicator and the Sogdian princess Apama. Soon after Seleucus's assassination in 281, Antiochus had to restore his father's empire by force of arms because of revolts in Syria and northern Anatolia and a war led by Antigonus II Gonatas of Macedonia. In addition, some 20,000 Galatians created havoc when they entered Asia Minor in 278. The victory that Antiochus won over them in 275 with the systematic use of war elephants led to his title "Soter" (savior). Antiochus also founded many new cities in Asia Minor and modern-day Iran, while at Babylon he rebuilt the ancient Esagila shrine.

At the end of 275, the continuous friction between the Seleucids and the Ptolemies over the regions of Coele-Syria and Phoenicia led to full-scale war (known as the First Syrian War). The war did not change the borders of the two kingdoms dramatically, and Coele-Syria and Phoenicia remained under Ptolemaic rule. Around 262 Antiochus tried to put an end to the growing power of Eumenes I of Pergamum by military force, but he was defeated near the city of Sardis and died soon afterward. Antiochus was succeeded in 261 by his second son, Antiochus II Theos.

IOANNIS GEORGANAS

See also
Eumenes I of Pergamum; Seleucid Empire; Seleucus I Nicator; Syrian-Egyptian Wars

References
Austin, Michel. *The Hellenistic World from Alexander to the Roman Conquest*. 2nd ed. Cambridge: Cambridge University Press, 2006.
Grainger, John D. *The Syrian Wars*. Leiden: Brill, 2010.
Gruen, Erich S. *The Hellenistic World and the Coming of Rome*. Berkeley: University of California Press, 1984.

Antiochus III Megas (ca. 241–187 BCE)

Antiochus III Megas (the Great) ruled the Seleucid kingdom between 222 and 187. Born around 241 BCE in Susa, Persia, Antiochus succeeded to the throne at the age of 20 following the death of his elder brother and predecessor Seleucus III. Antiochus put his cousin Achaeus in charge of Asia Minor west of the Taurus Mountains with the specific task of reconquering Seleucid lands seized by Attalus I, founder of the breakaway kingdom of Pergamum. Falsely accused by Antiochus's minister Hermeias of planning a rebellion, Achaeus had himself made king in 221/220.

At this time Antiochus was busy putting down the rebellion of Molon, the Seleucid satrap of Media and governor-general of the Upper Satrapies. Between 219 and 217, Antiochus fought the Fourth Syrian War against Ptolemy IV regarding Coele-Syria. Antiochus succeeded in conquering Tyre and Seleucia Pieria, among other places, but these acquisitions were lost when he was defeated at the Battle of Raphia in 217. Antiochus then turned to Achaeus and the war in Asia Minor. With the help of Attalus, Antiochus reconquered the Seleucid domains west of the Taurus and captured and executed Achaeus in 213.

In 212 Antiochus began his major offensive operation, a massive military expedition across his eastern empire to recover areas lost during the Seleucid civil wars of 245–225. First he brought Parthia and its king, Arsaces II, to heel. Antiochus next attacked the rebellious kingdom of Bactria, under the rule of Euthydemus I. Antiochus defeated Euthydemus in the Battle of Arius in 209 but was forced to make peace with him after the unsuccessful siege of Bactra, the Bactrian capital. Antiochus then pressed on into Afghanistan and India, crossing the Hindu Kush and renewing his friendship with Sophagasenus (Subhashsena) before returning west. It was probably during this military operation, which resembled that of Alexander the Great, that Antiochus began styling himself "the Great," in conscious imitation of Alexander.

After his return to the west, Antiochus resumed hostilities with the Ptolemaic kingdom over Coele-Syria. The Ptolemaic throne was now occupied by "a helpless infant," the five-year-old Ptolemy V Epiphanes, and the Roman historian Polybius records the striking of a secret pact by Antiochus and Philip V of Macedon in the winter of 203–202 to attack and dismember the Ptolemaic kingdom. The Fifth

Silver tetradrachm coin of Antiochus III the Great (r. 222–187 BCE), minted at Antioch. One of the most successful Diadochi, or successors of Alexander the Great, Antiochus ruled the Seleucid Empire of modern Syria and enjoyed success until he clashed with Rome. Defeated in the Syrian-Roman War (192–188 BCE), he was forced to surrender Asia Minor west of the Taurus Mountains to Rome. (Yale University Art Gallery)

Syrian War (202–195) saw Antiochus recover Coele-Syria from Ptolemy and win a major Seleucid victory at the Battle of Panium (200).

Beginning in 196, Antiochus began consolidating what he regarded as ancestral Seleucid territory in Asia Minor, attacking various Greek cities and Rhodian and Pergamene territory and crossing the Hellespont into European Thrace. Antiochus's relentless aggression, especially against Rome's eastern allies, and his formidable reputation as a "new Alexander" drew the attention of the Romans beginning in the late 200s. The Roman Republic established friendship with him in 200 during a failed Roman attempt to mediate the Fifth Syrian War. In 198 the Romans successfully intervened in the conflict between Antiochus and Attalus of Pergamum. After the Roman victory over Philip V in the Second Macedonian War, the Romans warned Antiochus not to harm the autonomous Greek cities of Asia Minor and to evacuate the former possessions of Ptolemy and Philip there.

At a conference at Lysimacheia in September 196, Antiochus effectively outmaneuvered the Romans, responding to their complaints point for point. Now firmly established in Thrace and Coele-Syria, Antiochus requested a treaty of alliance with Rome to clarify his status and authority relative to Rome's in the east. The Romans refused and demanded that the king abandon Thrace. Antiochus simply ignored the ultimatum.

In 192 the Aetolians, disgruntled by Roman treatment of them in the settlement of the Second Macedonian War, made Antiochus *strategos* of the Aetolian League, and the king crossed to Greece in 192. The Syrian-Roman War (192–188) broke out when Antiochus's soldiers attacked some Roman soldiers at Delium. The Romans defeated Antiochus twice in battle, at Thermopylae (191) and Magnesia in Asia Minor (190). The subsequent Peace of Apamea (188) compelled Antiochus to give up his territory west and north of the Taurus. Antiochus was killed in 187 while plundering the Temple of Baal at Susa.

Paul J. Burton

See also

Magnesia, Battle of; Ptolemy IV Philopator; Ptolemy V Epiphanes; Raphia, Battle of; Syria; Syrian-Egyptian Wars; Syrian-Roman War

References

Bevan, Edwyn R. *The House of Seleucus.* 2 vols. London: Edward Arnold, 1902.

Eckstein, Arthur M. *Rome Enters the Greek East: From Anarchy to Hierarchy in the Hellenistic Mediterranean, 230–170 B.C.* Oxford, UK: Blackwell, 2008.

Grainger, John D. *The Roman War of Antiochus the Great.* Leiden: Brill, 2002.

Ma, John. *Antiochus III and the Cities of Western Asia Minor.* Oxford: Oxford University Press, 1999.

Antiochus IV Epiphanes (ca. 215–164 BCE)

Antiochus IV Epiphanes was king of the Hellenistic Seleucid Empire from 175 to 164. Born around 215 BCE, he was the son of Antiochus III the Great. After his father's defeat by the Romans in 189, Antiochus was sent to Rome as a political hostage. He remained there until 175, when his brother Seleucus III managed to release him. Soon afterward Seleucus was assassinated, and Antiochus claimed the throne.

In 170 the Ptolemies demanded the return of Coele Syria, Palestine, and Phoenicia, which had been recently conquered by the Seleucids. Antiochus responded swiftly and with a preemptive attack took control of Egypt and Cyprus.

Because of Roman intervention, however, Antiochus was forced to yield these newly gained territories.

On his return from Egypt in 167, Antiochus sacked the city of Jerusalem. The Jewish religion was outlawed, and Antiochus enforced the establishment of an imperial cult; a statue of him portrayed as Zeus was erected in the Jewish temple. This move, in connection to a general effort for the Hellenization of the Jews, eventually led to the Maccabean revolt.

Antiochus returned in triumph to Antioch (166) but soon had to turn his attention to more serious problems on his eastern borders, where he was forced to face the Armenians and the Parthians. Antiochus fell ill and died while in Persia in 164.

IOANNIS GEORGANAS

See also
Antiochus III Megas; Judaea; Maccabean Revolt; Ptolemy VI Philometor; Seleucid Empire; Syrian-Egyptian Wars

References
Austin, Michel. *The Hellenistic World from Alexander to the Roman Conquest*. 2nd ed. Cambridge: Cambridge University Press, 2006.
Bevan, Edwyn R. *The House of Seleucus*. 2 vols. London: Edward Arnold, 1902.
Eckstein, Arthur M. *Rome Enters the Greek East: From Anarchy to Hierarchy in the Hellenistic Mediterranean, 230–170 B.C.* Oxford, UK: Blackwell, 2008.

Antiochus VII Sidetes (ca. 159–129 BCE)

Born around 159 BCE, Antiochus VII Sidetes was the last Seleucid king who might have held the empire together. When his older brother Demetrius II was captured in Parthia in 139, Antiochus occupied the northern part of the empire with a mercenary army and was then invited into the capital of Antioch by Demetrius II's wife Cleopatra. He then married her and took the title King Antiochus Euergetes (Benefactor). The nickname "Sidetes" (the Sidonian) came from his early life in Side in southern Asia Minor.

Antiochus vigorously suppressed the usurper Diodotus Tryphon who had been in control of the southern parts of the empire since the reign of Demetrius II. Antiochus also reasserted Seleucid control over Judaea-Palestine (135–134), took Jerusalem following a siege of the city, and then allowed the Jews religious autonomy.

With the western empire restored to its full extent, in 129 Antiochus launched an ambitious campaign to win back territory in present-day Iraq and Iran that had been lost to Parthia. He won several victories across these regions but could not bring the Parthian king to accept subjection to Seleucid rule. In 129 Antiochus's army, which had wintered in scattered camps, was caught by local uprisings. The main Parthian force ambushed his army near Ecbatana and destroyed it. Reportedly, Antiochus VII was killed in the battle and most of his army taken prisoner.

This disaster and the attendant great loss of manpower rendered permanent the loss of the eastern territories. The Seleucid realm was now restricted to Syria and the immediately adjacent territories.

DOUGLAS KELLY

See also
Demetrius II Nicator; Seleucid Empire

References
Austin, Michel. *The Hellenistic World from Alexander to the Roman Conquest*. 2nd ed. Cambridge: Cambridge University Press, 2006.
Bevan, Edwyn R. *The House of Seleucus*. 2 vols. London: Edward Arnold, 1902.
Sherwin-White, Susan, and Amélie Kuhrt. *From Samarkhand to Sardis: A New Approach to the Seleucid Empire*. London: Duckworth, 1993.

Antiochus Hierax (ca. 260–226 BCE)

Antiochus Hierax (The Hawk) was the younger brother of King Seleucus II, who reigned during 246–225 BCE. Placed in charge of Seleucid territory in Asia Minor with the backing of his mother Laodice, the late king's widow, he acted as a virtually independent ruler, supplying reinforcements in the Third Syrian War (246–242) but only on condition of being recognized by his brother as joint king.

Seleucus II moved against Hierax in the War of the Brothers (237–236) and defeated him in two battles but failed to capture Sardis, where Hierax had taken refuge. Hierax then made alliances with the Seleucids' enemies in Asia Minor: Ziaelas of Bithynia, Mithridates II of Pontus, and the Galatians. This coalition defeated Seleucus II at Ancyra and forced him to make peace.

Hierax had to pay indemnities to the Galatians and even so could not prevent them from plundering his territory. King Attalus I of Pergamum undertook a defensive war against the Galatians and, building on his successes, drove a discredited Hierax out of Asia Minor. Hierax fled to King Arsames of Armenia and induced him to provide forces for an attack on his brother. Hierax was defeated by a Seleucid reserve army in Mesopotamia, commanded by Seleucus II's uncle Andromachus and his cousin Achaeus. Seleucus II himself was forced to break off his campaign against the Parthians and drove Hierax out of Asia Minor, where he had attempted to reestablish himself, and into Thrace. There Hierax was murdered by some Galatians in 226 BCE.

Hierax's turbulent career illustrates the tenuous nature of the Seleucids' hold on Asia Minor and how prone the Seleucid family was to internal conflict.

DOUGLAS KELLY

See also
Parthian Empire; Seleucid Empire

References
Sherwin-White, Susan, and Amélie Kuhrt. *From Samarkhand to Sardis: A New Approach to the Seleucid Empire.* London: Duckworth, 1993.
Shipley, Graham. *The Greek World after Alexander, 323–30 BC.* London: Routledge, 2000.

Anti-Semitism

Anti-Semitism, defined as hostility toward the Jewish people, has played a significant role in history. European anti-Semitism, rooted in medieval culture, served as one of the principal motivations for the Zionist movement in the early 20th century and the initial migration of European Jews to Palestine. The murder of 6 million Jews during World War II represents the most heinous expression of European antipathy toward Judaism. Revulsion at the atrocities of the Nazis and sympathy for the victims of the Holocaust contributed significantly to international support for the founding of the State of Israel in 1948. However, the end of the Holocaust did not mean an end to anti-Jewish feelings in the world. The establishment of Israel resulted in the growth of anti-Jewish sentiment throughout the Arab world and the global Muslim community, sentiments that remain strong today.

Some of the roots of European anti-Semitism lie in Late Antiquity. Early Christian texts can be interpreted as placing blame on the Jews for the death of Christ. However, most of the familiar manifestations of anti-Semitism in Europe originated in the Middle Ages. A significant decline in European acceptance of Judaism took place in the second half of the 11th century as increasing centralization in the Roman Church reduced the religious autonomy of local authorities. The Gregorian reforms of the period and the writings of St. Peter Damian attacked the practice of Judaism in Central Europe as a danger to the Christian community. The Crusades also had disastrous implications for European Jews, as the pursuit of Christian orthodoxy was combined with the use of force in a systematic way. Following Pope Urban II's call in 1095 for a holy war to wrest Jerusalem from Muslim control, a number of riots and massacres aimed at the Jewish communities of Europe took place. Both the People's Crusade of 1096 and the more formal military expedition (the First Crusade) that followed engaged in numerous pogroms. In short, crusading zeal was directed against non-Christians in general. Following the conquest of Jerusalem in 1099, virtually the entire Jewish community of the city was slain by the victorious crusading army.

After the 11th century, anti-Semitism occupied a permanent place in medieval Christian culture. During the pontificate of Innocent III (1198–1216), such sentiments acquired an institutional character. Pope Innocent viewed Judaism and Christian heretical thought as significant threats to the orthodoxy of the church. The Fourth Lateran Council (1215), presided over by Innocent, required that Jewish communities be separated from those of Christians, thus creating Jewish ghettos. In addition, Jews were required to wear yellow symbols and were denied participation in various professions. Jewish customs also contributed to separation of peoples. These policies formed the foundation for centuries of anti-Jewish behavior on the European continent.

The crowned heads of Europe also adopted measures directed against the Jewish population during the High Middle Ages. Rulers often charged high taxes in return for granting protection to Jewish communities. Ultimately, Edward I of England and Philip IV of France expelled the Jewish populations from their kingdoms in the late 13th century, confiscating property in the process. These expulsions contributed to the concentration of Jews in Central and Eastern Europe. Widespread vilification of the Jews accompanied physical violence and forced isolation. Jews were accused of complicity in the death of Christ, using the blood of Christians in their rituals, and slaughtering Christian children.

The Jewish community of the medieval Iberian Peninsula had a more complex experience. While Jews suffered persecution in the Visigothic kingdom of the Early Middle Ages, they were quite well treated under the Arab Muslim rule that began in the early 8th century. Positive attitudes toward Jewish monotheism allowed for significant Jewish participation in the life of the Arab state in the 10th and 11th centuries. However, later Berber-dominated governments adopted a more hostile view of Judaism, and this prompted Jewish migrations to the Christian kingdoms of northern Iberia, which accepted the new migrants.

Conditions for the Jews of Iberia changed in the Late Middle Ages. After 1391 they came under significant pressure to convert to Christianity. The Spanish Inquisition, founded by King Ferdinand and Queen Isabella in 1478, viewed the enforcement of Christian orthodoxy among converts as one of its principal roles and inflicted considerable suffering on Jews and Jewish converts through the first half of the 16th century. In 1492, Spanish tolerance of the Jews waned altogether. Ferdinand and Isabella ordered them expelled from the kingdom, and Portugal followed suit in 1497. These expulsions ultimately led to the establishment of Jewish communities across the Mediterranean and in North Africa. Medieval anti-Semitism established patterns and policies that would persist into the 20th century: vilification, physical separation, exclusion from economic activity, stigmatization, forced conversion, and periodic violence.

Ultimately, the European Enlightenment of the 18th century and the liberal political agendas of the 19th century reduced the role of Christianity in European public life and produced a more secular society. In this atmosphere, many European Jews gradually began to assimilate into the economic, political, and cultural lives of the nations in which they lived.

However, the rise of modern European secular culture in the 18th and 19th centuries did not result in the disappearance of anti-Semitism. It remained an ugly part of the European cultural landscape. Theodor Herzl's Zionist movement grew as a response to the continued exclusion of Jews from late 19th-century European culture, an exclusion rooted in medieval tradition. His arguments for a separate Jewish state proceeded from his realization that Jews would always be regarded as alien in Europe. In *Der Judenstaat,* he argued that Jews would never be assimilated in European nations despite their service and patriotism. Only a state of their own would free the Jews from oppression and persecution. Herzl suggested Palestine (then part of the Ottoman Empire) as a possible site for a Jewish homeland, and he also considered parts of Argentina.

While Zionism provided an ideological basis for Jewish immigration to Palestine in the early 20th century, such immigration also proceeded from the harshly anti-Semitic policies adopted by Tsar Alexander III in his Russian and Polish territories after 1881. While most Russian and Polish Jews fled to the United States or Western Europe, some proceeded to Palestine. Significant Jewish migration to the Middle East began while the region was still controlled by the Ottomans. The initial reaction of Palestinian Arabs to Jewish settlement was mixed: resentment on the one hand, economic cooperation and land sales on the other. The Jewish population grew and acquired a distinctly Zionist character. By the early 20th century, Palestinians began to pressure Ottoman authorities to restrict Jewish immigration, with limited effectiveness. It is important to point out that Arab political action against Jewish ambitions did not necessarily have an anti-Semitic nature. However, as Jewish socialist agricultural collectives proliferated and largely ended the hiring of Arab farm workers, the increasing tensions resulted in mutual bitterness.

World War I had a profound effect on Arab-Jewish relations in Palestine. In an effort to secure local support for its war against the Ottomans, the British government made conflicting promises of autonomy or outright independence to the Jewish and Arab inhabitants of Palestine. When the British gained control of the region in 1918 at the end of World War I, they soon found themselves mediating an increasingly acrimonious dispute. The figure of Haj Amin al-Husseini, grand mufti of Jerusalem, serves as an excellent indication of growing anti-Jewish sentiment during this period. A significant leader of the Palestinian Arabs, al-Husseini moved incrementally toward anti-Semitism as he opposed Jewish ambitions in the region. He inspired and organized the growth of Arab paramilitary groups intent on thwarting the growth of Jewish power. When disputes over access to the holy places in Jerusalem led to open conflict in 1929, he proved unable to control his followers. Violence spread across the region, with hundreds of Jews and Arabs killed. A significant consequence of the riots was the formation of the irregular Jewish defense force, Haganah.

Unrest erupted again in 1936 as Arab attempts at economic and political action against the Jewish population turned violent. The 1936 Arab Revolt involved conflict among all three groups in the region: British, Arab, and Jewish. The outbreaks of 1929 and 1936 resulted in severe limitations on Jewish immigration to Palestine as the British responded to Arab pressure. In addition, the violence undermined efforts at Arab-Jewish cooperation and led to mutual vilification and recrimination. Arab political resistance to Zionist aims came to include anti-Semitic policy and rhetoric.

The rise of Nazism in Germany during the 1920s and 1930s forever changed the destiny of the Jewish people. Nazi ideology drew upon the historical anti-Semitic elements of European culture and amplified them through German ultranationalism, social Darwinist rhetoric, and industrial technology. The systematic killing of 6 million Jews apparently confirmed Herzl's ideas about the illusory nature of Jewish assimilation in Europe. The Arab-Jewish conflict in Palestine was also affected by the war, and the grand mufti of Jerusalem gained notoriety for his active courting of the Axis powers.

Before and after the war, Zionists from the Middle East, eager to attract additional Jewish immigrants, depicted Palestine as an obvious refuge for European Jews. On the other hand, Palestinian Arabs continued to oppose any increase in Jewish migration. However, the horrors of the Holocaust resulted in an increase in global support for a Jewish homeland in the Middle East. In 1947, the British agreed to refer the fate of Palestine to the newly formed United Nations (UN). The UN resolution partitioning Palestine and creating a Jewish state was bitterly opposed by the Arab states. When the new nation of Israel was proclaimed in May 1948, five of the newly formed Arab states—Egypt, Syria, Iraq, Transjordan, and Lebanon—immediately invaded, initiating half a century of Arab-Israeli warfare.

As Israel won successive wars with its Arab neighbors, anti-Jewish feeling among the Arabs increased. Anti-Zionism represented the core of the Arab position. Indeed, none of the Arab nations of the Middle East recognized the right of Israel to exist until the Israel-Egypt Peace Treaty of 1979, and they vowed to destroy the Jewish state. Anti-Zionism, however, was often combined with anti-Semitism, as Arab rhetoric attacked Judaism and the Jewish people. At the same time, some Israeli rhetoric vilified the Arab people. The existence of Arab refugees fanned the flames. Such refugees, mostly Palestinian Arabs who had fled Israel during 1948–1949, lived in a number of large camps located in Syria, Gaza, Jordan, and the West Bank. Dispossessed, the refugees seethed with anti-Jewish sentiment. The Palestine Liberation Organization (PLO), founded in 1964, drew its members largely from their ranks.

During the Cold War, varied forms of Arab nationalism dominated the viewpoints of many Arab governments. Socialist and anticolonialist in tone, Arab nationalism attacked Zionism and Judaism as racist and imperialist and denounced Israel as part of an American plot for global domination. With the Israeli victory in the 1967 Six-Day War and the occupation of Arab territories in the Sinai, the West Bank, and the Gaza Strip, such charges intensified. This resulted in widespread isolation of Israel. Global anti-Zionism and anti-Semitism continued to grow, and the Israeli invasion of Lebanon in 1982 accelerated its pace.

The Arab-Israeli struggle changed significantly in the 1980s as low-intensity local insurgency largely replaced large-scale confrontations between national armies. Islamist paramilitary groups—Hamas, Hezbollah, and Islamic Jihad—played a central role in this new conflict. In addition, the collapse of the Soviet Union in 1990 and the defeat of the Baathist regime in Iraq in 1991 resulted in a decline in the status of Arab nationalism. As a result, radical Islam has become an increasingly important ideological basis for Arab resistance to Israel. Anti-Zionist views in the Middle East and around the world have acquired a more religious character in the years since the end of the Cold War and often involve anti-Semitic rhetoric. Indeed, the conflict between Israel and Islamist groups has led to significant mutual vilification.

Robert S. Kiely

See also
Arab Revolt of World War I; Crusades in the Holy Land, Christian; Haganah; Hamas; Hezbollah; Husseini, Haj Amin al-; Israeli War of Independence; Jihad; Ottoman Empire; Palestine, British Mandate for; Palestine Liberation Organization; World War I, Impact on the Middle East; World War II, Impact on the Middle East; Zionism

References
Cantor, Norman. *Civilization of the Middle Ages*. New York: Harper Perennial, 1994.
Dimont, Max. *Jews, God and History*. New York: Simon and Schuster, 1962.
Lewis, Bernard. *The Middle East*. New York: Scribner, 1995.
Perry, Marvin, and Frederick Schweitzer. *Anti-Semitism: Myths and Hate from Antiquity to the Present*. New York: Palgrave Macmillan, 2005.

Aoun, Michel (1935–)

Lebanese Army general and politician who has served as Lebanon's president since October 31, 2016. Born into a poor Christian Maronite family in the Harat Hraik southern suburb of Beirut on February 17, 1935, Michel Aoun ended his secondary education at the Collège des Frères in 1956. In 1958 he graduated from the Lebanese Military Academy as an artillery lieutenant. He received additional military training in France at Châlons-sur-Marne during 1958–1959 and at the École Supérieure de Guerre in 1978–1980. He also received training at the U.S. Army Artillery School, Fort Sill, Oklahoma, in 1966.

During the Israeli invasion of Lebanon in 1982, Aoun commanded a battalion defending the presidential palace in Baabda. During the Lebanese Civil War, in September 1983 he commanded the 8th Mechanized Infantry Battalion in the Battle of Souq el Gharbo. In June 1984, he was promoted to brigadier general and appointed commander of the Lebanese Army.

In September 1988, outgoing president Amin Jumayyil dismissed the civilian government of Salim al-Huss and appointed a six-man interim military government of three Christians and three Muslims. The Muslims refused to serve, however, and al-Huss, supported by Syria, refused to step aside. There were thus two competing governments in Beirut: one largely Christian and military in East Beirut and the other Muslim-dominated in West Beirut.

From September 1988 to October 1990, Aoun was prime minister and president of the Christian-military government. In 1989, emboldened by support from both France and Iraq, he vowed to remove Syrian influence from Lebanon. Fighting between elements of the Lebanese Army, including Aoun's portion, and the Syrian Army began soon thereafter, leading to an air and ground campaign in which many Lebanese—civilian as well as military—perished. Syrian influence in Lebanon sharply increased upon Iraqi president Saddam Hussein's invasion of Kuwait in August 1990. Then on October 13, 1990, Syrian forces invaded Beirut, killing hundreds of soldiers and civilians. Aoun's forces were defeated, and he was driven from office. He sought refuge in the French embassy and was given safe passage to France and asylum in France in August 1991. Aoun vowed to remain abroad until the last Syrian soldier had departed Lebanon, and he did not return to Lebanon until early May 7, 2005, upon the withdrawal of Syrian troops.

In December 2006 Aoun, as head of the Free Patriotic Movement, signed an agreement to work with the militant Muslim Hezbollah against the government of Prime Minister Fuad Siniura and President Émile Lahoud, a pro-Syrian figure. Aoun and his supporters strongly believed that a new unity government was required, as the current system, particularly its cabinet structure, does not allow the opposition to block any motion. Critics charged that as part of his quest to become Lebanon's president, Aoun was aiding Hezbollah in its aim to gain veto power in the government. He did not deny his desire to be president but defended his alliance with Hezbollah because he claimed that it would help prevent the return of Syria to Lebanon. That alliance continues. On October 31, 2016, Aoun was finally elected president, garnering more than 65 percent of the vote. He favors a strong secular Lebanese state and is an avowed opponent of armed militias. Aoun now leads the Strong Lebanon bloc, which has 29 parliamentary representatives out of a total of 128.

Spencer C. Tucker

See also
Hezbollah; Lahoud, Émile Jamil; Lebanon; Lebanon Civil War; Lebanon-Israeli War; Siniura, Fuad

References
Fisk, Robert. *Pity the Nation: The Abduction of Lebanon.* 4th ed. New York: Nation Books, 2002.
Rabil, Robert G. *Embattled Neighbors: Syria, Israel and Lebanon.* Boulder, CO: Lynne Rienner, 2003.

Aqaba, Capture of (July 6, 1917)

Major victory for the Arab tribesmen fighting the Ottoman Turks in World War I. The capture of Aqaba was the most important victory to that point in the Arab Revolt of 1916–1918.

Captain T. E. Lawrence of the British intelligence staff, who was serving as British representative to the Arab commander in the field, Prince Faisal ibn Hussein (Feisal or Faysal) of the Kingdom of Hejaz, realized the value to the Arabs of securing a port through which to facilitate British support. The British Army preferred an Arab action that would help protect the eastern flank of the army moving into Palestine. As a consequence, in April 1917 Lawrence formulated a plan to capture Aqaba at the head of an arm of the Red Sea running along the eastern Sinai. This plan did not have the support of Lieutenant General Sir Archibald Murray, commander of the Egypt Expeditionary Force.

On May 9, nonetheless, Lawrence left Wejh with 1,000 men for Aqaba. He took a circuitous path, proceeding almost as far north as Damascus. In the process Lawrence made contact with Arab leaders in Jordan and secured an additional 4,000 fighting men. During their march, Lawrence and his men destroyed several miles of railroad tracks and fought the Turks at Fuweila and Aba-el-Lissan, completely destroying the Ottoman force on July 2. Lawrence convinced the Arabs to take prisoners and treat them well in an effort to encourage other Ottoman garrisons to surrender.

Lawrence and his army continued to push south in order to approach Aqaba from the land side. Ottoman garrisons along his route most often surrendered without fighting, surprised at the size of the growing Arab force. The Arabs overran the outermost defenses at Khadra, and on July 6 they swept into Aqaba. There was little fighting, and the Ottoman garrison of some 300 men and a few German advisers soon surrendered. Only with difficulty did Lawrence prevent a massacre by the Arabs.

Commander of the Egypt Station Vice Admiral Rosslyn Wemyss immediately rushed food and arms to Aqaba to enable the Arabs to hold it. Faisal moved his headquarters there, and a regular army of Arabs, formed in Egypt of Arab prisoners of war captured in Egypt by the British, was established there. Aqaba became the chief base for the Arab Revolt and served as the conduit of arms, propaganda, and money from the British to the Arabs for the remainder of the war. Lawrence was promoted to major for his success.

TIM J. WATTS

See also
Arab Revolt in Palestine; Faisal I, King of Iraq; Lawrence, Thomas Edward; Murray, Sir Archibald James; Sinai Campaign of 1916–1917

References
Erickson, Edward J. *Ordered to Die: A History of the Ottoman Army in the First World War.* Westport, CT: Greenwood, 2000.
Lawrence, T. E. *Revolt in the Desert.* New York: George H. Doran, 1927.
Mack, John E. *A Prince of Our Disorder: The Life of T. E. Lawrence.* Boston: Little, Brown, 1976.
Thomas, Lowell. *With Lawrence in Arabia.* New York: Century, 1924.
Wilson, Jeremy. *Lawrence of Arabia: The Authorized Biography of T. E. Lawrence.* New York: Atheneum, 1990.

Aqaba, Gulf of

The Gulf of Aqaba, also known as the Gulf of Eilat, is a branch of the Dead Sea running east of the Sinai Peninsula and west of the Arabian mainland. The Gulf of Aqaba, bordered by Egypt, Israel, Jordan, and Saudi Arabia, is roughly 120 miles long, has a maximum width of 15 miles, and passes through the Strait of Tiran at its junction with the Red Sea.

Strategically important, the Gulf of Aqaba has played a major role in the relationships between Israel and the Arab states that border it. The Gulf of Aqaba, with the Israeli port of Eilat at its mouth, was Israel's only accessible waterway to East Africa, Asia, and Australia when Egypt closed the Suez Canal between 1967 and 1975.

Egypt blockaded the Strait of Tiran leading into the gulf from 1949 until 1956 and then again on May 23, 1967, despite the fact that it had been declared an international waterway by the United Nations in 1958. The 1967 closing of the straits by the Egyptians was one of the key factors precipitating Israel's preemptive attack on Egypt that sparked the Six-Day War.

Following the 1967 war, Israel occupied the Sinai and the strategic points along the Strait of Tiran to ensure access to the Gulf of Aqaba. Israel withdrew from its positions on the Strait of Tiran following the signing of the Camp David Accords of 1978 and the subsequent Israel-Egypt Peace Treaty of 1979.

In the 1980s, the Gulf of Aqaba played a major role in the Iran-Iraq War (1980–1988), when it became a vital supply route for Iraq. During the Persian Gulf War in 1991, the Gulf of Aqaba also served as an important blockade point for coalition forces against goods bound for Iraq.

KEITH A. LEITICH

See also
Camp David Accords; Eilat, Israel; Iran-Iraq War; Israel-Egypt Peace Treaty; Persian Gulf War, Overview; Red Sea; Sinai Campaign of 1956; Sinai Peninsula; Six-Day War; Strait of Tiran Crisis; Suez Canal

References
Bloomfield, Louis M. *Egypt, Israel, and the Gulf of Aqaba in International Law.* Toronto: Carswell, 1957.
Hakim, Ali A. *The Middle Eastern States and the Law of the Sea.* Syracuse, NY: Syracuse University Press, 1979.
Halderman, John W., ed. *The Middle East Crisis: Test of International Law.* Dobbs Ferry, NY: Oceana, 1969.
Porter, Paul A. *The Gulf of Aqaba, an International Waterway: Its Significance to International Trade.* Washington, DC: Public Affairs, 1957.
Salans, C. F. "The Gulf of Aqaba and the Straits of Tiran." In *The Arab-Israeli Conflict*, ed. John N. Moore, 807–819. Princeton, NJ: Princeton University Press, 1975.

Arab Economic Boycott of Israel

The collective, national, and singular Arab economic boycott of Jewish-owned and Israeli businesses and products. In 1945, the newly formed League of Arab States (Arab League) initiated a formal economic boycott of Jewish goods and services in an attempt to assist the Palestinians in their struggle against Zionism. The Arab League formally declared the economic boycott when it passed Resolution 16 on December 2, 1945, calling on all member states to boycott Jewish goods and services in the British Mandate for Palestine. Following the Arab defeat in the Israeli War of Independence (1948–1949), the boycott was formalized against Israel. The boycott prohibited direct trade between Arab countries and Israel.

In 1950 a secondary boycott was expanded to include non-Israelis who maintained economic ties with Israel. The secondary boycott was aimed at individuals, businesses, and organizations that conducted trade with Israel. The boycott prohibited public and private Arab entities from engaging in business with any entity that does business in Israel directly or indirectly. Any firms found in violation were put on a blacklist maintained by the Arab League. A prime example of the secondary boycott concerned the U.S.-based Coca-Cola Company, which had operations in Israel. As a consequence of Coca-Cola's commercial activities in Israel, Arab countries refused to import Coca-Cola products and gave their business to rival Pepsi-Cola. A subsequent tertiary boycott prohibited any entity in a member country from doing business with a company or individual that had business dealings with the United States or other firms on the Arab League blacklist.

In 1951 the Arab League created the Central Office for the Boycott of Israel in Damascus, Syria, which operated under the aegis of the league's secretary-general. While the central office maintains a register of blacklisted companies with which member states cannot trade, the Arab League does not enforce the boycott itself, and the regulations are not binding on member countries. In fact, several Arab states have chosen not to follow the secondary and tertiary boycotts. International reaction to the boycott ranged from expressions of outrage by the United States to reluctance by Japan to engage in trade with Israel for fear of offending Arab countries.

The boycott was dealt a significant setback on March 26, 1979, when Egypt signed the Israel-Egypt Peace Treaty. The treaty formally ended Egyptian participation in the boycott. The boycott was further eroded when Oman and Qatar established trade relations with Israel following the October 1991 Madrid Conference and the subsequent implementation of the Israeli-Palestinian peace process. In 1993, the Palestinian Authority (PA) gave up the boycott in an attempt to advance the Israeli-Palestinian peace process. On October 26, 1994, Jordan signed the Israeli-Jordan Peace Treaty with the State of Israel that also formally ended Jordanian participation in the economic boycott. In addition, in 1996 member countries of the Gulf Cooperation Council—Bahrain, Kuwait, Oman, Qatar, Saudi Arabia, and the United Arab Emirates—announced that they would only enforce the primary boycott. In 2005 and 2006, Bahrain and Oman agreed to drop the boycott altogether as a provision of their free trade agreements with the United States.

The impact of the boycotts on the Israelis has not been great, although it has most clearly taken a toll. The Israeli Chamber of Commerce has issued estimates suggesting that Israeli exports are about 10 percent lower than they would be without the economic boycott. In addition, foreign investment in Israel is probably 10 percent lower with the boycott in place. Israeli trade relations with the Republic of Korea (South Korea) and Japan especially suffered as a result of the boycott. In spite of the Arab boycott, Israeli products made their way into the affected nations. In general, these products are shipped to a third party, which then ships them to the various Arab states. Cyprus has been the leading third-party nation through which boycotted products are sent.

Because the boycott has been sporadically applied and enforced, it has been less than effective in hindering the economic development of Israel and has largely failed to deter companies conducting business with Israel. Despite the failure of the boycott, however, the Arab League has thus far chosen not to repeal it, and the Central Office for the Boycott of Israel still exists. Today the boycott is only sporadically applied and enforced. Syria, Lebanon, and Iran (though not an Arab state) are the only states that actively enforce it. The boycott thus has little impact on the Israeli or Arab economies.

KEITH A. LEITICH

See also
Arab League; Israel-Egypt Peace Treaty; Israel-Jordan Peace Treaty; Madrid Conference

References
Feiler, Gil. *From Boycott to Economic Cooperation: The Political Economy of the Arab Boycott of Israel.* London: Frank Cass, 1998.
Sarna, Aaron J. *Boycott and Blacklist: A History of Arab Economic Warfare against Israel.* Totowa, NJ: Rowman and Littlefield, 1986.
Sharif, Amer A. *A Statistical Study of the Arab Boycott of Israel.* Beirut, Lebanon: Institute for Palestinian Studies, 1970.
Weiss, Martin A. *Arab Boycott of Israel.* Washington, DC: Congressional Research Service, Library of Congress, 2006.

Arabi, Ahmed (1841–1911)

Ahmed Arabi (Urabi), also known as Arabi Pasha, was a charismatic Egyptian Army officer and an ardent nationalist leader who challenged the authority of the khedive (viceroy) of Egypt. Arabi's actions eventually resulted in confrontation with the British and the defeat of the Egyptian Army.

Sayed Ahmed Bey Arabi was born on March 31, 1841. He claimed descent from Hussein, the grandson of Prophet Muhammad. The son of a small village sheikh, Arabi was conscripted into the Egyptian Army at age 14. Tall, intelligent, and hardworking, he soon caught the attention of his superiors. Three years later, Arabi was commissioned a lieutenant. Soon he became an aide-de-camp to the progressive ruler Mohammed Ali and was promoted to lieutenant colonel.

After Ismail became khedive in 1863, Arabi fell out of favor, and his once-promising military career stagnated. His personal discontent increased, especially during the debacle of the Egyptian Army's invasion of Abyssinia (1875–1876). The British persuaded the Ottoman sultan to depose Ismail and replace him with Tewfik, Ismail's son.

Loss of sovereignty to the British and French and indebtedness were keenly felt by many Egyptians. Arabi became a leader of the nationalists, who were trying to end foreign domination. On February 1, 1881, and again on September 9, Arabi and other colonels used the threat of a military coup to issue ultimatums to Tewfik for governmental and military reforms. On both occasions, the khedive gave in to Arabi's demands.

In February 1882, Arabi became minister of war. The British and French sent a joint naval squadron that arrived at Alexandria late in May 1882 and demanded the dismissal of Arabi. The khedive consented, and his entire government resigned in protest. The Egyptian Army was in open defiance, and the country was in chaos. Arabi was reinstated as war minister. Riots erupted in Alexandria on June 11, 1882; 68 Europeans were killed and many more injured, including the British consul, although more than that number of Egyptians also died.

When Arabi refused a British demand to halt strengthening the fortifications of Alexandria, British ships bombarded the city on July 11, the same day Arabi was appointed commander of the army. The British then landed troops under the command of General (later field marshal viscount) Sir Garnet J. Wolseley. The force landed at Ismailia.

Arabi attacked the British at Kassassin on September 9 and was repulsed. In the decisive Battle of Tel el-Kebir on September 13, the British were victorious and entered Cairo the next day. Arabi and other senior Egyptian Army officers surrendered that evening.

In December, Arabi was brought to trial before an Egyptian military court and charged with rebellion. He pleaded guilty and was sentenced to death. The British government, concerned about further unrest, recommended leniency, and the khedive commuted Arabi's sentence to "perpetual exile." Arabi was transported to Ceylon. In 1901 he was permitted to return to Egypt, where he died on September 21, 1911.

Harold E. Raugh Jr.

See also
Alexandria, Bombardment of; Egypt; Egypt under British Rule; Tel el-Kebir, Battle of

References
Barthorp, Michael. *War on the Nile: Britain, Egypt, and the Sudan, 1882–1898*. Poole, UK: Blandford, 1984.
Farwell, Byron. *Queen Victoria's Little Wars*. New York: Harper & Row, 1972.
Lehmann, Joseph H. *All Sir Garnet: A Life of Field-Marshal Lord Wolseley*. London: Jonathan Cape, 1964.
Maurice, J. F. *Military History of the Campaign of 1882 in Egypt*. London: HMSO, 1887.

Arabia, Roman

Roman Arabia was roughly contiguous with modern-day Saudi Arabia. It was divided into Arabia Deserta, the arid areas of the north Saudi Arabian Peninsula, and Arabia Felix, the southern end of the peninsula, termed "Felix" for its prosperity as a producer of incense and spices and as an entrepôt for the Red Sea trade with India. The Romans did not incorporate Arabia, which lay beyond the empire's eastern frontier, as a province before the reign of Emperor Trajan (98–117). The kingdom of the Nabataeans, a pre-Islamic Arab people, was employed as a buffer and Roman client.

Trajan's eastern conquests allowed the annexation of the Nabataean kingdom and the creation of a Roman province termed Arabia. Its main cities were Bostra, garrisoned by a legion, and Petra, the ancient capital of the Nabataeans. Controlling the overland routes to Arabia, Felix became less necessary owing to the development of the Red Sea ocean route to India.

Sara E. Phang

See also
Roman-Parthian Wars; Trajan

References
Al-Otaibi, F. M. *From Nabataea to Roman Arabia: Acquisition or Conquest*. Oxford, UK: Archaeopress, 2011.
Bowersock, G. W. *Roman Arabia*. Cambridge, MA: Harvard University Press, 1984.
Parker, S. T. 1986. *Romans and Saracens: A History of the Arabian Frontier*. Philadelphia: American Schools of Oriental Research, 1986.

Arabian Gulf

See Persian Gulf

Arab-Jewish Communal War (November 30, 1947–May 14, 1948)

Fighting that erupted on November 30, 1947, between Arabs and Jews in the British Mandate for Palestine is often included as part of the Israeli War of Independence (1948–1949), but this first phase of fighting between Arabs and Jews began well before the Jewish proclamation of independence on May 14, 1948. The war erupted on November 30, 1947, immediately following announcement of the United Nations (UN) General Assembly vote approving the partition plan for Palestine. The month before, the Arab League had urged its member states to begin training volunteers for a possible military campaign to prevent the establishment of a Jewish state.

The Jews found themselves facing a wave of violence by elements of the Arab Palestinian population, assisted by irregular Arab forces from the neighboring states. The Arab military effort was only loosely coordinated. The Arab Higher Committee announced a general strike, and Arab mobs soon responded by attacking Jewish buses and other vehicles. An Arab mob destroyed the old commercial center of Jerusalem, while Arabs also fired on and broke into Jewish shops in Haifa, Jaffa, and other places. By December, the Arab and Jewish sectors were clearly segregated. Marginal or mixed areas in the cities were quickly evacuated by one side or the other. Fighting to control the lines of communication was especially fierce.

The UN vote on partition was also the signal for violence against Jews within the Arab states. In Aleppo, Syria, Arab demonstrators torched 300 Jewish homes and 11 synagogues. In Aden, Yemen, 76 Jews were slain.

When the fighting began, the principal Jewish military force was Haganah. This self-defense force consisted of a small fully mobilized nucleus and a larger militia element. The Haganah high command could call on a standing military force of four battalions of Palmach (commando units) numbering some 2,100 men in all, along with 1,000 reservists who could be called up on short notice, and the Hel Sade (HISH, field army) of about 1,800 men, with another 10,000 reservists. Haganah could also count on perhaps 32,000 members of the Hel Mishmar (HIM, garrison army), most of whom were older persons assigned to the defense of fixed locations such as towns and cities. Finally, there were Gadna (Youth Battalions) consisting of young people who were receiving some military training with the plan that when they were older they would join the HISH or Palmach.

Military equipment was inadequate. Haganah could count on about 15,000 rifles of a bewildering number of types, some light machine guns, and several dozen medium machine guns and 3-inch mortars. Its secret arms workshops were also producing the largely stamped Sten submachine gun as well as hand grenades and explosives.

Two other organizations must be mentioned. These were the Irgun Tsvai Leumi (National Military Organization) of about 5,000 members and Lohamei Herut Israel (Fighters for the Freedom of Israel), also known as Lehi and the Stern Gang, with about 1,000. These two elements operated very much on their own at the start of the fighting. Indeed, there was no love lost between them and Haganah, with even armed clashes. During the fighting, however, both organizations disbanded, and their members joined Haganah to form the new Tz'va Haganah L'Yisrael (Israel Defense Forces, IDF). From the start David Ben-Gurion, chairman of the Jewish Agency Executive, had charge of both political and defense matters.

The British government manifested a pronounced partiality for the Arab side. This could be seen in its refusal to lift embargoes on Jewish immigration into Palestine and the acquisition of weapons. British authorities refused to recognize the right of Haganah to exist and disarmed its members when they could be found. At the same time, Britain continued to sell arms to both Iraq and Transjordan with the full knowledge that these might be used against the Jews in Palestine. Also, Arab leaders were occasionally notified in advance of British military evacuations, enabling Arab irregulars to seize control for themselves of such strategically located sites as police stations and military posts.

The early Arab military attacks of the Communal War within Palestine were uncoordinated. They took the form of hit-and-run raids against isolated Jewish settlements with the aim of destroying Jewish property. The attacks were mounted entirely by Palestinian Arabs, although they did receive some financial assistance and arms from the Arab states. Arab efforts early on were, however, handicapped by ongoing tensions between the Nashashibi and Husseini factions.

On September 16, 1947, the Political Committee of the Arab League, meeting in Sofar, Lebanon, had appealed for economic reprisals against both Britain and the United States and for arms and money for the Palestinian Arabs. Following the UN partition vote, Iraqi premier Salih Jabr called for a meeting of Arab leaders in Cairo on December 12. There he called on the Arab states to intervene militarily in Palestine, but Egypt and Saudi Arabia were opposed, and King Abdullah of Jordan disliked even the mention of Arab volunteers. Eventually the Arab leaders adopted a resolution

Atop the roof of a Jerusalem railroad station, members of the Arab Liberation Army guard the main rail corridor to Bethlehem and southern Palestine on May 7, 1948, seven days before the formal declaration of the state of Israel. (Bettmann/Getty Images)

calling for 10,000 rifles and other light weapons and 3,000 Arab volunteers to be sent into Palestine through Syria, with the sum of £1 million to be allocated for the defense of Palestine.

The Cairo decision led to the formation of the Arab Liberation Army (ALA), to be commanded by Iraqi staff officer General Sir Ismail Safwat Pasha, who immediately set up his headquarters outside of Damascus. Field command went to Fawzi al-Qawuqji, guerrilla leader of the Arab Revolt of 1936. Most ALA members were in fact mercenaries. They included a large number of Syrian Arabs along with some Yugoslav Muslims, Circassians from the Caucasus region, Poles, Germans, and Spaniards. In late January 1948, members of the ALA began infiltrating across the Syrian border into Palestine, and al-Qawuqji set up his headquarters in Tiberias in the Galilee region of north-central Palestine. By the end of February 1948 there were perhaps 5,000 members of the ALA in Palestine, and by the end of March their numbers had grown to perhaps 7,000.

In the spring the Arab forces, including the ALA, divided Palestine into three major fronts. The northern sector contained by far the largest Arab force, some 7,000 men under al-Qawuqji and the Syrian Adib al-Shishakli. Another 5,000 were in the central sector, the largest number of whom were under the command of Abd al-Qadr al-Husseini, a nephew of the mufti of Jerusalem. Some 2,000 Arab fighters, most of them Muslim Brotherhood volunteers from Egypt, were located in the southern sector of the Negev Desert.

In the winter and early spring of 1948, the Arab forces launched a series of largely uncoordinated military attacks. These fell on Jewish quarters in the cities, chiefly Jerusalem, as well as the more isolated kibbutzim in the Hebron Hills area. The outnumbered but disinterested British authorities did nothing to inhibit the Arabs, who were soon able to cut key roads, including those between Tel Aviv and Jerusalem, Haifa and western Galilee, Tiberias and eastern Galilee, and Afula and the Beit She'an Valley. The Jewish farms in the Negev were also soon isolated.

Jewish authorities, who had expected to have more time to prepare, were caught off guard by these Arab military moves. Perhaps the most ominous situation was that facing the Jews in Jerusalem, now without ammunition and other military supplies but also cut off from food. The Arabs controlled the low hills dominating the Tel Aviv–Jerusalem road into the city and were able to destroy at will the Jewish truck convoys attempting to reach Jerusalem. The difficulty of the military situation facing the Jews was compounded by the decision taken by Ben-Gurion and the Jewish Agency Executive to defend every bit of territory allocated to the future Jewish state under the partition plan as well as Jewish settlements, which in accordance with the plan would be allocated to the Arab state. This decision meant that already meager Haganah resources would have to be dispersed throughout Palestine in a defensive stance, making concentration into larger units for offensive operations impossible. Resupply operations of isolated Jewish settlements through Arab areas such as Galilee and the Negev would be particularly difficult, as would the resupply of Jewish enclaves in the cities, including Jerusalem.

On January 10, 1948, 900 members of the ALA attacked K'far Szold in Upper Galilee but were beaten back. The next day other attacks occurred throughout Palestine against isolated Jewish settlements in the same region but also in the Hebron Hills, the Judaean Mountains, and the Negev. The Arabs also managed to get car bombs into the Jewish quarters of Haifa and Jerusalem. Among their successful targets were the offices of the *Jerusalem Post* and the Jewish Agency headquarters in Jerusalem. Jewish road traffic was largely limited to armored cars or armed convoys. Despite efforts to send the convoys at odd times and by circuitous routes, Arab military action soon brought this traffic to a complete halt.

In view of their inability to capture even one Jewish settlement, in March the Arabs decided to concentrate the bulk of their military effort against Jewish road traffic while at the same time not entirely abandoning attacks on the Jewish settlements or enclaves. The Jews did manage to get an armored convoy to isolated Gat and to destroy an Arab armaments convoy near Haifa. At the same time, however, the Arabs registered success in their effort to isolate Jerusalem. From late March they employed land mines for the first time, completely cutting off the coastal road to the Negev. The Arabs also ambushed at Nebi Daniel a large armored Jewish convoy bound for Jerusalem, destroying or capturing all its vehicles. To the north they also destroyed a Jewish convoy bound from Haifa to the isolated Y'hi'am settlement.

By the end of March the situation facing the Jews appeared grim. The Jewish section of Jerusalem was cut off from the coast, and settlements near the city were isolated from Jerusalem. The Negev and settlements of western Galilee were similarly cut off. On the other hand, Jewish forces were now fully mobilized. Some 21,000 men between the ages of 17 and 25 were now under arms. Progress had also been made in the manufacture of light weapons and explosives, and additional weapons were en route to Palestine from Czechoslovakia. Some 50 light liaison aircraft were in service, performing reconnaissance and transport of some light weapons and key personnel to isolated areas. Arab strength was also increasing, however.

Worried about weakening UN and U.S. support for the implementation of partition, the Jewish leadership was determined to take the offensive. This was made possible by the increased strength of Haganah and the continued evacuation of British military personnel from Palestine. In considering their options, Ben-Gurion and the other Jewish leaders assigned top priority to opening the supply route to Jerusalem.

Code-named Operation NACHSHON, this plan to secure both sides of the Tel Aviv–Jerusalem supply corridor involved the concentration of some 1,500 Jewish troops, armed in large part with weapons that had arrived from Czechoslovakia on April 1, 1948. The operation commenced on April 6. Fighting was intense especially at Kastel, which changed hands several times before the Arabs finally abandoned it on April 10. Abd el-Kadr al-Husseini, the Arab commander of the Jerusalem area, was killed in fighting on April 9. The operation, which ended on April 15, saw three large Jewish convoys reach the city.

At the same time, the ALA attempted to take the Jewish settlement of Mishmar Ha'Emek. The Arabs opened artillery fire on the settlement on April 4, but the defenders repulsed subsequent ground assaults. On April 12 Haganah forces counterattacked, and the Arab forces retreated. This Arab artillery was then relocated to shell the Jewish sector of Jerusalem in early May. During April 12–14 a Druze mercenary battalion attempted, without success, to take the Ramat Yohanan settlement.

Emboldened by its successes, Haganah stepped up its offensive, cutting the port of Tiberias in two on April 18 and forcing an Arab evacuation there. On April 21 as British forces were evacuating Haifa, Haganah began an assault on that city, taking it in two days. Most of the Arab residents left for Lebanon by land and sea, their leaders promising a speedy return. Success here made possible the resupply of Jewish settlements in Upper Galilee, and contact was reestablished with Safed.

On May 1 Arab forces struck back with an assault on the Jewish settlement of Ramot Naftali, previously under siege. Lebanese artillery and tanks took part, but the attack was again halted. On May 6, Jewish forces opened an assault against the Arab part of Safed but were themselves repulsed. The assault was renewed on the night of May 9–10, and this time Jewish forces were successful. The Arab inhabitants fled the city, and Palmach fighters captured a key mountain citadel there. Many other Arab residents in the general area of Safed now also fled, with the result that by mid-May all the Jewish settlements in Upper Galilee were connected. On April 29, part of the Golani Brigade seized Tzemah as well as a nearby police fort. Other former British police installations were taken, and the city of Akko and villages north to the Lebanese border were also secured by May 17.

In Operation HAMETZ, so named because it began on the eve of Passover (*hametz* means "leaven"), Jewish forces cleared Arab villages around Tel Aviv–Jaffa. On April 29 following Jewish encirclement of Jaffa, which was to be included in the Arab part of Palestine under the partition plan, many of its 70,000 Arab residents fled. The city itself surrendered on May 13 after the final British evacuation.

With the British stepping up their final evacuation, Arab forces again seized control of the Tel Aviv–Jerusalem road. The Harel Brigade of Palmach was shifted to Operation JEBUSI to reopen the vital supply corridor. The Harel Brigade was forced by a British ultimatum, backed by artillery, to withdraw from initial captures, and a Jewish attempt to secure the Jericho road also failed. On the night of April 28–29, a struggle for control of the Monastery of St. Simon began. Jewish reinforcements from the Jerusalem Brigade tipped the balance. On May 11 in Operation MACCABEE another effort was made to open the road to Jerusalem, but only one convoy of several dozen vehicles made it through before the Arabs again closed the road on May 17.

With the last British forces quitting Jerusalem on May 14, Jewish forces began Operation KILSHON (PITCHFORK) to prepare for an attack by the Arab Legion. The operation succeeded to the extent that the Jewish area of the city was made into a continuous whole for the first time but also failed to cut a supply corridor to the Jewish quarter of the Old City. Meanwhile, isolated Jewish settlements near Jerusalem were abandoned as indefensible, and the Arab Legion also registered several successes, including the capture of the entire Etzyon block.

In six weeks of heavy fighting before the proclamation of the State of Israel and the invasion by regular Arab armies, Jewish fighters had secured Haifa, Jaffa, Safed, and Tiberias. They had also captured about 100 Arab villages and had surrounded Akko. Most of the main roads were again open to Jewish traffic. For all practical purposes, the Palestinian Arab military forces had been defeated. The ALA had suffered heavy losses, and Jewish armed strength had now increased to 30,000 men. The arms shipments from Czechoslovakia had filled many deficiencies, including antitank and antiaircraft weapons, but the Jews still lacked fighter aircraft, field artillery, and tanks. On May 15, 1948, moreover, regular Arab armies invaded Israel, beginning the Israeli War of Independence, which continued until July 20, 1949, and the signing of the last armistice agreement with Syria.

SPENCER C. TUCKER

See also

Abdullah I; Arab Liberation Army; Arab Revolt in Palestine; Baldat al-Shaykh Massacre; Ben-Gurion, David; Haganah; Irgun Tsvai Leumi; Israeli War of Independence; Lohamei Herut Israel; NACHSHON, Operation; Palmach; Qawuqji, Fawzi al-

References

Dupuy, Trevor N. *Elusive Victory: The Arab-Israeli Wars, 1947–1974.* Garden City, NY: Military Book Club, 2002.

Lucas, Noah. *The Modern History of Israel.* New York: Praeger, 1975.

Sachar, Howard M. *A History of Israel: From the Rise of Zionism to Our Time.* 3rd ed. New York: Knopf, 2007.

Smith, Charles D. *Palestine and the Arab-Israeli Conflict: A History with Documents.* 6th ed. New York: Bedford/St. Martin's, 2006.

Arab League

The Arab League, also known as the League of Arab States, is a voluntary organization of Arabic-speaking nations. It was founded at the end of World War II with the stated purposes of improving conditions in Arab countries, liberating Arab states still under foreign domination, and preventing the formation of a Jewish state in Palestine.

In 1943 the Egyptian government proposed an organization of Arab states that would facilitate closer relations between the nations. Each member would remain a sovereign state, and the organization would not be a union, a federation, or any other sovereign structure. The British government supported this idea in the hope of securing the Arab nations as allies in the war against Germany.

In 1944, representatives from Egypt, Iraq, Lebanon, Yemen, and Saudi Arabia met in Alexandria, Egypt, and agreed to form a federation. The Arab League was officially founded on March 22, 1945, in Cairo. The founding states were Egypt, Iraq, Lebanon, Saudi Arabia, Transjordan (now Jordan), and Syria. Subsequent members include Libya (1953), Sudan (1956), Tunisia (1958), Morocco (1958), Kuwait (1961), Algeria (1962), South Yemen (1967, now Yemen), Bahrain (1971), Oman (1971), Qatar (1971), the United Arab Emirates (1971), Mauritania (1973), Somalia (1974), the State of Palestine (1976), Djibouti (1977), and Comoros (1993). Four nations enjoy observer status: Eritrea, where Arabic is one of the official languages; Brazil and Venezuela, both of which have large Arab communities; and India.

The original goals of the Arab League were to liberate all Arab nations still ruled by foreign countries and to prevent the creation of a Jewish state in Palestine as well as to serve the common good, improve living conditions, and guarantee the hopes of member states. In 1946, Arab League members added to their pact a cultural treaty under which they agreed to exchange professors, teachers, students, and scholars in order to encourage cultural exchange among member nations and disseminate Arab culture to their citizens.

The Arab League's pact also stated that all members would collectively represent the Palestinians so long as Palestine was not an independent state. With no Palestinian leader in 1945, the Arab states feared that the British would dominate the area and that Jews would colonize part of Palestine. In response to these fears, the Arab League created the Arab Higher Committee (AHC) to govern Palestinian Arabs in 1945. This committee was replaced in 1946 by the Arab Higher Executive, which was again reorganized into a new Arab Higher Executive in 1947.

The State of Israel was declared on May 14, 1948. The next day Egypt, Iraq, Lebanon, Saudi Arabia, Syria, and Transjordan responded with a declaration of war on Israel. Yemen also supported the declaration. Secretary-General Abdul Razek Azzam Pasha declared that the Arab League's goal was to conduct a large-scale massacre and extermination. Although King Abdullah of Jordan (he officially changed the name of Transjordan to Jordan in April 1949) claimed to be the legitimate power in Palestine, the Arab League did not wish to see Jordan in control of the area and thus established its own government on behalf of the Palestinians, the All-Palestine State of October 1, 1948. The mufti of Jerusalem, Haj Amin al-Husseini, was its leader, and Jerusalem was its capital. Although ostensibly the new government ruled Gaza, Egypt was the real authority there. In response, Jordan formed a rival temporary government, the First Palestinian Congress, which condemned the government in Gaza. The Arab-Israeli war ended in 1949 with Jordan occupying the West Bank and East Jerusalem and Egypt controlling Gaza.

In 1950 the Arab League signed the Joint Defense and Economic Cooperation Treaty, which declared that the members of the league considered an attack on one member country to be an attack on all. The treaty created a permanent military commission and a joint defense council.

During the 1950s, Egypt effectively led the Arab League. In 1952 a military coup in Egypt nominally headed by General Muhammad Nagib overthrew King Farouk, but within two years Colonel Gamal Abdel Nasser assumed rule of the nation. A strong proponent of Arab unity, he called for a union of all Arab nations, including Palestine. Nasser ended the All-Palestine government in Palestine, formed the United Arab Republic with Syria, and called for the defeat of Israel.

In 1956 Nasser nationalized the Suez Canal, precipitating the Suez Crisis that brought an Israeli invasion of the Sinai followed by short-lived British and French invasions of Egypt. U.S. economic and political pressures secured the withdrawal of the invaders. Far from toppling Nasser as the allied British, French, and Israeli governments had hoped, these pressures both strengthened Nasser's prestige in the Arab world and raised the stature of Pan-Arabism and the Arab League.

In the 1960s the Arab League pushed for the liberation of Palestine, and in 1964 it supported creation of the Palestine Liberation Organization (PLO), which was dedicated to attacks on Israel. Following the Six-Day War of 1967, which ended in extensive territory losses for Egypt, Jordan, and Syria, the Arab League met at Khartoum that August and issued a statement in which its members vowed not to recognize, negotiate with, or conclude a peace agreement with Israel. Egypt also agreed to withdraw its troops from Yemen.

The Arab League suspended Egypt's membership in 1979 in the wake of President Anwar Sadat's visit to Jerusalem and agreement to the 1978 Camp David Accords. The league also moved its headquarters from Cairo to Tunis. When the PLO declared an independent State of Palestine on November 15, 1988, the Arab League immediately recognized it. Egypt was readmitted to the league in 1989, and the headquarters returned to Cairo.

During the prelude to the 1991 Persian Gulf War, the Arab League condemned Iraq's invasion of Kuwait, passing a resolution on August 3 demanding that Iraq withdraw its troops. The league also urged that the crisis be resolved within the organization itself and warned that failure to do so would invite outside intervention. Although somewhat ambivalent about forcing the Iraqis to withdraw by military force, the Arab League did vote—by the narrowest of margins—to allow Syrian, Egyptian, and Moroccan forces to send troops as part of the building international coalition. In the 1990s, the Arab League also continued its efforts to resolve the Israeli-Palestinian dispute in the Palestinians' favor. More recently, in 2003 the Arab League voted to demand the unconditional removal of U.S. and British troops from Iraq. The lone dissenting voice was the tiny nation of Kuwait, which had been liberated by the 1991 Persian Gulf War.

Currently, Libya is represented by the Government of National Accord. With the Syrian Arab Republic having been suspended from membership in November 2011, owing to the Syrian Civil War, the Syrian seat is currently held by the Syrian National Coalition. Yemen, also in civil strife, is represented by the Cabinet of Yemen, which is disputed by the Houthi Supreme Revolutionary Committee. In 2015, the Arab League voiced its support for the Saudi-led military intervention in war-torn Yemen. As of 2019, the Arab League had 22 member states.

AMY HACKNEY BLACKWELL

See also
Husseini, Haj Amin al-; Iraq War; Nasser, Gamal Abdel; Pan-Arabism and Pan-Arabist Thought; Persian Gulf War, Overview; Sadat, Anwar; Six-Day War

References
Hourani, Albert. *A History of the Arab Peoples.* Cambridge, MA: Harvard University Press, 1991.
MacDonald, Robert W. *The League of Arab States: A Study in Regional Organization.* Princeton, NJ: Princeton University Press, 1965.

Arab Legion

Police and combat force founded in 1920 and dominated by Arabs in the British Mandate for Palestine. The Arab Legion was originally organized as a 150-man Arab police force under the leadership of British Army lieutenant colonel Frederick Gerard Peake (later Peake Pasha, major general). The unit was increased in size to almost 1,000 men within the year and was renamed the Reserve Mobile Force.

When the British recognized Abdullah as emir of Transjordan, Abdullah's civil police force was combined on October 22, 1923, with the Reserve Mobile Force as the Arab Legion. Peake served as its first commander. For more than 30 years, British officers commanded the legion. It held primary responsibility for policing the capital of Amman and its environs, leaving border security for Transjordan to the newly created Transjordan Frontier Force.

In November 1930, British Army major John Bagot Glubb (later Glubb Pasha, lieutenant general) became Peake's assistant. In March 1931 Glubb created the Arab Legion's Desert Patrol, a motorized unit composed mostly of Bedouins, to end tribal opposition to Abdullah's authority across Transjordan's vast desert regions. Glubb assumed command of the 2,000-man legion upon Peake's retirement in March 1939.

During World War II Emir Abdullah assumed a pro-Allied stance, allowing the Arab Legion to support British military operations in the Middle East. The legion participated in the April–May 1941 British offensive against the recently proclaimed pro-Nazi government of Rahid Ali al-Gaylani in Iraq and also played a major role in the relief of the British garrison at the Royal Air Force base at Habbaniya and in the liberation of Baghdad. The legion then joined the Allied operation against Vichy French forces in Syria, playing major roles in the Palmyra and Sukhna offensives in June 1941. So impressed were the British with the legion's performance that it was greatly enlarged, eventually reaching 16,000 men.

The Arab Legion was stationed in the Sinai Desert in 1942 in anticipation of German field marshal Erwin Rommel's advance across Egypt but was not committed after the Afrika Korps was halted at El Alamein. Although several draft plans called for the legion to deploy to the Italian theater of operations, the command was largely used for the remainder of the war to guard vital communications and strategic resources in the Middle East.

On May 25, 1946, Transjordan became an independent kingdom under King Abdullah. The Arab Legion was then reduced in size to 4,500 men. Thirty-seven British officers under Glubb remained with the legion, while a group of Arab junior officers were groomed for the day that the British would leave the mandate.

As tensions grew between Jews and Arabs in the dissolving British Mandate for Palestine, most of the British officers in the Arab Legion temporarily withdrew their services. Although the legion had been designed primarily as a desert force, most of its action was around Jerusalem. Glubb opposed this, fearing that it would lead to house-to-house fighting. The legion defeated the Jewish Kfar-Etzion bloc settlements south of Jerusalem in May 1948.

When Israel declared its independence on May 14, 1948, King Abdullah ordered Glubb to enter the Old City of Jerusalem, seize the Jewish Quarter, and engage the armed Jewish Haganah in the fight for the New City of Jerusalem. Meanwhile, two regiments of the Arab Legion bypassed Jerusalem for Latrun to fend off enemy reinforcements and hold the hills of Judaea for the Arabs.

By far the most effective formation in the Arab forces, the legion nonetheless suffered heavy losses in the fighting for the New City of Jerusalem and finally was forced to withdraw. The legion managed to hold the Old City, where supply problems led to a surrender of the Jewish Quarter on May 28.

In June, the fighting shifted to the Latrun area. The Arab Legion successfully fended off heavy attacks by the elite Palmach intending to seize Latrun. By mid-July it was clear that the legion had held.

When the Rhodes negotiations finally established a permanent armistice on April 3, 1949, the Kingdom of Jordan could lay claim to East Jerusalem, Hebron, Nablus, and Judaea (commonly referred to as the West Bank) thanks to the efforts of Glubb and the Arab Legion. Of Arab forces, only Glubb's legion turned in an exemplary performance.

Following the Israeli War of Independence, the size of the Arab Legion was set at three brigades. Two legion brigades were assigned to the Jordanian-controlled West Bank in an effort to stop Palestinians from crossing over into Israel and to stop Israeli reprisal attacks against fedayeen harbored in the West Bank. The legion also dealt with internal disputes aimed at discrediting the young King Hussein of Jordan, who assumed power a few months after his grandfather, Abdullah, was assassinated on July 20, 1951.

Within the Arab Legion there was a rising tide of anti-British sentiment, known as the Free Officers Movement and led by a clique of young Arab officers. On March 1, 1956, King Hussein dismissed Glubb from his command along with all British officers in the legion. After more than 25 years of service to Abdullah, Hussein, and the legion, Glubb subsequently returned to Britain. Brigadier General Rade Einab became the first Arab commander of the legion but was soon replaced by Ali abu Nowar, a friend of the young king and a leader among the Free Officers. Later in 1956, the elite Arab Legion was amalgamated with Jordan's National Guard into the Royal Jordanian Army, a force that still retains many of its British traditions.

THOMAS D. VEVE

See also
Abdullah I; Fedayeen; Glubb, Sir John Bagot; Haganah; Hussein ibn Talal, King of Jordan; Israeli War of Independence; Jordan; Palmach

References
Glubb, John Bagot. *The Story of the Arab Legion*. London: Hodder and Stoughton, 1950.
Lunt, James. *The Arab Legion*. London: Constable, 1999.
Vatikiotis, P. J. *Politics and the Military in Jordan: A Study of the Arab Legion, 1921–1957*. New York: Praeger, 1967.
Young, Peter. *The Arab Legion*. London: Osprey, 2002.

Arab Liberation Army

Multinational Arab fighting force created in early 1948 by the Arab League. The Arab Liberation Army (ALA) was an all-volunteer organization dedicated to the destruction of a Jewish state in the Middle East. The ALA was founded as British forces evacuated the area at the end of the British mandate over Palestine. Initially, the ALA numbered some 5,000 Palestinian and Syrian volunteers. Also among its ranks were Iraqis, Lebanese, Transjordanians, and Egyptians, including some from the Muslim Brotherhood. There were also a few British deserters, Turks, and Germans. The organization's only stated political strategy was preventing the creation of Israel, although it also served as a hedge against the desire of Transjordan's King Abdullah to possess parts of Palestine.

The ALA was initially commanded by Iraqi general Taha al-Hashimi, although he proved to be a largely ineffective figurehead. The field commander and acknowledged leader of the ALA was Syria's Fawzi al-Qawuqji. Al-Qawuqji had served in the Ottoman Army. He had also led Arab irregulars during the Arab Revolt of 1936–1939, including service as the commander of guerrillas in the Nablus region. He proved to an inept commander of the ALA, however.

In the period prior to the end of British occupation, the ALA's primary opponent was the much larger and better-disciplined Jewish self-defense force known as Haganah, which included the highly trained Palmach strike force. Haganah had thousands of British Army and Jewish Brigade veterans from World War II. Like the ALA, Haganah sought to fill the void left by the departing British. After the declaration of Israeli independence in 1948, Haganah was incorporated into the Israel Defense Forces (IDF).

In January 1948, the ALA became the first Arab organization to attempt the capture of a Jewish settlement in attacking Kfar Szold, a small village near the Syrian border. British authorities refused to countenance such and sent a small armored column to oppose the ALA, forcing it to withdrew. The ALA soon launched attacks on Yehiam and Kibbutz Tirat Zvi, however. These were undertaken in part to secure Palestinian support for the ALA. At Tirat Zvi, Haganah routed the ALA forces, killing 60 and capturing a large amount of ALA equipment.

Despite its early reverses, on April 4 the ALA launched an ambitious offensive against Mishmar Haemek. It included more than 1,000 ALA troops supported by seven Syrian-donated artillery pieces. The Jewish defenders, who had only small arms, held off the ALA assault to a battle of attrition. Even with superior manpower and equipment, the ALA could not break the defensive lines. On April 12 al-Qawuqji increased the pressure on Mishmar Haemek, only to discover that a Haganah flanking counterattack had almost completely encircled his troops. Al-Qawuqji was able to break free with his men but then withdrew to Jenin. The ALA had again suffered a demoralizing defeat.

Following the British withdrawal from Palestine and the proclamation of the State of Israel on May 15, 1948, the ALA joined Egypt, Iraq, Lebanon, Syria, and Transjordan in an attempt to destroy the fledgling nation. In the first attacks of the Israeli War of Independence (1948–1949), the ALA's 10,000 soldiers, backed by 50,000 more volunteers, were charged with the defense of areas captured by Arab League forces. To assist in their mission, the ALA was provided armored cars and artillery. The ALA troops operated in the northern and central sectors, with their largest concentrations in Samaria, Galilee, and Jerusalem. Lebanese elements of the ALA worked in concert with the Lebanese Army, although other ALA units failed to coordinate their actions with those of the invading Arab armies.

On June 11, 1948, after four weeks of bloody combat, a truce brokered by the United Nations (UN) went into effect between Israel and the Arab armies. The ALA refused to honor the cease-fire and continued attacking Israeli positions for the first two days of the truce. With the end of fighting on other fronts, however, the IDF shifted forces and countered the ALA threat. During an assault on Sejera the ALA absorbed heavy casualties, and its ranks broke and fled the battlefield.

Following expiration of the truce, the ALA was stationed in central Galilee. This area was perceived by IDF commanders as the weakest part of the Arab lines. In Operation DEKEL, launched on July 8, IDF forces attempted to drive the ALA completely from Israeli territory. The ALA launched a simultaneous all-out effort against Sejera, employing armored vehicles, artillery, and close air support. Again, the assaults were repelled with heavy losses, and the ALA withdrew from Galilee to avoid encirclement.

With failure of the second UN truce (July 18–October 15, 1948), the ALA contained fewer than 4,000 troops in three brigades and required direct support from the Lebanese Army to stay in the field. The IDF decided to completely destroy the ALA while pushing the northern front of the war back into Lebanon. A series of furious Israeli attacks drove the ALA across the border. In Operation HIRAM (October 29–31, 1948), the IDF annihilated the remnants of the ALA, killing or capturing virtually the entire force. The Lebanese Army was also forced from the war, with the IDF occupying parts of Lebanon. By November 1948 the ALA, which had proven to be almost totally ineffective as a combat force, had virtually ceased to exist.

PAUL J. SPRINGER

See also
Arab League; Haganah; Israeli War of Independence; Palmach; Qawuqji, Fawzi al-

References
Herzog, Chaim. *The Arab-Israeli Wars: War and Peace in the Middle East from the War of Independence to Lebanon.* Westminster, MD: Random House, 1984.
Levenberg, Haim. *Military Preparations of the Arab Community in Palestine: 1945–1948.* London: Routledge, 1993.
Pollack, Kenneth M. *Arabs at War: Military Effectiveness, 1948–1991.* Lincoln: University of Nebraska Press, 2002.
Sayigh, Yezid. *Armed Struggle and the Search for State: The Palestine National Movement, 1949–1993.* New York: Oxford University Press, 2000.

Arab Nationalism

Arab nationalism arose as a response to European imperialism after World War II and stressed unity of purpose and mutual cooperation among the newly formed Arab countries of the Middle East. While respectful of Islam, Arab nationalist movements were generally secular and drew heavily on socialist economic principles and anti-imperialist rhetoric. Political and military opposition to the State of Israel served as a focal point of many Arab nationalist movements, although repeated Arab military defeats contributed to the decline of Arab nationalism. However, Arab nationalist parties continue to play a dominant role in the politics of Syria, Egypt, Jordan, and, until recently, Iraq.

Arab nationalism has its roots in the late 19th century as European ideas of nationalism affected the Ottoman Empire. Following World War I, as the British and French mandates over various Arab territories of the former Ottoman Empire ended, Arab nationalist sentiment was divided between unifying notions of Pan-Arabism and individual independence movements. Such thinking contributed to the formation of the Arab League and the growth of numerous groups such as the Society of the Muslim Brothers (Muslim

Brotherhood) in Egypt and the Étoile Nord Africaine (North African Star) in Algeria. These and similar groups combined anti-imperialism with strong Islamic identity in their drive for independence.

In the years following World War II, most Arab states had gained partial or full independence yet were generally ruled by governments sympathetic to European powers. Political crises in the late 1940s and 1950s resulted in the overthrow of many of those governments and the establishment of new regimes that challenged the West, particularly in Egypt, Syria, and Iraq. During the Cold War, these nations lay at the heart of the Arab nationalist movement. Ongoing conflict with Israel played a major role in the growth of Arab unity. The common Israeli enemy provided the Arab states with a unifying cause that overshadowed individual differences.

Opposition to Israel and support for the Palestinians also served to link the resources of the newly wealthy oil states of the Persian Gulf to the larger Arab cause. Finally, the conflict with Israel, combined with the importance of petroleum resources, made the Middle East a region of great interest to the United States and the Soviet Union, and the two Cold War superpowers would have a substantial effect on the development of Arab nationalism.

Arab nationalism after World War II stressed Arab unity. It included experimental state unions, such as Egypt's merger with Syria in the short-lived United Arab Republic. In addition, Arab nationalist movements fit into a broader picture of postcolonial political ideologies popular in the developing world. Such ideologies stressed national or cultural identity along with Marxist, socialist, or populist ideas.

The two most important Arab nationalist movements were Baathism and Nasserism. The Baath (Resurrection) Party grew to prominence in Syria after 1945. One of its founders, Michel Aflaq, conceived of a single Arab nation embracing all the Arab states and recapturing the glory of the Arabian past. While the movement was respectful of Islamic tradition, its rhetoric and agenda were largely secular and increasingly socialist. This socialism grew partly as a response to Western imperialism and partly as a result of increasing Soviet political and military support of Baathist states. The Baath Party increased in influence in Syria and Iraq throughout the late 1950s and early 1960s. In Syria, it came to dominate the country's politics by the early 1960s and has remained a potent force since then. In Iraq, the party rose to national control in the late 1970s and remained dominant until the overthrow of Saddam Hussein in 2003.

Nasserism reflected the agenda and the political prowess of Gamal Abdel Nasser, Egypt's leader during 1952–1970. Raised amid British domination in Egypt, Nasser combined his rejection of imperialism with secular Arab nationalism and socialism. Nasser stressed modernization, state ownership of industry, and Arab unity. His suspicion of the West and preference for socialist economic policies drew him toward the Soviet sphere, but he avoided domination by Moscow.

Israel was a focal point for Nasser's brand of Arab nationalism; he viewed the defeat of Israel as an expression of Arab unity and a rejection of imperialist interference in the Middle East. In addition, Egyptian leadership in the struggle with Israel contributed to his stature in the Arab world as a whole. His position in Egypt and among Arab nations was enhanced during the 1956 Suez Crisis. However, Egypt's attempted military intervention in Yemen (1962–1967) brought Nasser's vision of Arab nationalism and socialism into conflict with the royalist Islamic views of Saudi Arabia and demonstrated the limits of his influence. Furthermore, Egypt's disastrous defeat in the Six-Day War with Israel in June 1967 dealt a severe blow to his power and prestige. Nasser's authority survived the 1967 war, and the overwhelming rejection of his proffered resignation by ordinary Egyptians testified to the scope of his popular appeal, but the 1967 defeat signaled the end of Nasser's vision of Arab unity.

Arab nationalism has fallen on hard times. Egyptian president Hosni Mubarak, an ideological and political descendant of Nasser, was forced from office in 2011. Since then Egypt has been wracked by political infighting and a resurgence of Islamist groups less interested in Pan-Arabism and more interested in the establishment of a republic based on Islamic law. Libyan strongman Muammar Gaddafi, another proponent of Arab nationalism, was deposed and killed in 2011. Libya has since witnessed a major insurgency led by Islamic extremist groups. In Syria, Bashar al-Assad's Baathist regime has also been under siege since 2011 in the Syrian Civil War, where Islamic extremists, led by the Islamic State of Iraq and Syria (ISIS), have been waging a war against Syrian secularism. The older concept of Arab nationalism personified by Nasser, Saddam Hussein, and al-Assad now seems to be passé; in its place is a unity that revolves around fundamentalist Islam rather than nationhood or ethnicity.

Robert S. Kiely and Sherifa Zuhur

See also

Egypt; Hussein, Saddam; Iraq; Islamic State of Iraq and Syria; Jordan; Mubarak, Hosni; Muslim Brotherhood; Nasser, Gamal Abdel; Six-Day War; Suez Crisis; Syria; United Arab Republic

References
Dawisha, Adeed. *Arab Nationalism in the 20th Century.* Princeton, NJ: Princeton University Press, 2003.
Hourani, Albert. *A History of the Arab Peoples.* Cambridge, MA: Harvard University Press, 1991.

Arab Oil Embargo (October 17, 1973– March 18, 1974)

In October 1973, the Arab members of the Organization of Petroleum Exporting Countries (OPEC) manipulated their vast oil resources to protest U.S. support of Israel during the Yom Kippur War (Ramadan War). The Arab oil embargo consisted of three interrelated actions: production curtailments, a total embargo targeted against countries deemed supportive of Israel, and price hikes posted without the consent of the oil companies.

As a result, the price of a barrel of oil nearly quadrupled, from $3.01 in the middle of October 1973 to $11.65 by the end of December. The skyrocketing prices and ensuing chaos created rampant inflation and a global recession that would last throughout the 1970s. Although Arab leaders had attempted to wield the so-called oil weapon in previous Arab-Israeli conflicts, by 1973 a host of political, diplomatic, and economic conditions ensured the potency of their oil policies.

When the embargo took effect, worldwide fuel stocks were already strained as demand began to outpace supply. The economic boom of the 1950s and 1960s, created largely by plentiful and cheap oil supplies, vastly increased oil consumption in the industrialized countries. Yet as long as prices were low, conservation efforts remained unpopular, and energy companies had little incentive to invest the huge sums of money required to locate and pump oil from new fields. The liabilities inherent in these trends became obvious by the early 1970s, as U.S. oil production topped out while imports tripled.

Thanks to its enormous oil reserves and geologic qualities that made drilling there economical, the Middle East was quickly becoming the new global center of oil production. Whereas the so-called black gold from Texas and Oklahoma had once supplied the world market, by 1970 industrialized nations looked to the Middle East and North Africa to satisfy upwards of two-thirds of the new demand for oil. Arab leaders approached these changing market conditions in ways consistent with the founding purpose of OPEC in 1960. The Arab oil-producing countries demanded and received a larger share of the windfall profits enjoyed by the oil companies along with more control over the production process. They also realized that the staggering amount of money pouring into their treasuries surpassed what their developing economies could spend. The Arabs reasoned that a future embargo would be economically prudent and was sure to have major and prolonged impact because non-Arab oil production was operating at peak capacity. As tensions in the Middle East mounted in the early 1970s, Arab oil producers were well positioned to cut production across the board while retaining the ability to embargo target countries as a tool of diplomatic coercion against Israel and its allies.

Israel's crushing victory in the Six-Day War of June 1967 placed large tracts of Arab land, including the Sinai Peninsula, the Golan Heights, and the West Bank, under the Jewish state's occupation. From Israel's perspective, the occupied territories provided a security barrier against future Arab aggression.

The fact of Israeli military dominance narrowed Arab rhetoric from destroying the Zionist entity to the less ambitious goal of regaining the land lost in the war. The situation was a diplomatic conundrum, as represented by United Nations Resolution 242, which called for secure and recognized boundaries and the withdrawal of Israeli forces from the occupied territories. Israel stipulated that negotiations regarding land transfers must take place directly with the Arabs, as face-to-face diplomacy would signal Israel's legitimacy among its neighbors.

Following the leadership of Egyptian president Gamal Abdel Nasser, Arab leaders refused to engage in direct negotiations while Israel occupied Arab land. Low-level border clashes, which erupted periodically between Israeli and Arab forces, failed to push either side toward a negotiated peace. In the Arab view, a full-scale war launched with weapons shipped from the Soviet Union was the only solution, as Israel remained entrenched and firmly supported by the United States.

When Richard Nixon became president of the United States in 1969, U.S. foreign policy was focused on two basic objectives: creating a viable exit strategy from the war in Vietnam and improving relations with the Soviet Union and China. In the view of Nixon and his national security adviser, Henry Kissinger, maintenance of Israeli hegemony through military support was the best guarantor of regional stability. In this strategy, the Arabs would eventually realize that U.S. diplomacy, not Soviet weapons, would achieve their goals. Until then, Nixon and Kissinger could focus their attention elsewhere.

Anwar Sadat, who succeeded Nasser as president of Egypt in 1970, rejected these assumptions. Sadat believed that Israel could be challenged by a massive surprise attack launched in conjunction with Syrian forces. He also lobbied King Faisal of Saudi Arabia to augment Egypt's war chest with the oil weapon. Recognizing the economic and political benefits of an embargo, Faisal consented, and Sadat began devising his war plans with strong backing from the Arab oil producers. On October 6, 1973—Yom Kippur in the Jewish calendar—Egyptian and Syrian forces launched a two-front attack. Israel was caught unprepared, and in the first week of fighting Israel's war matériel was depleted to dangerously low levels.

Israeli prime minister Golda Meir implored Nixon to commence a military resupply airlift. Although Faisal had repeatedly warned that such blatant support would elicit Arab retaliation in the form of an embargo, Nixon complied with the Israeli request. The Arabs promptly responded with cutbacks in oil production and a complete embargo against the United States and the Netherlands, with Rotterdam the main port of entry for oil into Western Europe. For Nixon, who narrowly defined U.S. interests in Cold War terms, the preeminent objective was to ensure that U.S. arms defeated Soviet arms on the battlefield. He reasoned that an Arab military victory might radicalize the entire region and lead to communist control of Middle Eastern oil, a prospect far more threatening than the temporary disruption in oil supplies instituted by staunchly anticommunist oil sheikhdoms.

Although the Arab oil producers lifted the embargo in March 1974 and new Western investment in oil exploration succeeded in limiting OPEC's coercive power, the ripple effects of the energy crisis lingered long thereafter. The oil shortages—represented memorably by long lines of cars waiting at gas stations—effectively highlighted a major fracture within the global anticommunist alliance system. Western Europe and Japan, both far more dependent on Middle Eastern oil than the United States, adopted an explicitly pro-Arab stance following the embargo. Israel became increasingly isolated on the world stage, and the United States has forged much of its subsequent Middle East policy over the objections of its traditional allies.

DAVID ZIERLER

See also
Arab Nationalism; Golan Heights; Meir, Golda Mabovitch; Nasser, Gamal Abdel; Organization of Petroleum Exporting Countries; Sadat, Anwar; Sinai Peninsula; Yom Kippur War

References
El-Sadat, Anwar. *In Search of Identity*. New York: Harper and Row, 1978.

Garthoff, Raymond L. *Détente and Confrontation: American-Soviet Relations from Nixon to Reagan*. Washington, DC: Brookings Institution, 1985.
Smart, Ian. "Oil, the Superpowers, and the Middle East." *International Affairs* 53 (1977): 17–36.

Arab Revolt in Palestine (1936–1939)

General revolt among Arabs in the British Mandate for Palestine. Although the uprising was aimed primarily at British interests in the area, attacks against Jews were far from uncommon. And while it failed to redress immediate concerns, the revolt had a lasting impact on Britain's policies in the mandate and on the Arab and Jewish communities.

The revolt was the culmination of growing Arab unrest over Jewish immigration and land purchases in Palestine and economic dislocation from increased urbanization and industrialization. It was, in fact, the most severe of a number of communal disturbances between Jews and Arabs dating from the early 1920s. Despite its failure, the Great Revolt (as the Arabs call it) marked the dawn of a distinctive Palestinian Arab nationalism.

The problems that triggered the unrest grew in part from events outside the region. Growing anti-Semitism in Eastern Europe and Nazi control of Germany from 1933 led to an increase in Jewish immigrants entering Palestine. At the same time, growing land purchases by Zionists in Palestine had led to the expulsion of large numbers of Arab peasants from lands on which they had been tenant farmers. These dislocations were also part of a deepening economic crisis that gripped the region as Palestinian agricultural exports to Europe and America declined in the midst of the Great Depression (around 1930–1940).

The many landless Arabs, often forced into slums erected around large cities, formed the rank and file of the revolt. The leadership, however, existed on two levels. The first was a more politically conscious Arab elite dominated by two rival clans: the Husseini family led by Haj Amin al-Husseini, the mufti of Jerusalem, and their rivals, the Nashashibis, represented by Fakhri al-Nashashibi. The second element (and the true center of the revolt's leadership) resided among local committees that had emerged in Jerusalem, Nablus, Jaffa, Tulkarm, and elsewhere.

Tensions among Arabs, Jews, and British administrators in Palestine had been building for several months prior to the revolt's outbreak in April 1936. It was clear that a surge of Islamic extremism had accompanied growing economic dislocation among Palestinian Arabs. Sheikh Izz al-Din al-Qassam, a Syrian-born, Egyptian-educated cleric, had been preaching fundamentalist Islam and calling for a jihad (holy war) against both Britons and Jews. At the same time, he was assembling a host of devoted followers, mostly from landless Arabs in the Haifa area. After his followers murdered a Jewish policeman near Gilboa, al-Qassam died in a shootout with British troops on November 20, 1935. His death triggered major nationalist demonstrations among Arabs throughout Palestine. At the same time, discovery by the British of an arms cache in a shipment of cement barrels intended for a Jewish importer fed rumors among Arabs that the Jews were arming for a war against the Arabs. These developments essentially pushed the tension-ridden atmosphere in Palestine into outright rebellion.

The Arab Revolt officially began in April 1936 in the hill country around Tulkarm and spread rapidly. The young nationalists who formed the local committees took the lead. Anxious to gain control of the revolt and to maintain their own credibility, the Husseini and Nashashibi clans formed the Arab Higher Committee to provide rhetorical, financial, and material support for the uprising. During the first six months of the revolt, 200 Arabs, 80 Jews, and 28 British soldiers and policemen died in clashes.

Initially, British reaction was somewhat restrained. Indeed, London hoped that the disturbances would blow over without forcing recourse to measures that might scar Anglo-Arab relations. British authorities imposed no death sentences in response to any of the killings. Only in September 1936 did British authorities impose martial law. Eventually, the government sent 20,000 troops from Britain and Egypt and recruited 2,700 Jewish supernumeraries to contain and quell the disturbances.

The reaction of the Jewish community in Palestine was also restrained. The Jewish Agency for Palestine acted to strengthen its self-defense force, Haganah, and fortified settlements, leaving suppression of the revolt to the British. As the uprising continued and attacks on Jewish settlements increased, the Palestinian Jews resorted to aggressive self-defense, including ambushes of rebel Arab bands and reprisals against neighboring Arab villages suspected of harboring guerrillas. This doctrine of harsh reprisals developed by the Zionist leadership during the revolt became a permanent fixture of Zionist military policy.

In the first months of the revolt, the British succeeded—through the use of night curfews, patrols, searches, and ambushes—in pushing Arab rebels out of the towns. By mid-May 1936 rural Palestine had become the center of gravity of the revolt and would remain so until the revolt's end in 1939, and leadership remained centered in the local committees. The Arab Higher Committee was increasingly paralyzed by rivalries between the Husseini and Nashashibi clans and never asserted control over the rural bands, although it did provide money, arms, and rhetorical support.

By the autumn of 1937, 9,000–10,000 Palestinian fighters, augmented by non-Palestinians brought in and financed by the Arab Higher Committee, were roaming the countryside. They were often motivated as much by the desire for loot as by nationalist zeal. Internecine violence among rival families resulted in more deaths among the Arabs than action by the British or Zionists. The rebels' practice of extorting food and other valuables from Arab peasants damaged the rural economy and increasingly alienated the rebels from their base of support. To pacify the countryside, the British shrewdly exploited divisions among the Arabs and used combined British-Zionist Special Night Squads (the best known of which was commanded by Captain Orde Wingate) that ambushed rebel bands, launched retaliatory strikes against Arab villages suspected of harboring guerrillas, and carried out targeted assassinations against rebel leaders.

The Arab Revolt collapsed in 1939 in the face of eroding support in the countryside, the arrest or exile of the senior leaders (including Haj Amin al-Husseini, who eventually wound up in Nazi Germany), lack of cohesion in the revolt's organization and leadership, and mounting British pressure. Nevertheless, the revolt had profound consequences for the mandate and the Arab and Zionist camps. The intensity of the uprising stunned British officials in Jerusalem and London and led the government to send a commission chaired by Lord William Robert Peel to Palestine in late 1936. The Peel Commission Report, which appeared in July 1937, proposed the partition of Palestine into a Jewish area and a much larger Arab area. This marked the first time that partition had been proposed as a solution to the Palestine issue. The violence subsided for a time—nearly a year—as the Peel Commission did its work. But both sides essentially rejected the proposal, and fighting ramped up considerably in the fall of 1937. The British eventually backed away from the Peel Commission proposals in the face of opposition from both Arabs and Jews.

More shocking for Palestinian Jews was the implementation of the British government white paper of May 1939, which restricted Jewish immigration and land purchases over the next 5 years and promised an independent Palestinian Arab state in 10 years if the rights of the Jewish community were protected. From the Jewish perspective, the white paper represented a surrender to Arab violence and intimidation. It also closed Palestine to European Jews at a time when anti-Jewish violence in Germany and Eastern Europe was intensifying. Indeed, the measure permanently damaged relations between Britain and the Jews in Palestine.

The worst damage, however, was to Palestinian Arabs. Although the Great Revolt gained a permanent place in Arab nationalist mythology, in the short term the Arabs were left with the consequences of a failed revolt. Most of the political leadership was in prison, exiled, or had left politics disgusted and disillusioned. The end of the revolt relieved many Palestinian Arabs who could now resume their normal lives and recoup some of their economic losses. Even so, blood feuds between families that had supported the uprising and those that had opposed it were to disrupt society and paralyze political life for years. The Palestinians had to depend on the Arab states in the region with baneful consequences, leading up to the Israeli War of Independence (1948–1949).

The Arab Revolt spontaneously unraveled throughout 1939 so that by year's end clashes and armed violence had largely ended. Nevertheless, the casualty figures were grim indeed. It is estimated that some 5,000 Arabs, 400 Jews, and 200 British soldiers and officials died in the uprising. And despite the summoning of 20,000 additional British troops and as many as 15,000 Haganah fighters, it took the better part of three years to conquer the revolt.

The overall legacy of the Arab Revolt, then, was the further poisoning of relations between Arabs and Jews and the further alienation of the British from both communities. The revolt also led to the separation of the Arab and Jewish economies, which had previously been somewhat integrated. This would burden Palestinian Arabs with poverty, high unemployment, and homelessness for the succeeding two generations. The divisions among Arab, Jew, and Briton remained largely dormant during World War II but would resurface with even more violence in the postwar years.

WALTER F. BELL

See also
Haganah; Husseini, Haj Amin al-; Palestine, British Mandate for; Peel Commission; Qassam, Izz al-Din al-; White Paper of 1939; Wingate, Orde Charles

References
Gelvin, James L. *The Israel-Palestine Conflict: One Hundred Years of War.* New York: Cambridge University Press, 2005.

Morris, Benny. *Righteous Victims: A History of the Zionist-Arab Conflict, 1881–2001.* New York: Vintage Books, 2001.

Porath, Yehoshua. *The Palestinian National Movement, 1929–1939: From Riot to Rebellion.* London: Cass, 1974.

Stein, Kenneth W. *The Land Question in Palestine, 1917–1939.* Chapel Hill: University of North Carolina Press, 1984.

Swedenburg, Ted. *Memories of Revolt: The 1936–1939 Rebellion and the Palestinian National Past.* Minneapolis: University of Minnesota Press, 1995.

Arab Revolt of World War I (June 5, 1916–October 31, 1918)

Uprising during World War I by Arab peoples of north, central, and western Arabia against Ottoman rule. Since the 16th century, the Ottoman government in Constantinople had controlled Syria, Palestine, Iraq, the western provinces of Saudi Arabia, and part of Yemen. Much of the region's 6 million people were nomadic. In 1908 the Young Turks came to power in Istanbul (Constantinople) and promoted Turkish nationalism at the expense of other nationalities of the empire, which the Arabs and other peoples resented. The new government also sent troops into Arab lands and introduced conscription, both of which angered the Arabs.

Under the terms of the Ottoman constitution of 1909, the Arab peoples of the empire sent representatives to the Imperial Parliament at Istanbul, where they openly supported Arab rights. At the same time newspapers and political organizations, some secret, sprang up in the Arab lands promoting Arab nationalism. Damascus and Beirut were centers of this activity but were too close geographically to Anatolia to risk overt action. Arab power was in fact diffuse and largely wielded by local chieftains who had little ability to initiate hostilities against the Ottoman government on their own.

The center of the Arab nationalist movement was the Hejaz region of central Arabia, which contained the holy cities of Mecca and Medina. The region was connected to Anatolia by means of the Damascus-Medina (Hejaz) railway. Sharif of Mecca Hussein ibn Ali ibn Mohammed was nominal head of the Hejaz. His position was strengthened by his senior position in the Muslim religious hierarchy as a direct descendant of Prophet Muhammad. Hussein saw the railway as an infringement on his control and had long hoped for an independent Arab kingdom under his rule. World War I provided that opportunity.

As early as February 1914, Hussein had been in communication, through his son Abdullah, with British authorities in Cairo. Abdullah met with the British high commissioner in Egypt, Horatio Lord Kitchener, and told him that the Arabs were prepared to rebel against the Ottoman Empire in return for British support. The British were skeptical, but Ottoman entrance into the war on the side of the Central Powers changed this attitude. Both Sir Reginald Wingate, British governor-general of the Sudan, and Sir Henry McMahon, Kitchener's successor as high commissioner in Egypt, kept in touch with Hussein.

In the spring of 1915 Hussein sent his third son, Emir Faisal, to Damascus to reassure Ottoman authorities there of his loyalty but also to sound out Arab opinion. Faisal had favored the Ottomans, but the visit to Damascus and profound discontent of the Arab population he discovered there reversed this view.

Hussein then entered into active negotiations with McMahon in Cairo. Hussein promised to declare war on the Ottoman Empire and raise an Arab army to assist the British in return for British support for him as king of a postwar Pan-Arab state. The British agreed and soon were providing rifles and ammunition to the Arabs. Meanwhile, Ottoman leaders were endeavoring to stamp out Arab nationalism in Damascus, where they executed a number of Arab leaders. Many other Arab patriots fled south to Mecca, where they urged Hussein to take up arms. Ottoman authorities were well aware of the Arab preparations and from May 1916 blockaded the Hejaz from arms shipments and began a buildup of their forces in Damascus.

The actual revolt was initiated by the dispatch of Ottoman troops to reinforce their garrison at Medina. Hussein largely left leadership of the revolt to his four sons. Outside Medina on June 5, 1916, Hussein's eldest son Ali and Faisal officially proclaimed the start of the Arab Revolt.

Joined by 30,000 tribesmen, Faisal led an immediate assault on the Ottoman garrison at Medina but was repulsed. The Arabs did succeed, however, in cutting the railway north of the city. To the south, Hussein led an attack on the 1,000-man Ottoman garrison at Mecca, taking the city after three days of street fighting. Another Arab attack shortly thereafter against the port city of Jiddah was also successful,

Arab forces, as shown in this photograph, played an important role in assisting British and Imperial troops in the defeat of Ottoman Empire forces in Palestine and Syria in 1918. (Ridpath, John Clark. *Ridpath's History of the World*, 1921)

supported by the British Royal Navy seaplane carrier *Ben-my-Chree* based at Aden. Other cities also fell to the Arabs. In September, the 3,000-man Ottoman garrison at Taif, the last city in the southern Hejaz held by the Turks, surrendered to Arab forces supported by British-supplied artillery.

On November 2, Hussein proclaimed himself "king of the Arab Countries." This created some embarrassment for the British government with the French. Finally, the Allies worked out a compromise by which they addressed Hussein as "king of the Hejaz." A number of Arabs in the Ottoman Army, including officers, taken prisoner in the fighting helped provide a leadership cadre for the so-called Arab Army. Military strength of its four main forces commanded by Hussein's sons fluctuated wildly, and few of the men involved, who ranged widely in age, were trained.

In October 1916, the Ottomans managed to drive the Arab Army south of Medina and reopen the railway. The British sent a party of advisers to Hussein, and Arabist captain T. E. Lawrence became Faisal's official adviser, successfully urging Faisal to resume the offensive. Rather than meet Ottoman power head-on, the two men initiated a series of hit-and-run raids over northern Arabia that took advantage of local support and forced Ottoman leaders to divert increasing numbers of troops to the region.

In the spring of 1917, Faisal received pledges of Arab support from Syria once military operations reached there. In July 1917 Lawrence led an attack that captured Aqaba, which then became Faisal's chief base, while forces under Abdullah and Ali contained the Ottoman garrison at Medina and protected Mecca. Faisal's northern wing of the Arab Army was the revolt's chief military force and acted on the right flank of Lieutenant General Edmund Allenby's British Empire forces in Palestine. In the autumn of 1917 Lawrence, who understood and effectively practiced guerrilla warfare, led a series of successful attacks on Ottoman rail traffic. Allenby's calls for diversionary attacks by the Arab Army produced a series of raids that diverted some 23,000 Ottoman troops from participation in the fighting in Palestine. Faisal also cooperated closely with Allenby in the Megiddo Offensive and, with 30,000 men, led the revolt's climactic action, the entrance into Damascus in October 1918.

The Arab Revolt had immense repercussions in the Arab world in fueling Arab nationalism. It helped free the Arab lands from Turkish rule and led to the formation of Arab states. But the victorious Allies thwarted Hussein's ambitions. McMahon's pledge to Hussein preceded by six months the 1916 Sykes-Picot Agreement between the British and French governments, a breach of promises made to the Arabs that in effect set up British and French spheres of influence in the Middle East. Ultimately, much of the territory was awarded as mandates to Great Britain and France under the League of Nations. Faisal received Syria but was deposed and became king of Iraq under British protection. Abdullah became king of the newly created Transjordan. Hussein declared himself caliph of Islam in March 1924 but was forced to abdicate as king of the Hejaz to his son Ali when Abd al-Aziz al-Saud (Ibn Saud) conquered most of the Hejaz.

Spencer C. Tucker

See also

Allenby, Sir Edmund Henry Hynman; Hussein ibn Ali ibn Mohammed; Ibn Saud, King; Ottoman Empire; Palestine, British Mandate for; Sykes-Picot Agreement

References

Fromkin, David. *A Peace to End All Peace: The Fall of the Ottoman Empire and the Creation of the Modern Middle East.* New York: Avon, 1989.

Glubb, Sir John. *A Short History of the Arab Peoples.* New York: Dorset, 1969.

Hourani, Albert. *A History of the Arab Peoples.* Cambridge, MA: Harvard University Press, 1991.

Lenczowski, George. *The Middle East in World Affairs.* 4th ed. Ithaca, NY: Cornell University Press, 1980.

Tauber, Eliezer. *The Arab Movements in World War I.* London: Frank Cass, 1993.

Thomas, Lowell. *With Lawrence in Arabia.* New York: Garden City Publishing, 1924.

Arab Riots, Jerusalem (April 4–8, 1920)

By early 1920, relations between Arabs and Jews in Palestine had grown extraordinarily tense. In February 1920, Arab raiders attacked the Jewish settlements of Metulla and Tel Hai in the extreme north along the Palestine-Lebanese border. Among those killed at Tel Hai was Joseph Trumpeldor, a Zionist hero who had led the Zion Mule Corps in World War I. His death sent a shock wave through the Jewish community in Palestine. World Zionist Organization (WZO) president Chaim Weizmann warned British mandate authorities that even worse trouble was brewing. The next month, March 1920, the Syrian National Congress defied French authorities and offered Prince Faisal the throne of Syria, to include Palestine.

This was also the period of the Arab Festival of Nebi Musa, when devout Arabs traveled on the Jericho Road to make a pilgrimage to the tomb of Moses, a Muslim as well as Jewish patriarch. On April 4, a large number of these pilgrims gathered in Jerusalem to hear speeches by agitators who were promoting Faisal. Their apparent intention was to influence Allied deliberations regarding the determination of League of Nations mandates.

The crowd soon became unruly and was joined by Arab police. The rioters began attacking Jews, injuring some 160. Synagogues were also burned, and Jewish property was destroyed. Only after some three hours of rioting did the British police arrive and quell the disturbances, arresting some of the instigators. The next morning, however, British authorities released those they had arrested, and the attacks resumed and continued during the next two days until order was finally restored. By then, 6 Arabs and Jews had been killed, and the total of wounded had risen to several hundred.

Although British authorities dismissed the Arab mayor of Jerusalem and handed out stiff prison sentences to several of the instigators, the vast majority of those involved received only light sentences or went unpunished. At the same time, the British sentenced Vladimir Jabotinsky and several associates, who had organized a Jewish self-defense group during the riots, to 15-year prison terms.

The riots came as a great shock to the Jews, and the event and reaction to the disparity in sentences handed down by the authorities led to an official court of inquiry. The officers of the British military administration insisted that Zionist provocation was responsible for the rioting, while Jews accused the mandatory government of complicity and of doing little to halt the rioting once it had begun. Weizmann sent a telegram to British prime minister David Lloyd George in which he blamed the rioting on "poisonous agitation" and "inflammatory speeches" that the authorities had allowed to continue. Colonel Richard Meinertzhagen, chief British intelligence officer in Cairo, astonished his superiors by fully supporting the Jewish charges. The reaction to this was profound. The British military administration in Palestine was sufficiently compromised so that on April 29, less than a week after the Supreme Allied Council had assigned the Palestine mandate to Britain, London announced that the military administration in Palestine would be dissolved in favor of a civilian authority. The rioting of April 1920 also convinced Jews in Palestine of the necessity of forming a self-defense organization, Haganah, ready to fight for Jewish Palestine.

SPENCER C. TUCKER

See also
Faisal I, King of Iraq; Haganah; Jabotinsky, Vladimir Yevgenyevich; Palestine, British Mandate for

References
Sachar, Howard M. *A History of Israel: From the Rise of Zionism to Our Time.* 3rd ed. New York: Knopf, 2007.
Sanders, Ronald. *The High Walls of Jerusalem: A History of the Balfour Declaration and the Birth of the British Mandate for Palestine.* New York: Holt, Rinehart and Winston, 1983.
Shepherd, Naomi. *Ploughing Sand: British Rule in Palestine, 1917–1948.* New Brunswick, NJ: Rutgers University Press, 1999.

Arab Spring (December 17, 2010–Mid-2012)

The Arab Spring was a wave of prodemocracy uprisings that swept through North Africa and the Middle East beginning in December 2010. The protest movements, which were a mixture of both violent and nonviolent activities, were spurred mainly by dissatisfaction with local governments and economic inequalities that seemed to deepen after the global economic downturn in 2008. Essentially, the Arab Spring was propelled by a frustrated population contending with oppressive leaders, government corruption, and high levels of unemployment. The grassroots uprisings have had differing levels of success in each of the Arab nations.

On December 17, 2010, a Tunisian street vendor named Mohamed Bouazizi set himself on fire in the provincial city of Sidi Bouzid to protest police confiscation of his unregistered cart and vegetables. He died two weeks later, but the next day his act of self-immolation set in motion what would be the first of the Arab Spring's major movements, the Tunisian Revolution of 2011. Angry about what happened to Bouazizi and frustrated with the lack of jobs in Tunisia, among other issues, hundreds of disgruntled young adults took to the streets in Sidi Bouzid on December 18, destroying local shop windows and automobiles in their wake. The rioting gained momentum and soon spread throughout the country. By mid-January 2011, autocratic Tunisian leader Zine El Abidine Ben Ali had lost control of the national military and dissolved his police state in favor of a more democratic process.

The success of the Tunisian protest movement encouraged civil dissidence in other parts of the Arab world. In early January 2011, an Egyptian man set himself on fire outside of a parliamentary building in Cairo after loudly criticizing the government. The Egyptian government was perhaps even more restrictive than that of Tunisia and had outlawed any form of public protest or demonstrations. However, despite government control over most media, people began connecting through such social media outlets as Facebook to orchestra massive demonstrations.

Although the government cut Internet and text messaging services, the seed had been sown. Some 20,000 people gathered in Tahrir Square in Cairo on January 25, calling for an end to government repression in what was the beginning of the Egyptian Revolution. After a bloody standoff between security forces and crowds of demonstrators that swelled to the millions, Egyptian president Hosni Mubarak, pressed to do so by the U.S. government, stepped down as president on February 11.

The Arab Spring demonstrations did not stop with Egypt. Soon, disgruntled citizens in other countries were stepping forward to voice their grievances against authoritative rule. Through most of 2011, prodemocracy protests ensued in such nations as Libya, Yemen, Bahrain, and Syria.

The results were not nearly as swift as what had occurred in Tunisia and Egypt. In Libya, dictator Muammar Gaddafi implemented a brutal crackdown on protests that began in February. However, the protests soon became all-out rebellion. During the course of the next several months, rebel forces grew in size and controlled all of eastern Libya. As Gaddafi's military began forcibly taking back territories, the United Nations stepped in to establish a no-fly zone in order to protect Libyan residents from air attacks called by their own leader. Aided by North Atlantic Treaty Organization (NATO) airpower beginning on March 19, 2011, the Libyan rebels gradually took territory held by Gaddafi's forces and then set up a transitional government in August 2011. Gaddafi himself was captured and immediately executed on October 20. Widespread violence continued, however, as various factions vied for power.

In Yemen, large-scale protests began peacefully in February 2011 but turned violent by early February as police and military led a major crackdown on the demonstrators. Protests continued despite this hard-line stance, and longtime president Ali Abdullah Saleh eventually agreed to leave office in November 2011 in exchange for immunity from prosecution over the violent tactics employed to quell the protests. Prodemocracy antigovernment protests in Bahrain were complicated by religious tensions between the majority Shiite Muslim population and the Sunni Muslim ruling class.

Having lived with political uncertainty and strife since Syria's independence in 1946, Syrian citizens were inspired by the events that unfolded in Tunisia and Egypt to take matters into their own hands. In March 2011, demonstrations began in what was a remarkably peaceful protest against the government. The peace was not to last, however. Soon, Syrian president Bashar al-Assad cracked down hard with military force and martial law. Civil war erupted and continued to rage into 2017, with immense loss of life, the flight of millions of Syrians abroad, and widespread physical destruction.

In addition to these major uprisings, protests and demonstrations also took place in such states as Morocco, Iraq, Iran, and Jordan. Although the Arab Spring brought with it limited democratic change in parts of the Arab world, the political future of even these nations experiencing it remains uncertain.

Tamar Burris and Spencer C. Tucker

See also
Assad, Bashar al-; Egypt; Mubarak, Hosni; Saleh, Ali Abdullah; Shia Islam; Sunni Islam; Syria; Syrian Civil War; Yemen

References
Brownlee, Jason, Tarek Masoud, and Andrew Reynolds. *The Arab Spring: The Politics of Transformation in North Africa and the Middle East.* Oxford: Oxford University Press, 2013.

Dabashi, Hamid. *The Arab Spring: The End of Postcolonialism.* New York: Palgrave Macmillan, 2012.

Haddad, Bassam, Rosie Bsheer, and Ziad Abu-Rish, eds. *The Dawn of the Arab Uprisings: End of an Old Order?* London: Pluto, 2012.

Lesch, David W. *Syria: The Fall of the House of Assad.* New Haven, CT: Yale University Press, 2011.

Arafat, Yasser (1929–2004)

Palestinian nationalist and leader of the Palestine Liberation Organization (PLO) (1969–2004). Yasser Arafat was born Mohammed Yasser Abdel Rahman Abdel Raouf Arafat al-Qudwa al-Husseini on August 24, 1929. Arafat claimed to have been born in Jerusalem, but Israeli officials beginning in the 1970s claimed that he was born in Cairo to discredit him.

Arafat's father was a Palestinian Egyptian textile merchant. His mother, Zahwa, also a Palestinian, was from a family that had lived in Jerusalem for generations. She died when Arafat was five, and he then lived with his mother's brother in Jerusalem. Arafat remembered British soldiers invading his uncle's house one night, destroying possessions and beating its residents. When Arafat was nine his father brought him back to Cairo, where his older sister raised him.

As a teenager in Cairo, Arafat became involved in smuggling arms to Palestine to aid those struggling against both the British authorities and the Jews there. He attended the

University of Fuad I (later Cairo University) but left to fight in Gaza against Israel in the Israeli War of Independence (1948–1949). When the Arabs lost that war and Israel was firmly established, Arafat was inconsolable. He briefly attended the University of Texas but then returned to Cairo University to study engineering. He spent much time with fellow Palestinian students discussing hopes for a free Palestinian state.

Arafat was president of the Union of Palestinian Students during 1952–1956. He joined the Muslim Brotherhood in 1952. Finally graduating from college in 1956, he worked in Egypt for a short time. During the 1956 Suez Crisis he served as a second lieutenant in the Egyptian Army. In 1957 he moved to Kuwait, where he was an engineer and formed his own contracting company.

In 1958 Arafat founded al-Fatah, an underground guerrilla group dedicated to the liberation of Palestine. In 1964 he quit his job and moved to Jordan to devote all his energies to the promotion of Palestinian nationhood and to organize raids into Israel. The PLO was founded that same year.

In 1968, the Israel Defense Forces (IDF) attacked al-Fatah at the Jordanian village of Al Karameh. The Palestinians and the Jordanian Army eventually forced the Israelis back, and Arafat's face appeared on the cover of *Time* magazine as leader of the Palestinian movement. Palestinians embraced al-Fatah, and Arafat became a hero to many. He was appointed chairman of the PLO the next year and within four years controlled both the military (the Palestine Liberation Army, or PLA) and political branches of the organization.

By 1970, the PLO was in effect a state within the state of Jordan. King Hussein saw the PLO as a threat to Jordanian security and sent his army to evict the organization. The ensuing fighting during September 1970–July 1971 became known to the PLO as Black September. Finally, the PLO agreed to a cease-fire and to quit Jordan. Arafat moved the organization to Lebanon. Soon the PLO was attacking the Israelis across the Lebanese border.

Arafat opposed overseas attacks because they gave the PLO a bad image abroad. He publicly dissociated the group from Black September, the organization that killed 11 Israeli athletes at the 1972 Munich Olympics, although there is now evidence of his involvement. In 1974 he limited the PLO's attacks to Israel, the Gaza Strip, and the West Bank. Although Israel claimed that Arafat was responsible for the numerous terrorist attacks that occurred within the country during the 1970s, he denied responsibility. In 1974 he spoke before the United Nations General Assembly as the representative of the Palestinian people and condemned Zionism

Until his death in November 2004, Yasser Arafat was the leader of the Palestine Liberation Organization, the Palestinian Autonomous Region in the Gaza Strip, and the West Bank city of Jericho. (AFP/Getty Images)

but offered peace, which won him some praise from the international community.

During the Lebanese Civil War of 1975–1990, the PLO initially sided with the Lebanese National Front against the Lebanese forces. Thus, when Israeli forces invaded southern Lebanon in 1982, the PLO ended up fighting against the Israelis and then the Syrian militia group Amal. Thousands of Palestinians, many of them civilians, were killed during the war, and the PLO was forced to leave Beirut and relocate to Tunisia, where it remained until 1993.

During the 1980s, Iraq and Saudi Arabia donated millions of dollars to help Arafat rebuild the PLO. Arafat approved the First Intifada (1987) against Israel. In 1988, Palestinians declared Palestinian statehood at a meeting in Algiers. Arafat then announced that the Palestinians would renounce terrorism and recognize the State of Israel. The Palestinian

National Council elected Arafat president of this new unrecognized state in 1989.

Arafat and the Israelis conducted peace negotiations in Madrid in 1991. Although negotiations were temporarily set back when the PLO supported Iraq in the 1991 Persian Gulf War, over the next two years the two parties held a number of secret discussions. These led to the 1993 Oslo Peace Accords in which Israel agreed to Palestinian self-rule in the Gaza Strip and the West Bank. Arafat also officially recognized the existence of the State of Israel. Despite the condemnation of many Palestinian nationalists who viewed Arafat's moves as a sellout, the peace process appeared to be moving in a positive direction in the mid-1990s. Israeli troops withdrew from the Gaza Strip and Jericho in May 1994. Arafat was elected leader of the new Palestinian Authority (PA) in January 1996 with 88 percent of the vote in elections that were by all accounts free and fair (but with severely limited competition because Hamas and other opposition groups refused to participate).

Later that same year Likud Party leader Benjamin Netanyahu became Israeli prime minister, and the peace process began to unravel. Netanyahu, a hard-line conservative, did not trust Arafat, whom he charged was supporting terrorists. Arafat continued negotiations with the Israelis into 2000. That July, with Ehud Barak having replaced Netanyahu in office, Arafat traveled to the United States to meet with Barak and President Bill Clinton at the Camp David Summit. Despite generous concessions by Barak, Arafat refused to compromise, and a major chance at peace was lost.

On the collapse of the peace process, the Second (al-Aqsa) Intifada began in September 2000. From its beginning, Arafat was a besieged man who appeared to be losing influence and control within the Palestinian and larger Arab communities. His inability or unwillingness to arrest Palestinian terrorist attacks against Israel resulted in his virtual captivity at his Ramallah headquarters beginning in 2002. In declining health by 2004, Arafat increasingly looked like a man past his time.

Flown to France for medical treatment, Arafat died on November 11, 2004, outside Paris. For a time, there was much intrigue and conspiratorial conjecture concerning his illness and death. Rumors persist that he was assassinated by poisoning, although it is equally likely that he succumbed to unintentional food poisoning.

AMY HACKNEY BLACKWELL

See also
Barak, Ehud; Black September Organization; Camp David Accords; Fatah, al-; Hamas; Intifada, First; Intifada, Second; Jordan; Karameh, Battle of; Lebanon; Lebanon Civil War; Lebanon-Israeli War; Muslim Brotherhood; Netanyahu, Benjamin; Oslo Accords; Palestine Liberation Organization; Pan-Arabism and Pan-Arabist Thought; Terrorism

References
Aburish, Said K. *Arafat: From Defender to Dictator.* New York: Bloomsbury, 1998.
Gowers, Andrew. *Arafat: The Biography.* Rev. ed. London: Virgin Books, 1990.
Hart, Alan. *Arafat: A Political Biography.* Rev. ed. London: Sidgwick and Jackson, 1994.
Said, Edward W. *Peace and Its Discontents: Essays on Palestine in the Middle East Process.* New York: Vintage Books, 1995.

Ardashir I (180–240)

Founder and the first king of the Persian Sassanian dynasty (224–651), who ruled from 224 to 240. Also known as Ardashir the Unifier, he was the son of Papak or Pabag (New Persian: Babak) and founded the Sassanian dynasty after he defeated and killed the last Arsacid Parthian monarch, Artabanus IV on the battlefield.

Ardishir I was born in 180, and several accounts describe Ardashir's family lineage and his rise to power. An inscription of Shapur I, the son of Ardashir, identifies Ardashir's father as Papak and Sasan as the ancestor of the family after whom the dynasty was named. Another source states that Ardashir's father was Papak, with Sasan as his grandfather. Several sources have Sasan as the custodian of the temple of Anahid, the Iranian goddess of waters, in the district of Istakhr (Estakhr) in the province of Fars.

Papak was the vassal of Gochihr or Gozihr, ruler of Istakhr. Gozihr was himself a vassal of the ruling Arsacid dynasty. With permission and support from Gozihr, Papak had his son Ardashir appointed to a military post in Darabgerd, a town near present-day Darab in the province of Fars. After the commander of Darabgerd died, Ardashir succeeded him. Using Darabgerd as his operational base, Ardashir expanded the territory under his control by waging war and defeating several local rulers. With encouragement from Ardashir, his father, Papak, revolted against Gozihr and was able to remove him from the throne of Istakhr.

From Istakhr, Papak extended his rule to much of Fars Province. He may have requested that the ruling Arsacid monarch recognize his older son, Shapur, as the ruler of Istakhr. When the Arsacid king turned down this request, Papak proclaimed his independence.

The revolt of Papak and the subsequent rise of Ardashir to power took place in the context of a civil war within the Parthian Arsacid Empire between King Vologeses VI and his younger brother Artabanus, who seized the throne in 216, and a series of wars between the Arascid dynasty and the Romans, with the decisive battle occurring at Nisibis in present-day southeastern Turkey, where the Parthians scored an impressive victory. These events provided a golden opportunity for Ardashir to expand his territorial possessions from Fars into the present-day southwestern province of Khuzestan and territories along the northern shores of the Persian Gulf. Ardashir also pushed eastward and seized Kerman in southeastern Iran. These conquests allowed Ardashir to declare himself an independent king. To demonstrate his independence, he minted his own coins.

After these successful campaigns, Ardashir moved against Artabanus IV. The Arsacid monarch seems initially not to have taken this challenge from a petty vassal very seriously. As Ardashir expanded his territory, however, Artabanus had no other alternative but to respond. In April 224 the two armies joined battle, and Ardashir defeated and killed Artabanus, ending Arsacid rule in Persia.

Ardashir now ascended the throne as the *shahanshah* (king of kings) and founder of the new Sassanian dynasty. Soon all the provinces of the Parthian Empire were brought under the authority of the new ruler. Initially, Ardashir allowed local kings and governors who submitted voluntarily to his rule to retain their power, but he removed those who refused and replaced them with Sassanian princes, often his own sons. It seems that the majority of the powerful landowning families previously allied with the Arsacid dynasty submitted to Ardashir.

In sharp contrast to the Arsacids, who ruled a highly decentralized political system, Ardashir I established a centralized administrative structure, which concentrated enormous power in the hands of the Sassanian monarch, an absolutist king who ruled as the representative of God on Earth. Also unlike the Arsacids, who tolerated religious diversity and granted autonomy to the religious communities of their empire, Ardashir's successors imposed Zoroastrianism as the state religion of the Sassanian Empire.

Historians disagree on the territorial extent of Ardashir's empire. It seems, however, that he brought all the provinces ruled by the Parthians under his authority. In the east, the king of the Kushans, who ruled the area corresponding to Pakistan, Afghanistan, and the southern regions of Central Asia, submitted and accepted Sassanian suzerainty. Sassanian forces also seized the island of Bahrain and the nearby southern coast of the Persian Gulf. In 230 Ardashir shifted his focus westward and attacked Roman possessions in Mesopotamia. According to Roman historian Cassius Dio, Ardashir saw himself as the heir to the Persian Achaemenid dynasty and vowed that he would win back all the territorial holdings of the first Persian Empire as his rightful inheritance.

In his initial campaign against the Roman Empire, Ardashir laid siege to Nisibis (modern-day Nusaybin in southeastern Turkey near the border with Syria and Iraq). He also attacked Hatra, a major religious and commercial center of the Parthian Arsacid Empire in present-day northern Iraq but failed to capture it. Alarmed by the attacks on their eastern provinces, the Romans tried to conclude a peace agreement with Ardashir, but the negotiations failed.

In 232, Roman emperor Alexander Severus reluctantly went to war against the Sassanian state in a two-pronged attack where he targeted both Armenia in the north and Mesopotamia in the south. The Roman forces succeeded in seizing Armenia, but their campaign in Mesopotamia fizzled. Ardashir struck back. In 238 Sassanian forces attacked and captured Nisibis and Carrhae in present-day southeastern Turkey on the border with Syria. In 240 Ardashir again attacked Hatra and captured it that same year after a prolonged siege. This first military test between the Romans and Sassanian Persia ended with the Roman forces sent to Mesopotamia failing to achieve positive result.

Ardashir died in 240. He was succeeded by his son Shapur I who had ruled with his father as the coregent in the last years of Ardashir's reign.

Mehrdad Kia

See also
Parthian Empire; Sassanid Empire; Shapur I the Great

References
Agathias. *The Histories.* Translated and with an introduction by Joseph D. Frendo. Berlin: Walter de Gruyter, 1975.

Bundahish, ed. *Mehrdad Bahar.* Tehran: Tus Publications, 1991.

Cassius Dio. *Dio's Roman History.* Translated by Earnest Cary. London: William Heinemann, 1927.

Daryaee, Touraj. *Sasanian Persia: The Rise and Fall of an Empire.* London: I. B. Tauris, 2013.

Frye, Richard Nelson. *The History of Ancient Iran.* München: C.H. Beck'sche Verlagsbuchhandlung, 1984.

Frye, Richard Nelson. "The Political History of Iran under the Sasanians." In *The Cambridge History of Iran,* Vol. 3 (I), *The Seleucid, Parthian and Sasanid Periods.* Cambridge: Cambridge University Press, 1983.

Arif, Abd al-Salam (1921–1966)

Iraqi military officer, Baath Party leader, and president of Iraq from 1963 to 1966. Abd al-Salam Arif was born in Baghdad in 1921, the son of a rug and clothing merchant. Arif attended Iraq's military college during 1938–1941 and trained for a time with British troops. He sided with the rebels during the pro-Axis rebellion in Iraq in 1941 that prompted a British intervention and occupation that lasted for the remainder of World War II.

In 1942 Arif first met his mentor, Abdul Karim Qasim, who would go on to overthrow the British-installed Hashemite monarchy in 1958. By 1957 at the insistence of Qasim, Arif was a member of the Free Officers group, which was responsible for the 1958 revolution. Evidently, some questioned Arif's membership in this group, as he was just a colonel at the time.

With the success of the 1958 revolution, Arif, a Sunni Muslim, became Iraq's deputy prime minister and deputy supreme commander of the armed forces. Within months, however, Qasim had sacked Arif for his advocacy of Iraq's inclusion in Egyptian president Gamal Abdel Nasser's United Arab Republic of Egypt and Syria, which Qasim did not support. In November 1958 Arif was arrested and summarily sentenced to death, allegedly for trying to have Qasim assassinated. Arif was released from prison in 1961, and two years later he led a revolt that toppled Qasim's regime.

After solidifying his power and taking full charge of the Baath Party, Arif assumed the presidency, a position he held from 1963 to 1966. His power base came mainly from military officers with Pan-Arabist leanings. Arif signed a controversial agreement with Egyptian president Nasser in 1964 that called for the unification of Iraq and Egypt.

In keeping with his Baathist beliefs, Arif instituted a number of social and political reforms aimed at modernizing Iraq in keeping with Nasser's Pan-Arab visions. Included in these was the wholesale nationalization of Iraqi industries in an attempt to keep Western influence out of Iraq.

The planned unification of Iraq with Egypt was never realized, however, as Iraq went into a steep economic recession. Many Iraqis blamed Arif's aggressive Baathist policies and nationalizations for the downturn. At the same time, Arif was forced to deal with a Kurdish revolt in northern Iraq, the suppression of which was only partially successful.

On April 13, 1966, Arif was killed in a helicopter crash outside Baghdad. Given his unpopularity, some have posited that the accident was a successful assassination by disgruntled army officers and other high-ranking officials. Arif was succeeded in power by his older brother, Abd al-Rahman Arif. For all his mistakes, Arif had been a charismatic leader who helped bridge the gap between Iraq's Sunni and Shiite populations so that sectarian strife was kept to a minimum during his tenure in office. Arif's brother was ousted from power in July 1968 by General Ahmad Hassan al-Bakr.

Paul G. Pierpaoli Jr.

See also
Baath Party; Bakr, Ahmad Hassan al-; Iraq; Nasser, Gamal Abdel; Pan-Arabism and Pan-Arabist Thought; Qasim, Abdul Karim

References
Batatu, Hanna. *The Old Social Classes and the Revolutionary Movement of Iraq: A Study of Iraq's Old Landed and Commercial Classes and of Its Communists, Ba'athists, and Free Officers.* Princeton, NJ: Princeton University Press, 1978.

Tripp, Charles. *A History of Iraq.* New York: Cambridge University Press, 2002.

Armenians and the Armenian Genocide

Armenians claim descent from Hyak, grandson of the biblical Noah. For more than 3,000 years their homeland has been the region around Lake Van and Mount Ararat. Their greatest political empire came under Tigranes the Great in the first century BCE, whose realm stretched from the Caspian Sea to the Mediterranean.

In the fourth century CE, Armenia became the first state to convert to Christianity, and the Armenian Orthodox Church was instrumental in helping Armenians survive centuries of Ottoman rule. In the 1870s, nationalist movements within the Ottoman Empire stirred Armenians to press for greater rights. In response, the Ottoman government repressed them in various ways, including employing the Kurds as surrogates to harass the Armenians through violent means.

Prior to World War I, territorial aggrandizement by the Russian Empire had led to the creation of a Russian-controlled Armenia. In 1914 there were perhaps 2 million Armenians living in the Ottoman Empire, and during the war the Russian government recruited thousands of Armenians to join the army and fight against the Ottoman Empire. In 1915, Ottoman leaders in Istanbul (Constantinople), notably Interior Minister Mehmed Taalat Pasha, Minister of War Enver Pasha, and Minister of the Navy Djemal Pasha, concluded that the Armenians were a threat to the empire and needed to be eliminated. The Ottoman ruling triumvirate found justification for the massacre of Armenians in the claim that they were openly supporting the Russians.

Ottoman leaders planned to proceed in stages. First, they would kill the chief Armenian leaders. The Ottomans would then disarm Armenian soldiers in the Ottoman Army and place them in labor battalions on the railroads, where they might be killed off in small groups. Then the Ottomans would move against outlying Armenian villages, endeavoring to kill all their inhabitants. Finally, cities would be emptied of their Armenian populations. Those who remained, chiefly women and children, would be sent on forced marches to the eastern desert areas. Worn down by exhaustion and starvation, only a minority were expected to survive.

On the night of April 23, 1915, a coordinated Ottoman government operation led to the arrest of hundreds of Armenian leaders. Many were executed or soon died in confinement. A few, however, were saved by the intervention of U.S. ambassador Henry Morgenthau and others.

As further punishment for the Armenians allegedly supporting the Russians, the triumvirate ordered local authorities to relocate by force Armenians in Anatolia to Aleppo and then to remote mountainous or desert locations in the Mesopotamian desert, such as Deir ez-Zor on the Euphrates River. These "relocations" were actually death marches, during which most of the Armenians were murdered, beaten, or raped by Kurds or vengeful Turks. Estimates of the number of Armenians who died in what is known as the Armenian Genocide (Armenian Massacre, Armenian Holocaust) as a result range from 600,000 to 1.5 million people.

In some locations, Armenians resisted the removals. At Musa Dagh (Mount Moses) on the Mediterranean Sea near Antioch and the Orontes River in the late summer of 1915, Armenians held out against Ottoman forces for 50 days, and more than 3,000 Armenians in this location were eventually rescued by French Navy ships.

With evidence of the Armenian massacre widespread, the German and Austrian ambassadors in Istanbul warned the Ottoman authorities that this policy would provide the Allied Powers with strong propaganda material. When the Ottomans rejected appeals to curb their behavior, however, Berlin and Vienna took no further action for fear of alienating their ally. Secret negotiations between Djemal Pasha and

Armenian widows and children, ca. 1915. The Armenian Genocide of 1915–1916 during World War I was the first genocide of the 20th century and one of the largest in world history. It claimed the lives of some 600,000 to 1.5 million Armenians and the deportation of an estimated 1.75 million to 2 million Armenians living in the Ottoman Empire. The Turkish government today rejects all claims that a genocide occurred. (Library of Congress)

the Allies from December 1915 until March 1916 that might have ended the massacre came to naught, largely because of French and British desires to secure territory in the Middle East at Ottoman expense.

The March 3, 1918, Treaty of Brest Litovsk formally ended fighting between the Ottoman Empire and Russia, but the region remained in flux. The Transcaucasian Federative Republic of Georgia, Azerbaijan, and Armenia soon collapsed. The Ottomans recovered Erzincan, Erzurum, Kars, and Alexandropol to reach their 1914 border in the spring of 1918 and then attempted to drive eastward in order to establish a link with historic Turkistan and the Turkic peoples beyond the Caspian Sea. The Ottoman advance was halted on May 23, 1918, in the Battle of Sardarapat, and on May 28 an Armenian Republic was declared in Tiflis by the Armenian National Council. The Treaty of Batum of June 4, 1918, ended hostilities between Armenia and the Ottoman Empire.

Following the 1919 Paris Peace Conference, on August 10, 1920, the Allied Powers signed the Treaty of Sèvres with Turkey. The treaty recognized an independent Armenia with boundaries to be submitted to the U.S. president for arbitration. On November 22, 1920, the Woodrow Wilson administration drew the border between Turkey and Armenia from the Black Sea to include in Armenia the areas of Trebizond, Erzincan, Bitlis, Van, and all of Lake Van including the land to the south for about 25 miles, then eastward to the Persian border. Turkish leader Mustafa Kemal (Ataturk) rejected this provision of the treaty and mounted an operation that drove the Armenians eastward.

With a Turkish military victory, on December 2, 1920, the Armenians were forced to accept the terms of the Treaty of Alexandropol, which effectively placed the border at about its present location. Shortly afterward, Armenia became a republic in the Soviet Union.

To this day, the Turkish government denies the occurrence of a World War I massacre of Armenians, and no individuals were officially held to account. Efforts by the Turkish government to quash mention of the genocide have produced numerous scholarly, diplomatic, political, and legal controversies.

ANDREW J. WASKEY

See also
Ataturk, Mustafa Kemal; Djemal Pasha, Ahmed; Enver Pasha; Ottoman Empire; Sèvres, Treaty of; Taalat Pasha, Mehmed

References
Akçam, Taner. *From Empire to Republic: Turkish Nationalism and the Armenian Genocide*. New York: Zed, 2004.
Balakian, Peter. *The Burning Tigris: The Armenian Genocide and America's Response*. New York: HarperCollins, 2003.
Graber, G. S. *Caravans to Oblivion: The Armenian Genocide, 1915*. New York: Wiley, 1996.
Hovannisian, Richard G. *Remembrance and Denial: The Case of the Armenian Genocide*. Detroit: Wayne State University Press, 1998.
Hovannisian, Richard G., ed. *The Armenian Genocide: History, Politics, Ethics*. London: Macmillan, 1992.
Hovannisian, Richard G., ed. *Looking Forward, Moving Backward: Confronting the Armenian Genocide*. New Brunswick, NJ: Transaction, 2003.
Lewy, Guenther. *The Armenian Massacres in Ottoman Turkey: A Disputed Genocide*. Salt Lake City: University of Utah Press, 2007.
Morgenthau, Henry. *Ambassador Morgenthau's Story*. Detroit: Wayne State University Press, 2003.
Ternon, Yves. *The Armenians: History of a Genocide*. Translated by Rouben C. Cholakian. Delmar, NY: Caravan, 1990.

Army of Islam

An Ottoman-Azeri military unit active in the concluding years of World War I. The Army of Islam was established at Ganja in Azerbaijan following the treaty of friendship signed by the Ottoman Empire and the Azerbaijani Democratic Republic in 1918. The army eventually consisted of some 8,000 Ottoman regulars and about 10,000 Azeri and Dagestani irregulars under the command of Nuri Pasha, brother of Enver Pasha.

The Army of Islam played an important role in defeating the Baku soviet and capturing Baku in September 1918. After the signing of the Armistice of Mudros on October 30, 1918, the Ottoman Empire left the war; however, the unit was disbanded, and its members joined the newly established military forces of the Azerbaijani Democratic Republic.

ALEXANDER MIKABERIDZE

See also
Enver Pasha

References
Firuz Kazemzadeh. *Struggle For Transcaucasia (1917–1921)*. New York: New York Philosophical Library, 1951.
Swietochowski, Tadeusz. *Russian Azerbaijan, 1905–1920: The Shaping of National Identity in a Muslim Community*. Cambridge: Cambridge University Press, 1985.

ARROWHEAD RIPPER, Operation (June 19–August 19, 2007)

Multi-National Force–Iraq (MNF-I) assault against Al Qaeda in Iraq and other insurgents in and around the Iraqi city of Baquba during June 19–August 19, 2007. Baquba is some 30 miles northeast of Baghdad. As a result of the Baghdad

Security Plan developed in early 2007 and the American troop surge that accompanied it, Al Qaeda in Iraq and other Sunni insurgent forces withdrew from some areas of Baghdad and began operating in Diyala Province. The insurgents, who belonged to the Khalf al-Mutayibin group, established a strong presence in Diyala Province and especially in Baquba, a city of some half a million people, which they designated as the capital of their self-proclaimed "Islamic State of Iraq."

On June 19, 2007, 10,000 U.S. soldiers, along with more than 1,000 Iraqi police and Iraqi military personnel, launched ARROWHEAD RIPPER to clear the region of Al Qaeda militants. Three U.S. brigades participated in the opening days of the operation: the 1st Cavalry Division's 3rd Brigade Combat Team, commanded by Colonel David Sutherland; the 2nd Infantry Division's 4th Stryker Brigade Combat Team, commanded by Colonel John Lehr; and the 2nd Infantry Division's 3rd Stryker Brigade Combat Team, commanded by Colonel Steven Townsend.

For security reasons Iraqi leaders were not included in the initial planning, but as the operation progressed, the Iraqi 2nd Brigade and 5th Iraqi Army Division played sizable roles. By operation's end, the Iraqi 5th Army Division had particularly distinguished itself.

The operation began with a night air assault by Colonel Townsend's 3rd Stryker Brigade Combat Team. As the operation unfolded, it quickly became apparent that Al Qaeda units, estimated to number more than 1,000 fighters, had dug in to stay. In addition to Iraqi security forces (army and police), "concerned citizens" groups—also referred to as Iraqi police volunteers—cooperated with U.S. military personnel and Iraqi security forces in rooting out insurgents. These groups were instrumental in finding and exposing the safe houses where Al Qaeda militants were hiding.

Fighting was fierce throughout Diyala Province but especially in Baquba. The attacking forces, proceeding house to house, met heavy resistance. As troops entered neighborhoods, they found schools, businesses, and homes booby-trapped with homemade improvised explosive devices (IEDs). The heaviest fighting during the operation occurred within the first four weeks.

An important goal of ARROWHEAD RIPPER was to prevent insurgents fleeing Baquba from escaping and reorganizing elsewhere. The attacking forces therefore set up a series of blocking posts to the northwest of Baquba in the Khalis corridor and south of the city near Khan Bani Saad to deny insurgents passage through these areas.

Coalition and Iraqi forces also conducted operations to disrupt enemy lines of communication and deny Al Qaeda areas of safe haven. Following the initial push that cleared Baquba of insurgents, coalition forces began to reposition and destroy Al Qaeda positions northeast of Baquba in the Diyala River Valley. In spite of their efforts, many insurgents escaped capture and fled.

By the end of the operation on August 19, more than 100 insurgents had been killed, including the Al Qaeda leader in Baquba, and more than 100 insurgents had been captured. An additional 424 suspected insurgents were taken prisoner. A total of 129 weapons caches were captured or destroyed, and some 250 IEDs were found and rendered inoperable, including those in houses and vehicles. Coalition casualties were 18 Americans killed and 12 wounded; 7 Iraqi Army personnel were killed and 15 wounded. Two allied Iraqi militiamen and 3 Iraqi police were also killed. Civilian casualties were estimated at 350 killed and many more wounded.

One reason for the success of the operation was the newly formed Diyala Operations Center, established to coordinate coalition activities in the province. Through it, coalition forces, local police, the Iraqi military, and citizen informants sympathetic to the American military were all linked to one headquarters location. This enabled planners and leaders of the operation to react quickly to any situation.

RANDY JACK TAYLOR

See also
Al Qaeda in Iraq; Iraq Insurgency

References
Radcliffe, Woodrow S. *The Strategic Surge in Iraq: Pretense or Plan for Success?* USAWC Strategy Research Project. Carlisle Barracks, PA: U.S. Army War College, 2007.
Simon, Steven, and Council on Foreign Relations. *After the Surge: The Case for U.S. Military Disengagement from Iraq.* New York: Council on Foreign Relations, 2007.
Simons, G. L. *Iraq Endgame? Surge, Suffering and the Politics of Denial.* London: Politico's, 2008.
Woodward, Bob. *The War Within: A Secret White House History, 2006–2008.* New York: Simon and Schuster, 2008.

Arsacid Empire
See Parthian Empire

Arsuf, Battle of (September 7, 1191)
Battle fought during the Third Christian Crusade in the Holy Land (1189–1192) between armies commanded by King Richard I of England and Muslim forces under Saladin.

Following the capture of Acre (today Akko, Israel) in July 1191, Richard's next objective was Jaffa (today Tel Aviv–Yafo, Israel), the port nearest Jerusalem. Richard's 8,500-man crusader army set out on August 25. It became the classic demonstration of what is known in military terms as the fighting march, as the crusaders came under nearly constant Muslim attack. The crusaders' right was protected by the sea and by their fleet, which included Egyptian galleys captured in Acre. Aware of the danger of hit-and-run attacks, Richard kept the crusaders in tight formation. Half the crusader infantry screened the left flank of the knights, alternating with the other half, which marched with the baggage train between the knights and the sea. Heat and incessant harassing by Saladin's mounted archers meant that the pace was painfully slow, but so long as the crusaders stayed in formation they could not be halted.

Eventually Saladin realized that if he was to halt the crusaders, he would have to risk committing the main body of his own troops. At Arsuf (north of present-day Herzliyya, Israel) on September 7, Saladin attacked and finally provoked the crusader rear guard into launching a premature charge. Only Richard's prompt reaction in massively reinforcing the crusader rearguard attack, while still managing to hold other contingents in reserve, brought victory out of imminent chaos. Although the casualty figures are suspect, those of the crusaders are given at 700, the Muslims at 7,000.

Three days later the crusaders reached Jaffa, an important step in moving against Jerusalem. Realizing that he could not hold these, Saladin then evacuated and demolished most of his fortresses in southern Palestine, including Ascalon, Gaza, Blanche-Garde, Lydda and Ramleh. Richard went on to capture the fortress of Darum, the sole fortress that Saladin had garrisoned. While the Christian control of the seacoast threatened Saladin's hold on Jerusalem, Saladin soon rebuilt his forces, and Richard settled for negotiations with the Muslim leader.

JOHN GILLINGHAM AND SPENCER C. TUCKER

See also
Crusades in the Holy Land, Christian; Richard I, King; Saladin

References
Gillingham, John. *Richard I*. New Haven, CT: Yale University Press, 1999.
Verbruggen, Jan Evans. *The Art of Warfare in Western Europe during the Middle Ages*. Woodbridge, UK: Boydell, 1997.

Artah, Battle of (August 11, 1164)

Battle that pitted Frankish forces of northern Outremer and their allies against those of Muslim ruler of Aleppo Nur al-Din. After Nur al-Din sent part of his forces to Egypt under his general Shikuh to counter an invasion mounted by King Amalric of Jerusalem, he opened up a second front by besieging the town of Harenc, which had been retaken by the Franks in 1158.

Bohemund III of Antioch, Raymond III of Tripoli, and Joscelin III of Courtenay assembled a large force of their own men and the military orders together with Armenian and Byzantine contingents, amounting to some 600 knights plus infantry. Nur al-Din's numerically superior forces withdrew but then gave battle in the plain of Artah on August 11, 1164. Nur al-Din feigned flight and split the Christian forces, most of whom were killed or captured. Those taken prisoner included Bohemund, who was ransomed shortly after, and Raymond and Joscelin, who were to remain prisoners for a decade. Harenc capitulated one day after the battle, and Antioch's frontier was once more pushed back to the line of the Orontes River.

ALAN V. MURRAY

See also
Nur al-Din

References
Cahen, Claude. *La Syrie du Nord à l'époque des croisades et la principauté franque d'Antioche*. Paris: Geuthner, 1940.
Nicholson, Robert L. "The Growth of the Latin States, 1118–1144." In *A History of the Crusades*, Vol. 1, ed. Kenneth M. Setton, 410–447. Madison: University of Wisconsin Press, 1969.

Artaxerxes I (?–424 BCE)

Persian king of the Achaemenid (First Persian) Empire who ruled from 465 to 424 BCE. Little information is available on Artaxerxes I before his accession to the throne in 465. He was the second son of King Xerxes I (r. 486–465) and the grandson of Darius I. Artaxerxes's mother was Amestris, the daughter of the Persian commander Otanes who had supported Darius I when he seized the throne after the death of Cambyses II, the son of Cyrus the Great in 522 BCE. The Greek sources gave Artaxerxes the surname of Macrocheir, while his surname in Latin was Longimanus (Longhand), because his right hand was apparently longer than his left. Classical sources generally described the Persian king as brave, kind, benevolent, and handsome.

As the second son of his father, Artaxerxes was not in the main line of succession. The heir apparent was Darius, the oldest son of Xerxes I. Artaxerxes was installed on the Persian throne by Artabanus, the captain of the royal guard who murdered Xerxes in 465. Instead of admitting to his crime, Artabanus accused Darius of patricide, convincing Artaxerxes to order the execution of his brother. The ultimate objective of Artabanus was to remove Artaxerxes and seize the throne himself. Before he could carry this out, however, Artaxerxes moved against him and killed Artabanus himself.

The reign of Artaxerxes began with the rebellion of the king's brother who served as the governor of Bactria (present-day northern Afghanistan). This rebellion was quickly suppressed. Then in 460 BCE, a more significant rebellion broke out in Persian-controlled Egypt. Inaros, a Libyan who had requested assistance from Athens, led the insurrection. The Athenians agreed to support him and sent 200 ships to Egypt.

The confrontation between the rebels, backed by the Athenians, and the Persians, supported by pro-Persian Egyptians, was centered on Memphis south of modern-day Cairo. During a battle between the rebels and the Persian army at Papremis in the western Nile River delta, Achaemenes, the brother of Artaxerxes I, was killed, but the Athenians failed to capture Memphis. Artaxerxes I dispatched an army under the command of one of his generals, Megabyxos, who was the governor of Syria. The king's army relieved Memphis, defeated the rebels and their Greek supporters, and after a blockade of 18 months seized the island of Prosopitis. After the Greek fleet was destroyed, the rebel leader, Inaros, and 6,000 Greeks surrendered. The Athenians suffered another defeat when 50 of their ships sailed up the Nile and were attacked by the Persians and their Egyptian allies. The intervention in Egypt thus ended in a major disaster for Athens.

The defeat in Egypt and the ongoing conflict and warfare in mainland Greece forced Athens to gradually reconsider its confrontational policy vis-à-vis the Achaemenid Empire, although in 450, after concluding a five-year peace with Sparta, the Athenian Kimon attacked the island of Cyprus. A year later in 449, Athens sent a delegation to the Persian capital of Susa to negotiate a peace treaty with Artaxerxes I. The Peace of Callias between the Persian Empire and the Delian League, led by Athens, ended the so-called Persian Wars. The treaty granted autonomy to the Ionian states of Asia Minor. Persian ships were prohibited from sailing in the Aegean. In return, Athens withdrew its forces permanently from Egypt and Cyprus and agreed to not interfere with Persian Empire's territorial possessions in Asia Minor, Cyprus, Egypt, and Libya.

Artaxerxes I, the Persian Achaemenid dynasty king who ruled during 465–424 BCE, was praised for his kindness and compassion. He followed the tolerant policies of Cyrus the Great and Darius I, and lent support to the Jewish leaders trying to resettle their community in Palestine. (Borna Mirahmadian/Dreamstime.com)

War between the Achaemenid Empire and Athens had ended, but Artaxerxes's policy of fueling conflict among the Greek states continued with dramatic results during the reigns of his successors. Learning from the military blunders in Greece of his father, Xerxes I, Artaxerxes adopted the policy of utilizing his empire's enormous financial resources to encourage conflict and war among the Greek city-states, particularly Sparta and Athens. Instead of organizing large armies and marching long distances, the empire's new strategy called for forming alliances with Greek city-states that had sought its support against those that had adopted a hostile attitude toward the empire. As long as Artaxerxes I ruled, the Persians maintained a posture of neutrality in the Peloponnesian War, but during the reign of his successor, Darius II, Persian diplomacy backed by Persian gold played an important role in bringing about Sparta's devastating victory over Athens.

In the Jewish tradition, Artaxerxes I is portrayed as a king who continued with the tolerant religious and cultural policies of Cyrus the Great. As with Cyrus, Artaxerxes supported the efforts of the Jewish religious leadership to establish its authority over the Jewish community in Palestine. In 458, the Jews of Babylon requested from Artaxerxes that he allow the Jewish priest Ezra to visit Palestine, with full authority over the affairs of the Jewish community there, and to enforce the book of the law as the will of the king. Ezra was permitted to return to Jerusalem with 1,500 Jewish families who formerly had lived in exile. However, when disputes erupted among the Jews, Artaxerxes intervened and dispatched his cupbearer and trusted confidant, Nehemiah, to settle the quarrel. As a result, the temple and walls of Jerusalem were rebuilt in 441 BCE, and the Jewish high priest was proclaimed the ruler of Jerusalem and Judaea.

As had been the case with Cyrus the Great, Darius I, and Xerxes I, Artaxerxes I was an ambitious and accomplished builder. His royal inscription at Persepolis near Shiraz in southern Iran states that he completed the throne hall of his father, Xerxes, thus contributing to the construction of the palace complex, which was originally built by his grandfather, Darius, and then significantly expanded and enlarged by Xerxes. Artaxerxes I died in 424 BCE after a 40-year reign. His tomb is located at Naqsh-e Rostam near Persepolis in the southern Iranian province of Fars.

Mehrdad Kia

See also
Achaemenid Empire; Darius II; Xerxes I

References
Briant, Pierre. *From Cyrus to Alexander: A History of the Persian Empire.* Winona Lake, IN: Eisenbraun, 2002.
Burn, A. R. "Persia and the Greeks." In *The Cambridge History of Iran*, Vol. 2, *The Median and Achaemenian Periods*, ed. Ilya Gershevitch. Cambridge: Cambridge University Press, 1985.
Ghirshman, R. *Iran from the Earliest Times to the Islamic Conquest.* New York: Penguin Books, 1978.
Thucydides. *The History of the Peloponnesian War.* Translated by Richard Crawley and revised by Donald Lateiner. New York: Barnes and Noble Books, 2006.
Waters, Matt. *Ancient Persia: A Concise History of the Achaemenid Empire.* Cambridge: Cambridge University Press, 2004.

Artaxerxes II (435 or 445–358)

King of Persia. Artaxerxes II had the longest reign—46 years—of any Achaemenid (First Persian) Empire ruler. Born Arsames in 435 or 445 BCE, he was the eldest son of King Darius II and ruled from 404 to 359 BCE. Artaxerxes II ascended the Persian throne upon the death of his father. His title in Greek, *mnemon,* translates as "mindful." From the beginning of his reign there was tension between Artaxerxes and his younger brother, Cyrus, who was the favorite son of their mother.

Artaxerxes intended to kill his younger brother, but through the intercession of their mother the new king allowed Cyrus to return to Sardis in present-day western Turkey and remain the governor of the western provinces of the Persian Empire. Shortly after Artaxerxes II became king, a revolt in Egypt, which had been brewing since the latter part of his father's reign, finally erupted. Egypt broke away from the Achaemenid Empire and declared its independence. Persian authority would not be reestablished in Egypt until the reign of Artaxerxes III (r. 359–338).

A year after Artaxerxes II lost Egypt, Cyrus (also known as Cyrus the Younger), led a revolt. Cyrus raised an army that included a large unit of Greek mercenaries and marched to Mesopotamia, where Artaxerxes II was waiting for him with a large force. The two armies joined battle in 401 at Cunaxa on the left bank of the Euphrates River 50 miles north of Babylon in present-day southern Iraq. Cyrus was defeated and killed after he had attacked and wounded Artaxerxes. The bulk of Cyrus's army was routed, and the Greek commanders who had participated in the campaign were executed, but according to the Greek officer and author Xenophon, some 10,000 Greek mercenaries who had fought with Cyrus returned to their homeland by way of Asia Minor and the Black Sea. This epic withdrawal is detailed by Xenopohon in his *Anabasis* (March of the Ten Thousand).

Regarding Persian policy toward Greece, Artaxerxes II reversed the pro-Sparta policy of his father, Darius II, and lent his support to Athens and its allies. Artaxerxes recognized that the defeated and demoralized Athenians could no longer pose a threat to Persian rule, but a rejuvenated and confident Sparta could potentially cause trouble in the western provinces of his empire. The conflict with Sparta headed by its king, Agesilaos, did not go well at first, but through a combination of bribes and effective generalship, the Persians and their Greek allies seized the upper hand, destroying the Spartan fleet in the Battle of Cnidus off the southwestern coast of Asia Minor in the summer of 394 BCE.

The Persian and allied forces then moved against Spartan-occupied cities and liberated them. The Persian policy of playing Athens against Sparta exhausted the Greek cities and forced them to send their ambassadors to the Persian capital, where they agreed to the Peace of the King

(387–386). According to this agreement, Persia reestablished its rule over the Greek cities of Asia, including Ionia in Asia Minor, along with the island of Cyprus. Artaxerxes II achieved this result by the brilliant use of diplomacy and Persian gold. The Persian policy of inciting conflict between Athens and Sparta reignited the war between the two Greek states. When the two exhausted and war-torn city-states ended their war, Thebes, which dominated the region of Boeotia in central Greece, attacked them with support from Artaxerxes II and scored a decisive victory over both.

The overwhelming success of Artaxerxes in his Greek policies masked the growing weakness of the Achaemenid central government, which was facing an increasing number of revolts in its western provinces. There, satraps who had accumulated enormous power challenged the authority of the Persian king and formed their own armies and alliances. The revolt of these satraps throughout the decade of the 360s posed a serious threat to the security and survival of the Achaemenid state.

Among these revolts, the most menacing was that of Datames, satrap of Cappadocia in central Asia Minor. Equally alarming was the rebellion of Ariobarzanes, governor of Dascylium in northwestern Asia Minor. By 362 BCE, the revolts of the king's satraps in Asia Minor and an Egyptian attack on Syria and Phoenicia had brought the Persian state to the brink of defeat and disintegration. But at the very moment when everything seemed to be going against the Persian king, the tables were turned on his opponents, and the threats from the empire's western provinces as well as from Egypt disappeared.

In Asia Minor, Orontes, the aging son-in-law of Artaxerxes, organized the assassination of Datames. Orontes also arrested Ariobarzanes, governor of Dascylium. As for the threat from Egypt, a palace coup dethroned Egyptian pharaoh Takhos, who was at the time in Phoenicia. The humiliated Takhos was forced to seek refuge at the Persian court, while his ally, Straton, the king of Sidon (in present-day southern Lebanon) was murdered by his wife. King Agesilaos of Sparta, who had formed an alliance with Takhos, left Egypt and died on board ship as he sailed home.

By the time of his death in 359 BCE, Artaxerxes II ruled an empire temporarily freed from internal strife. He was succeeded as ruler by his son Ochos, who ascended the throne as Artaxerxes III.

MEHRDAD KIA

See also
Achaemenid Empire; Artaxerxes III; Cunaxa, Battle of; Cyrus the Younger; Darius II

References
Cook, J. M. *The Persian Empire.* New York: Schocken, 1983.
Curtis, John. *Ancient Persia.* Cambridge, MA: Harvard University Press, 1990.
Ghirshman, R. *Iran from the Earliest Times to the Islamic Conquest.* New York: Penguin Books, 1978.
Plutarch. *Plutarch's Lives: Volume Two.* New York: Barnes & Noble, 2006.
Xenophon. *The Persian Expedition.* Translated by Rex Warner. London: Penguin, 1950.

Artaxerxes III (359–338 BCE)

Persian king and the son of King Artaxerxes II. Artaxerxes became king in 359 BCE following the death of three brothers (respectively, executed for treason, driven to suicide, and murdered) and consolidated his position by eliminating other members of the royal family.

Artaxerxes's 20-year reign saw various successes. Satrapal dissidence in Anatolia was curbed, and the prospect of Persian retaliation for an incursion into Persian territory forced Athens to make peace with its rebellious allies. Both achievements reflected threats rather than military action, however, revealing the fear induced by a new and ruthless ruler. Artaxerxes suppressed rebellions in Cyprus and Phoenicia in the early 340s with military force, though the fall of Sidon was achieved by a sordid mixture of Sidonian treachery and Persian double-cross.

Artaxerxes's principal achievement came in Egypt. After a failure to reconquer Egypt in 351 (which perhaps helped to prompt the Cypriot and Phoenician revolts), a renewed attack in 343 (the seventh attempt since Egypt's rebellion in 404) proved successful. A substantial Persian army was drawn from imperial heartlands and Asia Minor, supplemented by Greek mercenary forces including some who, with their commander Mentor, had been involved in the treacherous surrender of Sidon to the Persians. When the attackers penetrated the Egyptian defensive line in the Eastern Delta in separate coordinated operations, Pharaoh Nectanebo II retreated to Memphis and then fled to Ethiopia. Remaining Egyptian resistance was at best local. As at Sidon, Persian victory was followed by extensive destruction and looting. The Persian victory saw Artaxerxes become the first pharaoh of the 31st dynasty of Egypt.

In Artaxerxes's final years a perceived Macedonian threat to Persian control of western Anatolia led to Mentor being appointed regional commander and the local satraps supporting Perinthus when it was besieged by Macedonian king Philip II. Artaxerxes was, however, dead before Philip's forces landed in northwest Anatolia and began the process that his son Alexander III (the Great) would so triumphantly complete. Artaxerxes III was succeeded by his youngest son, Artaxerxes IV.

CHRISTOPHER TUPLIN

See also

Achaemenid Empire; Artaxerxes II; Cyprus; Darius III; Egypt; Phoenicia

References

Briant, Pierre. *From Cyrus to Alexander: A History of the Persian Empire*. Winona Lake, IN: Eisenbraun, 2002.

Kuhrt, Amélie T. *The Persian Empire: A Corpus of Sources from the Achaemenid Period*. London: Routledge, 2007.

Ruzicka, Stephen. *Trouble in the West: Egypt and the Persian Empire, 525–332 BCE*. Oxford: Oxford University Press, 2012.

Waters, Matt. *Ancient Persia: A Concise History of the Achaemenid Empire*. Cambridge: Cambridge University Press, 2014.

Artemisia I (5th Century BCE)

Artemisia I was the queen of the ancient city-state of Halicarnassus and of the nearby island of Kos in the Achaemenid Persiua satrapy of Caria, located in far western Anatolia, during the reign of Persian king Xerxes I (r. 486–465 BCE) and served in his invasion of Greece in 480. She was the daughter of Lygdamis of Halicarnassus and a Cretan. Artemisia I has a reasonably prominent supporting part in Herodotus's *Histories*, perhaps because of the relative novelty of a female commander but also because Herodotus also came from Halicarnassus. Herodotus portrays Artemisia sympathetically as one of those who provided Xerxes with good-quality, honest advice, which he failed to follow.

Herodotus claims that Artemisia chose to personally command the five-ship contingent from her territories on the expedition because of her "manly courage." Prior to the important Battle of Salamis, she advised Xerxes not to attack and instead wait for the Greek fleet opposing him to disintegrate from internal dissension. In the battle she fought well but at one point came close to capture. To escape, she rammed one of her own ships, causing the pursuer to think that her ship was either Greek or a defector. From his hilltop vantage point Xerxes and his staff observed the incident and assumed that she had bravely rammed a Greek ship. Herodotus notes that the Athenians offered a price for her capture because they were so upset that a woman was fighting against them. Artemisia survived the battle and was selected to escort Xerxes's children home following the Persian defeat.

IAIN SPENCE

See also

Greco-Persian Wars; Xerxes I

References

Herodotus. *The Histories*. Translated by Robin Waterfield with an introduction and notes by Catherine Dewald. New York: Oxford University Press, 1998.

Lazenby, John F. *The Defence of Greece, 490–479 B.C.* Warminster, UK: Aris and Phillips, 1993.

Munson, Rosaria V. "Artemisia in Herodotus." *Classical Antiquity* 7 (1988): 91–106.

Artuqid Dynasty (1101–1408)

A Turkoman dynasty that at the height of its power in the 11th and 12th centuries ruled eastern Anatolia, northern Syria, and northern Iraq. It was founded by Artuq, a chief of the Döger clan of the Oghuz tribe. Artuq fought for Seljuk sultan Malik Shah, established a power base in Upper Mesopotamia, and governed Palestine from 1086 until his death in 1091. In the early 12th century, the Artuqids split into two branches: Artuq's son, Suqman, took power in Hisn Kayfa in 1102, and his direct line ruled there until 1232. This branch was eventually extinguished by the Ayyubids. Another descended from Suqman's brother, Ilghazi; members of this branch governed Mardin and Mayyafariqin until 1408, when their rule was terminated by the Turkoman Qarakoyunlu confederation. A third short-lived branch of the Artuqids (1185–1234) ruled at Kharput (modern-day Harput, Turkey).

Between 1100 and 1130 Suqman, his brother Ilghazi, and their nephew Balak ibn Bahram stood out as redoubtable opponents of the Franks. These nomadic Turkoman chiefs were still under the nominal suzerainty of the Seljuk sultan, whose main power base was in Persia and Iraq. The threat of punitive action from the sultan prevented them from operating as independently as they might have wished. Shortly before the beginning of the First Crusade (1096–1099), Suqman and Ilghazi were governing the city of Jerusalem on behalf of the Seljuks. Suqman rallied to Karbugha, the *atabeg* (governor) of Mosul, in his attempt to relieve Antioch in 1098. That same year the Fatimid vizier, al-Afdal, captured Jerusalem from Suqman and Ilghazi, who withdrew to Mesopotamia.

Suqman then became active against the Franks. In 1101 he tried unsuccessfully to take the town of Saruj from Baldwin I, count of Edessa. In May 1104 Suqman joined Jekermish, the governor of Mosul, in defeating the combined Frankish forces of northern Syria in battle near Harran. Although disunity between the two commanders prevented an expected attack on Edessa, their victory at Harran halted Frankish momentum and was a boost to Muslim morale. In 1105 Suqman again proceeded to Syria, but he died suddenly, allegedly of quinsy but possibly poisoned by Tughtigin, the *atabeg* of Damascus. Thus, a vigorous opponent had been removed too early in the conflict with the Franks for him to have real impact.

Ilghazi, however, came to the fore almost immediately after his brother's death. In April 1110 in the first military campaign sponsored by the Seljuk sultan Muhammad (Tapar) against the Franks, Ilghazi accompanied its commander Mawdud to Edessa. The following year Mawdud led a second expedition against the Franks with a new coalition, including Ayaz, Ilghazi's son, but not Ilghazi himself. Mawdud's neighbor, Suqman al-Qubi of Akhlat, died suddenly in the Syrian campaign, and Ilghāzī, attracted by the short-term prospect of gain, attacked his funeral cortege on its route home, a deed that earned him opprobrium. In 1114, Ilghazi again refused to join the next campaign from the east under Aq Sunqur al-Bursuqi.

In 1115 Ilghazi's disobedience to the Seljuk sultan became open hostility. When another campaign from the east came to Syria under Bursuq ibn Bursuq, it faced a Muslim-Frankish alliance among Ilghazi, Tughtigin, and Prince Roger of Antioch, forged to defend local territorial interests. Roger's subsequent victory over Bursuq at Tell Danith made this the last expedition sent by the Seljuk sultan. The cessation of this threat and the death of Sultan Muhammad in April 1118 emboldened Ilghazi to take more personal initiatives against the Franks and expand his power base. He followed his capture of Mardin and Mayyafariqin in 1118 by seizing Aleppo the following year. He then descended into the Orontes Valley. Tughtigin promised to join him, but Ilghazi did not wait for him. Nor did Roger of Antioch wait for other Frankish princes. Ilghazi won a resounding victory at the Battle of the Field of Blood (Ager Sanguinis) in May 1119, and the Franks sustained considerable losses.

This triumph in battle over Roger was the crowning achievement of Ilghazi's career, gaining him great prestige in the Muslim world. The caliph bestowed on him the honorific title Najm al-Din (Star of Religion); Ilghazi had succeeded where semiofficial Seljuk campaigns had not, and the glory fell exclusively to him. Yet the short attention span of his Turkomans—who, once satisfied with the plunder from a battle, were reluctant to embark straightaway on further fighting—and his own prolonged alcoholic celebration (which lasted three weeks) prevented him from following up this triumph in the obvious way with an attack on Antioch.

Ilghazi was above all opportunistic and would pursue whatever chances for plunder presented themselves. Accordingly, in 1121 he struck northward into the Caucasus. There he was roundly defeated by the Christian Georgian king David II and was lucky to escape to Mardin. Ilghazi died in November 1122, but there was a dramatic epilogue. Before his death was announced publicly, his widow ordered two men to hold his corpse upright on his horse as it entered Mayyafariqin so as to secure the citadel for his son Sulayman.

The Artuqid threat to the Franks of Syria was not, however, finished. Ilghazi's dynamic but overextended energies were now replaced by those of his intrepid nephew, Balak, who controlled Melitene (modern-day Malatya, Turkey) and Kharput. Balak captured Count Joscelin I of Edessa in 1122 and King Baldwin II of Jerusalem in 1123; both languished in his pit at Kharput. The seizure of the Frankish king gave Balak great prestige. He then took Aleppo, but on hearing that Joscelin had escaped from prison, he hastened to Kharput, seized the castle, and had all the inhabitants, except for Baldwin, thrown over the battlements. Balak was killed by a stray arrow while besieging Manbij in May 1124. He had indeed been a formidable opponent of the Franks in the north. The inscription on his tomb speaks of him as a martyr and carries a quotation from the Quran: "Think not of those who are slain in the way of God as dead. Nay, they are living."

The strength of the early Artuqids lay in the raiding skills of their bellicose Turkoman cavalry, and Ilghazi had relied latterly on his alliance with Tughtigin of Damascus. Between 1100 and 1130, the northern Syrian towns were under constant pressure; threatened by vigorous Frankish expansion, they turned for protection to Muslim commanders such as the Artuqids. But such protection was a mixed blessing. The proximity of the undisciplined Turkomans, whom the Artuqids could not always control, threatened the safety of the cities. Indeed, Ilghazi's troops had previously terrorized the citizens of Baghdad, and Balak's lieutenant in Aleppo forcibly (and illegally) turned churches into mosques.

With Balak's death, the Artuqids relinquished Aleppo and ceased to operate as vigorous, independent opponents of the Franks in northern Syria. Henceforth their role would be to answer calls to arms from more powerful Muslim rulers in Syria and Egypt. Otherwise, they entrenched themselves in their lands in Upper Mesopotamia, involved in local power struggles. Once the career of the Muslim leader Zangi, governor of Mosul, was fully launched in the 1130s, both Ilghazi's son Timurtash, who succeeded him at Mardin, and his Artuqid cousins at Hisn Kayfa lived in Zangi's shadow, threatened by his growing power and fearsome reputation. They had a stark choice: send troops to reinforce Zangi or risk his personal reprisals in their own territories. Their perceived misdemeanors were dealt with firmly on several occasions; for example, just before besieging Edessa in 1144, Zangi attacked the Artuqid ruler of Hisn Kayfa, Qara Arslan, who had allied himself with Joscelin II of Edessa.

By the time of Nur al-Din, Zangi's son, the Artuqids had learned their lesson and knew their place. When called upon, they provided troops for Nur al-Din, such as at the Battle of Artah in 1164. Saladin too relied on his Artuqid vassals, whom he kept under tight control and in whose domestic squabbles he sometimes intervened.

In 1182 Saladin captured Amid, handing it to Nur al-Din Muhammad, Artuqid ruler of Hisn Kayfa. Artuqid troops accompanied Saladin in his unsuccessful attack on Kerak in Transjordan in 1184. Under Saladin's direct successors, the Ayyubids, Artuqid power was further reduced, and they lost Amid, Hisn Kayfa, and Mayyafariqin in turn. In the 13th century the sole remaining Artuqids of the Mardin branch were successively vassals to the Seljuks of Rum, the Khwarazm shah Jalal ad-Din, and finally the Mongols. Karakoyunlu captured Mardin in 1409, ending Artuqid rule altogether.

Muslim medieval sources rarely mention the crucial fact that the Artuqids ruled predominantly Christian towns. However, as a small military elite, the Artuqids established a modus vivendi with local notables, giving the citizens military protection in exchange for the payment of taxes. Beginning as nomadic chiefs, the Artuqids, as early as the second generation, became attached to the territories they governed. In administration, they ruled a Seljuk successor state in microcosm. Timurtash was more interested in peace than war, and he invited scholars to Mardin. Artuqid copper coins, with figural imagery based inter alia on ancient Greek, Roman, and Byzantine models, have suggested a classical revival to some scholars. Moreover, the Artuqids were vigorous patrons of architecture, building mosques, bridges, tombs, and caravanserai and renovating the walls of their cities.

After the Artuqids lost Aleppo, their territories were situated too far from Outremer to pose a serious threat to the Frankish territories. But their early leaders had indeed proved to be tough opponents for the Franks, and the simulated cavalry flights and sudden raids of the Turkomans were justifiably feared. However, Ilghazi and Balak lacked the iron discipline of Zangī, and they came too early to benefit from the heightened atmosphere of jihad (holy war) and the support of the religious classes later enjoyed by Nur al-Din and Saladin.

Carole Hillenbrand

See also
Ager Sanguinis, Battle of; Artah, Battle of; Ayyubid Dynasty; Baldwin I of Jerusalem; Baldwin II of Jerusalem; Crusades in the Holy Land, Christian; Harran, Battle of; Ilghazi ibn Artuq, Najm al-Din; Malik Shah I; Nur al-Din; Rum, Sultanate of; Saladin; Zangi, Imad ad-Din

References
Cahen, Claude. "Le Diyar Bakr au temps des premiers Urtukides." *Journal Asiatique* 277 (1935): 219–276.
Hillenbrand, Carole. "The Career of Najm al-Din Il-Ghazi." *Der Islam* 58 (1981): 250–292.
Hillenbrand, Carole. "The Establishment of Artūqid power in Diyar Bakr in the Twelfth Century." *Studia Islamica* 54 (1981): 129–153.
Hillenbrand, Carole. *A Muslim Principality in Crusader Times.* Leiden: Nederlands Historisch-Archaeologisch Instituut te Istanbul, 1990.
Ilisch, Ludger. "Geschichte der Artūqidenherrschaft von Mardin zwischen Mamluken und Mongolen 1260–1410 A.D." Unpublished doctoral dissertation, Westfälische Wilhelms-Universität, 1984.

Asabiyya

Arab tribal or group solidarity in the face of external threats. The ties which bound early and medieval Muslim military classes together were separate from their family ties. Nevertheless, *asabiyya* (tribal solidarity) remained strong, if only within tribal armies. Meanwhile, *istina'* was the sense of obligation between soldiers and their commander or patron. In a more general sense, a feeling of group identity was called *sinf*. This could be based on economic class or cultural or ethnic background. It was often seen among leaders who had served in the same armies or who rose in rank and power together.

By the 10th century, the public swearing of mutual oaths of loyalty became an important, if not particularly effective, means of cementing relationships between rulers, officers, and men. Gifts of clothes, arms, armor, and horse harness similarly enabled a ruler to reward his followers, since social and military status was indicated by the richness of an individual's appearance.

The strongest sense of mutual obligation, however, was that among slave-recruited soldiers who had been purchased, trained, and freed by the same purchaser-patron, especially those freed at the same time. The loyalty binding such *ghulam* or mamluk soldiers together was again called *istina'*, as was the loyalty felt by a "client" or man from a humble family or tribal origin to the individual or tribe that had accepted him, and sometimes also his family, as members of the "superior" group. As such, *istina'* often linked up with the *asabiyya* feeling of family or tribal loyalty to form a broader group solidarity.

DAVID NICOLLE

See also
Sharia

Reference
Humphreys, R. S. "The Emergence of the Mamluk Army." *Studia Islamica* 45 (1977): 67–99, 147–182.

Ascalon, Battle of (August 12, 1099)

Battle fought near Ascalon (Askelon, modern-day Tel Ashqelon, Israel) between the Christian forces of the First Crusade (1096–1099) and those of the Fatimid caliphate of Egypt, resulting from the attempt by Emir al-Afdal, vizier of Egypt, to recapture the Fatimid territory in Palestine lost to the crusade in July 1099.

Al-Afdal's forces may have numbered as many as 20,000 men, with a core of heavily armored Ethiopian infantry and large numbers of Bedouin light horse and more heavily armored Seljuk Turk cavalry. On July 25 the new Frankish ruler of Jerusalem, Godfrey of Bouillon, sent word to Tancred and Eustace of Boulogne that a large Fatimid army was gathering at the coastal city of Ascalon. All three crusader leaders and their forces made for Caesarea and then pushed south, arriving at Ramla on August 7. There they were later joined by men under Robert of Normandy and Raymond of Saint-Gilles.

On August 11 the combined crusader army, numbering perhaps 1,200 knights and 9,000 infantry, marched toward Ascalon and there captured a large number of their enemy's cattle; these cattle played an influential role in subsequent battle, as the Egyptians mistook them in the distance for soldiers and consequently believed the crusader army to be much larger than was actually the case.

The main battle was fought on August 12, 1099, approximately three miles north of Ascalon. Raymond commanded the crusader right alongside the sea, Robert the center, and Godfrey the left. They were able to surprise the numerically superior Egyptians.

Al-Afdal pushed forward his heavy infantry into the center to allow time for his heavy cavalry to deploy and tried to outflank the crusader left with his Bedouin cavalry. The crusaders beat back both attacks, and as the Ethiopian infantry tired, Robert of Normandy led a charge that captured the Egyptian battle standard and overran their camp. Godfrey repulsed a counterattack, and thousands of Egyptian soldiers were killed trying to escape into Ascalon. The crusaders had won a decisive victory, but this did not prevent al-Afdal from successive subsequent efforts to recover Jerusalem.

ALEC MULINDER

See also
Al-Afdal; Crusades in the Holy Land, Christian; Fatimid Dynasty; Godfrey of Bouillon; Jerusalem, Crusader Siege of

Reference
France, John. *Victory in the East: A Military History of the First Crusade*. Cambridge: Cambridge University Press, 1994.

Ashkenazic Judaism

The larger of the two primary branches of Judaism. During the Middle Ages, Judaism diverged into two cultures differing in laws, customs, liturgy, and language. Ashkenazic Judaism evolved and flourished in Central and Eastern Europe, the environs of the Holy Roman Empire. Sephardic Judaism evolved and took root in the Moorish Iberian Peninsula, primarily Spain, and North Africa. Ashkenazic customs (traditions) and halakic (Jewish law) rulings are based on the Torah understood in the light of the Babylonian Talmudic and ritual tradition. Sephardic customs and halakic rulings are based on the Palestinian Talmudic and ritual traditions. This division of Ashkenazic and Sephardic Judaism can be seen in the structure of the chief rabbinate of Israel that represents all of Judaism in Israel and is the final arbiter of halakic and kashruth (Jewish food laws). The chief rabbinate has two chief rabbis, one Ashkenazic and one Sephardic. The Jewish community in Rome predates the destruction of the Solomonic Temple and the diaspora and, along with Yemenite, Ethiopian, and Oriental Jewry, is neither Ashkenazic nor Sephardic.

Ashkenaz was a son of Gomer (Genesis 10:3) and the grandson of Noah's son Japheth. German Jewry of the 10th century traced its lineage to Ashkenaz and applied that name to Germany. The Ashkenazim migrated eastward during the 15th and 16th centuries, shifting the center of Ashkenazic Judaism to Poland and Lithuania. Hasidic Judaism arose in the 17th century and emphasized personal spirituality and piety as opposed to the more academic study of Judaism emphasized by Ashkenazic Judaism.

The Ashkenazic academic approach to Judaism provided the fertile ground from which the Jewish Enlightenment (Haskalah) grew in concert with the West European Enlightenment of the 17th and 18th centuries. The Jewish Enlightenment fostered a neglect of halakah similar to the West European rejection of the absolutistic truths of supernaturalism in general and Christianity in particular.

The first Jewish immigrants to the Americas were Sephardic. However, by 1750 Ashkenazic Jews dominated the American Jewish community. Ashkenazic Jewish immigration to the United States in the mid-19th through the early 20th centuries was driven by the increase in religious persecution of Jews (pogroms) in Europe and the expanding American economy. Ashkenazic Jews represented a mere 3 percent of world Jewry in the 11th century. Ashkenazic Judaism expanded to comprise 92 percent of world Jewry by 1931 before being decimated by the Nazi-inspired Holocaust. Ashkenazic Jews now comprise approximately 85 percent of world Jewry. Today, the majority of contemporary Jewry in North America is descended from Ashkenazic immigrants from Germany and Eastern Europe.

Many of the Ashkenazic Jews who survived World War II immigrated to Israel, the United States, and France. Mizrahi Jews—Sephardic Jews of North African and Middle Eastern ancestry—comprise more than half of 21st-century Israel's population. Ashkenazic Jews descended from the World War II Holocaust refugee immigration, and the Zionist immigration of the late 19th and early 20th centuries comprises most of the remaining Israeli citizenry. Ethiopian Jews who came to Israel via Menachem Begin's Operations MOSES (1984) and SOLOMON (1991) constitute approximately 1 percent of the contemporary Israeli population.

In addition to the differences in Talmudic traditions, Ashkenazic and Sephardic Jews differ in their indigenous languages and in some legal and ritual practices. Yiddish (Judeo/Hebrew-German) is the traditional vernacular language of Ashkenazic Jews. Ladino (Judeo/Hebrew-Castilian/Spanish) is the traditional vernacular of Sephardic Jewry. Just as the Gileadites and the Ephramites of biblical times varied in their pronunciation of "Shibboleth," Ashkenazim and Sephardim vary in their pronunciation of one Hebrew consonant and some vowels. Ashkenazim and Sephardim also vary in some halakic and kashruth (kosher) practices. Ashkenazim do not eat rice, corn, peanuts, legumes, and millet during the observance of Passover (Pesach). Sephardic Jews do. Ashkenazim are generally not as strict as Sephardim in their understanding of which meats are kosher, and there are differences in the permissibility of specific slaughter practices as well.

Although they have much in common, Ashkenazic and Sephardic Torah services and worship practices also differ. The terms "Ashkenazic" and "Sephardic" are often used to refer to liturgical traditions (*nusakh*) that vary in the content of the prayers, the order of the prayers, the text of the prayers, the melodies of the prayers, and the prayer book (Siddur). Ashkenazic brides and grooms refrain from meeting for one week prior to their wedding. Sephardic brides and grooms do not. Ashkenazic Torahs lie flat during a Torah service, while Sephardic Torahs stand. The Ashkenazic understanding of the law is based on the writings of Rabbi Moses Isserles, and the Sephardic understanding of the law is based on the writings of Rabbi Joseph Caro.

Zionism and its dreams of the modern State of Israel were based in the European history of intolerance, discrimination, and persecution of the Ashkenazic Jewry. Ashkenazic Jewry founded and fueled the modern Zionist movement and immigration. It also set forth the correlative kibbutz movement in Ottoman Palestine in the late 19th and early 20th centuries. It was the Ashkenazic Zionists who prevailed on the British government to issue the Balfour Declaration (1917), expressing official British support for a Jewish homeland in Palestine. That ultimately led to the formation of the European Ashkenazic–dominated State of Israel by the United Nations in 1948. This domination of 21st-century Israel by Ashkenazic Jews of European descent now faces a burgeoning Mizrahi post-Zionist backlash. The Mizrahim assert that Mizrahi or Arab Jews (the word is also used for Iranian Jews and those from Kazakhistan, Uzbekistan, Afghanistan, and India) and their ancestors are and were discriminated against by Israel's European Ashkenazic Jewish political establishment. These Mizrahim contend that the Zionist immigration policies that promoted Ashkenazic Jewish immigration from the late 19th through the 20th centuries reduced Mizrahi Jews to second-class citizenship. This, they argue, created and promotes social, political, and economic discrimination that separates Ashkenazic Israelis from Sephardic and Mizrahi Israelis.

RICHARD M. EDWARDS

See also
Balfour Declaration; Holocaust; Zionism

References
Biale, David. *Cultures of the Jews: A New History.* New York: Schocken, 2002.
Dimont, Max. *Jews, God and History.* New York: Simon and Schuster, 1962.
Gross, N. *Economic History of the Jews.* New York: Schocken, 1975.
Haumann, Heiko. *A History of East European Jews.* Budapest: Central European University Press, 2001.
Seltzer, Robert. *Jewish People, Jewish Thought.* New York: Macmillan, 1980.
Vital, David. *A People Apart: A History of the Jews in Europe.* Oxford: Oxford University Press, 1999.

Ashurbanipal (ca. 693–627 BCE)

King of Assyria. Ashurbanipal (Assurbanipal or Sardanapal) was born sometime around 693 BCE. The younger son of King Esarhaddon, he developed an interest in history and literature. Unlike his predecessors, Ashurbanipal was able to read Sumerian and obscure Akkadian texts. He was also said to be athletic, skilled in archery and hunting. Ashurbanipal became crown prince in 672 on the death of his elder brother and showed sufficient qualities of statesmanship that his father left him in complete charge of the government when he was away.

Ashurbanipal became king on the unexpected death of his father at Harran while campaigning in Egypt in 669. For whatever reasons, Ashurbanipal was said to be unpopular at court and with the priesthood; reportedly, the assistance of his mother, Queen Naqi'a-Zakutu, proved vital in his accession.

As was the case throughout Assyrian history, Ashurbanipal's reign was marked by near-constant warfare. His first concern was a revolt in Egypt. He crushed this and captured Memphis (668–667 BCE). The year 667 saw the first of eight campaigns against Elam. During 664–663 he put down a second revolt in Egypt, sacking the city of Thebes. Around 665 he moved against Tyre, which had supported both Egyptian revolts, and captured it following a siege. This led to the submission of other Syrian cities.

In 652 Ashurbanipal went to war against his brother Shamash-shum-ukin, who led a coalition against him centered on Babylon. Following a two-year siege, Ashurbanipal retook Babylon (648). The coalition against him then promptly collapsed.

In 647 BCE Ashurbanipal renewed the campaigns against Elam, taking and destroying its capital of Susa (639). Details of the remainder of his rule are sketchy, but there are reports of court intrigues against him involving two sons. Reportedly, Ashurbanipal died in his capital of Nineveh in 627, but it may have been as early as 630 BCE. In any case, his death led to a protracted civil war between his two sons that proved catastrophic for Assyria.

A highly capable military leader and administrator, Ashurbanipal was also a patron of the arts. He caused to be collected or copied and then assembled at Nineveh the first cataloged library of the ancient Middle East. (The British Museum houses approximately 20,720 Assyrian tablets and fragments from this facility.) He also built and restored palaces. Known for his religious zeal, he rebuilt and raised new religious shrines throughout the Assyrian Empire. Whatever his failings, Ashurbanipal was certainly one of the great rulers of the ancient world.

Spencer C. Tucker

See also
Assyrian Empire

References
Olmstead, Albert T. E. *History of Assyria.* 1923; reprint, Chicago: University of Chicago Press, 1960.
Saggs, H. W. F. *The Might That Was Assyria.* London: Sidgwick and Jackson, 1984.

Assad, Bashar al- (1965–)

President of the Syrian Arab Republic (2000–present) and head of the Syrian Baath Party. Bashar al-Assad was born in Damascus, Syria, on September 11, 1965. His father was Hafez al-Asad, strongman and president of Syria from 1971 to 2000. The Alawite sect to which Bashar al-Assad belongs encompasses approximately 12 percent of the Syrian population, but under the Assads it controlled Syria politically. Assad's older brother, Basil, was a more popular figure than was Bashar before he was killed in an automobile accident in 1994.

Beginning in the mid-1980s, the younger Assad studied medicine at the University of Damascus, training in ophthalmology at the Tishrin Military Hospital and then the Western Eye Hospital in London. After the death of his older brother Basil, Bashar became the heir apparent and enrolled in the military academy at Homs. He became a colonel in the Syrian Army in 1999.

Although Syria is a republic, President Hafez al-Assad had groomed Basil, then Bashar, as his successor. Bashar

Bashar al-Assad, strongman of Syria, who became its president upon the death of his father, Hafez al-Assad, in June 2000. (Joseph Eid/AFP/Getty Images)

al-Assad's acquisition of both military and Baath Party credentials was imperative to his legitimacy, but most observers believed that the senior power brokers in the Syrian government assented to his succession as a matter of convenience. In 2000, he was elected secretary-general of the Baath Party and stood as a presidential candidate. The People's Assembly amended the Syrian Constitution to lower the minimum presidential age to 35, and Assad was elected president for a seven-year term. A general referendum ratified the decision.

A reform movement emerged during the first year of Assad's rule, which was dubbed the Damascus Spring. Many Syrians embraced their young president's stated goals of ending government corruption and introducing economic liberalization. Reformers also hoped for an end to the State of Emergency Law, which had been in place since 1963 and had led to human rights abuses. Political prisoners were released from the notorious Mezze Prison, and certain intellectual forums were permitted. However, by mid-2001 the president reined in the reformists, some of whom were imprisoned and accused of being Western agents.

Under Bashar al-Assad, Syria opened somewhat in terms of allowing more media coverage, although censorship remained a contentious issue. The government finally allowed access to the Internet. Assad made job creation, the lessening of Syria's dependence on oil revenues, the encouragement of private capital investments, and the mitigation of poverty key goals. The government created foreign investment zones, and private universities were permitted, as were private banks. Economic liberalization was too gradual to instill much confidence in Syrian modernization.

Syria's relations with Iraq had improved prior to the change of regime in that country in April 2003, and Syrian-Turkish relations were also less tense than in the past. However, the United States showed great irritation with the foreign fighters who were crossing into Iraq from Syria and with former Iraqi Baathists who were using Syria for funding purposes. The ensuing 2004 sanctions against Syria under the Syria Accountability Act, first enacted by the U.S. Congress in 2003, discouraged investors and the modernization of Syria's banking systems. More importantly, this situation provided a lever to force Syria out of Lebanon, finally put in motion after the assassination of former Lebanese prime minister Rafik al-Hariri.

Syria strongly opposed the American presence in Iraq after the Anglo-American–led invasion of that country in March 2003, and Syria's own Islamist movement reemerged as a threat. Assad also had to deal with a huge influx of Iraqi refugees to Syria, who posed an additional burden on the economy.

Assad inherited a hard-line position toward Israel. Yet internally, the public saw the president as promoting an honorable peace for Syria, deemed necessary for further economic development. This did not mean that Syria and Israel were any closer to a peace agreement, but Syria also was most likely to seek to avoid war, as during the Israeli invasion of southern Lebanon in 2006. Syria and Israel engaged in an exploration of peace talks, and by the end of 2008 there were signs of a Syrian-Israeli rapprochement that might return the Golan Heights, taken in the 1967 Six-Day War, to Syria. Israel's war against Hamas in Gaza, which began in late December 2008, probably led to their suspension.

Other important changes came with the shift in Syria's position in Lebanon. When Hariri was assassinated in a bombing in February 2005, many blamed the Syrian government. Anti-Syrian Lebanese demonstrated, as did such pro-Syrian groups as Hezbollah. The United Nations inquiry into Hariri's death as well as comments by former Syrian vice president Abdul Halim Khaddam implicated Syrians at the highest level and pro-Syrian elements in Lebanon intelligence services in the assassination. The Syrian government fought hard to postpone establishment of a tribunal to investigate Hariri's death but to no avail. Syrian troops finally withdrew from Lebanon in April 2005, thereby ending a long period of direct and indirect influence over the country. Additional important Lebanese figures were assassinated, including Pierre Gemayel, founder of the Kataeb Party. Lebanon was a key economic asset for Syria because of highly favorable trade terms, smuggling, and the absorption of large numbers of Syrian laborers. The U.S. government continued to charge Assad with aiding and bolstering Hezbollah in Lebanon, but Syria viewed the organization as a wholly Lebanese entity. Assad was reelected to an additional seven-year presidential term in 2007.

Assad sought to improve relations with his Arab neighbors, but his pro-Iranian policies and interference in Lebanese affairs led to tensions with such countries as Saudi Arabia, and Syria has sided with a new group joined by Qatar.

On January 26, 2011, protests began in Syria, part of the so-called Arab Spring. Demonstrators called for political reforms, the reestablishment of civil rights, and an end to the state of emergency in effect in Syria since 1963. Protests occurring on March 18–19 were the largest in the country in decades, and Assad responded with overwhelming force. In May 2011, U.S. president Barack Obama signed an executive order imposing sanctions, hoping to pressure Assad into moving toward a democratic system. Members of the European Union followed suit, as did other nations, particularly Turkey, the government of which called for international action to oust Assad from power.

Although Assad employed U.S. public relations firms and endeavored to project a positive image, nothing came of his frequent promises of dialogue and pledges of reform as he continued to blame the violence, which grew into full-scale civil war, as the work of a small number of "terrorists." Both Iran and Russia have been strong supporters of Assad, Iran because Alawites are considered part of Shia Islam and Russia because of its long-standing ties with Syria and its important Mediterranean naval base there.

The Assad regime has been accused of numerous atrocities, including torture and indiscriminate attacks on civilians. The United Nations subsequently confirmed that the Assad regime employed poison gas in March and August 2013, killing a large number of innocent civilians. This finding led the Obama administration to threaten military intervention, which forced Assad to agree to surrender his country's large stockpile of chemical weapons and see them destroyed in August 2014.

The extremist Islamic State of Iraq and Syria (ISIS) joined the fight against Assad, making the establishment of an anti-Assad coalition much more difficult. By 2014 ISIS controlled wide swaths of northern Syria and northern Iraq, determined to carve out an Islamist state under strict sharia law.

Although Assad was reelected to another presidential term in 2014, following the capture of four key Syrian government military bases in Raqqa Province in September 2014 and the massacre of Syrian government troops by ISIS at one of them in September, Assad came under increasing criticism from his Alawite base of support. The reversal of Syrian government fortunes in the civil war was a key factor in triggering active Russian military participation on behalf of the Syrian government forces, chiefly in the form of air strikes beginning in September 2015. These were an important factor in enabling government forces to win the long battle for control of Aleppo (2012–2016) and appeared to give them a strong upper hand in the war by the summer of 2018. Assad meanwhile vowed to fight on until "every inch" of Syrian territory had been recovered from those he called "terrorists."

In November 2017 Assad's government declared victory over ISIS, although pockets of resistance persisted in parts of Syria. By 2018 Assad had solidified his grip on power, aided by the Russian intervention and the Donald Trump administration's shift in policy, which no longer viewed Assad's removal from power as its chief goal in Syria. However, two chemical attacks allegedly perpetrated against Syrian civilians by Assad's forces in 2017 and 2018 resulted in two limited U.S. retaliatory punitive strikes on Syrian government targets. In the summer of 2018, peace negotiations involving Turkey, Iran, and Russia continued, but no agreement was reached.

SHERIFA ZUHUR AND SPENCER C. TUCKER

See also
Alawites; Gaza War of 2008–2009; Iran; Israel; Syria; Syrian Civil War

References
Darraj, Susan Muaddi. *Bashar al-Assad*. New York: Chelsea House, 2005.
Glass, Charles. *Syria Burning: A Short History of a Catastrophe*. New York: Verso, 2016.
Lesch, David W. *Syria: The Fall of the House of Assad*. New Haven, CT: Yale University Press, 2012.
Leverett, Flynt. *Inheriting Syria: Bashar's Trial by Fire*. Washington, DC: Brookings Institution Press, 2005.
McHugo, John. *Syria: A Recent History*. London: Saqi, 2015.

Assad, Hafez al- (1930–2000)

Syrian military officer, political leader, and president of Syria (1971–2000). Hafez al-Assad was born in modest circumstance at Qardaha in western Syria on October 6, 1930. A member of the minority Alawite sect of Shia Islam, at age 16 he began his political career by joining the Baath Party. As a secular organization, the Baath Party actively recruited members from all sects and branches of Islam as well as from Christian groups. Baathism opposed imperialism and colonialism and espoused nonalignment in foreign policy except with other Arab countries. As a youth, Assad participated in Baathist demonstrations against the French occupation of Syria and for Syrian independence.

With no resources to attend college, Assad secured a free education at the Syrian Military Academy. Graduating in 1955, he was commissioned an air force lieutenant pilot. After advanced fighter training, he was promoted to squadron leader in 1959.

Assad opposed the 1958 union of Syria with Egypt in the United Arab Republic (UAR), for which he was exiled to Egypt during 1959–1961. In Cairo, Assad worked with other Syrian military officers committed to the resurrection of the Syrian Baath Party. He favored Pan-Arabism but he was opposed to the union with Egypt, which had seen most power in the hands of Egyptian leader Gamal Abdel Nasser. Assad's outspoken opposition to the UAR led to his brief imprisonment in Egypt at the breakup of the UAR in 1961.

On March 27, 1962, the army seized power in Syria and abolished the parliament. Army leaders promised to introduce "just socialism." Then on March 8, 1963, the Baath Party, supported by allies from within the military, toppled this new regime. In 1964 Assad become commander of the Syrian Air Force. Although Amin al-Hafiz, a Sunni Muslim, was the nominal leader of Syria, in effect a group of young Alawites, including Assad, controlled affairs of state.

Rivalries within the leadership of the state brought yet another coup on February 23, 1966. Led by General Saleh al-Jadid, it entailed considerable bloodshed. Assad became one of the key members of the new government as minister of defense (1966–1970). Assad's political position was considerably weakened by the disastrous Six-Day War of June 1967 that saw Syria lose the Golan Heights to Israel. A protracted power struggle then ensued between Assad and his mentor Jadid, then chief of staff of the Syrian armed forces.

In the autumn of 1970 Jadid decided to intervene against King Hussein's government in Jordan, which had moved against the militant Palestinians there. Jordanian aircraft savaged the invading Syrian tanks, forcing them to withdraw. This fiasco cleared the way for Assad to seize power. In the so-called Corrective Revolution of October 17, 1970, Assad forced Syrian President Nureddin el-Atassi to resign. This was followed by the arrest of Premier Yussuf Zuayyen and Foreign Minister Ibrahim Makhous. On November 21, Assad became prime minister. Atassi and Jadid were imprisoned.

While his rivals had concentrated on neo-Marxist economic reform, Assad and his nationalist faction were more committed to Arab unity and the destruction of Israel than to socialism. In 1971 Assad was elected president, the first of five terms. The previous regime had been a military dictatorship, but on coming to power Assad increased its repressive nature. Political dissenters were subject to arrest, torture, and execution, although usually the regime achieved its ends through bribes and intimidation. The government became strongly totalitarian, with a cult of personality buttressing the all-powerful leader, in part an effort to end the sharp fractures in Syrian society.

The only major internal threat to Assad's rule came in the form of a rebellion in the small city of Hamah in February 1982. Members of the fundamentalist Muslim Brotherhood purged the city of Baathists, killing perhaps 50. Assad's reaction was out of all proportion to the actual events. He called up the army and special security forces and sent them into the city. Two weeks of fierce fighting followed in which large parts of Hamah were razed. The death toll has been estimated at 10,000 to 38,000 people.

With Soviet support, Assad dramatically increased Syrian military strength. Syrian educational curriculums were revised to stress Assad's position that Syria was the champion of the Arab cause against Israel and Western imperialism. In his foreign policy, Assad employed a strange mix of diplomacy, war, and state-sponsored terrorism.

In foreign affairs, Assad's chief immediate aim was to regain the Golan Heights from Israel. Six years after the 1967 war with no progress toward that return of territory captured by the Jewish state, Assad and Egyptian president Anwar Sadat carefully planned and then initiated a surprise attack on Israel that would force it to fight simultaneously on two fronts. The conflict began on October 6, 1973. Known as the Yom Kippur or Ramadan War, it caught Israel by surprise. Despite initial Egyptian and Syrian military successes, which included a Syrian drive into the Golan Height and Egyptian crossing of the Suez Canal, Israel secured the initiative and was on the brink of a crushing victory over its two opponents when a United Nations–brokered cease-fire took effect on October 22. Assad then falsely sought to shift the blame for the defeat on Sadat and Egypt, resulting in lasting enmity between the two men.

Assad's continued insistence on the unconditional return of the Golan Heights prevented any fruitful peace negotiations with Israel. Indeed, Assad opposed all peace accords between the Palestinians and the Israelis as well as Jordan's decision in 1994 to end the state of war between itself and Israel.

In 1976 Assad sent troops into Lebanon, ostensibly on a peacekeeping mission to end the civil war raging there but in reality to secure Syrian control. Israel's invasion and occupation of southern Lebanon (1982–1985) led Assad to impose changes in the constitution of Lebanon that granted Muslims equal representation with Christians in the Lebanese government while securing Syria's virtual control of Lebanon. Syrian forces in Lebanon became essentially an army of occupation, which did not end until 2005.

Assad regularly supported radical Palestinian and Muslim terrorist groups based in Lebanon and allowed them to establish bases and administrative centers in Syria, leading the United States to routinely accuse Syria of state-sponsored terrorism. Assad supported Iran in the Iraq-Iran War (1980–1988) and participated in the coalition formed to force Iraq from Kuwait in the Persian Gulf War (1991), but Assad and Iraqi dictator Saddam Hussein developed close ties in 1998 when Israel began to develop a strategic partnership with Turkey.

Hafez al-Assad died in Damascus of a heart attack on June 10, 2000. He was succeeded in power by his son, Bashar al-Assad.

RICHARD M. EDWARDS AND SPENCER C. TUCKER

See also
Assad, Bashar al-; Baath Party; Egypt; Hussein, Saddam; Iran-Iraq War; Iraq; Lebanon; Muslim Brotherhood; Pan-Arabism and Pan-Arabist Thought; Persian Gulf War, Overview; Sadat, Anwar; Syria; Terrorism; United Arab Republic

References
Patterson, Charles. *Hafiz Al-Asad of Syria.* Englewood Cliffs, NJ: Prentice Hall, 1991.
Seale, Patrick. *Asad of Syria: The Struggle for the Middle East.* Berkeley: University of California Press, 1990.

Assassins

"Assassins" (*ashishiyya*) is a pejorative term applied to the Nizaris, a sect of the Ismaili branch of Shiite Islam in the Middle Ages. In 1094 the Nizaris broke away from the main body of the Ismailis in Egypt in the course of a dispute between al-Mustali and Nizar, two rivals for the succession to the Fatimid caliphate. Although al-Mustali was invested as caliph in Cairo, Hasan al-Abba, an Ismaili anti-Seljuk agitator in Persia, declared his support for Nizar, who had disappeared under mysterious circumstances. In the late 11th and early 12th centuries the Nizaris enjoyed considerable support in the major towns of the Syrian interior and made determined attempts to take control in Damascus and Aleppo.

The Assassins frequently resorted to political murder in the furtherance of their aims; indeed, the English word "assassin" derives from the Arabic term *ashishiyya*. It was once thought that the *ashishiyya* were so called by their enemies either because their leader, "the Old Man of the Mountains," used drugs (hashish) to delude his followers into believing that they were being given a foretaste of Paradise in his garden or because the Assassins resorted to taking drugs to steel themselves to perform their bloody deeds. However, on balance it seems more probable that those who called them *ashishiyya* meant more vaguely to insinuate that the Assassins were the sort of low-life riffraff who might take drugs; in this period hashish use tended to be confined to city slums.

By the 1130s the Assassins' attempt to take control of the Syrian cities had failed, and they withdrew to a mountainous part of northwestern Syria, where they took possession of a group of fortresses in the Jabal Bahra region, notably Masyaf, al-Kahf, Qadmus, Khariba, Khawabi, Rusafa, Qulay'a, and Maniqua. Masyaf was the headquarters of the Syrian Assassins. In 1126 Ughtigin, the *atabeg* of Damascus, gave them the town of Banyas, but they held it for only a few years. Meanwhile, an Assassin attempt to seize power in Damascus failed. Although the Assassins also hoped to take control of Shaizar, several of their attacks on the place were unsuccessful; they held it only briefly in 1157 after an earthquake had leveled its walls. In 1090 radical Ismaili preacher Hasan al-Abba established himself at Alamut, a strong fortress in the northwestern Persian province of Daylam, and as noted, a few years later when the succession dispute broke out in Cairo, he declared his support for the Nizari line.

From their bases in Syria and Persia, the leaders of the Assassins masterminded a series of political murders. The list of their victims included Sunni, Shiite, and Frankish leaders. These included Niam al-Mulk, the Seljuk vizier (1092); Jana al-Dawla, emir of Homs (1103); Fatimid vizier al-Afdal (1121); al-Bursuqi, governor of Mosul and Aleppo (1126); Abbasid caliph al-Manur ibn al-Mustarshid (1135); and Count Raymond II of Tripoli (1152). The assassination of Raymond and other Franks notwithstanding, in general Assassin outrages and the divisions they caused worked to the advantage of the Frankish principalities. The assassinations posed a major threat to Saladin, and in 1174 several Assassins reached his tent before being struck down. In 1176 Assassins made another attempt on Saladin's life. He launched an abortive siege of Masyaf before reluctantly coming to terms with Sinan, leader of the Syrian Assassins.

In 1192 for reasons that remain unclear, the Assassins struck down Conrad of Montferrat in Tyre (modern-day Soûr, Lebanon), perhaps acting on the behest of Henry of Champagne. In 1194, the latter visited al-Kahf to confirm the alliance between what was left of the Kingdom of Jerusalem and the sect. Other 13th-century assassinations include Raymond, son of Prince Bohemund III of Antioch (1213), and Philip of Montfort (1270), undertaken at the behest of Sultan Baybars, as well as the wounding of Prince Edward of England (1272).

During the 13th century the Assassins paid tribute to both the Hospitallers and the Templars in northern Syria. According to the Christian chronicler Joinville, this was because the masters of those orders did not fear assassination, for the Nizaris knew they would be replaced by masters just as effective. It is more likely that the tributary relationship reflected the strength on the ground of the orders based in Margat (modern-day Marqab, Syria) and Tortosa (modern-day Tartus, Syria). In a series of campaigns from 1265 to 1271, Mamluk sultan Baybars I captured the Assassin castles and made the sect his tributaries. He and his successors also employed them as a kind of state assassination bureau to attack enemies in the Mongol Ilkhanate of Persia. However, after the 14th century this practice seems to have been discontinued, and one hears little of what had become a remote, rustic group of villages inhabited by harmless sectarians.

The end of the Assassins in Persia happened earlier. They were unwise enough to challenge the growing power of the Mongols, and in 1256 Mongol general Hulegu was dispatched by Mongke Khan to capture Alamut and the other Assassin castles nearby. Grandmaster Rukn al-Din surrendered on a pledge of safe conduct but was subsequently put to death. Alamut had been a major center of Ismaili learning and possessed an impressive library of esoterica, which the Persian historian Juvayni inspected on Hulegu's orders.

Although the Nizari Ismailis were quite widely feared and detested throughout the Muslim world, they survive today in India and elsewhere as a respectable and prosperous community under the *agha* khan.

Robert Irwin

See also
Al-Afdal; Baybars I; Hulegu; Ismailis; Mongol Invasion of the Middle East; Saladin

References
Daftary, Farhad. *The Isma'ilis: Their History and Doctrines.* Cambridge: Cambridge University Press, 1990.
Daftary, Farhad. "The Isma'ilis and the Crusaders: History and Myth." In *The Crusades and the Military Orders: Expanding the Frontiers of Medieval Latin Christianity*, ed. Zsolt Hunyadi and József Laszlovszky, 21–42. Budapest: Department of Medieval Studies, Central European University, 2001.
Hodgson, Marshall G. S. *The Order of the Assassins: The Struggle of the Early Nizârî Ismâ'îlîs against the Islamic World.* The Hague: Mouton, 1955.
Lewis, Bernard. *The Assassins.* London: Weidenfeld and Nicolson, 1967.

Assyrian Empire

The Assyrian Empire was a major power in the ancient Middle East and, at its greatest extent, the largest empire of the ancient world. Named for the city of Assur (Ashur), one of many Akkadian city-states in Mesopotamia as early as the 25th century BCE, it was centered on the Tigris River in Upper Mesopotamia (present-day northern Iraq, northeastern Syria, southeastern Turkey, and the northwestern edge of Iran). The Assyrian Empire came to include Cyprus and the eastern Mediterranean to Iran; what is now Armenia, Georgia, and Azerbaijan; much of the Arabian Peninsula; Egypt; and eastern Libya.

The Akkadian-speaking people who founded Assyria entered Mesopotamia during 3500–3000 BCE, eventually intermingling with the earlier Sumerian-speaking population. The cities of Assur, Nineveh, Gasur, and Arbela came into existence by 2600. Assyrian tradition holds that the first king of Assyria was Tudiya circa 2450, while around 2050 Assyrian king Ushpia dedicated the first temple to the god Ashur in the city of that name.

During the period of the Akkadian Empire (2334–2154), founded by Sargon the Great, the Assyrians and all other Akkadian-speaking Mesopotamian Semites (as well as the Sumerians) came under the rule of the city-state of Akkad in central Mesopotamia.

Following a period of civil war and attacks by the barbarian Gutian people in 2154, Assyria again became independent until 2112, when most of it became part of the Neo-Sumerian Empire (or third dynasty of Ur), founded around 2112.

What is known as the Old Assyrian Empire can be said to have begun with King Puzur-Ashur I (r. ca. 2025–ca. 1950), who apparently established an independent state and dynasty that survived until 1809. Ilu-shuma (r. ca. 2008–1975) secured control of the Sumerian city-states of Ur, Nippur, and Der. His son and successor Erishum I (r. ca. 1974–ca. 1935) secured colonies in Asia Minor and expanded Assyrian trade.

Around 1808 Shamshi-Adad I seized the throne, ruling until circa 1706. He moved the capital from Assur to Shekhna in present-day northeastern Syria, renaming it Shubat-Enlil. Around 1741 he took control of the Amorite city-state of Mari, which controlled the caravan route between Anatolia and Mesopotamia. This made Assyria an empire with control of central Mesopotamia, the northeastern Levant, and parts of eastern Asia Minor. Shamshi-Adad I subsequently conquered additional territory.

Shamshi-Adad's son, Ishme-Dagan I (r. ca. 1775–ca. 1750), became involved in a struggle for dominance of the Near East with Babylon, then ruled by Hammurabi (r. 1792–1750), who had made that city-state into the major regional power of Babylonia. Hammurabi defeated a number of other states, most notably Elam, before also defeating Ishme-Dagan's son and successor Mut-Ashkur (r. ca. 1749–ca. 1740). The Assyrian monarchy survived, but Mut-Ashkur and two of his immediate successors became vassals of the Babylonian ruler.

Assyria also underwent a period of civil war that lasted until around 1732. Rulers followed in quick succession until Adasi (r. ca. 1724–1706) was able to restore order and end Babylonian control. The Akkadian-speaking Sealand dynasty of southern Mesopotamia drove out both the Amorites and Babylonians, and Elam took territory in the southeast, leaving Babylonia restricted to around the city of Babylon itself. Bel-bani (r. ca. 1705–ca. 1696) succeeded Adasi as the Assyrian ruler and campaigned with success against the Babylonians and Amorites, after which Assyria enjoyed two centuries of relative calm and peace.

Little is known about the Assyrian kings who followed, but Assyria remained secure when Babylon was sacked and its Amorite rulers were toppled first by the Hittites and then the Kassites in 595. Puzur-Ashur III (r. 1521–1498) proved to be a strong Assyrian ruler. He undertook considerable building work in Assur, including the construction of temples, and refortification of the city. He also signed a treaty with Burna-Buriash I, Kassite king of Babylon, defining the borders of their two states.

In the latter half of the 15th century, the Assyrians came under threat from the Hurri-Mitanni Empire in Anatolia. King Ashur-nadin-ahhe I (r. 1450–1431) concluded a treaty with Egyptian pharaoh Amenhotep II against the Hurri-Mitannian Empire. This alliance probably prompted Emperor Saushtatar of Mitanni to invade Assyria and sack Assur, making Assyria a vassal state. Shaustatar deposed Ashur-nadin-ahhe I and replaced him with his own brother Enlil-nasir II (r. 1430–1425), who was then forced to pay tribute. Despite this, Mitannian influence appears to have been short-lived. Assyrian king Ashur-bel-nisheshu (r. 1417–1409) seems to have been independent of Mitannian influence. He and his immediate successor undertook extensive rebuilding work in Ashur.

The Middle period of the Assyrian Empire of 1392–934 saw a number of highly effective rulers as well as wars that transformed Assyria into a warrior society, with all male citizens obliged to serve time in the army. During this period, Assyria defeated the Hurri-Mitanni Empire as well as the Hittite Empire, the Egyptian Empire, Babylonia, Elam,

Canaan, and Phrygia to become the dominant power of the Near East.

Infighting in the Mitanni Empire court enabled Assyrian king Eriba-Adad I (r. 1392–1366) to reverse the arrangement with that empire and exert Assyrian influence over Mitanni affairs. Ashur-uballit I (r. 1365–1330) proved to be another strong ruler, combining Assyria with the Hittites to break Mitanni power. Ashur-uballit I defeated Mitanni king Shuttarna II in battle, making Assyria again an imperial power. The Kassite king in Babylon married Ashur-uballit's daughter. The Kassite faction at court in Babylon then murdered the king and placed another on the throne. Assur-uballit I invaded Babylonia to avenge his son-in-law and installed a new ruler there. He then attacked and defeated Mattiwaza, king of Mitanni, adding the Mitanni and Hurrian lands to Assyria's holdings.

The next Assyrian king, Enlil-nirari (r. 1329–1308), faced an attack by Kurigalzu II of Babylon, who had been installed by his father, but defeated him and annexed some Babylonian territory. King Arik-den-ili (r. 1307–1296) campaigned in the Zagros Mountains to the east, subjugating the Lullubi and Gutians. He also defeated Semitic tribes in Syria. King Adad-nirari I (r. 1295–1275) made Kalhu his capital and continued Assyrian expansion to the northwest, mainly at the expense of the Hittites and Hurrians. He also conquered Shupria in northeastern Asia Minor, and he made gains to the south by annexing Babylonian territory and forcing the Kassite rulers of Babylon into accepting a new frontier agreement that favored Assyria.

Shalmaneser I (r. 1274–1244) conquered the Hurrian kingdom of Urartu, encompassing most of eastern Anatolia and the southern Caucasus, as well as the Gutians of the Zagros. He then attacked the Mitanni-Hurrians and annexed what remained of the Mitanni kingdom. The Hittites, who had been unable to save Mitanni, then allied with Babylon in an unsuccessful economic war against Assyria. Also a great builder, Shalmaneser expanded the city of Kalhu at the juncture of the Tigris and Zab Rivers.

Shalmaneser's son and successor, Tukulti-Ninurta I (r. 1244–1207), won a major victory against the Hittites in the Battle of Nihriya (ca. 1237) and then conquered Babylonia, taking King Kashtiliash IV captive. The Assyrians demolished its walls of Babylon, massacred many of the inhabitants, and plundered much of the city including taking the statue of the god Marduk. Tukulti-Ninurta then ruled in Babylon himself for seven years, taking the title "King of Sumer and Akkad," which had first been used by Sargon of Akkad. Tukulti-Ninurta also defeated the Elamites and conquered the pre-Arab South Semitic kingdoms of Dilmun and Meluhha. Following a revolt in Babylon, he plundered its temples. He also built a new capital city in Kar-Tukulti-Ninurta. Tukulti-Ninurta's sons rebelled against their father and laid siege to the new capital where he was murdered.

Instability ensued during which Babylonia again secured its independence under Kassite kings. Ashur-Dan I (r. 1179–1133) ended Assyrian internal unrest. He captured much of northern Babylonia, but this brought him into a protracted war with Elam, which had secured what remained of Babylonia. Although the fighting seesawed back and forth, Ashur-Dan I eventually defeated Elamite king Shutruk-Nahhunte and forced a treaty on him.

A brief period of internal unrest followed in 1133 on the death of Ashur-Dan I. A son and successor was deposed that same year by another brother, who died shortly thereafter. A third brother, Ashur-resh-ishi I, then became king. His 17-year rule (1133–1116) began a new period of Assyrian expansion. As the Hittite Empire collapsed under attack from the Indo-European Phrygians, Babylon and Assyria vied for control of the former Hittite-controlled Aramaean regions in modern-day Syria. Ashur-resh-ishi's armies defeated those of Babylonian king Nebuchadnezzar I on several occasions. Assyria then invaded and annexed Hittite-controlled lands in Asia Minor, Aram (Syria), and the Gutian and Kassite regions in the Zagros.

Ashur-resh-ishi I's son, Tiglath-Pileser I (r. 1116–1077), ranks as one of the great Assyrian kings. His first campaign in 1112 was against the Phrygians who had occupied certain Assyrian districts in the Upper Euphrates region. After defeating and driving out the Phrygians, he overran the Luwian kingdoms of Commagene, Cilicia, and Cappadocia in western Asia Minor. He also forced the Neo-Hittites from the Assyrian province of Subartu, northeast of Malatia. Later Assyrian forces penetrated Urartu, reaching the mountains south of Lake Van before turning westward to receive the submission of Malatia. Still later Tiglath-Pileser again attacked Commagene, Cilicia, and Cappadocia. Next he attacked the Aramaeans of northern and central Syria, reaching as far as the sources of the Tigris. He then took the Canaanite/Phoenician city-states of Byblos, Tyre, Sidon, Simyra, Berytus (Beirut), Aradus, and Arvad.

Tigleth-Pileser I twice invaded and defeated Babylonia, now under an Elamite dynasty, and took the old title "King of Sumer and Akkad." A great builder as well as a warrior, he is believed to have ordered the restoration of the temple of the gods Ashur and Hadad in Assur. Certainly, during his rule Assyria became the most powerful state of the Middle East, a position it would hold for half a millennium.

In 1703 Ashur-bel-kala became king. He campaigned successfully against Urartu and Phrygia to the north and the Arameans to the west. He also invaded Babylonia and appointed its ruler as his vassal. Ashur-bel-kala built both zoological and botanical gardens in Ashur. Late in his reign, civil war occurred when a usurper sought the throne. Although Ashur-bel-kala prevailed, the Arameans invaded Assyrian-controlled territory from the west. Ashur-bel-kala counterattacked. Nonetheless, by the end of his reign in 1056, much of Syria and Phoenicia-Canaan as far as the Mediterranean were lost to Assyrian control.

After the death of Ashur-bel-kala in 1056 BCE, Assyria went into a comparative decline for the next century or so. The empire shrank in size significantly, and by 1020 BCE Assyria controlled only its indigenous territory (the present-day northern half of Iraq, northeast Syria, southeast Turkey, and northwest Iran) and regions close to the borders of Assyria, essential for maintaining trade routes.

Despite its apparent weakness Assyria remained a strong nation, with secure borders and perhaps the world's most powerful military establishment. It was certainly in a far better position than the rival states of Egypt, Babylonia, Elam, Phrygia, Urartu, Persia, Lydia, and Media. Kings such as Ashur-bel-kala (r. 1074/3–1056), Eriba-Adad II (r. 1056–1054), Ashurnasirpal I (r. 1049–1031), Ashur-rabi II (r. 1012–972), Tiglath-Pileser II (r. 967–935), and Ashur-Dan II (r. 935–912) successfully defended Assyria's borders.

The Neo-Assyrian Empire period is usually dated from the accession of Adad-nirari II in 911 and ended with the capture of Nineveh in 612 by an alliance of Babylonians, Chaldeans, Medes/Persians, Scythians, and Cimmerians. Adad-nirari II (r. 911–891) secured Assyria's borders and then expanded its territory into Anatolia, ancient Iran, the Levant, and Babylonia.

Assyrian expansion continued under Ashurnasirpal II (r. 883–859). He secured much of the Levant to the west, subjugated the newly arrived Persians and Medes in the east, annexed central Mesopotamia from Babylon to the south, and expanded Assyrian control deep into Asia Minor to the north. He also moved the capital from Ashur to Kalhu (Calah/Nimrud) and undertook major building projects throughout Assyria.

Shalmaneser III (r. 859–824 BCE) continued Assyrian expansion into the Caucasus, Israel, and Aram-Damascus, subjugating Persia and Arab lands south of Mesopotamia as well as driving the Egyptians from Canaan. Adad-nirari III (r. 811–783) embarked on a major campaign of conquest. He subjugated the Arameans, Phoenicians, Philistines, Israelites, Neo-Hittites and Edomites, Persians, Medes, and Manneans and projected Assyrian power as far as the Caspian Sea. He also invaded and subjugated Babylonia and made vassals of the Chaldeans and Suteans in southeastern Mesopotamia.

There was little additional Assyrian territorial expansion until the reign of Tiglath-Pileser III (r. 745–727). A great military reformer, he replaced the former militia system with a strong standing army. He also centralized authority in the monarchy, transferring to it powers formerly vested in the provincial governors. Tiglath-Pileser III conquered as far as the eastern Mediterranean, bringing the Greeks of Cyprus, Phoenicia, Judah, Philistia, Samarra, and the whole of Aramea under Assyrian control. Not content with Babylonia as a vassal state, he had himself crowned king there.

King Sargon II (r. 722–705) took Samaria, effectively ending the northern Kingdom of Israel and carrying off some 27,000 people. He was forced to drive out the Scythians and Cimmerians who had attempted to invade Assyria's vassal states of Persia and Media. Sargon conquered the Neo-Hittite states of northern Syria as well as Cilicia, Lydia, and Commagene and also defeated Elam and reconquered both Babylonia and Chaldea.

Sargon II also established a new capital city named Dur Sharrukin. His son Sennacherib (r. 705–681) moved the capital to Nineveh and put the deported peoples to turning it into one of the most beautiful and also the world's largest city of its day. Sennacherib defeated a revolt in Cilicia, abetted by the Greeks. He also reasserted Assyrian control of Corduene, Cilicia, and Phrygia in Asia Minor and defeated an alliance in 701 of the Egyptians, Judah, Sidon, Ascalon, and Ekron. He took many cities, including Jerusalem after a siege. Although he took tens of thousands of captives, he spared Jerusalem.

When Merodach-Baladan, the former ruler of Babylonia, returned there, Sennacherib attacked and defeated him near Kish in 703 and then plundered Babylonia and installed a puppet ruler. When the latter recommenced hostilities, Sennacherib returned to Babylon in 700, defeated him, and installed his own son Ashur-nadin-shumi as king. In 694 Sennacherib invaded Elam and ravaged it. Aided by the Chaldeans, the king of Elam then attacked Babylonia. In 689 Seenacherib again took Babylon and this time slaughtered its people and utterly destroyed the city, tearing down its walls and opening canals to turn what remained into a marsh. Those Babylonians who survived were scattered. In

681 Sennacherib was murdered by one or more of his own sons supposedly for the destruction of Babylon, which was held a sacred city for all Mesopotamians.

Esarhaddon (r. 681–669) had Babylon rebuilt. He also imposed vassalage on his Persian, Median, and Parthian subjects, and he again defeated the Scythes and Cimmerians. Deciding to conquer Egypt, he crossed the Sinai in 671 and took once mighty Egypt in less than a month, then declared himself "king of Egypt, Libya, and Kush." Esarhaddon could well boast that "I am without an equal among all kings."

Ashurbanipal (r. 669–627 BCE) was the last great Assyrian ruler. During his reign Assyria controlled the territory from the Caucasus Mountains (modern-day Armenia, Georgia, and Azerbaijan) in the north to Nubia, Egypt, Libya, and Arabia in the south and from the eastern Mediterranean, Cyprus, and Antioch in the west to Persia, Cissia, and the Caspian Sea in the east.

Shamash-shum-ukin, the brother of Ashurbanipal and ruler of Babylon on his behalf, became infused with Babylonian nationalism and attempted a rebellion that included many Assyrian vassal peoples. It ended in defeat in 648 BCE, when Babylon was sacked and Shamash-shum-ukin committed suicide in the palace. Ashurbanipal then set about invading and punishing the Elamites, Persians, Chaldeans, Medes, Arameans, Arabs, and Canaanites who had supported the revolt. Assyrian forces conquered Babylonia, Chaldea, Elam, Media, Persia, Urartu (Armenia), Phoenicia, Aramea/Syria, Phrygia, the Neo-Hittite States, the Hurrian lands, Arabia, Gutium, Israel, Judah, Samarra, Moab, Edom, Corduene, Cilicia, Mannea, and Cyprus and defeated and/or exacted tribute from Scythia, Cimmeria, Lydia, Nubia, Ethiopia, and others. At its height, the Assyrian Empire encompassed the whole of the modern-day nations of Iraq, Syria, Egypt, Lebanon, Israel, Palestine, Jordan, Kuwait, Bahrain, Palestine and Cyprus together with large swaths of Iran, Saudi Arabia, Turkey, Sudan, Libya, Armenia, Georgia and Azerbaijan.

Assyria appeared stronger than ever. However, the long, costly wars and pacifications found Assyria materially exhausted. Following the death of Ashurbanipal in 627, unrest broke out in Assyria itself, and the empire began to come apart.

A prolonged period of civil wars ensued involving rival kings Ashur-etil-ilani, Sin-shumu-lishir, and Sin-shar-ishkun. Egypt's Twenty-Sixth Dynasty, which had been installed by the Assyrians as vassals, broke free of Assyrian control. The Scythians and Cimmerians also took advantage of the situation to ravage Assyrian colonies in Asia Minor and the Caucasus, where the Assyrian vassal kings of Urartu and Lydia begged for assistance in vain. The Scythians also raided the Levant, Israel, and Judah (sacking Ashkelon) and even the coasts of Egypt. The Iranic peoples of the Medes, Persians, and Parthians also took advantage of the upheavals in Assyria to form a powerful Median-dominated force that destroyed the Assyrian vassal kingdom of Mannea and absorbed the remnants of the Elamites of southern Iran as well as the Gutians, Manneans, and Kassites of the Zagros Mountains and the Caspian Sea.

Cyaxares, which was technically an Assyrian vassal state, formed an alliance with the Scythians and Cimmerians and launched a surprise attack on Assyria in 615, sacking Kalhu and taking Arrapha (modern-day Kirkuk) and Gasur. Throughout 614 in bitter fighting the attackers gradually made inroads into Assyria itself. In 613, however, the Assyrians somehow rallied and won a number of victories against the Medes-Persians, Babylonians-Chaldeans, and Scythians-Cimmerians. A massive combined offensive by the attackers in 612, however, led to the capture of Nineveh late that year, with Assyrian king Sin-shar-ishkun dying in the battle for the city. Despite the odds against them and the capture of all their major cities, the Assyrians continued to resist under King Ashur-uballit II (r. 612–605). The remaining Assyrian forces coalesced around Harran (in modern-day southeastern Turkey), Carchemish (modern-day Jarablus in northeast Syria), and the vassal kingdom of Urartu in modern-day northeastern Turkey. Nonetheless, Assyria's enemies took Harran in 608 and Carchemish in 605 BCE.

Remnants of the Assyrian army then withdrew into western Assyria, where they may have held out for a time, but certainly no later than 599 Assyria disappeared as an independent political entity. It now fell under the successive control of the Median Empire, the Achaemenid Empire, the Macedonian Empire, the Seleucid Empire, the Parthian Empire, the Roman Empire (briefly), and the Sassanian Empire. The Arab Islamic conquest in the mid-seventh century, however, saw the end of Assyria as a geopolitical entity.

Although brutal in war, with captured soldiers tortured and slain and cities destroyed, Assyria was in many respects a liberal empire in that its cities and each nation it controlled had considerable autonomy. Conquered states were allowed to keep their own laws, religions, and rulers, provided that the set amount of tribute was paid promptly. Such a loose administration, however, fostered rebellions, and the subject states had to be conquered again and again. All in all the Assyrian Empire was an instrument of war, with its wealth derived from abroad. In the end, these nearly constant wars destroyed it, depleting its manpower and diluting the quality of its military with the necessary influx of foreign levies. Assyria on its own simply lacked sufficient numbers of men to garrison and control its vast empire. Another factor in the decline was the nature of the Assyrian economy, which relied on foreign tribute that could be cut off at any time.

SPENCER C. TUCKER

See also
Achaemenid Empire; Ashurbanipal; Babylonian Empire, Neo-; Babylonian Empire, Old; Cyrus II the Great; Hammurabi; Sargon of Akkad; Sennacherib; Tiglath-Pileser I; Tiglath-Pileser III

References
Bower, Susan Wise. *The History of the Ancient World from the Earliest Accounts to the Fall of Rome.* New York: Norton, 2007.
Bryce, Trevor. *The Routledge Handbook of the Peoples and Places of Ancient Western Asia: The Near East from the Early Bronze Age to the Fall of the Persian Empire.* London: Routledge, 2009.
Hackett, John. *Warfare in the Ancient World.* New York: Facts on File, 1989.
Healy, Mark. *The Ancient Assyrians.* London: Osprey, 2003.
Kriwaczek, Paul. *Babylon: Mesopotamia and the Birth of Civilization.* New York: St. Martin's Griffin, 2012.
Nardo, Don. *The Assyrian Empire.* Farmington Hills, MI: Greenhaven, 1998.
Olmstead, Albert T. E. *History of Assyria.* 1923; reprint, Chicago: University of Chicago Press, 1960.
Oppenheim, A. Leo. *Ancient Mesopotamia: Portrait of a Dead Civilization.* Chicago: University of Chicago Press, 2013.
Pollock, Susan. *Ancient Mesopotamia: The Land That Never Was.* Cambridge: Cambridge University Press, 2008.
Saggs, H. W. F. *The Greatness That Was Babylon: A Survey of the Ancient Civilization of the Tigris-Euphrates Valley.* London: Sidgwick & Jackson, 1988.
Smith, Sidney. *Early History of Assyria to 1000 B.C.* London: Chatto & Windus, 1928.
Van de Mieroop, Marc. *A History of the Ancient Near East, ca. 3000–323 BC.* Hoboken, NJ: Wiley-Blackwell, 2015.
Wise, Terrence. *Ancient Armies of the Middle East.* Oxford, UK: Osprey, 1984.

Ataturk, Mustafa Kemal (1881–1938)

Turkish general and statesman regarded as the father of modern Turkey. Born Mustafa Rizi in Salonika (Thessaloníki) on March 12, 1881, he was the son of a customs official and began military schooling at age 12. Ataturk proved so adept at mathematics that he earned the nickname "Kemal," meaning "The Perfect One." The young man liked the name and made it part of his own, preferring to be known as Mustafa Kemal and later Kemal Ataturk.

Commissioned a lieutenant in 1902, Ataturk served ably in a number of staff posts and combat commands. During the turbulent years before the outbreak of World War I, he became active in the emerging reformist Young Turk movement. In 1909 he took part in the march on Constantinople to depose Sultan Abdulhamid II but soon after turned his attention to military matters. Ataturk saw action as a major during the Italo-Turkish War (1911–1912), when the Italians invaded and seized Libya. A year later as a lieutenant colonel, he was chief of staff of a division based at Gallipoli during the Balkan Wars (1912–1913).

Ataturk was overshadowed during this period by the rise of Enver Pasha, a dashing politically minded officer who was leader of the reformist Young Turks and a remarkably inept general. Ataturk and Enver disagreed violently about the encouragement of German influence in the government and armed forces. Unlike his rival, Ataturk believed that the Ottoman Empire should remain neutral in World War I, doubted the chances of the Central Powers, and resented Enver's invitation to Berlin to send a

Mustafa Kemal Ataturk, credited as the founder of the modern Turkish state, served as the first president of Turkey from 1923 to 1938 and introduced numerous reforms in an effort to modernize his country. (Library of Congress)

military mission to not only advise but also actually command Ottoman forces.

Following a period of exile as military attaché in Sofia, Bulgaria, Ataturk was recalled and appointed to command the 19th Division at Rodosto on the Gallipoli Peninsula, with the rank of colonel. Although in charge only of the area reserves and subordinated to German general der kavallerie Otto Liman von Sanders, Ataturk established his military reputation during the Allied amphibious landings of April 1915. He immediately committed his troops and led a series of fierce counterattacks that pinned the invaders on the landing beaches.

When the Allies tried another landing at Suvla Bay (August 1915), Ataturk received command of that area as well. By early 1916 when the Allies had evacuated their forces, he was hailed as the "Savior of Constantinople." Subsequently promoted to general, he took command of the XVI Corps and continued his success against the Allies in defending Anatolia in March 1916. He was the only Ottoman general to win victories against the Russians.

Ataturk's accomplishments as well as his chafing at being subordinate to the Germans so threatened and angered Enver Pasha that the latter relieved him of command in 1917, placing him on sick leave. A year later with the German-Ottoman alliance facing defeat by the Allies, Enver recalled Ataturk to command the Seventh Army in Palestine. Outnumbered by Lieutenant General Sir Edmund H. Allenby's better-equipped British forces, Ataturk extricated the bulk of his command and withdraw first to Aleppo and then to the Anatolian frontier, an orderly retreat that nonetheless saved his army.

With the Allied victory and collapse of the Ottoman Empire, Ataturk used his assignment as inspector general of the armies in eastern and northeastern Anatolia to strengthen those elements working for a free and independent Turkish nation. On May 19, 1919, ignoring the sultan's attempt to remove him, Ataturk issued orders that all Turks fight for independence. In April 1920 he established a provisional government in Ankara. Ataturk became president of the National Assembly in Ankara and directed Turkish forces against Greek forces in eastern Anatolia during 1921–1922. In the Battle of Sakarya (August 23–September 13, 1921), Ataturk halted the Greek drive on Ankara. He then went on the offensive, taking Smyrna in bitter fighting that culminated in the burning and sacking of the Greek section of the city (September 9–23, 1922).

With the external threat ended, Ataturk advanced on Istanbul. The Allied Powers agreed to withdraw their troops there, and Ataturk ended the sultanate on November 1, 1922. The Treaty of Lausanne (July 24, 1923) granted almost all the concessions that Turkey demanded, and Ataturk proclaimed the Republic of Turkey (October 29, 1923), with himself as president.

Ataturk then set about implementing widespread reforms that limited the influence of Islam and introduced Western laws, dress, and administrative functions. Although an autocrat, Ataturk, the name he took in 1934, encouraged cooperation between the civil and military branches and based his rule on the concept of equality of all before the law. His achievements in every field of national life were extraordinary, and virtually single-handedly he inspired Turkey to take its place among the modern nations of the world. Ataturk died in Istanbul on November 10, 1938.

JAMES H. WILLBANKS

See also
Gallipoli Campaign; Greco-Turkish War; Turkey

References
Erickson, Edward J. *Ordered to Die: A History of the Ottoman Army in the First World War.* Westport, CT: Greenwood, 2001.
Fewster, Kevin, Hatice Basarin, and Vesihi Basarin. *Gallipoli: The Turkish Story.* London: Allen and Unwin, 2004.
Kinross, Patrick Balfour. *Atatürk: A Biography of Mustapha Kemal, Father of Modern Turkey.* London: William Morrow, 1992.
Macfie, A. L. *Atatürk.* New York: Longman, 1994.
Moorehead, Alan. *Gallipoli.* New York: Harper, 1956.

Attrition, War of
See War of Attrition

Auchinleck, Sir Claude John Eyre (1884–1981)

British Army general. Born at Aldershot, England, on June 21, 1884, Claude Auchinleck, known as "the Auk," graduated from the Royal Military Academy of Sandhurst in 1902. He saw extensive service in India and Tibet (1904–1912), in the Middle East (1914–1919), and in India again (1929–1940). In 1930, he was promoted to colonel; three years later he was appointed a temporary brigadier general. He became a major general in November 1935.

Auchinleck returned to England in January 1940, expecting to prepare British units for action in France. Instead, he was sent on May 7, 1940, to command British forces in Narvik in the disastrous Norwegian Campaign, which suffered from lack of air cover and inadequate forces and equipment. Just after Britain's evacuation of Norway, on June 14, 1940, Auchinleck took over the Southern Command to prepare for a possible German invasion. In this role, he worked effectively to improve the Home Guard.

As fears of invasion receded, Auchinleck was promoted to general and sent to India as commander in chief on November 21, 1940. British officials charged him with controlling pressures for independence while overseeing the training of Indian units for Allied use elsewhere.

Prime Minister Winston L. S. Churchill called on Auchinleck to take the same role in the critical Middle East Theater (June 21, 1941), replacing Archibald Wavell. While in Egypt, Auchinleck came under constant pressure from Churchill to undertake aggressive action against German general der panzertruppen Erwin Rommel's Afrika Korps. Auchinleck countered that he first had to train his force and overcome the difficulties of having inadequate supplies and armaments. Auchinleck began his offensive, Operation CRUSADER, against Libya on November 18, 1941, but it suffered from the lack of a strong Eighth Army commander in Lieutenant General Alan Cunningham. That effort would end on December 30. Auchinleck replaced Cunningham with Major General Neil Ritchie, and for a time the offensive went well. But Rommel struck back, leading to the fall of Tobruk on June 21, 1942, in which more than 30,000 men were taken prisoner.

Auchinleck then took direct control of the Eighth Army and stabilized his line at the First Battle of El Alamein (July 1–27, 1942) in Egypt later that month, thus saving Egypt from Axis control. However, Churchill, impatient for success from a more aggressive commander, relieved him of his command on August 5, 1942. Damning reports from Lieutenant General Bernard Montgomery about Auchinleck surely eased the skids.

Turning down a proffered command in Syria and Iraq, Auchinleck returned to India as commander in chief of the army there (1943–1947). Auchinleck was made a field marshal in June 1946, refusing a peerage a year later (he did not wish to be honored for helping to divide India and Pakistan, a result he abhorred). He retired in 1967 to live in Marrakesh, Morocco, and died there on March 23, 1981.

CHRISTOPHER H. STERLING

See also
El Alamein, First Battle of; Montgomery, Bernard Law; Rommel, Erwin Johannes Eugen

References
Connell, John. *Auchinleck: A Biography of Sir Claude Auchinleck.* London: Cassell, 1959.
Greenwood, Alexander. *Field-Marshal Auchinleck.* Durham, UK: Pentland, 1991.
Parkinson, Roger. *The Auk: Auchinleck, Victor of Alamein.* London: Grenada, 1977.
Warner, Phillip. "Auchinleck." In *Churchill's Generals*, ed. John Keegan. New York: Grove Weidenfeld, 1991.
Warner, Phillip. *Auchinleck: The Lonely Soldier.* London: Buchan and Enright, 1981.

Aurelian, Emperor (214–275)

Roman emperor who ruled 270–275 during the third-century crisis, Lucius Domitius Aurelianus was born in Dacia Ripensis in 214, the son of a tenant farmer. Aurelian joined the Roman Army, rising to the position of cavalry commander under Emperor Gallienus. Together with other leading officers, including the future emperor Claudius II Gothicus, Aurelian conspired to murder Gallienus at Milan in 268. Claudius II died less than two years later after contracting the plague, and Aurelian defeated Claudius's brother Quintillus to claim the throne for himself in September 270.

Aurelian's reign was not without its problems. He faced several rebellions from senators and other officials, including the moneyers' revolt at Rome in 271, led by the financial administrator Felicissimus. But Aurelian's reputation as a successful military leader was well deserved.

Shortly after his accession Aurelian repelled assaults on Italy by the Alamannis and Iuthungis and by the Vandals in Pannonia. In 272 he engaged in campaigns against the Goths, who had invaded the Balkans; this resulted in the decision to abandon the province of Dacia across the Danube that had been established by Trajan. In its place, Aurelian created two new Dacian provinces from the territory of Moesia.

Aurelian next turned his attention to Zenobia, queen of Palmyra, who had claimed authority over the eastern provinces, including Egypt. She was defeated in battle at Antioch and Emesa before being captured while trying to escape to Persia. In late 272, Aurelian traveled to the Balkans to fight the Carpis but was forced to return to the east to suppress a second Palmyrene rebellion in 273. Zenobia was brought back to Rome and exhibited at Aurelian's triumph there but was permitted to remain a free woman and even married into the senatorial aristocracy. In 274, Aurelian embarked on a campaign against the Gallic empire in the west. He defeated the forces of Gaius Esuvius Tetricus, the last ruler of this breakaway state, in battle at the Catalaunian plain. Tetricus surrendered and later became the governor of a region of Italy. In less than five years Aurelian had restored the Roman Empire to its former extent and became known as the *restitutor orbis* (restorer of the world).

Aurelian's legacy included construction of the Aurelian Wall, which enveloped the city of Rome. Flanked by impressive towers every 30 yards, the wall (parts of which still stand today) demonstrated Aurelian's ability to protect the citizens of the empire. Aurelian also constructed a new temple of Sol Invictus (the "Unconquered Sun") in Rome and attempted to reform the coinage.

Aurelian embarked on war against Persia in 275 but was murdered on the way to the front as a result of a plot hatched by one of his secretaries. Aurelian proved himself to be one of the most successful soldier emperors of the third century in his efforts to reunify the empire while tackling barbarian incursions. However, he earned a reputation as a harsh ruler, which was one of the factors prompting his assassination.

CAILLAN DAVENPORT

See also
Zenobia

References
Southern, Pat. *The Roman Empire from Severus to Constantine.* New York: Routledge, 2001.
Watson, Alaric. *Aurelian and the Third Century.* New York: Routledge, 1999.

Auspicious Incident (June 15, 1826)

The Auspicious Incident was the forced abolishment of the Janissaries in the Ottoman Empire by Sultan Mahmud II in 1826. The Janissary Corps, the first Ottoman standing army, was established during the 14th century and facilitated the expansion of the Ottoman Empire. Initially a force of about 1,000 infantrymen, by the 17th century the Janissaries were a powerful military force of 40,000 infantrymen but with significant political influence, able to dictate policy to the Ottoman government. By the 18th century, however, the size of the corps had increased to more than 100,000 infantrymen. By this time, the Janissaries had ceased to serve as an effective military unit and had repeatedly rejected attempts by the Porte to modernize the Ottoman Empire's military establishment. Indeed, in 1807 the Janissaries deposed Sultan Selim III, who tried to modernize the Janissary Corps.

In 1826, Mahmud II announced that he was about to form a professional army trained by West Europeans. The Janissary Corps, not unexpectedly, revolted. The sultan, however, was prepared for this and unleashed the Sipahis, the mounted Ottoman elite cavalry. The Janissaries around Constantinople retreated to their massive barracks in Thessaloniki. On June 15, 1826, the Sipahis opened an artillery bombardment of the Janissary barracks. This shelling and the ensuing fires resulted in the deaths of some 10,000 Janissaries. The remaining Janissaries were either killed (often by angry mobs) or exiled or escaped by blending into society, and the corps was disbanded.

The Auspicious Incident allowed the sultan to introduce a modernized Ottoman army, the Nizam-i Cedid.

MICHAEL R. HALL

See also
Janissaries; Mahmud II, Sultan

References
Finkel, Caroline. *Osman's Dream: The History of the Ottoman Empire.* New York: Basic Books, 2007.
Goodwin, Godfrey. *The Janissaries.* London: Saqi Books, 2006.

Austrian-Ottoman Wars
See Ottoman-Habsburg Wars

AUTUMN CLOUDS, Operation (November 1–8, 2006)

Operation conducted by the Israel Defense Forces (IDF) against the Gaza Strip during November 1–8, 2006. Operation AUTUMN CLOUDS followed Operation SUMMER RAINS (the 2006 Gaza War) in the summer of 2006. After the attempted Israeli assassination of a senior Hamas military figure in Gaza on October 12, 2006, Hamas launched a number of rocket and mortar attacks from the Gaza Strip against southern Israel that injured four Israelis. This in turn triggered Operation AUTUMN CLOUDS, a limited weeklong Israeli incursion into Gaza beginning on November 1.

The operation involved Israeli air strikes, the use of helicopter gunships, and tanks, as well as hundreds of infantrymen. The major fighting occurred near Beit Hanoun, a city on the northeast edge of the Gaza Strip that saw Israeli air strikes and the use of helicopter gunships and 60 armored vehicles, leading to the deaths of 6 Palestinians and 1 Israeli soldier and the wounding of 35 civilians.

IDF forces began withdrawing on November 7, ending the operation the next day. Israel claimed that the operation resulted in the deaths of 53 Palestinians, including 16 civilians, while 1 IDF soldier was also slain. Hamas claimed that 82 Palestinians had been killed, including 50 civilians, with

262 others wounded. The IDF leveled several homes and mosques. One IDF soldier was killed and 3 were wounded during ground clashes. Palestinians stepped up rocket fire into southern Israel during the incursion, wounding 8 Israelis.

SPENCER C. TUCKER

See also
Gaza Strip; Gaza War of 2006; Israel

Reference
"Israeli Military Operations against Gaza, 2000–2008." *Journal of Palestine Studies* 38, no. 3 (Spring 2009): 136.

Ayn Jalut, Battle of (September 3, 1260)

Major military engagement in which a Mongol army commanded by Ketbugha Noyon engaged a Mamluk army from Egypt near Ayn Jalut (Ayn Jalut, the Spring of Goliath), a village situated between the towns of Bethsan and Nablus (in the modern West Bank) on September 3, 1260.

Mongol armies under Chinggis (Genghis) Khan, his sons, and his senior commanders had invaded the northeastern regions of the Islamic world beginning in 1220. During the next 40 years they swept all before them, overthrowing or reducing to submission virtually every Muslim ruling dynasty in Central Asia, Persia, Afghanistan, and Anatolia, culminating in Hulegu's conquest and virtual destruction of Baghdad in 1258.

In January 1260 a Mongol army seized Aleppo in northern Syria and on March 1 entered Damascus, the governing center of Mamluk Syria. In response, a substantial Mamluk army set out from Egypt to halt the Mongol advance. Sultan Qutuz had command, while its vanguard was led by Baybars al-Bunduqdari, who would himself become sultan later that year.

Most sources agree that the Mongol army was outnumbered by that of the Mamluks, although the widely accepted figures of 120,000 Mamluks fighting a mere 10,000 Mongols is no doubt a great exaggeration. The Mongols were also supported by numerous Christian allies and auxiliaries. The Mamluks were a disciplined foe, and they understood that they were the last Islamic power capable of halting the Mongol advance. Ketbugha Noyon attacked and drove back the Mamluk left wing, perhaps relying on the Mongols' reputation for invincibility. Most of the Mamluk army then swept around to attack the advancing Mongols in the flank or rear, perhaps having lured them into a preplanned trap. The Mongols were crushed, and their commander, Ketbugha Noyon, was captured and executed.

Hulegu, the Mongol khan of Persia and other conquered Islamic territories in the Middle East, was infuriated by this unprecedented reverse and prepared a major punitive expedition. However, political problems at the heart of the Mongol Empire following the death of the Great Khan Mongke almost exactly a year earlier prevented this plan's execution.

DAVID NICOLLE

See also
Baybars I; Homs, First Battle of; Homs, Second Battle of; Homs, Third Battle of; Hulegu; Mamluk Sultanate; Mongol Invasion of the Middle East

References
Amitai-Preiss, Reuven. *Mongols and Mamluks: The Mamluk-Ilkhanid War, 1260–1281* Cambridge: Cambridge University Press, 1995.
Jackson, Peter. "The Crisis in the Holy Land in 1260." *English Historical Review* 175 (1980): 481–513.
Smith, J. Masson. "'Ayn Jalut: Mamluk Success or Mongol Failure?" *Harvard Journal of Asiatic Studies* 44 (1984): 307–347.
Thorau, Peter. "The Battle of 'Ayn Jalut: A Re-examination." In *Crusade and Settlement,* ed. Peter W. Edbury, 236–241. Cardiff: University College of Cardiff Press, 1985.

Ayyubid Dynasty

Muslim dynasty of Kurdish origin. Its name derives from Ayyub, the father of the great Kurdish Muslim leader Saladin (1138–1193), although it was the successes of Saladin himself that established the dynasty. After Saladin's death in 1193, the Ayyubids ruled Egypt until 1250 and Syria for another decade. They also had cadet branches in Mesopotamia and Yemen. As with the Buyids and Seljuks of Persia before them, they governed as a loose-knit and often discordant confederacy.

Ayyub and his brother Shirkuh both hailed from Dvin in Armenia; they fought for the Turkish warlords Zangi and his son Nur al-Din, Saladin's two great predecessors in warfare against the Franks. Saladin accompanied Shirkuh on three expeditions to Egypt in the 1160s. After Shirkuh's death in 1169, Saladin assumed power in Egypt in the name of Nur al-Din and overthrew the Shiite Fatimid regime there. Although a rift developed between the two men, it never grew to the extent of open warfare because of the death of Nur al-Din in 1174. That same year Saladin dispatched his brother Turan Shah to conquer Yemen.

During much of Saladin's first decade as an independent ruler (ca. 1174–1184), he was occupied with subjugating his Muslim opponents and creating a secure power base in Egypt and Syria for himself and his family. Then from 1185 onward he turned his full attention to the Franks. In 1187 he achieved his great victory against the army of the Kingdom of Jerusalem in the Battle of Hattin and reconquered the city of Jerusalem for Islam. The Third Crusade (1189–1192), launched in response to this loss, ended in truce and stalemate.

Saladin died in 1193. Despite his prestigious successes, he had failed to rid the Levant of the Franks, who regrouped at their new capital of Acre and still controlled crucial Mediterranean ports. Saladin's brother, the austere Sayf al-Din al-Adil (known to the Franks as Saphadin), had acted as his principal, indeed indispensable, helper in governing his empire, both administratively and militarily. His involvement in drawing up the peace treaty with King Richard I of England (Richard the Lionheart) in 1192 was especially valuable.

Saladin did not envisage a centralized state as his legacy. Instead, he bequeathed the three main provinces of his empire (Cairo, Damascus, and Aleppo) to his sons, hoping that this arrangement would ensure lasting Ayyubid power. But his desired father-son succession did not take root, nor did primogeniture prevail among Saladin's successors. Within the clan, might was right.

After Saladin's death, al-Adil's role as senior family member asserted itself; indeed, Saladin's sons were no match for al-Adil's long experience and diplomatic skills. By 1200, he had reorganized Saladin's inheritance plans in favor of his own sons, deposed Saladin's son al-Aziz Uthman in Cairo, and secured the overall position of sultan for himself. Only in Aleppo did Saladin's direct descendants continue to rule: Saladin's son al-Ðahir, after submitting to al-Adil, was allowed to keep his territory, which remained in his family until the Mongol invasion of 1260.

In the complicated power struggle after Saladin's death, a key role was played by the regiments of mamluks (slave-soldiers) recruited by Saladin (the *alaiyya*) and his uncle Shirkuh (the *asadiyya*). Al-Adil was greatly assisted by the *alaiyya*. Saladin's expansionist aims continued under al-Adil, who masterminded the Ayyubid acquisition of more Zangid and Artuqid territories. He secured his northeastern frontier in 1209–1210, established truces with the Franks that lasted for most of his reign, and traded with the Italian maritime states.

In 1218 shortly after the beginning of the Fifth Crusade (1217–1221), al-Adil died, allegedly of shock. He was succeeded by his son al-Kamil, whose brothers, al-Mu'aam and al-Ashraf, supported him in this crisis, but after Damietta was recovered, this short-lived family solidarity gave way to

Entrance ramp to the inner gate of the citadel of Aleppo, Syria. While a fortress had been on the site from the 10th century, the present citadel was built by Ayyubid-dynasty ruler al-Zahir (1186–1216), the son of Saladin. (Corel)

disunity and conflict. The main contenders in the long and convoluted power struggle that followed were al-Kamil and his brother al-Mu'aam at Damascus. By 1229 al-Kamil, with the help of al-Ashraf in Mesopotamia, emerged as principal ruler of the Ayyubids.

Already in 1226 al-Kamil, an astute politician, had begun negotiations with Holy Roman emperor Frederick II to bolster himself against al-Mu'aam and to deflect the imminent crusade. However, by the time Frederick arrived in Acre in 1228, al-Mu'aam had already died. Secret negotiations between al-Kamil and Frederick resulted in the Treaty of Jaffa (1229). In it al-Kamil ceded Jerusalem to Frederick, who was permitted to fortify the city, but al-Kamil kept a Muslim enclave, including the Aqsa Mosque and the Dome of the Rock. This piece of realpolitik caused widespread disapproval on both sides, and even al-Kamil's own preachers protested outside his tent.

The Muslim chronicler Sib Ibn al-Jawzi recorded that when al-Kamil gave Jerusalem to Frederick, "all hell broke loose in the lands of Islam." However, some modern scholars have interpreted the Treaty of Jaffa more positively, viewing al-Adil and Frederick as being farsighted in their attempts to obtain a more lasting peace and to maintain the holy sites of both Islam and Christianity under the protection of their own adherents.

Al-Kamil's death in 1238 ushered in another turbulent period. His dispossessed eldest son, al-Ali Ayyub, who had been sent to rule Upper Mesopotamia, disputed the succession in Egypt. He deposed his brother al-Adil II and took power in Cairo in 1240. While he was in Hisn Kayfa, al-Ali Ayyub had allied himself with a group of Qipchaq Turks: they were known as the Khwarazmians because they had fought in Central Asia for the ill-fated ruler of Khwarazm, Jalal ad-Din, against the Mongols in 1220s. After Jalal ad-Din's death (1231), the Khwarazmians joined the service of al-Ali Ayyub as mercenaries.

In 1244 under their infamous leader Berke Khan, the Khwarazmians sacked Jerusalem to general condemnation. They then joined Ayyub's army near Gaza and fought that same year against three Ayyubid princes as well as Frankish forces. The Battle of La Forbie (Harbiyya) resulted in a clear victory for al-Ali Ayyub and his Khwarazmian allies. Ayyub took Jerusalem (August 1244) and then Damascus (1245). The Ayyubid prince of Homs, however, destroyed the Khwarazmians in 1246.

Al-Ali Ayyub fell ill at the time of the crusade to the East of French king Louis IX (the Seventh Crusade of 1248–1254). The crusaders occupied the city of Damietta in 1249; later that year al-Ali Ayyub died while encamped at Mansurah in the Nile Delta. In 1250 the sultan's own slave troops (the Bariyya Mamluks) defeated the crusaders. Then in a coup d'état the Bariyya Mamluks murdered Turan Shah, son and heir of al-Ali Ayyub, and terminated Ayyubid rule, raising one of their own number to the rank of sultan and thereby inaugurating the Mamluk Sultanate.

CAROLE HILLENBRAND

See also

Al-Adil; Crusades in the Holy Land, Christian; Frederick II, Holy Roman Emperor; Hattin, Battle of; Louis IX, King of France; Mamluk Sultanate; Mongol Invasion of the Middle East; Nur al-Din; Richard I, King; Saladin

References

Eddé, Anne-Marie. *La principauté ayyoubide d'Alep (579/1183–658/1260)*. Stuttgart: Steiner, 1999.

Hillenbrand, Carole. *The Crusades: Islamic Perspectives*. Edinburgh, UK: Edinburgh University Press, 1999.

Holt, Peter M. *The Age of the Crusades*. London: Longman, 1986.

Humphreys, R. Stephen. "Ayyubids, Mamluks, and the Latin East in the Thirteenth Century." *Mamluk Studies Review* 2 (1998): 11–18.

Humphreys, R. Stephen. *From Saladin to the Mongols: The Ayyubids of Damascus*. Albany: State University of New York Press, 1977.

Lyons, Malcolm C., and David E. P. Jackson. *Saladin: The Politics of the Holy War*. Cambridge: Cambridge University Press, 1982.

Sib Ibn al-Jawzi. *Mir'at al-Zaman fi Ta'rikh al-A'yan*, Vol. 2. Hyderabad: Dayrat alMa'arif al-Uthmaniiyah, 1952.

Sivan, Emmanuel. *L'Islam et la Croisade: Idéologie et propagande dans les réactions musulmanes aux Croisades*. Paris: Maisonnneuve, 1968.

B

Baath Party

Political party that is currently the governing party of the Syrian Arab Republic and that ruled Iraq briefly in 1963 and then again from 1968 to 2003 and the end of Saddam Hussein's regime. The word *ba'ath* is Arabic for "rebirth," "renewal," or "renaissance," and the aim in founding the party was to promote unity among the Arab states of the Middle East by advocating Arab nationalism and to modernize the region by employing socialist economic principles. The Baath Arab Syrian Party (BASP) explains its ideology as "national (pan-Arab), socialist, popular and revolutionary," and its founding charter and constitution identifies its commitment to the "Arab Nation, the Arab homeland, the Arab citizen, the Arab people's authority over their own land and the freedom of the Arab people."

The Baath Party grew out of an ideological and political movement in Syria, promoted in the 1930s, to end French occupation of that country and, more generally, to end European colonialism and imperialism in the Middle East. French-educated Syrian intellectuals, including Michel Aflaq, a Greek Orthodox Christian, and Salah al-Din al-Bitar, a Sunni Muslim, were the principal founders of the Baath movement and party. The Baath Party has always been secular in nature, putting it in conflict with Islamic fundamentalism.

The Baath Party was formed at the first Baath Party Congress during April 4–6, 1947. The Iraqi Baath Party was founded in 1949 but, like its Syrian counterpart, remained an underground movement throughout the 1950s because it advocated the overthrow of the Iraqi monarchy. The Baath Party came to power in both Syria and Iraq in coup d'états in 1963. The coup in Iraq did not last out the year, however. Three years later, the Syrian and Iraqi parties split because of a series of ideological disputes including ties with the Soviet Union.

The Syrian Baath Party openly aligned itself with the Soviets, while Iraqi Baathists were more cautious regarding such close ties. Rivalries between different factions of the Syrian Baath Party led to an interparty coup in 1966 followed by another one four years later that brought General Hafez al-Assad to power. He remained in office until his death in 2000. His son, Bashar Assad, assumed leadership of the Syrian Baath Party and remains the president of Syria.

The rivalry between the respective leaders of Syria and Iraq, Assad and Hussein, became pronounced as each sought to be the preeminent leader of the Arab world. This rivalry became most evident when Syria supported Iraq's archenemy, Iran, a non-Arab country, during Iraq's eight-year war with its Persian neighbor.

Hussein joined the Iraqi Baath Party at age 21 in 1956 and steadily rose in the party's ranks, first as an assassin and then as vice president once the Baath Party had regained power in a 1968 coup. As vice president of Iraq, Hussein became responsible for protecting the party from internal and external threats as head of the party's secret police apparatus. In 1979, he assumed the presidency and ruled the country until March 2003. Hussein became infamous for his ruthless and authoritarian rule, which included waging wars against Iran (1980–1988) and Kuwait (1990–1991) and employing chemical weapons that killed thousands of Iraqi Kurds in 1988. As with Hussein, the two Assads of Syria presided over a brutal dictatorship.

The stated Baathist goal of Arab unity proved hollow. In both Iraq and Syria, Baathists supported repressive dictatorships focused on the preservation of power by virtually any means. Despite the dictatorial nature of both regimes, one notable accomplishment, particularly in Iraq, was the serious effort to modernize the economy and society by promoting literacy, education, and gender equality. As a result, in the 1970s Iraq possessed a highly educated population, including a large thriving middle class. Iraq could also point to a relatively high standard of living. Hussein's disastrous war with Iran and then the Persian Gulf War of 1991, which in turn led to an ongoing conflict with the United States and an American-led invasion of Iraq, largely destroyed these accomplishments and turned Iraq into an impoverished, unstable state.

The American-led invasion of Iraq in March 2003 and the overthrow of Saddam Hussein led to a ban of the Baath Party, the so-called de-Baathification of the country, under U.S. occupation forces. The postwar government of Iraq, dominated by Shiites who had been persecuted by Hussein's Sunni-dominated Baath Party, partially lifted the ban on the Baath Party in January 2008, which allowed former low-level Baath members to seek government jobs. Many critics of the U.S. occupation policy in Iraq claim that U.S. administrator Paul Bremer's decision, approved by Washington, to ban all Baathists from government posts hopelessly hamstrung the government and fueled the Iraqi insurgency, which was peopled by many bitter and disenfranchised Baathists.

In Syria, the result of Baathist rule was a brutal dictatorship and civil war beginning in 2011 that has seen massive destruction and casualties and the flight abroad of more than a quarter of the Syrian population.

STEFAN BROOKS

See also
Arab Nationalism; Assad, Bashar al-; Assad, Hafez al-; Hussein, Saddam; Iraq; Pan-Arabism and Pan-Arabist Thought; Syria

References
Hinnerbursch, Ray. *Syria: Revolution from Above*. New York: Routledge, 2001.
Hydermann, Steven. *Authoritarianism in Syria: Institutions and Social Conflict, 1948–1970*. Ithaca, NY: Cornell University Press, 1999.
MacKey, Sandra. *The Reckoning: Iraq and the Legacy of Saddam Hussein*. New York: Norton, 2003.
Tripp, Charles. *A History of Iraq*. New York: Cambridge University Press, 2002.

Babylon, Siege of (539–538 BCE)

Having absorbed Lydia, it was natural that King Cyrus II (the Great) of Persia would eventually move against Lydia's ally, Babylon. King Nabonidus's authority in Babylon was weak because he had secured the throne as a successful general rather than by right of inheritance, and he had further alienated his people by advancing the worship of Sin, the moon goddess, over Marduk, the national deity. He had also spent years away from his capital campaigning in distant lands including Harran, where he established a temple to Sin. In Arabia he secured a number of oases, and his journey reached as far as Medina.

Cyrus meanwhile seems to have established contact with Babylon's alienated religious leaders, assuring them of his support for their traditional religious practices. Too late, Nabonidus embraced Marduk and ordered all statues of the god to be assembled at Babylon to fortify it spiritually.

There are two very different accounts of how Cyrus secured Babylon. One has him defeating the Babylonians at Opis, the former capital of Akkadia, and then destroying that city. Learning this, the city of Sippar surrendered to Cyrus, whereupon Nabonidus fled Babylon and Cyrus made a peaceful entry into the city in October.

The second account is put forward by the Greek historian Herodotus and supported by the books of Daniel and Jeremiah in the Bible—although Daniel incorrectly identifies Darius as the king of Persia and Belshazzar as the king of Babylon. (The latter was the son of Nabonidus and ruled the city while his father was away on campaign.) This version tells of a great siege during 539–538.

In it, Cyrus arrived and quickly encircled the city with his army under the walls, cutting off Babylon from assistance. Riding on horseback, Cyrus personally inspected the troop dispositions and concluded that the city could not be taken by direct assault. He then ordered his troops to institute a siege.

Cyrus was either advised of or came up with on his own a stratagem to take Babylon. He ordered the construction of a circular system of trenches around the city and ditches to be dug sufficient to accommodate the water of the Euphrates River, which bisected Babylon through a break in the city walls. This work went forward into the winter, supervised by Persian engineers. The Euphrates was separated from the ditches by only a simple dam that could be easily opened. The Persians also constructed towers made of palm trees, which led the Babylonians to believe that their enemies intended to starve them out. The authorities in the city were not worried, though, as they had gathered sufficient food stocks to last for many years.

Early in 538 Cyrus was ready to unleash his attack, which he timed to coincide with the beginning of an important Babylonian festival. That evening, with the Babylonian rituals under way and the inhabitants distracted, Cyrus ordered the dam broken and the Euphrates diverted. Normally the river was so deep that the breaks in the walls where it flowed through Babylon did not represent a serious threat from outside enemies. When the river was diverted, however, the flow was so low that it was possible for Persian infantry and even cavalry to traverse the newly formed river banks into Babylon itself.

The Persian attack caught the Babylonians by surprise, and the city was soon taken. Cyrus was known for sparing the lives of kings he had defeated, and this may have been the case with Nabonidus, said to have been sent into exile. Reportedly Belshazzar and his principal followers were slain. Cyrus ordered that Babylon be destroyed. As the prophet Jeremiah notes in the Bible (51:29 and 51:37), "And the land shall tremble and sorrow: for every purpose of the Lord shall be performed against Babylon to make the land of Babylon a desolation without an inhabitant.... And Babylon shall become heaps, a dwelling place for dragons, an astonishment, and an hissing, without an inhabitant."

Following the reduction of Babylon, Cyrus took Jerusalem. He allowed those Jews of Babylon who wished to do so to return home to Jerusalem, ending the Babylonian Captivity of the Jews.

Spencer C. Tucker

See also
Babylonian Empire, Neo-; Cyrus II the Great; Diaspora

References
Cook, J. M. *The Persian Empire.* New York: Schocken Books, 1983.
Herodotus. *The History of Herodotus.* Ed. Manuel Komroff. Trans. George Rawlinson. New York: Tudor Publishing, 1956.
Lamb, Harold. *Cyrus the Great.* Garden City, NY: Doubleday, 1960.
Melegari, Vezio. *The Great Military Sieges.* New York: Thomas Y. Crowell, 1972.
Xenophon. *Cyropaedia.* Trans. Walter Miller. Cambridge, MA: Harvard University Press, 1979.

Babylonian Empire, Neo- (626–539 BCE)

The Old Babylon Empire had fallen under the control of the Neo-Assyrian Empire, but in the seventh century BCE Assyria itself underwent a series of costly internal civil wars that used up its manpower and contributed heavily to its demise. In approximately 627 BCE Sin-shar-ishkun (Sinsharishkun) seized the Assyrian throne amid continuing civil strife. He ruled until 612. In these circumstances, Nabopolassar, a previously unknown Chaldean chieftain, led a revolt in 620 in Babylon that would establish the Neo-Babylonian Empire (Chaldean Empire). It lasted from 626 to 539 BCE.

Nabopolassar received widespread Babylonian support in the revolt against Assyrian control. Only the city of Nippur and some northern regions of Babylonia were loyal to the Assyrian king. Nonetheless, in the course of the next four years Nabopolassar had to contend with Assyrian forces in Babylon endeavoring to drive him from power. Ongoing civil strife in Assyria, however, prevented Sinsharishkun from concentrating what were diminishing military resources against Nabopolassar.

In 615 BCE Nabopolassar concluded an alliance between the Babylonians and Chaldeans with Cyaxares, a vassal of Assyria but also king of the Iranian peoples of the Medes, Persians, Sagartians, and Parthians. Cyaxares had taken advantage of the Assyrian destruction of Elam and Mannea to free the peoples of what is present-day Iran from three centuries of Elamite domination. Now the chaos in Assyria and the alliance with the Chaldeans and Babylonians promised a means to end Assyrian control. The Scythians and Cimmerians from north of the Crimea and the Black Sea area also joined the alliance, as did regional Aramean tribes.

In 615 BCE while Sinsharishkun's army was fighting the rebels in Assyria and in Babylonia, Cyaxares launched a surprise attack on Assyria itself, taking and sacking the cities of Kalhu and Arrapha (modern-day Kirkuk). Its opponents' strength was simply too great for Assyria to overcome. Major Assyrian cities such as Ashur, Arbela (modern-day Irbil), Guzana, Dur Sharrukin (modern-day Khorsabad), Imgur-Enlil, Nibarti-Ashur, Gasur, Kanesh, Kar Ashurnasipal, and Tushhan all fell during 614. In 613, however, Sinsharishkun managed to overcome the odds against him and drive back his adversaries.

In 612 a renewed combined coalition offensive carried the day, and late that year after a prolonged siege, Nineveh was captured and sacked. Sinsharishkun died in the fighting for the Assyrian capital and was succeeded by Assyrian general Ashuruballit II (r. 612–605 BCE). Apparently offered the

Restored ruins of the palace of Nebuchadnezzar II in ancient Babylon, located just south of present-day Baghdad, Iraq. (Jukka Palm/Dreamstime.com)

possibility of a position of vassalage, he refused and managed to escape Nineveh and reach the northern Assyrian city of Harran in Upper Mesopotamia, where he established his capital. In 607 the coalition forces took Harran.

Meanwhile, Egyptian pharaoh Necho II, whose dynasty had been installed as vassals of Assyria in 671, belatedly attempted to aid the Assyrians. With Egyptian assistance, the Assyrians fought on until the coalition achieved final victory at Carchemish in northwestern Assyria in 605. Ashur-uballit II's fate is unknown.

Nabopolassar died in 605 and was followed by his son Nebuchadnezzar II (r. 605–562 BCE), during whose reign Babylonia again ruled Mesopotamia, taking part of the former Assyrian Empire, while the former Assyrian eastern and northeastern territories were secured by the Medes and the far north went to the Scythians. Babylonia's former allies of the Scythians and Cimmerians were now a threat, and Nebuchadnezzar II was forced to march into Anatolia and rout their forces. Nebuchadnezzar II also campaigned against the Egyptians who had advanced eastward, driving them back across the Sinai.

Nebuchadnezzar's subsequent effort to conquer Egypt itself failed, largely because of rebellions by the Israelites of Judah, the former kingdom of Ephraim, the Phoenicians of Caanan, and the Arameans in the Levant. Nebuchadnezzar crushed all of these. Following a long siege of Jerusalem, in 587 he razed much of the city, destroying the Temple of Solomon and removing a large number of the population to Babylon in what became known as the Babylonian Captivity of the Jews. The Babylonian king also took such cities as Tyre, Sidon, and Damascus, and he subjugated much of the Arab population to the south.

In 567 Nebuchadnezzar II again waged war against Egypt, this time invading Egypt proper. Having secured his realm, he married a Median princess and worked to maintain his empire while embarking on major building projects, including the Tower of Babel and the storied Hanging Gardens of Babylon.

Nebuchadnezzar's son Amel-Marduk succeeded him. Born in 581, he became king on his father's death in 562. His reign was brief, as he was deposed and murdered in 560 by Neriglissar, the son-in-law of Nebuchadnezzar II. Neriglissar's reign was also brief: 560–556. Neriglissar campaigned with success in Aram and Phoenicia, securing both. Neriglissar died young, apparently of natural causes, and was succeeded by his son Labashi-Marduk in 556. Still a boy, he was deposed and killed that same year in a palace conspiracy.

The last Babylonian king was Nabonidus (Nabu-na'id, 556–539), ironically the son of an Assyrian priestess, his father unknown. The population of Babylonia was at this point increasingly disenchanted with its rulers. Certainly some of this was owing to his Assyrian parentage, but Nabonidus also alienated much of the priesthood of the kingdom by removing the statues of gods from local temples and taking them to Babylon in an attempt to centralize the state's polytheistic religion in the temple of Marduk there. Also, Nabonidus was little interested in military affairs, leaving this to his son, Belshazzar (Belsharutsur), who while an able soldier, succeeded in alienating much of the political elite.

Despite what had happened so recently to several of his predecessors, Nabonidus seemed oblivious to any threat as he busied himself with archaeological research and the construction of new temples in the former Assyrian city of Harran and among his Arab lands.

In 546 Cyrus of the Persian dependency of Media became king of all Persia. He soon embarked on a campaign to put down a revolt in his Assyrian territories. Then in 539, Cyrus invaded Babylonia. Battle was joined in June at Opis, and the Persians were victorious. The Babylonian city of Sippar on the east bank of the Euphrates promptly surrendered, and Nabonidus fled to Babylon. The Persians then proceeded again Babylon. Accounts differ as to how the city was taken. Some have it falling two days after the capture of Sippar, the Persians having arrived at Babylon so swiftly that they caught the defenders by surprise, and their troops were able to enter the city without fighting, although Greek historian Herodotus claims that it fell only after a prolonged siege during 539–538. In any case, Nabonidus was dragged from a hiding place and taken prisoner. His fate is uncertain, although Cyrus is known to have spared the lives of kings taken prisoner, and this is believed to have been the case with Nabonidus. Belshazzar died in battle, however.

Cyrus arrived in Babylon after the city had fallen, with the Persian soldiers having been restrained from sacking the city. The Persian king claimed to be the legitimate successor of the ancient Babylonian kings and the avenger of Bel-Marduk, who was assumed to be wrathful at the impiety of Nabonidus in removing the images of local gods from their ancestral shrines to Babylon. Thus, one of Cyrus's first acts was to allow the Jewish exiles to return to their own homeland, carrying with them their sacred temple vessels.

The Neo-Babylonian or Chaldean Empire had come to an end, and Babylonia was now part of the Achaemenid Empire (First Persian Empire). A year before he died in 529, Cyrus elevated his son Cambyses II, who had accompanied his father in the invasion of Babylonia, as king of Babylon. Cyrus reserved for himself the fuller title "king of the (other) provinces" of the empire. It was only when Darius I came to the Persian throne and ruled it as a representative of the Zoroastrian religion that the old tradition was broken, and the claim of Babylon as a holy city that conferred legitimacy on the rulers of Western Asia came to an end.

SPENCER C. TUCKER

See also

Achaemenid Empire; Assyrian Empire; Babylonian Empire, Old; Cambyses II; Cyrus II the Great; Nebuchadnezzar II

References

Bower, Susan Wise. *The History of the Ancient World from the Earliest Accounts to the Fall of Rome.* New York: Norton, 2007.

Bryce, Trevor. *The Routledge Handbook of the Peoples and Places of Ancient Western Asia: The Near East from the Early Bronze Age to the Fall of the Persian Empire.* London: Routledge, 2009.

Healy, Mark. *The Ancient Assyrians.* London: Osprey, 2003.

Kriwaczek, Paul. *Babylon: Mesopotamia and the Birth of Civilization.* New York: St. Martin's Griffin, 2012.

Oates, Joan. *Babylon.* London: Thames and Hudson, 1979.

Oppenheim, A. Leo. *Ancient Mesopotamia: Portrait of a Dead Civilization.* Chicago: University of Chicago Press, 2013.

Pollock, Susan. *Ancient Mesopotamia: The Land That Never Was.* Cambridge: Cambridge University Press, 2008.

Saggs, H. W. F. *The Greatness That Was Babylon: A Survey of the Ancient Civilization of the Tigris-Euphrates Valley.* London: Sidgwick & Jackson, 1988.

Van de Mieroop, Marc. *A History of the Ancient Near East, ca. 3000–323 BC.* Hoboken, NJ: Wiley-Blackwell, 2015.

Babylonian Empire, Old (ca. 1894–911 BCE)

Babylonia was an ancient Akkadian-speaking state and cultural area situated in central and southern Mesopotamia in the land between the Tigris and Euphrates Rivers (in what is now present-day Iraq), the overflow of which provided the basis for rich agricultural production. Babylon furnished much to the world in the areas of language, medicine, astronomy, mathematics, philosophy, physics, and architecture. It also provided the Jews with much of their mythology. The city of Babylon itself is certainly the most famous urban center of ancient Mesopotamia.

Babylonia was the successor of the earlier kingdoms of Sumer and Akkad. Sumer was the first urban civilization in

Mesopotamia, flourishing around 3500–2000 BCE, while Akkad rose to prominence under its great ruler Sargon (r. 2334–2279), who established an empire with the conquest of such neighboring states as Elam and Gutian. Indeed, Akkad is sometimes referred to as the world's first empire. Under its rulers Akkadian largely replaced Sumerian as the spoken language of the region.

After the fall of the Akkadian Empire (the last ruler was Shu-turul during 2170–2154), the people of Mesopotamia eventually coalesced into two major Akkadian-speaking nations: Assyria in the north and, a few centuries later, Babylonia in the south.

With the end of the Akkadian Empire, the southern Mesopotamian region was dominated for a few decades by the Gutians, a people who originated in the Zagros Mountains to the northeast of Mesopotamia. They were followed by a brief period of Sumerian resurgence in the Third Dynasty of Ur. Their king Ur-Nammu (r. ca. 2047–2030) drove out the Gutians. He also built temples, including the ziggurat; regularized agriculture through improved irrigation; and issued a code of laws that preceded that of future Babylonian ruler Hammurabi by 300 years. The Third Dynasty of Ur ended circa 2004, its demise caused by an economic crisis perhaps brought on by climate change that led to an agricultural collapse.

Elam briefly held sway, but a number of seminomadic Semitic-speaking Amorite tribes migrated into southern Mesopotamia from the Levant and gradually established a number of small states. In the north the Assyrians reestablished their independence, and the already established southern states probably called on their fellow Akkadians in Assyria for assistance. An inscription details the intervention in the south of Assyrian king Ilu-shuma (ca. 2008–1975) of the Old Assyrian Empire (2025–1750). Sargon I, king of Assyria during 1920–1881, withdrew Assyrian forces from the south in preference of territorial expansion in Anatolia and the Levant.

During the first centuries of this Amorite period, the most powerful southern city-states were Isin, Eshnunna, and Larsa. However, one of the Amorite dynasties established the small kingdom of Kazallu, which included the then minor urban center of Babylon. Amorite chieftain Sumu-abum secured from the ruler of Kazallu a grant of land that included Babylon. Ruling during 1894–1877, Sumu-abum is considered the first king of Babylon and founder of its First Dynasty, although neither he nor his two immediate successors made any claim to be a king, suggesting that Babylon was then of little importance.

Sin-Muballit (r. ca. 1748–1729) was the first of the Amorite rulers to take the title of king. Still, the neighboring kingdoms of Isin and Larsa as well as Assyria to the north and Elam to the east in ancient Iran were far more important. Elam in particular occupied much of southern Mesopotamia. Babylon remained a small insignificant kingdom until its sixth ruler, Hammurabi (r. 1792–1750).

The first few decades of Hammurabi's reign were peaceful, enabling him to concentrate on major public works projects that greatly expanded Babylon into a major urban center. Assuring himself of priestly support through the construction of temples, Hammurabi raised the god Marduk as the dominant deity in Babylon, just as Ashur was supreme in Assyria. Babylon soon became known as a holy city. Hammurabi also greatly improved Babylon's defenses by heightening its walls. A gifted administrator, he centralized government, established an effective tax system, and published his now-famous code of laws. Under his rule, Babylon grew in size and population.

Hammurabi proved to be a great military leader. He defeated Isin, Larsa, Eshnunna, Kish, Lagash, Nippur, Borsippa, Ur, Uruk, Umma, Adab, Sippar, Rapiqum, and Eridu, forming all of southern and central Mesopotamia into one state and establishing the Babylonian Empire. Turning eastward, Hammurabi invaded what would become present-day Iran, conquering Elam as well as territory held by the Gutians, Lullubi, and Kassites. He also conquered the Amorite states of the Levant with the kingdoms of Mari and Yamhad.

The Assyrian Empire controlled much of southeastern Anatolia as well as the northeast Levant and part of central Mesopotamia. It was thus not unexpected that the Assyrians and Babylonians would enter into a protracted struggle for control of all of Mesopotamia and the Near East. After decades of war, Hammurabi forced Assyrian king Mut-Ashkur (r. 1730–1720) to pay tribute to Babylon circa 1751 BCE, thus giving Babylonia control over Assyria's Hattian and Hurrian colonies in Anatolia.

Southern Mesopotamia had no natural defensible borders, which rendered it vulnerable to attack. After the death of Hammurabi, his empire began to disintegrate. Under his successor Samsu-iluna (r. 1749–1712) the far south of Mesopotamia was lost to Akkadian-speaking king Ilum-ma-ili, and the south passed under control of the native Sealand dynasty. Babylonian rule in former Assyrian territory to the north was ended by Assyrian-Akkadian governor Puzur-Sin around 1740. After six years of civil war in Assyria, a native king named Adasi seized power circa 1735. He then took former Babylonian and Amorite territory in central Mesopotamia.

Amorite rule survived in a much-reduced Babylon. Samshu-iluna's successor Abi-Eshuh (r. 1648–1620) tried but failed to recapture the Sealand dynasty for Babylon. By the end of his reign, Babylonia had become a small and largely weak city-state. Abi-Eshuh's successors accomplished little. Samsu-Ditana (r. 1625–1595) was the last Amorite ruler of Babylon.

Early in Samsu-Ditana's reign, Babylon came under pressure from the Kassites, a people originating in the mountains of what is today northwestern Iran. But in 1595 Babylon was attacked and sacked by King Mursili I of the Anatolia-based Hittites, and Samsu-Ditana was overthrown. The Hittites did not remain in Babylon for long, but the destruction they had wrought there enabled the Kassites to take control.

Although some sources end the Old Babylonian Empire with 1595 BCE, it endured under Kassite rule. The period of their rule is also known as the Second, or Middle, Babylonian dynasty.

The Kassites renamed Babylon Karduniaš. They returned the statue of the god Marduk that had earlier been plundered by the Hittites from Babylon, solidifying Babylon's continued position as the religious capital of Mesopotamia. The Kassites did not rule from Babylon, however. Kassite king Kurigalzu I (r. 1415–1390 BCE) built a new capital city, Dur-Kurigalzu, named for himself, and transferred administrative rule there from Babylon. The new capital was near the confluence of the Tigris and Diyala Rivers, some 19 miles west of modern-day Baghdad. After a series of wars, around 1460 the Kassite rulers were able to secure control of the south from the Sealand dynasty. The Kassite state was thus about the size of the Babylonia of Hammurabi's day.

More intent on defending their existing territory than expanding it, the Kassites established diplomatic relations with Egypt. Trade between the two states flourished, and eventually the Babylonian and Egyptian dynasties even intermarried.

Assyria again became a threat when it conquered western Syria. Eventually, the Assyrians also intermarried with the Kassite rulers in Babylon. However, the latter were unwilling to accept rule by an Assyrian king, although the Assyrians did place a Kassite of their choosing on the Babylonian throne.

The Assyrian threat was a major reason why around 1297 the Kassites aligned with the Hittites. Assyrian king Tukulit-Ninurta I (r. 1244–1197) was determined to secure control over the lucrative trade routes. After taking the 28th Kassite king of Babylon Kashtiliash IV to Ashur as a captive in 1225, Tukulit-Ninurta I ruled Babylon himself during the next 32 years. Following his death, however, the Babylonians under King Adad-shuma-usur (r. 1216–1187) were able to drive the Assyrians from Babylon.

Elam was also a threat and frequently raided Babylon in an effort to weaken Assyria. Around 1157 the Elamites, led by Shutruk-Nahhunte I, took Babylon, carrying off the monument with Hammurabi's legal code and also the statue of Marduk. In 1155 the Elamites killed the last Kassite ruler of Babylon, Enlil-nadin-ahhe.

Nebuchadnezzar I, fourth king of the Second Dynasty of the Mesopotamian city of Isin and the Fourth Dynasty of Babylon, ruled Babylon during 1125–1104. He defeated Elam, capturing its capital and bringing back to Babylon the statue of Marduk. His younger brother, Marduk-nadi-ahhe, challenged Assyrian power by attacking the city of Ekallate. The Assyrians' response was brutal, and their ensuing destruction of much of Babylonia resulted in widespread famine.

During the next two centuries Babylon underwent considerable internal political instability. At the same time, nomadic Aramaean tribes became a serious threat to Babylon and Assyria. They may have attacked the cities of Mesopotamia, and there was at least one Aramaean king of Babylon, Adad-apla-iddina (r. 1069–1048). The only lasting legacy, however, was that Aramaic became the language of Babylonia until the Muslim conquest.

During 1025–1006, the Second Sealand dynasty became the dominant power in southern Mesopotamia. Simbar-Sipak ruled circa 1025–1008 before power shifted during 1005–986 to the House of Bazi from the Tigris region. Dynasty E of some five Babylonian kings ruled Babylon during the ninth century.

Although Assyria was the dominant regional power, its rulers were bent on external conquest, and thus Assyria maintained an uneasy peace with Babylon. The ruling dynasties of Babylon and Assyria actually intermarried, and there was a lengthy period of relative peace.

The reign of Assyrian king Assurnasirpal II (883–859) marked the beginning of the Neo-Assyrian Empire. He did not interfere in Babylon, then ruled by Nabu-apla-iddina who entered into a treaty with Assurnasirpal's son and successor, Shalmaneser III. Shalmaneser III's son, Shamshi-Adad, called on Babylon to honor the treaty in helping him put down an internal rebellion, after which the Babylonians insisted on a renegotiation of the treaty. Angered by its terms, Shamshi-Adad invaded and conquered Babylon and carried off its ruler. He then called himself "King of Sumer and Akkad."

Having created a vast empire, the Assyrians found themselves constantly quelling revolts and reconquering what they had already taken. The cost of this was high, and eventually Assyrian military strength was completely depleted. In an attempt to end chronic unrest in Babylon, Assyrian king Adad-nirari III (r. 811–783) agreed to honor Babylonian religious ceremonies and traditions as long as Assyria controlled its political affairs. The Babylonians considered the Assyrians to be their oppressors, however, and this provided the southern-based Chaldeans an opportunity to take the Babylonian throne.

Assyria soon descended into a series of costly internal civil wars that were to cause its downfall. Ashur-etil-ilani was deposed by one of his generals, Sin-shumu-lishir, in 623, who also set himself up as king of Babylon. After only one year on the throne amid continual civil war, he was ousted in 622 by Sinsharishkun, who ruled until 612. Sinsharishkun, however, faced constant civil war in Assyria. In these circumstances, in the year 620 Nabopolassar, a previously unknown Chaldean chieftain, led a revolt in Babylon that brought the establishment of the Neo-Babylonian Empire or Chaldean Empire (626–539 BCE).

Spencer C. Tucker

See also
Assyrian Empire; Babylonian Empire, Neo-; Hammurabi; Kassites

References
Bower, Susan Wise. *The History of the Ancient World from the Earliest Accounts to the Fall of Rome.* New York: Norton, 2007.
Bryce, Trevor. *The Routledge Handbook of the Peoples and Places of Ancient Western Asia: The Near East from the Early Bronze Age to the Fall of the Persian Empire.* London: Routledge, 2009.
Charpin, Dominique. *Hammurabi of Babylon.* London: Tauris, 2012.
Healy, Mark. *The Ancient Assyrians.* London: Osprey, 2003.
Kriwaczek, Paul. *Babylon: Mesopotamia and the Birth of Civilization.* New York: St. Martin's Griffin, 2012.
Oates, Joan. *Babylon.* London: Thames and Hudson, 1979.
Oppenheim, A. Leo. *Ancient Mesopotamia: Portrait of a Dead Civilization.* Chicago: University of Chicago Press, 2013.
Pollock, Susan. *Ancient Mesopotamia: The Land That Never Was.* Cambridge: Cambridge University Press, 2008.
Saggs, H. W. F. *The Greatness That Was Babylon: A Survey of the Ancient Civilization of the Tigris-Euphrates Valley.* London: Sidgwick & Jackson, 1988.
Van de Mieroop, Marc. *A History of the Ancient Near East, ca. 3000–323 BC.* Hoboken, NJ: Wiley-Blackwell, 2015.

Badr, Battle of (March 15, 624)

The Battle of Badr on March 15, 624, was small in terms of numbers of men engaged but had immense repercussions. It confirmed Muhammad as the leader of Islam and allowed the religion's expansion.

Inspired by what he believed to have been a series of divine revelations beginning in 610, Muhammad, a merchant in Mecca, began espousing a new monotheist and egalitarian religion known as Islam. In 622 he organized the tribes of Yathrib (now Medina) into a community under the will of God (Allah) as revealed in his teachings. Muhammad was both prophet and military commander, and he now sought to expand the faith by force of arms. His first actions were against Mecca.

Muhammad's first military actions were raids on Meccan caravans. In early 624 Muhammad ordered a dozen men to attack a small caravan from Yemen to Mecca. Acting as pilgrims bound for Mecca, his followers located the caravan and joined it. They faced one glaring problem: it was a holy month in Arabia during which warfare was forbidden. If they obeyed that stricture, then they would reach the holy city of Mecca, where fighting was forbidden. The raiders decided to violate the first rule and fell on the guards, killing one and capturing two others.

Muhammad was widely condemned for the raid. His response was that the merchants of Mecca were committing greater sins than any violation by his men of the holy month. The leaders of Mecca, however, were now determined to destroy Muhammad. They used as bait a rich caravan from Sinai to Mecca, tricking Muhammad into a battle in which he would be badly outnumbered.

Muhammad fell into the trap. In early March he led some 300 men from Medina to intercept the caravan. Most of his men were on foot. Reportedly they had only 70 camels and 2 horses. The Meccans meanwhile sent out almost 1,300 men. Led by Abu Jahl, they were far better armed and equipped and had some 700 camels and 100 horses. Half the men were supposedly wearing chain mail.

The caravan leader, Abu Sufyan, discovered the location of Muhammad's ambush force and diverted the caravan to another route. Abu Sufyan then informed Abu Jahl of its safe arrival at Mecca. This news caused some 400 of the Meccans, who now saw no need for battle, to desert. Abu Jahl was determined to destroy Muhammad, however, and told his remaining forces that they would travel to the wells at Badr, about 25 miles southwest of Mecca, and there celebrate the safe passage of the caravan.

Muhammad's men were lying in wait at Badr. Learning of Abu Jahl's approach, Muhammad called a council on the evening of March 14. When representatives of both his Mecca and Medina followers pledged their support,

Muhammad announced that they would indeed give battle. On the advice of his second-in-command, Abu Bakr, Muhammad had all the wells except one stopped up; he then positioned his men around this well. On March 15, Abu Jahl's men arrived, nearly out of water. They approached the one serviceable well on rising ground.

Muhammad, seated under a tent, instructed his men to hold their positions and advance only when ordered. In the meantime, they would meet the attackers with arrows. Reportedly a sandstorm struck the Meccans as they advanced and their attack faltered, whereupon Muhammad ordered his force forward. The Meccan force broke and ran, leaving 70 dead and another 70 as prisoners. Abu Jahl was wounded and taken prisoner. He was beheaded when he refused to acknowledge Allah as the real victor.

Many in Arabia saw the victory of Muhammad's badly outnumbered, poorly armed, and badly equipped force as a sign from God. It certainly added immensely to Muhammad's reputation, especially as a military leader. Defeat at Badr would probably have brought his death. The Medians were themselves defeated the next year at Ohod, however. This setback did not appear to damage Muhammad's reputation. The Meccans laid siege to Medina in 627 but were unable to take the city. Following a period of truce, fighting resumed, and Muhammad and his followers captured Mecca by assault in 630.

In 629 the Muslims had staged their first raid against the Byzantine Empire. War between these two would extend over the next thousand years. Muhammad died in 632, but he left a rapidly growing religion that would soon came to dominate the Middle East and North Africa.

SPENCER C. TUCKER

See also
Muhammad, Prophet of Islam; Quran

References
Balyuzi, H. M. *Mahammed and the Course of Islam*. Oxford, UK: G. Ronald, 1976.
Holt, P. M., Ann K. S. Lambton, and Bernard Lewis. *The Cambridge History of Islam*, Vol. 1. Cambridge: Cambridge University Press, 1970.
Irving, Washington. *Mahamet and His Successors*. Madison: University of Wisconsin Press, 1970.

Badr al-Jamali (1015–1094)

Fatimid vizier and military commander who was the virtual dictator of Fatimid Egypt for more than 20 years. An ethnic Armenian, Badr was purchased as a slave (mamluk) by Syrian emir Jamal al-Dawla. Demonstrating great administrative talent, Badr made his name in Syria, where he served twice as the Fatimid governor of Damascus and Acre and successfully repelled Seljuk invasions. In 1073–1074 Fatimid caliph al-Mustansir, facing increasing internal disorder and encroachment of tribal forces, invited Badr to help him restore order. Badr insisted on bringing his own army and during the next few years ruthlessly crushed all opposition, successfully subduing the delta region and Upper Egypt and repelling the Seljuk invasion of Egypt. His success resurrected the caliphate and enabled it to survive for another century.

After restoring central authority, Badr emerged as the virtual ruler of Egypt, holding the titles of commander in chief, vizier, and chief justice. Although notorious for his iron rule and harsh repression, Badr also brought order and prosperity to Egypt and left a rich legacy of buildings still visible in Cairo. In the 1080s he rejuvenated Cairo, reinforcing it with a second tier of fortifications that included three monumental gates (the Bab al-Futuh, Bab al-Nasr, and Bab al-Zuwayla).

Despite incessant campaigning (1078–1079, 1085–1086, and 1089–1090), Badr was less successful in Syria, where the Seljuks captured Damascus and much of Syria. Before his death just months before al-Mustansir, Badr managed to have his son al-Afdal Shahinshah designated as heir to all of his offices. As with his father, al-Afdal retained real authority in Egypt for almost three decades.

ALEXANDER MIKABERIDZE

See also
Fatimid Dynasty; Mamluk Sultanate; Seljuk Dynasty

References
Dadoyan, Seda B. *The Fatimid Armenians*. Leiden: Brill, 1997.
Walker, Paul Ernest. *Fatimid History and Ismaili Doctrine*. Aldershot, UK: Ashgate, 2008.
Williams, Caroline. *Islamic Monuments in Cairo: The Practical Guide*. Cairo: American University in Cairo Press, 2002.

Baghavard, First Battle of (June 14, 1735)

Decisive battle between Ottoman and Persian armies at Baghavard (also known as Eghvard or Murad-Tappa) near Yerevan on June 14, 1735. Following the Afghan invasion of 1722, Persia experienced over a decade of civil strife that saw the rise of several warlords. One of them, Nadir Khan, proved to be most successful and gradually secured much of the former Safavid empire. His attempts at restoring Persian authority, however, clashed with the Ottomans, who had exploited Iranian weakness to occupy much of Iraq and southeastern Caucasia. Nadir successfully campaigned in Iraq in late 1733 and Shirvan (southeastern Caucasia) and Armenia in 1734–1735. He besieged Ottoman-held Yerevan, forcing the Ottoman *serasker* Köprülü Abdullah Pasha to march against him with some 80,000 troops. As the Ottoman forces crossed the Arpa Chay River, Nadir left Yerevan with an advance guard of some 18,000 men while the main Iranian army of some 40,000 men followed behind him. Nadir found the Ottoman army deployed near Baghavard on June 14.

The battle began that same afternoon when Nadir, without waiting for the main army, launched an attack with some 3,000 men to lure the Ottomans out of their camp and threaten Ottoman artillery that was deployed unsupported. The Persian attack surprised the Ottomans and resulted in the Ottoman artillery being either captured or forced to withdraw, allowing Nadir to use his own artillery to target Ottoman troops. Nadir then exploited confusion among the Ottomans to charge with his cavalry. Köprülü failed to counter these attacks, and the Ottoman troops in general performed slowly and disjointedly; an Armenian who witnessed the battle wrote that the Ottoman cannon had fired only two or three times, while the Persian cannon had fired some 300 rounds or more.

The Ottoman army soon broke ranks and fled. Köprülü Abdullah Pasha was almost captured during his flight but fell from his horse and was then beheaded by a Persian soldier named Rustam. Contemporary sources claim that the Ottoman Army lost some 40,000 killed, wounded, or captured, but this number constituting half of the army seems exaggerated. Still, the Ottoman personnel casualties were heavy, coupled with the loss of 32 cannon and their enormous baggage train. And besides their commander in chief, several other prominent Ottoman commanders were also slain, as the retreating troops were pursued for several miles back to the Arpa Chay River.

Following his victory, Nadir was able to occupy parts of Armenia and Georgia, capturing Ganja (July 9), Tiflis (August 12), and Yerivan (October 3). Their defeat also made the Ottomans more receptive to Persian peace offers, and diplomatic negotiations soon followed.

ALEXANDER MIKABERIDZE

See also
Baghavard, Second Battle of; Nadir Shah

References
Axworthy, Michael. *Nader Shah: From Tribal Warrior to Conquering Tyrant.* New York: I. B. Tauris, 2006.
Shaw, Stanford. "Iranian Relations with the Ottoman Empire in the Eighteenth and Nineteenth Centuries." In *The Cambridge History of Iran*, Vol. 7, ed. Peter Avery et al., 297–314. Cambridge: Cambridge University Press, 1991.

Baghavard, Second Battle of (August 9, 1745)

Decisive battle between Ottoman and Persian armies at Baghavard (also known as Eghvard or Murad-Tappa) near Yerevan on August 9, 1745. In the 1740s, Nadir Shah of Iran mounted a series of campaigns to restore Persian influence following years of decline. After successful campaigns in Central Asia and Caucasus, Nadir made peace overtures to the Ottomans, which were rejected. In 1743 the Ottomans and Persians resumed hostilities, and Nadir besieged several Ottoman cities in Iraq but failed to gain any decisive results and agreed to a cease-fire.

Following a quick campaign in the Caucasus, Nadir Shah camped near Yerevan in 1745. To engage him, two Ottoman armies advanced, one toward Qars and the other farther south to Mosul. Nadir sent a part of his army to engage the latter army and prepared to fight the former himself.

On August 7 Nadir left Yerevan and camped on the battlefield of Baghavard, where he had secured a decisive victory against the Ottomans in 1735. By August 9, the Ottoman army of some 140,000 men led by Yegen Muhammad Pasha arrived and formed up for battle. To negate Ottoman superiority in firearms, Nadir instructed his infantry to fire one volley before engaging the enemy with their sabers.

Fighting was fierce, and victory was unclear until Nadir's cavalry charge on the Ottoman flank drove that army back to its fortified camp, where the Persians surrounded it and cut off its supplies. After several days, Ottoman *levends* (irregulars) mutinied and killed Yegen Muhammad Pasha before fleeing in utter confusion, leaving their artillery and baggage to the victors. The Ottomans lost up to 28,000 men, almost half of them dead. The Persian victory, which cost Nadir up to 8,000 men, compelled the Ottoman sultan to accept a peace treaty, which was signed in September 1746 in Kordan, northwest of Tehran. The sultan recognized Nadir as a shah and agreed to the proposed frontiers, exchange of ambassadors, and protection of religious pilgrims.

ALEXANDER MIKABERIDZE

See also
Baghavard, First Battle of; Nadir Shah

References

Axworthy, Michael. *Nader Shah: From Tribal Warrior to Conquering Tyrant.* New York: I. B. Tauris, 2006.

Shaw, Stanford. "Iranian Relations with the Ottoman Empire in the Eighteenth and Nineteenth Centuries." In *The Cambridge History of Iran,* Vol. 7, ed. Peter Avery, 297–314. Cambridge: Cambridge University Press, 1991.

Baghdad, Capture of (March 11, 1917)

Baghdad was one of the four most important cities in Islam, and although capturing it would have little real military value, a victory here by British forces would have an important psychological impact. The British had deployed troops to Mesopotamia in October 1914 to protect the oil fields and refineries there. For the British and the Indian Army that contributed the majority of the British Empire forces in this theater during World War I, securing Baghdad seemed to be the logical goal. Baghdad was the "City of the Caliphs" and a communications center with more than 140,000 people.

The first Allied attempt to capture Baghdad ended in disaster when Major General Charles Townshend's 12,000-man force had nearly reached the city but was forced to withdraw and then was surrounded and obliged to surrender at Kut al-Amara in April 1916. In September 1916 General Frederick Maude took command in Mesopotamia, and British Empire strength there was increased to five divisions. Maude also worked to improve logistical support.

Although warned to keep casualties at a minimum, that November Maude received permission to take the offensive. In December, enjoying a considerable numerical advantage, Maude advanced up the Tigris River toward Baghdad. He cleared the fortified Khadairi Bend by the end of January 1917 and then attacked Kut. Employing his greater numbers and mobility to good advantage, Maude crossed the Tigris upstream of Kut, threatening the Turkish line of retreat. Turkish commander General Kiazim Karabekir's XVIII Corps sustained significant losses in men and equipment but managed to withdraw to Baghdad. Maude halted his army at Aziziyeh on February 27. Then on March 5, he opened his drive on Baghdad. Three days later Maude's advance guard reached the Diyala River, 10 miles east of Baghdad. That night the British forces attempted a crossing, but the Ottoman defenders, part of Halil Pasha's Sixth Army, turned them back with heavy losses. A similar attempt the next night was also beaten back, with a small party of British soldiers trapped on the Ottoman side of the river. Halil Pasha had about 12,500 men, mostly in the XVIII Corps. Another 20,000 men of the XIII Corps were en route but failed to arrive in time for the battle. Most of the defenders were positioned along the Diyala River, which entered the Tigris River from the left bank. Although he considered destroying the irrigation system to flood the British positions, Halil chose not to do so. Blocked at the Diyala, in an attempt to surprise his opponent Maude moved two divisions to the right bank of the Tigris on March 9.

Ottoman reconnaissance in the form of German reconnaissance aircraft provided warning of the British move. Halil then ordered nearly all his troops to move to the left bank and take up a position to protect Baghdad from the south, leaving only one regiment to hold the Diyala line. In the predawn hours of March 10, the British attempted another river crossing to rescue their trapped comrades on the other side. The Ottoman position there now collapsed, and the British quickly threw a bridge across the Diyala. By morning, Halil could see British columns advancing on Baghdad. A sandstorm halted operations for the day, allowing Halil time to ponder his alternatives. That night he ordered Baghdad evacuated. The Ottoman forces destroyed those supplies they could not move. On the morning of March 11 the first British soldiers marched into Baghdad, while the Ottomans took up new positions to the north.

TIM J. WATTS

See also
Mesopotamian Theater, World War I

References

Barker, A. J. *The Bastard War: The Mesopotamian Campaign of 1914–1918.* New York: Dial, 1967.

Moberly, F. J. *The Campaign in Mesopotamia, 1914–1918.* 3 vols. Nashville: Battery Press, 1997–1998.

Baghdad, 812–813 Siege of (August 812–September 813)

The city of Baghdad came under siege during August 812–September 813 in the last phase of the civil war between al-Amin and al-Mamun, the sons of Caliph Harun al-Rashid who were vying for control of the Abbasid Caliphate. Following the defeat of Caliph al-Amin's forces in the Battle of Rayy on May 1, 811, and further defeats in Al-Ahwaz, al-Amin was forced to withdraw all his remaining forces on Baghdad. The troops of al-Mamun, commanded by Tahir ibn Husayn, arrived at Baghdad in August 812 and laid siege to the city. Although the city center was defended by a circular wall, the majority of the population lived outside these fortifications, and it was these suburbs that Tahir would have to capture first.

Tahir ordered construction of a large number of siege engines, including many stone-throwing mangonels. In response, al-Amin's troops built their own siege weapons for defense. Much of the fight for the city consisted of both sides bombarding each other's positions, resulting in the deaths of many civilians. Gradually Tahir pushed into the city, helped by the fire from mangonels he deployed on boats on the Tiber. His troops won a series of house-to-house battles at the al-Shammasiyyah gate and advanced closer toward al-Amin's palace.

By September 813 al-Amin tried to negotiate safe passage, but Tahir ordered that he must hand over his scepter and seal. Al-Amin refused to do this and tried to escape by boat. However, his vessel was intercepted. Al-Amin was killed and his head was placed on top of the Al-Anbar gate of the city. Tahir was now able to inform al-Mamun that the city had been taken in his name.

RALPH MARTIN BAKER

See also
Abbasid Caliphate

References
Al-Tabari, Abu Ja'far Muhammed Bin Jarir. *History of Al-Tabari*. Vol 31. Translated by M. Fishbein. Albany: State University of New York Press, 1992.

Kennedy, Hugh. *The Armies of the Caliphs: Military and Society in the Early Islamic State*. Oxford, UK: Routledge, 2001.

Kennedy, Hugh. *When Baghdad Ruled the Muslim World: The Rise and Fall of Islam's Greatest Dynasty*. New York: Da Capo, 2006.

Baghdad, 1258 Siege of

In 1352 the Ilkhanate Mongol army under Hulegu Khan besieged and then sacked Baghdad. The city of Baghdad had served as the center of the Islamic world for almost 500 years. Even though the once united Abbasid Caliphate had entered its twilight, Baghdad remained an important intellectual, cultural, and religious center.

Beginning in the 1220s, the Islamic world faced a grave threat from the east as the Mongol hordes of Genghis Khan conquered Central Asia and part of Persia. In 1251, the Great Khan Mongke resolved to extend his authority to the Abbasid Caliphate. His brother, Hulegu, was given command of a considerable army and tasked with extending Mongol power into Western Asia. Hulegu's army was drawn from various parts of the Mongol Empire and included military contingents from Georgia and Armenia and engineers from China.

In 1256, Hulegu directed his men against the infamous sect of Assassins (Hashashin) that had terrorized much of the Middle East since the 11th century. After destroying Alamut, the Assassins' stronghold, he then advanced on Baghdad. Abbasid caliph al-Mustasim (1242–1258) refused to recognize the nature of the threat posed by the Mongols and failed to make proper preparations for the invasion. Indeed, he sent the following message to Hulegu:

O young man who have barely entered upon your career and who, drunk with a ten day success, believe yourself superior to the whole world, do you not know that from the East to the Maghreb, all the worshipers of Allah, whether kings or beggars, are slaves to this court of mine, and that I can command them to muster?

In January 1258, the Mongols reached the Tigris River and approached Baghdad. Al-Mustasim tried to engage them, but his attack failed abysmally near Baghdad when the Mongols broke the dikes and flooded the Muslim camp, drowning many Muslim troops and slaying those who survived. By late January the Mongols had taken positions on both sides of the river, placing the city under siege. The Chinese engineers constructed siege engines and began bombarding Baghdad in early February. Lacking stone projectiles, the engineers improvised with stumps of palm trees and foundations from the occupied suburbs of Baghdad. Al-Mustasim tried to negotiate and offered to swear fealty to Hulegu, but it was too late. The Mongol leader would accept only unconditional surrender.

By February 10 Baghdad's walls were breached, and the Mongol army launched the final assault. What followed remains one of the most tragic examples in history of wanton destruction of human lives and property. For days the Mongols and their Christian auxiliaries murdered and plundered, destroying Baghdad's famous libraries, hospitals, palaces, and mosques. A Muslim chronicler lamented that "They swept through the city like hungry falcons attacking a flight of doves, or like raging wolves attacking sheep, with loose reins and shameless faces, murdering and spreading terror." None of the invaders set about their task with greater relish than the Georgian contingent, which desired to avenge centuries of harassment at the hands of caliphs.

Probably some 100,000 people died in Baghdad, although some accounts claim 800,000 to 1 million. Caliph al-Mustasim watched his citizens being slaughtered and then was killed on February 15. Out of respect for his position as a religious leader, Mustasim's blood was not shed visibly, but instead he was sewn up in a carpet and trampled to death by horses. Thus, after more than 500 years the Abbasid caliphate came to an end, even though Abbasid shadow caliphs survived in Egypt until 1517. Baghdad never recovered from this wholesale destruction and continued to linger in the shadow of its former glory for centuries to come.

ALEXANDER MIKABERIDZE

See also
Abbasid Caliphate; Assassins; Hulegu; Mongol Invasion of the Middle East

References
Chambers, James. *The Devil's Horsemen: The Mongol Invasion of Europe.* New York: Atheneum, 1979.
Curtin, Jeremiah. *The Mongols: A History.* Westport, CT: Greenwood, 1972.
Grousset, René. *The Empire of the Steppes: A History of Central Asia.* Translated by Naomi Walford. New Brunswick, NJ: Rutgers University Press, 1970.
Morgan David. *The Mongols.* Oxford: B. Blackwell, 1986.
Spuler, Bertold. *History of the Mongols.* Berkeley: University of California Press, 1972.

Baghdad, 1401 Siege of

During his campaigns in Persi and Iraq, Tamerlane (Timur) sought to reduce the influence of Sultan Ahmad Jalayir, who controlled territory from Azerbaijan to southern Iraq, with his capital in Baghdad. In 1393 Tamerlane led a surprise attack and, marching from Fars to Mesopotamia in just eight days, arrived at Baghdad on August 29. Caught unprepared, Sultan Ahmad could do nothing but abandon the city and retreat to Syria. Although the sultan destroyed the bridges over the river, Timur demonstrated his foresight by having equipped his troops with necessary materials such as beams and planks by means of which they crossed the river and took the city without a fight. The population of Baghdad was treated relatively leniently but had to pay a heavy indemnity. Upon his departure, Timur left a small garrison in Baghdad.

In 1394, Sultan Ahmad returned from Syria to reclaim the city. The sultan's ostentatious lifestyle, however, caused much resentment in the devastated city, and by 1397 a conspiracy was hatched against Sultan Ahmad, who called in Qara Qoyunlu tribesman to restore order in Baghdad.

In 1400 following his victorious campaign in Anatolia and Syria, Tamerlane turned his attention to Baghdad. In March 1401 he led his army to the city, which resisted his attacks for 40 days before falling to an assault on July 9, 1401. Enraged by the city's resistance, Tamerlane ordered the massacre of all of its residents except Muslim theologians and dervishes. In the subsequent bloodbath tens of thousands of people died and the city was largely destroyed, its fortifications and public buildings demolished.

ALEXANDER MIKABERIDZE

See also
Tamerlane

References
Fisher, William Bayne, et al., eds. *The Cambridge History of Iran.* Cambridge: Cambridge University Press, 1986.
Marozzi, Justin. *Tamerlane: Sword of Islam, Conqueror of the World.* Cambridge, MA: Da Capo, 2006.

Baghdad, 1638 Siege of

The Ottoman siege of Baghdad on 1638 was part of the prolonged Ottoman-Safavid struggle for control of Iraq. In 1504, Safavid shah Ismail captured Baghdad during one of his campaigns. Thirty-nine years later, the Ottomans conquered it during the reign of Sultan Suleiman the Magnificent and retained control of it for the next nine decades. The Persians managed to reclaim it only in 1624 and defended it against several Ottoman attacks.

Finally, in 1638 Sultan Murad IV organized an expedition to drive the Safavids out of Iraq. By then, Baghdad boasted massive fortifications. The Ottoman observer Ziyaeddin Ibrahim Nuri described city walls that were 50 cubits (25 meters) tall and between 10 and 7 meters wide, reinforced by earthen ramparts to withstand artillery bombardment and protected by a wide and deep moat. The city walls featured 114 towers (*kule*) between the North Gate (Imam-i Azam) and the South Gate (Karanlik Kapu), while another 97 towers ran westward parallel to the Tigris; in between these 211 towers, there were numerous crenels (*beden*). Safavid garrison commander Bektash Khan had carried out extensive repairs to fortifications that were damaged in previous sieges and built outworks to prevent enemy forces from approaching the walls.

The Ottoman army, with the sultan at its head, left the capital in May 1638 and, traveling through Konya, Aleppo, and Mosul, reached Baghdad in mid-November. To overcome the city's defenses, Sultan Murad IV brought with him

24,000 military laborers (*beldar*) and another 8,000 miners and sappers (*lagimci*). He deployed his infantry to trenches and placed cavalry on flanks and behind trenches to protect against Safavid sorties.

The Ottoman *beldar* and *lagimci* then commenced building a zigzag trench (*siçan yolu*) and defensive batteries that, once completed, directed their fire against the city defenses. At the same time, the miners dug underneath the walls, successfully opening a wide breach. After a siege of 40 days, the Ottomans stormed the city on December 25, massacring most of its inhabitants.

The next year Iran sued for peace and ceded Baghdad and much of Iraq to the Porte.

ALEXANDER MIKABERIDZE

See also
Ismail I, Shah; Ottoman-Safavid Wars; Suleiman I

References
Finkel, Caroline. *Osman's Dream: The History of the Ottoman Empire, 1300–1923*. New York: Basic Books, 2006.
Goodwin, Jason. *Lords of the Horizons: A History of the Ottoman Empire*. New York: Picador, 2003.

Baghdad, 1733 Battle of (July 19, 1733)

Major battle fought between Ottoman and Persian armies over the control of Iraq. In early 1733, Persian ruler Nadir Khan invaded Iraq seeking to reclaim lands formerly belonging to Persia. Leading an army of some 100,000 men (accompanied by up to 200,000 noncombatants), Nadir occupied Samarra, Najaf, Karbala, and other Iraqi towns before besieging Baghdad. Lacking heavy artillery, the Persians were unable to create a breach in the massive walls of the city, which was vigorously defended by the Ottoman garrison under Ahmad Pasha.

By mid-July Ahmad Pasha, however, was willing to negotiate surrender when he received news of the approach of an Ottoman relief army of some 80,000 men with 60 cannon, led by former grand vizier and experienced commander Topal Osman Pasha. Nadir left part of his army at Baghdad and set off with some 70,000 men to face Topal Osman. The decisive battle took place near the Tigris River not far from Baghdad on July 19, 1733. The Ottoman army was deployed on a rolling terrain with the river behind the troops, as was the wind, which blew the sand toward the Persian position.

Nadir began the battle by launching his cavalry against the Ottomans, who repulsed it. He then advanced with the main army organized in three groups and, after a fierce fight, forced the Ottoman center to fall back to its camp. Topal Osman then committed his reserves, who restored the tide of war while some Kurdish and Arab units changed sides and attacked Nadir Khan's flanks. After nine hours of fighting and as the Persians wavered in the face of the Ottoman surge, Nadir's horse was wounded, causing him to fall. Believing that their commander had been killed, many Persian troops panicked and withdrew from the battlefield, abandoning baggage and artillery (18 guns and 500 zanburaks).

Both sides suffered heavy casualties, with the Ottomans losing up to 20,000 men and the Iranians as many as 30,000. This victory allowed the Ottomans to relieve Baghdad on July 24 and protect Anatolia from a probable Persian invasion. Nadir's defeat in the battle negated most of his earlier accomplishments in Iraq and was the one of the worst setbacks in his brilliant military career.

ALEXANDER MIKABERIDZE

See also
Nadir Shah

References
Axworthy, Michael. *Nader Shah: From Tribal Warrior to Conquering Tyrant*. New York: I. B. Tauris, 2006.
Hammer-Purgstall, Joseph von. *Histoire de l'Empire Ottoman*, Vol. 14. Paris: Bellizard, Barthès, Dufour et Lowell, 1844.
Lockhart, Laurence. *Nadir Shah: A Critical Study Based Mainly upon Contemporary Sources*. London: Luzac, 1938.

Baghdad, 2003 Battle of (April 5–10, 2003)

On March 20, 2003, a coalition invasion ground force of 100,000 U.S., British, and Australian troops moved into southern Iraq from Kuwait in what became known as Operation IRAQI FREEDOM. The ultimate U.S. military goal was the capture of the Iraqi capital of Baghdad, a city of 5 million people, 300 miles to the north. Before the Iraq War, American planners operated under the assumption that removing Iraqi dictator Saddam Hussein from power would very likely require a ground attack on Baghdad. What everyone from U.S. president George W. Bush on down wanted to avoid, however, was grueling urban warfare that would devastate the city and lead to heavy casualties on all sides, the civilian populace included. To prevent this, the U.S. Army developed a plan to isolate Baghdad first, with the 3rd Infantry Division encircling the city from the west and the I Marine Expeditionary Force enveloping it from the east. Once a

Baghdad, 2003 Battle of 185

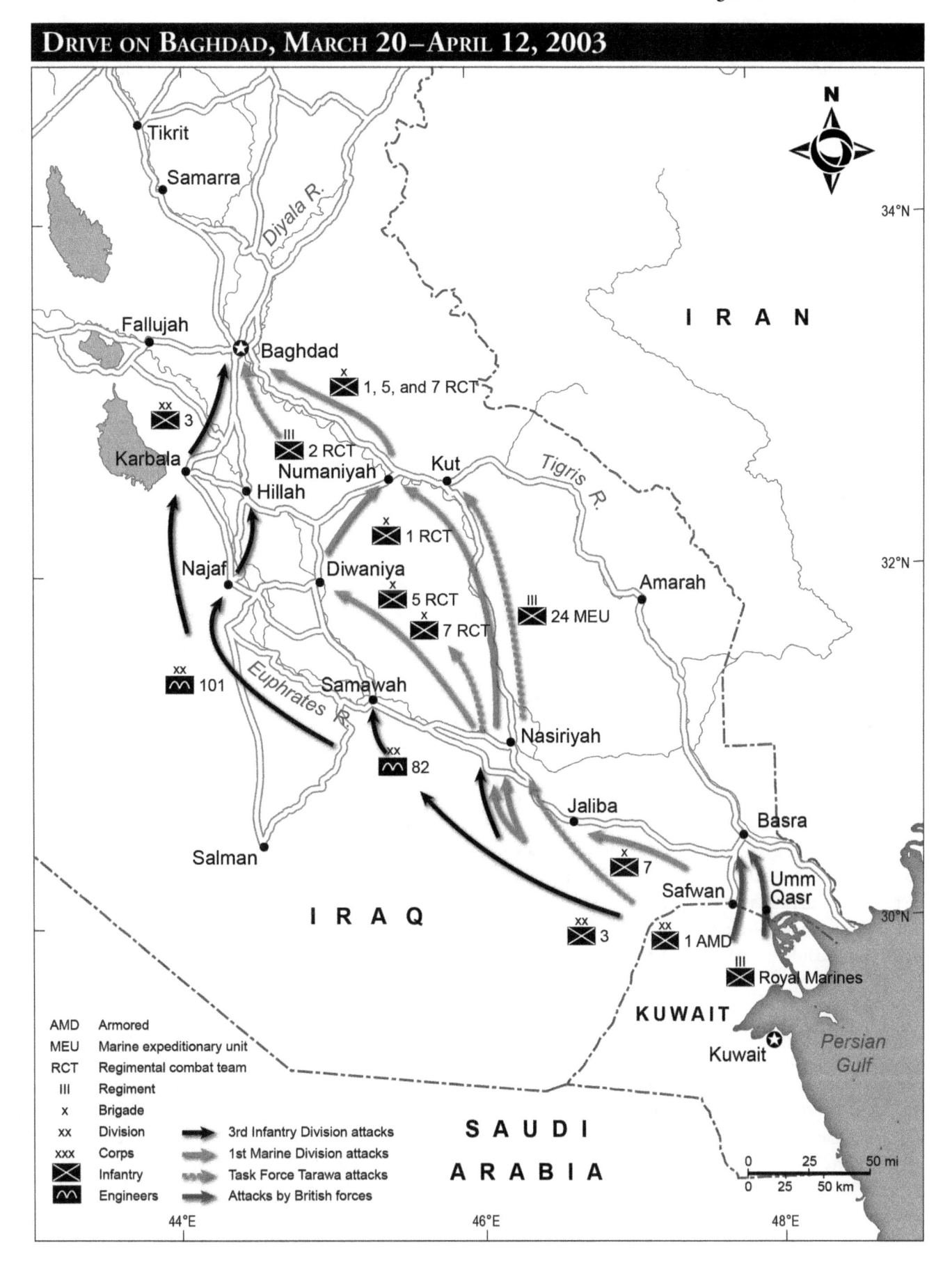

rough cordon had been established around Baghdad, the Americans intended to employ a combination of air strikes, armored and mechanized infantry raids, special forces incursions, and other small-scale operations to whittle away at the city's defenses and Baath Party control of the government, ideally reducing one or both to the breaking point.

The army never got the opportunity to test its operational concept for taking Baghdad, however, as the plan was scrapped once elements of the 3rd Infantry Division reached the outskirts of Baghdad just a little over two weeks into the campaign. By April 4, 2003, the division had secured two of the three objectives on its half of the cordon west of the Tigris River: Saddam International Airport, code-named Lions, and the crucial highway junction just south of the city, referred to as Saints. The third area, Titans, controlled the roads heading northwest out of Baghdad and remained in Iraqi hands. Meanwhile, the 1st Marine Division, which had a more difficult approach to the capital through the populated center of the country, was involved in fierce fighting with Republican Guard armor, Iraqi militia, and foreign irregulars and had yet to reach either of the two objectives on its side of the Tigris. Rather than wait for the encirclement of Baghdad to be completed, the 3rd Infantry Division commander, Major General Buford Blount, decided to begin probing the city's defenses immediately.

The battles on the approach to Baghdad suggested to Blount that Iraqi resistance was beginning to crumble, while the latest intelligence reports indicated that Baghdad was not the heavily fortified, stoutly defended deathtrap that some were expecting. In fact, the opposite proved to be true, as Hussein's paranoia had played directly into American hands. His fears of a coup had prevented him from undertaking military preparations of any kind in Baghdad, and he had entrusted defense of the capital to a relatively small cadre of loyal troops—the three brigades of the Special Republican Guard—supported by the irregulars known as Fedayeen Saddam.

Blount launched his first foray into Baghdad on April 5, sending an armored battalion from the 2nd Brigade Combat Team (BCT) on a thunder run (reconnaissance in force) from Saints into the city center and then out to the airport. The column of 29 Abrams tanks, 14 Bradley Fighting Vehicles, and assorted other vehicles met with a hail of small-arms fire, rocket-propelled grenades (RPGs), and mortar fire from the many hundreds of Iraqi fighters who took up positions along its route. A lucky shot from an RPG disabled one of the American tanks, and it had to be abandoned. Otherwise, the thickly armored Abrams and Bradley tanks were able to withstand multiple hits, and while the crews were exhausted at the end of the 140-minute mission, the vehicles themselves needed only minor repairs before again being ready for action.

The outcome of the April 5 thunder run confirmed Blount's suspicion that Baghdad's defenses were brittle. While the members of the 2nd BCT battalion received a day to catch their breath, Blount employed the 3rd BCT to tighten his grip on the city perimeter. On April 6, the brigade advanced to take control of objective Titans, an area that included the Highway 1 bridge across the Tigris, a crucial point of entry and exit from the capital. This move triggered an intense battle with Iraqi tanks and infantry seeking to regain control of the crossing. The Iraqi attack began on the evening of April 6 and continued into the next morning before it was finally broken up by a combination of concentrated artillery fire, direct fire, and low-level strafing attacks by U.S. A-10 Thunderbolt Warthog ground support aircraft.

The conclusion of the battle for the Tigris bridge to the northwest coincided with the launching of the second thunder run. Intended to be a limited raid much like the first, the April 7 operation developed into something altogether different, an armored strike into the heart of downtown Baghdad. Colonel Dave Perkins, commander of the 2nd BCT, took all three of his maneuver battalions on the mission. Blount and his superiors up the chain of command expected Perkins to pull back to the city's edge at the end of the thunder run. Instead, Perkins made the daring decision to lead his two armored battalions into the center of Baghdad and remain there. The battalions met with strong resistance on their drive into the city and afterward had to fend off repeated attacks by small bands of Iraqi fighters once they established their defensive perimeters in the downtown area. But it was the trailing infantry battalion, assigned the vital task of protecting the brigade's supply line into Baghdad, that found itself engaged in some of the heaviest and most desperate fighting. The battalion was assailed not only by Republican Guard and Fedayeen Saddam troops but also by hundreds of Syrian volunteers who had arrived in Iraq only days earlier. Despite some tense moments, the battalion kept the roadway open so that supply vehicles could reach the units parked downtown.

The thunder run of April 7 struck the decisive blow in the Battle for Baghdad. On the same day, the marines breached the Iraqi defenses along the Diyala River and began their advance into east Baghdad. Fighting continued on April 8, especially in the downtown area and in the 3rd BCT's sector at Titans. By April 9, however, resistance within the city had

Members of the 3rd Battalion 4th Marines during fighting for the Baghdad highway bridge, April 6, 2003. Members of the 3rd Battalion Marines were the first U.S. servicemen to enter Baghdad during the battle for the Iraqi capital. (Laurent Van Der Stockt/Gamma-Rapho via Getty Images)

become generally disorganized and sporadic, as increasing numbers of Iraqi fighters put down their weapons and melted into the general populace. The Baathist regime also dissolved, and some governing officials returned home. Others, most notably Saddam Hussein and his two sons, Uday and Qusay, slipped out of the capital and sought refuge elsewhere, leaving Baghdad to the U.S. Army and marines. Baghdad was considered secured by April 10. Two days later, the 101st Airborne Division relieved the marines and the 3rd Infantry Division in Baghdad, allowing them to deploy northwest to Hussein's ancestral home of Tikrit.

Casualty figures for the Battle of Baghdad are not terribly reliable, but it is believed that the coalition suffered 34 dead and at least 250 wounded. The number of Iraqis dying in the battle has been given as 2,300 killed, but the actual figure is undoubtedly much higher. There is no estimate of the number of Iraqi wounded.

JEFF SEIKEN

See also
Bush Doctrine; Hussein, Saddam

References
Fontenot, Gregory. *On Point: The United States Army in Operation IRAQI FREEDOM*. Fort Leavenworth: Combat Studies Institute Press, 2004.
Gordon, Michael R., and General Bernard Gordon. *Cobra II: The Inside Story of the Invasion and Occupation of Iraq*. New York: Pantheon Books, 2006.
Zucchino, David. *Thunder Run: The Armored Strike to Capture Baghdad*. New York: Grove, 2004.

Baghdadi, Abu Bakr al- (1971–)

Iraqi cleric and leader of the Islamic State of Iraq and Syria (ISIS). Abu Bakr al-Baghdadi was born near Samarra, Iraq, on July 28, 1971. He reportedly obtained a doctorate in Islamic or Quranic studies from the Islamic University of Baghdad. Those who knew al-Baghdadi before he became involved in radical Islamic ideology claim that he was a reserved, shy scholar who seemed to have no penchant for violence. By the mid-1990s, he was living in modest quarters attached to a mosque on the western edge of Baghdad. It would appear that al-Baghdadi became fully radicalized after the Anglo-American–led invasion of Iraq in March 2003.

That same year, 2003, al-Baghdadi cofounded Jamaat Jaysh Ahl al-Sunnah wa-I-Jimaah (JJASJ), a radical Islamic militant group dedicated to removing all foreign troops from Iraq and establishing a regime based on sharia law in the country. Al-Baghdadi served on the JJASJ's powerful sharia committee. In February 2004, U.S. occupation forces arrested and jailed him on suspicion that he was fomenting unrest and violence in Iraq. In December 2004, however, he was released from custody.

Al-Baghdadi subsequently joined the Mujahideen Shura Council (MSC) in 2006, which was soon redubbed Al Qaeda in Iraq (AQI). This group was the principal precursor of ISIS. The cleric then became head of AQI's sharia committee and a member of its consultative council. In May 2010 al-Baghdadi became the leader of AQI, which by now was also known as the Islamic State of Iraq (ISI).

However, al-Baghdadi's vision of founding an Islamic emirate in Iraq clashed with the more modest goals of AQI, so he began to assemble his own rebel group. Thereafter he co-opted several other jihadist organizations, most notably the MSC, and began recruiting followers who shared his vision. This was the genesis of ISIS. By 2013, ISIS had emerged as a distinct group and had virtually subsumed AQI. That same year, al-Baghdadi declared his intention to form an Islamic fundamentalist regime in both Iraq and Syria and began leading his followers in armed combat in both states. He also announced that the al-Nusra Front, then engaged in the Syrian Civil War, would be merged with ISIS. Not all al-Nusra members, however, wished to become part of ISIS, with the result that infighting occurred between the two groups, which only intensified the violence under way in Syria.

In 2014 ISIS ramped up its insurgency, especially in Iraq, where it began to seize large swaths of western and northern Iraq, threatening the viability of the Iraqi government in Baghdad. In February of that year Al Qaeda officially disavowed itself from ISIS activity, indicating that ISIS had become too radical even for Al Qaeda. In June, al-Baghdadi audaciously proclaimed the creation of a global caliphate, with him as the caliph and its capital at Raqqa in Syria. Meanwhile, ISIS was seizing and holding more territory in Iraq and Syria and had begun a series of gruesome public beheadings, some involving Westerners. The beheadings were depicted on video and released on the Internet. The group was also engaged in kidnappings, sexual slavery, and mass killings of minority groups in Iraq and Syria.

Al-Baghdadi has kept a low profile in recent years, earning him in some quarters the sobriquet "the invisible sheikh." There have been numerous reports of his death, but none have been substantiated. Reportedly he fled from Raqqa before its fall in December 2017 and may have been injured. Some observers claim that he is in hiding in Iraq, most probably at some place along the Euphrates River where ISIS sympathizers are known to be. Others claim that he is in Syria, Libya, or even Afghanistan. By 2016, the U.S. government had placed a $10 million bounty on his head. In February 2018, several media outlets claimed that al-Baghdadi had been wounded during an air raid in Iraq and was being treated in Syria. In July 2018, al-Baghdadi's son and heir apparent, Hudhayfah al-Badri, was killed in action in Syria.

Paul G. Pierpaoli Jr.

See also
Al Qaeda; Al Qaeda in Iraq; Iraq; Iraq Insurgency; Iraq War; Islamic State of Iraq and Syria; Sharia; Syria; Syrian Civil War

References
McCants, William. *The ISIS Apocalypse: The History, Strategy and Doomsday Vision of the Islamic State.* New York: Picador, 2016.
"Profile: Abu Bakr al-Baghdadi." BBC News, May 15, 2015, http://www.bbc.com/news/world-middle-east-27801676.
Rosenberg, Matthew. "Citing Atrocities, John Kerry Calls ISIS Actions Genocide." *New York Times,* March 17, 2016, http://www.nytimes.com/2016/03/18/world/middleeast/citing-atrocities-john-kerry-calls-isis-actions-genocide.html.

Baghdad Pact (February 4, 1955)

Treaty of mutual cooperation and mutual defense among the nations of Turkey, Iraq, Pakistan, Iran, and Great Britain agreed on February 4, 1955. The Baghdad Pact, also known as the Central Treaty Organization (CENTO) and the Middle East Treaty Organization, was part of Western efforts to establish regional alliances to contain the Soviet influence. In the end, the Baghdad Pact failed because Arab leaders saw it as an attempt by the West to continue its colonial domination over the region. As the Cold War developed in the late 1940s and early 1950s, the U.S. government adopted a policy of communist containment. In Europe, the North Atlantic Treaty Organization (NATO) was formed in 1949. President Dwight D. Eisenhower's administration continued this process along other borders of the Soviet Union. The Middle East was viewed as a key area, in large part because it was the main source of oil for the West. The British government was expected to be the key to the formation of an alliance here, since it already had extensive relations with the Arab states. As such, British diplomats laid the groundwork for regional defense agreements. The first attempts included Egypt, but the government of President Gamal Abdel Nasser was more interested in Pan-Arab agreements that excluded Britain. Indeed, Egypt refused to join a proposed Middle East defense organization in 1953, causing that initiative to collapse.

The United States and Britain therefore tried to create an alliance among the northern tier of Arab states. Turkey was already a NATO member, and its status as a Muslim nation helped to encourage other Muslim countries to consider defensive alliances with the Western powers. In February 1954, Turkey and Pakistan signed a pact of mutual cooperation, one of the first in the region. Following much diplomatic activity, on February 24, 1955, Turkey and Iraq signed the Pact of Mutual Cooperation, which became better known as the Baghdad Pact, aimed at preventing Soviet aggression. The treaty included language inviting members of the Arab League as well as other interested nations to join. Britain adhered to the alliance in April 1955, and the Royal Air Force received the right to base units in Iraq and to train the Iraqi Air Force. Pakistan joined in September, and Iran joined on October 12, 1955. The United States remained a shadow member of the group but did not officially join, since American relations with Israel might have prevented Arab members from joining. A permanent secretariat and permanent council for the alliance was created and headquartered in Baghdad.

Nasser viewed the Baghdad Pact as an attack on his own vision of Pan-Arabism, to be achieved under his leadership. He therefore immediately attacked the pact as Britain's way of continuing its colonial presence in the Middle East. At the time, Nasser had great prestige in the Arab world as a

Delegates at the Baghdad Pact conference, November 24, 1955. The pact, initially signed in 1955 by Iraq and Turkey, established a defense coalition between Iraq, Turkey, Pakistan, Iran, and the United Kingdom. Iraq withdrew from the pact shortly after the 1958 coup that brought down King Faisal II and put Abdul Karim Qasim in power. (Fox Photos/Getty Images)

nationalist and an opponent of Israel, and his condemnation of the treaty caused opposition to it among ordinary Arab peoples. Jordan had been expected to join the Baghdad Pact, but riots there convinced King Hussein I to withdraw his support for it. Syria refused to sign the treaty, instead forming a union with Egypt known as the United Arab Republic. Even Lebanon, which requested Western assistance to help settle a civil war in 1958, refused to join the pact. Saudi Arabia also opposed the pact because it feared that Iraq would become the dominant regional power. The Baghdad Pact received a serious blow in October 1956 when Britain joined France and Israel in an invasion of Egypt in reaction to the Suez Crisis. The U.S. government opposed the attack and helped force its allies to withdraw. The action discredited Britain across the Middle East. In an attempt to keep the Western orientation of the pact, the United States joined the Military Committee of the organization in 1958 and funneled military assistance and other funds through the pact's organizations.

The gravest threat to the Baghdad Pact occurred on July 14, 1958, when Iraqi officers overthrew King Faisal II and the Iraqi monarchy. The new Iraqi government, sympathetic to Nasser, withdrew Iraq from the Baghdad Pact on March 24, 1959. That same year, the United States officially joined the alliance, which changed its name to the Central Treaty Organization. The alliance proved to be weak, however. When Pakistan and Iran became involved in conflicts with India and then Iraq during the 1960s, they tried to invoke the alliance, but Britain and the United States refused to be drawn into the regional conflicts. As a result, Pakistan and Iran came to regard the alliance with considerable cynicism. CENTO declined in importance as the British Empire continued to contract. In 1968, Britain withdrew its forces from the Persian Gulf, making British bases on Cyprus the closest ones to the Middle East. In 1974, budget cutbacks forced Britain to withdraw specific troop commitments to CENTO. After that, CENTO became a chiefly symbolic structure rather than an effective defensive mechanism. In 1979, Iran left CENTO following the overthrow of Shah Reza Pahlavi. Pakistan withdrew in 1979 as well, and with it CENTO and the vestiges of the Baghdad Pact had collapsed entirely.

TIM J. WATTS

See also
Faisal II, King of Iraq; Nasser, Gamal Abdel

References
Dann, Uriel. *Iraq under Qassem: A Political History, 1958–1963.* New York: Praeger, 1969.

Kuniholm, Bruce. *The Origins of the Cold War in the Near East.* Princeton, NJ: Princeton University Press, 1980.

Podeh, Elie. *The Quest for Hegemony in the Arab World: The Struggle over the Baghdad Pact.* New York: Brill, 2003.

Bahrain

Bahrain, officially known as the Kingdom of Bahrain, is an archipelago of more than 30 islands on the western shores of the Persian Gulf. Bahrain continues to create artificial islands for economic and tourism purposes. Only five of the islands are permanently inhabited, however. Bordered on the west by the Gulf of Bahrain and by the Persian Gulf on the north, east, and south, Bahrain is about 20 miles from Qatar to the south, while a 16-mile-long causeway westward connects the Bahraini island of Umm al-Nasan to Saudi Arabia. Bahrain's area is only some 295 square miles. The nation's capital is Manama.

Bahrain's 2018 population numbered about 1.4 million. Those of Bahraini descent account for some 45.5 percent of the total. The remainder are 45.5 percent South Asian, 4.7 percent other Arabs, 1.6 percent African, 1 percent European, and 1.2 percent others. Islam is the religion of some 85 percent of the population, with 70 percent of the Muslim population being Shia. The remaining 15 percent practice Bahai, Christianity, and other religions. Arabic, English, and Farsi are the most commonly spoken languages.

Politically, the country consists of a constitutional monarchy ruled by Emir Khalifa bin Hamad al-Thani. Bahrain is a member of the Gulf Cooperation Council (GCC), a collective security organization consisting of six countries on the western side of the Persian Gulf. Bahrain also belongs to the Arab League, the United Nations, the Organization of Islamic Conference, the Organization of Arab Petroleum Exporting Countries, and other international organizations.

Although fixing the precise starting date of Bahraini civilization is difficult, Pakistan's Harappans and the Greeks traded their goods for Bahraini pearls in ancient times. Indeed, Bahrain's pearl fisheries were considered the finest in the world into the 19th century. Historically, Bahrain has been known as Dilmun, Tylos, and Awal. Pre-Islamic Bahrain's religions included both paganism and Nestorian Christianity, the latter having a bishopric located on Umm al-Nasan that lasted at least until 835 CE. Bahrain adopted Islam during the lifetime of Prophet Muhammad, and this soon become the dominant religion there. The Ismaili al-Qaramita Islamic sect dominated Bahrain between 900 and

BAHRAIN

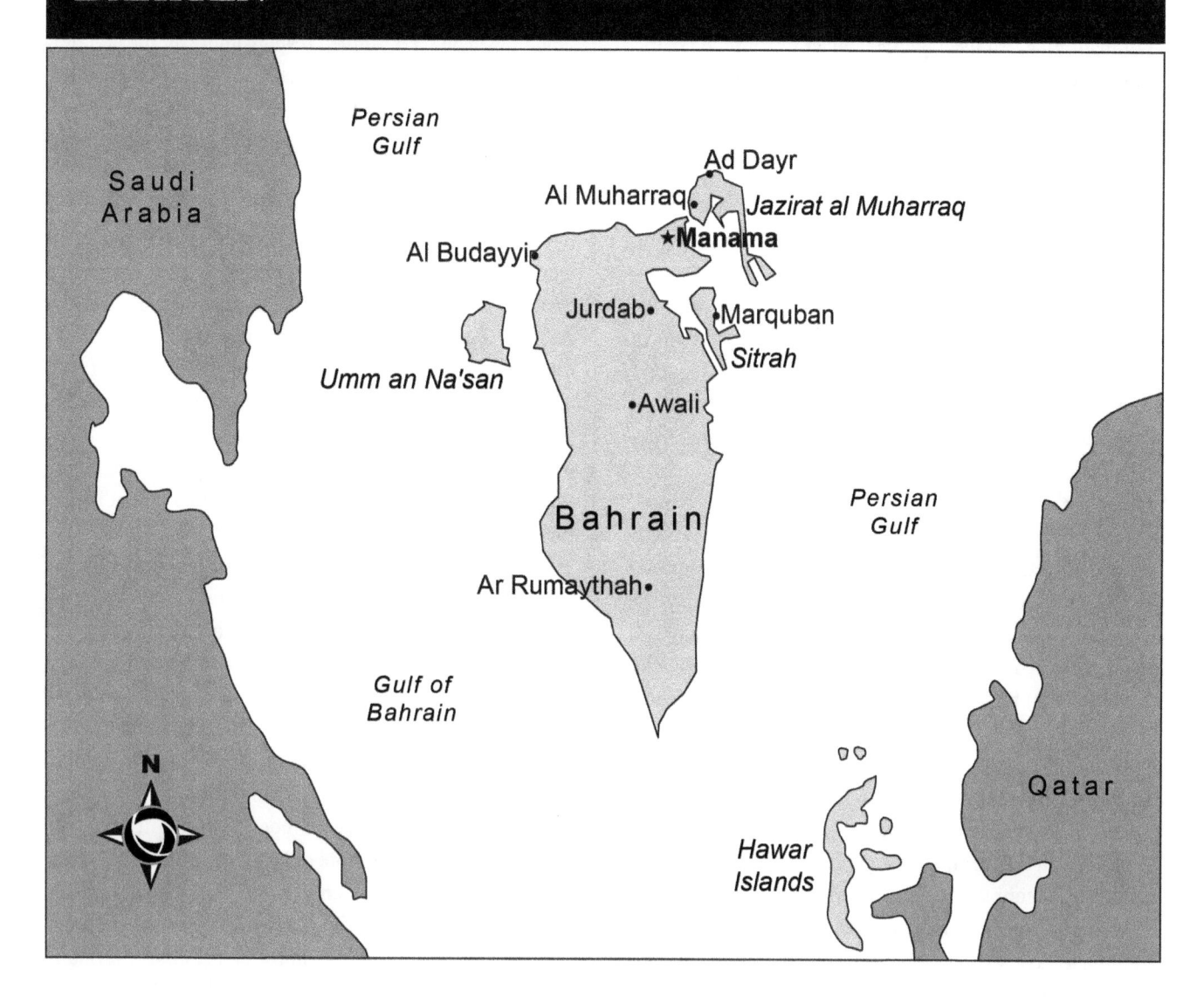

976. Afterward, the Shias eventually became the dominant force in Bahraini Islam.

Throughout Bahrain's history various empires have occupied the country, including those of Babylon, Assyria, Portugal, and Safavid Iran. Portuguese forces captured Bahrain in 1521 and controlled the country until 1602, when Bahrainis overthrew them. Iran's Safavid Empire quickly conquered Bahrain the same year and maintained control until 1717. Iran has used this fact to repeatedly claim Bahraini territory.

In 1783 the al-Khalifa clan, led by Ahmad ibn Mohammed al-Khalifa, invaded and conquered Bahrain. This family line has led the country ever since. The royal family is Sunni Muslim while, as noted, the majority of Bahrain's population is Shia Muslim.

In 1820 Bahrain signed a treaty with the British government pledging not to engage in piracy. Britain agreed to provide military protection for Bahrain and official recognition of the al-Khalifa family as the rulers. In exchange, Bahrain agreed not to cede its territory to any country except Britain and not to establish foreign relations with other nations without British consent. Meanwhile, British advisers encouraged the al-Khalifa rulers to adopt a series of social reforms. Iran continued to assert its rights to Bahrain, however. In 1927 Iranian ruler Reza Shah claimed sovereignty over the country in a letter to the League of Nations.

Discovery of oil in 1931 by the Bahrain Petroleum Company, a subsidiary of the Standard Oil Company of California, had immense impact. Production began the next year, and Bahrain soon was an early leading exporter of oil. Meanwhile relations with Britain became closer, especially after 1935 when London relocated a major naval base there from Iran. Bahrain allied itself with Britain at the onset of World War II, declaring war on Germany on September 10, 1939. During the war, Bahrain provided oil to the Allied Powers and served as a staging point for the protection of British colonies and oil-production facilities in Asia and Africa.

After India acquired its independence from Britain on August 15, 1947, British interest in the Persian Gulf region diminished markedly, eventually leading to London's decision in 1968 to withdraw from the treaties signed with the Persian Gulf states during the 1800s. Initial attempts to unite Bahrain with other Persian Gulf states failed, and on August 15, 1971, Bahrain declared its full independence.

By 1973, Bahrain's oil reserves were diminishing. Seeking an alternative source of revenue, Bahrain established a robust banking industry seeking to replace that of Lebanon, which had greatly suffered as a consequence of the long Lebanese Civil War (1975–1990). Bahrain soon was recognized as the banking center of the Middle East.

In 1973 Bahrain held its first parliamentary elections. Its members soon quarreled with Emir Isa bin Salman al-Khalifa (r. 1961–1999) regarding implementation of a security law, however. The emir responded by dissolving the assembly in 1975 and putting the law into force by decree. Despite his actions, Bahrain is regarded as quite liberal and tolerant compared to most other Islamic nations in the region.

In 1981 the government of the Islamic Republic of Iran sought to encourage Bahrain's large Shia population to carry out a revolution there. Although some Bahraini Shias attempted a coup d'état that same year, it was unsuccessful. Indeed, Iranian interference in Bahraini affairs encouraged the nation to establish collective security agreements that created the Gulf Cooperation Council on May 25, 1981, as well as efforts to improve diplomatic ties with the United States. On January 26, 1982, Bahrain joined Saudi Arabia, Kuwait, Oman, Qatar, and the United Arab Emirates in establishing a joint military command structure and integrated air defense system. This step was prompted by the perceived threats from Iran, the ongoing Iran-Iraq War (1980–1988), and the Soviet-Afghan War (1979–1989).

Acts against the Bahrainian government include attacks by external and internal sources. One such threat came from the Islamic Front for the Liberation of Bahrain (IFLB), a Shia Islamist militant group that sought to establish a theocratic government in Bahrain. Active from 1981 into the 1990s, it was based in Iran and trained and financed by Iranian intelligence and the Revolutionary Guards. With the failure of the 1981 coup attempt, The IFLB carried out a number of small terrorist attacks against Bahraini targets, mostly by bombings. The IFLB claimed responsibility for the bombing of the Diplomat Hotel on February 10, 1996, that wounded four people. The perception that the IFLB was closely linked to Iran, however, greatly diminished its support among the wider Bahraini Shia community, and the IFLB disbanded in 2002. Many of its members were amnestied and agreed to work within the political process, becoming active in the Islamic Action Party.

Political dissent within Bahrain grew during the 1980s and 1990s, abetted by the fact that the citizenry lacked the opportunity to actively participate in the governing of their country. Another threat came from the Bahrain Freedom Movement (BFM), formed by Bahraini dissidents. It too sought the establishment of an Iranian-style Islamic republic and toward that end engaged in bombings and other terrorist acts.

The death of Emir Isa ibn Salman al-Khalifa on March 6, 1999, led to significant changes in Bahrain, for his son and new emir Khalifa bin Hamad al-Thani instituted a series of social and political reforms designed to end the unrest associated with the uprising of the 1990s and meet demands for reform. In 2001 Hamad put forward his National Action Charter, among the provisions of which was the resumption of constitutional rule. A referendum on the charter during February 14–15 saw a reported voter turnout of 90 percent and a favorable vote of 98.41 percent. In 2002 King Hamad agreed to parliamentary elections in which women could vote for the first time and run for office, although none won election. Several parties, including the major religious party, the al-Wifaq National Islamic Society, boycotted the election.

Although the United States had sent warships to the Persian Gulf region during the 1800s, Washington had little interest in Bahrain until 1949, when it began leasing British bases there. The United States has maintained at least a minimal force in Bahrain since. Bahrain allowed U.S. forces to use its territory and facilities for launching military operations against Iraq during both the 1991 Persian Gulf War and the 2003–2011 Iraq War. Bahrain was also a major U.S. base for Operation ENDURING FREEDOM in Afghanistan.

Bahrain was also actively involved militarily in the Persian Gulf War. The country sent a small contingent of 400 troops to serve in the coalition as part of the Joint Forces Command East. Additionally, the Bahraini Air Force, employing F-16 Fighting Falcon fighters and F-5 Tiger II fighters, engaged in defensive sorties in the region and launched offensives against Iraqi assets.

Bahrain also provided limited military assistance in Operations ENDURING FREEDOM in Afghanistan with some naval units. Bahrain provided only a support role in IRAQI FREEDOM (the Iraq War, 2003–2011), although it did subsequently furnish assistance to the new Iraqi government to help stabilize that country.

The U.S. Naval Forces Central Command is headquartered in Manama, making it the home of the U.S. Navy's Fifth Fleet. Army and air force units operating in Bahrain include the 831st Transport Battalion, located at Mina Sulman, and the Air Mobility Command, which has a detachment at Muharraq Airfield. Additionally, the Sheik Isa Air Base serves as a military airfield for various U.S. military aircraft. U.S. military personnel in Bahrain total some 6,000. Flowing from this close Bahraini-U.S. cooperation, in 2004 Bahrain concluded a free trade agreement with the United States.

Discontent in Bahrain with the pace of reforms surfaced in 2011. Inspired by the events in Egypt that toppled Egyptian president Hosni Mubarak on February 11, late on February 15 demonstrators thronged into Pearl Square, the symbolic heart of Manama. They demanded greater political rights, but the upheaval also revealed the religious divide. The crowds demanded that the monarchy give up some powers and end discrimination against Shiites in key positions in the military and the government. Subsequent modest government concessions only served to embolden the demonstrators.

Although the crowds showed restraint and the government had promised to act with moderation, at 3:00 a.m. on February 17, police suddenly charged the demonstrators with tear gas and buckshot. Four people were killed, some 600 others were injured, and a reported 60 were missing in the worst violence in the kingdom in decades. The government then sent in tanks and demanded that the people vacate the streets.

This action inflamed the protestors, who vowed that they would not be intimidated. U.S. officials, stunned by the heavy-handed government action, expressed strong support for the U.S. military alliance with Bahrain but urged its government to act with restraint. On February 19 crowds again occupied the strategic center of the capital.

On February 22 in the largest demonstrations to date, tens of thousands marched in Manama, chanting "No Shia, no Sunni, only Bahraini." Demonstrations continued, and on February 26 Hassan Mushaima, leader of the banned Haq Movement, an opposition party, returned to Bahrain. Long a leader in calling for fundamental reforms, he urged the demonstrators to continue their protests until they had achieved a "successful revolution."

On March 12, U.S. defense secretary Robert Gates met with King Hamad and informed him that "baby steps" to reform were not sufficient to meet the political and economic unrest. In an ensuing press conference Gates told reporters that Iran was looking for ways to exploit the situation and that "time is not our friend."

On March 14, however, Saudi Arabia, acting on a request from Hamad, sent some 150 vehicles and 1,000 troops into Bahrain via the long causeway with the stated goal of protecting government offices and ending the demonstrations. While expressing concern, the Barack Obama administration refused to condemn the Saudi move, which was regarded as a sign on the part of Saudi leaders that concessions by the Bahrainian monarchy could empower Saudi Arabia's own Shia minority and benefit Iran. The government of the United Arab Emirates also supported the Saudi move and issued a statement in promising to honor Bahrain's appeal for assistance.

On March 15 Hamad proclaimed a three-month state of emergency, imposed martial law, and ordered the military to restore order. Soldiers and riot police employed tear gas and armored vehicles to drive hundreds of demonstrators from Pearl Square, resulting in the deaths of several demonstrators and police officers.

On June 4, 2012, Saudi Arabia and Bahrain held talks designed to strengthen their military and political ties in order to meet what they identified as a threat from Iran. Indeed, the Saudis sought common diplomatic and military approaches by all of the GCC states. The talks with Bahrain reportedly discussed the possibility of some sort of union of Bahrain and Saudi Arabia. Such a step, however, would be opposed by many Shias in Bahrain. Suggestions of this had resulted in demonstrations by tens of thousands of Shias in Bahrain on May 18.

Bahrain took part with Saudi Arabia and other Arab states in the campaign against the Islamic State of Iraq and Syria (ISIS). On September 23, 2014, cruise missiles and aircraft from the United States and the allied Arab nations struck ISIS targets in Syria. Bahrain also assisted Saudi Arabia in its military intervention in the Yemen Civil War that had begun on March 19, 2015. On March 26, Saudi Arabia and its Persian Gulf region allies launched air strikes in Yemen in an effort to counter Iran-allied Houthi rebel forces besieging the southern city of Aden, where U.S.-backed Yemeni president Abd-Rabbu Mansour Hadi had taken refuge. The close ties between Bahrain and Saudi Arabia were again demonstrated when on January 4, 2016, after rioters stormed the Saudi embassy in Tehran amid a row over the Saudi execution of prominent Shia Muslim cleric Sheikh Nimr al-Nimr and 46 others condemned for alleged terrorist activities, Bahrain promptly followed Saudi Arabia in breaking diplomatic relations with Iran.

A major world banking center and regarded as financially secure, Bahrain has one of the fastest-growing economies in the Arab world. Its economy is also recognized as the freest in the Arab world. Petroleum accounts for some 60 percent of exports and constitutes 70 percent of government income. Aluminum is the second most exported product. Tourism is an important source of revenue, with most tourists coming from other Arab states.

With little arable land, Bahrain is highly dependent on food imports. The depletion of its oil assets is another concern. Unemployment remains low, and the country is considered politically stable.

Bahrain has a small but well-equipped military. Known as the Bahrain Defence Force (BDF), it numbers some 13,000 personnel and is commanded by the emir. Most BDF equipment comes from the United States. This includes the F-16 Fighting Falcon and F-5 Freedom Fighter aircraft, UH-60 Blackhawk helicopters, M60A3 tanks, and an Oliver Hazard Perry–class former U.S. Navy frigate, RBNS *Sabha*.

In the years since the Arab Spring, Bahrain has made a concerted effort to crack down on and silence any form of dissent. This has resulted in the arrest and imprisonment of prodemocracy advocates and opposition leaders, including those who participated in the Arab Spring. These individuals have also been stripped of their citizenship. In August 2017, U.S. secretary of state Rex Tillerson chided Bahrain's government for its discrimination against Shia Muslims, but that did not stop the United States from concluding a $3.8 billion arms deal with Bahrain the following month.

Wyndham E. Whynot and Spencer C. Tucker

See also
Islamic State of Iraq and Syria; Saudi Arabia

References
Al-Baharna, Husain. *Legal Status of the Arabian Gulf States: A Study of Their Treaty Relations and Their International Problems*. Manchester, UK: Manchester University Press, 1968.
Faroughy, Abbas. *The Bahrein Islands (750–1951): A Contribution to the Study of Power Politics in the Persian Gulf*. New York: Verry, Fisher, 1951.
Jerry, Sampson. *History of Persian Gulf States, Kuwait, Bahrain, Oman, Qatar, United Arab Emirat: Government, Politics, Economy*. NP: CreateSpace Independent Publishing Platform, 2016.
Matthiesen, Toby. *Sectarian Gulf: Bahrain, Saudi Arabia, and the Arab Spring That Wasn't*. Stanford, CA: Stanford University Press, 2013.
McCoy, Eric Andrew. "Iranians in Bahrain and the United Arab Emirates: Migration, Minorities, and Identities in the Persian Gulf Arab States." Unpublished master's thesis, University of Arizona, 2008.
Mojtahed-Zadeh, Pirouz. *Security and Territoriality in the Persian Gulf: A Maritime Political Geography*. London: Routlege-Curzon, 1999.
Ochsenwald, William, and Sydney Nettleton Fisher. *The Middle East: A History*. 6th ed. New York: McGraw-Hill, 2004.
Palmer, Michael. *Guardians of the Gulf: A History of America's Expanding Role in the Persian Gulf, 1833–1992*. New York: Free Press, 1992.
Pridham, B. R. *The Arab Gulf and the West*. New York: Taylor & Francis, 1985.
Shehabi, Ala'a. *Bahrain's Uprising*. London: Zed Books, 2015.
Spencer, William J. *The Middle East*. 11th ed. Dubuque, IA: McGraw-Hill/Contemporary Learning Series, 2007.
Winkler, David. *Amirs, Admirals & Desert Sailors: Bahrain, the U.S. Navy, and the Arabian Gulf*. Annapolis, MD: Naval Institute Press, 2007.

Bakhchisarai, Treaty of (January 3, 1681)

Treaty between Russia, the Ottoman Empire, and the Crimean Khanate to end the Russo-Ottoman War of 1676–1681. Signed in January 2, 1681, at Bakhchisarai in the Crimea, the treaty proclaimed a 20-year truce and set the Dnieper River as the border between the Ottoman and Russian realms. The Porte then recognized Moscow's sovereignty in eastern (left-bank) Ukraine, including Kiev, and the Zaporozhian Cossack Sech, while Russia recognized Ottoman control of southern and southwestern Ukraine. Both sides agreed not to settle the territory between the Southern Bug and Dnieper Rivers. The Crimean Tatars and Nogai tribes retained the right to live as nomads in the southern steppes of Ukraine, while the Cossacks retained the right to fish in the Dnieper and its tributaries and to sail on the Dnieper and the Black Sea.

Alexander Mikaberidze

See also
Russo-Ottoman Wars

References
O'Brien, C. Bickford. "Russia and Turkey, 1677–1681: The Treaty of Bakhchisarai." *Russian Review* 12 (1953): 259–268.
Wojcik, Zbigniew. "From the Peace of Oliwa to the Truce of Bakhchisarai: International Relations in Eastern Europe, 1660–1681." *Acta Poloniae Historica* 34 (1976): 255–280.

Bakr, Ahmad Hassan al- (1914–1982)

Iraqi military officer, Baath Party leader, and president of Iraq (1968–1979). Ahmad Hassan al-Bakr was born in Tikrit (then part of the Ottoman Empire) on July 1, 1914, and was an elder cousin of future Iraqi dictator Saddam Hussein. After completing the equivalent of high school, Bakr taught secondary school for six years before enrolling in the Iraqi Military Academy in 1938.

Early in his military career, Bakr became involved with antigovernment activity culminating in the 1941 Rashid Ali al-Gaylani Revolt. On suppression of that uprising, he was arrested, jailed, and forced out of the army. Not until 1956, when he had sufficiently rehabilitated himself under the waning Hashemite monarchy, was he permitted to rejoin the army. That same year, he clandestinely joined the Iraqi Baath Party.

In 1957 Bakr, now a brigadier general, was part of a military cabal known as the Free Officers group that successfully overthrew the monarchy during the July 14 Revolution that brought General Abd al-Karim Qasim to power. In 1959 Bakr was again purged from the military for alleged ties to an antigovernment rebellion in Mosul, the goal of which was to draw Iraq closer to the United Arab Republic. Nevertheless, he retained his prominent position within the Baath Party hierarchy and in 1963 helped foment a putsch that ousted Qasim. Bakr then became prime minister and vice president but held these posts for only a few months before Abd al-Salam Arif launched another coup in November 1963. By January 1964 Bakr had been stripped of both his government positions. Arif's death in 1966 brought his brother, Abd al-Rahman Arif, to power.

Bakr's power base within the Baath Party was still considerable, and he plotted to oust Arif from power and return Baathist rule. Aided by the Egyptian government, in 1968 Bakr staged a coup that resulted in Arif's exile. That same year Bakr became president and prime minister of Iraq. Determined to implement his Baath Party platform, he named his cousin, Saddam Hussein, as his chief deputy and deputy head of the Revolutionary Command Council. Hussein later became vice president and was essentially the second most powerful man in Iraq.

As president, Bakr nationalized Iraqi oil concerns and instituted a wide array of economic and social reforms. After 1973, when world oil prices skyrocketed, Bakr pursued an aggressive industrial expansion program and funded a panoply of public works projects and infrastructure improvements. Increased oil revenues also allowed his government to purchase large quantities of weapons from the Soviets and significantly augment the Iraqi armed forces. During Bakr's tenure in power, Iraqi-Soviet relations improved dramatically.

Bakr suppressed a Kurdish uprising financed in part by Iran. When his government settled some long-standing differences with Iran in 1975, the Kurdish cause was dealt a crippling blow. In 1978 the Iraqi government banned all political parties except for the ruling Baath Party and made it a capital offense for any government or military official to belong to another party.

By the late 1970s Hussein had begun to consolidate his power and, with Bakr's health deteriorating, became the real power behind the throne. By early 1979 Bakr was leader in name only, and on July 16, 1979, he stepped down, allegedly because of health concerns. Hussein immediately took the reins of state and became the new president of Iraq. Bakr was allowed to live in quiet seclusion, but his paranoid cousin kept constant watch over him. On October 4, 1982, Bakr died in Baghdad, supposedly of natural causes, but some have speculated tha his death occurred on the orders of Hussein.

Paul G. Pierpaoli Jr.

See also
Arif, Abd al-Salam; Baath Party; Hussein, Saddam; Iraq; Qasim, Abdul Karim

References
Marr, Phebe. *The Modern History of Iraq.* 2nd ed. Boulder, CO: Westview, 2003.
Tripp, Charles. *A History of Iraq.* Cambridge: Cambridge University Press, 2007.

Balak ibn Bahram ibn Ortok (?–1124)

Artukid ruler who fought with great success against the Christian crusaders. Balak ibn Bahram ibn Ortok's birth date is unknown. As the ruler of Khartbirt (Khartpert, Harput) since around 1113, Balak conducted several successful operations against the crusader states. In 1120 he routed a crusader army near Arzangan, capturing its leader Theodore Habras, count of Trebizond. Two years later he besieged Edessa and captured Count Joscelin of Edessa, Count Galeran of Birejik, and 60 other prominent Edessan knights.

Balak's victory at Edessa prompted King Baldwin II of Jerusalem to take action, and in the spring of 1123 the Frankish Army embarked on a campaign against Balak, who was besieging the fortress of Karkar. Balak lifted his siege and swiftly marched against Baldwin, whom he surprised while the latter's forces were crossing a bridge over the Sendja

(Nahr al-Azrak, Bolam Su), a tributary of the Euphrates River. In the subsequent battle, Balak routed the Franks and captured the king himself. Balak refused to ransom Baldwin except in exchange for huge territorial concessions. Balak exploited the fact that the Franks in the Levant had become leaderless to consolidate his authority in the region. In May–July 1123 he captured Harran and Aleppo, emerging as the leader of the Artukid clan.

Balak then turned back to the Franks. He marched northward to Edessa, invading the region of Dalik and Tel Bashir, which he burnt and plundered. He chose to ignore the city of Edessa itself and targeted Antioch. In August 1123 he captured Albara and laid siege to the powerful fortress of Kafartab.

Meanwhile, Balak's crusader prisoners, including King Baldwin and Count Joscelin, languished in prison in Khartbirt. They managed to get a message out, and with the help of local Armenians, a daring raid was organized on the fortress that seized the imagination of contemporary chroniclers. Disguising themselves as peasants, the Armenians from Behesni managed to enter the castle, massacre the garrison, and deliver Khartbirt to Baldwin; Joscelin hastened to Antioch and Jerusalem in search of troops to aid Baldwin.

Balak learned about the loss of his capital, treasure, and harem just days later. He immediately lifted the siege of Kafartab and marched to Khartbirt, which he besieged in September. Aware that the impregnable fortress was built on a hill of limestone, he had his men dig several tunnels, propped up by wooden beams, beneath Khartbirt and then methodically destroyed the beams to bring down the walls. On September 16, 1123, the fortress was captured, and although Baldwin and a few other valuable prisoners were spared, the Armenian garrison and the few remaining local inhabitants were all massacred. The crusader relief army, led by Count Joscelin, arrived too late to rescue Baldwin, who was moved to Harran.

In the spring of 1124 Balak launched new offensives against the Franks, first targeting the mutinous ruler of Menbij who sided with Joscelin. Although Balak quickly captured the town proper, the citadel resisted his troops. Joscelin organized a relief army from Antioch and Edessa to rescue Menbij, but Balak defeated it and forced it back to Tel Bashir. Returning to Menbij, he was personally positioning the siege artillery on May 6, 1124, when he was mortally wounded by an archer from the citadel's wall. Balak is buried in a tomb at Aleppo.

ALEXANDER MIKABERIDZE

See also
Baldwin II of Jerusalem; Crusades in the Holy Land, Christian

References
Al-Athir, 'Izz al-Din ibn. *The Chronicle of Ibn al-Athir*, ed. D. S. Richards. Aldershot, UK: Ashgate, 2006.
Harari, Yuval N. *Special Operations in the Age of Chivalry, 1100–1550*. Rochester, NY: Boydell, 2007.
Sauvaget, J. "La Tombe de l'Ortokide Balak," *Ars Islamica* 5, no. 2 (1938): 207–215.

Baldat al-Shaykh Massacre (January 31, 1947)

Mass killing of Palestinian civilians carried out by Palmach, Haganah, and allied Jewish paramilitary members in the Palestinian town of Baldat al-Shaykh in the British Mandate for Palestine during January 30–31, 1947. The massacre was in retaliation for Arab violence against Jews at the Haifa Petroleum Refinery. Although the details of the melee at the refinery remain very sketchy, it ended with approximately 60 Jews dead or injured and an unknown number of Palestinian casualties.

Early on January 31, 1947, some 150–200 well-armed Jewish men mounted a retaliatory raid against the Palestinian town of Baldat al-Shaykh. The men were mostly members of the Palmach 1st Battalion, although a detachment from the so-called Carmelie Brigade of Haganah also participated. The assault began a bit after midnight on January 31 and lasted for just one hour. The attackers caught most of the town's residents asleep, bursting into the Palestinians' homes indiscriminately and firing machine guns and lobbing grenades. When the mayhem ended at about 1:30 a.m., approximately 60 Palestinians—many of them women, children, and elderly—lay dead.

The attack outraged Palestinians and brought international condemnation of Palmach. A later report by those Palmach members involved in the attack stated that "due to the fact that gunfire was directed inside rooms, it was not possible to avoid injuring women and children."

The Baldat al-Shaykh Massacre was part of the opening salvo in a series of mass killings involving both Jews and Palestinians that precipitated the Arab-Jewish Communal War (November 1947–May 1948) and was a precursor to the forthcoming Israeli War of Independence (May 1948–March 1949).

PAUL G. PIERPAOLI JR.

See also

Arab-Jewish Communal War; Haganah; Israeli War of Independence; Palmach

References

Hadawi, Sami. *Bitter Harvest: Palestine between 1914–1967.* New York: New World, 1967.

Rosenfield, Daniel. *Code Name Amnon: The Life and Times of a Haganah Fighter, 1943–1949.* New York: Rosenfield, 2003.

Segev, Tom. *One Palestine, Complete: Jews and Arabs under the British Mandate.* New York: Owl Books, 2001.

Baldwin I of Constantinople (1171–1206)

One of the leaders of the Fourth Christian Crusade in the Holy Land (1202–1204) and subsequently the first Latin emperor of the Kingdom of Constantinople (1204–1206). Baldwin was born in Valenciennes in July 1171, the son of Baldwin V, count of Hainaut, and Margaret, countess of Flanders. In 1192 he succeeded to Flanders and Hainaut (he is usually identified respectively in this context as Baldwin IX and VI). Baldwin I changed the direction of the foreign policy of Flanders. Allying himself with King Richard I of England, he succeeded in resisting the encroachments of Philip II Augustus of France, whom he defeated in a series of battles and recovered much of the territory annexed by Philip some years earlier.

Baldwin took the cross on February 23, 1200, together with his wife Mary, sister of Count Thibaud III of Champagne; his brother, Henry; and many knights. In 1201 Baldwin organized a fleet under the command of John of Nesle and left Flanders on April 14 (Easter) by the land route. He was one of the first crusaders to reach Venice (probably in July) and was also one of those who contributed plate and money to try to meet the debt to the Venetians before the fleet could sail. Baldwin is not mentioned in connection with the attack on Zara (modern-day Zadar, Croatia), but at Corfu (modern-day Kerkira, Greece) he joined with the other leaders in trying to convince the army to accept the offer of exiled Byzantine prince Alexios Angelos.

When the crusaders arrived at Constantinople (Istanbul), Baldwin took command of the vanguard, according to the chronicler Geoffrey of Villehardouin, because of the number of archers and crossbowmen among his men. Baldwin led his troops in the abortive encounter with Alexios III Angelos and his army outside the gates of Constantinople; when his men halted their advance at the sight of the much larger Greek army, Baldwin was accused of cowardice by the squadron of Hugh, count of Saint-Pol, and was told by his own men that they would no longer acknowledge him unless the advance continued. The Greeks withdrew while the crusaders were still in some confusion, but the incident shows that Baldwin had difficulty controlling his troops. Baldwin does not seem to have had a prominent role during the reign of the coemperors Isaac II and Alexius IV, but he was among those who negotiated the agreement with the Venetians on how to divide the empire once the crusaders had decided to attack Constantinople a second time.

Baldwin quickly emerged as the leading rival to Boniface of Montferrat in the election for a new emperor. On May 9, 1204, Baldwin was elected as Latin emperor, largely because the Venetians had no intention of allowing any increase in the power of their Italian neighbor Boniface. Eight days later Baldwin was crowned in the Church of St. Sophia, which made him the rightful emperor in the eyes of many Greeks. He reluctantly agreed to the request of Boniface that he should have Thessalonica (modern-day Thessaloniki, Greece) and its environs instead of Asia Minor. Baldwin then set out to campaign against Alexios V Doukas Mourtzouphlos and marched to Adrianople (modern-day Edirne, Turkey), where his brother, Henry, had preceded him. As Baldwin advanced, his advisers made trouble between him and Boniface by advising that he should insist on his right to go to Thessalonica, despite Boniface's request that he should not. On arriving in Thessalonica, Baldwin acted as overlord, renewing the privileges of the Greeks while a furious Boniface campaigned in Thrace for the recognition of his stepson Manuel (the son of Isaac II and Margaret of Hungary) as the rightful emperor. Open warfare was only avoided by the intervention of the other leaders of the crusaders and the tact of Geoffrey of Villehardouin.

With peace restored, Baldwin gave some attention at the beginning of 1205 to the administration of Flanders, while many of the knights departed to try to conquer the fiefs granted them in Thrace and across the straits in Asia Minor. At this point there was an influx of Franks from Palestine who came to join the crusaders, informing Baldwin that his wife Mary had died.

In March 1205 the Greeks in Thrace rebelled, supported by an invasion by Kalojan, the ruler of Bulgaria, whose overtures the crusading leaders had unwisely rejected. Baldwin summoned his men back to Constantinople, but the crisis in Thrace seemed so serious that he did not wait for the return of all of them and set off with whatever reinforcements he could muster. He besieged Adrianople with an inadequate number of men, and even the arrival of the doge of Venice with reinforcements added but few men to the army. Kalojan meanwhile was hastening to attack the besiegers, and the Cumans, his nomadic cavalry, lured the Franks into a disorderly attack on April 13 in which they suffered greatly and from which they had great difficulty extricating themselves. After the battle Baldwin held a council during which new battle orders were agreed upon, with the knights keeping their formation. Battle was resumed the next day (April 14), but Louis of Blois ignored the agreed-upon orders and charged the Cumans, calling on Baldwin to follow him. Louis was fatally wounded, and Baldwin refused to escape, as this would be dishonorable, and was captured and badly wounded. There was no definite news of him thereafter, but by 1206 the Franks were sufficiently certain that he was dead in captivity to crown his brother, Henry, as the new emperor. Rumors about Baldwin continued to circulate; in the 1220s an impostor had considerable success in Flanders, which had been misgoverned by Baldwin's daughter Jeanne and where his reign was remembered with affection. The impostor was exposed and executed by Jeanne.

Baldwin's position as emperor was fatally weakened by the presence of fellow crusaders such as Louis of Blois and Boniface, who in the West had been his equals in rank and were reluctant to accept his orders. The power of the Venetians also hindered his freedom to maneuver. Baldwin showed little of the military and political skill of his successor, Henry, and during his brief reign the new Latin Empire was almost constantly under very serious threat of extinction.

Peter S. Noble

See also
Alexios III Angelos; Alexios V Doukas Mourtzouphlos; Boniface I of Montferrat; Crusades in the Holy Land, Christian

References
Hendrickx, Benjamin. "Baudouin IX de Flandre et les empereurs byzantines Isaac II l'Ange et Alexis IV." *Revue Belge de Philologie et d'Histoire* 49 (1971): 482–489.
Longnon, Jean. *Les compagnons de Villehardouin*. Genève: Droz, 1978.
Moore, John C. "Count Baldwin IX of Flanders, Philip Augustus, and the Papal Power." *Speculum* (1962): 79–89.
Verlinden, Charles. *Les empereurs belges de Constantinople*. Bruxelles: Dessart, 1945.
Wolff, Robert Lee. "Baldwin of Flanders and Hainaut, First Latin Emperor of Constantinople: His Life, Death and Resurrection, 1172–1225." *Speculum* 27 (1952): 281–322.

Baldwin I of Jerusalem (ca. 1061–1118)

A participant in the First Crusade (1096–1099) and subsequently count of Edessa (1097–1100) and first king of Jerusalem (1100–1118). Baldwin was the third son of Eustace II, count of Boulogne, and Ida of Bouillon. Born sometime between 1061 and 1070, Baldwin was originally educated for the clergy and held benefices in the dioceses of Liège, Reims, and Cambrai, but by 1090 he had become a knight and married Godehilde, daughter of the Norman nobleman Ralph of Tosny. When his elder brother Godfrey of Bouillon decided to participate in the First Crusade (1096–1099), Baldwin and his wife accompanied him.

Baldwin played an important role as one of the leaders of Godfrey's contingent, but when the main crusading armies reached Cilicia in late 1097, he left them with a military force recruited primarily from his brother's followers, evidently intending to conquer lands for himself. Baldwin contested the possession of the coastal town of Tarsos with Tancred but in early 1098 moved farther east to conquer the area around Turbessel (modern-day Tellbasar Kalesi, Turkey) and Edessa (modern-day Sanliurfa, Turkey) in northern Syria, whose Armenian population had risen in revolt. He initially shared the government of the city of Edessa with the Armenian nobleman T'oros but soon supplanted him and by 1100 had extended Frankish rule more than 60 miles on either bank of the Euphrates. The county of Edessa—the first Frankish state to be established by the First Crusade—constituted an important buffer against the Seljuk Turks and was in a position to provide logistical help for the main crusader armies during their campaigns in the environs of Antioch in 1098. As Godehilde had died at Marash in 1097, Baldwin married the daughter of the Armenian prince Taphnuz.

When Godfrey of Bouillon died on July 18, 1100, his knights summoned Baldwin to succeed to the throne of Jerusalem. He bestowed the county of Edessa on his kinsman Baldwin of Bourcq and hurried south with a small force, which reached Jerusalem in November. Unlike his brother, Baldwin insisted on a royal coronation, which was performed in the Church of the Nativity at Bethlehem at Christmas 1100 by the patriarch of Jerusalem Daibert of Pisa, who had initially attempted to prevent Baldwin's succession. Two years later the king managed to have Daibert deposed and thereafter exercised an iron rule over the Latin Church in his kingdom, although it was not until 1112 that he was able to secure the appointment of his main clerical supporter, Arnulf of Chocques, as patriarch of Jerusalem.

Baldwin created few lordships, preferring to reward his nobles with fiefs of revenues rather than land.

Sometime after his accession Baldwin set aside his Armenian wife and in 1113 married Adelaide del Vasto, widow of Roger I of Sicily, agreeing to the condition that if they had no children the throne would pass to Adelaide's son Roger II of Sicily. The nobility and clergy of the kingdom were largely legitimist in sentiment and favored the succession of Baldwin's brother Eustace. When the king was thought to be in danger of dying during an illness in the winter of 1116–1117, opposition forced him to repudiate Adelaide and the marriage treaty.

Baldwin secured and greatly expanded the territory that he had inherited, defeating three major Fatimid invasions (1101, 1102, and 1105) and capturing the coastal towns of Arsuf and Caesarea (1101), Acre (1104), Beirut (1110), and Sidon (1110). Although his own forces were small, he was regularly able to enlist the military support of pilgrims from the West as well as the Italian merchant republics, which he rewarded with quarters and privileges in the conquered cities, thus bringing their trading interests to the new kingdom. Baldwin's status as the senior Frankish ruler in Outremer was manifested through his arbitration in the dispute over the county of Tripoli (1109), which recognized the claims of Bertrand of Toulouse and imposed a reconciliation on the rival parties.

In 1113 Baldwin managed to repulse an invasion of Galilee by the Seljuks of Mosul and Damascus, despite sustaining a defeat at al-Sannabra. In the period of relative peace that followed he attempted to secure the eastern and southern frontiers of the kingdom, which he had already explored with reconnaissances in force in 1100 and 1107. In 1115–1116 he constructed a great castle at Shaubak in the region of Edom, which he named Montréal, and he subsequently explored the country to the south as far as the Red Sea.

Baldwin's last campaign, in 1118, was directed against Egypt, but although the army captured the coastal town of Farama (March 22), it was unwilling to advance on Cairo. Baldwin became gravely ill due to the opening of an old wound, which worsened as the Franks withdrew toward Palestine. He died at El-Arish on April 2, having named his brother Eustace as his heir but recommending Baldwin of Bourcq as a successor if Eustace refused the inheritance. On April 7 Baldwin I was buried alongside his brother Godfrey in the Church of the Holy Sepulchre in Jerusalem.

Alan V. Murray

See also

Crusades in the Holy Land, Christian; Jerusalem, Latin Kingdom of; Ramla, First Battle of; Ramla, Second Battle of; Ramla, Third Battle of

References

Gindler, Paul. *Graf Balduin I. von Edessa.* Halle, Germanmy: Kaemmerer, 1901.

Hiestand, Rudolf. "König Balduin und sein Tanzbär." *Archiv für Kulturgeschichte* 70 (1988): 343–360.

Mayer, Hans Eberhard. *Mélanges sur l'histoire du royaume latin de Jérusalem.* Paris: Académie des Inscriptions et Belles-Lettres, 1984.

Murray, Alan V. *The Crusader Kingdom of Jerusalem: A Dynastic History, 1099–1125.* Oxford, UK: Prosopographica et Genealogica, 2000.

Baldwin II of Constantinople (1217–1273)

The last emperor of the Latin Empire ruling from Constantinople (1240–1261). Baldwin was born in Constantinople in 1217, the son of Peter of Courtenay and Yolande of Flanders. He was only 11 when his brother Emperor Robert died in 1228. The Latin barons of Constantinople appointed as regent first Baldwin's older sister Marie and then Narjot of Toucy before coming to an agreement with John of Brienne (d. 1237), the former king of Jerusalem. According to this agreement of March 1229, Baldwin was to marry Marie, John's daughter, and was to receive at age 21 the "kingdom of Nicaea." John dispatched Baldwin as his representative to the French royal court. A number of documents have survived referring to Baldwin's activities in the Low Countries and France. There during 1238–1239 he mortgaged the relic of the Crown of Thorns, along with the castle and marquesette of Namur and the county of Auxerre, to French king Louis IX in order to raise much-needed funds for his empire.

In July 1239 Baldwin returned with a small army to Constantinople, where he was crowned emperor, probably at Easter 1240. On his way to the capital, Baldwin concluded an alliance with the Cumans in Bulgaria. He returned to the West in 1244 to recruit further support, returning to Constantinople in 1248. In 1249 Baldwin accompanied Louis IX to Damietta during the French king's unsuccessful attempt to conquer Egypt. During that time, his wife Marie visited Cyprus and France, where she spent several years seeking financial support. Nine years later, the impoverished

Baldwin II was obliged to mortgage his own son Philip to the Venetian merchants John and Angelo Ferro (1258).

On the political and military fronts, the reign of Baldwin was as disastrous as the empire's financial situation. Nevertheless, in June 1241 Baldwin secured a truce with John III Vatatzes, emperor of Nicaea, for a period of two years. In 1244 he renewed this truce for another year. During 1240–1243 Baldwin also tried to secure an alliance with the Sultanate of Rum, and in August 1243 he even approached Blanche of Castile, queen of France, to give one of her nieces in marriage to the Seljuk sultan. In May 1246 he contacted King Alfonso X of Castile in order to obtain troops for Constantinople, and that August he concluded an agreement with Don Pelayo Pérez Correa, master of the Order of Santiago, to the same effect.

The situation changed dramatically after the deaths of John Vatatzes (1254) and Theodore II Laskaris (1258), as the usurper Michael VIII Palaiologos became emperor of Nicaea. Michael's policy was decidedly both more shrewd and more aggressive, having as final purpose the recovery of Constantinople, to which the Frankish defeat at Pelagonia (1259) was a prelude. Michael played for time in July 1261, agreeing to another truce with Baldwin while preparing the final onslaught. As a result, the same month (July 25), Michael's general Alexios Strategopoulos unexpectedly recaptured Constantinople. Baldwin fled via the Peloponnese to Italy, where he agreed to the Treaties of Viterbo (May 24 and 27, 1267), which granted the suzerainty of the Frankish Peloponnese and other regions to Charles I of Anjou, king of Naples. Baldwin died in Sicily in October 1273. His son Philip succeeded as titular emperor (r. 1273–1285).

BENJAMIN HENDRICKX

See also
Constantinople, Latin Empire of; John of Brienne; Louis IX, King of France; Michael VIII Palaiologos

References
Geneakoplos, Denos J. "Greco-Latin Relations on the Eve of the Byzantine Restoration: The Battle of Pelagonia." *Dumbarton Oaks Papers* 7 (1956): 101–141.
Lock Peter. *The Franks in the Aegean, 1204–1500.* London: Longman, 1995.
Longnon, Jean. *L'empire latin de Constantinople et la principauté de Morée.* Paris: Payot, 1949.
Wolff, Robert L. "The Latin Empire of Constantinople, 1204–1261." In *A History of the Crusades*, Vol. 2, ed. Kenneth M. Setton et al., 153–203. 2nd ed. Philadelphia: University of Pennsylvania Press, 2016.
Wolff, Robert L. "Mortgage and Redemption of an Emperor's Son: Castile and the Latin Empire of Constantinople." *Speculum* 29 (1954): 225–303.

Baldwin II of Jerusalem (1060–1131)

Count of Edessa (1100–1118) and second king of Jerusalem (1118–1131). Born in France in 1060, Baldwin was a son of Hugh I, count of Rethel, and Melisende of Montlhéry. In 1096 Baldwin joined the First Crusade (1096–1099), traveling in the army of his kinsman, Godfrey of Bouillon, and later took service with Godfrey's brother Baldwin (later Baldwin I of Jerusalem), who had established himself as count of Edessa in 1097–1098 and appointed Baldwin II as his successor there when he left to become ruler of Jerusalem after Godfrey's death (1100). Soon after his accession as count, Baldwin II married Morphia, daughter of the Armenian lord Gabriel of Melitene, by whom he would have four daughters.

Most of Baldwin's reign in Edessa was spent in defending the county from Seljuk Turk attacks. In 1104 he was captured by the Seljuks of Mosul while besieging the Muslim city of Harran; during his subsequent four-year captivity in Mosul, Edessa was governed by the Antiochene Normans Tancred (until late 1104) and Richard of the Principate (1104–1108), neither of whom attempted to ransom him. Baldwin's release in 1108 was secured through the efforts of his cousin and vassal Joscelin of Courtenay, Lord of Turbessel. However, his restoration to Edessa only came about after a short but intensive war against Richard and Tancred in which each side enlisted the aid of Seljuk allies against their Christian opponents. Hostility between Baldwin and Tancred persisted until 1110, when a reconciliation was imposed by King Baldwin I of Jerusalem. From around this time Count Baldwin was forced to abandon much of his territory east of the Euphrates River, owing to intensifying Seljuk pressure; fresh strife occurred in 1112, when he accused Joscelin of Courtenay (whose lands, situated west of the river, were safer from attack) of insufficient contributions to the defense of the county. Joscelin surrendered his fiefs and went to Jerusalem, where Baldwin I made him lord of Tiberias.

In 1114 the city of Edessa itself was besieged by a Seljuk army led by Aq Sunqur al-Bursuqi, *atabeg* (governor) of Mosul, but the threat ended owing to the victory of Roger of Antioch over a coalition organized by Seljuk sultan Muhammad at the Battle of Tell Danith (September 14, 1115). Baldwin used this opportunity to expand his territory through the conquest of several of the independent Armenian principalities to the north, including the strongholds of Raban, Kesoun, Bira, and Gargar (1115–1117).

By 1118 the security of the county of Edessa had been sufficiently established that Count Baldwin was able to visit Jerusalem, where he arrived to find that King Baldwin I had died on April 2 while campaigning in Egypt, having named his elder brother Eustace of Boulogne as successor. However, a powerful party led by the patriarch Arnulf and Joscelin of Courtenay promoted Count Baldwin's candidacy and succeeded in having him consecrated as king on April 14, 1118. As it was possible that Eustace or one of his descendants would claim the throne at a future date, Baldwin II attempted to secure his position through new appointments within the clergy and nobility of the kingdom. He also secured Joscelin's support by naming him as Baldwin's successor in Edessa.

Much of the first half of Baldwin II's reign was absorbed by the defense of the principality of Antioch after the defeat of Prince Roger at the Ager Sanguinis (Field of Blood, June 28, 1119). Baldwin marched north in August and was victorious at Zerdana against the Seljuk Turks of Mardin and Damascus, only returning to Jerusalem for his coronation at Christmas. Until 1126 he governed Antioch as regent for its underage heir, Bohemund II, and led further campaigns to defend the Frankish north in 1120, 1122, and 1123. During the last of these Baldwin was captured by the Seljuks and remained a prisoner until August 1124. The repeated campaigning in the north and the consequent disruption to government as well as the granting of lordships and offices to the king's relatives and their vassals led to opposition among the Jerusalem nobility, some of whom made an abortive attempt to depose Baldwin during his absence in favor of Count Charles of Flanders.

After his release from captivity Baldwin devoted himself to the defense of his kingdom, undertaking major campaigns against Damascene territory in 1126 and 1129. During this time he also arranged for his eldest daughter Melisende to marry Fulk V, count of Anjou; they and their son Baldwin III (born 1130) succeeded as joint rulers on the king's death on August 21, 1131. Baldwin II's second daughter, Alice, married Prince Bohemund II of Antioch, and the third, Hodierna, married Count Raymond II of Tripoli; the youngest, Yveta, who had served as a hostage for him after his second captivity, became a nun, ending her life as abbess of the convent of St. Lazarus at Bethany.

ALAN V. MURRAY

See also
Ager Sanguinis, Battle of; Baldwin I of Jerusalem; Edessa, County of; Godfrey of Bouillon; Harran, Battle of; Jerusalem, Latin Kingdom of

References
Mayer, Hans Eberhard. *The Crusader Kingdom of Jerusalem: A Dynastic History, 1099–1125.* Oxford, UK: Prosopographica et Genealogica, 2000.

Mayer, Hans Eberhard. "Jérusalem et Antioche au temps de Baudouin II." *Académie des Inscriptions et Belles-Lettres: Comptes-rendus* 4 (1980): 717–733.
Murray, Alan V. "Dynastic Continuity or Dynastic Change? The Accession of Baldwin II and the Nobility of the Kingdom of Jerusalem." *Medieval Prosopography* 13 (1992): 1–27.
Nicholson, Robert L. "The Growth of the Latin States, 1118–1144." In *A History of the Crusades,* Vol. 6, ed. Kenneth M. Setton, 410–447. Madison: University of Wisconsin Press, 1969.

Baldwin III of Jerusalem (1130–1163)

King of Jerusalem (1145–1163) and the eldest son of Queen Melisende and King Fulk. Born in 1130, Baldwin was still an infant when his grandfather Baldwin II died in 1131, having arranged that Fulk would have to share power with his wife and son. The chronicler William of Tyre noted that the boy was well educated in history, law, and war, as befitting a future king.

When Fulk died in 1143, Baldwin III was still a minor, and Melisende became regent. Clearly Melisende wanted to retain the power she had wielded since Fulk's reign, but she could not lead troops into battle, whereas military success would strengthen Baldwin III's hand. In 1144 at age 14, Baldwin III led his first campaign, at Wadi Musa in Transjordan. Yet at the end of that year when Imad ad-Din Zangi, ruler of Mosul, besieged Edessa (modern-day Sanliurfa, Turkey), Melisende did not allow her son to head north, sending instead men loyal to her. The queen had already built up supporters by dispensing lands, offices, and other privileges. Now these men could help her circumscribe Baldwin III's independence, even though they could not prevent Zangi from taking Edessa.

Zangi's victory, however, eventually prompted the Second Crusade (1147–1149), led by Conrad III of Germany and Louis VII of France. When these rulers arrived in Outremer in 1148, Baldwin III convinced Conrad to attack Muslim Damascus, a plan approved by the crusade leaders and Jerusalem's High Court in June of that year (although it is not clear that Melisende agreed to the proposal). The campaign failed miserably, and Damascus increasingly turned toward Nur al-Din, Zangi's younger son and lord of Aleppo from 1146. Nur al-Din became the foremost enemy of the Franks of Outremer, unifying Muslims under the banner of jihad (holy war).

Nur al-Din's success contrasted markedly with power struggles in Jerusalem. Although Baldwin III attained his majority in 1145, Melisende continued their joint rule with the support of her younger son Amalric, the higher clergy, and several great lords. Baldwin had some lesser nobles on his side, and he had to help both Antioch and the last Christian strongholds in Edessa. From 1149 until 1152, Outremer had to face the problems posed by Nur al-Din and essentially separate governments in Jerusalem run by the queen mother and the young king.

Matters came to a head at Easter in 1152, when the king forced Melisende to give up her formal role in government and retire to her lands in Nablus. In the following years, according to William of Tyre, Baldwin became undisputed overlord of all Outremer. Count Joscelin II of Edessa was captured by the Seljuk Turks in 1150, Count Raymond II of Tripoli was murdered in 1152, and Princess Constance of Antioch, widowed in 1149, did not remarry until 1153. The king headed north when danger threatened, simultaneously trying to prevent attack from the south by building a castle at Gaza. In 1153 he was finally free to besiege Ascalon. His victory following a nine-month siege brought vast amounts of plunder into the kingdom and toppled the last Fatimid stronghold in Palestine.

Baldwin III now set his sights on Egypt, although Nur al-Din's annexation of Damascus in 1154 and his subsequent attacks on the kingdom prevented an Egyptian campaign. Yet it seems likely that the king did not give up his designs there. He came to terms with Byzantine emperor Manuel I Komnenos after Reynald, the new prince of Antioch, and T'oros of Armenia attacked Byzantine-controlled Cyprus in 1156.

By 1157, the rulers agreed that Baldwin III would allow Manuel to punish Reynald, while Manuel would lend aid against Nur al-Din. Manuel also provided Baldwin his niece Theodora as queen, along with a rich dowry; the marriage took place in 1158. Manuel himself traveled to Antioch, where he humbled Reynald and treated with Baldwin III. Then Manuel concluded a truce with Nur al-Din.

These arrangements among Jerusalem, Byzantium, and Aleppo changed the balance of power in the eastern Mediterranean. Nur al-Din no longer had to fear an imperial attack and in return promised to aid Manuel against the Seljuk Turks. Manuel also managed to exert influence over northern Syria for some two decades. This would not have been possible if Nur al-Din had not threatened the Latin Christians. In this new situation, neither Christians nor Muslims could destroy the other.

Despite heightened imperial claims over Antioch, the status quo did not change. Baldwin III remained the undisputed sovereign over all Outremer; for the medieval chronicler William of Tyre, Baldwin was the greatest ruler of the Kingdom of Jerusalem. Taken ill in Tripoli, Baldwin III insisted on being carried within his own borders before he died childless on February 10, 1163. He was succeeded by his brother Amalric, count of Jaffa and Ascalon.

DEBORAH GERISH

See also
Amalric of Jerusalem; Conrad III, King of Germany; Crusades in the Holy Land, Christian; Jerusalem, Latin Kingdom of; Louis VII, King of France; Manuel I Komnenos, Emperor; Nur al-Din; Zangi, Imad ad-Din

References
Edbury, Peter W., and John G. Rowe. *William of Tyre, Historian of the Latin East.* Cambridge: Cambridge University Press, 1988.
Forey, Alan J. "The Failure of the Siege of Damascus in 1148." *Journal of Medieval History* 10 (1984): 13–23.
Mayer, Hans Eberhard. "Studies in the History of Queen Melisende." *Dumbarton Oaks Papers* 26 (1972), 95–182.
Mayer, Hans Eberhard. "The Succession to Baldwin II of Jerusalem: English Impact on the East." *Dumbarton Oaks Papers* 39 (1985): 139–147.
Mayer, Hans Eberhard. "The Wheel of Fortune: Seignorial Vicissitudes under Kings Fulk and Baldwin III of Jerusalem." *Speculum* 65 (1990): 860–877.

Baldwin IV of Jerusalem (1161–1185)

King of Jerusalem (1174–1185) known as the Leper King. Born in the early summer of 1161, Baldwin was the son of Amalric, then count of Jaffa, and his first wife, Agnes of Courtenay. Although Amalric's marriage was annulled when he became king of Jerusalem in 1163, Baldwin and his sister Sibyl were legitimized by Pope Alexander III. In 1170 the chronicler William of Tyre was appointed Baldwin's tutor and observed that the prince suffered from a loss of feeling in his right hand and arm. Although leprosy could have been considered a possible cause, there would have been no visible symptoms during Baldwin's childhood, so no positive diagnosis could have been made then.

When King Amalric died, Baldwin was 13 years old and was crowned king on July 15, 1174. At first the seneschal Miles of Plancy ruled in Baldwin's name, but when Miles was assassinated in October 1174, the High Court of the kingdom appointed Amalric's cousin Raymond III of Tripoli as regent. Because of these crises in Jerusalem, Saladin, ruler of Egypt, was able to annex Damascus without any opposition from the Franks. In 1175 Raymond made peace with Saladin, thus leaving him free to make further gains in

Muslim Syria. Consequently Outremer faced the prospect of encirclement by a single Islamic power.

Baldwin assumed direct rule in the summer of 1176 at the age of 15. He was beginning to show the symptoms of lepromatous leprosy, perhaps triggered by the onset of puberty: his hands and feet and face were disfigured by nodules. Because of his illness, Baldwin could not marry, and his mother, Agnes of Courtenay, took on the role of queen mother and became an influential member of his court. The king's chief advisers were his uncle, Joscelin III of Courtenay, who was made seneschal, and Reynald of Châtillon, former prince of Antioch. Baldwin was alarmed by the growth of Saladin's power and refused to renew the peace that Raymond III of Tripoli had made with him when regent. Whenever his health permitted, the king took an active part in the wars that followed. Despite his disabilities, he was a skilled rider and had been taught to fight left-handed. On November 25, 1177, his forces inflicted a crushing defeat on Saladin's invading army at the Battle of Mont Gisard, at which Baldwin was present and during which he relied heavily on the military expertise of Prince Reynald.

In 1176 Baldwin's sister Sibyl had married William Longsword, son of William V of Montferrat, a union arranged by Raymond of Tripoli while regent. However, William died a few months later, leaving his wife pregnant. Their son was named Baldwin after the king, and the succession was thus ensured, but it was essential that Sibyl should marry again so that a new husband could take over the government when the king became too ill to rule. In 1179 Hugh III, duke of Burgundy, agreed (with the assent of King Louis VII of France) to resign his duchy to his son and come to Jerusalem to marry Sibyl. In Holy Week 1180 before Hugh's arrival, the king's cousins Bohemund III of Antioch and Raymond III of Tripoli invaded the kingdom with an army, intending to depose Baldwin and marry Sibyl to a husband of their choice. The king outwitted them by arranging Sibyl's marriage to the French nobleman Guy of Lusignan, who was present in Jerusalem, before his cousins reached the city. This decision, made without consulting the High Court, caused resentment in the long run but frustrated the attempted coup. Baldwin then arranged a two-year truce with Saladin and used the time to try to restore unity among the Franks.

When the truce expired in 1182, Saladin launched a series of attacks on the kingdom but met with determined opposition and withdrew his forces to campaign against the Zangid princes of Iraq. During his absence Baldwin led a raid on the desert city of Bosra, during which he recaptured the great cave fortress of Cave de Suète east of the Jordan. During 1183

Detail of a depiction of the coronation of Baldwin IV, king of Jerusalem during 1174–1185, from *Histoire d'Outremer* by William of Tyre, 15th century. (The British Library)

Baldwin's health deteriorated severely. The leprosy attacked his hands and feet so that he could no longer ride but had to be carried in a litter, and he became functionally blind. Saladin returned to Damascus in August 1183 and prepared to invade Galilee. Baldwin mustered the host there but ran a high fever and could not accompany it, so he appointed his official heir, Guy of Lusignan, as his regent. Guy did not offer battle, and Saladin's forces were free to plunder at will. Nevertheless, because the Frankish army was undefeated, Saladin had no option but to withdraw to Damascus, having made no territorial gains.

Although Guy's strategy had been effective, Baldwin was informed that he had only adopted it because many of the crown vassals refused to obey his orders. The king considered this too dangerous a situation to tolerate, and he convened the High Court, dismissed Guy as regent, and resumed power himself. In order to bar Guy from the succession, Baldwin had his five-year-old nephew Baldwin (V) crowned as coruler. Saladin attacked Prince Reynald's chief castle, Kerak, at this time, and the king accompanied his army in his litter to aid the defenders. As the royal army approached, Saladin's forces withdrew. Baldwin then tried to have the marriage of Sibyl and Guy annulled, but they refused to cooperate and withdrew to Guy's county of Ascalon, where they defied the king.

For most of the year 1184, Baldwin lived in seclusion; his uncle, Joscelin the Seneschal, ruled in his name. Early in 1185 Baldwin IV developed a high fever that proved fatal. He summoned the High Court to his deathbed and on its advice appointed Raymond III of Tripoli as regent for the eight-year-old coruler, Baldwin V, to whom the crown vassals did homage. Baldwin IV died at age 24 on March 16, 1185, and was buried in the Church of the Holy Sepulchre at the foot of Mount Calvary, the most holy place in Christendom, which he had spent his life defending.

BERNARD HAMILTON

See also
Amalric of Jerusalem; Jerusalem, Latin Kingdom of; Mont Giscard, Battle of; Saladin

References
Hamilton, Bernard. "Baldwin the Leper as War Leader." In *From Clermont to Jerusalem: The Crusades and Crusader Societies, 1095–1500,* ed. Alan V. Murray, 119–130. Turnhout, Belgium: Brepols, 1998.
Hamilton, Bernard. *The Leper King and His Heirs: Baldwin IV and the Crusader Kingdom of Jerusalem.* Cambridge: Cambridge University Press, 2000.
Lyons, Malcolm C., and David E. P. Jackson. *Saladin: The Politics of Holy War.* Cambridge: Cambridge University Press, 1982.
Vogtherr, Thomas. "Die Regierungsdaten der lateinischer Könige von Jerusalem." *Zeitschrift des deutschen Palästina-Vereins* 110 (1994): 51–81.

Balfour Declaration (November 2, 1917)

The Balfour Declaration of November 2, 1917, was a promise by the British government to support the creation of a national homeland for the Jewish people in Palestine. The British government issued the declaration in an effort to gain the support of Jews around the world for the Allied war effort. The promise apparently contradicted an earlier pledge by London to the Arabs to support the establishment of an independent Arab state after World War I. The Balfour Declaration helped encourage Jewish immigration to Palestine during the 1920s and 1930s but alienated Arabs from the British mandate government there. Indirectly, the Balfour Declaration led to the creation of the State of Israel in 1948 and ongoing conflict between Arabs and Jews in the Middle East.

Before World War I, Palestine had been a part of the Ottoman Empire. Palestine included the Sinai Peninsula and parts of present-day Lebanon and Syria. A small number of Jewish settlements were located in Palestine, with a total population of about 50,000 people. The Zionist movement, developed in the 19th century, taught that Judaism was not only a religion but was also a national group. Zionists called for Jewish immigration to traditional Jewish lands to establish a Jewish state for Jews from around the world. Zionism was formally organized in 1897 when smaller groups came together to create the World Zionist Organization at Basel, Switzerland. Supporters of Zionism included influential Jews and non-Jews throughout Europe and America.

When World War I began, Zionists urged the various governments to support their movement. The most fertile ground was in Great Britain. Although the total number of Jews in Britain was small, they included influential individuals such as Sir Herbert Samuel and the Rothschild banking family. The leader of the Zionists in Britain was Dr. Chaim Weizmann, an eminent chemistry professor at Manchester University. Events during the spring of 1917 aided Weizmann's campaign for British support for a Jewish homeland in Palestine.

The first such event was the March Revolution in Russia. Some of the more prominent leaders of the revolution were Jews, and Weizmann argued that they were more likely to keep Russia in the war if an Allied goal was a Jewish homeland. Another important event was the entry of the United States into the war in April 1917. The large Jewish population in America could campaign for greater and more immediate U.S. contributions to the war effort. Jewish financial contributions toward the war effort might be increased with support for a homeland as well. Weizmann also told his friends in the British government that support for a Jewish homeland might prevent German Jews from giving their full support to the kaiser's war effort.

Arthur James Balfour, who was foreign secretary, supported a promise of a Jewish homeland after the war. On a trip to the United States, he conferred with U.S. Supreme Court justice Louis Brandeis, a Zionist. Brandeis was an adviser to President Woodrow Wilson and told Balfour that the president supported a homeland for the Jews. At the time, however, Wilson was reluctant to give it open support. Other prominent Americans, such as former presidential candidate William Jennings Bryan, supported a Jewish homeland, many because they believed that it would fulfill biblical prophecies.

Members of the Zionist movement in Britain helped draft a declaration that was approved by the British cabinet and released by Balfour on November 2, 1917. The key sentence in the document was "His Majesty's Government views with favour the establishment in Palestine of a national home for the Jewish people." The declaration went on to state that the civil and religious rights of the existing non-Jewish peoples in Palestine were not to be prejudiced. In response to fears by some Jews that a homeland in Palestine would harm their efforts to assimilate into other societies, the declaration also called for nothing that would harm those efforts. The French government pledged its support for the declaration on February 11, 1918. Wilson finally gave open approval in a letter to Rabbi Stephen Wise on October 29, 1918.

The declaration did indeed win Jewish support for the Allied war effort but had unintended effects as well. Correspondence between British high commissioner in Egypt Henry McMahon and Sharif Hussein of Mecca in 1915 had promised the establishment of an independent Arab state upon the defeat of the Ottomans. It was understood that this state would include Palestine. The declaration was also a violation of the Sykes-Picot Agreement between Great Britain and France that provided for joint rule over the area directly after the war. The apparent double-dealing by the British government alienated many Arabs and caused them to doubt whether they could trust British promises.

At the end of World War I, the League of Nations granted a mandate over Palestine to Great Britain. Language from the Balfour Declaration was incorporated into the mandate's wording. Over the next 30 years, the Jewish population of Palestine increased from 50,000 to 600,000 people. This dramatic increase of Jews in Palestine led to numerous clashes with Palestinians already living there. Ultimately, the task of trying to keep conflicting promises to Arabs and Jews proved too much for the British. They gave up their mandate in 1948, and the State of Israel was created. The result has been hostility and sporadic wars between Jews and Arabs ever since.

Tim J. Watts

See also
Arab Revolt of World War I; Ottoman Empire; Palestine and Syria Campaign, World War I; Sykes-Picot Agreement; Zionism

References
Egremont, Max. *Balfour: A Life of Arthur James Balfour*. London: Collins, 1980.
Sanders, Ronald. *The High Walls of Jerusalem: A History of the Balfour Declaration and the Birth of the British Mandate for Palestine*. New York: Holt, Rinehart and Winston, 1983.
Stein, Leonard. *The Balfour Declaration*. 1961; reprint, London and Jerusalem: Magnus Press, Hebrew University, 1983.

Balkans, Ottoman Conquest of the (1350s–1593)

Ottoman expansion into the Balkans began early in its excursions against the Byzantine Empire in the 14th century. Okhan, son of Osman (founder of the Ottoman dynasty), was stationed in northeastern Anatolia across the Dardanelles from Constantinople, putting him in an advantageous strategic position to strike the capital of Byzantium. However, he sometimes cooperated in joint ventures with the Byzantines in military engagements against common enemies from Europe.

In one of these western sojourns into the Balkans, Ottoman forces began their expansion into the Slavic Balkan states surrounding the Byzantine Empire. Ottoman attacks on Serbia, particularly the Battle of Maritsa (1371), broke that kingdom up into various states. Moreover, Ottoman forces had also met initial stubborn resistance by local Slavic states, such as Bosnia, but these states were unable to replenish their troop numbers during the long term. In contrast, Ottoman forces were able to muster troops from their conquered territories to offset their losses. During the next several centuries after endemic warfare in the Balkan region, Ottoman forces were able to wear down and eventually conquer all the major Slavic states piecemeal, with the exception of Croatia.

The first important engagements involving a major Balkan state came between Ottoman Empire forces and Serbia. Despite a series of losses against Slavic states in the Battle of Plocnik against the Serbs (1386) and the Battle of Bileca against the Bosnians (1388), Ottoman sultan Murad I moved his forces toward Serbia, arriving in Pristina on June 14, 1389. On June 28, 1389, Ottoman and Serbian forces met on the battlefield at Kosovo. Despite having the initial advantage after a first charge, the Serbians were defeated by a crushing Ottoman cavalry and infantry counterattack. Murad, however, died in the battle. Prince Lazar, commanding the Serbian forces, also was killed, as were most of his men. The annihilation of their forces in the battle obliged the Serbians to concede Ottoman dominance to include the payment of tribute and supplying men for the Ottoman Army.

The Ottomans then concentrated on destroying the remnants of Byzantium. Murad's successor, Bayezid, laid siege to Constantinople in 1395. Hungary then took the lead in forming a coalition against the Ottomans. These forces were, however, utterly defeated by Bayezid at the Battle of Nicopolis (1396), giving the Ottomans regional hegemony. The Ottomans then transferred their capital from Bursa to Edina in Thrace. Despite losses in the Middle East, the Ottomans were able to expand in the Balkans at the expense of the Byzantine Empire, now in protracted decline.

When Mehmet II became Ottoman sultan in 1451, he pursued the final conquest of the Byzantine Empire, taking Constantinople in 1453 after a protracted siege. It became the capital city of the Ottoman Empire. Mehmet II then secured the outlying regions of Greece not under Ottoman control.

The remaining independent Balkan states were subsequently conquered piecemeal by the Ottomans during the course of the next century. In 1459, the Ottomans secured the Serbian city of Smederevo. Bosnia was finally taken in 1463. Montenegro was conquered in 1499, and Belgrade was secured in 1521 along with adjacent territories in Hungary. Despite the steady depletion of its personnel strength, Croatia was able to resist the Ottoman forces far longer than other Slavic state in large part because of its fortified cities. After the Battle of Sisak (1593), when Ottoman forces fought against the Croatians and their Habsburg allies, Croatia was able to maintain its independence from further Ottoman incursions. The Ottomans then chose to move against Central Europe, threatening the Habsburg domains.

Abraham O. Mendoza

See also
Bayezid II; Byzantine-Ottoman Wars; Mehmed II, Sultan; Nikopolis, Crusade in

References
Kinross, Patrick. *The Ottoman Centuries.* New York: Morrow, 1977.
Shaw, Stanford. *The History of the Ottoman Empire and Turkey.* New York: Cambridge University Press, 1977.
Wheatcroft, Andrew. *The Ottomans.* London: Viking, 1993.

Balkan Wars (1912–1913)

Part of the decline of the Ottoman Empire, the Balkan Wars of 1912–1913 were a series of sharp and bloody conflicts in Southeastern Europe that led to World War I. Most of this region had come under Ottoman domination by the end of the 14th century. During the 19th century, nation-states emerged from the weakened structure of the Ottoman Empire. These states, including Bulgaria, Greece, Montenegro, and Serbia, all harbored irredentist aspirations against the Ottomans, and many of these aspirations overlapped, especially in Macedonia. For some time these rivalries precluded the formation of a Balkan alliance directed against the Ottomans. The Young Turk revolution in 1908 and its objective of an Ottoman revival, however, engendered closer cooperation among these Balkan states. An opportunity for the realization of their nationalist objectives arose when the weakness of the Ottomans became apparent during the Italo-Ottoman War of 1911–1912.

With the support of Russia, the leaders of which sought to regain the position lost in Southeastern Europe during the Bosnian Crisis of 1908–1909, Bulgaria and Serbia signed an alliance in March 1912. This alliance contained provisions for the rough division of Ottoman territories, including a partition of Macedonia into a Bulgarian zone and a contested zone to be arbitrated by the Russian tsar. Bulgaria and Serbia then signed bilateral agreements with Greece and Montenegro during the spring and summer of 1912. Other than the Bulgarian-Serbian agreement, the Balkan allies made little effort to arrange division of any territories conquered from the Ottomans.

The fighting, between Montenegro and the Ottoman Empire, began on October 8, 1912. Bulgaria, Greece, and Serbia entered the war on October 18. Each of the Balkan allies separately confronted their common enemy. The most important theater was in Thrace, where a strong Bulgarian offensive overcame Ottoman resistance at Kirk Killase (Lozengrad) and at the massive battle raging from Buni Hisar to Lyule Burgas. At the same time, the Bulgarians surrounded and besieged the Ottomans at Adrianople (Edirne). The Bulgarian offensive thrust the Ottomans to the final defensive positions at Chataldzha (Çatalca), about 20 miles outside of Constantinople. Only on November 16–17 did Ottoman forces rally to defeat a Bulgarian attempt to cross the Chataldzha lines and seize their capital. Smaller Bulgarian units meanwhile proceeded against little opposition into western Thrace and toward Salonika.

Elsewhere, the Greek Army advanced in two directions against slight opposition. The northwesterly thrust moved into Epirus and besieged Janina (Ioannina). The northeasterly push overran Thessaly and entered Salonika only a day ahead of the Bulgarian unit moving south from Bulgaria with the same objective. An uneasy condominium ensued in that city. The Greek Navy held the Ottoman fleet at bay and seized the Aegean Islands. One section of the Montenegrin Army advanced into the Sandjak of Novibazar, while most of the rest of the Montenegrin force besieged the northern Albanian town of Scutari (Shkodër). The main part of the Serbian Army easily defeated the Ottomans at Kumanovo in northern Macedonia and then proceeded to take most of the rest of Macedonia. Meanwhile, other Serbian units occupied Kosovo. By the time

A photograph of the battlefield during the Siege of Adrianople, November 3, 1912–March 26, 1913, during the Balkan Wars. (Library of Congress)

the warring parties agreed to an armistice on December 3, the only territories in Europe remaining to the Ottomans were the besieged cities of Adrianople, Janina, and Scutari; the Gallipoli Peninsula; and that part of eastern Thrace behind the Chataldzha lines.

While the Balkan allies and the Ottomans assembled in London on December 16 to negotiate a peace settlement, the ambassadors of the Great Powers convened nearby to direct the course of the peace settlement and to protect their own interests. This ambassadors conference, on the insistence of Austria-Hungary and Italy, recognized the independence of an Albanian state that some Albanian notables had proclaimed in Vlorë on November 28. This state blocked Serbian and Montenegrin claims to territories on the eastern shore of the Adriatic Sea. These claims had the strong support of Russia. At the same time, the Austrians demanded that Serbian troops evacuate those portions of northern Albania occupied that autumn. Talks between the Balkan allies and the Ottomans soon stalled, mainly over the issue of Adrianople, and hostilities resumed on February 3, 1913.

On March 6, Janina fell to the Greeks. On the 26th the Bulgarians, with Serbian help, took Adrianople. The Montenegrins and assisting Serbian units bogged down around Scutari. Only on April 23, after the departure of the Serbs under pressure from the Great Powers, did the Montenegrins succeed in entering the city. Nevertheless, the major powers, especially Austria-Hungary, refused to sanction a Montenegrin occupation of Scutari because the London Ambassadors Conference had assigned it to the new Albanian state. After threats and a show of force, together with the promise of generous subsidies, the Montenegrins evacuated Scutari. On May 30, 1913, the Balkan allies and the Ottomans signed a peace treaty in London. With the Treaty of London, the Ottoman Empire ceded its European territories west of a straight line drawn between Enos and Media (Enez-Midye).

By then, however, the loose Balkan alliance was disintegrating. The Serbs sought compensation for Albania in Macedonian areas assigned to Bulgaria by the alliance treaty but occupied by Serbia during the previous autumn fighting. At the same time, the Bulgarians and Greeks were skirmishing over Macedonia. On May 5, 1913, the Greeks and Serbs signed an agreement directed against the Bulgarians. A feeble Russian attempt at arbitration in June failed. On the night of June 29–30, the Bulgarians launched probing attacks against Serbian positions in Macedonia. The Greeks and Serbs utilized these attacks to implement their alliance, and the Second Balkan War resulted.

Greek and Serbian counterattacks thrust the Bulgarian forces back. Taking advantage of the situation, Romanian and Ottoman troops joined in the attack on Bulgaria. The Romanians objected to the establishment of a strong Bulgaria on their southern frontier and sought compensation in the town of Silistra and in southern Dobrudzha. The Ottomans sought to recover Adrianople. The Bulgarians found themselves attacked on all sides. The result was a Bulgarian catastrophe. With no aid forthcoming from any Great Power, the Bulgarians had to seek terms. In the Treaty of Bucharest (August 10, 1913) with Greece, Montenegro, and Serbia and the Treaty of Constantinople (September 30, 1913) with the Ottoman Empire, the Bulgarians acknowledged complete defeat and the loss of much of the gains from the First Balkan War.

The two Balkan wars changed the map of Southeastern Europe. A fragile Albanian state emerged, largely dependent on the Great Powers. Serbia acquired Kosovo and much of Macedonia, almost doubling its territory. Serbia and Montenegro divided the Sandjak of Novibazar between them. Montenegro also gained small areas on its southern border with the new Albanian state. Greece obtained clear title to Crete and also obtained Epirus, including the city of Janina; a large portion of southern and western Macedonia, including Salonika; and the Aegean Islands. Bulgaria, even after defeat in the Second Balkan War, gained central Thrace, including the insignificant Aegean port of Dedeagach, and a piece of Macedonia around Petrich. Romania obtained southern (Bulgarian) Dobrudzha. The Ottomans managed to regain eastern Thrace, which remained its only European possession.

The Balkan wars were the first armed conflicts on European soil in the 20th century and presaged World War I. Mass attacks against entrenched positions, concentrated artillery barrages, and military use of airplanes made their first appearances in European warfare. The two wars resulted in at least 150,000 military dead, with the Bulgarians and Ottomans suffering the heaviest losses. Many more soldiers were wounded or missing. These wars also brought about the deaths from disease of tens of thousands of civilians, and many more were displaced. The Balkan wars left a legacy of frustration for the Bulgarians and Ottomans, providing a basis for continued conflict in World War I. They also imparted a sense of inflated success among the Greeks, Romanians, and Serbs. On two occasions during the Balkan Wars, Austria-Hungary had resorted to threats of force against Serbia to protect Albania. The Austrians would make one more such threat in October 1913 before finally resorting to force. Less than a year after the signing of the Treaty of Bucharest war again erupted in Southeastern Europe, but this time the Third Balkan War metamorphosed into World War I. Within the next five years, all of the participants in the Balkan wars would become involved in further disastrous and costly conflicts. Many of the same battlefields of the Balkan wars, such as Salonika, Gallipoli, and Dorian, saw new fighting. During World War I, the populations of Southeastern Europe again made great sacrifices for nationalist aims.

Richard C. Hall

See also
Constantinople, 1913 Treaty of; Italo-Ottoman War; London, 1913 Treaty of; World War I, Impact on the Middle East; Young Turks

References
Hall, Richard C. *The Balkan Wars, 1912–1913: Prelude to the First World War.* London: Routledge, 2000.
Helmreich, E. C. *The Diplomacy of the Balkan Wars, 1912–1913.* Cambridge, MA: Harvard University Press, 1938.
International Commission to Inquire into the Causes and Conduct of the Balkan Wars. *The Other Balkan Wars.* Washington, DC: Carnegie Endowment, 1993.
Király, Béla K., and Dimitrije Djordevic, eds. *East Central European Society and the Balkan Wars.* Boulder, CO: Social Science Monographs, 1987.

Balta Liman, Convention of (May 1, 1849)

Treaty signed on May 1, 1849, in Balta Liman between Russia and the Ottoman Empire in response to the revolutions that had swept through much of continental Europe in 1848–1849. In the convention, Russia and the Ottoman Empire pledged themselves to regulate the internal politics of the Danubian principalities of Walacia and Moldavia in order to prevent revolutionary movements there. The hospodars, who ruled these principalities, would be nominated by the Ottoman sultan and approved by Russia, thus replacing the former system by which the principalities selected their own leaders. The convention remained in effect for seven years.

Alexander Mikaberidze

See also
Hunkar Iskelesi, Treaty of; Russo-Ottoman Wars

Reference
Jelavich, Barbara. *Russia's Balkan Entanglements, 1806–1914.* New York: Cambridge University Press, 1991.

Baltim, Battle of (October 12–13, 1973)

The Battle of Baltim was a naval engagement during the 1973 Yom Kippur War (Ramadan War). It took place off the Egyptian port of Baltim on the night of October 12–13 and was fought between Egyptian and Israeli missile boats.

The Israeli Navy had been seeking an opportunity to replicate with the Egyptian Navy its victory over the Syrians in the October 6 Battle of Latakia (Ladhakiyya). That chance presented itself on October 12 when four Egyptian Osa-class missile boats sortied from Port Said, Egypt. This move was anticipated. The Israeli Army had launched a ground counterattack in the area that day against Egyptian forces in the hope of regaining the Suez Canal. The Israeli Navy command believed that the missile boats at Port Said would then attempt to flee to the naval base at Alexandria, 110 miles to the west. The Israeli ground attack stalled, however, and Israeli Navy leaders decided to try to draw out the boats by shelling land targets in the Nile Delta area.

Commander Michael Barkai had charge of the flotilla of 10 Israeli missile boats dispatched from Haifa. At 9:00 p.m. local time the missile boats picked up radar contacts and charged in line abreast at 40 knots toward the Egyptian coast, only to discover that they had been chasing a phantom, no doubt the result of freak atmospheric conditions. The Israeli missile boats had been dispatched in a hurry, and 2 had been on station for some time, so 4 of them had fuel barely sufficient to return to Haifa.

Barkai informed Israeli Navy commander Rear Admiral Biny-a-min Telem of the situation, and Telem suggested that Barkai send to Haifa only the four boats that were low on fuel and remain on station with the six remaining. Barkai agreed and shifted his flag from the *Miznak* to the *Herev*. As Barkai was transferring to the *Herev*, the Israelis learned that the four Egyptian boats had sortied from Alexandria and were headed east.

At 11:00 p.m. Barkai immediately ordered his six remaining missile boats to intercept the Egyptians. The Israeli boats moved in pairs on parallel tracks. To the north were the two large Israeli-manufactured Reshef-class boats: the *Reshef* and the *Keshet*. In the center were the *Eliat* (named for the Israeli destroyer sunk by an Egyptian Styx missile in 1967) and the missileless *Misgav*. On the south were the *Herev* and the *Soufa*. The Israelis did not know if the Egyptian boats were aware of their presence.

Just before midnight, Barkai took the *Herev* and the *Soufa* in close to shore to shell Damietta in the Nile Delta. As they were preparing to open fire, the crew of the *Herev* picked up readings off Baltim to the west. In order to determine if it was another false reading, Barkai ordered his northern boats to send up chaff rockets and see if these would draw missile fire. The chaff cloud immediately drew two pairs of Styx rockets, and Barkai responded by ordering his own boats, which were within the 27-mile range of the Egyptian Styx missiles but well beyond the 12 miles of the Israeli Gabriel missiles, to charge what were soon identified as four Egyptian Osa-class missile boats. At 12:15 a.m. the Egyptians began launching their Styx missiles. The situation was tense, for while electronic countermeasures on the Israeli boats would help, the boats themselves would remain one of many targets identified by Styx radar. The Egyptian boats then fired their last barrage of missiles at a range of 18 miles, still well beyond effective Gabriel range, and turned to run back into Alexandria.

The chase was on, with the Israelis endeavoring to close to within their own firing range. Barkai divided up the targets and ordered none of his boats to fire until they had closed to within 10.5 miles. After a 25-minute chase, the *Keshet* closed to within Barkai's imposed range and fired a Gabriel missile that hit one of the Egyptian missile boats, setting it alight. With the *Keshet* taking on water from a burst pipe, the *Misgav* dashed in to finish off the Egyptian missile boat with cannon fire. Meanwhile, the *Reshef* had also fired at and hit another Egyptian missile boat. The *Reshef* then closed with the *Eilat*, which had also fired a missile at the same Egyptian boat, and they sank the Egyptian boat with cannon fire. A third Egyptian missile boat was sunk by the *Herev* and the *Soufa*. The last Egyptian Osa-class boat managed to escape to the protection of the guns and missile defenses of Alexandria. At 1:30 a.m. on October 13, the Israeli boats began turning northeast and ran for Haifa.

The Battle of Latakia and the Battle of Baltim were the two major naval engagements of the war.

Spencer C. Tucker

See also
Latakia, Battle of; Yom Kippur War

References
Erell, Shlomo. "Israeli Saar FPBs Pass Combat Test in the Yom Kippur War." *U.S. Naval Institute Proceedings* (September 1974): 115–118.
Rabinovich, Abraham. *The Boats of Cherbourg: The Secret Israeli Operation That Revolutionized Naval Warfare.* New York: Seaver, 1988.

Bapheus, Battle of (July 27, 1301)

important battle between the Byzantine Empire and the rising Ottoman state led by Osman I. In Ottoman chronicles, the conflict is often described as the Battle of Yalak-Ovasi. Fought in the summer of 1301, the battle is sometimes considered the starting point for Ottoman sovereignty. The battle was part of Osman's campaign to capture Nicaea (modern-day Iznik), a key Byzantine town in western Asia Minor that was the interim capital city of the Byzantine Empire after the Fourth Crusade of 1204 until the Byzantine recapture of Constantinople in 1261.

By the late 13th century the rising Ottoman state, seeking to expand its territory, repeatedly clashed with the Byzantines, who had suffered a number of Ottoman raids. During 1300–1301 Osman, leader of the Ottoman Turks who declared his independence from the Seljuk Turks in 1299, laid siege to Nicaea. Under blockade and suffering from a famine, the defenders finally got a messenger to Emperor Michael IX Palaiologos in Constantinople, who dispatched Hetaireiarches Mouzalon with some 2,000 men.

Both the Byzantine and Ottoman sources provide some details on what happened next. Byzantine historian George Pachymeres described Osman as surprising the Byzantines with an ambush at Telemaia and then engaging the enemy at Bapheus, where the numerical superiority of Osman's troops, the failure of support by the local Byzantine militia, and the lack of discipline among the Byzantine soldiery led to a decisive Byzantine defeat. According to Ottoman chronicles, the Byzantine emperor had sent a relief force by sea to Nicaea. The force had arrived at Yalak-Ovasi (the coastal plain on the southern shores of the Gulf of Izmit [Nicomedia]) and began to land for a surprise attack on Osman's troops. Informed through a Greek spy of the plan, Osman, who had received aid from the sultan of Konya and local Turkoman lords, set an ambush and was victorious.

The date of the battle is often given as June 27, 1302, but this date has been rejected by the Byzantinists, most of whom agree on July 27, 1301. The Ottoman victory of Bapheus was the first major military success for Osman, securing his sovereignty and bringing him renown among the Turkoman lords.

ALEXANDER MIKABERIDZE

See also
Byzantine-Ottoman Wars

References
Bartus, Mark C. *The Late Byzantine Army, Arms and Society, 1204–1453*. Philadelphia: University of Pennsylvania Press, 1997.

Inalcik, Halil. "Osman Ghazi's Siege of Nicaea and the Battle of Bapheus." In *The Ottoman Emirate: 1300–1389*, ed. Elizabeth Zachariadou, 77–99. Rethymnon: Crete University Press, 1993.

Barak, Ehud (1942–)

Israeli Army officer, chief of the General Staff, and prime minister (1999–2001). Ehud Barak (Borg) was born on February 12, 1942, in Kibbutz Mishmar Ha-Sharon, Palestine (now northern Israel). The kibbutz had been founded in 1932 by his Lithuanian immigrant father. Barak earned a degree in physics and mathematics at Hebrew University in 1976 and a master's degree in economic engineering systems at Stanford University in 1978. His studies were persistently interrupted by the demands of military service.

In 1959 Barak joined the Israel Defense Forces (IDF), serving first as a soldier and then rising to become chief of the General Staff (1991). He served in and commanded elite special forces units and was a reconnaissance group commander in the 1967 Six-Day War. In 1972 he led the successful rescue of hijacked Sabena Airlines hostages at Ben-Gurion Airport in Tel Aviv during which future prime minister Benjamin Netanyahu was wounded. In 1973 in the covert operation SPRING OF YOUTH against the organization that murdered Israeli athletes at the 1972 Munich Olympics, Barak disguised himself as a woman in order to gain access to Palestine Liberation Organization (PLO) terrorists in two seven-story buildings in Muslim West Beirut. He served as a tank battalion commander in the Sinai during the 1973 Yom Kippur War. He next commanded a tank brigade and then an armored division.

Barak was a principal planner for the Entebbe raid (1976) that rescued Israeli hostages and an Air France aircrew. In 1982 Barak was appointed as head of the IDF Planning Branch and promoted to major general. He served as deputy commander of Israeli forces in Lebanon during Operation PEACE FOR GALILEE. He was appointed head of the IDF's Intelligence Branch (April 1983), then headed the IDF Central Command (January 1986) and was deputy chief of staff (May 1987). He assumed the position of chief of the General Staff in April 1991, being promoted to lieutenant general, the highest rank in the IDF.

During 1994, Barak participated in the signing of the Gaza-Jericho Agreement (also known as the Cairo Accord) with the Palestinians and negotiations that led to the Treaty

General Ehud Barak, former chief of staff of the Israel Defense Forces (1991–1995), became head of the Labor Party in 1997 and was prime minister of Israel during 1999–2001. He remains the most decorated soldier in Israeli history. (Israeli Government Press Office)

of Peace with Jordan as well as Syrian-Israeli negotiations. In 1995 he resigned as chief of staff and began his political career as Prime Minister Yitzhak Rabin's interior minister (July–November 1995). Barak replaced Shimon Peres as minister of foreign affairs (November 1995–June 1996) after Peres became prime minister following the assassination of Rabin on November 4, 1995. Barak assumed the leadership of the Labor Party after Peres was defeated by Likud's Benjamin Netanyahu in the May 1996 elections following a series of Palestinian suicide bombings that killed 32 Israeli citizens.

Barak served on the foreign affairs and defense committees after being elected to the Knesset in 1996. In 1999 he meshed factions of the Labor, Gesher, and Meimad Parties into the One Israel Party. It was under this banner of a softer approach to the Palestinians that he was elected prime minister (May 17, 1999) and assumed the office of minister of defense (July 6, 1999).

As prime minister, Barak renewed peace talks with the PLO's Yasser Arafat in September 1999 and agreed to finalize peace accords by September 2000 that would transfer more Israeli-occupied territory in the West Bank to Palestinian control. Barak withdrew all Israeli forces from a narrow security zone established by Peres and thereby ended Israel's 17-year occupation of southern Lebanon. Additionally, Barak renewed peace talks with Syria that had been stalemated for 3 years.

All of these efforts to establish peace between Israel and its Arab neighbors began to unravel in the summer of 2000. Barak's frustration over the lack of progress in confirming a framework for peace with the Palestinian side led him to call on the aid of U.S. president Bill Clinton. This resulted in the Camp David Summit of July 2000. The summit was a failure, and even though Clinton and Prince Bandar of Saudi Arabia openly blamed Arafat for the failure to reach an agreement, Barak came under heavy criticism from Israeli right-wing politicians as having offered Arafat too much and by Israeli left-wing politicians as having offered too little.

Three parties resigned from Barak's coalition government, leaving him with a minority government that barely survived a confidence vote in the Knesset. The death knell of his peace process and premiership was sounded when violence erupted in September 2000 in the West Bank and in Gaza and when Arafat openly disregarded the cease-fire agreement he made with Barak. In December, Barak called for special elections for February 2001. Following his defeat in this election, he resigned the prime ministership on May 7, 2001. The Likud Party's Ariel Sharon succeeded him.

Barak then worked as senior adviser with the U.S. firm Electronic Data Systems and also helped found a private firm emphasizing security work. In 2005 he announced his intention to reenter Israeli politics. He made a bid for the leadership of the Labor Party late that same year, but his poor standing in the polls caused him to drop out of the race early and throw his support to Peres, who failed to win the post. Barak remains the most decorated soldier in Israeli history, having been awarded the Distinguished Service Medal and four citations for courage and operational excellence. In 2013 Barak officially retired from Israeli politics. His retirement, however, did not mean that he remained aloof from Israeli affairs. Indeed, in May 2018 he lamented the state of Israeli political affairs and the continuing failures to reach consensus on the Palestinian-Israeli impasse. He also stated that Prime Minister Benjamin Netanyahu should resign his office.

RICHARD M. EDWARDS

See also
Arafat, Yasser; Camp David Accords; Entebbe Hostage Rescue; Intifada, Second; Lebanon-Israeli War; Netanyahu, Benjamin; Rabin, Yitzhak; Sharon, Ariel; Six-Day War; Yom Kippur War

References
Gelvin, James L. *The Israel-Palestine Conflict: One Hundred Years of War*. New York: Cambridge University Press, 2005.

Lévy, Paule-Henriette. *Ehud Barak: Le Faucon de la Paix*. Paris: Plon, 1999.

Maddy-Weitzman, Bruce, and Shimon Shamir. *The Camp David Summit—What Went Wrong? Americans, Israelis, and Palestinians Analyze the Failure of the Boldest Attempt Ever to Resolve the Palestinian-Israeli Conflict*. Sussex, UK: Sussex Academic, 2005.

Swisher, Clayton E. *The Truth about Camp David: The Untold Story about the Collapse of the Middle East Peace Process*. New York: Thunder's Mouth, Nation Books, 2004.

Barkiyaruq (1079/1080–1105)

Sultan of the Great Seljuk Empire (1092–1105). Born in 1079 or 1080, the eldest son of Sultan Malik Shah I, Barkiyaruq came to power at the age of 13 after defeating his brother, Sultan Mamud I (r. 1092–1094). Barkiyaruq's reign was characterized by continuous civil wars with his uncles and brothers throughout his vast empire. These occurred as the First Christian Crusade of the Holy Land (1096–1099) was penetrating his dominions in Syria.

Barkiyaruq's uncle Tutush I, king of Syria, disputed his claim to the sultanate and occupied western Persia, having won the recognition of the Abbasid caliph in Baghdad. However, in February 1095 Barkiyaruq killed Tutush in battle at Dashlu in Persia, which had devastating consequences for Seljuk unity in Syria. A long civil war broke out between Tutush's sons Riwan, who ruled Aleppo and northern Syria, and Duqaq, who ruled Damascus and southern Syria. Barkiyaruq himself was occupied by another rebellion led by his uncle, Arslan Arghun, in Khurasan in 1097. This was followed by another challenge to power by the sultan's younger brother Muhammad Tapar in 1098 that continued for the rest of the reign, exhausting Seljuk military power and crippling the empire's economy.

The struggle between Barkiyaruq and Muhammad took place mostly in Iraq, Persia, and Transoxania. Seljuk Syria was neglected to such an extent that when a Syrian delegation traveled to Baghdad to urge the sultan and the caliph to intervene after Jerusalem fell to the crusaders, the caliph pleaded helplessness, as Barkiyaruq was fighting in Khurasan. When his cousin Duqaq was killed in 1104, Barkiyaruq was unable to prevent the *atabeg* Tughtigin from seizing control of Damascus from the Seljuk dynasty. Barkiyaruq died of tuberculosis in January 1105 after designating his son, Malik Shah II, as his successor.

Taef El-Azhari

See also
Seljuk Dynasty; Seljuk War of Succession

References
Boyle, John Andrew, ed. *The Cambridge History of Iran*, Vol. 5, *The Saljuq and Mongol Periods*. Cambridge: Cambridge University Press, 1968.

Lambton, A. K. S. *Continuity and Change in Medieval Persia*. London: Tauris, 1988.

Bar Kochba Revolt (132–135)

The Bar Kochba Revolt was the second Roman-Jewish war and was fought during 132–135 in the Roman province of Judaea. The causes of this war were rooted in the political situation that followed the first Jewish War of 66–70. After that revolt the Romans annexed Judaea, making it into a Roman province and stationing the Tenth Legion (Legio X Fretensis) in Jerusalem. In the 120s another legion was brought into Palestine, replaced in 130 by Legio VI Ferrata, stationed in southern Galilee.

In 130 CE, Emperor Hadrian visited Judaea and ordered the city of Jerusalem to be refounded as the pagan city Aelia Capitolina. He ordered built a temple to Jupiter Capitolinus, the chief Roman god, on the site of the Jerusalem Temple. This was presumably the main cause of the rebellion. Another literary source, the highly tendentious Historia Augusta, suggests that Hadrian banned circumcision and that he precipitated the revolt, though most historians consider this unlikely. This could have incited a revolt among the Jews, because the rite of circumcision was fundamental to Jewish identity. Other factors may have been resentment from the first war and messianic, apocalyptic fervor, as evidenced in Jewish literature.

Simon Bar Kochba led the revolt, styling himself the *nasi*, the rank below king among the Jews. The course of the revolt is impossible to reconstruct based on the extant sources. Initially Bar Kochba's army enjoyed some success, routing the forces of Roman governor Tinnieus Rufus. To crush the rebellion, Hadrian sent seven more legions to join the two already in place. These were commanded by Julius Severus, the former governor of Britain who was transferred to quell the rebellion.

Bar Kochba's name means "son of a star," suggesting that the rebellion had messianic overtones. His army built a vast array of underground caves and fortifications, such as those found at Beth Guvrin, from which they harried the Romans. Some of Bar Kochba's letters have been discovered, revealing him to be a petty, cruel, ineffective leader. In Christian literature, Bar Kochba is portrayed as a persecutor of the early church. No doubt the revolt had other leaders, but they remain unknown.

The Roman Army virtually annihilated Judaea. Archaeological evidence suggests that most of the population was either slain or enslaved. The war culminated with the siege of Betar, a city southeast of Jerusalem, where Bar Kochba died. In rabbinic literature, the Bar Kochba Revolt is remembered as a catastrophe on par with the destruction of the Temple during the First Revolt.

This rebellion had massive costs in manpower and money for the Roman Empire. Legio XXII Deiotariana appears to have been disbanded because of its heavy losses. The suppression of the revolt was celebrated widely by the Romans, and a triumphal arch honoring Hadrian was erected at Tel Shalem, south of the city of Scythopolis at the edge of Judaea. To punish the Jews, Hadrian renamed Judaea as Palestine.

NATHAN SCHUMER

See also
Hadrian, Emperor; Jewish-Roman War, First; Judaea

References
Bloom, James. 2010. *Jewish Revolts against Rome, AD 66–135: A Military Analysis.* Jefferson, NC: McFarland, 2010.
Gambash, Gil. 2015. *Rome and Provincial Resistance.* New York: Routledge, 2015.
Schafer, Peter, ed. *The Bar Kokhba War Reconsidered: New Perspectives on the Second Jewish Revolt against Rome.* Tubingen: Mohr Siebeck, 2003.
Yadin, Yigael. *Bar Kokhba: The Rediscovery of the Legendary Hero of the Second Jewish Revolt against Rome.* New York: Random House, 1971.

Bar-Lev Line

Early warning line constructed by the Israelis to stop or blunt a sudden Egyptian offensive across the Suez Canal. The line was located on the Sinai Peninsula running north to south along the eastern shore line of the canal from the Mediterranean Sea to the Red Sea. The Bar-Lev Line was begun after the 1967 Six-Day War, when it became apparent to Israeli leaders that no long-term peace settlement with Egypt was imminent.

Egyptian artillery and commando attacks in 1968 led Israel Defense Forces (IDF) chief of staff Lieutenant General Haim Bar-Lev to seek a means of protecting IDF observation points that would provide immediate warning of any Egyptian Army attack across the Suez Canal while at the same time preventing Egyptian observation of Israeli defenses. After much internal discussion, the IDF sanctioned the construction of an early warning line, which was then named after the chief of staff.

Built at a cost of some $500 million and largely completed by March 1969, the line consisted of some 20 concrete observation posts running north and south along the east bank of the Suez Canal for nearly 100 miles. Approximately 500 IDF military personnel manned the line. The line was not designed as a static defense. Rather, the IDF remained committed to a flexible mobile counterattack for its primary response to a cross-canal attack. Occasionally, the strongpoints were abandoned and later reopened. The IDF normally stationed garrisons of 15–20 men at the strongpoints.

A sand embankment of 20–25 yards high built at water's edge at an angle of 45 degrees ran the length of the line. A secondary sand embankment was constructed about 1.5 miles behind the main defense line. Dedicated artillery fire and armored patrols using embankment access roads provided additional security to the strongpoints. Mobile armored units were situated behind the front lines to repel any canal crossing. Prepositioned equipment behind the line provided support to units arriving to defend the line. Pipes were installed to carry oil to the canal, to be ignited upon an attack. All plans operated on the presupposition that the IDF would have sufficient early warning to allow the shifting of units forward.

During the 1969–1970 War of Attrition, the Bar-Lev Line came under constant artillery barrage and regular commando attacks. Although these attacks exposed the weakness of the line, the IDF remained committed to the ability of the Bar-Lev Line to provide sufficient early notification of an impending attack.

In January 1973, Egyptian president Anwar Sadat ordered his military leadership to begin secret planning for a cross-canal attack. The Egyptian Army conducted detailed planning and training to penetrate the Bar-Lev Line and move quickly into the Sinai Desert. Repeated Egyptian training for the upcoming attack came to be interpreted as routine military maneuvers by IDF intelligence. Thus, the IDF failed to detect the warning signs of an impending attack. Only in the final hours immediately prior to the Egyptian assault did IDF intelligence finally recognize an abnormal situation. This led to a limited call-up of reserves. The Egyptian deception plan and IDF overconfidence in the Bar-Lev Line had set the stage for a successful Egyptian crossing of the canal.

A massive artillery barrage signaled the start of the Egyptian attack launched on October 6, 1973, with much of the IDF on leave for Yom Kippur. Egyptian surface-to-air missiles (SAMs) protected the bridging operations. Water cannon mounted on Egyptian pontoons blasted openings in the sand berms of the Bar-Lev Line, allowing for the passage of armored vehicles and troops. The Israeli plan to burn oil on the canal failed because sand weight had collapsed the oil pipes, rendering them useless. Under cover of Soviet-supplied air defenses and new antiarmor weaponry, the Egyptians passed 80,000 men across the canal.

With the exception of only Strongpoint Budapest, located at the northern end of the Bar-Lev Line, Egyptian forces overran all IDF strongpoints. The surrounded garrisons either managed spectacular escapes or suffered heavy casualties and were captured. On October 9, the IDF admitted that the Bar-Lev Line had been completely breached.

Although the IDF later brought about a stunning reversal of fortune, the successful Egyptian crossing of the canal demonstrated a complete breakdown of the Israeli early warning system. The Bar-Lev Line placed too much reliance on signals intelligence and technology. The IDF had become overconfident and failed to identify the emerging capabilities of the Egyptian Army. Ironically, the IDF, which had long achieved success from its rapid mobile units backed by local initiative and boldness, in the end believed that it had gained military security in the Bar-Lev Line. Although the Bar-Lev Line was not originally designed as a static defensive line, it came to be relegated to membership in military history's long list of failed defensive lines.

Thomas D. Veve

See also
Sadat, Anwar; Six-Day War; Suez Canal; War of Attrition; Yom Kippur War

References
Dunstan, Simon. *The Yom Kippur War, 1973.* 2 vols. Westport, CT: Praeger, 2005.
Herzog, Chaim. *The Arab-Israeli Wars: War and Peace in the Middle East from the War of Independence to Lebanon.* Westminster, MD: Random House, 1984.
Rabinovich, Abraham. *The Yom Kippur War: The Epic Encounter That Transformed the Middle East.* New York: Schocken, 2005.

Basian, Battle of (1203)

Decisive battle fought between the Georgians and a Muslim coalition at Basian near Erzurum in modern-day northeastern Turkey. The reign of Queen Tamar of Georgia (1178–1213) underscored Georgian might after a large Muslim coalition was crushed in battle at Shamkhor in 1195. This Georgian success led Rukn al-Din Sulayman Shah II, sultan of Rum (r. 1196–1204), to rally the Muslim principalities of Asia Minor against Georgia.

A massive Muslim army advanced toward the Georgian borders in 1203 and was met at Basian by a much smaller Georgian force under David Soslani, king consort to Tamar. The Georgians initially made an unexpected attack with their advance guard and spread confusion among the Muslim troops. The sultan managed to rally his forces and counterattacked but was surprised by coordinated flanking attacks, which routed his forces. The bitterly contested battle produced heavy casualties on both sides.

The Georgian victory at Basian secured its preeminence in the region. Exploiting the success, Queen Tamar annexed Arran and Duin and then subdued the emirate of Kars, the Armen-Shahs, and the emirs of Erzurum and Erzincan. In 1204, she provided military and political support to the grandsons of Byzantine emperor Alexios I Komnenos in establishing the empire of Trebizond. The Georgians then invaded Azerbaijan, advancing as far as Ardabil and Tabriz in 1208 and Qazvin and Khoy in 1210. These victories brought Georgia to the summit of its power and glory, establishing the Pan-Caucasian Georgian Empire stretching from the Black Sea to the Caspian and from the Caucasus Mountains to Lake Van.

Alexander Mikaberidze

See also
Alexios I Komnenos; Rum, Sultanate of

Reference
Allen, William. *A History of the Georgian People: From the Beginning Down to the Russian Conquest in the Nineteenth Century.* New York: Barnes & Noble, 1971.

Basil II Bulgaroctonos (958–1025)

Byzantine emperor. Born in Constantinople in 958, the son of Emperor Romanus II (959–963), Basil II Bulgaroctonos (Bulgar-butcher) was nominally the emperor on his father's death in 963, but others exercised effective rule. In 976 he was formally recognized as coemperor with his brother Constantine. In response to inroads by Tsar Samuel of Bulgaria into Byzantine territory, in 981 Basil invaded Bulgaria but met defeat that same year in the Battle of Sofia.

Basil then returned to Constantinople to deal with internal matters, and because his brother had no interest in affairs of state, from 985 Basil was sole emperor. In 987 several of his generals led a revolt against him. Gaining control of most of Anatolia, they marched on Constantinople. Basil called on Kiev for aid and defeated the rebels in the Battle of Chrysopolis (988) and achieved final victory over them at Abydos (April 13, 989).

In 991 Basil again campaigned against Bulgaria but was forced to break this off on the invasion of his eastern territory by the Egyptian Fatimids in 995. Taking personal command, Basil raised the siege of Aleppo that same year, then managed to regain all the territory lost earlier. While Basil was campaigning against the Fatimids, Tsar Samuel invaded Greece, laying waste to it as far as the Peloponnese. Basil then moved into the Balkans, defeating Samuel in the Battle of Spercherios (996), then retaking Greece and Macedonia. By 1001 Basil had seized forts around Sardica (modern-day Sofia), cutting off Samuel from Bulgarian territory along the Danube. Samuel then invaded Macedonia and sacked Adrianople before being defeated by Basil in a battle near Skopje in 1004.

Basil then drove the Bulgars from Thrace and Macedonia and invaded Bulgaria itself in 1007. Finally, in the Battle of Balathista (Kleidion) of July 29, 1014, Basil gained a decisive victory over the Bulgars, although Tsar Samuel managed to escape. Basil ordered all Bulgar prisoners taken to be blinded and led to Samuel in groups of 100, each by a man left with only one eye. Reportedly Samuel was so shaken by this that he collapsed and died several days afterward.

With these events, Bulgar resistance soon ended and Basil incorporated Bulgaria into the Byzantine Empire. He then turned east, annexing Armenia and building defenses against the Seljuk Turks in 1020. He was preparing an expedition to take Sicily from the Arabs when he died on December 15, 1025.

Basil II grew to be a highly effective general. Bold, daring, and ruthless, he was also an excellent administrator and certainly one of the most competent of Byzantine emperors.

Spencer C. Tucker

See also
Byzantine Empire; Fatimid Dynasty; Seljuk Dynasty

References
Browning, Robert. *The Byzantine Empire.* New York: Scribner, 1980.
Franzius, Enno. *History of the Byzantine Empire: Mother of Nations.* New York Funk & Wagnalls, 1988.
Gregory, Timothy E. *A History of Byzantium.* Boston: Blackwell Publishing, 2005.
Holmes, Catherine. *Basil II and the Governance of Empire (976–1025).* New York: Oxford University Press, 2005.

Basra, Battle for (March 23–April 7, 2003)

Battle fought between British and Iraqi forces during the Iraq War of 2003 at the Iraqi city of Basra in southeastern Iraq near the Shatt al-Arab waterway and the Persian Gulf. The battle began on March 23 and ended with the British capture of the city on April 7. At Basra, the British pursued a strategy considerably different from that followed by their American coalition partners. While this British strategy sharply limited loss of life, it also allowed many Iraqi soldiers and officials to escape and fight in the subsequent insurgency.

At the beginning of the Iraq War, British forces, supported by U.S. marines and offshore coalition naval units, seized the Faw Peninsula and the deepwater port of Umm Qasr. The British then took over occupation of the Rumaylah oil fields from American units that were needed elsewhere. The next major task for the British was the capture of Basra, Iraq's second-largest city and its principal port, with a population of more than 1.25 million people.

The capture of Basra was assigned to Major General Robin Brims's 1st Armoured Division. Iraqi forces in the city were commanded by General Ali Hassan al-Majid, otherwise known as "Chemical Ali" for his role in the Iraqi nerve gas attack on the Kurdish town of Halabja in 1988. Ali commanded a mixed force of Iraqi regulars and Baathist militia.

Brims decided on a strategy to limit civilian deaths and mitigate physical damage to the city buildings and infrastructure. The population was primarily anti–Saddam Hussein Shiites, and Basra had suffered greatly during Hussein's suppression of the 1991 southern Shiite rebellion that had followed the 1991 Persian Gulf War. Brims did not wish to turn the city against the coalition.

Brims order his men to surround Basra beginning on March 23. The siege was a loose one that allowed anyone who wanted to leave the city to do so, hoping to encourage desertion among Iraqi conscripts, which did occur. Brims also avoided the use of indirect artillery fire against Iraqi positions in Basra, thereby minimizing civilian casualties. Ali meanwhile sought to draw the British into battle in the narrow city streets where the British advantage in armor would be nullified, but Brims refused to engage in street fighting.

Frustrated, the Iraqis attempted to provoke the British into launching a major attack on the city. On the evening of March 26, Ali sent out a column of T-55 tanks to attack the British. The 120mm gun of the British Challenger tanks of the Royal Scots Dragoon Guards outranged the T-55's main gun, resulting in the destruction of 15 T-55s without British loss.

On March 31 British reconnaissance, intelligence, and sniper teams began infiltrating Basra, gathering intelligence, sniping at Iraqi officers and Baathist officials, making contact with anti-Hussein resistance circles, and directing artillery and air strikes. Beginning in early April, the British initiated a series of devastating yet limited raids against Iraqi positions using Warrior armored vehicles equipped with 30mm cannon and capable of speeds of more than 50 mph.

On April 5, an American F-16 fighter-bomber dropped two satellite-guided Joint Direct Attack Munition (JDAM) bombs on a building thought to be Chemical Ali's headquarters. The building was destroyed, but Ali survived the bombing and was not captured until after the war, although reports that he had died were widely believed by Iraqi defenders, whose morale now plummeted.

Following a successful British probe into northern Basra on the morning of April 6, Brims decided that the time had come to move in force. At 11:00 a.m. on April 6, he ordered British troops into the city. Despite heavy fighting, most of Basra was under British control by nightfall. The British suffered only three soldiers killed. Some additional fighting continued the next day, but by the evening of April 7 the battle was officially over, and Basra was secure.

Although loss of life was minimized and further damage to the city's infrastructure was avoided, many Baathists were able to escape from Basra and join the postwar Sunni insurgency. Basra also experienced a wave of immediate looting and violence similar to that in Baghdad.

PAUL WILLIAM DOERR

See also
Hussein, Saddam; Iraq War; Majid al-Tikriti, Ali Hassan al-; Shia Islam; Sunni Islam

References
Gordon, Michael R., and Bernard E. Trainor. *Cobra II: The Inside Story of the Invasion and Occupation of Iraq.* New York: Pantheon, 2006.
Keegan, John. *The Iraq War.* Toronto: Key Porter, 2004.

Bassorah, Battle of (November 7, 656)

Major battle, also known as the Battle of the Camel and the Battle of Jamal, that took place on November 7, 656, at present-day Basra, Iraq. It was fought between the forces of Rashidun caliph Ali ibn Abi Talib and his opponents on the outskirts of present-day Basra, Iraq.

While on a pilgrimage to Mecca in 656, Aisha, one of Prophet Muhammad's wives, learned of the slaying of the third caliph, Uthman. She was so angered by this and the naming of Ali ibn Abi Talib as fourth caliph and his refusal to punish those responsible that she led a revolt against him. For the first time, Muslims had taken up arms against one other. This struggle is now known as the First Fitna, or Muslim civil war.

Aisha gained the support of prominent figures Zubayr and Talha. The rebels set out from Mecca with such funds and support as they could muster and headed for Basra, where the rebels were met by the new caliph's supporters. The rebels were victorious over the caliph's supporters, and Ali's governor was driven out of the city. Those inhabitants of Basra who had participated in the siege of Uthman's home and his murder were put to death. In response, Ali marched from Medina to Kufa to rally support and then moved on Basra, where he arrived with some 12,000–20,000 fighters. Talha, Zubayr, and Aisha met the caliph reportedly with 30,000 men. However, many Basrans remained neutral or were swayed by Ali's appeal to them and abandoned the rebel cause, tipping the scales in Ali's favor.

Some accounts state that the two sides agreed on a truce prior to the battle. However, those in Ali's army who had participated in Uthman's murder launched a surprise attack on the rebel army at dawn because they were afraid that a peace agreement would bring their deaths. Talha and Zubayr then retaliated, believing that Ali had betrayed them, while Ali thought likewise and ordered a full attack.

The ensuing battle of November 7 saw the rebel army defeated, with both Talha and Zubayr killed. Aisha was captured, but Ali honored her and allowed her to retire in Medina with a pension. The battle is also know as the Battle of the Camel because Aisha urged her followers on in the midst of the battle while mounted on a camel.

Caliph Ali ibn Abi Talib's victory cemented his hold on power. He made Kufa his capital and then turned his attention to dealing with his opponents in Syria.

ADAM ALI AND SPENCER C. TUCKER

See also
Ali ibn Abi Talib; Islamic Civil War, First; Siffin, Battle of

References
Glubb, John Baggot. *The Great Arab Conquests.* London: Hodder and Stoughton, 1963.
Hodgson, Marshall G. S. *The Venture of Islam: Conscience and History in a World Civilization.* Chicago: University of Chicago Press, 1977.

Madelung, Wilferd. *The Succession to Muhammad: A Study of the Early Caliphate.* New York: Cambridge University Press, 1997.

Baybars I (1223–1277)

Mamluk sultan of Egypt and Syria (1260–1277). Baybars (Baibars) was by origin a Qipchaq Turk. He was born at Cumania, on the southern Russian steppe, on July 19, 1223. As a 14-year-old, he was enslaved and sold to Aydakin al-Bunduqdar, an emir of the Ayyubid sultan al-ali Ayyub. In 1246, Baybars's master fell into disgrace, and Baybars became one of the Bariyya mamluks (military slaves) of al-ali Ayyub. After Ayyub's death, the mamluks killed his successor Turan-Shah and seized power in 1250, establishing the Mamluk Sultanate. The new Mamluk sultan built up his own military household so that from this point the history of the sultanate was marked by continuing power struggles of the different Mamluk groups. After the victory of the Mamluks over the Mongols at the Battle of Ayn Jalut (1260), Baybars killed Sultan Quuz and was elected by the leading officers of the Bariyya as the new sultan.

Having usurped the sultanate from the Ayyubids, the Mamluk regime had from the start a problem of legitimacy. Thus, when descendants of the Abbasid family arrived in Cairo in 1261, Baybars took the opportunity to revive the caliphate, which had been ended by the Mongols when they conquered Baghdad in 1258. The newly installed caliph, al-Mustanir Billah, invested Baybars as the sole universal sultan of all Islamic territories and of lands yet to be conquered. This investiture not only served Baybars as a means of legitimating his rule but was also the announcement and authorization of a program of expansion. The ulema also bolstered Baybars's authority by highlighting his services to Islam, since he supported them financially by the establishment of pious foundations for mosques and schools.

After the Battle of Ayn Jalut the Mongols had fled back across the Euphrates, and Baybars's predecessor Quuz made the first arrangements for Mamluk rule in Syria and Palestine. While the Ayyubid emirs of Hama, Homs, and Kerak were confirmed in their principalities, governors were appointed for the two most important cities, Aleppo and Damascus. Yet since the Mongols had not given up their aspirations of conquering Syria, Baybars had to strengthen his regime internally and integrate his conquests into his domains. Thus, in 1263 he placed Homs and Kerak under direct Mamluk control. He continued the Ayyubid policy of

Baybars was the most important of the Mamluk sultans of Egypt. Ruling Egypt during 1260–1277, he turned back Mongol invasions of Egypt and inflicted a decisive defeat on the Christian forces during the 7th Crusade led by King Louis IX of France. He is also noteworthy for his important military and administrative reforms. (Pictures from History/Bridgeman Images)

destroying the fortifications of the conquered Frankish cities of Outremer on the coast to prevent their being used as bridgeheads for future crusades. Farther inland, he captured the Frankish strongholds one after another.

The Mamluk regime was based mainly on its powerful army, which Baybars had strengthened. During his reign the Egyptian Army was greatly enlarged by the purchase of large numbers of slaves for the sultan's military household (the so-called Royal Mamluks) and the households of the emirs. Baybars also improved the army by emphasizing training and inspecting his troops regularly.

By 1260–1261, Baybars had also organized a postal system with post stations at regular intervals along the routes between Egypt and Syria where horses could be changed. This service was primarily intended for military purposes and was restricted to use by the sultan. Since the Mamluk Army was concentrated in Cairo when not on campaign, rapid word of any Mongol or Frankish attack would enable it to react effectively. Baybars also restored and built roads and bridges in Syria and Palestine to improve the infrastructure of his realm.

Baybars also consolidated his hold on power through far-reaching diplomatic activities. The Mamluks were always endeavoring to weaken their opponents by securing allies. Thus, Baybars formed an alliance with Berke, khan of the Golden Horde, against their mutual enemy, the Ilkhanate of Persia. Baybars also established good relations with Byzantine emperor Michael VIII Palaiologos to prevent any threat to the import of military slaves from the Caucasus.

In 1261, Mamluk rule in Syria and Palestine was still unstable. The Franks at Acre tried to take advantage of this situation and set out to attack a group of Turkomans on the Golan Heights. Severely beaten, they thereafter did not dare launch a major attack against the Mamluks. Nevertheless, in the first years of his reign, Baybars had to come to some kind of understanding with the Franks to pursue his war against the Mongols. For this reason, in 1261 he concluded a treaty with the Franks of Acre. Largely a renewal of the agreement of 1254 between the ruler of Damascus, al-Nair Yusuf, and the Franks, it provided that the territory extending to the Jordan River was a Frankish tributary. However, Baybars pursued a quite different policy toward the principality of Antioch. Prince Bohemund VI had remained a close ally of the Mongols even after the Battle of Ayn Jalut, so Baybars raided his territory regularly to both punish him for his cooperation with the Mongols and wear down his military strength.

In 1265, having repulsed another Mongol attack on Bira, Baybars averted the danger from the Mongols for the time being, and he turned his attention to the Frankish states. Conquering Caesarea and Arsuf, he destroyed their fortifications and harbors. From that point on, Baybars launched attacks against the Franks nearly every year to reduce their power and territory. In 1266, the Mamluk Army invaded Cilicia as a punishment for its support of the Mongols. The Mamluks inflicted a major defeat on the Armenians, devastating their capital of Sis. This marked the end of the political importance of the kingdom of Cilicia. In 1268 the Mamluks secured Antioch, and the Frankish states of Outremer were reduced to the county of Tripoli and the residual Kingdom of Jerusalem around Acre.

In 1271, Baybars was at the height of his power when he undertook his last great campaign against the Frankish states. He took Krak des Chevaliers, a crusader citadel in Syria, from the Hospitallers and was about to attack Tripoli. At this moment the last crusader army arrived in Palestine, led by Prince Edward of England, who had arranged with Abagha, Ilkhan of Persia, for a joint attack against Baybars. However, Edward's contingent numbered only a few hundred men, and the force sent by Abagha was also modest in size. As soon as Baybars extended a truce to Bohemund VI of Antioch and sent an army against the Mongols, they withdrew from Syria. Thus ended the only attempt of Franks and Mongols to act together against the Mamluks. Edward remained in Outremer until 1272 without achieving anything, departing Acre after narrowly escaping an assassination attempt arranged by Baybars.

At the end of his reign, Baybars sought to secure a decisive advantage over the Ilkhanate by conquering the Seljuk sultanate of Rum, which was a Mongol protectorate. He defeated the Mongols in the Battle of Elbistan (April 1277) and was then made sultan of Rum. However, lacking local support, he had to withdraw only a few days later. Baybars died on July 1, 1277.

JOHANNES PAHLITZSCH

See also
Ayn Jalut, Battle of; Mamluk Sultanate; Mongol Invasion of the Middle East; Qalawun

References
Amitai-Preiss, Reuven. *Mongols and Mamluks: The Ilkhanid War, 1260–1281.* Cambridge: Cambridge University Press, 1995.
Holt, Peter M. *The Age of the Crusades: The Near East from the Eleventh Century to 1517.* London: Longman, 1986.
Thorau, Peter. *The Lion of Egypt: Sultan Baybars I and the Near East in the Thirteenth Century.* London: Longman, 1992.

Bayezid I (1360–1403)

Ottoman sultan (r. 1389–1402). Born in 1360, Bayezid I came to the throne on the death of his father, Murad I, who was killed at the Battle of Kosovo Polje (June 23, 1389). Bayezid I's reign was one of great territorial expansion. The Byzantines were then reduced to a position of dependency, with Emperor Manuel II Palaiologos being forced to accompany Bayezid on campaign while the Ottoman state continued to be a center of commerce, particularly with Genoa and Venice, with which there was constant diplomatic contact.

Bayezid campaigned effectively against his various rivals in Anatolia, annexing the states of Aydin and Menteşe on the western coast, defeating the İsfendiyaroğlari in the north, and successfully defeating his major rival, the state of Karaman, based around Konya (Ikonion). Farther east, Bayezid defeated Burhan al-Din, the ruler of Sivas (Sebasteia), and took Malatya (Melitene) from the Mamluks, the rulers of Egypt and Syria. Bayezid represented a grave danger for the Byzantines, whose capital city of Constantinople was now under Ottoman threat, and for the European powers, in particular King Sigismund of Hungary. A Christian crusader force composed of troops from Hungary, England, Germany, and France was assembled to do battle with the Ottomans, but Bayezid administered a crushing defeat on it in in 1396 in the Battle of Nikopolis on the Danube, west of Ruse (in modern-day Bulgaria).

By the end of Bayezid's reign, the Ottomans had taken Bulgaria; they controlled Walacia, had advanced into Hungary, and had moved into Albania, Epiros, and southern Greece. Their advance was greatly aided by the divisions between the Frankish and Greek lords in the Peloponnese. In the east, Ottoman control stretched over most of what is modern-day Turkey.

Bayezid's whirlwind conquests were not to last, for in 1402 he was defeated in the Battle of Ankara by Timur, the founder of the Timurid dynasty in eastern Persia and Central Asia, who had invaded from the east. Bayezid was taken prisoner and died on March 8, 1403, in captivity. With his capture, the Ottoman state was plunged into a period of civil war.

KATE FLEET

See also
Ankara, Battle of

References
Alexandrescu-Dersca, M. M. *La Campagne de Timur en Anatolie (1402)*. London: Variorum, 1977.
Imber, Colin. *The Ottoman Empire, 1300–1481*. Istanbul: Isis, 1990.
İnalcık, Halil. *The Ottoman Empire: The Classical Age, 1300–1600*. London: Weidenfeld and Nicolson, 1973.
Vatin, Nicolas. "L'ascension des Ottomans (1362–1429)." In *Histoire de l'Empire Ottoman,* ed. Robert Mantran, 222–275. Paris: Fayard, 1989.

Bayezid II (1447–1512)

Ottoman sultan (r. 1481–1512). Born on December 3, 1447, Bayezid II was the eldest son and successor of Mehmed II. Bayezid ruled as sultan of the Ottoman Empire from May 14, 1481, to April 24, 1512. He was immediately faced with discontent caused by the fiscal rule of his father, Mehmet II, and by civil war with his brother Cem (Djem). Cem, once defeated, fled to the Hospitallers on Rhodes, who later moved him to France and then in 1489 handed him over to the pope.

From 1483, Bayezid II paid an annual sum, first to the Hospitallers and then to the pope, to ensure that Cem was kept in safe custody. With Cem in Christian hands, Bayezid was forced to adopt a pacific policy toward the West, ratifying a treaty in 1479 with Venice, concluding a five-year truce in 1482 with King Matthias Corvinus of Hungary, and in 1490 undertaking not to attack the Papal States, Venice, or Rhodes. This was not entirely a period of peace, however. In 1483 the Ottomans annexed Hercegovina, in 1484 they invaded Moldavia, and from 1485 to 1491 they were at war with the Mamluk Sultanate.

In 1494, Cem fell into the hands of King Charles VIII of France who, after his invasion of Italy and capture of Rome, announced a crusade against the Ottomans in January 1495. Cem, however, died in February, and Charles's crusade came to nothing. From this time on Bayezid was freer in his dealings with the West. In 1498 the Ottomans raided into Poland, and in 1499 they attacked Venetian territories, taking Naupaktos (1499); Modon, Coron, and Navarino (1500), and Durrës (1502), all of which remained lost to Venice under the peace treaty of 1503. From that point on, Ottoman attention turned to the east and to the Safavids of Persia.

Bayezid's reign ended in April 1512 when he was forced to abdicate by his son Selim. Not a warlike man, Bayezid tended to be more conciliatory than his father. He established the Ottomans as a major Mediterranean naval power, introduced a systematic codification of customary law, and instituted fiscal reform.

KATE FLEET

See also
Mamluk Sultanate; Mehmed II, Sultan; Selim I, Sultan; Venetian-Ottoman Wars

References
Brummett, Palmira. *Ottoman Seapower and Levantine Diplomacy in the Age of Discovery*. Albany: State University of New York Press, 1993.
Imber, Colin. *The Ottoman Empire 1300–1481*. Istanbul: Isis, 1990.
İnalcık, Halil. *The Ottoman Empire: The Classical Age, 1300–1600*. London: Weidenfeld and Nicolson, 1973.
Vatin, Nicolas. *L'Ordre de Saint-Jean-de-Jerusalem, l'Empire Ottoman et la Méditerranée orientale entre les deux sièges de Rhodes, 1480–1522*. Louvain: Peeters, 1994.

Bedouins

A nomadic and seminomadic desert-dwelling peoples generally located in the Arabian peninsula, North Africa, the Levant, Iraq, the Negev Desert, and the Sinai Peninsula. Bedouin territories include present-day Jordan, Saudi Arabia, Kuwait, Yemen, Oman, the Arab Emirates, Israel, Egypt, Sudan, Syria, Iraq, Lebanon, Algeria, and Libya. Bedouins are of Arab origin and practice Islam. The Bedouins are organized by clans into tribes. Individual households, or *bayts* (tents), are composed of three or more adults: a man and his wife or wives and his parents or siblings plus their children. A tribe, or *hamula*, is presided over by a sheikh, which is a patrilinear position usually handed down from elder brother to younger brother and sometimes from father to son. While the sheikh has status and commands great respect, he is not a ruler in the ordinary sense of the word.

For centuries the Bedouins have been nomads who engage in light agriculture, usually animal husbandry, and live off of the land. As they have been forcibly settled by governments since the 19th century, those retaining their traditional ways are mostly seminomadic. They move throughout their prescribed lands seasonally, following freshwater sources or moving to take advantage of various plant supplies. Many have herded sheep, goats, and camels. Traditionally, Bedouins move in groups containing several families and live in tents, which aid in their ability to pick up stakes and move when the situation warrants. However, beginning in the 1950s, more and more Bedouins have given up their lifestyle to work and live in cities and towns throughout much of the region. Indeed, expanding population, urban sprawl, government policies, and the shrinking of suitable grazing lands have pushed many Bedouins into sedentary urban lifestyles. It is difficult to determine the precise number of Bedouins in the Middle East, although estimates vary from as little as 750,000 to well over 1 million. While Bedouins are noted for their generous hospitality, they are also fiercely territorial and take violations of their land rights seriously.

Bedouin culture is a complex and fascinating one and has been many centuries in the making. Bedouin tents are functional and well designed. Most are divided in two by a cloth curtain (*ma'nad*), which separates the tent into a seating/living area for men and a place to entertain guests, and another area (the *maharama*) in which women cook, socialize, and receive female guests. Bedouins have their own unique poetry, storytelling, music, and dance, much of which is reserved for the reception of guests, special occasions, and the like. Both Bedouin men and women wear traditional and prescribed clothing that can often indicate the status or age of the wearer, especially in the case of their head wear. Clothing also varies depending on the area or nation the Bedouins inhabit. The Bedouins have their own tribal, or customary, law, and thus disputes may be solved and punishment meted out according to those laws rather than resorting to civil courts of a state or locality.

Currently, Bedouins make up about 12 percent of the total Arab population in Israel. As part of the Arab minority, they face many of the same hurdles as their Arab brethren, including institutional and societal discrimination, reduced socioeconomic opportunities, substandard education, and poor health care. However, they have come under additional pressure as the Israeli government has tried to impose settlement policies on them and reduce or eliminate their traditional land areas. A fair number of Bedouins (5–10 percent of Bedouin males) serve in the Israeli military. Their intricate knowledge of the local terrain makes them valuable rangers and trackers.

Bedouins have faced similar pressures even in Arab states, however, as governments have purposely adopted land-use and settlement policies that are at odds with traditional Bedouin culture and lifestyle. Nevertheless, Bedouins have held fast to their tribal and cultural identities even after they have settled and adopted modern urbanized lifestyles. For others, the restrictions and pressures on them have meant the abandonment of a truly nomadic way of life. Now they are at best seminomadic and have adopted some of the trappings of urbanization. Agricultural pursuits, including animal husbandry, are the main livelihoods for these Bedouins in transition.

PAUL G. PIERPAOLI JR.

See also
Israel

References
Alotaibi, Muhammad. *Bedouin: The Nomads of the Desert*. Vero Beach, FL: Rourke, 1989.

Ingham, Bruce. *The Bedouin of Northern Arabia*. London: Kegan Paul International, 1986.

Losleben, Elizabeth. *The Bedouin of the Middle East*. Minneapolis: Lerner, 2002.

Nevins, Edward, and Theon Wright. *World without Time: The Bedouin*. New York: John Day, 1969.

Beersheba, Battle of (October 31, 1917)

In World War I during March 26–27 and April 17–19, 1917, British and Dominion troops of the Egyptian Expeditionary Force (EEF) commanded by Lieutenant General Sir Archibald Murray were defeated in two attempts to storm Ottoman lines at Gaza in Palestine. These defeats led to the replacement of Murray by Lieutenant General Edmund Allenby, who was ordered to take Jerusalem before Christmas.

Allenby insisted on and received immediate reinforcements. Ultimately, he had seven infantry divisions and the Desert Mounted Corps of three cavalry divisions, centered on the Australian Light Horse Division. Opposing Allenby,

German colonel Friedrich Kress von Kressenstein commanded the Ottoman Fourth Army of nine infantry divisions and a single cavalry division.

Lieutenant General Philip Chetwode, new commander of the XX Corps under Allenby, developed the British operational plan, which Allenby adopted upon assuming command in July. Chetwode rejected yet another frontal assault on Gaza and noted that the weakest point in the Ottoman defenses was their extreme left flank at Beersheba, 30 miles inland from the Mediterranean. The Ottomans believed that it would be impossible for the British to attack Beersheba because of the shortage of water in the region. Beersheba was therefore held by only one Ottoman division. If the British could somehow take Beersheba and its water wells, they could then move west behind Gaza and sever its rail and road communications.

For the British, securing adequate water was the key. British engineers refilled old Roman cisterns and repaired wells damaged by the Ottomans. They also worked to improve the flow of others.

At the same time, the British made every effort to convince the Ottomans that they were planning yet another frontal assault on Gaza. An intelligence officer allowed false but apparently credible documents outlining an attack on Gaza to fall into Ottoman hands. While Lieutenant General Edward Bulfin's XXI Corps of three divisions "demonstrated" against Gaza, on October 29 Lieutenant General Henry Chauvel's Desert Mounted Corps and Chetwode's XX Corps began their movement toward Beersheba, leaving their camps entirely in place as if they still occupied them.

In all, the force assigned to take Beersheba numbered some 40,000 men to attack a position held by only 4,400 defenders. Although the Ottomans detected the British movement, the deception was so successful that the Ottomans assumed that it involved only one infantry and one mounted division and that the main EEF attack would still occur at Gaza.

The success of Allenby's entire offensive operation hinged on capturing Beersheba in only one day. The British struck on October 31. The XX Corps attacked from the west, while the Desert Mounted Corps swung wide east and attacked from the south, east, and north. The infantry enjoyed initial success with the capture of the Ottoman outposts at a cost of 1,200 casualties, with British artillery superiority a key factor.

The mounted attack that began east of Beersheba did not go as planned, however. The Anzac Mounted Division was stopped at the Ottoman Tel el Saba redoubt, and by the time it was taken the attackers were well behind schedule, and it looked as if it would not be possible to secure Beersheba before dark. Faced with this situation, Chauvel asked Allenby for permission to retire for the night to water his horses, which had not had water for 24 hours. Allenby refused and ordered Chauvel to take Beersheba that very day to secure both water and prisoners. Chauvel then ordered the Australian 4th Light Horse Brigade to make a mounted attack. The 4th and 12th Regiments of the brigade formed in three lines and charged across four miles of open terrain against Ottoman small-arms and machine-gun fire. Caught by the audacity of the attack, the Ottoman gunners failed to adjust their sights and fired too high. Surprisingly, the attackers incurred few casualties as the horsemen leapt over the barbed wire and trenches and entered Beersheba itself. Ottoman resistance promptly collapsed, and many of the garrison were taken prisoner. More important from the attackers' standpoint, the Turks succeeded in destroying only 2 of the town's 17 wells. Two reservoirs of 90,000 gallons of water were also taken, and a sudden downpour that left pools of water provided immediate replenishment for the horses.

Although more hard fighting lay ahead, the EEF was able to secure Jerusalem on December 9.

Spencer C. Tucker

See also
Allenby, Sir Edmund Henry Hynman; Gaza, First Battle of; Gaza, Second Battle of; Gaza, Third Battle of; Kress von Kressenstein, Friedrich Sigismund Georg; Murray, Sir Archibald James

References
Bullock, David L. *Allenby's War: The Palestine-Arabian Campaigns, 1916–1918.* New York: Blandford, 1988.
Gardner, Brian. *Allenby of Arabia: Lawrence's General.* New York: Coward-McCann, 1966.
Great Britain, War Office. *Brief Record of the Egyptian Force under the Command of General Sir Edmund H. H. Allenby: July 1917 to October 1918, Egyptian Expeditionary Force.* 2nd ed. London: HMSO, 1919.
Hughes, Matthew. *Allenby and British Strategy in the Middle East, 1917–1919.* London: Cass, 1999.

Begin, Menachem (1913–1992)

Prime minister of Israel (1977–1983). Menachem Wolfovitch Begin was born to an Ashkenazic Jewish family in Brest-Litovsk (Brisk), Russia (now Belarus), on August 16, 1913. He fled with his family to Vilnius, Poland, to escape fighting in World War I. Begin's father was an ardent Zionist, and

Begin joined the Hashomer Hatzair scout movement and then Vladimir Jabotinsky's Betar youth movement at age 16. Betar was committed to the creation of a Jewish state on both sides of the Jordan River. Begin took up the leadership of the Organization Department of Betar for Poland in 1932.

Begin graduated from the University of Warsaw with a law degree in 1935 and assumed the leadership of Betar Czechoslovakia in 1936. He returned to Warsaw in 1937 and was imprisoned for a short time for his Zionist activities. He became head of Betar in Poland in 1938. Some 100,000 members engaged in self-defense, weapons, agricultural, and communications training. Betar also transported to Palestine immigrants declared illegal by the British government. Begin advocated the establishment of a Jewish national homeland in Palestine by conquest and pushed this position at the 1938 Betar convention.

Begin fled Warsaw when the Germans invaded Poland in September 1939, moving into eastern Poland and thus avoided the subsequent roundup of Jews by the Nazis. Both his parents and a brother died in Nazi concentration camps during the war. Two weeks later Soviet forces invaded eastern Poland, and in 1940 Begin was arrested and sent to a concentration camp in Siberia. He was released following the establishment of a Polish army to fight the Germans that followed the German invasion of the Soviet Union in June 1941.

Begin enlisted in the Free Polish Army in exile. Sent in 1942 to the British Mandate for Palestine for training, he left the army there in 1943 and joined the Jewish national movement in Palestine. Begin openly criticized the Jewish Agency for Palestine and worldwide Zionism as being too timid in their approach to a Jewish state. In 1942 he had joined Irgun Tsvai Leumi (National Military Organization) and commanded it from 1943 to 1948. Under Begin's leadership, in 1944 Irgun declared war on the British and resumed attacks on Palestinian Arab villages and British interests. The British classified Irgun as a terrorist organization, and the Jewish Agency for Palestine, Haganah, and Histadrut all declared its operations to be terrorist acts.

British authorities launched an extensive manhunt for Begin, but he avoided capture. Begin directed the Irgun bombing of the British military, police, and civil headquarters at Jerusalem's King David Hotel on July 22, 1946, that killed 91 people. He and Irgun claimed to have issued three warnings in an attempt to limit casualties.

Following the Israeli declaration of independence on May 15, 1948, Irgun was incorporated into the Israeli national military, the Israel Defense Forces (IDF), that September.

Menachem Begin was a militant Zionist who was prime minister of Israel during 1977–1983. He is perhaps best remembered for his part in the Camp David Accords (1978), which established the basis for peace between Egypt and Israel. (Israeli Government Press Office)

Begin led Israel's political opposition from 1948 to 1977, reforming what remained of Irgun into the rightist Herut (Freedom) Party. In 1965 Herut merged with the Liberal Party, creating the Gahal Party, which formed the understructure of the future Likud (Unity) Party. Just prior to the June 1967 Six-Day War, Begin joined the National Unity Government's cabinet as minister without portfolio. That government was dissolved on August 1, 1970.

Likud's May 17, 1977, victory in the national elections for the ninth Knesset allowed Begin, chairman of Likud since 1970, to form the new government. On June 21 he became prime minister. Domestically, Begin moved to turn the Israeli economy away from the centralized, highly planned enterprise that characterized it under Labor. He also actively promoted immigration to Israel, especially from Ethiopia and the Soviet Union. Begin also sought infrastructure improvements, advances in education, and the renewal of Israel's poorest neighborhoods.

Begin particularly asserted himself in foreign policy. One of his first acts as prime minister was to challenge King Hussein of Jordan, President Hafez al-Assad of Syria, and President Anwar Sadat of Egypt to meet with him to discuss peace. Sadat alone accepted the challenge and arrived in Israel on November 19, 1977. Following intermittent negotiations, Begin and Sadat met with U.S. president Jimmy Carter at Camp David, Maryland, and signed the Camp David Accords after nearly two weeks of negotiations (September 5–17, 1978).

The accords included two framework agreements that established guidelines for both the Israel-Egypt Peace Treaty and a potentially wider Middle East peace agreement. The bilateral treaty was signed in Washington, D.C., on March 26, 1979, and Begin and Sadat were awarded the 1978 Nobel Peace Prize.

Despite Begin's willingness to seek peace with Egypt, the other Arab states remained hostile toward Israel. And Begin was uncompromising on the place of the West Bank and the Gaza Strip, seized by Israel during the Six-Day War, in the modern State of Israel. He considered them part of the historical lands given to Israel by God. Indeed, he promoted and oversaw the expansion of Jewish settlements in the West Bank and the Gaza Strip that continue to be an impediment to Palestinian-Israeli peace.

From May 28, 1980, to August 6, 1981, Begin served concurrently as Israel's prime minister and defense minister. When Israeli intelligence notified Begin that Iraq was close to producing weapons-grade nuclear fuel at its Osiraq/Tammuz nuclear reactor, he ordered the Israeli Air Force's successful destruction of that facility on June 7, 1981. Shortly thereafter he enunciated the Begin Doctrine, which held that Israel would act preemptively to counter any perceived threat from weapons of mass destruction (WMD).

On June 30, 1981, Begin was reelected prime minister. It was soon apparent to the second Begin government that the Lebanese government was unable or unwilling to stop terrorist attacks launched from its soil. As such, in June 1982 Begin authorized Operation PEACE FOR GALILEE, the Israeli invasion of southern Lebanon. Its stated aim was to drive Palestine Liberation Organization (PLO) Katyusha rockets out of the range of Israel's northern border and to destroy the terrorist infrastructure that had developed in southern Lebanon, but Begin and Defense Minister Ariel Sharon pushed far beyond that and the IDF aid siege to Beirut.

Although the PLO was driven from Lebanon, the Israeli presence in the country lasted three years. (A limited Israeli force remained until 2000.) It also brought great worldwide negative public opinion against Israel. Tired and still mourning the recent death of his wife, Begin resigned as prime minister on September 15, 1983. Begin died of heart failure in Tel Aviv on March 9, 1992, in Tel Aviv.

RICHARD M. EDWARDS

See also

Camp David Accords; Gaza Strip; Haganah; Irgun Tsvai Leumi; Lebanon-Israeli War; Osiraq Raid; Sadat, Anwar; Sharon, Ariel; Sinai Peninsula; Zionism

References

Begin, Menachem. *The Revolt.* Los Angeles: Nash Publishing, 1972.

Perlmutter, Amos. *The Life and Times of Menachem Begin.* Garden City, NY: Doubleday, 1987.

Seidman, Hillel. *Menachem Begin: His Life and Legacy.* New York: Shengold, 1990.

Sofer, Sasson. *Begin: An Anatomy of Leadership.* New York: Blackwell, 1988.

Temko, Ned. *To Win or to Die: A Personal Portrait of Menachem Begin.* New York: Morrow, 1987.

Belisarius (ca. 505–565)

Great Byzantine general. Probably born in present-day southwestern Bulgaria around 505, Belisarius is presumed to be of Thracian ancestry. He entered the Byzantine Army as a youth. Rising rapidly in the ranks, he served in the bodyguard of Emperor Justin I, whose successor, Justinian I, entrusted him with command of an army sent against Persia in 530. With 25,000 men, Belisarius defeated a Persian army of 40,000 men in the Battle of Dara. Although then narrowly defeated by a numerically vastly superior Persian army in the Battle of Callinicum near Urfa on the Euphrates River (531), he was able to prevent further Persian inroads that year, which encouraged the Persians to make peace.

Belisarius received command of an expedition against the Vandals in North Africa but, fortunately for Justinian I, had not yet departed Constantinople when the great Nika uprising occurred there in 532. Belisarius played a key role in putting down the rioting that claimed as many as 30,000 lives. In the process he probably saved Justinian's throne.

In 533 Belisarius sailed with 15,000 land troops to engage the Vandals. Using Sicily as a base of operations, he arrived in Africa that September and defeated the Vandals under their leader Gelimer at Ad Decimum that same month. He then captured the city of Carthage and again, this time outnumbered as much as 10 to 1, surprised and defeated Gelimer in the Battle of Tricamerum in December. Capturing Gelimer (March 534), he returned with him to Constantinople in triumph.

In 535 Emperor Justinian gave Belisarius command of an expedition to Italy in the hopes of reuniting the two halves of the former Roman Empire. Never provided sufficient manpower resources by Justinian, Belisarius nonetheless performed brilliantly. With only 8,000 men, he invaded Sicily and besieged and took Palermo (autumn of 535). Distracted from his design by an uprising among Byzantine troops in North Africa, he sailed there with only 1,000 men and put it down (spring of 536). He then landed in southern Italy, taking Naples that summer and Rome in December. Rebuilding the defenses of Rome, he withstood a siege by the Goth army under Vitiges (March 537–March 538), then with the arrival of reinforcements forced Vitiges to end the siege. Belisarius then moved to Ravenna, where Vitiges had taken refuge, and laid siege to that city (538–539), inducing Vitiges to surrender (late 539). Belisarius was forced to break off plans for the conquest of all of Italy when he was recalled to Constantinople by a jealous Justinian, who feared that his great general would accept proffered offers to become king of Italy. Despite Justinian's poor treatment, Belisarius always remained completely loyal to the emperor.

Commanding against the Persians in 542, Belisarius drove them out of Lazica in present-day southeastern Anatolia (542–544) and then invaded Persia itself. With the achievement of a truce with the Persians in 545, secured by the payment of tribute by the Byzantines, Justinian again sent Belisarius to Italy. Because of inadequate resources, Belisarius was unable to prevent the capture of Rome by Goth leader Totila. Nonetheless, Belisarius soon retook that city and held it against repeated Goth attacks in 546. Despite his successes, Belisarius was never able to accomplish much in Italy because of Justinian's failure to provide him with adequate resources.

Justinian recalled Belisarius to Constantinople in 549, where he again retired. Called from retirement in 554, Belisarius secured southwest Spain for the Byzantine Empire. Again called from retirement in 559 to confront a major Bulgar invasion across the Danube into Moesia (today northern Bulgaria) and Thrace, Belisarius was victorious over a much larger Bulgar force under Zabergan in the Battle of Melanthius, after which he drove the Bulgars back across the Danube.

Brought to trial on Justinian's orders on undoubtedly trumped-up charges of corruption in 562, Belisarius was found guilty and stripped of his honors and property. Justinian evidently had second thoughts, for Belisarius was restored to favor the next year. Largely responsible for having increased the size of the Byzantine Empire by some 45 percent, Belisarius died in Constantinople in 565.

Brave, resourceful, a brilliant tactical commander, and entirely loyal to Justinian, despite the latter's poor treatment of him, Belisarius was certainly the last great Roman general.

SPENCER C. TUCKER

See also
Byzantine Empire; Justinian I the Great, Emperor

References
Gibbon, Edward. *The History of the Decline and Fall of the Roman Empire.* Vol. 4 of 7. London: Methuen, 1909.
Mahon, Lord [Stanhope, Philip Henry]. *The Life of Belisarius: The Last Great General of Rome.* 1848; reprint, Yardley, PA: Westholme Publishing, 2005.
Oman, C. W. C. *The Art of War in the Middle Ages.* Ithaca, NY: Cornell University Press, 1953.
Presland, J. *Belisarius, General of the East.* 1916; reprint, New York: Hesperides, 2006.

Ben-Gurion, David (1886–1973)

Zionist leader, defense minister (1948–1954 and 1955–1963), and prime minister of Israel (1948–1953, 1955–1963). Celebrated as Israel's "Father of the Nation," David Ben-Gurion was born David Grün in Plonsk, Poland, on October 16, 1886. Educated in his Zionist father's Hebrew school, as a teenager he joined the Zionist youth group Erza. He then taught at a Hebrew school in Warsaw and joined the Poalei Zion (Workers of Zion). Grün believed that Zionism would be achieved by Jewish settlement in Palestine and by collective farming and industrialization of the land.

Grün moved to Jaffa, Palestine, in 1906 and established the first Jewish workers' commune there. He then began organizing other workers into unions. In Jerusalem in 1910 he began writing for the newspaper *Ahdut*, writing under the name Ben-Gurion ("son of the lion" in Hebrew).

Ben-Gurion then moved to Jerusalem and joined the editorial staff of another newspaper. He left Palestine in 1912 to earn a law degree from Istanbul University during 1912–1914. Returning to Palestine to take up his union work, he was expelled by the Ottomans—who still controlled Palestine—in March 1915.

Settling in New York City, Ben-Gurion met Russian-born Paula Munweis, whom he married in 1917. Buoyed by the 1917 British Balfour Declaration that proposed a

Jewish homeland in Palestine, Ben-Gurion joined the Jewish Legion, a volunteer British military unit formed to fight the Ottomans. In 1920 he returned to union organizing and helped found the Histadrut, a powerful federation of Jewish labor unions. During 1921–1935 he served as its secretary-general. The Histadrut became in effect a state within British-controlled Palestine. Ben-Gurion was also a driving force behind the establishment of Haganah, the paramilitary force of the Zionist movement that helped facilitate illegal Jewish immigration to Palestine and protect the Jewish settlements there. Within the Zionist movement in Palestine, however, he was known as a moderate who opposed the radical approach advocated by Ze'ev Jabotinsky and Menachem Begin. Briefly Ben-Gurion cooperated with Begin's Irgun Tsvai Leumi (National Military Organization) but only rarely supported violence, and then only against military targets. While Ben-Gurion agreed to Begin's plan to bomb the King David Hotel, it was only with the aim of humiliating the British. When it became apparent that the effort would result in loss of life, Ben-Gurion ordered Begin to call off the bombing, which Begin refused to do.

When it became clear after World War II that Britain was not sympathetic to the establishment of a Jewish state in Palestine, Ben-Gurion pursued other avenues to achieve Jewish statehood. He supported the United Nations (UN) 1947 partition plan that called for separate Jewish and Arab states in Palestine. In May 1948 the UN formally partitioned Palestine, and the State of Israel was born.

Ben-Gurion was concurrently both prime minister and defense minister. He insisted that the new state be marked by full social and political equality without regard to race, religion, or sex. As defense minister, he immediately consolidated all the Jewish paramilitary organizations into the Israel Defense Forces (IDF), enabling them to effectively fight both the Arab Palestinians and the surrounding Arab nations.

As Israel's prime minister, Ben-Gurion promoted Jewish immigration from the Arab states (Operation MAGIC CARPET). He also oversaw establishment of the Jewish state's governmental institutions, advocated compulsory primary education, and urged the creation of new towns and cities. Deeply involved in rural development projects, he urged the establishment of new settlements, especially in the Negev. He was also one of the founders of Mapai, the political party that held power in the first three decades of the Jewish state.

Ben-Gurion retired from politics in 1953, only to return as prime minister and defense minister in 1955. His second period as prime minister coincided with the 1956 Suez Crisis in which the Israeli government worked secretly with the French and British governments to seize control of the Suez Canal and topple Egyptian president Gamal Abdel Nasser from power. Although the IDF performed admirably, heavy pressure from the U.S. government brought the withdrawal of the British, which in turn forced the French and Israelis to remove their own forces.

The last years of Ben-Gurion's premiership were marked by general Israeli prosperity and stalled secret peace talks with the Arabs. He resigned his posts in June 1963 but retained his seat in the Knesset (Israeli parliament). In 1965 he broke with the Mapai Party over Prime Minister Levi Eshkol's handling of the Lavon Affair. Ben-Gurion then formed a new party, Rafi. When it voted to merge with Mapai to form the Labor Alignment in 1968, he formed another new party, the State List. He resigned from the Knesset and left politics altogether in 1970. Among his books are *Israel: An Achieved Personal History* (1970) and *The Jews in Their Land* (1974). He spent his last years on his kibbutz. Ben-Gurion died in Tel Aviv–Jaffa on December 1, 1973.

RICHARD M. EDWARDS

See also
Balfour Declaration; Begin, Menachem; Eshkol, Levi; Suez Crisis; Zionism

References
Bar-Zohar, Michel. *Ben-Gurion: The Armed Prophet.* Translated by Len Ortzen. London: Barker, 1967.

Kurzman, Dan. *Ben-Gurion: Prophet of Fire.* New York: Simon and Schuster, 1983.

Zweig, Ronald W., ed. *David Ben-Gurion: Politics and Leadership in Israel.* Jerusalem: Y. I. Ben-Zvi, 1991.

Bernadotte, Folke (1895–1948)
United Nations (UN) mediator in 1948 in the Israeli War of Independence. Born in Stockholm, Sweden, on January 2, 1895, Folke Bernadotte, count of Wisborg, was the son of Prince Oscar of Sweden who, by marrying without the consent of his father King Oscar II, left the royal family. Following military training, Bernadotte became a cavalry officer in the Royal Horse Guards. During 1930–1931 he studied banking in New York and Paris, but given his deep religious faith, humanitarian work was a more natural pursuit.

Bernadotte represented Sweden in 1933 at the Chicago Century of Progress Exposition, and in 1939 he was Swedish commissioner-general at the New York World's Fair. As vice chairman of the Swedish Red Cross during World War II, Bernadotte, who spoke six languages, facilitated the exchange of British and German prisoners of war and the release of many concentration camp internees.

On November 29, 1947, the Arab states rejected the UN General Assembly vote to partition Palestine into Arab and Jewish states. Five Arab armies moved into Palestine the day after Israel unilaterally proclaimed its establishment as a state on May 14, 1948. Six days later on May 20, the UN Security Council agreed to the appointment of Bernadotte, a proven diplomat, as mediator to seek a peaceful solution to the conflict. Ten days later Bernadotte initiated discussions with Arab and Jewish leaders, and he succeeded in securing agreement to a 30-day truce commencing on June 11, 1948. Drawing upon his experience in Red Cross work, he also initiated the humanitarian relief program for Palestinian refugees.

Bernadotte presented two consecutive plans to restore peace. The first (on June 27, 1948) suggested that Palestine (defined as the British mandate for 1922 and thus including Transjordan) would comprise a union of the two peoples. Bernadotte considered the original UN partition plan untenable. Instead of establishing individual states, he proposed that Arabs and Jews form a union consisting of a small Jewish entity and an enlarged Transjordan. There would also be a free port at Haifa and a free airport at Lydda (Lod). Israel would receive western Galilee and unlimited immigration for two years, after which the UN would assume control. Between 250,000 and 300,000 Arab refugees would be permitted to return to Arab lands with compensation, and Transjordan would control the Negev and Jerusalem, despite Israeli claims to exclusivity in the latter. Bernadotte also proposed a reconciliation committee as the first step toward achieving a lasting peace.

Both sides rejected the plan. The Arabs opposed a Zionist entity in Palestine, while Jews opposed the reduction in the size of their state and circumscription of its sovereignty in several important aspects. The Israelis found especially objectionable the handing over of Jerusalem to the Arabs, and it was perhaps this that sealed Bernadotte's fate. Fighting resumed on July 8 until a second UN cease-fire was declared on July 18.

Bernadotte's second plan, of September 16, formally recognized the Jewish state. He proposed that the whole of Galilee be defined as Jewish territory. Arab Palestine was still to be merged with Transjordan, and the whole of the Negev was to be given to the Arab state. Jerusalem now would be placed under UN control. Major changes had been made to reconcile the Israelis, but the principal winner was still King Abdullah of Transjordan. The Jewish state still would have covered only some 20 percent of Palestine.

One organization that saw Bernadotte's efforts as a threat was the Fighters for the Freedom of Israel (Lohamei Herut Israel, or Lehi), a Jewish underground group that had waged a terrorist campaign to drive the British from Palestine. Lehi considered Bernadotte a British agent and saw his plan as a threat to its goal of Israeli control of both banks of the Jordan River. It is now generally accepted that the Central Committee of Lehi took the decision to assassinate Bernadotte. On September 17, 1948, Bernadotte and Colonel André Serot of the French Air Force were assassinated in Jerusalem by a group of armed men led by Avraham Stern. Three days after Bernadotte's death, his final report on his peace efforts was published in Paris. While it gave the UN General Assembly a formula for peace, the plan was never implemented.

PETER OVERLACK

See also
Israeli War of Independence; Israeli War of Independence, Truce Agreements; Lohamei Herut Israel

References
Bernadotte, Count Folke. *Instead of Arms: Autobiographical Notes.* Stockholm: Bonniers, 1948.
Marton, Kati. *A Death in Jerusalem.* New York: Arcade, 1996.
Persson, Sune O. *Mediation & Assassination: Count Bernadotte's Mission to Palestine in 1948.* London: Ithaca, 1979.

Beth-Horon, Battle of (October 66 CE)

The Jewish victory over Roman forces in the Battle of Beth-Horon prompted a general uprising against Rome and what became known as the First Jewish-Roman War (CE 66–73), with fatal consequences for the Jewish nation. Modern Israel occupies a small land area, slightly less than the U.S. state of New Jersey. In ancient times the region was poor, bereft of natural resources and barely able to provide for itself. It could hardly resist Roman power. The area was important because of its location, for it formed a highway between the larger empires of the Assyrians, Babylonians, and the Persians to the east and the Egyptians, and finally the Greeks and Romans on the west.

The unique contribution of the Jews to the West was their development of an exclusive monotheism, the belief in a single all-powerful god, Jehovah, who watched over his "chosen people" but also demanded a high standard of ethical conduct on pain of severe punishment. No people in history were to fight more tenaciously for their liberty against greater odds. The belief of Jews in their uniqueness and their intolerance of other religions created in the ancient world a sense of separation and widespread animosity against them.

In 63 BCE Roman consul Pompey Magnus (Pompey the Great), fresh from defeating Mithridates VI of Pontus and Tigranes I of Armenia, moved to annex Syria, making it a Roman province. He next laid siege to Jerusalem and took it. Roman soldiers secured the Temple there, cutting down its priests with the sword. Although he preserved the Temple treasury, Pompey dared to visit the Holy of Holies, where only the high priest was allowed. This typified Roman rule thereafter.

Jews constituted only a small proportion of the Roman Empire's population—about 6–9 percent—but this did not keep them from being a constant problem. Roman insensitivity, sacrilege, and plain stupidity produced riots and uprisings that brought savage reprisals. Consequently, this part of the empire attracted only the dregs of the Roman civil service. A string of maladroit decrees and a succession of inept Roman administrators fed Jewish extremism and convinced many Jews that a day of reckoning was inevitable. These determined Jews came to be known as Zealots.

Matters came to a head in May 66 CE under Roman procurator Gessius Florus. His tactless decisions led to rioting, and the Zealots seized control of Jerusalem. Promised amnesty, the Roman forces holding the Antonia Fortress that overlooked the Temple precinct were nonetheless slaughtered. Gessius soon lost control of all of Judaea and appealed to the Roman governor of Syria, legate Cestius Gallus at Antioch, who had available a much larger force of four legions.

Despite the urgency of the situation in Judaea, Cestius took three months to assemble an expeditionary force. Centered on the XII Fulminata (Thunderbolt) legion of 4,800 men, it included another 6,000 legionnaires (2,000 from each of the other three legions). Cestius also had some 2,000 cavalry and 5,000 auxiliary infantry in six cohorts. Rome's allies, King Antiochus IV of Commagene and King Sohamemus of Emesa, furnished slingers and javelin throwers—perhaps another 32,000 men. Some 2,000 Greek militias of Syria also joined, eager to participate in any action against Jews.

In October 66, Cestius easily subdued Galilee; his men unleashed a terror campaign of widespread destruction in the expectation that this would both remove any threat to his rear area and intimidate the Jewish population along the route to Jerusalem. Leaving moderate forces to hold Galilee, Cestius also detached units to secure the seaport of Joppa. The Romans razed Joppa and slew perhaps 8,000 people there. Additional Roman columns secured other potential rebel strongholds.

These coastal columns rejoined the main force at Caesarea, and Cestius moved against Jerusalem. He expected to conclude the campaign in a few weeks, before the heavy autumnal rains could make quagmires of the roads. To this point, Jewish resistance was sporadic and apparently disorganized.

Cestius believed that his terror campaign had worked. On his approach to Jerusalem through the Beth-Horon gorge (named for two villages 10 and 12 miles northwest of Jerusalem), he therefore failed to follow standard procedure and make an adequate reconnaissance. As a result, the Jews were able to lay an ambush and attack the head of his column before the Romans could deploy from march formation. According to Jewish sources, the Romans sustained some 500 dead, the Jews only 22.

Cestius recovered, however; he resumed the advance and set up camp on Mount Scopus, less than a mile from Jerusalem. Here he waited for expected internal Jewish divisions to do their work. The Zealots refused, however, to treat with any emissaries and even put one to death. After several days of waiting, on October 15 Cestius sent his men into Jerusalem. The Jews fell back to the inner city wall. The Romans burned the suburb of Betheza, expecting that this would bring submission. It did not. The Romans then launched full-scale attacks but failed to penetrate the Jewish defenses. Following a week of this, Cestius suddenly withdrew. Stiffer than expected Jewish resistance, the approach of winter, and shortages of supplies and mules for transport were the factors in his decision.

Cestius decided to return to the coast through the Beth-Horon gorge. Again he failed to post pickets on the hills, allowing the Jews to attack his forces in the narrow defile. Other Jewish forces moved to block the Roman escape. This running engagement, known as the Battle of Beth-Horon, turned into a rout. Cestius and the bulk of his force escaped but at the cost of all of their baggage and nearly 6,000 men killed. The XII Legion also lost its eagle standard. The siege equipment that the Jews captured would serve them effectively in combating Roman siege operations four years later.

The battle had serious consequences. One immediate effect was the massacre of Jews by Greeks in Damascus; the leaders there were now confident that this action would have Cestius's support. The Battle of Beth-Horon meant that the Jewish revolt would not immediately be put down, however. Jews hitherto reluctant to commit themselves now joined the Zealots. Many were convinced that the victory was a sign that God favored their cause. By November the Jews had set up an independent secessionist government in Jerusalem.

The Romans could not allow this, however. Emperor Nero appointed Vespasian (Titus Flavius Vespasianus) as commander of an expeditionary force to bring Judaea to heel. Vespasian moved south from Antioch with two legions, while his son Titus came up with another legion drawn from the garrison of Egypt. The invasion began in 69, and following some delays, in 70 the Romans took Jerusalem without difficulty, thanks to internal divisions among the Jews themselves. The sack of the city was terrible (the Jewish historian Josephus gives a figure of 1.1 million for the number of dead in the siege), and the Romans burned the Temple. Some isolated Jewish fortresses managed to hold out for several more years, but the Jewish state was no more. The Romans renamed it Syria Palestina. It was not until 1948 that there would again be a Jewish nation-state.

SPENCER C. TUCKER

See also
Jerusalem, Roman Siege of; Jewish-Roman War, First; Vespasian, Emperor

References
Grant, Michael. *The Jews in the Roman World.* New York: Scribner, 1973.
Jones, A. H. M. *The Herods of Judea.* Oxford, UK: Clarendon, 1967.
Lendon, J. E. "Roman Siege of Jerusalem." *MHQ: The Quarterly Journal of Military History* 17, no. 4 (Summer 2005): 6–15.
Lendon, J. E. *Soldiers and Ghosts: A History of Battle in Classical Antiquity.* New Haven, CT: Yale University Press, 2005.

Bible

The Bible is a compilation of ancient documents now accepted as the sacred canon for, among others, Christianity and Judaism. It has served as the seed text for several other religions. The Bible (from the Latin *biblia sacra*, or "holy books") is commonly divided into two sections, the 33 canonical works of the Hebrew Bible (Tanakh) and the 27 books of the New Testament.

The Tanakh, or what Christians refer to as the Old Testament, is the primary Jewish canonical scripture consisting of three main sections. The Torah (teaching or law) is the most important document of Judaism and is composed of five books: Genesis, Exodus, Leviticus, Numbers, and Deuteronomy. These are often referred to as the Pentateuch (Greek for "five containers"). The Nevi'im (Prophets) encompasses 17 books that tell of the rise of the Jewish monarchy and the empowerment of the children of Israel. The Ketuvim (Writings) are made up of 11 books containing material ranging from the poetry of the Psalms to the Five Scrolls, which include the prophecies of the book of Daniel.

The books of the Torah were fixed about 400 BCE, and the remainder of the Jewish canon was fixed over a period of time between 200 BCE and CE 100. Around 250 BCE Greek-speaking Jews, most probably in Alexandria, produced the Septuagint, a Greek translation of Jewish sacred writings. Not all of the books of the Septuagint were accepted into the Jewish canon, however, because some were never written in Hebrew originally or because the Hebrew original versions were lost. Those excluded books now comprise the Jewish Apocrypha and include First and Second Maccabees, which tell the Hanukkah story.

The books of the Jewish Apocrypha are included in the Old Testament canon of the Greek Orthodox version of the Bible. In many other Christian denominations the books of the Jewish Apocrypha have a semicanonical status and are often included in a separate section between the Old Testament and the New Testament. The writings that now make up the Pseudepigrapha, on the other hand, consist of early Hebrew religious texts not recognized as part of either the Jewish or the Christian canons or the Jewish Apocrypha.

The term "New Testament" was likely coined by Tertullian from the Latin phrase "Novum Testamentum" and implies "the new covenant." This refers to the belief that in the Tanakh, the first covenant was made between God and man through Moses. Jesus Christ established a new covenant, which was documented in a new set of scriptures that became the New Testament.

The New Testament is a collection of works by Christ's apostles. Many texts from various sources were used during the early stages of the developing Christian Church. In 367 CE St. Athanasius, the bishop of Alexandria, drew up the list of the 27 books of the New Testament canonical works that was confirmed by the Third Council of Carthage in 397. The debate over the canon continued, however, until the New Testament canon was confirmed once and for all by the Roman Catholic Church at the Council of Trent (1545–1563).

The early Christian texts that did not make it into the canon comprise the Christian Apocrypha. Although the mainstream church considered such writings heretical, they nonetheless remained popular and influential for many years after their exclusion from the canon and were widely represented in literature and art. Ironically, the books of the Jewish Apocrypha have greater theological status among Christians than do those of the Christian Apocrypha, which have a status similar to the books of the Pseudepigrapha.

The King James Version of the Bible recognizes five divisions of New Testament works. The first section is made up of the Gospels (Good News), and in each of the four gospels (Matthew, Mark, Luke, and John) one of Christ's apostles tells the life story of Christ and details his ministry. Next is the Acts of the Apostles, where the narrative continues and details how each apostle continued to spread Christ's ministry. The Pauline Epistles are 14 epistolary writings generally attributed to Paul. These letters provide instruction in moral guidance, church doctrine, and the nature of the church itself. The General Epistles, 7 epistolary books written by apostles other than Paul, targeted a more universal audience of churches.

Revelation (also known as the Apocalypse of John) refers to its author as John "of the Island which is called Patmos" (1:9), whom early theologians believed was the apostle John. Revelation's importance lies in the fact that the text has been interpreted by most Christians as prophesying a terrifying apocalyptic scenario known to them as Armageddon, or the end of days.

The Bible remains relevant to ongoing warfare in the Middle East and especially the Arab-Israeli conflict for many reasons. One is ethnic monotheism, which holds that there is only one God who belongs only to his chosen people. This concept creates a cultural dichotomy in that the world is automatically divided into the One God's chosen people in the Promised Land and those on the outside, who are to be converted, saved, or destroyed. Islam recognizes the sacred message of Judaism but rejects the notion that the Jews are God's chosen people.

B. Keith Murphy

See also
Quran

References
Asimov, Isaac. *Asimov's Guide to the Bible*. 2 vols. New York: Avenel, 1981.
Lamsa, George M. *Holy Bible: From the Ancient Eastern Text*. San Francisco: Harper and Row, 1957.
Nicholson, Adam. *God's Secretaries: The Making of the King James Bible*. New York: Perennial, 2004.
Panati, Charles. *Sacred Origins of Profound Things: The Stories behind the Rites and Rituals of the World's Religions*. New York: Arkana Penguin, 1996.

Bin Laden, Osama (1957–2011)

Islamic militant and exponent of terror as a means of political communication. Osama bin Laden was born on March 10, 1957, in Riyadh, Saudi Arabia, into a wealthy Saudi family that had made its fortune in the construction business. At the time of the Soviet war with Afghanistan (1970–1989), he underwent a religious awakening to militant Islamic fundamentalism, specifically Saudi Arabia's Wahhabi sect. After a period devoted to raising funds for the struggle against the Soviet Union, bin Laden traveled to Afghanistan and used his family's wealth and equipment in support of the resistance against the Russians.

After the war, bin laden became a regular speaker in mosques throughout Saudi Arabia. Recordings of his powerful speeches were widely circulated. He argued that the victory over the Russians showed that a jihad (holy war) could not be stopped and that Islam was the wave of the future. The Saudi regime initially supported bin Laden but subsequently distanced itself following the Iraqi invasion of Kuwait in 1990. Bin Laden called for the liberation of Kuwait by means of a religious jihad, but the Saudi government preferred to join the United States and accomplish the task through a more conventional campaign. A staunch critic of the Saudi government for allowing U.S. (infidel) troops on Saudi soil, bin Laden

Saudi Arabian Osama bin Laden was a founder of the pan-Islamic militant Al Qaeda organization that carried out the September 11, 2001, terrorist attacks on the United States as well as many other terrorist actions in the Middle East and elsewhere in the world. (AFP/Getty Images)

became persona non grata and relocated to the Sudan. He now considered the United States the epicenter of evil.

Sudan was the base for a number of Islamic militant organizations with which bin Laden became associated. In Sudan, bin Laden also organized the terrorist activities of Al Qaeda, which were in place by 1989. Its goals were to incite all Muslims to join in a defensive jihad against the West and to help overthrow secular Muslim secular governments. Bin Laden established an Al Qaeda training camp at Soba, north of Khartoum, and in 1992 he sent advisers and equipment to Somalia to aid the fight against the Western mission to restore order in that country. He also began terrorist activities directed against Americans in Saudi Arabia.

Bin Laden made adroit use of the fax and the Internet to extend his reach. He moved frequently. Although his campaign included religious-based arguments against the United States, Israel, and the pro-Western governments of Egypt and Saudi Arabia, he increasingly looked to dramatic acts of terrorism to publicize his message and humiliate his enemies. Early incidents associated with bin Laden include a 1995 car bombing in Riyadh. Bin Laden also issued a declaration of war against the United States.

The first major blow in this war fell in August 1998 when bombs exploded at the U.S. embassies in Kenya and Tanzania, killing 224 mostly local people. This simultaneity, which multiplied the psychological impact of the attacks, became a trademark of bin Laden's activities. Foiled plans included plots to hijack and destroy 2 planes in Hong Kong and 11 planes in U.S. airports. He also sought out prestige targets, with plans to attack the World Cup soccer match in France in 1998. Successful operations ascribed to bin Laden included a suicide attack on the U.S. Navy destroyer *Cole* at Aden.

In 1996 bin Laden returned to Afghanistan, where the ultrareligious Taliban regime offered a safe haven to Al Qaeda to construct and operate terrorist training camps. Bin Laden's political activities within Afghanistan included one of the most potent acts in the region: intermarriage with the family of Taliban leader Mullah Mohammad Omar. In the wider Middle Eastern region, bin Laden became a folk hero to the poor and disenfranchised: his picture appeared in bazaars in Pakistan and was placed in the hands of demonstrators in the Gaza Strip. No Arab leader had commanded such popular appeal since Gamal Abdel Nasser in the 1950s.

On September 11, 2001, Islamic terrorists crashed hijacked planes into prestige targets in the United States: the World Trade Center in New York City and the Pentagon in Arlington, Virginia. Initially bin Laden denied direct responsibility but later admitted it. As a U.S.-led coalition mounted a war on terrorism against his Afghan strongholds, bin Laden issued statements to the outside world in the form of video messages, broadcast on the Qatar-based satellite TV channel Al Jazeera. Bin Laden escaped from the cave complex of Tora Bora across the border into Pakistan, where his presence was known to government authorities.

The U.S. government having finally established bin Laden's location, early on May 2, 2011, U.S. Navy SEALs, without the knowledge or permission of the Pakistani government, stormed bin Laden's compound in Abbottabad, Pakistan, and killed him in the resulting firefight.

NICHOLAS J. CULL AND SPENCER C. TUCKER

See also
Terrorism

References
Bergen, Peter L. *Holy War, Inc.: Inside the Secret World of Osama bin Laden.* New York: Touchstone, 2002.
Bodansky, Yossef. *Bin Laden: The Man Who Declared War on America.* Rockilin, CA: Forum, 1999.
Gunaratna, Rohan. *Inside Al Qaeda: Global Network of Terror.* New York: Columbia University Press, 2002.
Randal, Jonathan. *Osama: The Making of a Terrorist.* New York: Knopf, 2004.
Reeve, Simon. *The New Jackals: Ramzi Yousef, Osama Bin Laden and the Future of Terrorism.* Boston: Northeastern University Press, 1999.

Bithynia

Bithynia in modern-day Turkey was a kingdom in northern Asia Minor on the southern end of the Euxine (Black Sea) to the east of Chalcedon. The area was mountainous and forested although with fertile river valleys. It was a Thracian area but subject to early Greek influence from several colonies, the largest of which were Chalcedon and Heraclea. The local tribes often fought the colonists, but in the sixth century BCE Croesus of Lydia conquered the area. When Cyrus the Great conquered Lydia in the mid-sixth century BCE, Bithynia became part of the Persian Empire, although the region gained some measure of autonomy. In 298–297 Zipoetes, a local dynast who had been ruling Bithynia since 326, proclaimed himself its first king. He maintained Bithynian independence under Alexander III the Great's successors, notably Lysimachus and the Seleucids, and in 301 defeated Chalcedon and Astacus.

While the early history of Bithynia is characterized by successful resistance to invasion, the kingdom became progressively weaker during the next 200 years. By the early third century BCE, the dynastic names such as Nicomedes I

(Zipoetes's successor) demonstrate a Hellenizing influence in the court—perhaps in similar fashion to Pontus where the court took on a distinctly Greek character. At this time also Bithynia came under considerable pressure from the Celts (Galatians). Nicomedes I originally brought them to Asia Minor (278–277) to use as mercenaries against his brother Zipoetes II, resist Antiochus I Soter, and expand his territory.

Although successful in this, the Celts later seized the opportunity to expand their own power. Nicomedes I's heir was killed in battle against them, and they were only finally defeated (228) by his grandson, Prusias I. Prusias further expanded Bithynia at the expense of neighboring Pergamum and Heraclea Pontica. Despite giving refuge for a time to Hannibal, Prusias astutely remained out of Rome's war with Antiochus III (the Great).

However, in the second century BCE under Prusias II, Bithynia was defeated by both Pontus and Pergamum. Prusias sent his son Nicomedes II to seek Roman assistance, partly to get the popular prince out of the country, but the Romans instead supported Nicomedes's overthrow of his father. Nicomedes III succeeded his father in 127 and after some successes in Paphlagonia and Cappadocia was forced to withdraw under Roman pressure. His successor, Nicomedes IV Philopator (r. ca. 94–74), was forced out by his brother and Mithridates VI Eupator of Pontus but was restored by Rome. However, taking advantage of Rome's distraction during the Social War (90–88), Mithridates conquered the whole of Bithynia and exiled Nicomedes IV. Although the Romans restored him again soon after (85), he was effectively a client-king and formally recognized Roman control by leaving his country to Rome in his will. When he died in 74, Bithynia became a Roman province.

IAIN SPENCE

See also
Antiochus I Soter; Croesus of Lydia; Cyrus II the Great; Lysimachus; Seleucid Empire

References
Cohen, Getzel M. *The Hellenistic Settlements in Europe, the Islands, and Asia Minor.* Hellenistic Culture and Society, 17. Berkeley: University of California Press, 1995.

Madsen, Jesper M. *Eager to Be Roman: Greek Response to Roman Rule in Pontus and Bithynia.* London: Duckworth, 2009.

Black September (September 6, 1970–July 1971)

Armed conflict between the Jordanian Army and various factions of the Palestine Liberation Organization (PLO) that began in September 1970. The confrontation also led to fighting between Jordan and Syria. The struggle did not end until July 1971, when the PLO was permanently expelled from Jordan and relocated to Lebanon.

Relations between Jordan and the PLO had steadily deteriorated during the late 1960s for two primary reasons. First, PLO attacks on Israel launched from Jordanian territory frequently resulted in Israeli retaliation against Jordan. Second, the PLO sought to create a state within a state in northern Jordan. For obvious reasons, Jordan's King Hussein did not look favorably on such a scheme and came to believe that the PLO threatened his hold on the country and, as a result, directly threatened the monarchy. Hussein and PLO chairman Yasser Arafat were unable to resolve the dilemma as fighting escalated during the spring and summer of 1970.

Tensions increased when the Popular Front for the Liberation of Palestine (PFLP) hijacked four Western airliners on September 6, 1970, and a fifth airliner three days later. One plane was forced to land in Cairo and another hijacking failed, but the three other planes were taken to Dawson Field, an abandoned air base in northern Jordan. The passengers survived the ordeal, but the aircraft did not. They were deliberately destroyed on September 12, 1970, in a theatrical event staged for the media. The hijackings and their aftermath, which seemed to prove that King Hussein did not have control over his own country, deeply embarrassed him.

Sensing that he now had to take strong and decisive action, Hussein ordered the army to launch an offensive against PLO guerrilla organizations. The operation began on September 17, 1970. The ensuing conflict pitted the Jordanian Army of 70,000 troops with heavy weapons against the PLO, which had approximately 12,000 regulars and 30,000 militiamen armed with light weapons. The offensive was supposed to take two days but quickly bogged down into a war of attrition because of stiff Palestinian resistance and Jordanian tactical errors. Fighting was concentrated in northern Jordan, especially around Amman and Irbid.

On September 19, 1970, Syria sent a task force with 300 tanks and 16,000 troops, but no air cover, to assist the PLO. The Syrians won the initial engagement against the Jordanians. However, that prompted the Jordanian Air Force to attack Syrian forces on September 22, 1970. Syria suffered 600 casualties and lost 120 armored vehicles, prompting its subsequent withdrawal within a few days. Fighting between Jordan and the PLO subsided after Arab leaders compelled Hussein and Arafat to reach a cease-fire agreement during a meeting in Cairo on September 27, 1970. Hostilities resumed in November 1970, however, and continued until the final

PLO defeat in July 1971, at which point the PLO withdrew and reestablished itself in Lebanon. Approximately 600 Jordanians died in the fighting, while more than 1,200 were wounded. Palestinian casualties ran into the thousands, but the exact figures are unknown.

Black September produced numerous aftershocks. The stressful negotiations undertaken by Egypt may well have precipitated President Gamal Abdel Nasser's fatal heart attack on September 28, 1970. Afterward Anwar Sadat took power, eventually reversed many of Nasser's policies, and made peace with Israel. In Syria, Minister of Defense Hafez al-Assad used the events of Black September to seize power in a bloodless coup d'état on November 13, 1970. In so doing, he swept aside the civilian leadership in what has been termed the Corrective Revolution and established an authoritarian regime. PLO forces relocated to Lebanon, where they contributed to the Lebanese Civil War (1975–1990) and the 1982 Israeli invasion of Lebanon. Those events led to U.S. involvement in Lebanon and the beginning of an anti-Western terrorism campaign. Black September also spawned a terrorist group of the same name whose attacks included the 1972 Munich Olympics massacre of Israeli athletes. Finally, Black September further discredited the idea of Arab and Palestinian nationalism, thus encouraging the rise of militant Islamist organizations.

CHUCK FAHRER

See also
Arab Nationalism; Arafat, Yasser; Assad, Hafez al-; Hussein ibn Talal, King of Jordan; Jordan; Lebanon Civil War; Lebanon-Israeli War; Nasser, Gamal Abdel; Palestine Liberation Organization; Popular Front for the Liberation of Palestine; Syria

References
Cooley, John K. *Green March, Black September: The Story of the Palestinian Arabs.* London: Frank Cass, 1973.
Dobson, Christopher. *Black September: Its Short, Violent History.* New York: Macmillan, 1974.
Mishal, Shaul. *The PLO under Arafat: Between Gun and Olive Branch.* New Haven, CT: Yale University Press, 1986.
Pollack, Kenneth M. *Arabs at War: Military Effectiveness, 1948–1991.* Lincoln: University of Nebraska Press, 2002.

Black September Organization

Palestinian terrorist group founded in the autumn of 1971, named for the conflict between Palestinians and Jordanian armed forces that began in September 1970 (Black September) and saw the forced expulsion of Palestinians from Jordan. The Black September organization was said to be an offshoot of Fatah, the wing of the Palestine Liberation Organization (PLO) controlled by Yasser Arafat, because some Palestinians who identified with Fatah joined Black September. Soon other Palestinian militants also joined, including certain members of the Popular Front for the Liberation of Palestine (PFLP).

The extent to which the Black September organization was tied to Fatah or even to Arafat remains somewhat murky. Nevertheless, it is more than probable that Black September received monetary aid and intelligence information via the PLO. If Arafat did indeed acquiesce to the formation of the Black September organization and if he did funnel resources to the group, he took considerable pains to disguise this.

The first significant act taken by Black September occurred in November 1971 when several members attacked and killed Jordanian prime minister Wasfi Tal in Cairo, Egypt. The assassination was said to be retribution for Tal's hard-line policies toward the Palestinians and the PLO's subsequent eviction from Jordan. A month later the group struck again with an unsuccessful assassination of a Jordanian ambassador. Black September was also likely responsible for two acts of sabotage on foreign soil: one in West Germany and the other in the Netherlands. Three months later members of Black September hijacked Sabena Airlines flight 572, a Belgian jetliner that had departed Vienna for Tel Aviv. A daring Israeli commando raid ended the crisis. Two of the Black September hijackers were killed, and two more were taken prisoner by the Israelis. One of the passengers also died.

Without a doubt, Black September's most spectacular terrorist scheme unfolded during the 1972 Olympic Games in Munich. There when members murdered 11 Israeli athletes, 9 of whom they had previously kidnapped. The terrorists also shot and killed a West German police officer during an abortive rescue attempt of the hostages. The murders shocked the world, but the Black September organization undoubtedly achieved its aim of international exposure and notoriety, thanks to the venue in which the killings occurred and the concentration of print and broadcast journalists in Munich at the time. The Munich massacre saw the Israelis take immediate and bold steps to crush the Black September organization and apprehend or kill those responsible for the attacks.

Despite Israeli reprisals and an international hunt for Black September members, the organization carried out another terrorist attack, this time on the Saudi embassy in Khartoum, Sudan, in March 1973. In the course of the assault, two American diplomats and the Belgian chargé d'affaires were killed. In the autumn of that year around the time of the Yom Kippur War, Arafat allegedly pressured the Black September organization to disband. The following year he would only sanction terrorist attacks in Israel proper, in the West Bank, and the Gaza Strip. It is likely that the Black September organization persisted for a time thereafter.

PAUL G. PIERPAOLI JR.

See also
Arafat, Yasser; Black September; Fatah, al-; Palestine Liberation Organization; Popular Front for the Liberation of Palestine; Terrorism

References
Dobson, Christopher. *Black September: Its Short, Violent History.* New York: Macmillan, 1974.
Livingstone, Neil C., and David Haley. *Inside the PLO.* New York: William Morrow, 1990.
Yodfat, Aryeh Y., and Yuval Arnon-OHannah. *PLO Strategy and Tactics.* New York: St. Martin's, 1981.

Bohemund I of Antioch (ca. 1054–1111)

Leader of the Italian Norman contingent in the First Crusade (1096–1099) and subsequently prince of Antioch (1098–1111). Bohemund was born around 1054 in San Marco Argentano, Calabria, the son of Robert Guiscard, the Norman conqueror of southern Italy, by his marriage to the Norman Alverada. Baptized Mark, his name Bohemund was actually a nickname taken from a legendary giant. In 1058 Guiscard repudiated this first marriage in order to marry the Lombard princess Sikelgaita, and thus Bohemund lost his right of inheritance to the duchy of Apulia in favor of Guiscard's sons by Sikelgaita.

As a young adult Bohemund engaged in warfare at his father's side, including his father's attacks on the Dalmatian coast of the Byzantine Empire in the 1080s. These were intended to provide Bohemund with his own lands, but after Guiscard died in 1085 the Dalmatian conquests were soon lost. Bohemund was left to fight his half brother and his paternal uncle, the count of Sicily (both called Roger), for a small territorial inheritance in Apulia, including the cities of Taranto and Bari. It was therefore widely assumed at the time that Bohemund took part in the First Crusade because of territorial ambition.

Bohemund's contingent, which was not large, crossed the Adriatic in October 1096 ahead of the other major armies and landed near Dyrrachion (modern-day Durrës, Albania), which Bohemund and his father had besieged during the winter of 1081–1082 and was betrayed into their hands. The Byzantines were, however, wary of their old antagonist; indeed, one source reported a secret approach by Bohemund to Godfrey of Bouillon suggesting an attack on Constantinople (modern-day Istanbul, Turkey).

Emperor Alexios I Komnenos endeavored to contain the potential threat from Bohemund by extracting an oath from him in return for which the emperor would give Bohemund lands "beyond Antioch." The exact terms of this oath have been much discussed. Byzantine fears were justified when in the summer of 1098 following a long siege the crusaders took Antioch (modern-day Antakya, Turkey) and Bohemund kept the city, which had been part of the Byzantine Empire and of immense importance to it strategically, economically, and symbolically.

Bohemund's actions in the spring of 1098 suggest that he was actively maneuvering to secure Antioch for himself. Having identified a traitor within the city, he encouraged first the withdrawal of the Byzantines under Tatikios and then that of Stephen of Blois, who held overall command within the barons' war council. Bohemund extracted a

Detail of historiated initial "E" depicting Bohemund I of Antioch and Daimbert, patriarch of Jerusalem, sailing for Apulia in a ship flying the cross of St. George. (The British Library)

promise from the other crusade leaders that the city should be granted to whichever of them could effect its capture. Thus, when the city was betrayed to the crusaders, Bohemund laid claim to it, and although there was considerable subsequent wrangling over his possession, especially with Raymond of Saint-Gilles, he remained in Antioch when the rest of the leaders marched south to Jerusalem early in 1099. Bohemund did not visit that city until Christmas 1099.

While campaigning in Cilicia in August 1100, Bohemund was captured by the Danishmendid emir and held for ransom. Bohemund's nephew Tancred assumed the regency of Antioch during Bohemund's absence (1101–1103) but was unwilling to raise the enormous sum demanded to release him. Bohemund meanwhile persuaded his captor to refuse an offer by Byzantine emperor Alexios to ransom him, which would have ended his ambitions, in favor of a smaller sum and an alliance with the Franks. This ransom was raised by King Baldwin I of Jerusalem and Patriarch Bernard of Antioch. Remarkably, Bohemund reclaimed Antioch from Tancred. Bohemund and Joscelin I of Edessa profited from the alliance with the Danishmendid emir to secure Marash (modern-day Kahramanmaraſl, Turkey) in 1103, while a Byzantine attempt to reclaim Cilician cities was unsuccessful. In the following year, however, Bohemund and Tancred found themselves fighting both Muslims and Byzantines, and in September 1104 Bohemund announced that he would sail for Europe to secure reinforcements. He left Tancred as regent.

Bohemund headed first for his lands in southern Italy, where he spent some months putting his affairs in order after a nine-years absence and in recruiting Normans for an expedition. In Rome he persuaded Pope Paschal II that the Byzantines were inimical to the Latin settlements in Outremer and secured crusading status for a planned attack on the Byzantine Empire. From there Bohemund traveled to France, where King Philip I gave him permission to recruit, and to Normandy, where he met King Henry I of England and his sister Adela, widow of Stephen of Blois. They brokered a marriage for Bohemund with Constance, daughter of Philip of France and the divorced countess of Champagne. Although Constance accompanied Bohemund no farther than Italy, the marriage served as an impressive mark of favor and a boost to recruitment.

Bohemund returned to Italy in 1106 and spent much of the following year planning his crusade. He and his army landed on the Dalmatian coast of the Byzantine Empire in October 1107 and marched on Dyrrachion. This time too he was unable to take the city by assault, and Emperor Alexios moved swiftly to impose a blockade by sea. In the spring of 1108 the Byzantine Army moved up to encircle the crusaders, who suffered from both famine and disease that summer. In September, Bohemund was forced to surrender. The Treaty of Devol made him the emperor's liegeman, governing Antioch under the emperor's suzerainty, while his Cilician conquests were forfeited to the emperor. Also, a Greek patriarch was to be restored in Antioch. Finally, Tancred was obliged to comply with the treaty as well. Bohemund withdrew to his Italian lands, where he died a broken man on March 3, 1111, leaving two infant sons by his French wife to inherit his claim to Antioch. One of these was Bohemund II of Antioch.

Susan B. Edgington

See also
Antioch, Sieges of; Baldwin I of Jerusalem; Crusades in the Holy Land, Christian; Godfrey of Bouillon; Joscelin I of Edessa

References
Asbridge, Thomas. *The Creation of the Principality of Antioch, 1098–1130*. Woodbridge, UK: Boydell, 2000.
Gadolin, Anitra R. "Prince Bohemund's Death and Apotheosis in the Church of San Sabino, Canosa di Puglia." *Byzantion* 52 (1982): 124–153.
Rice, Geoffrey. "A Note on the Battle of Antioch, 28 June 1098. Bohemond as Tactical Innovator." *Parergon* 25 (1979): 3–8.
Rowe, John Gordon. "Paschal II, Bohemond of Antioch and the Byzantine Empire." *Bulletin of the John Rylands Library* 49 (1966): 165–202.
Yewdale, Ralph B. *Bohemond I, Prince of Antioch*. Princeton, NJ: Leonaur, 2010.

Bohemund VI of Antioch-Tripoli (ca. 1237–1275)

Prince of Antioch and count of Tripoli (1252–1275). The son of Bohemund V of Antioch-Tripoli and Lucienne of Segni, Bohemund VI was born around 1237 and succeeded to both principalities on the death of his father in 1252, when, although still a minor, he seized power from his mother with the help of crusader king Louis IX of France. It was Louis who arranged Bohemund's marriage to Sibyl, daughter of King Het'um I of Cilicia, ending years of hostilities between these two neighboring states. With Het'um, Bohemund allied with the Mongols and received back the port of Laodikeia (modern-day AlLādhiqīyah, Syria), which had been lost since 1188. However, the Mongols required Bohemund to admit the Greek patriarch Euthymios into the city of Antioch (modern-day Antakya, Turkey), earning Bohemund a papal excommunication.

Following the Mongol defeat by the Mamluks in the Battle of Ayn Jalut (September 3, 1260), Bohemund's lands were again threatened. The Mamluks invaded the county of Tripoli in 1266, capturing Arqah and dividing the county in two. Ten years later in 1268, Mamluk sultan Baybars I captured Antioch, massacring its inhabitants; although Bohemund survived in Tripoli, most of the principality of Antioch was lost. In 1270 the important Hospitaller castle of Krak des Chevaliers fell to Baybars, but Bohemund managed to secure a 10-year truce with the sultan. Bohemund VI died in 1275, passing his much-reduced lands to his son Bohemund VII.

CHRISTOPHER MACEVITT

See also
Ayn Jalut, Battle of; Baybars I; Louis IX, King of France

References
Cahen, Claude. *La Syrie du Nord à l'époque des croisades et la principauté franque d'Antioche.* Paris: Geuthner, 1940.
Runciman, Steven, *History of the Crusades.* 3 vols. Cambridge: Cambridge University Press, 1954.
Sourdel, Dominique. "Bohémond et les chrétiens à Damas sous l'occupation mongole." In *Dei gesta per Francos,* ed. Michel Balard, Benjamin Z. Kedar, and Jonathan Riley-Smith, 295–299. Aldershot, UK: Ashgate, 2001.

Bohemund VII of Antioch-Tripoli (1261–1287)

Prince of Antioch and count of Tripoli (1275–1287). Born in 1261, Bohemund VII succeeded to his much-reduced domains on the death of his father, Bohemund VI, in 1275 but remained in Cilicia with his mother's relatives until he came of age in 1277. On his return Bohemund faced opposition from Guy II Embriaco, lord of Gibelet, and the Templars, which led to civil strife for the next five years. In 1282, Bohemund captured Guy and his two brothers and had them buried in sand up to their necks until they starved to death.

In 1281 Bohemund abandoned the long-standing alliance with the Mongols and signed a truce with the Mamluks shortly before a Mongol invasion. However, in March 1287 Mamluk sultan Qalawun captured Laodikeia (modern-day Al-Lādhiqīyah, Syria), the last portion of the principality of Antioch. Bohemund died that same year on October 19. He was succeeded in the county of Tripoli by his sister Lucia. Two years later Tripoli itself fell, and the long line of Norman princes of Syria came to an end.

CHRISTOPHER MACEVITT

See also
Bohemund VI of Antioch-Tripoli; Qalawun

References
Cahen, Claude. *La Syrie du Nord à l'époque des croisades et la principauté franque d'Antioche.* Paris: Geuthner, 1940.
Runciman, Steven. *History of the Crusades.* 3 vols. Cambridge: Cambridge University Press, 1954.

Bonaparte, Napoleon (1769–1821)

French general and emperor who campaigned in Egypt during 1799–1801. Napoleon Bonaparte was born Napoleone di Buonaparte in Ajaccio, Corsica, on August 15, 1769. His parents, Carlo and Letizia Buonaparte, were members of the lesser nobility. Genoa had ceded Corsica to France the year before, so Bonaparte was born a citizen of France. He was a student at the Brienne military school in France during 1779–1784. Considered a foreigner by his classmates and alone much of the time, there he developed his prodigious powers of concentration and memory.

Bonaparte studied at the École militaire in Paris during 1784–1785 and was commissioned in the army at age 16 and assigned to an artillery regiment. He secured a leave with pay to return to Corsica in September 1786, which he extended, returning to his regiment in June 1788.

The French Revolution of 1789 made possible Bonaparte's rapid advancement and brilliant military career. War began in the spring of 1792, and with but two brief exceptions (1802–1803 and 1814–1815) 23 years of war followed, 17 of them dominated by Bonaparte. Except for two periods (February–September 1791 and May–September 1792), he was in Corsica for most of the next three years (late 1789–June 1793). He and his brothers Joseph and Lucien hoped to advance the family position in Corsica, but running afoul of Corsican nationalist Pascal Paoli, the family fled to France.

The collapse of his Corsican ambitions in June 1793 was undoubtedly the turning point in Bonaparte's career. He now had to provide for his family (including his mother and six brothers and sisters). Finding employment in the siege by the French Army of the Royal Navy and French Royalists of Toulon (September 4–December 19), Bonaparte developed the artillery plan that drove the British from the port. In the final stage of the attack, he was wounded slightly by a bayonet.

Recognized for this success, Bonaparte was advanced from captain to brigadier general in December 1793 and given command of the artillery in the French Army of Italy in February 1794. Briefly arrested and imprisoned as a suspected Jacobin, Bonaparte secured appointment to the Topographical Bureau in Paris. He was then second-in-command of the Army of the Interior and in this capacity put down the royalist uprising of 13 Vendémaire (October 5, 1795). His "whiff of grapeshot" killed several hundred people but saved the Convention. In reward, Bonaparte received command of the Army of the Interior until given command of the Army of Italy in March 1796. Before his departure for Italy, he married the widow Josephine de Beauharnais.

Taking the offensive on his arrival in Italy in April 1796, Bonaparte showed his motivational abilities. He forced an armistice on the Piedmontese and defeated the Austrians at Lodi (May 10) and entered Milan (May 15). He secured all of Lombardy and then won a series of other battles against the Austrians, including those at Arcole (November 15–17) and Rivoli (January 14–15, 1797). Advancing into Austria, he imposed on the Austrians the preliminary Peace of Leoben (May 12).

From Italy, Bonaparte instigated General Pierre Augereau's coup of 18 Fructidor (September 4, 1797) against Royalists who sought to overthrow the Directory. He then dictated the terms of the Treaty of Campo Formio with Austria (December 17) that secured the Austrian Netherlands (Belgium and Luxembourg) for France and Austrian recognition of a northern Italian (Cisalpine) republic under French influence.

Bonaparte's reward for his brilliant success was command of an expedition against Egypt, the plan being to march overland and threaten the British position in India. Bonaparte stopped at Malta en route, seizing that island and its large treasury on June 10, 1798. Landing at Alexandria on July 1, Bonaparte defeated the Mamluks in the Battle of the Pyramids on July 21 but was then cut off in Egypt by the destruction of most of his fleet by Admiral Horatio Nelson in the Battle of Aboukir Bay on August 1 (called by the British the Battle of the Nile).

Bonaparte's forces overran all of Egypt and set up headquarters in Cairo. After reorganizing and modernizing the Egyptian government, in February 1799 Bonaparte invaded Syria to forestall a Ottoman attack but failed to take the city of Acre by siege (March 15–May 17).

Returning to Egypt, Bonaparte defeated an Anglo-Turkish force in the First Battle of Aboukir (July 25, 1799). Learning of unrest in France, however, he abandoned his army in Egypt and, with a small party, sailed in a fast frigate on August 1, eluding British ships. Returning to France on October 9, Bonaparte took the leading role in the coup d'état of 18 Brumaire (November 9, 1799).

Elected first consul under the Constitution of the Year VIII in February 1800, Bonaparte solidified his still-precarious position in France and abroad by invading Italy and defeating the Austrians in the narrowly won Battle of Marengo (June 14, 1800). Following General Jean Moreau's brilliant victory over the Austrians in Germany at Hohenlinden (December 3), Austria sued for peace in the Treaty of Lunéville on February 3, 1801.

Bonaparte ended hostilities with England at Amiens in March 1802. Europe was now at peace for the first time in a decade, and Bonaparte was rewarded by being made consul for life in May. He refused to work to secure a lasting peace; indeed, his actions gave Britain every excuse to resume the war in May 1803. Bonaparte then prepared for an invasion of Britain. He was crowned emperor of the French in Paris as Napoleon I on December 2, 1804, and king of Italy on May 26, 1805.

On the opening of hostilities with Austria in July, Napoleon broke up the camp at Boulogne and marched his forces across Germany, surprising the Austrians and forcing the surrender of an entire army at Ulm (October 20, 1805), then captured Vienna (November 13). Advancing against a larger Austrian and Russian force in Moravia, Napoleon tricked the allies into attacking him and won his most brilliant victory, at Austerlitz (December 2). He then forced peace terms on Austria at Pressburg (modern-day Bratislava, Slovakia) on December 26.

Napoleon dissolved the Holy Roman Empire and reorganized much of Germany into the Confederation of the Rhine under French control in July 1806. His passage of French troops through Prussian territory (Ansbach) in 1805 on the way to attack the Austrians and his offer to cede back Hanover to England without first consulting Prussia led the latter to declare war on France in September 1806. Napoleon advanced into Germany along two main axes to meet the Prussian forces moving to attack him. Marshal Louis Davout defeated the main Prussian army under the duke of Brunswick at Auerstädt, while the same day, October 14, Napoleon defeated another Prussian army at Jena. These two battles decided the campaign, although other engagements followed. Russian support for Prussia drew Napoleon into Poland, where he did battle with the Russians, suffering a check at Eylau (February 8, 1807) and then achieving success at Friedland (June 14), which led Tsar Alexander I to conclude the Peace of Tilsit (July 7).

As part of the treaty, Russia agreed to join Napoleon's Continental System, designed to prohibit British exports to Europe. Napoleon promulgated the system in his Berlin Decree in November and Milan Decree in December. His efforts to impose this economic system on all of Europe led to unrest in Portugal and Napoleon's decision to take over both Portugal and Spain. This in turn created a popular uprising in Madrid against the French (May 2, 1808) and brought the Peninsular War, with Britain sending an expeditionary force. Napoleon now began to feel the effects of strategic overreach.

Austrian leaders decided to go to war against France again, believing that all of Germany would join it. This did not happen. Napoleon took Vienna but suffered defeat at Aspern-Essling (May 21–22), which he reversed with a decisive victory at Wagram (July 5–6). He then dictated peace in the Treaty of Schönbrunn in October. Desperate for an heir, he set aside Josephine and married Archduchess Marie Louise on April 1, 1810. She gave birth to their son, Napoleon Francis Joseph Charles, the king of Rome, in 1811.

Russian tsar Alexander I meanwhile was unhappy with the fruits of his alliance with France and Napoleon's demands regarding the Continental System. Russia then withdrew from the Continental System in December 1810. Napoleon resolved to punish the tsar and all through 1811 put together the Grand Army, invading Russia with half a million men (June 24, 1812). He took Smolensk (August 7) but ignored the warnings of his advisers and decided to push on for Moscow, which he believed would bring the tsar to terms. At Borodino (September 7), Napoleon fought the bloodiest battle of the century. The Russians were able to withdraw in good order, however. Although Napoleon captured Moscow (September 14), Alexander refused to treat with him. Napoleon waited too long—six weeks—before withdrawing. The winter, lack of provisions, and Russian Army attacks destroyed his Grand Army.

Napoleon left the army and returned to Paris to raise a new force on December 16. He could secure men but was not able to recover from the loss of officers, noncommissioned officers, and trained horses in the Russian fiasco. Napoleon then advanced into Germany in 1813 to fight what became known as the German War of Liberation. He won costly battles at Lützen (May 2) and Bautzen (May 20–21), but a prolonged truce during June–August, when he did not negotiate seriously, allowed his enemies to become stronger, especially with the addition of Austria, which joined the coalition against him. Although Napoleon won the Battle of Dresden (August 26–27), he was defeated in the largest battle of the Napoleonic Wars, at Leipzig (the Battle of the Nations, October 16–19). Napoleon then rejected peace terms that would have given France a Rhine frontier.

In the winter of 1813–1814 Napoleon waged a brilliant campaign, winning a number of battles with dwindling resources but being unable to stop the allies from occupying Paris (March 30, 1814). Napoleon prepared to fight on, but his marshals united against this and demanded his abdication at Fontainebleau on April 4. Exiled to Elba by the Treaty of Fontainebleau, he busied himself with his small kingdom. With France in some unrest over decisions by the new government of Bourbon king Louis XVIII and the allies in sharp disagreement over the peace settlement at the Congress of Vienna, Napoleon escaped from Elba and arrived back in France (March 1, 1815). Troops sent to arrest him rallied to their former commander, and Napoleon returned to Paris and issued yet another more liberal constitution in an effort to win popular support. Resolved to strike before his enemies could again coalesce against him, he invaded Belgium on June 1 and defeated the Prussians at Ligny (June 16) and the British at Quatre Bras (June 16). He then detached a large body to pursue the withdrawing Prussians who, however, marched to aid the British at Waterloo, enabling the Allies to win that battle (June 18) and bring the Napoleonic Wars to a close.

Napoleon abdicated for a second time and surrendered to the English, who sent him to the island of St. Helena in the South Atlantic on October 15, where he died from gastric cancer on May 5, 1821. In 1840 his remains were returned to France and entombed at Les Invalides in Paris.

Spencer C. Tucker

See also
Aboukir, First Battle of; Aboukir Bay, Battle of; Acre, 1799 Siege of

References
Chandler, David G. *The Campaigns of Napoleon*. New York: Macmillan, 1966.
Cole, Juan. *Napoleon's Egypt: Invading the Middle East*. New York: Palgrave Macmillan, 2008.
Connelly, Owen. *Blundering to Glory: Napoleon's Military Campaigns*. Wilmington, DE: Scholarly Resources, 1990.
Herold, J. Christopher. *Bonaparte in Egypt*. Tucson, AZ: Fireship, 2009.
Stratham, Paul. *Napoleon in Egypt*. New York: Bantam, 2009.
Thompson, J. M. *Napoleon Bonaparte*. New York: Oxford University Press, 1952.

Boniface I of Montferrat (ca. 1150–1207)

Marquis of Montferrat (1192–1207), titular leader of the Fourth Crusade (1202–1204) and subsequently marquis of Thessalonica (1204–1207). Born around 1150, the third son of William V "the Old," marquis of Montferrat, and Judith of Austria, Boniface succeeded to the marquesette of Montferrat in northwestern Italy in 1192 when his elder brother Conrad was assassinated in the Holy Land. In June 1201 the leading barons of the Fourth Crusade, perhaps on the advice of King Philip II of France, offered the leadership of the enterprise to Boniface, who accepted. After visiting the king in Paris and the monks of Cîteaux, Boniface traveled to Haguenau in Alsace, where he spent Christmas with his cousin, Philip of Swabia, king of Germany. There Boniface spoke with young Alexios Angelos, the brother of Philip's wife, Irene, and son of the deposed Byzantine emperor, Isaac II Angelos. Alexios had just arrived in the West and was seeking an army to help him obtain the throne by overthrowing his uncle, Emperor Alexios III Angelos. The plan was commended by Philip, although given his own struggle for the German throne, he could offer no material support. Boniface promised to do all that he could to help. He later tried but failed to convince Pope Innocent III to allow the crusade to divert to Constantinople.

The crusade fleet left Venice in early October 1202 without Boniface, who had matters to attend to elsewhere. He also wanted to avoid the conquest of Zara (modern-day Zadar, Croatia), which the crusaders had agreed to undertake in return for the suspension of their debt to the Venetians, and did not arrive at Zara until mid-December. A few weeks later envoys from Philip of Swabia arrived, promising rich rewards for the crusaders if they would help the young Alexios claim his throne in Constantinople.

Boniface naturally supported the plan, as did most of the other barons, conscious of the crusade's lack of funds. Alexios joined the crusaders on April 25, 1202, and remained under the marquis's care thereafter. After the crusaders had successfully placed their claimant on the throne of Byzantium as Emperor Alexios IV (July 1203), Boniface became an important member of the imperial court; it was probably at this time that Alexios granted him the island of Crete. Boniface led an expeditionary force with the new emperor to capture Alexios III and extend control over Thrace in the autumn of 1203, but soon after the marquis was edged out of court by a growing anti-Latin faction.

Given their experience with the Montferrat clan, the Greek citizens of Constantinople believed that the crusader attack on the city in April 1204 was an attempt to place Boniface on the throne of the caesars. After the city's fall, people on the streets would greet Latins with the Greek phrase *ayos vasileas marchio* (holy emperor the marquis). Boniface certainly aspired to the position, and he looked the part. He had already occupied the Great Palace of Constantinople and married the widow of Isaac II, Margaret of Hungary. However, the crusaders elected Count Baldwin IX of Flanders instead, and a dispute between the two men soon broke out over possession of the city of Thessalonica, which Boniface insisted should be given to him at once. War was avoided only by the quick work of Doge Enrico Dandolo and Geoffrey of Villehardouin. Boniface took the city and, with the help of his wife and her son Manuel, extended his holdings throughout Thessaly and into central Greece. From 1205 onward Boniface, allied with the new emperor, Henry, waged war against the Bulgarian emperor, Kalojan. Boniface was killed on September 4, 1207, in a Bulgarian ambush near Mosynopolis, leaving a young son, Demetrius, as heir to Thessalonica.

Thomas F. Madden

See also

Alexios III Angelos; Baldwin I of Constantinople; Crusades in the Holy Land, Christian

References

Brader, David. *Bonifaz von Montferrat bis zum Antritt der Kreuzfahrt (1202)*. Berlin: Ebering, 1907.

Queller, Donald E., and Thomas F. Madden. *The Fourth Crusade: The Conquest of Constantinople*. 2nd ed. Philadelphia: University of Pennsylvania Press, 1997.

Usseglio, Leopoldo. *I Marchesi di Monferrato in Italia ed in Oriente durante i secoli XII e XIII*. 2 vols. Milano: Miglietta, 1926.

Border War (1949–1956)

Persistent series of clashes between Israel and bordering Arab states that involved civilians as well as organized armed forces. The struggle of the State of Israel over the determination of its borders following the Israeli War of Independence (1948–1949) constituted the basis for its rationale of retaliation. This ongoing struggle was shaped by the continuing hostility of the Arab states toward Israel.

Following the Israeli War of Independence, many difficult and controversial problems remained to be resolved between Israel and its neighbors. Neither the Arab States nor the United Nations (UN) recognized as permanent borders the cease-fire lines that had been drawn. Hundreds of thousands of Arab refugees, most of them Palestinians, were

Armor and infantry units of the Israel Defense Forces's Armored Corps conducting training exercises in the Negev Desert on October 9, 1954. (Israeli Government Press Office)

living in temporary crowded camps along Israel's borders, often in full view of their former homes and fields. But they were unable to return to their lands and possessions.

For the Arab states, the border issue was not of paramount importance. In 1947 they had rejected the UN partition plan of Palestine and thus did not recognize Israel's right to exist. They were indeed waiting for an opportune moment to commence a second round of fighting, which, they hoped, would reverse the previous military failure and restore the alleged stolen lands to their owners.

Israeli leaders, for their part, sought to preserve the relative tranquility attained by the Jewish state's successful completion of the 1948–1949 war and to establish the cease-fire lines as the state's permanent borders. During the first few years following the war the Israeli government stuck to the territorial status quo, demarcated by the demilitarized zones adjoining the cease-fire lines and their status as delineated in Israel's interpretation of the truce agreements. The Israelis were initially prepared to overlook the many border incursions affecting daily life along its borders with Egypt and Jordan, as long as they did not see in these violations a threat to the state's survival.

Nevertheless, the persistent problem of infiltrations into Israeli territory was quite bothersome to the security and military establishments during these years. The war along the borders took place between Arab refugees and newly settled Israelis in these frontier areas. The Arabs freely crossed the cease-fire lines in order to return to their homes, cultivate their fields, or reap their crops. In the initial phase, these infiltrations were carried on quite innocently and were largely motivated by a desire on the part of the Arabs to return to their homes. However, as the border crossings became increasingly accompanied by theft, smuggling, and the like, they quickly degenerated into armed and violent incursions.

With time, infiltrators became more adept at executing these forays. Soon, border violations became economically profitable. In the refugee camps and Arab villages stretched along the Israeli border, bands of robbers organized and operated nightly within Israeli territory. In the earliest stages at least, these infiltration activities did not receive support from the Arab host nations. They were essentially regarded as a localized affair, a conflict between frontier settlers and refugee infiltrators intent on smuggling and theft.

In the first phase of the Border War (1950–1953), the retaliatory actions of the Israel Defense Forces (IDF) targeted civilians with the objective of harming those Arab villages from which the infiltrators set out. These reactive operations, which were justified as an eye for an eye, sought to inflict property damage in the appropriate villages and pressure the Arab governments to stop the raids. Despite widespread actions by the IDF, infiltration activity continued, unaffected by the large number of trespassers who were killed or wounded in clashes. Penalizing actions by the IDF against the Arab villages did not bring about the hoped-for results, and it appeared that Israel had no adequate response to the problem of border incursions.

Israel now came to regard infiltration as a threat to its sovereignty. The government feared a situation in which an increasing stream of returning refugees would endanger the demographic balance of the new Jewish state. In addition, the return of refugees and their control over grazing lands and cultivable fields raised the specter of a loss of Israeli territory along the unrecognized borders. This would also blur potential demarcation lines for state borders. However, the greatest peril was the serious threat to which residents in the frontier settlements, mostly new immigrants, were subjected. Many residents abandoned the settlements for safer havens in the central part of Israel, thereby weakening the settlements' social infrastructure. At the same time, this population loss would make the settlements even more vulnerable to murderous attacks and robbery.

In August 1953 the IDF created Unit 101 to deal with the incursions. This occurred against the background of military failure during 1951–1953. The inability of the IDF to cope with infiltration activities and the terror of the fedayeen led to the decision for a nonconventional solution. Unit 101, commanded by Ariel Sharon and numbering about 40 men, carried out the vast majority of reprisal operations, more than 70 in all, from the end of 1953 until the Sinai Campaign in 1956. In January 1954, Unit 101 was merged into the Israeli Paratroop Battalion.

The Qibya Raid in October 1953 was a turning point and marked a change in IDF policy with regard to the Border War. On the night of October 12–13, 1953, Arab infiltrators tossed a hand grenade into a house in the Israeli village of Yahud. A woman and two of her children were killed, while a third child was slightly injured. The footprints of the perpetrators led directly to the Jordanian border.

On October 15, men of Unit 101 entered the Jordanian village of Qibya, occupied it, and blew up 45 buildings. An inquiry into the operation revealed that Unit 101 had killed 69 civilians, half of them women and children. The Israeli government then ordered the IDF to refrain from attacking civilian targets and to concentrate on military objectives in retaliatory cross-border operations.

It should be noted that among the consequences of the Qibya operation was a significant reduction in infiltration into Israel along the Jordanian border. Establishment of an Israeli border guard unit within the Israeli police also made a notable contribution to pacifying Israel's eastern border. In addition, Jordanian forces assumed responsibility for closing that long border to infiltrators and restoring calm along it.

Until 1954 Jordan was the center of infiltration activities against Israel, but in that year leadership passed to Egypt. In May and June 1954 alone, the Israeli government registered some 400 complaints of infiltration activities with the Israel-Egypt Mixed Armistice Commission. Egyptian groups of infiltrators backed by Haj Amin al-Husseini, the former grand mufti of Jerusalem, and the Muslim Brotherhood operated from the Gaza Strip to mine roads, bridges, and water pipelines and steal equipment and livestock. The infiltrators were soon organized into a fedayeen battalion, and their activities came to be a direct threat to the Israeli settlement program in southern Israel.

Following some 45 incidents in February 1955, Israel responded with an operation in the Gaza Strip on February 28, only six days after David Ben-Gurion returned as Israeli prime minister. A turning point in Israeli-Egyptian relations, this devastating IDF military strike involved a reprisal raid of brigade strength against the Egyptian military headquarters in Gaza. It saw IDF units blowing up a number of buildings. In the raid, 38 Egyptian soldiers were killed and another 24 were wounded, a humiliation for the Egyptians and a blow to President Gamal Abdel Nasser. The Israeli raid served as the justification for Nasser's arms deal with Czechoslovakia. In response to the raid, the fedayeen mounted dozens of terrorist attacks, and by midyear the Egyptian-directed guerrilla campaign was in high gear. Receiving reinforcements from the regular Egyptian Army, the fedayeen grew into a select military unit. Egyptian intelligence operatives went on to establish similar units in Jordan, Syria, and Lebanon.

Growing Pan-Arab sentiment stoked by Nasser led to the expulsion of British officers from Jordan in early March 1956. They were replaced by radical anti-Israeli officers, again opening the way to infiltration activities from Jordan into Israel and raising the level of violence and interstate tensions.

Israel now adopted a policy of restraint. From September 1954 until September 1956, the IDF did not carry out any military operations against Jordan. Despite the Jordanian government's stated intention to halt terrorist activities originating from its territory, hostile acts continued to increase during July and August 1956. The situation along the borders continued to deteriorate, and it was clear to all that the Jordanian Legion was responsible for these provocations. In September 1956 Jordan joined the Syrian-Egyptian Defense Pact, placing its armed forces under Egyptian command. An escalation in shooting incidents along the Jordanian border followed.

On September 10, 1956, the Jordanian National Guard attacked a group of IDF cadets undergoing orientation training some 300 feet from the Jordanian border. Six of the cadets were killed, and their bodies were dragged across the border and mutilated. In reprisal, on the night of September 11–12 the IDF Paratroop Battalion launched operation JONATHAN, a raid on the al-Rahwa police station in Jordan. More than 29 Jordanian soldiers died in the attack, and the police compound was blown up. The paratroopers suffered 1 killed and 3 wounded.

That same evening, 3 Druze guards were killed inside Israel at an oil rig site at Ein Ofarim in the Arabah region bordering Jordan. Israel took revenge for these murders in Operation GARANDAL. On the night of September 13–14, Israeli paratroopers raided the police station at Garandal, Jordan, blowing up the stronghold and those inside as well as an empty school nearby. Jordanian casualties were 16 killed and 6 wounded. The raiders sustained losses of 1 killed and 12 wounded.

On September 22, 1956, machine-gun fire from Jordanian Legion positions opposite Kibbutz Ramat Rahel was directed at a crowd of archaeological conference attendees. Four were killed and 20 others injured. A day later, shots were fired by a Jordanian soldier at a woman and her daughter as they were gathering firewood beside their house at Aminadav inside Israel. The daughter died, and her hand was cut off. Another incident occurred on the same day at Kibbutz Maoz Haim in the Beit She'an Valley. A member of the kibbutz working in the fields was killed, and his body was dragged across the border.

On the night of September 25–26, Israeli paratroopers attacked a Jordanian police station in the sector and outposts of the National Guard located in this sector. The paratroopers occupied and demolished the police station as well as three military positions close by. The Jordanians sustained 39 killed and 12 wounded.

On October 9, 1956, 2 Israelis died while working in an orchard near the village of Even Yehuda. This time, the victims' ears were cut off. On October 10, Israeli paratroopers demolished the Qalqilya police station. Casualties among the IDF forces were 8 killed and 29 wounded. Overall, the frenzy of violence that began on September 10 claimed 18 IDF soldiers dead and 68 injured. Israeli reprisals claimed the lives of 100 Jordanian policemen, National Guard soldiers, and civilians.

Meanwhile, another border war emerged in northern Israel. In May 1951 a border incident took place on the crest of the heights dominating an area in northern Israel where the Jordan River enters the Sea of Galilee. This small-scale clash quickly grew into a five-day battle.

Initial tensions started in March 1951 when Israel began to drain the swamps of the Chula Lake. The Syrians fired on the tractors that entered the demilitarized zone. Israel had persisted in the swamp-draining project in order to assert sovereignty over its sector of the zone. The demilitarized areas had been delineated in the cease-fire agreement between Syria and Israel at the end of the war in 1949. They straddled both sides of the border at a breadth of between 15 and 30 miles. Israel regarded the zone as its sovereign territory, with the attendant obligation to keep it free of military personnel but legitimately open to development for civilian purposes. The Syrians, on the other hand, maintained that the zone was a no-man's-land with no entry rights to either side and that it was certainly not for development or agricultural cultivation.

At the beginning of April, Israel sought to assert its sovereignty over the demilitarized zone at al-Hama, where the Jordanian, Syrian, and Israeli borders met. On April 4, an IDF patrol set out for the zone and encountered a Syrian ambush. Seven Israeli soldiers were killed in the incident, and the IDF responded with an air strike against the Syrian police station close to where the hostilities took place. Two women were killed and six additional civilians were wounded in the attack.

The Battle of Tel Mutila occurred against this backdrop of rising tensions and the shooting incident with the Syrians. The battle began when a number of IDF soldiers from the Golani Brigade ascended the Tel to capture a herd of cattle grazing on the heights. The force was caught in a Syrian cross fire, and four soldiers were killed. Tel Mutila had strategic military importance because it dominated the area where the Jordan River enters the Sea of Galilee. The peak of the Tel was 1,200 feet above ground level and gave the IDF a commanding position over the entire demilitarized zone in an area controlled by Syrian military positions situated above on the Golan Heights.

On May 2, a reserve force from the 3rd Brigade, augmented by two squads from the Golani Brigade's 13th Battalion, attacked and secured Tel Mutila. The Syrians were concentrated in nearby military posts on the ridge overlooking Tel Mutila. On May 3, the 13th Battalion was reinforced by a company of officer trainees and succeeded in occupying the post where the Jordan enters the Sea of Galilee. The Syrians continued to harass IDF forces in the area with intermittent gunfire. Golani Brigade units continued in their efforts to occupy the entire area that had been penetrated by Syrian forces. However, repeated attacks during May 4–6 failed to dislodge the Syrians. In the end, Israeli Air Force planes fired a few rounds at the Syrian command post. This brought the withdrawal of Syrian forces from the positions. Five days of fighting resulted in the deaths of 40 IDF soldiers. It was the first major military encounter with the Syrians since the 1948–1949 war.

In 1955 Israel dominated most of the demilitarized zone in the area of the Sea of Galilee, but the Syrians more than once directed gunfire on Israeli fishing vessels from the fortified heights overlooking the water basin. Despite the arrangement by which the international border passed inland from the east bank of the Sea of Galilee, there was no way of preventing Syrian farmers and fishers from using the waters for irrigation and fishing. Syrian emplacements were located at the water's edge and provided protection for them. For years, the Syrians demanded a change in the border westward to the middle of the Sea of Galilee or at least an arrangement that would permit joint use of the lake. The Israeli government, however, was not prepared to compromise regarding control of water sources that it deemed vital for Israel's economic development and agriculture.

From the end of 1953 to the beginning of 1954, firefights periodically occurred between Syrian posts and Israeli patrol vessels on the Sea of Galilee. The Syrians wanted to fish in the northwestern sector of the sea. When they were chased away by Israeli police patrols, the Syrian military responded with gunfire, often directed at the Israeli fishers in the area. Israeli police patrols were then replaced by armored patrol vessels outfitted with antitank weapons and machine guns.

The Israelis executed a reprisal operation on the Sea of Galilee, code-named ALEIZAYIT (OLIVE LEAVES), on the night of December 11–12, 1955. During the fight, 6 IDF soldiers were killed and 5 were seriously wounded, while the Syrians lost 54 killed and 30 taken prisoner. The Israelis demolished most of the Syrian positions and fortifications in the sector and razed a number of structures. In spite of the heavy blow sustained by the Syrian military, it resumed operations the next day. Within a short time the destroyed emplacements were reconstructed, and shooting at Israeli fishers and farmers resumed.

Following the 1956 Sinai Campaign, the Israeli borders were largely quiet. The Israelis undertook a policy of restraint, even in those cases in which infiltrators and terrorists penetrated the borders during the 1960s. For all intents and purposes, the Suez Crisis and the resultant Sinai Campaign brought the Border War to an end.

MOSHE TERDIMAN

See also
Arab Legion; Ben-Gurion, David; Expellees and Refugees, Palestinian; Fedayeen; Gaza Strip; Golan Heights; Husseini, Haj Amin al-; Israeli War of Independence; Israeli War of Independence, Truce Agreements; Jordan River; Muslim Brotherhood; Nasser, Gamal Abdel; Sinai Campaign of 1956; Suez Crisis; Terrorism

References
Drori, Ze'ev. *Israel's Reprisal Policy, 1953–1956: The Dynamics of Military Retaliation.* London: Frank Cass, 2005.
Morris, Benny. *Israel's Border Wars, 1949–1956: Arab Infiltration, Israeli Retaliation, and the Countdown to the Suez War.* Oxford, UK: Clarendon, 1993.
Shalev, Aryeh. *The Israel-Syria Armistice Regime, 1949–1955.* Tel Aviv: Tel Aviv University, 1993.

Bremer, Lewis Paul, III (1941–)

U.S. diplomat, career U.S. State Department official, and administrator of the Coalition Provisional Authority in Iraq (2003–2004). Lewis Paul "Jerry" Bremer III was born in Hartford, Connecticut, on September 30, 1941. He received a BA from Yale University in 1963 and an MBA from Harvard University in 1966. Later that same year, he joined the Foreign Service.

Bremer's tenure with the State Department featured posts as an assistant to National Security Advisor and then Secretary of State Henry Kissinger (1972–1976), ambassador to the Netherlands (1983), and ambassador-at-large for counterterrorism (1986). In 2002 in the aftermath of the September 11, 2001, terrorist attacks, Bremer was appointed to the Homeland Security Advisory Council. Considered an expert on terrorism, he spent much of his career advocating a stronger U.S. position against states sponsoring or harboring terrorists.

After Iraqi forces had been defeated in the March–May 2003 war, on May 6, 2003, President George W. Bush named Bremer U.S. presidential envoy in Iraq. Bremer thus became the top executive authority in Iraq. As administrator of the Coalition Provisional Authority, he oversaw the beginning of the transition from the U.S.-led military coalition governing Iraq to Iraqi self-governance. Bremer was to serve as the top civilian leader of Iraq until such time that the nation was stable enough to govern itself.

Bremer's first move was to increase the number and visibility of U.S. military police in Baghdad while making reconstruction of the Iraqi police force a high priority. Bremer also sought to speed up the rebuilding of Iraq's infrastructure and to make certain that government workers were being paid. Despite his efforts, violence—both sectarian and by insurgents—continued to mount, and Iraqi citizens became increasingly frustrated with the U.S.-led coalition. Bremer was also forced to postpone establishing an Iraqi-led transitional government.

Bremer is credited for making some critically important decisions in his role as envoy. Among these were removal of all restrictions on freedom of assembly, suspension of the death penalty, and the establishment of a central criminal court. Some of Bremer's decisions have been highly criticized, however, particularly his decision to disband the Iraqi Army and remove members of Saddam Hussein's Baath Party from government positions.

The decision to disband the Iraqi Army has been called a major blunder. Bremer presented it via video hookup from Baghdad during a meeting of the National Security Council (NSC) convened by President Bush in Washington on May 22, 2003. Bremer's decision caught those in the room by surprise. Bush endorsed it during the meeting, and the decree was issued the next day. This reversed a plan approved by Bush of 10 weeks earlier that would have relied on the Iraqi Army to help keep order and rebuild the country. Bremer's decision was taken without consultation with Secretary of State Colin Powell (then in Paris) or senior American commander in Iraq Lieutenant General David D. McKiernan.

Bremer responded to his critics that there was, in truth, no Iraqi Army left for him to dissolve, as that task had already been accomplished by the war. He also claimed that his Baath Party purge was directed at only the top 3 percent of the party leadership.

During his tenure in Iraq, Bremer was the target of numerous failed assassination attempts. At one point, Al Qaeda leader Osama Bin Laden placed a bounty of 10,000 grams of gold on the ambassador's head. Despite the violence and the assassination attempts, Bremer was able to achieve many of his goals. On July 13, 2003, the Iraqi Interim Governing Council, chosen from prominent Iraqis, was approved, and on March 8, 2004, the interim constitution was signed after being approved by the governing council. Then on June 28, 2004, the U.S.-led coalition formally transferred limited sovereignty to the interim government. In a move that surprised many, Bremer left Iraq the same day. After his departure, U.S. ambassador to Iraq John Negroponte became the highest-ranking U.S. civilian in Iraq.

After leaving Iraq, Bremer embarked on speaking tours and coauthored a book, *My Year in Iraq*, published in 2006. He is currently chairman of the advisory board for the GlobalSecure Corporation, a firm that deals with homeland security issues.

B. Keith Murphy

See also
Baath Party; Bin Laden, Osama; Iraq Insurgency; Iraq War; Terrorism

References
Bremer, L. Paul, and Malcolm McConnell. *My Year in Iraq: The Struggle to Build a Future of Hope.* New York: Simon & Schuster, 2006.

Ricks, Thomas E. *Fiasco: The American Military Venture in Iraq.* New York: Penguin, 2006.

Scheuer, Michael. *Imperial Hubris: Why the West Is Losing the War on Terror.* Dulles, VA: Potomac Books, 2004.

Bubiyan Island, Battle of (January 29–30, 1991)

Bubiyan is an island off the northern coast of Kuwait, close to the Iraqi border. The Battle of Bubiyan Island (also known to the coalition forces as the Bubiyan Turkey Shoot) was the major naval engagement of the Persian Gulf War. It took place between that island and the Shatt al-Arab marshlands.

The battle began on the night of January 29 when an A-6E Intruder from the U.S. Navy aircraft carrier *Ranger* piloted by Commander Richard Noble with Commander Richard Cassara as bombardier/navigator, having just completed an attack on Iraqi Silkworm missile site at Umm Qsabah in Kuwait, commenced patrolling along the coast of Bubiyan Island. Just off the Al Faw Peninsula they picked up by radar four identified vessels without lights proceeding in line at 15–18 knots and headed east, apparently toward Iranian waters. As with his air force, Iraqi president Saddam Hussein hoped that his navy might find refuge in Iran and had issued orders for them to depart.

Decreasing the altitude of their plane, Noble and Cassara identified the four as Iraqi missile boats. An E-2C Hawkeye confirmed the sighting and authorized an attack. Noble and Cassara then dropped two laser-guided 500-pound bombs that scored direct hits on two of the boats, while another A-6E, its bomb guided by Noble, hit a third. All three boats were soon on fire and dead in the water.

The remaining Iraqi boat continued to make for Iranian waters, but with both A-6Es low on fuel, the E-2C control aircraft assigned the task of finishing it off to two Royal Canadian Air Force CF-18 Eagle aircraft, flown by Major David W. Kendall and Captain Stephen P. Hill, the combat air patrol for the Intruders. The CF-18s strafed the fourth vessel, clearly identified as an Osa II missile boat, with cannon fire. Its superstructure was badly damaged, but it nonetheless managed to make it to an Iranian port.

The next day, January 30, a large number of Iraqi Navy craft were reported at the Umm Qasr, Kuwait, and al-Zubayr, Iraq, sortieing for Iran. Coalition naval aircraft carried out 21 separate attacks on these vessels between Bubiyan Island and the Shatt al-Arab marshlands. Three Royal Navy Sea Lynx helicopters used Sea Skua missiles to destroy 8 vessels before U.S. Navy aircraft arrived. The battle raged over the course of 13 hours. Twenty of the 22 Iraqi ships identified as attempting to escape were either destroyed or badly damaged: 7 missile boats, 3 amphibious ships, a minesweeper, and 9 other vessels. Only 2 Iraqi ships—a missile boat and am amphibious ship—made it to Iranian waters, but both were cut up.

As with the planes of the Iraqi Air Force that made it to Iran, the vessels were seized by the Iranian government and not returned to Iraq after the war. The Battle of Bubiyan Island effectively destroyed the Iraqi Navy.

SPENCER C. TUCKER

See also
Persian Gulf War, Air Campaign; Persian Gulf War, Naval Operations

Reference
Marolda, Edward, and Robert Schneller. *Shield and Sword: The United States Navy and the Persian Gulf War.* Annapolis, MD: U.S. Naval Institute Press, 2001.

Burqan, Battle of (February 25, 1991)

Battle on February 25, 1991, the second day of ground combat during the Persian Gulf War (Operation DESERT STORM), fought between the U.S. 1st and 2nd Marine Divisions and elements of the Iraqi III Corps. Burqan is in Kuwait, part of the vast Al-Burqan oil fields. For the initial defense of occupied Kuwait, the Iraqis relied on a defensive works known as the Saddam Line to stymie a coalition attack. Behind this, the Iraqis had placed infantry and mechanized divisions to contain any coalition breakthrough. Counterattacks would be carried out by divisions of the elite Republican Guard positioned farther north.

The six-week-long coalition air offensive had significantly degraded Iraqi capabilities by the time the ground offensive was launched on February 24. That same day the 1st and 2nd Marine Divisions broke through the Saddam Line and headed for Kuwait City. Major General Salah Aboud Mahmoud, commander of the Iraqi III Corps located in southeastern Kuwait, realized that a counterattack was essential to save the Iraqi army in Kuwait.

Mahmoud employed two brigades from the Iraqi 5th Mechanized Division with about 250 tanks and armored vehicles, along with smaller supporting units. These were to attack out of the cover of the Burqan oil field and catch the 1st Marine Division on its right flank as it advanced north, hopefully achieving surprise. The Iraqi attack was partially concealed by heavy morning fog and smoke from oil fields that the Iraqis had set ablaze to provide battlefield cover from coalition aircraft.

The marines received some intelligence that an Iraqi attack could be expected, and they began reorienting their defenses and calling in artillery during the early morning hours of February 25. The Iraqi attack began at 8:00 a.m., and the fighting continued for three hours. The attack had been preceded by the arrival of an Iraqi major at a U.S. marine outpost who rolled up with his T-55 tank, surrendered, and then informed his captors that the vehicles coming into view were about to open fire.

The Iraqis mounted a furious attack in conditions of minimal visibility. The marines held, however, assisted by AH-1 Cobra attack helicopters firing Hellfire missiles. After the morning fog lifted, coalition fixed-wing aircraft were also called in. The marines were also helped by poor Iraqi tactical skills, with the attackers proceeding in predictable head-on patterns, making little effort to maneuver, and demonstrating abysmal marksmanship.

Marine casualties at the Battle of Burqan were negligible, although the Iraqis did manage to down a U.S. Marine Corps OV-10 Bronco observation aircraft and an AV-88 Harrier jet. The marines destroyed 50 Iraqi tanks along with 25 armored personnel carriers and took 300 prisoners. Additional Iraqi tanks and armored vehicles were destroyed in air strikes.

After the failure of Mahmoud's attack, the Iraqi General Staff ordered the III Corps to pull out of its positions in southeastern Kuwait, an order that precipitated a general rout of remaining Iraqi forces in Kuwait. While it ended in a decisive Iraqi defeat, the Battle of Burqan represents one of the few examples during the Persian Gulf War of the Iraqi Army taking the initiative.

PAUL WILLIAM DOERR

See also
Kuwait, Liberation of; Saddam Line, Persian Gulf War

References
Gordon, Michael R., and Bernard Trainor. *The General's War: The Inside Story of the Conflict in the Gulf.* New York: Little, Brown, 1995.

Pollack, Kenneth. *Arabs at War: Military Effectiveness, 1948–1991.* Lincoln: University of Nebraska Press, 2002.

Bush Doctrine

Foreign/national security policy articulated by U.S. president George W. Bush in a series of speeches following the September 11, 2001, terrorist attacks on the United States. The Bush Doctrine identified three threats against U.S. interests: terrorist organizations, weak states that harbor and assist such terrorist organizations, and so-called rogue states. The centerpiece of the Bush Doctrine was that the United States had the right to use preemptory military force against any state that is seen as hostile or that makes moves to acquire weapons of mass destruction, be they nuclear, biological, or chemical. In addition, the United States would "make no distinction between the terrorists who commit these acts and those who harbor them."

The Bush Doctrine represented a major shift in American foreign policy from the policies of deterrence and containment that characterized the Cold War and the brief period between the collapse of the Soviet Union in 1991 and 2001. This new foreign policy and security strategy emphasized the strategic doctrine of preemption. The right of self-defense would be extended to use of preemptive attacks against potential enemies, attacking them before they were deemed capable of launching strikes against the United States. Under the doctrine, furthermore, the United States reserved the right to pursue unilateral military action if multilateral solutions could not be found. The Bush Doctrine also represented the realities of international politics in the post–Cold War period: that is, that the United States is the sole superpower and that it aimed to ensure American hegemony.

A secondary goal of the Bush Doctrine was the promotion of freedom and democracy around the world, a precept that dates to at least the days of President Woodrow Wilson. In his speech to the graduating class at West Point on June 1, 2002, Bush declared that "America has no empire to extend or utopia to establish. We wish for others only what we wish for ourselves—safety from violence, the rewards of liberty, and the hope for a better life."

The immediate application of the Bush Doctrine was the U.S.-led invasion of Afghanistan in early October 2001 (Operation ENDURING FREEDOM). Although the Taliban-controlled government of Afghanistan offered to hand over Al Qaeda leader Osama bin Laden if it was shown tangible proof that he was responsible for the September 11 attacks and also offered to extradite bin Laden to Pakistan where he would be tried under Islamic law, its refusal to extradite him to the United States with no preconditions was considered justification for the invasion.

The administration also applied the Bush Doctrine as justification for the Iraq War, beginning in March 2003 (Operation IRAQI FREEDOM). The Bush administration did not wish to wait for conclusive proof of presumed Iraqi weapons of mass destruction (WMD), so in a series of speeches, administration officials laid out the argument for invading Iraq. To wait any longer was to run the risk of having Iraqi president Saddam Hussein employ or transfer the alleged WMD. Thus, despite the lack of any evidence of an operational relationship between Iraq and Al Qaeda, the United States, supported by Britain and a few other nations, launched an invasion of Iraq.

The use of the Bush Doctrine as justification for the invasion of Iraq led to increasing friction between the United States and it allies, as the Bush Doctrine repudiated the core idea of the United Nations (UN) Charter. The charter prohibits any use of international force that is not undertaken in self-defense after the occurrence of an armed attack across an international boundary or pursuant to a decision by the UN Security Council. Even more vexing, the distinct limitations and pitfalls of the Bush Doctrine were abundantly evident in the inability of the United States to quell sectarian violence and political turmoil in Iraq. The doctrine did not place parameters on the extent of American commitments and viewed the consequences of preemptory military strikes as a mere afterthought. The Bush Doctrine was virtually abandoned as a foreign policy tenet with the advent of the Barack Obama administration, which began in 2009.

KEITH A. LEITICH

See also
Al Qaeda; Bin Laden, Osama; Chemical Weapons and Warfare; Hussein, Saddam; Iraq War; September 11, 2001, Attacks on the United States; Terrorism

References
Buckley, Mary E., and Robert Singh. *The Bush Doctrine and the War on Terrorism: Global Responses, Global Consequences.* London: Routledge, 2006.

Dolan, Chris J. *In War We Trust: The Bush Doctrine and the Pursuit of Just War.* Burlington, VA: Ashgate, 2005.

Gurtov, Melvin. *Superpower on Crusade: The Bush Doctrine in U.S. Foreign Policy.* Boulder, CO: Lynne Rienner, 2006.

Heisbourg, Francis. "Work in Progress: The Bush Doctrine and Its Consequences." *Washington Quarterly* 6, no. 22 (Spring 2003): 75–88.

Jervis, Robert. *American Foreign Policy in a New Era.* New York: Routledge, 2005.

Schlesinger, Arthur M. *War and the American Presidency.* New York: Norton, 2004.

Byzantine Empire (330–1453)

The Byzantine Empire, or Byzantium, is the conventional modern name for the medieval Christian Greek-speaking empire that was created after the division of the Roman Empire into western and eastern parts, Byzantium being the eastern part of the empire. Contemporary Byzantines referred to their empire in Greek as *Romaike autokratoria* (Roman Empire) or *autokratoria ton Romaion* (empire of the Romans), regarding it as the continuation of the ancient Roman Empire; Westerners called it the "Greek Empire" or "Empire of the Greeks." The name Byzantium was only used by the people of the empire to describe the city of Constantinople (modern-day Istanbul, Turkey), which was founded in the seventh century BCE by Byzas, a Greek from Megara; the name Byzantium never referred to the empire itself. The term "Byzantine" was introduced by Hieronymus Wolf in 1562.

The Byzantine Empire was a multinational empire, composed primarily of Greeks, Armenians, Jews, and Slavs. Initially the official language of the empire was Latin, but in the seventh century it was replaced by Greek, which was the vernacular used by the various peoples of the empire.

The history of the empire, the longest lived of Western civilization, spans more than 11 centuries. There is no generally agreed date for the beginning of Byzantine (as opposed to Roman) history. Some modern scholars have suggested that it began in 324, when Emperor Constantine I the Great became *monokrator* (sole ruler) of the Roman Empire, or in 330, when Constantine transferred the capital of the empire from Rome to the city of Byzantium. Others suggest 395, when Emperor Theodosios the Great died and the empire was divided into western and eastern parts. Other suggested dates are the year 284, when Diocletian became emperor; the year 610, when Heraclius I became emperor; and the year 717, when the Isaurian dynasty ascended the throne of Constantinople. Most scholars agree, however, that the fourth century should be considered as the beginning of Byzantine history. The fall of Constantinople to the Ottoman Turks (1453) can be regarded as its end, in spite of the fact that two Byzantine territories, the despotate of Mistra and the empire of Trebizond, fell to the Turks only in 1460 and 1461, respectively.

At the beginning of its existence, the borders of Byzantium coincided with those of the eastern Roman Empire. In the 6th century Emperor Justinian I extended its frontiers to the Atlantic, capturing the southern part of Spain as well as North African lands. In the following centuries the Arabs, Lombards, Slavs, and Normans deprived Byzantium of most of its territories outside the Balkan Peninsula and Asia Minor. In the last centuries of its existence, the empire was confined to the southern Balkans and western Asia Minor. At the beginning of the 14th century, it lost Asia Minor to the Turks; in the middle of that century, it had only eastern Macedonia and Thrace under its authority; and at the beginning of the 15th century, it was confined to Constantinople, a few islands in the Aegean Sea, and the despotate of Mistra in the Peloponnese.

The Early Byzantine Period (330–717)

The early Byzantine period has also been called proto-Byzantine, referring to the period of Late Antiquity. In this period, the administrative and legal systems of the empire were influenced significantly by those of the Roman Empire in the previous centuries. Until 476 the Byzantine emperor also ruled the western half of the empire, part of which Justinian I managed to recover briefly in the first half of the sixth century. This period is characterized by the transfer of the capital to Constantinople and the toleration of Christianity and subsequent adoption of the Christian faith as the official religion of the empire, by the gradual adoption of the Greek language as the official language of the empire, and by the defeat of invaders who appeared at the borders of the empire.

Constantinople, or New Rome, was strategically located at the crossroads of Europe and Asia and was protected by the sea on three sides. The city controlled the land route that joins Europe and Asia Minor and also the sea route connecting the Black Sea and the Aegean Sea. Constantinople was

Byzantine Empire, 1355

also closer than Rome to the Danube area, which had been invaded by Germanic peoples, and to the eastern borders of the empire, which were under threat from the Persian Empire. Constantinople was thus the perfect choice for a capital city from a strategic point of view.

In 313 Emperor Constantine I (r. 306–337) recognized Christianity as a legal religion. Emperor Theodosios I (r. 379–395) proclaimed it the official state religion in 380. During this period, the first rift between the church of Constantinople and the church of Rome took place, while in six ecumenical synods, all of which took place in the eastern half of the empire and in all of which the Byzantine emperors were involved, the doctrine of the Christian faith was defined, and various heresies (including Arianism and Nestorianism) were proscribed.

When Constantine I transferred the capital of the empire, the new state administration in Constantinople was Latin-speaking. The adoption of Greek as the official language of the state was a slow process. From the fourth century, court judgments could be recorded in Greek. In the fifth century wills written in Greek were considered valid, and in the sixth century a new series of laws, the Novellae, were written in

Greek; however, it was only in the seventh century that Greek became the sole official language of the state. The church, however, only ever used the Greek language, since the eastern part of the empire was Hellenized to a large extent and Greek was the language understood by most of the citizens there. In this period, the empire successfully turned back the waves of Goths, Franks, and Lombards on its northern and western borders, the early Turkish-speaking peoples in the north, and the Persians in the east; however, by 642 the Arabs had succeeded in depriving the empire of all of its provinces in the Near East and Egypt, and in the 670s and 710s the Arabs' Umayyad Caliphate even besieged Constantinople.

The Middle Byzantine Period (717–1204)

In 717–718 in one of the great sieges in history, large Muslim land and sea forces of the Umayyad Caliphate, led by Maslama ibn Abd al-Malik, besieged Constantinople, only to be turned back by capable Byzantine emperor Leo III the Isaurian (r. 717–741).

During the middle Byzantine period, a number of significant ecclesiastical, political, and military events occurred that affected the power and prestige of the empire. A religious controversy known as iconoclasm (or iconomachy) arose as a result of disputes among the Christians of the empire over the veneration of icons, beginning in 726. By its end in 843, it had devastated the empire financially and cost a number of emperors their thrones because their views on iconoclasm did not coincide with those of the majority of the population at that time. In the ninth century, systematic Byzantine missionary expeditions led to the Christianization of the Slavic peoples and the invention of the Cyrillic alphabet by two missionary brothers, Saints Constantine (Cyril) and Methodios.

On Christmas Day 800, the Frankish king Charlemagne (Charles the Great) was crowned by the pope in Rome as emperor and governor of the Roman Empire. From this time the Byzantine Empire, haven been an (ecumenical) "Roman" Empire, became a "Greek" empire in the political and ecclesiastical perceptions of Western Europe.

In the 860s, dogmatic and ritual differences between the church of Constantinople and the church of Rome, together with a clash of personalities of their leaders, led to a rift, which was healed, however, in 886. In 1054 during the reign of Emperor Constantine IX Monomachos (r. 1042–1055), the patriarchate of Michael Keroularios, and the pontificate of Leo IX, the Greek Orthodox and Latin Churches separated because of their ecclesiastical and theological differences, which were triggered by the intervention of the pope in bishoprics under the jurisdiction of the patriarch of Constantinople.

In the middle Byzantine era, the empire succeeded in repelling a number of attacks by Arabs and Bulgarians. In 1071, however, it suffered severe territorial losses on two fronts. In eastern Anatolia, Emperor Romanos IV Diogenes (r. 1068–1071) suffered a disastrous defeat at the hands of the Seljuk Turks at the Battle of Manzikert, which resulted in the loss of a large part of the Byzantine lands in Asia Minor. In Italy, the Normans seized Bari, the last Byzantine territory on the peninsula.

During the reign of the first two emperors of the Komnenoi dynasty, Byzantium managed to recover some of its territorial losses of the previous decades. Emperor Alexios I Komnenos (r. 1081–1118) succeeded in recovering part of Asia Minor with the help of the crusaders, and he defeated his enemies in the Balkans, while his son John II Komnenos (r. 1118–1143) extended the dominion of the empire in the Balkans at the expense of the Pecheneg and Cuman peoples. These successes were reversed when the Byzantines suffered another crushing defeat at the hands of the Seljuk Turks at Myriokephalon in Asia Minor (September 17, 1176).

During the rule of the Komnenoi (1081–1185) and Angeloi (1185–1204) dynasties, the presence of Westerners in the eastern Mediterranean changed the political, military, and financial status quo in the region. The Norman conquerors of southern Italy, with their many attacks against Byzantine lands, posed a serious threat to the empire, and the Italian port cities, thanks to the commercial privileges they had been granted by the Byzantine emperors, gained control of trade in the eastern Mediterranean and thus reduced Byzantium's financial resources. The first commercial privileges were granted to Venice in 1082 as the direct result of the military pressure by the Normans on the Byzantines. In the treaty of May 1082 between Byzantium and Venice, the latter promised to support the Byzantine Empire against the Normans and in return received, among other privileges, an annual tribute and tax-free trading privileges in the empire. In his struggle against Norman imperialism, Alexios I also approached the Holy Roman (Western) emperor, Henry IV, and Pope Gregory VII, but only Venice supported him militarily against the Normans.

In the 1090s it was the Seljuk Turks who posed the greatest threat to the Byzantine Empire. After the crushing defeat at Manzikert, the Byzantines were unable to halt the Seljuk Turkish advances, which led to the capture of the town of Nicaea (modern-day Iznik, Turkey) in 1081, the establishment of the sultanate of Rum in Bithynia, and the loss of the important city of Antioch on the Orontes (modern-day Antakya, Turkey) in Syria in 1085. In March 1095, a Byzantine embassy sent by Alexios I Komnenos to Pope Urban II appealed for military aid in the struggle against the Turks. In November 1095 at the Council of Clermont, Urban II appealed for a campaign to liberate Jerusalem from the Muslims, to pass through Asia Minor. The series of expeditions now known as the First Crusade (1096–1099) was the help that the Byzantines were offered by the West against the Turks.

The first crusaders who reached Constantinople in the summer of 1096 under the leadership of Peter the Hermit and Walter Sans-Avoir were well received by Emperor Alexios, despite having raided the Byzantine countryside and clashed with Byzantine forces in the central Balkans because of their attacks against locals. Alexios arranged for the crusaders to be transferred hastily across the Bosporus to Asia Minor for fear of further adverse incidents if they stayed in the empire any longer. On October 21, 1096, however they were ambushed by the Seljuk Turks and annihilated.

Between the summer of 1096 and May 1097, a more disciplined crusader army assembled at Constantinople composed of the different contingents that had traveled by several routes from the West. The arrival of the crusaders in the Byzantine Empire brought its authorities and the local population face to face with unfamiliar and threatening attitudes and practices. Violent clashes between the crusader armies and their Byzantine escorts on their way to Constantinople, raids on its suburbs, foraging in the countryside, looting, the destruction of a small town in Macedonia, and an attack on Constantinople itself on Maundy Thursday 1097 shocked the Byzantines and worried Alexios. Another source of worry was the presence of armed Norman crusaders under Bohemund of Taranto, when only a few years earlier the emperor had appealed to the West for help against Norman attacks.

More importantly, since no provision had been made at the launch of the crusade regarding dominion over the lands that the crusaders might liberate from the Muslims, the Byzantines were concerned about the fate of their former territories in the East. For that reason, Alexios demanded from the leaders of the crusade two oaths: the first was a promise to hand over to the Byzantines all the lands they liberated from the Turks that had once belonged to Byzantium; the second was an oath of homage and fealty. In return, the Byzantine emperor gave them a large financial subsidy but did not promise to take on the leadership of the crusade, something most of its leaders were hoping for.

The Byzantines did help the crusaders militarily, however. After transporting them to Asia Minor, they joined them in besieging Nicaea, the capital of the sultanate of Rum, which in June 1097 surrendered to the Byzantine emperor. Next, the Byzantine Army liberated Smyrna, and Alexios himself advanced toward Phrygia while the crusaders moved east to Syria and Mesopotamia. In June 1098 the city of Antioch was captured, although it was not handed over to the Byzantines as had been agreed, and on July 15, 1099, Jerusalem fell to the crusaders.

The newly established Norman principality of Antioch, under Bohemund I (of Taranto), proved to be a constant source of worry to the Byzantines. When they reoccupied Tarsos, Adana, Misis, and Laodikeia in Syria, Bohemund went to Europe to organize a crusade against the Byzantine Empire. In 1107, the army that he assembled in the West landed in Valona and marched on Dyrrachion (Durazzo), where Byzantines and Normans met again outside the walls of the city, 25 years after their last encounter there. Bohemund was defeated and in 1108 signed a treaty with Emperor Alexios at Devol, according to which he was to rule over the principality of Antioch as the Byzantine emperor's vassal. However, Bohemund did not return to Antioch, and the terms of the treaty were never implemented by Tancred, his regent there.

The disputes between Byzantium and Antioch continued after the deaths of Alexios I and Bohemund I. In 1137, Emperor John II Komnenos subjugated Cilicia (Lesser Armenia), which lay between the Byzantine Empire and the principality of Antioch. In August 1137 Antioch surrendered to him after a short siege, and its ruler, Raymond of Poitiers, offered John an oath of vassalage. In 1142 Raymond annulled his agreement with John II, leading the Byzantine emperor to plan an expedition against him. But John II died unexpectedly in April 1143.

Manuel I Komnenos (r. 1143–1180), John's son and successor, achieved a temporary success against the Frankish states. During his reign, the armies of the Second Crusade (1147–1149) passed through the empire. Once again, there were violent skirmishes between the crusaders and the locals (the bishop of Langres's party proposed an attack against Constantinople) but on a lesser scale than those of the First Crusade. Adopting his grandfather's policy toward the crusaders, Manuel transferred them to Asia Minor as soon as possible. He also demanded an oath of homage from their leaders and a promise that they would hand over to him all the former Byzantine lands that they captured.

The first wave of crusaders who were transported to Asia in 1147 consisted of Germans under the leadership of King

Conrad III (r. 1138–1152). Manuel had recently become his kinsman, having married Bertha, a relative of the German king. He also had an alliance with Conrad against the Normans of Sicily. However, the German crusaders were defeated in their first encounter with the Seljuk Turks.

The second wave, of French crusaders under King Louis VII, joined forces with the surviving Germans and marched through Byzantine lands along the coast, but in January 1148 at Antalya they suffered severely from Seljuk attacks. Short of supplies and with little assistance from the Byzantines, only a small number of exhausted crusaders reached Antioch. On his way back to the West, Conrad III stopped in Constantinople, where he was received warmly and committed himself to an expedition against Roger II, the Norman king of Sicily, who had captured Corfu, Corinth, and Thebes while the Byzantines were preoccupied with the crusade in the East.

Manuel's achievements with regard to Outremer after the end of the Second Crusade were impressive. In 1158 he marched against the principality of Antioch and Cilicia, which in 1156 had attacked Byzantine Cyprus. Manuel forced the rulers of both states, Prince Reynald of Antioch and Prince T'oros II of Armenia, to pay homage to him. In the same year, King Baldwin III of Jerusalem put himself under the protection of the Byzantine emperor and married one of Manuel's nieces, Theodora. In April 1159 Manuel entered Antioch in triumph, riding a white horse with Reynald walking alongside him, and two years later he sealed the special relationship that he had established with Antioch by his marriage to Princess Maria of Antioch.

The issue of the nationality and confession of the patriarch of Antioch was a source of constant friction between the Latin principality and Byzantium during the period of the Komnenian emperors. The Greek emperors considered themselves protectors of the Orthodox population of the area, and the Greek Orthodox Church refused to accept the Latinization of the church of Antioch. After the expulsion of the Greek patriarch John of Oxeia from Antioch in 1100, the Byzantines appointed another Greek as (titular) patriarch of Antioch, thus refusing to accept John's Latin successor. In 1136–1137 during the successful Byzantine expedition against Cilicia and Antioch, there seemed to be a real prospect of restoring the Greek patriarch of Antioch to his throne, but in the end that goal was not realized because of Emperor John II's withdrawal to Europe in order to deal with the Normans of southern Italy. During Manuel I's successful campaign against the principality of Antioch in 1159, the issue of the restoration of the Greek patriarch of Antioch to his throne was not raised, mainly because Manuel did not want to jeopardize the de facto recognition of his overlordship by the rulers of the Latin East by upsetting the religious sentiment of the Latins there. Prince Bohemund III agreed to restore the Greek patriarch in 1165 in return for the money that the Byzantine emperor offered to pay the ransom he owed Nur al-Din for his freedom. In 1170 after an earthquake killed the Greek patriarch of Antioch, the Latin patriarch was brought back, thus forcing the next two Greek patriarchs to live in exile in Constantinople.

In 1189, the Byzantines were reassured by Holy Roman emperor Frederick I Barbarossa that the passage of the crusaders of the Third Crusade (1189–1192) through Byzantine lands would be peaceful. The Byzantines in return promised to supply provisions and guides. In the same year, however, Byzantine emperor Isaac II Angelos (r. 1185–1195) renewed the treaty of alliance that his predecessor Andronikos I Komnenos (r. 1183–1185) had signed with Saladin with the purpose of impeding the German crusaders' passage to Jerusalem. The reason Isaac sided with Saladin was the close relationship that Emperor Frederick had established with the Serb, Bulgarian, and Turkish enemies of Byzantium.

Frederick responded to the treaty with Saladin as well as to Isaac's demand that he should hand over to Byzantium half of his future conquests from the Muslims by capturing the city of Philippopolis, plundering the Byzantine countryside, and starting preparations to march against Constantinople. The threat to the Byzantine capital forced Isaac to sign a treaty with Frederick in 1190, providing for the transfer of the crusaders to Asia Minor and their provisioning. The only event of the Third Crusade that had a lasting impact on Byzantium was the capture of Cyprus in 1191 by one of the leaders of the crusade, King Richard I of England (r. 1189–1199).

The aim of the Fourth Crusade (1202–1204) was the liberation of the Holy Land from the Ayyubids by means of an invasion of Egypt, but the lack of funds to pay the Venetians the agreed costs of naval transport to the Levant was the main reason for the diversion of the crusade against the town of Zara (modern-day Zadar, Croatia), which the crusaders captured and plundered. An exiled Byzantine prince, the future Alexios IV, then invited the crusaders to turn against Byzantium to restore his father, Isaac II Angelos, who had been deposed in 1195. Alexios IV Angelos promised the crusaders and the Venetians a large sum of money, committed himself to assist the crusade after his father had been restored to the throne, and promised to work toward the reunification of the Greek Orthodox and Latin Churches. A few months later after Alexios had failed to fulfill his promise to pay the crusaders, they besieged Constantinople, capturing the city in April 1204. For three days the crusaders ruthlessly sacked the Byzantine capital.

The diversion of the Fourth Crusade to Constantinople and the atrocities committed by the crusaders and the Venetians after the capture of the city can be fully explained if Byzantine-Latin relations of the recent past are taken into consideration. There is no doubt that the crusaders and the Venetians wanted their debts to be paid by the Byzantines, but apart from this a significant role in the events of 1204 was played by the antipathy that had been cultivated for decades in the West against Byzantium because of the lack of commitment of the emperors to the aims of the crusaders. Further contributory factors were the schism between the Latin and Greek Orthodox Churches, the imperialistic policy of Emperor Manuel I toward the West, the anti-Latin policy of Emperor Andronikos I, and finally long-standing Western ambitions to conquer Constantinople, which had been an aim of the Norman kings of Sicily in the 11th century and may well have been considered by Emperor Frederick I Barbarossa and his son Emperor Henry VI in the 12th century.

The Later Byzantine Period (1204–1453)

The period after 1204 saw the decline and collapse of the Byzantine Empire, which apart from external enemies now also faced civil wars and rebellions. Around the time of the Latin conquest of Constantinople in 1204, a number of independent Greek states were established in the lands of the former Byzantine Empire, three of which played a dominant role in the political developments in the area in the first decades of the 13th century: the empire of Nicaea, the principality of Epiros, and the empire of Trebizond. The empire of Nicaea fought against the other two states in its struggle to be recognized by Greeks as the legitimate successor state of the Byzantine Empire. It achieved this aim in 1230, when the Bulgarian army of Ivan Asen II crushed the Epirote army at the Battle of Klokotnitsa. The empire of Trebizond had already been a vassal state to the Seljuk sultanate of Rum since 1214.

The Nicaean Army liberated Constantinople from the Latins in 1261, and the Nicaean emperor Michael VIII Palaiologos (r. 1259–1282) himself entered the city in triumph in August 1261, thus restoring the Byzantine Empire. However, in the 1270s popular uprisings took place in the empire because the vast majority of Byzantines disagreed with Michael's policy of forcing the Orthodox Church to accept reunification with the Church of Rome on papal terms in return for political benefits for the empire.

Further internal restlessness occurred during the reigns of Michael's successors. Emperor Andronikos II Palaiologos (r. 1282–1328) fought for seven years (1321–1328) against his grandson Andronikos III. In the mid-14th century the religious movement known as Hesychasm (Quietude) led to an open conflict among members of the church and also between the church and the emperor. A civil war (1341–1347), which initially did not seem to have social causes but eventually became a violent manifestation of the hostility between the lower classes and the landed aristocracy, was the worst civil conflict and destroyed almost everything, according to Emperor John VI Kantakouzenos (r. 1347–1354).

After the end of the civil war, John VI ruled in place of the young John V Palaiologos (r. 1379–1390), thus interrupting for seven years the rule of the Palaiologoi dynasty (1261–1453). Finally, when John V was restored to the throne, he had to face the rebellion of his son Andronikos IV (1376–1379) and then of his grandson John VII (1379–1390).

In this period, the empire was surrounded only by enemies. The continuing commercial privileges enjoyed by Italian maritime cities (principally Venice and Genoa) posed a threat to the existence of the empire: the privileges enabled those cities to intervene at will in its internal affairs by means of the fleets they had stationed in Byzantine waters. The Angevin dynasty that ruled southern Italy and Sicily was a serious threat to the integrity of the Byzantine Empire throughout the reign of Michael VIII Palaiologos (r. 1259–1282).

In order to reduce this danger, Michael submitted the Greek Orthodox Church to the Latin Church, believing that the pope would be willing and able to hold back an Angevin attack against Byzantium. At the same time, the Ottoman Turks were consolidating their position in Asia Minor at the expense of the Seljuks of Rum and later of the Byzantines themselves, who by the beginning of the 14th century had lost most of Bithynia (in northwestern Asia Minor) to them. In the 14th century, the Byzantine lands in northern and central Greece were captured by the Serbs, who under Tsar Stephan Dušan deprived the Byzantine Empire of almost half of its lands, and by the Catalan Company, which established control over the duchy of Athens and Thebes (1311–1388) after the Byzantine emperor had been unable to pay it for its mercenary services.

In 1354, the Ottomans crossed over to Europe for the first time and captured the Gallipoli Peninsula. By the end of the century a number of Byzantine cities in the Balkans had succumbed, and in 1390 the last Byzantine stronghold in Asia Minor was captured by Ottoman sultan Bayezid I. A

Western-Balkan coalition against the Seljuk Turks, the so-called Crusade of Nikopolis, ended in disaster in 1396. It was mainly thanks to the defeat of the Turks by the Mongols at the Battle of Ankara in 1402 that the Byzantine Empire managed to survive for a further 50 years.

The empire desperately needed aid from abroad, but the means that were employed to achieve this occasionally caused more problems in the empire. Attempts to heal the schism between the Orthodox and Latin Churches at the Council of Ferrara-Florence (1438–1439) were followed by internal unrest in the Byzantine Empire, whose population was divided into unionists and antiunionists. As at the Second Council of Lyons in 1274, the motivations of the Byzantines in signing the agreement on the reunification of the churches were mainly political, hoping for military aid from the West. Pope Eugenius IV appealed to Western rulers for a crusade against the Ottoman Turks, and in the summer of 1443 about 25,000 crusaders, Hungarians, Serbs, and Vlachs were assembled. In November 1443 they captured Niš and entered Sofia; in June 1444 King Ladislas of Hungary signed a 10-year truce with Ottoman sultan Murad II, which, however, lasted for only a few months.

In November 1444 the Hungarians and the crusaders renewed their military activities and besieged Varna but were defeated by the Turks there on November 10. The Crusade of Varna was the last attempt in the Byzantine era for a coordinated Christian offensive against the Ottomans. With the Ottomans threatening a new assault on the Byzantine capital, Emperor Constantine XI Palaiologos (r. 1448–1453) did what he could to prepare the city defenses but concluded that only military assistance from the West could offer the empire any hope of survival. To that end, he again tried to implement the reunification of the churches agreed to in Ferrara-Florence. The much-needed aid from the West did not arrive on time, and Constantinople fell to the Ottomans on May 29, 1453, with the emperor dying in its defense. The loss of Constantinople was followed by that of the despotate of Mistra in 1460 and the empire of Trebizond in 1461.

APHRODITE PAPAYIANNI

See also
Alexios I Komnenos; Ankara, Battle of; Antioch, Sieges of; Baldwin III of Jerusalem; Bayezid I; Bohemund I of Antioch; Byzantine Empire Civil War; Byzantine-Muslim Wars; Byzantine-Ottoman Wars; Byzantine-Sassanid War; Byzantine-Seljuk Wars; Conrad III, King of Germany; Constantine I; Constantine XI Palaiologos; Constantinople, Crusader Siege and Capture of; Constantinople, Latin Empire of; Constantinople, Muslim Siege of; Constantinople, Ottoman Siege of; Crusades in the Holy Land, Christian; Frederick I or Frederick Barbarossa; Jerusalem, Roman Siege of; Leo III the Isaurian; Manuel I Komnenos, Emperor; Manzikert, Battle of; Myriokephalon, Battle of; Nicaea, Empire of; Nikopolis, Crusade in; Nur al-Din; Richard I, King; Rum, Sultanate of; Saladin; Seljuk Dynasty; Umayyad Caliphate; Varna Crusade

References
Angold, Michael. *The Byzantine Empire (1025–1204): A Political History.* London: Longman, 1997.
Brown, Peter. *The Making of Late Antiquity.* Cambridge, MA: Harvard University Press, 1978.
Browning, Robert. *The Byzantine Empire.* London: Weidenfeld and Nicolson, 1980.
Harris, Jonathan. *Byzantium and the Crusades.* London: Hambledon, 2003.
Jenkins, Romilly. *Byzantium: The Imperial Centuries, A.D. 610 to 1071.* London: Weidenfeld and Nicolson, 1966.
Lilie, Ralph-Johannes. *Byzantium and the Crusader States (1096–1204).* Oxford, UK: Clarendon, 1993.
Nicol, Donald. *The Last Centuries of Byzantium (1204–1453).* Cambridge: Cambridge University Press, 1993.
Ostrogorsky, Georg. *History of the Byzantine State.* Oxford, UK: Blackwell, 1984.
Stratos, Andreas N. *Byzantium in the Seventh Century.* 5 vols. Amsterdam: Hakkert, 1968–1980.
Vryonis, Spyros. *The Decline of Medieval Hellenism in Asia Minor and the Process of Islamization (11th–15th Centuries).* Berkeley: University of California Press, 1986.

Byzantine Empire Civil War (1341–1347)

The Byzantine Empire, also known as the Eastern Roman Empire, was established by Roman emperor Constantine I (Constantine the Great). Having become Roman western emperor, he embarked on a series of campaigns that ended in 324 with the reunification of the Eastern and Western Roman Empires. In 330, however, Constantine formally transferred the capital to Byzantium (later known as Constantinople and now Istanbul). Predominantly Christian and Greek speaking with its capital city strategically situated on the Bosporus, the empire survived the fifth-century collapse of the Western Roman Empire and stood as a barrier to Muslim expansion into Eastern Europe until it was finally conquered by the Ottoman Turks in 1453.

For most of its more than 1,100-year existence, the Byzantine Empire was the most powerful state in Europe. In addition to extensive lands in the Balkans, at its height under Emperor Justinian II (527–565 CE) the empire controlled most of the territory around the Mediterranean Sea, including much of North Africa, part of southern Spain, all of Italy, the Mediterranean islands, Bulgaria, Greece, the southern Crimean Peninsula, Anatolia (present-day Turkey), Syria, Palestine, and Egypt. During the long period of its existence the empire was frequently at war, both in Europe and in Asia and the Middle East. During the course of the centuries its territory contracted considerably until 1360, when it was restricted to a few holdings in the Balkans. Its decline was advanced by frequent political upheavals and civil strife. The empire experienced dozens of civil wars, especially regarding succession to the throne. Such struggles invariably weakened the empire, making it vulnerable to foreign conquest.

In 1282 Andronicus (Andronikos) II Palaeologus (Palaiologus) became sole Byzantine emperor on the death of his father, Michael VIII, with whom he had been coemperor. In 1294 or 1295 Andronicus II made his son coemperor as Michael IX. When the Byzantines suffered a major defeat in 1302 at the hands of the Ottomans in the Battle of Bapheus, Andronicus hired Catalonian mercenaries, but their brutal tactics alienated those they were supposed to liberate and led to a major disagreement with Michael and Catalonian devastation of parts of Thrace, Thessaly, and Macedonia. The Ottomans meanwhile continued to make gains at the expense of the Byzantines in Asia Minor, and by the end of Andronicus II's reign in 1331 the Ottomans controlled much of Bithynia. Other invaders also made strategic inroads as the Serbs, Bulgarians, Venetians, and Genoese all sought to take advantage of Byzantine weakness.

Bulgarian ruler Theodore Svetoslav defeated Byzantine forces under Michael IX and secured much of northeastern Thrace during 1305–1307. The dissolute behavior of Michael IX's son, also named Andronicus, created a major schism in the ruling family, and after Michael IX's death at only 43 in 1320, Andronicus II disowned his grandson and barred him from succession to the throne.

Andronicus II had alienated much of the nobility because of heavy taxes he had imposed in order to expand the army. The younger Andronicus took advantage of this disaffection to declare himself emperor as Andronicus III. The ensuing civil war of 1321–1328 saw numerous small engagements that nonetheless devastated stretches of the empire and led Andronicus II to agree in 1315 to a power-sharing arrangement whereby the younger Andronicus would become coemperor and sole ruler of Thrace and Macedonia as Andronicus III.

The compromise arrangement was not sufficient for Andronicus III. In 1328 when he tried to enter Constantinople and was refused, he seized Salonika, the empire's second-largest city. Most of the Byzantine forces in the west declared for him, and in May Andronicus III was able to enter Constantinople in triumph and force the abdication of his grandfather, becoming sole ruler. His grandfather died as a monk at Constantinople in 1332.

This protracted turmoil and attendant weakness brought foreign incursions. Indeed, some scholars have suggested that Andronicus III had actually invited in the foreign invaders as a means of weakening Andronicus II. In 1330 King Stefan Dušan of Serbia defeated a Byzantine and Bulgarian army in the Battle of Velbûzhd (modern-day Küstendil, Bulgaria), giving the Serbs control of most of the Vardar Valley, with Bulgaria briefly under Serbian suzerainty. Despite this setback, Andronicus III led Byzantine forces in the field and was subsequently generally successful in expanding Byzantine territory in Europe at the expense of his neighbors. Victorious over the Despotate of Epirus, he reintegrated it into the empire in 1337. He also secured the submission of the Latin barons in the Peloponnese and took steps to reattach Trabzon to the Byzantine Empire.

Andronicus III did not enjoy similar success in Asia, however. In 1329 the Byzantines lost the Battle of Pelekanon (Pelecanum, or Maltepe) in Anatolia to Orkhan I, principal organizer of the Ottoman Empire. Orkhan then secured almost all the Byzantine strongholds in Anatolia, including Nicaea (1331) and Nicomedia (1337).

Andronicus III Paleologus died suddenly in June 1341 at only age 45 following a short illness, possibly malaria. His death touched off a complicated but highly important successionist struggle, the Byzantine Civil War of 1341–1347 (sometimes known as the Second Palaeologan Civil War).

Andronicus III's heir was his nine-year-old son, John V Palaeologus. The accession of such a young boy to the throne necessitated a regency under General John Cantacuzenus (Kantakouzenos), a close friend of the late emperor who was related to him through his mother and had aided him in securing the throne and served as chief minister. Although it was customary Byzantine practice for an empress to be regent, Andronicus had insisted that on his death Cantacuzenus be made either coemperor or regent.

Cantacuzenus now demanded that John V marry his daughter, but any plans Cantacuzenus may have had to be coemperor were blocked by powerful opposition at court in the form of John III's mother, Empress Anna of Savoy; patriarch of Constantinople John Calecas (Kalekas); and governor of Constantinople Alexius Apocaucus (Apokaukos). The presence in Constantinople of troops loyal to Cantacuzenus and a demonstration by them in the city on June 20 ensured him the regency, however.

The Serbs, Bulgars, and Ottomans immediately sought to take advantage of the infighting in Constantinople to secure Byzantine territory in Europe for themselves. Forces of the emir of Saruhan raided the coast of Thrace, while Tsar Ivan Alexander of Bulgaria threatened war. Attempting to recover territory lost to Andronicus III, Serbian ruler Stefan Dušan invaded Macedonia and mounted a new assault on the city of Thessalonica.

Had Cantacuzenus remained in Constantinople he would no doubt have been able to secure his hold on power, but he departed the city to lead the fight against the Serbs. After enjoying some success in his military efforts against the empire's myriad enemies, he returned to Constantinople in early September to deal with an abortive effort to kidnap John V. Cantacuzenus and then left the city again soon thereafter to return to Thrace in order to lead a military campaign into the Peloponnese.

Cantacuzenus's decision to leave Constantinople a second time was a major mistake, for that same month, September 1341, his opponents there staged a coup and overthrew him. His relatives and friends were forced to flee, and their properties were confiscated. Although his wife and children were safe at his headquarters in Demotika (Didymoteicho), Cantacuzenus's mother was imprisoned, and privations ultimately led to her death. A mob, egged on by the conspirators, also attacked and burned Cantacuzenus's residence. Patriarch Calecas meanwhile excommunicated John VI. The civil war was on.

Cantacuzenus's attempt to negotiate with the new leaders in Constantinople failed, and on October 26, 1341, the army, which had remained loyal to Cantacuzenus, in the fashion of the Roman legions proclaimed him emperor as John VI. Repeated efforts at negotiation came to naught, with Cantacuzenus's envoys imprisoned. In November, the regency in Constantinople proclaimed the formal coronation of John V as emperor.

The empire's enemies took sides. The Ottomans backed John VI, while the Serbs tried to play both sides, publicly pledging support for John VI while secretly informing the leaders in Constantinople that they were really backing John V. The empire itself split largely along lines of class but also along the lines of rural areas against the cities. The aristocrats, who owned the great landed estates, tended to support John VI, who was one of their own, and their influence carried much of the rural poor with them. There was really no Byzantine middle class, and the leaders of the coup in Constantinople effectively mobilized the urban poor against the rich. The numbers of poor had swelled in recent years, owing to the many refugees who had escaped the territorial inroads by various invaders and settled there. The poor harbored great resentment against the aristocrats, who greatly benefited from the endemic Byzantine corruption to evade taxes. In the civil war most of the cities opted for John V, along with almost all the provincial governors. Demotika was a notable exception among the cities; it remained Cantacuzenus's stronghold throughout the long civil war.

There was also a religious split. A political party known as the Zealots seized power in Thessalonica, then persecuted those opposing their religious beliefs. The Zealots would control Thessalonica for the next seven years.

In the first several years of the civil war, Cantacuzenus made little progress against the regency in Constantinople. It came to control much of Thrace and Macedonia, and a number of Cantacuzenus's men switched sides and joined the regency forces. In July 1342 Cantacuzenus met with Serb leader Dušan in an effort to conclude an alliance. Dušan was not so inclined but was forced into it by his leading nobles, who saw a chance to regain territory to the south lost to the Byzantines earlier. Apparently the Serbs were granted most of Macedonia. The Serbs duly secured most of western Macedonia and also all of Albania. Several military efforts by Cantacuzenus meanwhile met failure, and rumors circulated that he planned to give up the struggle and enter a monastery. Meanwhile, Cantacuzenus's wife called on Bulgarian tsar Ivan Alexander to relieve the regency blockade of Demotika. The Bulgarian forces duly arrived but chose to ravage the countryside around the city instead.

Cantacuzenus's fortunes began to turn in 1343, however. In this he was greatly aided by his former Ottoman ally, Umur I, emir of Aydin. In early 1343, Umur sailed up the Evros River (which forms the boundary between present-day Greece and Turkey and flows into the Thracian Sea) with some 300 ships and 15,000 men and then relieved the siege of Demotika, chasing out both the regency forces and the Bulgars in the countryside. Although Umar withdrew with the onset of cold weather that fall, his intervention saved Cantacuzenus and left him less dependant on Dušan and the Serbs. Cantacuzenus also persuaded several key forts to surrender to him rather than to the Serbs, a step that angered Dušan and caused him to open negotiations with the regency and openly ally with it that summer.

Although Cantacuzenus failed in his effort to take Thessalonica, Ottoman assistance allowed him to concentrate on Thrace. By the end of 1344 he had secured most of Epirus and Thrace. In 1345, his forces captured Adrianople. The change in Cantacuzenus's fortunes brought a number of prominent Byzantine officials over to his side.

At the same time, Serb successes placed a great strain on the regency's financial situation. The Serbs came to control virtually all of Macedonia and Epirus. This cut off substantial revenue to the regency, which was now essentially bankrupt. Empress Anna was forced to pawn her jewels to the Venetians, but this made little difference. At the same time, the Ottoman presence in Thrace cut off that source of grain to Constantinople. The situation was so desperate that the empress appealed to the pope, promising to submit to his authority in return for aid. Meanwhile, Cantacuzenus was able to turn back attacks by both the Serbs, led by Dušan, and regency forces, under Apocaucus, until the return of Umur and 20,000 Ottomans in the spring of 1345. Cantacuzenus and Umur then took the offensive into Bulgaria and also defeated an army under Momchil, a former outlaw whom Cantacuzenus had made governor of Merope.

Early in 1345 Cantacuzenus again appealed to the regency to open negotiations for a peace settlement, only to see this rejected. With the regency hold on Constantinople slipping, Apocaucus ordered the arrest of a number of nobles considered politically unreliable. On June 11 while he was inspecting a new prison built to house these individuals, Apocaucus was set upon by the prisoners and lynched. This was a major blow to the regency, as Apocaucus's adroit administrative skills and firm hand had been key to the regency remaining in power.

On hearing the news Cantacuzenus immediately marched on Constantinople, his supporters hopeful that the death of Apocaucus would topple the regency. The regency restored order, however, and Cantacuzenus was rebuffed. Concurrently, Cantacuzenus sustained a number of setbacks. John Apocaucos, governor of Thessalonica, had announced his allegiance to Cantacuzenus and intention to surrender the city to him, but this led to an uprising by the Zealots, and Apocaucos was slain along with many in the city who supported Cantacuzenus. Most upsetting was the departure of Umur in order to deal with Christian crusaders in Smyrna. Then in September 1345, the Macedonian city of Serres fell to Dušan's Serbs after a long siege.

With the Serbs now controlling about half of the territory of the pre-1341 Byzantine Empire, on Easter Sunday, April 16, 1346, Dušan had himself crowned in Skopje "Emperor of the Serbs and Romans." This event led Cantacuzenus, who had only been acclaimed emperor, to have himself crowned. This occurred on May 21, with patriarch of Jerusalem Lazaros presiding. Lazaros then convened a synod of bishops and excommunicated patriarch of Constantinople Calecas. Not long afterward, the alliance between Cantacuzenus and Umur was cemented in the marriage of Cantacuzenus's daughter Theodora to Umur.

The regency in Constantinople was now on the verge of collapse. Empress Ana had been largely unsuccessful in her efforts to secure foreign aid. Those few troops secured were defeated in battle or turned to pillage. On May 19, 1346, part of Hagia Sophia cathedral in Constantinople collapsed, a bad omen for the faithful.

The circumstances were now ripe for a peace deal. Cantacuzenus left his son Matthew in charge in Thrace and moved the bulk of his forces to Selymbria, close to Constantinople but did not attack. Although criticized for the lack of action and having thereby prolonged the war, Cantacuzenus claimed in his memoirs that he did not want to see the Ottoman troops among his forces enter the city.

The situation in Constantinople continued to deteriorate, with major food shortages. After two attempts mounted by the regency to assassinate Cantacuzenus failed, Empress Anna and the patriarch had a falling-out, and on February 2, 1347, a synod removed Calecas from his position. That same night, Cantacuzenus and some 1,000 of his men entered the city. Meeting no resistance, they surrounded the imperial residence. Fearing the worst, Empress Anna refused to surrender. After a standoff of several days Cantacuzenus's troops became impatient and stormed the residence, whereupon Emperor John V persuaded his mother to accept what was in fact a generous settlement. Half a decade of strife had come to an end.

Under the terms of the peace agreement of February 8, 1347, Cantacuzenus was to be senior emperor for a period of 10 years with responsibility for administering the empire as a whole. Upon coming of age, John V would be coemperor as equal. The agreement was sealed by the marriage of Helena, a daughter of Cantacuzenus, to John V. Such a generous settlement could have been reached in 1341, of course, but for the obstinacy of the empress and her cabal. Still, there was considerable distrust of the settlement on both sides and strong opposition to it from Cantacuzenus's eldest son Matthew, who resented being passed over by John V.

Emperor John VI ruled until 1355. He not only recovered his personal lands in Thrace but also distributed large tracts of land to his two sons. Matthew governed land in Thrace, protecting against further encroachments on Byzantine territory by Serbia, while Michael Cantacuzenus secured holdings in the Peloponnese. Thessalonica refused to recognize the settlement but was conquered by Cantacuzenus in 1350.

Efforts by John VI to secure other land lost by the empire in the civil war had little success. The Black Death (plague) brought major depopulation and was a major factor in Dušan's successful conquest of both Epirus and Thessaly during 1347–1348. The Serbs now effectively controlled all of mainland Greece. Yet when Serbia went to war with Bosnia, John VI campaigned in Macedonia. However, much of this recovered territory was again lost to Serbia in subsequent fighting, although John VI did hold on to Thessalonica.

By 1352 John V demanded a greater role in the government. Instead John VI ceded to him the lands in Thrace held by Matthew Cantacuzenus, compensating the latter with lands to the east around Adrianople. But this led to a renewal of fighting between the Palaeologus and Cantacuzenus families after border disputes between Matthew, who held western Thrace, and John V, in eastern Thrace. Foreign powers were soon drawn in. John V received help from the Serbs, while Matthew was aided by the Ottomans. Although John V enjoyed some initial success, the Ottomans defeated the Serbs in the Battle of Demotika in October 1352, the first victory for the Ottomans in Europe.

John V escaped to the Venetian-held island of Tenedos, and from there in March 1353 he launched an unsuccessful attempt to seize Constantinople. John VI declared John V deposed and invested his son Matthew as coemperor in February 1354. John V then allied with the Venetians. Blamed for having admitted the Ottomans into the empire, John VI on December 10, 1354, abdicated and became a monk.

John V entered Constantinople in November 1354, and the next year he defeated Matthew and forced him to relinquish his claims. Matthew then joined his brother in the Morea. A subsequent attempt by John V to conquer the Morea failed.

The civil war and its aftermath greatly weakened the ability of the Byzantine Empire to stand against outside pressures. In the course of the war the Byzantine economy and bureaucracy collapsed, and neither was ever properly restored. Indeed, the Byzantine Empire was an empire in name only, having lost most of its remaining territory. Serbia had nearly doubled in size, and its ruler claimed the title of tsar. The Ottomans had entered Europe and seized the Dardanelles. They established their first permanent European settlement at Gallipoli in 1354 in what was the first step in their conquest of the Balkans. The Ottomans then expanded into Thrace, and in 1365 they captured Adrianople, which Murad I made his capital.

In 1371 the Ottomans invaded Macedonia. John Ugljesa, Serbian ruler of the Serres region, sought Byzantine assistance, but only his brother Volkasin, king of Prelip in Macedonia, lent assistance. On September 26, 1371, they confronted the Ottoman Army at Cernomen on the Maritza River west of Adrianople and were routed, with both Serbian leaders among the dead. The Serbs and the Bulgars were then forced to recognize Ottoman suzerainty, pay tribute, and provide military assistance if requested. Serbia and Bulgaria, the two Christian states of the Balkans, as well as what remained of the Byzantine Empire now were all vassals of the Ottomans.

During 1376–1392 another dynastic struggle further weakened the Byzantine Empire, with the consequence of the Ottomans taking most of its territory. Constantinople itself fell in 1453. The Byzantine Empire was no more.

Spencer C. Tucker

See also
Bapheus, Battle of; Constantine I; Pelekanon, Battle of

References
Bartusis, Mark C. *The Late Byzantine Army: Arms and Society, 1204–1453*. Philadelphia: University of Pennsylvania Press, 1997.

Mango, Cyril, ed. *The Oxford History of Byzantium*. New York: Oxford University Press, 2002.

Nicol, Donald M. *The Last Centuries of Byzantium, 1261–1453*. 2nd ed. New York: Cambridge University Press, 1993.

Norwich, John Julius. *Byzantium: The Decline and Fall*, Vol. 3. New York: Knopf, 1996.

Treadgold, Warren T. *A History of the Byzantine State and Society*. Stanford, CA: Stanford University Press, 1997.

Byzantine-Muslim Wars (629–1035)

In 629, the Byzantine Empire successfully concluded a long series of wars with Sassanian Persia by which the Byzantines recovered territory in Palestine, Lebanon, and Syria. The empire had little time, however, to organize administration or defenses there before the Muslim incursions. The initial Muslim Arab invasion in 629 was defeated by Byzantine forces at Mutah, but in 630 a Muslim expedition forced the submission of the town of Aqaba.

A more earnest Arab effort at conquest occurred in 633–634, when Caliph Abu Bakr sent four armies, totaling perhaps 20,000 men, into Syria. By the end of 634 the Arabs had won a series of victories, most notably at Bosra, Ajnadain, Marj-al-Rahit, and Fahl. In 635, the Muslim armies occupied Damascus and Homs for the first time but were forced to abandon the cities in the face of a Byzantine counteroffensive led by Emperor Heraclius (r. 610–641). This counteroffensive came to an end on August 20, 636, when Byzantine forces suffered a catastrophic defeat in the Battle of the Yarmouk River. As a result of this victory, Muslim armies overran most of Palestine and Syria except for a portion of Syria granted a one-year truce, which allowed Christian Arabs to flee into Byzantine territory before the resumption of hostilities.

With expiration of the truce, Muslim forces resumed the offensive, taking over the remainder of Syria and Palestine. In December 639, Arab forces began an invasion of Egypt and Mesopotamia and raided Cilicia and Anatolia. The deaths in 641 of Byzantine emperors Heraclius and Constantine III (r. 641) and then the removal, through a coup, of Emperor Heraclonas (r. 641) created political instability in Constantinople, resulting in no effective aid being given to isolated Byzantine forces in Egypt. Arab armies were able to complete their invasion of Egypt and moved on Cyrenaica in 642.

After these initial disasters the Byzantines turned to positional warfare, attempting to hold the major cities while letting interior areas go. While this policy slowed the Muslims' advance by forcing their armies to take the time to seize fortified points, in the long term the strategy was doomed to failure. The cities could not be held without also securing the agricultural hinterland that supplied them. In 642, the Arab invasion of Armenia began. Within 20 years, despite constant Byzantine efforts to control Armenia, the Muslims had successfully converted the region into a client state.

In 650 the Arabs invaded Cyprus, which later became a Byzantine/Arab codominion by treaty. In the 650s, the Arabs turned their attention to the Persian Empire and to further conquests in North Africa. While raids remained frequent, the Byzantine Empire was able to gain control of the Taurus mountain passes leading into Anatolia. Further Arab conquests there were thus blocked.

In 648, an initial Arab invasion of the Byzantine province of Africa was bought off by local officials. The years 653–654 saw further Arab assaults on Cyprus, Crete, and Rhodes. At the same time Muawiyah, Arab governor of Syria, developed the first Muslim naval fleet, and in 655 a Muslim fleet under Abdullah bin Sa'ad bin Abi'l Sarh defeated a Byzantine fleet commanded by Emperor Constans II (r. 641–668) in the Battle of Masts (Battle of Phoenix) off the coast of Lycia. This Byzantine defeat opened the eastern Mediterranean to further Muslim expansion. However, by 656 the Muslim offensive stalled, as the ascension of Ali ibn Abi Talib to the caliphate split the Muslim community and led to a Muslim civil war that lasted until 661.

After the assassination of Caliph Ali in 661, Caliph Muawiyah launched a new offensive against the Byzantine Empire, seizing the city of Calcedon on the Bosporus in 668.

The following year, the Muslims crossed the Bosporus to attack the Byzantine capital of Constantinople itself but were repelled by the Byzantines at Amorium. In 670, the Muslim invasion of Africa began in earnest but met with firm resistance. In 674, the Muslims attempted to seize Constantinople, beginning a four-year-long siege. In 677, the Byzantine Navy decisively defeated the Muslims in the Battle of Syllaeum in the Sea of Marmara, which greatly contributed to the lifting of the siege of Constantinople the following year. As a result, the Muslim advance in Asia Minor and the Aegean was halted, and an agreement to a 30-year truce was concluded soon after.

During the next two decades both the caliphate and the Byzantine Empire were occupied securing their domains and waging minor skirmishes against each other. Full-scale war occurred in 696–699 when a second Arab expedition to Africa led to the seizure of Carthage and Utica, ending the Byzantine presence in North Africa. The Byzantines' efforts to recover their possession there proved unsuccessful, and this led to further political instability in Constantinople, where three emperors were overthrown between 711 and 717. At the same time, in 711 the Muslims breached the Taurus barrier and advanced into Anatolia. Unable to stop the Arab advance, Emperor Anastasius II (r. 713–715) began preparing the defenses of the capital. In 716 another Muslim assault on Constantinople failed, but in 717 an Arab force of 120,000 men and 1,800 ships besieged the capital. The Bulgarians, hoping to take the city for themselves, attacked the Arabs, who were forced to build two sets of siege works to contain the Byzantines on one side and to keep out the Bulgarians on the other. In September, the Muslim fleet appeared but was driven off by the Byzantines using Greek fire. The Muslim army thus remained trapped in its siege works during an unusually harsh winter. The Arabs sent a relief force of 600 ships, which landed near Chalcedon to avoid the Byzantine fleet. The crews of the Muslim fleet, mostly Egyptian Christians, defected en masse to the Byzantines. After a Muslim reinforcing column was destroyed near Nicaea and an epidemic had broken out among the Muslim forces near Constantinople, Caliph Umar finally ordered a retreat in August 718. The Muslim retreat was not opposed, but surviving Muslim ships were attacked, and the Muslim fleet was further damaged by storms.

Between 718 and 741, a series of raids and counter-raids ravaged Anatolia. In this period, Byzantine strategy embraced not only positional defense but also a policy of intercepting Muslim raids returning from plundering expeditions. These tactics proved moderately successful. In 739,

Emperor Leo III gained a major victory at Akroinon over Muslim forces led by Sulayman, the brother of Umayyad caliph Hisham ibn Abd al-Malik (723–743).

In 741, Emperor Constantine V (r. 741–775) took advantage of political instability in the Umayyad Caliphate to begin a campaign to regain lands lost to Muslims. In the mid-740s he gradually pushed the Byzantine frontier forward, recapturing parts of Syria, and in 746 his fleet defeated a Muslim fleet near Cyprus and took control of the island. As the Ummayad dynasty fell to the Abbasid attacks, Constantine campaigned in southern Caucasia, reclaiming parts of Armenia in 751–752. The Byzantine expansion continued under Constantine's successor, Leo IV (r. 775–780), who defeated the Muslims at Germanicopolis in 778 and reclaimed most of Anatolia. Nevertheless, Muslim attacks and raids on the Byzantine territories continued. The death of Leo IV in 780 saw the Byzantine crown pass to his nine-year-old son Constantine VI, whose mother Irene served as a regent.

Caliph al-Mahdi (r. 775–785) initiated new offensive operations, and in 783 the Abbasid army reached the Bosporus, near which it defeated the Byzantines at Nicomedia (Izmit or Kocaeli). Irene was forced to sue for peace and accept a three-year truce and pay tribute. In 786, new caliph Harun al-Rashi (r. 786–809) began fortifying his borderland territories in preparation for an invasion of the Byzantine Empire. In 797 Abbasid forces advanced to the Byzantine cities of Ephesus and Ancyra (Ankara), forcing Empress Irene to reinstate the previously agreed tribute.

In 802, Nicephorus I (r. 802–811) seized the Byzantine throne and broke the truce with the Abbasids agreed to by Empress Irene. In response, Harun al-Rashid led an army across the Taurus Mountains of Anatolia in 803 and seized the Byzantine city of Heraclea Cybistra (Eregli). Although Nicephorus sued for peace, he soon broke the truce, provoking another Abbasid retribution. Harun al-Rashid's armies won victories on land and at sea, defeating the Byzantines at Krasos in 805, capturing Tyana and Ancyra (Ankara) in 806, and ravaging Rhodes and Cyprus between 805 and 807. Nicephorus was again compelled to sue for peace. The subsequent death of Harun al-Rashid in 809 and successionist struggle enveloping the caliphate allowed Nicephorus to concentrate on other threats to his power before being killed in battle against the Bulgars in 811.

During the next two decades, both sides were occupied with internal turmoil. Besides the Abbasid threat, the Byzantine Empire came under attack from other Muslim states. Thus, in 824 Crete fell to Abo Hafs Omer al-Baloty's Iberian Muslims who were exiled from Spain by Umayyad emir Abd-ar-Rahman I (r. 796–822). Three years later Ziyadat Allah, the Aghlabid emir of Tunisia, attacked Sicily. Meanwhile, Abbasid caliph al-Mamun (813–833), having secured his authority, resumed attacks against the Byzantine territories in 830–832. Palermo fell in 831, and Emperor Theophilos (r. 829–842) was forced to agree to heavy tribute in 833.

After al-Mamun's death, Theophilos sought to recover lost ground and led a Byzantine army into northern Iraq in 837, capturing several Abbasid fortresses. Caliph al-Mutasim (r. 833–842) retaliated in 838, and his army, led by Khaydar ibn Kavus-Afshin, defeated Theophilos in the Battle of Dazimon on the Halys River in July 838 and sacked the Byzantine stronghold of Amorium. However, al-Mutasim's plan to besiege Constantinople failed when the Abbasid fleet was destroyed in a storm. In 841, the Byzantine emperor and caliph agreed to a truce. But sporadic attacks continued. The Muslims sacked Messina in 842 and Enna in 859, while the Byzantines, led by Petronas, uncle of Emperor Michael III (836–867), attacked Damietta in 853 and defeated Muslims near Amida (Diyarbakir) in 856. However, four years later Emperor Michael III suffered a defeat on the Euphrates River in northern Syria, and the two sides soon concluded a truce.

The armistice lasted three years only, and in 863 Omar, emir of Melitene, invaded Anatolia, sacked Samsun, and campaigned in Paphlagonia and Galatia. But the Byzantines intercepted him on his return, and in the decisive Battle of Poson the Muslim army was almost entirely destroyed and Omar was slain. This victory was celebrated with great pomp at the Hippodrome in Constantinople.

The victory at Poson produced a seven-year lull in the Byzantine-Muslim hostilities. The Abbasid Caliphate meanwhile suffered a major domestic turmoil, which the Byzantines immediately exploited. Emperor Basil (813–886) launched a major campaign into Syria and Iraq, defeating the Abbasid forces on the upper Euphrates River at Samosata (Samsat) in 873 and capturing Zapetra. Although he later suffered defeat at Melitene, he launched an expedition to drive Muslims from Sicily and southern Italy, where Bari was besieged and captured in 875. But Basil failed to drive the Muslims out of Sicily, where Syracuse was in the Muslim hands, but he secured Tarentum (Taranto) in 880 and Calabria in 885.

In the 10th century, Byzantine defense efforts began to show real results. In 900, Leo VI (r. 886–912) invaded the emirate of Tarsus and campaigned in Armenia. In 926, Romanus Lecapenus (r. 920–944) renewed the attack on the Arabs and sacked Melitene. In 927 the emir of Melitene submitted to the empire, and in 928 the city received

Depiction of the Battle of Poson in 863, fought between Byzantine Empire forces and an invading Arab army in Paphlagonia (modern northern Turkey). The Byzantines were victorious, paving the way for their subsequent territorial conquests. (Biblioteca Nacional, Madrid, Spain/Photo copyright AISA/Bridgeman Images)

a Byzantine garrison. The Abbassids initially expelled it, but in 933 and 934 the Byzantines systematically occupied the fortresses around Melitene and the city of Samosata. Melitene was eventually taken, and all non-Christians were forced to leave. Samosata was taken and razed in 936.

In 940 Saif al-Dawlah, the gifted Hamdanid general, successfully campaigned in Armenia and raided Byzantine territory up to Colonia before John Curcuas, Grand Domestic, drove him back. During 941–943 Curcuas launched a counteroffensive, sacking a number of cities in Armenia and Mesopotamia and besieging the city of Edessa. He withdrew only after the governor of the city had agreed to surrender the Mandilyon, a cloth said to bear the imprint of the face of Christ. The relic and Curcuas were accorded a triumphal entry into Constantinople.

In late 944, however, the Byzantines were soundly beaten by Saif al-Dawlah near Antioch. Constantine VII (r. 913–959) assumed full power in 944 and, with his generals Nicephorus Phocas, John Tzimisces, and Basil the Grand Chamberlain, conducted a successful raiding war against Saif al-Dawlah, who repelled the first Byzantine invasion in 948 but was forced to give ground in subsequent attacks. Byzantine efforts to recapture Crete, Sicily, and Italy were less successful, and Muslim forces repeatedly defeated forces sent to those places. Encouraged by Byzantine losses, Saif al-Dawlah organized an ambitious raid from Tarsus to the Theme of Charsianum, where he defeated the Byzantines in the valley of the Lycus. But on the return trip, Saif al-Dawlah was ambushed and defeated by Leo Phocas in a mountain pass between Lycandus and Germanicea. Rejecting the Byzantine offer of truce, Saif raided Melitene and Lycandus in 951. He successfully campaigned in the border regions in 953–954 and rebuilt the strategic fortress of Adata and Samosata. In the spring 956, Saif defeated the rising Byzantine general John Tzimisces but suffered a naval defeat at the hands of Cibyrrhaeots. Three years later John Tzimisces raided southern Armenia and northern Mesopotamia, sacking Dara and Samosata and decisively defeating

Saif's main army. The Byzantines fared worse in Italy, where their attacks failed in Calabria and Sicily in 958–959.

Constantine's successor, Romanus II (r. 959–963), reorganized Byzantine forces in an effort to intensify the war against the Arabs. In 960, a massive expedition under Nicephorus Phocas landed on Crete. Phocas's army killed thousands of Muslims and besieged the principal city of Chandax from 960 until the spring of 962, when it finally fell. A raid into Syria by Saif in that year was defeated by Byzantine forces in a pass through the Taurus. After capturing Chandax, Nicephorus Phocas attacked and defeated the emir of Tarsus and took several towns in Anatolia and Syria. Phocas then marched against Saif al-Dawlah in Aleppo and, evading Saif's main force, fell upon the poorly prepared defenses of Aleppo, which he overcame. Upon his return to Constantinople, Phocas found that Romanus II had died in a hunting accident, and Phocas assumed imperial power.

Nicephorus Phocas (r. 963–969) continued the war against Saif, taking the town of Mopsuestia as well as Tarsus in 965. The following year, Saif al-Dawlah asked for a truce and an exchange of prisoners, which the Byzantines accepted. In 967 Saif al-Dawlah, the dauntless Muslim commander who fought the Byzantines for decades, died. Nicephorus exploited this opportunity to expand Byzantine control of Armenia and Syria, clearing Cyprus of its Arab garrison. Yet the Byzantine emperor was murdered in a coup in 969 when John Tzimisces seized power. During his reign of 969–976, Aleppo ceded control of its coastal territory to Byzantium, which now bordered the Fatimid Caliphate of Egypt and the Hamdanid emirate of Mosul, both of which were willing to expand at the expense of Byzantine or Arab neighbors. Tzimisces thus found himself fighting against the Fatimids in 971 and in 975 and the Hamdanids from 972 to 974. Tzimisces was able in the end to subject most of Syria and Lebanon to either direct Byzantine government or tributary status. He died before these conquests could be followed up and was succeeded by Basil II (r. 976–1025).

The greatest ruler of medieval Byzantium, Basil II faced civil disorder in the early part of his reign, but his Arab neighbors were too weak to take advantage. By the 990s, Basil was strong enough to drive off Fatimid attacks on the emirate of Aleppo, now a Byzantine client state. Fatimid attempts at naval warfare were equally unavailing. An Egyptian fleet burned in 996 in a mysterious fire, and the Byzantines defeated a second fleet off Syria. Fatimid caliph al-Aziz then died, and rebellions broke out over the succession.

Basil II turned his attention to Byzantine territories in Europe. He signed a 10-year truce with the Fatimids in 1001, which he renewed periodically for the rest of his reign. Basil refused to respond to Fatimid and Hamdanid attacks on Aleppo. That city fell to the Fatimids in 1015, only to be lost to them in a revolt in 1025. At this point Byzantine attentions became fixed elsewhere, with few exceptions. Romanus III (r. 1028–1034) forced the surrender of Edessa in 1031 and attempted to purchase the city of Aleppo. This offer was refused. The Fatimids renewed the 10-year truce in 1036, and the Byzantine frontier was secured by the presence of a client state, the Mirdanid emirate, in what is now modern-day Syria and Iraq. Though raids would occasionally continue, the initiative in Muslim expansion had passed from the Arabs to a group of Islamic mercenaries brought in by the Arabs, the Turks.

ALEXANDER MIKABERIDZE

See also

Abbasid Caliphate; Byzantine-Seljuk Wars; Constantinople, Muslim Siege of; Fatimid Dynasty; Muawiyah I; Saif al-Dawla; Yarmouk River, Battle of

References

Kaegi, Walter. *Byzantium and the Early Islamic Conquests*. New York: Cambridge University Press, 1992.

Treadgold, Warren. *A History of the Byzantine State and Society*. Stanford, CA: Stanford University Press, 1997.

Whittrow, Mark. *The Making of Byzantium, 600–1025*. Berkeley: University of California Press, 1996.

Byzantine-Ottoman Wars (1280–1479)

Founded in the late 13th century in northwestern Anatolia by Osman (d. ca. 1324), the Ottoman Empire developed rapidly from a small and insignificant polity into a powerful state. The Ottomans expanded quickly against the Byzantines, defeating them near Nikomedia (modern-day Izmit, Turkey) in 1302 and capturing various Byzantine towns. Under Orhan (d. 1362), the Ottomans took Bursa (1325), which became the Ottoman capital until the conquest of Adrianople (modern-day Edirne, Turkey), followed by Lopadion (modern-day Ulubat) in 1327, Nicaea (modern-day Iznik) in 1331, and Nikomedia in 1337.

The Ottomans crossed onto European soil when they were called in by Byzantine emperor John VI Kantakouzenos to assist him in the civil war (1341–1347) with his rival John V Palaiologos. Kantakouzenos, whose daughter Theodora married Orhan, kept his alliance with the Ottomans throughout his reign, and several times Ottoman forces were called in to fight for him. In 1354 the Ottomans took Gallipoli (modern-day Gelibolu) and other towns in Thrace.

Under Murad I (1362–1389), the Ottoman advance into Europe was swift and effective. The defeat of the Serbian despots of Macedonia, Vlkašin, and Ugleša in the Battle of Çirmen on the Maritsa River (1371) opened the way into the Balkans. The Ottomans took Philippopolis (modern-day Plovdiv, Bulgaria), Zagora, and probably much of Bulgaria. The tsardom of Turnovo also fell under Ottoman suzerainty, and Serbia and Bosnia came under Ottoman attack. In Greece, the Ottomans took Thessalonica (modern-day Thessaloniki) in 1387.

In 1365 Byzantine emperor John V, worried by the Ottoman advance, attempted without success to negotiate an alliance with the king of Hungary. John did, however, receive help from his cousin, Amadeus VI, count of Savoy, who seized Gallipoli in 1366. John also sent an embassy to Pope Urban VI and went himself to Rome in 1369, prepared in return for help to offer union of the Greek Church with the Roman. Western concern was evident in 1372 when Pope Gregory XI proposed an anti-Ottoman alliance between the Byzantine emperor, the king of Hungary, and the Latin lords of Greece. Concern was not sufficient, however, and an alliance was reached between the Ottomans and the Byzantines in 1373.

From that point on, the Ottomans played more and more of a role in internal Byzantine politics as the Byzantines descended into civil war between John V and his son Andronikos IV, backed by the Ottomans and the Genoese. Andronikos paid heavily for this support, both in financial terms and by having to return Gallipoli to Murad. Murad next supported John, who reentered Constantinople. By the time of the settlement, negotiated through the Genoese in 1381, the Byzantine emperor had been reduced to the position of a vassal of the Ottoman ruler.

After the death of Murad at the Battle of Kosovo Polje (June 23, 1389), Bayezid I (1389–1402) began a whirlwind expansion into Southeastern Europe. Bayezid moved into Bulgaria, which became an Ottoman possession by 1395. The Byzantines too found themselves increasingly under Ottoman domination. Manuel II Palaiologos, who became emperor in 1391, was forced to accompany the Ottoman ruler on campaign a year later. Constantinople itself came under Ottoman siege in 1394 and was to remain so until 1402.

Fear of growing Ottoman might caused increasing consternation in Europe. King Sigismund of Hungary, engaged in a power struggle with the Ottomans over control of Serbia, sought allies among the Western rulers for a united offensive. A crusade was organized involving forces from Hungary, Germany, France, and England. At the Battle of Nikopolis (1396), the Ottomans destroyed the European crusading force.

Byzantine emperor Manuel II turned in desperation to the West. In 1397 he approached the pope and the kings of France, England, and Aragon. The only response was the arrival of Marshal Boucicaut, sent by Charles VI of France to Constantinople with a force of 1,200 soldiers in 1399. In the same year Manuel set off for England and France in an attempt to drum up support. He was not to return for three years. The Ottomans moved into Albania, Epiros, and southern Greece, while at sea they harassed the Aegean islands and attacked Venetian shipping. What ultimately saved the West was not a crusading movement or European unity but rather the rise of a major military power to the East.

Sweeping out of Central Asia, the nomad conqueror Timur crushed the Ottoman forces at the Battle of Ankara in 1402, capturing Bayezid and plunging the Ottoman state into civil war. Timur's victory was a great relief for the European powers, including the Byzantine Empire. Bayezid's son Süleyman, who had fled to the European territory of the Ottoman state immediately after the battle, was forced to negotiate a peace treaty, concluded in early 1403, with the Byzantines, Venice, Genoa, and the Hospitallers of Rhodes. Although undoubtedly weakened, Süleyman remained a major player in the Balkans, while the European powers were still rent by internal divisions and, like Süleyman, threatened by Timur. Nevertheless, Süleyman did make considerable concessions to the various signatories of the treaty.

In 1411 Prince Süleyman was defeated and killed by his brother Musa, who was himself killed by another son of Bayezid I, Mehmet I (1413–1421). Mehmet I followed a peaceful policy, concluding a treaty with Serbia and with the Byzantines, who had supported him during his struggle with his brother. At the same time, Emperor Manuel tried to interest the Venetians in a scheme against the Ottoman ruler. Venice, out to conclude its own agreement with the Ottomans, refused to be drawn in. At this point Manuel appears to have released an Ottoman pretender, the son of Süleyman, a tactic he had apparently adopted earlier in the civil war between Musa and Mehmet. The son was captured by Mehmet and blinded.

Ottoman raiding in European territories continued through 1415. Negotiations began to form an anti-Ottoman league in the Aegean involving Emperor Manuel, the Genoese rulers of Chios and Mytilene, the Hospitallers, and Venice, but nothing came of it. In 1416 the Venetians secured a significant victory over the Ottoman naval forces, defeating and killing the Ottoman admiral. With the sea now somewhat safer, the Venetians had no real interest in Manuel's proposal in 1417 for a naval alliance with the Genoese and the Hospitallers, although the Byzantines tried again in 1420 to organize an anti-Ottoman alliance.

Gradually Mehmet gained control in western Anatolia and northeast Bulgaria. In 1420 he took the Genoese colony at Samsun on the Black Sea coast. In Europe he captured Valona (modern-day Vlorë, Albania) and a large part of southern Albania, and he reduced Mircea of Walacia to vassal status. Successfully surviving the challenge of his uncle Mustafa, backed by Byzantium, Murad II (1421–1444 and 1446–1451) laid siege to Thessalonica, which ultimately fell in 1430, and to Constantinople in 1422. The emergence of a fresh challenge to the throne, in Murad's brother Mustafa who was supported by Emperor Manuel, saved the Byzantine capital.

Murad defeated and killed Mustafa in January 1423. Late in the same year the new Byzantine emperor John VIII Palaiologos set off to Venice in an attempt to win Western support against the Ottomans. During his absence, his regent Constantine concluded a treaty with Murad (February 1424). Venice was more interested in a potential anti-Ottoman alliance with Hungary, proposed by Sigismund in 1425, but suffering from the considerable expense involved in defending Thessalonica, which it had received from Andronikos Palaiologos, Venice sought peace with Murad.

An agreement was concluded between the governor of Gallipoli and the Venetian Andrea Mocenigo, captain general of the sea, but was not ratified by Murad. Once again civil war in Byzantium, this time between John VIII and his brother Demetrios, drew the Ottomans into Byzantine politics. Demetrios called in Ottoman help for an attack on Constantinople, which lasted until August 1442.

Through the later 1420s and 1430s Murad campaigned in Serbia and Albania, which were brought under direct Ottoman rule. Hungary, weakened by a civil war following the death of King Albert II, saw its fortunes improved after the victories in Walacia in 1441 and 1442 of John Hunyadi, the *voivod* of Transylvania. Although in themselves of no great significance, they gave a great psychological boost to Murad's enemies, who now entered into an anti-Ottoman alliance.

At the Council of Florence (1439), Byzantine emperor John VIII had already accepted the union of the Latin and Greek churches in return for an attack by Christian forces against the Ottoman Empire. Pope Eugenius IV, for whose prestige a successful crusade would have been most advantageous, backed the enterprise, which also offered much to Hungary, Serbia, and Venice, ensuring the security of its territories in Greece and of its shipping in the Aegean Sea. In preparation for this crusade, peace was organized between the warring factions in Hungary, and Karaman, the perennial Ottoman enemy in Anatolia, was brought in. In 1443 Ibrahim, the ruler of Karaman, attacked Murad, apparently urged to do so by the Byzantine emperor, but with no help forthcoming from John VIII, Ibrahim made peace the same year.

During the winter of 1443–1444, the Ottomans clashed with the forces of Hungary, Serbia, and Transylvania. Although the Christian forces did not win a great victory, the winter campaign was viewed as a success in Europe and gave further encouragement to the crusade movement. In November 1444 Murad met the crusader forces at Varna and routed them. A further attempt at a crusade was made along the Danube in 1445 involving the Byzantines, Burgundy, Walacia, Hungary, and Transylvania. Nothing much came of this campaign. An attempt the following year by the pope to persuade Venice to provide galleys for a new campaign was unsuccessful, Venice having concluded a treaty with Mehmet II in early 1446. Mehmet II's second reign (1451–1481) began dramatically for the Europeans with the conquest of Constantinople (1453).

The Genoese settlements of Old and New Phokaia (on the western coast of Anatolia) and Enez in western Thrace fell in 1455 and 1456. Mehmet campaigned in the Peloponnese in 1458 and took Athens. Serbia fell in 1459 and Bosnia in 1464, and in 1461 Mehmet extinguished the Byzantine Empire of Trebizond on the Black Sea coast of northeastern Turkey.

KATE FLEET

See also
Bayezid I; Bayezid II; Constantinople, Ottoman Siege of; Mehmed II, Sultan; Nikopolis, Crusade in; Suleiman I; Varna Crusade

References
Bisaha, Nancy. *Creating East and West: Renaissance Humanists and the Ottoman Turks.* Philadelphia: University of Pennsylvania Press, 2004.
Imber, Colin. *The Ottoman Empire 1300–1650: The Structure of Power.* Basingstoke, UK: Palgrave Macmillan, 2002.
İnalcik, Halil. *The Ottoman Empire: The Classical Age, 1300–1600.* London: Weidenfeld and Nicolson, 1973.
İnalcik, Halil. "The Ottoman Turks and the Crusades, 1329–1451." In *A History of the Crusades*, Vol. 2, ed. Kenneth Setton. 2nd ed. Philadelphia: University of Pennsylvania Press, 1969.
İnalcik, Halil, and Donald Quataert, eds. *An Economic and Social History of the Ottoman Empire, 1300–1914.* Cambridge: Cambridge University Press, 1994.
McCarthy, Justin. *The Ottoman Turks: An Introductory History.* Harlow, UK: Longman, 1997.

Byzantine-Sassanid War (602–628)

The most important of the Byzantine Sassanid wars. In 602 Byzantine general Phocas seized power in Constantinople from Emperor Maurice. Narses, governor of the Byzantine province of Mesopotamia, rebelled against Phocas and seized the city of Edessa. Phocas then ordered his general Germanus to retake Edessa, prompting Narses to request help from Persian shah Khosrau II. Khosrau saw this as a chance to recover Armenia and Mesopotamia and used the death of Maurice, his "friend and father," to go to war.

Germanus died in fighting against the Persians, while Byzantine forces sent by Phocas against Khosrau were defeated near Dara in Upper Mesopotamia, leading to the loss of that important Byzantine fortress in 605. Narses meanwhile endeavored to discuss peace terms with Phocas who, however, ordered him seized and burned alive. The death of Narses and Phocas's military failures against the Persians as well as inroads by the Avars and Slavs against the western Byzantine Empire in Southeastern Europe all greatly weakened Phocas's rule.

In 608 Byzantine general Heraclius the Elder, Exarch of Africa, led another revolt against Phocas. The Persians took advantage of civil strife in the Byzantine Empire to conquer the border areas of Armenia as well as Upper Mesopotamia. In 609 they captured Mardin and Amida (Diyarbakir). Edessa fell in 610.

In 610 Heraclius defeated Probus and became emperor. By that time, the Persians had conquered all the Byzantine territory east of the Euphrates and Armenia. They then moved into Cappadocia, where their general Shahin took Caesarea but was then besieged there.

Heraclius attempted to make peace with Persia, pointing out to them that Phocas, whose actions were the stated cause of the war, had been overthrown. Given that he was enjoying great military success and was perhaps hopeful of restoring the territorial extent of the Achaemenid Empire, Kosrau refused.

In 613 the Persians took Damascus, Apamea, and Emesa. The next year Jerusalem fell after a siege of three weeks. Reportedly some 60,000 inhabitants were killed there and another 35,000 were exiled to Persia. Many churches in the city (including the Church of the Resurrection or Holy Sepulchre) were burned, and numerous relics, including the True Cross, the Holy Lance, and the Holy Sponge, were carried off to the Persian capital of Ctesiphon.

In 617 Persian general Shahin secured Chalcedon (just across the Bosporus from Constantinople and today a suburb of Istanbul). Heraclius again sent out peace feelers, but Khosrau rejected them. Nonetheless, the Persian forces soon withdrew, no doubt to concentrate on their invasion of Egypt in 618. Alexandria fell after a yearlong siege of more than a year. The loss of Egypt's grain shipments was a severe blow to the Byzantines.

The Persians also captured Ancyra, an important military base in central Anatolia, and in the early 620s they took Rhodes and several other islands just off Anatolia. The Slavs had also moved in large numbers into Greece and Albania, while the Avars pressed into Thrace and Bulgaria. The Byzantine Empire appeared caught in a vice. The situation seemed so dire that Heraclius considered moving the government to Carthage in North Africa.

The rejection of peace terms caused Heraclius to consider a desperate action. Since coming to power, he had concentrated on rebuilding the Byzantine Army. Pronouncing his forces ready to take the offensive, Heraclius landed an army by sea in Cilicia in southern Anatolia in April 622 and defeated the Persians in the Battle of Issus that October. He then marched north into Pontus on the south shore of the Black Sea and was victorious over the Persians at Halys in the spring of 623. He next invaded Media (today central Iran), laying waste to much of it, then moved across Mesopotamia into Cilicia, defeating a Persian army at the Sarus River in the autumn of 625. Heraclius hoped to force the Persians to shift their attention north to defend Ctesiphon.

Khosrau II now sought to force Heraclius to withdraw from Persian territory by ordering an all-out offensive against Constantinople. To increase the pressure, the Persians secured an alliance with the Avars to move against the city from the west. During June–August 626 the Persians and Avars laid siege to the Byzantine capital. The city's defenses were strong, and Heraclius, trusting that Constantinople's land defenses and Byzantine naval strength would hold, refused to withdraw from Armenia. This strategy worked, with his opponents dissipating their forces in a futile effort to take Constantinople, and the Avars and Persians withdrew their greatly weakened forces that fall. Avar strength was further sapped by a revolt of the Slavs.

With Persian military strength having been greatly reduced, Heraclius pursued the war in Anatolia, securing an alliance with the Khazars, a Turkish people in the Caucasus, who supplied forces against the Persians. The Byzantines and Khazars then laid siege to Tiflis.

In mid-September 627 as the Byzantine-Khazar siege of Tiflis continued, Heraclius invaded Mesopotamia. Moving southwest with more than 25,000 men, he was pursued by Persian general Rhahzadh with some 12,000 men. On

December 12, Heraclius defeated the Persians in the Battle of Nineveh. The Persians withdrew after having suffered some 6,000 killed, including Rhahzadh.

The Battle of Nineveh proved decisive in the war. Heraclius went on to take Dastagard, securing significant treasure as well as recovering a reported 300 Byzantine/Roman standards lost in previous warfare. Heraclius then raided in the vicinity of Ctesiphon, while a coup d'état ousted Shah Khosrow II, beginning a bloody civil war in Persia. Persian general Shahrvaraz then struck a bargain with Heraclius in which he agreed to return Egypt, Palestine, Syria, and the other conquered territories to Byzantium in return for permission to march on Ctesiphon and take power. By 630 Heraclius had recovered all of Egypt and western Asia Minor. The ancient Byzantine boundaries had been restored, and the empire was at peace.

It was not to last, however. The long struggle between the Persians and Byzantines had exhausted and rendered both susceptible to pressure from the new threat posed by Islam. Within little more than a decade the Arabs had taken the entire Middle East, which they held from that point forward.

Spencer C. Tucker

See also
Heraclius

References
Haldon, J. F. *Byzantium in the Seventh Century*. Cambridge: Cambridge University Press, 1990.
Kaegi, Walter Emil. *Byzantium and the Early Islamic Conquests*. Cambridge: Cambridge University Press, 1995.
Kaegi, Walter Emil. *Heraclius, Emperor of Byzantium*. Cambridge: Cambridge University Press, 2003.
Pourshariati, Parvaneh. *The Sasanian Era*. London: I. B. Tauris, 2010.
Treadgold, Warren. *A History of the Byzantine State and Society*. Stanford, CA: Stanford University Press, 1997.

Byzantine-Seljuk Wars (1048–1308)

The wars between the Seljuk Turks and the Byzantine Empire aided by European crusaders saw a shift in the balance of power from the Byzantines to the Seljuk Turks and later the Ottoman Turks. First utilized as mercenary troops by the Abbasid caliphs, the Seljuks came to dominate political life of the caliphate by the mid-11th century. After two decades of raids on the Byzantine territories, the Seljuk Turks attacked the town of Caesarea in 1067, and they captured Iconium two years later.

Although they were driven back from both places soon afterward, the Seljuks continued their attacks, leading to the decisive battle fought near Manzikert (modern-day Mantzikert, Turkey) on August 19, 1071. There a Seljuk army under Sultan Alp Arslan defeated Byzantine forces under Emperor Romanos IV Diogenes.

The Battle of Manzikert led to a civil war in the Byzantine Empire between the potential successors, which allowed the Seljuk Turks to conquer parts of Asia Minor (Anatolia) and Palestine, including Jerusalem, during 1071–1096. Their success compelled Emperor Alexios I Komnenos to appeal for help to Western Europe, which eventually contributed to Pope Urban II in 1095 proclaiming a crusade to recapture Jerusalem and protect the Byzantine Empire in 1096. The crusaders were able to defeat the Seljuk Turks at Dorylaeum in July 1097 and capture Antioch in 1098 and Jerusalem in 1099. The crusaders eventually established small kingdoms in the Holy Land that were uncomfortable allies of the Byzantines.

Their wars against the Seljuk Turks did allow the Byzantines to retake some of their lost territories in Asia Minor. In 1117 Emperor Alexios I Komnenos defeated Seljuk sultan Malik Shah in the Battle of Philomelion. Alexios's successor, John II Komnenos (1118–1143), conducted numerous campaigns in Asia Minor that forced the Seljuks onto the defensive and secured Byzantine control of much of western Asia Minor. However, his successor Emperor Manuel Komnenos proved unable to maintain this territorial expansion. Leading an attack on the Seljuk capital of Iconium, he suffered a defeat at the Battle of Myriokephalon in September 1176 and was forced to halt his campaign. Nevertheless, the Byzantines still remained a force to be reckoned with as shown in their victory at the Battle of Hyelion and Leimocheir in 1177.

The death of Emperor Manuel led to a long period of political struggle. In 1183 Emperor Alexios II Komnenos was deposed by Andronikos I Komnenos, who was in turned killed in 1185. After years of weak rulers, the Byzantine Empire faced a major crisis with an assault on Constantinople itself by the crusaders of the Fourth Crusade in 1204. The crusaders sacked the city, and although it was rebuilt afterward, it was only a shadow of its former self.

The Byzantine Empire splintered into three main parts: the Latin Empire, the Empire of Nicaea, and the Despotate of Epirus. This fragmentation allowed the Seljuks to take advantage, and in 1207 the Seljuks of Rum captured Antalya. Nevertheless, the Nicaean Empire managed to survive and gradually reclaimed some parts of the Byzantine

Empire. In 1211, Emperor Theodore I Laskaris of Nicaea secured a decisive victory over the Seljuks of Rum, whose sultan Kaykhuisraw I was killed in the battle.

Forces of the Empire of Nicaea recaptured Constantinople in 1261 and regained control of Greece in later years, restoring the Byzantine Empire. But in Asia Minor, Byzantine success proved limited. Meanwhile, the Seljuk Turks were so weakened by Mongol attacks that their empire collapsed in the early 14th century. Their decline led to the rise of the Ottoman Turks, who resumed attacks on the Byzantine Empire and ultimately destroyed it in 1453.

ALEXANDER MIKABERIDZE

See also

Alexios I Komnenos; Alp Arslan; Byzantine-Muslim Wars; Byzantine-Ottoman Wars; Crusades in the Holy Land, Christian; Manzikert, Battle of; Rum, Sultanate of

References

France, J. *Victory in the East: A Military History of the First Crusade.* Cambridge: Cambridge University Press, 1994.

Haldon, John. *Byzantium at War: AD 600–1453.* Oxford, UK: Osprey, 2002.

Mango, Cyril. *The Oxford History of Byzantium,* New York: Oxford University Press, 2002.

Runciman, Stephen. *A History of the Crusades.* Harmondsworth: Pelican Books, 1971.

C

Caesar, Gaius Julius (100–44 BCE)

Roman general and political figure whose dictatorship ended the Roman Republic. Born in Rome on July 12–13, 100 BCE, into a prominent Roman family that was however no longer in the ruling circle, Julius Caesar was related by marriage to Roman military reformer Gaius Marius. Caesar served as a praetor in Spain in 61. Returning to Rome, in 60 he joined with two others to oppose the ruling faction in the Roman Senate. This First Triumvirate (60–51) consisted of Caesar, popular general Gnaeus Pompeius Magnus (Pompey the Great), and wealthy businessman Marcus Licinius Crassus. The alliance was cemented by Pompey's marriage to Caesar's daughter Julia.

Under the First Triumvirate, Caesar became one of two consuls in 59, followed by a military command for 5 years, later increased to 10 in Illyricum (Yugoslavia) and Gaul on both sides of the Alps (France and north Italy). Employing innovative attacks and utilizing his cavalry to good advantage, Caesar also relied heavily on Roman military engineering. He quickly subjugated the disunited tribes of northern France and Belgium during 58–57 and then conducted amphibious operations on the Atlantic seaboard in 56. In a memorable engineering feat, in June 55 Caesar caused a bridge to be built across the Rhine and then marched into Germany to intimidate the German tribes. Receiving the submission of several tribes, he returned to Gaul, destroying the bridge.

With two legions, Caesar invaded Britain in 55 and spent three weeks there. He returned in 54 with five legions, taking the capital at Wheathampstead. He received the submission of the British but effected no conquests.

Caesar returned to Gaul to confront a powerful coalition of tribes. He now proved himself a master of both rapid offensive movement and siege warfare. The culmination of the campaign was the great siege of Alesia during July–October 52, stronghold of Gallic leader Vercingetorix. Caesar's victory there broke Gallic resistance to Roman rule and added a rich and populous territory, indeed one of the largest territorial additions in Roman history. During the conquest of Gaul, Caesar's army grew from 2 to 13 legions.

Pompey had received the governorship of Spain but exercised it from Rome. In 53 Crassus was killed campaigning in Mesopotamia, and the Triumvirate ended. In 52 amid increasing civil unrest, Pompey became sole consul. His wife, Caesar's daughter, had died in 54, and Pompey was now pressed by a conservative group of senators to break with Caesar, whom they feared.

By 49 BCE Caesar and Pompey and their legions were fighting for control of Rome. The Senate had demanded Caesar give up his command and return to Rome. Caesar proposed a general disarmament, but the Senate insisted he give up his command or be declared an enemy of the state. On January 10, 49, Caesar crossed the Rubicon River, bringing his legions from Gaul to Italy. Caesar quickly occupied Rome and Italy, and Pompey withdrew with a number of senators to the Balkans. Caesar pursued him there after a rapid expedition to Spain, and in 48 at Pharsalus in

A charismatic figure and one of history's foremost military commanders, Julius Caesar (100–44 BCE) established the dictatorship that effectively ended the Roman Republic. (Corel Corporation)

northern Greece, Caesar defeated Pompey and the Senate forces. Pompey escaped with only a few followers, reached the coast, and sailed to Egypt, where he was murdered by some of his supporters.

Caesar then campaigned in Egypt and Asia Minor, accompanied by the beautiful 22-year-old Cleopatra, whom he confirmed as queen. Cleopatra bore Caesar a son, Caesarian. Caesar returned to Rome and then in two rapid campaigns crushed Pompey's sons in North Africa in 46 and Spain in 45.

In 46 BCE Caesar secured appointment by the Senate as dictator for 10 years. Although the formality of elections continued, Caesar in fact held power. What he intended is unclear. In 44 he caused his dictatorship to be extended for life and secured deification. A month in the calendar was renamed July after him. He seems to have wanted the kingship, but the public apparently opposed this step, and he was not to have the time to convince the people otherwise.

Rational and logical, Caesar carried out extensive reforms. He began projects to restore Corinth and Carthage, the destruction of which had marked the end of Mediterranean trade, and he believed that this would employ the Roman urban poor. He reformed local government by moving toward decentralization, and he also reformed the calendar. Caesar made many provincials citizens, including the entire province of Cisalpine Gaul.

Not all Romans approved of Caesar's reforms. Many traditionalists, powerful vested interests, and republicans were upset by his changes and cosmopolitan attitude. Shortly after he extended his dictatorship to life, Caesar was assassinated on March 15, 44 BCE, stabbed to death in Rome by a group of men who had once been his loyal supporters. Believing they had killed a tyrant and were restoring liberty, they brought anarchy instead.

Although he was not a great military innovator, Caesar was certainly one of history's great captains. He possessed an offensive spirit, a sense of the moment to strike, a perfect comprehension of supply problems, and the ability to make maximum utilization of the forces at his disposal.

Spencer C. Tucker

See also
Caesar's Campaign in Egypt; Cleopatra VII; Crassus, Marcus Licinius; Pompeius Magnus, Gnaeus

References
Caesar, Julius. *War Commentaries of Caesar.* Translated by Rex Warner. New York: New American Library, 1960.
Gelzer, M. *Caesar: Politician and Statesman.* Cambridge, MA, 1985.
Goldsworthy, Adrian. *Caesar: Life of a Colossus.* New Haven, CT: Yale University Press, 2006.
Grant, Michael. *The Army of the Caesars.* New York: Scribner, 1974.
Grant Michael. *Julius Caesar.* New York: M. Evans, 1992.

Caesar's Campaign in Egypt (48–47 BCE)

On August 9, 48 BCE, Julius Caesar was victorious over his rival Gnaeus Pompeius Magnus (Pompey the Great) in the Battle of Pharsalus during the Great Roman Civil War (49–45). Pompey, however, escaped and sailed for Egypt. Caesar pursued with only some 4,000 men and there learned that Pompey had been assassinated by his own subordinates on September 29. Caesar is said to have mourned the death of Pompey and subsequently put to death those who had murdered him.

Pompey's lieutenants in Egypt meanwhile convinced young Ptolemy XII, coruler of Egypt with his sister Cleopatra VII, to resist Caesar. With a force of some 20,000 men,

Ptolemy besieged Caesar at Alexandria. Although Caesar controlled only some of the eastern harbor of the city, he refused to flee. Sending an appeal for assistance, Caesar ably defended the small part of the city and seafront that he controlled. Although the former Pompeians dominated at sea, land and naval reinforcements for Caesar slowly arrived. Victorious in two desperate naval battles outside the harbor, Caesar lost a land battle on the harbor mole and a third naval battle nearby.

In January 47 Caesar's position again appeared desperate, however, but his luck held. Learning of the arrival of forces sent overland by his ally Mithridates of Pergamum, Caesar left only a small force to hold his existing positions in Alexandria and joined Mithridates outside the city for a battle with his opponents. Each side numbered about 20,000 men.

In this Battle of the Nile on February 27, 47 BCE, Caesar and Mithridates utterly defeated the Egyptians. Ptolemy XII was among the dead. After relieving his forces in Alexandria, Caesar established firm control over Egypt, placing on the throne Cleopatra's still-younger brother, Ptolemy XIII. At the same time, Caesar became involved romantically with Cleopatra and with her fathered his only known biological son, Ptolemy XV Caesar, known as Caesarian. Caesar and Cleopatra never married, however, owing to Roman law prohibiting marriage with a non-Roman citizen.

In April 47, Caesar sailed from Egypt With part of his army to do battle with Pharnaces, king of Pontus, who had taken advantage of the civil war to reclaim territory lost by his father, Mithridates VI. Securing reinforcements in Syria, Caesar moved overland to meet Pharnaces and defeated him in the Battle of Zela in May 47. This victory was the subject of his famous message to Rome "Veni, vidi, vici" ("I came, I saw, I conquered"). Caesar then reorganized the eastern part of the empire, giving Mithridates of Pergamum nominal rule over Pharnaces's territory.

Returning to Rome from the East, Caesar put down a mutiny among his troops who sought back pay, then campaigned with success against Pompey's supporters, first in North Africa, where he was victorious in the Battle of Thapsus in February 46, and then in Spain, where he inflicted a final defeat on the Pompeians in the Battle of Munda in March 45.

In July 45 Caesar returned to Rome, where he was now recognized as ruler and in effect uncrowned monarch. He secured appointment by the Senate as dictator for 10 years, then caused this to be extended for life and secured deification. He probably sought the kingship but did not have the opportunity to bring this to fruition. After carrying out a number of reforms, he was assassinated in a conspiracy of traditionalists and vested interests on March 15, 44.

Spencer C. Tucker

See also
Cleopatra VII; Mithridates VI Eupator Dionysius; Pompeius Magnus, Gnaeus

References
Fields, Nic. *Julius Caesar.* New York: Osprey, 2010.
Goldsworthy, Adrian. *Caesar: Life of a Colossus.* New Haven, CT: Yale University Press, 2006.
Goldsworthy, Adrian. *Caesar's Civil War, 49–44 BC.* New York: Osprey, 2002.
Grant, Michael. *Julius Caesar.* New York: M. Evans, 1992.
Jimenez, Raymond. *Caesar against Rome: The Great Roman Civil War.* Westport, CT: Praeger, 2000.

Cairo Accord (May 4, 1994)

Accord signed by Israeli officials and representatives of the Palestine Liberation Organization (PLO) on May 4, 1994, in Cairo, Egypt, that led to the creation of the Palestinian Authority (PA) and to promises of land transfers by Israel. Sometimes called the Gaza-Jericho Agreement, the accord was publicly signed by Israeli prime minister Yitzhak Rabin and PLO chairman Yasser Arafat. It was a direct result of the 1993 Oslo Accords and showcased the concept of land for peace whereby the Israelis agreed to turn over land to the Palestinians in return for certain guarantees. These guarantees usually took the form of security for Israel.

The accord was actually a follow-up to the Cairo Agreement of 1969, designed to regulate Palestinian activity and more clearly determine the status of the refugees in Lebanon. The agreement allowed the PLO, or the Palestinian Resistance Movement as it was known at the time, the freedom to organize resistance within the camps as long as Lebanese sovereignty was maintained. In 1987 during one of the lulls during the Lebanese Civil War (1975–1990), a new Lebanese government abrogated the agreement, as the Palestinian leadership had been exiled to Tunis.

Terrorists continued to operate against Israel from southern Lebanon, the occupied territory of Gaza, and the West Bank. Palestinian resentment toward Israel was especially strong in both the West Bank and the Gaza Strip. Palestinians who had been displaced had always argued for the right of return to their homes, whether in Israel or the West Bank and Gaza. With the possibility of a two-state solution, many hoped that refugees could negotiate a return to their original homes in Jericho and the Gaza Strip. Palestinians knew that there was great opposition to this in Israel but hoped that a set number might be resettled or compensated. However, the Oslo Accords had postponed the refugee issue until a later stage of negotiation.

The Cairo Accord laid the groundwork for the PA, which would become the governing body of the Palestinians in the occupied territories. The accord also stipulated that the Israelis turn land over to the Palestinians. In this case, they were bound to withdraw from most of the Gaza Strip and all of Jericho. Per the agreement, Israeli forces left Gaza by the end of May 1994. Subsequent withdrawals would eventually give 95 percent of the Palestinians living in Samaria and Judaea (West Bank) control over their own affairs. In return, the Palestinians were to end any support for terrorism against Israel or Israeli citizens and actively participate in an antiterrorism campaign designed to deter rogue elements from engaging in acts of violence. Other particulars of the agreement included joint Palestinian-Israeli civic and security arrangements and economic protocols.

Immediately after the signing of the Cairo Accord, the Palestinians made preparations for the PA's first elections, which were a prerequisite to Palestinian self-government. These were held in January 1996, and a legislative assembly was elected and seated. In those same elections, Arafat became the PA's first president.

Since May 1994 the peace process has remained volatile, disappointing, and unpredictable. In many ways, the Cairo Accord marked the high point of Israeli-Palestinian cooperation. In November 1995, Rabin was assassinated by an Israeli right-winger. The Palestinians have been unable to stem the tide of attacks on Israel, and Israel has not moved forward with its withdrawals according to the agreed-upon timetables. Subsequent agreements have also been abrogated by both sides. By the late 1990s, Israel's hard-line Likud Party, generally disdainful of the land-for-peace formula, had placed any further movement toward accommodation with the Palestinians on hold. For their part, the Palestinians have not done enough to curb violence, which accelerated dramatically after the start of the Second (al-Aqsa) Intifada in September 2000, provoked in part by Likud leader Ariel Sharon's visit to the Temple Mount. The Cairo Accord remains only partly realized, and only time will tell if the peace process regains the momentum it had in the early 1990s.

CHARLES FRANCIS HOWLETT AND PAUL G. PIERPAOLI JR.

See also
Arafat, Yasser; Gaza Strip; Intifada, Second; Israel; Oslo Accords; Palestine Liberation Organization; Palestinian National Authority; Rabin, Yitzhak; West Bank

References
Brown, Nathan J. *Palestinian Politics after the Oslo Accords: Resuming Arab Palestine.* Berkeley: University of California Press, 2003.
Freedman, Robert Owen, ed. *The Middle East and the Peace Process: The Impact of the Oslo Accords.* Gainesville: University Press of Florida, 1998.
Weinberger, Peter. *Co-opting the PLO: A Critical Reconstruction of the Oslo Accords, 1993–1995.* New York: Rowman and Littlefield, 2006.

Cairo Agreement (November 3, 1969)

Agreement brokered by Egyptian president Gamal Abdel Nasser regarding Lebanon and signed in Cairo on November 3, 1969, by Yasser Arafat, chairman of the Palestine Liberation Organization (PLO), and Lebanese Army commander General Emile al-Bustani. Al-Bustani was acting under the authority of Lebanese president Charles (Sharl) Hilu. The negotiations took place in Cairo in the presence of Egypt's minister of foreign affairs, Mahmud Riyadh, and minister of war, Muhammad Fawzi. The agreement allowed the PLO to operate in refugee camps in southern Lebanon and to recruit, arm, train, and employ fighters against Israel while using Lebanon as its primary base of military operations. The Cairo Agreement was an attempt to regulate Palestinian political and military activity in Lebanon while respecting Lebanese sovereignty.

Following the end of the June 1967 Six-Day War, more than 400,000 Palestinian refugees had settled in refugee camps in southern Lebanon as well as in the coastal cities of Tyre and Sidon. Within the refugee population, various Palestinian political factions were eager to establish a new front for attacks against Israel particularly after the revolution of 1969. The Lebanese government and its army sought to restrain the Palestinians from such activities. Palestinians in Lebanon, whether arriving before or after 1967, had no rights. They were not allowed to join the army or government service, as were Palestinians in Jordan. Instead, Palestinians in Lebanon were attacked by the Lebanese Army, repressed by the Deuxième Bureau government agents, and typically denied permits for work and travel.

Most Palestinians lived in extreme poverty, existing on day labor if available. Those who could obtain education tried to emigrate or began political information work, while camp Palestinians supported the armed struggle. Some Lebanese factions feared that the presence of the Palestinians would endanger the fragile communal and political balance in Lebanon and that raids into Israel would prompt retaliatory Israeli raids into Lebanon. Other groups saw the Palestinians as an ally in the process of political transformation. Non-Palestinians in southern Lebanon joined the fedayeen, or freedom fighters. As such, relations between Lebanon and the PLO deteriorated when Palestinian fedayeen, supported by the Muslim and Druze communities, openly clashed with the Maronite-dominated government forces throughout southern Lebanon in October 1969. In an effort to mediate the conflict between PLO forces and the Lebanese Army, Nasser brokered the Cairo Agreement, which defined the extent to which Palestinian commando, military, and political activities could be carried out in Lebanon.

The Cairo Agreement granted the PLO virtual autonomy in southern Lebanon. While the PLO was allowed to carry out attacks against Israel from Lebanese soil, the PLO agreed to fire on Israel from within the Jewish state. The accord also stipulated that the various Palestinian factions were free to train and carry arms within the confines of their refugee camps. The Palestinians were also granted unimpeded transit to Lebanon's border with Israel. In addition, PLO camps were to be located away from Lebanese towns. The Cairo Agreement ultimately resulted in the establishment of an autonomous area within Lebanon under PLO control. Arafat and the PLO were successful in gaining diplomatic recognition from a number of states while establishing diplomatic missions in more than 100 countries.

Although the aim of the Cairo Agreement was to control Palestinian military and political activity in Lebanon, it failed to accomplish this. PLO guerrillas enjoyed free rein in southern Lebanon, which lay beyond Beirut's control. Many of the most infamous Palestinian terrorist attacks of the 1970s were planned or originated in Lebanon. The border area soon became a launching site for Palestinian attacks against Israel and Israeli reprisals. Some Lebanese were unhappy with the terms of the accord because PLO attacks from Lebanon against Israel caused the Israelis to retaliate. The Israelis argued that it was Beirut's responsibility to secure its own borders, yet the Lebanese had virtually no control over PLO actions in southern Lebanon. Thus, the Cairo Agreement proved to be a bane to the Lebanese, who were constantly caught between the Palestinians and Israelis, but its advocates believed that it prevented a Black September–type organization from emerging in Lebanon.

In the long term, the Cairo Agreement was significant in that it legitimized an armed Palestinian presence in Lebanon and established the PLO as a state within a state. The agreement also prevented the Palestinians from assimilating into Lebanese society, and they were both discriminated against and suffered economically. Both sides broke the terms of the agreement when it suited their own interests. Following the June 1982 Israeli invasion of southern Lebanon, which resulted in the PLO's expulsion from Beirut, the Cairo Agreement became virtually meaningless. Another effect of the accord was increased tensions within Lebanon between Christians and Muslims as well as between Lebanese and Palestinian Arabs. This eventually led to civil war.

KEITH A. LEITICH

See also
Arafat, Yasser; Fedayeen; Lebanon; Lebanon Civil War; Lebanon-Israeli War; Nasser, Gamal Abdel; Palestine Liberation Organization; Six-Day War

References
El-Khazen, Farid. *The Breakdown of the State in Lebanon, 1967–1976.* Cambridge, MA: Harvard University Press, 2000.
Gresh, Alain, and Dominique Vidal. *The New A–Z of the Middle East.* New York: Tauris, 2004.
Khalaf, Samir. *Civil and Uncivil Violence in Lebanon: A History of the Internationalization of Communal Conflict.* New York: Columbia University Press, 2004.
Sayigh, Rosemary. *Palestinians: From Peasants to Revolutionaries.* London: Zed, 1979.

Cairo Declaration, Palestine Liberation Organization (November 7, 1985)

Official declaration by Palestine Liberation Organization (PLO) chairman Yasser Arafat on November 7, 1985, denouncing terrorism. As the late 1970s and early 1980s progressed, the PLO found itself in a rather isolated position diplomatically. While it enjoyed the support of many non-Palestinian Arabs and more than a few Arab governments, it was having a difficult time currying favor among Western nations. Also, the PLO's forced move to Tunis in 1982 diminished the organization's effectiveness, and the 1979 Egyptian-Israeli peace agreement made Arab rapprochement with Israel an attainable goal. The organization also knew that it would have to soften its rhetoric considerably in order to engage in discussions with U.S. policy makers. Thus, by 1985 Arafat and much of the PLO leadership decided that a fresh approach to the Palestinian dilemma was needed.

Arafat knew that securing entrance to Western diplomatic circles would be an enormous boost to the PLO's standing and would build legitimacy for the Palestinian cause. However, the United States had made it an official policy not to engage in any discussions with the PLO unless it abandoned terror tactics, recognized Israel's right to exist, and accepted United Nations Resolution 242 of 1967. Thus, Arafat and the Palestinian Legislative Council decided to alter their tactics.

Critics charged that Arafat's declaration amounted to rhetorical sleight of hand. Affirming an earlier pledge to eschew terrorism outside Israel and Palestine, Arafat now went further and vowed that henceforth the PLO would take "deterrent" steps against individuals or groups who violated this pledge. However, in the very same declaration, the PLO affirmed that the struggle against the "Israeli occupation" would continue "by all means possible," to include "armed struggle." While "terrorism" was now off limits, the continuing armed struggle against Israel would not end. Without such a declaration, the PLO would have lost its popular support. Many in the West, not necessarily understanding Palestinian fatigue with victimhood, saw "armed struggle" as merely a euphemism for "terrorism" in the occupied territories or elsewhere. As such, the Cairo Declaration brought the PLO no new diplomatic openings with the West. Yet it did seem to signal the beginning of a change in the organization's modus operandi.

Arafat had to move slowly and incrementally. Indeed, there was a hard-line constituency within the PLO that would not have been satisfied with sudden compromise and grand diplomatic overtures. Many on the Arab Left would likewise not have taken in good stride a great tactical turn on the part of the PLO. Three years later, the PLO would meet the West halfway by officially recognizing the State of Israel in the Algiers Declaration (1988). Yet rhetorical window dressing aside, there is ample evidence to suggest that some individuals within the PLO had not abandoned terrorism and clandestinely supported such activity during and after the Oslo Accords of 1993.

PAUL G. PIERPAOLI JR.

See also
Algiers Declaration; Arafat, Yasser; Palestine Liberation Organization

References
Abbas, Mahmoud. *Through Secret Channels: The Road to Oslo; Senior PLO Leader Abu Mazen's Revealing Story of the Negotiations with Israel.* Reading, UK: Garnet, 1997.
Aburish, Said K. *Arafat: From Defender to Dictator.* New York: Bloomsbury, 1998.
Livingstone, Neil C., and David Haley. *Inside the PLO.* New York: William Morrow, 1990.
Rubin, Barry. *Revolution until Victory? The Politics and History of the PLO.* Reprint ed. Cambridge, MA: Harvard University Press, 2003.

Cambyses II (?–522 BCE)

King of the Achaemenid (First Persian) Empire. Cambyses II ruled during 529–522 BCE. He was the elder son of Cyrus II the Great, founder of the Persian Achaemenid Empire. Cambyses's mother was Cassandane. As the elder son of his father, Cambyses accompanied Cyrus the Great during his campaign against the Neo-Babylonian Empire. After his conquest of Babylon, Cyrus appointed Cambyses as king of Babylon. Toward the end of Cyrus's reign, for a short time Cambyses acted as a coregent and shared the titles "king of Babylon" and "king of the lands" with his father.

Cambyses II ascended the Persian throne in 530 after his father was killed in a campaign against the Massagetae, a Scythian group in Central Asia. In 525, having restored order in the vast empire he had inherited from his father, Cambyses marched against Phoenicia (modern-day Lebanon) and Egypt. The Phoenicians submitted voluntarily. The conquest of Egypt, however, required a major military campaign and the personal participation and leadership of the Persian monarch.

In moving against Egypt, Cambyses II was continuing his father's policy of expanding the boundaries of the Persian Empire to North Africa. His principal objective was the conquest of the agriculturally rich Nile River Valley, which could provide the Persian state with an important strategic foothold in Africa while at the same time significantly enhancing and augmenting the economic and political power of the Persian king.

The Persian army first established a foothold on the eastern frontiers of Egypt. Scrambling to craft a military coalition capable of deterring the Persians from invading his country, Amasis, the pharaoh of Egypt, formed an alliance with Polycrates, the tyrant of the Greek island of Samos off the coast of Asia Minor in the eastern Aegean. This unreliable ally, however, abandoned the pharaoh shortly before the invasion of Egypt by the Persians. Worse, the commander of the pharaoh's forces also deserted his royal master and defected to Cambyses. Before the Persians invaded his country, Amasis died in 525, succeeded by Psammetichus III, who was left with the task of defending Egypt against the invaders.

When the two armies joined battle the Persians scored two quick victories, first at Pelusium and then at Memphis, where the new pharaoh was captured. Following the policy of his father, which was to retain a defeated ruler as a tribute-paying vassal, Cambyses spared Psammetichus III. The relationship between the two monarchs, however, deteriorated quickly when Cambyses was informed that the defeated pharaoh was involved in a conspiracy to create a rebellion against Persian rule. Cambyses ordered Psammetichus III executed. Ancient historians Herodotus and later Strabo described Cambyses as a brutal and cold-blooded murderer and madman who looted Egyptian temples and insulted Egyptian gods and priests. According to them, the brutality and savagery of Cambyses reached its climax when the Persian king killed Apis, the Egyptian sacred bull. Egyptian sources refute these fantastic stories and indicate that Persian rule did not leave an adverse impact on Egypt and that Cambyses behaved with respect regarding Egyptian religious beliefs, customs, and traditions. Herodotus also claimed that Cambyses invaded Nubia (southern Egypt and northern Sudan). This campaign was aborted, however, as a result of inadequate provisions.

Cambyses departed Egypt for Iran in 522 BCE after he was informed that an individual claiming to be his brother Bardiya, younger son of Cyrus the Great, had proclaimed himself king. On his inscription at Bisotun in western Iran, Achaemenid king Darius I (r. 522–480), who at the time served as an officer in Cambyses's army, claimed that the man who had revolted against Cambyses was not Bardiya but rather a priest named Gaumata. Darius stated that before leaving for Egypt, Cambyses II had secretly ordered the execution of his brother in order to prevent a palace coup in his absence. The murder of the king's brother was, however, kept secret, and was only known to a handful of individuals within the royal court.

Before he could reach Persia and quell the rebellion, Cambyses died suddenly in 522.

MEHRDAD KIA

See also
Achaemenid Empire; Babylonian Empire, Neo-; Cyrus II the Great; Darius I

References
Bresciani, E. "The Persian Occupation of Egypt." In *The Cambridge History of Iran*, Vol. 2, *The Median and Achaemenian Periods*, ed. Ilya Gershevitch. Cambridge: Cambridge University Press, 1985.
Briant, Pierre. *From Cyrus to Alexander: A History of the Persian Empire*. Winona Lake, IN: Eisenbrauns, 2002.
Ghirshman, R. *Iran*. New York: Penguin Books, 1978.
Herodotus. *Histories.* Translated by Aubrey De Sélincourt. Revised with Introduction and Notes by John Marincola. New York: Penguin Books, 1996.
Kent, Roland G. *Old Persian: Grammar, Texts, Lexicon*. New Haven, CT: American Oriental Society, 1950.

Camel, Battle of the
See Bassorah, Battle of

Camp David Accords (September 17, 1978)

Peace agreement reached between Egypt and Israel during talks held from September 5 to September 17, 1978, at Camp David, the U.S. presidential retreat in rural Maryland. During 1977 and 1978, several remarkable events occurred that set the stage for the Camp David negotiations. In the autumn of 1977, Egyptian president Anwar Sadat indicated his willingness to go to Israel in the cause of peace, something that no Arab leader had done since creation of the Jewish state in 1948. On November 19, 1977, Sadat followed through on his promise, addressing the Knesset (Israeli parliament) and calling for peace between the two nations. The Israelis welcomed Sadat's bold initiative but took no immediate steps to end the state of belligerency, instead agreeing to ministerial-level meetings in preparation for final negotiations.

In February 1978 the United States entered into the equation by hosting Sadat in Washington, with both President Jimmy Carter and Congress hailing the Egyptian president as a statesman and a courageous leader. American adulation for Sadat led to greater cooperation by the Israelis, and they agreed to a summit meeting in September at Camp David.

During September 5–17, 1978, Carter hosted a conference that brought together Sadat and Israeli prime minister Menachem Begin and their respective staffs. Carter participated as an active player in the resultant talks. As was expected, the discussions proved difficult. Begin insisted that Sadat separate the Palestinian issue from the peace talks, something that no Arab leader had been willing to do before. Israel also demanded that Egypt negate any former agreements with other Arab nations that called for war against Israel.

Sadat bristled at Begin's demands, which led to such acrimony between the two men that they met in person only once during the entire negotiation process. Instead, Carter shuttled between the two leaders in an effort to moderate their positions. After several days of little movement and accusations of bad faith directed mostly at Begin, however, Carter threatened to break off the talks. Faced with the possibility of being blamed for a failed peace plan, Begin finally came to the table ready to deal. He agreed to dismantle all Jewish settlements in the Sinai Peninsula and return it in its entirety to Egypt. For his part, given Begin's absolute intransigence on it, Sadat agreed to put the Palestinian issue aside and sign an agreement separate from the other Arab nations. On September 15, 1978, Carter, Sadat, and Begin announced that an agreement had been reached on two frameworks, the first for a peace treaty between Egypt and Israel and the second for a multilateral treaty dealing with

U.S. president Jimmy Carter locks hands with Egyptian president Anwar Sadat (left) and Israeli prime minister Menachem Begin (right) after the signing of the Camp David Accords on September 17, 1978. (Jimmy Carter Library)

the West Bank and the Gaza Strip. The treaty was signed by the principals at the White House in Washington, D.C., on September 17, 1978.

The framework regarding Egypt and Israel had 11 major provisions: (1) the two nations would sign a peace treaty within three months; (2) this treaty would be implemented within two to three years after it was signed; (3) Egypt would regain full sovereignty of the Sinai to its pre–Six-Day War (1967) borders; (4) Israeli would withdraw its forces from the Sinai, with the first such withdrawal to occur nine months after signature of the treaty; (5) Israeli was to have freedom of navigation through the Suez Canal and the Strait of Tiran; (6) a highway would be built between the Sinai and Jordan to pass near Eilat with the guarantee of free passage through Israeli territory for both nations; (7) Egyptian forces in the Sinai would be limited to one division in the area 50 kilometers (30 miles) east of the Gulf of Suez and the Suez Canal; (8) there would be no other Egyptian forces in the Sinai; (9) Israeli forces would be restricted to four infantry battalions in the area 3 kilometers (1.8 miles) east of the international border with Egypt; (10) United Nations (UN) forces would be positioned in certain areas; and (11) the peace between the two nations would be complete, including full diplomatic recognition and an end to any economic restrictions on the other nation's goods, with free movement of goods and people.

The second framework, officially known as the "Framework of Peace in the Middle East," was far more general and skirted major issues. It contained seven major provisions: (1) UN Security Council Resolutions 242 and 338 were recognized as holding "in all their parts" the basis for a peace settlement; (2) the peace settlement would be negotiated by Egypt, Israel, Jordan, and "the representatives of the Palestinian people"; (3) residents of the West Bank and Gaza would secure "full autonomy"; (4) Egypt, Israel, and Jordan were to agree on "modalities for establishing the elected self-governing authority" in these areas, and the Egyptian and Jordanian delegations "may include Palestinians from the West Bank and Gaza or other Palestinians as mutually agreed"; (5) a withdrawal of Israeli forces would occur, with remaining forces grouped in certain agreed-upon locations; (6) as soon as the self-governing authority ("administrative council") had been established, a five-year transitional period would begin by the end of which the final status of the West Bank and Gaza would have been agreed to, understanding that there would be recognition of "the legitimate rights of the Palestinian people and their just requirements"; and (7) in the transitional period, representatives of Egypt, Israel, and Jordan as well as those of the self-governing authority "will constitute a continuing committee" to agree on "the modalities of admission of peoples displaced from the West Bank and Gaza in 1967."

Despite a feeling of euphoria in the United States and an upward spike in Carter's approval ratings, the agreement in fact was a retreat from the president's own program in 1977 that called for Israeli withdrawal from the occupied lands with only minor territorial adjustments and a homeland for the Palestinian people based on self-determination rather than on autonomy under Israeli administrative control. Much was also simply left out. There was no mention in the framework of the future of Jerusalem and the Golan Heights or about Israeli settlements in the West Bank and the future of the Palestine Liberation Organization (PLO), which the United States steadfastly refused to recognize.

During the next several months, Secretary of State Cyrus Vance made numerous trips to the Middle East to finalize the agreement. The United States promised that it would help organize an international peacekeeping force to occupy the Sinai following the Israeli withdrawal. Washington also agreed to provide $2 billion to pay for the relocation of an airfield from the Sinai to Israel and promised economic assistance to Egypt in exchange for Sadat's signature on a peace treaty.

Finally, on March 26, 1979, in a White House ceremony, Sadat and Begin shook hands again and signed a permanent peace treaty, normalizing relations between their two nations. Hopes that other Arab nations, particularly the pro-Western regimes in Jordan and Saudi Arabia, would soon follow Egypt's lead were quickly dashed. Indeed, the Camp David Accords produced a strong negative reaction in the Arab world, where other states and the PLO denounced the agreement and condemned Sadat for having "sold out" the Arab cause. Egypt was expelled from the Arab League, and several Middle Eastern nations broke off diplomatic relations with Cairo. Not until the mid-1990s would another Arab nation, Jordan, join Egypt in normalizing relations with Israel. Nonetheless, the Camp David Accords were without doubt President Carter's greatest foreign policy success.

Brent Geary and Spencer C. Tucker

See also
Begin, Menachem; Egypt; Israel; Palestine Liberation Organization; Sadat, Anwar; Sinai Peninsula

References
Brzezinski, Zbigniew. *Power and Principle: Memoirs of the National Security Adviser, 1977–1981.* New York: Farrar, Straus and Giroux, 1985.
Carter, James E. *Keeping Faith: Memoirs of the President.* New York: Bantam, 1982.
Lenczowski, George. *The Middle East in World Affairs.* 4th ed. Ithaca, NY: Cornell University Press, 1980.
Quandt, William. *Camp David: Peacemaking and Politics.* Washington, DC: Brookings Institution, 1986.
Telhami, Shibley. *Power and Leadership in International Bargaining: The Path to the Camp David Accords.* New York: Columbia University Press, 1990.

Camp Speicher Massacre (June 12, 2014)

Mass killing of Iraqi Air Force cadets at a military training camp near Tikrit, Iraq, on June 12, 2014. Jihadists associated with the Islamic State of Iraq and Syria (ISIS) massacred as many as 1,700 men. The Iraqi government claimed that members of the Arab Socialist Baath Party–Iraqi Region were also complicit in the attack, but this has not been substantially proven.

At the time of the killings, ISIS was on the offensive and was about to seize the Iraqi city of Tikrit. At nearby Camp Speicher, which housed several thousand air force cadets, commanders decided to vacate the post, sending the men home in civilian attire. In the late morning of June 12, 2014, as the cadets were beginning to leave the area, dozens of well-armed ISIS fighters appeared in trucks and buses, kidnapping numerous cadets. Other cadets were cornered within the compound and forced to stand in shallow graves, where they were mowed down by assault weapons. Some of the kidnapped cadets were similarly executed, while others were forced into the Tigris River, where they were shot en masse. A number were also beheaded. As the killing spree progressed ISIS took videos, which were later put on the Internet. These depicted hundreds of Iraqi men clothed in orange jumpsuits being led to their deaths by masked fighters.

The Iraqi government initially tried to claim that the massacre was not sectarian based, but videos clearly showed

ISIS fighters singling out Shia Muslims and non-Muslims for execution. The Iraqi government also asserted that no more than 1,095 cadets had died, but the more likely figure is between 1,500 and 1,700. Clearly, Iraqi officials were deeply embarrassed by the tragedy and sought to downplay its severity. At the time, the Iraqi government was about to transition from Prime Minister Nuri al-Maliki's tenure to that of Haider al-Abadi. Certainly the loss of Tikrit and the Speicher massacre represented a stinging indictment of Maliki's inept and corrupt leadership.

Although a few suspects were arrested in the months after the massacre, Iraqi officials did not secure large numbers of purported perpetrators until its forces had retaken Tikrit in April 2015. Meanwhile, the Iraqi government mandated that the families of those cadets who had perished would receive death benefit payments equivalent to $8,600 per individual.

The legal process that ensued against the alleged participants in the massacre was evidently hasty and haphazard. An Iraqi court handed down the majority of the death sentences in August 2015 and February 2016. Thirty-six individuals were executed by hanging on August 21, 2016. Some of them—all Iraqi citizens—claimed innocence, and some alleged that they had not been anywhere near Tikrit in June 2014. Human rights organizations, including Amnesty International and the United Nations High Commissioner for Human Rights, lamented the executions, claiming that some defendants were denied access to lawyers or were forced to confess under duress or torture. Others warned that the executions, far from serving as a deterrent, might actually fuel more violence.

Paul G. Pierpaoli Jr.

See also
Iraq; Islamic State of Iraq and Syria; Maliki, Nuri Muhammed Kamil al-

References
Damon, Arwa, Hamdi Alkhshali, and Ralph Ellis. "Mass Graves in Tikrit Might Contain 1700 Bodies." CNN, April 8, 2015, http://edition.cnn.com/2015/04/06/middleeast/iraq-mass-graves/index.html.

"Iraq Hangs 36 Men Convicted of Speicher Massacre." *The Guardian*, August 21, 2005, https://www.theguardian.com/world/2016/aug/21/iraq-hangs-men-convicted-speicher-massacre-shia-tikrit.

Carrhae, Battle of (June 9, 53 BCE)

Battle between forces of the Roman Republic led by Marcus Licinius Crassus and those of the Parthian (Arsacid) Empire under General Surena on June 9, 53 BCE (some sources have the date as May 6), near Carrhae (Harran, near modern-day Altınbaşak, Turkey) in Upper Mesopotamia.

Roman leader Marcus Licinius Crassus was nearly 60 when he undertook the campaign against the Persians. His military experience was limited, going back to the 80s BCE and against Spartacus in 72–71, but Crassus may have wanted a victory to equal those of Pompey and Caesar: only a victory over a major enemy would bring the necessary prestige. In hindsight, Crassus's ambition was overreaching and motivated by greed.

Crassus secured a command in Syria to follow his second consulship in 55. It is not clear whether his *provincia* included the right to make war on the Persians. The size of his army—probably seven legions and about 4,000 cavalry—would suggest that it did. There was also instability on Rome's eastern frontier with which the Romans may have wanted to deal.

Crassus arrived in the spring of 54. He crossed the Euphrates and spent time reconnoitering and establishing garrisons, especially along the Belikh River. He returned to winter in Syria, train his troops, and organize his supply lines by extorting large sums of money and plundering temples (taken as a sign of his greed). In the following spring Crassus crossed the Euphrates again and traveled along the river. Support promised by Armenian king Artavasdes failed to materialize, as he had been diverted by a Persian attack. The claim of Abgar (or Ariamnes), an Arab chieftain and guide, that tracks heading southeast from the Euphrates indicated a retreating Persian force induced Crassus to head away from the Euphrates toward the garrisons along the Belikh.

After a desert crossing, Crassus did not rest his troops but pressed on, not wanting the supposedly retreating Persians to escape. At this point Abgar deserted, but Crassus kept going. The Persians were led by Surena, who devised tactics suited to his troops of heavily armed cavalry and a camel train to keep his archers supplied with arrows.

The two sides met near Carrhae on June 9, 53. Hemmed in by the heavy cavalry, the Romans fell to the continuous hail of arrows. Crassus's son Publius, who had brought 1,000 horsemen from Caesar, led a rash cavalry action away from the main battle and was killed. The battle was one of the most notorious defeats in Roman history. Rome may have lost between 35,000 and 40,000 men in the battle. Rome had not experienced a defeat of this magnitude since the Battle of Cannae in 216 BCE during Hannibal Barca's invasion of Italy in the Second Punic War. The loss at Carrhae had a powerful impact on the Roman psyche.

The Roman survivors headed for Carrhae, but staying there was untenable, so they moved north toward Sinnaca, another garrison. Near there, Surena offered a parley. Crassus reluctantly agreed, but he was taken prisoner and killed.

A number of Romans escaped, some to Syria, which they capably defended, while around 10,000 prisoners became mercenaries in the Persian Army. Some of these gradually worked their way east, one group even ending up settling in western China. The standards lost by Crassus's army were eventually recovered during the principate of Augustus in 20 BCE.

Losers usually receive bad press: Crassus was no exception. His loss is credited to his greed, but he did attempt to make adequate military preparations. Nor did he lead his army through a trackless and waterless desert: he had reconnoitered the area the year before, and the snowmelt meant that rivers would have had water. Where he can be blamed is his reliance on untrustworthy guides and his failure to learn enough about the tactics and resources of a better opponent.

Bruce Marshall

See also
Parthian Empire; Roman-Parthian Wars

Reference
Marshall, Bruce A. *Crassus: A Political Biography*. Amsterdam: Hakkert, 1976.

Carter Doctrine (January 23, 1980)

Foreign policy precept enunciated by U.S. president James "Jimmy" Carter in 1980 that pledged the nation to protect American and Allied interests in the Persian Gulf. By 1980 the Carter administration, which had been engaged in an ongoing debate over the direction of U.S. foreign policy as détente faded, declared its determination to use any means necessary, including military force, to protect American interests in the Persian Gulf. These interests mainly involved Persian Gulf oil and regional shipping lanes.

On January 23, 1980, Carter, in his State of the Union message, declared that "an attempt by any outside force to gain control of the Persian Gulf region will be regarded as an assault on the vital interests of the United States of America, and such an assault will be repelled by any means necessary, including military force." This emphasis on American military power marked a fundamental reorientation in Carter's foreign policy. Since 1977, in response to public disillusionment regarding the Vietnam War and disgust over the Watergate scandal, Carter had attempted to fight the Cold War with different weapons. While not ignoring the Soviet Union, he determined that U.S.-Soviet relations would not be allowed to dominate foreign policy formulation, a stance that he saw as having led to the costly containment policy and the tragedy of Vietnam. Instead, other nations, especially those in the developing world, would be considered in a regional rather than a global context. Additionally, the United States would assert its international predominance by emphasizing moral rather than military superiority by focusing on human rights and related humanitarian concerns.

By January 1980, however, the international climate had changed drastically. The Islamic Revolution in Iran had displaced America's longtime ally, Shah Mohammed Reza Pahlavi. On November 4, 1979, Iranian students seized the American embassy in Tehran and took 70 Americans hostage. This precipitated a 444-day crisis during which the Carter administration could do little to free the hostages. Also, on December 26, 1979, the Soviet Union invaded Afghanistan, sparking a bloody nine-year war there. Faced with these twin crises—religious fundamentalist terrorism and communist advancement by military force—during an election year, Carter reoriented his foreign policy. Although he did not abandon his commitment to human rights, the issue was accorded a much lower priority in policy formulation and was no longer used as a major weapon with which to wage the Cold War. Instead, the administration's official posture reflected a more customary Cold War policy that emphasized the projection of military power and communist containment. In addition, a globalist perspective began to supplant the regionalist outlook, with increased emphasis on East-West issues. These trends were accelerated considerably under President Ronald Reagan, Carter's successor. The Carter Doctrine is still operative in American foreign policy, almost three decades after it was enunciated. Indeed, it was used as a partial justification for the 1991 Persian Gulf War and the 2003 invasion of Iraq.

Donna R. Jackson

See also
Iran, Islamic Revolution in; Iran Hostage Crisis

References
Brzezinski, Zbigniew. *Power and Principle: Memoirs of the National Security Adviser, 1977–1981*. New York: Farrar, Straus and Giroux, 1983.

Carter, Jimmy. *Keeping Faith: Memoirs of a President*. Fayetteville: University of Arkansas Press, 1995.

Vance, Cyrus. *Hard Choices: Critical Years in America's Foreign Policy*. New York: Simon and Schuster, 1983.

CAST LEAD, Operation

See Gaza War of 2008–2009

Caucasus Front, World War I

Caucasia, also known as the Caucasus, is a geopolitical region marking the border between Europe and Asia and located between the Black Sea and the Caspian Sea. During World War I, this region saw fighting between the Ottoman Empire and Russia. The 300-mile-wide area of mountain ranges and high plateaus constituting the Ottoman-Russian frontier in Caucasia, in spite of its forbidding nature, had long been the primary battlefield of those two powers. Yet in 1914, Russian leaders did not regard this as a major theater of war. They rightly expected the war to be decided by the clash of mass armies on the battlefields of Europe.

Ottoman leaders, especially Minister of War Enver Pasha, nourished fantastic Pan-Turkic schemes and devoted a major military effort to offensives in the Caucasus region, forcing Russia to follow suit. A four-year struggle ensued in which the Ottoman Empire suffered some bitter defeats but also scored its most spectacular success of the entire war.

The two opposing armies entered the war on the Caucasus front insufficiently prepared for major operations. Russia normally maintained three corps in the area in peacetime, but with the war starting and the Ottoman Empire still neutral, two had redeployed to the Eastern Front. The I Caucasus Corps that remained had been reinforced only by the II Turkistan Corps and some Cossack divisions. Split in five separate groups, this Russian army of about 100,000 infantry, 15,000 cavalry, and 256 guns, commanded for all practical purposes by its chief of staff, the capable Major General Nikolai Yudenich, guarded the major communications across the frontier and maintained a general reserve around Tiflis (Tblisi). The Ottoman Empire's Third Army opposed the Russians. Commanded by Hasan Izzet Pasha, it contained the IX, X, and XI Corps. These were under-strength and desperately short of munitions.

Even before the Russian declaration of war on November 2, 1914, weak Russian forces advanced across the frontier to secure better defensive positions. Within a week, Izzet Pasha had concentrated four divisions of the IX and XI Corps against the main Russian body on the Kars-Erzurum road. He checked the Russians with heavy losses in fighting around Köprüköy, pushing the attackers back toward the frontier where they consolidated their position after being reinforced. The Russians were more successful on their left flank, where they encountered only weak Ottoman forces. On the other hand, Russian defenses on their right flank, around the Black Sea port of Batum, collapsed under the pressure of Ottoman irregulars.

This situation encouraged Enver Pasha to order the Third Army to undertake a major offensive, in spite of approaching winter that would cover the area with 10 to 12 feet of snow and drop temperatures to −50°F. The Third Army was reinforced to 120,000 men, outnumbering the Russians, who had about 80,000 men, by 50 percent. Enver's plan was a single encirclement with the IX and X Corps moving through the Oltu River Valley to place them in the right rear of the Russian salient, while the XI Corps pinned the Russians in front. But the grandiose operation that began on December 22, 1914, resulted in disaster. Although the flanking force advanced rapidly, taking Oltu within two days and the key city of Sarikamish within four days, the XI Corps failed to pin the Russian army.

With the aid of fresh reinforcements, Yudenich trapped the Ottoman left wing in the Turnagel Woods north of Sarikamish. On January 4, 1915, the Ottoman IX Corps surrendered wholesale. Having suffered 50,000 casualties to Yudenich's 28,000, the remnants of the Third Army withdrew in confusion.

Fortunately for the Ottomans, the Russians were too exhausted to follow up their victory with a rapid advance on Erzurum. During the spring, the battered Third Army, having been additionally reduced by a typhus epidemic to about 20,000 men, was slowly rebuilt to combat strength. By June 1915 it numbered more than 50,000 effectives, not counting the Erzurum fortress garrison, while Yudenich, now formally commander of the Russian Caucasus Army, had about 80,000 men.

Assuming that the Third Army was still weakest on its right, as it had been in 1914, Yudenich resumed the offensive in June 1915 by pushing his new IV Caucasian Corps down the northwestern shore of Lake Van for a drive on the key city of Muş. The Ottomans, however, succeeded in concentrating in the area a total of 70,000 effectives, formed around the rebuilt IX Corps as a new wing under Abdul Karim Pasha, a fact that the Russians failed to detect. Caught in the restricted terrain by superior Ottoman forces, the Russians' advance ground to a halt.

the ensuing battle focused on the city of Malazgirt, which the Ottomans captured on July 26. Intoxicated by this success, Abdul Karim pressed on into the Eliskirt Valley but, repeating the Sarikamish pattern, was then checked by a Russian counteroffensive that recaptured Malazgirt on

Russian soldiers display Ottoman standards taken in the capture of Erzurum, capital of Ottoman Armenia, on February 16, 1916. Russian army and navy forces then moved against the Black Sea port of Trebizon (Trabzon), which fell on April 18. (Reynolds and Taylor. *Collier's Photographic History of the European War*, 1916)

August 15. This indecisive military operation cost the Ottomans more than 80,000 casualties, with the unlucky IX Corps again almost being wiped out.

Both armies used the remainder of 1915 to rebuild their strength. Then, taking the Ottomans by surprise, Yudenich struck on January 10, 1916, with the I Caucasian Corps and the II Turkistan Corps down the Kars-Erzurum road, actually where the Ottoman lines were strongest. (Following the fight for Malazgirt, both armies had stripped the Muş sector of all but the bare minimum of troops.) Still, the attackers vastly outnumbered the defenders, who had tasked three understrength corps (IX, X, and XI Corps), with each holding 20 miles of front line. Within a week, the Russians had carried the fortified lines of Köprüköy. Badly mauled and reduced to some 50,000 effectives, the Ottoman Third Army retreated to the Erzurum fortress area.

As the second-largest Ottoman fortress (after Adrianople), Erzurum was regarded as an almost impregnable stronghold by the Ottoman General Staff. That belief may have been one reason it failed to send much-needed reinforcements quickly to the Third Army. On February 11, 1916, the Russians attacked the Ottoman lines around Erzurum. Yudenich concentrated more than 250 guns on a small sector of the line. Losses were heavy, but the Russians' three-to-one numerical superiority told. On February 16, the Third Army withdrew from Erzurum just in time to escape total envelopment. Along with the loss of the fortress, the Ottomans sustained 25,000 casualties and lost 327 guns, their hospitals, and substantial stocks of supplies. Additionally, on April 16, 1916, the only large Black Sea port in the area, Trabzon, fell to the Russians, a logistical disaster for the Ottomans in this mountainous area not serviced by railroads. Reinforced by the veteran V Corps from Gallipoli, the shaken Third Army was barely able to avoid annihilation.

During the spring, the Ottoman General Staff devised a new grand design. On the right flank of the Third Army, a new Second Army under Ahmed Izzet Pasha appeared, formed of crack divisions no longer needed for the defense of the Gallipoli Peninsula. While the Third Army remained seriously understrength and could not effectively oppose a renewed Russian offensive in July 1916, which cost the Ottomans the cities of Bayburt on July 17 and Erzincan on July 25, the Second Army was slowly brought up to a strength of 10 infantry divisions with ample cavalry and heavy artillery for a total of 100,000 effectives.

On August 2, Izzet Pasha launched his offensive against the Russian left flank. A month earlier such an attack might have saved the Third Army from disaster, but now Yudenich could devote his full attention to this new threat to his flank. Izzet Pasha's offensive was poorly planned and was carried out by three widely separated columns against a Russian army that enjoyed interior lines and superior communications. Still, the Second Army's crack troops were initially successful until they were checked by Russian counterattacks in late August. By September 26, Izzet Pasha's offensive was over. For little ground gained, he had sacrificed 30,000 irreplaceable well-trained infantry.

This proved to be the Ottoman Empire's penultimate major offensive. Soldiers on both sides on the Caucasus front spent the remainder of 1916 and most of 1917 in the trenches with almost no action on either side. The Ottoman Second and Third Armies had exhausted their offensive potential. In the second half of 1917 the Russian forces, plagued by revolutionary discontent, began to disintegrate. Caucasia became for all practical purposes a political and military vacuum.

On the Ottoman side, the Second Army was dissolved, and the entire front again was put under the authority of the Third Army. With its former corps and divisions consolidated into new ones but still far under authorized strength, the army was hardly capable of offensive operations. However, the disappearance of any organized opposition in its front, except the National Army of the newly independent Armenia, seemed to warrant another offensive, the last by the Ottoman Empire.

The final Ottoman offensive commenced on February 12, 1918, and was a great, if short-lived, success. Erzincan fell immediately, and Trabzon fell within a fortnight. On March 12 Vehip Pasha was in Erzurum, and on March 25 he crossed the prewar frontier. The Ottomans were in Sarikamish on April 3, on in Van April 6, and in Batum on April 14, having reconquered within two months all the ground lost since 1914. On April 25 the 10,000-strong Armenian garrison surrendered the fortress city of Kars, which had been Ottoman territory until 1878, along with more than 200 guns and substantial quantities of supplies.

Finally assuming a grandiose scale, the Ottoman offensive then fanned out into northern Persia and Azerbaijan. Amid chaotic peace talks with Russian, British, German, Armenian, and Georgian envoys, the Ottomans took the major Caspian Sea port of Baku on September 15, 1918. Finally, on November 8 their 15th Infantry Division captured Petrovsk, 180 miles north of Baku. By that time, however, the Armistice of Mudros on October 30 and the Ottoman Empire's departure from the war had already rendered the vast territorial gains of its last offensive entirely meaningless.

DIERK WALTER

See also
Enver Pasha; Erzurum Offensive; Gallipoli Campaign; Mesopotamian Theater, World War I; Persian Front, World War I; Sarikamish, Battle of; Yudenich, Nikolai Nikolaevich

References
Allen, W. E. D., and Paul Muratoff. *Caucasian Battlefields: A History of the Wars on the Turco-Caucasian Border, 1828–1921.* Cambridge: Cambridge University Press, 1953.
Erickson, Edward J. *Ordered to Die: A History of the Ottoman Army in the First World War.* Westport, CT: Greenwood, 2000.
Shaw, Stanford J., and Ezel Kural Shaw. *History of the Ottoman Empire and Modern Turkey,* Vol. 2, *Reform, Revolution, and Republic: The Rise of Modern Turkey, 1808–1975.* Cambridge: Cambridge University Press, 1977.

Cezayirli Gazi Hasan Pasha (1713–1790)

One of the greatest Ottoman admirals (*kapudan pasha*) and military commanders, Hasan Pasha was born in 1713 at Tekirdag in Eastern Thrace. Bought as a slave by a merchant from Rodosto (Terikdagh), he subsequently obtained his freedom and became a janissary and participated in the Habsburg-Ottoman War of 1737–1739, distinguishing himself at the Battle of Krozka (Hisarjik) in 1739. After the war he served in Algiers (hence his name Cezayirli, meaning "from Algiers"), and later he became beg of Tlemcen. However, he soon quarreled with the governor of Algiers and had to flee to Spain, where he was well received by King Charles IV.

After brief service in Spain and Naples, Hasan returned to the Porte, where Sultan Mustafa III gave him command of a warship; in 1766 Hasan already commanded a flagship. He participated in the Russo-Ottoman War of 1768–1774 and distinguished himself at the Battle of Chesme, where he was able to save the ships under his command and was the only Ottoman commander to emerge with his reputation intact. In 1770, he conducted a daring attack on the Russian-controlled island of Lemnos, for which he was accorded the rank of *kapudan pasha* and the title of *ghazi*.

In 1773 to improve the Ottoman Navy, Hasan Pasha opened a naval school that eventually became the storied Muhendishane-i Bahri Humayun (Imperial Naval Engineer School) in 1784. In 1773–1774 Hasan was sent to the Danubian front, where he served as the *serasker* of Ruse and fought against Russian armies. After the war ended in 1774, he returned to his post of *kapudan pasha*.

Hasan conducted successful operations against mutinous lords in Syria in 1775–1776 and the Morea in 1779. In 1780 he sailed to Egypt, where he forced the Mamluks to resume payment of tribute, which they had been refusing to do for years. In the 1780s, Hasan Pasha was preoccupied with the reorganization of the Ottoman Navy and laid the foundation for career naval service. In 1786–1787 he once again led the Ottoman Navy to Egypt, where the Mamluks rebelled against the Ottoman governor. He successfully subdued the Mamluk revolt and forced its leaders to continue paying tribute. As soon as he restored order in Egypt, he was sent to the Black Sea to participate in the Russo-Ottoman War (1787–1791). However, he failed to break the Russian siege of the Ottoman fortress of Ochakov, while the reinforcements he delivered were routed on land. Returning to Constantinople, Hasan Pasha became the *serasker* of Izmail and took command of the Danubian front, becoming the grand vizier in January 1790. He died of illness on March 19, 1790, and is buried in Shumla. The city of Chesme features a statue of Hasan Pasha along with that of the lion that he had domesticated while in Africa and took with him on campaigns.

ALEXANDER MIKABERIDZE

See also
Ottoman Empire

Reference
Zorlun, Tuncay. *Innovation and Empire in Turkey: Sultan Selim III and the Modernisation of the Ottoman Navy*. New York: Tauris, 2008.

Chaldean Empire
See Babylonian Empire, Neo-

Chaldiran, Battle of (August 23, 1514)
A major battle between forces of the Ottoman Empire and those of rising Safavid Persia. The conflict leading to the battle was prompted by Safavid shah Ismail's support for the Turkmen tribes, who were in open revolt against the Ottomans, and the spread of the Shiism in Anatolia. In 1514 Sultan Selim I launched a campaign against Ismail, and the two armies finally met at Chaldiran, northeast of Lake Van in eastern Anatolia, on August 23.

Deployed behind a barrier of wagons, the Ottomans exploited their superiority in artillery and firearms to repel the repeated charges of Ismail's traditional cavalry, which suffered heavy losses and fled from the field. The magnitude of the defeat can be discerned from the fact that Ismail's entire harem, including his wives, fell into Ottoman hands. After the battle Selim captured Tabriz on September 7, but he was unable to press on owing to discontent among the Janissaries.

Still, the victory at Chaldiran marked Ottoman expansion into eastern Anatolia and the halt of the Safavid expansion to the west. For Shah Ismail personally, this defeat also meant the loss of the aura of invincibility and certain divinity claimed by him. The battle seems to have shattered his military confidence, for he never again participated in a military campaign.

ALEXANDER MIKABERIDZE

See also
Ismail I, Shah; Ottoman-Safavid Wars; Selim I, Sultan

References
Jackson, Peter, and Lawrence Lockhart, eds. *The Cambridge History of Iran: The Timurid and Safavid Periods*, Vol. 6. Cambridge: Cambridge University Press, 1986.

Murphey, Rhoads. *Ottoman Warfare, 1500–1700*. New Brunswick, NJ: Rutgers University Press, 1999.

Chamoun, Camille (1900–1987)
Lebanese politician and premier. Camille Chamoun (Kamil Shamun) was born on April 3, 1900, into a prominent Maronite Christian family at Deir al-Qamar in Lebanon. Although a Maronite Christian, he came from the Shuf district where many Muslin Druzes lived. The Druzes, largely concentrated in Lebanon's Shuf Mountains and western Beirut, had once dominated Mount Lebanon and the Maronites. The latter, however, gained social ascendancy, as a number became wealthy through commerce. Maronites opposed the unification with Syria preferred by some Muslims and other Christian groups. Each sect possessed feudal lords who commanded the political loyalties of peasants or residents of urban areas.

Chamoun attended a Catholic elementary school in Deir al-Qamar and a high school in Beirut. During World War I, the Chamoun family was exiled for anti-Ottoman and Lebanese nationalist activities on the part of Chamoun's father. Following the war Lebanon became a French mandate, and Lebanese nationalists then attacked French colonialism. Chamoun meanwhile graduated from the Faculty of Law at the University of Saint Joseph in Beirut. Securing his law license in 1923, he became a successful lawyer, businessman, and property holder. He also began expressing his political views in newspaper articles.

Although the economy had expanded during the French mandate, there was much about French-dominated governance that the Lebanese disliked, including press censorship and preference for French investors. Chamoun wanted this situation changed. In 1929 he won his first election campaign and became an elector, whose duty it was to help choose delegates to Lebanon's National Assembly. That year, he also married Zalfa Thabit, whose family had important connections in British social circles. Chamoun subsequently learned English and developed contacts with British politicians.

Chamoun's nationalism subsequently intensified, and upon winning election to the Chamber of Deputies in 1934 he sided with the Constitutional Bloc led by Sheikh Bishara al-Khuri that sought to end French domination. Chamoun won reelection in 1937 and was appointed minister of finance. During World War II, he emerged as one of the architects of Lebanese independence. In 1941, Free French and British forces invaded Lebanon and ousted the colonial government controlled by Vichy France, which had collaborated with Nazi Germany. Britain supported Lebanese independence, and Chamoun lobbied to ensure continued British support for Lebanese nationhood.

Such activities led to Chamoun's arrest and imprisonment by the French authorities in November 1943, along with al-Khuri and Riad al-Sulh. Massive public demonstrations brought their release 11 days later, however, on November 22, now celebrated as Lebanon's Independence Day. The French government-in-exile also agreed to Lebanonese independence.

Elections in 1943 made the Constitutional Bloc the majority party in the National Assembly, and al-Khuri became president, al-Sulh prime minister, and Chamoun minister of finance. Then, because of his close ties to the British, Chamoun was made ambassador to Great Britain. He held this post during 1944–1946.

Chamoun's political acumen helped bring British support for the withdrawal of French troops when the French government had developed second thoughts about relinquishing total control of Lebanon. Chamoun also secured Lebanese membership in the United Nations. Now enormously popular, he planned to become president, but al-Khuri moved to amend the Lebanese Constitution to allow himself another term. Chamoun subsequently resigned his ministerial post and cooperated with the opposition National Socialist Front Party led by Kamal Jumblat (Junblat), a Druze leader. Al-Khuri remained president, but widespread discontent over charges of corruption led to his resignation in 1952.

With Jumblat's support, Chamoun won election by the National Assembly as president. Chamoun now ran into a formidable problem. He had antagonized his Constitutional Bloc followers and many Maronites by having cooperated with Jumblat, and when he tried to win back these people, he antagonized Jumblat and many Druzes, who opposed his pro-Western, conservative politics and alleged corruption. Nevertheless, Chamoun initiated several reforms: a change in the election system that weakened the domination of public offices by landholding aristocrats and urban elites, the implementation of suffrage for women and an independent judiciary. The economy expanded, and Chamoun promoted a free exchange of ideas, including relative freedom of the press.

Yet many members of the politically disadvantaged Muslim communities objected to Chamoun's refusal to let Lebanon join the United Arab Republic in 1958, and Pan-Arabists who favored Egyptian president Gamal Abdel Nasser held demonstrations that threatened to overthrow the government in June 1958. Chamoun believed that both his own power and Lebanese unity were imperiled. He then called on the United States for assistance, and President Dwight D. Eisenhower dispatched U.S. marines to Beirut. This action brought charges that Chamoun was a tool of Western imperialism and was too close to the pro-Israeli United States. U.S. diplomat Robert Murphy helped persuade Chamoun to resign in 1958. He was succeeded by General Fuad Shihab, a Christian who nonetheless was popular with Lebanese Muslims.

Chamoun remained politically active. In 1959 he formed a new opposition organization, the National Liberal Party (al-Ahrar), and he won election to the National Assembly in 1960 but was defeated in 1964 amid charges of gerrymandering. He again won election to the National Assembly in 1968 and 1972. He successfully maneuvered Suleiman Franjieh into the presidency in 1970. Chamoun held a succession of ministerial posts in the 1970s and 1980s.

In 1975, however, Lebanon's long-standing political and sectarian tensions erupted in civil war, and Chamoun obtained Israeli support for the Maronite forces. He helped found the Lebanese Front, heading it during 1976–1978.

It was a mostly Christian grouping of different parties. Its united militia was known as the Lebanese Forces (LF). Chamoun was initially inclined toward Syria but then opposed the growing Syrian presence in Lebanon. In 1980 the LF was largely destroyed in a surprise attack by the Phalangists, the militia headed by Christian rival Bashir Gemayel.

The bloodshed in Lebanon continued. Following the Israeli invasion of Lebanon in 1982, Chamoun entered into tacit cooperation with Israel against Syria, which was then occupying much of Lebanon and controlling its affairs. In 1984 Chamoun entered the National Unity Government as deputy prime minister, but the civil war, which by the end of the decade had claimed some 130,000 lives, overwhelmed this effort. Chamoun died in office in Beirut on August 7, 1987. Four years later a peace accord was signed, although it took several more years for peace to return to most of Lebanon.

SPENCER C. TUCKER

See also
Lebanon; Lebanon, First U.S. Intervention in; Lebanon Civil War; Lebanon-Israeli War; Maronites; Nasser, Gamal Abdel; United Arab Republic

References
Cobban, Helena. *The Making of Modern Lebanon*. London: Hutchinson, 1985.
El-Khazen, Farid. *The Breakdown of the State in Lebanon, 1967–1976*. Cambridge, MA: Harvard University Press, 2000.
Laffin, John. *The War of Desperation: Lebanon, 1982–1985*. London: Osprey, 1985.

Chancellor, Sir John Robert (1870–1952)

British Army officer, colonial administrator, and high commissioner for Palestine (1928–1931). John Robert Chancellor was born in Edinburgh, Scotland, on October 20, 1870. At age 20 he joined the British Army's Royal Engineers. He served in the Dongola Expedition in 1896 and the 1897–1898 Tirah Expedition. In 1902 he graduated from the Army Staff College, then served with the Intelligence Department of the War Office and held successive important military appointments, including liaison to civilian authorities.

Chancellor began his long career as a colonial administrator in 1911 when he was named governor of Mauritius, a post he held until 1916. In 1913 he received a knighthood. From 1916 to 1921 he was governor of Trinidad and Tobago, and from 1923 to 1928 he was governor of Southern Rhodesia. He arrived in Palestine to serve as high commissioner of the British mandate there in 1928, just prior to the Arab Uprising of 1929–1930.

Chancellor began his tenure in Palestine with no publicly stated position on the Arab-Jewish conflict. In private, however, he seemed to favor the Arab position, and he certainly was no great proponent of a Jewish state in Palestine. Furthermore, he suspected the loyalty of the Palestinian Jews to Great Britain. When Arab Palestinians pushed for more democratic representation, Chancellor appeared eager to take the issue up with London. Among other things, he hoped that the formation of an indigenous legislative council would empower Palestinian Arabs, who could curtail further Jewish immigration to Palestine.

In 1929 Chancellor traveled to London to discuss Palestinian self-government issues but was called back when Arab rioting broke out regarding Jewish immigration and land purchases. Upon his return, he publicly and sharply denounced the rioting but in a later proclamation took a much softer stance against the Arab violence.

In 1930 Chancellor played a significant role in the crafting of the white paper prepared by Colonial Secretary Sidney Webb, Lord Passfield. The Passfield White Paper was designed to discourage Zionist aspirations, revoke the 1917 Balfour Declaration's support for a Jewish homeland in Palestine, and curtail future Jewish immigration to the region. The white paper caused a storm of protest among Zionists worldwide, and in February 1931 British prime minister Ramsay MacDonald was compelled to issue a letter of conciliation to Zionists. That same year, Chancellor was recalled from Palestine.

As high commissioner, Chancellor was never popular with Jews, including those already living in Palestine and Jews among the larger diaspora. While it is undeniable that he was never a proponent of the Zionist vision in Palestine and favored tough restrictions on Jewish immigration, he was also acting in the larger interests of Great Britain. Indeed, as a mandatory power Britain was duty bound to treat both the Arabs and Jews in Palestine equally.

Chancellor largely left public life after 1931, but in 1945 he penned a letter to the London *Times* in which he embraced the partitioning of Palestine to stem the animosity and bloodshed that had plagued the area for years. He believed that an independent Jewish state would be virtually self-sufficient thanks in large part to donations and subsidies from wealthy Jews in Western Europe and the United States. An Arab-Palestinian state, however, would likely require monetary assistance initially, he concluded. Chancellor died on July 31, 1952, in Lanark, Scotland.

PAUL G. PIERPAOLI JR.

See also
Balfour Declaration; Palestine, British Mandate for; White Paper of 1930

References
Sachar, Howard M. *A History of Israel: From the Rise of Zionism to Our Time.* 3rd ed. New York: Knopf, 2007.
Shepherd, Naomi. *Ploughing Sand: British Rule in Palestine, 1917–1948.* New Brunswick, NJ: Rutgers University Press, 1999.

CHANGE OF DIRECTION, Operation

See Lebanon, Israeli Operations against

Chemical Weapons and Warfare

Chemical weapons utilize the toxic effects from man-made substances to kill or incapacitate enemy forces. Chemical weapons range from riot control agents such as tear gas and pepper spray, which cause short-term incapacitation, to lethal nerve agents such as tabun and sarin, which can kill humans with only a minuscule exposure. The use of living organisms, such as bacteria, viruses, and spores, is not classified as chemical warfare but rather is considered biological warfare. However, certain chemical weapons such as ricin and botulinum toxins use products created by living organisms.

Chemical weapons are typically described by the effects they have on victims. The major classes of chemical weapons are nerve agents, blood agents, vesicants, pulmonary agents, cytotoxic proteins, lachrymatory agents, and incapacitating agents. Nerve agents quickly break down neuron-transmitting synapses, resulting in the paralysis of major organs and quick death. Blood agents cause massive internal bleeding or prevent cells from using oxygen, leading to anaerobic respiration, seizures, and death. Vesicants, also known as blistering agents, burn skin and respiratory systems, either of which can be fatal. Pulmonary agents suffocate victims by flooding the respiratory system. Cytotoxic agents prevent protein synthesis, leading to the failure of one or more organs. Lachrymatory agents cause immediate eye irritation or blindness, although the effects are deliberately temporary. Incapacitating agents, also temporary, cause effects similar to drug intoxication.

The most important characteristics of an effective chemical weapon are its ability to be delivered accurately and its ability to persist as a danger to enemy troops. Throughout history, delivery methods for chemical weapons have evolved from simple dispersion, often by releasing a gas into the wind, to artillery shells or missile warheads containing chemical agents and to aerodynamic dispersal from aircraft. Since World War II, binary chemical weapons have been developed that contain two substances that are harmless by themselves but when combined form a weapons-grade chemical agent.

Primitive chemical weapons were used as early as the Stone Age, when hunter-gatherer societies used poison-tipped weapons for hunting. Sources of poisons included animal venoms and vegetable toxins. Undoubtedly, poison-tipped weapons were also used in intertribal warfare. Ancient writings describe efforts to poison water systems to halt invading armies. Chinese texts from approximately 1000 BCE describe methods to create and disperse poisonous smoke in war. Ancient Spartan and Athenian armies both used chemical weapons by the 5th century BCE. The Roman Army, however, considered the use of poisons abhorrent, and Roman jurists condemned enemies for poisoning water supplies. With the dawn of the gunpowder era, besieging armies launched incendiary devices and poisonous projectiles into enemy fortifications. By the 19th century, inventors in Britain and the United States proposed the development of artillery shells containing toxic gasses.

During World War I (1914–1918), more chemical weapons were used than during any other war in history. At the Second Battle of Ypres (April 22, 1915), German troops opened canisters of chlorine gas and utilized the wind to push the gas into Allied trenches. Soon both sides were using artillery shells to deliver chemical attacks, incorporating a wide variety of chemical agents.

Although they caused a great deal of panic and disruption on the battlefield and caused more than 1 million mostly nonlethal casualties in World War I, chemical weapons were never decisive by themselves. The chemical weapons of the period were relatively weak by modern standards, and no army of the time had developed nerve agents. Although early gas masks and other countermeasures were relatively primitive, they did neutralize the chemical effects to some degree. The Germans, under their artillery genius Colonel Georg Bruchmüller, came the closest to achieving decisive breakthroughs with chemical weapons during the 1918 offensives, but the German Army didn't have the operational mobility to exploit the tactical advantage.

The Italians employed chemical weapons against the Ethiopians (Abyssinians) during the Second Italo-Ethiopian War (1935–1936). In World War II (1939–1945), chemical

Victims of a gas attack attributed to the government of Syrian president Bashar al-Assad, at Douma, the last rebel-held area in Eastern Ghouta, Syria, on April 7, 2018. At least 78 civilians died in the attack, including women and children. (White Helmets/Handout/Anadolu Agency/Getty Images)

weapons were used in a few isolated instances, most notably by the Japanese in China. Both the Axis and the Allies had developed large arsenals of extremely toxic agents, but both sides feared retaliation by the other, acting as a deterrent to their widespread use. Chemical agents were used by the Germans in the gassing of large numbers of Jews during the Holocaust, however.

In the Middle East, the first modern large-scale use of lethal chemical agents occurred during the Iran-Iraq War (1980–1988). Early in the war, Iraq dropped bombs containing mustard agent and tabun on Iranian troops, causing an estimated 100,000 casualties including 20,000 deaths. Iraq accused Iran of having used chemical weapons first, but the allegations were never confirmed by United Nations investigators. Near the end of the war, the Iraqi government also employed chemical weapons against rebellious Kurdish Iraqi citizens.

During the Persian Gulf War (1991), Iraq was accused of launching Scud missiles with chemical warheads against Israel, although no traces of chemical weapons were found. Iraq did not strike the attacking coalition forces with chemical weapons. One possibility is that the Iraqis feared that the coalition would retaliate with its own chemical weapons or perhaps even tactical nuclear weapons. A more likely possibility, however, is that the Iraqis never had the planning and coordination time necessary to employ chemical weapons. Virtually every successful use of chemical weapons in the 20th century was in an offensive operation, where the attacker had the initiative and necessary time to plan and tightly control the use of such weapons and their effects. Being on the defensive from the start, the Iraqis never had that flexibility.

Chemical weapons in the hands of terrorist groups pose a significant threat. On March 20, 1995, Aum Shinrikyo, a Japanese apocalyptic cult, released sarin gas on a Tokyo subway, killing 12 commuters and injuring more than 5,000. In 2002 the terrorist organization Al Qaeda released a videotape purportedly showing the deaths of dogs from a nerve agent. Al Qaeda has repeatedly announced its intention to obtain chemical, biological, and nuclear weapons.

There have been many attempts to prohibit the development and use of chemical weapons. In 1874 the Brussels

Declaration outlawed the use of poison in warfare. The 1900 Hague Conference banned projectiles carrying poisonous gasses, as did the Washington Arms Conference Treaty of 1922 and the Geneva Protocol of 1929. None of the prohibitions proved sufficient to eradicate chemical warfare, however. The most recent effort to eliminate chemical weapons was the multilateral Chemical Weapons Convention (CWC) of 1993. The CWC came into effect in 1997 and prohibited the production and use of chemical weapons. Numerous nations known to maintain or suspected of maintaining chemical weapons stockpiles refused to sign or abide by the treaty, including several in the Middle East. Egypt, Libya, and Syria, all known to possess chemical weapons, each refused to sign the CWC, although Libya acceded to the treaty in early 2004 and has vowed to dismantle its chemical weapons program.

Israel, long suspected of having a sophisticated chemical weapons capability, signed the CWC but never ratified the agreement. Iran signed and ratified the CWC but refused to prove that it had destroyed known stockpiles of chemical weapons and does not allow international inspectors to examine its facilities.

Chemical weapons are not easy to use. They are difficult and awkward to store, transport, and handle; their use requires detailed and expensive planning and lead times; once released, their effects are difficult to predict and control; and one's own troops require specialized equipment and extensive training to operate in a chemical environment.

Syria possessed one of the world's largest stockpiles of chemical weapons, and the Syrian government of President Bashar al-Assad employed chemical weapons in the Syrian Civil War that began in March 2011. These were used indiscriminately against largely civilian areas in 2013. Confirmation of this by international inspection teams led U.S. president Barack Obama to draw a "red line," threatening military action. When Assad ignored the warning, the Obama administration said that air strikes might be averted only if the Syrian government agreed to the destruction of all of its chemical weapons stocks. The Russian Federation, allied with Assad, pledged its support and oversight. All chemical weapon stockpiles were then supposedly destroyed under international supervision.

Perhaps emboldened by statements from the new administration of President Donald Trump that in Syria the extremist Islamic State of Iraq and Syria (ISIS) rather than Assad was the enemy, the Syrian government again employed chemical weapons, dropped from aircraft in April 2017. Press coverage of this led the Trump administration to launch Tomahawk missiles against the airfield from which the attacking Syrian aircraft had flown, in what was the first overt U.S. military strike of the war against Syrian government assets. In April 2018, Syrian government forces perpetrated another chemical attack against civilians in Douma. In response, U.S., French, and British forces retaliated by launching missiles against Syrian government targets. The targets were said to have been facilities involved in the manufacturing and storage of chemical weapons.

Paul J. Springer and Spencer C. Tucker

See also
Assad, Bashar al-; Iran-Iraq War; Iraq; Kurds; Persian Gulf War, Overview; Syrian Civil War

References
Butler, Richard. *The Greatest Threat: Iraq, Weapons of Mass Destruction, and the Crisis of Global Security*. New York: PublicAffairs, 2000.

Morel, Benoit, and Kyle Olson. *Shadows and Substance: The Chemical Weapons Convention*. Boulder, CO: Westview, 1993.

Solomon, Brian. *Chemical and Biological Warfare*. New York: H. W. Wilson, 1999.

Torr, James D. *Weapons of Mass Destruction: Opposing Viewpoints*. San Diego: Greenhaven, 2005.

Tucker, Jonathan B. *War of Nerves: Chemical Warfare from World War I to Al-Qaeda*. New York: Pantheon, 2006.

Chesma, Battle of (July 5–7, 1770)

The naval Battle of Chesma was fought on July 5–7, 1770, in and near Çesme (Chesme or Chesma) Bay, between the western tip of Anatolia and the island of Chios. It was the most significant battle of the Russo-Ottoman War of 1768–1774 and the worst naval defeat suffered by the Ottomans since Lepanto in 1571. When war between Russia and the Ottoman Empire began in 1768, Russian naval squadrons were sent to the Mediterranean for the first time. By the summer of 1770, nine ships of the line and three frigates, along with lesser vessels, were operating against the Ottomans. The Ottoman fleet, commanded by Kapudan Pasha Hüsameddin, was at least twice as large but suffered from a lack of aggressiveness and training. The Ottomans assumed a defensive position north of Chesma.

The Russian fleet under Admiral Aleksei Orlov attacked the Ottomans on July 5. Ten Ottoman ships of the line were anchored in a first line, with six others in a second line covering the gaps. The Russian plan was to sail from the south and engage the first line. Ottoman fire was heavy but aimed high at the Russian ships' rigging. The leading Russian ship drifted into the Ottoman ship opposite. Both ships quickly caught fire and then blew up. The remaining Ottoman ships cut their anchor cables and fled into Chesma Harbor.

Determined to destroy the Ottoman fleet, Orlov began a bombardment of the harbor. After a day of preparations, three Russian ships of the line and two frigates entered the harbor in the early morning of July 7. Their cannon fire set one Ottoman ship of the line on fire. Meanwhile, four fireships also attacked the Ottoman fleet. Two of the fireships failed in their intent, but the other two each set fire to an Ottoman ship of the line. Fire from the two burning Ottoman ships soon spread to others in the crowded harbor. Russian landing parties were able to save one Ottoman ship of the line, but the remaining ships of the line were destroyed. At least six frigates and many smaller vessels were also burned, completely destroying the Ottoman fleet. The Russians remained in control of the Mediterranean for the rest of the war.

TIM J. WATTS

See also
Lepanto, Battle of; Russo-Ottoman Wars

Reference
Mitchell, Donald W. *A History of Russian and Soviet Sea Power.* New York: Macmillan, 1974.

Chinese Farm, Battle of the (October 14–18, 1973)

Pivotal battle on the Egyptian front during the Arab-Israeli Yom Kippur War of 1973. The battle was fought to secure the gap between the Egyptian Second and Third Armies and the crossing site over the Suez Canal used by the Israel Defense Forces (IDF) during Operation GAZELLE (October 18–23). The incorrectly named Chinese Farm was a failed experimental station that had been run by a Japanese agricultural assistance mission to Egypt. Israeli soldiers mistook the Japanese lettering on signs and building walls for Chinese. The farm dominated the intersection of two critical roads through the Sinai. The Lexicon Road was the main route parallel to the canal, running roughly north and south from the Great Bitter Lake to Lake Timsah. The Tirtur Road ran roughly east and west, from the canal back into the interior of the Sinai, and was a main axis of advance for the IDF. The two roads crossed just north of the Great Bitter Lake and just south of Chinese Farm.

Following the surprise Egyptian crossing of the Suez Canal on October 6, the IDF committed two hastily mobilized reserve divisions: the 162nd Reserve Armored Division under Major General Avraham Adan and the 143rd Reserve Armored Division under Major General Ariel Sharon, recently retired from the IDF and called back for the mobilization. Sharon from the start pushed his forces toward the enemy, and he had to be restrained constantly by the commander of the IDF Southern Command, Major General Shmuel Gonen. Sharon's last assignment before retiring only months earlier had been commanding general of Southern Command, and there was constant friction between the two generals.

As early as October 9, reconnaissance elements from Sharon's 14th Armored Brigade, commanded by Colonel Amnon Reshef, penetrated to the Chinese Farm sector and discovered a gap between the two Egyptian armies. Sharon continued to push for permission to cross the canal and exploit the gap. On October 10, former IDF chief of staff Lieutenant General Chaim Bar-Lev was brought out of retirement and made an adviser to Gonen, effectively superseding the latter in command. Apparently the real reason for the change in command was to keep Sharon under control. Although many in the IDF and the Israeli government considered Sharon to be a loose cannon, all recognized that they desperately needed his fighting abilities at this point in the war.

On October 14, Egyptian forces on the east bank of the canal launched a major offensive along a 100-mile front. More than 1,000 Egyptian tanks faced 750 Israeli tanks. But the Egyptians committed the fatal mistake of moving out beyond the protective umbrella of their relatively immobile surface-to-air missile (SAM) batteries, becoming easy prey for the Israeli Air Force. In the ensuing combat, the Egyptians lost more than 250 tanks and hundreds of men. The IDF lost only 25 tanks.

Driving along the Tirtur Road and just south of Chinese Farm, Sharon reached the canal on the night of October 15. He established a bridgehead with his 247th Reserve Paratroop Brigade, under Colonel Dani Matt. Meanwhile, major elements of the Egyptian 16th Mechanized Division under Brigadier General Fuad Aziz Ghali and the 21st Armored Division under Brigadier General Ibrahim Urabi reached Chinese Farm and dug in. Both divisions had been badly mauled in the fighting on October 14 but still had significant remaining combat power. Initially unaware of the size of the Egyptian force at Chinese Farm, Sharon sent a company of the 14th Armored Brigade's 40th Armored Battalion to secure the crossroads and clear the area. The IDF company was decimated, and the Egyptians closed the corridor behind Sharon.

On the night of October 15, the remainder of the 40th Armored Battalion and a paratroop unit designated Force

Shmulik resumed the attack on Chinese Farm, where they encountered withering interlocking fire from Egyptian armored vehicles dug into the farm's old irrigation ditches. By morning the Israelis held the crossroads but still had not taken Chinese Farm. The 14th Armored Brigade lost 60 tanks and more than 120 men in the fighting up to this point.

Although cut off, Sharon continued to push to be allowed to exploit his crossing, while the IDF high command insisted that Chinese Farm first be cleared. Leaving one battalion to hold the line west of Chinese Farm, Sharon nonetheless disengaged the remainder of the 14th Armored Brigade and started to cross the canal in force. By early on October 16 he had managed to get 27 tanks and 7 armored personnel carriers (APCs) across the waterway on improvised rafts. Adan meanwhile pushed forward with his division to break through the corridor and move up a pontoon bridge. He also committed one battalion from the 35th Paratroop Brigade to clear Chinese Farm. This battalion, under Lieutenant Colonel Amir Jaffe, battled for more than 14 hours, suffering 40 dead and 80 wounded, but the Egyptians still held the farm.

Ignoring IDF high command orders, Sharon continued to exploit his crossing, moving his headquarters to the west bank of the canal. Adan managed to reach the canal with the bridge on October 17. Finally, after Sharon and Adan clashed sharply over who had the responsibility to take Chinese Farm, Sharon redirected the 14th Armored Brigade to clear out the Egyptians once and for all. At the same time, the Egyptians made one final effort to close the corridor again, pushing from the north with the 16th and 21st Divisions and from the south with the Third Army's 25th Independent Armored Brigade. Sharon and Adan concentrated three armored brigades against the Egyptians. After a day and a half of savage fighting, the Egyptians had lost another 250 tanks.

The Chinese Farm finally fell on October 18. By that time, Adan's division had two brigades on the west side of the canal. The Israelis expanded the bridgehead as the 146th Reserved Armored Division under Brigadier General Kalman Magen started to cross behind Adan. By October 19 the Israelis had about 350 tanks across. They broke out the next day, with Adan's division heading south toward the port of Suez, Magen's division following behind that of Adan, and Sharon's division heading north toward Ismailia. Within days the 63,000 soldiers of the Egyptian Third Army, commanded by Major General Muhammad Abd al-Munim Wasil, were completely cut off.

DAVID T. ZABECKI

See also
Adan, Avraham "Bren"; Sharon, Ariel

References
Dunstan, Simon. *The Yom Kippur War, 1973*. 2 vols. Westport, CT: Praeger, 2005.
Herzog, Chaim. *The War of Atonement: The Inside Story of the Yom Kippur War*. London: Greenhill, 2003.

Cleopatra VII (69–30 BCE)

Cleopatra VII (r. 51–30 BCE), the last reigning member of the Ptolemaic dynasty of Macedonian Greeks, ruled Egypt during 51–30. She is famous for her connections to Julius Caesar and Mark Antony and for her attempt to preserve the independence of Egypt against the Roman Empire. She played an important role in the last stage of the civil war that brought Octavian to power as ruler of the Roman world.

Born in 69 BCE, Cleopatra was the daughter of Ptolemy XII Auletes (r. 80–58) and an unknown Greek minor noblewoman. When Ptolemy XII died, Cleopatra married her younger brother, Ptolemy XIII (r. 51–47?; sibling marriage was a traditional Pharaonic and Ptolemaic custom), but his ministers soon overthrew and briefly imprisoned her. Cleopatra escaped, probably after being tortured. When the defeated Pompey fled to Egypt expecting the already deceased Ptolemy XII to protect him, the Ptolemaic general Achillas persuaded Ptolemy XIII to order the murder of Pompey because he was deemed too dangerous. When Caesar arrived in Egypt in pursuit of Pompey, he learned of Pompey's murder and the civil war between Ptolemy and Cleopatra.

Caesar ordered Ptolemy XIII and Cleopatra to submit to Roman arbitration according to the alliance with Ptolemy XII. However, Pothinus, another minister of Ptolemy XIII, refused and encouraged Achillas to attack Caesar. Caesar thereupon executed Pothinus and seized Ptolemy XIII. Cleopatra's younger sister Arsinoe then joined another general, Ganymede, and proclaimed herself queen of Egypt. Ganymede killed Achillas, and later Caesar killed Ganymede.

Cleopatra won Caesar over with her charm (according to legend, she was smuggled to him in a carpet or large sack). Ptolemy XIII died in the fighting; Arsinoe was captured and later executed at Cleopatra's request. Caesar recognized Cleopatra as queen of Egypt and made her marry her younger brother Ptolemy XIV (r. 47–44). Caesar then departed Egypt. After his departure Cleopatra gave birth to a boy, Caesarion (later Ptolemy XV), whom she claimed

Silver tetradrachm of Cleopatra VII (69–30 BCE). She was the last active ruler of Ptolemaic Egypt before its annexation by Rome. (Yale University Art Gallery)

was the son of Caesar. Modern scholars have speculated that Caesarion was the product of rape during her brief captivity rather than Caesar's illegitimate son.

Despite the notorious Ptolemaic dynastic conflict, Cleopatra appears to have been a highly effective monarch of Egypt, ruling for the good of her subjects. She was an intelligent, well-educated woman who impressed those she met with her charm and wit rather than with her beauty, the latter being emphasized by later, more remote sources. If Cleopatra had an affair with Caesar, as the sources concur, it was calculated to establish a favorable relationship with Rome. For his part, Caesar secured Egypt as a client monarchy providing wealth and grain for Rome.

In 44 Cleopatra joined Caesar in Rome, a matter of chagrin for Cicero. Cleopatra hastily departed right after Caesar's assassination and never returned. In 42, Mark Antony ordered Cleopatra to appear in Tarsus to apologize for assisting Brutus and Cassius before Philippi. However, Cleopatra charmed Antony with her wit (and also seduced him with a display of Egypt's wealth). Antony began an affair that lasted more than a decade and fathered three children with Cleopatra. However, Antony agreed to marry Octavian's sister Octavia in the Treaty of Brundisium and never formalized his relationship with Cleopatra with marriage.

Thus, Antony appears to have attempted to play Roman commander and triumvir as well as Hellenistic monarch. He gained by doing so; Cleopatra helped fund his unsuccessful invasion of Persia. In the ceremony termed the "Donations of Alexandria" in 34, Antony held a quasi-triumph at Alexandria, and he and Cleopatra appeared on lofty thrones and garbed as "Dionysus" and the "New Isis," respectively. Antony proclaimed Cleopatra "Queen of Kings" and her son Caesarion "King of Kings"; their mutual children Alexander Helios, Cleopatra Selene, and Ptolemy Philadelphus. Alexander Helios was named king of Armenia, Media, and Parthia; his twin Cleopatra Selene received Cyrenaica and Libya; and Ptolemy Philadelphus was granted Syria and Cilicia. These "Donations of Alexandria" led to a fatal break with Rome, however, where the prevailing view held Antony's conduct as arrogant and un-Roman. Also, many of these areas were provinces governed by Romans and not his to give away.

Octavian exploited Antony's un-Roman behavior (and his slighting of Octavia) to justify a civil war against him. In Octavianic propaganda, the war was depicted as a foreign war against the Egyptian queen, depicting Antony as having lost his Roman identity from infatuation with Cleopatra. War was declared in 32. Cleopatra persuaded Antony to risk a naval battle over the advice of his more experienced commanders, who urged him to wait or fight on land. During the ensuing Battle of Actium (September 2, 31), Cleopatra and the fleet with the treasure sailed off to Egypt, and Octavian's forces destroyed or captured most of Antony's fleet.

Octavian's forces closed in on Egypt. Unable to resist for long, Antony committed suicide on September 1, 30 BCE, and Cleopatra surrendered to Octavian, hoping to remain a client monarch. Later realizing that she would be displayed in Octavian's triumph, she committed suicide. There are multiple versions of her death, but the most common is that an asp was smuggled in on a plate of figs and delivered a fatal bite. Many scholars have suggested that Cleopatra took poison by the normal route or that Octavian had her assassinated, though his attempts to revive her argue against the latter. Octavian allowed Antony and Cleopatra to be buried with traditional Egyptian and Ptolemaic pomp and in 29 BCE had an effigy of Cleopatra paraded in his triumph.

GAIUS STERN

See also
Actium, Battle of; Caesar, Gaius Julius; Egypt, Ancient; Pompeius Magnus, Gnaeus; Ptolemaic Kingdom

References

Ashton, Sally-Ann. *Cleopatra and Egypt*. Malden, MA: Blackwell, 2008.
Burstein, Stanley. *The Reign of Cleopatra*. Norman: University of Oklahoma Press, 2004.
Schiff, Steffie. *Cleopatra: A Life*. New York: Little, Brown, 2010.

Clermont, Council of (1095)

Catholic Church council held at Clermont (modern-day Clermont-Ferrand, France) in the Auvergne during November 18–28, 1095, at which Pope Urban II called on Christians to liberate the Holy Land from the Seljuk Turks. This expedition, which has since come to be known as the First Christian Crusade in the Holy Land (1096–1099), is generally regarded as inaugurating the crusade movement.

Urban II was able to return to Rome in 1093 after his imperialist rival, Clement III (Guibert of Ravenna), withdrew from the city. Two years later Urban left Rome on an extended journey to France, planned at least since 1091 as part of a wider plan of calming the unsettled state of affairs in the church in the aftermath of the death of Pope Gregory VII (1085). The Council of Clermont had originally been planned for Vézelay and then for Le Puy, but by the summer of 1095 Urban had summoned the bishops of France and some of the surrounding areas to meet at Clermont. All of the sessions except the final one took place either in the cathedral of Clermont or in the suburban church of Notre-Dame-du-Port. Among the ecclesiastical participants were many representatives from French sees, but the Italian delegation (which included the papal entourage) and the Spanish delegation were also very numerous.

Urban II focused on reform of the French church. Also of prime importance was settlement of the marital problems of King Philip I of France. The assembly decided at least 61 decrees, or canons, and concluded several lawsuits, as was usual at councils of this period.

The crusade to the East was not proclaimed until the speech with which Urban concluded the council on November 27, 1095. It was made outdoors in order to accommodate the great throngs of clergy and laity of all ages and classes who had come to hear him. No official record of the papal address has been preserved, although there are numerous accounts of it by chroniclers of the period.

It is nonetheless clear that Urban called on Christians of the West to come to the aid of fellow Christians in the East who were victims of the invading Seljuk Turks and whose churches had been destroyed. Like his immediate predecessors, Urban had long been interested in the relationship between the Greek and Latin churches, a problem that was urgent as far as southern Italy and Sicily were concerned, but the idea of military assistance for the Byzantines probably had not arisen before an embassy from Byzantine emperor Alexios I Komnenos approached the pope at the Council of Piacenza in March 1095. There can be no doubt, though, of the overwhelming and unexpected success of Urban's call.

The canons of the council would have been recited in one of the closing sessions, and some of them have survived in different forms. The majority confronted issues regarding church reform, such as the prohibition of liege homage by bishops or priests to the king or any layman, of investiture with ecclesiastical honors by kings or laymen, and of the possession of altars by laymen as well as the prohibition of simony (the payment of money for spiritual gifts) and of clerical marriage or concubinage; the sons of such unions were not to be promoted to ecclesiastical offices unless they became monks. To the faithful in general the eating of meat during Lent was prohibited, traditional rights of asylum were upheld, and marriages were prohibited within seven degrees of consanguinity. It is obvious that Urban set out to reform the moral as well as institutional life of Christianity in general.

The call for the armed pilgrimage to Jerusalem formed only part of Urban's program yet had the widest echo. One canon promulgated a "Peace and Truce" regulation for monks, clerics, women, and those who accompanied them. A second was the famous decree granting a penitential indulgence to all those having undertaken the journey to Jerusalem who "purely on the grounds of faith, not for the sake of glory or money, set out for Jerusalem in order to free the church of God." Another decree placed the goods of crusaders under the protection of the Peace of God.

UTA-RENATE BLUMENTHAL

See also

Alexios I Komnenos; Crusades in the Holy Land, Christian; Seljuk Dynasty

References

Le Concile de Clermont de 1095 et l'appel à la croisade: Actes du Colloque universitaire international de Clermont-Ferrand (23–25 juin 1995). Rome: L'Ecole Française de Rome, 1997.
Somerville, Robert. "The Council of Clermont and the First Crusade." *Studia Gratiana* 20 (1976): 325–337.
Somerville, Robert. *The Councils of Urban II, I: Decreta Claromontensia*. Amsterdam: Hakkert, 1972.
Somerville, Robert. *Papacy, Councils and Canon Law in the 11th–12th Centuries*. London: Variorum, 1990.

Climate of the Middle East

The climate of the Middle East is surprisingly variable, with great temperature extremes and considerable variances in precipitation. Nevertheless, a good deal of the region is known for its blazing hot summers and great dust storms that can markedly reduce visibility, making land travel difficult at best and air travel impossible. Except in mountainous regions and on high plains, the region's winters range from cool and rainy to mild and relatively dry.

Syria's climate is mostly characterized as that of a desert. There are three principal climate zones in Syria, however. These include a somewhat humid Mediterranean-style climate in the west, a semiarid central steppe, and a torrid desert environment in the east and southeast. The coastal climate experiences mild, short, rainy winters and hot, relatively dry summers. Because of its elevation, the highlands experience cold winters punctuated by occasional snow. Sometimes this weather affects areas as far south and west as Damascus. The eastern deserts receive 10 inches or less of rainfall a year and are characterized by hot summers with temperatures as high as 120 degrees. High winds blowing from the south can create dust storms, particularly in the desert.

Lebanon, with its long Mediterranean coastline, enjoys a fairly typical Mediterranean climate, characterized by hot, sunny summers and mild, wet winters. Along the coast, which is warm and humid, there is rain but not snow. Heavy snow falls in Lebanon's mountain areas in the winter. Lebanon's climate may be the most moderate of the Middle East countries owing to its small size and proximity to the coast. Rainfall is greatest from December to April.

Israel enjoys a moderately temperate climate. It features very hot and dry summers in the southern and western deserts. Elsewhere, the climate is similar to that of Lebanon, with long, dry, hot summers and short, rainy, cool winters. Some 70 percent of the nation's rain occurs from November to April, with rainfall slackening the farther south one goes. Only about one-third of the small country is capable of agricultural pursuits that do not require heavy irrigation. In the winter, light snow is not uncommon at higher elevations.

The climate of Jordan, like that of Syria, is largely desert. In the west, a rainy season from November to April brings most of an entire year's rainfall. Aside from that the area is very dry. Jordan's summers are quite hot, with average high temperatures over 100 degrees, higher still in the desert. The winters are moderately cool with snow occasionally at higher elevations. In the late spring and early fall, the country is subject to periodic hot, dry winds from the southsoutheast, which can drive relative humidity to 10 percent or less. These winds sometimes produce dust storms that can greatly impede transportation, pose health dangers, and force vehicles to halt.

The Egyptian climate is characteristic of a true desert environment. There are two seasons: a hot, dry summer from May to October and a moderate, slightly wet winter from December to March. Most of the country's rain falls near the northern coast. Owing to the moderating influence of the Mediterranean Sea, northern Egypt is slightly cooler. For this reason, Alexandria on the Mediterranean coast is a popular tourist destination, particularly in the summer months. There are, however, some variations. In the Nile Delta and the North Nile Valley, occasional winter cold snaps can bring light frosts and even small amounts of snowfall. In the south, near Aswan, there are great temperature fluctuations in the summer. Temperatures can be as high as 126 degrees or better during the day and dip as low as 48–50 degrees at night. From mid-March through May, howling dust storms sometimes occur, precipitated by southerly winds that can reach 90 miles per hour.

Saudi Arabia has a dry, hot, harsh climate characterized by great temperature extremes. Except for Asir Province, which is subject to monsoons from the Indian Ocean region and is more temperate, and the sometimes humid conditions of the coast of the Hejaz, the nation's climate is all desert. The desert areas experience dry summers with high temperatures of 120 degrees and higher. During times of drought, which are not infrequent, the southern two-thirds of Saudi Arabia can go for two years or more without measurable rainfall. In the late spring and summer, strong winds often create sand and dust storms. Other Persian Gulf states with climates very similar—or identical—to Saudi Arabia's include Qatar and the United Arab Emirates.

The Persian Gulf states of Bahrain, Oman, and Yemen feature more diverse climates. Bahrain's climate is extremely hot and dry, but because Bahrain is an island archipelago in the Persian Gulf, coastal areas tend to be very humid in the summer months, producing oppressive dew points. Oman has three main climates: hot desert in the north and west, a tropical zone in the south with plentiful rainfall, and a cold, mountainous zone where snow is not infrequent in the winter. Yemen's west coast is very hot and dry; the western highlands are more temperate, receiving as much as 39 inches of rain per year in some areas. Yemen's eastern and northern areas have a climate similar to that of southern Oman.

Iraq's climate is similar to that of the southwestern United States. Iraq is mostly a semiarid desert that experiences hot, dry summers and mild to cool winters with periodic rainfall. The mountainous regions along the Iranian and Turkish borders have cold winters with periodic heavy snowfalls. The great majority of Iraq's precipitation comes in the winter, while the northern areas receive slightly more rainfall over a slightly longer time span. From June to September, winds from the north and northwest can whip up heavy dust storms that cause plummeting humidity and decreased visibility. As in the American Southwest, the southern two-thirds of Iraq is prone to flash flooding. Kuwait, immediately south of Iraq, has a virtually identical climate to that of southern Iraq.

Iran's climate may be the most varied of all the major nations in the Middle East. It has arid and semiarid climate zones and even a subtropical climate along the Caspian Sea coast. In the northwest, summers are hot and dry, the autumn and spring are mild, and the winters are cold and frequently snowy. Most of the country's rainfall occurs from October to April, with the most falling near the coast. In the south, particularly near the Persian Gulf, average summer high temperatures are 112 degrees. Tehran, shielded by the Alborz Mountains, is more temperate, with average summer high temperatures of 96 degrees.

In Turkey, areas bordering the Mediterranean and Aegean Seas (including the small island of Cyrus) feature a Mediterranean climate, with hot, dry summers and mild, wet winters. In northern Turkey along the Black Sea, the climate is categorized as oceanic, with warm, wet summers and cool to cold, wet winters. Although snow is relatively rare along the southern coastal areas, it is common in northern and central Turkey and in the mountains. Turkey's large interior has a continental climate, with four distinct seasons and cold, snowy winters similar to those in the American Midwest. Rainfall in Turkey varies greatly, ranging from as little as 12 inches per year to nearly 90 inches per year.

Despite the many variations in the region's climate, almost all of the Middle East nations feature extremely hot summers and dust and sand storms. From a military perspective, the region can be daunting for troops as well as equipment. The searing heat of the summers is dangerous for troops, who can quickly succumb to heat-related illnesses and dehydration. For this reason, military action in the dead of summer is avoided, particularly on the Arabian Peninsula. The heat can also take a heavy toll on military equipment and vehicles.

Another perilous weather phenomenon is the region's frequent dust and sand storms. Greatly reduced visibility of a mile or less can ground aircraft. Moving a large number of troops in the midst of one of these storms is ill-advised. Airborne sand and dust can also foul the engines of ground vehicles as well as aircraft. Operation EAGLE CLAW, launched by the Jimmy Carter administration (April 25–25, 1980) and intended to rescue U.S. embassy personnel being held hostage in Iran, serves as a stark example of this. The operation ended in disaster when the engines of several U.S. helicopters were fouled with sand. Another helicopter struck an MC-130 transport aircraft on the ground amid low visibility, killing eight servicemen.

The general lack of rainfall throughout much of the region may also serve as the flashpoint for future Middle East conflicts as nations there scramble for increasingly precious water supplies.

PAUL G. PIERPAOLI JR.

See also
Iran Hostage Rescue Mission

References
Gleick, P. H. "Water, War and Peace in the Middle East." *Environment* 36, no. 3 (1994): 6–11.
Gribbin, John. *Weather Force: Climate and Its Impact on Our World.* New York: Putnam, 1979.
Riley, Dennis, and Lewis Spolton. *World Weather and Climate.* New York: Cambridge University Press, 1982.

Cold War in the Middle East

The Cold War between the communist world under the Soviet Union and the Western powers led by the United States began at the end of World War II, with most of the Middle East controlled directly or indirectly by the United Kingdom and France with a strong U.S. presence. As elsewhere, the region became a pawn in the Cold War. By the early 1960s the West European empires no longer existed, and the United States and the Soviet Union were the major players in the region, vying for influence over and control of resources and strategic locations. Yet the countries in the Middle East were often able to use this competition to their benefit by bidding for economic, political, and military support. They did this by allying with the highest bidder, changing sides as circumstances warranted, or advocating neutrality as a means of presenting the world an alternative to superpower domination.

In 1946, Iran became the first major Cold War hotspot in the Middle East. Even before the end of the war the Soviet Union had backed the leftist Tudeh Party, which supported Iranian oil concessions to the Soviets. The Soviets controlled much of northern Iran and after the war supported establishment of communist republics there. While both Britain and the United States withdrew their forces from Iran after the war, the Soviets remained, preventing Iran from reestablishing control of all of its territory and demanding oil concessions in return for withdrawal. Iran agreed. The United States and Britain took the issue to the United Nations (UN), and this along with the oil concessions convinced the Soviets to withdraw troops in May 1946. The communist governments collapsed, and Iran cancelled the concessions and curtailed Tudeh influence. The Soviet Union also put considerable pressure on Turkey and Greece.

This episode was a prelude to many confrontations between the Cold War powers in the Middle East. Iran continued as a front in the Cold War for many years, including the U.S. Central Intelligence Agency's successful effort in 1953 to overthrow the government of Mohammad Mossadegh in Iran because of supposed Soviet influence. Iran then became a member of the Baghdad Pact, one of the links in worldwide alliances opposing the Soviet Union. Iran continued to be a close ally of the United States until the overthrow of Shah Mohammad Reza Pahlavi in 1979, toward the end of the Cold War. After that Iran under Ayatollah Ruhollah Khomeini was almost equally opposed to both the United States and the Soviet Union, one being named the "Great Satan" and the other the "Little Satan."

After Iran, the next Cold War arena in the Middle East was the British mandate of Palestine. After World War II, Britain reduced its presence outside Europe. France would do the same but more reluctantly. The Arab Middle East sensed the possibility of independence from the European empires. The United States and the Soviet Union viewed the region as a future arena of competition.

In tandem with the British removal of forces and the failure of a UN partition plan, Jewish leader David Ben-Gurion declared Israeli independence on May 14, 1948. The United States recognized the new state on May 18, the same day as the Soviet Union. The declaration of independence brought immediate war with the Arab states. This resulted in an Israeli victory and a cease-fire in early 1949, with Israeli admission to the UN in May 1949. At this time, Israel enjoyed support from both the United States and the Soviet Union.

The two superpowers had varying motivations; the United States realized that a strong presence in the Middle East would be crucial as the West European powers began to withdraw to secure vital petroleum resources and prevent the Soviet Union from exercising strong influence. Both sides provided substantial aid to Israel. Israel continued to be a focal point during the Cold War, but over time the United States prevailed.

The Cold War continued to shape the Middle East until the collapse of the Soviet Union in 1991. Egypt was the focus of a Cold War struggle that began with the end of British control in the early 1950s. As elsewhere, local leaders played both sides for their national and regional goals. Key players were Gamal Abdel Nasser and Anwar Sadat, both of whom courted both sides, changing allegiances or professing neutrality as opportunities arose. The construction of the Aswan Dam on the Nile and the ensuing Suez Crisis provide an insight into the complexity and intense nature of the Cold War in the Middle East. After the Cold War, the Middle East faced an entirely different set of circumstances. The United States and its allies were the most powerful force in the area, but regional conflicts took on a greater importance to the peoples of the Middle East.

Daniel E. Spector

See also
Baghdad Pact; Ben-Gurion, David; Cyprus; Iran; Iraq; Israeli War of Independence; Jordan; Khomeini, Ruhollah; Nasser, Gamal Abdel; Sadat, Anwar; Saudi Arabia; Six-Day War; Syria; Turkey; Yom Kippur War

References
Levering, Ralph B. *The Cold War: 1945–1987.* Arlington Heights, IL: Harlan Davidson, 1988.
Powaski, Ronald E. *The Cold War: The United States and the Soviet Union, 1917–1991.* Oxford: New York, 1988.

Cole, USS, Attack on (October 12, 2000)

The attack on the destroyer USS *Cole* in Yemen on October 12, 2000, marked the first time a modern U.S. Navy warship was successfully targeted by terrorists. On October 12, 2000, the guided-missile destroyer *Cole* (DDG-67), commanded by Commander Kirk Lippold, was in the Yemeni port of Aden for refueling. At 11:18 a.m. local time, 2 men in a small harbor skiff pulled alongside the anchored ship. Crew members aboard the *Cole* saw the craft approach, but the men appeared friendly and made no untoward moves. Some aboard the *Cole* assumed that the men were harbor service workers, collecting trash or performing other routine tasks. The detonation of the explosives in their craft by the 2 suicide bombers thus came as a complete surprise. The blast killed both bombers and 17 members of the *Cole*'s crew; another 39 crew members were injured. It also tore a gaping hole in the ship's hull 35 feet high and 36 feet long.

The remaining crew members were able to keep the *Cole* afloat, and three days later it was taken aboard the Norwegian heavy lift salvage ship *Blue Marlin* and transported to the United States, where it underwent extensive repairs that lasted a year and cost more than $240 million.

The terrorist organization Al Qaeda claimed responsibility for the attack. Coordination between U.S. and Yemeni officials investigating the incident was aided by a counterterrorism agreement signed by Yemen and the United States in 1998, and the trial of 12 suspects formally commenced in June 2004. In late September 2004, Abd al-Rahim al-Nashiri and Jamal Mohammed al-Badawi both received the death penalty for their participation in the terrorist act. Four other participants were sentenced to 5–10 years in jail.

A U.S. judge subsequently held Sudan liable for the attack, while another judge released more than $13 million in Sudanese frozen assets to the relatives of those killed. An investigation into the bombing found that Lippold had acted reasonably and that the facts did not warrant any punitive action against him or any other member of the *Cole*'s crew. The U.S. Navy has, however, reconsidered its rules of engagement in response to this attack.

PAUL G. PIERPAOLI JR.

See also
Al Qaeda; Terrorism; Yemen

References
Williams, Paul. *The Al Qaeda Connection: International Terrorism, Organized Crime, and the Coming Apocalypse.* Amherst, NY: Prometheus Books, 2005.

Wright, Lawrence. *The Looming Tower: Al-Qaeda and the Road to 9/11.* New York: Vintage Books, 2007.

Confederates, Battle of the
See Khandaq, Battle of

Conrad III, King of Germany (1093–1152)

The first king of Germany (r. 1138–1152) of the Hohenstaufen dynasty and one of the leaders of the Second Crusade (1147–1149). Born in 1093, Conrad was the son of Duke Frederick I of Swabia and Agnes, daughter of Holy Roman emperor Henry IV. It is probable that Conrad made a pilgrimage to the Holy Land before the Second Crusade in 1124–1125; certainly he is known to have made a vow to go to Jerusalem, and he was not present at the election of a new German king in 1125, when his elder brother Duke Frederick II of Swabia (d. 1147) was one of the candidates. Conrad himself made a bid for the crown from December 1127 onward, probably shortly after his return from the East. He was eventually elected king in March 1138 after the death of Emperor Lothar III.

Conrad took the cross at Speyer at Christmas 1146. His initial reluctance was overcome by the persuasion of Abbot Bernard of Clairvaux, who had come to the Rhineland to end the anti-Jewish agitation stirred up by Cistercian monk Rudolf. The abbot reportedly gave the king a banner to carry on the expedition. Preparations were made speedily. A diet of the imperial princes was held at Frankfurt am Main in March 1147, from which Conrad wrote to Pope Eugenius III apologizing for taking the cross without notifying him. The crusaders set out from Regensburg in May 1147.

Despite some mishaps on the way, including the flooding of the army's camp shortly after it had entered Byzantine territory, Conrad arrived at Constantinople (modern-day Istanbul, Turkey) early in September. He already enjoyed close diplomatic relations with Byzantine emperor Manuel I Komnenos, not least through their common hostility to King Roger I of Sicily, and in 1145 Manuel had married Conrad's sister-in-law, Bertha of Sulzbach.

The crusaders crossed the Bosporus and set out from Nicaea (modern-day Iznik, Turkey) into Seljuk Turk–held territory on October 15, 1147. By now Conrad had split his forces, sending most of the poorer pilgrims and noncombatants along the coast of Asia Minor under the command of his half brother Otto, bishop of Freising. The main army soon ran short of food and suffered severely from Seljuk attacks before linking up with the French crusading forces under King Louis VII at the beginning of November.

On arrival at Ephesus, Conrad was forced to halt due to illness, and he subsequently returned with most of his surviving forces to Constantinople. Many of the German troops then returned home. Conrad himself was nursed back to health by Manuel Komnenos. He and a number of his princes eventually sailed directly to the Holy Land in Byzantine ships, landing at Acre (modern-day Akko, Israel) in April 1148. Manuel had provided him ample funds, and Conrad used these to recruit pilgrims to augment the forces that remained to him.

The French army, which had succeeded in crossing Asia Minor, marched south from Antioch (modern-day Antakya,

Turkey), and the reunited crusade, along with forces of the Kingdom of Jerusalem, attacked Damascus at the end of July 1148. The decision to pursue this attack, often criticized, had been settled in a conference among the three kings (Conrad, Louis VII, and Baldwin III of Jerusalem) near Acre a month earlier, although it has been suggested that Conrad and Baldwin had already decided on this before Louis's arrival. However, after five days of heavy fighting and with Muslim reinforcements approaching, the siege was abandoned. A subsequent proposal to attack Ascalon (modern-day Tel Ashqelon, Israel) came to naught, with Conrad blaming the crusaders from Jerusalem for their failure to arrive.

Conrad left Acre by sea on September 8, 1148, and returned to Germany via Thessalonica and Constantinople, where his friendly relations with Byzantium were strengthened by the marriage of his other half brother, Henry Jasomirgott, duke of Bavaria, to Manuel's niece, Theodora.

Conrad's health had been undermined by his experiences on the crusade, and he died on February 15, 1152. His eldest son had predeceased him, and he was succeeded as king of Germany by his nephew Frederick I Barbarossa, the son of Frederick II of Swabia. Conrad's reign in Germany was seen even at the time as a failure. He never secured his imperial coronation at Rome, and his crusade was a major setback. Certainly he must bear some responsibility for the indiscipline that hampered his army, and the attempt to follow the route of the First Crusade (1096–1099) across Anatolia in midwinter and not to wait for the French was misguided. Yet he preserved good relations with Byzantium, which the French did not, and the attack on Damascus was by no means as ill-conceived as some modern historians have claimed.

GRAHAM A. LOUD

See also
Baldwin III of Jerusalem; Crusades in the Holy Land, Christian; Louis VII, King of France; Manuel I Komnenos, Emperor

References
Berry, Virginia. "The Second Crusade." In *A History of the Crusades,* Vol. 1, ed. Kenneth M. Setton et al., 463–512. 2nd ed. Madison: University of Wisconsin Press, 1969.
Hiestand, Rudolf, "'Kaiser' Konrad III., der zweite Kreuzzug und ein verlorenes Diplom für den Berg Thabor." *Deutsches Archiv für Erforschung des Mittelalters* 35 (1979): 82–126.
Hiestand, Rudolf. "Kingship and Crusade in Twelfth-Century Germany." In *England and Germany in the Middle Ages: Essays in Honour of Karl J. Leyser,* ed. Alfred Haverkamp and Hanna Vollrath, 235–265. Oxford: Oxford University Press, 1996.
Vollrath, Hanna. "Konrad III. und Byzanz." *Archiv für Kulturgeschichte* 59 (1977): 321–365.

Constantine I (ca. 277–286–337)

Roman emperor who reunified the empire; also the first Christian emperor. Born in Naissus, Moesia (modern-day Niš, Serbia), sometime during the years 277–286, Constantine (Flavius Valerius Constantinus) was the eldest son of future emperor Constantius I (r. 305–306). Under the administrative system established by Emperor Diocletian, there were two senior emperors with the title of augustus and two deputy emperors with the title of caesar. On the death of an augustus, the caesar was to succeed him. After his father was appointed caesar in the east in 293, Constantine was made a tribune in Diocletian's court. In 302 he was made tribune in the east. He campaigned with his father in Britain when the latter became senior emperor of the Western Roman Empire in 305.

On his father's death in July 306, the army proclaimed Constantine western emperor. For five years Constantine concentrated on defending the frontier against the Germans. Then civil war ensued, for Diocletian's administrative system had proven inadequate, and seven rivals contested for power in the two halves of the empire. Constantine's chief rival in the western part of the empire was his brother-in-law, Marcus Aurelius Valerius Maxentius. Constantine took the offensive, and although his army was half the size of that of Maxentius, it was better organized and trained. In the battles at Turin and Verona (early 312) and then the Milvian Bridge on the Tiber River (summer 312), Constantine was victorious, establishing his control over the western empire.

Prior to the Battle of the Milvian Bridge, Constantine had been partially converted to Christianity under the influence of his mother Helena. According to Christian tradition, Constantine had a vision of a flaming cross prior to the battle and had ordered that the first two letters of Christ's name be marked on his soldiers' shields to bring victory. Constantine arranged an alliance with the eastern emperor, Licinius, and in 313 met with him at Milan. There they jointly issued the Edict of Milan granting toleration to all religions, including Christianity. Constantine made Christianity a favored religion, however, whereas Licinius soon reverted to persecuting it.

Both emperors sought to control the Balkans, and in 323 they went to war over that region. Constantine invaded Thrace and defeated Licinius in battles at Adrianople (Edirne, July 3) and Chrysopolis (Üsküdar, September 18). Licinius surrendered, and Constantine had him executed two years later in 325.

Constantine now reunited the two halves of the Roman Empire. He claimed that he was God's chosen instrument, and he personally presided over the great Council of Nicaea (modern-day Iznik, Turkey) in May 325, which dealt with the Arian heresy and established official church doctrine in the Nicaean Creed. Dissident Christians were punished. Constantine ordered the construction of numerous Christian churches and officially decreed that Sunday was to be a day of rest.

Constantine shifted the center of the empire to the east, to the Bosporus. There at Byzantium, in 216 he began construction of a new capital, Constantinople, which was officially dedicated in May 330. Among his many administrative reforms was to restructure the military into two branches: a garrison force to guard the frontier and a mobile field army ready to react to threats anywhere along the frontiers. He also continued Diocletian's policy of separate civil and military administrations.

Following successful military campaigns against the Franks and Goths, Constantine was preparing to campaign in Persia when he fell ill and died on May 22, 337, near Nicomedia, Bithynia (modern-day Izmit, Turkey). He left the empire to his three sons, Constantius II, Constans, and Constantine II. Constantine had intended that Constantinople would be the capital of an undivided empire, but given the vast distances involved and the primitive transportation of the day, it was perhaps inevitable that the reunited empire would break apart and the western portion would be let go.

One of the truly great later Roman emperors, Constantine was both a thoroughly competent strategist and a general who emphasized offensive action. His embrace of Christianity was a watershed in the spread of that religion.

SPENCER C. TUCKER

See also
Byzantine Empire

References
Burckhardt, Jacob. *The Age of Constantine the Great.* New York: Pantheon Books, 1949.
Eusebius. *Life of Constnatine.* New York: Oxford University Press, 1999.
Grant, Michael. *Constantine the Great: The Man and His Times.* New York: Barnes & Noble, 1998.

Constantine XI Palaiologos (1405–1453)

The last Byzantine emperor (r. 1448–1453), who died childless while defending the city of Constantinople (modern-day Istanbul, Turkey) against the Ottoman Turks. Born on February 8, 1405, Constantine was the son of Emperor Manuel II Palaiologos and became emperor in 1448 when his brother John VIII died without an heir. At the time of his accession to the throne, only Constantinople and the Peloponnese remained under Byzantine control. In 1428 he married Maddalena Tocco, niece of the Italian ruler of Epiros and Cephalonia. After her death Constantine married Caterina Cattilusio, daughter of the Genoese lord of the island of Lesbos.

Although he faced problems in making the union of the Greek Orthodox and Latin Churches acceptable in the Byzantine Empire, Constantine remained an advocate of the agreement that Emperor John VIII had concluded with the Roman church at Florence in 1439, since he believed that if union was brought about, the West would send the military aid that the Byzantines desperately needed in their fight against the Turks. In 1452 he asked for military reinforcements from Venice and various other Italian towns, King Alfonso V of Aragon (I of Naples), the Genoese rulers of Chios, and the pope but to no avail. The pope demanded from the Byzantines union with the Church of Rome before he would authorize the dispatch of military aid. In October 1452, 400 archers arrived in Constantinople, together with the papal legate Cardinal Isidore, who came to celebrate the union of the churches in a ceremony in the Church of Hagia Sophia on December 12 that same year. In January 1453, the Genoese Giovanni Longo arrived in Constantinople with 700 troops. This aid, however, was too little and arrived too late to save Constantinople, which fell to the Turks at dawn on May 29, 1453. Constantine died in the fighting the same day.

APHRODITE PAPAYIANNI

See also
Byzantine Empire; Constantinople, Ottoman Siege of; Manuel II Palaiologos, Emperor

References
Malherbe, Jacques. *Constantine XI, dernier empereur des Romains.* Louvain-la-Neuve: Academia Bruylant, 2001.
Mijatovich, Chedomil. *Constantine, the Last Emperor of the Greeks, or the Conquest of Constantinople by the Turks (1453).* London: Low, Marston, 1892.
Nicol, Donald. *The Immortal Emperor: The Life and Legend of Constantine Palaiologos, Last Emperor of the Romans.* Cambridge: Cambridge University Press, 1992.

Constantinople, Crusader Siege and Capture of (April 8–13, 1204)

The capture of Constantinople by the Christian crusaders, also known as the Sack of Constantinople and the Siege of Constantinople. In 1199 Pope Innocent III appealed for a new crusade to regain Jerusalem. Although the kings of

England and France ignored this, a new crusader force assembled under Theobald III, count of Champagne. Venice agreed to transport a force of 25,000 crusaders to Egypt and maintain them there for three years in exchange for a cash payment and half the crusader conquests.

When Theobald died in 1201, Boniface of Montferrat was chosen the new leader. In a meeting at Hagenau in December 1201, the crusaders decided to proceed not to the Holy Land by way of Egypt but rather via Constantinople. When they assembled in the summer of 1202, however, the crusaders were unable to raise the sum promised to Venice. They then arranged to pay half the sum in exchange for retaking the Venetian dependency of Zara. The pope condemned this attack on other Christians, but the crusaders proceeded to take and sack Zara. For this they were excommunicated.

The crusaders then intrigued with Alexios, son of deposed Byzantine emperor Isaac II, and most agreed that in return for a promised large cash payment, they would proceed to Constantinople and overthrow Emperor Alexios III. Some, notably Simon de Montfort of England, went directly to Palestine instead.

Sailing into the Bosporus, the crusaders set up camp near Constantinople. Meanwhile, a Venetian fleet forced its way into the Golden Horn at the city. On July 17, 1203, the crusaders attacked Constantinople. They were repulsed, but the Venetians were able to secure a portion of the seawall and part of the city. That night Alexios III fled Constantinople; notables then released former emperor Isaac II from prison and elected his son Alexios coemperor as Alexios IV. The new Byzantine leaders then endeavored to raise the money promised by Alexios IV for a successful military effort in the Holy Land.

The inability to raise the money greatly strained relations with the crusaders. On August 18, Greeks in Constantinople rioted against Latin residents there. The next day some crusaders attacked a mosque in the city and began a major fire. By December the situation in the city had greatly deteriorated, with crusaders plundering the city suburbs and residents of the city attempting to burn the crusader ships.

In January 1204 resentment against both the new rulers and the crusaders had grown to the point that Alexios Doukas Mourtzouphlos, son-in-law of Alexios III, led a major revolt. Isaac II was again imprisoned, and Alexios IV was executed. Mourtzouphlos then took the imperial throne as Alexios V. Once in power, Alexios V was not reluctant to engage the crusaders, and a number of skirmishes occurred.

This situation gave the crusaders the excuse to take Constantinople. The defenders turned back the initial assault on April 8, 1204, by crusader ships against the city walls. Although the defenders, especially the Varangian Guard, fought well, catapults on the Venetian ships hurled incendiaries into the city and started a major conflagration, causing the defenders to lose heart. On April 12, the crews of several ships were able to capture a tower on the harbor walls, and the crusader forces were able to secure a toehold in the northern part of the city. Another fire, set by the crusaders to fortify their position, raged out of control. That night Mourtzouphlos fled, and on April 13 the crusaders took control of Constantinople and subjected it to three days of rape and pillage. Many civilians were slain, and women, including nuns, were raped. Christian churches and religious establishments were looted, and bronze statues were melted down for their metal value.

This first successful assault of Constantinople effectively signaled the end of the Byzantine Empire. Although it continued in Christian hands for the next two centuries, the empire never really recovered from this blow inflicted by fellow Christians.

SPENCER C. TUCKER

See also
Alexios V Doukas Mourtzouphlos; Crusades in the Holy Land, Christian

References
Madden, Thomas F. "The Fires of the Fourth Crusade in Constantinople, 1203–1204: A Damage Assessment." *Byzantinische Zeitschrift* 84–85 (1992): 72–93.

Queller, Donald E., and Thomas F. Madden. *The Fourth Crusade: The Conquest of Constantinople.* 2nd ed. Philadelphia: University of Pennsylvania Press, 1997.

Constantinople, Latin Empire of (1204–1261)

An empire under Latin (Frankish) domination established in April 1204 after the overthrow of the Byzantine Empire by the Fourth Crusade (1202–1204). The territory of the Latin Empire was much smaller than that of Byzantium. At its greatest extent it comprised the city of Constantinople (modern-day Istanbul, Turkey), Thrace, eastern Macedonia, and northwest Asia Minor, although the Latin emperor was often, at least in theory, recognized as the suzerain of the other Frankish states in Greece.

Establishment and Early History (1204–1216)
The Latin Empire of Constantinople was the direct result of the deviation of the Fourth Crusade. While encamped before the walls of Constantinople in March 1204, the Frankish

crusaders and the Venetians agreed between themselves to replace the Byzantine emperor with a Latin one, and after the capture of the city, Count Baldwin IX of Flanders (VI of Hainaut) was crowned emperor (as Baldwin I) in the Cathedral of Hagia Sophia on May 16, 1204.

Baldwin I's first task was to safeguard the empire against the Greek and Vlacho-Bulgarian alliance in Thrace. On April 14, 1205, a battle occurred near Adrianople (modern-day Edirne, Turkey), where Tsar Kaloyan (Johannitsa), who had received the pope's blessing for his Vlacho-Bulgarian Empire, defeated Baldwin's army, which retreated toward Constantinople. Baldwin was taken prisoner and died in captivity.

Baldwin's brother Henry of Flanders became regent of the empire and was crowned emperor on August 20, 1206. He was the only "great" emperor of Latin Constantinople. On the military front he broke the Greco-Bulgarian alliance by ceding, by the end of 1205, Apros to the Greek Theodoros Branas, who also received Adrianople from the Venetians. After Kaloyan's death (1207), his empire disintegrated. Using diplomacy as well as military means, Henry met the internal and external threats. In February 1207 he married Agnes, daughter of Boniface I of Montferrat, king of Thessalonica. Around September 1208 Henry gave his natural daughter in marriage to the Bulgarian prince Aleksii Slav, and his brother, Eustace of Flanders, took as his wife a daughter of Michael of Epiros in 1209.

Henry supported David Komnenos, the coemperor of Trebizond, against Theodore I Laskaris, emperor of Nicaea, and four Latin military expeditions (1206–1207) strengthened the Latin position in the eastern part of the empire. By 1211 Boril and Theodore Laskaris once again were able to attack the Latin Empire. Boril first retreated deep into Bulgaria and was then defeated by Eustace and Slav. Strez was also defeated by Eustace, and on October 15, 1211, Henry won a victory over Theodore Laskaris. After the early death of his wife Agnes, Henry himself married the daughter of the new Bulgarian tsar, Boril (ca. 1212).

Emperor Henry also normalized relations with the principality of Achaia in June 1209, thus putting an end to the confusion of suzerainty over the Frankish Morea. Geoffrey I of Villehardouin, prince of Achaia, became Henry's vassal, but Venetian rights were preserved. Understanding that the empire could neither prosper nor even function without the support of the Greek population, Henry tried to accommodate Greek aspirations, especially those of religion, by initiating dialogue between the Latin and Greek Orthodox Churches. Although these negotiations proved unsuccessful, Henry gained the respect of his Greek subjects. His biggest challenge, however, came from the Lombards of the kingdom of Thessalonica. After Boniface's death (in 1207), the Lombard regent of the kingdom, Count Oberto of Biandrate, was unwilling to recognize the suzerainty of the emperor and planned to unite Thessalonica with the Italian territory of William of Montferrat, Boniface's brother, thereby hoping that William would supplant Henry as emperor. Henry, however, supported by Maria (Margaret) of Hungary, widow of Boniface, crowned her son Demetrios as king of Thessalonica in January 1209 and subdued the Lombards.

To keep enough manpower available, Henry wisely restored the rebellious Lombards to their fiefs, generally winning their loyalty. During the last years of Henry's reign (1214–1216), the political landscape again altered. Michael of Epiros was murdered and succeeded by his brother Theodore (1214–1230), who was an ally of Theodore Laskaris and gave his niece in marriage to Slav (whose wife, Henry's daughter, had died). When Henry suddenly died on June 11, 1216, in Thessalonica, he left a relatively well-organized empire.

Decline and End, 1216–1261

The sudden and unforeseen death of Emperor Henry was the catalyst for a series of catastrophes for the Latin Empire. While the Fleming Conon of Béthune proved to be an able regent, the same cannot be said about Henry's successors. Emperor Peter of Courtenay, husband of Yolande of Flanders (Henry's sister), unwisely decided to travel from the West to Durazzo (modern-day Durrës, Albania) and proceed from there to Constantinople by land. Ambushed by Michael of Epiros in 1217, he died in captivity. Yolande died in Constantinople in October 1219 and was succeeded by her second son, Robert of Courtenay (1221–1228), who was crowned emperor in Constantinople on March 25, 1221. He left the city after an unfortunate love affair and secret marriage with a French woman and died in the Morea in 1228.

The empire was by now in full crisis. In early 1224, Nicaean emperor John III Vatatzes had crushed the Latins in battle near the castle of Poimanenon (Poemanenum) and imposed humiliating conditions on the Latin Empire. In the west, Theodore, despot of Epiros, had extended his power, and in 1222 Thessalonica fell to the Epirote, who had himself crowned emperor. After Robert's death, the Frankish barons of Constantinople offered the throne to John of Brienne (former king of Jerusalem), whose daughter was to marry the future Baldwin II, Robert's young brother. John's election had alienated the Bulgarian tsar, Ivan Asen II, who had hoped that the crown would be offered to him. John of Brienne arrived in Constantinople during the summer of 1231 but waited until 1233 before attacking John Vatatzes. Once again, the political landscape had altered. In 1230, Theodore of Epiros-Thessalonica had broken his alliance with Asen and invaded Bulgaria but was defeated and captured. His brother Manuel, who was Asen's son-in-law, now ruled over Thessalonica (1230–1236). Between 1232 and 1235, Asen tried to build up a coalition of orthodox nations to recover Constantinople, and in 1235 his daughter was engaged to the future Theodore II Laskaris. But Asen's policy was unstable, and he again allied himself with the Franks, only to change camps once more after the sudden death of his wife. After his death (in 1241), Bulgaria suffered from internal weakness.

After the death of John of Brienne in 1237, Baldwin II returned to Constantinople from the Low Countries in July 1239 with a small army, concluded an alliance with the Cumans, and was crowned emperor in 1240. He spent several years in the West trying to find financial and military support for his impoverished and collapsing empire. He signed a truce with John Vatatzes (June 1241) for a period of two years, which was renewed for another year in 1244.

The military situation became untenable for the empire following the deaths of John Vatatzes of Nicaea (1254) and his successor Theodore II Laskaris (1258). The usurper Michael VIII Palaiologos became emperor of Nicaea, and his troops heavily defeated the Franks of the principality of Achaia at the Battle of Pelagonia in 1259. By now the empire had been effectively reduced to Constantinople and its environs.

In July 1261 Michael Palaiologos agreed to a truce, but on July 25 his general Alexios Strategopoulos took Constantinople by surprise, thus putting a de facto end to the existence of the Latin Empire. Emperor Baldwin II fled to Italy. By the Treaties of Viterbo (May 24 and 27, 1267), he ceded the suzerainty of the Frankish Peloponnese and other Latin regions to Charles I of Anjou, king of Naples. Baldwin died in Sicily in October 1273. His reign in Constantinople had been marked by poverty. He was even obliged to mortgage his own son, Philip, to Venetian merchants in 1258. In exile, Baldwin II and Philip of Courtenay maintained their claims as titular emperors, which passed to the dynasties of Valois and Taranto. They were extinguished with the death of Philip's great-great-grandson James of Baux (1285).

The manpower of the Latin Empire had been extremely limited by the fact that the Frankish states in Outremer had the same needs. Therefore, the creation and existence of the Latin Empire weakened the Frankish presence and manpower in the East. It also awakened Greek nationalism, especially since the rulers of the Byzantine successor states after 1204 were national Greek princes, ruling an indigenous, homogenous Greek population. Neither did the empire's existence help the Christian cause versus the progress of Islam: its existence caused the total breakdown of the traditional Byzantine political structures as well as of commerce and agriculture and left Constantinople and many other cities in ruins. The Latin Empire of Constantinople not only was unable to replace the Byzantine civilization as a Christian bulwark but actually destroyed that bulwark, thus contributing to the weakening of the Christian cause in Palestine and Syria and finally paving the way for the eventual disappearance of the Byzantine Empire.

BENJAMIN HENDRICKX

See also
Baldwin I of Constantinople; Baldwin II of Constantinople; Boniface I of Montferrat; Byzantine Empire; Henry of Constantinople; John of Brienne; Theodore I Laskaris

References
Geneakoplos, Denos J. "Greco-Latin Relations on the Eve of the Byzantine Restoration: The Battle of Pelagonia." *Dumbarton Oaks Papers* 7 (1956): 101–141.
Harris, Jonathan. *Byzantium and the Crusades.* 2nd ed. London: Bloomsbury, 2014.
Langdon, John S. *Byzantium's Last Imperial Offensive in Asia Minor: The Documentary Evidence for and Hagiographical Lore about John III Ducas Vatatzes' Crusade against the Turks, 1222 or 1225 to 1231.* New Rochelle, NY: A.D. Caratzas, 1992.
Ostrogorsky, George. *History of the Byzantine State.* New Brunswick, NJ: Rutgers University Press, 1969.
Setton, Kenneth M. *The Papacy and the Levant (1204–1571),* Vol. 1. Philadelphia: American Philosophical Society, 1976.
Wolff, Robert L. "Baldwin of Flanders and Hainaut, First Latin Emperor of Constantinople: His Life, Death and Resurrection, 1172–1225." *Speculum* 27 (1955): 281–322.
Wolff, Robert L. "The Latin Empire of Constantinople, 1204–1261." In *A History of the Crusades,* Vol. 2, ed. Kenneth M. Setton et al., 153–203. 2nd ed. Philadelphia: University of Pennsylvaniua Press, 1969.

Constantinople, Muslim Siege of (August 15, 717–August 15, 718)

The chief Muslim goal throughout the seventh and eighth centuries remained the acquisition of Constantinople. That great city controlled the Bosporus and thus access between the Mediterranean Sea and the Black Sea. It also guarded the entrance to Southern and Central Europe. The Muslims first attempted to take the city in 655, when Caliph Othman (r. 644–656) sent out a naval expedition. Although the Byzantine fleet met decisive defeat, the subsequent assassination

View of the Theodosian Walls, Constantinople (formerly Byzantium and now Istanbul) on the Bosporus. These defenses were built during the reign of Emperor Theodosius II (r. 408–450 CE) and withstood all but two invasions: that of the Fourth Crusade in 1204 and the conquest by Mehmed II in 1453. (design-ist/iStockphoto.com)

of Othman and war of succession provided a respite. In 669 the Muslims mounted a second attempt, and thereafter Constantinople came under intermittent attack. Several attempts in the 670s were turned back when the Byzantines defeated the attackers at sea.

The greatest threat to the city and to Byzantium came in the siege of 717–718. Caliph Suleiman (r. 715–717) prepared a great effort to attack the city, ending the short reign of Byzantine emperor Theodosius III (r. 716–717) and bringing to the throne a successful general, Leo the Isaurian (Isauria is in Asia Minor, today's Konia). Leo (r. 717–741), who had been born a poor peasant, took the title Leo III. He immediately ordered the granaries of Constantinople restocked and repairs made to the city's walls. He also secured weapons and ordered siege engines installed.

Constantinople was secure as long as its sea communications remained open. The city was built on a promontory flanked on the north by the so-called Golden Horn, an inlet of the Bosporus forming a natural harbor, and on the south by the Sea of Marmora. The city was protected on its western, or landward, side by both inner and outer walls; the inner wall had been built under Emperor Constantine the Great. The outer wall was constructed under Emperor Theodosius II and was some four miles in length. Normally the city population numbered about half a million people, but in 717 it must have swelled from refugees.

Until the invention of gunpowder, the only practical way to take a strongly held city was by blockading and starving its population. This meant closing both the Bosporus and the Dardanelles—a difficult feat because Constantinople flanked the Bosporus from the south. Everything depended on the Byzantine fleet, which was markedly inferior in numbers to that of the attackers.

Maslama, brother of the caliph, commanded the operation against Constantinople. Maslama took personal command of the land force of some 80,000 men and gave command of the 1,800-ship fleet transporting another 80,000 men to Suleiman the General. The attackers also had some 800 additional ships preparing in African and Egyptian ports, while the caliph was assembling a reserve army at Tarsus.

Maslama crossed over the Dardanelles to Europe, probably in July 717, and then moved overland to Constantinople, arriving there on August 15. Maslama ordered his troops to entrench before the city. He attempted a land attack, but the Byzantines beat it back. Maslama then ordered his men to surround his camp with a deep ditch and decided to reduce the city by blockade. He therefore instructed Suleiman the General to divide his fleet into two squadrons, one to cut off supplies from reaching Constantinople via the Aegean and Dardanelles and the other to move through the Bosporus and sever communications with the city from the Black Sea.

In early September, the second fleet got under way to sail north of the Golden Horn, where Leo III had his fleet. The entrance to the harbor was protected by a great chain suspended between two towers that could be raised or lowered. When the blockading squadron approached, the strong current in the Bosporus threw the leading ships into confusion. Leo immediately ordered the chain lowered, stood out with his galleys, and attacked the broken Muslim formation with Greek fire, destroying 20 ships and capturing others before retiring to the Golden Horn on the approach of the main body of Suleiman's fleet.

Suleiman the General made no further attempt to force the strait, and Leo was thus able to bring in supplies and prevent Constantinople's surrender through starvation. To add to Maslama's difficulties, his brother, Caliph Suleiman, suddenly died, and his successor, Omar II, turned out to be a religious bigot but no soldier. Omar continued the siege by land, but then winter set in and was unusually severe with snow. Many of the besiegers died in these conditions, among them Suleiman the General.

In the spring of 718, an Egyptian squadron of 400 ships arrived. Passing Constantinople at night, it closed the Bosporus. It was followed by a squadron from Africa of 360 ships and the reserve army to reinforce the land troops, who had reportedly been reduced to cannibalism. Although the closure of the Bosporus would in time have forced Constantinople to surrender, a large number of the crewmen on the Egyptian ships were impressed Christians, and many were able to desert and provide accurate intelligence regarding Muslim strength and dispositions.

Choosing an opportune time when his enemy was unprepared, Leo again ordered the boom lowered and came out of the Golden Horn to engage and defeat the Egyptian ships. The Christian crewmen deserted en masse; many Muslim vessels were destroyed by Greek fire, and others were captured. This naval victory gave Leo control of the Bosporus. He followed it up by ferrying over to the Asiatic side a sizable land force. There it trapped and routed a number of Muslim troops.

Leo was also active diplomatically. He arranged an alliance with Terbelis, king of the Bulgars, who then marched against Maslama, defeating him, probably in July 718, somewhere south of Adrianople. Some 22,000 Muslim troops are said to have been killed. Leo made adroit use of disinformation as well, scattering reports that the Franks were preparing to send large forces to the aid of Constantinople.

The caliph finally recalled Maslama, who raised the siege on August 15. It had lasted exactly one year. The fleet embarked the army, landing the troops on the Asiatic shore of the Sea of Marmora. The ships then sailed for the Dardanelles, but en route they encountered a great storm. Reportedly only 5 galleys out of some 2,560 in the siege returned to Syria and Alexandria. Of the land forces, which some estimates place at more than 200,000 men, no more than 30,000 made it home.

Leo's victory was decisive. In 739 Leo won a land victory that compelled the Muslims to withdraw from western Asia Minor. Leo's leadership was the key to the Byzantine victory. In the process, he may have saved not only his empire but all of Western European civilization.

SPENCER C. TUCKER

See also
Leo III the Isaurian

References
Gibbon, Edward. *The History of the Decline and Fall of the Roman Empire,* Vol. 6. Ed. J. B. Bury. London: Methuen, 1912.
Runciman, Steven. *Byzantine Civilization.* New York: Barnes & Noble, 1994.
Vasiliev, Alexander Alexandrovich. *History of the Byzantine Empire, 324–1453.* Madison: University of Wisconsin Press, 1990.

Constantinople, 1590 Treaty of (May 21, 1590)

Treaty that officially ended the Ottoman-Safavid War of 1578–1590. Also known as the Treaty of Ferhad Pasha for the Ottoman statesman, the Treaty of Constantinople was signed on May 21, 1590, at Constantinople (Istanbul). The war had seen the Ottomans secure from the Safavids the southern Caucasus, along with the important city of Tabriz. The shah of Persia, Abbas I, entered into the treaty largely because of civil strife at home and a war against the Uzbeks.

The Treaty of Constantinople recognized the Ottoman gains in the war to include most of the southern Caucasus, Tabriz, and northwestern Persia. Abbas also agreed to pay obeisance to Sunni Muslim religious leaders.

Although the treaty represented a considerable triumph for the Ottomans, Abbas soon restored order at home, reorganized his army, and went to war with his external enemies. In the ensuing fighting of the Ottoman-Safavid War of 1603–1612, Abbas defeated the Ottomans and regained the territory lost earlier as confirmed in the Treaty of Nasuh Pasha of 1612.

SPENCER C. TUCKER

See also
Abbas I the Great; Nasuh Pasha, Treaty of; Ottoman-Safavid Wars

References
Eskander Beg Monshi. *History of Shah Abbas the Great*. 2 vols. Trans. Roger M. Savory. Boulder, CO: Westview, 1978.

Nahavandi, H., and Y. Bomati. *Shah Abbas, empereur de Perse (1587–1629)*. Paris: Perrin, 1998.

Newman, Andrew J. *Safavid Iran: Rebirth of a Persian Empire*. London: I. B. Tauris, 2006.

Savory, Roger. *Iran under the Safavids*. Cambridge: Cambridge University Press, 2007.

Constantinople, 1700 Treaty of (July 3, 1700)

Treaty signed at Constantinople (Istanbul) on July 3, 1700, between Russia and the Ottoman Empire confirming the provisions of the 1699 Peace of Karlowitz. Russia retained control of the strategic fortress-cities of Azov, Taganrog, Pavlovsk, and Mius. Both sides agreed to maintain a military-free zone in their border regions. The treaty ended the tribute from Russia to the Crimean Khanate (and the Porte) and obligated the Porte to restrain Crimean khans from raiding into Russian territory. The Ottomans also agreed to accept a Russian government representative at Constantinople and to free all Russian prisoners of war.

Alexander Mikaberidze

See also
Karlowitz, Treaty of; Russo-Ottoman Wars

Reference
Matveyev, Vladimir. *The Karlowitz Congress and the Debut of Russia's Multilateral Diplomacy*. London: Centre for the Study of Diplomacy, University of Leicester, 2000.

Constantinople, 1720 Treaty of (November 16, 1720)

A treaty between Russia and the Ottoman Porte signed in Constantinople on November 16, 1720. The two powers pledged to maintain "permanent and perpetual peace, and true and sincere friendship." Russia recognized Azov and the surrounding territories as Ottoman possessions and agreed to demolish the fortress of Taganrog. Russia also agreed to recognize the Ottoman authority in the Crimea and promised not to interfere in Poland's affairs, while both powers pledged to guarantee sovereignty and territorial integrity of the Polish state. The two states also pledged to allow merchants of both nations to trade and travel safely from one state to another. The Porte allowed the Russians to make pilgrimages to Jerusalem and other holy places, without paying any taxes.

Alexander Mikaberidze

See also
Adrianople, 1713 Treaty of; Pruth, Treaty of; Russo-Ottoman Wars

References
Shaw, Stanford Jay. *History of the Ottoman Empire and Modern Turkey: Empire of the Gazis; The Rise and Decline of the Ottoman Empire, 1280–1808*. Cambridge: Cambridge University Press, 1991.

Treaties between Turkey and Foreign Powers. London: Foreign Office, 1855.

Constantinople, 1832 Treaty of (July 21, 1832)

Treaty signed on July 21, 1832, at the Constantinople Conference of the Great Powers (Britain, France, and Russia) and the Ottoman Empire. The treaty in essence marked the end of the Greek War of Independence that led to the establishment of modern-day Greece as an independent state free of the Ottoman Empire. The treaty outlined the boundaries of the new Greek Kingdom that were recognized by major powers. The Porte had agreed to recognize the kingdom of Greece and to evacuate Greek regions that were still under Ottoman occupation in return for an indemnity of 4 million Ottoman piastres.

The Ottomans retained the Fort of Punta, a key point in their defenses of Prevesa, but pledged to permit safe passage of Greek vessels through the Gulf of Arta. Individuals wanting to quit Greek or Ottoman territories and sell their estates were given 18 months to so. The Great Powers guaranteed a Greek loan of 2.4 million pounds and recognized King Otto's accession to the ranks of European monarchs.

Alexander Mikaberidze

See also
Ottoman Empire

Reference
Clogg, Richard. *A Concise History of Greece*. Cambridge: Cambridge University Press, 2002.

Constantinople, 1913 Treaty of (September 29, 1913)

Treaty concluded in Constantinople (Istanbul) on September 29, 1913, between Bulgaria and the Ottoman Empire to conclude the Second Balkan War (1913). During the war, the

Ottomans took advantage of Bulgaria's weakness to reclaim territory lost in the First Balkan War. The two countries agreed to resume diplomatic relations, exchange prisoners, and establish a general amnesty. The treaty compelled Bulgaria to accept Ottoman control of Adrianople (Edirne) and surrender territory up to the Maritsa River.

ALEXANDER MIKABERIDZE

See also
Balkan Wars

References
Hall, Richard C. *The Balkan Wars, 1912–1913: Prelude to the First World War.* London: Routledge, 2000.
Helmreich, E. C. *The Diplomacy of the Balkan Wars, 1912–1913.* Cambridge, MA: Harvard University Press, 1938.

Constantinople, Ottoman Siege of (April 6–May 29, 1453)

The successful 1453 Ottoman siege of the city of Constantinople marked the end of the Byzantine Empire. Throughout the course of the 14th century, the Ottomans had expanded their power over Anatolia. In 1352, Ottoman forces crossed the Bosporus from Asia and established a foothold in Europe in Rumelia. From there the Ottomans moved into Thrace. Soon they controlled the land around Constantinople, although this great Christian city on the Bosporus, capital of the once great Byzantine Empire, remained free of their control.

Mehmed II (Muhammad II), who became sultan in 1451, made it his principal goal to take Constantinople. In 1452 he completed construction of the Rumili Hisar (Castle of Europe) at the eastern outlet of the Bosporus on the European shore, opposite the older Anadoli Hisar (Castle of Asia) in Anatolia. These two fortresses ensured Mehmed's control of the passage across the straits from Anatolia to Rumelia and gave him the ability to block shipping from the Black Sea to Constantinople. In addition, artillery at Rumili Hisar could bombard Constantinople itself. In June 1452 Mehmed II's action brought war with Byzantine emperor Constantine XI.

In addition to the highly trained Janissary Corps, Mehmed II could call on substantial mercenary and irregular troops. The force he took to Constantinople has been variously estimated at between 100,000 and 200,000 men. He also brought some 70 artillery pieces. Many of the

A 16th-century Byzantine fresco depicting the 1453 Ottoman siege of Constantinople, from the Church of the Annunciation, Moldovita, Romania. Taken by Ottoman forces under Sultan Mehmed II, it was renamed Istanbul. (Ilona Budzbon/iStockphoto.com)

Siege of Constantinople, April 6–May 29, 1453

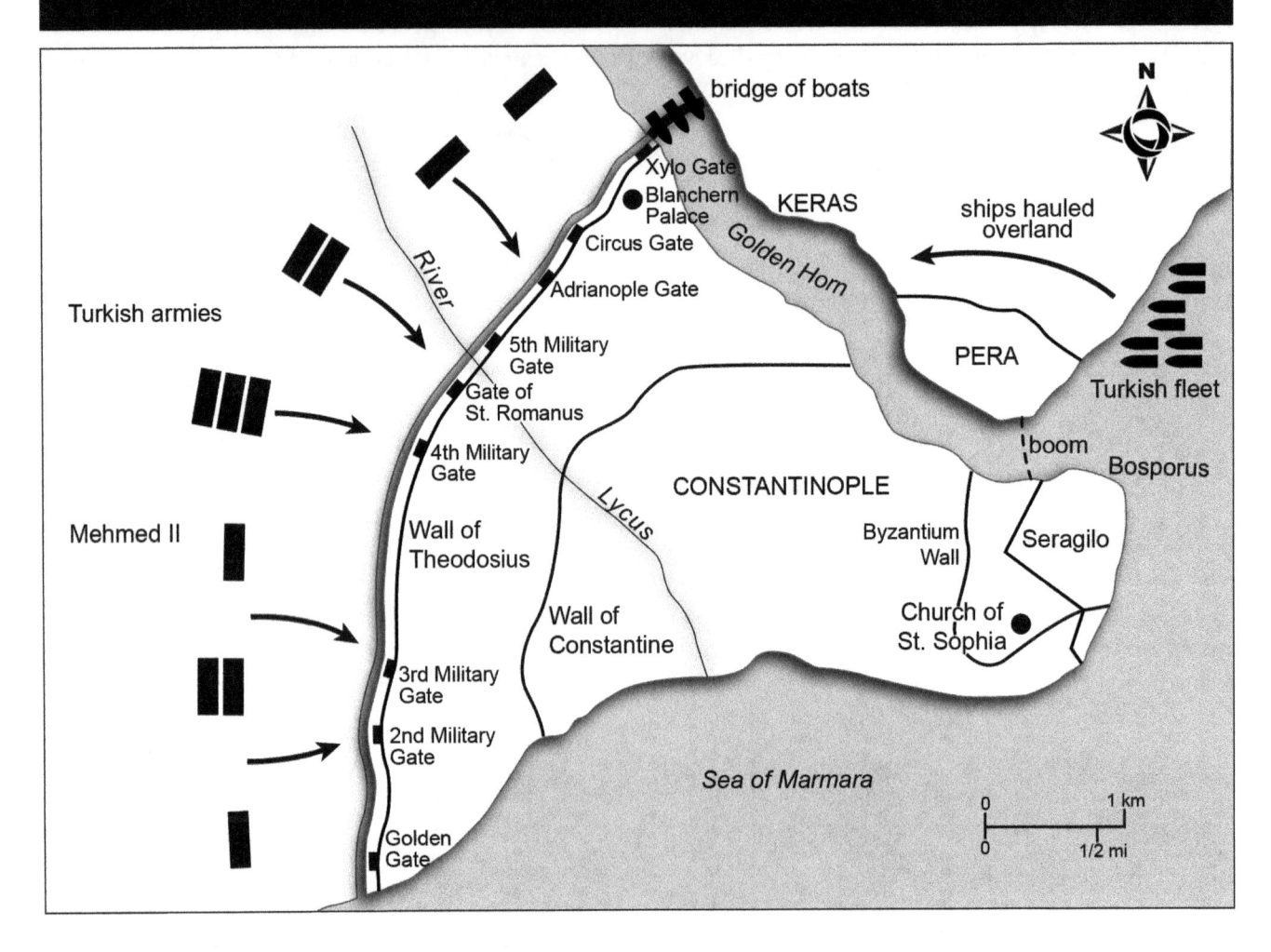

Ottoman guns were cast by an experienced Hungarian cannon founder and renegade named Urban. They included a dozen large bombards and one bronze gun nearly 27 feet in length with a 2.5-foot-diameter barrel that fired a 1,300-pound projectile.

During the winter of 1452–1453 Mehmed II ordered the assembly of some 125 naval vessels of various types. He was well aware that previous sieges of Constantinople had failed because they were from the land only. In the spring of 1453, his fleet sailed from Gallipoli into the Sea of Marmara. With a naval force five times that of the Byzantines, Mehmed II was confident that he had command of the sea and could block any relief attempt. At the same time, he began moving his vast land force from Thrace.

The Ottoman army arrived before the walls of Constantinople on April 2, 1453. Mehmed II then sent messengers to offer the inhabitants freedom of life and property under Ottoman protection if they would surrender. These terms were rejected, and on April 6 Mehmed II's heavy guns commenced fire.

Constantinople received limited aid from Venice and Genoa. To defend the city, Constantine had only 26 ships guarding the sea approaches and a small regular force of fewer than 10,000 men; 2,000 of them were foreigners. The city's chief defense was its 14 miles of nearly impregnable walls, but this translated into 1 defender per 7.5 feet of wall. Actual command of the defense fell to the leader of the Genoese mercenaries and expert in siege warfare, Giovanni Giustiniani. With news of the Ottoman approach, Constantine XI ordered the gates to the city closed, bridges over the moat demolished, and a great chain stretched across the mouth of the city harbor known as the Golden Horn.

The Ottoman artillery bombardment of the western walls of the city continued for six weeks without letup, but each time there was a breach the defenders managed to fill it in and drive back the Ottoman infantry. Superior Byzantine seamanship and armaments enabled them to repulse attacks by the Ottoman fleet, but Mehmed II had 70 galleys hauled overland to the Golden Horn on great greased rollers, bypassing the closed harbor entrance. When these were launched in the Golden Horn, the defenders knew that the battle was lost. Still, the Ottomans might have been repulsed had the major European powers made an effort to help defend the Christian city, but they did nothing.

By May food in Constantinople was in short supply, and the population was starving. Toward the end of that month the Ottomans managed to create a breach in the wall that the defenders could not completely block, and early on the morning of May 29 the Ottomans launched a great attack, accompanied by trumpets, drums, and war cries. Following human-wave assaults, the Ottoman troops forced an entry. Although many of the defenders took refuge in the ships, Constantine XI refused to flee. He removed his insignia, plunged into battle with the oncoming Janissaries, and was promptly slain.

After a disciplined march into Constantinople, the conquerors broke ranks and for three days subjected the city to an orgy of slaughter and pillage, carrying off not only the contents of palaces and houses but also their attractive young inhabitants as well. Mehmed II entered the city on horseback with a guard of Janissaries the evening it was taken and made his way to the great Church of Hagia Sophia, which he ordered transformed into a mosque.

Regarded as a seminal event in the history of the West, the fall of Constantinople was a great psychological and strategic blow to the European powers. It ended the Byzantine Empire, which had been the last buffer between Europe and the Ottomans. Mehmed II, now known as "The Conqueror," renamed the city Istanbul and made it his capital. The city faced both Asia and Europe, and during the next several decades Mehmed II directed from it the extension of Ottoman power to include Serbia, Greece, Albania, the Aegean, and even Otranto in southern Italy. Mehmed II died in May 1481. During the next two centuries his successors mounted repeated offensives to push Ottoman control west into the Mediterranean and north into Central Europe.

SPENCER C. TUCKER

See also
Byzantine Empire; Mehmed II, Sultan; Ottoman Empire

References
Browning, Robert. *Byzantine Empire.* New York: Scribner, 1980.
Gibbon, Edward. *The Decline and Fall of the Roman Empire, 1185–1453.* New York: Modern Library, 1983.
Kinross, John Patrick. *The Ottoman Centuries: The Rise and Fall of the Turkish Empire.* New York: William Morrow, 1977.
Norwich. John Julius. *Byzantium: The Decline and Fall.* New York: Knopf, 1996.

Constantius II, Emperor (317–361)

Roman emperor. Born Flavius Julius Constantius on August 7, 317, at Sirmium, Pannonia, Constantius was the third child and second son of Constantine I and Fausta and was named after his grandfather, who had been coaugustus with Galerius. At the time of Constantius's birth, his father was coaugustus with Licinius. In 324 Licinius was defeated in civil war, and Constantine raised Constantius to caesar. As a young man his father sent him to the east to resist the incursions of the Sassanid Empire. Constantius conducted a successful campaign there that was, however, cut short by news of his father's ill health. Constantius was with his father near Constantinople when he died in 337.

Constantine divided the Roman Empire among his sons. Constans and Constantius II became coaugustus in the east. Constantius immediately returned to the east to fight a new invasion by Shapur II. While Constantius waged a generally successful war against the Sassanians in the east, his brothers Constantine II and Constans fought a civil war. Constantine II was killed in 340, and Constans became sole augustus in the west.

Constantius still was fighting Shapur II in the east when the usurper Magnentius declared himself emperor in the west and had Constans murdered in 350. Constantius refused to recognize Magnentius and prepared for war. He elevated his cousin Gallus to caesar in the east and moved west against Magnentius. Constantius defeated Magnentius at Mursa Major in 351 and Mons Seleucus in 353. Magnentius committed suicide, and Constantius gained control of the entire Roman Empire. Constantius at once turned his attention to fighting Germanic incursions along the Danube and the Rhine.

After Gallus's short but turbulent reign as caesar, Constantius had Gallus executed for suspected conspiracy in 354. It was now clear to Constantius that the empire faced too many threats for just one man to handle. He turned to his last remaining cousin, Julian (the younger brother of Gallus), and in November 355 made him caesar in the west. While Julian fought the Franks and Alamans in Gaul, Constantius campaigned against the Sarmatians and Quadi along the Danube.

By 359, however, war was renewed against Shapur in the east. For his war against the Sassanians, Constantius ordered a large portion of Julian's Gallic army to move east. The soldiers rebelled and hailed Julian as emperor in 360. Constantius found himself trapped between the serious threat of Shapur in the east and Julian's rebellion in the west. Constantius began to move west to face Julian, but the two never met in battle because Constantius died of fever on November 3, 361, at Mobsucrenae in Cilicia. On his deathbed he was baptized an Arian Christian and named Julian his successor.

NIKOLAUS LEO OVERTOOM

See also
Constantine I; Shapur II the Great

References
Bowder, Diana. *The Age of Constantine and Julian.* New York: Barnes & Noble, 1978.
Browning, Robert. *The Emperor Julian.* Berkeley: University of California Press, 1976.
Cameron, Averil. *The Later Roman Empire.* Cambridge, MA: Harvard University Press, 1993.
Wienand, Johannes, ed. *Contested Monarchy: Integrating the Roman Empire in the Fourth Century A.D.* Oxford: Oxford University Press, 2015.

Copts

Copts are Christian descendants of the ancient Egyptians. The term "Coptic" is used to refer to race, religion, and language. As far as religion is concerned, the Copts, like the members of the Syrian Orthodox Church (Jacobites), are non-Chalcedonian—that is, they are monophysites who deny the doctrine of Christ's two natures.

The religious differences between the Coptic population of Egypt and their Byzantine rulers, who supported the diophysite doctrine of the Greek Orthodox Church, are part of the background to the Muslim conquest of Egypt in the seventh century, when many Copts actually welcomed their new masters. The Coptic patriarch of Alexandria was the leader of the community and acted as its representative to the Muslim authorities.

Throughout the period of the crusades, the largest concentrations of Copts were found in Upper Egypt. There were also Coptic communities in Ethiopia and Nubia as well as in the delta region of Lower Egypt. As late as the 12th century, Coptic Christians may have outnumbered Muslims in Egypt. Fustat was overwhelmingly a Coptic city, whereas the newer Fatimid foundation of Cairo was predominantly Muslim.

Copts were especially powerful in the administrations of the successive Egyptian regimes, and many Copts served the Fatimids, Ayyubids, and Mamluks as viziers, although the heyday of the Copts came during the Fatimid period. The Copts' prominent role as financial advisers and tax gatherers as well as the sultans' tendency to use them as cat's paws for unpopular measures contributed to their unpopularity with the Muslim community. Muslim hostility to the Copts flared up from time to time and increased during the crusade period, when many Muslims believed that the Copts were operating as a kind of fifth column for the Franks, supplying their coreligionists with intelligence and committing acts of sabotage. The burning of Fustat by Shawar to prevent King Amalric of Jerusalem from occupying it in 1168 was a disaster for the Copts.

In the course of the 13th century Copts came under increasing pressure to convert to Islam, but even then some of those who had converted were still suspected of being crypto-Christian spies and were persecuted still further. In fact, there is little evidence of any Coptic enthusiasm for the crusading cause, and those crusade theorists in the West who thought that the Copts might provide any effective assistance to a crusader invasion of Egypt were deluding themselves. In 1237 negotiations began for a union of the Coptic Church with the Latin Church, although nothing came of this.

All evidence suggests that the Coptic community suffered a catastrophic decline in numbers in the course of the 14th century as its members came under increasing pressure to convert. The Arabic chronicles of the period are peppered with accounts of anti-Christian riots, the destruction of churches, and senior Coptic officials being forced to renounce their faith.

Today Copts constitute some 9 percent of Egypt's population of 97 million, and St. Mark's Coptic Orthodox Church of Alexandria is the largest Christian church in Egypt, Northeast Africa, and the Middle East. The rise of Islamic extremism has affected the Copts, with terrorist actions having been carried out against them and their churches. One of these occurred on April 9, 2017, in twin bombings of St. George's Coptic Church in Tanta and outside St. Mark's in Alexandria. Together the blasts killed 49 people. Later that year, an attack on a Coptic church outside Cairo on December 29, 2017, killed 9 people. The Islamic State of Iraq and Syria (ISIS) claimed responsibility. Such terrorist attacks have left the fiercely nationalistic Coptic community feeling unprotected by the government on which it had relied for deliverance from the Islamist regime of Egyptian president Mohamed Morsi in 2012–2013.

ROBERT IRWIN AND SPENCER C. TUCKER

See also

Crusades in the Holy Land, Christian; Egypt; Islamic State of Iraq and Syria

References

Atiya, Aziz S. *History of Eastern Christianity.* Notre Dame, IN: University of Notre Dame Press, 1968.

Wilfong, Terry G. "The Non-Muslim Communities: Christian Communities." In *The Cambridge History of Egypt,* Vol. 1, *Islamic Egypt, 640–1517,* ed. Carl F. Petry, 175–197. Cambridge: Cambridge University Press, 1998.

Corupedium, Battle of (281 BCE)

A battle fought between the generals of Alexander III the Great seeking to control the vast territories he had conquered. The Battle of Corupedium between two of these successors (Diadochi) was fought in February 281 BCE in western Asia Minor near Magnesia on the plain of Corupedium, west of Sardis. It was the last battle between men who had served with Alexander: Lysimachus was more than 80 years old, and Seleucus was 77.

Lysimachus had killed his own son, the popular Agathocles, apparently at the instigation of his new wife, Agathocles's stepmother, Arsinoe. Agathocles's widow, Lysandra, fled to Seleucus's court, accompanied by another of Lysimachus's sons, Alexander (born to an Odrysian mother). They appealed to Seleucus, who took advantage of the unrest and defections after Agathocles's murder and invaded.

Very little is known of the battle itself other than that Lysimachus was killed and his army defeated. After the battle, Lysimachus's son Alexander had some difficulty in persuading Lysandra to return Lysimachus's body for burial. Although the battle seemed decisive at the time, Seleucus's assassination by Ptolemy Ceraunus less than a year later undid his success.

IAIN SPENCE

See also

Diadochi, Wars of the; Lysimachus; Seleucus I Nicator

References

Green, Peter. *Alexander to Actium: The Historical Evolution of the Hellenistic Age.* Berkeley: University of California Press, 1990.

Lund, Helen S. *Lysimachus: A Study in Early Hellenistic Kingship.* London: Routledge, 1992.

Crassus, Marcus Licinius (ca. 115–53 BCE)

Roman politician and military leader. Marcus Licinius Crassus was born circa 115 BCE, the son of Roman politician Publius Licinius Crassus. Marcus Licinius Crassus may have begun his military training under his father in Spain. Crassus's father and older brother were executed by the Marians when Marius's supporters seized control of Rome. Crassus fled and went into hiding in Spain. When Crassus learned that Sulla was heading back to Italy, he raised a small army and crossed first to Africa and then to Greece, where he joined Sulla. Crassus played an important role in Sulla's ultimate victory, in particular the Battle of the Colline Gate in November 82.

The beginnings of Crassus's large fortune came from the Sullan proscriptions. After his praetorship, probably in 73, Crassus offered to take over command of the war against Spartacus when others had failed. Crassus received command of a large army, eventually defeating Spartacus (72–71) and ordering large-scale crucifixion of the defeated slaves along the Appian Way.

Though a rival of Pompey, who had also advanced under Sulla and had even claimed credit for ending the slave war, Crassus joined with Pompey in running for the consulships of 70. In the mid to late 60s Crassus was involved in various schemes to counteract Pompey's growing military fame and influence. As censor in 65 Crassus tried to give citizenship to the Transpadani and annex Egypt, but these attempts came to naught, and he ended up resigning.

Crassus also promoted Julius Caesar. On Caesar's return from Spain, Pompey and Crassus supported Caesar for the consulship of 59, forming the First Triumvirate. This arrangement was inherently unstable. when Caesar left for his Gallic command, Crassus turned to supporting Clodius, who was threatening attacks on Caesar's consular legislation and on Pompey's interests. But Clodius was too ambitious to be a reliable ally. When attacks on the triumvirate increased and there were threats to replace Caesar in his Gallic command, Caesar met with Crassus at Ravenna in the winter of 56, and all three then met at Luca to forge a new agreement. Pompey and Crassus were to become consuls for 55, with subsequent five-year commands in Spain and in Syria, respectively, and a five-year renewal of Caesar's command. Crassus probably sought a military victory to keep up with his younger rivals, although he was now nearly 60 years old.

Before the end of 55 Crassus left for Syria. It is not clear whether the law proposing all the commands authorized him to attack the Persians, but that was certainly his intention, as he needed a major victory to secure the prestige he desired. Ancient authors regard Crassus as motivated by greed, but there were valid reasons for the campaign: continual bickering between Armenia and Persia was likely to upset Roman interests in the area following Pompey's settlements in 62. The probable size of Crassus's command of seven legions and 4,000 cavalry suggests that the Senate contemplated war against Persia.

Crassus spent his first campaigning season in 54 crossing the Euphrates, reconnoitering and establishing garrisons and depots, especially along the Belikh River. He returned to winter in Syria, train his troops, and complete financial preparations for the next campaigning season by plundering temples, including that at Jerusalem, and extorting large sums of money (attributed to his greed). In the spring of 53 Crassus again crossed the Euphrates. He then moved away from the river, persuaded by Abgar, an Arabian guide, that the Persian force, led by the Surenas, was heading southeast. After a desert crossing to the Belikh River, Crassus caught up with the Persians near Carrhae on June 9, 53 BCE, but the Romans suffered heavy losses at the hands of the Persian archers. The Roman army fled to Carrhae, then toward Sinnaca; invited to a parley, Crassus was treacherously captured and killed.

Carrhae was a disastrous loss, and the death of Crassus had repercussions for the growing rift between Pompey and Caesar. Crassus suffered from bad press because he ultimately lost in battle, but he was certainly a master of the game of politics. He was reputedly the richest man in Rome until Pompey returned from his victories in the East.

BRUCE MARSHALL

See also
Caesar, Gaius Julius; Carrhae, Battle of; Pompeius Magnus, Gnaeus

References
Marshall, Bruce A. *Crassus: A Political Biography.* Amsterdam: Hakkert, 1976.
Ward, Allen M. *Marcus Crassus and the Late Roman Republic.* Columbia: University of Missouri Press, 1977.

Cresson, Battle of (May 1, 1187)

Battle fought at the spring of the Cresson, a site near the town of Nazareth (modern-day Nazerat, Israel), on May 1, 1187, between Christian knights of the Kingdom of Jerusalem, including Templars and Hospitallers and Muslims under emir Muaffar al-Din Kukburī.

In April 1187, Saladin's son al-Afdal obtained permission from the lord of Tiberias, Raymond III of Tripoli, to pass through the lordship in order to raid the royal domain around Acre. The Muslims were to withdraw the same day and do the lordship no harm. Entering the lordship on May 1 north of Lake Tiberias, Kukburī followed the shore south to Tiberias (modern-day Teverya, Israel) itself before turning west. A Latin account, the *Libellus de expugnatione Terrae Sanctae per Saladinum expeditione,* indicates, however, that other Muslim groups had already crossed the Jordan the night before and were thus able to reach as far west as Shafa Amr before returning through the Wadi Saffuriya and Battauf Valley, respectively.

Gerard of Ridefort, master of the Temple, and Roger of Les Moulins, master of the Hospital, were on their way north to mediate between Raymond and King Guy and received warning of the raid from Raymond on April 30 while they were at the Templar castle of La Fève (al-Fula) in the Jezreel Valley. Disregarding Raymond's instructions not to interfere with the Muslims, they decided to attack them. Reinforced by Templars from Caco, their force of 80–90 Templars and 10 Hospitallers moved north to Nazareth, where they were joined by 40 knights of the king.

The crusader force then proceeded northeast toward Tiberias and came upon the main Muslim force returning toward the Jordan at the spring of the Cresson. In the ensuing battle, some 140 Christian knights were defeated by a force of perhaps 7,000 Muslims under Emir Muaffar al-Din Kukburī. Roger of Les Moulins and all the knights of the military order were killed, apart from Gerard of Ridefort and two other Templars; the secular knights were taken prisoner.

DENYS PRINGLE

See also
Guy of Lusignan; Saladin

References
Prawer, Joshua. *Histoire du royaume latin de Jérusalem.* 2nd ed. 2 vols. Paris: C.N.R.S., 1975.
Pringle, Denys. "The Spring of the Cresson in Crusading History." In *Dei gesta per Francos: Etudes sur les croisades dédiées à Jean Richard,* ed. Michel Balard, Benjamin Z. Kedar, and Jonathan Riley-Smith, 231–240. Aldershot, UK: Ashgate, 2001.

Crimean War (1853–1856)

See Russo-Ottoman Wars

Croesus of Lydia (ca. 595–547 BCE)

King of Lydia, a kingdom in western Asia Minor with its capital at Sardis. The son of Alyattes, Croesus was born circa 595 BCE. The Greek historian Herodotus fixes the beginning of his reign in 560 and identifies Croesus as the first to exact tribute from the Greeks of Asia Minor. Solon of Athens was reputed to have visited Croesus in Sardis, at the height of the Lydian Empire. His indifference to Croesus's wealth annoyed Croesus, as did his suggestion that one cannot judge a man to be happy until he is dead. However, Solon's advice was demonstrated when Croesus's eldest son, Atys, was killed in a hunting accident.

Croesus is famous for consulting the Delphic Oracle as to whether he should attack Persia and being told that if he fought Persia, a great empire would fall. Thinking that the oracle meant the Persian Empire and not his, he made alliances with the Egyptian king Amasis and then the Spartans and invaded Cappadocia, part of the Persian Empire. The first battle at Pteria was inconclusive, and Croesus withdrew to Sardis to await reinforcements.

Persian king Cyrus II the Great, founder of the Achaemenid Empire, pursued immediately and attacked before this could happen, placing his camels in front of the army to spook the Lydian cavalry. The Lydians ended up besieged in Sardis, which fell because an observant soldier detected a scalable point on the acropolis.

Croesus was sentenced to death but was reprieved at the last minute and became an adviser to Cyrus and later his successor Cambyses (at least according to Herodotus). It is possible that Croesus was the ruler under whom electrum was separated into gold and silver for minting coins.

ABIGAIL DAWSON

See also
Achaemenid Empire; Cyrus II the Great; Lydia

References
Harrison, Thomas. *Divinity and History: The Religion of Herodotus.* Oxford, UK: Clarendon, 2000.
Lang, Mabel L. *Herodotean Narrative and Discourse.* Cambridge, MA: Harvard University Press, 1984.

Crusades in the Holy Land, Christian (1096–1291)

In the great age of faith there many military efforts said to be primarily motivated by Christian fervor and dubbed "crusades." These included the Reconquista in Spain of 722–1492, the Albegensian Crusade in France during 1209–1229, the Aragonese Crusade of 1284–1285, and the Northern Crusade conducted by the Teutonic Knights in the Baltic region during the 12th and 13th centuries. But certainly the best known, most ambitious, least successful, and yet most lastingly influential of military efforts cloaked in religion were those advanced by the Latin Roman Catholic Church and supported by the Latin West to wrest control from the Muslims of Jerusalem and the Holy Land of Palestine. The term "crusade" comes from the Spanish *cruzada,* meaning "marked by the cross."

Apart from the stated religious goals of spreading the faith and reclaiming the Holy Land from the "infidel," there were many purely secular motivations behind the Christian crusades. One was the advance of the Seljuk Turks. In 1070 they had captured Jerusalem, and palmers—those Christians who had undertaken a pilgrimage to Palestine and then wore crossed palm leaves as a sign of their accomplishment—began to tell of repression of Christians there. Reportedly, one Peter the Hermit brought a letter from Simeon, patriarch of Jerusalem, to Pope Urban II bearing witness to this.

The Byzantine Empire was then weak. This important Christian state guarded access to South-Central Europe and for seven centuries had held back would-be invaders from crossing the narrow straits that separated Asia from Europe. If Constantinople were to fall, this would open the floodgates to Muslim expansion into Europe, and the victory of Tours in 732 would be undone. The threat was such that Byzantine emperor Alexius I Comnenus (r. 1081–1118) sent emissaries to Pope Urban II urging that theological and political differences be set aside and that Latin Europe join him in driving back the Seljuks. Alexius argued that it would be better to fight the Seljuks in Asia than in Europe.

There was also the ambition of the rising Italian city-states of Venice, Genoa, and Pisa. Their leaders sought to extend their commercial reach into the eastern Mediterranean, expanding trade and opening new markets and increasing their wealth and influence. Finally, there was also the quest for military glory and political advantage by kings and nobles.

The decision rested with Urban II. During March–October 1095 he toured northern Italy and southern France, meeting with leaders and enlisting support. Urban then called a church council at Clermont in France and, in what has been called the most influential speech in medieval history, addressed the faithful and proclaimed a crusade to reclaim the Holy Land. Certainly personal ambition played a role, for Urban hoped thereby to unite the Christian West under his leadership.

THE CRUSADES

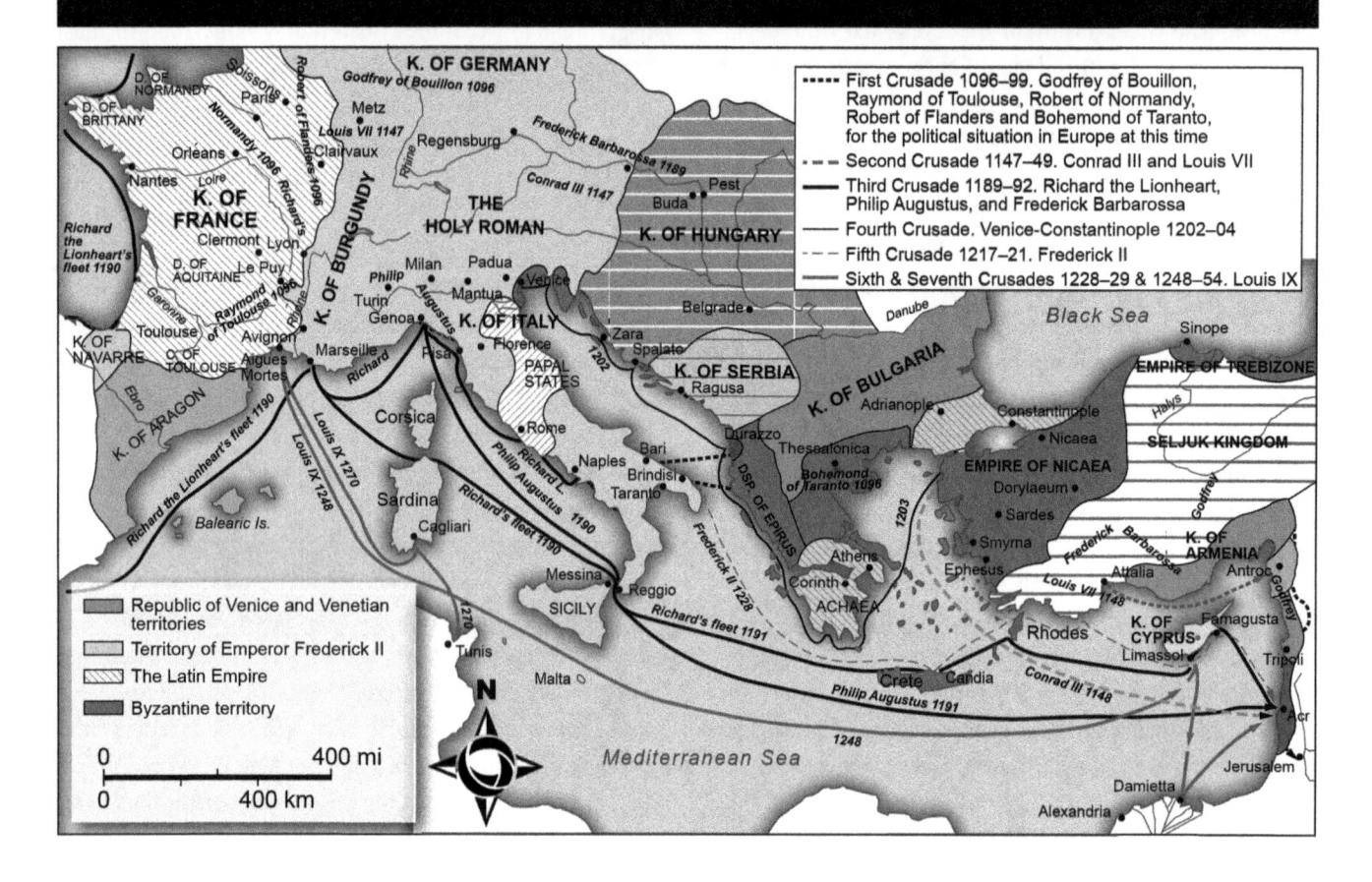

Extraordinary inducements were offered to participants. These included a plenary indulgence remitting all punishment for sin to those who might fall in the war, remission of criminal punishments, and exemption from feudal dues and taxes. Religious frenzy now swept Christian Europe, unfortunately bringing with it the murder of thousands of Jews, chiefly in Germany.

The First Crusade (1096–1099)

Urban set August 1096 as the date for the crusaders' departure. This was the age of faith, and many mostly unarmed peasants responded enthusiastically. In what became known as the People's Crusade or Popular Crusade—yet considered part of the First Crusade—some 40,000 people, including women and children, assembled, many of them under Peter the Hermit, then left from Cologne. There was some violence on their trek south in which the crusaders murdered Jews. At the end of July the crusaders arrived at Constantinople (modern-day Istanbul) and set up camp outside of the city. Some violence ensued, and Alexius was glad to provide transport for the crusaders across the Bosporus to Asia Minor, where he instructed them to wait for the arrival of the main crusader armies of knights. The crusaders were determined to proceed, however. Their numbers having dwindled to some 20,000 and under the leadership of Peter the Hermit, they ventured too far into Seljuk territory, and most were killed or taken prisoner by the Seljuk Turks in battle near Nicaea that October. Perhaps only 3,000 returned to Constantinople.

Meanwhile, the various state military contingents, ultimately numbering as many as 50,000 men, moved largely by land toward the agreed-upon assembly point of Constantinople, arriving there in the autumn of 1096 and the spring of 1097. Alexius was interested only in securing his Asiatic objectives and not the crusader objective of capturing Jerusalem. Rightly fearful of their intentions, Alexius insisted that the crusaders camp beyond the city walls of Constantinople. Finally, with the arrival of the remaining contingents in the spring of 1097 and aided by bribes, Alexius secured the fealty of the crusaders and a pledge that they would help him recover Nicaea (modern-day Iznik) from the Seljuks as well as hand over to him any other former Byzantine possessions they should conquer. Alexius then provided passage across the Bosporus as well as food and escorts to get the crusaders to the Holy Land and attempt to prevent plundering.

The crusaders and Byzantines laid siege to Nicaea during May 14–June 19, 1097. Alexius secured the surrender of the city to him and was able to keep the crusaders from sacking it. The crusaders then continued their march southeast. On July 1 in the Battle of Dorylaion, Seljuk cavalry under the personal command of sultan of Rum Kilij Arslan attacked the outnumbered lefthand crusader column under Norman duke Bohemund of Taranto and was on the brink of destroying it when crusader heavy cavalry under duke of Lower Lorraine Godfrey of Boullion and Count Raymond of Toulouse fall on the Seljuk left and rear. Some 3,000 Seljuks and 4,000 crusaders died in the battle.

Continuing their advance, the crusaders captured Kilij Arslan's capital of Iconium (modern-day Konya, Turkey), while Alexius and the Byzantine forces reoccupied much of western Anatolia. Following the Battle of Heraclea (modern-day Eregh), the crusaders advanced on Antioch, winning a hard-fought battle at Tarsos (modern-day Tarsus, Turkey) on the way. A number of crusaders under Baldwin of Lorraine then left the main column to cross the Euphrates and take Edessa in Mesopotamia, which was secured in March 1098.

On October 21, 1097, crusader forces led by Bohemund laid siege to Antioch. Emir Yaig Siyan mounted a skillful defense with skirmishing outside the walls. Twice the Christians drove off relief forces in battles at Harenc (December 31 and February 9, 1098). Close to starvation themselves, the poorly organized besiegers were saved only by the timely arrival of small English and Pisan supply flotillas and the capture of several small ports to allow access. Antioch fell on June 3, 1098, just before the arrival of a 75,000-man Seljuk relief force under Karbugha, lord of Mosul.

On arriving at Antioch, Karbugha commenced his own siege of the now Christian-controlled city. The Christians were cut off from their supply ports, and Yagi Siyan still held out in the city's citadel. Alexius was advancing with a Byzantine army on Antioch, but informed that the situation there was hopeless, he withdrew into Anatolia.

Spurred by the alleged sudden and miraculous appearance of the Holy Lance (the weapon used to pierce Jesus's side during the crucifixion), the crusaders risked everything in a sally from Antioch on June 28, 1098, by 15,000 men, only 1,000 of them mounted. The crusaders succeeded in engaging the larger Muslim force where it could not maneuver and after repeated charges broke it, causing the Muslim besiegers to flee.

Most of the crusaders survived an outbreak of plague in Antioch during July and August 1098 (one notable victim was Bishop Adhemar du Pay, papal legate and nominal crusader leader), but the leaders argued among themselves as to their next course of action. Some chose to honor their oath to Alexius and returned to Constantinople, but the vast majority decided to continue on to Jerusalem, the most holy city for Christians, who believe it to be the site of Christ's death and resurrection. The city had been controlled by the Muslims for 500 years and in 1099 was under the rule of the Fatimid Caliphate of Cairo.

The crusader advance began in mid-January 1099. The 400-mile march south from Antioch along the eastern Mediterranean coast proceeded through Sidon, Acre, and Caesarea, with the crusaders arriving at Jerusalem on June 7, 1099. They then commenced a siege of that place. Duke Godfrey of Bouillon commanded the Christian force of some 13,000 men, including 1,300 knights. Fatimid governor of Jerusalem Emir Iftikhar ad-Dawla could count on 20,000 men.

With the defenders having poisoned the nearby wells and cisterns and with the heat oppressive, the crusaders knew that they had to work quickly. As early as June 12 they attempted an assault, but lacking sufficient scaling ladders and war machines, they were easily repulsed. Siege equipment came on June 17 when six supply ships arrived at Jaffa, which has been abandoned by the Egyptians. Within several weeks the crusaders had constructed a large number of mangonels and scaling ladders and two large wooden siege towers.

On the night of July 13–14 the crusaders braved defensive fire to push the towers against the city walls, and on the morning of July 15 Duke Godfrey led an attack from one of the towers by means of a wooden drawbridge, while other crusaders employed scaling ladders to enter the city. Many of the Muslims sought refuge in the al-Aqsa Mosque, where Tancred de Hauteville, one of the crusader leaders, promised that their lives would be spared. Once the Christian forces had taken the city, however, they embarked on an orgy of destruction, slaughtering all Muslims, including women and children, who could be found. This included those within the al-Aqsa Mosque. Estimates of the number of Muslims slain in Jerusalem reach as high as 70,000. The surviving Jews fared no better; the Christians herded them into a synagogue and then burned them alive. Their bloodlust spent, the victors proceed to the Church of the Holy Sepulchre, the grotto of which they believed once held the body of the crucified Christ, and there gave thanks to the God of Mercies for their victory.

Learning of the advance on Jerusalem from Egypt of a 50,000-man Turkish army under Emir al-Afdal, Duke Godfrey led out some 10,000 crusaders against it. In the August 12, 1099, Battle of Ascalon, the Fatimids found themselves at great disadvantage against the more heavily armed and armored crusaders, who won a crushing victory.

Following the capture of Jerusalem, most of the crusaders still alive returned home. Those who remained set up small states in the Holy Land. Duke Godfrey died in July 1100, and Baldwin became king of Jerusalem. Near that city, in the First Battle of Ramla on September 7, 1101, Baldwin and only 1,100 men defeated an army from Egypt that may have numbered as many as 10,000. In the Second Battle of Ramla on May 17, 1102, however, an overconfident Baldwin with only 200 men attacked some 30,000 Egyptians and was soundly defeated, although he himself managed to escape. Putting together a new army of 8,000 men, Baldwin was victorious over the Egyptians in the Battle of Jaffa and pursued them into Anatolia.

A protracted multifaceted struggle then ensued for control of Mesopotamia from among the crusaders, various Seljuk sultanates, and other Muslim principalities. Kalij Arslan of the sultanate of Rum in Anatolia captured Mosul in 1102. He was subsequently defeated and killed in the Battle of the Khabur River of 1107 by forces led by Ridwan, emir of Aleppo. Although the crusaders continued to control the coast, they lacked the numerical strength to hold the interior.

During 1116–1117, King Baldwin of Jerusalem led a crusader expedition to the Gulf of Aqaba, where he built the fortress of Ailath (Eilat). In 1118 he led fewer than 1,000 men across the Sinai against Egypt but died during the campaign, and without its leader the expedition returned to Palestine.

The Second Crusade (1147–1149)

The principal figures on the Christian side in the Second Crusade of 1147–1149 were Emperor Conrad III of Germany and King Louis VII of France. Proceeding by land, the Germans ran out of food near Dorylaeum and were overwhelmed by a Seljuk Turk attack. Conrad and a few followers managed to make it back to Nicaea and then proceed to the Holy Land by ship. The French, who took a longer route, were halted by the Seljuks in battle near Laodicea. Louis and the cavalry then traveled to the Holy Land by ship. The infantry, continuing on by land, were annihilated by the Seljuks.

In 1148 the two Christian kings and their remaining men, joined by Baldwin III of Jerusalem, mounted an overland expedition against Damascus, which they invested.

Depiction of French king Louis VII leading a contingent of knights during the Second Crusade (1147–1149) in the Holy Land, from the *Chroniques de France ou de St. Denis*, mid-14th century. (The British Library)

Dissension among the Christian forces led to abandonment of the siege, however. This ended the disastrous Second Crusade.

In 1153 Baldwin III captured Ascalon, bringing the entire coast of Palestine under his control. In 1169 King Amalric of Jerusalem led a joint crusader-Byzantine expedition against Egypt, which was repulsed. The Muslims had long fought among themselves, but in 1171 Seljuk general Salah-al din Yusuf ibn Ayyub, better known as Saladin, established the Ayyubid dynasty in Egypt. Thanks in large part to dissension among the crusaders, Saladin was able to expand his influence from Egypt into Syria and northern Mesopotamia. He eventually conquered all the territory once held by Nur-ed-din, *atabeg* of Mosul.

Crusader Reynald of Châtillon, lord of the castle at Kerak on the road between Damascus and Mecca, carried out a series of attacks on Muslim caravans and towns along the Red Sea. When King Guy de Lusignan of the Latin Kingdom of Jerusalem failed to punish his rival Reynald for these actions, Saladin vowed revenge. In June 1187 Saladin proclaimed a jihad (holy war) against the crusaders and mounted an invasion of Palestine.

On June 26, Saladin crossed the Jordan River at the head of some 20,000 men and laid siege to the crusader stronghold of Tiberius. King Guy's advisers called on him for an immediate effort to raise the siege. Count Raymond of Tripoli, the ablest of the crusader generals whose wife was then in Tiberius, nonetheless urged Guy to wait. Tiberius was well supplied, and Raymond argued that it would be to the crusader advantage to delay any relief effort until Saladin's forces had experienced supply problems in the countryside. The extreme heat of summer would also make campaigning difficult. Guy ignored this wise advice. Instead, he ordered Christian castles and strongpoints to contribute much of their garrisons, and in late June he led a relief force of approximately 1,200 mounted knights and 18,000 infantry toward Tiberius.

On July 2 the Christian force reached Sephoria, about equidistant between Acre and Tiberius. Raymond again urged caution on Guy and again was rebuffed. Although Raymond warned Guy that there was only one spring accessible to the crusaders along the planned route of march, the army continued east. Saladin was pleased to learn of the crusader approach. He knew the impact of a lack of water on the heavily armored and armed crusader force.

Saladin immediately sent light cavalry to attack the Christians, bringing them to a halt on July 3 in the parched and barren land. The Muslim attack and the heat of the day forced the Christians to take up position near the village of Hattin, seven miles west of Tiberius and the Sea of Galilee and next to two mounds known as the Horns.

Saladin's men surrounded the crusaders and kept up constant arrow fire on their camp during the night of July 3–4. What little water the Christians had with them had by now been consumed. Saladin also had his men set fire to nearby brush upwind of the crusader camp, blowing smoke into it and making it even more difficult for the men and horses.

The next morning, July 4, Saladin still refused to close with the heavily armored Christians. Bringing up fresh stocks of arrows, he had his bowmen continue their harassing fire. In an effort to end this, the Christian cavalry charged the Muslims, but this action separated the cavalry from the infantry and enabled the Muslims to destroy the crusader forces piecemeal.

At the very end of the battle, Raymond and a small number of crusader horsemen succeeded in cutting their way out, but they were the only ones to escape. (Raymond later died of wounds sustained in the battle.) The remainder of the crusaders, out of water, their horses dying of thirst, and under constant harassing arrow fire, were forced to surrender. Guy was among the prisoners. Exact casualty totals in the Battle of Hattin are not known, but certainly the vast majority of the Christians were either taken prisoner or killed. While Saladin ordered Reynald executed, he treated Guy well and subsequently released him on the latter's pledge that he would not again take up arms against the Muslims.

Saladin's victory at Hattin on July 4, 1187, had tremendous consequences. It led directly to the Muslim conquest of most of Palestine, the Christian garrisons of which had been badly depleted in putting together the expeditionary force. Only at Tyre, where Christian reinforcements arrived just in time by sea, did Saladin suffer repulse. Saladin then turned against Jerusalem. Laying siege to it on September 20, he took the city on October 2. Fighting then centered on Acre, to which the Christians laid siege. Although they were blockaded by Saladin from the land, the Christians were able to receive supplies from the sea and continue their siege operations. Nine major land battles and numerous other small engagements occurred in the vicinity between the crusader and Muslim forces.

The Third Crusade (1189–1192)
The Muslim capture of Jerusalem shocked all of Europe and led Pope Clement III to appeal for a new crusade in the Holy Land. Three of Europe's most powerful rulers answered the call: Emperor Frederick I Barbarossa of Germany, King Philippe II Augustus of France, and King Richard I the Lionheart of England. The Third Crusade lasted from 1189 to 1192.

Frederick led 30,000 men in a protracted march by land from Constantinople, but in June 1190 he was drowned in the Salef River in Cilicia, and his army soon disintegrated under his less capable son and successor, Frederick of Swabia. Little more than 1,000 men of the original force managed to join the Christian forces at Acre. Philip and Richard arrived in the Holy Land by sea, with Philip stopping en route to capture Cyprus, which he turned into a base for future military operations.

The central event of the Third Crusade was the great Siege of Acre (August 28, 1189–July 12, 1191). King Guy of the Latin Kingdom of Jerusalem, who had been freed by Saladin following the Battle of Hattin on a pledge that he would not again fight against the Muslims, secured a ruling by the church that proclaimed his oath null and void. Guy, however, was now without a kingdom. But the Third Crusade brought to Palestine Christian reinforcements under Archbishop Ubaldo of Pisa as well as Sicilian mercenaries. Guy now took charge of them.

On August 28, 1189, Guy began an ineffectual siege of Acre. Following a failed assault several days later, he appealed to the Christian powers for additional assistance. In September a Danish fleet arrived and placed Acre under blockade from the sea. Ships from other European states also joined the effort. Conrad of Monferrat, who had established a Christian kingdom at Tyre, also landed troops. In October the reinforced crusaders again assaulted Acre but in bitter fighting were again repulsed.

Saladin sought reinforcements from other Muslim powers as far away as Spain. With this support, in October and December he was able to pass ships through the Christian naval blockade and bring supplies and men into Acre. He also began a land countersiege of King John's forces. Both sides constructed extensive trench systems and fortifications, with the crusaders having lines of both contravallation and circumvallation. Conrad was able to get past the Saracen fleet and deliver vital supplies to Guy.

Utilizing these supplies, during the winter of 1189 the Christians built three large siege towers and moved them against the city walls on May 1, 1190. On May 11, however, Saladin launched an attack on the Christian siege lines. The fighting was intense, and Saladin's attacks forced the crusaders to fight on both fronts, allowing the defenders of Acre to burn the siege towers.

During the summer of 1190 more Christian reinforcements arrived, chiefly from France. The most important figure among them was Henry of Troyes, count of Champagne, who took command of siege operations. In October the remaining Germans of Holy Roman emperor Frederick Barbarossa's forces arrived. The besieging crusaders now constructed both rams and trebuchets for another assault on Acre, but the defenders employed incendiary devices to destroy these siege engines and beat back several major Christian assaults.

In November the crusaders succeeded in opening a land supply route, although Saladin was able that winter to close it off again and isolate the crusaders. The winter of 1190–1191 was especially severe and hard on the crusaders, who also suffered extensively from disease and famine. Among the victims were Guy's wife Sybelle and their daughters. The Christians would have broken off the siege had it not been for the hope of English and French reinforcements in the spring.

As promised, additional Christian manpower, ships, supplies, and funds arrived on April 20, 1191, under French king Philip II Augustus and on June 8 under English king Richard I (the Lionheart). These created a new sense of hope and enthusiasm among the crusaders. With the additional warships, the crusaders were at last able to cut off Acre entirely from the seaborne resupply. They also constructed a great many trebuchets and other artillery pieces as well as a large siege tower, then concentrated their attacks on one tower, known as The Accused.

With Acre in dire straits, on July 3 Saladin attempted to draw off the crusaders. The attack, led by his nephew, failed. The crusaders opened a number of breaches in the city walls, and although the defenders repulsed three assaults, Acre surrendered on July 12, 1191. The Christian success here helped ensure the survival of a truncated crusader kingdom in the Holy Land for another century.

King Philip II Augustus returned to France, although most of his forces remained behind. Richard was now in sole command of the crusader army. Saladin meanwhile began gathering resources to ransom the Acre garrison and conduct a prisoner exchange. Angered by the exclusion of certain Christian nobles, Richard refused Saladin's first payment and on August 20, believing that Saladin was delaying, ordered 2,700 Muslim prisoners executed. Saladin retaliated in kind, killing Christian prisoners in his own possession.

Acre served as the chief military base for Richard in his effort to reconquer much of the coastal area of Palestine. Departing from there on August 22, he moved southward with fewer than 50,000 men intent on taking Jerusalem. A highly effective leader, Richard imposed considerable discipline on the unruly Christian commanders and their men.

The crusaders moved along the coast by easy marches, resupplied by sea. Saladin paralleled the march inland. Richard dispersed crossbowmen among his force to keep Saladin's horsemen at bay and prevent him from breaking apart the Christian column. He also ordered that the column not be drawn into battle with Saladin's harassing forces.

As the crusaders made their way down the coast, on September 7, 1191, Saladin ambushed them at Arsuf, opening with an attack on Richard's rear guard to try to get the Christians to retaliate so they could be cut off and destroyed. Richard refused battle until Saladin committed a larger force, then turned and mounted a coordinated cavalry charge that destroyed the Muslim force. On Richard's express command, the crusaders did not pursue. In the battle the Muslims suffered some 7,000 casualties against only 700 for the Christians. Saladin never again attempted to engage Richard in pitched battle.

After spending the winter of 1191–1192 at Ascalon, the crusaders resumed their advance on Jerusalem. Saladin initiated a scorched-earth policy and poisoned the wells. The shortage of provisions and always present but growing dissension among the crusader leaders convinced Richard that he would not be able to take Jerusalem without risking the loss of his army, and he withdrew to the coast. Following numerous small engagements in which he distinguished himself militarily, Richard concluded a treaty with Saladin in 1192 that granted special rights and privileges to Christian pilgrims to Jerusalem. Saladin died the next year, ensuring the crusader states a short period of relief.

In 1197 Holy Roman emperor and king of Sicily Henry VI sent a preliminary small German force to the Holy Land. It captured Beirut and other coastal cities in 1198. Henry died in 1197, however, temporarily shelving plans for a larger effort.

The Fourth Crusade (1202–1204)

In 1199 Pope Innocent III appealed for a new crusade to regain Jerusalem. Although the English and French kings did not participate, a crusader force assembled under Theobald III, count of Champagne. Venice agreed to transport 25,000 crusaders to Egypt and maintain them there for three years in exchange for a cash payment and half of the crusader conquests. When Theobald died in 1201, Boniface of Montferrat became the new leader. In a meeting at Hagenau in December 1201, the crusaders decided to proceed to the Holy Land not by way of Egypt but rather via Constantinople.

When the crusaders assembled in the summer of 1202, they were unable to raise the sum promised to Venice and arranged to pay half the original sum in exchange for retaking the Venetian dependency of Zara. The pope condemned this attack on other Christians, but the crusaders captured and sacked Zara, bringing a papal excommunication.

The crusaders then intrigued with Alexius, son of deposed Byzantine emperor Isaac II. Most agreed that in return for a promised large cash payment, they would proceed to Constantinople and overthrow reigning emperor Alexius III. Some, notably Simon de Montfort of England, went on to Palestine instead.

Most of the crusaders now sailed into the Bosporus and set up camp ashore near Constantinople. Meanwhile, the Venetian fleet forced its way into the Golden Horn. On July 17, 1202, the crusaders attacked Constantinople. They were repulsed, but the Venetians captured a portion of the seawall and secured part of the city. That night Alexius III fled; notables released former emperor Isaac II from prison and elected his son Alexius coemperor as Alexius IV. The new Byzantine leaders then attempted to raise the money promised by Alexius IV for a successful military effort.

In January 1204 resentment against both their new rulers and the crusaders produced a revolt in Constantinople led by Alexius Ducas Mourtzouphlos, son-in-law of Alexius III. Isaac II was again imprisoned, and Alexius IV was executed. Alexius Ducas took the imperial throne as Alexius V.

This action, however, gave the crusaders the excuse to take Constantinople. They assaulted the city in early April 1204. Although the defenders, especially the Varangian Guard, fought well, catapults on the Venetian ships hurled incendiaries into the city, starting a major conflagration and causing the defenders to lose heart. After taking the city, the crusaders subjected it to rape and pillage. Many scholars believe that this first successful assault of Constantinople effectively signaled the end of the Byzantine Empire. Although it would continue in existence for another two centuries, the Byzantine Empire never really recovered from this blow inflicted by fellow Christians.

The empire's territory was now divided between Venice and the crusader leaders, with the establishment of the Latin Empire of Constantinople. On April 14, 1205, however, in the Battle of Adrianople, Tsar Kaloyan of Bulgaria ambushed a Latin crusader army under new Latin emperor Baldwin I of Flanders. Kaloyan's Cuman allies feigned an attack on the crusader camp and then withdrew. The crusaders foolishly pursued the Cumans some distance, only to be ambushed by the main Bulgarian force. In the fighting the Bulgarians killed some 300 crusader knights. Baldwin was taken prisoner and then blinded. He died in captivity. The Bulgarians overran much of Thrace and Macedonia.

The Children's Crusade (1212)

The Children's Crusade is the name given to events said to be a crusade in 1212. These are probably largely apocryphal, but some people came to believe that only innocence could reclaim the Holy Land. Reportedly in 1212 a German boy by the name of Nicholas claimed that God had commissioned him to lead a crusade of children to the Holy Land, where they would peacefully convert the Muslims. The story has it that some 30,000 children, many of them girls in boy's clothing proceeded southward and found their way over the Alps, with many perishing en route. The survivors reached Genoa, where Pope Innocent III told them to go home but reminded them that since they had taken the oath, they would have to go to the Holy Land later. At the same time, a 12-year-old shepherd named Stephen went to King Philippe II Augustus and told him the same story. The king told Stephen to go home, but Stephen persisted, and some 20,000 children followed him to Marseille, where some ship captains promised to take the children to the Holy Land. Two of the ships are said to have been wrecked off Sardinia, but the other five proceeded to Tunis, where the children were sold into slavery.

A number of historians of the crusades have cast doubt on all of this, pointing out that these were likely not mostly children but rather wandering poor peasants in France and Germany, swept up in the age of faith and with only some seeking to go to the Holy Land.

The Fifth Crusade (1218–1221)

Pope Innocent III urged a new military effort in the Holy Land, insisting that it proceed by way of Egypt. To win the support of the pope against his rival Holy Roman emperor Otto IV, Frederick II—king of Germany, Italy, and Burgundy—agreed to lead it. In 1218 the crusaders proceeded to Acre, where they joined contingents from Christian states in the Holy Land under John of Brienne, king of Jerusalem. They landed near Damietta, and while a Genoese fleet defeated an Egyptian fleet, the crusaders laid siege to the city, capturing it after a year and a half in November 1219. The crusaders rejected Egyptian peace offers, waiting for more than a year for the arrival of additional forces under Frederick II. He never appeared, but reinforcements finally arrived in early 1221.

Ultimately the crusaders fielded some 46,000 men, including 10,000 cavalry. Egyptian sultan Malik al-Kamil had some 70,000 men. In June 1221 papal legate Cardinal Pelagius, who had insisted on taking command, ordered a crusader march on Cairo, which proceeded under difficult conditions. Al-Kamil offered to cede Jerusalem and other locations in the Holy Land in return for the crusader evacuation of Damietta. John urged acceptance, but Pelagius chose to reject the offer, insisting on an indemnity and other additional concessions. The crusaders then resumed their march but were repulsed in their attempt to cross the Ashmoun Canal.

At the same time, an Egyptian fleet cut off the crusaders from their base at Damietta. Facing starvation, Pelagius agreed to a face-saving arrangement whereby the crusaders would evacuate Damietta in return for safe passage home and some religious relics. The Fifth Crusade was a complete failure.

The Sixth Crusade (1228–1229)

Holy Roman emperor Frederick II, under considerable pressure from Pope Gregory IX because of his failure to deliver on his promise to lead the Fifth Crusade, sailed from Sicily with a crusader force in 1227. Once at sea, however, Frederick and many of the crusaders fell ill with a fever, and the expedition returned to port. With relations already strained and assuming that this was simply a ploy to delay, Pope Gregory excommunicated Frederick.

Frederick II set out again in 1228, but Gregory reiterated the excommunication. He also declared Frederick's lands in southern Italy forfeit and proclaimed a crusade against them. Mercenaries in the pay of Gregory then invaded and devastated Apulia.

In the Holy Land, Frederick discovered that the other crusaders would not cooperate with him because of the excommunication. Frederick nonetheless opened talks with Sultan al-Kamil and, through astute diplomacy, secured the cession of Jerusalem, Nazareth, and Bethlehem and a corridor connecting Jerusalem to the coast. Traveling to Jerusalem, Frederick crowned himself its king on February 18, 1229. Returning to Italy, he drove out the papal forces from southern Italy in May and made peace with Pope Gregory that August. Despite the lack of fighting in the Sixth Crusade, Frederick II was more successful than any other crusader except Godfrey de Bouillon in the First Crusade.

The Seventh Crusade (1248–1254)

The Seventh Crusade was sparked by the destruction of Jerusalem by the Khwarezmians in 1244. Endeavoring to escape the Mongols, who had taken their territory, the Khwarezmians took Jerusalem from the crusaders, sacked the city, and left it in ruins. The Khwarezmians then allied with Egypt against the crusaders, who themselves allied with the emir of Damascus. The two sides met in battle at Gaza later that same year, and the Khwarezmians and Egyptians were victorious, with Mamluk leader Baybars (Baibars) playing an important role.

King Louis IX of France (later canonized as Saint Louis) led the Seventh Crusade, departing France in 1248 with 1,800 ships carrying 60,000 troops (20,000 of them cavalry). After spending the winter in Cyprus, he occupied Damietta in Egypt in June 1249.

Not wishing to repeat the error of the Fifth Crusade by advancing on Cairo in summer, Louis delayed until autumn, which gave Sultan Malik al-Salih time to prepare. The crusaders set out in November but advanced slowly and, as in the Fifth Crusade, were halted at the Ashmoun Canal by an Egyptian force commanded by Fakr-ed-din of perhaps 70,000 men centered on 10,000 Mamluks.

During December 1249–January 1250 the crusaders attempted to construct a causeway across the Ashmoun Canal to enable them to continue their drive on Cairo, but the Egyptians responded by widening the waterway at that point from the opposite bank. After locating a ford near the causeway, Louis IX finally got his cavalry across, surprised the Egyptians, and won the Battle of Mansurah (February 8–11, 1250). Emir Fakr-ed-din was among those killed.

The battle might have been decisive in favor of the crusaders, but Robert of Artois threw away the possibility.

Instructed to seize the canal bank and hold it for the main body of cavalry and the infantry, he instead chose to pursue the fleeing Egyptians into Mansurah. In street fighting there, the Egyptians were able to offset the impact of the crusader heavy cavalry and almost annihilated Robert's force. Louis was saved only because the French infantry was able to cross to the opposite bank by means of a hastily constructed bridge from the end of the causeway.

On February 11 the crusaders withstood a large Egyptian attack against the bridgehead. By March, however, the crusader situation was desperate, and Louis ordered a withdrawal. Harassed by the Egyptians, the crusaders were decisively defeated in a pitched battle at Fariskur on April 8, 1250. Most of Louis's army was annihilated, and he was captured. Louis agreed to pay a ransom of 800,000 gold livres and to abandon Damietta. Sending most of the surviving crusaders home, he sailed to Acre. Louis's subsequent efforts in the Holy Land during 1250–1254 ended in failure.

The Eighth Crusade (1270)
The Mongols, led by Hulegu, conquered most of Syria, and the Christian crusaders found themselves caught between the Mongols and Mamluks of Egypt. Although most of the other crusader leaders remained neutral, Bohemund VI of Antioch-Tripoli allied with Hulegu's general Kitbuqa and the Mongols against the Mamluks. The two sides came together in battle at Ayn Jalut near Nazareth on September 3, 1260. The Mamluks won, and Kitbuqa was among the prisoners and was executed.

Baybars subsequently killed Qutuz and established himself as sultan. Although unsuccessful in his subsequent efforts to restore the Abbasid Caliphate in Baghdad, Baybars has been acclaimed as the greatest of the Mamluk sultans and recovered most of the crusader territory in Palestine and Syria.

The Christian reversals prompted King Louis IX of France to again take up the cross in 1270 in the Eighth Crusade. Intrigues by Baybars convinced Louis that he might convert the bey of Tunisia to Christianity, then proceed eastward to Egypt. Charles of Anjou, the new king of Sicily, reluctantly agreed to accompany his brother Louis to North Africa.

Meeting opposition, Louis commenced siege operations against Tunis. However, a plague swept the crusader camp, and Louis was among its victims. Charles then assumed command and negotiated an end to the crusade in return for tribute for both France and himself. Prince Edward of England (later king as Edward I) then arrived, only to find the Eighth Crusade at an end.

The Ninth Crusade (1271–1272)
Edward campaigned in the Holy Land during 1171–1172. With some 1,000 crusaders, he mounted raids in Palestine, one of which reached Nazareth. Edward's forays had no major impact, however.

In 1289 Mamluk sultan Kala'un captured Tripoli from the crusaders, and two years later the final disaster occurred. After some Christian adventurers robbed a Muslim caravan in Syria, killed a number of Muslim merchants, and attacked several towns, Mamluk sultan Khalil demanded satisfaction. Receiving none, he marched against the Christian stronghold of Acre. Laying siege to it, he took Acre after 43 days and allowed his men to massacre or enslave the 60,000 prisoners. Tyre, Haifa, and Beirut soon fell, bringing finis to the crusader kingdoms of the Latin East.

In the two centuries of crusading effort, Muslim civilization had clearly proven superior to Christian civilization in war. While the Crusades in the Holy Land had failed in their religious purpose of securing that territory for Christianity, they nonetheless had major and far-reaching impacts. They had, for example, helped delay the capture by the Turks of Constantinople. The Crusades also had a major role in bringing about the end of medieval Europe. Many knights had sold or mortgaged properties to take part in the Crusades, while peasants had secured remission of feudal dues and obligations. Serfs who participated had been able to leave the land, and many failed to return there afterward.

The coming together of two civilizations had a profound impact on both. Muslims, once tolerant of religious diversity, were made intolerant by the Crusades, while the Christians discovered that another civilization could be as refined as their own. This certainly helped weaken the hold of the Catholic Church on the faithful. Certainly the power of the Catholic Church, enhanced by the First Crusade, was greatly diminished by those that followed.

Arabic words and Arabic science came to the West, as did probably the reintroduction of public baths and private latrines and a revival of the Roman custom of shaving the beard. Gunpowder, the compass, and printing were all known in the East and may have come to the West as a consequence of the Crusades. Certainly the crusaders brought back to Europe with them advanced glass-making techniques that would find their way into the stained glass of many Gothic cathedrals.

The Crusades brought home to Europeans the vastness of the world and the opportunities posed for trade. This led to the voyages of discovery and exploration. The crusaders may have lost the Holy Land, but the Italian cities greatly benefited from significantly increased trade in the eastern Mediterranean. This in turn influenced banking and produced the wealth that made possible the Renaissance.

SPENCER C. TUCKER

See also
Abbasid Caliphate; Acre, 1189 Siege of; Acre, 1291 Siege of; Al-Afdal; Alexios I Komnenos; Antioch, Sieges of; Arsuf, Battle of; Ascalon, Battle of; Ayn Jalut, Battle of; Baldwin I of Jerusalem; Baldwin II of Constantinople; Baldwin II of Jerusalem; Baldwin III of Jerusalem; Baldwin IV of Jerusalem; Baybars I; Bohemund I of Antioch; Bohemund VI of Antioch-Tripoli; Conrad III, King of Germany; Dorylaion, Battle of; Edward I, King of England; Frederick I or Frederick Barbarossa; Gaza, Battle of; Godfrey of Bouillon; Guy of Lusignan; Hattin, Battle of; Jerusalem, Crusader Siege of; Karbugha; Louis VII, King of France; Louis IX, King of France; Maliki, Nuri Muhammed Kamil al-; Mansurah, Battle of; Pelagius of Albano; Peter the Hermit; Philippe II, King; Ramla, First Battle of; Ramla, Second Battle of; Richard I, King; Saladin; Seljuk Dynasty

References
Asbridge, Thomas. *The Crusades: The Authoritative History of the War for the Holy Land*. New York: Ecco, 2010.
Asbridge, Thomas. *The First Crusade: A New History; The Roots of Conflict between Christianity and Islam*. New York: Oxford University Press, 2005.
Findley, Carter Vaughan. *The Turks in World History*. New York: Oxford University Press, 2005.
Hillenbrand, Carole. *The Crusades: Islamic Perspectives*. Edinburgh, UK: Edinburgh University Press, 1999.
Hindley, Geoffrey. *A Brief History of the Crusades*. New York: Constable and Robinson, 2013.
Hindley, Geoffrey. *The Crusades: Islam and Christianity in the Struggle for World Supremacy*. New York: Carroll and Graf, 2004.
Hindley, Geoffrey. *Saladin: Hero of Islam*. Barnsley, South Yorkshire, UK: Pen and Sword Military, 2007.
Jackson, Peter. *The Seventh Crusade, 1244–1254: Sources and Documents*. Burlington, VT: Ashgate, 2007.
Madden, Thomas F. *The New Concise History of the Crusades*. Lanham, MD: Rowman and Littlefield, 2005.
Mayer, Hans Eberhard. *The Crusades*. 2nd ed. Oxford: Oxford University Press, 1988.
Nicolle, David. *The First Crusade, 1066–99: Conquest of the Holy Land*. New York: Osprey, 2003.
Nicolle, David. *The Fourth Crusade, 1202–04: The Betrayal of Byzantium*. New York: Osprey, 2011.
Phillips, Jonathan. *Holy Warriors: A Modern History of the Crusades*. New York: Random House, 2010.
Riley-Smith, Jonathan. *The Crusades: A Short History*. 2nd ed. New Haven, CT: Yale University Press, 2005.
Riley-Smith, Jonathan. *The First Crusaders, 1096–1131*. New York: Cambridge University Press, 1997.
Riley-Smith, Jonathan. *The Oxford History of the Crusades*. New York: Oxford University Press, 2002.
Runciman, Steven. *A History of the Crusades: The Kingdom of Acre and the Later Crusades*. 1951; reprint, New York: Cambridge University Press, 1977.
Tyerman, Christopher. *God's War: A New History of the Crusades*. Cambridge, MA: Belknap, 2006.

Ctesiphon, 363 Battle of (May 29, 363)

Important battle fought between Roman Empire forces led by Emperor Julian (r. 361–363) and those of the Sassanid Persian Empire led by Spahbod Merena. Invading Sassanid territory with a sizable land force and fleet, Emperor Julian advanced down the Euphrates to destroy Pirisabora and Maiozamalcha, then moved east against the Persian capital of Ctesiphon on the Tigris. For Persian king Shapur II the Great (r. 309–379), having ordered a scorched-earth policy and withdrawal, there were few engagements en route.

In late May the Romans reached the vicinity of Ctesiphon, although a large part of the army closing from another direction had not yet arrived. Nonetheless, Julian had his troops ferried across the Tigris by night. On May 29, 363, the army was formed up before the gates of the city facing the Persian army. Sources vary, but the Romans probably had something on the order of 65,000 men. The Persians had more men, along with war elephants. Although some of his subordinate commanders reportedly expressed reservations about engaging the larger and apparently well-organized Persian force so far from home, Julian did not.

Julian formed his army in a great crescent, which closed on the Persians from the two wings. Surprisingly, the battle was over quickly and resulted in a great Roman victory that forced the Persians to withdraw into Ctesiphon. Reportedly the Romans lost only 70 men to some 2,500 for the Persians. The triumph proved hollow, however. Julian lacked the equipment to lay siege to heavily fortified Ctesiphon, and Shapur was quickly closing with the principal Sassanid army, which was far larger than the army just defeated. Also critical were the failure of Julian's subordinate Procopius to arrive with his 30,000-man detachment and the fact that supplies for the army were dwindling, with little available in the surrounding countryside. Although Julian was in favor of advancing farther into Persian territory, opposition from his subordinates in a council of war on June 16 led to the decision to withdraw northward.

In a fateful decision, Julian burned his fleet. The Romans soon found themselves isolated and outmaneuvered as the Persians harassed them at every turn. In one of these engagements Julian was fatally wounded in the liver with a spear thrust; he died on June 26, 363.

Spencer C. Tucker

See also

Julian, Emperor; Roman-Sassanid Wars; Sassanid Empire; Shapur II the Great

References

Bowder, Diana. *The Age of Constantine and Julian.* New York: Barnes & Noble, 1978.

Bowersock, G. W. *Julian the Apostate.* Cambridge, MA: Harvard University Press, 1978.

Browning, Robert. *The Emperor Julian.* Berkeley: University of California Press, 1976.

Daryaee, Touraj. *Sasanian Iran (224–651 BCE): Portrait of a Late Antique Empire.* Costa Mesa, CA: Mazda Publishers, 2008.

Murdoch, Adrian. *The Last Pagan: Julian the Apostate and the Death of the Ancient World.* Rochester, VT: Inner Traditions, 2008.

Ctesiphon, 1915 Battle of (November 22–25, 1915)

World War I British victory over Ottoman forces in Mesopotamia. The Battle of Es Sinn (September 26–28, 1915) had left the British in control of Kut. Ottoman general Nur al-Din's defeated the Sixth Army, then withdrew to Ctesiphon, only 20 miles from Baghdad. There Nur al-Din received reinforcements, including the veteran 51st Division, and established a strong defensive position.

British forces in the area were centered on the 6th Poona Division of the Indian Army, which had been badly depleted by fighting, heat, and sickness during the summer campaign. Its commander, Major General Charles V. F. Townshend, had misgivings about continuing the offensive. British commander in Mesopotamia General John E. Nixon, however, was determined to take Baghdad, one of the four major cities of Islam, and ordered Townshend to continue the advance. The Indian government supported this decision, while the British government in London appeared largely unconcerned about events in Mesopotamia.

Seven weeks passed before Townshend had accumulated sufficient supplies at Kut to permit an advance, which began on November 11. Townshend was short of transport, however, and was dependent largely on shallow-draft riverboats. Townshend's flotilla included a new river monitor and several gunboats, but he did not have sufficient other craft to move all his troops and supplies. Daytime temperatures were moderate, making the march easier on Townshend's infantry, but the nights were freezing cold. With attached troops, Townshend had around 11,000 men. The British force arrived near Ctesiphon and was ready for battle on November 22.

Nur al-Din commanded some 18,000 men and 52 artillery pieces. Ottoman forces were established in strong positions, their trenches well camouflaged and nearly invisible to the attacking British. One trench line was located two miles east of a ruined arch, while the second position was a mile west. Both lines had been strengthened with redoubts. While the Ottomans were entrenched on both sides of the Tigris River, most of Nur al-Din's troops were on the northern side. The ground in front of the trench line on the southern bank was nearly impassable to an attacking force. Townshend's gunboats were also not able to provide support, as a sunken obstacle and Ottoman guns along the Tigris kept them from advancing to Ctesiphon.

Lacking sufficient manpower to attack on both sides of the river, Townshend decided to concentrate on the stronger Ottoman left on the north bank. He now decided to use a variation of his successful plan at Kut. Townshend divided most of his infantry into three columns; two were to make fixing attacks against the defenders, while the third would then break through and roll up the Ottoman trenches. Townshend's cavalry with attached infantry would outflank the Ottomans on their left. Creating havoc in the rear areas, the cavalry would then follow up by occupying Baghdad. This plan depended on coordination and good luck, both of which failed to materialize.

On November 22 the first British column attacked late at 8:00 a.m., and the soldiers quickly went to the ground when fire from the concealed Ottoman trenches swept through their ranks. The second column also sustained heavy casualties but was able to overrun the first line of trenches. The final column lagged behind but was able to break through as well. The men in two of the British columns believed that the entire first line of trenches had collapsed, so they pushed on toward their second objective. While the defenders were shaken, they were not ready to concede the battle. Holding their positions, they inflicted heavy casualties on the attackers, and the British did not take the entire first trench line until near the end of the day.

Meanwhile, the British cavalry failed to move far enough north, and when they turned east they ran into both Ottoman infantry and cavalry. Retreating behind the rightmost British infantry column, the cavalry contributed little to the course of the battle.

At dusk Townshend put an end to the attacks and reorganized his men. He lacked the reserves to continue and hoped that the Ottomans would withdraw during the night. Instead, they remained in place and even counterattacked the next day. Only halfhearted, their attack achieved nothing. Early on November 24 the Ottomans did begin a withdrawal on a false report of British reinforcements, but when Nur al-Din learned of his error the Ottomans returned ready to fight. Townshend meanwhile ordered a retreat. He had suffered 4,500 men killed or wounded; Nur al-Din had sustained more than 9,600 casualties.

The Ottomans and local Arabs closely followed and harassed the British withdrawal. Three of the supporting British gunboats were also lost, grounding in the Tigris. After a grueling week, Townshend's command returned to Kut on December 3. By then, Townshend surmised that his exhausted troops could go no farther. He sent his cavalry and wounded away along with his boats, expelled many of the inhabitants of Kut, and prepared for an Ottoman siege.

Tim J. Watts

See also
Kut al-Amara, Siege of; Mesopotamian Theater, World War I; Nixon, Sir John Eccles; Townshend, Sir Charles Vere Ferrers

References
Barker, A. J. *The Bastard War: The Mesopotamian Campaign of 1914–1918.* New York: Dial, 1967.
Davis, Paul K. *Ends and Means: The British Mesopotamian Campaign and Commission.* Toronto: Associated University Presses, 1994.
Erickson, Edward J. *Ordered to Die: A History of the Ottoman Army in the First World War.* Westport, CT: Greenwood, 2000.
Townshend, Charles. *Desert Hell: The British Invasion of Mesopotamia.* Cambridge, MA: Belknap Press of Harvard University Press, 2011.

Cunaxa, Battle of (401 BCE)

The Battle of Cunaxa (probably modern-day Tell-al-Kenisa, approximately 28 miles north of Babylon) was fought in the late summer of 401 BCE between the armies of Artaxerxes, King of Persia, and his younger brother Cyrus.

Cyrus, advancing from the north, placed some 12,900 Greek mercenaries on his right flank and took up the center position next to the Greeks with his personal regiment of 600 cavalry. His 100,000 Asiatic infantry, 20 scythed chariots, and the rest of his 3,000 cavalry were on his left. Artaxerxes had some 6,000 cavalry and 150 scythed chariots. Reports of the size of his infantry vary, reflecting the usual Greek difficulty with such large numbers, from 400,000 to 900,000. In any case, the forces of Artaxerxes far outnumbered those of Cyrus. Cyrus relied on his Greek infantry to break their opponents. Immediately before the armies engaged he ordered them to move obliquely to their left, apparently to attack Artaxerxes, who was stationed in the center of his army and was thus outside the Greeks' direct line of attack.

Cyrus's order was not carried out. The Greek charge cleared away the troops opposite them, and in their advance they lost contact with Cyrus. Cyrus himself made a brave but ill-judged attempt to strike at Artaxerxes with his 600 cavalry, wounding his brother before himself being cut down and killed. At his death his Asiatic army gave up. Artaxerxes's right wing attacked Cyrus's encampment to the rear of the army but was beaten off from the Greek section by the guards stationed there. The Greeks, who had pursued their defeated opponents for some three miles, returned to find themselves isolated.

The Battle of Cunaxa again demonstrated the superiority of Greek hoplites against Persian infantry. This and the success of Greek mercenaries in fighting their way home (their epic journey is recorded in Xenophon's *Anabasis*) led to renewed Greek military activity against the Persians, beginning with Agesilaus II of Sparta and culminating in Alexander III the Great's conquest of the Persian Empire.

Douglas Kelly

See also
Achaemenid Empire; Artaxerxes II; Cyrus the Younger; Xenophon

References
Anderson, John, K. *Xenophon.* London: Duckworth, 1974.
Prevas, John. *Xenophon's March into the Lair of the Persian Lion.* Cambridge MA: Da Capo, 2002.

Cunningham, Sir Alan Gordon (1887–1983)

British Army general and last British high commissioner in Palestine (1945–1948). Born in Dublin, Ireland, on May 1, 1887, Alan Cunningham was the younger brother of future British admiral of the fleet Andrew Browne Cunningham. The younger Cunningham graduated from the Royal Military College, Sandhurst, in 1906 and was commissioned in the army. He served with distinction in the artillery in France during World War I, then was a staff officer at the Straits Settlements during 1919–1921. Promoted to brigadier general, he commanded the 1st Division of the Royal Artillery from December 1937 until September 1938, when he assumed command of the 5th Antiaircraft Division.

During 1940, Cunningham commanded three infantry divisions in succession in Britain. In October 1940 he assumed command of British forces in Kenya, and in January and February 1941 he led three divisions in the conquest of Italian Somalia (Somaliland). He then rapidly advanced into Ethiopia and, in cooperation with General William Platt's forces from the Sudan, forced the surrender of the remaining Italian forces in Italian East Africa. Cunningham then took command of the British Eighth Army in Egypt in September 1941.

Two months later in November 1941, the Eighth Army began Operation CRUSADER, which was designed to relieve the siege of Tobruk. Having had little time to prepare, Cunningham was outmaneuvered by Afrika Korps commander General Erwin Rommel at Sidi Razagh, near Tobruk. In the resulting Battle of Totensonntag, the Eighth Army sustained heavy losses, and General Sir Claude J. A. Auchinleck relieved Cunningham of his command at the end of the month. Cunningham then commanded the Staff College, Camberley (1942–1943); was general officer commanding Northern Ireland (1943–1944); and headed the Eastern Command (1944–1945).

In the fall of 1945, Cunningham was promoted to full general and appointed the British high commissioner for Palestine. While he himself was not hostile to the Jews there, British Palestinian policy was decided in London rather than in Jerusalem. Cunningham's principal task was to keep order in the mandate during the sessions there of the Anglo-American Committee of Inquiry and the United Nations Special Commission on Palestine. Cunningham had his hands full in the face of Jewish opposition to British policy, illegal immigration by Jews into Palestine, and acts of terror and sabotage by Arabs against Jews and by Jewish militant organizations against the Arabs and British.

Cunningham endeavored to enforce British immigration policy and to oust the Jewish Agency from control. His policy included mass arrests of Jewish leaders in June 1946. In January 1947 London granted Cunningham authority to proclaim martial law in any part of the mandate he saw fit, but British military resources were not sufficient to halt the growing violence between Arabs and Jews, and Cunningham was able to maintain security only in British enclaves and main lines of communication. On May 8, 1948, he was able to secure a truce between the two sides in Jerusalem. A week later, on May 14, the State of Israel was proclaimed, and the same day Cunningham departed the country from Haifa. Knighted on his return to Britain, he died on January 30, 1983.

SPENCER C. TUCKER

See also
Anglo-American Committee of Inquiry; United Nations Special Commission on Palestine

References
Barnett, Correlli. *The Desert Generals.* New York: Viking, 1961.
Sachar, Howard M. *A History of Israel: From the Rise of Zionism to Our Time.* 3rd ed. New York: Knopf, 2007.
Sherman, A. J. *Mandate Days: British Lives in Palestine, 1918–1948.* Baltimore: Johns Hopkins University Press, 2001.

Cyprus

The island of Cyprus is both the third-largest and third most populous Mediterranean island. Situated in the eastern Mediterranean Sea, it is about 40 miles south of Turkey and 60 miles west of Syria. Because of its location, Cyprus is considered part of the Middle East. Inhabited by both Greeks and Turks, Cyprus covers a landmass of 3,572 square miles. Its 2018 population was some 1,175,000. Greeks constitute some 77 percent of the total, Turks account for 18 percent, and others make up 5 percent.

Archaeological remains date human activity on Cyprus to around 9000 BCE, but the early Bronze Age saw significant immigration from Asia Minor to the island and the development of cities. Cyprus was blessed with rich deposits of copper, and the Bronze Age was a period of prosperity for the island. Indeed, it has been suggested that the name of the island is derived from the Sumerian word for copper (*zubar*) or for bronze (*kubar*). Cyprus was also an important trading entrepôt, with archaeological remains identifying trading partners as Egypt, Phoenicia, Syria, Crete, and much of the Greek world.

The Phoenicians arrived in the ninth century, although the island retained its Greek character. Indeed, 8 of the 10 kings of the island in the seventh century BCE bear Greek names, despite this being a period of Assyrians domination. It is unclear whether the Assyrians actually conquered the island, however.

By the sixth century BCE the Egyptians had gained domination, and in 545 the island was conquered by the Persians under Cambyses II. It was then combined with Syria and Palestine to form the fifth satrapy of the Achaemenid (First Persian) Empire. Despite this, the island's monarchies seem to have survived, retaining a degree of autonomy and prosperity within the Persian satrapal system.

All of the Cyprian kingdoms—with the notable exception of Amathus—joined with the Greeks and rebelled against Persia during the Ionian Revolt (499–493 BCE). The

Cyprus

rebellion was swiftly and decisively crushed by Persia but had a long-lasting impact on the social fabric of the island, reinforcing the Hellenism of its inhabitants and leaders. After the Persian Wars, Cyprus was briefly freed by Athenian statesman and general Cimon.

Much of the fifth century was spent with Athens and Persia fighting for control over the island. In 411 Evagoras, king of Salamis, swept the Persians from the island and promoted Greek culture, language, and art at the expense of Phoenician influences. This Hellenism did not survive Evagoras, who was defeated in 380 and then assassinated in 374 in a court intrigue.

The struggle for independence from Persia lasted until Alexander the Great's victory over the Persians at the Battle of Issus in 333 BCE. The Cypriot fleet then assisted Alexander in his siege of Tyre in 332. In 294 the island became part of Ptolemaic Egypt under Ptolemy I Sotar before being annexed by the Romans in 58. Julius Caesar restored Cyprus to Egypt between 46 and 44, but the island passed back under Roman control when Egypt was annexed to Rome in 30 BCE.

With the division of the Roman Empire in 395 CE, Cyprus became part of the Eastern Roman or Byzantine Empire. Byzantine rule ensured a strengthening of the Greek orientation on the island. Beginning in 649 and continuing for some three centuries, Cyprus was subjected to devastating Muslim raids. Thousands of Cypriots perished in the raids, and much of the island's wealth was carried off. Byzantine rule was firmly restored in 965.

In 1191 during the Third Christian Crusade, King Richard I the Lionheart of England captured the island. It then survived as a Christian supply base. A year later, however,

Richard sold Cyprus to the Knights Templar who, after a bloody revolt, sold it to a French nobleman, Guy of Lusignan. James II, the last Lusignan king of Cyprus, died in 1473, and the Republic of Venice assumed control of the island, which it formally annexed in 1489. The Venetians heavily fortified Nicosia, which became an important commercial center for their eastern trade.

The Ottoman Turks frequently raided Cyprus during the period of Venetian rule, however. In 1570 during the Venetian-Ottoman War (1570–1573), the Ottomans mounted a full-scale invasion of the island with a force said to have numbered between 85,000 and 150,000 men and conquered it the next year, despite strong Cypriot resistance. Many islanders were massacred, and in the first major demographic change since antiquity, the Ottomans established a strong Muslim Turkic community on the island, settling there soldiers who had taken part in the conquest along with craftsmen and peasants from Anatolia. The Ottoman government also ordered the transport to Cyprus of a number of its citizens it deemed "undesirable."

After three centuries of their rule, the Ottomans ceded Cyprus to Britain in 1878 in return for British support against Russia. The British formally annexed the island outright in 1914, and in 1925 it became a crown colony. Until 1960, Cyprus was under British rule. The island served as an important strategic base for defense of the Suez Canal in both World War I and World War II. During the Cold War the West used Cyprus to monitor Soviet activities in the Middle East, and Britain launched its 1956 abortive Suez invasion from here.

Greece and Turkey had long been bitter adversaries, and following World War I and the breakup of the Ottoman Empire, the Greeks sought to secure control of Smyrna (modern-day Izmir), the sizable part of western Anatolia that had been home to a large Greek population since ancient times. Although Greece had been late to join the Allied side in World War I and then only under considerable pressure, the Western Allies, particularly the British government of prime minister David Lloyd George, had promised the new Greek government territorial gains at the expense of the Ottoman Empire.

The ensuing Greco-Turkish War (War of Turkish Independence, 1919–1922) saw Greek forces land in Smyrna and take control of the western and northwestern parts of Anatolia as well as eastern Thrace. As it turned out, however, the Turkish forces were far better led, organized, and motivated and halted the Greek advance, then took the offensive and won the war. The Greeks were forced to evacuate all Turkish territory and return to its prewar borders. A major relocation of populations followed.

The outcome of the Greco-Turkish War did not affect the status of Cyprus but did add impetus for the Greek demand for enosis (union) of the island with Greece, which developed among the majority Greek population of Cyprus and came to a head following the end of World War II. The sizable minority Turkish population on the island vowed to resist any such step and in this had the strong support of the Turkish government. At first Greek agitation was aimed at ending British control. Greek Orthodox archbishop Makarios III became the leader in this effort, condoning terrorism and reprisals against the British.

Greek general Georgios Grivas led the actual terrorist campaign to expel the British. Born in Cyprus, Grivas had fought in the defense of Greece following the 1940 Italian invasion and during the subsequent German invasion and occupation established his own guerrilla group, named X. After the end of the Axis occupation in 1944 the group was disbanded, and Grivas rejoined the regular army, seeing duty during the civil war against the communists from 1946 to 1949.

Following the Greek Army victory over the communists, Grivas had several meetings with Makarios to advance the cause of enosis. In November 1954 Grivas returned to Cyprus and fomented a violent campaign against the British occupation of the island. Taking the name Dighenis, a legendary Byzantine hero, he organized the National Organization of Cypriot Fighters (EOKA) with direct military support from Greece. EOKA's terrorist campaign commenced on April 1, 1955, and reached its climax in 1956 when British authorities exiled Makarios to the Seychelles Islands in the Indian Ocean.

Negotiations in 1955 among Britain, Greece, and Turkey broke down completely, abetted by the Turkish government's demands that Cyprus be partitioned. A total of 504 people were killed in the EOKA campaign, including 142 Britons and 84 Turks. At the same time, Turks on the island called for partition and toward that end formed the Turkish Resistance Organization (TMT). The British encouraged the TMT as part of a divide-and-rule effort.

The British government eventually concluded, albeit reluctantly, that Cyprus should become independent, and Prime Minister Harold MacMillan called for negotiations on the matter. On February 11, 1959, Greece and Turkey reached agreement at Zurich on a plan for the independence of Cyprus. On February 19 following a conference at Lancaster House in London, the British government reached final agreement regarding independence in talks with the

British soldiers in front of a barbed-wire barricade during an imposed curfew in Nicosia, Cyprus, in 1956. (Hulton-Deutsch Collection/Corbis via Getty Images)

governments of Greece and Turkey as well as Archbishop Makarios, recalled from exile, for the Greek Cypriot community, and Dr. Fazil Küçük, representing the Turkish Cypriots.

Following the Zurich and London agreements, Grivas ordered a cease-fire on March 13. A constitution for Cyprus was drafted and agreed to, and the Republic of Cyprus became independent on August 16, 1960, as a member of the British Commonwealth of Nations. The British retained two military bases on Cyprus but had no executive authority. Greek and Turkish troops on Cyprus were reduced to token forces of only a few hundred men. Britain, Greece, and Turkey all retained limited rights to intervene in Cypriot affairs in order to guarantee the basic rights of both ethnic communities there.

The constitution for the new state contained a power-sharing arrangement. It provided for a Greek Cypriot president elected for a five-year term by the ethnic Greeks, a Turkish Cypriot vice president elected for a similar term by the Turks on the island, and a parliament to reflect the island's 80-20 ethnic split, with each community electing its own representatives. The Council of Ministers consisted of 10 members, 3 of whom had to be Turks. The House of Representatives could not modify the constitution in any respect insofar as it concerned its basic articles, and any other modification required a majority of two-thirds of both the Greek Cypriot and the Turkish Cypriot members. To protect the Turkish minority, the vice president was vested with veto power over any legislation vitally affecting interests of the Turkish population.

Elected the first president of the Republic of Cyprus, Archbishop Makarios took office on August 16, 1960. On September 20, the island state became a member of the United Nations (UN). Independence only meant the beginning of a new phase of violence on the troubled island, however. In 1962 and 1963, Greek and Turkish leaders held a series of meetings but were unable to resolve their differences in matters of taxation, municipal councils, and local government. In 1963, the Green Line was established in the capital city of Nicosia to separate the two ethnic communities.

In November 1963, Makarios proposed a series of constitutional amendments designed to restrict the rights of the Turkish community. Understandably, Turkish Cypriots opposed these changes, and consequently, widespread intercommunal fighting began on December 21, 1963. This ushered in the most violent phase of the Cypriot conflict, with hundreds of casualties on each side. Turkish participation in the central Cypriot government also came to an end.

Makarios rejected mediation efforts by Britain and the United States, and on March 4, 1964, the UN Security Council authorized Secretary-General U Thant to establish a peace force and appoint a mediator. Despite the presence of this UN force, Greeks attacked Turkish villages. In response, during August 7–9, 1964, the Turkish Air Force strafed Greek Cypriot positions. With the situation spiraling out of control and Greece and Turkey on the brink of war, the UN was able to secure a cease-fire on August 9.

Although the Turkish parliament voted in 1964 in favor of occupying Cyprus, Turkey was unable to secure support for this from either the UN or the North Atlantic Treaty Organization (NATO). Indeed, U.S. president Lyndon B. Johnson warned Turkish premier Ismet Inönü that his country would resist any Turkish occupation. Turkey did not make good on its threat.

In March 1964 the UN Security Council established the UN Peacekeeping Force in Cyprus (UNFICYP) to ward off potential trouble, although fighting continued between the Greeks and Turks. The Turks then formed their own Turkish Cypriot provisional administration. Unhappy over the situation of its countrymen in Cyprus, in August 1966 the Turkish government again threatened military intervention. Following an appeal by U Thant, Makarios relaxed restrictions imposed on the Turkish minority. Another round of intercommunal violence began in November 1967, however, when Makarios attempted to eliminate the veto power vested in the Turkish vice president. War between Greece and Turkey was only narrowly averted by pressure brought by the United States on both countries.

The Greek Army had seized power in Athens in April 1967. With strong U.S. public opposition to providing military assistance to the Greek junta, the Greek generals authorized Grivas to return to Cyprus in 1971 and resume terrorist activities there. The implication was clear: if the United States refused aid to the junta, there would be no peace on Cyprus and new problems for the North Atlantic Treaty Organization (NATO). Washington found itself caught in a dilemma. The junta was a dictatorship, but Greece was of considerable importance to NATO and to the security of the eastern Mediterranean.

Makarios meanwhile shifted from supporting enosis to becoming a Cypriot nationalist. Winning reelection to the presidency in February 1974, he was increasing reconciled to a Makarios republic. Grivas, who now opposed the Greek junta in Athens and had taken up arms against his former ally, died of heart failure at Limassol, Cyprus, on January 27, 1974. His supporters continued the struggle against Mikarios, however.

On July 15, 1974, the Greek Cypriot National Guard seized power. The ruling Greek junta in Athens had fully supported this step to secure enosis and thereby shore up its fast-diminishing popularity within Greece. The coup ousted Makarios, who fled the island. The new president was proenosis nationalist Nikos Sampson, a former EOKA fighter. Meanwhile Rauf Denktaş, the Turkish Cypriot leader, called for joint military action by the United Kingdom and Turkey in order to prevent the unification of Cyprus with Greece. The British government could not be persuaded to agree, and Ankara decided to act alone.

On July 20, the Turkish government carried out its long-standing threat to intervene in the island. Turkey claimed that this action was completely justified under terms of the agreements establishing an independent Cyprus that gave it the right to protect its compatriots there. This justification, however, has been rejected by both the UN and the international community.

The Turkish Air Force bombed Greek positions in Cyprus, and Turkish paratroopers were dropped into the area between Nicosia and Kyrenia, the site of a number of long-established armed Turkish Cypriot enclaves. Turkish troopships then landed some 6,000 men as well as tanks and other vehicles, and the Turkish forces easily defeated the Greek Cypriot National Guard. By July 23 when a cease-fire had been agreed to, there were 30,000 Turkish troops on the island, and Turkish forces had captured Kyrenia, the corridor linking Kyrenia to Nicosia, and the Turkish Cypriot quarter of Nicosia. The Turkish military intervention also brought the collapse of the proenosis Greek Sampson regime.

The Greek junta in Athens seriously miscalculated both internationally and the situation in Greece itself when it encouraged the Greeks of Cyprus to seize power there. Junta leaders had believed that this event would rally the mainland Greek population behind their rule. Much to the surprise of the generals, there was little enthusiasm in Greece for war with Turkey. Indeed, widespread discontent regarding the previous seven years of ham-fisted junta rule now came to the fore. The junta leadership—shaken and unsure of itself—disavowed the Greeks in Cyprus, a step that further discredited the generals, who were driven from power on July 24, 1974.

In Cyprus meanwhile, Glafkos Clerides assumed the presidency of the Republic of Cyprus government in Nicosia, and constitutional order was restored. This removed the pretext for the Turkish invasion, but following negotiations between the sides in Geneva, the Turkish government reinforced its Kyrenia bridgehead and began a second invasion on August 14, quickly seizing Morphou, Karpass, Famagusta, and the Mesaoria Plain in north-central Cyprus. Although international pressure brought a cease-fire, by then the Turks had seized control of some 37 percent of the island and had evicted some 180,000 Greeks from their homes in the northern part of the island. Some 50,000 Turkish Cypriots moved to the areas under the control of the Turkish forces and took over the properties of the displaced Greek Cypriots. Subsequently, the Turkish government brought in some 20,000 Turks, mainly subsistence farmers from mainland Turkey, to settle and work the underpopulated land. Those who stayed more than five years were granted citizenship in the Turkish Federated State. In the Karpaz region, located on the Turkish side of Cyprus, a Greek-speaking minority remains under UN supervision.

The fighting itself had claimed some 568 Turkish military personnel killed in action. Another 270 Turkish civilians were killed, and 803 were missing. Greek casualties totaled some 1,378 killed an as many as 1,100 missing. Many others on both sides were wounded. The UNFICYP lost 9 killed and 65 wounded.

The U.S. government voiced its displeasure regarding the Turkish action, which had employed U.S.-supplied military equipment. In mid-1975 the U.S. Congress imposed a number of sanctions against Turkey, including an arms embargo. This step badly strained Turkish-U.S. relations. The embargo lasted until 1978, when it was lifted by U.S. president Jimmy Carter.

Since that time the Cyprus situation has remained frozen, with the island divided along a line that runs through the center of the city of Nicosia. Ankara retained some 25,000 troops on the island. With the stalemate continuing, on November 15, 1983, Denktaş, president of the Turkish Cypriot Federal State, unilaterally proclaimed the Turkish portion of the island to be independent as the Turkish Republic of Northern Cyprus. But it was only recognized as a legitimate independent state by Turkey and members of the Organization of the Islamic Conference. The UN has refused to recognize this political entity. Southern Cyprus is governed by the Republic of Cyprus, which the international community recognizes as having jurisdiction over the entire island and its territorial waters. Negotiations occurred, with the Turkish side prepared to cede some territory taken by Turkish forces in Cyprus in return for recognition of the self-proclaimed Turkish state. But the negotiations soon broke down, with the Greek Cypriots and the government in Athens firmly rejecting partition. An uneasy peace prevails, with the two sides kept apart by some 2,000 UN peacekeeping troops in a buffer zone. Britain retains its military bases in southern Cyprus as sovereign British territory.

On February 19, 1978, terrorists claiming to be members of the Palestine Liberation Organization (PLO) killed an Egyptian newspaper editor and took 30 people hostage in Cyprus. Egyptian president Anwar Sadat authorized a commando raid to take out those responsible. The Egyptian commandos killed the terrorists but then ran afoul of the Cypriot National Guard, who killed 15 of the Egyptians and captured others. Egypt responded by breaking off diplomatic relations with Cyprus.

In the period since the Turkish invasion, the northern third of Cyprus has become almost exclusively Turkish while the southern two-thirds is almost exclusively Greek, so the territories are now sometimes referred to as the "Greek part" and the "Turkish part" of Cyprus. Except for occasional demonstrations and infrequent confrontations between border soldiers, few violent conflicts have occurred since 1974. Turkey continued to maintain a significant troop presence in northern Cyprus, although their numbers have been somewhat reduced.

In November 1993 following the election of Cypriot president Glavkos Klerides, Greek Cypriots formed a joint defense pact with Greece. The Turkish Cypriots responded by entering into a joint defense and foreign policy program with Turkey. On January 1, 2004, the Republic of Cyprus was admitted to the European Union.

With Britain having retained its two bases as sovereign territory, on December 3, 2015, Royal Air Force Tornado aircraft carried out their first air strikes in Syria against the Islamic State of Iraq and Syria (ISIS). Taking off from Akrotiri Air Base, the jets struck an oil field in eastern Syria. The raid occurred only hours after British lawmakers had voted in favor of bombing ISIS strongholds there.

Today the Republic of Cyprus is recognized by the international community as having de jure sovereignty over the island of Cyprus and its surrounding waters except for the British Overseas Territory of Akrotiri and Dhekelia, which the British administer as sovereign base areas. However, the Republic of Cyprus remains de facto partitioned into two main parts: the area under the effective control of the republic, comprising some 63 percent of the island's area, and the north, with about 37 percent of the island's area and administered by the self-declared Turkish Republic of Northern Cyprus, which is recognized by the international community as territory of the Republic of Cyprus occupied by Turkish forces.

Despite these circumstances, Cyprus remains a major tourist destination. It also boasts a high-income economy and a very high Human Development Index. On January 1, 2008, the Republic of Cyprus joined the Eurozone.

RUSSELL BUZBY, SEDAT CEM KARADELI, LUCIAN N. LEUSTEAN,
AND SPENCER C. TUCKER

See also
Achaemenid Empire; Alexander III the Great; Caesar, Gaius Julius; Cyprus, Athenian Expedition to; Cyprus, Ottoman Conquest of; Diadochi, Wars of the; Greco-Turkish War; Grivas, Georgios; Ionian Revolt; Issus, Battle of; Makarios III, Archbishop; Phoenicia; Ptolemy I Soter; Suez Crisis

References
Anastasiou, Harry. *Broken Olive Branch: Nationalism Ethnic Conflict and the Quest for Peace in Cyprus.* Syracuse, NY: Syracuse University Press, 2008.
Asmussen, Jan. *Cyprus at War: Diplomacy and Conflict during the 1974 Crisis.* York, UK: I. B. Tauris, 2008.
Brewin, Christopher. *European Union and Cyprus.* Tallahassee, FL: Eothen, 2000.
Durrell, Lawrence. *Bitter Lemons.* New York: Dutton, 1957.
Holland, R. F. *Britain and the Revolt in Cyprus, 1954–1959.* New York: Oxford University Press, 1998.
Faustmann, Hubert, and Nicos Peristianis. *Britain and Cyprus: Colonialism and Post-Colonialism, 1878–2006.* Mannheim, Germany: Bibliopolis, 2006.
Hannay, David. *Cyprus: The Search for a Solution.* New York: I. B. Tauris, 2005.
Hill, George. *A History of Cyprus.* 4 vols. Cambridge: Cambridge University Press, 1949–1972.
Hitchens, Christopher. *Hostage to History: Cyprus from the Ottomans to Kissinger.* New York: Verso, 1997.
Joseph, Joseph S. *Cyprus: Ethnic Conflict and International Politics: From Independence to the Threshold of the European Union.* New York: St. Martin's, 1997.
Karageorghis, Vassos. *Cyprus from the Stone Age to the Romans.* London: Thames and Hudson, 1982.
Ker-Lindsay, James, and Hubert Faustmann. *The Government and Politics of Cyprus.* New York: Peter Lang, 2009.
Mallinson, William. *Cyprus a Modern History.* New York: I. B. Tauris, 2005.
Mirbagheri, Farid. *Cyprus and International Peacemaking.* London: Hurst, 1989.
Nicolet, Claude. *United States Policy towards Cyprus, 1954–1974: Removing the Greek-Turkish Bone of Contention.* Mannheim, Germany: Bibliopolis, 2001.
Reyes, Andres T. *Archaic Cyprus: A Study of the Textual and Archaeological Evidence.* Oxford, UK: Clarendon, 1984.
Richmond, Oliver. *Mediating in Cyprus: The Cypriot Communities and the United Nations.* Portland, OR: Frank Cass, 1998.
Richter, Heinz. *A Concise History of Modern Cyprus, 1878–2009.* Mainz: Rutzen, 2010.
Yiorghos, Leventis. *Cyprus: The Struggle for Self-Determination in the 1940s.* New York: Peter Lang, 2002.

Cyprus, Athenian Expedition to (450–449 BCE)

The Athenian expedition to clear the Persians from Cyprus in 450–449 BCE was one of several in the fifth century demonstrating continuing Athenian interest in the island. In 478 the Hellenic league fleet had freed a large part of Cyprus from Persia, and in 460 a 200-strong fleet headed to Cyprus was diverted to Egypt to take advantage of Inaros's revolt there. Probably in 450 (although some historians, Meiggs for example, have argued for 451). Cimon, recently returned from exile, led a 200-strong fleet to Cyprus.

The details of the expedition are difficult to recover. Accounts by Thucydides, Plutarch, and Diodorus have irreconcilable differences. The most plausible reconstruction of events is that Cimon captured Marium and raided Phoenicia in the first year of the campaign. He died in the second year (probably of illness) while besieging Citium—either just before or just after a major victory over the Persians on land and sea, resulting in the capture of 100 Persian ships.

There were sound strategic reasons for Athens's interest in a friendly, or Athenian-dominated, Cyprus. This would provide a check on the resurgence of Persian naval power and give Athens a firm base in the eastern Mediterranean to assist in its influence over the Greek cities of Asia Minor and also Egypt. The earlier expeditions suggest that this was an ongoing Athenian interest after the Second Persian War of 480–479.

IAIN SPENCE

See also
Cyprus; Egypt, Athenian Intervention in

Reference
Meiggs, Russell. *The Athenian Empire.* Oxford, UK: Clarendon, 1972.

Cyprus, Ottoman Conquest of (1570–1571)

The Ottoman conquest of Cyprus during 1570–1571 was the centerpiece of the Venetian-Ottoman War of 1570–1573. Even before he became sultan, Selim II (r. 1566–1574) had made taking the island his top priority, this despite a peace treaty with Venice that had been renewed as recently as 1567. Popular legend has ascribed this to his love of Cypriot wines, but contemporary accounts have Joseph Nasi, a Portuguese Jew who had become the sultan's close friend, as the prime instigator. Nasi hoped to become king of the island after it had been secured.

Despite considerable opposition to the plan, chiefly from Grand Vizier Sokollu Mehmed Pasha, those favoring the effort prevailed. Abrogation of the treaty was justified by a ruling declaring that because it was a "former land of Islam" (briefly in the seventh century), Cyprus had to be retaken. The campaign was financed in part by the confiscation and resale of Greek Orthodox monasteries and churches. Lala Mustafa Pasha had command of the Ottoman expeditionary land forces, while Müezzinzade Ali Pasha was the naval commander.

The Venetians were well aware of the Ottoman preparations and did what they could to prepare. They strengthened the defenses not only of Cyprus but also those of Crete, Corfu, and others of their Mediterranean holdings. Efforts were undertaken to make these vulnerable locations less reliant on outside support, both by increasing the size of their garrisons and with the establishment of gunpowder mills and foundries for the manufacture of cannon. (Despite this effort, shortages of gunpowder and other key supplies played a major role in the fall of the island in 1571.) Venetian leaders were well aware that Cyprus, only some 40 miles from Anatolia, could not hold for long unaided. Venice were also handicapped in that the government of Spain, the major Christian power in the Mediterranean, was then preoccupied with the Dutch Revolt and the Moriscos in Spain itself. Also, the Cypriots themselves were not happy with the heavy-handed Venetian rule and high taxes that accompanied it.

In March 1570, the Porte demanded that Venice cede Cyprus. Although some Venetian leaders suggested an effort to exchange the island for Ottoman territory in Dalmatia and trading concessions, hopes of foreign assistance against the Ottomans stiffened Venetian resolve, and the ultimatum was rejected.

On June 27, the Ottoman expeditionary force set sail. It was said to number 350–400 ships with as many as 85,000–150,000 men. On July 3 the Ottomans came ashore unopposed at Salines, near Larnaca on the island's southern shore, then marched on the capital city of Nicosia. Given the overwhelming Ottoman strength, the Venetian leaders decided that their own course of action was to withdraw into their fortifications and await relief forces.

The Ottomans began their siege of Nicosia on July 22. Although the newly constructed walls withstood the Ottoman artillery bombardment well, the Ottomans, covered by steady small-arms fire, dug trenches and steadily advanced these toward the walls, gradually filling in their surrounding ditch. After dozens of failed assaults and with the defenders having exhausted their ammunition, on September 9 the attackers breeched the walls and took the city.

The Ottomans then commenced a massacre of Nicosia's 20,000 inhabitants. Only women and boys, captured to be sold as slaves, were spared. A Christian fleet of 200 Venetian, Papal, and Neapolitan ships that had belatedly assembled at Crete and was sailing toward Cyprus, turned back on learning of Nicosia's fall. The same news also brought the prompt surrender of the northern fortress of Kyrenia.

On September 15, Ottoman cavalry arrived at the last Venetian stronghold of Famagusta. There Marco Antonio Bragadin commanded some 8,500 men with 90 artillery pieces. Ultimately virtually the entire Ottoman invasion force was concentrated on siege operations here, supported by 145 guns.

The Ottoman siege of Famagusta began on September 17. Although the Ottomans were able to surround the city from the land side, the Venetians were able to deliver some supplies and reinforcements from the sea. News of this caused Sultan Selim to relieve Piyale Pasha in January and give Lala Mustafa command of the Ottoman naval forces as well.

The continuing siege led to an offer by Grand Vizier Sokollu Mehmed Pasha to allow the Venetians a trading station at Famagusta if the republic would cede the island, but the Venetians were encouraged by their capture of Durazzo in Albania and negotiations to establish a league of Christian states against the Ottomans and refused.

On May 12, 1571, the Ottomans began what would be a continuing intense bombardment of Famagusta's fortifications. Finally, on August 1, 1571, their ammunition and supplies exhausted, the Famagusta garrison surrendered. The siege had reportedly claimed some 50,000 Ottoman casualties. The victors allowed the Christian residents and surviving Venetian soldiers to depart Famagusta peacefully, but when Lala Mustafa learned that the Venetians had killed some Muslim prisoners during the siege, he had Bragadin mutilated and flayed alive and other senior Venetian officers executed.

Cyprus would remain an Ottoman possession until 1878, when the Porte ceded it to Great Britain.

SPENCER C. TUCKER

See also
Cyprus

References
Hill, George. *A History of Cyprus,* Vol. 3, *The Frankish Period, 1432–1571.* Cambridge: Cambridge University Press, 1948.
Tofallis, Kypros. *A History of Cyprus: From the Ancient Times to the Present, an Illustrated History.* London: Greek Institute, 2002.

Cyprus, Turkish Invasion of (1974)
See Cyprus

Cyprus, War of
See Venetian-Ottoman Wars

Cyrus II the Great (ca. 601/590–530 BCE)

Persian king Cyrus II (also known as Cyrus the Great and to the Greeks as Cyrus the Elder) was the founder of the Achaemenid Empire (First Persian Empire). Much of Cyrus's early life is shrouded in legend, and his lineage is obscure. He was born sometime around 601–590 BCE, probably in Persis, the son of King Cambyses I of Anshan. Some have suggested that Cyrus was the son of a daughter of Astyages, king of Media. Reportedly Cyrus became king of Anshan in 558. The kings of Anshan were vassals of the Median Empire until Cyrus led a rebellion against Media beginning in 553. It ended in 550 in a battle on the Plain of Pasargadae, with Astyages taken prisoner (Cyrus spared him) and with Ecbatana plundered, after which point Cyrus took the title "king of the Persians."

Shortly after taking over Media, Cyrus found himself under attack by a coalition of Babylon, Lydia, and Egypt, joined by the Greek city-state of Sparta. In 547 BCE Cyrus took the field against King Croesus of Lydia and in 546 defeated Croesus in the Battle of Thymbra. Cyrus then captured the Lydian capital of Sardis in western Anatolia, making Lydia into a Persian province. One of Cyrus's generals extended Persian control over the Greek Ionian cities along the Mediterranean coast. During 546–540 Cyrus campaigned in the east, conquering considerable territory there in Parthia, Bactria, and Scythia and establishing fortified cities there to defend against nomad raids.

Cyrus next took the field against the Babylonian Empire, which had been in decline. He defeated the Babylonian army in the Battle of Opis in 539. The city of Sippar surrendered almost immediately thereafter. Babylon was either taken by surprise several days later or underwent a prolonged siege during 539–538; accounts differ. Cyrus reportedly spared Babylonian king Nabonidus, who spent his remaining years in exile.

From early 538 BCE, Cyrus styled himself "king of Babylon and king of the countries" (i.e., of the world). With the surrender of Babylon, its provinces in Syria also fell under Persian control. Known for his toleration of the religions of the peoples he conquered, Cyrus was welcomed by the peoples of Syria and Palestine. In 538 he permitted the Jews who wished to do so to leave Babylon where they had been removed and return to Jerusalem to rebuild the city and its temple that had been destroyed by the Babylonians in 538. He also returned temple vessels that had been removed by the Babylonians.

The wealth secured by the conquest of Babylon, the most opulent city of the ancient world, fueled further expansion of Cyrus's realm. His armies conquered territories extending deep into the tribal regions of Central Asia and built frontier settlements along the Jaxartes River. Throughout his empire, Cyrus established several different capitals, including Babylon and a new city called Pasargadaes. Moreover, his empire was connected by an efficient postal service and was governed by a document of law now considered to be the initial charter of human rights, first read out by Cyrus himself at his coronation at Babylon.

There is some confusion about the death of Cyrus, but most modern historians support the report of Greek historian Herodotus, who wrote that Cyrus was killed around 529 by Tomyris, the nomadic leader of the Massagetai in Central Asia. She reportedly killed Cyrus after he defeated her people, captured her son, and drove him to suicide. Cyrus left several children, including his successor, Cambyses II, and another son named Bardiya as well as at least one daughter.

In a very short span of time, Cyrus had built the mighty Persian Empire, reaching from the Indus and Jaxartes Rivers west to the Aegean Sea and the Egyptian frontier. A great warrior who led a loyal army, Cyrus was benevolent in his rule. He was certainly humane in his treatment of the conquered, a rarity in the ancient Middle East, which probably explains a good deal of his military success. He was also adroit in his rule, forming the leading princes into a royal council in which he was considered the first among equals. The Persian people acknowledged Cyrus as the founder of their empire, and even his enemies widely respected him.

Spencer C. Tucker and Nancy L. Stockdale

See also
Achaemenid Empire; Babylon, Siege of; Babylonian Empire, Neo-; Cambyses II; Lydia

References
Briant, Pierre. *From Cyrus to Alexander: A History of the Persian Empire*. Winona Lake, IN: Eisenbrauns, 2002.

Curtis, John, ed. *Forgotten Empire: The World of Ancient Persia*. Berkeley: University of California Press, 2005.

Herodotus. *The History of Herodotus*. Edited by Manuel Komroff. Translated by George Rawlinson. New York: Tudor Publishing, 1956.

Yamauchi, Edwin. *Persia and the Bible*. Grand Rapids, MI: Baker Book House, 1990.

Cyrus the Younger (ca. 423–401 BCE)

Persian prince and general. One of the four sons of Darius II (r. 423–404 BCE) and the first born after his father became king. His mother's suggestion that (like Xerxes) Cyrus should therefore be his father's successor was rejected, but she did save him when the Persian general Tissaphernes accused him of plotting to assassinate the new king, Artaxerxes II. Cyrus's royal ambitions were undiminished by this episode and, reinstated in the Anatolian satrapies he had held since 407, he planned a military challenge. The experience and personal connections gained from funding Spartan fleets in 407–405 helped him assemble the largest Greek mercenary army yet seen in the Aegean world and, with this and Anatolia-based non-Greek forces, he marched east in 401.

Belatedly warned of the danger by Tissaphernes (who had been fighting Cyrus for control of Miletus), Artaxerxes confronted Cyrus six months later at Cunaxa in northern Babylonia. Cyrus's mercenaries easily defeated their opponents, but the battle's outcome was settled by a cavalry encounter in which Cyrus wounded Artaxerxes but died in the ensuing melee.

The fullest source for these events is Xenophon's *Anabasis*, Book 1 of which conveys a distinctive picture of Cyrus through detailed narrative and a laudatory obituary chapter. A model product of court education, Cyrus displayed physical courage, had mastered the technical skills of a Persian aristocrat (horsemanship and use of weaponry), and knew how to exercise leadership by keeping his word, punishing wrongdoing (the spectacle of mutilated criminals allegedly kept Anatolian roads safe for travelers), and above all taking pleasure in rewarding loyalty and success generously.

Cyrus's politic empathy with subordinates even supposedly extended to suggesting that it would have been better to have been born a free Greek than a powerful Persian. In short, according to Xenophon, "all who can claim to have known him agree that no Persian since the Elder Cyrus was more like a king or more deserving of the throne" and "I have heard of nobody whom I judge to have been loved by more Greeks or barbarians."

Cyrus's fratricidal ambition, overconfidence immediately before Cunaxa (Artaxerxes's appearance caught him unawares), and fatal impetuousness during the battle perhaps undercut Xenophon's praise. But Cyrus's successful cooperation with the equally ambitious Lysander and ability to mount a credible military challenge to Artaxerxes suggest that he had remarkable qualities. Nor should we forget that he was at most 22 years old when he died.

Christopher Tuplin

See also
Artaxerxes II; Cunaxa, Battle of; Xenophon; Xerxes I

References
Briant, Pierre. *From Cyrus to Alexander: A History of the Persian Empire*. Winona Lake, IN: Eisenbraun, 2002.

Kuhrt, Amélie. T. *The Persian Empire: A Corpus of Sources from the Achaemenid Period*. London: Routledge, 2007.

Waters, Matt. *Ancient Persia: A Concise History of the Achaemenid Empire*. Cambridge: Cambridge University Press, 2014.

D

Damascus, Allied Capture of (October 1, 1918)

Turning point in the Palestine-Syria Campaign and an important event for Arab nationalism. Damascus (Syria) was an ancient Arab political, economic, and cultural center, and Arab nationalists had long regarded its possession as vital in the establishment of a sovereign Arab state.

After virtually destroying German general of cavalry and Ottoman field marshal Otto Liman von Sanders's Ottoman-German Army Group F (Yildirim, or Thunderbolt) in the Battle of Megiddo (September 1918), Lieutenant General Sir Edmund Allenby, commander of the British Egypt Expeditionary Force (EEF), issued orders for the rapid seizure of Damascus by Lieutenant General Sir Harry Chauvel's Desert Mounted Corps of three cavalry divisions.

The terms of the secret May 1916 Sykes-Picot Agreement between France and Britain, however, as well as consideration for Britain's Arab allies made it advisable to avoid prejudicing future possession of the city. Hence, Allenby's orders provided for the encirclement of Damascus, trapping any Ottoman troops defending it. British forces were not to enter the city before the forces of Prince Faisal's Northern Arab Army except in the event of compelling tactical reasons.

Some 40,000 Ottoman and German troops, principally of the Ottoman Fourth Army, defended Damascus, but they were widely dispersed and unable to offer effective resistance. On September 29 the Australian 3rd Light Horse Brigade drove some 5,000 of the defenders from their positions about nine miles southwest of the city. Only the eastern route from Damascus remained open when the EEF arrived on October 1. The Ottomans had already begun to evacuate, under fire from some of the city inhabitants as they did so, although 12,000 troops remained in their barracks awaiting capture.

Despite Allenby's orders, Damascus was in fact entered by Allied troops at least three times within a 24-hour period. Charged with cutting the Ottoman retreat route north by occupying the Homs road, men of the 3rd Australian Light Horse Brigade, commanded by Major A. C. N. "Harry" Olden, found it impossible to reach their objective without crossing the northern part of the city. Thus, early on October 1 the Australian troopers were in Damascus itself. They captured the Dummar train station and several hundred Ottoman soldiers.

Later in the afternoon on October 1, a detachment of the 4th Light Horse Brigade under Lieutenant Colonel M. W. J. Bourchier that had reached the southern outskirts of Damascus was notified of apparent unrest in the city upon the withdrawal of the Ottoman Fourth Army. Bourchier sent troops to protect public property but that evening was ordered to withdraw his men from the city.

Before Ottoman forces marched out of Damascus, they had entrusted its administration to a group of leading citizens who acknowledged King Hussein ibn Ali, sharif of the Hejaz and Prince Faisal's father, as their ruler. These individuals formed a committee that surrendered the town at least twice on the morning of October 1: once to the Australian

Light Horse and once to Sharif Nasir, the sharifian leader in the Damascus area. Later, Lieutenant Colonel T. E. Lawrence drove into Damascus and accepted its surrender from Shukri al-Ayyubi, a high-ranking Ottoman officer and Arab nationalist whom Lawrence immediately appointed military governor. Lawrence wrote in his book *Seven Pillars of Wisdom* that sharifian troops were the first forces into Damascus, but this seems highly unlikely.

On October 2, Chauvel was forced to order troops into the city to quell unrest. He discovered a confusing situation brought on by different Allied authorities supporting competing Arab factions. Only after the restoration of order was the Syrian capital finally handed over to Arab authority. Faisal did not arrive in Damascus until October 3.

The EEF took almost 20,000 Ottoman troops prisoner in and around Damascus, virtually eliminating the Ottoman Fourth Army as a fighting force. Only some 4,000 German and Ottoman troops remained in the area south of Aleppo.

DIERK WALTER

See also
Allenby, Sir Edmund Henry Hynman; Arab Revolt of World War I; Faisal I, King of Iraq; Hussein ibn Ali ibn Mohammed; Lawrence, Thomas Edward; Liman von Sanders, Otto; Megiddo, Battle of; Ottoman Empire; Ottoman Empire, Post–World War I Revolution in; Palestine and Syria Campaign, World War I; Sykes-Picot Agreement

References
Erickson, Edward J. *Ordered to Die: A History of the Ottoman Army in the First World War*. Westport, CT: Greenwood, 2000.
Falls, Cyril. *Military Operations: Egypt and Palestine, from June 1917 to the End of the War*. London: HMSO, 1930.
Kent, Marian, ed. *The Great Powers and the End of the Ottoman Empire*. 2nd ed. Portland, OR: Cass, 1996.
Lawrence, Thomas E. *Seven Pillars of Wisdom: A Triumph*. Garden City, NY: Doubleday, Doran, 1935.
Tauber, Eliezer. *The Arab Movements in World War I*. London: Cass, 1993.
Wavell, Colonel A. P. *The Palestine Campaigns*. London: Constable, 1928.

Damascus, Siege of (634–635)

The Siege of Damascus was part of the Muslim conquest of Syria during the Arab-Byzantine Wars. Dates for the siege vary widely. Some sources say that it lasted for six months and the city fell to the Arabs in January 635, while others give a far shorter period of August 21 to September 19, 634.

Abu Bakr, the first Rashidym caliph, was determined to expand Muslim control beyond the Arabian Peninsula. In 634 he sent four armies totaling perhaps 20,000 men into Syria, then controlled by the Byzantine Empire. These forces proving inadequate, Abu Bakr dispatched reinforcements under his capable general Khalid ibn Walid. These forces captured Bosra and then won a notable battle at Ajnadain (July 30). Having secured his flank, Khalid then proceeded against the key city of Damascus. The city was heavily fortified, with much of it surrounded by a wall 36 feet high.

The Byzantine Army commander of Damascus was an officer named Thomas, son-in-law of Byzantine emperor Heraclius. The senior civilian official was Mansur Ibn Sarjan, a Christian Arab. The Arabs had no siege equipment and so, reportedly on August 21 (again, dates for the siege differ), surrounded the city with the intention of starving it into submission. Lacking sufficient manpower to surround the city completely, Khalid concentrated his men at the six city gates, sufficient in numbers to repulse any Byzantine sorties. He also sent detachments to cut the Byzantine lines of communication to Damascus and dispatched cavalry to Thaniyat al-'Uqab (Eagle's Pass), some 20 miles northeast of the city on the Emesa to Damascus road, in order to provide warning of the approach of the anticipated Byzantine relief force and defeat it if possible.

Heraclius was at the city of Antioch when the siege of Damascus commenced and ordered a relief force there. Numbering only about 12,000 men, it encountered the Arab force at Eagle's Pass and was on the brink of defeating it when Khlaid arrived with reinforcements and turned the tide of battle. The Byzantine relief force then withdrew northward.

The besiegers had been greatly weakened by the removal of Arab forces to meet the Byzantine relief column, and if the defenders had attempted a major sortie at that time, it probably would have broken through. The opportunity soon passed, however, as after his victory at Eagle's Pass Khalid hurried back to Damascus.

Realizing that relief was now unlikely, Thomas concentrated manpower for a breakout attempt from Thomas Gate. The attempt by infantry covered by archers on the walls failed, and the infantry was driven back into the city. Thomas, who led the attack in person, was wounded in the eye by an arrow. Undaunted, he tried again that evening, this time in an attempt from four of the city gates, with three of these designed to draw off Muslim forces from the main assault from the East Gate, again led by Thomas in person. The fighting was heavy, but the Byzantine breakout attempt failed, and Thomas ordered it ended.

There are several versions of how Damascus actually fell. Reportedly an informant told Khalid about a celebration planned in the city for the night of September 19, and Khalid ordered a surprise attack to occur when the walls were likely to be lightly defended. That night the Arabs entered the city from two directions. Khalid's troops were first into the city, reportedly using ropes to get some men over the undefended wall at the East Gate and breaking through there, while another force, under Abu Ubaidah, breached Jabiyah Gate on the west.

Although it was traditional Arab practice to slay all the inhabitants of a city that had refused to surrender, Khalid's terms were generous in that only the Rumi or Byzantines of Greek origin were excluded from a general amnesty. Damascus, largely Christian in population, now became the capital city of Islamic Syria.

SPENCER C. TUCKER

See also
Byzantine-Muslim Wars; Heraclius; Khalid ibn al-Walid

References
De Goeje, M. J. *Memoire sur le conquête de la Syrie.* Leiden: Brill, 1900.

McGraw Donner, F. *The Early Islamic Conquests.* Princeton, NJ: Princeton University Press, 1981.

Damascus Agreement (December 28, 1985)

Agreement signed on December 28, 1985, intended to end the Lebanese Civil War (1975–1990) by revising the Lebanese political system with a more equitable distribution of power on behalf of ethnic Arabs and Muslims. The agreement was also meant to bring Lebanon into a closer relationship with Syria and to achieve the expulsion of Israeli forces from southern Lebanon. Although the agreement failed to end the Lebanese Civil War, in some ways it prefigured the Taif Accords of 1989 that would bring the civil war to a close in 1990.

Muslim frustration with the constitutional arrangement on Lebanon's independence based on the 1932 census, when Christians were in the majority, had encountered Lebanese Christian intransigence, triggering civil war in 1975. Given the fighting and absence of central government authority over much of the country, the Palestine Liberation Organization (PLO) was able to step up its raids on northern Israel from southern Lebanon.

The PLO raids brought an Israel invasion in 1982. It and the ensuing Israeli siege of Beirut brought the departure of the PLO but also heightened Lebanon's ethnic and religious tensions. In addition, the Israeli invasion provided a pretext for Syria to send its own forces into eastern Lebanon, ostensibly to protect the Lebanese from Israel but also to exert Syrian influence there.

Under intense international pressure, in 1985 the Israelis withdrew but retained about 10 percent of southern Lebanon as a buffer zone to reduce further attacks on their territory. The withdrawal of Israeli forces and the departure of foreign troops that had overseen the PLO departure left the Christian government of Lebanon isolated. President Amin Gemayel sought Syrian support in his war against Shiite and Druze armed militias, and the Syrians moved sizable forces into Lebanon to support him. With some 40,000 of its troops in Lebanon, the Syrian government was in position to exert considerable pressure on the Lebanese factions to agree to a return to the peace table and conclude the Damascus Agreement of December 28, 1985.

The agreement called for continued resistance to Israeli occupation in Lebanon and outlined the basic constitutional form of government for Lebanon, which was to remain both republican and democratic. The agreement did address the basic demographic problem. It reduced the power of the Christian president by requiring the approval of the Muslim prime minister for most major decisions. In addition, the agreement expanded the Chamber of Deputies and called for equality among the sects there. Most importantly, at least from the Syrian perspective, it outlined a close relationship between Lebanon and Syria, calling for mutual coordination of military strategy, foreign policy, security measures, economic relations, and education policy. Syria thus gained unparalleled power within Lebanon.

The Damascus Agreement failed to bring peace to Lebanon, however. Shiite forces in southern Lebanon, particularly Hezbollah, sought a strictly Islamic state. Other militias throughout the country meanwhile continued their conflicts with one another and the government. After the end of Gemayel's presidency, his successor Michel Aoun turned against the Syrians in 1989, resulting in conflict between Aoun's Christian forces and the Syrians and their militias and Aoun's defeat. A workable peace plan would not emerge until 1989 under the auspices of the Arab League at Taif in Saudi Arabia. It, however, built on much that had been contained in the Damascus Agreement. The new plan weakened the Lebanese presidency and strengthened the premiership, expanded the Chamber of Deputies, and delivered more power to the Muslim majority by shifting the old six-to-five ratio in favor of the Christians to equal representation for both Christians and Muslims. The Taif Accords differed from the Damascus Agreement most dramatically by requiring a two-thirds vote by the Council of Ministers to change the implementation of the agreement, providing protection for minority rights, and omitting much of the language binding Lebanon to Syria.

MICHAEL K. BEAUCHAMP

See also
Hezbollah; Israel; Lebanon; Lebanon, Second U.S. Intervention in; Lebanon Civil War; Lebanon-Israeli War; Palestine Liberation Organization; Syria; Taif Accords

References
Cleveland, William L. *A History of the Modern Middle East.* Boulder, CO: Westview, 2004.
Deeb, Marius. *Syria's Terrorist War on Lebanon and the Peace Process.* New York: Palgrave Macmillan, 2003.
Long, David E., and Bernard Reich. *The Government and the Politics of the Middle East and North Africa.* Boulder, CO: Westview, 2002.
Picard, Elizabeth. *Lebanon, a Shattered Country: Myths and Realities of the Wars in Lebanon.* New York: Holmes & Meier, 2002.

Damietta

Damietta (modern-day Dumyât, Egypt) is a port city on the eastern portion of the Nile Delta. During the Christian crusades in the Holy Land it boasted triple walls and a tower that controlled access to the upper Nile by means of a chain stretched across the river to the city walls.

In 1169 King Amalric of Jerusalem and Byzantine emperor Manuel I Komnenos besieged Damietta during their attempt to seize control of the Fatimid realm. Regarded as the "key to all Egypt," Damietta became the initial target of the Fifth Crusade (1218–1221), although the crusaders' intentions toward the city appear to have evolved during the course of their campaign. Some seem to have considered it and other potential acquisitions in Egypt as pawns to be traded for territory lost in the Kingdom of Jerusalem, while others saw Damietta as a beachhead for the permanent conquest and colonization of Egypt.

After a siege of 15 months, the crusaders captured the city in November 1219, a plague having ravaged its inhabitants. The port and its spoils, including the towers guarding its walls, were partitioned among the regional groups present in the army, although not without serious dispute. The overlordship of the city sparked a struggle between papal legate Pelagius, who wanted to reserve it for the titular, albeit absent, head of the crusade, Emperor Frederick II, and John of Brienne, who claimed it for the Kingdom of Jerusalem. After John was granted temporary custodianship, the city's mosques were converted into churches, including a cathedral for a newly created archbishopric.

The crusaders repeatedly rejected truces proposed by Ayyubid sultan of Egypt al-Kamil, offering the return of Jerusalem and major fortresses west of the Jordan in return for the Christian army's withdrawal, partly due to his exclusion of the castles of Kerak and Montréal, considered essential to hold Jerusalem. However, after the crusader army advanced toward Cairo, it suffered devastating losses and was forced to surrender Damietta to al-Kamil in 1221.

Perhaps influenced by the advice of John of Brienne, King Louis IX of France also made Damietta the initial goal of his crusade against Egypt (1248–1254), taking it in 1249. After Louis and his army were taken prisoner by the Egyptians in the spring of 1250, however, the city was returned to Muslim hands as part of the staggering ransom demanded for the crusaders' release. It was razed shortly thereafter to prevent the vulnerable port from being used as a foothold for future crusader offensives.

JESSALYNN BIRD

See also
Amalric of Jerusalem; Crusades in the Holy Land, Christian; Fatimid Dynasty; Frederick II, Holy Roman Emperor; John of Brienne; Louis IX, King of France; Manuel I Komnenos, Emperor

References
Phillips, Jonathan. *Defenders of the Holy Land: Relations between the Latin East and the West, 1119–1187.* Oxford, UK: Clarendon, 1996.
Powell, James M. *Anatomy of a Crusade, 1213–1221.* Philadelphia: University of Pennsylvania Press, 1986.
Richard, Jean. *Saint Louis. Crusader King of France.* Cambridge: Cambridge University Press, 1992.

Danishmendid Dynasty (1071–1178)

A Turkish dynasty (in Turkish, Danişmendliler) ruling an emirate in central and northeastern Anatolia in the period 1071–1178. Several of the dynasty's rulers were involved in conflicts with Byzantines, crusaders, and Franks as well as the rival dynasty of the Seljuks of Rum, who eventually annexed the Danishmendid territories shortly before the mid-12th century.

The Danishmendids were the first pre-Ottoman Turks to employ on their coinage (with Greek and Arabic inscriptions) the terms "Romania" and "Rum" shortly before the Seljuks of Rum, with whom they struggled for domination over Anatolia in the 12th century. Their first two leaders,

Malik Danishmend Ghazi (r. ca. 1071/1085–1104) and Amir Ghazl Gumushtegin (r. 1104–1134), distinguished themselves in protracted wars against Byzantium, the Franks, and the Rupenids of Cilician Armenia as well as interfering successfully in Seljuk internal affairs.

Cappadocia and north-central Anatolia as far west as Ankara constituted the initial Danishmendid center of power. Their first emir, Malik Danishmend Ghazī (from the Persian *danishmand*, for "wise, learned man" or "scholar"), prevailed in central Anatolia in the period of confusion that followed the death of the founder of the Sejuk sultanate of Rum, Sulayman I ibn Qulumush (in 1085 or 1086). During 1097–1105, Malik Ghazi formed an alliance of necessity with Qilij Arslan I of Rum against the various crusading armies that were arriving from the West, and the two allies defeated the crusaders in 1101 at Mersivan and Herakleia (modern-day Ereğli, Turkey). Malik Ghazi had previously captured Prince Bohemund I of Antioch, imprisoning him at Neocaesarea until he was ransomed following negotiations with King Baldwin I of Jerusalem in 1103. In that year Malik Ghazi took Melitene (modern-day Malatya, Turkey) from its Armenian ruler, Gabriel, although it was captured by Qilij Arslan I following Malik Ghazi's demise (ca. 1106).

A period of further conquests ensued under Amir Ghazi Gumushtegin. Intervening in the Seljuk struggle for succession, he helped Mas'ud I seize power in Ikonion (1116). Ghazi also defeated and held for ransom the Byzantine duke of Pontic Chaldia, Constantine Gabras (ca. 1120), and captured Melitene from Mas'ud's rivals (1124–1125). The conquest of Caesarea in Cappadocia (modern-day Kayseri, Turkey), Ankara, and Kastamoni (modern-day Kastamonu, Turkey) in the Pontos (1126–1127) alarmed the Byzantine emperor, John II Komnenos, who prepared for war. In 1129–1130 Amir Ghazi invaded Cilician Armenia, taking several strongholds and defeating Bohemund II of Antioch, who had come to assist the Rupenid prince Leon I. John II Komnenos repeated campaigns against the Danishmendids in 1130–1135. The Greeks seized Kastamoni (1131–1132), which, however, was lost again in 1133. Amir Ghazi was honored by the Abbasid caliph al-Mustarshid and the Great Seljuk sultan Sanjar with the title of *malik* (prince) for his struggles against the infidels, although Ghazi's premature death bestowed that title on his successor, Malik Muhammad (r. 1134–1142).

Muhammad refortified Caesarea and continued the war against Byzantium, raiding Cilicia and the Sangarios River region as far as Neocaesarea (modern-day Niksar, Turkey) in 1138–1139. John II eventually managed to repel the Danishmendids from eastern Bithynia and Paphlagonia in 1139–1140, although part of his army was defeated by Muhammad's forces in 1141.

Upon Muhammad's death in 1142, the dynasty split into two branches descending from his brothers: one under Yaghibasan at Sebasteia (modern-day Sivas, Turkey) and another under Ayn al-Dawla at Melitene and Elbistan; the latter's son Dhu'l-Nun established himself at Caesarea. Yaghibasan (r. 1142–1164) became an ally of Byzantine emperor Manuel I Komnenos against the Seljuks of Rum and even issued seals with Greek inscriptions designating him as the latter's servant (in Greek, *doulos*). Following Yaghibasan's death and the ensuing decline of his emirate, Qilij Arslan II of Rum invaded Danishmendid territory but was temporarily halted by the fact that Dhu'l-Nun, ruling at Caesarea, was the son-in-law of the powerful Nur al-Din of Damascus, who threatened to attack the Rum Sultanate. It was only after Nur al-Din's death in 1174 that Qilij Arslan II had a free hand to launch his decisive attack on the Danishmendids, annexing the territories of both branches of the dynasty: first that of Sebasteia in 1174 and then that of Melitene and Elbistan in 1177–1178. A 13th-century Persian chronicler at the court of Ikonion (modern-day Konya, Turkey), Ibn al-Bibī, recorded that the surviving Danishmendids entered Seljuk service.

ALEXIOS G. C. SAVVIDES

See also
Bohemund I of Antioch; Manuel I Komnenos, Emperor; Nur al-Din; Seljuk Dynasty

References
Cahen, Claude. *Pre-Ottoman Turkey: A General Survey of the Material and Spiritual Culture and History, c. 1071–1330.* London: Sidgwick and Jackson, 1968.

Mercil, Erdoğan, "The Danishmendid Principality." In *A Short History of the Turkish-Islamic States (Excluding the Ottoman State)*, ed. M. D. Yıldız, E. Mercil, and M. Saray, 187–188. Ankara: Turkish Historical Society, 1994.

Oikonomidès, Nicolas. "Les Danishmendites entre Byzance, Baghdad et le Sultanat d'Iconium," *Revue numismatique* 25 (1983): 189–207.

Runciman, Steven. *History of the Crusades*. 3 vols. Cambridge: Cambridge University Press, 1954.

Daoud, Abu (1937–2010)

Palestinian militant and mastermind of the Black September organization terrorist attack on Israeli athletes at the 1972 Munich Summer Olympics. Muhammad Daoud, more commonly known as Abu Daoud, was born in the Jerusalem community of Silwan on May 16, 1937. Little is known of his early life, but from the time he was a youth he demonstrated a penchant for militancy.

Black September refers to a violent struggle in September 1970 when Jordan's King Hussein expelled the Palestinians and the Palestine Liberation Organization (PLO) from the country. In the process, many Palestinians were killed or imprisoned before the conflict ended in July 1971, with the PLO forced out of Jordan to Lebanon. Daoud was first an operative and then a leader of the Black September organization, named in commemoration of this event. The organization's original goal was to avenge the events of Black September and gain the release of Palestinians imprisoned in Jordan.

The alleged purpose of the Munich attack was to protest the exclusion of the Palestinians from the 1972 Summer Olympic Games. Daoud planned the attack and led it during its initial phases. In response to the attacks, Israeli prime minister Golda Meir authorized, in Operation WRATH OF GOD, the assassination of those known to be responsible for the Munich massacre, and the 1973 Operation SPRING OF YOUTH, led by Ehud Barak, an attack on Popular Front for the Liberation of Palestine (PFLP) headquarters in Beirut. Daoud's role in the Munich event was well known to Mossad, the Israeli intelligence agency, and he contended that it was Mossad that inflicted 13 wounds to his body when he was shot at close range in a Warsaw, Poland, hotel on July 27, 1981.

Daoud was arrested late on 1972 while leading a team into Jordan with the goal of taking hostage the Jordanian prime minister and members of his cabinet, then exchanging them for Palestinians imprisoned for actions committed during Black September. Daoud was convicted and sentenced to death in March 1973. King Hussein commuted the sentence to life in prison and later released him along with 1,000 other prisoners in a September 1973 general amnesty. Daoud then moved to Lebanon and remained there until the onset of the Lebanese Civil War in 1975, at which time he returned to Amman.

In January 1977 Daoud was arrested in Paris. Although the Jerusalem Magistrates Court issued a warrant on January 10 seeking his extradition on charges relating to the Munich attack, a French court released him when the government of the Federal Republic of Germany failed to expeditiously request his extradition. Daoud then returned to Jordan. He was allowed to move from Jordan to the West Bank city of Ramallah in 1993 following the Oslo Accords. He became a member of the Palestinian National Council (PNC) in 1996, and in 1999 he publicly and unrepentantly admitted his role in the Munich attack and the subsequent Lufthansa hijacking in his book *Palestine: From Jerusalem to Munich*. Daoud also asserted that PLO chairman Yasser Arafat had granted prior approval for the Munich attack, which Arafat and others denied.

Daoud's admissions led to the issuance of a German arrest warrant. Denied reentry into the Palestinian Authority (PA) territories on June 13, 1999, Daoud moved to Syria, the one country that would allow him residence. He died in Damascus on July 3, 2010.

RICHARD M. EDWARDS

See also

Arafat, Yasser; Black September; Black September Organization; Oslo Accords; Palestine Liberation Organization; Palestinian National Authority; Terrorism

References

Daoud, Abu. *Memoirs of a Palestinian Terrorist*. New York: Arcade, 2002.

Daoud, Abu [Muhammad Daoud Audeh], with Giles du Jonchay. *Palestine: De Jerusalem à Munich*. Paris: Éditions Anne Carriere, 1999.

Jonas, George. *Vengeance: The True Story of an Israeli Counter-Terrorist Team*. New York: Simon and Schuster, 2005.

Klein, Aaron. *Striking Back: The 1972 Munich Olympics Massacre and Israel's Deadly Response*. New York: Random House, 2005.

Roman, Michael. *Black September*. Orlando: Northwest Publishing, 1995.

Dar al-Islam and Dar al-Harb

Two basic categories—the Abode of Islam and the Abode of War—of political space in Islamic law. Dar al-Islam designates the area under Muslim rule in which Islamic law operates and war is neither necessary nor permissible; Dar al-Harb is territory not under Muslim control. The inhabitants of the Dar al-Harb, the harbis, are non-Muslims who have received a call to convert to Islam.

This conception of political space reflects the political unity of the Muslim community (the umma) under Muhammad and the early caliphs. Muhammad and his successors offered their non-Muslim neighbors the choice of conversion or warfare. Since the most fundamental roots of sharia are the Quran and the hadith, the findings of the jurists inevitably reflected the early decades of Islam rather than the eighth and ninth centuries when Islamic jurisprudence developed.

The jurists clearly regarded the expansion of the Dar al-Islam to absorb the entire Dar al-Harb as a fundamental duty of Muslim rulers, but they did not envision continuous warfare, given the severe restrictions on the waging of offensive jihad. Two of the four major schools of Sunni law, the Hanafis and the Shafi'is, both envision intermediate territories, Abodes of Truce (Dar al-Muwada'ah or Dar al-Sulh), where the rulers have reached a truce with the Muslims, generally in return for the payment of tribute.

Although the concepts of Dar al-Harb and Dar al-Islam form the basis of political space in Islamic law, they have had little impact on actual statecraft. While Muslim rulers have occasionally referred to or made use of these concepts, they have not and do not make them the basis of their external policies. Even contemporary states that claim to govern in accord with sharia, the Kingdom of Saudi Arabia and the Islamic Republic of Iran, have routine diplomatic relations with non-Muslim states.

DOUGLAS E. STREUSAND

See also
Sharia

References
Bonner, Michael. *Jihad in Islamic History: Doctrines and Practices.* Princeton, NJ: Princeton University Press, 2006.
Cook, David. *Understanding Jihad.* Berkeley: University of California Press, 2005.
Khadduri, Majid. *War and Peace in the Law of Islam.* Baltimore: Johns Hopkins University Press, 1955.

Dardanelles, 1807 British Expedition to
See Anglo-Ottoman War

Dardanelles Campaign (February–March 1915)

The World War I Dardanelles Campaign was an Allied effort to open the straits connecting the Black Sea with the Mediterranean and drive the Ottoman Empire from the war. One of the war's most controversial operations, it was also one of its great missed opportunities.

The Ottoman Empire's entry into the war on the side of the Central Powers severed French and British access to the Black Sea and greatly increased the difficulty of sending military supplies to Russia. It also denied Russia a means of exporting goods to the West, thus exacerbating that country's financial difficulties.

Reopening the Dardanelles was not initially a priority for the Allies; their attention was fixed on the campaign in

The French battleship *Bouvet*, shown here, was sunk by an Ottoman mine on March 18, 1915, during the Allied naval effort to force the Dardanelles and proceed to Istanbul. The pre-dreadnought battleship went down in only two minutes with the loss of 660 of its 710-man crew. (Reynolds, Francis J. and C. W. Taylor. *Collier's Photographic History of the European War*, 1916)

France. Stalemate there, however, led to increased interest in a flanking movement elsewhere. First Lord of the Admiralty Winston Churchill was also anxious to employ British sea power.

At the end of December 1914, Lieutenant Colonel Maurice Hankey, secretary of the War Council in London, submitted a plan for a Dardanelles campaign. He argued that Britain should use its navy and three corps of troops to attack the Ottoman Empire. Churchill embraced the plan and became its avatar. First Sea Lord John Fisher was persuaded to go along, as was secretary of state for war Field Marshal Horatio Kitchener, moved by a Russian plea for a diversionary attack to relieve Ottoman pressure in the Caucasus.

With Kitchener opposed to drawing troops from France, after much debate the War Council decided on a purely naval operation. It assumed that once the fleet had reached Constantinople, its threat of naval bombardment would drive the Turks from the war. Fisher and the admirals of the War Staff Group saw what Churchill did not—the need for a properly mounted combined-arms operation. Churchill also did not appreciate the vulnerability of ships to shore fire.

Vice Admiral Sackville Carden, commander of the blockading squadron off the Dardanelles, had charge of the operation. Carden was less than enthusiastic and requested a considerable force, including battle cruisers, to deal with the powerful German battle cruiser *Goeben* that had escaped to Constantinople at the beginning of the war. France agreed to send a squadron commanded by Vice Admiral Émile Paul Guépratte.

Carden's force was the strongest ever assembled in the Mediterranean. It consisted of the superdreadnought *Queen Elizabeth* (flagship), the battle cruiser *Inflexible*, 16 old battleships (4 of them French), and 20 destroyers (6 French). A flotilla of 35 minesweeping trawlers and a seaplane carrier were also dispatched, and cruisers and submarines were available if needed.

The Ottomans had some 100 guns defending the Dardanelles, 72 of which were in fixed emplacements in 11 different forts. The Germans supplied several dozen 5.9-inch (15cm) howitzers and some other modern pieces. The heaviest guns, along with searchlights and minefields, guarded the entrance of the Dardanelles. The defenders were, however, short of shells.

Although Carden came to believe that a naval bombardment alone would not be sufficient to force the Dardanelles, the War Council ordered him to commence operations. Bad weather delayed bombardment of the outer Ottoman forts until February 19. The weather then closed in, forcing a six-day interruption.

The bombardment recommenced on February 25. Naval gunfire silenced all four outer Ottoman forts, and minesweepers began clearing a path for the larger ships. Demolition parties also went ashore to complete destruction of the outer forts. The fleet then sailed into the straits and began bombarding the inner forts. Carden hoped to be off Constantinople in two weeks.

Carden's optimism proved unfounded. Although the forts could be hit, damage was not that great. In any case, the mobile Turkish howitzers, firing behind the crests of the hills, were not easily accessible to the flat-trajectory high-velocity naval guns, and they scored a growing number of hits on Allied vessels. This fire did not bother the battleships, but it did affect minesweeping operations. Until troops could be landed to destroy the mobile howitzers, their fire prevented sweeping the minefields.

On March 3, Rear Admiral Sir John de Robeck reported that the operation would not succeed unless troops were landed to control the shores of the straits, but Churchill had assured the War Council that the navy would be able to force the straits alone. He had even failed to send out the Royal Naval Division, which was available.

Captain Roger Keyes, Carden's chief of staff, took charge of the minesweeping, which went forward day and night. Churchill meanwhile kept up pressure on Carden, urging speed before the Germans sent submarines. Despite his near total lack of losses, Carden was fearful of taking responsibility for the destruction of any ships. On March 16 his health broke, and de Robeck assumed command of the grand assault planned for two days later.

The naval effort to force the narrows began on schedule on March 18, when the Allied battleships bombarded the land batteries in the narrows. Three ships (two British and one French) sustained damage, but most shore batteries were hit hard. Then disaster struck. The French battleship *Bouvet* took a hit in one of its magazines and blew up, sinking with the loss of 640 men. Allied shelling of land batteries continued throughout the afternoon, and de Robeck ordered his minesweepers forward, but they fled after coming under fire. Then the British battle cruiser *Inflexible* struck a mine, and it withdrew from action. A few minutes later the battleship *Irresistible* also was disabled by a mine. De Robeck then ordered a withdrawal for the night but instructed Keyes to stay in the straits with the destroyers and organize a tow for the *Irresistible* with the help of two other battleships, the *Ocean* and *Swiftsure*.

Instead of concentrating on the salvage operation, the *Ocean* shelled shore installations. It was then torn by an internal explosion, its steering disabled. Keyes ordered the *Swiftsure* to retire with the crew of the *Ocean*. He then secured permission to sink the *Irresistible* by torpedo and determine if the *Ocean* could be salvaged. As Keyes returned, there was a great explosion. No trace of the two battleships was found. Later, it was learned that all three battleships had run into a new and very small minefield, which Allied seaplane patrols had failed to detect.

Keyes and other senior officers believed that one more determined push by the fleet would be decisive. In fact, the Ottoman shore batteries had used up half of their supply of ammunition in that one day and were down to their last armor-piercing shells. They were also virtually out of mines.

A great storm now blew up, damaging some British and French ships. Still, preparations for renewal of the offensive went forward, and a message from the Admiralty ordered de Robeck to renew the assault. On March 20 de Robeck had 62 vessels ready as minesweepers and said that the offensive would be renewed in a few days. Two days later, however, after meeting with newly arrived land force commander British Army general Sir Ian Hamilton, de Robeck changed his mind. In an acrimonious session, the War Council decided to let the views of its commanders on the spot prevail.

The attempt to force the Dardanelles with warships alone cost the British and French 700 lives, three battleships sunk and two crippled, and damage to other ships. The naval offensive was not renewed. The campaign now shifted to land operations on the Gallipoli Peninsula, and naval activities from this point consisted of gunfire support and resupply.

SPENCER C. TUCKER

See also
Gallipoli Campaign

References
Churchill, Winston S. *The World Crisis.* Vol. 2. New York: Scribner, 1923.
James, Robert Rhodes. *Gallipoli: The History of a Noble Blunder.* New York: Macmillan, 1965.
Moorehead, Alan. *Gallipoli.* New York: Harper and Row, 1956.

Darius I (ca. 549–486 BCE)

King of Persia. The son of Hystaspes and born around 549 BCE, Darius (Dariash, Dareios, Dariavaush) took the throne in 521 following a period of civil war during 522–521. Parts of the empire had taken advantage of the turmoil to attempt to break free, and Darius spent the first several years of his reign quashing revolts in Persia, Media, Babylonia, and other places in the empire during 521–519.

One of the greatest of Persia's kings, Darius I (Darius the Great) reformed his vast empire administratively, dividing it into 20 provinces, or satrapies. As the satrap of each province usually inherited his position, this allowed considerable autonomy and the maintenance of local customs and traditions. Indeed, Darius sought to win the support of the many different peoples of the empire by allowing them a good deal of local autonomy so long as tribute was paid promptly. He also revised the legal code and encouraged the peoples' religions; for example, he permitted the Jews to build their temple at Jerusalem. However, each satrapy was required to remit regular tribute in the form of gold or silver. The satrap was answerable only to the Great King himself, but in addition to him there were in each province two imperial officials who reported directly to the king: a financial officer and a military coordinator. They served to help prevent the satraps from becoming too powerful. Darius standardized weights and measures, fixed the coinage, and introduced the gold daric. He also reformed the Persian military by introducing conscription, pay for the soldiers, and a program of regular training.

Darius was a great builder, his chief project being the construction of the new Persian capital at Persepolis. The city itself was surrounded by walls 60 feet high. Darius also caused to be built a canal that connected the Nile to Suez, and Persian ships were able to sail from the Nile through the Red Sea and then to Persia. Darius was also responsible for the construction of the system of royal roads throughout the empire. As with other Persian rulers, he did not permit slavery, and all royal workers were paid.

When Darius came to the throne the Persian Empire was well established, and although he embarked on a number of lengthy campaigns, these were only to extinguish a perceived threat or to round out natural frontiers. Toward that end, Darius campaigned in the area of the Black Sea and Armenia and fought on the Iranian steppe as well as along the Indus River. During his rule the empire reached its greatest territorial extent.

Following operations against the Scythians east of the Black Sea in 512 BCE, Darius personally campaigned in Southeastern Europe in 511. Supervising construction of a floating bridge across the Bosporus, he took Thrace and Macedonia. He also caused to be constructed another large floating bridge over the Danube and then campaigned for several hundred miles north, largely living off the land.

Fatefully for Persia and Europe, Darius also waged war with the Greeks. Ionians (Greeks living in Asia Minor), mistakenly believing that Darius had been defeated by the Scythians to the north, revolted against Persian rule but were quickly crushed in 510 BCE. Rising against Persia again in 499, the Ionians requested aid from the Greek city-states. Sparta declined, but Athens and Eritrea sent an expeditionary force by sea. The rebels then attacked and burned Sardis, the capital city of Lydia (498), but the satrap Artaphernes quickly reestablished control. Darius also assembled a large fleet and defeated the Greeks in the Battle of Lade (494).

Again master of Asia Minor, Darius was determined to punish Athens and Eritrea. He dispatched a naval expedition, but it encountered a storm and the fleet was wrecked off Mount Athos in 492 BCE. The second expedition reached Greece, only to meet defeat on land in the important Battle of Marathon (September 490). Darius died in 486 while preparing yet another expedition against Greece. This enterprise was taken up by his son, Xerxes I. Temporarily diverted by a revolt in Egypt during 486–484, Xerxes then sent perhaps the largest land force assembled to that time along with powerful naval forces, which nonetheless met defeat at sea in the Battle of Salamis in 480 and on land in the Battle of Plataea in 479.

The greatest Persian ruler after Cyrus the Great, Darius reformed the empire administratively and advanced it to its greatest territorial extent. His son was less successful.

Spencer C. Tucker

See also
Achaemenid Empire; Greco-Persian Wars

References
Abbott, Jacob. *Darius the Great.* New York: Harper & Brothers, 1904.

Rowley, H. H. *Darius the Meade and the Four World Empires in the Book of Daniel: A Historical Study of Contemporary Theories.* Cardiff: University of Wales Press, 1964.

Darius II (?–404 BCE)

Darius II was a king of the Persian Achaemenid dynasty who ruled from 423 to 404 BCE. He did not succeed his father, Artaxerxes I (r. 465–424), when the latter died. Artaxerxes I was succeeded first by his son Xerxes II, who ruled for only 45 days when he was murdered by his brother Sogdianos. The usurper, however, quickly alienated the elite palace guards when he executed their commander. Recognizing a golden opportunity to seize the throne, another son of Artaxerxes I, Ochos, who was governor of Hyrcania (modern-day Gorgan), on the southeastern shores of the Caspian Sea, organized an army, marched against his brother, defeated Sogdianos, and had him put to death after only six and half months on the throne.

Ochos then ascended the throne as Darius II in 423. Sometime after becoming king, Darius II was forced to fight his brother Arsites, who was backed by Artyphios, the son of capable Persian military commander Megabyxos. After suffering two defeats, the king's army managed to overcome the rebel prince and suppress the revolt. Both Arsites and Artyphios were executed. A revolt in Media in western Iran in 409–408 was also put down, but another uprising on the southern shores of the Caspian Sea in the region of present-day Gilan in northern Iran continued for some time.

The most serious challenge to Persian rule during the reign of Darius II came from Sardis in western Anatolia. Sometime around 416 BCE, the Persian governor of Sardis, Pissouthnes, revolted against the authority of the Persian king. As the satrap since 440 BCE, Pissouthnes had established deep-rooted ties with the local population and had organized an army that included Greek mercenaries. Darius II sent one of his commanders, Tissaphernes, to suppress the revolt. Tissaphernes crushed the revolt and restored order. As a reward for his performance, Darius II appointed Tissaphernes the satrap (governor) of Sardis.

The threat continued, however. During 414–412 Amorges, the son of Pissouthnes, resumed his father's revolt with assistance from Athens. This miscalculation by an overconfident Athens proved disastrous for them. Darius II responded by dropping any pretense of neutrality in the Peloponnesian War (431–404) and threw all of his support behind the Spartan alliance, which was fighting Athens and its allies. The Persian backing ultimately allowed Sparta to defeat Athens and emerge as the supreme power in mainland Greece. After the Athenian fleet, which had been sent to capture Syracuse, was destroyed in 413 BCE, the Spartan Navy also imposed its domination over the eastern half of the Aegean Sea. Meanwhile, the Persian governor, Tissaphernes, used the war between Sparta and Athens as an opportunity to reestablish Persian control over the Greek cities on the western coast of Asia Minor and to arrest the rebellious Amorges.

Seeking a positive outcome in Asia Minor, Darius II appointed his second son, Cyrus (Cyrus the Younger), as commander of Persian forces in the west. Cyrus, who nurtured a dream of becoming the ruler of the Persian Empire after the death of his father, was determined to cultivate the friendship of the Greeks, particularly the Spartans, who could provide him with troops in his impending confrontation with his older brother, Artaxerxes (future king Artaxerxes II), in the succession to the Persian throne. Not surprisingly, Cyrus was anxious to bring finis to the Peloponnesian War so he could recruit Greek mercenaries seeking new employment. Thus, Cyrus contributed generously to the Spartan war efforts, a key factor in enabling the Spartans to defeat the Athenians and end the war in 404 BCE.

Shortly after the conclusion of the Peloponnesian War, Darius II died in 404. He was succeeded by his oldest son, Artaxerxes.

Some historians of Achaemenid Persia have identified the reign of Darius II as the period when the gradual decline of the Persian Empire began. These scholars point to the growing restlessness in various provinces of the empire. They also cite the mounting influence of court eunuchs and their involvement in palace intrigues and plots.

Mehrdad Kia

See also
Achaemenid Empire; Artaxerxes I; Artaxerxes II; Cyrus the Younger

References
Burn, A. R. "Persia and the Greeks." In *The Cambridge History of Iran,* Vol. 2, *The Median and Achaemenian Periods,* ed. Ilya Gershevitch. Cambridge: Cambridge University Press, 1985.
Cook, J. M. *The Persian Empire.* New York: Schocken, 1983.
Curtis, John. *Ancient Persia.* Cambridge, MA: Harvard University Press, 1990.
Ghirshman, R. *Iran from the Earliest Times to the Islamic Conquest.* New York: Penguin Books, 1978.

Darius III (ca. 380–330 BCE)

Darius III, the last king of the Persian Achaemenid dynasty, ruled from 336 to 330 BCE. He was a cousin of Artaxerxes III, who ruled the Persian Achaemenid Empire from 359 to 338 BCE.

In 338 Achaemenid king Artaxerxes III was murdered together with most of his sons by Bagoas, a close confidant of the king who had performed brilliantly in the Persian reconquest of Egypt. Bagoas was not only an intelligent and capable commander but also a ruthless and ambitious individual who dreamed of ruling the Achaemenid Empire. He kept alive Arses, one of the sons of Artaxerxes III, to use him as a puppet king. Arses, however, discovered the truth about the role of Bagoas in the murder of his father and brothers and tried to remove him, but Bagoas murdered Arses and his sons as well. Thus, the Achaemenid royal house was destroyed several years before the invasion of the Persian Empire by Alexander III the Great of Macedon. In a desperate search for a legitimate heir to the throne who could claim a direct link to the Achaemenid male line, the satrap or governor of Armenia, Artashata (Ochos), known to the Greeks as Codommanos, was chosen as the new king. Artashata ascended the throne as Darius III (Old Persian, Daryavaush III).

The ambitious Bagoas retained his position and power, but soon the king and the minister were on a collision course. Darius III and Bagoas were not strangers. During the reign of Artaxerxes III, Bagoas had been sent by the king to subdue the rebellious Cadusii, a nomadic Iranian group that inhabited the southwestern shore of the Caspian Sea. The young Darius III had participated in this campaign and had displayed conspicuous valor on the battlefield, which won him great praise and recognition. Bagoas suppressed the Cadusii revolt successfully, and Ochos was appointed the satrap of Armenia. Now the prince and the minister were fighting over who should rule the Achaemenid Empire. When Darius III tried to wrest the reins of power from the ambitious courtier,

King Darius III, depicted here in the Alexander Mosiac recovered from Pompeii, was the last Achaemenid ruler of Persia and ruled during 336–330 BCE. Defeated in battle by King Alexander III the Great of Macedon, he was slain by his own generals. (alfiofer/iStockphoto.com)

Bagoas planned to poison the king, but Darius was informed of the plot. The king forced the conspirator to drink the poisoned cup himself and end his own life.

With the death of Bagoas, Darius III could then have focused on the chaotic situation in the western provinces of his empire in an effort to restore the authority of the central government there, but he did not have sufficient time to do this, as a threat to the empire was presenting itself to the west. The rise of a powerful and aggressive Macedonia posed a direct threat not only to the Achaemenid state but also to the Greek city-states, which were on the verge of being swallowed up by a superior military force. Toward the end of Artaxerxes III's reign, King Philip II had established a strong Macedonian state. In 340 he attacked Perinthos in northern Greece with the goal of establishing himself as the master of the straits (Bosporus and Dardanelles) connecting the Black Sea to the Aegean Sea. Alarmed by this Macedonian aggression, the Athenians sent an embassy to Artaxerxes III and requested an alliance with the Persian king. With support from Athens, Artaxerxes III sent an army that ejected the Macedonians from Perinthos, but Philip persisted nonetheless. He marched with a large force against Greece and defeated the armies of Athens and Thebes in the decisive Battle of Chaeronea in 338, establishing Macedonian control over Greece. Then in 337, Philip organized the League of Corinth and declared the goal of liberating the Greek cities under Persian rule in Asia Minor. In 336, Philip dispatched an army to Asia Minor as the first step toward a full-fledged invasion of the western provinces of the Achaemenid Empire. The planned invasion, however, came to a sudden end when Philip was assassinated in July 336.

The news of Philip's death provided temporary relief to Persia, but Philip's son Alexander now assumed the throne and was determined to employ his father's well-trained and well-organized army to attack the Persian Empire. In the spring of 334 BCE, Alexander crossed the Hellespont and began his conquest of Asia Minor. Darius had failed to prepare his armies adequately for a Macedonian attack. The Macedonians therefore defeated an Achaemenid force at Granicus. The Macedonian victory allowed Alexander to capture Sardis in western Asia Minor. The next confrontation between the two sides occurred in 333 at Issus in present-day southern Turkey near the city of Iskandarun. The battle resulted in another defeat for Darius III and his army. Darius fled the battlefield, and Alexander's men took captive the Persian king's mother, wife, infant son, and two of his daughters as well as several noble Persian ladies. Moving south along the present-day Lebanese coast, Alexander then seized Tyre in southern Lebanon following a lengthy siege of seven months. While Alexander was in Syria, Darius appealed to him for the release of his family as well as an alliance, both of which Alexander rejected.

From Syria and Phoenicia, Alexander marched against Gaza and then Egypt before turning east once again to confront Darius and his army in the Battle of Gaugamela in present-day northern Iraq in 331. The Achaemenid army was again defeated after Darius III again fled the battlefield.

Alexander now moved against Babylon and Susa, while Darius sought refuge in the summer capital of Hagmatana/Ecbatana (modern-day Hamedan). Meanwhile, Alexander seized Babylon, Susa, and Persepolis, destroying the palace there. After Alexander departed Persepolis, Darius and the Persian nobles accompanying him left Ecbatana for eastern Iran. They probably planned to connect with loyal units and commanders in the eastern provinces of the empire, particularly Bactria and Sogdiana, and then raise an army and strike back. It is not certain what happened at this point. Some historians maintain that Darius refused to flee any farther, forcing his loyal commanders to imprison him. Regardless, by the time Alexander caught up with Darius, the Achaemenid king was already dead, probably murdered by Bessus, the governor of Bactria, and the other Persian nobles who were fleeing with him. With the death of Darius III in the summer of 330 BCE, the Persian Achaemenid Empire came to an end.

MEHRDAD KIA

See also

Achaemenid Empire; Alexander III the Great; Alexander III's Invasion of the Persian Empire; Artaxerxes III; Gaugamela, Battle of; Granicus, Battle of the; Issus, Battle of; Tyre and Gaza, Sieges of

References

Briant, Pierre. *From Cyrus to Alexander.* Winona Lake, IN: Eisenbrauns, 2006.

Burn, A. R. *The Cambridge History of Iran,* Vol. 2, *The Median and Achaemenian Periods,* ed. Ilya Gershevitch. Cambridge: Cambridge University Press, 1985.

Cook, J. M. *The Persian Empire.* New York: Schocken, 1983.

Diodorus Siculus. Translated by C. H. Oldfather. London: William Heinemann, 1933.

Wiesehöfer, Josef. *Ancient Persia.* London: I. B. Tauris, 2011.

Dawud Pasha (1767–1851)

The last of the powerful Mamluk governors of Iraq. From the early 18th century, a succession of powerful Georgian mamluks ruled from Baghdad, often extending their authority to southern Iraq. Presiding over a tributary system, the mamluks maintained a fragile political order, extracted the revenues, and defended the region against internal or external challengers. Although the Ottoman sovereignty was acknowledged, the mamluks usually refused to accept material limitations on their rule. Beginning in 1749, however, Iraq had been under the rule of mamluks who nominally recognized Ottoman authority.

Born in Georgia in 1767, Dawud was kidnapped and sold into slavery in his youth. He was eventually bought by Suleyman Pasha, governor of Baghdad. Dawud's good looks, learning, and ostentatious piety contributed to his rapid advance, as did his marriage to the governor's daughter. Enjoying the patronage of Suleyman Pasha, Dawud became *daftardar* (treasurer) and *kahya* (deputy governor). In 1817, he obtained the title of pasha and ruled Iraq for the next 15 years.

Dawud Pasha proved to be a capable administrator and manipulative politician who exploited factional and tribal rivalries to his advantage. Emulating Mehmet Ali of Egypt, Dawud Pasha endeavored to modernize Iraq. He developed a strong central administration and restored peace to the country by ruthlessly subduing rebellious tribes. He removed or exiled tribal leaders not loyal to him, and he placed a number of his supporters at the heads of the tribes. His conflict with the Kurdish tribes, however, faced opposition from Iran and contributed to mounting tensions between the Porte and Persia that led to a war in 1821. Although he failed to end the system of capitulations owing to British pressure on the Porte, Dawud Pasha pursued comprehensive plans for the economic revival of Iraq.

Dawud Pasha carried out numerous public works, including the construction of canals and various buildings. In 1826 he completed the al-Nil canal and irrigation system that revived Iraqi agriculture. He facilitated the establishment of new manufactures (many of them designed to meet the needs of his army) and promoted trade and commerce. His actions ensured the safety of highways and facilitated the transport of goods by land and water.

Dawud Pasha also hired European experts to modernize his military forces. In 1823 during the Ottoman-Persian War, he stopped the Iranian invasion of Iraq and later helped Ottoman authorities quell the Janissary revolt. However, his persistent insubordination, particularly his delay in sending the military contribution demanded by the Ottoman government after the Russo-Ottoman War of 1828–1829, caused Sultan Mahmud II to remove him from power. In 1831 as Iraq was reeling from the terrible plague and drought, the Ottoman Army, under Ali Pasha of Aleppo, defeated Dawud Pasha and ended the era of mamluk rule in Baghdad. Taken prisoner and delivered to Istanbul, Dawud Pasha was well treated and later appointed to important offices in the Ottoman Empire. In 1843 he was appointed guardian of the holy shrines of Medina, a position he held until his death in 1851. He was buried opposite the tomb of Caliph Osman (Othman).

Alexander Mikaberidze

See also

Mahmud II, Sultan; Mehmed Ali; Ottoman-Persian Wars of the 18th and 19th Centuries; Russo-Ottoman Wars

References

Huart, Clément. *Histoire de Bagdad dans les temps modernes.* Paris: Leroux, 1901.

Nieuwenhuis, Tom. *Politics and Society in Early Modern Iraq: Mamlūk Pastias, Tribal Shayks and Local Rule between 1802 and 1831.* The Hague: M. Nijhoff, 1982.

Silagadze, Beniamin. *Eraqi Mamluktha gamgeblobis khanashi, 1749–1831.* Tbilisi: Metsniereba, 1978.

Dayan, Moshe (1915–1981)

Israeli general and political leader during the formative years of the State of Israel. Moshe Dayan was born on May 20, 1915, in Degania Kibbutz near the Sea of Galilee. His parents had emigrated to Palestine from Russia. At age 14 Dayan joined Haganah, the Jewish self-defense militia in the British mandate of Palestine. At the beginning of the Arab Revolt of 1936–1939 Dayan was studying at the London School of Economics, but he returned to Palestine in 1936 and rejoined Haganah. He served in ambush and patrol units and trained under British Army captain Orde Wingate. In 1939 because of his membership in Haganah, which had been banned by the British, Dayan was sentenced to five years in prison.

Released in February 1941, Dayan led reconnaissance forces into Vichy France–controlled Syria to support the subsequent British invasion there. During one mission in Syria on June 8, 1941, Dayan was shot by a sniper and lost his left eye. From then on, he became well known for his trademark black eye patch.

Posted to the Haganah General Staff, Dayan worked to gather intelligence on Arab military capabilities. In May 1948, Israel proclaimed its independence and was immediately attacked by the neighboring Arab nations. In the ensuing Israeli War of Independence (1948–1949), Dayan led the defense of the Deganya settlements during May 19–21, 1948. He then raised the 89th Commando Battalion, a mobile unit in jeeps and half-tracks, leading it in capturing Lod and Ramallah (July 9–19). Named commander in the Jerusalem vicinity on July 23, he proved to be an exceptional strategist and tactician. As such, he rose rapidly through the ranks of the Israel Defense Forces (IDF). In 1950 he became head of the Southern Command, and two years later he assumed control of the Northern Command. In 1953, General Dayan was named chief of army operations and then chief of staff of the IDF.

Dayan remained chief of staff from 1953 until 1958. In this post he reinvigorated the IDF. He ordered the best officers into the fighting units and toughened training, leading the way by completing a parachute and commando course himself. The IDF's proportion of combat to noncombat forces of 50 percent was probably the world's highest. Dayan also insisted that officers lead from the front. During the 1956 Suez Crisis, Dayan planned and oversaw the so-called Lightning Campaign that saw Israeli forces advance quickly through the Sinai toward the Suez Canal.

In 1958 Dayan retired from the IDF and joined the Mapai Party led by David Ben-Gurion, Israel's first prime minister. Dayan was elected to the Knesset (Israeli parliament)

Moshe Dayan (1915–1981) was an important Israeli general and chief of staff of the Israel Defense Forces during 1953–1958. As minister of defense during 1967–1974, he presided over the highly successful 1967 Six-Day War but his reputation was greatly tarnished by the Yom Kippur War of 1973 and he resigned the next year. Dayan last held office as foreign minister during 1977–1979. (Israeli Government Press Office)

in 1959 and served in the cabinet as minister of agriculture during December 1959–November 1964. In 1964 he left Mapai and helped form Rafi, Ben-Gurion's separatist party. Dayan was reelected to parliament, and in June 1967 Prime Minister Levi Eshkol named him minister of defense as part of the prime minister's unity government. The members of Rafi rejoined Mapai to form the Labor Party in 1968.

While defense minister, Dayan presided over the June 1967 Six-Day War. He was not an integral part of IDF planning for the conflict, but his presence contributed to military morale and confidence in the Eshkol government. The quick war included conquest of the Golan Heights, the West Bank, and the Sinai Peninsula. Dayan's prominent public role in the conflict inflated his popularity within Israel. He pushed for open annexation of the occupied territories and used his position to create Jewish settlements in the West Bank and on the Golan Heights. He remained minister of defense under Golda Meir, who became prime minister after Eshkol's death on February 26, 1969.

Dayan's image was greatly tarnished by the Yom Kippur War (1973), which began with surprise Egyptian and Syrian attacks and heavy losses in troops, equipment, and territory by the IDF. Although later exonerated by an official inquiry, Dayan's ministry clearly ignored the signs of impending hostilities. Despite Israel's eventual victory, the toll of the war led Meir to resign along with her entire cabinet in May 1974.

The war had deeply depressed Dayan, who went into a political eclipse for a time. Despite his ties to the Labor Party, he joined Prime Minister Menachem Begin's Likud Party government in 1977, serving as foreign minister. In this capacity, Dayan assisted in negotiating the 1978 Camp David Accords and the 1979 Israel-Egypt Peace Treaty. Soon after the treaty was signed, however, Dayan disagreed with Begin over the status of Palestinian territories occupied by Israel and the construction of Jewish settlements. Dayan believed that Israel should disengage entirely from the territories seized in the 1967 war. In 1981 he formally left the Labor Party to form a new party, Telem, which won only two seats in the 1981 parliamentary elections. One of Telem's positions was that Israel should withdraw from the occupied territories.

Dayan was an amateur archaeologist, and he also wrote four books. He died on October 16, 1981, of colon cancer in Tel Aviv. An able and resourceful military commander, Dayan was, however, somewhat less successful as a politician.

PAUL J. SPRINGER

See also
Begin, Menachem; Camp David Accords; Eshkol, Levi; Haganah; Israel-Egypt Peace Treaty; Israeli War of Independence; Meir, Golda Mabovitch; Sinai Campaign of 1956; Six-Day War; Suez Crisis; Wingate, Orde Charles; Yom Kippur War

References
Dayan, Moshe. *Moshe Dayan: The Story of My Life*. New York: Morrow, 1976.
Slater, Robert. *Warrior Statesman: The Life of Moshe Dayan*. New York: St. Martin's, 1991.
Teveth, Shabtai. *Moshe Dayan: The Soldier, the Man, the Legend*. Boston: Houghton Mifflin, 1973.

Debecka Pass, Battle of (April 6, 2003)

Engagement that unfolded in northern Iraq on April 6, 2003, during the Iraq War (Operation IRAQI FREEDOM). U.S. strategy for the Iraq War called for the major thrust against Iraq to come from the south. A secondary offensive featuring the 4th Infantry Division would move through Turkey and invade northern Iraq. When the Turkish government refused permission for the 4th Division to operate from its territory, however, strategists revised the plan for a northern thrust. The new plan called for a joint force consisting of the 173rd Airborne Brigade, the 26th Marine Expeditionary Unit, and U.S. Army Special Forces operating in cooperation with Kurdish fighters known as Peshmerga ("those who face death").

The 10th Special Forces Group, commanded by Colonel Charlie Cleveland, opened the second front in northern Iraq. Its mission was to destroy training camps used by Ansar al-Islam terrorists and to prevent Iraqi forces in northern Iraq from reinforcing the units defending Baghdad. The particular objectives of the 10th Special Forces Group were the cities of Mosul and Kirkuk and the northern oil fields near these cities.

The basic unit of the special forces was the Operational Detachment A, or A-Team. A captain commanded the 12-man A-Team with a warrant officer serving as second-in-command. Noncommissioned officers composed the balance of the team, with two each possessing specialty training in one of the five special forces functional areas: weapons, engineering, medical, communications, and operations and intelligence.

For the push into northern Iraq, the special forces utilized specially modified Humvees (high-mobility multipurpose wheeled vehicles). The Humvees served as a mobile headquarters and fighting platform, and they had sophisticated communications equipment to enable the troops to call in air strikes. Each vehicle carried several machine guns, Mark 19 grenade launchers, sniper rifles, side arms, Stinger shoulder-fired antiaircraft missiles, and the new Javelin fire-and-forget antitank missile. The Stinger launcher and missile weighed about 50 pounds. Consequently, a single soldier could carry and operate it. The Javelin had a range of about 2,750 yards. The missile used an internal guidance system to fly to the target and then dive down to strike the top of an armored vehicle, its most vulnerable spot because top armor was thinner than front or side armor. The Javelins figured prominently in the April 6, 2003, Battle of Debecka Pass.

Two special forces A-Teams and forward air controllers (26 personnel in all) were given the task of securing a key intersection on Highway 2 near the town of Debecka in northern Iraq between the cities of Irbil to the north and Kirkuk to the south. Accompanied by as many as 80 Peshmerga fighters, the team deployed to block Iraqi troop movements along Highway 2 in either direction. However, a surprise Iraqi counterattack featuring some 150 infantry, eight armored personnel carriers, and four T-55 tanks with 100mm main guns struck the special forces, forcing them to withdraw to a nearby ridge line.

From their new position the Americans engaged the approaching Iraqi armored forces with Javelin antitank missiles, .50-caliber machine guns, and Mark 19 40mm grenade launchers. One Javelin destroyed an armored personnel carrier from a distance of 2,950 yards, 200 yards beyond the rated maximum engagement range. During this phase of the battle, of eight Javelins fired by the special forces, seven struck their intended targets, destroying five armored personnel carriers and two trucks. The Javelin strikes stopped the momentum of the Iraqi attack. The Iraqis then moved the tanks behind an earthen berm where they could not be targeted by the Javelins, because the Javelins required the operator to have a clear line of sight to the target. The Iraqis did not know that the Americans had only three Javelins remaining.

Meanwhile, a request for air support brought U.S. Navy Grumman F-14 Tomcat fighters. U.S. Air Force forward air controllers operating with the special forces directed the Tomcats to attack the Iraqi armor at the intersection. In a case of mistaken identify, an F-14 Tomcat bombed friendly Kurdish fighters operating behind the special forces, killing 16 Kurds and wounding another 45. A British Broadcasting Corporation (BBC) film crew was present and broadcast a description of this incident as it occurred.

The special forces were holding their position until an Iraqi battery of D-20 towed 152mm howitzers opened fire. The special forces had no answer to this fire and were again compelled to relocate. In their new position they received a resupply of Javelin missiles. The Americans were also able to see more clearly the Iraqi T-55 tanks as well as the surviving armored personnel carriers. The special forces again opened fire with the Javelins. When an Iraqi tank tried to change positions it emerged into the open, where it was promptly destroyed by a Javelin. This event broke the morale of the Iraqi forces.

At 12:45 p.m. local time, about 15 Iraqi soldiers appeared from a ravine indicating that they wished to surrender. Suddenly, two white Toyota Land Cruisers appeared and disgorged Iraqi security personnel, who began shooting down the surrendering soldiers. A laser-guided bomb dropped from an American airplane then destroyed the Land Cruisers. During the final phase of the combat, another Javelin missile destroyed another Iraqi T-55 tank. The remaining Iraqi soldiers then abandoned their vehicles and fled.

In a telephone interview in the autumn of 2003, one of the special forces sergeants in the battle attributed the American victory to the Javelin missiles. Without them, the special forces would not have been able to hold off the Iraqi tanks. The Americans suffered no casualties, but the Peshmerga sustained 16 dead and 45 wounded from the friendly fire incident; 1 civilian was also killed. Iraqi killed and wounded are unknown, but 20 were taken prisoner. The Iraqis also lost at least two T-55 tanks, eight armored personnel carriers, and four trucks. The Battle of Debecka Pass was an example of how small highly trained well-led units with sophisticated weaponry can defeat larger conventional units.

JAMES ARNOLD

See also
Iraq War; Peshmerga

References
Antenori, Frank, and Hans Halberstadt. *Roughneck Nine-One: The Extraordinary Story of a Special Forces A-Team at War.* New York: St. Martin's, 2006.

Gordon, Michael R., and General Bernard E. Trainor. *Cobra II: The Inside Story of the Invasion and Occupation of Iraq.* New York: Pantheon Books, 2006.

Murray, Williamson, and Robert H. Scales Jr. *The Iraq War: A Military History.* Cambridge, MA: Belknap, 2005.

Stilwell, Alexander. *Special Forces Today: Afghanistan, Africa, Balkans, Iraq, South America.* Dulles, VA: Potomac Books, 2007.

DEFENSIVE SHIELD, Operation (April 3–May 10, 2002)

An Israeli military operation launched against Palestinian militant groups in the West Bank between April 3, 2002, and May 10, 2002. Numerous suicide bombings and Israeli reprisal attacks had taken place since the late summer of 2001. A particularly horrifying suicide bombing occurred at a hotel where a group had gathered to celebrate the religious holiday of Passover.

In response to the bombings, Israeli prime minister Ariel Sharon directed the Israel Defense Forces (IDF) to launch Operation DEFENSIVE SHIELD. The goals of the operation were to enter the West Bank, locate villages and towns harboring or aiding terrorists, arrest the terrorists and their supporters, seize weapons, and destroy secret bases and camps (as well as any matériel of use to the terrorists), all while minimizing civilian casualties.

IDF forces began the operation on April 3, rolling into the West Bank towns of Nablus, Ramallah, Jenin, and Bethlehem, all identified as terrorist centers. Hebron and Jericho were not targeted. The IDF imposed strict curfews on the civilian population, which according to Palestinian sources resulted in numerous civilian deaths, as did the denial of emergency medical services during the curfew hours. IDF troops encountered mixed opposition, with action taking place in Jenin, in Bethlehem, and at the Palestinian Authority (PA) compound in Ramallah.

In Bethlehem, 26 Palestinian gunmen seized the Church of the Nativity, holding the clergy there hostage. The IDF finally negotiated their release by allowing the gunmen safe passage to Cyprus or the Gaza Strip and releasing 24 terror suspects from a hospital where they were being detained. In Ramallah, the IDF engaged in a siege of the PA compound, trapping Arafat and others, that lasted nearly a month and involved additional attacks all through Ramallah. The siege was lifted when U.S. negotiators arranged for 6 men wanted by the IDF in the compound to be placed in a PA jail in Jericho. The Israelis captured numerous documents at the PA compound, which purportedly demonstrated the PA knowledge of and collusion with many of the terrorist organizations attacking Israel.

Significant fighting occurred in Jenin and the refugee camp in its environs. In order to minimize civilian deaths, the Israelis decided to forgo air strikes in favor of a ground attack. Thousands of booby traps had been set, and the IDF employed heavily armored bulldozers to demolish houses suspected of harboring terrorists and any places that might have been rigged with explosives. The Israelis claim that fair warning was given before the bulldozing, but Palestinian sources refute this and claim that no warning was given. The fighting in Jenin was heavy at times, and running gun battles with armed militants were common. The IDF claims that it destroyed 10 percent of the houses in the Jenin refugee camp through offensive action. IDF sources claim 52 Palestinian dead including 22 civilians. The Palestinians accused the IDF of perpetrating a massacre in Jenin, but investigation by both the United Nations and independent human rights organizations could find no evidence of a mass killing.

The operation officially ended on May 10, 2002. The IDF claimed more than 5,000 small arms and explosives captured along with computers, chemicals, cell phones, and weapon-making components. The IDF also claimed that intelligence documents captured at Arafat's compound vindicated the operation. These documents provided ample evidence of PLO collusion with the radicals and identified key figures of interest to the Israelis. Palestinian casualties during the operation included 188 dead, 599 wounded, and 425 others detained. Israeli casualties included 29 dead and

129 wounded. Total civilian casualties were 632 for the Palestinians and 135 for the Israelis.

Officially, the Israeli government viewed the operation as a success. In a public opinion survey, most Israelis held that the operation had been necessary. However, at least 54 percent believed that it damaged Israel in the realm of world opinion.

RODERICK VOSBURGH

See also

al-Aqsa Martyrs Brigades; Arafat, Yasser; Fatah, al-; Hamas; Palestinian Islamic Jihad; Palestinian National Authority; Sharon, Ariel; Suicide Bombings; Terrorism

References

Dor, Daniel. *The Suppression of Guilt: The Israeli Media and the Reoccupation of the West Bank.* London: Pluto, 2005.

Finkelstein, Norman G. *Image and Reality of the Israel-Palestine Conflict.* New York: Norton, 2003.

Reinhart, Tanya. *Israel/Palestine: How to End the War of 1948.* New York: Seven Stories, 2004.

Definitive Treaty (March 14, 1812)

Treaty of alliance between Persia and Great Britain. Also known as the Treaty of Friendship and Alliance between Great Britain and Persia and the Tehran Treaty of 1812, it marked a major change in Persia's foreign policy following the failed Treaty of Finckenstein (1807) between Persia and France. The Definitive Treaty, signed in the Persian capital city of Tehran on March 14, 1812, was based on the Preliminary Treaty negotiated by London and Tehran in March 1809.

Under the terms of the Definitive Treaty, Persia pledged to declare all alliances formerly contracted with European powers null and void and promised to stop any European power that might attempt to cross Persian territory to reach India. Britain pledged financial aid (200,000 *tomans*) or troop reinforcements if a European power attempted to invade Persia. The treaty also made provisions for the training of the Persian Army by British officers and for an increased Persian naval presence in the Caspian Sea. Britain promised not to interfere in any conflicts between Persia and Afghanistan, while the shah pledged to provide military aid should the Afghans attack British interests.

The treaty soon became problematic, since during the Russo-Persian War of 1804–1813 the British government found itself in the difficult position of having to assist Persia against Russia, with which Britain was allied against Napoleonic France. While British officers, serving as observers, assisted the Persian Army against Russia, the British government pushed for renegotiating the Definitive Treaty. This led to the conclusion of the Tehran Treaty (also known as the Definitive Treaty) of November 1814.

ALEXANDER MIKABERIDZE

See also

Russo-Persian Wars; Tehran Treaty

References

Aitchison, C. U., ed. *A Collection of Treaties, Engagements, and Sanads Relating to India and Neighbouring Countries*, 10:48–52. Calcutta: Office of the Superintendent of Government Printing, 1892.

Daniel, Elton L. *The History of Iran.* Westport, CT: Greenwood, 2001.

Degania, Battle of (May 20, 1948)

A hard-fought battle on May 20, 1948, between Israeli and Syrian forces for control of the Jordan River Valley during the Israeli War of Independence (1948–1949). Degania was Palestine's first collective settlement, or *kvutzah*. It was located in the Jordan Plain west of the Sea of Galilee (Lake Kinneret). Degania means "cornflower" and comes from the Arab designation of the land, Umm Juni.

Arthur Ruppin purchased uncultivated land here in 1909 for the Jewish National Fund, and that same year a group of Jewish immigrants attempted to farm the land along conventional lines but failed. The next year 36 others asked to farm the area on a collectivist basis, and Ruppin agreed. He also provided the settlers with two mud-brick dormitories, basic farm equipment, and half a dozen mules. Although conditions were difficult and malaria took a heavy toll, the effort succeeded and in 1911 brought in a successful harvest.

Degania was organized along strict collectivist lines with full equality among the sexes. Degania Alif (A) became the designation for this first settlement and was known as the "Mother of the Kvutzah." Its members wanted to keep the same arrangement rather than be organized along the lines of the larger collective settlement, or kibbutz. Thus, in 1920 with the arrival of another group of settlers, Degania Bet (B) was organized just to the south. In 1932 a portion of the land was given to a third collective settlement, Kibbutz Afikim.

The two Deganias were the scene of heavy fighting during the Israeli War of Independence. On May 18, 1948, the Syrian Army's 1st Brigade, commanded by Brigadier General Husni al-Zaim, attacked Zemach, about a mile due east of Degania A on the Sea of Galilee. Al-Zaim had at his disposal some 30 armored vehicles including Renault tanks. The Jewish Haganah defenders had only small arms and two 20mm antitank guns. Part of the Syrian brigade swept around to the south of Zemach, outflanking the defenders who also lost one of their antitank guns to Syrian fire. Most of the defenders were killed, and the remainder withdrew.

It now looked as if the way was open for the Syrians to overrun the entire Jordan Valley. The two villages of Degania A and B became the new front line. That night, the Israelis rushed up reinforcements but also evacuated the villages of Shaar HaGolan and Masada to the east. At the same time, the Syrians beat back an attempt by Palmach forces to retake the police post in Zemach.

The Syrian attack on the two Deganias opened at dawn on May 20 with an artillery bombardment. The thrust of the attack was against Degania A, which was defended by only 70 men and the one remaining 20mm gun. The attacking Syrian infantrymen were preceded by five tanks and some armored cars. The Syrian tanks easily overcame the defensive fire and broke through the Israeli outer perimeter. The one Israeli antitank gun crew knocked out one Syrian armored car. Israeli fire also damaged one of the Renault tanks, which then withdrew. Still, the remainder of the Syrian tanks proceeded and came up against the Israelis' last trenches. There the defenders, who were fighting for their homes, attacked the tanks and armored cars with both Molotov cocktails and British World War II PIAT (Projector Infantry Anti-Tank) hollow-charge explosives. The leading Syrian tank was disabled by a Molotov cocktail but continued to fire until it was destroyed by other gasoline bombs. (This tank has never been removed and is kept in situ as a permanent memorial to the defenders.) The bulk of the Syrian infantry had not kept up with the tanks and thus fell prey to Israeli small-arms fire. At midday, having lost two more armored cars, the Syrians withdrew from Degania A and concentrated on Degania B to the south.

Here the Syrians committed eight tanks and armored cars and two infantry companies. All were driven back. At the same time and for the first time in the war, Israeli artillery came into battle. The guns had been received only a few days before at Tel Aviv and were immediately sent north, where they were positioned in the hills overlooking the Sea of Galilee. Their shells caused the Syrians to withdraw from Remesh, Shaar HaGolan, and Masada, which were then reoccupied by the Israelis. By May 23, the Israelis had won the battle for control of the Jordan Valley.

Today the two Deganias have a population of some 1,200 people. In addition to farming, there is also a metal factory there.

Spencer C. Tucker

See also
Israeli War of Independence

References
Herzog, Chaim. *The Arab-Israeli Wars: War and Peace in the Middle East from the War of Independence to Lebanon.* Westminster, MD: Random House, 1984.

Lustick, Ian. *From War to War: Israel vs. the Arabs, 1948–1967.* New York: Garland, 1994.

Pollack, Kenneth M. *Arabs at War: Military Effectiveness, 1948–1991.* Lincoln: University of Nebraska Press, 2002.

Deir Yassin Massacre (April 9–11, 1948)

A massacre of Arab civilians in the British Mandate for Palestine by Jewish forces during April 9–11, 1948. The incident occurred just one month prior to the declaration of the State of Israel and the beginning of the Israeli War of Independence (1948–1949). Since the 1930s, there had seen increasing violence between Arabs and Jews for control of Palestine. In one sense, Deir Yassin (Dayr Yasin) was a continuation of that struggle.

Beginning on April 9, 1948, Jewish forces attacked the Arab village of Deir Yassin. Located near Jerusalem, the village of about 750 persons overlooked the important Tel Aviv–Jerusalem Road and was slated for occupation under Plan Dalet. The forces involved included members of the paramilitary Palmach organization, which was part of the Jewish self-defense organization Haganah, and members of the Jewish terrorist organizations Irgun Tsvai Leumi (National Military Organization) and Lohamei Herut Israel (Lehi or Stern Gang). The raiders killed somewhere between 96 and 254 Arab villagers, mostly elderly, women, and children. Their bodies were dumped into the village well or left in the streets. In addition, some survivors were paraded naked in West Jerusalem and then returned to Deir Yassin, where they were killed. About 100 orphaned village children were left outside the wall of the Old City in Jerusalem.

The massacre, which was widely publicized in official Jewish radio broadcasts intended to terrify Arabs, was the major impetus in the flight of hundreds of thousands of Arabs from Palestine.

Arabs claim that what happened at Deir Yassin was a premeditated and deliberate act of terrorism by Jews. The flight of terrified villagers from their homes served to facilitate Jewish efforts to secure Arab lands and create a Jewish state in Palestine. Jews defended the attack on Deir Yassin as part of Operation NACHSHON, meant to break the Arab siege of Jerusalem, but according to Arabs, Deir Yassin had remained neutral in the growing violence between armed Arab and Jewish groups. Villagers had even made a pact with Haganah that they would not aid armed Arab groups on the understanding that their village would not then be targets of Jewish attacks. Some Israeli officials dispute these claims, contending that armed Arabs along with Iraqi volunteers from the Arab Liberation Army (ALA) were given sanctuary and stationed in the village, thus violating any pact that may have existed.

Also in dispute is whether villagers fought the attackers and whether a truck equipped with a loudspeaker warned the villagers of the impending attack in Arabic before it began. Most accounts, even from Israelis, claim that the truck either never arrived or arrived after the fighting had already begun. Irgun leader Menachem Begin, who was not a participant in the massacre but shared in the responsibility for it, disputed both of these claims. In his book *The Revolt* (1951), he insisted that the Deir Yassin massacre was a fabrication by anti-Semites.

The number of villagers killed is also in dispute. The initial death toll was said to be 254, publicized by an Irgun commander who later admitted that he exaggerated to force the Arabs to panic and flee their homes. One subsequent and disputed study concluded that the number of Arabs slain did not exceed 120. Yet International Red Cross representative Jacques Reynier counted 150 maimed bodies (including disembowelments and decapitations) in the cistern, while others were scattered through the streets of the village. That testimony and survivors' reports supported the higher figure of dead originally given. Arab League president Azzam Pasha pointed to the massacre at Deir Yassin as the principal reason for the Arab states' invasion of Palestine following the proclamation of the State of Israel in May 1948.

STEFAN BROOKS

See also
Abdel-Rahman, Omar; Arab-Jewish Communal War; Arab League; Begin, Menachem; Haganah; Irgun Tsvai Leumi; Lohamei Herut Israel; NACHSHON, Operation; Palmach

References
Begin, Menachem. *The Revolt.* Los Angeles: Nash Publishing, 1972.
Collins, Larry, and Dominique Lapierre. *O Jerusalem!* New York: Simon and Schuster, 1972.
Kanaana, Sharif, and Nihad Zeitawi. *The Village of Deir Yassin.* Monograph No. 4, Destroyed Palestinian Villages Documentation Project. Birzeit, Palestine: Documentation Center of Birzeit University Press, 1988.
Khalidi, Walid, ed. *All That Remains: Palestinian Villages Occupied and Depopulated by Israel in 1948.* Washington, DC: Institute for Palestine Studies, 1992.

McGowan, Daniel, and Marc Ellis. *Remembering Deir Yassin: The Future of Israel and Palestine.* Brooklyn, NY: Olive Branch, 1998.
Morris, Benny. *The Birth of the Palestinian Refugee Problem Revisited.* 2nd ed. Cambridge: Cambridge University Press, 2004.

Demetrius I Poliorcetes (336–282 BCE)

Known as Poliorcetes (the Besieger), Demetrius I Poliorcetes was the son of Antigonus I Monophthalmus. Of all the successors (Diadochi) of Alexander III of Macadeon (Alexander the Great) who battled after his death in 323 BCE to secure the territory he had conquered, Demetrius most resembled Alexander in talent, looks, and charisma. Born in 336 and raised in Phrygia, Demetrius received his first independent command from Antigonus at age 22 in 314, when he was charged with the defense of Syria. Although Demetrius suffered defeat in the Battle of Gaza in 312, he was responsible for a number of successful campaigns against the generals of Ptolemy I Soter and Seleucus I Nicator in 311–310.

By 307, Demetrius and his father were being hailed as savior gods by the Athenians after their liberation of the city, and cults were established for them. Eventually, Demetrius was effectively deified by the Athenians. He distinguished himself particularly by his naval victory against Ptolemy at Salamis in 306, which was later commemorated on examples of his coinage.

Shortly afterward, Demetrius and his father at last crowned themselves kings, making them the first of Alexander's successors to claim the title. This set a precedent for the other successors, who quickly followed suit. Another career highlight was Demetrius's yearlong siege of Rhodes. His important innovations there in this form of warfare and in siege engines earned him his nickname "the Besieger"—a somewhat ironical name as the siege of Rhodes was at great cost and he was ultimately unable to take it.

Demetrius was also well known for debauchery and scandalous, excessive behavior, particularly in Athens where he was said to have inflicted a great number of indecencies on the Parthenon. He was polygamous, like many of the early Hellenistic kings, marrying at least five times and keeping many mistresses. A coalition of the other Diadochi defeated Demetrius at the Battle of Ipsus in 301, where Antigonus lost his life and Demetrius was forced to flee.

Despite this reversal of fortune, Demetrius retained his huge fleet and title and effectively ran his kingdom from the sea for a number of years as he campaigned to regain his territories. He spent time in 299 attacking Thrace at Lysimachus's expense, and the two were to become lifelong enemies. In 296 Demetrius was able to take back Athens and then campaigned against Sparta. The death of Cassander in Macedon and the subsequent succession crisis then allowed Demetrius the opportunity to seize the Macedonian throne.

Demetrius was, however, poorly received as king, and by 288 he was expelled by another coalition, headed by Lysimachus and Pyrrhus. Demetrius once again set about rebuilding his empire and left for Asia with his force, but being in poor health and facing numerous desertions from his supporters, he was soon forced to surrender to Seleucus. Demetrius was from then on detained in honorable captivity and appears to have refused to cooperate with his son Antigonus II Gonatas's attempts to liberate him. Demetrius died within three years of his captivity, his poor health no doubt accelerated by the excessive drinking and depression of his final years.

CHARLOTTE M. R. DUNN

See also
Alexander III the Great; Antigonus I Monophthalmus; Diadochi, Wars of the; Ipsus, Battle of; Lysimachus; Ptolemy I Soter; Seleucus I Nicator

References
Billows, Richard A. *Antigonus the One-Eyed.* Berkeley: University of California Press, 1990.
Bosworth, A. Brian. *The Legacy of Alexander: Politics, Warfare and Propaganda under the Successors.* Oxford: Oxford University Press, 2002.

Demetrius II Nicator (ca. 160–125 BCE)

Demetrius II ruled the Seleucid Empire in two separate reigns: circa 145–138 and 129–125 BCE. The son of Demetrius I Soter, he was born around 160. At about 15 Demetrius II led a mercenary army to drive out the usurper Alexander I Balas. Demetrius then showed further military capacity by reasserting Seleucid control over Judaea-Palestine and defeating the usurper Diodotus, who had taken the regal name King Tryphon.

In 139, Demetrius II launched an ambitious offensive to regain territories in Mesopotamia lost to the Parthians. He won victories but was taken prisoner, allegedly falling into a trap under a deceitful peace treaty. In his absence the kingdom passed into the hands of his younger brother, Antiochus VII Sidetes.

When Antiochus VII attacked Parthia in 129, Demetrius was released to create the diversion of a civil war in the Seleucid Empire. With the death of Antiochus VII in Parthia, Demetrius reestablished himself as king and ruled to 125, when he attacked Egypt and was killed and defeated near Tyre by Egyptian forces supporting a pretender, Alexander II Zabinas.

Demetrius II's early military successes gained him the title Nicator, "the Conqueror." He showed great gifts for leadership at the head of his troops in the tradition of Alexander the Great but was too harsh to be popular, and in his second rule he suffered from the discredit of his captivity in Parthia.

DOUGLAS KELLY

See also
Antiochus VII Sidetes; Seleucid Empire

References
Sherwin-White, Susan, and Amélie Kuhrt. *From Samarkhand to Sardis: A New Approach to the Seleucid Empire.* London: Duckworth, 1993.
Shipley, Graham. *The Greek World after Alexander.* New York: Routledge, 2000.

DESERT FOX, Operation (December 16–19, 1998)

Four-day American and British air campaign against Iraq during December 16–19, 1998, conducted in response to Iraqi resistance to United Nations Special Commission (UNSCOM) weapons inspectors carrying out their duties in searching for weapons of mass destruction (WMD). The UNSCOM visits were being held under agreements reached at the end of Operation DESERT STORM in 1991.

U.S. president William J. (Bill) Clinton ordered the attacks with the objectives of degrading Iraqi WMD development and delivery capabilities, limiting the Iraqi ability to threaten neighboring states, and punishing President Saddam Hussein's regime for not supporting the United Nations inspection requirements. The DESERT FOX strikes occurred within the context of Operations NORTHERN WATCH and SOUTHERN WATCH, which had imposed no-fly zones in Iraq north of the 36th parallel and south of the 33rd parallel (originally the 32nd). These operations began after Operation DESERT STORM in February 1991 and lasted until the commencement of Operation IRAQI FREEDOM in March 2003. U.S. Marine Corps general Anthony Zinni, commander of U.S. Central Command (CENTCOM), planned and commanded Operation DESERT FOX, using U.S. Air Force, Navy, and Marine Corps resources as well as assets from the British Royal Air Force.

Operation DESERT FOX consisted of a brief, intense, and highly focused series of strikes against a carefully selected set of 100 targets in Iraq, including sites capable of WMD production and delivery, command and control centers, intelligence service and Republican Guard facilities, airfields, components of the integrated air defense system, and a petroleum site associated with illegal exports under the existing UN sanctions.

The attack force included 325 sea-launched Tomahawk cruise missiles, 90 conventional air-launched cruise missiles fired from American B-52 bombers, and 600 bomb strikes conducted by B-1 bombers (carrying out their first combat operation) and fighter aircraft flown from aircraft carriers and bases in Kuwait and neighboring Persian Gulf states. Saudi Arabia chose not to support direct combat missions against Iraq, and the French Air Force, which had been participating in the no-fly zone enforcement, also did not participate and subsequently withdrew from the theater.

The strikes were an impressive tactical success with substantial target damage and no allied aircraft lost. However, the strategic results were less conclusive, and the impact of the strikes was debated until the Iraqi WMD issue was resolved by the invasion and occupation of Iraq during Operation IRAQI FREEDOM.

Some critics have charged that the operation was designed by President Clinton as a distraction from the impeachment process stemming from the Monica Lewinsky affair, which was then under way in the U.S. Congress, but there is no substantial evidence to support such an allegation. Additionally, some analysts believe that the operation was not a strong enough blow to achieve substantial results, and others noted that it created diplomatic challenges for the United States with selected diplomatic partners.

Although Operation DESERT FOX did not force Iraq to resume cooperation with the UNSCOM inspection program, it nonetheless significantly damaged elements of the targeted Iraqi capabilities, and although Saddam Hussein remained highly belligerent in his public comments, the strikes demonstrated American resolve and in general contributed to a strengthened containment of Iraq.

JEROME V. MARTIN

See also
Chemical Weapons and Warfare; Iraq; Iraq War; NORTHERN WATCH Operation; SOUTHERN WATCH, Operation

References
Byman, Daniel, and Matthew C. Waxman. *Confronting Iraq: U.S. Policy and the Use of Force since the Gulf War.* Santa Monica, CA: Rand Corporation, 2002.
Clancy, Tom, with Anthony Zinni and Tony Kolz. *Battle Ready.* New York: Putnam, 2004.
Cordesman, Anthony H. *The Military Effectiveness of Desert Fox: A Warning about the Limits of the Revolution in Military Affairs and Joint Vision 2010.* Washington, DC: Center for Strategic and International Studies, 1999.
Ricks, Thomas E. *FIASCO: The American Military Adventure in Iraq.* New York: Penguin, 2006.

DESERT SHIELD, Operation
See Persian Gulf War, Overview

DESERT STORM, Operation
See Persian Gulf War, Overview

DESERT THUNDER I, Operation (1998)
The U.S. plan to deploy more troops and equipment to the Persian Gulf region in 1998 to deter Iraqi belligerency and to force Iraq to comply with United Nations (UN) weapons inspectors. In late 1997, Iraq had begun to take aggressive action that threatened to destabilize the region. Worse, Iraq continued to interfere with UN weapons inspection teams. In response, the United States initiated Operation DESERT THUNDER I to increase its military presence during negotiations between the UN and Iraq over its alleged weapons of mass destruction program.

Initially DESERT THUNDER referred to potential military operations against Iraq but later became the nomenclature for several troop deployments during 1998. Ultimately there were two main DESERT THUNDER deployments (I and II), with DESERT VIPER designated as the actual strike plan if one was to occur.

Early in 1998 the U.S. Central Command (CENTCOM) commenced the dispatch of land, sea, and air assets, including more than 35,000 U.S. and coalition forces to the Persian Gulf region. Concurrently, General Anthony C. Zinni, CENTCOM commander, established a permanent Coalition/Joint Task Force (C/JTF) based at Camp Doha, Kuwait, commanded by Lieutenant General Tommy R. Franks, commander of Army Central Command's (ARCENT) Third Army.

Even as these forces took up positions, officials also deployed a brigade task force from the 3rd Infantry Division at Fort Stewart, Georgia, to Kuwait. On January 18, 1998, the task force left Hunter Army Airfield, Georgia, with 4,000 personnel and 2,900 short tons of equipment on 120 aircraft, landing at Kuwait City International Airport 15 hours later. They men then drew prepositioned equipment and were in battle positions 48 hours afterward.

By February 28, 1998, 9,000 troops of the C/JTF-Kuwait were in fortified positions ready to defend Kuwait. Allies including Argentina, Australia, Canada, the Czech Republic, Hungary, New Zealand, Poland, Romania, the United Kingdom, and Kuwait provided liaison teams, aircraft support, special operations elements, chemical/biological units, base defense units, and field medical personnel and facilities.

Offshore in the Arabian Gulf, a Maritime Preposition Force waited with equipment sufficient for one army and one marine brigade. Plans called for soldiers and marines to obtain their equipment from the ships near shore and deploy to the front if necessary. In addition, U.S. Navy, U.S. Air Force, and coalition air assets were stationed at ground bases and on aircraft carriers nearby.

During three weeks in February and March, the U.S. Transportation Command supported the deployment by flying more than 300 airlift missions and nearly 200 air-refueling missions, transporting 10,000 passengers and 11,000 short tons of cargo. Simultaneously, the U.S. Navy aircraft carrier *George Washington* arrived in the gulf to join the carrier *Nimitz* battle group. Later in the spring, the Forrestal-class *Independence* battle group relieved the *Nimitz*, leaving two carrier battle groups in the region. These Fifth Fleet assets joined coalition ships such as the British carrier *Invincible*, an antisubmarine warfare carrier, and the *Illustrious*, a light aircraft carrier, for a total of 50 ships/submarines and 200 naval aircraft.

During February as the 366th Air Expeditionary Wing (366 AEW) from Mountain Home AFB, Idaho, prepared to deploy to Bahrain, the 347th Air Expeditionary Wing (347 AEW) from Moody AFB, Georgia, deployed to Bahrain as the first true Air Expeditionary Wing in the air force. The 347 AEW was replaced by the 366th AEW on April 1, 1998. As this initial deployment wound down, the Third Army ARCENT moved its headquarters to Riyadh, Saudi Arabia. It had moved thousands of troops and civilian technicians and a massive amount of equipment.

During the buildup, UN secretary-general Kofi Annan flew to Baghdad to meet with Iraqi president Saddam Hussein. Annan convinced Hussein to allow uninterrupted weapons inspections. This meant an end to tensions for the time being. In June 1998 a drawdown of most of the U.S. forces occurred.

DESERT THUNDER I was the largest multinational force assembled in the Persian Gulf region since the conclusion of the 1991 Persian Gulf War. The operation demonstrated allied resolve and an ability to rapidly deploy combat troops when and where needed in short order. If an actual attack had been ordered, it would have code-named Operation DESERT VIPER.

On November 11, 1998, Iraq again refused to allow UN weapons inspections, resulting in the initiation of Operation DESERT THUNDER II. Again, CENTCOM moved its forces into position to initiate strikes into Iraq. During this operation an additional 2,300 troops were deployed, and once more Hussein backed down.

By December 1998, however, continued Iraqi intransigence prompted Operation DESERT FOX, during which allied forces destroyed several important Iraqi facilities during this brief engagement. DESERT FOX reportedly set back the Iraqi ballistic missile program by several years.

WILLIAM P. HEAD

See also
DESERT FOX, Operation; DESERT THUNDER II, Operation; Franks, Tommy

References
Raduege, Major General Harry D., Jr., USAF, and Lt. Col. Jerry L. Pippins Jr., USAF. "Operation DESERT THUNDER: New Dimensions for C4I in Expeditionary Warfare." In *New Dimensions for C4I in Expeditionary Warfare*. Washington, DC: Chief of Information, Dept. of the Navy, 1999.
Woodward, Bob. *Plan of Attack*. New York: Simon & Schuster, 2004.
Zinni, Tony, and Tom Clancy. *Battle Ready*. New York: Putnam, 2004.

DESERT THUNDER II, Operation (1998)

U.S.-led troop buildup begun in November 2008 in the Persian Gulf designed to end Iraqi intransigence regarding United Nations (UN) weapons inspections. Less than three months after the end of Operation DESERT THUNDER I, Iraqi president Saddam Hussein again refused to allow UN weapons inspectors to conduct unhindered inspections of Iraqi weapons development facilities. This refusal to abide by UN Security Council resolutions led to the initiation of Operation DESERT THUNDER II on November 11, 1998. At the direction of the National Command Authorities (NCA), the U.S. Central Command (CENTCOM) began the deployment of forces and positioned in-theater assets in expectation of strike operations.

Specifically, DESERT THUNDER II was the U.S. deployment of an additional 2,300 troops to Kuwait, including advance parties from the 3rd Infantry Division and two marine expeditionary units, in mid-November in support of the Central Command Joint Task Force, Kuwait. By November 13, 1998, there were 23,500 troops in the area, including 2,600 soldiers, 14,300 sailors and marines, 5,600 air force personnel, and joint headquarters and other joint units comprising some 1,000 people.

By the beginning of December when the buildup had been halted, there were some 25,000 military personnel in the area. Air assets included 267 land and carrier-based aircraft as well as attack helicopters and fixed-wing gunships.

Other units comprised a cruise missile force, surface warships, a marine expeditionary unit, a Patriot missile battalion, a mechanized battalion task force, and a mix of special operations forces.

In late November the impact of this second deployment resulted in Iraq's eventual, albeit short-lived, compliance with the UN weapons inspections. After only two weeks, however, the situation worsened again, and between December 16 and 19, 1998, Operation DESERT FOX then occurred, during which actual military attacks were carried out. In it U.S. Air Force, Navy, and Marine Corps aircraft, British Royal Air Force aircraft, and cruise missiles were employed against military targets in Iraq to force a recalcitrant Iraq to allow the inspection of its weapons research facilities as provided for in UN Security Council Resolution 687, agreed upon at the end of the 1991 Persian Gulf War.

Operation DESERT THUNDER II officially ended on December 22, 1998. A number of U.S. Defense Department officials were critical of the William J. Clinton administration's reluctance to pursue a more aggressive military option in the seemingly endless conflict with the Iraqi dictator. Yet the immense difficulties involved with invading and occupying Iraq would later be revealed during the Iraq War beginning in 2003.

WILLIAM P. HEAD

See also
DESERT FOX, Operation; DESERT THUNDER I, Operation

References
Raduege, Harry D., Jr., and Jerry L. Pippins Jr. "Operation DESERT THUNDER: New Dimensions for C4I in Expeditionary Warfare." In *New Dimensions for C4I in Expeditionary Warfare*. Washington, DC: Chief of Information, Department of the Navy, 1998.
Zinni, Tony, and Tom Clancy. *Battle Ready*. New York: Putnam, 2004.

Devshirme System

As Ottoman conquests spread across the southeastern Balkan peninsula in the 1360s, the Ottomans enlisted numerous prisoners of war as soldiers, just as previous Islamic rulers including those of pre-Ottoman Turkish Anatolia had done. Yet it was the remarkable *devshirme* system of recruitment that caught the attention of outsiders. This effectively enslaved some of the sultan's own non-Islamic subjects and was therefore illegal under Islamic law, which stipulated that conquered non-Muslims should be demilitarized and protected. The *devshirme*—in practice if not in theory—also involved virtually enforced conversion to Islam, which was certainly contrary to Islamic law.

The *devshirme* system probably began in the 1380s, though the word itself did not appear in written records until 1438, around the time that infantry and cavalry recruited in this way became military elite. For the next two centuries or more the *devshirme* supplied the Ottoman state with its most dedicated servants, both military and administrative. The principle was based on recruiting 1 child from every 40 non-Muslim households roughly once every five years. In its fully developed form it enlisted between 1,000 and 3,000 youths per year. It would begin with an edict from the sultan. Not all *devshirme* conscripts entered the Janissary Corps, however. The best were trained for government service as administrators and bureaucrats. The next best were selected for the Kapi Kulu (Palace) cavalry regiments, while the remainder became Janissary or Bostanci infantry, though those of lowest ability may have been employed as government laborers.

Many families actually volunteered their children for what could potentially be a good career, with both Christian and Muslim parents reportedly offering bribes so their children would be accepted. Officially, however, the only Muslims included in the *devshirme* were Bosnian Slavs whose families had converted to Islam. They normally skipped the first stage of training and went directly into an elite Bostanci unit. In 1568 a few sons of retired Janissaries were allowed into the corps, and from 1582 onward freeborn men were permitted to become protégés of the Yeniceri Agasi (commander of Janissaries). By the mid-16th century many soldiers apparently favored phasing out the *devshirme*, thus opening up opportunities for their own offspring, and within a few generations the majority of recruits were probably such sons of Janissaries. Finally, in 1594 the ranks were officially opened to all Muslim volunteers, and the *devshirme* system was effectively stopped in 1648.

The accompanying training system remained in place, however, and a final though unsuccessful European *devshirme* was attempted in 1703. By then, the main source of human booty was from the Crimean Tatar Khanate of the Ukraine and southern Russia, but even that ended with the Russian annexation of the Crimea in 1783.

DAVID NICOLLE

See also
Janissaries; Ottoman Empire

References
Gross, M. L. *The Origins and Role of the Janissaries in Early Ottoman History.* Amsterdam: Middle East Research Association, 1969–1970.
Ménage, V. L. "Devshirme." In *Encyclopedia of Islam.* 2nd ed., 2:210–213. Leiden: Brill, 1965.
Miller, B. *The Palace School of Mohammed the Conqueror.* Cambridge, MA: Harvard University Press, 1941.
Wittek, Paul. "Devshirme and Sharia." In *Selected Readings on Ottoman History,* Vol. 2, ed. Stanford Shaw, 645–653. Cambridge, MA: Harvard University Library, 1965.

Dhahran, Scud Missile Attack on (February 25, 1991)

At 8:32 p.m. on February 25, 1991, during the Persian Gulf War, sirens sounded at Dhahran in eastern Saudi Arabia warning of an approaching Iraqi scud missile. This was by no means the first such attack, so by now U.S. Army personnel in the sprawling base complex there were well acquainted with the air raid procedures. Thirteen minutes later a Scud missile slammed into a barracks housing members of the 475th Quartermaster Group, killing 28 and seriously injuring 110. Some 100 others were slightly injured. This was among 46 such missiles launched from Iraq into Saudi Arabia during the war. Iraq targeted Dhahran not only because of the important U.S. military facilities there but also because the city was the administrative headquarters for the Saudi oil industry and a significant seaport.

Six surface-to-air Patriot missile batteries had failed to track and intercept the Scud. A postattack investigation found that the Patriot's software system, which helped track the trajectory of incoming missiles, had malfunctioned. Prior to DESERT STORM, the Patriot system had never before been used to intercept missiles, and it was not designed to operate continuously for many hours at a time. Its extended operation may have been a contributing factor to the failure of its software guidance system. Crew inexperience in engaging missiles may also have been a factor.

The Scud attack at Dhahran represented the single greatest loss of life for coalition forces during all of Operation DESERT STORM and spurred U.S. Defense Department efforts to improve the Patriot and develop purpose-designed antimissile systems.

PAUL G. PIERPAOLI JR.

See also
Persian Gulf War, Overview

References
Brenner, Elliott, and William Harwood, eds. *Desert Storm: The Weapons of War.* London: Orion Books, 1991.
Time Magazine, eds. *Desert Storm: The War in the Persian Gulf.* Boston: Little, Brown, 1991.
Zaloga, Steven J. *Scud Ballistic Missile and Launch Systems, 1955–2005.* New York: Osprey, 2006.

Dhofar Rebellion (1962–1976)

The Dhofar (Duhfar) Governorate is the largest in area of the four governorates constituting the Sultanate of Oman, which is located on the southeast coast of the Arabian Peninsula at the strategically important mouth of the Persian Gulf. Dhofar is in southern Oman and borders Yemen. Dhofar had a centuries-long tradition of defying its rulers. Geographically remote from the Omani capital city of Muscat, Dhofar features difficult terrain combining desert and forbidding mountain ranges. Its population is culturally distinct from the rest of Omani society, sharing an affinity with the tribal cultures of the Arabian Peninsula's desert interior. This orientation was fundamentally at odds with the more cosmopolitan cultural outlook of Oman's northern communities, the history of which had been shaped by their interactions with the maritime commercial world of the Indian Ocean and the Persian Gulf. A heritage of political autonomy reinforced the geographical and cultural distinctions.

Until 1959, when Dhofar was formally united with the Sultanate of Oman, Dhofar's formal status was that of an autonomous region, reflecting a 19th-century arrangement that split temporal power in Oman between the secular sultanate based in Muscat and the religious Islamic Imamate based in the tribal communities of Dhofar. During the passage of time, the institution of the Imamate became the rallying point for opponents of the successive sultans, generating the momentum for several uprisings against the sultanate throughout the 19th and early 20th centuries.

The tensions between these two centers of power flared up during the reign of Sultan Said bin Taimir (r. 1931–1970). A conservative ruler determined to insulate Oman from Western ideas and institutions, Said presided over a repressive regime that had little tolerance for Dhofar's traditions of autonomy. Said implemented a limited program of internal improvements designed to raise his subjects' standard of living, education, and health, but most of these initiatives benefited Oman's northern communities, not the Dhofar region. Said's failure to provide a meaningful response to an extended drought that ravaged Dhofar's agriculture- and livestock-based economy in the late 1950s further alienated the region's population from their ruler. This ecological and economic crisis forced hundreds of Dhofaris to seek work in neighboring nations' booming oil industries. While abroad, many were influenced by Arab nationalism and Marxist-inspired notions of national liberation and class struggle, concepts providing Dhofaris with an ideological framework for their resentment of Said's regime.

In 1962, Dhofari opposition groups united under the umbrella of the Dhofar Liberation Front (DLF). Led by Mussalim bin Nafl, the DLF's composition reflected the fragmented character of Said's Dhofari opponents. Though the DLF espoused regional autonomy, modernization, and internal development as its principal goals, it remained essentially conservative, affirming a strong commitment to perpetuating traditional tribal and Islamic religious values.

Fighting commenced in December 1962 with hit-and-run raids against the British air base at Salalah. Warfare intensified in 1964 with hit-and-run rebel assaults on government installations and oil industry facilities. Following a failed assassination attempt on his person in April 1966, Sultan Said bin Taimur retired to his palace and was never again seen in public.

But while the insurgents enjoyed limited support from Saudi Arabia and Yemen, the DLF never succeeded in gaining the support of a critical mass of the Dhofari population. At the same time, Said's small military establishment, though increasingly benefiting from British-led reorganization and training, lacked the capacity to eradicate the insurgency, which continued inconclusively throughout the mid-1960s.

The insurgency gained a new lease on life in 1967, when the DLF's radical leftist elements seized control of the insurgent movement. Led by Muhammad bin Ahmad al-Ghasani, the insurgency's Marxist wing renamed itself the Popular Front for the Liberation of the Occupied Arabian Gulf (PFLOAG). This signaled a fundamental shift in the nature of the insurgency from a tribally oriented struggle for regional autonomy to a mass revolutionary movement that aspired to overthrow the sultanate, replace it with a Marxist state, and transform Oman into a springboard for leftist revolutionary activity throughout the Arabian Peninsula. In keeping with its ideological orientation, the PFLOAG received weapons and training from the newly independent People's Democratic Republic of Yemen (PDRY) as well as from the Soviet Union, China, Iraq, and the Palestine Liberation Organization (PLO).

By 1970, the PFLOAG had grown to a force of approximately 3,000–4,000 active fighters who dominated the interior of Dhofar. Oman's counterinsurgent strategy was heavy-handed and unimaginative, focusing on kinetic methods that stressed search-and-destroy tactics and virtually ignored civic action and political and economic reform.

With the PFLOAG on the threshold of victory and the counterinsurgency efforts in tatters, Said's son Qaboos bin Said al-Said mounted a coup that removed his father from the throne in 1970 and dramatically altered the strategic course of the war. Qaboos radically reoriented the government's strategy by making civic action, modernization, and internal reform integral elements of the counterinsurgency campaign. These initiatives sought to deprive the PFLOAG of popular support among Dhofaris, many of whom were growing disenchanted with the insurgent movement's attempts to eradicate Islam and impose Marxist socioeconomic norms in areas "liberated" from government control. By targeting the insurgency's root causes, Qaboos's civic action plan drove a wedge between the PFLOAG fighters and the people on whose behalf they claimed to be fighting, seriously undercutting the insurgents' political legitimacy.

In parallel with these initiatives, Qaboos revived the military elements of the counterinsurgency. Using revenues from Oman's nascent oil industry, he expanded and modernized the country's armed forces. New equipment and training, in combination with the assistance of British military advisers, enhanced the effectiveness of the sultan's military. Airpower in the form of helicopters, airlift assets, and light ground-attack aircraft provided the counterinsurgents with mobility and firepower that negated the insurgents' ability to exploit the Dhofar region's rugged terrain. In addition, British Special Air Service teams seconded to the Omani military trained former insurgents, known as Firquats, to assist with the counterinsurgency effort. Intimately familiar with Dhofar's terrain, they provided valuable intelligence and proved highly effective in fighting their former comrades.

At the strategic and policy level, the Dhofar Development Committee, composed of military commanders and members of Qaboos's government, ensured that military action would function in support of the civic action program. By

1976, the combination of the two elements had completely eradicated the insurgency.

Sebastian Lukasik

See also
Popular Front for the Liberation of the Occupied Arabian Gulf; Qaboos bin Said al-Said

References
Akehurst, John. *We Won a War: The Campaign in Oman, 1965–1975*. Wiltshire, UK: M. Russell, 1982.
Allen, Calvin H., and W. Lynn Rigsbee. *Oman under Qaboos: From Coup to Constitution, 1970–1976*. London: Routledge, 2000.
Gardiner, Ian. *In the Service of the Sultan: A First-Hand Account of the Dhofar Insurgency*. London: Pen and Sword, 2007.
Peterson, John. *Oman's Insurgencies: The Sultanate's Struggles for Supremacy*. London: Saqi, 2007.

Diadochi, Wars of the (323–275 BCE)

King Alexander III (Alexander the Great) of Macedon died in Babylon in 323 BCE, the result of a fever and possibly malaria after a drinking bout. Only 32 years old at the time of his death, Alexander did not have the time necessary to consolidate his vast and very diverse empire, which encompassed some 2 million square miles and extended from Greece eastward to parts of India. It included the Greek world, the former Persian Empire, Egypt, Syria, Mesopotamia, Bactria, and the Punjab.

As he lay dying, Alexander was asked to whom he left the empire and reportedly replied "to the strongest." The vastness of the empire, its very different component parts, and the political vacuum created by Alexander's death led to a series of wars within the empire by his lieutenants, who sought to succeed him. These civil wars lasted from 323 until 275 BCE and are collectively known as the Wars of the Diadochi (*diadochi* is Greek for "successors").

The list of the principal figures vying for control is a long one. It includes Perdiccas (ca. 355–320), Alexander's chief minister; Antipater (ca. 397–319), who was regent in Greece and Macedon during 335–320; Eumenes (ca. 362–316), private secretary to Philip of Macedon and then to Alexander; Ptolemy I Soter (ca. 367–283), a personal aide and general under Alexander and subsequent ruler of Egypt; Lysimachus (ca. 360–281), a Macedonian officer and aide to Alexander who became a basileus (king) in 306 BCE and ruled Thrace, Asia Minor, and Macedon; Craterus (ca. 370–321), a Macedonian general who would be killed in battle; Alexander Polyperchon (?–314), a leading general in the Wars of

A silver tetradrachm of Ptolemy I Soter, ruler of Egypt during 323–282 BCE. Ptolemy is depicted wearing a diadem, with an *aegis* (the symbol of protection by Zeus and Athena) around his neck. The reverse depicts an eagle with a thunderbolt. The coin symbolizes royal power and divine protection and links him to Alexander the Great, whose coins also showed him with the *aegis*. (The J. Paul Getty Trust)

the Diadochi; Antigonus Monophthalmus (382–301), "The One Eyed," so called because he had lost an eye in battle, an infantry division commander and later satrap under Alexander; Cassander (358–297), also an infantry division commander under Alexander and subsequently king of Macedon during 305–297; and Demetrius (337–283), subsequently king of Macedon during 294–288.

Conflict among Alexander the Great's strong-willed generals following his death was virtually inevitable. Meleager, a leading infantry general, ordered Perdiccas, whom Alexander had designated as regent, to be killed, but Perdiccas was too quick for him. Part of the cavalry and most of the generals sided with Perdiccas, and they quit the city of Babylon and established a camp outside its walls. Negotiations then occurred. Meleager and his supporters advanced the candidacy of Arrhidaeus, Alexander the Great's half brother, who was also intellectually disabled. Perdiccas and his faction favored waiting until the birth of Alexander's child (the future Alexander IV) by his wife, Bactrian princess Roxana.

With Eumenes playing a key role, a compromise was hammered out. Arrhidaeus became king as Philip III of Macedon and was to rule jointly with Roxana's child, assuming it was a boy. Perdiccas meanwhile was confirmed as regent for the entire empire, with Meleager to assist him.

The power-sharing arrangement between Perdiccas and Meleager did not last. Perdiccas lulled his rival into a false sense of security while he worked to secure control of Arrhidaeus. This accomplished, Perdiccas assembled the army, supposedly for the purpose of a military review, during which on the prompting of Perdiccas, Arrhidaeus demanded the surrender and punishment of all those who had been involved in the recent turmoil. Some 300 alleged mutineers were seized and summarily executed. Although not singled out, Meleager understandably was alarmed and sought refuge in a temple, where on the order of Peridccas he was apprehended and killed.

Having eliminated his rival, Perdiccas endeavored to maintain the unity of the empire, rewarding those generals who had supported him by making them satraps throughout the empire. Ptolemy ruled in Egypt; Laomedon received Syria and Phoenicia; Philotas secured Cilicia; Peithon took Media; Antigonus received Phrygia, Lycia, and Pamphylia; Asander received Caria; Menander took Lydia; Lysimachus received Thrace; Leonnatus secured Hellespontine Phrygia; and Neoptolemus received Armenia. Macedon and Greece were under the joint rule of Antipater, who had governed them for Alexander, and Craterus, Alexander's most able lieutenant. Eumenes received Cappadocia and Paphlagonia.

In the eastern portion of the empire, Perdiccas largely left Alexander's arrangements intact. Thus, Taxiles and Porus governed kingdoms in India; Oxyartes, Alexander's father-in-law, had charge of Gandara; Sibyrtius had control of Arachosia and Gedrosia; Stasanor ruled Aria and Drangiana; Philip ruled Bactria and Sogdiana; Phrataphernes governed Parthia and Hyrcania; Peucestas governed Persis; Tlepolemus had charge over Carmania; Atropates governed northern Media; Archon ruled Babylonia; and Arcesilas had charge of northern Mesopotamia.

Lamian War (322 BCE)

This power sharing did not last. Revolt came first in Greece. The news of Alexander's death inspired a revolt in Athens and other Greek cities, which had long chafed under Macedonian rule. The ensuing Lamian War of 322 pitted the city-states of the Greek confederation against the Macedonians. It took its name from the fortress of Lamia, where Antipater was besieged. With few forces of his own available, Antipater called for reinforcements from Asia. A Macedonian relief force led by Leonnatus raised the siege of Lamia, although Leonnatus himself was killed in the fighting.

Craterus arrived with reinforcements, and he and Antipater then moved south with their combined forces to force a decisive action. In the ensuing Battle of Crannon of September 5, the Macedonians had perhaps 40,000 infantry, 3,000 slingers and archers, and 5,000 cavalry. Forces of the Greek confederation, led by Athenian general Antiphilus, numbered only 25,000 infantry and 3,500 cavalry. Superior Macedonian numbers told, and the battle ended with a Greek withdrawal. Although the Greeks had suffered only about 500 dead (some 130 Macedonians also fell), Antiphilus asked for terms the next day. The Macedonians rejected a general settlement, instead insisting on reaching agreement with each member state separately, and, following their capture of several Thessalian cities, achieved their end. Abandoned by most of its allies, Athens was forced to surrender unconditionally. Antipater then imposed terms on Athens that included a Macedonian military garrison and replacement of its democracy with an oligarchy. Meanwhile, Peithon suppressed a revolt by Greeks in the eastern parts of the empire, while Perdiccas and Eumenes did the same in Cappadocia.

First War of the Diadochi (322–320 BCE)

An intense period of intrigue, bribery, and outright murder among the leaders of the empire followed. When Perdiccas attempted to marry Alexander's sister Cleopatra, Antipater, Craterus, Antigonus, and Ptolemy joined forces to oppose him. The outbreak of fighting in what became the First War of the Diadochi (322–320) was caused by Ptolemy's theft of Alexander's body and shipment of it to Egypt. Eumenes, who made common cause with Perdiccas, defeated the rebels in Asia Minor, during which Craterus was killed, but this came to nothing because Perdiccas was unsuccessful militarily against Ptolemy in Egypt. Ptolemy then bribed his generals Seleucus, Peithon, and Antigenes, leading to a rebellion of Perdiccas's troops at Pelusium and Perdiccas's murder there in 320. Antipar was now dominant in Europe, while Antigonus held sway in Asia.

Ptolemy then replaced Perdiccas as regent with Peithon and Arrhidaeus, but opposition to this chiefly from Antipater led not long afterward to a general reshuffling of territorial assignments in the Treaty of Triparadisus, which was concluded at that place in 321. Under its terms,

Antipater became regent of the empire, while Kings Philip III and Alexander IV were relocated to Macedon. Antigonus remained ruler of Phrygia, Lycia, and Pamphylia but also secured Lycaonia. Ptolemy continued to rule Egypt, while Lysimachus ruled Thrace. Seleucus, Peithon, and Antigenes, the murderers of Perdiccas, received the provinces of Babylonia, Media, and Susiana, respectively. Arrhidaeus received Hellespontine Phrygia. That same year, 321, Seleucus retook the eastern provinces of Alexander's old empire in Bactria and Parthia.

Second War of the Diadochi (319–315 BCE)

Despite the Treaty of Triparadisus, fighting soon resumed. Antipater died in 321. Before he died he passed over his own son, Cassander, and named Polyperchon as regent. Fighting in the Second War of the Diadochi (319–315) occurred in Macedon and Greece pitting Polyperchon against Cassander, who enjoyed the support of both Antigonus and Ptolemy. Although Eumenes in Asia supported him, Polyperchon was forced out of Macedonia by Cassander and fled to Epirus with the boy king Alexander IV and his mother Roxana. In Epirus, Polyperchon joined his own forces with those under Olympias, Alexander III's mother. They then jointly invaded Macedon. King Philip III Arrhidaeus and his wife Eurydice met them there in 317 with an army, but the troops promptly defected. Philip III and Eurydice were taken prisoner, and Olympias had them killed. Soon thereafter, however, Cassander was victorious over the invaders, capturing and killing Olympias and securing control of Macedon as well as Alexander IV and Roxana. In Asia, Eumenes was gradually forced eastward by Antigonus, leading to battles in present-day Iran at Paraitacene in 317 and Gabiene in 316. Both were indecisive, but after Gabiene his own men, bribed by Antigonus, handed Eumenes over, and Antigous had him executed in 315.

Third War of the Diadochi (314–311 BCE)

Antigonus now had undisputed control of the Asian territories of Alexander the Great's old empire. Believing that he had become too powerful, Ptolemy, Lysimachus, and Cassander now formed a coalition to unseat Antigonus. In 314 the Third War of the Diadochi began when Antigonus invaded Syria, then part of Ptolemy's territory, and besieged the port city of Tyre for more than a year. Antigonus allied with Polyperchon, but the war went against him. A general sent by Antigonus to subdue the Nabatameans failed to accomplish this, while Ptolemy invaded Syria and there defeated Antigonus's son, Demetrius Poliorcetes, in the Battle of Gaza in 312. That same year Seleucus, whom Antigonus had expelled as satrap of Babylon in 316, received troops from Ptolemy and recaptured Babylon in 311, regaining control of his satrapy. Antigonus then concluded the Peace of Dynasta in December 1311 with Ptolemy, Lysimachus, and Cassander. This arrangement in effect recognized the division of Alexander's former empire between Antigonous (Asia), Cassander (Macedon and Greece), Lysimachus (Thrace), Ptolemy (Egypt), and, by omission, Seleucus (the eastern satrapies).

The Babylonian War (311–309 BCE)

Antigonus continued war against Seleucus in what is known as the Babylonian War (311–309). Seleucus had retaken the city of Babylon in May 311, all except its principal fortress, held by a garrison loyal to Antigonus. Seleucus then dammed the Euphrates, creating an artificial lake. That August, with the lake having grown quite large, he broke the dam, and the resulting flood waters crumbled the fortress walls.

Nicanor, the new satrap of Media, and Evagoras, the satrap of Aria, now invaded on behalf of Antigonus. His own forces outnumbered by more than three to one, Seleucus concealed his men in marshes near the Tigris where Nicanor was planning to cross and then launched a surprise night attack. Evagoras was killed early in the battle, and Nicanor was cut off from his forces. News of the death of Evagoras caused most of his Persian soldiers to surrender and then agree to switch sides. Only Nicanor and a few of his men escaped.

His own forces greatly increased, Seleucus took the offensive and captured first Ecbatana, capital of Media, and then Susa, capital of Elam. These victories gave him control of what is now southern Iraq and most of Iran.

With the defeat of Nicanor and Euagoras, Antigonus ordered his son Demetrius Poliorcetes to reverse the situation. He arrived at Babylon in the spring of 310 while Seleucus was campaigning to the east. Although Demetrius managed to enter Babylon and hold it for a time, resistance was such that he soon departed and returned to Syria. Antigonus himself invaded that autumn and also managed to enter Babylon, but he abandoned it in March 309. Returning to the northwest, he encountered Seleucus's army in what turned out to be a decisive battle. Details are sketchy, but one source has the battle lasting an entire day without result, and that night while Antigonus's men slept, Seleucus mounted a night attack and was victorious.

Antigonus now accepted Seleucus's control of Babylonia, Media, and Elam. Seleucus also campaigned to the east and reached the Indus Valley. There he concluded a treaty with Chandragupta Maurya in which the latter was recognized as controlling part of Afghanistan, Pakistan, and western India, while Seleucus received recognition of control of all of present-day Iran and most of Afghanistan as well as 500 war elephants. Seleucus now controlled all of the eastern part of Alexander III's old empire, making him the most powerful ruler since Alexander. Seleucus's campaigning also firmly established the Seleucid Empire (312–363).

The peace settlement ending the Third War of the Diadochi had recognized the rights of King Alexander IV and held that when he came of age he would succeed Cassander as ruler. The boy was now nearly 14 years old. In order to preserve his throne, Cassander ordered one Glaucias to secretly assassinate the boy and his mother. Carried out in 309, this deed ended the Argead dynasty that had ruled Macedon for several centuries.

Fourth War of the Diadochi (308–301 BCE)

In 308 there was another general war. With Ptolemy seeking to expand his territory in the Aegean islands and Cyprus and Seleucus occupied in the east, Antigonus dispatched his son Demetrius to secure Greece. Demetrius captured Athens in 307 and restored the city's democratic government. In 306 Demetrius decisively defeated Ptolemy's fleet near the island of Salamis and invaded and took Cyprus.

In 306 Antigonus attempted to invade Egypt, but major storms in the eastern Mediterranean prevented Demetrius's fleet from supplying him, and he was forced to withdraw. With Seleucus still campaigning in the east and Cassander and Ptolemy both materially weakened, during 305–304 Demetrius Poliorcetes, son of Antigonus I, laid siege to the island of Rhodes in order to cause it to break its neutrality and close relationship with Ptolemy I. Ptolemy was later known as "Soter" (savior) for assisting Rhodes during the siege of that island in 305–304 BCE, one of the most notable sieges of antiquity. Ptolemy, Lysimachus, and Cassander all dispatched reinforcements there. Ultimately the leaders of Rhodes concluded an agreement with Demetrius whereby they would support Antigonus and Demetrius against all enemies except Ptolemy. This, however, left Demetrius free to attack Cassander in Greece. Demetrius duly defeated Cassander in Greece and formed a new Hellenic League under himself. Cassander sued for peace, but Antigonus rejected the overture. Demetrius then invaded Thessaly. Inconclusive engagements between his forces and those of Cassander followed. Cassander then secured assistance from Lysimachus, who invaded Anatolia, thereby forcing Demetrius to quit Thessaly for Asia Minor to assist Antigonus. Although Lysimachus was able to conquer much of western Anatolia, in 301 he was cornered near Ipsus in Phrygia by Antigonus and Demetrius. There he was saved by the timely arrival of Seleucus. Plutarch gives the strength of the two sides as follows: Antigonus and Demetrius had 70,000 infantry, 10,000 cavalry, and 75 war elephants, while Lysimachus, Cassander, and Seleucus had 64,000 infantry, 15,000 cavalry, 400 war elephants, and 300 scythed chariots. The Battle of Ipsus ended in a decisive victory for the invaders. Antigonus and some 22,000 of his men were killed, and Demetrius fled to Greece with some 4,000 infantry and 5,000 cavalry in order to preserve his rule there. Lysimachus and Seleucus divided up Antigonus's former Asian territories between them. Lysimachus took western Asia Minor and Seleucus took the remainder, although Cilicia and Lycia were given to Cassander's brother Pleistarchus.

The Struggle over Macedon (298–285 BCE)

The next contest was for control of Macedon itself. Cassander, king of Macedonia, died in 297. His sons Antipater and Alexander proved inept and fell to quarreling. Alexander called in both Pyrrhus, king of Epirus, and Demetrius, who controlled Cyprus, the Peloponnese, and many of the Aegean islands. After Pyrrhus captured the border region of Ambracia, Demetrius invaded, killed Alexander, and seized control of Macedon for himself in 294. While Demetrius was busy establishing control of Macedon, Lysimachus conquered Demetrius's outlying territory of western Anatolia, Seleucus secured most of Cilicia, and Ptolemy recovered Cyprus, eastern Cilicia, and Lycia.

Demetrius was soon forced to flee Macedon following a rebellion fomented by Lysimachus and Pyrrhus, who then divided Macedon between them. Leaving Greece under his son, Antigonus Gonatas, Demetrius invaded the east in 287 but after some initial success was taken prisoner by Seleucus in 286. Demetrius died two years later.

Struggle between Lysimachus and Seleucus (285–281)

Although Lysimachus and Pyrrhus had cooperated in driving Antigonus Gonatas from Thessaly and Athens, they soon fell out, and Lysimachus drove Pyrrhus from the lands he had acquired in Macedon. In Egypt Ptolemy I Soter passed over his eldest son, Ptolemy Cearunus, and named as heir his younger son Ptolemy Philadelphus. Ceraunus fled to Seleucus. Ptolemy I Soter died peacefully at age 84 in 282 and was succeeded by Ptolemy II Philadelphus.

Lysimachus meanwhile had his son Agathocles murdered, apparently on the instigation of his second wife, Arsinoe. Agathocles's widow, Lysandra, fled to Seleucus, who then went to war against Lysimachus. In the last great battle of the Diadochi, Corupedium (Corus) in Lydia in 281 BCE, Seleucus defeated Lysimachus, reportedly killing him in hand-to-hand combat. Seleucus now ruled all of Alexander's former empire except for Egypt. He did not live to enjoy his triumph for long. For reasons that are obscure, Seleucus was almost immediately murdered by Ptolemy Ceraunus.

Celtic Invasions and Consolidation (280–275 BCE)

Ptolemy Ceraunus also did not rule Macedon for long. Soon the Gauls invaded Macedon and Greece as well as Asia Minor. Ptolemy Ceraunus died fighting the invaders, and several years later Antigonus Gonatas emerged as ruler of Macedon. In Asia, Seleucus's son Antiochus I, who now ruled his father's vast Asian territories, defeated the Celts, who then settled down in central Anatolia in the part of eastern Phrygia henceforward known as Galatia. The Wars of the Diadochi were over.

The end of the Wars of the Diadochi confirmed, almost a half century after the death of Alexander the Great, that his empire could not be reestablished. There was at last some semblance of order, as the contenders thought themselves strong enough to claim the title of king in their own areas of the Hellenistic world. The three major power centers of the Hellenistic world were now Egypt, the Seleucid Empire, and Macedon.

Ptolemy II Philadelphus ruled Egypt during 283–246 BCE. Ptolemaic Egypt also came to include southern Syria (known as Coele-Syria) and various territories on the southern coast of Asia Minor. Ptolemy II's predecessor Ptolemy I had built new cities and settled his soldiers in them throughout Egypt. He established his capital in the port city of Alexandria, founded by Alexander the Great in 331. Alexandria became a major center of Greek culture and trade as the principal export point on the Mediterranean for grain. Alexandria's great library was one of the wonders of the ancient world, and the Ptolemies encouraged scholars to reside there and carry on scientific as well as cultural endeavors.

Egypt underwent several revolts against the Ptolemies, but Ptolemaic rule was eased by the new rulers taking on many of the traditions of the pharaohs. This included the practice of marrying a sibling, adopting Egyptian style and dress, and participating in Egyptian religious practice, which included treating the ruler as a god. Temples to the Ptolemies were erected throughout Egypt. The Ptolemies also created a vast new bureaucracy to both administer Egypt more effectively and extract as much revenue from the people as possible.

Ptolemy II and his successors fought a series of six wars with the Seleucids for control of the area of Coele-Syria. These so-called Syrian Wars occurred during 274–168. In 217 Ptolemy IV (r. 221–204) defeated the Seleucids in the great Battle of Raphia. The Ptolemies ruled Egypt until it was conquered by the Romans in 30 BCE.

The Seleucid Empire existed from 312 to 63 BCE and was a major center of Hellenistic culture, buttressed by the immigration of numerous Greeks. Antiochus I Soter was king of the vast Asia territories constituting the Seleucid Empire during 281–261 and the end of the Wars of the Diadochi. His realm included almost all of the Asian portions of Alexander's old empire, but having to contend with Antigonus II Gonatas of Macedon and Ptolemy II in Egypt, he failed in efforts to conquer the European portions of Alexander's old empire.

During 175–164 Antiochus IV Epiphanes ruled the empire. With the guardians of Egyptian king Ptolemy VI Philometer demanding the return of Coele-Syria in 170 BCE, Antiochus decided to invade Egypt before the Egyptians could attack him. His preemptive strike brought the conquest of all of Egypt except the city of Alexandria. King Ptolemy VI was taken prisoner, but fearful of encouraging intervention by Rome, Antiochus permitted him to remain on the throne as a puppet ruler. Alexandria, however, promptly elected Ptolemy's brother as King Ptolemy VIII Euergetes. In order to avoid a potentially disastrous civil war, the two brothers reached agreement to rule jointly.

In 168 BCE, Antiochus IV mounted a second invasion of Egypt and also sent a fleet to capture Cyprus. Before reaching Alexandria, he was met by the Roman ambassador, who promptly informed him that unless he withdrew his forces from both Egypt and Cyprus, Rome would declare war. Antiochus chose the first option.

The Seleucids held suzerainty over Judaea, and while they had for the most part respected Jewish culture and Jewish institutions, Antiochus IV reversed this sound policy, bringing the Maccabean Revolt of 167–160. King Mithridates I of Parthia took advantage of the preoccupation of Antiochus in the west to attack from the east in 167 and seize the important city of Herat. Antiochus left one of his generals to deal with the Maccabees while he himself marched with the main

Seleucid army against the Parthians. Mithridates I enjoyed some success in the east, especially in Armenia, but died suddenly of disease in 164.

Macedonia, the other major power center following the Wars of the Diadochi, dominated Greece. The Antigonid dynasty ruled Macedon. Antigonus II Gonatas was king during 277–274 and 272–239. A highly effective ruler, he solidified Antigonid rule following a long period of civil strife and near anarchy dating from 297. Antigonus restored order and prosperity. Although he was to lose control of many of the Greek city-states, he twice defeated invasions mounted by Ptolemy II of Egypt and won lasting fame for defeating an invasion of the Balkans by the Gauls. Antigonus III Doson (r. 229–221) built on these gains by reestablishing Macedonian power across the region.

Unlike the Ptolemies and the Seleucids, the Macedonians never did adopt the trappings of Hellenistic monarchy. Under Philip V (221–179) and his son Perseus (179–168), Macedon was forced to deal with the Roman Republic. Two major Macedonian battlefield defeats, in 197 and 168, brought the end of the Antigonid dynasty and the dismantling of the Macedonian kingdom. In 148 BCE Rome established direct rule, and Macedonia became a Roman province.

SPENCER C. TUCKER

See also
Alexander III the Great; Antigonus I Monophthalmus; Antiochus I Soter; Antiochus IV Epiphanes; Corupedium, Battle of; Demetrius I Poliorcetes; Eumenes of Cardia; Gabiene, Battle of; Lysimachus; Maccabean Revolt; Paraetacene, Battle of; Perdiccas; Ptolemy Ceraunus; Ptolemy I Soter; Ptolemy II Philadelphus; Ptolemy IV Philopator; Ptolemy VI Philometor; Seleucid Empire; Seleucus I Nicator; Syrian-Egyptian Wars

References
Bennett, Bob, and Mike Roberts. *The Wars of Alexander's Successors, 323–281 BC.* 2 vols. Barnsley, UK: Pen and Sword Military, 2008, 2009.
Chamoux, François. *Hellenistic Civilization.* Malden, MA: Blackwell, 2003.
Parker, Victor. *A History of Greece, 1300 to 30 BC.* Malden, MA: Wiley, 2014.
Shipley, Graham. *The Greek World after Alexander.* Routledge History of the Ancient World. New York: Routledge, 2000.
Troncoso, V. Alonso, and Edward Anson. *After Alexander: The Time of the Diadochi (323–281 BC).* Oakville, CT: Oxbow Books, 2013.
Walbank, F. W. *The Cambridge Ancient History,* Vol. 7, Part 1, *The Hellenistic World.* Cambridge: Cambridge University Press, 1984.
Waterfield, Robin. *Dividing the Spoils: The War for Alexander the Great's Empire.* New York: Oxford University Press. 2011.

Diaspora

Greek term for the dispersion of the Jews. It is generally dated from the Babylonian exile of 587–586 BCE, when Babylonian ruler Nebuchadnezzar sacked Jerusalem and removed the elites to Mesopotamia. The term "diaspora" also describes all Jews residing outside of Israel. Diaspora today means the dispersion of any people, including the Palestinians, but for a long time it was applied only to the Jews.

The Jews who were deported to Mesopotamia originally thought of this as exile (*galut* in Hebrew). When it became possible for the Jews to return to Palestine, however, only a few thousand of the Babylonian Jews took advantage of the opportunity to do so. By the time the Romans crushed the Great Jewish Revolt of 66–70 CE, captured Jerusalem, and destroyed its Temple, there were already thriving Jewish communities in Babylonia, Syria, Egypt, Asia Minor, Greece, and Rome. Nonetheless, the end of the Great Jewish Revolt and Bar Kokhba's Revolt of 132–135 greatly increased the numbers of diaspora Jews. Many Jews fled, while others were sold into slavery and dispersed throughout the empire.

When the Romans expanded their empire north in Europe, Jews established new communities in those lands, and the spread of the Byzantine Empire also saw some limited Jewish communities established as well. Jews settled as far as India, Central Asia, and even China. Persecutions in one place brought new Jewish diasporas in other areas. Jews also found their way to North and South America and Australia. Indeed, as a result of the persecutions (pogroms) in Russia and Poland, the United States came to have the world's largest Jewish population.

The two key elements of Jewish consciousness came to be the diaspora and a longing for Israel, but only rarely until after the proclamation of the State of Israel in 1948 were most Jews able to return. Even then many Jews living in the Soviet Union found it impossible to move to Israel because of Soviet restrictions on emigration. The awareness of Jews that they lived in the diaspora was certainly the prime motivator in the birth of Zionism at the end of the 19th century.

SPENCER C. TUCKER

See also
Jewish-Roman War, First; Zionism

References
Barclay, John M. G. *Jews in the Mediterranean Diaspora: From Alexander to Trajan (323 BCE–117 CE).* Berkeley: University of California Press, 1999.
Comay, Joan. *The Diaspora Story: The Epic of the Jewish People among the Nations.* New York: Random House, 1980.

Gold, Steven J. *The Israeli Diaspora.* Seattle: University of Washington Press, 2002.

Grant, Michael. *The Jews in the Roman World.* New York: Scribner, 1973.

Djemal Pasha, Ahmed (1872–1922)

Ottoman naval minister (1913–1914) and military governor of Syria (1915–1917). Born on May 6, 1872, in Istanbul (Constantinople), Ahmed Djemal graduated from the Ottoman War Academy and in 1898 was posted as a staff officer to the Third Army at Salonika. He joined the Committee of Union and Progress (CUP), also known as the Young Turk movement, in 1904.

Following the 1908 revolt of the Third Army and a brief civil war that led to the deposition of Sultan Abdul Hamid II, Djemal became part of the new military administration. In 1911 he was appointed governor of Baghdad, but in 1912 he resigned to serve in the First Balkan War (1912–1913). In support of the coup against Grand Vizier Mehmed Kamil led by Enver Pasha on January 23, 1913, Djemal, then a lieutenant general, assumed emergency powers as military governor of Istanbul.

After holding various senior command positions during the Balkan Wars of 1912–1913, Djemal became naval minister and minister for public works in Enver's cabinet in 1913. Unlike Enver, Djemal was disposed favorably toward the Entente and looked to both France and Great Britain for assistance to train and equip the badly neglected Ottoman Navy. His diplomatic approaches to the Entente Powers met with no result, however, chiefly because the two Western allies were not prepared to jeopardize their cooperation with Russia, which harbored plans for substantial expansion at the expense of the Ottoman Empire.

Although Djemal eventually submitted to Enver's pro-German policy, he remained opposed to a full-fledged alliance with Germany. Only under Enver's pressure and after Germany had offered substantial amounts of money to the Ottoman government did Djemal finally acquiesce and permit Vice Admiral Wilhelm Souchon, commander of the German Mediterranean Squadron and supreme commander of Ottoman naval forces, to launch a preemptive attack against the Russian Black Sea ports in October 1914.

In January 1915 shortly after the Ottoman Empire entered the war, Djemal became military governor of Syria and commander of the Ottoman Fourth Army stationed in Damascus. That same month he launched an ill-conceived offensive with his 80,000-man army across the Sinai Peninsula, toward the Suez Canal. Following the collapse of the offensive, Djemal confined himself to his governorship of Syria, where his harsh repression of Arab resistance and his persecution of the Armenian minority earned him the nickname "The Blood Shedder."

With the disintegration of the Palestinian front and the fall of Jerusalem in December 1917, Djemal returned to Istanbul as a cabinet member of the CUP administration. When the government was forced from office, Djemal and other CUP leaders fled the Ottoman capital aboard a German ship on November 1, 1918.

Djemal thereafter served as a liaison officer in talks between the new Bolshevik government of Russia and the postwar Turkish government. He then served as a military adviser to Afghanistan. Tried in absentia by a military tribunal in Istanbul on war crimes charges, he was found guilty and sentenced to death. On July 21, 1922, Armenian assassins attacked and killed Djemal in Tbilisi, Georgia, in retribution for his role in the 1915–1916 Armenian Genocide.

Dirk Steffen

See also

Arab Revolt of World War I; Armenians and the Armenian Genocide; Enver Pasha; Ottoman Empire; Ottoman Empire, Entry into World War I; Ottoman Empire, Post–World War I Revolution in; Palestine and Syria Campaign, World War I; Sinai Campaign of 1916–1917; Taalat Pasha, Mehmed

References

Akçam, Taner. *From Empire to Republic: Turkish Nationalism and the Armenian Genocide.* New York: Zed, 2004.

Cleveland, William. *A History of the Modern Middle East.* Boulder, CO: Westview, 2004.

Kent, Marian, ed. *The Great Powers and the End of the Ottoman Empire.* London: Allen and Unwin, 1984.

Palmer, Alan. *The Decline and Fall of the Ottoman Empire.* London: Murray, 1992.

Doha Agreement (May 21, 2008)

Diplomatic agreement reached on May 21, 2008, and signed in Doha, Qatar, that ended an 18-month-long political crisis in Lebanon. On November 21, 2006, Lebanese minister of industry Pierre Germayel was assassinated, the fourth high-level outspoken Lebanese critic of Syria to be slain since the murder of former prime minister Rafik Hariri in 2005. After repeated calls for changes in the government and the cabinet, six ministers resigned from the cabinet in November, bringing about a constitutional and governmental crisis. This was followed beginning on December 1, 2006, by huge public demonstrations and picketing directed against Prime Minister Fuad Siniura. The demonstrations were sponsored by the pro-Syrian parties of Amal, Hezbollah, and the Free Patriotic Movement of Michael Aoun with the goal of securing veto power in the government.

Lebanese affairs were further paralyzed when the opposition refused to attend the parliament and vote for a new president on the expiration of Émile Lahoud's term of office. Siniora was thus acting president until a new president could be voted into office. This state of affairs and the demonstrations continued for 17 months until May 7, 2008, when Hezbollah, Amal, the Syrian Social Nationalist Party, and other groups mounted an effort to take power in Beirut. The Rafik Hariri International Airport and a number of other locations came under siege, and some 200 people were killed in the few days of fighting.

Qatari emir Sheikh Hamad bin Khalifa Al Thani invited the leaders of the Lebanese political parties to come to Doha and there work to resolve their differences. The ensuing Doha Agreement of May 21, 2008, ended the confrontation between the Hezbollah-backed minority, supported by Iran and Syria, and the Lebanese majority, supported by the West. The agreement received firm support from the United Nations Security Council in a vote of 15 to 0.

The parties agreed to convene the parliament and elect as president the consensus candidate Suleiman. They also agreed to the formation of a national unity government composed of 30 ministers: 16 ministers from among the majority, 11 from the opposition, and 3 by the president. All parties committed not to resign or obstruct government actions. The agreement also set electoral constituencies in conformity with the 1960 law. All parties to the agreement committed to abstain from recourse to weapons and violence in order to secure political gain. They also accepted the Lebanese state's authority over all Lebanese territory.

SPENCER C. TUCKER

See also
Hezbollah; Lebanon; Lebanon Civil War; Siniura, Fuad

References
Harris, William. *Lebanon: A History, 600–2011.* New York: Oxford University Press, 2014.
Levitt, Matthew. *Hezbollah.* Washington, DC: Georgetown University Press, 2016.
Traboulsi, Fawwaz. *A History of Modern Lebanon.* 2nd ed. London: Pluto, 2012.

Donkey Island, Battle of (June 30–July 1, 2007)

Military engagement in Iraq between U.S. forces and Al Qaeda in Iraq insurgents during June 30–July 1, 2007. The Battle of Donkey Island occurred on the banks of a canal leading from Ramadi to Lake Habbaniyah near the city of Tash, south of the city of Ramadi in al-Anbar Province, Iraq. The island is named for the wild donkeys native to the region. This skirmish pitted elements of the U.S. Army Task Force 1–77 Armor Regiment and the 2nd Battalion, 5th Marines, against a force of Al Qaeda in Iraq insurgents, who outnumbered the Americans.

The insurgent force had gathered in the area to launch a planned assault on Ramadi employing daytime suicide attacks to break the shaky peace that had been recently established in the city. American forces discovered the company-size insurgent force while conducting a routine patrol in Hummvee vehicles on the evening of June 30. The insurgents had opened fire on the convoy. Despite being outnumbered, a U.S. platoon-size element, along with the original patrol group, counterattacked with superior firepower a short while later and defeated the insurgent group after what turned out to be a 23-hour on-again, off-again gun battle. Although a clear military victory for the American forces, the engagement demonstrated that Al Qaeda in Iraq, along with other insurgent groups, still had the ability to organize forces effectively in an attempt to destabilize the Anbar region.

American forces suffered 2 dead and 11 wounded, while an estimated 32 insurgents were killed out of an estimated force of 40–70 fighters. U.S. forces also managed to destroy two trucks operated by the insurgents that had carried considerable numbers of arms and ammunition.

RICHARD B. VERRONE

See also
Al Qaeda in Iraq; Iraq Insurgency

References
Cockburn, Patrick. *Muqtada: Muqtada al-Sadr, the Shia Revival, and the Struggle for Iraq.* New York: Scribner, 2008.
Ricks, Thomas E. *The Gamble: General David Petraeus and the American Military Adventure in Iraq, 2006–2008.* New York: Penguin, 2009.

Dorylaion, Battle of (July 1, 1097)

Battle on July 1, 1097, during the First Crusade (1096–1099). It was fought between crusading forces and troops of Qilij

Arslan I, Seljuk sultan of Rum, and his allies on the edge of the Anatolian plateau near the city of Dorylaion (modern-day Eskişehir, Turkey) and probably north of modern-day Bozüyük.

Qilij Arslan had been absent from his capital of Nicaea (modern-day Iznik, Turkey) when the crusader siege there began on May 14, 1097, and his attempt to relieve it two days later failed. On June 19 Nicaea surrendered, and on June 26 the crusaders began their march across Anatolia.

Neither the reasons for the crusaders choice of direction nor the precise nature of their route are known. The sources make clear that as a result of divided command, their army split into a vanguard, led by Bohemund of Taranto, and a larger main force, with substantial elements straggling between the two. This gave Qilij Arslan the opportunity to defeat the crusaders in detail by first attacking the vanguard, which his army of around 6,000 men outnumbered.

On July 1, the Seljuks ambushed the vanguard. Bohemund rallied his men sent for help, but the cavalry was driven back on their camp in a confused mass. The Seljuks were then drawn into a close-quarter fight lasting from early morning till noon, when the main crusader force arrived and routed them.

JOHN FRANCE

See also
Qilij Arslan I of Rum; Rum, Sultanate of; Seljuk Dynasty

Reference
France, John. *Victory in the East: A Military History of the First Crusade.* Cambridge: Cambridge University Press, 1994.

Druze-Ottoman Wars

Series of conflicts between the Ottoman imperial authorities and the Druze population in present-day Syria and Lebanon. The Druzes trace their origins to the Ismaili sect of Shiism and venerated the Fatimid caliph al-Hakim (d. 1021) as an incarnation of God. After the caliph's death, the sect was persecuted by the later Fatimid rulers and scattered throughout Lebanon and Syria, where it became politically important in the mid-11th century. The Ottoman-Mamluk War of 1516–1517 and the subsequent Ottoman occupation of Syria-Lebanon brought the Druzes under Ottoman authority. Sultan Selim I (1467–1520) initially placated the Druzes by naming Fakhr ad-Din (d. 1544) of the House of Ma'n the emir (native ruler) of the Druzes in the Ottoman Empire.

Throughout the Ottoman period (1516–1918), the Druzes constituted a thorn in the side of the Ottomans. In 1584 while a convoy of Janissaries was passing through Lebanon, they were attacked and robbed of a large sum of money that had been collected as taxes in Egypt and Palestine. Infuriated by such a brazen action, Sultan Murad III (r. 1574–1595) organized a punitive expedition against Yusuf Sayfa in whose district the convoy was robbed. The sultan then accused the Druze leader, Fakhr ad-Din's son Qurqumaz (r. 1544–1585), of organizing the attack and sent Ibrahim Pasha, *wali* of Egypt, to exact punishment.

Ibrahim acted with particular savagery, slaughtering the some 600-man Druze delegation that greeted him at Ayn Sawfar and then sacking dozens of villages, killing thousands more. Qurqumaz took refuge in the mountains near Jazzin, where he died after being poisoned by an agent of the Ottoman sultan. Qurqumaz left a teenage son, Fakhr ad-Din II, who assumed the title of emir of Jabal al-Duruz (mountain of the Druzes, as part of Lebanon was then known) in 1590.

Despite his youth and diminutive stature, Fakhr proved to be a rather capable statesman who desired to expand his authority to greater Lebanon and sever ties with the Porte. A consummate practitioner of diplomacy, he reconciled with the Ottoman authorities and used their support to consolidate his power in northern Lebanon. He continued to maintain friendly relations with Constantinople while also cultivating relations with European states that opposed the Ottomans. Taking advantage of the Ottoman preoccupation with fighting in Europe and eastern Anatolia, Fakhr expanded his authority to southern Lebanon and negotiated an alliance with Grand Duke Ferdinand I of Tuscany in 1608; the agreement contained a secret military provision directed against the Ottoman Empire.

Alarmed by this development, Ottoman sultan Ahmed (r. 1589–1617) sent Hafiz Pasha, *wali* of Damascus, on a punitive expedition against the rebellious Druzes in 1613. At first Hafiz Pasha was unable to penetrate deep into the mountains of Lebanon where Fakhr was established, but the Ottoman blockade of the coast soon forced Fakhr to flee to Italy. He spent five years there, seeking in vain to secure European support against the Porte.

In 1618 Fakhr reconciled with new Ottoman sultan Osman II (1604–1622), who allowed him to return to Lebanon even though Fakhr continued to maintain close relations with Tuscany. Fakhr quickly reclaimed his authority in northern and southern Lebanon and even gained new territories that the Porte granted to him in 1622. Two years later the sultan acknowledged him as the lord of "Arabistan" that stretched from Aleppo to Egypt. Yet, Fakhr's continued political ambitions soon led to renewed tensions with the Ottoman authorities, although the Druze leader was able to prevent Ottoman military action in 1625 through a generous bribery to the Ottoman officials at Constantinople (Istanbul).

By the early 1630s Ottoman sultan Murad IV (1609–1640), while planning a campaign against the Safavid Iran, could no longer ignore the presence of a rebellious Druze leader whose allegiance was questionable. In 1633 the sultan ordered Kuchuk Ahmad Pasha, *wali* of Damascus, to launch a land expedition against Fakhr while an Ottoman fleet under Jafar Pasha blockaded the Lebanese coast. Fakhr's son died gallantly in battle at Wadi al-Taym in 1634, while Fakhr himself withdrew deep into the mountains, his calls for European assistance unheeded. Fakhr was finally captured and beheaded in Constantinople in April 1635.

Alexander Mikaberidze

See also
Fatimid Dynasty; Lebanon; Mamluk-Ottoman Wars

References
Firro, Kais. *A History of the Druzes.* Leiden: E. J. Brill, 1992.
Hitti, Philip K. *History of Syria Including Lebanon and Palestine.* London: Gorgias, 2002.
Hitti, Philip K. *Origins of the Druze People and Religion.* London: Saqi, 2007.
Swayd, Samy. *Historical Dictionary of the Druzes.* Lanham, MD: Scarecrow, 2006.

Druzes

People who adhere to an Islamic sect derived from Ismaili Shia Islam. The name "Druze" is a misnomer, probably derived from the 11th-century figure Nashtakin al-Darazi, regarded as the first Druze, or heretic. The Druzes call themselves *muwahhidun,* or believers in monotheism (*tawhid*), a central principle of Islam, meaning unicity or strict monotheism. They are also known as Ahl al-Tawhid and Bana Maruf.

Historically, some other Muslims treated the Druzes as an extremist sect or disclaimed their Islamic beliefs, as today some discredit all of Shia Islam. The Druzes number about 1 million people and are most numerous in Syria (400,000), Lebanon (196,000), and Israel (140,000). Smaller communities exist in the United States (63,000), Colombia (50,000), Jordan (32,000), Australia (20,000), Canada (20,000), and Germany (14,000).

The Druzes are Arabs and tribal in origin. They are divided between the Qays and Yaman, or northern and southern traditional family rivalries. Their esoteric teachings were not revealed to all Druzes, meaning that the common folk (*juhhal*) were excluded from some of the secrets of the faith possessed by the *uqqal,* or wise elders, although commoners may seek initiation into the sect's esoteric teachings.

The Druzes are an endogamous group, marrying within the faith, and no longer accept converts. The earliest *muwahhidun* were followers of the Fatimid caliph al-Hakim (966–1021) who developed into a reform movement under Hamza ibn Ali and others. The group proselytized and established a community in the Levant among 12 Arab Tanukhi tribes.

An intra-Druze war in 1711 spelled defeat for one faction, some of whom moved to the Hawran and Suwaida districts of Syria. Maronite Christians moved from northern Lebanon into some formerly Druze areas in Lebanon at this time.

The Druze religion is an offshoot of Ismaili Islam that developed in the 10th century. Druzes adhere to five articles of faith and seven acts of worship that correspond to the so-called Five Pillars of Islam (actually seven pillars including jihad [striving] and *walaya* [allegiance]). However, the esoteric interpretation of the acts of worship differs, or goes beyond the exoteric (outward) practice in Sunni Islam. The articles of faith include (1) *tawhid,* or unicity of God, and the idea that he has no opponents (Satan is not a separate force); (2) veneration (*taqdis*) of seven who preached a message (including Abraham, Muhammad, and Muhammad ibn Ismail) and their divine helpers as well as five luminaries, or key principles; (3) metempsychosis (*taqamus*), the rebirth of souls in a new body; (4) the need for initiation (*ta'aqul*), as faith should be pursued through reason; and (5) erudition or esoteric knowledge, known as *ma'rifa.*

In addition, the required acts of worship must include key principles that correspond to pillars of the Druze faith. These are speaking truth to attain unicity; supporting fellow believers with pure hearts; abandonment of old (polytheistic) ways and of sin; self-purification, or fleeing from evil nature and oppression; declaring the unity of God (true declaration of the *shahada* following esoteric understanding); being content and patient (*ridha*) with God's will as the expression of jihad; and submission to God's will.

For purposes of self-protection, the Druzes, like other Shia Muslims, may practice *taqiyya* (dissimulation, or not admitting that one is a Druze). However, in their home areas, Druzes are identified by their family names and their more classical pronunciation of Arabic.

The Druzes belief in *taqamus,* a doctrine meaning transmigration of the soul after death, and tolerance of other faiths, or races. Their esoteric teachings sparked other sects' suspicion of their beliefs. These suspicions were politically promoted at times, as in Ibn Taymiyya's fatwa against them when the Mamluk forces aimed to reconquer local dynasties cooperating with the Mongols.

The Druzes abstain from alcohol, tobacco, and pork. The five-pointed multicolor star of the Druze religion represents the five luminaries referred to above, or five seminal principles: reason and intelligence, the universal soul, the word, historical precedence, and immanence (*al-tali'*, or the following).

The Druzes in Lebanon—mainly found in Mount Lebanon, the Wadi Taym area, and Beirut—became involved in the Lebanese Civil War (1975–1990). Under the leadership of Kamal Jumblat, their participation in the Lebanese National Movement pitted them against establishment Christian forces. The Druzes fought effectively against the Christian Maronite Phalangist militia. Since the end of the war, certain Druzes and Maronites have reconciled. In Lebanon, Israel, and Syria, the Druzes are officially recognized by the respective governments and maintain their own religiously based court system.

In Syria, the Druzes were leaders in the nationalist resistance to the French. Later, some were involved in a coup attempt against the Hafez al-Assad government and were subsequently treated poorly by the central government. Their region remains underdeveloped and poorly funded to this day. Nonetheless, some key Druze politicians were supporters of the Baath Party.

In Israel, the Druzes live mainly in the Galilee and Carmel regions. The Druzes of the Golan Heights suffered from expulsion from their villages or actual separation of territory. In all, the Druzes have had about 80 percent of their former lands confiscated by Israel. The Israeli government treated the Druzes more favorably than other Arabs as part of a policy aimed at dividing Arabs and creating loyalty to the state. The Druzes routinely serve in the Israel Defense Forces (IDF) but nevertheless experience discrimination as non-Jews.

Sometimes the Israeli, Syrian, and Lebanese Druze communities have tried to support one another. When the IDF attempted to establish Christian domination in Lebanon over the Shuf area, Palestinian Druzes vocally opposed this policy, which may have partially prompted Israeli withdrawal from the area. Some Druze officers have in recent years risen to general officer rank in the IDF.

PAUL G. PIERPAOLI JR. AND SHERIFA ZUHUR

See also
Assad, Hafez al-; Lebanon; Lebanon Civil War

References
Abu Izzeddin, Nejla M. *The Druzes: A New Study of Their History, Faith, and Society.* Leiden: Brill, 1993.
Betts, Robert Brenton. *The Druze.* New Haven, CT: Yale University Press, 1990.
Dana, Nissim. *The Druze in the Middle East.* Eastbourne, East Sussex, UK: Sussex Academic, 2003.
Swayd, Samy S. *The Druzes: An Annotated Bibliography.* Kirkland, WA: ISES Publications, 1998.

E

EAGLE CLAW, Operation
See Iran Hostage Rescue Mission

EARNEST WILL, Operation (1987–1989)

U.S. military operation designed to provide oil tanker escorts in the Persian Gulf from 1987 to 1989 during the last stages of the Iran-Iraq War. During the Iran-Iraq War (1980–1988), both the Iranians and Iraqis carried out attacks on tankers and other merchant shipping in the Persian Gulf. This became known, informally, as the Tanker War. The Tanker War was essentially designed to inflict economic damage on the enemy. Iraq, lacking a significant navy, used planes to attack Iranian tankers and ports. Iraq did not have a tanker fleet, so Iran targeted the shipping of countries that favored Iraq, such as Saudi Arabia and Kuwait. Iran used a variety of methods in its attacks, including small boats, mines, frigates, and aircraft. Kuwait was a nonbelligerent yet feared Iranian attacks on its tankers, which were critical to its status as a major oil and natural gas exporter.

In December 1986 and January 1987, Kuwait asked both the United States and the Soviet Union to protect 11 of its oil tankers from potential Iranian attacks. After much discussion, the United States agreed to place all 11 of the Kuwaiti-owned tankers under the U.S. flag and escort them with warships through the Persian Gulf. The Ronald Reagan administration had three main motivations for agreeing to the escorts: to keep the Soviet Union out of the oil-rich Persian Gulf, to improve diplomatic relations with Middle East allies, and to ensure the flow of oil to the West. Kuwait secretly agreed to provide free fuel for the escort operation.

Low-key planning for the operation, code-named EARNEST WILL, began in the spring of 1987. At the time, the United States had only a small naval contingent called the Middle East Force, consisting of seven ships, stationed in the Persian Gulf. Rear Admiral Harold Bernsen was the commanding officer of the Middle East Force. These ships were originally set to carry out the escorts with no augmentation. On May 17, 1987, during the EARNEST WILL planning stages, an Iraqi plane on a tanker attack mission mistakenly fired two missiles into the U.S. Navy Perry-class frigate *Stark,* one of the Middle East Force ships. This attack, held to be accidental, killed 37 U.S. sailors, drew increased public and congressional scrutiny to the upcoming escort operation, and led to increased coordination with Iraq in hopes of avoiding another such incident. The United States now sent more ships to the Persian Gulf and upgraded the capability of the Middle East Force in preparation for the late July start of EARNEST WILL.

The first official escort mission began on July 24, 1987, amid Iranian threats to disrupt the operation. The first Kuwaiti tankers to be reflagged and escorted were the *Bridgeton* and *Gas Prince.* Three U.S. warships accompanied the two tankers from the Gulf of Oman to a position

Reflagged Kuwaiti oil tankers transiting the Persian Gulf under U.S. Navy escort in 1987 during Operation EARNEST WILL. (U.S. Department of Defense)

near Farsi Island in the northern Persian Gulf. At that point, *Bridgeton* struck a submerged sea mine on July 27, 1987. The explosion caused little damage to the massive tanker, which continued on to Kuwait after a short delay. The United States quickly determined that the Iranians had laid the mines in the path of the convoy. Iran denied any involvement but continued to make veiled threats. Despite criticism from Congress and even from segments of the U.S. military, the Reagan administration ordered EARNEST WILL to continue. The escorts were temporarily suspended while minesweeping operations began. The escorts resumed in early August, with improvised minesweepers leading the way.

The mine threat prompted the United States to bring in special forces units and to increase intelligence-gathering efforts to prevent further mining. On the night of September 21, 1987, U.S. helicopters spotted an Iranian ship, the *Iran Ajr*, laying mines and took the ship under fire. Navy SEALs boarded the *Iran Ajr* the next morning and took the surviving crew members as prisoners. The Reagan administration presented the mines seized from *Iran Ajr* as proof of the Iranian mining campaign.

In early October 1987, U.S. special forces outfitted the first of two oil barges converted into heavily armed mobile sea bases in the northern Gulf. Small boats and helicopters based on the barges patrolled the area watching for Iranian minelayers and other activity that might threaten the convoys. These efforts virtually stopped the mining campaign in that area of the Persian Gulf. Iran periodically fired Silkworm missiles, and on October 16, 1987, one of the missiles struck a U.S.-flagged Kuwaiti tanker. The explosion blinded the captain, a U.S. citizen, and wounded several other members of the crew.

The United States retaliated with a naval bombardment of an offshore Iranian oil platform on October 19, 1987. According to intelligence reports, Iran used this platform along with others as command and control bases for tanker attacks. This bombardment was code-named Operation NIMBLE ARCHER and was commanded by Rear Admiral Dennis Brooks, who was stationed with a carrier task force in the Arabian Sea.

Following NIMBLE ARCHER, there were no confrontations between the United States and Iran for almost six months. The escorts continued with only minor problems throughout the winter of 1987–1988. In February 1988, the United States combined the forces in the Persian Gulf and the Arabian Sea into a joint command led by Vice Admiral Anthony Less.

On April 14, 1988, the U.S. Navy Oliver Hazard Perry–class guided missile frigate *Samuel B. Roberts* hit a mine while transiting through the central Persian Gulf alone. The mine severely damaged the ship and wounded 10 sailors. Only excellent damage control kept the ship afloat while it steered clear of the area. Further investigation found an extensive minefield with the same type of mines found on *Iran Ajr* and in other Iranian-laid minefields.

The United States planned a significant retaliatory measure, which took place on April 18, 1988. This daylong running battle was code-named Operation PRAYING MANTIS and involved nine American surface ships and a carrier air wing from the *Enterprise*. One of the mission's goals was to sink an Iranian warship. The operation began with bombardments of two Iranian oil platforms. Iran sent various ships, boats, and planes to confront the U.S. ships throughout the day. Most of the Iranian force, including two frigates, were sunk or disabled by the Americans. The United States lost one helicopter with a two-man crew to an accident early in the evening. PRAYING MANTIS was the largest U.S. military combat operation to date in the Persian Gulf and the largest sea-air battle since World War II. Shortly after, the United States extended protection to all non-Iranian shipping in the Persian Gulf.

By the summer of 1988, Iraq clearly had the upper hand in the undeclared war with Iran. On July 3, 1988, the U.S. Navy Ticonderoga-class AEGIS guided missile cruiser *Vincennes* accidentally shot down an Iranian passenger jetliner in the Strait of Hormuz. This incident was seen in Iran as further evidence that the United States was taking sides with Iraq, and it was no doubt one of the reasons the Iranian government decided to seek an end to the Tanker War and the Iran-Iraq War.

The Iran-Iraq War finally ended in August 1988, but the EARNEST WILL escorts continued until December 1989. Operation EARNEST WILL was mostly successful and laid the groundwork logistically and diplomatically for subsequent U.S. Persian Gulf operations.

HAROLD WISE

See also
Iran; Iran Air Flight 655, Downing of; Iran-Iraq War; Iraq; Persian Gulf; PRAYING MANTIS, Operation; *Stark* Incident

References
Palmer, Michael A. *Guardians of the Gulf: A History of America's Expanding Role in the Persian Gulf, 1833–1992.* New York: Free Press, 1992.

Wise, Harold L. *Inside the Danger Zone: The U.S. Military in the Persian Gulf 1987–1988.* Annapolis, MD: Naval Institute Press, 2007.

Edessa, County of

A Frankish state in northern Syria and Upper Mesopotamia (1097–1150). The first of the Christian principalities established in Outremer in the course of the First Crusade (1096–1099), the county of Edessa was also the first to be conquered by the Turks. The brevity of Edessa's history has left it the least studied of all the principalities of Outremer, but its many distinctive qualities make it more important than the duration of Frankish political authority might suggest. Edessa was the training ground for many leaders of Outremer, including two kings of Jerusalem (Baldwin I and Baldwin II). Another distinctive feature of Edessa was that the county was entirely landlocked.

At its greatest extent, the county of Edessa covered a large portion of what is now southeastern Turkey as well as parts of modern-day Syria. The county stretched from Marash (modern-day Kahramanmaraş, Turkey) in the west to Tell-Mawzan (modern-day Viranflehir, Turkey) in the east and from Gargar (modern-day Gerger, Turkey) in the north to Azaz in the south. The Euphrates River cut through the center of the county, providing both a line of communication and a line of defense. The town of Bira (modern-day Birecik, Turkey) commanded the crossing of the Euphrates between the city of Edessa (modern-day Şanlıurfa, Turkey) and Antioch on the Orontes (modern-day Antakya, Turkey) and was the farthest point north that river traffic from the Persian Gulf could travel.

Most of the land within the county was dry high plateau, suitable for raising horses, cattle, and sheep. The fertile areas around the Euphrates and other rivers, such as the Khabur, the Sadjur, and the Balikh, allowed the cultivation of wheat and other grain crops. The wealth of the county was based largely on its agricultural products. Unlike the Holy Land, Edessa had only minimal pilgrim traffic and never attracted dependencies of Italian merchant republics.

Frankish domination was established in the course of the First Crusade. The first important conquest was Turbessel (modern-day Tellbasar Kalesi, Turkey), an important fortress and later residence of the counts, captured in the fall of 1097 by Baldwin of Boulogne, a younger brother of Godfrey of Bouillon. The city of Edessa, however, did not come under Baldwin's authority until March 1098. Baldwin established the county through a strange combination of conquest and political subterfuge. After having shown himself to be an effective fighter against the Turks by capturing Turbessel and other fortresses, Baldwin came to Edessa to help protect the city from Turkish attacks, invited by either the city's T'oros, a Melkite Armenian, or by the citizens. T'oros adopted the crusader, but within 15 days of Baldwin's arrival a mob had killed T'oros and proclaimed Baldwin the new leader of the city. Baldwin I soon added Saruj (modere-day Suruç, Turkey) and Samosata (modern-day Samsat, Turkey) to his domains and married the daughter of an Armenian lord. In October 1100 Baldwin left Edessa to claim the throne of Jerusalem, which had been left vacant by the death of his brother Godfrey. The county he left behind was a patchwork of castles, cities, and rural areas, some directly under Frankish authority but most under local Armenian leaders. Some were allied with Baldwin, but others were opposed to the new Frankish influence. Baldwin directly ruled a core of territory on the western bank of the Euphrates River, but in the eastern area his authority only extended to Edessa, Saruj, and Samosata.

Baldwin I's successor was Baldwin II of Bourcq, a distant cousin. Soon after becoming count, Baldwin II installed his cousin Joscelin I of Courtenay as lord of Turbessel, which effectively gave authority over the western half of the county to Joscelin, leaving Baldwin free to concentrate on establishing Frankish authority over the eastern portion. But more importantly, Baldwin had an ally on whom he could rely. Baldwin's marriage to Morphia, the daughter of Gabriel of Melitene, temporarily brought that city under his influence sometime between 1100 and 1104, but it was conquered soon after by the emir of Sivas.

When Baldwin and Joscelin fell captive to different Turkish emirs at the Battle of Harran in 1104, Tancred of Antioch and Richard of the Principate, Normans from Antioch, assumed authority over the county, which they were loath to relinquish when Baldwin and Joscelin were eventually released in 1108. Armenian and Syriac chroniclers denounce Richard as a vile usurper who exploited the county for financial gain and did nothing to protect Baldwin's interests. The intervention of Baldwin I of Jerusalem was necessary to force Tancred and Richard to return the county to Baldwin II.

Baldwin II had scarcely reestablished his authority when the county fell under attack by Mawdud, the *atabeg* of Mosul. Mawdud was the first to employ the ideology of jihad (holy war) to rally Muslims against the Frankish settlers. While failing to conquer any significant portion of Frankish territory, Mawdud did establish a model of Islamic leadership that would later prove very effective against the Franks in the time of Zangi and Nur al-Din. It was perhaps these attacks that spurred Baldwin to establish his authority over all the Christian areas of northern Syria, seeking to replace local Armenian leaders with Franks loyal to him. Taking advantage of the death of Kogh Vasil in 1113, Baldwin seized his territory, capturing the important towns of Kesoun (modern-day Keysun, Turkey), Raban, and Behesni (modern-day Besni, Turkey). The important crossing point of Bira on the Euphrates came into Frankish hands in 1117, when Baldwin's cousin Waleran of Le Puiset married the daughter of its lord, the Armenian Ablgharib, thereby resolving the siege under which the Franks had placed the fortress. By 1118, many of the more independent-minded Armenian leaders had either died or been forced out by the Franks, though some still held important fortresses within the county.

In 1118, Baldwin II succeeded Baldwin I as king of Jerusalem. Baldwin II subsequently established Joscelin as count of Edessa. Joscelin I proved to be a vigorous leader and was particularly admired for his military prowess and his close relations with local Christian communities. He first married a daughter of the Armenian lord Rupen, who was the mother of his only son, Joscelin II; he later married Maria, the sister of Roger of Antioch. Joscelin and Baldwin II, acting as regent of Antioch, gained a significant victory over Ilghazi ibn Artuq, Artuqid ruler of Mardin and Aleppo.

This triumph was short-lived. Soon after Ilghazi's death in 1122, his nephew Balak ibn Bahram captured Joscelin and Waleran of Bira. Baldwin II was also taken prisoner not long after that, leaving northern Syria leaderless. A resourceful band of Armenians infiltrated the fortress where Joscelin and Baldwin II were imprisoned, allowing Joscelin to escape. Once free, he sought to force Balak to free Baldwin by continuously attacking his former captor's territories. Balak's death in May 1124 led to Baldwin II's release, but Joscelin continued his attacks on Aleppo, now ruled by Aq Sunqur al-Bursuqi. Most of the conflict consisted of raids along Edessa's border with Aleppo that probably did not affect the remainder of the county.

Joscelin died in 1131 and was succeeded by his son, Joscelin II. Edessa was relatively untroubled during the first few years of his reign, since Zangi, son of Aq Sunqur, was concentrating on subduing his Turkish opponents. Joscelin resided chiefly in Turbessel, perhaps because of its proximity to Antioch. By 1135, however, Zangi had united much of Muslim Syria and Mesopotamia behind him and began to focus his considerable military resources on the Franks, first attacking Antioch. Little effort was made to defend the principality, however, as a result of political conflict within Antioch.

Within two years, the threat posed by Zangi was recognized throughout Outremer. A combined Frankish army was assembled under the leadership of King Fulk of Jerusalem that temporarily halted Zangi's attacks, but Edessa and

Antioch could not always rely on the military aid of Jerusalem. Joscelin and Raymond of Antioch turned to the Byzantine emperor, John II Komnenos, and both leaders swore an oath of fealty to him in return for protection. The price of Byzantine military support came largely at the expense of Antioch, but Joscelin feared that John's ambitions extended to Edessa as well. In the spring of 1138 the emperor led a Frankish-Byzantine army to Syria, capturing Kafartab and Atharib from Zangi with Frankish assistance. The siege of the independent Arab city of Shaizar, however, failed because of Joscelin and Raymond's failure to cooperate with the Byzantines and also because of the approach of Zangi's army.

While John Komnenos was alive, his army deterred Zangi's attacks. In 1143 John again returned with his army to Syria and demanded hostages to ensure Joscelin's cooperation. Following John's death later that year, however, the Byzantine army withdrew, leaving Zangi unopposed. While Joscelin II was aiding a Seljuk enemy of Zangi in late 1144, Zangi attacked and captured the city of Edessa. The loss of the city was a blow to the economy and prestige of the county but, more importantly, signaled to locals and foreigners alike that the Frankish presence in the Levant was by no means permanent. Joscelin, however, still controlled important towns and castles on the western side of the Euphrates that together formed a viable principality. His attempt to recapture Edessa in 1146 was briefly successful, but within a month the Frankish and Armenian forces were again expelled, and the city's Christian population was massacred.

Although it was launched as a response to the fall of Edessa, the Second Crusade (1147–1149) did little to aid Joscelin or the much-diminished county. Instead of attacking Nur al-Din, Zangī's son and successor in Aleppo, the crusaders attacked the independent Muslim state of Damascus, which had the paradoxical effect of pushing it into Nur al-Din's growing empire. Joscelin secured a truce with Nur al-Din to protect the remnants of his county and thus did not aid Raymond of Antioch when the latter attacked him in 1148 and 1149. Following the death in battle of Reynald, lord of Marash, Reynald's lands fell to Mas'ud, the sultan of Rum, despite Joscelin's attempts to defend the lands. Gargar similarly fell to Joscelin's erstwhile ally, Kara Arslān, and in 1150 Joscelin himself was captured on his way to Antioch. He was blinded and imprisoned in Aleppo and died in 1159. His wife, Beatrix, defended Turbessel against Nur al-Din's attacks, but on the advice of Baldwin III of Jerusalem, she sold the remaining portion of the county to the Byzantine emperor, Manuel I Komnenos. The strongholds there fell to the Turks by the end of 1151.

The history of the county of Edessa has often been portrayed as the struggle of an embattled island of Christianity striving to maintain itself in a surrounding sea of Islam. Yet the conflicts cannot be so neatly separated into Christian against Muslim. The county of Edessa relied on Muslim allies to maintain their position; Joscelin II was aiding a Muslim emir when Zangi captured Edessa. Similarly, Franks turned to Muslims for support, as both Baldwin II and Tancred did during their feud over control of Edessa. The victories of Zangi and Nur al-Din were opposed not only by the Franks but also by Turkish and Arab rulers who sought to maintain their independence. Frankish authority over Edessa thus fit into a Levantine world of fragmented local authority, whether Christian or Muslim, which could not survive in the united world of Nur al-Din and Saladin.

Christopher MacEvitt

See also
Balak ibn Bahram ibn Ortok; Baldwin I of Jerusalem; Baldwin II of Jerusalem; Byzantine Empire; Harran, Battle of; Ilghazi ibn Artuq, Najm al-Din; Manuel I Komnenos, Emperor; Mawdud; Nur al-Din; Rum, Sultanate of; Saladin; Zangi, Imad ad-Din

References
Amouroux-Mourad, Monique. *Le comté d'Edesse, 1098–1150.* Paris: Bibliothèque de l'Institut français de Beyrouth, 1988.
Cahen, Claude. *La Syrie du nord à l'époque des croisades et la principauté franque d'Antioche.* Paris: Geuthner, 1940.
Gardiner, Robert. "Crusader Turkey: The Fortifications of Edessa." *Fortress: The Castles and Fortifications Quarterly* 2 (1989): 23–35.
MacEvitt, Christopher. "Christian Authority in the Latin East: Edessa in Crusader History." In *The Medieval Crusade*, ed. Susan J. Ridyard, 71–83. Woodbridge, UK: Boydell, 2004.
Nicholson, Robert L. *Joscelyn I, Prince of Edessa.* Urbana: University of Illinois Press, 1954.
Runciman, Steven. *A History of the Crusades.* 3 vols. Cambridge: Cambridge University Press, 1951–1954.
Segal, Judah B. *Edessa, The Blessed City.* Oxford, UK: Clarendon, 1970.

Edward I, King of England (1239–1307)

King of England, also known as Longshanks, the Law-giver, and Hammer of the Scots. Born in the Palace of Westminster, London, on June 17, 1239, Edward was the eldest son of King Henry III and Eleanor of Provence. In 1254 Edward traveled to Castille to marry Eleanor, half sister of King Alfonso X.

Edward returned to encounter unrest in his Welsh lands but was unsuccessful in putting down the revolt there because of a lack of support from Henry III and the border nobility in 1255. Edward quarreled with his father, who sent him to Gascony during 1260–1263. During the Barons' War of 1263–1265, Edward's ill-advised pursuit of the withdrawing enemy in the Battle of Lewes (May 14, 1264) led to his own capture and that of Henry III. Edward then escaped and assumed leadership of the royalist forces.

Edward then began a brilliant campaign, defeating forces under his uncle, Simon de Montfort, earl of Leicester (whom he had initially supported), in battle at Newport (July 8, 1264) and then those of his son, Simon the Younger, at Kenilworth (August 1). Edward then marched back and, despite the exhaustion of his men, defeated Montfort again at Evesham (August 4), rescuing his father.

Henry III had repeatedly stated his intention to go on crusade, but it was Edward, known as the Lord Edward, who finally took the cross in 1268, the crusade being closely linked to the political settlement following the defeat of the earl of Leicester and his partisans. The papal legate Ottobuono promoted the crusade as part of the peace process, although in fact Edward was to be accompanied largely by his own allies from the civil war period.

The expedition was intended to join the second crusade of Louis IX of France, whom Edward seems to have admired; the English were to join Louis at the port of Aigues Mortes in southern France for the departure of the main expedition. However, Edward's fleet sailed after that of Louis. Edward arrived in Tunis in North Africa in the autumn of 1270, only to find that Louis had died and that his brother, Charles I of Anjou, had declared the crusade at an end. Edward wintered in Charles's kingdom of Sicily before sailing to Acre (modern-day Akko, Israel). Arriving there in May 1271, he found the Christians of Outremer in a perilous position following Mamluk successes in the north. Edward lacked a sizable army to stem the tide of Mamluk pressure and agreed to an 11-year truce with Sultan Baybars I on the advice of the local barons. Edward also caused a tower to be built at Acre and arranged for a garrison to defend it. Having survived an assassination attempt while in the East, Edward sailed for home in September 1272. He returned as king, his father having died in his absence (November 16, 1272).

Edward was never to go on crusade again, despite his stated intentions to do so. He always maintained that his crusading intentions were sincere but that his prior duty to God was the defense of his own kingdom, using crusade taxation to fund his wars. He reaffirmed his crusade vow in 1306 and made arrangements in his will for the maintenance of a force of crusading knights and for his heart to be buried in the Holy Land.

Formally crowned king of England as Edward I on August 19, 1274, Edward I spent much of his early reign on matters of administrative and legal reform. He crushed revolts by the Welsh during 1276–1277, 1282–1283, and 1294–1295 and banished from the kingdom 16,000 Jews on charges of usury in 1290.

During 1286–1289 Edward was in Gascony, reforming it administratively; later he fought France over Gascony during 1297–1299. Meanwhile, he had become involved in affairs in Scotland, where the throne had fallen vacant. Asked to arbitrate among the claimants, he demanded that the Scottish nobles submit to his suzerainty, which they did in 1292. He then chose John de Baliol as king in 1292, but when the nobles forced Baliol into alliance with France, Edward invaded and conquered Scotland in 1296. Following a brief campaign in France in 1297, he defeated a revolt in Scotland led by William Wallace, winning the Battle of Falkirk (July 22, 1298). Although he continued to campaign there during 1298–1303, Edward never completely subdued Scotland. Revolt broke out anew in Scotland under Robert Bruce in 1306. Edward raised an army to return there but died en route at Burgh-upon-the-Sands, near Carlisle, Cumberland, England, on July 7, 1307.

Certainly one of England's greatest kings, Edward was a highly effective lawmaker and a wise and just ruler who picked capable officials to advise him. A brilliant tactician and strategist, he was also one of the greatest generals in British history.

Spencer C. Tucker and Michael R. Evans

See also
Baybars I; Crusades in the Holy Land, Christian; Louis IX, King of France

References
Lloyd, Simon. *English Society and the Crusade 1216–1307.* Oxford, UK: Clarendon, 1988.
Lloyd, Simon. "The Lord Edward's Crusade, 1270–72." In *War and Government in the Middle Ages: Essays in Honour of J. O. Prestwich,* ed. John Gillingham and J. C. Holt, 120–133. Woodbridge, UK: Boydell, 1984.
Prestwich, Michael. *Edward I.* London: Edwin Methuen, 1988.
Tyerman, Christopher. *England and the Crusades.* Chicago: Chicago University Press, 1988.

Egypt

Egypt is a North African and Middle Eastern nation encompassing 387,048 square miles of territory and thus is the third-largest African nation. Officially the Arab Republic of Egypt, the country is bounded by the Mediterranean Sea to

EGYPT

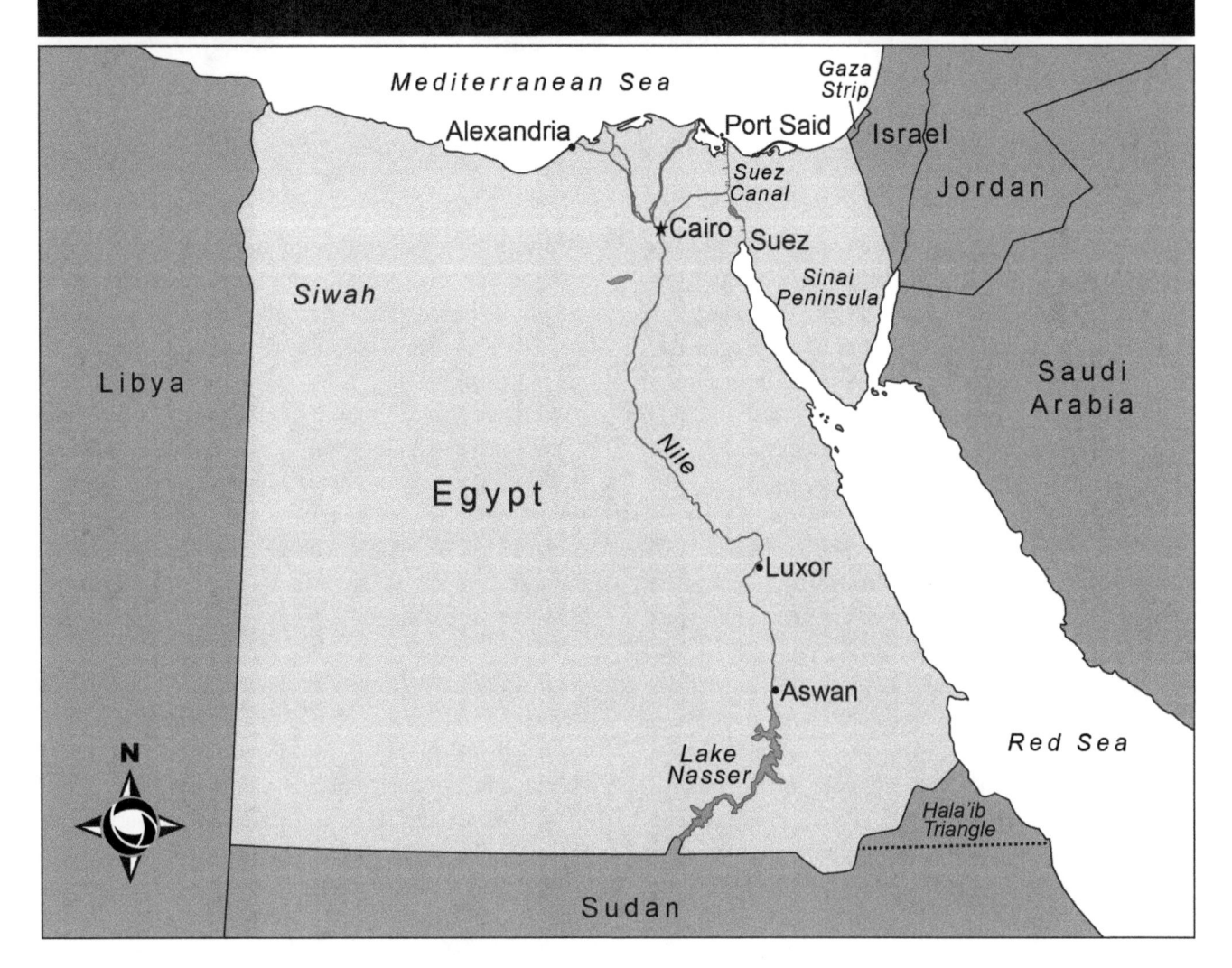

the north, Libya to the west, Sudan to the south, and the Red Sea, the Gulf of Aqaba, and Israel to the east and northeast.

Egypt's 2018 population of some 96 million gives the country the largest population in the Arab world and ranks it 14th in the world by population. Cairo is its capital city. Ethnic Egyptians constitute some 91 percent of the population. Minorities include Abazas, Turks, Greeks, Bedouin Arab tribes in the eastern deserts and the Sinai Peninsula, and Nubian communities along the Nile.

President Anwar Sadat made Islam the official state religion. Muslims constitute some 90 percent of the population, the vast majority of them Sunnis. Perhaps 15 million Egyptians follow native Sufi orders, while Shia Muslims could number as many as 3 million, and Salafis (ultraconservatives) are perhaps 5 million to 6 million. Although before the Arab conquest Christians were a majority of the Egyptian population, today they make up only about 10 percent (9 percent are Coptic Christians, and 1 percent are other Christian denominations).

Egyptian civilization is one of the world's oldest. Egypt is considered a cradle of civilization, and Egyptians call their country the "mother of the world." Egypt's ancient civilization was closely tied to the Nile River, which runs from south to north through the country and empties into the Mediterranean Sea. Ancient Egypt presents some of the world's earliest forms of writing, agriculture, organized religion, and central government. Ancient Egyptian monuments, including the pyramids, are some of the world's greatest archaeological treasures, and tourism is a major source of revenue for the country.

The Achaemenid Persians conquered Egypt in the sixth century BCE. Following a series of native revolts, the

Persians again took control of Egypt in the fourth century BCE. Alexander III (Alexander the Great) of Macedon conquered Egypt in 323 BCE. Following his death and rule by the Ptolemies, Egypt was a tributary province of the Roman Empire. Arab armies conquered the country in the seventh century CE. Various Muslim nonindigenous dynasties including the Mamluks then ruled Egypt. In 1517 the Ottoman Turks took control of Egypt.

In 1798 French forces under Napoleon Bonaparte invaded the country. Upon the French departure Muhammad Ali Pasha (Mehmed Ali), an Ottoman military envoy, held control during May 1805–March 1848. He developed a disciplined army and was the self-proclaimed khedive of Egypt, recognized by the Ottomans in return for his having suppressed rebellions in other Ottoman territories, the Arabian Peninsula, and Syria. Ali's descendants ruled Egypt and modernized Cairo, while Egypt remained nominally an Ottoman province. In 1867, Egypt secured the status of an autonomous vassal (khedivial) state of the Ottoman Empire; this continued until 1914.

In 1869 a French company headed by Ferdinand de Lesseps completed construction of the Suez Canal, which became immediately important to the British as a considerably shorter passage to India. The canal construction led to enormous debt to European banks and caused popular discontent in Egypt because of the onerous taxation required. Khedive Ismail's profligate spending abetted the situation, and he was forced to sell Egypt's share in the canal, purchased by the British government. Within three years this brought British and French controllers, who in effect became the real power in Egypt. Ismail and his successor Tewfik Pasha governed Egypt as a quasi-independent state under Ottoman suzerainty until the British occupation of 1882.

Egyptian popular dissatisfaction with foreign control brought formation of nationalist groups in 1879, and in February 1881 Ahmet Arabi (Urabi) led a revolt, proclaiming "Egypt for the Egyptians." Arabi becomes minister of war and the key figure in the government. Their position in Egypt threatened, the British and French governments planned a joint military intervention in Egypt, but a change of government in France led to a belated decision in Paris not to participate. London then proceeded alone.

On June 11, 1882, antiforeign riots in Alexandria brought the deaths of 68 Europeans and provided the British with the excuse for action. When Arabi rejected British demands to disarm Alexandria's defenses, British warships shelled the city on July 11 and inflicted considerable damage on the largely antiquated Egyptian shore defenses, while fires, some set by Egyptians, burned much of the city. British marines and seamen sent ashore drove Egyptian troops from the city.

Following the landing of a British expeditionary force, in the Battle of Tel el-Kebir of September 13, British troops under Lieutenant General Garnet Wolseley defeated Arabi's forces in strong defensive positions between Cairo and the Suez Canal. Arabi lost some 2,000 men killed and 500 wounded, while British losses were 58 killed, 379 wounded, and 22 missing.

British cavalry entered Cairo on September 15, almost without opposition. Arabi surrendered, and the revolt quickly collapsed. The British then reinstalled Ismail's son Tewfik as figurehead of a de facto British protectorate. Although British prime minister William Gladstone's government formally notified other powers that the British Army would be withdrawn "as soon as the state of the country, and the organization of the proper means for the maintenance of the Khedive's authority, will admit of it," British troops remained in Egypt. The real ruler of the country for the next 23 years was British consul general and high commissioner Lord Cromer.

When war erupted between the Allied and Central Powers in August 1914, Egypt was still technically an Ottoman tributary, with Khedive Abbas Hilmi II subject to the authority of Sultan Mehmed V. On October 31, 1914, the Ottoman Empire officially entered the war on the side of the Central Powers, and Abbas Hilmi II declared his support for the Ottoman Muslim caliphate. The British then made the protectorate official, and the title of head of state was changed from khedive to sultan, effectively ending Ottoman control. The British replaced Abbas II with his uncle, Hussein Kamel.

During World War I, Alexandria was the chief support base for the unsuccessful Allied 1915 Gallipoli Campaign. Egypt was threatened by Ottoman forces operating in Sinai, Gaza, and Palestine and from the Libyan desert to the west, where the Germans succeeded in persuading the Senussis, the warlike Bedouin tribesmen of Cyrenaica, to rise up against Britain. In the winter of 1915–1916 the Senussis, with German and Ottoman money and arms, invaded Egypt. They then surrounded the garrison at Sollum and forced it to surrender. The British assembled the special Western Desert Force, and operations in early 1916 ended in major defeat for the Senussis and the retaking of Sollum. However, continued raids and incursions from the Libyan desert through the summer of 1916 forced the British to maintain significant forces on the Egyptian western frontier.

In the east, two large Ottoman operations against the Suez Canal were mounted and defeated on February 3, 1915, and August 3, 1916. The British then went over to offensive operations in Palestine. After several rebuffs at Gaza, new British commander Lieutenant General Sir Edmund Allenby prevailed against Gaza in October, and by December 11, 1917, his forces had taken Jerusalem.

Although rising Egyptian nationalism led the British to cede nominal independence to Egypt in 1922 (making Hussein Kamel king), in effect the British retained considerable control over the Egyptian government and also maintained substantial military bases there. During World War II, Egypt was again an important Allied base. Its importance can be seen in that during the 1940 Battle of Britain, Prime Minister Winston Churchill diverted desperately needed military assets there.

Axis and British forces clashed following an Italian invasion of Egypt in 1940, and the ensuing campaigns and battles in Libya and Egypt were some of the most critical of the entire war, especially the First Battle of El Alamein (July 1–27, 1942), in which the British halted the Axis advance on Alexandria and then Cairo and the Suez Canal, and the Second Battle of El Alamein (October 23–November 11, 1942), which saw British forces break through the Axis defenses and begin pushing the Germans and Italians back on Tripoli, where the Allies were victorious in May 1943.

The expanded presence of Western troops in Egypt during the war, however, fueled the fires of Egyptian nationalism and especially angered the Muslim Brotherhood, an antisecularist party that sought to dominate the country.

The Egyptian government strongly opposed the creation of an independent Jewish state, and Egyptian forces constituted the largest contingent of the Arab armies that fought in the Israeli War of Independence (May 14, 1948–January 7, 1949). Although enjoying success at first, the extended and widely dispersed Egyptians were ultimately driven back by the Israelis.

Frustration over the defeat was one factor driving the coup of July 23, 1952, when a group of Egyptian Army officers known as the Free Officers overthrew King Farouk and seized power. They called this event a revolution because it dislodged from power the former regime and the upper class and also because they claimed legitimacy in the name of common Egyptians in place of the elite. Military and security considerations dominated political life thereafter, and the armed forces grew considerably. In fact, since that date all four Egyptian presidents have been military officers.

The Free Officers chose as their leader Muhammad Najib, but he was outmaneuvered by another officer, Gamal Abdel Nasser, who became president of Egypt on June 23, 1956.

Nasser preached a populist and anti-imperialist philosophy that called for Arab unity and became known as Nasserism. Starting in 1961, he also promoted certain policies of Arab socialism.

Soon after becoming president, Nasser suppressed Egyptian Marxists, the labor movement, and the Muslim Brotherhood. In 1955 he signed an agreement with Czechoslovakia to purchase Soviet arms. This, his 1955 refusal to sign the pro-Western Baghdad Pact, and his association with the Non-Aligned Movement ran counter to British aims and also concerned policy makers, who did not differentiate local nationalisms from communism, which they hoped to contain in the region.

Angered with Nasser's policies, especially his courting of the Soviet Union, the United States rescinded its pledge to help fund his ambitious plan to build a high dam on the upper Nile at Aswan. To secure the needed funds, Nasser then nationalized the Suez Canal. This step greatly angered British leaders. The French government was already upset over Nasser's support for insurgent forces in Algeria who were fighting for independence from France, and the Israelis were angered over his decision to blockade the Gulf of Aqaba (Israel's access to the Indian Ocean) and Egyptian sponsorship of Palestinian fedayeen raids into the Jewish state. The British, French, and Israeli leaders then secretly colluded to precipitate what became known as the 1956 Suez Crisis.

On July 29, Israeli forces invaded the Sinai. When Egypt refused to allow the British to intervene to "protect" the Suez Canal, Britain and France attacked Egypt and landed troops. The Soviet Union openly supported Egypt, but the key factor was strong financial pressure by U.S. president Dwight D. Eisenhower on Britain. He demanded that the British, French, and Israelis withdraw, which they did. Although Israel benefited from the crisis, Britain and France did not. And far from overthrowing Nasser, the three nations in effect made him a hero in the Arab world. Nasser now expelled many foreigners and minorities from Egypt and seized their property.

Nasser's government turned increasingly to the Soviet bloc, receiving both technical advisers and weaponry. Some 17,000 Soviet advisers eventually arrived in Egypt, and Egyptians were sent to the Soviet Union to receive advanced military training.

In 1958 Syrian officers and politicians prevailed on Nasser to join their two countries in what was known as the United Arab Republic. Seen as a first step toward a larger Pan-Arab state and established on February 1, 1958, it was, however, completely dominated by Egypt. Displeasure in Syria with this brought an army coup in Syria on September 28, 1961. The new Syrian leaders declared Syria's independence. Although the coup leaders expressed their willingness to renegotiate a union under terms that would have placed Syria on a more equal basis with Egypt, Nasser refused. Indeed, he considered military action against Syria, only rejecting this option when he learned that his allies there had all been removed.

In 1961, the Egyptian government also pursued more aggressive Arab socialist policies in the form of land reform, government seizure of private holdings, and further nationalizations. After 1962 the Arab Socialist Union, a single political party, dominated Egypt's bureaucratic and governmental structures. The party became even more important for a time after 1965.

The Egyptian military expanded throughout the Cold War and was equipped primarily by the Soviets. Egypt's chief military challenge was Israel's better-funded and far better-trained armed forces. A struggle developed between more progressive Arab states such as Egypt and Western-aligned monarchies such as Saudi Arabia; some scholars termed this the Arab Cold War. It undoubtedly led Nasser to pursue secondary aims by supporting the Yemeni republicans against the Saudi proxies of the Yemeni royalists in 1962. During the Yemen Civil War (1962–1970), the Egyptian forces there, which grew to some 55,000 men in late 1965, were not highly successful. They were also bogged down there and thus not available to Egypt during the short 1967 Six-Day War with Israel.

By 1967 with Israeli's chief supporter, the United States, mired in the Vietnam War, Soviet leaders saw an opportunity to alter the balance of power in the Middle East that would favor their client states of Egypt and Syria. On May 13, the Soviets provided Egypt with false information that Israel was mobilizing troops on the Syrian border. In consequence, on May 16 Nasser declared a state of emergency, and the next day the Egyptian and Syrian governments proclaimed a state of combat readiness. Jordan also mobilized.

Nasser's belligerency caused his popularity to soar in the Arab world with profound impact. On May 16, Nasser demanded that the United Nations Emergency Force (UNEF) in the Sinai depart immediately. Since 1956 UNEF had served as a buffer between the Egyptian and Israeli forces. UNEF complied on May 19. The day before, Syria and Egypt placed their armed forces on maximum alert while Iraq and Kuwait mobilized.

Nasser then announced Egypt's intention to close the Strait of Tiran to Israeli shipping. The strait was the principal avenue for Israel's trade with Asia and the transit point for 90 percent of its oil imports. Israel's economy would be adversely impacted immediately, and Israel had already let it be known that it would consider such a step a cause for war. Nasser knew that Israel would probably react militarily, but he assumed that the United States would not support this and that Egypt and its allies could count on the Soviet Union. The Kremlin, however, reacted negatively. Having stirred the pot, it now urged restraint. Following a hotline call from U.S. president Lyndon Johnson, Moscow insisted on May 27 that the Egyptians not strike first.

Nasser's announcement regarding the Strait of Tiran was in fact largely a bluff. He assumed that the threat of closing the strait would force Israel to withdraw its supposed increased forces along the Syrian border. On May 22, however, Egyptian minister of defense Field Marshal Abdel Hakim Amer ordered Egyptian forces to close the strait the next day. A countermanding order would have signaled weakness, and Nasser now ordered the Egyptian military to prepare for war.

On May 26, Nasser had announced that if Israel were to strike either Egypt or Syria, this would result in a general war, with the Arab goal being "the destruction of Israel." On May 30 Jordanian king Hussein arrived in Cairo and there concluded a mutual security pact with Egypt.

On paper, the balance of forces heavily favored the Arab states. The Israel Defense Forces (IDF) had 230,000 troops, 1,100 tanks, 200 artillery pieces, 260 combat aircraft, and 22 naval vessels. Egypt and Syria together had 263,000 men, 1,950 tanks, 915 artillery pieces, 521 combat aircraft, and 75 naval vessels. Counting Iraqi and Jordanian forces, the Arab advantage swelled to 409,000 men, 2,437 tanks, 1,487 artillery pieces, 649 combat aircraft, and 90 naval vessels.

Now certain of war and despite strong U.S. opposition, on June 4 Israeli prime minister Levi Eshkol authorized a preemptive strike against Egypt. The Six-Day War began on June 5, 1967, with carefully planned and brilliantly executed Israeli strikes that first destroyed much of the Egyptian Air Force. The Israelis then repeated the process against Syria and Jordan. Israeli ground forces went into action simultaneously, and at the end of only six days Egypt had lost the Sinai and the Gaza Strip, Jordan lost Old Jerusalem and the entire West Bank of the Jordan River, and Syria lost the Golan Heights.

The debacle led Nasser to make the gesture of resigning, but wide-scale popular demonstrations by the Egyptian people blocked this. Marshal Amer was made the scapegoat. Allegedly approached by high-ranking Egyptian officers, he was given a choice to stand trial for treason, which would inevitably have ended with his conviction and execution, or face an honorable death by taking poison. Apparently he chose the latter and received a full military burial.

Recovering politically, Nasser then mounted what became known as the War of Attrition against Israel, consisting largely of artillery fire across the Suez Canal into the Sinai that continued from July 1, 1967, until August 7, 1970. Meanwhile, Nasser pursued his Arabist ideals and supported the Palestinian cause. Growing Palestinian and Syrian pressures on Jordan led to an inter-Arab crisis known as Black September in 1970 when the Jordanian Army expelled the militant Palestinians from that country. Nasser was personally involved in negotiating the aftermath of this crisis just prior to his death on September 28, 1970.

Anwar Sadat, another member of the officer group that had come to power in 1952, succeeded Nasser as president. Under Sadat, Egypt moved toward the West. Sadat expelled communist bloc advisers and purged Nasserists from the governmental elite. Egypt also received more Arab aid, and Sadat gradually opened the economy to foreign investment and joint partnerships.

Sadat opened negotiations with Israel in the hopes of securing the return of the Sinai. Disillusionment with the lack of progress in 1971, however, led him to begin planning a military operation to break the political stalemate. Sadat believed that even a minor Egyptian military success would change the military equilibrium and force a political settlement. Israel's strength was in its air force and armored divisions in maneuver warfare. Egyptian strengths were the ability to build a strong defense line and new Soviet-supplied surface-to-air missiles (SAMs) deployed in batteries along the canal and deep within Egypt. Sadat hoped to paralyze the Israeli Air Force with the SAMs and counter the Israelis' advantage in maneuver warfare by forcing them to attack well-fortified and well-defended Egyptian strongholds.

In an attempt to dilute the Israeli military forces on the Sinai front, Sadat brought in Syria. A coordinated surprise attack by both states would place maximum stress on the IDF. The key to success was secrecy. Were Israel to suspect an imminent attack, it would undoubtedly launch a preventive attack, as in 1967. That part of Sadat's plan, at least, was successful.

A combination of effective Egyptian deceptive measures and Israeli arrogance contributed to Israel's failure to comprehend the threat. One deception consisted of repeated Egyptian drills along the Suez Canal, simulating a possible crossing. The Israelis thus interpreted Egyptian preparations for the actual crossings as just another drill. Even the Egyptian soldiers were told as much. Only when the actual crossing was under way were they informed of its true nature.

On the Israeli-Egyptian front, Egypt amassed nearly 800,000 soldiers, 2,200 tanks, 2,300 artillery pieces, 150 SAM batteries, and 550 aircraft. Along the canal, Egypt deployed five infantry divisions with accompanying armored elements, supported by additional infantry and armored independent brigades and backed by three mechanized divisions and two armored divisions. Israel had only a single division supported by 280 tanks. Not until the early morning hours of October 6 did Israeli military intelligence conclude that an Egyptian attack was imminent, but Prime Minister Golda Meir decided against a preemptive strike.

The Yom Kippur War of October 6–25, 1973, also known as the Ramadan War, the October War, and the 1973 Arab-Israeli War, commenced at 2:00 p.m. on October 6 on Yom Kippur, the holiest day for Jews, when Egypt launched a massive air strike against Israeli artillery and command positions. At the same time, Egyptian artillery shelled the Bar-Lev Line fortifications. Egyptian commandos crossed the canal followed by engineers, who quickly constructed bridges, allowing the Egyptians to pass across sizable numbers of infantry and armor. By October 8 Egyptian infantry and some 500 tanks had pushed three to five miles east of the canal, defended by the SAM batteries.

The Israelis meanwhile mobilized two armored divisions and on October 8 launched a quick counteroffensive to repel the Egyptians. These encountered the far larger and well-equipped Egyptian force protected by handheld antitank missiles. The Egyptians crushed the Israeli counteroffensive. Israeli ground support aircraft suffered heavy losses against Egyptian antiaircraft defenses, especially from SAMs. Following this setback, the Israeli General Staff decided to halt offensive actions on the Suez front and give priority to the Syria front.

Sadat now overruled his ground commander, Field Marshal Ahmed Ismail Ali, and, following Syrian pleas for assistance, ordered a resumption of the offensive on October 11. This, however, took Egyptian forces out of their prepared defensive positions and removed them from the effective SAM cover on the other side of the canal. On October 14 the Israelis threw back the Egyptians, inflicting on them heavy losses.

Concurrent with the initial Egyptian assault, Syrian armor and mechanized forces moved in force against the Golan Heights and almost broke through. The Syrian drives were contained, however, and Israeli forces then began their own offensive action and occupied a portion of Syria. Meanwhile, the Israelis crossed the Suez Canal themselves, defeated the Egyptians in the Battle of the Chinese Farm (October 14–18), and cut off Egyptian forces on the east bank. Heavy pressure from the United States, the Soviet Union, and the United Nations (UN) brought a cease-fire agreement on October 25.

Although Egyptian forces had been driven back, they had fought well, and Egyptians regarded the 1973 war as an affirmation of the nation's strength. Sadat knew that his country could not afford another costly war, however. He took the dramatic step of traveling to Tel Aviv in 1977 to address the Israeli parliament and lay the groundwork for a peace agreement with Israel. This was ultimately achieved, with the assistance of U.S. president Jimmy Carter, in the September 17, 1978, Camp David Accords. The settlement returned the Sinai Peninsula to Egyptian control. Egyptian participation in the bilateral agreement with Israel was very unpopular with other Arab governments, however. They promptly cut off aid and tourism to Egypt for a time and expelled Egypt from the Arab League. Because of other political issues, including Sadat's failure to open the political system, the peace agreement also soon became unpopular with many Egyptians.

New Islamic fundamentalist groups began to emerge in Egypt in the 1970s. Sadat had pardoned and released from jail members of the Muslim Brotherhood and allowed Islamist student groups to organize. One of these groups attempted to kill Sadat during a visit to the Military Technical Academy. On October 6, 1981, however, the radical organization Islamic Jihad succeeded in assassinating Sadat in the course of a military review.

Sadat's successor as president, Hosni Mubarak, Egyptian air chief marshal and head of the air force during 1972–1975, continued Egypt's economic opening to the West via privatization and joint ventures, all the while maintaining a large military establishment. The most important challenge to the state internally in the 1980s and 1990s came from Islamist groups that mounted attacks against local officials and tourists. These groups as well as many professionals opposed normalized relations with Israel.

Mubarak joined the international coalition to oppose Iraqi control of Kuwait, and Egyptian troops participated in the liberation of Kuwait during the Persian Gulf War of January–February 1991. As a result of its support, Egypt also received loan waivers from the United States, Western Europe, and several Persian Gulf states in excess of $20 billion.

In the aftermath of the September 11, 2001, terrorist attacks against the United States, the Egyptian government voiced its support for the U.S. global war on terror but declined to deploy any troops to the U.S.-led invasions of Afghanistan and Iraq. Indeed, Egypt voiced its displeasure regarding the latter. However, following the overthrow of Iraqi president Saddam Hussein, Egypt publicly supported the Iraqi Governing Council.

Since 2003, U.S.-Egyptian relations have been periodically strained because of disagreements regarding the war in Iraq and the Israeli-Palestinian conflict, U.S. calls for increased Egyptian democratization in Egypt, and suggestions that U.S. aid might be cut off. In December 2006 Egypt's foreign minister called for an end to what he termed "nuclear double standards," which saw economic sanctions imposed against Iran because of its alleged program to acquire nuclear weapons but allowed Israel to develop and deploy nuclear weapons with complete impunity.

Egypt, on U.S. insistence, helped in isolating the radical Palestinian organization Hamas in the Gaza Strip, which after 2007 was under an economic blockade mounted by Israel and Western nations. Egypt closed its borders with Gaza, yet widespread smuggling occurred into Gaza from Egypt through an extensive system of tunnels. Although Egypt took a tougher line with Hamas than that organization expected, Egypt also played a key role in negotiations with Hamas and has hosted various meetings aimed at securing a new truce between it and Israel and ending the economic boycott.

Israeli's all-out attack on the Gaza Strip during December 2008–January 2009 imposed serious strains on Egyptian-Israeli relations. In the spring of 2008 a series of attacks and attempted attacks on tourists in Egypt occurred, and there was mounting discontent in the Egyptian military, both of which were attributed to the Gaza debacle.

As part of the wider Arab Spring movement—a demand for democratic reform that swept much of the Arab world from late 2010 through mid-2012—in January 2011 protesters staged massive street demonstrations in Egypt against the repressive Mubarak government. When Egyptian government forces attempted to quash the rebellion, civilians were killed, and Mubarak's grasp on power quickly diminished. This placed the U.S. government in a delicate situation, as it had supported Mubarak for many years. Nevertheless, the Barack Obama administration reluctantly signaled that the Egyptian strongman should step down, which he reluctantly did on February 11, 2011. After that, the Egyptian military took effective control of the country, suspended the constitution and parliament, and promised to hold democratic elections in the near future.

Parliamentary elections occurred during November 28, 2011–January 11, 2012, and in June 2012 Mohamed Morsi was elected president. In August, it was announced that several members of the Muslim Brotherhood would join the government, which caused many Egyptians to question the validity of the new regime. When the Islamist Muslim Brotherhood openly embraced Morsi, most secular and liberal parliament members walked out of the assembly in protest, plunging Egypt into another government crisis. In November 2012, Morsi defended the new constitution and declared his actions to be legal and free from the actions of what he called "reactionaries." This prompted more mass protests. These continued into the summer of 2013, virtually paralyzing Egypt and its economy.

On July 3, 2013, the Egyptian military ousted Morsi from power, and in January 2014 a new constitution was established, receiving more than 98 percent approval (although just 38.6 percent of Egyptians participated in the vote). Egypt's government was then dominated by the military under the aegis of an interim government. In May 2014, nationwide elections resulted in the selection of Abdel Fattah el-Sisi as president. The former head of Egypt's armed forces, he took office on June 8, 2014. El-Sisi's election meant that the Egyptian government would continue to be dominated by the military.

Sisi's government declared the Muslim Brotherhood a terrorist organization and imprisoned scores of Morsi supporters. Then on August 14, Egyptian security forces opened fire on and killed more than 800 pro-Morsi protesters in Rabaa in what is known as the Rabaa Massacre. The U.S. government then halted major weapons transfers to Egypt in protest. (At $1.3 billion, Egypt ranked second in U.S. military aid in 2014, behind only Israel at $3.1 billion. The ban on major weapons transfers was lifted by the Obama administration on March 31, 2015.) Morsi, Egypt's first democratically elected ruler, was brought to trial and found guilty of membership of the now-banned Muslim Brotherhood but acquitted of espionage. He was sentenced to 25 years in prison.

Ongoing violence in Egypt, especially in the Sinai against the government, remains a sizable problem, as does the depressed Egyptian economy, partly owing to a drop in tourism. Terrorism is a constant threat. On October 31, 2015, a Russian Metrojet Airlines Airbus A321 bound for St. Petersburg crashed in the Sinai after takeoff from Sharm El Sheikh, killing all 224 people on board. A little-known terrorist group, calling itself Ansar Beit al-Maqdis and operating in the Sinai, is believed to have planted a bomb on the aircraft. Then on May 19, 2016, EgyptAir Flight MS804 from Paris to Cairo crashed into the Mediterranean, killing all 66 people on board. The cause of that crash has yet to be determined.

Egypt's Coptic Christians have also come under attack from Islamic extremists. On April 9, 2017, twin bombings occurred at St. George's Coptic Church in Tanta and outside St. Mark's Coptic Cathedral in Alexandria, the largest Christian church in Egypt, Northeast Africa, and the Middle East. The blasts killed 49 people. In December 2017 another Egyptian Coptic church was attacked, killing 9 people. The Islamic State of Iraq and Syria (ISIS) claimed responsibility for the attacks. Such terrorist attacks have left the fiercely nationalistic Coptic community feeling unprotected by the government on which it had relied for deliverance from the Islamist regime of President Mohamed Morsi. After the April assault, President el-Sisi declared three days of mourning and announced plans to impose a three-month state of emergency. He also pledged creation of a council to develop means to counter terrorism and extremism.

Egypt's Muslims have not been immune from terrorist attack either. In the deadliest such attack in modern Egyptian history, on November 24, 2017, ISIS militants attacked a packed Sufi Muslim mosque at Bir al-Abed in the Sinai Peninsula. The militants detonated a bomb inside the mosque and then shot down panicked worshippers as they endeavored to flee, killing 305 people and wounding at least 128 others. Sufi Muslims practice a mystical form of Islam that ISIS and other Sunni extremist groups deem heretical.

The attack sent shock waves across Egypt and put great pressure on the Sisi government. Although Egyptian aircraft immediately struck ISIS targets and the government claimed that these had destroyed the terrorist vehicles and killed their occupants, the mosque attack highlighted the inability of Sisi's government to halt terrorism in the Sinai, with Sisi having justified his harsh crackdown on political freedom in Egypt in the name of crushing Islamic militancy.

Egyptian-Russian relations vastly improved under Sisi. Following President Obama's 2013 temporary halt in arms shipments to Egypt, in September 2014 Sisi traveled to Russia and concluded a deal to purchase $3.5 billion in arms from Moscow. The closer relations between Moscow and Cairo continued during the presidency of Donald Trump. On December 1, 2017, Sisi allowed Russian military aircraft access to Egyptian air space and bases. That same month Russian president Vladimir Putin received a warm welcome in Cairo and concluded a $21 billion contract to build Egypt's first nuclear power plant. These developments marked the greatest Russian influence in Egypt since 1973, when President Sadat expelled Soviet military advisers.

Sisi easily won the March 2018 presidential election, having faced only token opposition. During his tenure relations with Turkey have deteriorated, but relations with Saudi Arabia have become markedly better. Meanwhile, Egypt continues its participation in the Saudi-led military intervention in Yemen. Sisi's government has tried to mediate disputes between the Israelis and Palestinians, although it has rebuked Israel's hard-line policies toward Hamas in the Gaza Strip. Since the advent of the Trump administration, U.S.-Egyptian relations have generally improved. When Sisi visited Washington in the spring of 2017, Trump heaped praise on him. Meanwhile, since 2016 Sisi has cultivated closer relations with the Syrian government of Bashar al-Assad, and by 2018 this development had morphed into open support for Syrian government forces in the long-running Syrian Civil War.

JAMES B. MCNABB, SHERIFA ZUHUR, AND SPENCER C. TUCKER

See also

Achaemenid Empire; Alexander III the Great; Alexandria, Bombardment of; Allenby, Sir Edmund Henry Hynman; Amer, Abdel Hakim; Aqaba, Gulf of; Arabi, Ahmed; Arab Spring; Bar-Lev Line; Black September; Black September Organization; Bonaparte, Napoleon; Camp David Accords; Chinese Farm, Battle of the; Copts; El Alamein, First Battle of; El Alamein, Second Battle of; Eshkol, Levi; Gallipoli Campaign; Gaza Strip; Hamas; Ismail, Khedive; Ismail Ali, Ahmad; Jordan; Mamluk Sultanate; Mehmed Ali; Mubarak, Hosni; Muslim Brotherhood; Ottoman Empire; Ottoman Empire, Entry into World War I; Nasser, Gamal Abdel; Ottoman Empire, Post–World War I Revolution in; Persian Gulf War, Overview; Ptolemaic Kingdom; Sadat, Anwar; Six-Day War; Strait of Tiran Crisis; Suez Canal; Suez Canal, World War I Ottoman Operations against; Suez Crisis; Syria; Tel el-Kebir, Battle of; United Arab Republic; Yemen, Civil War in the North; Yom Kippur War

References

Abdel-Malek, Anouar. *Egypt: Military Society*. New York: Random House, 1968.

Aburish, Said. *Nasser: The Last Arab*. New York: St. Martin's and Thomas Dunne Books, 2004.

Beattie, Kirk J. *Egypt during the Sadat Years*. New York: Palgrave, 2000.

Binder, Leonard. *In a Moment of Enthusiasm: Political Power and the Second Stratum in Egypt*. Chicago: University of Chicago, 1978.

Cooper, Chester L. *The Lion's Last Roar: Suez, 1956*. New York: Harper & Row, 1978.

Daly, M. W., ed. *The Cambridge History of Egypt*, Vol. 2. Cambridge: Cambridge University Press, 1998.

Ford, Roger. *Eden to Armageddon: World War I in the Middle East*. New York: Pegasus, 2010.

Gordon, Joel. *Nasser's Blessed Movement: Egypt's Free Officers and the July Revolution*. New York: Oxford University Press, 1992.

Hinnebusch, Raymond A., Jr. *Egyptian Politics under Sadat: The Post-Populist Development of an Authoritarian-Modernizing State*. Cambridge: Cambridge University Press, 1985.

Korn, David. A. *Stalemate: The War of Attrition and Great Power Diplomacy in the Middle East, 1967–1970*. Boulder, CO: Westview, 1992.

Telhami, Ghada. *Palestine and the Egyptian National Identity*. Westport, CT: Praeger, 1992.

Waterbury, John. *The Egypt of Nasser and Sadat*. Princeton, NJ: Princeton University Press, 1983.

Zuhur, Sherifa. *Egypt: Security, Political and Islamist Challenges*. Carlisle, PA: Strategic Studies Institute, 2007.

Egypt, Ancient

Egyptian civilization remains one of the greatest in world history. It is also one of the oldest. It seemed ancient even to the ancients. Greeks and Romans of 2,000 years ago viewed it much the way we view the ancient Greeks and Romans.

As with civilization in Mesopotamia, that of Egypt originated in a river valley. The annual floods of this river, the Nile, enriched the land with a fresh layer of silt. Coupled with intensive irrigation, this made possible the growing of crops in an otherwise largely arid land. The White Nile starts at Lake Victoria, and the Blue Nile starts at Lake Tana. The two come together just north of present-day Khartoum in the Sudan. The Nile then proceeds northward through a series of cataracts, which prevented navigation. From the last of these (or the first from the Egyptian side) the river passes through a plateau some 600 miles in length to reach the Mediterranean Sea. In its final 100 miles or so the river splits into different streams, forming a great triangular-shaped delta. The population of Upper Egypt was crowded into a thin ribbon of land along the river. The delta region of Egypt, known as Lower Egypt, lies open to the sea, but in ancient times it was thinly populated.

Unlike ancient Mesopotamia, which occupied an open plain, Egypt was favored by geography. Deserts on both sides formed a natural protective barrier against invasion. As a result, although not entirely free of outside influences, ancient Egypt was able to develop more or less independently for much of its history, which had profound influence on that civilization.

As in Mesopotamia, ancient Egyptian civilization was preceded by several thousand years in which smaller communities coalesced into larger population centers along with the development of the complicated irrigation systems that fostered agriculture. About 3000 BCE, the rulers of the First Dynasty united Upper and Lower Egypt from the first cataract to the Mediterranean into one political entity.

Historians divide the history of ancient Egypt into 31 dynasties. The First Dynasty lasted some 550 years from

Ancient Egypt

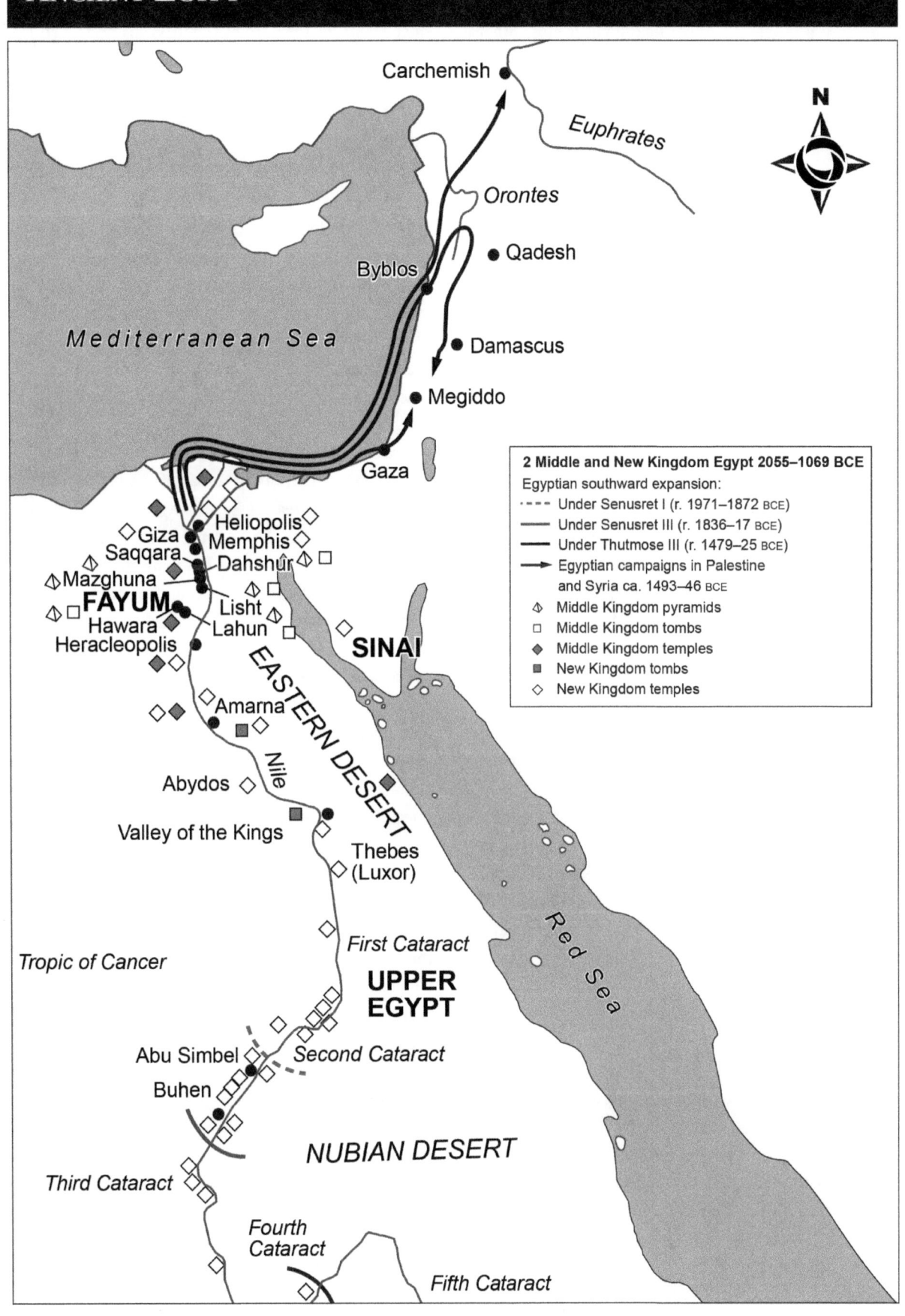

2 Middle and New Kingdom Egypt 2055–1069 BCE

Egyptian southward expansion:
- ---- Under Senusret I (r. 1971–1872 BCE)
- —— Under Senusret III (r. 1836–17 BCE)
- —— Under Thutmose III (r. 1479–25 BCE)
- → Egyptian campaigns in Palestine and Syria ca. 1493–46 BCE
- △ Middle Kingdom pyramids
- □ Middle Kingdom tombs
- ◆ Middle Kingdom temples
- ■ New Kingdom tombs
- ◇ New Kingdom temples

about 3100 to 2686 BCE. Known as the Archaic period in Egyptian history, it saw the Egyptian rulers, known as pharaohs, acquire a degree of power unknown in most other civilizations, for the Egyptian religion held that the pharaoh was not only an absolute monarch but also a living god, the son of Ra the sun god, and the source of all power. In theory at least, the land belonged entirely to the pharaoh, as did the wealth of the state. Although there was a powerful priestly class as well as provincial administrators and a small artisan middle class, peasants constituted the vast bulk of the population. They lived highly regimented lives and were at the service of the state whenever required.

With ancient Egypt being a very religious land, much of the wealth of the state went into the construction by tens of thousands of men over many years of great stone temples and tombs to hold the bodies of mummified pharaohs and nobles, for the ancient Egyptians believed in immortality. Egyptian engineering was quite advanced, indeed superior to that of the Greeks and Romans. The great pyramid at Giza built to house the remains of Khufu (Cheops), the second pharaoh of the Fourth Dynasty (ca. 2680–2560), is 775 feet square at its base and 481 feet high. It contains more than 2 million blocks of stone, each weighing some 2.5 tons. This pyramid was regarded as one of the Seven Wonders of the Ancient World. The Egyptians also led in the fields of medicine and astronomy and were responsible for the solar calendar of 365 days in a year. As the extensive irrigation systems expanded from the Nile so did Egypt's material wealth, and by 2600 Egyptian trading vessels were plying the eastern Mediterranean and the Red Sea.

The Old Kingdom, with its capital at Memphis, lasted from about 2925–2775 BCE and is regarded as one of the high points of Egyptian civilization. It came to an end with the passing of the Sixth Dynasty. Evidently too much power in the hands of provincial governors greatly weakened the authority of the central government and brought on a period of civil strife.

Order was restored by the pharaohs of the Eleventh and Twelfth Dynasties. These formed what is called the Middle Kingdom from about 2050 to 1800. Perhaps the greatest pharaoh of the Middle Kingdom was Amenemhet I (r. 1991–1962). He moved the capital from Memphis to Thebes. After putting down a conspiracy among high officials whom he had raised to office, Amenemhet established a strong centralized administrative system that lasted for several centuries and brought a revival of Egyptian energy and prosperity.

Egypt again experienced a second prolonged period of disorder with the arrival of the Hyksos from the area of present-day Syria in Lower Egypt beginning about 1650. Evidently civil war in Egypt between rival claimants for the Egyptian throne allowed the Hyksos to invade and conquer Egypt for themselves. The Hyksos destroyed many of Egypt's cities and much of its accumulated art. These so-called Shepherd Kings ruled Egypt from about 1650 to 1550. The Hyksos introduced both the horse and wheeled chariot into Egypt.

Finally, around 1550 the Egyptians rose up and expelled the Hyksos, establishing what is known as the New Kingdom. It consisted of the Eighteenth through Twentieth Dynasties of rulers and lasted from about 1550 to 1077. The New Kingdom marked the zenith of Egyptian power. No doubt in large part prompted by the period of Hyksos rule, the pharaohs of the New Kingdom sought to establish a buffer between their kingdom and the Levant, and under their rule, Egypt reached its greatest territorial extent. Also in response to attacks by the powerful Kingdom of Kush, the Egyptian rulers expanded their territory to the south, into Nubia.

Thutmose III (r. 1479–1425) of the Eighteenth Dynasty was one of the greatest Egyptian pharaohs. Having rebuilt the Egyptian Army, he embarked on the first in a series of some 15 campaigns. In the Battle of Megiddo (c. 1457) he won a great victory by defeating the army of the King of Kadesh. Thutmose went on to make Egypt the master of the Mediterranean world. He not only conquered; he also reorganized the territory he had secured, leaving capable governors in charge and garrisons to secure the peace. He was the first ruler in known history to recognize the importance of sea power, building a large fleet to control the eastern Mediterranean. The vast wealth secured in tribute from his conquests led to a flowering of Egyptian art.

Ikhnaton (or Akhenaten, who began his reign as Amenhotep IV) ruled during 1353–1336. He was determined to restore the power of the pharaohs as under the Old Kingdom. To accomplish this he had to destroy the clergy, and this meant destroying their gods. After reining in these for half a decade, he undertook a drastic step against the powerful Egyptian priesthood and the old religion. He ordered the construction of a new capital some 200 miles south of present-day Cairo near present-day Tell el Amarna. Here, far from Thebes, he sought to dramatically change Egypt's religion, abandoning traditional Egyptian polytheism in favor of worship of Aton (Aten), the sun god or "solar disk" and source of life and light. Indeed, he changed his own name from Amenhotep to Ikhnaton, meaning "Aton fulfilled." Some scholars regard this as the world's first great expression of monotheism. He also named his new capital Akhetaton, "the horizon of Aton."

Ikhnaton's effort failed, however, perhaps in part because he did not allow the people direct access to Aton. Indeed, they were to worship Aton through him, the god king. After his death, traditional pantheistic Egyptian religious practices were restored, the capital was returned to Thebes, his monuments were dismantled and hidden, his statues were destroyed, and his name was excluded from the list of pharaohs. The army had helped Ikhnaton carry out his failed revolution, and it now made peace with the priests and civil service, all three of which in fact shared power with the pharaohs, careful to respect the rights and privileges of each.

The later part of the New Kingdom, under the Nineteenth and Twentieth Dynasties (1292–1069 BCE), is also known as the Ramesside period, so named for the 11 pharaohs who took the name of Ramesses I, founder of the Nineteenth Dynasty. In 1279 Ramesses II, the fourth ruler of that dynasty, became pharaoh. Ruling Egypt for 67 years until 1213, he is regarded by many scholars as Egypt's greatest pharaoh.

Ramesses proved to be an able military leader. At the beginning of his realm he defeated the Sea People, pirates who had been preying on Egyptian trade in the eastern Mediterranean. He then embarked on a program to take back land in Asia Minor that had been lost earlier to the Hittites and secure Egypt's borders. One of his most memorable battles was that of Kadesh in Syria. In addition to extensive campaigns in the Levant, Ramesses also campaigned south of the first cataract of the Nile into Nubia. Egyptian forces may have also ventured as far as 200 miles into coastal Libya, at least as far as Zawiyet Umm el-Rakham. A great builder, Ramesses ordered construction of a new city, Pi-Ramesses in the Nile Delta, to serve as his new capital and advance base for his military operations to eastward. Certainly, he did everything on a grand scale to include colossal statues of himself throughout the realm. Half of ancient Egypt's surviving edifices are said to date from his reign.

Only one power exceeded that of the pharaoh, and that was the clergy. In the recurring struggle throughout history between church and state, the church won out, and Egypt became a stagnant theocracy with the decay of institutions that had protected the state.

New nations arose in Assyria, in Babylonia, and in Persia. These now challenged the Egyptians. One by one its rivals invaded and conquered Egypt, laying it to waste. In 954 BCE the Libyans invaded from the west, while in 722 the Ethiopians invaded from the south. In 674, it was the turn of the Assyrians.

The Twenty-Fifth Dynasty or Nubian dynasty came up against the Assyrians. In 667 BCE, under assault by Assyrian king Ashurbanipal's army, Pharaoh Taharqa (r. 690–664) abandoned Lower Egypt and fled to Thebes. After his death three years later his nephew Tantamani (Tanutamun), pharaoh of Egypt and the Kingdom of Kush in northern Sudan, seized Thebes, invaded Lower Egypt, and laid siege to Memphis but abandoned his effort to secure Egypt in 663 BCE and withdrew southward. The Assyrians pursued and took and sacked Thebes, the name of which was now added to the long list of cities plundered and destroyed by the Assyrians.

The wealth of ancient Egypt can be gleaned from the record of the vast treasure that Ashurbanipal took from Thebes back to Assyria. It included precious jewels, temple doors, and two great obelisks of electrum, an alloy 75 percent gold, 22 percent silver, and 3 percent copper, the two weighing 2,500 talents (166,650 pounds, with 124,988 pounds of this gold).

In 525 it was the turn of the Persians. The Egyptian Twenty-Sixth Dynasty, alarmed by the expansion of the Persian Empire under Cyrus the Great, hired Greek mercenaries and expanded the Egyptian fleet. It was for naught. Following Persian sieges of Gaza and Memphis, a decisive battle occurred at Pelusium in the eastern Nile Delta region. It transferred the throne of the pharaohs to Cambyses II of Persia, the first ruler of the Twenty-Seventh Dynasty. Egypt was now reduced to a satrapy.

Egypt, however, frequently revolted against Persian rule, first in 487 when it took two years for Xerxes to quell the revolt. On Xerxes's death in 465 the Egyptians revolted again, appealing for help from Athens. In 460 the Athenians dispatched a significant force of soldiers and 200 ships in 460 and had early successes, leaving only the citadel of Memphis in Persian hands. But by 454 the Persians had gained the upper hand and surrounded the Greek forces, who were forced to flee across the Libyan desert with few survivors.

In 404, Egypt again declared its independence and, despite frequent dynastic struggles and internecine strife, was not reconquered until Artaxerxes III recaptured the province in 343. On his death in 338, Egypt again revolted, but Darius III regained control in 336, only to lose it to Alexander the Great in 332. Alexander left Egypt under local governors. After his death in 323 one of his generals, Ptolemy, swiftly moved to seize control of Egypt and eventually (in 304) established the Ptolemaic dynasty as Ptolemy I Soter (Savior).

In the third century Ptolemaic Egypt exercised considerable power in the Aegean and the Levant, and it fought a series of wars with Seleucid Syria. After the end of the Fifth Syrian-Egyptian War in 195, however, the Ptolemies were once and for all pushed back within Egypt itself, while the

Sixth (and final) Syrian-Egyptian War, which ended in 168, made it clear that even in the east the dominant power was now Rome. Nevertheless, Egypt remained independent until the last Ptolemaic ruler, Queen Cleopatra VII, was defeated by Rome and committed suicide in 30. Egypt then became a Roman province.

RUSSELL BUZBY AND SPENCER C. TUCKER

See also

Achaemenid Empire; Alexander III the Great; Artaxerxes III; Cleopatra VII; Darius I; Egypt, Athenian Intervention in; Kadesh, Battle of; Megiddo, Ancient Battle of; Pelusium, Battle of; Ptolemaic Kingdom; Ptolemy I Soter; Ptolemy II Philadelphus; Ptolemy V Epiphanes; Raphia, Battle of; Syrian-Egyptian Wars; Thutmose III, Pharaoh; Xerxes I

References

Aldred, Cyril. *Akhenaten, King of Egypt.* London: Thames and Hudson, 1991.

Clayton, Peter A. *Chronicle of the Pharaohs: The Reign-by-Reign Record of the Rulers and Dynasties of Ancient Egypt.* London: Thames and Hudson, 1994.

Dodson, Aidan, and Dyan Hilton. *The Complete Royal Families of Ancient Egypt.* London: Thames & Hudson, 2004.

Lewis, Napthali. *Greeks in Ptolemaic Egypt.* Oxford, UK: Clarendon, 1986.

Shaw, Ian. *The Oxford History of Ancient Egypt.* Oxford: Oxford University Press, 2003.

Tyldesley, Joyce A. *Ramesses: Egypt's Greatest Pharaoh.* Harmondsworth, UK: Penguin, 2001.

Walbank, Frank William. *The Cambridge Ancient History.* Cambridge: Cambridge University Press, 1984.

Egypt, Arab Conquest of (640–642)

Egypt had been part of the Byzantine Empire since the division of the Roman Empire into the Western Empire, ruled from Rome, and the Eastern Empire, including Egypt, ruled from Constantinople. The Persians under Khosrau II managed to capture it in the early seventh century, but Byzantine emperor Heraclius retook it soon afterward. Under the Byzantines, Egypt was ruled from the port city of Alexandria and was important in the early history of Christianity. However, after the death of Prophet Muhammad in 632, Abu Bakr became caliph and united Arabia under his authority. He then sought to expand his rule through Syria and then Egypt by military conquest and conversion. After capturing Palestine and Syria, Muslim leaders considered it feasible to attack Egypt from Palestine. This was made easier by the Byzantines having divided their forces into a number of garrisons.

In December 639 some 4,000 Arab soldiers marched to Rafah and there received messengers from the caliph. The local commander, Amr ibn al-As, decided not to read these communications, fearful that they would probably order him to call off the invasion. The story was that he crossed into Egypt and then read the communications, which told him that if he was still in Palestine he should not attack, but if he was already on Egyptian soil, then he should proceed.

The Arabs continued their offensive operations through Sinai and then laid siege to Fayoum before proceeding southward. In June 640 Amr ibn al-As received reinforcements from Arabia, and in the following month he defeated the Byzantines in the Battle of Heliopolis. With that success he turned back to Fayoum, captured it, and then occupied most of Egypt, entering into a treaty with Cyrus of Alexandria, the Byzantine administrator.

Byzantine emperor Heraclius repudiated the treaty, and this caused problems for the Copts, the Egyptian Christians, some of whom supported the Byzantines and others the Muslims. In February 641 the Muslim forces marched on Alexandria, capturing it in September. Subsequently they took Nubia. Once Egypt was secured in 642, they used it as a base of operations to secure all of North Africa.

ALEXANDER MIKABERIDZE

See also

Amr ibn al-As

References

Hamblin, William James. *The Fatimid Army during the Early Crusades.* Ann Arbor, MI: University Microfilms International, 1985.

Johnson, Allan Chester, and Louis C. West. *Byzantine Egypt: Economic Studies.* Princeton, NJ: Princeton University Press, 1949.

Egypt, Athenian Intervention in (460–454 BCE)

The Athenian expedition to Egypt in 460–454 BCE was part of Athens's aim to extend its influence in the eastern Mediterranean. The fleet was originally bound for Cyprus and diverted to Egypt to capitalize on the revolt of Prince Inaros there. The 200-ship Athenian fleet (including perhaps 100 allied ships from the Delian League) eliminated the Persian naval presence in the Nile. Memphis was captured, except for its citadel of the White Tower. Continuing military action occurred during the next few years, although the first Persian counteroffensive was diplomatic. Persian general

Megabazus went to Sparta in an unsuccessful attempt to bribe the Spartans to invade Attica and cause an Athenian withdrawal from Egypt. In 455 a large Persian navy and army under Megabazus arrived in Egypt, defeated the rebel army, relieved Memphis, and trapped the Greek fleet at the island of Prosopitis. In the summer of 454, the Persians diverted the water around Prosopitis and took it by land.

The extent of the defeat has been the subject of debate. Greek historian Thucydides clearly suggests that the defeat was major, with almost the entire expedition lost, including a relief force of 50 ships surprised on arrival just after the fall of Prosopitis. However, Diodorus, another Greek historian, states that the Athenians withdrew under truce. Modern historians have argued that the loss of 200 triremes and their crews would have crippled Athens for some time, but Athens was clearly able to field large fleets in the years following the defeat. However, if half the fleet was allied and not Athenian and the loss was not complete, this would not necessarily have been crippling. In any event, the losses were apparently serious enough to encourage Athens to look to a negotiated end to the First Peloponnesian War.

IAIN SPENCE

See also
Cyprus; Cyprus, Athenian Expedition to; Egypt, Ancient

References
Meiggs, Russell. *The Athenian Empire.* Oxford, UK: Clarendon, 1972.
Ruzicka, Stephen. *Trouble in the West: Egypt and the Persian Empire, 525–332 BCE.* Oxford Studies in Early Empires. Oxford: Oxford University Press, 2012.

Egypt, British Invasion of (1807)

A failed expedition to Egypt undertaken by the British Army and the Royal Navy during the Anglo-Ottoman War of 1807–1809. Following the French invasion of Egypt in 1798, Britain played an active role in expelling the French from the region. In 1801 British forces landed in Egypt and defeated the French Army of Egypt. Following the Treaty of Amiens in 1802, the British returned the survivors of the French expeditionary force to France.

When hostilities between Britain and France resumed in 1803, the British government was greatly concerned about Ottoman sultan Selim III's alliance with French emperor Napoleon I. In March 1807, British forces commanded by General Alexander MacKenzie-Fraser landed near Alexandria and captured it after a four-day siege. The British then endeavored to create an alliance with the Egyptian ruler Muhammad Ali (Mehmed Ali). As the British gradually took control of the delta region, Muhammad Ali conducted an effective campaign against the British occupation forces, which faced daunting logistical problems and suffered defeats at al-Hamad and Rosetta. By the end of September 1807, the British had withdrawn their troops from Egypt.

ALEXANDER MIKABERIDZE

See also
Anglo-Ottoman War; Dardanelles Campaign; Mehmed Ali

References
Douin, Georges, and E. C. Fawtier-Jones. *L'Angleterre et l'Egypte: La campagne de 1807.* Cairo: l'Institut français d'archéologie orientale, 1928.
Fahmy, Khaled. *Mehmed Ali: From Ottoman Governor to Ruler of Egypt.* Oxford, UK: Oneworld, 2009.
Fortescue, John W. *A History of the British Army, 1807–1809: From the Expedition to Egypt, 1807, to the Battle of Coruña, January 1809.* London: Macmillan, 1921.

Egypt, French Invasion and Occupation of (1798–1801)

An effort by the French to gain control of Egypt, remove British influence from the area, and then proceed overland to threaten British rule in India. After Napoleon Bonaparte's successful campaign in Italy (1796–1797), the French government sought to use his talents elsewhere. Stymied in their wish to invade Britain by the failure to control the English Channel, the revolutionary government decided to send an expeditionary force under Bonaparte to Egypt. That country was especially important to the British trade system, and removal of British influence there would deal both an economic and psychological blow to France's archenemy. In addition, France claimed that it would liberate Egypt from the often oppressive rule of the Mamluks and return control to the Ottoman Empire, a French ally.

Bonaparte's subordinates for the expedition included Generals Alexandre Berthier, Jean Lannes, Joachim Murat, Louis Charles Desaix, and Jean-Baptist Kléber. These generals led an army of between 35,000 and 40,000 soldiers, almost 200 cannon, and more than 1,000 horses, ferried on the 2,000-mile trip to Egypt by 335 ships. On May 19, 1798, Bonaparte's forces departed Toulon. Three weeks later they landed at Malta, an island critical to control of the Mediterranean sea routes.

In a week at Malta, Bonaparte deposed the ruling Knights of St. John, eliminated the feudal system, granted religious

British rear admiral Horatio Nelson's decisive victory over the French in the Battle of the Nile on August 2, 1798, cut off French general Napoleon Bonaparte's army in Egypt and firmly established Royal Navy dominance in the Mediterranean. (Clarke, James Stanier and John McArthur. *The Life and Services of Horatio, Viscount Nelson . . . from his Lordship's Manuscripts*, 1840)

freedom to Jews, wrote a modern constitution, reorganized the legal and educational institutions, and improved the island's defenses. He also confiscated the treasury. Bonaparte then set sail for Egypt.

In July, Bonaparte's forces landed near Alexandria and quickly took that city. Bonaparte then marched with the main force across the desert. Reaching al-Rahmaniya, they were on the Nile. After defeating the Mamluk forces of Murad Bey near Shubra Khit (July 13), Bonaparte proceeded toward Cairo. On July 21 near the famous Pyramids of Giza, Bonaparte famously addressed his men: "Forty centuries of history look down on you." In the Battle of the Pyramids, the French defeated the Mamluk forces.

With the Mamluk army defeated, the campaign, however, suffered a major blow with the discovery that Admiral Horatio Lord Nelson's warships had destroyed the French fleet near Alexandria in what the British called the Battle of the Nile on August 2. Furthermore, Sultan Selim III, refusing to accept French claim of protecting Ottoman interests in Egypt, declared war on France and mobilized two armies for expedition to Egypt. Then on October 21 and 22, many citizens of Cairo rose up in violent opposition to the French occupation. The revolt was put down, but it was clear that the French position was somewhat precarious.

Nevertheless, French operations in Upper Egypt met some success as Desaix pursued the Mamluks of Murad Bey. On October 7, 1798, the French defeated a force of Mamluks in a savage battle at al-Lahun but were unable to completely remove Murad Bey's influence in the region. Always elusive, Murad Bey learned lessons from prior engagements and refused to be brought to battle, leading the French on a chase through Upper Egypt. On January 20, 1799, Murad Bey finally engaged Desaix's army in open battle at Samhud but suffered another defeat and retreated as far as Aswan. By the summer, the French extended their authority to the Red Sea port of al-Qusair.

Meanwhile, facing an Ottoman invasion of Egypt, Bonaparte chose to attack first, turning his attention to the Ottoman army approaching through the Holy Land. The French army marched into Palestine, capturing El Arish and

Jaffa, and then laid siege to the fortified city of Acre (Acco). During the siege Bonaparte's forces scored important victories over the Ottoman and Mamluk forces near Nazareth and Mt. Tabor but were unable to take Acre, owing to the capture of his heavy siege guns, sent by sea and seized there by the British. On May 20, Bonaparte ended the siege and returned to Egypt. When the second Ottoman army arrived by sea at Aboukir, near Alexandria, Bonaparte was ready, and his victory there on July 25 removed the Ottoman threat for the foreseeable future.

Made aware of the political turmoil in France by French newspapers passed to him by the British, Bonaparte left Egypt without orders to do so, sailing in a fast frigate on August 23, 1799. He left command to General Kléber. The French repelled a second landing of Ottoman troops at Damietta in early November but then faced combined Anglo-Ottoman forces, which included the European-style Nizam-i Cedid troops of the Ottoman Army. Kléber negotiated a French withdrawal with the Ottoman grand vizier at El-Arish on January 24, 1800, but the agreement depended on the availability of British ships to transport the French army back to France. Upon the British refusal to accept the treaty, fighting resumed.

On March 20, 1800, Kléber scored a decisive victory over the Ottomans at Heliopolis and reclaimed Cairo and much of Lower Egypt. In late March, the French faced another major uprising in Cairo but brutally suppressed it by the end of April. Kléber, looking for new troops, organized the Coptic Legion that was equipped and trained along European lines. Yet on June 14, Kléber was accosted and stabbed to death by a young Syrian while walking down the street without an escort.

Kléber's successor was General Jacques Menou, who converted to Islam and took the name Abdallah Menou. A less capable leader than Kleber, Menou was disliked in the army and failed to make preparations for the British invasion in the spring of 1801.

On March 8, 1801, British forces came ashore at Aboukir Bay and defeated the French forces near Alexandria, which was soon surrounded by the Ottoman and British forces. Another Ottoman army marched through Syria to Egypt, while a new uprising against the French began in Cairo. Although Murad Bey died of the plague, his Mamluk forces also continued to harass the French throughout Lower Egypt. In June 1801 the French garrison of Cairo surrendered, and Menou capitulated in Alexandria in September. By the terms of Franco-British agreement, the British fleet evacuated the surviving French troops back to France.

Bonaparte had arrived in Egypt with some 34,000 land troops and some 16,000 sailors. Of this number only about 23,000 (3,000 of them sick or wounded) returned to France. The French Egyptian adventure was over.

One positive by-product of Napoleonic imperialism was the discovery of the Rosetta Stone, a carved black granodiorite stele found in July 1799 by a French soldier near the Rosetta mouth of the Nile. It is inscribed with three versions of a decree issued at Memphis, Egypt, in 196 BCE on behalf of King Ptolemy V. The top and middle texts are in ancient Egyptian using hieroglyphic script and Demotic script, respectively, while the bottom is in ancient Greek. As the decree is the same (with some minor differences) in all three versions, the Rosetta Stone proved to be the key to deciphering Egyptian hieroglyphs and unlocking the secrets of ancient Egyptian civilization. Upon the capitulation of the French in Egypt in 1801, the stone came into British possession and was transported to London. On public display since 1802, it is the object most visited in the British Museum.

J. David Markham and Spencer C. Tucker

See also

Aboukir, First Battle of; Aboukir, Second Battle of; Aboukir Bay, Battle of; Acre, 1799 Siege of; Bonaparte, Napoleon; Mamluk Sultanate; Pyramids, Battle of the

References

Chandler, David G. *The Campaigns of Napoleon*. New York: Macmillan, 1966.

Herold, J. Christopher. *Bonaparte in Egypt*. New York: Harper & Row, 1962.

Markham, J. David. *Napoleon's Road to Glory: Triumphs, Defeats & Immortality*. London: Brassey's, 2003.

Schur, Nathan. *Napoleon in the Holy Land*. London: Greenhill, 1999.

Strathern, Paul. *Napoleon in Egypt*. New York: Bantam, 2007.

Egypt, Ptolemaic and Roman Periods

The Twenty-Sixth Dynasty of Egypt, alarmed by the expansion of the Persian Empire under Cyrus the Great, hired Greek mercenaries and expanded the fleet. Nevertheless, in 525 BCE Persian king Cambyses II defeated the inexperienced pharaoh Psammetichus III and became the first Persian ruler of the Twenty-Seventh Dynasty; Egypt was reduced to a Persian satrapy. Egypt frequently revolted against Persian rule, first in 487 when it took two years for Persian king Xerxes I to quell the revolt. On Xerxes's death in 465 the Egyptians again revolted, appealing for help from Athens.

The Athenians dispatched a significant force of soldiers and 200 ships in 460 and had early successes, leaving only the citadel of Memphis in Persian hands. But by 454 the Persians had gained the upper hand and surrounded the Greek forces, who were forced to flee across the Libyan desert with few survivors.

In 404, Egypt again declared its independence and, despite frequent dynastic struggles and internecine strife, was not reconquered until Artaxerxes III recaptured the province in 343. On his death in 338 Egypt again revolted, but Darius III regained control in 336, only to lose it to Alexander III the Great of Macedon in 332. Alexander left Egypt under local governors.

After Alexander's early death in 323 one of his generals, Ptolemy, swiftly moved to seize control of Egypt and eventually (in 304) established the Ptolemaic dynasty as Ptolemy I Soter (savior). In the third century Ptolemaic Egypt exercised considerable power in the Aegean and the Levant and fought a series of wars with Seleucid Syria. After the end of the Fifth Syrian-Egyptian War in 195, however, the Ptolemies were once and for all pushed back within Egypt itself, while the Sixth (and final) Syrian-Egyptian War, which ended in 168, made it clear that even in the east the dominant power was now Rome.

Egypt remained independent nevertheless until after the Battle of Actium (September 2, 31 BCE) in which Octavian defeated the forces of Antony and Cleopatra VII, the last Ptolemaic ruler. In 30 BCE Egypt became a province of Rome. Owing to its strategic importance as a supplier of grain to the Roman Empire, the province of Egypt was governed by an equestrian prefect rather than by a senator. Egypt's other high-ranking administrators and commanders, including commanders of legions, were also equestrian, appointed by the emperor. In the early first century CE it was unthinkable that an equestrian would attempt to usurp the imperial power. Later this was not the case. A usurper, Firmus, claimed the role of emperor in the mid-third century, and the revolt of another claimant was put down by Diocletian in circa 297.

Egypt was garrisoned by three and later two legions, a fleet, and various auxiliary units. Two legions and the fleet were stationed at Alexandria. There were no significant foreign invasions or wars in Egypt during the Roman period (before the seventh-century Byzantine-Muslim conflict). The tribal peoples to the south, the Nobatae and Blemmyes, were not a serious threat. The main role for the Roman soldiers was policing. The fleet patrolled the Nile River, which was the main north-south route through the province. Minor garrisons occupied mines and quarries in the Eastern Desert and patrolled the land routes through the Eastern Desert to seaports on the Red Sea coast, guarding the lucrative Red Sea trade from Arabia and India. Soldiers might be called on to suppress rioting in Alexandria or banditry in the Nile Delta.

Romans tended to have a poor opinion of Egyptians, regarding them as animal worshippers and depreciating Egyptian immigrants to Rome. Alexandria, however, was a major center of Greek cultures. The Greek-speaking elite of Alexandria and the Jews of Alexandria were hostile to one another, breaking out into violent conflict during the reign of Claudius (41–54). The emperor Caracalla (211–217) also had trouble with the Alexandrians.

Roman Egypt was a highly hierarchical society, with Roman citizens and Greek-speaking Alexandrians at the top followed by the Greek-speaking inhabitants of other cities and towns; at the bottom were the Egyptian peasants. Egypt was also intensively exploited by the Romans. However, whether social conflict was worse in Egypt than in other provinces is uncertain; conflict may only be better attested.

Egypt became heavily Christianized and was one of the first areas to practice monasticism. The Christian Church adapted a written version of the Egyptian language, Coptic, that is still used today by the Coptic Church.

Russell Buzby and Sara E. Phang

See also

Achaemenid Empire; Actium, Battle of; Alexander III the Great; Artaxerxes III; Caesar's Campaign in Egypt; Cambyses II; Cleopatra VII; Darius I; Egypt, Athenian Intervention in; Ptolemaic Kingdom; Ptolemy I Soter; Ptolemy II Philadelphus; Ptolemy III Euergetes; Ptolemy IV Philopator; Ptolemy V Epiphanes; Ptolemy VI Philometor; Raphia, Battle of; Syrian-Egyptian Wars; Xerxes I

References

Alston, Richard. *Soldier and Society in Roman Egypt*. New York: Routledge, 1995.

Bagnall, Roger S. *Egypt in Late Antiquity*. Princeton, NJ: Princeton University Press, 1993.

Fuhrmann, Christopher J. *Policing the Roman Empire: Soldiers, Administration, and Public Order*. New York: Oxford University Press, 2012.

Lewis, Napthali. *Greeks in Ptolemaic Egypt*. Oxford, UK: Clarendon, 1986.

Lewis, Naphtali. *Life in Egypt under Roman Rule*. Oxford, UK: Clarendon, 1983.

Egyptian-Arab Wars (1811–1840)

Wahhabism, founded by Muhammad ibn Abd al-Wahhab, a theologian from Nejd, sought to return Muslims to pure

Islam by removing false beliefs and the regimes that supported them. By the 1790s, the Wahhabist movement extended over most of the Arabian Peninsula and gained many adherents, including Emir Muhammad ibn Saud in 1774. The Saudi-led Wahhabis displayed their growing confidence by attacking Iraq, Syria, and the Hejaz. By 1800, the Wahhabist movement was dominated by Abd al-Aziz ibn Saud, who raided the Shia holy city of Karbala in 1802. A year later ibn Saud laid waste en route to Mecca during the hajj. Sacred tombs and sites were destroyed, and those who refused to adhere to the Wahhabist doctrines were slain. In 1804, Wahhabists returned to seize Mecca, ousting Sharif Ghalib and closing pilgrimage routes to the city for all non-Wahhabists. The Wahhabists went so far as to remove Sultan Selim III's name from Friday prayers and replace it with that of the Sauds, therefore usurping a privileged position in the Islamic world.

Unable to defeat the Wahhabists and return the Hejaz to Ottoman control, Selim III turned to Mehmed Ali (Muhammad Ali) Pasha, governor of Egypt. Mehmed Ali used this opportunity to resolve his domestic problem by inviting the Mamluk leaders, who posed great threat to his authority in Egypt, to join his campaign against the Wahhabis. As the Mamluk leaders arrived at the Cairo Citadel on March 1, 1811, the governor's Ottoman troops attacked them from atop the high walls that flanked the roadway and massacred them all. Mehmed Ali then dispatched some 15,000 infantry to the Arabian port of Yanbu under the command of his young son Tussun, whose inexperience brought disaster. Tussun led his army into a Wahhabi ambush at Wadi Safra, where the Egyptian/Ottoman forces suffered heavy losses and were forced to withdraw.

The Egyptians, however, regrouped and returned later that year. In October 1811 Tussun led his men through the mountain passes into Hejaz and besieged Medina, which he took after a siege of several weeks. By January 1812 Mecca was taken without resistance, and the pilgrimage was resumed. For more than a year Tussun's forces sought to win the loyalty of the local chieftains, many of whom sided with the Wahhabists. In September 1813 Mehmed Ali sent reinforcements that launched two unsuccessful expeditions against Taraba, the principal settlement of the Baqum Arabs who supported the Wahhabists. The second expedition proved to be particularly disastrous, as the Egyptian retreat through waterless territory turned into a rout. Mehmed Ali's attempt to capture the Hejaz port of Qunfidah also failed, while the Wahhabis defeated an 1814 expedition led by Abdin Bey.

Exasperated by these failures, Mehmed Ali took personal charge of the operations against the Wahhabis in 1815. Bringing new reinforcements, he lured the Wahhabi forces into an ambush and defeated them near Taif. He then captured Taraba and Qunfidah, clearing much of Hejaz of the Wahhabi presence. Returning to Mecca, Mehmed Ali had a few dozen prisoners impaled outside the city gates and left Tussun to govern the region.

The Wahhabi resistance continued, however. Their hit-and-run tactics inflicted considerable losses on the Egyptian troops. In the spring of 1815, an Egyptian detachment led by Thomas Keith was ambushed and its force of more than 200 slaughtered. Late the same year Tussun, unbeknownst to his father, and Abdullah ibn Saud, Abd al-Aziz ibn Saud's grandson, negotiated a compromise by which the Wahhabis recognized the authority of the Ottoman sultan, renounced their claims to Mecca and Medina, and agreed to give safe passage to caravans crossing their territory; Tussun agreed to relinquish control of the Qasim region and recognize Wahhabi control of the northern tribes of Arabia. Upon learning about this agreement, Mehmed Ali refused to ratify it, while ibn Saud made no effort to pledge an allegiance to the Ottoman sultan.

In the fall of 1815 Mehmed Ali organized a new expedition to Arabia to put an end to the Wahhabi threat. He recalled Tussun to Egypt and replaced him with his much more capable son Ibrahim, who launched a methodical campaign against the Arab tribes using bribery, threats, or force. In 1817 his troops inflicted a major defeat on ibn Saud's tribesmen near the wells of Mawiyah, and the following year they captured the Wahhabi stronghold of Dariiyah, where they seized ibn Saud as well. When attempts to reform the Wahhabist ulema failed, dozens were slaughtered in the Dariyah mosque, while Abdullah ibn Saud and members of his family were imprisoned and later executed.

The Egyptian influence in Hejaz continued throughout 1820, although Saudi detachments raided Medina, Mecca, and al-Taif in late 1827. By mid-1830s, Mehmed Ali decided to impose his authority in Nejd (central Arabia). In July 1836, Egyptian troops with artillery, commanded by Ismail Bey, invaded Arabia. The Saudi ruler Faisal tried to avoid fighting by offering to deliver 5,000 camels to Mehmed Ali, but the Egyptians demanded three times that number, which Faisal could not provide.

Landing at Yanbu, Ismail marched to Medina and attacked Saudi forces at al-Rass, driving Faisal back to Anaiza by April 1837. The Egyptian army then proceeded deep into central Arabia, capturing Qasim and Jabal Shammar, while

Faisal fled to Hufuf in eastern Arabia. In May 1837 Ismail Bey occupied Riyadh, ending Faisal's reign there and putting his rival Khalid ibn Saud on the throne. Although the Egyptian Army tried to extend its authority to southern Arabia, it suffered a crushing defeat near al-Hilwa in July 1837, losing hundreds of men and all of its artillery.

Seeking to exploit this victory, Faisal besieged Riyadh, where the remaining Egyptian forces was garrisoned, but could not capture it after two months. The arrival of Egyptian reinforcements in early 1838 convinced Faisal that he would not be able to prevail militarily. Choosing to compromise, he agreed to divide Arabia into two parts: eastern Arabia and southern Nejd remained under his authority, while central and northern Nejd submitted to pro-Egyptian Khalid ibn Saud.

The agreement proved short-lived, since Mehmed Ali rejected compromise and dispatched Khurshid Pasha to complete the conquest of Arabia. Khurshid Pasha and his reinforcements reached Nejd in May 1838 and proceeded to subdue defiant sheikhs in the region. In the fall of 1838 Khurshid, with some 4,000 men with 10 guns, surrounded Faisal's forces at Dilam and took the town after a monthlong siege on December 10, 1838. Faisal was captured and sent to Egypt as a prisoner.

The victory at Dilam marked the start of an Egyptian occupation of Nejd that continued for 18 months. Although Khalid ibn Saud remained on the throne at Riyadh, real authority was in the hands of Khurshid Pasha and his Egyptian troops. In Asia (southwestern Arabia), Egyptian forces defeated Arab tribesmen in several clashes but could not conquer them and faced continued revolts that lasted until 1840.

Khurshid tried to exert Egyptian influence in southeastern Arabia as well, but his attempts to compel local rulers to pay tribute failed and instead alarmed the British, who ordered their local naval commander to use force if necessary to protect Bahrain from the Egyptians. In 1839–1840, British residents visited the Trucial Coast and signed agreements with local sheikhs promising British support in case of Egyptian attack. Also concerned about Egyptian expansion into Yemen, the British seized the port of Aden in 1839. But by then Egypt was no longer in position to continue its military involvement in Arabia. Under the pressure of European powers, Mehmed Ali ordered the evacuation of Nejd and Yemen in March 1840.

ALEXANDER MIKABERIDZE AND ROBERT W. MALICK

See also
Bahrain; Egypt; Mehmed Ali; Saudi Arabia; Wahhabism; Yemen

References
Allen, Charles. *God's Terrorists: The Wahhabi Cult and the Hidden Roots of Modern Jihad.* Cambridge, MA: Da Capo, 2006.
Finkel, Caroline. *Osman's Dream: The History of the Ottoman Empire.* Cambridge, MA: Basic Books, 2006.
Kinross, Lord. *The Ottoman Centuries: The Rise and Fall of the Turkish Empire.* New York: Perennial, 2002.
McGregor, Andrew. *A Military History of Modern Egypt: From the Ottoman Conquest to the Ramadan War.* Westport, CT: Praeger Security International, 2006.
Vassiliev, Alexei. *The History of Saudi Arabia.* London: Saqi Books, 1998.

Egyptian-Ottoman Wars (1831–1833 and 1838–1841)

Two major conflicts between the Ottoman Empire and its nominally vassal Muhammad Ali Pasha al-Mas'ud ibn Agha of (Mehmed Ali) Egypt. In 1821, the Ottoman Empire saw the start of the Greek Revolt that threatened Ottoman rule in the Balkan Peninsula. Struggling to contain the rebellion, Sultan Mahmud II asked for help from his vassal Muhammad Ali of Egypt, promising him control of Syria and Crete as a reward for military aid. The Egyptian ruler delivered army and navy aid but could not defeat the Greeks, who had the support of the major European powers.

First Egyptian-Ottoman War (1831–1833)

Falling out with the sultan over terms of compensation for his considerable military efforts in Greece, Muhammad Ali decided to claim the territories by force and used a personal quarrel with the pasha of Acre as a pretext for war that began in October 1831. In November 1831, Muhammad Ali's son Ibrahim Pasha invaded Ottoman Palestine and scored one quick victory after another, capturing Jaffa (November 12) and Haifa (November 17), while the residents of Jerusalem, Nablus, Tyre, and Tripoli pledged their allegiance to the Egyptians.

On December 4, Ibrahim laid siege to the formidable fortress costal city of Acre, which withstood Napoleon Bonaparte's attacks 32 years earlier, and captured it on May 27, 1832, following a brief siege. With its road into Syria now open, the modernized Egyptian army occupied Damascus on June 16 and routed one Ottoman army under Mehmed Pasha at Homs on July 8 and a second Ottoman army under Huseyin Pasha at Bilan (the Syrian Gates) on July 29. Crossing the Taurus Mountains, Ibrahim occupied the strategic cities of Tarsus and Adan on July 31, halting there to regroup.

Confronted with these defeats, Mahmud II raised a new army of some 80,000 men under Grand Vizier Rescid Mehmed Pasa, but on December 21, 1832, Ibrahim Pasha crushed the Ottomans at Konya and advanced on Bursa, only a short distance from the Ottoman capital of Istanbul. Desperate for help, the Porte turned to its historic enemy, Russia, and a Russian naval squadron arrived in Istanbul in February 1833. At the same time, alarmed by Egyptian victories and anxious to arrest Russian influence and access to the Mediterranean, France and Britain quickly intervened to mediate the conflict.

The Kutahya Convention (May 4, 1833) required Ibrahim Pasha to pull back from Anatolia but recognized Egyptian control of Greater Syria, Crete, and the Hejaz. Although immediately the threat to his authority was gone, Sultan Mahmud II chose to negotiate a separate defensive accord with Russia at Hunkiar Iskelesi (July 8, 1833). This guaranteed Russian assistance in the event of a future war.

Second Egyptian-Ottoman War (1839–1841)

The Kutahya Convention was more a truce than a peace treaty. Muhammad Ali used it to secure his authority throughout Greater Syria, Arabia, Crete, Cyprus and much of the Sudan, creating the largest Egyptian empire in history. In 1838 he ended its tribute payments to the Porte, effectively proclaiming Egypt's independence.

In 1839 Sultan Mahmud II then assembled an army to invade Syria, but both land and sea expeditions failed. On June 24, Ibrahim Pasha routed the Ottoman army under Hafiz Pasha at Nezib. At the same time, the commander of the Ottoman Navy sold out to the Egyptians and surrendered his fleet to Muhammad Ali in Alexandria. With the Ottoman Empire seemingly on the verge of collapse, the major European powers once again rushed to intervene in what became known as the Oriental Crisis of 1840.

By the Treaty of London (July 1840), Britain, Austria, Prussia, and Russia pressured new Sultan Abdulmecid I to recognize the hereditary rights of Muhammad Ali and his heirs to rule Egypt and parts of Palestine, provided that they would continue to recognize Ottoman suzerainty and restore Syria and Lebanon to the sultan. Believing that he had the support of France, Muhammad Ali vacillated on accepting this compromise, prompting a combined European effort against him. In the fall of 1840, the Great Powers moved from diplomacy to military action. British and Austrian warships cut Ibrahim Pasha's seaborne lines of communication, blockaded the Nile Delta, and bombarded and destroyed Egyptian forts at Beirut and Acre, where British, Austrian, and Ottoman troops landed in early November. With the European powers then threatening Alexandria itself with bombardment, Muhammmad Ali decided to compromise, in effect accepting the terms of the London Convention in the Alexandria Convention of November 17, 1840.

Muhammad Ali renounced his claims to Crete and the Hejaz (western Arabia) and agreed to return the Ottoman fleet and downsize his remaining naval forces and army. In return, he and his descendants were granted hereditary rule over Egypt and Sudan.

ALEXANDER MIKABERIDZE

See also
Hunkar Iskelesi, Treaty of; Ibrahim Pasha; Konya, Battle of; Kutahya Convention; London, 1840 Treaty of

References
al-Sayyid-Marsot, Afaf Lufti. *Egypt in the Reign of Muhammad Ali.* Cambridge: Cambridge University Press, 1984.
Fahmy, Khaled. *All the Pasha's Men: Mehmed Ali, His Army, and the Making of Modern Egypt.* Cambridge: Cambridge University Press, 1997.

Egyptian Revolution of 2011

On January 25, 2011, a series of massive demonstrations against the 30-year rule of Egyptian president Hosni Mubarak began in Cairo and other Egyptian cities amid the larger Arab Spring movement. Protesters were inspired by similar demonstrations in Tunisia that had forced Tunisian president Zine El Abidine Ben Ali from office on January 14, 2011. The Egyptian protesters were angered by high unemployment, high food prices, and a corrupt and autocratic government that stifled many basic civil liberties.

The Egyptian Revolution commenced when 20,000 protesters took to Tahrir Square on January 25. Police were immediately called to quell the demonstrations, and there were reports that three people were killed. Protests continued the next day, and on January 27 the government began shutting down cell phone and Internet services in an attempt to disrupt the protesters. That same day, the Muslim Brotherhood began asking its members to join the protests. Some observers expressed concerns about a prominent Muslim Brotherhood presence in a post-Mubarak government, because it is an Islamist group that seeks a government established along Islamic religious lines.

On January 29, Mubarak dismissed his cabinet and acknowledged the "legitimate demand" for reforms. He appointed Omar Suleiman, his intelligence chief, as vice president, and in the following days Suleiman announced that the government would negotiate reforms with opposition leaders. Protests nevertheless continued, despite government-imposed curfews and shows of force by the military. Mubarak announced on February 1 that he would not be a candidate in presidential elections scheduled for September 2011 but would remain in office until after those elections to ensure an orderly transition of power. Protests continued amid increasing international demands—including from U.S. president Barack Obama—that Mubarak leave office as soon as possible. On February 2 protesters clashed with groups of Mubarak loyalists, largely off-duty police officers and government workers paid to be there. On that date, arrests and the harassment of foreign journalists commenced as well.

As the protests grew, Suleiman began holding talks on February 6 with representatives from opposition groups, including the Muslim Brotherhood, to discuss reforms and ending the official state of emergency that had been in effect since Mubarak assumed power in 1981. At the same time, some banks reopened for the first time since January 27. Still, protests continued, and many Egyptians and international observers characterized the government's efforts as window dressing meant to reduce the anger of the demonstrators. On February 10, Mubarak prepared to make a televised address amid widespread speculation that he would announce his resignation. Protesters reacted angrily, however, when he said that he would delegate unspecified powers to Suleiman and repeated that he would serve out his term.

On February 11 following 18 days of protests and violence that had brought some 300 deaths, Suleiman announced Mubarak's resignation, and protest crowds erupted in cheers and chants of "Egypt is free!" Suleiman now declared that authority over the country would be temporarily ceded to the military.

The military junta that now assumed power dissolved parliament, suspended the constitution, and announced that national elections would be held within six months. Mubarak meanwhile was jailed, awaiting trial for having ordered the murder of protesters. Elections were held in May and June of 2012, with Mohamed Morsi, a leader in the Muslim Brotherhood, being elected president of Egypt. He took office on June 30, 2012, and was proclaimed the first democratically elected president in Egypt's long history.

This was not to last, for Morsi's election created as many problems as it solved. Many secular Egyptians, particularly military officers, deeply distrusted and resented Morsi, believing that he intended to impose sharia (Islamic) law. Morsi did his regime no favors when soon after taking office he gave himself unlimited extrajudicial powers, including the right to draft and enact legislation. He claimed that he did so to purge the government of Mubarak's influences, but many Egyptians saw it as a power grab. In November 2012, Morsi backed a plan that would have resulted in an Islamist constitution. These moves sparked fresh protests in Egypt that lasted for nearly seven months.

On June 30, 2013, with mass protests again crippling Egypt's cities and with calls for Morsi to resign, the powerful Egyptian military establishment, led by General Abdel Fattah El-Sisi, issued an ultimatum to Morsi: he was to resign within 48 hours if he did not immediately accede to the demands of popular will and attempt to resolve the crisis peacefully. Morsi scoffed at the request and accused the military of fomenting a coup against him. On July 3, the Egyptian military establishment ousted Morsi. The new military junta immediately cracked down on the Muslim Brotherhood, suspended the constitution, and charged Morsi with inciting deadly violence. He would later be tried, convicted, and imprisoned on that charge.

Unrest in Egypt persisted, however, and during late 2013 and into 2014 mass protests against military rule occurred. The Egyptian government has since periodically resorted to deadly force to scatter or intimidate protesters, and for a time the nation remained more unstable than it was when Mubarak left office in 2011. More recent protests have frequently been dominated by the Muslim Brotherhood and other Islamist groups. On January 18, 2014, a new Egyptian constitution was overwhelmingly approved by popular vote. The document retained Islam as the official state religion, but the government would not be set up along religious lines, or according to sharia law.

National elections were held in May 2014, and el-Sisi won in a landslide, taking office in June 2014. Parliament was subsequently reconstituted, although the office of the president holds much of Egypt's governing powers. El-Sisi won reelection easily in March 2018. His election and reelection all but guarantee the continued dominance of the Egyptian military in the nation's affairs, a situation that had persisted in Egypt under Mubarak and his predecessors. Meanwhile, Egypt's economy continues to struggle, while the Sinai Peninsula has been plagued by a persistent Islamist insurgency.

DENNIS MORAN

See also
Egypt; Mubarak, Hosni

References

Amin, Galal, and Jonathan Wright. *Whatever Happened to the Egyptian Revolution?* Cairo: American University in Cairo Press, 2013.

Culbertson, Shelly. *The Fires of Spring: A Post-Arab Spring Journey through the Turbulent Middle East.* New York: St. Martin's, 2016.

Egyptian-Soviet Arms Deal (Summer 1955)

The first of many Egyptian-Soviet arms deals in which Egypt purchased tanks and other weapons systems from the Soviet Union. Because some of the purchases involved Czech-manufactured goods and given the fact that the Soviets hoped to obscure their involvement in the arms deal, this first Egyptian purchase of Soviet bloc military hardware was referred to as the Egyptian-Czechoslovakian arms deal. Nevertheless, it clearly had the Soviet imprimatur, and the Czechoslovakians could not have sold arms to Egypt without the prior and express consent of Moscow. The 1955 arms deal delivered to the Egyptians some 200 tanks and other weapons and amounted to about $325 million (in 1955 dollars).

The deal was consummated after several high-level Soviet figures visited Egypt in the summer of 1955. This marked the start of a major Soviet effort to insert its influence in the Middle East. It was also the beginning of an Egyptian-Soviet alliance that would last until the mid-1970s and paved the way for similar Soviet arms deals with Syria and Iraq.

The arms deal had implications far beyond the actual transfer of military goods to Egypt. First, the deal threatened to disrupt the regional Middle East military balance. In so doing, it essentially nullified the 1950 Tripartite Declaration, enunciated by the United States, France, and Great Britain, that among other things instituted a virtual arms embargo against all nations in the Middle East. Second, the deal strengthened the hand of Pan-Arab Egyptian president Gamal Abdel Nasser in the region and most certainly emboldened him to nationalize the Suez Canal less than a year later. Finally, from a larger geostrategic standpoint, the Egyptian-Soviet arms deal brought the Cold War rivalry to the Middle East in a very significant way. Indeed, the arms purchase helped induce both the United States and Great Britain to withdraw their financial support for the construction of the Aswan High Dam project in Egypt. This in turn precipitated Nasser's nationalization of the Suez Canal and the Suez Crisis of 1956 that followed.

When the Israelis learned of the arms purchases they immediately began lobbying the West, and the United States in particular, to sell them arms as a countermeasure. The Americans stalled and then referred the Israeli government to France and other Western countries. Not until 1962, however, would the United States engage in an arms deal with the Israelis. The French were more than willing to oblige and sold about 200 tanks to Israel in early and mid-1956. Helping Israel was just one incentive for the French, however. They also saw the arms deal as retribution for Nasser's vocal support of Algerian nationalists fighting the French in the Algerian War, which had begun in earnest in 1954.

To pay for the arms shipment the Egyptians incurred considerable debt, and in 1956 nearly 40 percent of Egypt's cotton production went to the Soviet Union as payment. Just two years earlier, it had been only 15 percent.

PAUL G. PIERPAOLI JR.

See also

Egypt; Nasser, Gamal Abdel; Suez Canal; Suez Crisis; Tripartite Declaration

References

Jabber, Paul. *Not by War Alone: Security and Arms Control in the Middle East.* Berkeley: University of California Press, 1981.

Louis, William R., and Roger Owen, eds. *Suez, 1956: The Crisis and Its Consequences.* New York: Oxford University Press, 1989.

Varble, Derek. *The Suez Crisis, 1956.* London: Osprey, 2003.

Egypt under British Rule (1882–1936)

Technically part of the Ottoman Empire, Egypt in the 19th century enjoyed de facto independence after Muhammad Ali Pasha (1769–1848) became ruler in 1805. In 1869 the Suez Canal opened, greatly increasing Great Britain's interest in Egypt, for the canal significantly shortened the trade route to India. Under Ismail Pasha (r. 1863–1879), the nation accumulated a tremendous foreign debt that peaked at £91 million in 1875. Even after negotiations reduced this amount, Ismail had to allocate 66 percent of government revenues to pay European banks and bondholders.

Desperate for ready cash, Ismail sold Egypt's share of the Suez Canal to the British government in 1875. This was hardly sufficient to cover even a year of expenditures but greatly increased Britain's interest in Egypt. Four years later, Britain and France forced Ismail to accept dual control, under which British and French administrators supervised the collection and disbursement of all Egyptian revenues. Opposition to this loss of sovereignty led to

Ismail's replacement by his son Muhammad Tewfiq Pasha (r. 1879–1892) that same year.

Under Tewfiq, Egypt's leaders sought to appease the Great Powers by paying down the debt as quickly as possible. This entailed massive cutbacks in government spending plus a significant increase in the number of French and British "advisers" to the Egyptian government. A nationalist reaction fueled the rise of Egyptian Army colonel Ahmad Arabi (1841–1911), whose 1881 coup established a new government under the popular slogan "Egypt for the Egyptians." With Arabi's government calling for renegotiation of the foreign debt and following the massacre of a number of foreigners, the British and French planned to send a joint naval task force to Egypt. A change of government in France, however, led that country to back out, and the British proceeded alone, although supported by smaller Austrian and Ottoman contingents. In the 1882 Anglo-Egyptian War, the British bombarded Alexandria (July 13), then sent forces ashore to secure the city. An expeditionary force then landed and defeated the Egyptian Army in the Battle of Tel el-Kebir (September 13) before taking control of Cairo.

Although British prime minister William Gladstone's government formally notified other powers that British forces would be withdrawn "as soon as the state of the country, and the organization of the proper means for the maintenance of the Khedive's authority, will admit of it," British troops remained in Egypt. The real ruler of the country for the next 23 years was British consul general and high commissioner Evelyn Baring, Lord Cromer.

The period of British rule during 1882–1914 is often referred to as the "veiled protectorate," for Britain closely controlled Egyptian affairs behind a veneer of native Egyptian politicians and civil servants. This veil lifted at the beginning of the Great War, when Great Britain openly declared its domination of Egypt.

Outright colonial status for Egypt, without the support of at least one other Great Power, would have placed Britain in a difficult position, and the French objected to British control. This ended in 1904, however, with the establishment of the Entente Cordiale, by which Britain recognized French control of Morocco and the French government recognized that of Britain in Egypt.

The fiction that Egypt was still part of the Ottoman Empire and that British officials were simply advisers allowed room to maneuver in the complex world of late 19th-century Great Powers diplomacy. It also helped to diffuse local opposition, thus necessitating a garrison of only 5,000 soldiers.

Britain's success is also in large part attributed to a string of energetic and capable proconsuls: Evelyn Baring, Lord Cromer (1841–1917); Eldon Gorst (1861–1911); and Horatio Kitchener (1850–1916). Challenged with paying off the debt by cutting government expenditures while supporting economic expansion and maintaining order, this trio was markedly successful.

The British focused on expanding agricultural production through improved irrigation plus a strenuous anticorruption campaign. By 1889 the Egyptian government produced a surplus; six years later this reached the very considerable figure of £1 million. The debt crisis was over.

Despite economic improvement, Britain's hold over Egypt was never popular outside select financial circles and certain non-Muslim groups. Egyptian Muslims were at best neutral and more frequently were hostile. Native opposition to British domination centered on Abbas II Hilmi (1874–1944) and his protégé, Mustafa Kamil (1874–1908). The former was Egypt's khedive, heir to Tewfiq, but very much under the thumb of Baring, Gorst, and Kitchener. The latter, an up-and-coming lawyer, became a powerful nationalist leader and editor of the popular newspaper *Al-Liwa* (The Standard).

Egyptian nationalists were drawn mainly from the ranks of the Egyptian elites: educators, lawyers, writers, and government officials. While divided by competing visions for an independent Egypt, most could agree on the need to end British control. Mustafa Kamil argued that this could best be accomplished through nonviolent opposition and diplomacy. The latter tactic involved seeking support from France. After 1904's Entente Cordiale, however, the focus shifted to the Ottoman Empire.

In a peculiar move for a nationalist leader, Mustafa Kamil convinced his supporters to side with Ottoman authorities regarding the Taba boundary question (1906), even though this would mean the loss of Egyptian territory. Mustafa Kamil argued that this would be an act of solidarity with fellow Muslims that was worth the cost of some Sinai desert. Other Egyptian nationalists formed rival political groups in the Party of the Nation and the Constitutional Reform Party. Mustafa Kamil's own Nationalist Party survived Taba but not his death, splintering over leadership issues.

Divided over foreign policy, Egyptian nationalists were also split on the position of Abbas Helmi II Pasha (r. 1892–1914), who reduced his support for nationalists while becoming more accommodating to the British. Both Gorst and Kitchener fueled this division, allowing limited political power to a Legislative Assembly that they hoped would pit the khedive against the nationalists.

A growing anti-British stance led the British to depose Abbas Helmi II on December 19, 1914, while he was abroad. The British also ended the khedivate by terminating the nominal ties between Egypt and the Ottoman Empire. Abbas Helmi II's half uncle Hussein Kamel became Egypt's ruler as sultan, with the title placing him on equal footing with the Ottoman sultan. This did not mean a lessening of British control, which remained in the hands of the British high commissioner.

On February 28, 1922, the United Kingdom issued a declaration unilaterally ending the protectorate. On March 14 that same year, Sultan Fuad I issued a decree whereby he took the title of king of Egypt. British influence was nonetheless pervasive. The Anglo-Egyptian Treaty of August 26, 1936, officially ended 54 years of British occupation in Egypt. Nevertheless, Egyptian sovereignty remained circumscribed, for the treaty established a 20-year military alliance that allowed Great Britain to impose martial law and censorship in Egypt in the event of international emergency. The treaty also permitted the stationing of as many as 10,000 British troops and 400 Royal Air Force pilots in the Suez Canal Zone until the Egyptians were capable of protecting the area and permitted Great Britain to retain its naval base at Alexandria for up to 8 years. In October 1951, the Egyptian parliament approved decrees unilaterally abrogating the Anglo-Egyptian Treaty of 1936 and proclaiming Farouk I king of Egypt and the Sudan (which had been governed as an Anglo-Egyptian condominium since 1899). The last British troops did not leave Egypt until June 1956.

JOHN P. DUNN AND SPENCER C. TUCKER

See also
Alexandria, Bombardment of; Anglo-Egyptian War; Suez Canal; Tel el-Kebir, Battle of

References
al-Sayyid-Marsot, Afaf Lutfi. *Egypt and Cromer: A Study in Anglo-Egyptian Relations.* London: John Murray, 1968.
Hunter, F. Robert. *Egypt under the Khedives, 1805–1879: From Household Government to Modern Bureaucracy.* Cairo: American University in Cairo Press, 2000.
Tignor, Robert L. *Modernization and British Colonial Rule in Egypt, 1882–1914.* Princeton, NJ: Princeton University Press, 1966.
Tollefson, Harold. *Policing Islam: The British Occupation of Egypt and the Anglo-Egyptian Struggle over Control of the Police, 1882–1914.* Westport CT: Praeger, 1999.

Eilat, Israel

Israel's southernmost city. Located on the Gulf of Aqaba, the eastern arm of the Red Sea, and near the Sinai region, Eilat has a population of some 50,000 people. Here the southernmost extensions of the Arabah savanna zone and the Negev Desert meet.

Eilat is a major port city with both economic and military significance. Dry savanna/desert flora and fauna that can withstand long periods of drought predominate. Indeed, the name "Eilat" is derived from the Hebrew word for "trees." Eilat's nearby neighbors are the Egyptian city of Taba and the Jordanian port of Aqaba, all providing access to Africa and the East.

Historically, Eilat is thought to be close to the site of Ezion-Geber, a key port during the reign of King Solomon some 3,000 years ago. The city of Eilat was reestablished in 1949, and a modern deepwater harbor opened there in 1965.

Eilat was strategically significant for Israel from the very inception of the Jewish state in 1948. When Egypt refused to allow passage of Israeli and non-Israeli ships headed for Israeli ports from traversing the Suez Canal, Eilat became the only viable entry port for the movement of goods into and out of Israel. The Egyptians had barred Israeli access to the canal as a result of the Israeli War of Independence (1948–1949). Essentially, Eilat became Israel's main artery. Especially critical were oil imports that now had to go through the city's port.

After the Egyptians shut off the Suez Canal to Israeli interests, Eilat became Israel's only direct way to access markets and resources in Southeast Asia and East Africa. Indeed, were it not for Eilat, Israeli ships would have had to embark on a tortuous trip through the Mediterranean and around the African continent and the Cape of Good Hope to reach East Asia.

Keeping the port open became an absolute necessity for Israel. This became even more apparent in 1967 when the Egyptians blocked the Strait of Tiran to Israeli shipping. In so doing, they effectively blockaded Eilat. Among other provocations, the Israelis cited the closure of the straits as a reason for going to war against Egypt in 1967. Israel continues to take access to Eilat very seriously. Eilat became a free trade zone in 1985.

ANTOINETTE MANNION

See also
Red Sea; Six-Day War; Suez Canal

References
Orni, Ephraim. *Geography of Israel.* Philadelphia: Jewish Publication Society of America, 1977.

Parker, Richard B., ed. *The Six-Day War: A Retrospective.* Gainesville: University Press of Florida, 1996.

Eilat, Sinking of (October 21, 1967)

The sinking of the Israeli destroyer *Eliat* by the Egyptian Navy was the first time a warship was sunk by a missile. Beginning in 1962, Egypt received several Osa- and Komar-class missile boats from the Soviet Union. Armed with radar-guided Styx missiles that carried a 1,000-pound high-explosive and had a shaped charge warhead to a maximum range of 48 miles, these missile boats posed a serious threat to Israel's aging warships, but outside the Soviet bloc little was known about this new weapons system, and Egypt did not deploy them in the 1967 Six-Day War.

Following the Six-Day War, Israeli defense minister Moshe Dayan ordered Israeli military forces to demonstrate along the Sinai coast to assert Israeli possession of the newly occupied territory. Some of these warships approached Egypt's 12-mile territorial limit.

On July 11, 1967, while on patrol north of the Sinai desert, the Israeli destroyer *Eilat*, a veteran of World War II purchased from Britain, and two motor torpedo boats engaged and sank two Egyptian torpedo boats in a running gun battle. Fearing a missile attack, *Eilat* captain Commander Yitzhak Shoshan engaged the Egyptians cautiously until lookouts determined that the Egyptian ships were older vessels armed with torpedoes rather than missiles.

This incident, however, encouraged Egyptian leaders to respond to Israel's naval patrols and test the Styx missile in combat. Three months later on October 21, 1967, on another such patrol the *Eilat* approached Egypt's 12-mile territorial limit. At 5:30 p.m. local time roughly 13.5 miles north of Port Said, lookouts spotted an approaching missile. Shoshan ordered the engines full ahead and turned his ship to present its stern to the missile. Israeli machine-gun fire had no effect on the missile, which struck the ship and severely damaged the engine room. While the crew fought the resulting fires, the *Eliat* continued to turn broadside toward Port Said, whereupon lookouts spotted a second and then a third incoming missile. Both of these hit, leaving the *Eilat* severely damaged and listing. Two hours after the first missile hit, Shoshan ordered his crew to abandon ship and radioed for help. A fourth missile struck the ship as it sank, wounding many sailors struggling in the water. Rescue aircraft reached the survivors within the hour, and helicopters brought the survivors home. Of the 190-man crew, 47 died and 90 suffered injury.

The following May, Egyptian missile boats struck again, sinking the *Orit*, a small wooden fishing vessel, off El Arish. The attack demonstrated the effectiveness of the Styx against even very small ships. The Israeli Navy had thought the Styx's guidance system too primitive to locate small ships, but the sinking of the *Orit* convinced its leaders of the need to develop electronic countermeasures.

The sinking of the *Eilat* gave new impetus to other nations to develop antiship guided missiles. Israel, already developing its Gabriel missile, rushed it to completion to equip its own French-built missile boats. Other nations also developed antiship missiles. These soon included the U.S. Harpoon, the French Exocet, and the Italian Otomat.

Israel retaliated for the attack on the *Eilat* by air strikes against Egyptian oil refineries at Suez. Egypt responded in kind, and raids along the Suez Canal soon escalated into the War of Attrition.

STEPHEN K. STEIN

See also
Dayan, Moshe; Six-Day War; War of Attrition

References
Colvin, R. D. "Aftermath of the Eilat." *U.S. Naval Institute Proceedings* 95 (October 1969): 60–67.

Rabinovich, Abraham. *The Boats of Cherbourg: The Secret Israeli Operation That Revolutionized Naval Warfare.* New York: Seaver, 1988.

Tzalel, Moshe. *From Ice-Breaker to Missile Boat: The Evolution of Israel's Naval Strategy.* Westport, CT: Greenwood, 2000.

Eisenhower Doctrine (1957)

Major Cold War foreign policy tenet regarding U.S. policy toward the Middle East enunciated by President Dwight D. Eisenhower on January 5, 1957, in the course of a special joint session of the U.S. Congress in which he addressed recent developments in the Middle East. Since the mid-1950s, both the United States and the Soviet Union had increasingly treated that area as a theater of Cold War competition. As the region decolonized, in 1950 Great Britain, the United States, and France had issued a statement expressing their hopes for continuing peace and stability in the Middle East and their desire to avoid an ever-escalating arms race there, especially between the Arab nations and the newly founded State of Israel. Such proclamations proved fruitless. When nationalist regimes resentful of their former colonial overlords won power in the region, most notably in Egypt, they increasingly looked to the Soviet bloc for economic and military aid, while Israel received substantial assistance from the United States. With American backing, in February 1955 Iraq, Turkey, Pakistan, Iran, and the United Kingdom signed the Baghdad Pact, a mutual security treaty widely perceived as a mechanism for preserving Western influence.

In the summer of 1956, American resentment of the fact that Egypt's nationalist young president, former army officer Gamal Abdel Nasser, had accepted substantial amounts of Soviet bloc weaponry led the United States to cancel economic assistance previously promised for a showpiece Egyptian development project, the Aswan Dam. Nasser decided to meet the projected funding shortfall by nationalizing the Suez Canal, which was owned and managed by the British and French governments, a constant source of irritation to Egyptian nationalist pride. This strategically and commercially valuable waterway linked the Mediterranean with the Red Sea, enabling shipping to move between Europe and Asia without circumnavigating Africa. In November 1956 a brief war, usually called the Suez Crisis, erupted when Britain, France, and Israel invaded Egypt and tried to retake control of the canal, only to withdraw when Eisenhower and his secretary of state, John Foster Dulles, exerted heavy financial and diplomatic pressure to compel them to retreat.

During the Suez Crisis, the Soviet Union made what could be interpreted as threats of military action against Britain and France unless they removed their forces from Egypt. Soviet leader Nikita Khrushchev had also recently sent troops to the East European Soviet satellite Hungary to prevent its secession from the Warsaw Pact. Shortly afterward, Khrushchev also indulged in somewhat threatening proclamations that his country would win the Cold War and "bury the Western powers." The Middle East contained the world's most substantial oil reserves, resources that were increasingly essential to the heavily energy-dependent American domestic economy and also to U.S. military capabilities. Convinced that the Middle East, where rising anti-Western nationalism and Arab resentment of Israel compounded the tumultuous political situation, had become a Cold War battleground, Eisenhower advocated a high level of U.S. involvement in the region and demanded that Congress grant him military and financial resources to aid Middle Eastern powers attempting to fend off communism. Eisenhower also asserted that when required, the United States would deploy American military forces in the region to oppose "overt armed aggression from any nation controlled by International Communism." In March 1957 Congress passed a joint resolution endorsing Eisenhower's request, the beginning of extensive American involvement in the Middle East that would continue into the 21st century.

The Soviet Union was predictably hostile to the Eisenhower Doctrine, attacking it as a colonialist effort by the United States to replace British and French imperialism with its own hegemony, in defiance of the aspirations to national independence of the Arab peoples. Soviet officials were particularly incensed by the possibility of future American military interventions in the Middle East. In the Soviets' view, the real objective of the United States was to impose "a kind of military protectorate and protect its petroleum interests, especially the near-monopolistic position of American oil companies." The Soviet Union reminded Arab countries of its own support for Egypt over Suez and urged them to look to itself for protection against attempts at domination by outside powers. Clearly, the two Cold War superpowers now viewed the Middle East as a significant arena for strategic and economic competition, its various states constituting a potential sphere of influence from which each sought to exclude the other.

Many Arab states and radical nationalist elements were equally hostile to the Eisenhower Doctrine, condemning it immediately as a new form of Western colonialism. Proclamation of the Eisenhower Doctrine effectively dissipated any credibility that American actions during the Suez crisis had won the United States with Arab nationalist forces. The United States proved unable to prevent a brutal coup in Iraq in July 1958, when radical army officers overthrew the Hashemite monarchy, killing King Faisal II and several of his relatives. The Eisenhower administration did, however, intervene successfully in both Lebanon and Jordan in 1958 to shore up pro-Western governments that it feared might follow suit and succumb to radical leftist coups. These actions helped to reinforce the prevailing image of the United States in the Middle East as a conservative power wedded to the status quo and committed to supporting traditionalist and often illiberal regimes to resist more radical, progressive, and modernizing political forces.

Priscilla Roberts

See also
Arab Nationalism; Baghdad Pact; Eisenhower Doctrine; Faisal II, King of Iraq; Lebanon, First U.S. Intervention in; Nasser, Gamal Abdel; Suez Crisis

References
Brands, H. W. *Into the Labyrinth: The United States and the Middle East 1945–1993*. New York: McGraw-Hill, 1994.
Salt, Jeremy. *The Unmaking of the Middle East: A History of Western Disorder in Arab Lands*. Berkeley: University of California Press, 2008.

Stivers, William. *America Confrontation with Revolutionary Change in the Middle East, 1948–83.* London: Macmillan, 1986.

Yaqub, Salim. *Containing Arab Nationalism: The Eisenhower Doctrine and the Middle East.* Chapel Hill: University of North Carolina Press, 2004.

Eitan, Rafael (1929–2004)

Israeli military officer and politician. Rafael "Raful" Eitan was born on January 11, 1929, in Afula in the British Mandate for Palestine. He was brought up and educated in the kibbutz Tel Adishim. During the Israeli War of Independence (1948–1949), he fought as a junior officer in Palmach during the defense of Jerusalem and was wounded in the fight for the San Simon Monastery (Operation YEVUSI, April–May 1948).

Eitan remained with the Israel Defense Forces (IDF) after the war, and in 1954 he was promoted to captain in command of a paratroop company in Unit 101. He was again wounded in Operation KINERETH, a 1955 raid on Syria. In 1956 he was a lieutenant colonel in command of the 890th Paratroop Battalion. On October 29, 1956, his paratroopers began the Sinai Campaign by securing the eastern approach to the strategic Mitla Pass in the Sinai Peninsula.

In 1967 during the Six-Day War, Colonel Eitan commanded the Paratroop Brigade on the Gaza front and received a severe head wound during the advance on the Suez Canal. Promoted to brigadier general in 1968, the next year he headed IDF infantry troops. He next commanded a division, and during the Syrian attack on the Golan Heights in the Yom Kippur War of October 1973, his division played a vital part in blunting the Syrian attack. During an advance of Syrian tanks, Eitan personally employed a bazooka to destroy several of the tanks. Immediately following the 1973 war, he was promoted to major general and assumed command of the northern front.

In April 1978 Eitan was promoted to lieutenant general and appointed chief of staff of the IDF. In this role he approved the plans for Operation OPERA, the Israeli air attack that destroyed Iraq's nuclear facilities at Osiraq in June 1981. He also created the Raful Youth Project, which sought to encourage underprivileged Israelis to join the IDF and train there for professions. At the same time, he took measures to increase discipline and efficiency in the IDF. However, his most important role as chief of staff was to oversee the Israeli invasion of Lebanon in 1982. Despite some dramatic military successes, including the destruction of Syrian air defenses in the opening days of the conflict, the Israeli forces became bogged down in guerrilla warfare and were held responsible for the massacres at the Sabra and Shatila Palestinian refugee camps near Beirut. Eitan received some of the blame for this in the report of the Kahan Commission, charged with investigating the events at Sabra and Shatila. This report ultimately compelled his resignation.

Eitan retired from the IDF in 1983. He turned to politics and was elected to the Knesset (Israeli parliament) in 1984. A conservative, he formed his own party, Tsomet, that took a hard-line stance on national security and defense issues but a more liberal approach to domestic social issues. Between 1989 and 1991 he served as minister of agriculture. He published his memoirs, *A Soldier's Story,* in 1992.

Tsomet failed to gain in influence even after the 1996 elections that brought conservative Benjamin Netanyahu to power. Between 1996 and 1998 Eitan served as the environment and agriculture minister, and he was deputy prime minister from 1998 to 1999. He retired from politics in 1999. On November 23, 2004, while on the breakwater at the Mediterranean port at Ashod where he was working on a port renewal project, Eitan drowned when a large wave swept him out to sea.

RALPH MARTIN BAKER

See also

Expellees and Refugees, Palestinian; Lebanon-Israeli War; Osiraq Raid; Palmach; Sinai Campaign of 1956; Six-Day War; Yom Kippur War

References

Eitan, Rafael. *A Soldier's Story: The Life and Times of an Israeli War Hero.* New York: S. P. I. Books, 1992.

Gabriel, Richard. *Operation Peace for Galilee: The Israeli-PLO War in Lebanon.* New York: Farrar, Straus and Giroux, 1985.

Rabinovich, Abraham. *The Yom Kippur War: The Epic Encounter That Transformed the Middle East.* New York: Schocken, 2005.

El Alamein, First Battle of (July 1–27, 1942)

Crucial battle of World War II that helped determine the outcome of fighting in North Africa and the Middle East. The First Battle of El Alamein, also known as the Battles of Ruweisat Ridge, was fought in western Egypt during July 1–27, 1942. German field marshal Erwin Rommel and his Axis forces had already won spectacular victories in far eastern Libya at Gazala (May 26–June 13, 1942) and the capture of Tobruk (June 20–21). Driving his troops hard, Rommel hoped to rout the retreating British imperial forces, capture

A British 25-pounder gun firing against German and Italian positions during the First Battle of El Alamein in Egypt, July 1–27, 1942. (Daily Mirror/Mirrorpix via Getty Images)

Cairo, and seize the Suez Canal. The British defeat at Mersa Matruh on June 28 appeared to confirm this course of action.

After months of heavy fighting, however, Axis forces were exhausted and understrength. At the end of June, the three German divisions of 2,000 infantrymen possessed only 55 tanks, 77 field pieces, and 63 antitank guns. Italian forces included 8,000 infantrymen, 70 tanks, and 200 field pieces. Axis forces were at the end of a rapidly lengthening supply and reinforcement line. Rommel had also outrun his air support, with the Axis air forces struggling to establish new forward bases.

On June 25, General Sir Claude Auchinleck, British commander in the Middle East, took personal control of the Eighth Army. Its defensive positions were almost 100 miles west of Alexandria, Egypt, and ran south for 38 miles from the coastal town of El Alamein to the impassable salt marshes of the Qattara Depression. These positions formed a natural choke point, as they could be penetrated but not outflanked. The terrain was largely flat except for two low east-west ridges—Miteiriya in the north and Ruweisat in the center.

The 1st South African Division occupied the northern positions, the 18th Indian Brigade held the center, and the 2nd New Zealand Division deployed in the south. Rommel planned to have his 90th Light Division attack in the north, driving eastward and then swinging left to the sea, encircling the South Africans. The 21st and 15th Panzer Divisions were to move east in the center and then strike right, attacking the New Zealanders in the rear.

Confident of victory, Rommel began the attack on July 1. The panzers found their path blocked by the 18th Indian Brigade. The Indian defenses were incomplete, and the troops were short of ammunition and even water. Luckily, the day before artillery units had arrived with some 40 guns, and the defenders fought tenaciously until overrun that evening. They had, however, destroyed 18 German tanks and stopped the German advance. To the north, the 90th Light Division encountered heavy fire from the South Africans and an artillery reinforcement. Panic erupted among the long-suffering German soldiers, and the officers were fully occupied restoring control.

On July 2, Rommel attempted to use his panzers to renew the attack in the north. Auchinleck now inserted the 1st Armoured Division. Two of its three brigades with 38 Grant medium tanks thrust into the open southern German flank and fought the panzers until nightfall. Rommel resumed the offensive on July 3, sending his tanks forward along both sides of Ruweisat Ridge. The Italian Ariete and Trieste Divisions, which had excellent fighting records, were to attack south. But the 1st Armoured Division barred the panzers' path. In the south, the Trieste Division failed to move, and the Ariete was split, its tanks entangled in the armor battle. The remaining units were struck by the New Zealanders, and the Ariete Division fled, with the loss of 531 men and 44 guns.

Auchinleck now unleashed a series of counterstrokes, relying heavily on information garnered through Ultra intercepts. Reinforcements from the 9th Australian Division came into play. In the north on July 10, the 2nd South African and 26th Australian Brigades attacked positions west of El Alamein held by Italian infantry. This assault overran the Italian lines and netted 1,500 prisoners and 30 guns before it was halted.

Auchinleck then mounted an assault in the center of the line, sending two New Zealand brigades and an Indian brigade against some 4,000 Italian troops on Ruweisat Ridge. Between July 14 and 15 they seized the ridge, but it was impossible to dig into the rocky terrain, and no tanks came forward to assist. In addition, corps commander Lieutenant General William H. Gott failed to coordinate his infantry and armor. In a devastating counterattack, German armor recovered the ridge, and 1,405 New Zealanders were lost.

On July 17, two Australian battalions attacked south against Italian positions on Miteiriya Ridge. The Australians captured 700 prisoners, but they came under fire by Italian guns and were halted by a German task force. Rommel now reluctantly concluded that he must go over to the defensive. German engineers laid extensive minefields and erected strongpoints, where troops were armed with automatic weapons and antitank guns.

In his report of July 21, Rommel exaggerated his losses in order to accelerate reinforcement. This report, decoded by Allied Ultra radio intercepts, strengthened Auchinleck's resolve to crush Rommel. Strong pressure also came from British prime minister Winston L. S. Churchill, whose government was under parliamentary attack occasioned by a series of military defeats.

Auchinleck planned a three-pronged assault for the night of July 21–22. The 161st Indian Brigade was to seize the western end of Ruweisat Ridge, while the newly arrived 23rd Armoured Brigade (less one regiment supporting the Australians) was entrusted with the major objective of attacking the center and overrunning Rommel's headquarters. The 6th New Zealand Brigade was to attack from the south in a northwest direction. The 2nd and 22nd Armoured Brigades were to join the New Zealanders by daybreak.

The Indians met stiff resistance from German and Italian infantry, incurring substantial losses in their failure. In the south, the New Zealanders secured their objective, but the 2nd and 22nd Armoured Brigades failed to link up with them. On the morning of July 22, the 15th and 21st Panzers destroyed the 6th Brigade, inflicting 904 casualties. That same morning, the 23rd Armoured Brigade unleashed two regiments of infantry tanks in a determined assault. Encountering vicious antitank gunfire and blundering into uncleared minefields, the British had 40 tanks destroyed and another 40 damaged. Only 7 tanks remained intact. This attack did cause serious concern for the defenders, as it had penetrated German defenses and overrun a key strongpoint.

Auchinleck's last effort came in the northern sector in an attack against Miteiriya Ridge on July 26–27. One battalion from the 24th Australian Brigade and two battalions from the British 69th Brigade were to seize the ridge, whereupon the 2nd Armoured Brigade would move through gaps cleared in the minefields to support the infantry. The infantry troops gained their objectives, overrunning two Axis battalions. The mine clearing went awry, however, and the Australians and British fell victim to swift German armored counterattacks, losing 1,000 men.

Commonwealth infantrymen, particularly the New Zealanders, emerged from these battles bitter about the lack of British armor support and what they regarded as incompetent British commanders. Although 7,000 Axis prisoners were captured in the Ruweisat battles, British/Commonwealth casualties totaled 13,250. On August 8, Churchill removed Auchinleck from command.

SHERWOOD CORDIER

See also
Auchinleck, Sir Claude John Eyre; Mersa Matruh, First Battle of; Rommel, Erwin Johannes Eugen; Suez Canal and Egypt, World War II Campaigns for Control of

References
Greene, Jack, and Alessandro Massignani. *Rommel's North Africa Campaign: September 1940–November 1942.* Conshohocken, PA: Combined Publishing, 1994.
Playfair, I. S. O. *British Fortunes Reach Their Lowest Ebb.* London: HMSO, 1960.
Scouller, J. L. *Battle for Egypt: The Summer of 1942.* Wellington: War History Branch, Department of Internal Affairs, 1955.

El Alamein, Second Battle of (October 23–November 11, 1942)

Watershed battle in the campaign for the western desert of North Africa in World War II. The battle was fought at El Alamein in north-central Egypt when British Eighth Army commander Lieutenant General Bernard Montgomery initiated the final contest for control of North Africa. By the fall of 1942 there were signs that the war in North Africa was turning in favor of the British. Axis forces under Field Marshal Erwin Rommel driving eastward toward the Suez Canal had failed to break through the British lines at Ruwiesat Ridge in July and at Alam-el-Halfa Ridge in September. British prime minister Winston Churchill repeatedly pressed for an earlier offensive, but Montgomery carefully gathered the resources he thought necessary for success and held off Churchill's demands. Generals Sir Alan Brooke, chief of the Imperial General Staff, and Harold Alexander, British commander in chief in North Africa, managed to placate Churchill.

Montgomery set the operation, code-named LIGHTFOOT, to begin on the night of October 23–24 under a full moon. When LIGHTFOOT began, Montgomery had an overwhelming advantage of 195,000 men, 1,029 tanks (including 300 U.S.-built M-4s), 2,311 artillery pieces, and 750 aircraft. Opposing these, Rommel commanded 104,000 men (50,000 Germans and 54,000 Italians), 489 tanks, 1,219 guns (80 of them 88mm), and 675 aircraft. Rommel had no confidence that his forces could hold against the anticipated British offensive.

The restricted front from the Mediterranean Sea to the Qattara Depression could not be turned. It was heavily fortified in depth, with the defenders relying on an estimated 450,000 mines. Montgomery hoped to catch the Axis defenders off guard with a feint to the south while the main thrust was delivered in the north, against the strength of the Axis line, by Lieutenant General Sir Oliver Leese's XXX Corps; indeed, elaborate British deceptions led the Germans to expect the major offensive to come in the south.

The Battle of El Alamein began under a full moon at 9:40 p.m. on October 23, when 1,000 British guns bombarded a six-mile sector of the German left flank near the Mediterranean. Twenty minutes later the XXX Corps moved out, while Lieutenant General Sir Brian Horrocks's XIII Corps began the southern diversionary attack near the Qattara Depression to fix Axis forces there. Infantry of the XXX Corps managed to clear two corridors in the German minefields, and Lieutenant General Herbert Lumsden's X Armored Corps then moved through them. The Italians, who held this sector, fought well, and a counterattack by the 15th Panzer Division nearly halted the British advance. Rommel, in Germany on sick leave when the attack began, hurried back to North Africa and on the 25th resumed command of Axis forces in the battle.

Montgomery soon halted the southern diversion and concentrated his effort along the coast. During the next week both sides flung armored units into the main battle sector south of the coastal road and railroad. The Eighth Army enjoyed air superiority, and the German tanks, which came into the battle piecemeal, were steadily reduced in number. Rommel's lack of armor reserves and his chronic shortages of fuel and ammunition were influential in the battle's outcome. Rommel did manage to extricate his 164th Division, which had been pinned against the coast by the Australian 9th Division; on November 1 he withdrew to new positions three miles to the west.

The next day the 2nd New Zealand Division managed to clear a path through the minefields for the British tanks. Rommel mounted a Panzer counterattack, but by the end of the day he had only 35 tanks remaining. British tactical air and artillery fire neutralized the German 88mm antitank guns. Hitler now held up the general westward withdrawal of Afrika Korps for two days with an order that Rommel hold in place.

British forces broke cleanly through the German lines, however, and Rommel disregarded Hitler's command, disengaged his forces, and withdrew to the west. The ever-cautious Montgomery delayed the pursuit for 24 hours.

Casualty figures for the battle vary. The British claimed to have inflicted 55,000 casualties, but the Axis forces probably sustained something on the order of 2,300 killed, 5,500 wounded, and 27,900 captured. Rommel also lost almost all his tanks and many of his artillery pieces. For the British Eighth Army, casualties were 4,600 killed and 9,300 wounded. Montgomery had 432 tanks destroyed or disabled.

The Battle of El Alamein was one of the decisive engagements of the war. Churchill wrote of it that "Before Alamein we never had a victory. After Alamein we never had a defeat." Despite the outcome, military historians have criticized Montgomery for attacking the strength of the German line and for the high cost of the victory. Also, Montgomery's assertion that everything went according to plan is simply not true. The chief negative for the Allies, however, came in the Eighth Army's leisurely pursuit of Axis forces after the battle. Despite Montgomery's plans to keep constant pressure on the Germans, during November 5–December 11 Rommel made good his escape. Rommel's forces repeatedly eluded Montgomery's lethargic encirclement attempts again and again.

SPENCER C. TUCKER

See also

Alam el Halfa, Battle of; Montgomery, Bernard Law; Rommel, Erwin Johannes Eugen

References

Carver, Michael. *El Alamein*. London: Batsford, 1962.

Greene, Jack, and Alessandro Massignani. *Rommel's North Africa Campaign, September 1940–November 1942*. Conshocken, PA: Combined Publishing, 1999.

Guingand, Francis de. *Operation Victory*. London: Hodder & Stoughton, 1946.

Hamilton, Nigel. *Monty: The Battles of Field Marshal Bernard Montgomery*. New York: Random House, 1994.

Rommel, Erwin. *The Rommel Papers*. Ed. B. H. Liddell Hart. London: Collins, 1953.

Elazar, David (1925–1976)

Israel Defense Forces (IDF) general and chief of staff from 1971 to 1974. David Elazar was born of Sephardic heritage on August 27, 1925, in Sarajevo, Yugoslavia (now Bosnia). In 1940 he immigrated to Palestine. He was briefly sent to a British internment camp where he was confined until March 1941, after which he was released to work on Kibbutz Ein Shemer. He joined Palmach, the Jewish underground military organization, in 1946 and was initially assigned to a scout company. He saw action in a number of important engagements in the 1948–1949 Israeli War of Independence including the Battle of San Simon Monastery in Jerusalem, where he saw extremely heavy combat. In July 1948 he rose to become commander of the 4th Battalion (Raiders) and a major in the new IDF.

Following the war, Elazar elected to remain in the IDF. He attended a battalion commanders' course and then served in the Training Command as an instructor. He was promoted to lieutenant colonel and appointed as a senior military instructor in 1950. In June 1952 he was appointed operations officer at the IDF's Central Command. In 1954 he became head of the Combat Doctrine Department of the Training Branch, and in late 1955 he received a secondary appointment as the commander of a reserve unit, the reinforced 12th Infantry Brigade. In June 1956 he was appointed commander of the Infantry School and promoted to the rank of colonel.

Elazar fought in the Gaza Strip during the 1956 Suez Crisis and the Sinai Campaign as the commander of the 12th Infantry Brigade, which had been mobilized for the fighting. He transferred to the newly created armor corps in July 1957 at his own request out of a belief that tank warfare was the wave of the future for the IDF. In March 1958 he was appointed commander of the 7th Armored Brigade, the IDF's regular armor unit. In April 1959 he became deputy commander of the Armored Corps. In June 1961 he was promoted to major general and appointed as commander of the Armored Corps.

In 1964 Elazar took charge of Israel's Northern Command, where he remained for five years. During the June 1967 Six-Day War, he led Israeli troops to victory over the Syrians and seized the Golan Heights in the last major campaign of the war. In 1969 he was appointed chief of the General Staff's Operations Division, the traditional stepping-stone to becoming chief of staff.

Elazar became a lieutenant general and chief of staff of the Israeli Army in December 1971. He spent the first part of his tenure focused on fighting terrorists and Palestinian guerrillas. During his watch the 1972 Munich Olympics massacre took place. In retaliation, Elazar ordered the largest Israeli attack on terrorist enclaves in the country's history to that point. Artillery and air attacks pounded terrorist camps in both Lebanon and Syria. Operation SPRING OF YOUTH resulted in the deaths of dozens more terrorists in Beirut in April 1973.

Elazar's career and reputation suffered a crippling setback as a result of the 1973 Yom Kippur War when the Israeli military was caught off guard by the Egyptian and Syrian attack. Although Elazar became convinced at 5:00 a.m. on October 6 (Yom Kippur) that an attack would occur that day, the chief of Israeli military intelligence, Major General Eli Zeira, and the minister of defense, Moshe Dayan, did not believe it likely. That morning Elazar requested both a general mobilization and a preemptive attack by the Israeli Air Force against Syria scheduled for 11:00 a.m., but Dayan rejected both, although he agreed to take Elazar's recommendations to Prime Minister Golda Meir. On his own authority, however, Elazar ordered the partial mobilization of several thousand essential army and air force reservists.

Elazar was nevertheless held responsible for the early Israeli reverses in the war. In April 1974 the Agranat Commission board of inquiry recommended his dismissal. Elazar resigned from the Israeli Army shortly after the report's release. Later historians have been much kinder to Elazar than the Agranat Commission, noting that he remained calm and effective during the early stages of the war, in sharp contrast to both Dayan and the Israeli political leadership. Meir depended heavily on Elazar and called him "a rock" during the 1973 war. Nevertheless, Elazar was at least partially responsible for accepting and propagating a military doctrine that was largely dismissive of Arab military capabilities prior to the attack.

After he left the army, Elazar became director-general of the Israeli Navigation Company. He died in Tel Aviv of heart failure on April 22, 1976.

W. ANDREW TERRILL AND MARY J. ELIAS

See also

Gaza Strip; Golan Heights; Palmach; Sinai Campaign of 1956; Six-Day War; Suez Crisis; Yom Kippur War

References

Bartov, Hanoch. *Dado: 48 Years and 20 Days.* New York: Ma'ariv Book Guild, 1981.

Herzog, Chaim. *The War of Atonement: October, 1973.* Boston: Little, Brown, 1975.

Insight Team of the Sunday Times. *The Yom Kippur War.* New York: Simon and Schuster, 2002.

Rabinovich, Abraham. *The Yom Kippur War: The Epic Encounter That Transformed the Middle East.* New York: Schocken, 2005.

Elbistan, Battle of

See Abulustayn, Battle of

Entebbe Hostage Rescue (July 3–4, 1976)

The rescue of hostages aboard a French jetliner in Entebbe, Uganda, by the Israel Defense Forces (IDF) on July 3–4, 1976. Around noon on June 27, 1976, hijackers commandeered Air France Flight 139, in route from Tel Aviv to Paris. The hijacking occurred shortly after a brief stopover in Athens, Greece. The plane carried 246 passengers and 12 crew members. Four hijackers had boarded the aircraft in Athens. The hijackers were led by Wilfred Bose, a West German Red Army Faction terrorist, and Fayez Abdul-Rahim Jaber. The operation was carried out in the name of the Popular Front for the Liberation of Palestine (PFLP).

The hijacked plane left the Athens radar screen and flew to a preplanned stop in Libya, a nation that had long harbored terrorists. As the aircraft refueled at the Benghazi airport, one passenger, an Israeli woman claiming to be pregnant, was freed. Departing Libya around 9:30 p.m., Flight 139 flew to Entebbe Airport in Uganda, in accordance with the hijacking plan. It arrived at Entebbe at 3:15 a.m. on June 28. Three additional terrorists joined the hijackers at Entebbe.

All evidence suggests that the Ugandan government was complicit in the hijacking of Flight 139 from the very beginning. It also clearly demonstrates that Ugandan president Idi Amin Dada assisted the terrorists once the hijacked plane had arrived. Uganda had long been friendly to Israel, and Amin had once been tutored by the Israelis. In 1972, however, the mercurial Amin turned on the Israelis and ordered all Jews out of Uganda. He then promptly turned Uganda into a Palestinian terrorist training ground. Although Amin visited the hostages several times during their ordeal, he did not discourage the hijackers' actions and seemed to be pushing their demands. Throughout the crisis, Ugandan troops at Entebbe Airport assisted the terrorists in guarding the Jewish hostages.

On June 29 the hijackers issued their demands, which included the release of 40 terrorists held by the Israelis and another 13 terrorists languishing in jails in France, Germany, Switzerland, and Kenya. In two stages the hijackers released many hostages, almost all non-Jews, who were flown to Paris. The hijackers continued to hold the remaining 105 hostages, all identified as Jews. The entire French air crew bravely refused to take advantage of the release and stayed behind with the remaining hostages.

An extremely distressed Israeli cabinet initially rejected any hope of mounting a military rescue operation. It did so chiefly because of the great distance between Israel and Entebbe, more than 2,000 air miles one way. Instead, Prime Minister Yitzhak Rabin's government concentrated on negotiations that they hoped would free the hostages. Because the hijacked aircraft was French owned, Israeli diplomats traveled to Paris to arrange a trade of terrorists for hostages, most likely in either Paris or Djibouti. The Israeli cabinet faced added pressure from relatives of the hostages, who demanded that the government seek a deal at the earliest opportunity.

Israeli defense minister Shimon Peres subsequently ordered the IDF General Staff to review any reasonable military option. Peres's military staff was nearly as pessimistic as the cabinet about a successful rescue operation. Under the direction of IDF chief of staff Mordechai Gur and Israeli Air Force chief Benny Peled, a planning committee led by General Dan Shomron began to plot the suitability of any and all military options. The military planning was done in great secrecy, while Rabin continued to use diplomatic channels to negotiate a possible end to the situation.

The intense planning and training period for Israeli military personnel was backed by a massive intelligence-collection effort to learn everything possible about Entebbe Airport. Military planning was enhanced by the Israelis' knowledge of the construction of Entebbe Airport, which

One of the injured hostages from a hijacked Air France flight being transported by the Israeli military to Tel Aviv on July 7, 1976. The plane had been taken over by pro-Palestinian terrorists on June 27 and landed at Entebbe in Uganda. Non-Jewish passengers were released, but 103 Jews were held captive until released in a daring hostage rescue mission by the Israel Defence Forces on July 4. (AFP/Getty Images)

they had built years before. Israeli agents traveled to Paris to interview the released hostages, which provided sharp insights into both the hostage and terrorist situations. On July 1 a final plan was presented to the IDF General Staff and Defense Minister Peres, and the plan was approved. A reluctant Rabin, appalled by the possibility of having to yield to terrorism, agreed to the plan, subject to cabinet approval. He convened a cabinet meeting for the afternoon of July 3 while military rehearsals continued.

In order to arrive at Entebbe at the desired time of 11:00 p.m. on July 3, the rescue operation left Israeli airspace in midafternoon prior to final approval by the cabinet. When the cabinet unanimously backed the plan, the rescue operation proceeded. Four C-130 aircraft carrying approximately 200 IDF personnel landed on schedule at Entebbe. The rescue force was commanded by Lieutenant Colonel Jonathan Netanyahu, brother of future prime minister Benjamin Netanyahu.

The initial assault team was charged with seizing the old terminal building and releasing the hostages. Jonathan Netanyahu, on the lead aircraft, drove up to the old terminal in a black Mercedes-Benz, an exact replica of the official car of the Ugandan dictator. The Ugandan troops guarding the terminal were initially duped into believing it was a surprise late-night arrival of Amin. One assault element commandeered the air traffic center at the new terminal while another team prepared emergency beacons for the runways. A fourth team refueled the Israeli aircraft using Entebbe's own fuel tanks. A final assault team was to destroy Ugandan aircraft on the ground that might threaten the Israelis' escape. One Israeli aircraft was dispatched to Nairobi, Kenya, to assist in the medical care for the hostages and IDF personnel, while another aircraft flew over Lake Victoria providing electronic support to rescuers.

The IDF force secured the hostages after a brief firefight during which Netanyahu was fatally wounded. The first C-130, carrying the hostages, left the airport within 40 minutes. The entire operation lasted less than an hour on the ground. The Israelis destroyed 11 MiG-17 and

MiG-21 aircraft, probably half of the Ugandan Air Force. The Kenyans welcomed the IDF planes to the Nairobi airport largely because of their hatred for Amin. The planes then refueled before returning to Israel. By midday on July 4 even before the former hostages had reached Israel, most of the world was aware of the successful rescue.

At least 6 terrorists involved in the hijacking were killed, and approximately 20 to 40 Ugandan soldiers supporting the terrorists were believed killed resisting the Israeli rescuers. One IDF soldier was wounded, while the number of wounded terrorists and Ugandan soldiers remains unknown. Three hostages were either killed during the operation or died of wounds later on. One hostage had been removed from the Entebbe old terminal prior to the rescue operation because of illness and was taken to a local hospital and is believed to have been murdered there on Amin's orders. Four Ugandan air traffic controllers from the airport were executed by order of Amin after the rescue operation's success had been revealed to the world.

RALPH MARTIN BAKER

See also
Allon, Yigal; Netanyahu, Benjamin; Popular Front for the Liberation of Palestine; Rabin, Yitzhak

References
Ben-Porat, Yeshayahu, Eitan Haber, and Zeev Schiff. *Entebbe Rescue*. New York: Delacorte, 1977.
Herzog, Chaim. *Heroes of Israel: Profiles of Jewish Courage*. London: Little, Brown, 1989.
Stevenson, William. *90 Minutes at Entebbe*. New York: Bantam, 1976.

Enver Pasha (1881–1922)

Ottoman Empire political leader and army general. Born on November 22, 1881, in Istanbul (Constantinople), Ismail Enver was among those Ottoman military officers who underwent experimental training in Germany and became convinced that the future of their empire lay in modernization.

Graduating from the military academy at Istanbul, Enver entered the army and, as a major serving in the Third Army headquarters in Salonika, was part of the Young Turk movement that overthrew Ottoman sultan Abdul Hamid in 1908. Enver then served as military attaché in Berlin (1909–1911), where he made valuable German contacts. During the 1911–1912 Tripolitan War between the Ottoman Empire and Italy, Enver organized Ottoman defenses in coastal cities before being named governor of Benghazi in 1912.

During the First Balkan War of 1912–1913, Enver led the coup of January 23, 1913, that gave the Young Turks full power. As one of the triumvirate who controlled the Ottoman state (along with Mehmed Taalat Pasha and Ahmed Djemal Pasha), Enver took the title of pasha. He cemented his popularity as chief of staff of the Ottoman armies by recapturing Adrianople on July 22, 1913, during the Second Balkan War of that year. Promoted to brigadier general, Enver became minister of war in February 1914 and conducted a broad purge of the Ottoman officer corps. On October 31, he ordered that all men of military age report for services. The administration was unable to handle this vast influx of personnel, and the ensuing shortfall in agricultural workers had the effect of greatly reducing the crop harvest that fall. In 1915 this grain shortage produced famine conditions in the cities.

The most pro-German of the new Ottoman leaders, Enver favored Ottoman intervention in World War I on the side of the Central Powers. He thus worked closely with German vice admiral Wilhelm Souchon to bring that about by sending Souchon and the ships of the Ottoman Navy to shell Russian ports on the Black Sea. As the chief architect of Ottoman military policy during the war, Enver sought to expand the empire territorially by offensives in the Caucasus region and Russian Central Asia.

Early in the war, Enver assumed personal command of the Ottoman Third Army against Russian forces in the Caucasus region under General Nikolai Yudenich in a brutal campaign through the mountains of eastern Anatolia that culminated in a disastrous Ottoman defeat at Sarikamish on December 29, 1914. In the campaign Enver lost all but 18,000 men of his original force of 95,000. Along with other Ottoman leaders, Enver blamed the defeat on the Armenians, and he supported a program of genocide that diverted resources and eventually led to the deaths of more than 1 million Armenians.

Enver's interest in the Caucasus region intensified following the 1917 revolutions in Russia, and his diversion of military resources there deprived the Ottomans of forces to face the British in Palestine. Enver and the other Young Turks were ousted from power at the end of the war in October 1918, with Enver fleeing to Germany.

In July 1919, a Turkish military tribunal found Enver guilty in absentia of war crimes (the Armenian Genocide) and sentenced him to death. Enver plotted from Turkistan to overthrow the emerging government of Mustafa Kemal (Ataturk) but died on August 4, 1922, while leading Basmachi ethnic troops against Bolshevik Red Army forces.

MARGARET D. SANKEY

See also

Armenians and the Armenian Genocide; Balkan Wars; Caucasus Front, World War I; Djemal Pasha, Ahmed; Italo-Ottoman War; Ottoman Empire; Ottoman Empire, Post–World War I Revolution in; Sarikamish, Battle of; Taalat Pasha, Mehmed; Yudenich, Nikolai Nikolaevich

References

Allen, W. E. D., and Paul Muratoff. *Caucasian Battlefields: A History of the Wars on the Turco-Caucasian Border, 1828–1921*. 1953; reprint, Cambridge: Cambridge University Press, 1969.

Masayuki, Yamauchi, ed. *The Green Crescent under the Red Star: Enver Pasha in Soviet Russia, 1919–1922*. Tokyo: Institute for the Study of Languages and Cultures of Asia and Africa, 1991.

Okay, Kurt. *Enver Pascha: Der grosse Freund Deutschlands*. Berlin: Verlag für Kulturpolitik, 1935.

Ramsaur, Ernest Edmonson. *The Young Turks: Prelude to the Revolution of 1908*. Princeton, NJ: Princeton University Press, 1957.

Shaw, Stanford J., and Ezel Kural Shaw. *History of the Ottoman Empire and Modern Turkey*, Vol. 2, *Reform, Revolution, and Republic: The Rise of Modern Turkey, 1808–1975*. Cambridge: Cambridge University Press, 1977.

Trumpener, Ulrich. *Germany and the Ottoman Empire, 1914–1918*. Princeton, NJ: Princeton University Press, 1968.

Erdoğan, Recep Tayyip (1954–)

Turkish politician, prime minister (2003–2014), and president (2014–). Recep Tayyip Erdoğan was born on February 26, 1954, in Istanbul. As a teenager he became interested in politics, joining the youth group of the Welfare Party, an Islamic fundamentalist political group, at age 15.

After graduation from Istanbul's Marmara University in 1981, Erdoğan embarked on a professional soccer career. Nonetheless, his involvement with the Welfare Party grew deeper, and after a few years as a professional athlete he embarked on a political career, progressing quickly in the 1980s through the ranks of the Welfare Party.

In 1994, Erdoğan was elected mayor of Istanbul. Often thought of as one of Turkey's most charismatic politicians, he earned praise from some of his opponents as well as his followers. Despite their dissatisfaction with his ban on alcohol in Istanbul's cafés, many of Erdoğan's secular critics admitted that he did a good job of cleaning up the city.

As his political career progressed, Erdoğan's pro-Islamist leanings made him popular with devout Muslims who felt slighted by Turkey's secular government; however, this also brought him controversy and legal trouble. In 1998, Erdoğan was convicted of inciting religious hatred after he read a controversial Islamic poem aloud at a public function. The poetry reading earned him a jail sentence; however, he was released after having served just 4 months of his 10-month sentence. That same year the government banned the Welfare Party for allegedly undermining the government's secular policies.

After Erdoğan was released he joined the reformist wing of the Virtue Party, the pro-Islamic party that had been founded on the ruins of the Welfare Party. Working alongside his friend and fellow Virtue Party member, Abdullah Gul, Erdoğan sought to disavow his hard-line religious views. When the Virtue Party was banned in 2001, Erdoğan and Gul formed the Justice and Development Party (AKP).

With pledges that it would not espouse hard-line Islamist ideology, Erdoğan's new party soon gained a larger following, and in the November 2002 legislative elections the AKP won a surprise landslide victory, placing Erdoğan at the forefront of national politics. However, because his previous conviction barred him from holding government office, he was not permitted to become prime minister. Gul took office instead, promising to step down once the law was changed. In February 2003, the Turkish national electoral board ruled that Erdoğan was able to participate in by-elections, and on March 11 Gul tendered his resignation, paving the way for Erdoğan to take office on March 14, 2003.

While there was concern about the AKP's Islamic-based policy, Erdoğan initially focused on economic reform and Turkey's entrance into the European Union. Turkey's economy not only weathered the 2007–2009 recession but also continued to grow, contributing to election victories for it and Erdoğan in 2007 and 2011. Despite protests in 2013 over the AKP's Islamist influence in the government, Erdoğan was elected president by popular vote in August 2014.

Erdoğan agreed to maintain Turkish troops in Afghanistan during the U.S.-led invasion of that country, Operation ENDURING FREEDOM (2001–2014), and more than 500 Turkish troops remained there until 2017 as part of Operation RESOLUTE SUPPORT. However, Erdoğan's government refused to support the Iraq War, which began in March 2003. Nor would he permit coalition forces to utilize Turkish military bases, which complicated U.S. military operations early in the war and badly strained U.S.-Turkish relations. Those relations were further strained beginning in late 2007 when Turkey launched air strikes and then ground incursions against the Kurdistan Workers' Party (PKK) in northern Iraq.

Erdoğan's long tenure in office has not been without problems or controversies. Many critics have decried his increasingly dictatorial ways, which have included strict censorship of the press, crackdowns against political

Recep Tayyip Erdoğan (1954–) has been the president of Turkey since 2014 and previously served as prime minister during 2003–2014. Erdoğan founded the Justice and Development Party (AKP) in 2001. As president, he has increasingly suppressed democratic institutions and moved toward one-man rule. (Mikhail Palinchak/Dreamstime.com)

opponents, judicial tampering, police brutality, and a general drift toward Islamist policies. In late 2012, Erdoğan's government entered into negotiations with the PKK. Those talks yielded a cease-fire in 2013, but by 2015 the deal had unraveled, and the PKK began launching conventional and terrorist raids against Turkish targets, leading Erdoğan to renew military action against it.

Erdoğan only reluctantly entered the fight against the Islamic State of Iraq and Syria (ISIS), and there were credible claims during 2015 that his government was in fact aiding the group in an effort to topple Syria's Bashar al-Assad regime, long a thorn in Turkey's side. Also in 2015, Erdoğan's government finally permitted the United States and its allies to utilize Incirlik Air Base to launch sorties against ISIS. Erdoğan angered the U.S. government during 2015–2018, however, by carrying out raids against Syrian Kurds who had been engaged in the fight against ISIS. In November 2015 Turkey shot down a Russian warplane that it claimed had strayed into its airspace, drawing an angry response from Moscow and causing major concerns that the incident might escalate into a NATO-Russia conflict. Meanwhile, a series of bloody terrorist attacks in Turkey during 2015 and 2016 led to charges that Erdoğan's government was not adequately protecting the country.

The Turkish military had long regarded itself as the guardian of secular democracy in Turkey and had staged several coups to ensure that end. Despite Erdoğan's earlier purges of the officer corps (which included a number being sentenced to prison for long terms on what many allege to be trumped-up charges) to prevent it from interfering against his government, on July 15, 2016, a small number of army officers attempted to oust Erdoğan. The attempted coup failed within 24 hours, with Erdoğan calling for and receiving large public demonstrations of support. Erdoğan's government then rounded up more than 6,000 people, including members of the military, political critics, and the press. Many observers feared that Erdoğan would use the attempted coup to strengthen his grip on power and to move his nation away from moderate secularism. Some of Erdoğan's critics even suggested that he had engineered the coup himself in order to purge his detractors and political enemies.

The abortive coup also precipitated a deterioration in U.S.-Turkish relations when Erdoğan demanded that the American government extradite Turkish cleric and Erdoğan detractor Fethullah Gulen to Turkey to stand trial for sedition. Erdoğan's government claimed that the cleric, who had been living in the United States for many years, had played a major role in fomenting the attempted putsch. At the same time Erdoğan reached out to Moscow, seemingly healing the rift between Turkey and Russia.

Following several terrorist attacks in Turkey, which Ankara blamed on ISIS, on August 20, 2016, Erdoğan launched Operation EUPHRATES SHIELD, a major military operation by Turkey's army and air force across the Euphrates River into northern Syria. He vowed that this would continue until the threat to Turkey was ended.

Although early in his presidency Erdoğan had loosened many restrictions on Kurdish culture, he clamped down again beginning in 2015 after the collapse of negotiations with the Kurds. This accelerated during the state of emergency he declared after the failed coup against him in 2016.

Clearly, Erdoğan used the failed 2016 coup to consolidate his growing power. By the spring of 2017 some 47,000 people had been jailed (including some 120 journalists, more than in any other nation in the world), and 120,000 others had been fired or suspended from their jobs in what can only be described as a naked power grab by Erdoğan. A national referendum held on April 18, 2017, approved 18 amendments to the Turkish Constitution by a margin of 51.5–48.5 percent. In effect, this replaced Turkey's existing parliamentary government with a presidential system in which the president enjoys greatly expanded powers. The state of emergency proclaimed after the failed coup also remained in place, with Erdoğan announcing on May 22 that it would be extended indefinitely until the country achieved "welfare and peace." This allowed Erdoğan to issue sweeping decrees without parliamentary oversight or review by the constitutional court. By late July 2017 Erdoğan's government had seized more than 950 Turkish businesses worth more than $10 billion, all of them purportedly linked to Fethullah Gullen, the Muslim cleric said by the government to have been behind the 2016 coup.

Erdoğan handily won the June 2018 presidential election, which made him both head of state and head of government. At the same time, Turkey has been gripped by a serious debt and currency crisis, precipitated largely by Erdoğan's profligate deficit spending and his highly unorthodox regulation of interest rates. The result of this, which continued as of August 2018, has been high inflation and anemic economic growth. Although President Donald Trump has periodically praised Erdoğan for his strong leadership, relations between Washington and Ankara continued to erode during 2018.

A main irritant in the relationship was Erdoğan's treatment of U.S.-backed Kurds in Syria and Iraq and Turkey's military operations in northern Syria during 2018. The latter was designed to stop Kurdish incursions into Turkey from Syria. A second contentious issue between the two nations was Turkey's temporary alliance with Moscow vis-à-vis the Syrian Civil War, which Ankara has cynically used mainly to defeat its Kurdish foes. A third issue was Turkey's long-term detainment of a U.S. pastor. Ankara insisted that the clergyman had engaged in anti-Erdoğan activities, which the U.S. government flatly refuted. In August 2018 when negotiations between Washington and Ankara broke down over the clergyman's release, the Trump administration turned up the heat and slapped huge tariffs on Turkish steel and aluminum imports. On August 10, 2018, the Turkish lira hit an all-time low of 6.24 liras per U.S. dollar. The precipitous drop was blamed largely on the collapse of the negotiations and the announcement of more U.S. tariffs targeting Turkish exports. On August 15 Erdoğan retaliated against the latest U.S. tariffs, placing tariffs on a variety of goods imported from the United States, including automobiles. Erdoğan continues to poursue an independent course in foreign policy and consolidate his power within Turkey, silencing the press and carrying out purges of the opposition.

Tamar Burris, Paul G. Pierpaoli Jr., and Spencer C. Tucker

See also
Iraq; Kurds; Syria; Turkey

References
Mango, Andrew. *The Turks Today.* New York: Overlook, 2004.
Pope, Nicole, and Hugh Pope. *Turkey Unveiled: A History of Modern Turkey.* New York: Overlook, 2011.
Segal, David. "Turkey Wages War on 'Enemies' in Business." *New York Times,* July 12, 2017.
Vatandas, Aydogan. *Hungry for Power: Erdogan's Witch Hunt and Abuse of State Power.* Clifton, NJ: Blue Dome, 2015.

Erzincan, 1230 Battle of (August 10–12, 1230)

A decisive military engagement, also known as the Battle of Yassi Chemen, fought between Seljuk Turk forces and the Khwarazmian army of Jalal ad-Din in August 1230. Following the Mongol conquest of Khwarazm, Jalal ad-Din, the son of the last Khwarazmian ruler, fled to India and then to Persia, where he was recognized as a sultan by local tribal leaders.

Rallying his forces, Jalal ad-Din sought to expand his sphere of influence by threatening the territory of the Abbasid caliph of Baghdad in 1224. This led to three attacks on Georgia during 1225–1228. Jalal ad-Din captured the strategically important fortress of Khilat (northwest of Lake Van) from al-Ashraf, the Ayyubid sultan of Damascus. In response, al-Ashraf concluded an alliance with Seljuk sultan Ala ad-Din Kayqubad (Kai-Qobad, r. 1220–1237) I of Konya.

During August 10–12, 1230, al-Ashraf and Kayqubad decisively defeated Jalal ad-Din in battle near Erzincan. The victory proved to be bittersweet. Although al-Ashraf and Kayqubad removed the immediate threat to their territories, they had also largely destroyed the last army that served as a buffer between them and the Mongols.

While attempting to escape in disguise, Jalal ad-Din was discovered and killed in 1231. His short-lived sultanate was conquered by the Mongols. After the death of Ala ad-Din Kayqubad in 1237, the Seljuks suffered the same fate in 1243.

Alexander Mikaberidze and Spencer C. Tucker

See also
Abbasid Caliphate; Seljuk Dynasty

Reference
Grousset, René. *The Empire of the Steppes: A History of Central Asia.* Rutgers, NJ: Rutgers University Press, 1988.

Erzincan, 1916 Battle of (July 25–26, 1916)

Important World War I battle on the Caucasus front. The city of Erzincan (today the capital of Erzincan Province) is located in Turkish Armenia in northeastern Turkey about a mile from the Euphrates River. Erzincan was not only a center for the production of civilian goods but also served as the headquarters for an Ottoman Army corps. The facilities at Erzincan, which included a barracks and factories geared to military production, made the city a lucrative target for the Russian Army, which in the summer of 1916 appeared to have the momentum following several earlier successes. The Battle of Erzincan pitted the Russian Caucasus Army commanded by General Nikolai Yudenich against the recently reinforced Ottoman Third Army led by Abdul Kerim and was the last major action on the Caucasus front.

Erzincan was a key objective of the Russian offensive that began on July 12, 1916, with the capture of Mama Khatun. In this operation, Russian forces gained control of the heights of Naglika and took an Ottoman position near the Durum Darasi River. Also, their cavalry pierced the Boz-Tapa-Mertekli Line.

The Russians reached Erzincan on July 25, 1916, and took the largely evacuated city in only two days. Erzincan was relatively untouched by battle and yielded a considerable amount of supplies and equipment. Ottoman forces then retreated to the southeast to Mosul and Sivas. With their victory at Erzincan, Russian forces had advanced 80 miles and were well placed to strike at Sivas, Angora, and Istanbul (Constantinople). They could also threaten the Mediterranean port of Adana and were even in position to sever communications and trade between the Ottoman Empire and Europe. The capture of Erzincan also provided proof positive of the execution there of Armenian civilians by the Ottomans.

Yudenich pursued the withdrawing Ottomans until the end of August. The siphoning off of his forces owing to Russian reversals inflicted by the Central Powers on the Eastern Front precluded further offensives on this front, however.

ANTHONY J. SCHMAUS

See also
Armenians and the Armenian Genocide; Caucasus Front, World War I; Yudenich, Nikolai Nikolaevich

References
Erickson, Edward J. *Ordered to Die: A History of the Ottoman Army in the First World War.* Westport, CT: Greenwood, 2000.
Halsey, Francis Whiting. *The Literary Digest: History of the World War,* Vol. 8, *Turkey and the Balkans, August 1914–October 1918.* New York: Funk and Wagnalls, 1920.
Havannisian, Richard G. *Remembrance and Denial: The Case of the Armenian Genocide.* Detroit: Wayne State University Press, 1998.
Weber, Frank G. *Eagles on the Crescent: Germany, Austria, and the Diplomacy of the Turkish Alliance, 1914–1918.* Ithaca, NY: Cornell University Press, 1970.

Erzurum, First Treaty of (July 28, 1823)

Peace agreement between Persia and the Ottoman Empire. In 1821, the Qajar dynasty of Persia decided to take advantage of the Ottoman preoccupation with the Greek Revolt against that empire (1821–1832) to claim some of territories in Iraq and eastern Anatolia. The ensuing Persian in Iraq stalled but was successful in the north, where Persian crown prince Abbas Mirza won the Battle of Khuy (May 1822).

On July 28, 1823, the two sides negotiated a peace accord that restored the border as determined by the Treaties of Zuhab (Qasre-Shirin) in 1639 and Kuran in 1746. The treaty recognized Iraq (including Baghdad and the Shatt al-Arab), western Caucasia, and Kurdish territories as part of the Ottoman Empire but granted southeastern Caucasia to Persia. The sultan allowed Iranian merchants to enter the Ottoman territory and recognized Persian claims to sovereignty over some border tribes.

ALEXANDER MIKABERIDZE

See also
Abbas Mirza; Mahmud II, Sultan; Zuhab, Treaty of

References
Kashani-Sabet, Firoozeh. *Frontier Fictions: Shaping the Iranian Nation, 1804–1946.* London: I. B. Tauris, 2000.
Masters, Bruce. "The Treaties of Erzurum (1823 and 1848) and the Changing Status of Iranians in the Ottoman Empire." *Iranian Studies* 24 (1991): 3–15.

Erzurum, Second Treaty of (May 31, 1847)

Peace agreement between Persia and the Ottoman Empire on determining the international boundary between the two states. The treaty came in the wake of the 1823 Treaty of Erzurum that established the border along the lines set by the Treaty of Zuhab (1639). However, in the 1830s both sides routinely violated its provisions, and in 1843 under the auspices of Britain and Russia, a joint Ottoman-Persian commission was established to discuss the border question and eventually produced the 1847 Treaty of Erzurum.

Signed on May 31, 1847, the agreement made Iran cede its claim to Sulaymaniyya (northeastern Iraq), while the Ottomans recognized Persian sovereignty over the city and port of Muhammara (Khoramshahr, in southwestern Iran) and the island of Khidhr (Abadan). Although the strategically important Shatt al-Arab remained in Ottoman hands, Persia secured the right to navigate it from its mouth to the point of contact of the two countries' frontiers. The Delimitation Commission, on which Britain and Russia served as mediators, functioned during 1848–1876.

ALEXANDER MIKABERIDZE

See also
Erzurum, First Treaty of; Zuhab, Treaty of

References
Kashani-Sabet, Firoozeh. *Frontier Fictions: Shaping the Iranian Nation, 1804–1946.* London: I. B. Tauris, 2000.
Masters, Bruce. "The Treaties of Erzurum (1823 and 1848) and the Changing Status of Iranians in the Ottoman Empire." *Iranian Studies* 24 (1991): 3–15.

Erzurum Offensive (January 10–March 25, 1916)

Russian World War I offensive on the Caucasus front. Compared with the towering Pontic Alps to the north and the forbidding highlands to the east, the Erzurum area in present-day eastern Turkey is comparatively accessible geographically. In 1916, the Kars-Erzurum road was the only important land communication between Anatolia and Caucasia. After its abortive advance on Sarikamish in the winter of 1914–1915, the battered Ottoman Third Army had withdrawn to a fortified line on the hills east of Köprüköy, about 60 miles from Erzurum.

Following the Ottoman victory over the Allied expeditionary force at Gallipoli, General Nikolai Yudenich, commander of the Russian Caucasus Army, rightly assumed that the Ottomans would reinforce the Caucasus front with divisions from Thrace. He calculated that these reinforcements could arrive from the early spring of 1916. Accordingly, Yudenich decided to preempt the expected Ottoman strike with a Russian winter offensive that he hoped would destroy the Ottoman Third Army. The attack would focus on breaking the Ottoman lines east of Köprüköy and advancing on the fortress city of Erzurum.

While Yudenich selected favorable terrain for his offensive, ground that could be negotiated by troops even in the middle of the terrible Caucasian winter, he also chose the point where the Ottoman lines were strongest. Abdul Kerim Pasha, commander of the Third Army who was charged with defending the entire 300-mile-long Caucasus front, had all his divisions but one concentrated in the defense of the Erzurum area. Still, the length of the front meant that his 65,000 men and 100 guns were insufficient for anything but a thin screen along the entire front. Yudenich had only 80,000 infantry himself, but he concentrated vastly superior numbers at the point of attack (35,000 men against 13,000 Ottomans). With more than 230 guns, he also had a decisive advantage in artillery.

During the last months of 1915, the Russian Caucasus Army carefully and secretly prepared for the offensive. Its assault on the Köprüköy lines on January 10, 1916, took the Ottoman defenders by surprise, although a diversionary attack by the II Turkistan Corps over the heavily broken ground of the Karadag mountain range on the Russian right was checked by the Ottomans, who enjoyed the protection of deep trenches and well-placed machine guns.

On January 12 the I Caucasian Corps attacked over the plains in the center but was repelled with serious loss. Yet the Ottoman lines were too weak to resist for long. On January 14 Yudenich launched a general attack, and the superior Russian numbers overran the Ottoman defenders.

On January 16 a Russian drive around the northern flank of Cilligül Hill threatened to cut off the Ottoman defenders in the Aras Plain. That night Abdul Kerim ordered a general retreat to the Erzurum fortified area. The Russians failed to pursue vigorously, and the Third Army reached its fallback position in comparatively good order. It had sustained some 20,000 casualties, almost a third of its strength, and lost about 30 guns. Russian casualties were some 12,000.

The next obstacle facing the Russians was the Erzurum fortified area proper. Nature rendered Erzurum an impressive stronghold. All approaches from the north, east, and south ran over or cut through mountain ranges considered impassable, especially in winter.

This natural protection had been improved since the 1880s with a series of 15 independent forts arrayed in two lines, extending in a semicircle. These forts were of modern construction and could withstand everything except the newest heavy siege guns of German or Austrian manufacture; the Russian Caucasus Army had no such guns, however.

Bristling with more than 300 artillery pieces and connected with carefully prepared fieldworks, the Erzurum forts constituted a formidable obstacle. Fully manned, however, they required about 75,000 men, and the Third Army's

Ottoman army soldiers captured by the Russians during their Erzurum Offensive of January 10–March 25, 1916. (Bettmann/Getty Images)

effective strength did not exceed 50,000 after Köprüköy. Still, the Ottoman General Staff considered Erzurum an impregnable stronghold and believed that it would hold out for months, as it had in fighting against the Russians in 1877–1878. That may have been one reason the Ottomans did not quickly reinforce Erzurum; another was the primitive state of communications in Anatolia.

Yudenich was not a man to be discouraged by the formidable but undermanned fortifications that his army faced. He enjoyed a significant numerical advantage, and he knew that Ottoman morale was low. Yudenich also chose the weakest spot in the defensive perimeter for his attack.

Due north from Erzurum, the Gürcü-Bogaz Defile opened on to the plains of the Karasu River. The area was enclosed by mountain ranges considered impassable in winter and defended by only two unsupported forts. Yudenich concentrated three rifle divisions in this sector. The assignment was to scale the slopes of the Kargapazar and Dumlu Mountains and encircle the forts, then break through to the plains beyond. The remainder of the army would attack frontally the main fortified lines on the Deve-Boyun Ridge and the Palandšken Mountain in order to pin the Ottomans and force them to commit their few reserves.

On the afternoon of February 11, the Russians launched their offensive. In spite of tough Ottoman resistance, the attack progressed favorably. The defenders at Fort Dalangšz on Deve-Boyun were surprised and fell to the Russians at dawn on February 12. Furious Ottoman counterattacks failed to retake it. The defenders at Forts Çoban-Dede, Kaburga, Ortayuk, and Gez repelled the attackers, but the main Russian attack in the Gürcü-Bogaz Defile succeeded.

The Ottoman X Corps was poorly led, and its three divisions fought widely separated. The Russians encircled and captured Fort Kara-Gšbek, the northernmost of the Erzurum strongholds, on February 12. The next day the flanking columns, passing over the supposedly impassable mountains, converged on Fort Tafet, which fell on February 14. The way to the Karasu Plain was now open.

On February 15, the Ottomans began to withdraw from Erzurum. Russian aircraft detected their rearward movement, but the II Turkistan Corps failed to cut their retreat. What remained of the Ottoman Third Army escaped the trap in some semblance of order. It had lost 10,000 killed or wounded, 5,000 captured, and perhaps another 10,000 as stragglers during the retreat. The Russians captured 327 guns in Erzurum; their own casualties in the battle totaled about 9,000 men.

Erzurum had held out for only four days. Its loss had a disastrous effect on the Third Army's logistics and morale. Yet the Russians failed to follow up their spectacular success with a vigorous pursuit. Following the defeat, the Ottomans were able to recover and stiffen their resistance. By the end of March 1916, the Russian offensive was over.

DIERK WALTER

See also
Caucasus Front, World War I; Gallipoli Campaign; Ottoman Empire; Sarikamish, Battle of; Yudenich, Nikolai Nikolaevich

References
Allen, W. E. D., and Paul Muratoff. *Caucasian Battlefields: A History of the Wars on the Turco-Caucasian Border, 1828–1921*. Cambridge: Cambridge University Press, 1953.

Erickson, Edward J. *Ordered to Die: A History of the Ottoman Army in the First World War*. Westport, CT: Greenwood, 2000.

Reynolds, Michael A. *Shattering Empires: The Clash and Collapse of the Ottoman and Russian Empires, 1908–1918*. New York: Cambridge University Press, 2011.

Eshkol, Levi (1895–1969)

Israel's first minister of defense (1948–1951) and its minister of finance (1952–1963) and prime minister (1963–1969). Levi Eshkol was born Levi Shkolnik on October 25, 1895, in Oratova village near Kiev in Ukraine. Following a traditional Jewish education in Oratova, he attended a Hebrew high school in Vilna, Lithuania. At age 16 he joined the Zionist youth group Tzeirei Tzion (Youth of Zion), and in 1914 he immigrated to Palestine, where he worked as an agricultural laborer and political activist.

In 1918 Eshkol joined the Jewish Legion of the British Army. After World War I he helped found Degania Beth, one of the first kibbutzim in Palestine. He was elected to the first three sessions of the Assembly of Palestine Jewry. In 1921 he took part in the founding of Histadrut (the General Confederation of Labor). He joined the Mapai, the left-of-center workers' party, in 1929, eventually becoming a member of its central committee. During the 1930s he worked to bring Jewish immigrants from Germany to Palestine. He also helped found the Mekorot Water Company, Israel's water utility, in 1937 and served as its chief executive until 1951.

In 1940 Eshkol joined Haganah, the Jewish self-defense military organization. In 1947 he was responsible for recruiting what became the Israel Defense Forces (IDF). Upon Israeli independence he played an important role in helping to secure arms from abroad during the ensuing Israeli War of Independence (1948–1949). During 1950–1951 he was director-general of the Ministry of Defense. He then became minister of agriculture and development, and in 1952 he became minister of finance, a post he held for 12 years. In this key position he helped secure funds for economic development, absorb the many Jewish refugees who immigrated to Israel, and secure modern military equipment for the IDF. He served briefly as deputy prime minister and was favored by many Israelis to replace Prime Minister David Ben-Gurion when the latter temporarily left the government in late 1953. The Mapai Party chose Moshe Sharett as party leader instead.

Ben-Gurion returned as prime minister following the 1961 elections but resigned on June 16, 1963. Eshkol followed him as prime minister and remained in the post until his death in 1969. Among his accomplishments was the opening of diplomatic relations with West Germany. He also established cultural ties with the Soviet Union, which then allowed some Jews to immigrate to Israel. In May 1964, Eshkol was the first Israeli prime minister to visit the United States.

Eshkol's most important accomplishment was undoubtedly that of guiding the nation through the period just before and during the 1967 Six-Day War. His initial reluctance to accept his own military leaders' calls for a preemptive strike was at the time seen as timid. His decision to delay proved prescient, however, for it served to increase Egyptian president Gamal Abdel Nasser's provocations and created diplomatic support for Israel's position, especially in the United States, when the government did indeed launch the war. On the commencement of the June 1967 war, Eshkol created a government of national unity by giving the post of minister of defense to Moshe Dayan and by bringing Menachem Begin of the Herut Party into the cabinet. Eshkol also worked to find new sources of supplies after France initiated a military boycott of Israel. Eshkol died of a heart attack in the prime minister's residence in Jerusalem on February 26, 1969.

JOHN DAVID RAUSCH JR. AND SPENCER C. TUCKER

See also
Begin, Menachem; Ben-Gurion, David; Haganah; Israeli War of Independence; Nasser, Gamal Abdel; Six-Day War

References
Hammel, Eric. *Six Days in June: How Israel Won the 1967 Arab-Israeli War*. New York: Scribner, 1992.

Oren, Michael B. *Six Days of War: June 1967 and the Making of the Modern Middle East*. Novato, CA: Presidio, 2003.

Prittie, Terence. *Eshkol: The Man and the Nation*. New York: Pitman, 1969.

Eumenes of Cardia (ca. 361–316 BCE)

Macedonian general and one of the Diadochi (successors) who fought for control of the empire created by Alexander III the Great. Eumenes was born in Cardia in Thrace circa 361 BCE. At around the age of 19 he became the personal scribe (*grammateus*) to Philip II of Macedon and then Philip's son Alexander. Eumenes took part in Alexander's invasion of the Persian Empire beginning in 334 and was given a minor military command in 326 during Alexander's Indian Campaign. After the death of Hephaestion in 324, Eumenes was promoted to the position of cavalry commander within the Companion Cavalry, replacing Perdiccas, who was promoted to Hephaestion's former office.

After Alexander's death in 323, Eumenes was appointed as governor (satrap) of Paphlagonia and the yet unconquered Cappadocia. Calls for support in securing Cappadocia were ignored owing to Eumenes's non-Macedonian heritage. Eventually, however, Perdiccas came to his assistance and helped him secure the region.

During the ensuing Wars of the Diadochi, Eumenes allied with Perdiccas against a coalition that included Antipater, Antigonus I Monophthalmus, Craterus, and Ptolemy I Soter. When Perdiccas was killed in Egypt, Eumenes assumed the leadership of the faction and continued campaigning in Asia Minor. He fought two indecisive battles with Antigonus, at Paraetacene in 317 and then again at Gabiene in 316. During the latter battle, however, Antigonus had captured Eumenes's camp along with its baggage, treasure, and families of the soldier. Antigonus was able to turn some of Eumenes's officers, who gave him to Antigonus in return for their baggage, treasure, and families. Antigonus respected Eumenes as a general but nonetheless had him executed.

EVAN M. PITT AND SPENCER C. TUCKER

See also
Alexander III the Great; Antigonus I Monophthalmus; Demetrius I Poliorcetes; Diadochi, Wars of the; Gabiene, Battle of; Paraetacene, Battle of; Perdiccas; Ptolemy I Soter

References
Anson, Edward M. *Eumenes of Cardia: A Greek among Macedonians*. Leiden: Brill, 2004.
Waterfield, Robin. *Dividing the Spoils: The War for Alexander the Great's Empire*. New York: Oxford University Press, 2011.

Eumenes I of Pergamum (r. 263–241 BCE)

Eumenes was the nephew and adopted heir of Philetaeru, ruler of the kingdom of Pergamum located in the Aeolis region of western Asia Minor. Eumenes, who succeeded his uncle to the throne in 263, took further steps toward the independence of Pergamum from the Seleucid Empire than his predecessor and ruled for 22 years until his death in 241.

An inscription suggests that Eumenes (or possibly his predecessor) had established mercenary garrisons at Attalia in Lydia and Philetaerea-under-Ida in war with the Seleucid Empire in 262 that saw Eumenes defeat the Seleucid king Antiochus I in a battle at Sardis.

Celtic tribes of Gauls had crossed from Europe to Asia in the first quarter of the third century BCE and settled on both sides of the Halys River (the modern-day Kızılırmak). They levied tribute on the whole of Asia Minor as far as the Taurus Mountains from their territory known as Galatia. Eumenes too appears to have paid them tribute.

During his rule Eumenes appears to have concentrated on securing and consolidating his possessions in Asia Minor and never adopted the title of king. Allegedly dying of drunkenness, he was succeeded by Attalus I.

DAVID HARTHEN

See also
Antiochus I Soter; Lydia; Pergamum; Seleucid Empire

References
Evans, Richard. *A History of Pergamum: Beyond Hellenistic Kingship*. London: Bloomsbury Publishing, 2012.
Hansen, Esther V. *The Attalids of Pergamon*. Ithaca, NY: Cornell University Press, 1971.

Eumenes II of Pergamum (r. 197–159 BCE)

Eumenes was the eldest son of Attalus I, king of Pergamum; the brother of Attalus II; and the father of Attalus III. During Eumenes's reign the Pergamene kingdom in the Aeolis region of far western Asia Minor rose to the height of its power. Eumenes II was born sometime before 220 BCE and became king in 197. As ruler, he embarked on an extensive building program, making his capital of Pergamum one of the beautiful cities of the Hellenistic world.

Eumenes inherited his father's alliance with Rome and, in refusing an alliance with Seleucid king Antiochus III the Great, provoked the Syrian-Roman War (196–188), playing a decisive role in the Battle of Magnesia in 190. With the Peace of Apamea in 188, Eumenes was given most of the Seleucid territories in Asia Minor and the Thracian Chersonese, including the city of Lysimacheia.

Eumenes's Roman allies gave him diplomatic support in his war against King Prusias I of Bithynia. War between Eumenes and Pharnaces of Pontus between 182 and 179 resulted in victory for Eumenes and more territorial gains.

In 172 Eumenes denounced Perseus of Macedon to the Roman Senate, which led to the outbreak of the Third Macedonian War (171–168) against Perseus, during which Eumenes sacked Abdera. However, political maneuvering by Eumenes during the conflict aroused the suspicion of Rome, which lost trust in him. Eumenes died in 159 and was succeeded by his brother Attalus II of Pergamum.

DAVID HARTHEN

See also
Antiochus III Megas; Magnesia, Battle of; Pergamum; Syrian-Roman War

References
Evans, Richard. *A History of Pergamum: Beyond Hellenistic Kingship*. London: Bloomsbury Publishing, 2012.
Hansen, Esther V. *The Attalids of Pergamon*. Ithaca, NY: Cornell University Press, 1971.

Euphrates River

The Euphrates River is one of the two great rivers of Mesopotamia, the other being the Tigris. Located west of the Tigris River, the Euphrates originates in the mountains of Armenia and first flows in a southwest direction toward the Taurus Mountains before it proceeds southward. It is the longest river of Western Asia. From its source of the Murat River to the confluence with the Tigris, the Euphrates is some 1,900 miles. Of these, 760 miles are in Turkey, 440 miles in Syria, and 660 miles in Iraq. The Shatt al-Arab, which connects the Euphrates and the Tigris with the Persian Gulf, is some 120 miles in length.

"Mesopotamia" is a Greek term meaning "lands between the two rivers" and was generally used as a reference to the actual region and at times as a generic term for the earliest civilizations that developed along these two rivers. The region was then fought over between a succession of empires, with the last of these being the Ottoman. With the defeat of the Ottoman Empire in World War I, the region's borders were redrawn in the Treaty of Lausanne (July 24, 1923).

Clause 109 of the Treaty of Lausanne stipulated that the three states of the Euphrates region (Turkey, France for its mandate of Syria, and the United Kingdom for its mandate of Iraq) were to reach a mutual agreement on the use of its water and construction of any hydraulic installation. A 1946 agreement between Turkey and Iraq required Turkey to report to Iraq on any hydraulic changes it made on the Tigris-Euphrates river system and allowed Iraq to construct dams on Turkish territory to manage the flow of the Euphrates.

Turkey and Syria completed their first dams on the Euphrates River within a year of one another: the Tabqa Dam (better known as the Euphrates Dam) by Syria in 1973 and the Keban Dam by Turkey in 1974. Concurrently with filling the reservoirs, the region underwent a severe drought, sharply reducing the river flow. An international crisis ensued during which the Iraqi government threatened to bomb the Tabqa Dam. Iraq and Syria eventually reached agreement. Another crisis, although devoid of military threats, occurred in 1981 when Turkey almost emptied the Keban Dam reservoir to temporarily increase its hydroelectricity production.

In 1984, the Turkish government pledged to ensure a flow of water amounting to at least 18,000 cubic feet per second into Syria. A treaty to that effect was signed between the two states in 1987. Another such agreement in 1989 between Syria and Iraq set the amount of water flowing into Iraq at 60 percent of the amount Syria receives from Turkey.

In 2008, Turkey, Syria, and Iraq established the Joint Trilateral Committee to manage the water in the Tigris-Euphrates basin. On September 3, 2009, another agreement was signed to this effect. On April 15, 2014, concurrent with a deterioration in Syrian-Turkish relations following the beginning of the Syrian Civil War (2011–), Turkey began to reduce the flow of the Euphrates into Syria and Iraq. The flow was cut off completely on May 16, 2014, with the result that the Euphrates now effectively terminates at the Turkish-Syrian border in what is a clear violation of the 1987 treaty.

SPENCER C. TUCKER

See also
Iraq; Lausanne, Second Treaty of; Mesopotamia; Shatt al-Arab Waterway; Syria; Syrian Civil War; Tigris River; Turkey

References
Hillel, Daniel. *Rivers of Eden: The Struggle for Water and the Quest for Peace in the Middle East*. New York: Oxford University Press, 1994.
Kliot, Nurit. *Water Resources and Conflict in the Middle East*. New York: Routledge, 1994.
Shapland, Greg. *Rivers of Discord: International Water Disputes in the Middle East*. New York: Palgrave Macmillan, 1997.

Eurymedon, Battle of (ca. 468–466 BCE)

The Battle of Eurymedon was a major Greek naval victory over the Persians near Phaselis in Pamphylia (southern Asia Minor) that occurred in 468–466 BCE. The Athenian Cimon commanded the Delian League fleet of 300 triremes (200 Athenian and 100 allied ships); the Persians probably had around 350 ships. This was Persia's last direct attempt to challenge Athenian naval superiority in the operations following the Second Persian War (480–479).

Cimon attacked the Persian fleet while it was mustering, supported by an army, at the mouth of the Eurymedon River before the imminent arrival of 80 Phoenician warships en route from Cyprus to reinforce it. The Athenian ships were carrying more hoplite marines than previously, reflecting a greater emphasis on amphibious operations. The ships had also been modified to make it easier for the marines to move around in an engagement. The Persians were quickly driven onto the shore and sought refuge with their forces ashore. Cimon landed his marines and defeated the Persian troops, then intercepted and destroyed the Phoenician reinforcements. The scale of the Persian disaster was great: 200 ships captured, in addition to an unknown number sunk, and the battle gave Athens naval control in the Aegean for most of the rest of the century.

IAIN SPENCE

See also
Greco-Persian Wars

References
Cawkwell, George. *The Greek Wars: The Failure of Persia.* Oxford: Oxford University Press, 2005.

Meiggs, Russell. *The Athenian Empire.* Oxford, UK: Clarendon, 1972.

Eustace III of Boulogne (ca. 1058–1125)

Count of Boulogne (ca. 1089–1125) and participant in the First Crusade (1096–1099). Born around 1058, Eustace was the eldest son of Eustace II, count of Boulogne, and Ida of Bouillon. Eustace III succeeded to his father's county of Boulogne in northern France; his younger brothers, Godfrey of Bouillon and Baldwin, were to become the first two Frankish rulers of the Kingdom of Jerusalem.

Eustace led a contingent of his own in the First Crusade, although it is unclear whether he traveled to Constantinople with his brothers or with others; he and Godfrey often campaigned together. At the siege of Nicaea (modern-day Iznik, Turkey), Eustace helped lead the initial crusader attack, and he aided in the rescue of Bohemund of Taranto's beleaguered troops at the Battle of Dorylaion (July 1, 1097). At Antioch (modern-day Antakya, Turkey), Eustace and Godfrey defeated an ambush early in the siege. Later, Eustace, Robert of Normandy, and Adhemar of Le Puy defended the crusader camp while the other leaders attacked the Turkish reinforcements. In the final assault on the city, Eustace led one of the crusader divisions. He participated in the Council of Princes that sought to resolve the conflict between Raymond of Saint-Gilles and Bohemund (November 1098). Shortly thereafter, Eustace assisted Raymond in sacking Ma'arrat an-Nu'man in December 1098.

In July 1099 Eustace and Tancred successfully raided Nablus. Eustace gained great fame at the capture of Jerusalem (July 15). It was he, Godfrey, and their men who breached the walls of the city while the other crusaders despaired of victory. Shortly after Godfrey's election, Eustace and Tancred received the surrender of Nablus, and on their return they took an Egyptian scouting party by surprise. At the Battle of Ascalon (August 12, 1099), Eustace commanded one of the crusader divisions.

Eustace returned home a few months later. On Godfrey's death, Baldwin I became king of Jerusalem, and when he died in 1118 Eustace was elected as his successor by a group of the magnates of the kingdom. Eustace set off for the Holy Land, but upon his arrival in Apulia a few weeks later he learned that Baldwin II (of Bourcq) had been crowned king. Without attempting to contest this second election, Eustace returned to Boulogne. Twelfth-century histories and the early crusade epics depict Eustace III as one of the campaign's heroes. In his epitaph, written at Cluny, he is called "the captor of Jerusalem and the dread of the Eastern empires."

HEATHER J. TANNER

See also
Ascalon, Battle of; Baldwin I of Jerusalem; Dorylaion, Battle of; Godfrey of Bouillon; Jerusalem, Crusader Siege of

References
Murray, Alan V. *The Crusader Kingdom of Jerusalem: A Dynastic History, 1099–1125.* Oxford, UK: Prosopographica & Genealogica, 2000.

Tanner, Heather J. "In His Brothers' Shadow: The Crusading Career and Reputation of Eustace III of Boulogne." In *The Crusades: Other Experiences, Alternate Perspectives*, ed. Khalil J. Semaan. Binghamton, NY: Global Academic Publishing, 2003.

Evagoras I (ca. 435–374 BCE)

King of Salamis in Cyprus circa 411–374 BCE who was instrumental in achieving Cypriot independence from Persian rule in the late fifth century. Despite being nominally a part of the Persian (Achaemenid) Empire throughout the fifth century after its conquest by Cyrus, the larger cities of Cyprus retained a degree of independence with their own ruling dynasts.

Evagoras I was born around 435. During his youth Salamis had fallen under Phoenician domination, and Evagoras was exiled to Cilicia. While there, he gathered loyal followers and in 411 returned to the island and seized the Salaminian throne. As king, he orchestrated a period of Hellenization on Cyprus and encouraged ties with Athens. During the next two decades he extended his control over almost the entire island. In 391 the remaining free cities appealed to Persian king Artaxerxes II for assistance. The Athenians sent 10 triremes to support Evagoras, but they were captured en route by the Spartans.

Persia had no interest in seeing a unified and Hellenized Cyprus, but Evagoras's revolt lasted a decade, with assistance from Egypt. In this time he extended his power to parts of Cilicia and Phoenicia. Eventually in 382 the Persians sent an overwhelming force. The Persians destroyed his fleet in the Battle of Citium, and Evagoras was forced to come to terms. He was permitted to retain the throne of Salamis but was forced to give up designs on the rest of Cyprus. Evagoras was assassinated in 374 in a court intrigue and was succeeded by his son Nicocles.

RUSSELL BUZBY

See also

Achaemenid Empire; Cyprus

References

Costa, Eugene A. "Evagoras I and the Persians, ca. 411 to 391 B.C." *Historia* 23 (1974): 40–56.

Spyridakis, Konstantinos. *Evagoras I von Salamis*. Stuttgart: W. Kohlhammer, 1935.

Exodus Incident (July 11–August 22, 1947)

The ill-fated voyage of the ship *Exodus 1947* (July 11–August 22, 1947) highlighted the plight of Jewish refugees attempting to immigrate to Palestine after World War II and helped shape world opinion in favor of the creation of a Jewish state. The British government had from 1939 continued to limit Jewish immigration to Palestine. Indeed, during the war and in the midst of the Holocaust, Britain had maintained warships off Palestine to intercept ships bound for Palestine carrying Jewish refugees fleeing the Holocaust.

British policies of blocking illegal Jewish immigration to Palestine continued after the war. Jewish leaders responded by encouraging and facilitating illegal immigration (Aliya Bet). From 1945 to 1948 Mossad Le-Aliya Bet, a branch of Haganah headed by Shaul Avigur, organized 65 voyages transporting in all some 70,000 displaced Jews to Palestine. One of the vessels involved in this effort was the former *President Warfield*.

The *President Warfield* was a Chesapeake Bay ferry that had been transferred to the British under Lend-Lease and had participated in ferrying operations to Normandy after the June 6, 1944, Allied invasion. It had been returned to the United States after the war. This worn-out ship was then sold as scrap to the Jewish immigration effort for slightly more than $8,000.

Renamed the *Exodus 1947* and packed with 4,515 refugees for Palestine, the ship departed Sète, France, on July 11, 1947. Eight British warships—the cruiser *Ajax*, five destroyers, and two minelayers—eventually trailed the ship. Twelve miles beyond Palestinian territorial waters, the British surrounded the *Exodus 1947* on July 18 and boarded it.

Hand-to-hand fighting ensued. In the melee that lasted several hours, the British finally resorted to small-arms fire. Two passengers and 1 crewman died, and 32 others were injured. The crewmen surrendered only when the British began ramming the *Exodus 1947*, threatening to sink it.

The British towed the *Exodus 1947*, now listing badly, to Haifa. Ordinarily the refugees would have been sent to camps in Cyprus, but these were now packed with 26,000 people, and the British sought to make an example. They embarked the passengers on three troopships and sent them to Marseille, France, in effect returning them to their point of debarkation. There the deportees rejected orders to go ashore, and French officials, who were willing to see them reenter France, refused to remove them by force. Only 130 passengers, most of them sick or pregnant, disembarked.

The remaining passengers, including many orphaned children who were Holocaust survivors, began a hunger strike. French authorities offered supplies, which the refugees rejected despite desperate sanitary conditions and extreme heat.

After 24 days and fearing the outbreak of an epidemic, the French ordered the three ships to depart. The British government, reeling from growing adverse worldwide public outrage over what had transpired, ordered the ships on to Hamburg in their zone of Germany. There, British soldiers forcibly removed the refugees, who were then sent on to two displaced persons (DP) camps near Lübeck. Demonstrations and protests occurred in DP camps throughout Europe over the events.

International outrage brought a change in British policy in which Britain ended the effort to return illegal immigrants to Palestine to their port of origin. Instead, Britain sent them to Cyprus. Media coverage of the events also led to a swing in public opinion in favor of the Jews and establishment of a Jewish state in 1948.

Many of the passengers on the *Exodus 1947* continued to try to reach Palestine. Although some gained illegal entry, more than half of them were detained again and deported to Cyprus. There they remained until they were allowed to immigrate to Israel after its founding in May 1948. The *Exodus 1947* itself burned at Haifa in August 1952 and was scrapped in 1963.

Writer Leon Uris loosely based his novel *Exodus* (1958) on the *Exodus 1947* incident and the lives of David Ben-Gurion and Menachem Begin. Paul Newman received an Academy Award for best actor for his portrayal of the fictional Ari Ben Canaan in the film *Exodus* (1958), directed by Otto Preminger.

Richard M. Edwards and Spencer C. Tucker

See also
Haganah; Palestine, British Mandate for; Zionism

References
Gruber, Ruth. *Exodus 1947: The Ship That Launched a Nation.* New York: Crown, 1999.
Halamish, Aviva. *The Exodus Affair: Holocaust Survivors and the Struggle for Palestine (Religion, Theology and the Holocaust).* Translated by Ora Cummings. Syracuse, NY: Syracuse University Press, 1998.
Kaniuk, Yoram. *Commander of the Exodus.* New York: Grove, 2001.

Expellees and Refugees, Palestinian

The plight of the Palestinian refugee community remains one of the most tragic and controversial aspects of the Israeli-Palestinian conflict since the Israeli War of Independence (1948–1949). In the violent events of that time, hundreds of thousands of Palestinians within what was to become the Green Line of Israel fled or were driven from their homes to escape the encroaching violence. This event is known as the Nakba (Catastrophe). United Nations (UN) General Assembly Resolution 194 of 1948 called in vain for these exiles to be returned to their homes.

According to the UN Relief and Works Agency for Palestine Refugees in the Near East (UNRWA), more than 914,000 individuals became refugees during this time. Put another way, from 1.4 million Palestinians in 1948, only 60,000 were counted in the first Israeli census inside Israel. Some 360,000 refugees settled in the West Bank, and 200,000 went to the Gaza Strip. They also went to surrounding Arab states, including Jordan (100,000), Lebanon (104,000), Syria (82,000), and Iraq, Egypt, Saudi Arabia, and Kuwait. Most of the remaining two-thirds settled either in or around major cities of their host countries or near the camps themselves. Following the 1967 Six-Day War in which Israel took administrative and military control of East Jerusalem, the West Bank, and Gaza, the refugee camps swelled with a new influx of displaced persons. In 2016 more than 1.5 million people, nearly one-third of the some 5 million registered Palestine refugees, lived in 58 recognized Palestine refugee camps in Jordan, Lebanon, the Syrian Arab Republic, the Gaza Strip, and the West Bank, including East Jerusalem.

The status of the Palestinian refugee community has changed dramatically even as its future has remained consistently uncertain. The most obvious shift in the refugees' plight has been the gradual acknowledgment of a semipermanent status to what was once assumed a temporary issue. Shabby concrete blocks have replaced tent city camps around the region, while most of the refugees' former homes have been razed or subsumed and reinhabited within Israeli townships.

The number of registered refugees grew to more than 4.1 million in 59 official camps by 2004. More than 1.7 million are in 10 camps in Jordan alone. Jordan remains the only primary host country to offer some Palestinian refugees national citizenship. Many but by no means all of the refugees in Jordan have managed to participate in wider national socioeconomic life, often successfully. In the remaining areas, including camps in the West Bank and Gaza, refugees linger in semipermanent ghettos that tend to be overcrowded, with poor sanitation and infrastructure, extremely high unemployment, and a general situation of grinding poverty and malaise. This state of affairs has played a key role in significant regional events of the past several decades, including Jordan's Black September uprising (1970), the Lebanese Civil War (1975–1990), and the First and Second Intifadas in the West Bank and Gaza (1987–1993 and 2000–2004, respectively).

Initially, relief functions were undertaken by Palestinian charitable organizations. UNRWA, created in 1948 (although its operations in the area did not effectively commence until 1951), has been responsible for the refugees' education, health, and general social services. Its specific mandate has been to assist this population, an acknowledgment by the international community of the scale of the humanitarian crisis.

Behind such statistics, the fact remains that the status of Palestinian refugees, past and future, is still an issue as contentious and politically complex as the future status of East Jerusalem and the fate of Jewish settlements. For the tenuous Palestinian leadership, the refugees make up a majority of its wider constituency, and more importantly, their claim of the right of return represents a call for the acknowledgment of and restitution for their wrongful exile during the Nakba of 1947–1948. They point out that the Palestinians who fled their homes at that time were the victims of a Zionist strategy designed to make way for a clear Jewish majority. Many of the refugees themselves cling to keys, deeds, identity cards, and other remnants of their ancestral claims within Israel in the hopes that any eventual final status agreements will allow them to return or receive compensation. Although there have been a number of legal rulings on the illegal seizure of lands and property, finding in favor of Palestinians, no land has been returned.

For Israel to accept a role of responsibility in the refugee crisis would imply by extension that Palestinian exiles have ancestral rights within what is now Israel, therefore weakening the long-standing argument that these refugees should be subsumed into their sister ethnic communities within the Arab states. Furthermore, accepting a right of return for these refugees would shake the foundations of the Israeli state. For its population of 6.7 million, ideologically dependent on a clear Jewish majority of 73 percent (5.1 million people), the addition of 4.1 million Palestinian Arabs would mean a practical end to modern Zionism.

The fate of the Palestinian refugee community, then, represents more than a present humanitarian crisis. It is also a linchpin of the Israeli-Palestinian conflict around which turn some enormously complex issues. Any proposed solution will have real and significant ideological, demographic, and humanitarian consequences. It is thus unsurprising that by the time of this writing, few genuine solutions to the refugee issue have been seriously considered or approached.

Kurt Werthmuller

See also

Black September; Expellees and Refugees, Palestinian; Gaza Strip; Intifada, First; Intifada, Second; Israel; Israeli War of Independence; Lebanon Civil War; Right of Return, Palestinian; West Bank; Zionism

References

Ateek, Naim, Hilary Rantisi, and Kent Wilkens. *Our Story: The Palestinians.* Jerusalem: Sabeel Ecumenical Liberation Theology Center, 2000.

Fischbach, Michael R. *Records of Dispossession: Palestinian Refugee Property and the Arab-Israeli Conflict.* New York: Columbia University Press, 2003.

Masalha, Nur. *Expulsion of the Palestinians: The Concept of "Transfer" in Zionist Political Thought, 1882–1948.* Washington, DC: Institute for Palestine Studies, 1992.

Morris, Benny. *The Birth of the Palestinian Refugee Problem Revisited.* 2nd ed. Cambridge: Cambridge University Press, 2004.

Shlaim, Avi. *The Iron Wall: Israel and the Arab World.* New York: Norton, 2001.

Smith, Charles D. *Palestine and the Arab-Israeli Conflict: A History with Documents.* 6th ed. New York: Bedford/St. Martin's, 2006.

United Nations Relief and Works Agency. *UNRWA: The United Nations Relief and Works Agency for Palestine Refugees.* Pamphlet. Amman, Jordan: UNRWA Public Information Office, 2003.

United Nations Relief and Works Agency. *UNRWA in Figures.* Pamphlet. Gaza City: UNRWA Public Information Office, March 2004.

F

Fahd, ibn Abd al-Aziz al-Saud (1922–2005)

King of Saudi Arabia (1982–2005) and son of the founder of Saudi Arabia, Abd al-Aziz ibn Abd al-Rahman al-Saud (commonly known as Ibn Saud). Fahd ibn Abd al-Aziz al-Saud was born in 1922 or 1923 in Riyadh. At the time of his birth his father was in the process of building modern Saudi Arabia, and during the 1920s Ibn Saud gained control over the Hejaz, the western region with the Holy Cities of Mecca and Medina.

Fahd was the 11th of Ibn Saud's 37 officially recognized sons. According to the Kingdom of Saudi Arabia's 1992 Basic Law, only sons and grandsons of monarchs are eligible to be kings of Saudi Arabia. Fahd was the eldest of the so-called Sudayri Seven, the seven sons fathered by Ibn Saud with his favorite wife, Hussah bint Ahmad al-Sudayri. These seven formed a close-knit group within the Saudi royal family and occupied key positions in the government.

Fahd was educated at the Princes' School, established by Ibn Saud for members of the royal family, and from 1953 to 1960 Fahd served as minister of education. In 1959 he led the Saudi delegation to the meeting of the League of Arab States. In 1964 he became interior minister. In this capacity, he ordered mass arrests after several terrorist attacks on oil facilities and government ministries. He also reportedly put down a coup attempt in 1968. Later he assumed the post of second deputy prime minister.

Following the assassination of King Faisal by his nephew on March 25, 1975, Fahd was named crown prince. He assumed full control of daily management of the government that same year. It was assumed that Saudi king Khalid would abdicate in 1978 after hip and open heart surgery, but his health then improved. Nonetheless, by 1981, because of King Khalid's incapacitating illness, Fahd became de facto ruler of Saudi Arabia. In August 1981 he advanced an eight-point plan to solve the Israeli-Palestinian-Arab dispute, which, however, was rejected by the Israeli government.

Following the death of King Khalid on June 13, 1982, Fahd formally assumed the throne. As king, he pursued a policy of open friendship with the United States while also attempting to take a leading role in Islamic and Arab issues in the Middle East. He encouraged economic development based on the nation's vast oil wealth and consistently sought to develop plans for economic diversification. Although Saudi Arabia remained one of the most traditional Islamic societies during Fahd's rule, advancements were nevertheless realized in technology, infrastructure, and education.

Within Saudi Arabia, Islamic fundamentalists were the king's greatest critics, and on November 22, 1979, heavily armed ultra-Wahhabists, led by Juhayman Utaybi, seized the Haram, or Grand Mosque, at Mecca and held hostages there for two weeks until they were ousted. Utaybi and 62 others were subsequently beheaded. The rebels had accused the Saudi royal family of bowing to secularism and had proclaimed one of their leaders to be the Mahdi.

In August 1990 after Iraqi forces invaded and occupied Kuwait, Fahd allowed U.S. and coalition forces into his kingdom in what became Operation DESERT SHIELD. He took this step mainly out of concern that Iraq now posed a direct military threat to the kingdom. Fahd and Iraqi leader Saddam Hussein became implacable enemies. Fahd's decision, however, earned the condemnation of many Saudi Islamic conservatives, including Osama bin Laden.

Fahd was an avid supporter of the United Nations. Indeed, that organization's backing of the plan to expel Iraqi forces from Kuwait by force helped Fahd in his decision to allow U.S. troops into the kingdom. Faud also actively supported the Palestinian cause and repeatedly criticized Israeli government policies toward the Palestine Liberation Organization (PLO).

After Fahd suffered a debilitating stroke in 1995, many of his official duties were delegated to his brother, Crown Prince Abdullah. Although Fahd still attended government meetings, he spent increasing time on his 200-acre estate in Marbella, Spain. After the terrorist attacks of September 11, 2001, Fahd's government fully supported the global war on terror and mounted its own counterterrorism campaign against the Al Qaeda in the Arabian Peninsula movement within Saudi Arabia. Fahd died of pneumonia in Riyadh on August 1, 2005. At the time of his death, he was considered one of the world's richest men, with an estimated personal fortune of more than $20 billion. Fahd was succeeded by his brother Abdullah.

MICHAEL R. HALL

See also
Bin Laden, Osama; Ibn Saud, King; Persian Gulf War, Overview; Saudi Arabia

References
Farsy, Fouad. *Custodian of the Two Holy Mosques: King Fahd bin Abdul Aziz*. New York: Knight Communications, 2001.

Henderson, Simon. *After King Fu'ad: Succession in Saudi Arabia*. Washington, DC: Washington Institute for Near East Policy, 1994.

Faisal I, King of Iraq (1885–1933)

Leader of the Arab Revolt of 1916–1918, then king of Syria and then Iraq. Born on May 20, 1885, in Taif near Mecca, Prince Faisal ibn Hussein of the Kingdom of Hejaz was the third son of Hussein bin Ali. Faisal's early childhood was spent in Arabia. From 1891 he was educated in Istanbul (Constantinople), where his father lived under house arrest at the order of the Ottoman sultan, who was trying to control Arab nationalist leaders. In 1908 Faisal's family returned to Mecca after his father had been appointed sharif of Mecca.

Gathering support from nationalists and the British, Sharif Hussein proclaimed the Arab Revolt against the Ottoman Empire on June 10, 1916.

As part of that revolt, Faisal served as his father's principal military commander. His brother Ali ibn Hussein attacked Medina. That attack and another on Wadi Safra were both repulsed. Faisal moved with the Northern Arab Army, utilizing Bedouin irregular forces as well as deserters from the Ottoman Army. Lieutenant Colonel T. E. Lawrence, who fought with him against the Ottomans, described Faisal as an excellent leader. By dint of his leadership and demonstrated personal courage, Faisal was accorded the fierce loyalty of the Arab fighters drawn to his cause.

In early 1917 Faisal led the Northern Arab Army of some 10,000 men north to Wajh. With Faisal's authorization, Lawrence then led the raid that captured Aqaba, which became the next staging area for the army. In the autumn of 1917 Faisal was made a British general under commander of the Egyptian Expeditionary Force British Army lieutenant general Edmund Allenby, who had been charged with carrying the campaign from the Transjordan region to Damascus.

As the fighting in 1918 progressed, Faisal moved his headquarters from Aqaba northward and then to Azraq. Meanwhile, the Southern Division of the Arab Army immobilized the Turkish garrisons at Medina. The Arab forces were successful in the north at Maan and easily triumphed over the remaining resistance blocking the way to Damascus. Faisal entered Damascus in triumph on October 3, 1918, then headed a provisional Syrian government. Because the British had promised him a united Arab state, he was angered to learn that Britain had agreed to the French Mandate for Syria. At the 1919 Paris Peace Conference he declared, "We desire, passionately, one thing—independence."

In March 1920 the Syrian National Congress proclaimed Faisal king, but the French expelled him, defeating his forces in the Battle of Maysalun on July 24. With British intervention, Faisal was then made king of Iraq in 1921. King Faisal died on September 8, 1933, in Bern, Switzerland, while undergoing treatment for heart problems.

ANDREW J. WASKEY

See also
Allenby, Sir Edmund Henry Hynman; Arab Revolt of World War I; Bedouins; Hussein ibn Ali ibn Mohammed; Iraq; Lawrence, Thomas Edward; Maysalun, Battle of

References
Erskine, Beatrice. *King Faisal of Iraq*. London: Hutchinson, 1933.

Lawrence, T. E. *Revolt in the Desert*. Herefordshire, UK: Wordsworth Editions, 1997.

Faisal II, King of Iraq (1935–1958)

King of Iraq from 1939 to 1958. Faisal was born in Baghdad on May 2, 1935, the only son of the second king of Iraq, Ghazi II, who died in an automobile accident in 1938. Until Faisal turned 18 in 1953, his uncle, Abd al-Ilah, served as regent of Iraq and de facto head of state.

Faisal meanwhile studied at the Harrow School in Great Britain with his cousin, the future King Hussein of Jordan. The two men enjoyed a close relationship, and both would subsequently face growing militant Pan-Arab nationalism in the Middle East. In 1952, Faisal graduated and returned to Iraq.

Following World War I, the British received a League of Nations mandate over Iraq. The British were soon confronted with a fierce rebellion against their rule during 1920–1922, however. In restoring order and stability in Iraq, they installed on the Iraqi throne a member of the Hashemite family, Faisal I (the grandfather of Faisal II), to whom they had earlier promised the throne of Syria. Some Iraqis viewed the members of the Iraqi royal family as foreigners, as they hailed from the Hejaz, a western area of the Arabian Peninsula. Others supported Faisal I, who had symbolized the Arab cause for independence in the Arab Revolt. Many political followers of Faisal I accompanied him from Syria to Iraq, including Iraqi former Ottoman Army officers who provided a base of power for him. His son Ghazi was popular with Iraqis but was not an adept ruler. The royal family's pro-British policies and those of Nuri al-Said Pasha, who had held as many as 48 cabinet positions, including repeated stints as prime minister, caused Faisal II and the regent to be viewed by Iraqis as puppets of the British government.

By 1940 the most powerful group in Iraqi politics was the Golden Square of four army colonels, led by Colonel Salah al-Din al-Sabagh, an Arab nationalist who supported the Palestinian cause. The British regarded the Golden Square as a distinct threat and as being sympathetic to the Axis cause. In April 1941 Colonel Rahid Ali al-Gaylani, part of this group, engineered a military coup in Iraq, sent Abd al-Ilah into exile, and proclaimed himself regent. Rashid Ali sought to pursue a foreign policy independent of the United Kingdom. The young King Faisal went into seclusion outside of Baghdad. Within a month, however, a combined force of the Iraqi Air Force, Jordan's Arab Legion, and a contingent of British troops defeated Rashid Ali's forces and restored Abd al-Ilah as regent. Faisal II then returned to Baghdad. In May 1953 upon his 18th birthday, he assumed full governing responsibility over Iraq.

In his policies, Faisal II was guided by his mentor and uncle, Abd al-Ilah, and pro-British prime minister Nuri al-Said. Many Iraqis became disillusioned with Faisal's foreign policy during the 1950s, however. Arab nationalists opposed the government's pro-Western stance on diplomatic issues. In 1955, Iraq joined the U.S.-inspired anti-Soviet Middle East Treaty Organization (also known as the Baghdad Pact). Its members included Iraq, the United States (as an associate member), the United Kingdom, Turkey, Pakistan, and Iran. The Arab nationalist president of Egypt, Gamal Abdel Nasser, strongly opposed the pact, arguing that threats to the Middle East originated in Israel, not the Soviet Union. During the 1956 Suez Crisis, Iraqis supported Egypt's resistance to the coordinated attack undertaken by Great Britain, France, and Israel. The Iraqi government's relationship with Great Britain, however, caused tensions concerning the rise of Nasserists and Pan-Arabists in Iraq after this crisis.

In response to Egypt's February 1, 1958, union with Syria known as the United Arab Republic, the Hashemite monarchs of Jordan and Iraq created the Arab Federation of Iraq and Jordan on February 14, 1958. Faisal II became head of state of the new federation.

In June 1958, King Hussein of Jordan requested military assistance from Iraq to quell disturbances fueled by Arab nationalists. Faisal ordered troops to Jordan, including a division of the Iraqi Army under the command of General Abdul Karim Qasim, a staunch opponent of British ambitions in the Middle East. On July 14, 1958, using the troop movements as a cover, Qasim overthrew the monarchy and proclaimed a republic. Members of the royal family, including King Faisal II, were murdered and their bodies mutilated. Prince Zayid, the youngest brother of Faisal I, was in London at the time of the coup and became the heir-in-exile to the Iraqi throne. When Zayid died in 1970, he was succeeded as heir-in-exile by his son, Raad, an adviser to Jordan's King Abdullah.

MICHAEL R. HALL AND SHERIFA ZUHUR

See also

Baghdad Pact; Hussein ibn Talal, King of Jordan; Nasser, Gamal Abdel; Nuri al-Said; Pan-Arabism and Pan-Arabist Thought; Suez Crisis; United Arab Republic

References

Eppel, Michael. *Iraq from Monarchy to Tyranny: From the Hashemites to the Rise of Saddam.* Gainesville: University Press of Florida, 2004.

Marr, Phebe. *The Modern History of Iraq.* 2nd ed. Boulder, CO: Westview, 2003.

Fallujah, First Battle of (April 4–May 1, 2004)

A U.S. military operation, the principal goal of which was to retake the Iraqi city of Fallujah after insurgents had seized control. Code-named VIGILANT RESOLVE, it occurred during April 4–May 1, 2004. Sunni insurgents, including Al Qaeda fighters, had steadily destabilized Anbar Province in Iraq in the aftermath of the 2003 U.S.-led invasion. Fallujah, located some 42 miles west of Baghdad in the so-called Sunni Triangle, emerged as a focal point for anticoalition attacks. The town was dominated by Salafist groups who were extremely suspicious of all outsiders, particularly foreigners; family and clan ties dominated personal relationships. The collapse of Iraqi president Saddam Hussein's regime had left some 70,000 male inhabitants in the city unemployed, providing a major source of recruits for the Iraqi insurgency movement.

Growing violence in Fallujah in March 2004 led the U.S. military to withdraw forces from the city and conduct only armed patrols. On March 31 insurgents ambushed four contractors working for Blackwater USA, a private contracting company that provided security personnel to the Coalition Provisional Authority (CPA). The insurgents dragged the bodies through the streets and then hanged them from a bridge. Television cameras transmitted the grisly images around the world, prompting a strong response to offset the perception that coalition forces had lost control of the area.

In an effort to regain control of the city and the surrounding province, the U.S. military launched a series of operations against suspected insurgent groups and their bases. The lead unit was the I Marine Expeditionary Force (I MEF), which had been deployed to Anbar in March. The ground forces were supported by coalition aircraft and helicopter units. U.S. lieutenant general James Conway had overall command of the operation. On April 4 some 2,200 marines surrounded Fallujah. They blockaded the main roads in and out of the city in an effort to allow only civilians to escape the fighting. The commanders on the ground believed that the marines should remain outside of the city because they lacked the troops to effectively control the area and the population; nevertheless, they were ordered to seize the city.

In the opening days of the operation, U.S. forces conducted air strikes on suspected targets and undertook limited incursions into Fallujah, including a strike to take control of its main radio station. At least one-quarter of the

U.S. marines during the First Battle of Fallujah (April 4–May 1, 2004). (U.S. Marine Corps)

civilian population fled the city as insurgents used homes, schools, and mosques to attack the marines, who responded with devastating firepower that often produced high collateral damage and civilian casualties.

Within the city there were an estimated 15,000–20,000 insurgent fighters divided among more than a dozen insurgent groups of various origins. Some were former members of Hussein's security forces. They were armed with a variety of weapons, including light arms, rocket-propelled grenades (RPGs), mortars, and improvised explosive devices (IEDs). The insurgents used guerrilla tactics against the marines, including ambushes, mortar attacks, and mines and IEDs. Sniper fire was common throughout the operation. U.S. forces responded with artillery and air strikes, including the use of heavily armed Lockheed AC-130 gunships. Support from Bell AH-1W Super Cobra attack helicopters, however, was limited because of significant ground fire. Meanwhile, the marines attempted to secure neighborhoods one or two blocks at a time using air support and tanks.

There were problems coordinating movements in the dense urban environment, especially because maps were not standardized between the various units. Meanwhile, many of the remaining Iraqi security forces within the city either joined the insurgents or simply fled their posts. After three days of intense fighting, the marines had secured only about one-quarter of Fallujah.

In response to the escalating violence, the failure of the marines to make significant progress in the city, growing pressure from Iraqi political leaders, and increasing domestic pressure on the George W. Bush administration that was largely the result of media coverage, the U.S.-led CPA ordered a unilateral cease-fire on April 9 and initiated negotiations with the insurgent groups. The marines allowed humanitarian aid into the city; however, in spite of the cease-fire, sporadic fighting continued. Throughout the negotiations, it was decided that the United States would turn over security for the city to a newly formed ad hoc Iraqi militia force, the Fallujah Brigade. The United States agreed to provide arms and equipment for the brigade, which included former soldiers and police officers of the Hussein regime.

On May 1 U.S. forces completely withdrew from Fallujah, but they maintained a presence outside of the city at an observation base. More than 700 Iraqis had been killed in the fighting (the majority of these, perhaps as many as 600, were civilians), while 27 U.S. marines were killed and 90 were wounded.

The Fallujah Brigade failed to maintain security and began to disintegrate during the summer of 2004. Many of its members joined or rejoined the insurgency, and the military announced that Abu Musab al-Zarqawi, the leader of Al Qaeda in Iraq, was headquartered in Fallujah. The coalition undertook a second campaign in Fallujah in the autumn of 2004, code-named Operation PHANTOM FURY.

Tom Lansford

See also
Fallujah, Second Battle of; Fallujah, Third Battle of; Iraq Insurgency; Iraq War; Sunni Triangle

References
Afong, Milo. *Hogs in the Shadows: Combat Stories from Marine Snipers in Iraq.* New York: Berkley, 2007.
Cockburn, Patrick. *The Occupation: War and Resistance in Iraq.* New York: Verso, 2007.
O'Donnell, Patrick K. *We Were One: Shoulder to Shoulder with the Marines Who Took Fallujah.* New York: Da Capo, 2007.
West, Bing. *No True Glory: A Frontline Account of the Battle for Fallujah.* New York: Bantam, 2006.

Fallujah, Second Battle of (November 7–December 23, 2004)

Major battle fought in and around the city of Fallujah, some 42 miles west of Baghdad, between U.S., Iraqi, and British forces and Iraqi insurgents (chiefly Al Qaeda in Iraq but also other militias). Following the decision to halt the coalition assault on Fallujah in Operation VIGILANT RESOLVE (the First Battle of Fallujah, April 4–May 1, 2004), the U.S. marines had withdrawn from the city and turned over security to the so-called Fallujah Brigade, an ad hoc force of local men who had formerly served in the Iraqi Army. The Fallujah Brigade failed dismally in this task, giving the insurgents another chance to claim victory and attract additional recruits. During the summer and autumn months, the Fallujah police turned a blind eye as the insurgents fortified positions inside Fallujah and stockpiled supplies. The Iraqi interim government, formed on June 28, 2004, then requested new efforts to capture and secure Fallujah.

In preparation for the ground assault, coalition artillery and aircraft began selective strikes on the city on October 30, 2004. Coalition ground forces (American, Iraqi, and British) cut off electric power to the city on November 5 and distributed leaflets warning people to stay in their homes and not use their cars. This was a response to insurgent suicide bombers who had been detonating cars packed with explosives. On November 7 the Iraqi government announced a 60-day state of emergency throughout most of Iraq. Because of all these warnings, 75–90 percent of Fallujah's civilian population abandoned the city before the coalition ground offensive began. Many of these fled to Syria, where they remain as refugees.

The Americans initially labeled the assault Operation PHANTOM FURY. Iraqi prime minister Ayad Allawi, however, renamed it AL-FAJR (NEW DAWN). The operation's main objective was to demonstrate the ability of the Iraqi government to control its own territory, thereby bolstering its prestige. The American military focused on the important secondary objective of killing as many insurgents as possible while keeping coalition casualties low. About 10,000 American soldiers and marines and 2,000 Iraqi troops participated in Operation AL-FAJR. Some Royal Marines also took part. The American forces involved had considerable experience in urban combat.

The assault plan called for a concentration of forces north of Fallujah. Spearheaded by the army's heavy armor, army and marine units would attack due south along precisely defined sectors. The infantry would methodically clear buildings, leaving the trailing Iraqi forces to search for insurgents and assault the city's 200 mosques, which coalition tacticians suspected would be used as defensive insurgent strongpoints. Intelligence estimates suggested that some 3,000 insurgents defended the city, one-fifth of whom were foreign jihadists. Intelligence estimates also predicted fanatical resistance.

Ground operations associated with the Second Battle of Fallujah commenced on November 7, 2004, when an Iraqi commando unit and the Marine 3rd Light Armored Reconnaissance Battalion conducted a preliminary assault. The objective was to secure the Fallujah General Hospital to the west of the city and capture two bridges over the Euphrates River, thereby isolating the insurgent forces inside the city. This preliminary assault was successful, allowing the main assault to commence after dark the following evening. The American military chose this time because it knew that its various night-vision devices would provide it a tactical advantage over the insurgents. Four marine infantry and two army mechanized battalions attacked in the first wave. M-1A2 Abrams tanks and M-2A3 Bradley Fighting Vehicles provided mobile firepower for which the insurgents had no answer. The Abrams tanks exhibited the ability to absorb enormous punishment and keep operating. The speed and shock of the massed armor overwhelmed the insurgents, enabling the American soldiers to drive deep into Fallujah. Iraqi forces also performed surprisingly well. After four days of operations, coalition forces had secured about half the city.

By November 11 the methodical American advance had driven most of the insurgents into the southern part of Fallujah. Three days of intense street fighting ensued, during which time the Americans reached the southern limits of the city. On November 15 the Americans reversed direction and attacked north to eliminate any insurgents who had been missed in the first pass and to search more thoroughly for insurgent weapons and supplies. For this part of the operation, the ground forces broke down into squad-size elements to conduct their searches. By November 16 American commanders judged Fallujah secured, although the operation would not end officially until December 23, by which time many residents had been allowed to return to their homes.

U.S. casualties in the Second Battle of Fallujah were 95 killed and 560 wounded; Iraqi Army losses were 11 killed and 43 wounded. Insurgent losses were estimated at between 1,200 and 2,000 killed, with another 1,000 to 1,500 captured. The disparity in the casualties indicated the extent of the coalition's tactical advantage. Indeed, postbattle army and marine assessments lauded the tremendous tactical skill in urban warfare displayed by American forces. However, the intense house-to-house fighting had caused the destruction of an estimated 20 percent of the city's buildings, while another 60 percent of the city's structures were damaged. The tremendous damage, including that to 60 mosques, enraged Iraq's Sunni minority. Widespread civilian demonstrations and increased insurgent attacks followed the Second Battle of Fallujah. Although the 2005 Iraqi elections were held on schedule, Sunni participation was very low partially because of the Sunnis' sense of grievance over the destruction in Fallujah.

JAMES ARNOLD

See also
Allawi, Ayad; Al Qaeda in Iraq; Fallujah, First Battle of; Fallujah, Third Battle of; Iraq Insurgency; Sunni Islam; Sunni Triangle

References
Ballard, John R. *Fighting for Fallujah: A New Dawn for Iraq.* Westport, CT: Praeger Security International, 2006.
Bellavia, David. *House to House: An Epic Memoir of War.* New York: Free Press, 2007.
Gott, Kendall D., ed. *Eyewitness to War: The U.S. Army in Operation Al Fajr; An Oral History.* 2 vols. Fort Leavenworth, KS: Comba.

Fallujah, Third Battle of (May 23–June 28, 2016)

On May 23, 2016, Iraqi forces began the Third Battle of Fallujah, also known as Operation LLUJA. General Abdul Wahab al-Saadi had command of the operation to retake the city from the Islamic State of Iraq and Syria (ISIS). Iraqi prime minister Haider al-Abadi addressed the nation over television to announce the start of the long-planned operation. Abadi's announcement followed by several hours an effort by the Iraq military urging residents of the ISIS-held city to flee their homes ahead of the operation. Fallujah, in Sunni-dominated Anbar Province, was the scene of two major battles during the Iraq War and had been under ISIS control since January 2014. In the operation the Iraqi Army was accompanied by Shia Muslim militia groups and—worrying to the United States—senior Iranian military and intelligence personnel as well as members of the Iranian Quds Force.

In all, the attacking forces numbered some 11,000 to 14,500 men. The ISIS defenders are believed to have numbered about 4,500. Well aware of the Iraqi government's intentions, they had constructed strongpoints as well as ambush positions and communication and escape tunnels. U.S. air strikes also greatly assisted the Iraqi forces on the ground.

On May 30, the Iraqis retook a handful of settlements near Falluja itself, including the town of Saqlawiya some 6.5 miles northwest of the city and the villages of al-Buaziz, al-Bu Efan and al-Shiha north and west of it.

Fighting was intense and the advance slowed at times, but on June 26 al-Saad announced on Iraqi state TV that the Iraqi forces had secured the al-Jolan neighborhood, the last ISIS stronghold in the city. Fighting continued in the western outskirts of the city for several more days, however. In the five-week battle, the government claimed that 2,500 ISIS militants were killed and 2,186 captured. Estimates of the attackers' casualties range from 394 to 900 killed and 3,308 wounded. Meanwhile, civilians who had fled the fighting were in dire straits, grouped in hastily prepared refugee camps where even the basic amenities were lacking. Most of these people were Sunni Muslims, the very group the Shia-dominated Iraqi government was seeking to win over.

With Fallujah completely secured, the Iraqi military could begin to prepare for its long-awaited drive to recapture from ISIS Iraq's second-largest city of Mosul. Mosul was cleared of ISIS fighters in July 2017. In December of that year, the Iraqi government officially declared victory over ISIS in Iraq. In the summer of 2018, a full year after the recapture of Mosul, much of the city remained badly damaged or destroyed. In July 2018, Iraqi prime minister al-Abadi warned that it would take perhaps years to rebuild the city; he also cautioned that isolated ISIS cells continued to operate near Mosul, which would require additional military efforts to subdue them completely.

Spencer C. Tucker

See also
Abadi, Haider al-; Fallujah, First Battle of; Fallujah, Second Battle of; Islamic State of Iraq and Syria

References
Adel, Loca. "80 PC Areas to West and South of Fallujah Liberated." *Iraqi News,* June 30, 2016, http://www.iraqinews.com/iraq-war/80-pc-areas-to-west-and-south-of-fallujah-liberated/.

al-Sudani, Thaier, and Ahmed Rasheed. "Iraqi Forces Assess the Damage to Fallujah As They Secure the City." Huffington Post, June 27, 2016, http://www.huffingtonpost.com/entry/iraq-closes-in-on-isis-west-of-fallujah_us_57712ef9e4b0dbb1bbbb1212.

Fao Peninsula

Strategically important peninsula located in southeastern Iraq, adjacent to the Persian Gulf. The Fao (al-Faw) Peninsula lies to the south and east of Basra, Iraq's principal port and second-largest metropolis, and west of the Iranian city of Abadan. The peninsula separates Iraq from Iran and lies to the immediate west of the critical Shatt al-Arab waterway, which is Iraq's only access to the sea and only seagoing route to the port at Basra. Control of the Fao Peninsula has thus been strategically essential to Iraq, as loss of control there likely means being cut off from access to the Persian Gulf.

The Fao Peninsula is also important because is has been home to some of Iraq's largest oil installations, including refineries. The country's two principal terminals for oil tankers are also located here—Khor al-Amaya and Mina al-Bakr. The only significant population center on the peninsula is Umm Qasr, the base of Iraqi former dictator Saddam Hussein's navy.

The Fao Peninsula was a center of attention during the 1980–1988 Iraq-Iran War and was the site of several pitched battles as both nations struggled to control the Shatt al-Arab. In February 1986, Iranian forces were able to overwhelm the poorly trained Iraqi forces charged with guarding the peninsula. Despite desperate fighting, the Iraqis were unable to dislodge the Iranians from the area, even in the face of numerous offensives. The Iranians were then able to threaten Basra and Umm Qasr and use the Fao Peninsula as a base from which to launch missiles into Iraq, into naval and merchant assets in the Persian Gulf, and into Kuwait, which was backing Iraq in the war. In April 1988, the Iraqis launched a new and determined effort to dislodge the Iranians from the peninsula. With almost 100,000 troops, heavy artillery, and aerial bombing that included chemical weapons, the Iraqis finally drove the Iranians out after a 35-hour offensive.

In the lead-up to the 1991 Persian Gulf War, the Fao Peninsula and the Shatt al-Arab became a bone of contention between Iraq and Kuwait, as both nations jockeyed to control access to Umm Qasr as well as two small adjacent islands. Hussein used the dispute as part of his justification for the August 1990 Iraqi invasion of Kuwait. When Operation DESERT STORM began in January 1991, coalition air forces heavily bombed the Fao Peninsula, wiping out much of Iraq's naval assets and oil facilities. Although no significant ground actions occurred here, Iraqi shipping was closed down by the bombardment, meaning that Iraq was cut off from any seaborne trade or resupply efforts.

During the Iraq War, which began in March 2003, American and British plans called for the immediate seizure and occupation of the Fao Peninsula to deny Iraq access to the Persian Gulf and to open Umm Qasr and Basra to humanitarian and military resupply missions. Military planners also hoped to secure the peninsula before Iraqi troops could damage or destroy its oil facilities.

The coalition attack on Umm Qasr, led by U.S. and British Marines and Polish special land forces, began on March 21, 2003, but ran into unexpectedly heavy Iraqi resistance. After four days of sporadically heavy fighting, however, Umm Qasr and the Fao Peninsula had been largely secured and the adjacent waterway cleared of Iraqi mines. Pockets of Iraqi resistance endured in the "old city" of Umm Qasr until March 29, when the entire peninsula had essentially been occupied and secured. Almost immediately coalition forces opened the port at Umm Qasr, which then became the primary entrepôt for humanitarian and civilian aid to Iraq.

PAUL G. PIERPAOLI JR.

See also
Iran-Iraq War; Iraq War; Kuwait; Persian Gulf; Persian Gulf War, Overview; Shatt al-Arab Waterway

References
Keegan, John. *The Iraq War*. New York: Knopf, 2004.
Tripp, Charles. *A History of Iraq*. New York: Cambridge University Press, 2000.

Fariskur, Battle of (April 8, 1250)
See Crusades in the Holy Land, Christian

Farouk I, King of Egypt (1920–1965)

King of Egypt from 1936 until 1952, when he was ousted by a military coup. Born on February 11, 1920, in Cairo, Faruq al-Awwal (Farouk) was the son and successor of King Ahmad Fuad I. Farouk was just 16 years when his father died and he ascended the throne, although a regency council ruled for him until July 1937. As king, Farouk continued his father's policy of opposing the popular Wafd Party and was usually successful in keeping it from power.

During World War II Farouk, who was anti-British, sought to keep Egypt neutral. Nevertheless, the British government pressured him to honor Egypt's 1936 treaty obligations to lend Britain wartime support and to dismiss profascist sympathizers from the government and army officer corps. In 1942 the British forced him to accept as prime minister Mustafa an-Nahhas Pasha, a Wafd Party leader sympathetic to British interests. In October 1944 an-Nahhas helped to negotiate the Alexandria Protocol as a step toward the creation of an Arab league of states. Farouk, who sought to head the movement himself, promptly dismissed an-Nahhas.

Farouk's reign and reputation were seriously compromised by defeat in the 1948 Arab-Israeli War of Independence. Revelations of rampant corruption in the palace and in the Egyptian bureaucracy also discredited him with the Egyptian military. Farouk's position was further damaged by his reputation as an inveterate womanizer and playboy who amassed fantastic wealth but was never quite satisfied with what he had. He owned hundreds of thousands of acres of land, dozens of palaces, and hundreds of automobiles. He was known as a hard-driving gambler and a man of the nightclub circuit, and his apparent kleptomania earned him the nickname "the Thief of Cairo." These excesses were a major catalyst to his downfall.

In 1952 Farouk sponsored unpopular candidates for minister of defense and other key positions. On July 23 the clandestine Free Officers organization, led by General Muhammad Nagib and Colonel Gamal Abdel Nasser, forced Farouk to abdicate and sent him into exile in Monaco. His infant son was immediately proclaimed King Fuad II, but the monarchy was formally abolished in 1953 when Egypt was declared a republic.

In exile, Farouk continued to lead the high life. His love of food and drink rendered him dangerously obese, and by the time he collapsed after a heavy meal on March 3, 1965, he weighed almost 300 pounds. He died in Rome on March 18, 1965.

ANDREW J. WASKEY

See also

Egypt; Israeli War of Independence; Nasser, Gamal Abdel

References

McLeave, Hugh. *The Last Pharaoh: Farouk of Egypt.* New York: McCall, 1970.

Stadiem, William. *Too Rich: The High Life and Tragic Death of King Farouk.* New York: Carroll and Graf, 1991.

Fatah, al-

Palestinian guerrilla organization and political party, the name of which means "conquest"; its full name in Arabic is Harakat al-Tahrir al-Watani al-Filastini (Palestine National Liberation Movement). Founded in exile in 1957 by Yasser Arafat and Khalil al-Wazir, al-Fatah sought full independence for the Palestinians in a state that would include Gaza between Egypt and Israel and the West Bank between Israel and Jordan. The organization was founded to win back the land lost to the Jews in the 1948–1949 War of Israeli Independence.

Al-Fatah became increasingly important in the 1960s and joined the Palestine Liberation Organization (PLO) in 1967. In 1969 Arafat secured full control over the PLO, and eventually al-Fatah became the largest faction within that organization. Al-Fatah carried out guerrilla attacks inside Israel and then attacked Israeli interests worldwide. Originally based in Damascus, it was forced to relocate several times before the attainment of a political agreement with Israel in 1993.

From the late 1960s to 2006, al-Fatah remained the most powerful group within the PLO and dominated Palestinian politics. During that period al-Fatah policies changed dramatically, from the military and terrorist actions of the 1960s to the pragmatic politics of a democratic Palestine. In 1994 the Palestinian Authority (PA) was established, and al-Fatah dominated the governing body for the next 12 years. However, a number of factions within al-Fatah rejected the goal of peace with Israel and split from the main organization.

Farouk Kaddoumi, the remaining living cofounder of al-Fatah, became its leader after Arafat's death in 2004. On November 12, 2006, Mahmoud Abbas became the president of the PLO. In the 2006 elections for the Palestinian Legislative Council, the rival organization Hamas unexpectedly defeated al-Fatah and formed its own government. Since then, al-Fatah and Hamas have fought each other for control of the Palestinian Authority, especially in Gaza.

ROBERT B. KANE

See also

Arafat, Yasser; Palestine Liberation Organization; Terrorism

References

Aburish, Said K. *Arafat: From Defender to Dictator.* New York: Bloomsbury, 1998.

Jamal, Amal. *The Palestinian National Movement: Politics of Contention, 1967–2005.* Bloomington: Indiana University Press, 2005.

Kurz, Anat N. *Fatah and the Politics of Violence: The Institutionalization of a Popular Struggle.* Eastbourne, East Sussex, UK: Sussex Academic, 2006.

Mishal, Shaul, and Avraham Sela. *The Palestinian Hamas Vision, Violence and Coexistence.* New York: Columbia University Press, 2000.

Rubin, Barry. *The Transformation of Palestinian Politics: from Revolution to State-Building.* Cambridge, MA: Harvard University Press, 2001.

Zuhur, Sherifa. *Hamas and Israel: Strategic Interaction in Group Based Politics.* Carlisle, PA: Strategic Studies Institute, 2008.

Fatimid Dynasty (909–1171)

An Arab dynasty that ruled Egypt during 969–1171. The Fatimids belonged to the Ismaili branch of Shiite Islam, which recognized the descendants of the two sons of Prophet Muhammad's daughter Fatima and Ali, the fourth caliph, as the legitimate rulers of the Muslim community. By the mid-ninth century, the Ismailis were engaged in subversive and revolutionary activities against the Abbasid caliphs in Baghdad. In 909, the establishment of a Fatimid state in Tunisia caused a rupture in the Ismaili movement when the Carmathians of Bahrayn opposed the Fatimid claim to be the imams, that is, divinely chosen and rightly guided rulers of Islam.

The Fatimids ruled Tunisia and Sicily until 973, when they transferred their state to Egypt after the conquest of that country by their general Jawhar in 969. The North African phase of the Fatimid state was marked by the establishment of new cities reflecting their deep involvement in trade with Muslim Spain, Italy, and Byzantium and with its naval activities against these. The Fatimids also maintained a network of commercial relations with sub-Saharan Africa, where they procured gold and black slaves.

The Fatimid efforts to conquer Egypt were inspired not only by their difficulties in ruling North Africa (exemplified by the rebellion of Abu Yazid in 944–947, which posed a serious challenge to the Fatimid rule) but mainly by their desire to reach Baghdad and supplant the Abbasid caliphs. Immediately after the conquest of Egypt the Fatimids invaded

Al-Azhar mosque and university in Cairo, founded under the patronage of the Fatimid dynasty in the year 972. (Paul Cowan/Dreamstime.com)

Palestine and Syria, but their dream of reaching Baghdad never materialized, and their always precarious hold over Damascus and Palestine collapsed in the second half of the 11th century with the arrival of the Seljuk Turks.

The impact of Fatimid rule on Egypt was manifold and outlived the Fatimids in two areas. The establishment of Cairo proved to be a great success. It became the seat of the Fatimid rulers, a religious and cultural center and a magnet for local and foreign merchants. During Fatimid rule, a commercial network that connected India and the Mediterranean emerged and lasted well into the late Middle Ages, declining only during the Ottoman period. Egyptian trade flourished, with merchants from the Muslim areas of the Mediterranean (Spain, North Africa, and Sicily), Italy, and Byzantium visiting Alexandria and Cairo in pursuit of spices and goods from India and the East Indies.

The majority of the Egyptian population were Sunni Muslims, with Christian and Jewish minorities. There were few Shiite Muslims. The Fatimid regime depended largely on its control of the army, which was mostly made up of non-Egyptian elements. Although the Fatimid caliph was nominally the head of state, from the second half of the 11th century the actual control of government was usually in the hands of a vizier. The Fatimids used missionaries outside the empire to spread Shiite doctrines, especially among the urban populations of Seljuk-controlled Syria, but there was no attempt to spread Shiite Islam within Egypt, as this would have aroused antagonism within the majority Sunni population.

The Fatimids misunderstood the intentions of the First Crusade (1096–1099) and initially tried to form an alliance with the crusaders for cooperation against the Seljuks, who supported the rival Abbasid caliphate. As it was the Seljuk territories that came under attack first, the Fatimids were able to take the opportunity to seize Jerusalem from Seljuk control (June 1099). However, they were slow to recognize that Jerusalem itself was the main goal of the crusade, and their relieving army arrived too late to prevent the fall of the city to the crusaders (July 15, 1099). The Fatimid army that camped around Ascalon (modern-day Tel Ashqelon, Israel) suffered a humiliating defeat at the hands of the crusaders in the Battle of Ascalon (August 12, 1099), allowing the crusaders to consolidate the territorial achievements.

During the first decade of the 12th century, the Fatimids lost the towns of Arsuf, Haifa, Beirut, Sidon, and Tripoli to the Franks of Jerusalem and Tripoli. Fatimid land and naval efforts were uncoordinated and their armies hesitant and unable to mount a serious military challenge to the Franks. The fall of Tyre (modern-day Soûr, Lebanon) in 1124 came about as the result of lack of cooperation between the Fatimids and the rulers of Damascus, while a contributory factor to the fall of Ascalon in 1153 was a coup that took place in Cairo while the Franks were besieging the town.

An examination of the fighting between the Fatimids and the Franks shows that the Fatimids failed militarily because their army collapsed in crucial battles fought in Palestine (1099, 1105, and 1123) owing to a lack of cooperation between the cavalry and the infantry. This reflected a sociomilitary problem deriving from the inherent weakness of Muslim multiethnic armies. Traditionally, the Fatimid Army was a multiethnic force dominated by a very large component of black slave infantry with a much smaller but ethnically diverse cavalry element. In the mid-11th century the strength of the Fatimid Army was probably over 100,000 soldiers, but the numbers dwindled from that point, and during the 1060s the army consisted of only 40,000 African infantry and over 10,000 cavalry. The Fatimid multiethnic army was very difficult to handle on the battlefield, since such a heterogeneous force was ridden with ethnic animosities, exacerbated by the different status of freeborn troops and military slaves (Arab mamluks).

On three occasions (at Ramla in 1105, Ibelin in 1123, and Ascalon in 1153) the navy performed better than the army, but the navy on its own, without the support of the army, achieved nothing. The small Fatimid Navy was vastly outnumbered by the European fleets that operated in the eastern Mediterranean in support of the crusades, and its ability to ship supplies and reinforcements was limited. For this reason the Fatimids were very hesitant to commit their naval forces to the support of coastal towns that were besieged by the Franks and European naval forces, as happened at Acre in 1104, Tripoli in 1109, and Tyre in 1124. In any case, naval battles were quite rare events, and only in the summer of 1123, off the south Palestinian coast, was the Fatimid Navy involved in a disastrous naval battle with a Venetian fleet. Naval raids were more common, but the shipping lanes used by the European fleets on their way to the Levant were beyond the range of Fatimid warships operating from the Egyptian ports of Alexandria and Damietta. The Fatimid naval failure was a result of European naval superiority combined with geographical and naval factors characteristic of the eastern Mediterranean.

During the 1160s the Fatimids became entangled in the conflict between Nur al-Din, the ruler of Muslim Syria, and the Franks. Shawar, an ousted Fatimid vizier, managed to involve both Nur al-Din and the king of Jerusalem in the internal affairs of the Fatimid state. Each power coveted Egypt and was ready to do anything to prevent its rival from gaining control of Egypt. Politically the Fatimid state was weak and divided, and the Fatimid Army was no match for either the Franks or the forces of Nur al-Din.

In economic terms Egypt was a valuable prize, with its rich agricultural output and flourishing long-distance international trade. The Franks were well informed about Egypt's agricultural potential and possessed a list of Egyptian villages and the incomes derived from them. The participation of Italian maritime republics in the crusades also posed a serious dilemma for the Fatimids, since the Italians stimulated trade with India because of their demand for spices and their presence in Egypt was crucial to maintain the momentum of this trade. Egypt was also dependent on its Mediterranean partners for supplies of timber, iron, and pitch. The Fatimids, like Saladin later on, continued to maintain commercial relations with the Europeans and allowed the presence of Italian and Byzantine merchants in their ports in spite of the wars of the crusades.

Between 1164 and 1171 the armies of Nur al-Din and the Kingdom of Jerusalem fought their wars on Egyptian soil, with the Fatimids unable to influence the course of events. Eventually the Franks withdrew from Egypt, and Egypt came under the control of Nur al-Din's general, Shirkuh. On Shirkuh's death his nephew Saladin became vizier. The Fatimid regime had failed to strike deep roots among the Muslim population of the country during the two centuries of its rule in Egypt, and Saladin overthrew it easily. He broke up the Fatimid Army and on the death of the caliph al-Aid (1171) recognized the religious authority of the Abbasid caliph in Baghdad, which effectively ended Fatimid rule.

YAACOV LEV

See also
Abbasid Caliphate; Crusades in the Holy Land, Christian; Jawhar; Kafur, Abu al-Misk; Nur al-Din; Seljuk Dynasty

References
Brett, Michael. *The Rise of the Fatimids: The World of the Mediterranean and the Middle East in the Tenth Century CE.* Leiden: Brill, 2001.

Ehrenkreutz, Andrew S. "The Fatimids in Palestine—The Unwitting Promoters of the Crusade." In *Egypt and Palestine,* ed. A. Cohen and G. Baer, 66–77. New York: Palgrave Macmillan, 1984.

Halm, Heinz. *Die Kalifen von Cairo: Die Fatimiden in Ägypten, 973–1074.* München: Beck, 2003.

Halm, Heinz. *The Empire of the Mahdi: The Rise of the Fatimids.* Leiden: Brill, 1996.

Lev, Yaacov. *State and Society in Fatimid Egypt.* Leiden: Brill, 1991.

Lev, Yaacov. *Saladin in Egypt.* Leiden: Brill, 1999.

Walker, Paul E. *Exploring an Islamic Empire: Fatimid History and Its Sources.* London: Tauris, 2002.

Fatwa

The fatwa (sing. *responsa;* pl. fatawa, or *responsae*) is a question-and-answer process referred to in the Quran (4:127, 176) beginning in early Islam as a means to impart knowledge about theology, philosophy, hadith, legal theory, religious duties, and, later and more specifically, sharia, or Islamic law. Fatawa may deal with a much broader series of subjects than did the Islamic courts, and a fatwa, unlike a court ruling, is not binding. The reason it is not binding is that in a court, a qadi (judge) is concerned with evidentiary matters and may actually investigate these and hear two sides to an argument, but a cleric or authority issuing a fatwa is responding instead to just one party, should the question involve a dispute, and thus the question might be formulated in a particular way.

In modern times, a fatwa is usually defined as a legal opinion given by someone with expertise in Islamic law. However, so long as a person mentions the sources he uses in a legal opinion, other Muslim authorities or figures may issue fatawa. A modern fatwa usually responds to a question about an action, form of behavior, or practice that classifies it as being obligatory, forbidden, permitted, recommended, or reprehensible.

Traditionally, a fatwa could be issued by a Muslim scholar knowledgeable of both the subject and the theories of jurisprudence. These persons might be part of or independent from the court systems. However, other persons might issue fatawa as well. Muslim governments typically designated a chief mufti who had the role of the sheikh of Islam in the Ottoman Empire.

In the colonial period, the Islamic madrassas, or institutes of Islamic education, began to include a fatwa-issuing office, Dar al-Ifta, in some cases. Muslim governments continued in efforts to control and limit the issuing of fatawa, as in the Higher Council of Ulema and the Permanent Council for Scientific Research and Legal Opinions in Saudi Arabia and the Council of Islamic Ideology in Pakistan. However, many Muslim authorities—from lesser-trained sheikhs to political figures to legal specialists classified as *fuqaha* (specialists in jurisprudence), *mujtahids,* and muftis—issue fatawa. Some are no more than a short response to the inquiry, whereas others are recorded, published, or circulated along with explanations.

For many reasons, including the development of differing legal schools within Islam and the history of opinions concerning religious requirements as opposed to mere duties, fatawa may conflict with each other. For example, the legal opinions concerning women's inheritance under Jafari, or Twelver Shia, law and that given by a Hanafi Sunni jurist would differ. At times, even councils of jurists from a single sect may issue a complex opinion with, for instance, each indicating their agreement with or reservations about different implications or subquestions of a fatwa. Muslim countries today may govern with civil laws that are partially dependent on principles of Islamic law or are derived in part from Ottoman law. When matters of civil legal reform are discussed, then the opinions of religious authorities might be consulted. Or a fatwa may be issued by popular figures outside of the venue of civil authorities. Other countries, however, operate on the basis of uncodified Islamic law. At the supranational level, there is no single authoritative person or body that can settle conflicting issues or declare binding fatawa in Islamic law (as the pope and the Vatican issue religious decrees for Roman Catholicism).

In 1933 clerics in Iraq issued a fatwa that called for a boycott of all Zionist-made products. In 2004 the very popular Egyptian Sunni Muslim cleric and scholar Yusuf al-Qaradawi declared a fatwa similarly calling for a boycott of goods manufactured in Israel and the United States.

Other much-disputed questions have concerned the necessary resistance of Palestinians to Israeli rule and the actual status of Palestine. One set of questions, mainly affecting the right to wage jihad (holy war), concerns the land's status the (dar al-Islam) or an Islamic territory that is the generally agreed condition resting on the presence of the Bayt al-Maqdis, the holy sites at the al-Aqsa Mosque complex, from which Prophet Muhammad experienced the Miraj and the Isra (the Night Journey and Ascent to Heaven). Because the country is an Islamic land and Muslims cannot visit their holy sites or practice their religion and have had their lands and properties seized, some fatawa assert that jihad is an individual duty incumbent on Muslims. Divergent fatawa say that the country, now Israel, is *dar al-kufr,* a land of unbelief (somewhat like India under British rule) from which Muslims should flee, as in a highly disputed fatwa by Sheikh Muhammad Nasir al-Din al-Albani. While Palestinian Islamic Jihad issued a lengthy fatwa in 1989 that legitimated suicide attacks by Palestinians in the context of jihad, no leading clerics actually signed this document. It could be countered by a statement by the grand mufti of Saudi Arabia made on April 21, 2001, that Islam forbids suicide attacks, which is referred to as if it were a formal fatwa. Sheikh Qaradawi issued a fatwa in 2002 that said women could engage in martyrdom operations in conditions when jihad is an individual duty.

PAUL G. PIERPAOLI JR. AND SHERIFA ZUHUR

See also
Khomeini, Ruhollah; Religious Sites in the Middle East, Muslim; Shia Islam; Sunni Islam

References
Coulson, Noel J. *A History of Islamic Law.* Edinburgh, UK: Edinburgh University Press, 1994.
Esposito, John L. *Islam: The Straight Path.* New York: Oxford University Press, 1991.
Messick, Brinkley. *The Calligraphic State: Textual Domination and History in a Muslim Society.* Berkeley: University of California Press, 1993.

Fedayeen

Term used to refer to various (usually Arab) groups that have engaged in either armed struggle or guerrilla tactics against civilians and sometimes governments. The term "fedayeen" is the plural of the Arabic word meaning "one who is ready to sacrifice his life" and has for centuries referred to Muslim fighters, including Egyptians who fought against the British in the Suez Canal Zone, Palestinians who waged attacks against Israelis in the 1950s and 1960s, Iranian guerrillas opposed to Mohammad Reza Shah Pahlavi's regime in the 1970s, and a force loyal to Iraqi dictator Saddam Hussein during the Iraq War of 2003.

Following the rejection by Arab leaders of the 1947 United Nations (UN) partition plan that would have created a Palestinian state in the West Bank and the Gaza Strip and the resulting declaration of the State of Israel the following year, Palestinian refugees were driven from their homes and flooded into the areas surrounding the new Jewish state. Anti-Israel activity became prevalent, particularly in West Bank and Gaza Strip areas. Supported by money and arms from a number of Arab states, Palestinians carried out attacks against Israeli military forces and also Israeli settlers, and in 1951 the raids became more organized. These fighters were referred to as fedayeen since they were an irregular rather than a government force. The fighters created bases in Egypt, Jordan, and Lebanon, with Egyptian intelligence training and arming many of them. Between 1951 and 1956 the fedayeen orchestrated hundreds of raids along the Israeli border, killing an estimated 400 Israelis and injuring 900 others.

The fedayeen operated primarily out of Jordan, and this caused that country to bear the brunt of the retaliation campaign carried out by the Israel Defense Forces (IDF) and paramilitary groups. Fedayeen attacks and subsequent retaliations were significant factors in the outbreak of hostilities during the 1956 Suez Crisis. The fedayeen continued to be active after that, now launching attacks into Israel from Jordanian territory. The fighters included those associated with the Palestine Liberation Organization (PLO), the Popular Front for the Liberation of Palestine (PFLP), and various other militant groups.

King Hussein of Jordan was initially supportive of the groups, but by 1970 he deemed their presence detrimental to Jordan and a threat to his own political power. Although based in refugee camps, the fedayeen were able to obtain arms and financial support from other Arab countries and therefore clashed with Jordanian government troops who attempted to disarm them beginning in 1968. The civil war that erupted in 1970 during what has been called Black September saw the eventual defeat and removal of the fedayeen from Jordanian soil.

The fedayeen were forced to recognize Jordanian sovereignty via an agreement reached between PLO leader Yasser Arafat and King Hussein on October 13, 1970. Although its members often participated in fedayeen raids, the PLO denied playing a role in several terrorist attacks. After being ousted from Jordan, the PLO and the fedayeen relocated to Lebanon, where they continued to stage attacks on Israel. At present, the term "fedayeen" is still used by many Palestinian militants who see them as freedom fighters seeking the establishment of a Palestinian state in the region.

Fedayeen-e Khalq was the name taken by a radical Islamic group opposed to the reign of Reza Pahlavi of Iran. Between 1971 and 1983 these Iranian fedayeen carried out numerous attacks, including political assassinations, against people supportive of the shah. Most recently, the name was used for a group loyal to ousted Iraqi leader Saddam Hussein. The Fedayeen Saddam was most likely named to imply association with anti-imperialism and freedom fighters as well as the example of the Palestinians. Although established by Hussein's son Uday in 1995, the group drew international attention only with the outbreak of the 2003 Iraq War. Like their Palestinian counterparts, members of the Fedayeen Saddam were mostly young unemployed men and did not constitute part of Iraq's regular army. These irregular soldiers became part of the Iraqi resistance, or *muqawama*. Following the March 2003 U.S.- and British-led invasion, the fedayeen turned their attention to coalition troops, attacking them with rocket-propelled grenades, machine guns, and mortars.

SPENCER C. TUCKER

See also
Black September; Expellees and Refugees, Palestinian; Gaza Strip; Hussein, Saddam; Hussein ibn Talal, King of Jordan; Iran; Iraq; Israel; Jordan; Palestine Liberation Organization; Popular Front for the Liberation of Palestine; Reza Shah Pahlavi; Suicide Bombings; Terrorism; West Bank

References
Laqueur, Walter, and Barry Rubin, eds. *The Israel-Arab Reader: A Documentary History of the Middle East Conflict.* London: Penguin, 2001.
Nafez, Nazzal, and Laila A. Nafez. *Historical Dictionary of Palestine.* Lanham, MD: Scarecrow, 1997.
O'Neill, Bard E. *Revolutionary Warfare in the Middle East: The Israelis vs. the Fedayeen.* Boulder, CO: Paladin, 1974.
Rubin, Barry. *Revolution until Victory? The Politics and History of the PLO.* Reprint ed. Cambridge, MA: Harvard University Press, 2003.

Finckenstein, Treaty of (May 4, 1807)

Agreement between France and Persia concluded in the castle of Finckenstein in East Prussia on May 4, 1807. The treaty was signed in the midst of the Russo-Persian and Russo-French wars and was undertaken to create a Franco-Persian alliance against Russia. French emperor Napoleon I guaranteed the territorial integrity of Iran, recognized eastern Georgia and other south Caucasian polities as Fath Ali Shah's possession, and agreed to assist the shah in reclaiming them from Russia. Napoleon pledged to provide arms and military experts to modernize the Persian armed forces. The shah agreed to declare war against France's enemy, the United Kingdom, and to expel all Britons from Persia. Persia also undertook to gain Afghan cooperation for a joint invasion of India, then under British rule.

The treaty proved short-lived, since Napoleon ended the war with Russia with the Treaty of Tilsit of July 1807 that established a Franco-Russian alliance and recognized Russian claims to southern Caucasia. Thus, none of the terms of the treaty were realized. Feeling betrayed by the French, Persia turned to Britain and signed a treaty of cooperation with that nation in 1809.

ALEXANDER MIKABERIDZE

See also
Definitive Treaty; Russo-Persian Wars; Tehran Treaty

References
Amini, Iradj. *Napoleon and Persia: Franco-Persian Relations under the First Empire.* Washington, DC: Taylor & Francis, 2000.
Karsh, Inari. *Empires of the Sand: The Struggle for Mastery in the Middle East, 1789–1923.* Cambridge, MA: Harvard University Press, 2001.

Fitna, First and Second
See Islamic Civil War, First; Islamic Civil War, Second

Forbie, Battle of (October 17, 1244)

A battle fought on October 17, 1244, at Forbie (Harbiyah) near Gaza. The Battle of Forbie, also known as the Battle of Harbiyah, involved the Franks of Jerusalem allied with the Ayyubids of Damascus, Kerak, and Homs against the Ayyubids of Egypt.

The battle resulted from disputes among the Ayyubids after the death in 1238 of Sultan al-Kamil. His son al-Adil II was recognized in Egypt, while another son, al-ali Ayyub, seized Damascus, which was soon taken from him by his uncle al-Ali Ismail.

After al-Adil had been deposed, Ayyub was able to install himself in Egypt and plan the reconquest of Damascus. This led to a coalition among Ismail of Damascus, al-Nair Dawud of Kerak, al-Manur Ibrahim of Homs, and the Franks, all of whom were determined to prevent the unification of Damascus and Egypt under one ruler. Ayyub allied himself with the Khwariazmians, a people displaced from Iraq by the Mongol offensives. In 1244 the Khwariazmians captured Jerusalem and joined Ayyub's troops near Gaza, where they made contact with the Franks and their allies on October 17.

Contrary to the advice of their allies, the Franks followed the leadership of Count Walter of Jaffa and attacked because they outnumbered their opponents but were defeated. More than 5,000 Franks were casualties in the battle, among them the archbishop of Tyre and almost all participating members of the military orders, and 800 prisoners were taken to Egypt. The Battle of Forbie was considered the worst Frankish defeat since that of Hattin in 1187.

JOCHEN BURGTORF

See also
Hattin, Battle of

References

Bulst-Thiele, Marie Luise. "Zur Geschichte der Ritterorden und des Königreichs Jerusalem im 13. Jahrhundert bis zur Schlacht bei La Forbie am 17 Oktober 1244." *Deutsches Achiv für Erforschung des Mittelalters* 22 (1966): 197–226.

Runciman, Steven. *A History of the Crusades*. 3 vols. Cambridge: Cambridge University Press, 1951–1954.

Franco-Lebanese Treaty (November 13, 1936)

A mutual agreement of friendship negotiated between the government of France and the mandate government of Lebanon that granted Lebanon considerable autonomy. The Franco-Lebanese Treaty was signed on November 13, 1936, and was intended to clarify France's relationship to Lebanon in light of the Franco-Syrian Treaty of September 1936 that had essentially begun Syria's course toward independence. At the time, both Lebanon and Syria were part of a French mandate authorized by the League of Nations. The French parliament, however, did not ratify the treaty. With the Franco-Lebanese Treaty coming so close on the heels of the treaty with Syria, many French politicians were leery of setting Lebanon on its own course of independence. Be that as it may, the spirit of the treaty guided Franco-Lebanese relations right up until the fall of France in 1940.

Most notably, the Franco-Lebanese Treaty granted Christian Maronites preferential treatment in terms of politics and economic matters. Indeed, the Maronites had enjoyed a long and beneficial connection with the French that had furthered France's commercial interests, and the French hoped to capitalize on this. The privileges granted within an unwritten document known as the Mithaq al-Watani (National Pact) angered the Muslim and Druze populations, however, and created animosities that would plague Lebanon into the 21st century. Indeed, by the early 1930s the Maronites no longer constituted a majority of the Lebanese population. There was a rough parity between Christians and Muslims. (Druzes can also be included in this category, although they are not actually Muslim.)

The Muslims decried the continuation of French rule via the mandate and did not wish to be part of a secular, independent Lebanon. Rather, they hoped to either form their own Arab Muslim state or become part of a greater Syrian state. Needless to say, Lebanon's Muslims and Druzes were not enamored of the treaty with the French.

When France fell to invading Nazi German armies in June 1940, the Lebanese mandate fell under the control of the collaborationist Vichy government. In 1941, however, Free French troops occupied Lebanon and took control of the country politically and militarily. Soon thereafter Free French officials proclaimed Lebanese and Syrian independence, which the British underwrote. Nevertheless, Free French policy makers were reluctant to hand over complete control to the Lebanese. And in 1943 when the new democratically elected Lebanese government moved to purge Lebanon of any French influences, Free French forces promptly jailed most of the Lebanese officials, including President Bishara al-Khuri. This precipitated a Lebanese rebellion that had to be handled via diplomatic intervention on the part of the British. Not until 1946 would the last of French (and British) troops be withdrawn from Lebanon. That same year, the Lebanese achieved complete independence. French preferential treatment of the Maronites via the treaty and their heavy-handedness during World War II most certainly led to the balkanization of Lebanese politics in the postwar era.

PAUL G. PIERPAOLI JR.

See also
Lebanon

References

Gaunson, A. B. *The Anglo-French Clash in Lebanon and Syria, 1940–1945*. New York: St. Martin's, 1987.

Odeh, J. B. *Lebanon, Dynamics of Conflict: A Modern Political History*. London: Zed, 1985.

Franco-Syrian Treaty (September 9, 1936)

Treaty signed on September 9, 1936, between the French government and the Syrian government, which at the time was under a French-administered League of Nations mandate. Like the Franco-Lebanese Treaty of November 1936, the Syrian treaty was not ratified by the French parliament. The treaty was designed to begin the process toward Syrian independence and pledged both governments to mutual friendship and alliance. The treaty also stipulated that Syria and Lebanon would retain their separate statuses and that Syria would attain its independence by the close of 1939. At that point, it would join the League of Nations as an independent state.

This was not the first time that the French had attempted to negotiate an independence treaty with the Syrians. Two years earlier in 1934, the French had tried to impose a treaty on the Syrian government, which at the time was headed by pro-French president Muhammad Ali Bey al-Abid. Al-Abid was extremely pro-French, in sharp contrast to many of the Syrian leaders who were nationalists. When word of the proposed treaty leaked out, Syrian nationalists were outraged. The treaty was heavily pro-French, and while eventual independence would have been granted, the French wanted to control the Syrian Mountains themselves, apparently in perpetuity.

Syrian nationalist leader and parliament member Hashim al-Atasi almost immediately mobilized his forces to stage countrywide protests. These included a 60-day general strike that soon crippled the economy. Mass protests ensued, as did several riots in urban areas. Within weeks, al-Atasi's National Bloc had seized the upper hand, and the proposed 1934 treaty was scrapped.

When al-Atasi and the National Bloc had proven themselves to be the favored ruling coalition in Syria, France's recently inaugurated Popular Front government agreed to enter into negotiations with al-Atasi. On March 22, 1936, al-Atasi arrived in Paris to begin talks with the Paris government. For almost six months al-Atasi, who had not yet assumed the Syrian presidency (he would do so in December), led the Syrian delegation in the negotiations. The final treaty draft guaranteed immediate recognition of a Syrian Republic and a 25-year transition to complete independence. It also stipulated that the Syrian government would control both the Druze and Alawite populations, that France would gradually reduce its military presence in Syria, and that Paris would not involve itself in the internal political affairs of the Syrian Republic.

Although the treaty was less than al-Atasi and other nationalists had hoped for, it was nevertheless an important step toward independence and was far less slavish to French interests than the aborted 1934 treaty. The treaty bolstered the National Bloc and the political fortunes of al-Atasi, who was elected to the presidency in late November 1936. He is considered Syria's first modern head of state.

The French soon proved recalcitrant, however. The treaty was put before the French parliament on more than one occasion, and each time it came up for a vote it fell short of the required majority. There were two major factors driving France's backtracking on the Franco-Syrian Treaty. First, as Nazi Germany became stronger as the 1930s progressed, French policy makers became increasingly reluctant to cede any of France's colonial territories. The fear, of course, was that Germany would move against the Middle East and gain access through weak ex-colonial holdings there. Also driving French hesitance was a rising tide of procolonial forces in French politics. These individuals vowed not to relinquish any of France's colonial possessions.

As 1939 dawned, it had become patently obvious that the French were indeed not going to ratify the treaty. By the spring of 1939, protests and riots again wracked Syria as the public grew resentful of what they considered to be French duplicity. Al-Atasi was greatly angered and embarrassed by the turn of events but was in no position to alter the situation in any meaningful way. When France unilaterally ceded to Turkey the Syrian province of Alexandretta, which the French had guaranteed would stay under Syrian control, Syrian nationalists had enough. After mobilizing more demonstrations and strikes, they were successful in driving al-Atasi and the National Bloc from office. Al-Atssi resigned the presidency on July 9, 1939. Thereafter, several years of political unrest and French military engagements ensued. Syria would finally achieve independence in 1946.

PAUL G. PIERPAOLI JR.

See also
Franco-Lebanese Treaty; Lebanon; Syria; World War I, Impact on the Middle East; World War II, Impact on the Middle East

References
Harvey, John. *With the French Foreign Legion in Syria.* London: Greenhill, 1995.

Pipes, Daniel. *Greater Syria: The History of an Ambition.* New York: Oxford University Press, 1990.

Shambrook, Peter A. *French Imperialism in Syria, 1927–1936.* Reading, Berkshire, UK: Garnet Publishing/Ithaca Press, 1999.

Franco-Turkish War (1920)

The Ottoman Empire collapsed amid political and military turmoil at the end of World War I, and many of its former provinces became battlegrounds for new conflicts. Under the Sykes-Picot Agreement of 1916, Britain and France agreed to a postwar partition of former Ottoman domains, with Cilicia in south-central Asia Minor (along the southern coast of Anatolia) granted to France. At the same time, the French government had negotiated an agreement with the leaders of the Armenian national liberation movement who promised to provide military support against the Ottomans.

When the Ottoman Empire left the war as a consequence of the Armistice of Mudros (October 30, 1918), the French government dispatched a military force to secure Cilicia. On November 17, some 15,000 French troops landed at the port of Mersin. Most of these were Armenians who had organized the French Armenian Legion to fight for the creation of the

Armenian state. Two days later additional French troops came ashore at Tarsus to establish their headquarters at Adana. Gradually France took over the Ottoman provinces of Antep, Maras, and Urfa, even briefly—during one day—taking the city of Mardin.

The French, however, faced increasing resistance from the local Turkish population, which was particularly incensed by the French Armenian Legion's actions. The Sütçü İmam Incident, in which the Armenian troops mistreated the local Turkish populace, provoked clashes in Maras (Kahramanmara) in late 1918 and eventually contributed to the outbreak of open hostilities.

In the Franco-Turkish War (Cilicia War), the Battle of Maras saw almost a month of fighting between the Association for the Defense of National Rights, a group established by former Ottoman Army officers, and the Franco-Armenian forces, which were ultimately forced to evacuate that city in February 1920. Facing intensifying resistance, the French authorities gradually pulled their troops from Cilicia and in October 1921 signed the Treaty of Ankara with the Turkish Grand National Assembly. France acknowledged Turkish control of Cilicia, while the Turkish authorities accepted the French mandate in Syria.

ALEXANDER MIKABERIDZE

See also
Ottoman Empire; Sykes-Picot Agreement

References
Güçlü, Yücel. *Armenians and the Allies in Cilicia, 1914–1923*. Salt Lake City: University of Utah Press, 2010.
Nevakivi, Jukka. *Britain, France and the Arab Middle East 1914–1920*. London: Athlone, 1969.

Franks, Tommy (1945–)

U.S. Army general who commanded coalition forces in the invasions of both Afghanistan and Iraq. Tommy Ray Franks was born in Wynnewood, Oklahoma, on June 17, 1945, and grew up in Oklahoma and Midland, Texas. Attending the University of Texas at Austin for two years, Franks dropped out owing to lack of motivation and poor grades, joining the U.S. Army in 1965. He was later able to attend the University of Texas at Arlington through the army, earning a BA in business administration there. He also earned a master's degree in public administration at Shippensburg University in 1985.

After entering the army in 1965, Franks attended basic training at Fort Leonard Wood, Missouri, and advanced training at Fort Devens, Massachusetts. Selected to attend the Artillery and Missile Officer Candidate School at Fort Sill, Oklahoma, upon graduation he was commissioned a 2nd lieutenant in 1967. He then served in Vietnam in the artillery and was wounded.

In 1968 Franks returned to Fort Sill, where he commanded a battery in the Artillery Training Center. After finishing his BA in 1971 under the army's Book Strap Degree Completion Program, he attended the Artillery Advanced Course at Fort Sill before being assigned to Germany, where he commanded an artillery battery. From 1976 to 1977, he attended the Armed Forces Staff College in Norfolk, Virginia, and in 1984–1985 he attended the U.S. Army War College at Carlisle Barracks, Pennsylvania.

In the 1991 Persian Gulf War, Franks was a colonel and an assistant division commander of the 1st Calvary Division. He was promoted to brigadier general in July 1991 and to major general in April 1994. From 1994 to 1995 he was assistant chief of staff for combined forces in Korea, and during 1995–1997 he commanded the 2nd Infantry Division in Korea. From 1997 to 2000 he was commander of the Third

U.S. Central Command (CENTCOM) commander General Tommy Franks led the successful toppling of the Taliban in Afghanistan in 2001 and the invasion of Iraq in 2003. (U.S. Department of Defense)

Army/Army Forces Central Command, Atlanta, Georgia. He was promoted to lieutenant general in May 1997 and to general in July 2000, when he assumed command of the United States Central Command (CENTCOM).

Following the September 11, 2001, terrorist attacks on the United States, Franks headed planning for and then commanded the U.S.-led invasion of Afghanistan (Operation ENDURING FREEDOM). In 2003 he headed planning for and then commanded the U.S.-led invasion of Iraq (Operation IRAQI FREEDOM).

Denied additional forces by Secretary of Defense Donald Rumsfeld, who believed that the invasion could be accomplished with fewer men, Franks's plan in Iraq involved five ground prongs into that country with two main thrusts, one by the 1st Marine Expeditionary Force up the Tigris River and one through the western desert and up the Euphrates by the army's 3rd Armored Division. The plan allowed for great flexibility, and even though CENTCOM advertised a shock-and-awe bombing campaign, in fact there was never any such intention, as Franks's plans called for a near-simultaneous air and ground assault.

Franks emphasized speed and bypassing cities and Iraqi strongpoints. Contrary to media reports that coalition forces were bogged down and had not occupied many population centers, Franks maintained that this was by design: CENTCOM did not want the Iraqis to see the method and tactics by which coalition forces planned to take Baghdad demonstrated in Basra or Najaf.

The campaign was an unprecedented success, going farther and faster with fewer casualties than any other comparable military campaign in history. This reflected what Franks called "full-spectrum" war, in which not only were the enemy's military forces engaged, but there were also simultaneous attacks on computer/information facilities and the banking/monetary structure. Franks expanded the concept of C3I (Command, Control, Communications, and Intelligence) to include Computers in C4I. American forces operated in true joint operations, wherein different service branches could speak directly to units in other service branches, and featured true combined-arms operations, in which air, sea, and land assets were all simultaneously employed by commanders in the field to defeat the enemy.

Franks's tenure as commander of CENTCOM was not without controversy, however. Some critics blamed him for not committing 800 U.S. Army rangers who were available for the Battle of Tora Bora in Afghanistan. They claim that had this been done, it could have resulted in the capture of Osama bin Laden and other members of Al Qaeda who were then able to escape into Pakistan and from there mount an insurgency in Afghanistan.

During the Iraq War, Franks was forced by Rumsfeld to operate with fewer troops in the invasion than he had hoped. Franks therefore concentrated almost exclusively on the immediate tasks of defeating the Iraqi Army and capturing Baghdad. Forces were simply not available for occupation tasks and addressing postinvasion requirements. Still, the 4th Infantry Division (Mechanized) sealift ships were kept at sea (the division was to have operated from Turkey, but Ankara refused at the last minute to grant the anticipated approval) instead of landing the equipment in Kuwait, which would have permitted the division to take part in the early postinvasion operations. Franks maintained that keeping the ships at sea deceived the Iraqis into believing that U.S. forces would invade from yet another direction. Critics have also charged that Franks was slow to realize the threat of an Iraqi insurgency.

Although reportedly offered by Rumsfeld the position of army chief of staff, Franks chose to retire in July 2003. General John Abizaid succeeded him as CENTCOM commander. In 2004, President George W. Bush awarded Franks the Presidential Medal of Freedom.

Franks subsequently wrote his memoirs, *American Soldier* (2004). In 2003 he established his own consulting firm, specializing in disaster recovery. He has also sat on a number of corporate and nonprofit boards of directors, including those of Bank of America and the National Park Foundation.

LARRY SCHWEIKART AND SPENCER C. TUCKER

See also
Abizaid, John Philip; Bush Doctrine; Iraq Insurgency; Iraq War

References
Cordesman, Anthony. *The Iraq War: Strategy, Tactics, and Military Lessons.* London. Center for Strategic and International Studies, 2003.
Fontenot, Gregory, et al. *On Point: The United States Army in Operation Iraqi Freedom.* Washington, DC: Office of the Chief of Staff, 2004.
Franks, Tommy R. *American Soldier.* New York: HarperCollins, 2004.
Gordon, Michael R., and Bernard E. Trainor. *Cobra II: The Inside Story of the Invasion and Occupation of Iraq.* New York: Pantheon Books, 2006.
Ricks, Thomas E. *Fiasco: The American Military Adventure in Iraq.* New York: Penguin, 2006.
Woodward, Bob. *Plan of Attack.* New York: Simon & Schuster, 2004.

Frederick I or Frederick Barbarossa (1122–1190)

German emperor. Born in 1122, the eldest son of Frederick, duke of Swabia, Frederick succeeded his father in 1147. His Italian name "Barbarossa" came from his red beard. Frederick accompanied his uncle, Emperor Conrad III, on the Second Christian Crusade in the Holy Land during 1148–1149. On Conrad's death, Frederick was elected emperor on March 4, 1152. Because the nobles exercised considerable authority in Germany and imperial power was weak there, Frederick concentrated his attention on Italy and Burgundy. Indeed, during most of his rule he concentrated on Italian affairs.

In 1154 Frederick began the first of six campaigns in Italy, restoring Pope Eugenius III to authority in Rome. Returning to Germany in 1155, Frederick showed himself adroit in managing affairs there by playing off potential rivals. In 1156 he married Beatrice of Burgundy and, through her, laid claim to Burgundy.

Frederick campaigned in north Italy in 1156, crushing a revolt in Milan and firmly establishing his authority over the other cities. He then called the diet of Roncaglia, which acknowledged him as king of Italy in November. On the death of Pope Adrian IV in 1159, Frederick supported antipope Victor IV, earning an excommunication from Pope Alexander III in March 1160. Harsh rule led Milan to again rebel, and Frederick retook and then burned the city in 1162. Italy again revolted, and he returned there again in October 1166, taking Rome and installing Pope Paschal III. This triumph was cut short by the outbreak of plague in his army. Cities in north Italy took advantage of Frederick's military weakness to form the League of Lombardy against him, and he was forced to return to Germany in the spring of 1168.

Frederick then occupied himself with German affairs and extending his authority over Bohemia, Hungary, and part of Poland. Finally, in 1174 he led an army into northern Italy for a fifth time and a showdown with the Lombard League but suffered a major defeat in the Battle of Legnano (May 29, 1176). Frederick then concluded a treaty with Pope Alexander in June 1177 and a six-year truce with the Lombard League.

Returning to Germany in the autumn of 1177, Frederick again busied himself with German affairs. His powerful cousin, Henry the Lion, had refused assistance in his Italian campaign, and Frederick now deprived him of his holdings, giving Bavaria to Otto of Wittelsbach in 1179. Frederick concluded a definitive treaty with the Lombard League at Constance in June 1183, although this obliged him to give up some of his Italian holdings.

In 1184 he betrothed his son Henry to Constance, heiress presumptive to the Norman kingdom of Sicily. With a new Italian war threatening, Frederick embarked with a large force of as many as 4,000 knights on the Third Crusade to the Holy Land in 1189. His forces departed from Regensburg in May. The early stages of the crusade proceeded smoothly with the cooperation of King Béla III of Hungary. However, problems developed once the army crossed into Byzantine territory at the end of June. Byzantine emperor Isaac II Angelos had made an alliance with Saladin some years earlier and had promised the sultan to try to prevent the expedition from crossing his territory. He was also suspicious of Frederick's negotiations with the rulers of Serbia and with the Turks of Asia Minor—indeed, he arrested the envoys whom Frederick had sent to the Sultanate of Rum on their return journey. When the German army reached Philipopolis (modern-day Plovdiv, Bulgaria) at the end of August, relations were already breaking down, and while the expedition remained in this fertile region for some 11 weeks, they grew worse. By the time the Germans had moved on to Adrianople (modern-day Edirne, Turkey) in mid-November, there was open warfare with the Greeks. Indeed, there was strong pressure from within the army for an attack on Constantinople (modern-day Istanbul), not least because there appears to have been knowledge of Isaac's alliance with Saladin. But although Frederick was prepared to threaten Isaac with such an attack and even to open negotiations for the assistance of the Bulgarians in this, he was anxious that the crusade should proceed to its intended destination and restrained his men.

After wintering with his forces in Adrianople, Frederick reached agreement with the Byzantines on February 14, 1190. The army crossed the Hellespont from Gallipoli (modern-day Gelibolu, Turkey) at the end of March without incident, transported in Pisan and Byzantine ships. Frederick kept his army well in hand as they marched southeast through Byzantine territory, but attacks on them began almost immediately after they crossed into Turkish territory at the end of April. Frederick had hoped that his negotiations with Qilij Arslan II, which had continued while the army was at Adrianople, would have prevented this. However, during the winter of 1189–1190 the sultan's authority had been usurped by his eldest son, Qutb al-Din Malik-Shah, who was reluctant to allow the Christian army to pass through Seljuk territory, not least since he had recently married a daughter of Saladin. Furthermore, the latter's disputes with his brothers had led to a breakdown of the Seljuk state, which would have made restraining attacks on the crusaders difficult even if the rulers had been so minded.

The crusaders beat back a series of attacks but soon began to run short of food for themselves and fodder for their animals. After defeating a major attack on May 14, Frederick decided to attack the Seljuk capital of Ikonion (modern-day Konya, Turkey), which he took four days later. The Seljuks then agreed to provide supplies if the army moved on, and while the expedition proceeded toward the friendly territory of Cilician Armenia, attacks on the column were limited to minor harassment from Turkoman nomads. The army reached the plain of Seleucia (modern-day Silifke, Turkey) on the morning of June 10, 1190, but here disaster struck. The emperor, who insisted, despite the pleas of his entourage, was thrown from his horse, suffered a heart attack, and drowned while crossing the Suleph (Göksu) River.

Command devolved upon the emperor's son, Duke Frederick V of Swabia. The crusaders arrived at Antioch (modern-day Antakya, Turkey) on June 20. Yet casualties in Asia Minor had been heavy, and the loss of horses and baggage animals, many of which were eaten, posed serious problems. At Antioch, the Germans were also ravaged by disease. Some of the survivors then went home; others accompanied Frederick of Swabia to the siege of Acre (modern-day Akko, Israel), but disease in the crusader camp continued its ravages there. Frederick of Swabia died in January 1191, and despite further reinforcements arriving by sea, the German contribution to the Third Crusade was thereafter relatively minor. It was disease rather than Frederick's death that ruined the German expedition. Its suffering also showed that the land route across Asia Minor was no longer practical for crusader forces.

SPENCER C. TUCKER AND GRAHAM A. LOUD

See also
Crusades in the Holy Land, Christian; Frederick V, Duke of Swabia; Rum, Sultanate of; Saladin; Seljuk Dynasty

References
Eickhoff, Ekkehard. *Friedrich Barbarossa im Orient: Kreuzzug und Tod Friedrichs I.* Tübingen: Wasmuth, 1977.
Hiestand, Rudolf. "Kingship and Crusade in Twelfth-Century Germany." In *England and Germany in the Middle Ages: Essays in Honour of Karl J. Leyser*, ed. Alfred Haverkamp and Hanna Vollrath, 235–265. Oxford: Oxford University Press, 1996.
Munz, Peter. *Frederick Barbarossa: A Study in Medieval Politics.* London: Eyre & Spottiswood, 1969.
Opll, Ferdinand. *Friedrich Barbarossa.* Darmstadt, Germany: Wissenschaftliche Buchgesellschaft, 1990.

Otto of Freising. *The Deeds of Frederick Barbarossa.* Translated by Charles Christopher Mierow. New York: Norton, 1953.
Pacaut, Marcel. *Frederick Barbarossa.* London: Collins, 1970.

Frederick II, Holy Roman Emperor (1194–1250)

Holy Roman emperor, called by contemporary chronicler Matthew Paris "Stupor Mundi" (Wonder of the World). Frederick Hohenstaufen was born in Jesi, near Ancona, on December 26, 1194, the son of Emperor Henry VI and Constance, daughter of Norman king Roger II of Sicily. Frederick's father arranged for his son's election as king of Germany in 1196.

Henry's unexpected death in September 1197 led, however, to a series of wars for control not only of the Holy Roman Empire but also of the Kingdom of Sicily, which included southern Italy. On his mother's death in November 1198, Frederick became king of Sicily. Pope Innocent III became his guardian, and on reaching his majority Frederick assumed control of Sicily in December 1208. The next year he married Constance, daughter of King Peter II of Aragon.

In August 1209 Otto IV, the son of Henry the Lion (the great rival of Frederick's grandfather, Frederick Barbarossa), invaded Italy, but Pope Innocent III persuaded the German princes to depose him and name Frederick as emperor in his stead in September 1211. Frederick paid homage to Innocent (by proxy) and traveled to Germany in 1212, where he was well received. He arranged an alliance with France against Otto and King John of England and was formally crowned emperor at Mainz on December 9, 1212. Frederick's position as emperor was made secure by the French defeat of his rival Otto in the Battle of Bouvines (July 26, 1214). Frederick was then recrowned in Otto's former stronghold of Aachen on July 25, 1215. Pope Honorius III crowned Frederick as Holy Roman emperor in Rome on November 22, 1220.

Frederick had agreed in 1215 to participate in the Fifth Crusade in the holy land (1218–1221), but distracted by Italian affairs that included a revival of the Lombard League against imperial authority in northern Italy, he delayed his participation. In March 1223 Frederick had sworn that he would depart by June 1225. This was coupled with an undertaking that he would marry Isabella II (also known as Yolande), daughter of John of Brienne and queen of Jerusalem through succession to her mother, Maria of Montferrat (la Marquise).

In July 1225 a papal delegation met Frederick in San Germano and extracted from him a new pledge to lead 1,000

Holy Roman emperor Frederick II (1194–1250) enthroned with a falcon at his side, from his treatise on falconry, ca. 1220–1250. (Stefano Dulevant for Alinari/Alinari via Getty Images)

knights and 150 ships and galleys to the Holy Land, on pain of excommunication, by August 1227. On November 9, 1225, Frederick married Isabella II in Brindisi and claimed the title and rights of king of Jerusalem. For the first time a crusade was to be the obligation of a single monarch, one who would go not merely as a crusader but instead as the first Western ruler to wear the crown of Jerusalem.

Honorius III died in March 1227 and was succeeded by Gregory IX, whose choice of papal name signaled his intention to assert papal interests against the empire. When August 1227 came, Frederick's fleet began to leave Brindisi. Frederick himself sailed on September 8 with Landgrave Ludwig IV of Thuringia but returned to land within two days when an epidemic broke out on board, from which Ludwig died. Gregory excommunicated the emperor for his technical breach of the agreement reached at San Germano. When Frederick embarked again on June 28, 1228, the pope renewed the ban, and the emperor reached Acre an excommunicated crusader.

Frederick immediately took up earlier preparatory contact with Sultan al-Kamil of Egypt. Without fighting a single battle, on February 11, 1229, Frederick concluded with the sultan a treaty that ceded to the Christians most of Jerusalem along with Bethlehem, Nazareth, and a land corridor to Acre. The treaty also provided that Jerusalem and Montfort could be refortified and established a 10-year truce. On March 17 Frederick entered Jerusalem, where he crowned himself king in the Church of the Holy Sepulchre, though the papal ban disqualified him from hearing mass. Frederick also issued an imperial encyclical extolling himself as soldier of Christ and divinely ordained instrument of God's plan of salvation.

On May 1, 1229, Frederick departed the Holy Land never to return, although he kept the title of king of Jerusalem until his death and continued to support the kingdom financially and diplomatically. Gregory IX responded to Frederick's defiance by releasing his subjects in Sicily from their allegiance to their king and invading the kingdom.

Gregory was determined to prevent firm German control of southern Italy. When papal forces invaded Frederick's realm and devastated Apulia, Frederick returned to Italy in June 1229 and expelled them. As a consequence of the resultant Treaty of San Germano on July 23, 1230, Frederick was absolved of his excommunication in August. Frederick now endeavored, with intermittent success, to secure northern Italy. He assisted Gregory IX in putting down a revolt at Rome in 1234, and a rebellion by his son Henry VII in Germany collapsed when Frederick's army crossed the Alps in September 1234, whereupon Frederick confined Henry to a castle in Apula until his death in 1244.

A series of confusing wars followed in which Gregory IX allied with Genoa and Venice against him. Although Frederick won a number of victories, including the Battle of Cortenuova (November 17, 1237), and annexed Tuscany in 1241, his forces could not overcome the Italian city's defensive fortifications. On Pope Gregory's death at the age of 100 in August 1241, the new pope, Innocent IV, continued the struggle against Frederick and then ordered him deposed in 1245.

In 1244 Frederick invaded Campagna. He also faced intrigues from within his own court and revolts in Germany. During his siege of Parma in 1248 a sudden sally from that place scattered his army while he was away hunting. Frederick was, however, generally successful, and the situation was gradually improving until his sudden death at Castle Florentino, Apulia, on December 13, 1250. Although his son Conrad IV continued the struggle, Hohenstaufen control of Italy was irretrievably lost.

Frederick was a capable military commander. Highly intelligent, he was also a major patron of the arts. As a ruler he sacrificed German interests to those of Italy.

Spencer C. Tucker

See also
Crusades in the Holy Land, Christian; John of Brienne

References
Abulafia, David. *Frederick II: A Medieval Emperor.* Oxford: Oxford University Press, 1992.

Jacoby, David. "The Kingdom of Jerusalem and the Collapse of Hohenstaufen Power in the Levant." *Dumbarton Oaks Papers* 40 (1986): 83–101.

Lomax, John Philip. "Frederick II, His Saracens and the Papacy." In *Medieval Christian Perceptions of Islam,* ed. John Victor Tolan, 175–198. London: Routledge, 2000.

Ross, Linda. "Frederick II: Tyrant or Benefactor of the Latin East?" *Al-Masāq: Islam and the Medieval Mediterranean* 15 (2003): 149–159.

Stürner, Wolfgang. *Friedrich II.* 2 vols. Darmstadt: Wissenschaftliche Buchgesellschaft, 1994–2000.

Van Cleve, Thomas Curtis. *The Emperor Frederick II of Hohenstaufen: Immutator Mundi.* Oxford: Oxford University Press, 1972.

Frederick V, Duke of Swabia (1167–1191)

Commander of the German crusaders in the Third Crusade (1189–1192) during 1190–1191. Born at Modigliana in Romagna (central Italy) in February 1167. Frederick was the third son of Emperor Frederick I, known as Frederick Barbarossa, and Beatrix of Burgundy. Frederick V was originally called Conrad but received the traditional forename of the Staufen (Hohenstaufen) family after the death of his elder brother, also called Frederick, in 1169. As the second brother, Henry, was intended as future king of Germany and the Holy Roman emperor, Frederick was given the duchy of Swabia, which had become vacant on the death of his cousin Frederick IV (of Rothenburg).

Frederick V of Swabia took the cross in March 1188 in Mainz at the gathering known as the Court of Jesus Christ along with his father and numerous other German nobles and prelates. Unlike the other contingents that joined the crusade, Barbarossa's army traveled overland to the East. Frederick of Swabia was entrusted with many important diplomatic and military responsibilities during the march, and he led the crusader assault that captured Ikonion (modern-day Konya, Turkey), capital of the Seljuk Sultanate of Rum, on May 18, 1190.

When Emperor Frederick I was drowned on June 10, 1190, while attempting to swim his horse across the Suleph (Göksu) River, Frederick V was unanimously recognized as the commander of the German crusader force. Disease and hardship attended the march, and a large number of German crusaders died or returned home, but Frederick led the remainder via Tarsos (modern-day Tarsus, Turkey) and Antioch (modern-day Antakya, Turkey) to Tripoli (modern-day Trâblous, Lebanon), from where they traveled to Palestine by sea, arriving in October. There they joined the other crusader contingents engaged in the siege of Acre (modern-day Akko, Israel), but Frederick V succumbed to a pestilence and died on January 20, 1191.

Alan V. Murray

See also
Crusades in the Holy Land, Christian; Frederick I or Frederick Barbarossa; Rum, Sultanate of

References
Eickhoff, Ekkehard. *Friedrich Barbarossa im Orient: Kreuzzug und Tod Friedrichs I.* Tübingen: Wasmuth, 1977.

Hiestand, Rudolf. "Precipua tocius christianismi columpna: Barbarossa und der Kreuzzug." In *Friedrich Barbarossa: Handlungsspielräume und Wirkungsweisen des staufischen Kaisers,* ed. Alfred Haverkamp, 51–108. Sigmaringen, Germany: Thorbecke, 1992.

Opll, Ferdinand. *Friedrich Barbarossa.* Darmstadt, Germany: Wissenschaftliche Buchgesellschaft, 1990.